ECONOMICS

SHOREY PETERSON
The University of Michigan

New York
HENRY HOLT AND COMPANY

Preface

When a new textbook appears, especially a book that enters an occupied area, its particular aims should be stated at the outset. This volume emerges from a decade of local evolution in which certain goals of instruction came to be looked on as properly controlling in a basic course in economics.

It is unavoidable that such a course should have a dual character in the liberal-arts college. It must serve that majority of students who will not study economics any further in a formal way. It must also provide a suitable foundation for students who will major in economics. Few of the latter have selected their special field until they have studied in it, and thus a specialized introductory course is not a feasible expedient. For each of these groups there are alternative ways of proceeding, but, if both are to be served, the path to be followed seems to be quite well marked, at least in the main features to be sought and to be avoided.

One end to be striven for is that the principles of economics, the abstract statements of relationships, should appear in the role of working tools, developed in the setting of their applications. There can be little place for dangling theories whose only hope of application is in some later course, or even in some remote section of the first course. The instructor should be able at all times to meet the challenge that what he is teaching is significant to the intelligent citizen. At the same time his text material should aid him in promoting a scholarly appreciation of the analytical structure on which the thinking of the intelligent citizen should rest. For example, the teacher cannot expect to evoke any serious concern in his students over the operation of markets in fixing prices in each of a dozen hypothetical situations. But he should get them to sense and understand how markets are relied on in the American economy to coordinate the activities of numerous producers and consumers and how such policies as the antitrust laws, public-utility regulation, and farm-price supports fit into the structure of an economy so organized.

When principles are taught in a beginning course with an eye to their application in problems and policies, it is easy to be diffuse and superficial. But the chief aim of instruction, it seems—for the general student no less than for the prospective specialist—should be disciplined and critical thinking. Rigor may be pursued abstractly, and often is, through detailed formulation of hypotheses and examination of them. But if instruction is to be vital to the majority of students, it seems for the most part that rigor is better sought in other ways. With only a little sacrifice of neatly classified assumptions, ideas can be hammered into sharp and useful tools by applying them to current ways of thinking and to the matters on which businessmen, workers, legislators, and ordinary observers are continually reaching judgments. Economics is not then an aggregate of concepts and analyses to be remembered but the active use of disciplined ways of thinking.

A different aim, but no less important, is to give the student a balanced view of the requirements of economic well-being and of the problems faced by modern economies. Economists may not agree fully as to what constitutes a proper proportioning of emphasis, but the author of a basic textbook should strive for a reasonable balance, not being sidetracked by the easier ways of catching student interest nor by the current focus of theorists and investigators. Anyone who has taught economics for a quarter-century or more is fully aware of the succession of swings in emphasis that have occurred and will probably feel that the pendulum is still moving. For the general student, a balanced approach seems a primary duty of the teacher, but perspective is no less important to the student who is laying a foundation for further study.

The earlier preoccupation of textbooks with price and distribution theory, often in an artificial framework, has been corrected in various ways in recent years. Competition and monopoly have been viewed more realistically, but the correction, unfortunately, has sometimes appeared in an elaborate "economics of the firm" that neither tells the businessman how his firm should be run nor throws much light for the student of society on the critical aspects of its operation. Variations on the marginal theme easily burst the bounds of significance for the beginning student. The newer hypotheses can be examined as abstractly and disproportionately as the older ones.

During the 1930s the customary textbook chapter on business cycles came to seem perfunctory and inadequate in dealing with prevailing views on the employment problem. In the local situation in which the present book was developing, this difficulty was attacked through earlier versions of the material on national-income measurement and aggregate demand that now appears herein in Chapters 3 and 14. The problem of unemployed resources should unquestionably receive major attention, but here again a question of balance must be faced to avoid a distorting, disproportionate emphasis and the introduction of theories more appropriate in a senior course for economics majors. Well-being still depends fundamentally on the conditions of economic power and progress, as well as the use made of that power. It rests heavily on the direction and coordination of activities through markets and in other ways and on the sharing of total product and income. These are all major problems that should have appropriate weight both in basic analysis and in the applications of that analysis in institutional and policy situations. It seems hardly enough that balance should be implicit in the treatment of them. Considerable conscious effort is necessary in developing breadth and judgment in the student so that he will see particular matters in the perspective of the whole economy.

The present book does not deal ambitiously with theoretical questions over which economists are still struggling, though it departs from convention here and there. But it may be thought fairly ambitious, both for student and teacher, in its general conception of elementary instruction. In trying to convey the practical meaning of basic ideas, especially in the policy sphere, it may go further at some points than elementary instruction should. Occasional sections may thus serve their purpose best through interpretation by the teacher without the requirement of technical understanding by the student.

To facilitate instruction, the handling of topics has been governed in one important respect by the principle of progression in difficulty. In the elementary course in which this book evolved, Parts I through IV have constituted the work of the first semester, Parts V through VII of the second semester. Effective analysis of markets and income distribution requires much of the student, and these subjects, with related policies, can be handled to better advantage when the training and sifting of the first semester have been completed. But partly because some understanding of the role of markets and prices is needed at earlier points, a preliminary sketch of these matters appears in the survey of competitive capitalism in Chapter 4.

Since useful study is never a passive process but one of active mastery and application, no formal summaries are included that might invite rote learning. Instead review questions are inserted at frequent intervals; and many of these questions consist of a restatement of central ideas for students to explain.

For a textbook to succeed as a teaching instrument, it needs sympathetic handling by teachers who share its aims. But to aid them properly it should have grown out of considerable teaching experience along the lines it advocates. For any merit this book may possess, a large debt is owed the numerous instructors who have worked with the writer over a long period and have threshed out problems of content and method with him in weekly meetings. Of these associates

William B. Palmer of the University of Michigan and Floyd A. Bond, now of Pomona College, have labored over much of the manuscript and have made numerous valuable suggestions. Similar help has come from George R. Anderson, Daniel B. Suits, Harold M. Levinson, Robert W. Stevens, and others of the Michigan staff. For the defects of the book only the writer is responsible.

The part played by I. L. Sharfman in friendly encouragement and practical assistance, as well as in earlier training and guidance, is gratefully acknowledged. For help both general and specific, an immense debt has accumulated to the writer's wife Eleanor Shipp Peterson.

S. P.

Ann Arbor, Michigan
November 22, 1948

Contents

List of Tables

PART I

The Economy
as a Whole

Every businessman, worker, and plain citizen has ideas on economic matters. But modern economic life is so complicated that, for these ideas to be coherent and meaningful, much critical sifting and systematizing must be done from a standpoint broader than the personal experience of any individual.

The first task, then, in studying economics is to see clearly what this broad standpoint involves and to achieve a framework of study, a scheme of orientation, into which the analysis of more detailed problems and relationships can be fitted. So, after an introductory chapter dealing with some preliminary questions about the nature of the subject, we shall look at the economy as a whole from three comprehensive viewpoints. First, in Chapter 2, we shall examine the occupational structure of the United States to see, in its historical setting, the logic of the complex organization of production that now prevails in advanced economies. Next, in Chapter 3, we shall consider the primary dependence of economic welfare on production and income, and with the necessary concepts in mind, we shall trace the course of the national, or aggregate, income of the people of the United States in recent decades. Thirdly, in Chapter 4, we shall turn to the broad arrangements which the phrase "economic system" implies and, in light of the tasks that systems must perform, examine in a preliminary way the distinctive features and problems of the American economic tradition. This is the tradition that we find expressed most commonly in such phrases as "free enterprise" and "competitive capitalism."

These four chapters will constitute Part I of this volume. Brief introductions similar to this one will precede the other main divisions

1

of the book and will serve, it is hoped, to outline its general plan and bind its numerous topics into a coherent whole. Economics, after all, is concerned with a small number of major questions; and, after the bird's-eye approach that Part I provides, the succeeding parts will deal systematically with these major matters.

- 1 -

Economics as
a Field of Study

BECAUSE the fundamentals of economics affect the
lives of all of us, they need to be more widely understood. To appreciate
this need, one must learn what economics is about, what its aims are,
what sort of knowledge and understanding it can hope to convey. These
matters are discussed in this opening chapter.

Economics deals with a large segment of human life and social organization—that segment in which, in the popular phrase, people are engaged in "making a living." About 40 percent of us in the United States,
if we exclude housewives from our statistics, are so engaged. As jobholders and as operators of factories, farms, and other businesses, we give to
our work from a third to a half of our waking hours and much of our
thought and energy. All 145,000,000 of us in the United States are consumers, and our welfare, from infancy to old age, rests heavily on the
goods which "making a living" provides. These goods include not only
the food, clothing, and shelter necessary to living but also most of the
comforts of life and many of the means of recreation and culture; books,
music, travel, the services of artists, teachers, and preachers depend on
income and how we use it. As preachers and philosophers view these
matters, making a living is not the most important part of life but it is
certainly the most obtrusive and demanding.

We are doomed to this economic role because the things it provides
us cannot be had freely and abundantly in Garden-of-Eden fashion.
Vast activity is required in getting them, and great care—which we call
economizing—is necessary in making the most of them and of the resources used in getting them. This is the central fact of economic life;
and it is this activity and this economizing with which the study of
economics is concerned.

3

While economics deals with the behavior of people in making a living; it does not tell them how to make a living; it provides no code of instructions for the individual jobholder, businessman, and consumer. At the same time, economics deals with matters of fundamental importance to the economic welfare of everyone. To reconcile these statements, one must appreciate the nature and aims of economics as a field of study.

A social approach to individual interests

The key to the matter is that the welfare of the individual depends largely on factors outside his control—on underlying economic conditions and forces and on relationships among many people over wide areas and through long periods. This is not to deny that personal success depends on being a good workman in one's chosen field or an astute businessman in dealing with problems of production and markets. But it implies that personal success arises also through skillful adaptation to these broader conditions and relationships and that it is limited by them. This is an abstract statement. What does it mean?

Part of its meaning appears if one ponders the economic position of the average American in comparison with that of the typical Russian, Chinese, or Hottentot. Whatever his individual merit, the American is peculiarly fortunate in his opportunities for personal economic achievement and well-being. His opportunities spring from an environment of favorable natural resources, advanced technology, accumulated equipment, efficient production arrangements, and political and other institutions which are the essential conditions of his achievements.

More of the meaning appears if one examines the nature of American capitalism and the position of the individual within it. The individual, let us assume, is an excellent carpenter; and it happens that he is anxious to have a new automobile. But whether he can have it will depend on the construction of houses, on the wages received by carpenters, and on the price of automobiles. He cannot make people decide to buy new houses; and he may, in consequence, be unemployed. As an individual, he cannot change the wage of carpenters, and even through his union he cannot do very much. Higher wages will mean that houses cost more, that fewer people can afford new houses, and that more people will buy prefabricated houses. Certainly he cannot change the price of automobiles. Even the building contractor and the automobile manufacturer are not much better off in these respects. They cannot make people buy houses and automobiles, and they cannot do very much about the wages they pay and the cost of materials and supplies. Like every person engaged in making a living—and we need not limit this statement to capitalism—they are caught in a network of factors beyond their personal control.

Broad effects of private actions. But the dependence of the individual on his economic environment is only part of the picture. Along with other producers and consumers, he is the source of pressures and influences of far-reaching effect. Especially is this true under capitalism. Though he may have only private ends in view, his decisions and actions are integral elements in the working of the economy as a whole, the economy on which the living of everyone depends.

As an ordinary jobholder, he may think mainly of the money he earns and the living it gives him; but the quality of his work and the amount he accomplishes contribute to the living of numerous others. It is the total of such contributions which determines the level of living that prevails throughout the nation. As a consumer, he is probably unaware of the effect his spending has. If, let us suppose, he has laid aside a sum for use either in buying a new car or as downpayment on a new house, the decision he reaches will affect the operations of two distinct industries and the opportunities of the workers and suppliers who depend on them. Or, if he rejects both of these purchases and keeps his bank deposit instead, he creates the need of equivalent spending by someone else, perhaps a borrower from the bank, to maintain the flow of buying that is a condition of prosperity. The bank may lend to an industrialist who, thinking mainly of his probable profit, uses the loan to purchase and install a new machine, thereby stimulating the machinery industry—with benefit to those who serve it—and expanding his capacity to supply his product to the public. The banker, making and refusing loans according to standards of sound and profitable banking, exerts an influence on prices and the value of the dollar and on the variations in general prosperity.

So one might go on with instances of the broadly public effect of private action. Taken singly, the impact of the consumer or worker may be slight. Or, as in the case of the union leader or corporation head, it may be relatively great. But, even so, it is likely to appear only as the by-product of pursuing a private end. The union leader may decide what wage rates to demand or whether to call a strike without regard for the probable effects on prices, production policies, or public convenience. The head of a dominant firm may decide, on narrow grounds of business policy, whether his product should be priced for higher unit profit on smaller volume or lower unit profit on larger sales. But whatever the extent of individual influence or the aim behind it, the working of the economy in its entirety must be the composite result of innumerable private decisions and pressures.

Government in economic life. But the significant decisions and pressures are not all private. Some are governmental. The environment to which the individual must adapt himself in making a living depends at many points on the general legal framework of the nation and on specific enactments. Laws regarding the ownership and use of property and the contractual relationships among individuals create such fundamental differences as exist between the United States and Russia. Laws regarding competition and monopoly in markets, laws regulating specific lines of business such as banking and railroads, laws to protect labor and aid agriculture, laws to promote security of income despite unemployment and inability to work, tax laws which divert purchasing power to government and public spending on government services and projects—these and other policies are powerful influences even though the economy depends mainly on voluntary private action to provide goods.

When public policies are influential, no one questions that economic welfare is a social and not just an individual matter. All would agree that, when government invades the economic sphere, it should act with an eye to all the probable consequences, near and remote, of what it does. Even so, people are prone to take a limited view of public actions just as they do of private actions. Perhaps this is most likely when public policies result directly from the political pressures of interested groups. It is easy, for instance, when American manufacturers want a protective tariff that will shut out foreign competition, to look no farther than the anticipated direct effect on the manufacturers' prosperity and that of their immediate employees—neglecting the interest of American consumers in low prices and of American exporters in enabling foreign nations to buy from us. It is easy, similarly, to regard labor legislation or farm legislation merely as means of giving direct benefit to workers or farmers and not as far-reaching influences that must be incorporated in a complex economic structure.

Economics an analysis from the social viewpoint. These paragraphs have mentioned a number of factors in economic organization, not to throw light on them specifically but to make clear that economic welfare is an intricate matter that must be viewed broadly and socially and not merely from the limited viewpoint of individual consumers, jobholders, and businessmen. When viewed thus broadly, the business of making a living becomes the subject matter of economics.

Economics undertakes to describe and analyze the leading conditions and relationships on which economic well-being depends. It is concerned with the main factors in productive power and progress, with markets and prices and the forces governing the behavior of producers and consumers, with incomes and the sharing of economic well-being, with money and the use of credit, with the flow of purchasing power as it affects general prosperity, with government as a taxing and spending agency and a controlling influence in many connections. Economics tries especially to trace the major relationships which enable one to see the actions of all producers and consumers as an interconnected whole. Insofar as this end is achieved, one can view specific practices and policies critically in an orderly setting.

For want of a better word, the viewpoint of economics is said to be *social*. It is not social in the sense that it is concerned with an abstract society apart from the welfare of individuals. Economic welfare is individual welfare. It is not comprehensively social, since it largely neglects matters which are not economic. But its approach is social (1) in the sense that it stresses relationships beyond the individual, extending widely throughout society, and (2) in the sense that its critical judg-ments are rendered from a viewpoint broader than that of particular economic groups. Its usefulness must lie largely in pointing out and analyzing matters that extend beyond the experience of persons in their private capacities, and sometimes in stressing matters that special in-terests would prefer to ignore.

Purposes in studying economics

Why should one study such a field? To the person of scholarly bent, the intricate ordering of modern economic life offers a challenging field of inquiry simply for the sake of understanding it. Sheer curiosity may lead as appropriately to an investigation of economic matters as to a study of prehistoric mammals or the remoter constellations. Doubt-less most persons who study economics intensively are spurred by a curiosity incentive.

To the majority of people whose interest remains on a more casual level, some understanding of the subject can render ordinary economic experiences and observations more meaningful than they otherwise would be. Just as the factory worker takes more interest in his narrow task when he sees it in relation to the whole plant and the completed product, so the making of that product, or the doing of any kind of work, gains significance when seen in a broad setting as the source and the result of many impacts. As an observer of events—of the shifting course of prices and prosperity, the onrush of organized labor, the financial expedients of government, the state of trade with other coun-tries, the requirements and effects of modern war—one is likely to find that every gain in insight is rewarding.

One should not study economics to learn techniques of production or of money-making. Certainly the ordinary businessman may prosper and the jobholder perform his usual task without understanding the principles of economics, just as one may learn to walk on stilts or a tight rope without the physicist's knowledge of gravitation. A common-sense or rule-of-thumb application of unrecognized principles is usually enough. Indeed, money may sometimes be made in ways that, from the standpoint of economics, are deplorable. But there are, nevertheless, many practical roles in the economy in which the broader approach of economic analysis has a definite place. Responsible judgments in banking and finance, in the direction of large firms, in the contacts of business with government, and in applying government policies in the economic sphere often require such an approach. In the intensive study of many business problems, business and economics tend to merge.

The economist, however, is mainly interested in applications of economics not as they affect private money-making but as they may improve the operation of the whole economy. To some extent these beneficial applications may come about through ordinary private action. It is generally assumed under capitalism—and probably under any workable economic system—that most people most of the time will be governed by fairly narrow private interests. But it is also true that most people like to believe that their actions are in harmony with the public interest and that they are serving others as well as themselves. If one knows where the public interest lies, there is some latitude in almost any job to promote it a little. In the more influential positions, as noted above, the heads of large corporations and labor unions may have considerable latitude within which they can modify action in the public interest. Perhaps their decisions will seldom be altruistic; but, if they realize the remoter effects of their decisions and are persuaded that no one can prosper in the long run except as part of an entire system that works effectively, they may find it easier to reconcile private advantage and public interest to the benefit of everyone. There is need of a developing ethics of economic behavior that sees private prosperity in the light of the social conditions on which its continuance depends. The study of economics may be said to have some such end in view.

But it is largely in his role as citizen that the individual must contribute to the improvement of economic life. Certainly it is in this role that wide understanding is most necessary. Government now touches the economy at so many points, indeed basic institutions are so largely in the hands of government, that economic responsibilities must be discharged with the ballot as well as on the job. Comprehension of economic issues is far too low even among educated persons, and catch phrases and loose observations too largely pass for understanding. Even an informed citizenry, it is true, cannot become expert on complex problems; but a wider grasp of fundamentals promotes general soundness of judgment and holds legislators and public officials to a higher level of performance.

Perhaps most important is the inculcation in the citizenry of a viewpoint that embraces the whole economy. Pressure groups with numerous interested votes have grown in power, and the lobbying of businessmen is matched by that of farmers and ordinary workers in supporting or opposing proposals that affect them. The danger of all such partisan emphasis is that it obscures the common interest of everyone in high production and in a smoothly working economy. To some extent, people are bound to vote as their short-run interest lies; but intelligent members of the rank and file are likely to take more moderate positions than do the partisan leaders who feel that their jobs depend on the vigor of their demands. Thus, more general understanding of the working of the economy should improve the outlook for sound policies.

Dependability of conclusions in economics

On beginning the study of a subject such as economics, one naturally wonders how confidently one should accept its teaching. Are its analyses dependable? Are the propositions it lays down well founded? Economists are known to disagree fairly often on questions of policy, and their predictions of coming events may diverge. While this is not the place to discuss methods of analysis in economics, certain comments should be made.

To the student with a background in the physical sciences, many generalizations in economics may seem inexact and some of the applications of them incautious. How buyers and producers of goods will act under given conditions is not as predictable and measurable as the behavior of expanding gases and falling bodies. Nor may the "given conditions" remain as obligingly fixed. Human activities must be studied as they actually take place and not under the neat laboratory conditions that simplify much physical research. Moreover, it is unfortunately the case that new policies—say a reduction of the gold equivalent of the dollar or the establishment of old-age annuities—cannot be tried out on an economic proving ground before they become the law of the land. Understanding of them must come slowly—and often painfully.

For much of economics, however, the difficulties are not so great as these statements suggest. Of all the aspects of behavior on which the conduct of human affairs must rest, probably the economic are the most dependable and manageable. Economic objectives are fairly clear and economic procedures fairly definite. Such matters as production, capital, income, prices, money, purchasing power, and so on can be analyzed more confidently and precisely than most of the factors in social and political organization. Some of the more important ideas in economics, moreover, require no elaborate analysis to support them, but rest on a simple logic that needs stressing only because it involves a viewpoint broader than individual experience. Thus, without statistical research, a reasonable person can easily agree that giving more money to people will not enable them to buy more goods than are produced. But such points must often be stressed, since the complexities of economic life obscure them.

Questions on which competent students disagree will occupy only a small part of this volume. We shall not be concerned with predicting what prices or employment will do in the next six months or whether foreign trade will move more freely fifteen years from now. The art of short-run economic prediction has not reached a high state and may not do so. Nor do economists view it as their function to predict expertly the political developments on which government policies depend.

Necessarily we shall consider some questions of public policy that are controversial, and on which economists may hold divergent views. Policy questions are usually a tangle of numerous economic, political, and general social factors that cannot be weighed in the way that physical forces can often be measured and compared. The very goals of policy may even be debatable. But though comprehensive agreement on a policy is difficult even among persons supposed to be expert, insight into it is furthered by ordinary economic analysis. One may find it hard to decide, for instance, whether government should spend large sums during depressions to promote prosperity; but a useful conclusion is more likely if one is able to break the problem into its elements and to analyze the effect of public spending on the buying power of labor, on the activity of producers of materials, on costs that private business encounters, on taxes and the public debt, on business attitudes and confidence.

A constructive attack on public problems must proceed along these lines. While some debated problems will be discussed in the present study, the object will not be to promote particular policies. Instead, the aim will be to clarify issues and especially to develop the key ideas of economics in a setting of useful application. The tools of economic analysis seldom depend on particular social philosophies. On the contrary, they afford avenues of insight to all honest observers of the current scene, whether they speak for management or labor or believe in capitalism or socialism.

Review Questions [1]

1. Definitions seldom help one to understand anything, but they may sum up in a useful way something that is already understood. With this end in view, how might the subject of economics be defined so as to bring out its resemblances to, and differences from, sociology, political science, and business administration?

2. "The economic position and behavior of the individual are both result and cause of influences that extend throughout the economy, and largely determine its character." Explain and illustrate.

3. Make a list of public problems in the United States which you regard as essentially economic in character. Do they involve noneconomic elements?

4. Of what importance is it that people who have no intention of becoming economists should have some knowledge of economics? Distinguish several reasons. As a prospective businessman, lawyer, engineer, teacher, physician, government worker, bring out any special connection between the study of economics and your field of work.

5. Compare economics and physics with respect (a) to the kinds of data with which they are concerned; (b) the methods of reaching generalizations; (c) the means of arriving at solutions of practical problems.

6. What is a scientific attitude? Is it limited to situations in which scientific methods are used? Is it possible in economics? Do most people who generalize on economic matters have it?

7. "I am interested in facts, not in theories." Show that facts have little significance until conclusions have been drawn from them and the relationships between them have been stated.

8. "Only theorists say a protective tariff is bad. As a practical man interested only in facts, I know it is good for my business, and that it is also good for the country." Show that the speaker is theorizing. Does it seem likely that he has evidence to support his conclusions? Do you think that intelligent supporters and opponents of a tariff should be able to agree on the main factors and relationships that ought to be considered in reaching a decision from the public standpoint?

[1] Questions based on the text will appear systematically throughout the chapters of this book. These questions reflect the belief that all learning is an active process and that nothing is really understood until it is thought through and, where possible, applied. Questions will be included that involve most of the important ideas in the chapters, but without the reformulations that drill sometimes requires. They are called "review questions," with the idea that positive reconsideration rather than purely verbal repetition must be the only effective summary and review.

- 2 -

The Occupational
and Industrial Structure

As CONSUMERS, each of the 145,000,000 of us in the
United States depends on thousands, even millions, of the 60,000,000 of
us who are producers—indeed on many other producers in foreign
countries. The simplest product we use—the book we are reading, the
pencil in our hand, the chair we sit on—reflects an intricate process.
We sense this process if we fix attention on the materials of which the
product is made, the places these materials come from, the factories that
shape them, the ships and railroads and motor vehicles that move them,
the middlemen that handle them, and, farther back, on the activities
through which the factories, the means of transport, and all the other
instrumentalities become available—a receding vista without end.
There are thousands of such products, and in getting them we are enmeshed in a network of prices and financial operations.

In these respects, the life of the Eskimo and the Australian bushman,
and of all primitive people past and present, is simple. Typically, the
few products that they use they provide directly, as individuals and
within small groups. Their pattern of production is easy to describe and
understand.

Complexity is certainly not in itself the essence of progress, but it
seems to be an aspect of progess in the economic sense. The complicated
modern organization provides people more abundantly with the things
they want, not only with the essentials of food and bodily protection
but with these essentials in a variety and on a scale the body does not
require; in addition it offers numerous means of enjoyment, improvement, and relief from backbreaking toil in a measure beyond the reach
of primitive man.

This developing complexity, then, is an evolution, reflecting an internal logic of adapting means to ends. The aim of this chapter is to disclose, in a preliminary way, the logic in the organization of modern production, and at the same time to show, in major categories, how the people of the United States make a living.

Wants, resources, products

In essentials all economic organization, primitive and modern, is alike. It arises from two conditions: (1) human desires for things which are not naturally abundant and available—in the way that air is available for breathing; and (2) resources, in human abilities and in nature, for obtaining at least part of these things. Whether the economy is that of the South Sea Islander exploiting his environment for fish and coconuts or that of the modern American lost in a maze of occupations, markets, and products, the main framework of economic organization is the same. It consists in arrangements for using resources to provide the goods that people want. Economic progress is to be judged mainly by the flow of products, the size and variety of this flow, and the nicety with which it fits the desires of the people.

Wants are not static. Food, clothing, and shelter serve needs that continue with little change; and the desires for adornment and ostentation, for entertainment, recreation, and self-improvement seem to lie deep in human nature. But within these broad channels, human wants change and expand endlessly as cultures evolve and producers enlarge the array of available goods.

Nor are resources static. Populations increase, human abilities develop, and nature reveals expanding possibilities as knowledge grows. To the primary productive power in man and in nature is added the power of tools and machines and engines and structures of all kinds, instrumentalities that man contrives and makes from materials that nature provides.

Fully as changing is the organization itself through which resources are used. Through technical advance and through many elusive but cumulative shifts in ways of doing things, the pattern alters and becomes more intricate. But, however elaborate it gets to be, it should be viewed analytically as a scheme of using resources to provide goods to meet human wants.[1]

Occupational classes in the United States

To the discerning eye, much can be learned about modern economic organization, and about economic life in the United States, from a

[1] The next chapter, which focuses attention on the flow of products, will begin with a brief critical examination of the adequacy of this approach.

statistical summary of occupations. In 1946 the persons, in millions, engaged in production in the United States were distributed over the major fields as the accompanying table shows.[2]

TABLE 1—PERSONS ENGAGED IN PRODUCTION, BY INDUSTRY, 1946
(In millions)

Farming, forestry, and fishing	7.3
Mining—including extraction of petroleum	.9
Construction—including buildings, roads, dams, etc.	2.3
Manufacturing—to be viewed in some detail presently	14.6
Trade, wholesale and retail	10.4
Transportation—all fields, including pipe lines	3.0
Finance, insurance, and real estate	1.8
Communication and public utilities—including radio	1.1
Services—including personal, professional, household, hotel	6.8
Government—federal, state, and local	8.9
Total	57.3

There is little point in memorizing statistics, but a sound sense of approximate sizes and relationships in leading connections can be of great value in giving definiteness to one's knowledge of economic life and in avoiding mistakes in thinking. "Many of the people concerned with legislation," one Washington observer wrote during the recent war, "have not the wildest idea of relative economic magnitudes." [3] One need not remember exact figures from the above table to recall, for instance, that factory employees are now about one fourth of all workers. That is a significant fact. City folk who watch employees pour from factory gates at quitting time may easily believe that most of working America is found at bench and machine and assembly line. In the dark days of the 1930s a common view held in high circles was that unemployment could be ended if factories reduced the working week. Apart from the other defects, the unreality of this view is apparent from the above facts, because much of the unemployment was in other fields. The same idea appeared again in discussions of postwar employment; and, though the point should be commonplace, a leading magazine saw fit to publish an opening article under the title "Factories Can't Employ Everybody!" [4] Certainly both policy makers and job seekers, in-

---

[2] Department of Commerce, *National Income, Supplement to Survey of Current Business,* July 1947, p. 40. Figures are for man-years of full-time employment and exclude unpaid family workers. The usual total of 60,000,000 or more includes all gainful workers of fourteen and over, including the currently unemployed. Because of the rounding of figures in this and subsequent tables, totals are not always equal to the sum of the items.

[3] Walter S. Salant, *American Economic Review Supplement,* June 1944, p. 24.

[4] C. Hartley Grattan in *Harper's Magazine,* September 1944.

cluding young persons planning their fields of work, should have some knowledge of the occupational structure of the country.

But the reason for introducing these occupational data here is neither to analyze the employment problem nor to provide job guidance. The purpose is to show, in proportion, the main lines of activity in an advanced economy and to provide a basis for seeing how these activities are related and why such an economy is advanced. In considering these matters it will be useful to examine simpler economies, as well as that of the United States, and to look for the main lines of evolution.

The Evolving Organization of Production

From such occupational statistics as the foregoing, and without examining actual techniques of production, what can be learned about the economic life of a nation and about the progress it has achieved? What functional relations exist among the major fields of activity which explain why economic development has followed the lines it has in such nations as the United States? Consideration of these questions will reveal some of the logic of the organization of production, very broadly regarded.

The primary industries, especially food production

The very first item in the table is one of the most significant. Of the 57,000,000 gainfully occupied persons in 1946, 7,300,000 were in the farming-forestry-fishing category, with slightly under 7,000,000 in agriculture. Most of the farmers provided foodstuffs—cereals, vegetables, fruits, meat, and dairy products—but they also provided cotton and other textile fibers and some other raw materials. If we add in the miners and oilfield workers, we have a total of slightly over 8,000,000 then producing foodstuffs, fuels, and materials for industry.

These activities, in which human labor is applied directly to external nature, are known as the *primary industries.* It is a striking fact that they employ only 15 per cent of the working population. It is striking because a large and varied output of goods, necessary to a high level of living, is possible only when a very minor fraction of total productive effort is absorbed in the primary lines, especially in getting foodstuffs. Where the fraction in the primary fields is small, a varied and complex occupational structure, such as that in the United States, is enabled to develop.

Food production in backward economies. Food is the first of human requirements. It is the mark of primitive economies that they are mainly concerned with providing food. Indeed, at its most primitive level, the economic life of men, as of animals, is solely concerned with food and consists merely of the direct taking from nature of flesh and fruit and other edible things. Domestication of animals, with controlled raising of sheep and hogs and cattle, represented a marked advance above the hunting and foraging level; and cultivation of the soil, with the growing of grain and root crops, was a still greater advance. These great steps enabled more people to live better, and with greater security, in given areas. But despite these advances, the bulk of humanity throughout all history, or at least until recent times, has been occupied mainly in providing enough food for itself.

Clothing and shelter claimed some effort of early peoples, especially as they drifted into regions of severe climate. But skins of animals, by-products of the pursuit of food, made both the tepee of the Indian and the warm garments of the Eskimo and afforded bodily protection quite generally; and means of shelter could also be found readily in earth and forests. Although the food getting remained the principal activity in primitive economies, the getting and processing of other materials was carried on after hours and in off seasons and by dependent members of the family.

We need not linger over historical detail. Even in ancient times there were complex economies, such as that of the Greeks, with luxury and variety for a few people. Nor need primitive economic organization, dominated by the pursuit of food, imply a primitive culture. China and India have ancient civilizations, but farming, mainly food raising, still absorbs 70 or 80 percent of their effort. It has been said that if all the Chinese raised food at their present rate of output they would scarcely maintain a satisfactory dietary level. Countries have risen in the economic scale to the extent that they have solved the food problem in particular and the raw-material problem in general. With this background in mind, one can appreciate how fortunate the United States is in being able to obtain its food and other primary products with so small a fraction of its working force.

Food production in the United States. This is not the full story of the production of basic products in this country. We import some foods from abroad, especially such things as sugar and coffee; but we export foodstuffs also. We also import other raw materials, and to some extent exported manufactures must pay for them; but only a very small part of the labor force is so used. In comparing the United States with primitive food-dominated economies, more important is the fact that here much effort is expended off the farm in providing food. Over a million people in manufacturing are processing foods and beverages, and several million are transporting them and handling them as middlemen. About one third of all personal expenditure is for food—a figure which includes much outlay of a luxury nature, just as much of the spending for clothing and shelter is not dictated by requirements of health and comfort. On the basis of a total that includes industrial equipment and other products not bought for personal use, probably from a fifth to a fourth of all productive effort in the United States is devoted to feeding people—a fraction whose small size is of utmost significance in understanding both the effectiveness and the complexity of the nation's economy.

The lines of economic development

An organization of production that comprises mainly the primary industries is necessarily simple. It is simple in the fact that products are few and uncomplicated. It is simple in the small number of occupations to be entered and in the crudity of the operations carried on. It is simple, further, in the small number of people who are dependent upon each other and the small size of the areas within which people are interdependent. There are no great concentrations of people but rather a wide dispersion that is based on the dominant and direct place of the natural environment in all production.

Historians, in tracing the evolution of modern economic life, often start with the situation in the late Middle Ages. The English manor was typical of the period. The manor was a small, nearly self-contained agricultural community. Food was the main product, and farming the main occupation. There might be a few part-time specialists in other trades, such as a miller and a smith; and a few goods, such as salt and iron, might be obtained through outside trade. But these departures from the basic pattern were slight. The towns of the period, apart from agricultural villages, contained only a small part of the total population. They performed military, governmental, and religious functions, and served as centers of trade and handicraft. But most townsmen were also farmers, deserting their tasks at planting and harvest time to get food from the surrounding countryside.

Modern economies have evolved from their simple manorial forerunner within a period of five hundred years, and, in important respects, in much less time than that. Various applications of science to agriculture expanded farm output and released labor to other lines of work. This was fundamental, but by no means all. Other major developments have come in fields that we shall call secondary and tertiary and in the performance of services essential to better living.

Secondary industries, especially manufacturing

Secondary industries are those that process materials and put them into useful forms, from packaged foods to automobiles and skyscrapers.

They include all manufacturing and construction activities. In 1946 over 14,000,000 people were engaged in manufacturing in the United States and over 2,000,000 in construction, a total of 17,000,000 or 30 percent of the working population—a proportion somewhat expanded to overcome wartime arrears. Adding the people in primary lines, we observe that less than half of all workers were engaged in getting materials from the earth and putting them into shape to use. This is another striking fact in analyzing the occupational structure of this country.

Handicraft and the domestic system. The story of the development of manufacturing has often been told. In the most primitive economies, making things is the almost incidental home activity of persons chiefly engaged in primary pursuits. Gradually, in all instances of notable economic advance, specialists in *handicraft* have appeared and have often attained an admirable skill. In the medieval and early modern town, the master craftsman was a specialist in making things of a certain material, as of wool or wood or leather or of copper or iron, or he might specialize in a certain product, as in the hatters' trade. But he was not a specialist in particular processes as is the modern factory worker. He not only made the entire product, perhaps assisted by an apprentice or two, but he owned the tools, the materials, the finished product, and probably the shop, and he served as merchant also in disposing of the product.

A degree of functional specialization entered—and with it a suggestion of modern capitalism—when enterprising persons began to buy materials and handle products on a larger scale and to hire artisans to do the processing, and only that. This was the *domestic system,* so called because fabricating could be done at scattered points, even in rural homes, by persons unacquainted with the ways of markets.

The factory system. The bigger break, the sensational change that has been called the Industrial Revolution, came late in the eighteenth century as manufacturing entered the factory. There had been earlier instances of factory production in which perhaps a hundred or more workers were organized to produce cooperatively under a single roof. But modern factory production appeared only as three notable elements were combined: (1) the application to materials of machine techniques in place of manually controlled tools; (2) the specialization of labor in performing limited processes repetitiously; and (3) the use of non-human power, especially the steam engine, in driving the machines. The ordinary worker not only has no responsibility as buyer of materials and seller of products, but he does not own the instruments he uses—the shop and the machines. His work is controlled, and it may be monotonous; but its physical strain has been reduced and its productivity enormously increased.

These fundamentals have changed little since the factory system began. Progress has been great in devising better machines, in providing more effective power (especially electricity), in chemical improvements of materials, and in developing the arts of management. Minor revolutions have come, as when, in mass production, such principles as the interchangeability of parts and the moving assembly line have been introduced. Factories have become much larger, and numbers of plants have sometimes been brought together in single enterprises. But the main lines of development were marked out before 1800.

Little is told of the variety and volume of factory output by counting the persons in the main manufacturing fields. But some light is cast on the kinds of products and activities merely by noting the numbers working on the main types of materials. Thus summarized, the 14,-500,000 in manufacturing in this country in 1946 were engaged as shown in Table 2.[5]

TABLE 2—PERSONS ENGAGED IN MANUFACTURING, 1946
(In millions)

Foods, beverages, tobacco	1.6
Textiles and clothing	2.4
Lumber, furniture, related products	1.1
Paper, paper products, printing, publishing	1.1
Chemical products, products of petroleum and coal	.9
Leather and rubber products	.7
Iron and other metal products—machinery, automobiles, other transportation equipment	5.7
Stone, clay, glass, and miscellaneous products	1.0
Total	14.6

Construction. Outside of manufacturing, the working of materials is mainly the business of the construction industry. Progress in this field has varied widely. Modern steel and concrete construction—as applied to factory and office buildings, to bridges and dams—is a sharp break from the methods that gave rise laboriously to the castles and cathedrals of the past. Holes are dug, hills moved, fields leveled with a power and speed that armies of workmen could not equal. But much of the building of today, especially of ordinary dwellings, is the product of hammer and saw and the laying of brick on brick as it has been for centuries.

[5] Supplement to *Survey of Current Business,* cited in note 2.

Specialization and exchange; tertiary industries

References to specialization have been frequent. Specialization underlies most of the complexity of modern economic organization. A Robinson Crusoe, a complete nonspecialist producing for himself all that he consumes, is part of no organization at all. But if a Friday appears, and if by arrangement Friday catches fish and Crusoe raises vegetables for their common use, specialization has entered and organization is present.

As more different products are produced, each one by specialists, larger numbers of people come to depend upon each other for the goods they use, and organization becomes more involved. As these specialists are located farther and farther apart, greater areas become subject to a single organization. As specialization goes further and the individual performs only a limited operation on a product, as in a factory, the number who are interdependent expands greatly; and problems of organization arise in turning out particular products as well as among the people turning out different products. As greater quantities of products are produced at given points, materials usually have to be brought longer distances and customers served over wider regions.[6]

Thus arises the problem of exchange of goods. Crusoe and Friday pool their efforts in a direct and simple way, and so may the few specialists in a small, closely knit community. But as the exchange involves many people over wide areas, it becomes extremely intricate and constitutes, of necessity, an important segment of the whole organization of production, comparable to the procuring of materials and their fabrication. Thus it is necessary to have specialists in what may be called tertiary industries.

Trade and transportation. In particular, there must be middlemen who assist in transferring goods into the hands of people who will use them and transporters whose function it is to overcome the distance factor in production. In the United States in 1946 more than 10,000,-000 people were middlemen in wholesale and retail lines, and over 3,000,000 were engaged in transportation. Exchange required about half as many people as the primary and secondary lines taken together.

Middlemen become necessary because products are numerous, because each consumer must obtain goods from many different sources, because distance makes difficult knowledge of markets and sources of supply. Direct exchange of limited scope between specialized producers in close contact with each other requires no intermediary. There was no place for a merchant within the manor, though an occasional peddler might bring salt in and take hides away. Artisans in early towns

---

[6] Specialization will be discussed more fully in Chapter 7

could do their own limited selling. As surpluses for trade developed, occasional fairs brought town and country folk into direct contact for the exchange of goods. But as specialization became more complex, professional traders were needed to market the products of shop and farm and to provide ready sources of supply for consumers. The Industrial Revolution was preceded by a century or two of expanding commerce that prepared the way for factory production, both as a general stimulus to enterprise and as an outlet for goods. As production has developed along modern lines, merchants have had a growing place, not only absolutely but in relation to the economy as a whole. Methods of merchandising, moreover, have developed, as is evidenced at the retail level by the appearance of chain stores, mail-order houses, and great department stores.

Transport of goods on backs of men and beasts can serve local needs and be carried on incidentally to other work. Such transportation may even serve a limited trade in luxury goods over wider areas, as over the caravan routes of the East. But for long distances water provided the only satisfactory early avenue of movement, mainly on rivers and between such ports as those of the Mediterranean, and water probably occupied the first transport specialists. A scattering of ships that traversed the oceans typified the spirit and met the needs of the early modern period. Greatly enlarged demand for effective inland transport induced the canal and turnpike building of the late eighteenth and early nineteenth centuries. But only with the adaptation of the steam engine that brought the railroad—and with it a network for the ubiquitous low-cost carriage of all ordinary goods—were the needs of modern industry met. More recently, motor vehicles and modern roads have provided a flexible medium superior for many uses, and airplanes have given swift but costly service to a small tonnage.

It is essential to sense the full logic of this expansion of exchange activities. Trade and transportation are the necessary counterpart of the modern specialized production of natural and manufactured products. Without their development, great regions could not be supplied with foodstuffs, raw materials, and manufactured goods that are produced in places and by methods that are outstandingly productive. Consumer desires could not be met with the fullness and the nicety that modern living implies. Primary, secondary, and tertiary activities are inseparable parts of a single economic whole.

Capitalistic production; finance

At most points specialization is the key word in explaining the growing complexity of production and the occupational structure. Products and processes are multiplied, and more people and places become interdependent, through an unfolding specialization. But further light is thrown on modern organization if we note its capitalistic as well as its specialized character. Production is capitalistic in so far as it involves the use of produced wealth—wealth of human origin—in turning out final products for consumption.

Specialization and capitalistic production must not be confused. Crusoe and Friday specialize when they concentrate, respectively, on growing vegetables and catching fish. But if Friday had never appeared on the island, Crusoe would still have produced capitalistically if he devoted part of his time not directly to obtaining fish and vegetables but to making nets and a boat to help him in fishing or tools and storage places for his gardening. Production becomes capitalistic through the provision of such productively useful forms of wealth.[7]

Plainly wealth of this sort is enormously important in modern production. It includes all the plant and equipment used in manufacturing, all the transport facilities, all the buildings and structures used in merchandising and other fields. It also includes great stocks of materials and fuels and goods-in-process that are necessary in production. Most of the technical ideas that have revolutionized industry in the last two centuries have been usable only as they were embodied in billions of dollars' worth of productive wealth.

The occupational structure of the United States is far more complex than it would be if all workers were engaged in providing goods for final consumption. Millions of persons in manufacturing are involved in producing machines and transport facilities, and numerous construction workers are producing factories, stores, power dams, highways, and other means of modern production. Activities are thus multiplied; and, what is more, the functional picture is complicated by the fact that some goods are produced so that other goods can be produced, perhaps in a lengthy series.

Finance enters the organization of production in promoting its capitalistic character. Large amounts of labor and materials must be brought together to produce buildings and equipment and other capital goods, and they must be paid for before these facilities are ready to produce products to sell. Providing these preliminary funds is the work of finance, and it is a big industry in itself. It comprises various kinds of banks—commercial, savings, and investment—and other institutions that lend money and help in marketing the stocks and bonds of corporations. In 1946 more than half a million people were engaged in these activities in this country. Finance, like trade and transportation, may be classed as a tertiary industry.

[7] Chapter 6 will be devoted to explaining the capitalistic process of production.

Services, public utilities, government

So far, in sketching the organization of production, we have been concerned with physical commodities and the activities that provide them. Most products are of a material, tangible nature, but not all. Quite a number of very important products are transmitted from producer to user without physical embodiment and thus must be consumed at the moment they are made available. Of such nature are the *services* of preachers and teachers, of doctors, dentists, and nurses, of actors and musicians. In this category, also, may be placed the services of barbers, beauticians, and household employees.

In the classification of occupations followed here, the nearly 7,000,000 who were described in 1946 as engaged in the service fields included not only the above but a broad miscellany of other workers. Were it important to insist that the word "services" should be applied strictly to nonmaterial final products, we would exclude some of them and probably quibble about others; but discussion of the niceties of classification can easily become a sterile exercise. Hotel workers may be thought of merely as providing food and shelter or as aiding travel and recreation. Motion-picture workers present a similar difficulty. But some of the included services, as of automobile and house repair, as of auditing and other business aids, as of engineers and many lawyers, are plainly involved, though perhaps indirectly, in making physical commodities available for use.

Another category not previously discussed are the million or more workers in the *public-utility* field outside of transportation. They include the employees of companies providing gas and electricity, telephone and telegraph services, and also radio broadcasts. In part these workers are providing final products to consumers, and in part they are supplying fuel and power and communication service to industry. Their contributions may be analyzed, if one pleases, as belonging partly each in the primary, secondary, and tertiary fields and partly among the services which are nonmaterial final products.

A final group—and now a very important one—is that of *government* employees. The employees of all divisions of government in the United States numbered nearly 9,000,000 in 1946. This was more than three times the number in 1929 but little more than half the wartime peak, when the armed services reached the highest point in history. Such government services as national defense and the maintenance of an orderly society may be thought of as final products. So may educational services, which are performed in this country mainly by persons on government pay rolls. But government also provides aids to business and other economic groups. Its highway workers belong functionally in the transportation field. Employees of government-owned power plants do the same work as the public-utility employees included above, who, despite the use of the word "public," are employees of private industry.

These service, utility, and government activities add greatly to the variety of products. In part they lie within the complex aggregate of primary, secondary, and tertiary functions whose interrelations are the main object of study in any attempt to understand the general organization of production. But in part they lie outside the central maze, attached to it in various incidental ways.

Economic Progress and the Occupational Structure

Colin Clark, an Australian economist, has compared statistically the productive systems of most of the world's nations and has observed a striking relationship between their productivity, the level of living they make possible, and the proportions of the workers in various fields. The most backward nations, where output per person is lowest, show the largest percentage of persons, perhaps 75 or 80 percent, in the primary fields. The most advanced nations, on the other hand, show the lowest fraction in the primary lines and the highest, perhaps as much as half of the whole working force, in tertiary, service, and related activities.[8] This conclusion has been implied in the preceding discussion. It is worth while to look further into the reasons for it and to note what may be called the costs of complexity in the organization of production.

The logic of occupational shifts

Plainly a nation cannot rise in the economic scale simply by shifting workers from farms to stores and railroads. China and India cannot progress by raising less food. Occupational changes are a reflection of progress, not the progress itself. But there is progress in the fact that farming becomes more productive, so that fewer people are needed to feed the population, and thus more people can engage in manufacturing, construction, and the services and thereby expand the variety and volume of products.

Certainly it is not the fact that many persons engage in the tertiary fields, in trade, transportation, and finance, that accounts directly for

---

[8] This analysis appears in his book, *The Conditions of Economic Progress*, Macmillan & Co. Ltd., 1940. Not being quite so much concerned with the functional relationships of activities as we are here, he classifies them a little differently. He uses the word tertiary to cover the whole range of activities which are not primary and secondary, and he puts mining in the secondary category, presumably because of the close relationship of minerals to manufacturing. We shall make further use of Mr. Clark's findings in Part II, where the factors that govern productivity will be examined.

the high level of output in Canada, New Zealand, and the United States. Moving things about and financing their production may easily seem less important than getting materials from the earth and putting them in shape to use. But the point is that, if the primary and secondary industries are to provide goods in the most effective way, they must be served by an elaborate organization in the tertiary fields. Foods and raw materials must be produced in the most suitable areas, and much transporting must be done. Manufactured goods must be produced in quantity by modern methods, and materials and products must often travel far. If consumers everywhere are to have ready access to numerous products from many areas, middlemen have a major task. If great wealth is to be accumulated in the facilities of modern production, much financing must be done. Thus such figures as Mr. Clark's, which show the proportion of workers in tertiary fields, are symptomatic of the degree of progress.

Large numbers in the main service fields are, however, *direct* evidence of high productivity. Poor economies, in which food and other essentials are hard to get, usually allow only a small part of their productive power to be used in promoting health and education or in providing means of recreation and entertainment. The modern utilities that provide light and power and heat and communication to the home are conspicuous only in advanced economies. Transportation, a tertiary field in the organization of commodity production, is prominent also as a means of luxury travel in countries where production averages high. Even merchandising may be expanded beyond the bare requirements of the exchange of goods and cater, in a rich economy, to a love of fine displays and flattering services.

Of course, in an advanced economy the primary and secondary industries also do many things that they cannot do in a backward economy. Varied and costly foods are produced, houses and clothing are provided far beyond bodily needs, cars and radios and numerous other ingenious manufactured goods are made available. It is therefore still more striking that, despite the expansion of output in these commodity lines, an increasing fraction, a larger relative part, of the working force is found in the service fields.

The costs of complex organization

Although the tertiary lines are indicative of progress, they also represent costs that progress entails. If goods could be produced without a great expenditure of effort in exchanging them, modern methods would yield a larger product than they do. To compare the older handicraft with modern machine methods is to derive a first impression that output per man must be hundreds of times greater than it formerly was. But actually only a very small part of the working force is directly engaged in operating power-driven machines. Millions of people must be used in providing the necessary supplementary services in the fields of trade, transportation, and finance.

Millions must be engaged also right within the primary and secondary fields in maintaining the conditions, the general structure, under which modern methods can be used. Especially in manufacturing companies, numerous employees are concerned with transporting and marketing, with record-keeping and planning, with supervision and personnel. Indirect labor is an important part of total labor. Much of manufacture and construction, moreover, is devoted to producing instrumentalities of production—the facilities of modern industry—and to keeping them in shape rather than to providing final products for consumers. Even the provision of fuel and electrical energy for factories, farms, and transportation is an important task.

Thus, despite the miracle of machines, an output per person that is five or ten or twenty times as great as in backward economies, rather than hundreds of times as great, may be all that can be expected. And when it is recognized that the personal and professional services which are increasingly demanded as the level of living rises are the least mechanized of all productive fields, the impact of mechanization is seen to be restricted further.

The effort involved in providing a modern organization is, moreover, not its only cost. Costs of a less definite sort arise from the difficulties of coordination that every complex structure entails. Coordinating forces operate in the *markets* through which the producers and users of goods are brought together, and they are manifest in the use of *money* and in the *pricing* of products and of the means of producing them. The processes and problems of coordination and control are among the most challenging in the study of modern economic life.

This phase of the subject will be set forth in a preliminary way in Chapter 4, in which the main features of capitalism, or of a free-enterprise system, will be examined and the problems that beset it introduced. But it will be useful, first, to examine with care not the structure through which goods are made available but the flow of goods itself, which is the main object of economic effort. This will be the subject of Chapter 3.

The Historical Side of Economics

This chapter will be concluded with a brief aside, a sort of parenthesis, on the historical approach to economics. The chapter has aimed to convey a general sense of the organization of production under modern conditions, together with some data on occupations in the United States. In showing the functional relations of activities, it has seemed useful to suggest how the modern organization has evolved from simpler arrangements. Perhaps the chief aim in studying history is to show the basis and the logic of present arrangements. The past, if viewed imaginatively, can set off the present with dramatic effect. On the well-known idea that no creature knows less about water than the fish, we must somehow get outside our own environment if we are to appreciate it. History serves this purpose. So also does an examination of the present economies of other, especially of backward, countries.

This is said not because a great deal of economic history will be included in this volume but because very little of it will be included. Time and space are lacking. There will be some description of present arrangements, and many pages will be devoted to explaining them and the problems growing out of them. But history will be neglected. If supplementary reading is done, some of it can well be done in the economic annals of this and other lands.[9]

It is true that economists differ in the value they see in approaching economic problems historically. Often historical introductions to present problems are annoying because their purpose seems largely decorative. They promote erudition but not insight. If the aim is to understand the present, time can easily be wasted on historical detail. We build fences, as one fine old teacher loved to declare, not because our grandfathers did but to keep the cows in.[10] Certainly the facts and logic of a present situation are more revealing in discovering how to handle it than any examination of the past can be.

But judicious use of history can greatly enrich one's understanding of present institutions and problems. Beyond the uses made of it in this chapter, it often provides a sort of laboratory in which the behavior of people can be examined under conditions so closely paralleling the present that much light is shed on present problems. Thus wartime inflation can be better understood through close acquaintance with similar inflation in the past. Labor disputes can be approached more

[9] The literature in this field is extensive. The following books represent a variety of approaches to it: Russell A. Dixon and E. Kingman Eberhart, *Economics and Cultural Change*, McGraw-Hill, 1938; Herbert Heaton, *Economic History of Europe*, Harper & Bros., 1936; Clive Day, *History of Commerce*, Longmans, Green, 1926; Chester W. Wright, *Economic History of the United States*, McGraw-Hill, 1941; Harold F. Williamson, *The Growth of the American Economy*, Prentice-Hall, 1944; John George Glover and William Bouck Cornell (editors), *The Development of American Industries*, Prentice-Hall, 1946.

[10] The late Professor Fred M. Taylor, whose knowledge of history greatly exceeded that of most economists.

constructively through knowledge of the labor movement and the basis of the attitudes of contending parties. Matters of monopoly, employment, taxation and public debt, indeed nearly all the economic problems that concern us, can be grasped more fully and judged more accurately if the lessons of experience have been studied in their historical setting.

Moreover, in a more general way, acquaintance with the past brings balance and maturity of view. For both the blind reactionary and the callow revolutionary, a generous dose of history is excellent medicine. The wise individual senses keenly both the elements of continuity and of change in economic life. He sees that existing arrangements are too deep-rooted to be wiped away; but that they are neither so excellent nor so inevitable that they should be accepted reverently and without question. While freely critical, he will not expect perfection in human affairs and will not, therefore, enlarge the deficiencies of an imperfect present by setting it against the blueprint of a Utopian future. He will appreciate the human side of human arrangements and not look upon the reform of economic institutions as a problem in mechanical reconstruction, as some technically minded reformers appear to do. He will see that economic, political, and social factors are inseparable and will not attempt to solve economic problems by the direct application of economic logic alone.

With these cautions, if not with the historical study that would support them, we shall proceed now with an examination of the flow of products toward which progress in the organization of production is directed.

Review Questions

1. "Economic organization, whether primitive or modern, rests on two underlying sets of facts." Explain.

2. "Ten million unemployed out of fifty million workers is a serious matter. But if factory executives would reduce working hours moderately, the situation could be taken care of quite well." Show that the speaker was poorly informed regarding the size of occupational classes in this country.

3. "The prominence of manufactured goods in modern living is, in part, the result of progress in manufacturing; but it is also the result of progress in agriculture." Explain the second clause.

4. From 1870 to 1930 the working population of the United States increased from 12,925,000 to 48,830,000 persons. At the same time the number of agricultural workers increased from 6,850,000 to 10,472,000. Show percentagewise what happened to the absolute and the relative position of agriculture in the American economy. What light is thrown on the economic development of the country?

5. Trace the principal stages in the evolution of manufacturing, bringing out the distinctive features of each stage.

6. "The story of economic development may be told, very largely, in terms of increasing specialization." Show clearly the elements in economic organization that are related in one way or another to specialization; show how they are related.

7. Between 1870 and 1930 persons engaged in trade in the United States increased from 6.8 to 12.5 percent of the working population, and persons in transportation and communication from 4.2 to 7.9 percent. To have a high volume of physical commodities per consumer, would it not have been better if the high relative growth had taken place in providing materials and fabricating them?

8. "It is a corollary of economic progress that increasing numbers of people should have come to live in towns and cities." Explain.

9. Distinguish sharply between specialization and capitalistic production. In what connection are they linked together?

10. At what point in the organization of production does finance enter?

11. Distinguish the main classes of occupations in the "service" category. What is the point of considering whether or not they are related to the production of physical commodities?

12. "The relative numbers of workers in the primary, secondary, tertiary, and service fields throw much light on the stage of economic progress that a nation has achieved." Explain carefully.

13. One writer observes that each of us, on the average, is today served by forty mechanical slaves not possessed by our forefathers of a few centuries ago. He goes on to express surprise that, with this multiplication of working power, we have not raised the level of production by a great deal more than we have. Show that such a surprise indicates a superficial view of the organization of production. Bring out clearly the matters that need to be taken into account in appraising the total effectiveness of modern methods.

14. Distinguish the historical and the analytical approach to contemporary problems. What seem to be their respective merits?

15. "A keen sense of the elements both of continuity and of change in economic life should improve the thinking and attitudes both of radicals and conservatives." What is meant? Do you agree?

‒ 3 ‒

Production and Income—
Individual and National

Between the Civil War and the depression of the 1930s the total product of the United States expanded eightfold. With population nearly tripling, output per person also nearly tripled. The same idea is expressed by saying that the national income of this country was multiplied by eight and the per-capita income almost by three.[1]

The flow of products and income—from the social standpoint, a single stream—is of central importance in the study of economics. It is on this flow that economic welfare depends. The principal mark of economic progress is a rising plane of living made possible by an expanding flow of goods.

In the preceding chapter we looked broadly at the developing occupational structure characteristic of economic progress. Now, after a brief inspection of the idea of progress, we shall consider the meaning and the measurement of production and income, examining certain relationships necessary to an understanding of them. Somewhat incidentally at the end of the chapter we shall examine the concept of wealth and its relation to income.

Economic Aims and Standards

Are we justified in assuming that goods for consumption, which determine the level of living, are the *actual* object of economic effort,

[1] See Simon Kuznets, *National Income: A Summary of Findings*, pp. 31–39. This book is one of a series by the National Bureau of Economic Research. Part of the eightfold expansion, perhaps one-third of it, represents not an increase in productivity in particular fields but the shift from agriculture to other fields that was discussed in the preceding chapter. Production statistics are corrected for changes in the value of the dollar from one year to another but not for shifts from industries in which output per worker has a low value to industries in which the value is greater. See *Ibid.*, pp. 48–49. For other corrections in interpreting this figure, see note 3 below.

and then in proceeding on that basis to analyze economic behavior? More important, are we right in viewing the level of living as the *proper* economic goal, and thus in judging economic practices and policies by their effects on production and income? Both assumptions have been questioned and deserve comment.

Varied motives but similar behavior

Economic aims become more complex as people rise in the economic scale. If the most that can be achieved is a bare subsistence, then goods to live on—essential food, clothing, and shelter—are the unavoidable goal. Likewise, when a surplus above subsistence becomes available, the conception of satisfactory living—what is known in economics as the *standard of living*—rises, and a larger quantity of goods is sought. But with rising productivity there is room also for some diversity of aims.

Goods may be sought not only for the direct satisfaction of consuming them but through vanity in being seen to consume them—"conspicuous consumption," as Thorstein Veblen called it. The real aim may not even be consumption in the sense of use but sheer possession or accumulation—whether in the money of the miser, the jewels of the Indian prince, or the securities of the American capitalist. Or satisfaction may be found in winning an economic game in which dollars are the counters. Or the aim in part may be the prestige and power that accompany success. Or, again, it may be a desire to improve the lives of other people.

The motives behind economic behavior undoubtedly differ, but probably actual economic behavior does not differ greatly because of them; the several ends call for about the same course of action. In a modern specialized economy, all of these purposes require effective production for the market in order to get money income and the power to obtain goods. Whether adequate consumption is the only goal, or whether producers are also influenced by love of the game or of power or of mere accumulation, the same road for the most part must be traveled. It is behavior along this road with which economics is mainly concerned and not the reasons why people travel it.

This is something of an oversimplification, since account must be taken of the satisfactions people get from their work and the conditions under which they work, as well as of their output and their return. But in economics attention centers mainly on production and income.

Judgments of economic achievement

Production and income are the focus of attention in economics not only in explaining economic behavior but also in judging it. Progress is seen to lie in an increasing command over goods, and economic practices and policies are judged accordingly.

But progress in this economic sense, it is important to recognize, is not always accepted as progress in the broadest social sense. Economic achievement is often belittled as standing low in the full scale of human values or even as a positive obstacle to higher types of achievement. From the Biblical dictum regarding love of money as the root of all evil, through Thoreau's view of business as the meanest of pursuits, to more recent blasts at a civilization preoccupied with streamlined cars and bathtubs and with keeping up with the Joneses, many social critics have found little to commend in economic aims and behavior.

Accordingly it should be borne in mind that economics, in dealing with things exchangeable for money, does not hold economic welfare to be equivalent to human welfare as a whole. Of course the "good life" involves much more than making a living. And economics does not oppose the belief that many things in the economic sphere are out of harmony with a higher set of human values. It welcomes the efforts of moralists, philosophers, and religious leaders to apply these higher values to economic institutions and merely asks that the critics make a responsible effort to understand the matters they discuss. The love of money, for example, may be condemned without denying the essential role of money in a specialized society.

As much as it can, economics tries to avoid rendering ethical judgments, but one basic ethical assumption, nevertheless, is present. It is the assumption that more goods are preferable to fewer goods; that when labor is expended and materials are used, it is better to have a large product than a small one. The very word *economy* implies a primary concern over the ratio of output to input. The word *progress* is applied to an expanding production and to a higher level of living resting on economic goods. Business methods, labor practices, public policies are criticized when they obstruct the flow of goods and approved when they further it.

Even here some economists would be careful to say that they are merely examining the implications of the economic goal and not really endorsing it. But most economists undoubtedly believe that economic welfare is not only consistent with human welfare in the broadest sense but can positively further it. Certainly the critics who dismiss all economic striving as purely materialistic miss much of the point of economic achievement. The real materialism is that of backward peoples who grind their lives away in getting the bare essentials of living and have neither time nor energy for anything else. Perhaps increased productivity is often absorbed in gadgets and crude display, but it need not be. The quest for increased income may be the quest for freedom from the demands of animal existence, for the infusion of ordinary living with esthetic elements, for adequate medical care, for education and the arts, for opportunities to travel and to participate in community affairs. All rest on an economic basis. Much can be done in improving the uses made of economic progress; but here the higher criticism must be careful lest, in demanding for people what they ought to have, it lose touch with what they really want.[2] Into this we need not go.

Of course, the very idea that people are better off with more goods can be denied. Poverty, the complete lack of worldly things beyond the barest essentials, may be thought necessary to virtue. Self-denial, even self-chastisement, have been looked upon as holy. Or work itself may be thought good, even ennobling, and "the fruits of work," as Hindu scripture has it, "should never be your motive in working."

In the face of such beliefs, economics offers no defense of its conception of progress. One may have one's beliefs. Merely as observers of human behavior now and in the past, economists may generally question the bent toward saintliness of average human beings. Some, but not because they are economists, may even lean a little to the view with which Dr. Johnson has been charged that "there are few ways in which a man can be more innocently employed than in getting money." But their basis of judgment, economists would insist, is not money but the goods money will buy, the flow of products on which economic welfare depends. Economics assumes without proof that such welfare is worth while and attempts to analyze its nature and the conditions of its achievement.

The economic standard amplified. The present chapter will go into the nature of the flow of goods and its measurement, viewed both as product and as income. But this primary emphasis must not convey the impression that only the size of the flow is important. Economic welfare has other aspects.

Production should be steady and income should be dependable. Instability of output means not only loss of output but also a sense of insecurity that in itself reduces well-being. *Income security* has been increasingly stressed in recent years as a major goal. This chapter will contain some data on income variation.

Important, along with the flow of products, is their division, their *distribution* among the people. Economic welfare implies that all

[2] It is charged that capitalism both causes undue preoccupation with economic ends and distorts tastes as between economic ends. These criticisms will be noted in the discussion of demand and consumer problems in Chapter 19.

people should live on an acceptable plane and not merely that the aggregate income should be high.

Important, also, is the make-up of the aggregate. Progress consists in part in extending the *variety of goods,* especially as total output expands well beyond the physical requirements of people. There must be adequate provision in economic organization for adapting the kinds of goods to the wants of the people, providing them in the most *satisfactory proportions.*

But the flow of products, even when these several requirements are fully covered, does not meet all the tests of economic welfare. There are at least two others. One is that there should be *adequate leisure* to enjoy the products and to pursue other human interests. As productivity increases, progress should take the joint form, in suitable balance, of additional products and additional leisure.

The other is that the *conditions of work* should be made as satisfactory as possible. When eight hours a day or thereabouts are devoted to making a living, these eight hours are part of living; and the effectiveness of economic arrangements must be judged in part by the pleasure which the job affords and by the fatigue and irksomeness that it entails. Workmen want the opportunity to act and to develop; they require a sense of harmony in their relationships. Industry must be judged not only by its productivity but by its effect on the lives of the people who work in it.

Immediately, however, we are concerned with understanding the flow of products and the income it provides.

Economic Goods and Production

Thus far, in speaking of goods, production, and income, it has been sufficient to rely on everyday meanings of these terms or on the context to convey the intended meaning. But terms—and the concepts behind them—are instruments of analysis, and real understanding of economics required precision in using them. If concepts are approached not as mere verbal formulations to be memorized but as tools of thinking, the learning of them requires much insight into the situations to which they apply and their application to those situations. When terminology is fully understood, much of economics will have been learned. It is from this standpoint that we now approach the main concepts used in discussing the flow of goods on which economic welfare depends.

First we should look more closely at this word *economic*. Not everything in the world, indeed by no means everything of human importance, is economic. It is sometimes said that things that are economic are exchangeable for money; but this is only a superficial earmark. Why are some things exchangeable for money and others not? What, in short, are *economic goods?*

The flow of economic goods, which is the basis of economic welfare, results from a process called *production.* In ordinary discourse, activities are viewed favorably when they are called productive, unfavorably when called unproductive. For purposes of analysis, what meaning should be attached to the word production?

These questions set the task of the present section. In the section that follows, production will be examined quantitatively and with reference to the income it yields.

Economic goods

There is need in economics for a term to cover the whole area of economic things—for a common term to use in speaking of the results of production, of the means of production, of possessions and accumulations. All such things, which are to economics what matter is to the physical sciences, are called *economic goods.*

Goods and utility. Many things in the world are not *goods* at all, let alone being economic goods. Elements in the earth unknown to man, sand and rock and vegetation to which man is indifferent, weeds and pests and diseases hateful to man, are not goods. But the word *good,* as here used, does not imply virtue or benefit. To be a good, the only test a thing must meet is that it must be *wanted* by human beings. Whisky, for example, is a good, however bad many people think it is. The quality of a good which causes it to be wanted is said to be its *utility*—a word that does not imply usefulness in any workaday sense but only *wantedness.* If terms are to be used in describing and explaining the economic life of man as it is, they must not be limited in scope by tests of what ought to be.

Scarcity. Not all goods are economic. Air, the most immediately essential good to man, is not economic under the ordinary circumstances of its use. Economic goods must not only have utility; they must also be *scarce.* If goods are available, like air, without human effort and in quantities so great that people can directly consume all they want, then they are not scarce. If nature does not provide them directly in such abundance, all desires for them cannot be satisfied, and decisions have to be made as to how to use them and how to get the most out of them. Then they are scarce—and economic—and the process of getting the most out of them is the essence of *economizing.* Most goods are not provided directly by nature at all, but various steps have to be taken to make them available. If the resources used in getting them are scarce, if work must be done—effort put forth other than in the spirit of play—in order to get them, the resulting goods will be scarce —and economic. Scarcity, in this sense, must underlie every economic situation.

The meaning of scarcity should be noted carefully, since there has been some confusion regarding it. It has been said, for instance, that we are now able to enjoy an "economy of abundance," in contrast with the "economy of scarcity" of the past, and references have been made to a "scarcity economics" that is said to be outmoded, if not positively vicious. These phrases may seem impressive, but in fact they are only a fancy way of saying that productive power is greater than it used to be, and that a fairly high level of living is possible for everyone if we use that power sensibly, avoiding practices that restrict its use, or promote scarcity artificially.

Such phrases cannot mean that we are no longer confronted with scarcity, as that word has always been used in economics. For if scarcity in the usual sense were absent, all goods would be as freely available as air is. All the wants of modern Americans would be met on the Garden-of-Eden principle, and excellent food and clothing, fine homes, cars, yachts, medical service, an abundance of everything desired, would be available just for the taking. This is what abundance must mean if abundance is the opposite of scarcity, and scarcity is used in the economist's sense. But with this meaning, the idea of an "economy of abundance" would be nonsense. With abundance, there would be no economizing, no economic activity, and no economics. Scarcity is the distinctive feature of economic situations; and economics is concerned with human behavior in the face of it.

Transferability. We have almost defined the boundaries of economic goods when we say that they are scarce—which implies, incidentally, that they must be wanted, must have utility. But the boundaries must still be contracted and tightened somewhat to exclude a variety of things, both wanted and scarce, that do not belong in the economic realm. Examples would include the occasional sunshine in a generally cloudy region, the friendship we prize but find too rare, the smile that is said to be worth a million dollars but is not economic at all. To be economic, a good must have a certain manageable quality which enables individuals to take definite possession of it and transfer possession to others. For one reason or another, the examples just given lack this quality. For want of a more exact term, we may call it *transferability*.

Precise terminology is not so important that a test need be inserted to exclude smiles and sunshine from the economic realm; but a test is necessary to distinguish human services which are economic goods from human abilities which are not. In doing an operation, a surgeon performs a service that is transferred in the sense that any product is transferred from producer to consumer. But the ability or the skill of the surgeon, however important and however scarce it may be, still belongs to him after the operation is performed and does not itself enter into the activities and the transactions of economic life. This distinction between human capacities and the use made of those capacities is of general application.

One may argue that it is arbitrary to exclude human abilities from the category of economic goods. Abilities enter into economic calculations, as when one considers whether it is worth while to incur the cost of education necessary to develop a skill. They are part of the nation's productive power, and it is arguable that they should be counted in the nation's wealth, just as natural resources and plant and equipment are counted. But the practice, nevertheless, is to exclude them. An immediate reason is that any statistical measure of them would be largely guesswork—a difficulty arising from the fact that the market places no value on goods which are not transferred. A deeper reason lies in the dual relation of human beings to economic life. People are producers; but they are also the beneficiaries of production, the occasion for all economic activity. There is a suggestion that they are merely means, rather than ends, in the idea that their personal qualities, inseparable from them, are economic goods. Only in a slave society, in which human beings are bought and sold, can human abilities have full recognition as economic goods.

Value. Economic goods, being wanted, scarce, and transferable, have *value* in the economic sense. In wide areas of economic analysis, value is their chief attribute. If economic concepts were to be ranked in importance, doubtless value, along with income, would stand at the top. *Prices,* which provide the basis for the exchange of goods in markets, express values in money terms. When we say, then, that economics is concerned with things that are exchangeable for money, we are saying that it is concerned with all the things that people want that are scarce and can be transferred.

Production

Any act or process is productive that *helps to make economic goods available*. Or we may define production as adding utility to economic goods. The productive act may be performed by people, as in mining coal or making textiles, or it may be an act of material resources, as of land in growing crops or supporting a factory building, or of a machine shaping metals or an engine pulling a train. The product may be any kind of economic good. It may be a tangible, material thing, like a loaf of bread or an automobile, or it may be a nonmaterial service, like the music of an orchestra or the sermon of a preacher. The productive process may be related to the product directly or indirectly and may or may not alter its physical nature. In producing the loaf of bread, farming contributed by raising the wheat, manufacturing by milling the flour and baking the bread, transportation by moving wheat and flour and bread, merchandising by furthering a succession of exchanges, banking by providing funds to mobilize resources. Behind these activities were others that helped to make them possible, especially the production of equipment.

All of these processes perform necessary roles, and it should not be said, therefore, that one of them is more productive than another. This point is worth stressing, because it is often implied that the farmers and miners and lumbermen who take materials from the earth or the manufacturers who put them into useful forms are the only true producers, whereas others, like transporters and middlemen, merely shift products about without adding to them. Such a view misses the real nature of production. The essence of production lies in making goods available to satisfy wants, not in adding to matter—that cannot be done—nor in manipulating matter. To satisfy your desires for an orange for breakfast, it is as necessary that the orange be transported from the orange grove as that it be grown.

"Production and distribution." It may be convenient, however, in talking about production to distinguish its various aspects—as we did in the preceding chapter in speaking of primary, secondary, and tertiary activities. Often businessmen speak of the "production and distribution" of goods in order to distinguish marketing processes from the getting and shaping of materials. But when used in this way, the phrase implies that marketing is not a part of production, though the businessmen who use it would not accept the idea that merchants and transporters are not producers.

The phrase may also mislead in its use of the word *distribution*. In its principal use in economics, distribution refers to a division or sharing, as when we speak of inequality in the distribution of income or wealth. Distribution in this sense has nothing to do with the tertiary lines of production to which the businessman is referring. No confusion need arise from these varied usages as long as people are clearly aware of them. Economic terms have not been mastered until there is an almost habitual awareness of meanings in such circumstances.

Making money without producing. But while the term production should be used broadly, one should not conclude that every way of making a living is productive. Theft is not productive, nor are those means of acquisition known as racketeering. Goods so obtained have utility to the people who acquire them; but the means of getting them does not add to their utility or expand the total flow of goods.

Likewise monopoly income that comes from arbitrary restriction of supply cannot be credited to production. Those medieval spice importers who, after sounding out the market, dumped part of their cargo into the harbor to increase the price, may have managed to expand their money return, but the process by which they did it should be described as destruction not as production. Positive destruction of goods is unusual; but whenever industrialists or their employees, through some form of market control, restrict output to expand income, their additional income does not reflect added production.

These are clear cases. Others are not so clear. It has been debated, for instance, whether advertising as now carried on is productive. Certainly its productivity should not be questioned in so far as it informs buyers regarding products and how to get them. But when the public is bombarded with the baseless, or wholly unilluminating, claims of rival products, the contribution of advertising—if there is one—is obscured.

Or one may ask what the product is of the paid employees of pressure groups organized solely to divert income to their members. The services of these people are not final products wanted on their own account, nor do they seem to add indirectly to the total of such products. Perhaps the best case that can be made for them, from the standpoint of production—and the same can be said for the more dubious part of advertising—is that they are an incidental but unavoidable part of an entire system of institutions that, on the whole, is accepted and approved. In specific situations this may be a perfectly valid line of reasoning.

Much more dubious are incomes from products that are salable only through misrepresentation—the patent medicine that no informed person would buy or the repair performed on the automobile to remove a nonexistent defect. But even here, a sharp distinction is not easy to draw between what is and what is not productive. It will be remembered that economics does not set up a standard of what people ought to want but counts as goods all the things that they do want. Thus the patent medicine may be desired, whether or not it should be, and providing it may thus be deemed productive. But this reasoning is not conclusive. It may still be said that there is no contribution to utility when the sole basis of the want is the false claims of the supplier of the article.

These examples of the shady margin between productive and non-productive activities are presented for two reasons. One purpose is to induce a critical attitude toward ways of making a living to supplement the broad conception of production previously developed. The other purpose is to illustrate a common difficulty in all definition and classification. In the study of society, as in the study of nature, material can seldom be analyzed, distinctions can seldom be made, without running into borderline cases that are difficult to place. Most items fall easily into one category or another, but a few items fall between. The latter scarcely detract at all from the usefulness of concepts and are harmful only when they cause senseless quibbling and divert attention from the main theme. Definition is never an end in itself, but concepts should be developed that will be useful tools of analysis. The concept of production is such a tool.

Measurement of production. Some statistics of production in the United States will appear in the following section on income. These statistics should be interpreted in light of the difficulties in measuring production to be noted now.

Products are actual economic goods, but for most purposes they cannot be measured in *physical units* related to their nature and use. It is possible to compare in bushels the production of wheat in 1940 and 1948; but there is no useful physical unit in which wheat production can be compared with beef production in 1948 or with the production of automobiles or of men's clothing. Even for the same product, output in two periods cannot be compared in physical units unless the product is standardized. For example, to count the number of machine tools produced would scarcely provide a significant fact.

A physical factor common to different products is the *amount of labor* employed in producing them. Thus, in Chapter 2 comparisons were made by saying that 7,000,000 workers were engaged in producing farm products, 3,000,000 in transportation, 6,000,000 in metal manufacturing, over 2,000,000 in making textiles and clothes. But while measurement on a worker basis is useful in explaining the occupational structure of the United States, it is not appropriate in the measurement of output. For one thing, the type and quality of labor differ greatly among industries—as between textile mills and building construction, for instance. For another, labor is aided quite unequally by natural resources in different fields and by equipment of all kinds. Output per worker is high where production is highly mechanized.

For these reasons, and perhaps others, statistics of production commonly rest on *value units* rather than on physical units. Value is the universal economic characteristic of goods, and, when expressed in money terms, it provides a suitable basis for all sorts of summations and comparisons involving different products, groups of products, and different years.

Value, however, is not a perfect basis for production statistics. Value measures have several defects that should be borne in mind:

1. Value measures may include some ways of getting private income which are not genuinely productive. The activities of the thief may not be reflected in the statistics, but those of the monopolist are. In industries in which artificial restriction of output has raised the prices of goods, these prices are the basis of measuring output.

2. Entirely apart from artificial price raising, value measures may give a poor impression of the utilities created in different fields. The reason, again, is that scarcity as well as utility affects value. Take an extreme example. Suppose that in one year the potato crop is worth $200,000,000 (representing 400,000,000 bushels at 50 cents each) and the wheat crop is worth $600,000,000 (representing 600,000,000 bushels at $1 each). Thus the potato crop is worth one third as much as the wheat crop. Then suppose that in the next year the potato crop falls off by 25 percent and the price doubles to $1, whereas the wheat situation remains unchanged. Now the value of the potato crop is $300,000,-000 (representing 300,000,000 bushels at $1). Potatoes, by becoming less plentiful, have risen from one third to one half of the value of the wheat crop. It is true, from a want-satisfying standpoint, that each bushel of potatoes is more important than before, but it is not true that the potato crop, by becoming smaller, came closer to the wheat crop in total want-satisfying importance.

3. Value measures are also defective in comparing the production of different years, because of changes in the value—or purchasing power—of the money unit in which values are expressed. Statistics can be corrected for this defect, but it is important to be aware when using them whether they have been corrected or whether they rest directly on the current prices of the years to which they apply.

4. Products may escape the statistics altogether when they are not sold and the market never puts a value on them. In some cases, such as the production of food that is consumed right on the farm, estimates are likely to be made. But such activities as the preparation of food and the laundering of clothes in the home are not recognized, though like activities in restaurants and commercial laundries are.[3]

[3] Omission of nonmarketed products distorts some statistical comparisons. For example, the fact that baking, canning, and sewing were once done extensively in the home and

These defects in the measurement of production appear also in the measurement of income.

Review Questions

1. "It is much too simple to say that people engage in economic activity because they want the satisfactions from consuming goods. Economic motivation is more complex." Do you agree? Explain.

2. "The task of the economist is simplified by the fact that diverse motives often lead to similiar behavior." Explain.

3. What is the main ethical assumption of economics? Does it fit in with the prevailing attitude of people in this country? Does it seem objectionable from the standpoint of the highest human interests? What do you think of the charge that our society is unduly materialistic? If you agree with this charge, would you argue that economics should alter its basic assumption?

4. "Abundance of goods is the primary economic goal. But for production and income to be satisfactory, more is required than a high aggregate output." Explain.

5. What else does economic welfare involve beside goods?

6. Is each of the following a good: influenza, a roulette table, air, bread, a surgeon's skill, the services of a surgeon? Explain why or why not. Is each of them an economic good? Explain.

7. "The emphasis of economics is pernicious. It is concerned only with things that are scarce, whereas human betterment is promoted by abundance." Explain the relationship of economics to scarcity.

8. "If abundance is the opposite of scarcity, and scarcity is used in the economic sense, the phrase 'economy of abundance' is a contradiction in terms." Explain.

9. It may be convenient to say that economics is concerned with things exchangeable for money, but what are the characteristics that things must have to possess this earmark? How is the value concept related to your answer?

10. "The baker of bread is more productive than the maker of jewelry, and he is certainly more productive than the retailer who handles his bread or the banker who lends him money." Comment critically. For purposes of economic analysis, what should production mean?

11. "I would call the farmer and the manufacturer productive, and perhaps even the railroad that moves their product. But certainly the barber and the actor and the doctor produce nothing. They merely share in the income from other people's products." What is the specific error in this view?

12. "When the business phrase 'production and distribution' is examined according to the use of these words in economics, the meaning of production

now are done commercially for the most part means that statistics of production show a rate of growth which exaggerates the real expansion in the flow of products. The same defect appears in comparisons of output between advanced and backward nations. For a discussion of the problems of interpreting production and income statistics, see Simon Kuznets, *op. cit.*, Part IV.

seems to be narrowed and the meaning of distribution seems to be broadened." Explain.

13. What points need to be considered in judging the productivity of advertising? Of monopolists? Of lobbyists?

14. Why must production ordinarily be measured in value terms? Why may value not always be a perfect basis of measurement? Point out several necessary cautions in interpreting production statistics.

Income—Individual, Business, and National

Product and income are opposite sides of the same coin. The word "product," or "output," implies that something is being put forth or made available. The word "income" implies that something is coming in or becoming available. As seen by the whole community of interdependent producers and consumers, the same stream of goods is both product and income.

Looked at in detail, the production-income process is less simple. It proceeds through countless transactions of a variety of types and through the intervention of money. And it appears in different light when viewed from the standpoint of individual producers and consumers, of business enterprises, and of the nation as a whole. Since economic welfare must be judged in terms of this process, it is one of the first things to be grasped in studying economics.

Flows of services, products, and money

The complexities are quite manageable if we admit them gradually. The simplest case, of course, is that of the Crusoe who applies his labor to the production of a few goods which, in turn, directly become his income. There is no difficulty in seeing that the same stream of goods is both product and income.

The identity is also apparent in the case of a small, primitive community in which a few *specialists* apply their labor to different products and then *exchange* them through direct barter. Now the particular product of the individual does not constitute his income. We may say, instead, that his income consists of the products of others which his product commands in exchange. Or we may say that it consists in the *command over goods* that his product gives him. But certainly, if we view the situation from the standpoint of all the specialists together, the total product of all of them constitutes the income of them all.

When *money* is introduced into this situation as a medium of exchange, it does not change the essentials of the production-income process at all, but it may cause people to think of their incomes in a different way. Since money is received for products and used to buy products, money received is likely to be thought of as income. It measures very simply the command over goods that the producer enjoys. From the collective standpoint, moreover, it may be convenient to think of the aggregate of these money receipts as *measuring* the total product and the total income. But, very clearly, the plane of living depends on the goods and not the money.

The next complicating factor is the *business firm,* or producing organization. When an individual produces the complete product himself and sells it, the firm does not enter. But when an individual, as a businessman or enterpriser, hires the labor of several other persons, buys materials and supplies, perhaps leases land and borrows capital, and combines all these elements together in producing a product that he sells, a new entity has entered the income picture. We may say that the product is produced by the firm, but actually it is a cooperative result of all these combined elements. The money received from the sale of the product cannot now be viewed as income to the firm but only as gross receipts or sales revenue. Most of it will be paid out for labor, for the use of land and capital, for materials and supplies. Selling products and receiving income from them are now not quite identical. The product is sold by the firm; the income is received by suppliers of services to the firm.

The purchase of materials and supplies introduces the further complication that some products enter other products and that goods may pass through a *series of transactions* before they reach the final user. A farm grows wheat and sells it to an enterprise that operates grain elevators; this firm sells it to a miller; the miller, after processing it, sells it in the form of flour to a distributor who passes it on to a baker; the bakery turns it into bread which it sells to a retailer; and the retailer finally gets the fully processed wheat to the consumer. In addition, transportation services must be purchased at several stages and also the services of banks, insurance companies, power companies, and others. Moreover, equipment bought from still other companies will be used by all these parties to the production of a loaf of bread.

Opposite flows of goods and money. This complex production-income process may be thought of as consisting of two circular flows: one of productive services and products and one of money. In the former, individuals provide labor and the services of wealth which, through a series of stages, go into products, and the products, also after several steps, go to consumers. These consumers who get the products are, broadly, the same people who provided the productive services.

The money circuit moves in the opposite direction. Consumers, the final buyers of products, make payments to the firms that sell them, and these payments sift back through antecedent firms. At each stage part of the payments lodges in the hands of workers and business owners and lenders of capital as income for their contribution to the productive process. But, again, the suppliers of these services are, broadly, the very people who as consumers buy the final product. The money they receive as producers they spend as buyers of goods.

Transactions *versus* **income.** Care is necessary to see the relationship of these money payments to the value of products and the amount of income. Transactions may add up to $5 or more in getting a $1 product produced from beginning to end; but the $1 still sets the limit to the total value of productive services all along the line and to all the incomes received from them. It is the nature of money to circulate as goods change hands, and some of the elements in final products change hands several times. Not literally, but essentially, the same $1 is moving back and being divided up to reward all the participants.

But it is equally important to see the separateness of products and incomes when they are separate. The farmer uses some of his income from the wheat to buy a radio. The miller uses some of his income from the flour to pay his butler. The money may be the same, but these purchases are being made with true money income, not just with sales revenue. Radios and butler services are independent final products, and no part of the wheat-flour-bread productive process. That the money is the same is an irrelevant fact in measuring product and income.

Whatever the complications, the essentials of the production-income process remain the same. Goods flow from producers to consumers, and these goods are products from the one viewpoint and income from the other. But to sense this over-all picture is only one purpose in the present study. More specific problems as to the nature and measurement of income must be considered in the way they appear to the individual, the firm, and the nation as a whole.

Income to the individual

Individuals receive income from a number of services and in a number of forms. The largest part of it comes from labor service as performed by employees of business firms. Labor is paid for in wages and salaries, and sometimes in commissions and fees. Individuals also get income in the form of interest by lending their savings and in the form of rent for the use of land and other wealth. Or they may use their wealth and energies as enterprisers in some undertaking and receive their income in the form of business profits, a residual after expenses are met. If the enterprise is organized as a corporation, it is said to receive the profit; and the income turned over to the owners, or stockholders, is called dividends. These sources and forms of income will be analyzed in Part VI.

Income, whatever the form, must be measured in relation to *time*. The workman may be paid so much per piece or unit of performance; but his wage is significant primarily as the return for his services for a specified period and as his means of support for that period. Income payments may be expressed on an hourly, weekly, or monthly basis, but for most purposes income per year is the more useful expression.

From the individual standpoint, is it sufficient to view income simply as a net *money* return per unit of time? We have seen that receipt of money is a distinctly subordinate part of the process by which individuals in a complex society obtain goods for the satisfaction of their wants. But the money-income form provides an easy, convenient way to express one's economic reward and to measure the quantity of goods of all kinds that one is able to obtain. It is quite acceptable for most purposes; but its two serious deficiencies should be appreciated.

Defects of money-income concept. One of these deficiencies appears in the case of people who receive part of their income *in kind*—that is, directly in the form of goods. Certainly the food that farm families grow and consume is part of their income, even though it is obtained without the intervention of money. The preacher should include in his income the rental value of the parsonage that he is supplied. Men in the armed services who receive food, clothes, and lodging without charge have incomes much larger than the money they are paid. Even in our money-using economy, not all income is received in money form.

The other deficiency arises from the *changing value of money*. A person who received a $3000 salary in 1940 and a $4000 salary in 1948 has enjoyed a rise in income in money terms, but actually his income has fallen. With prices rising by more than 70 percent during this period, the $4000 will buy less in 1948 than the $3000 would in 1940. The final test of income is the goods that can be obtained, and money-income expressions must often be corrected to allow for the changing value of money.

Real income; command over goods. To overcome these defects of the money-income concept, economists have often substituted the concept of *real income*. The word "real" is used extensively in economics to focus attention not on money and money measures but on the things for which money stands and for which it can be exchanged. Real income, as usually interpreted, consists of the goods for which money income is spent and of goods received directly as payment for services.

It is better, however, not to go quite this far in departing from the concept of money income—at least in thinking of individual and business income. An intermediate way to think of income is as the *command over goods,* or power to acquire them, obtained during a period. In this sense, income includes payments in kind, and it also allows for the changing value of money. A $4000 income commands fewer goods in 1948 than a $3000 income did in 1940 and is thus a smaller income. But attention is focused not on the goods actually obtained but on the power to obtain them.

One reason for preferring the command-over-goods idea is that individuals commonly do not convert all of their money income directly into goods. They save part of it, put it in the bank, or invest it somewhere, and it is awkward to think of this part of their income in real terms.[4] But they have the command over goods, however they use the money. Another reason is that a very important part of economic analysis is concerned with the spending of income; and it would be obvious nonsense to speak of the spending of income if the word "income" were used to mean the actual goods for which money is spent. The concept of command over goods distinguishes income and the use of income. When we turn to the collective view of income, or national income, this distinction need not be important; and we shall often speak of the national income as consisting of actual products.

Further income concepts. Both the real-income idea and the command-over-goods idea have the advantage, not present when income is thought of as money, of relating income closely to the conditions of economic welfare. Our plane of living depends on products, not on money. But neither of these concepts gives us an adequate basis of measuring income when money is used to buy durable goods, goods that we continue to use over a period of years. In the case of such products as automobiles, furniture, and household equipment, it is sometimes necessary to distinguish the goods themselves and the services they yield throughout their lifetime of use. A man may use $1500 of his $5000 income to buy a car in 1947; but the services of that car will contribute to his level of living not only in 1947 but through several succeeding years. The final test of income lies in human satisfactions, and satisfactions depend in part on the *services of durable goods.*[5]

[4] Writers who insist that income is the actual goods have to say, when money is saved and banked, that the saver, in effect, acquires ownership of goods bought by the person who borrows from the bank. This is going a little far. Moreover, there is no assurance that loans by banks will equal the funds they receive.

[5] Undoubtedly we think of income in two ways: (1) as a measure of economic performance and achievement, and (2) as a measure of the well-being we currently achieve. From the former standpoint, the $1500 spent for the car should be credited to the year in which it is received. But from the latter, it should be spread over the years in which the car is used.

The logical outcome of this approach would be to define income in terms of satisfactions, and this is done sometimes. Income may be viewed not as money, not as ability to command goods, not as goods actually obtained, but as the stream of satisfactions which is the final aim of economic activity. This stream is known as *psychic income*. It is much too elusive a concept for ordinary use. No way has been found of measuring quantities of satisfaction. But in dealing with problems of inequality of income, it is sometimes necessary to take account of the unequal satisfactions obtained from given quantities of goods; and then the psychic-income idea has some use.

Income to the firm

Few individuals in these days produce a complete product and sell it—as a housemaid does her services—to the final consumer. Most products, as we have seen, require the cooperation of the labor and wealth of more than one person, including the persons from whom materials, supplies, and equipment are bought. Thus the revenue from the sale of the product is not income to the one who sells it but a composite return that must provide income to a number of people. From the seller's standpoint, it is a gross return from which he must deduct his expenses to get his income. This is the situation of the business firm.

Accountants analyze this situation and summarize the result in a report called an *income statement*. The aim of the accountant is to disclose the outcome of the firm's operations, regarding it from the standpoint of its owners or stockholders. Starting with the revenue from the sale of its product, he must make deductions for its purchases from other firms, for taxes, and for income payments to other participants in its operations, mainly employees and lending capitalists. In addition, adjustments are called for by the changing value of its inventories, or stocks of goods, and by the loss of life of its durable facilities such as buildings and machines. Since our interest here is in income in general and not merely in owners' income, we shall depart somewhat from the conventional form of statement.

Let us assume that the XYZ Corporation, a manufacturing concern, sells its product to the extent of $5,000,000 in a given year. To measure the operations of this firm as distinct from other firms, it is necessary first to deduct the value of all purchases from other firms that went into this $5,000,000 product. In doing so, we arrive at a figure often called by the statisticians "value added by manufacture." In this particular year the sum of $2,500,000 was spent for materials, fuel, supplies of various kinds, electric power, and other items. But, unfortunately, we cannot arrive at the "value added" simply by deducting this sum.

Much of the material that went into this year's product was already in stock at the beginning of the year, and part of this year's purchases remain in stock at the end of the year. Thus the purchased items that should be charged against this year's product may amount to more or less than $2,500,000. Let us assume that the inventory of goods on hand was $1,000,000 on January 1 and that it is $1,100,000 on December 31. Accordingly, only $2,400,000 has to be deducted for purchased items, and the "value added" is $2,600,000.

In obtaining this year's product, changes also took place in the fixed plant and equipment of the *XYZ* Corporation. Some machines were bought and some were scrapped, but the sums involved do not directly affect the income statement at all. They affect the property accounts which record the wealth, or capital, of the enterprise. But this year's product must be charged with the wearing out of these fixed facilities, the yielding up of a fraction of their service life, during the current year. Thus, if a machine is used that cost $10,100, that was estimated to be good for 10 years, and that would bring $100 when scrapped, $1000 should be charged against this year's product to cover its use. This deduction, which distributes the cost of durable facilities over the whole lifetime of their use, is known as a *depreciation* charge. In the present year, depreciation is estimated to be $200,000 for all of the buildings and equipment of the corporation. Deducting this sum from the previous remainder of $2,600,000, we get a figure of $2,400,000 which the statistician, not the accountant, might call the *net product* of the firm's operations.

Not all of the value of this net product is available as income to the participants in the operations. Governments—federal, state, and local —assert their claims, and $400,000 is paid in *taxes*. In part these taxes may be thought of as payments for services, such as the protection of property, that the business requires, just as it requires materials and insurance. In part they are contributions to general public purposes, such as national defense and care of the indigent. When taxes are deducted, $2,000,000 remains out of the revenue of $5,000,000 as income to the several participants.

Of this $2,000,000, we shall assume that $1,500,000 went in *wages* and *salaries* to employees at all levels, including the officers of the corporation. $100,000 was paid in *interest* on outstanding bonds. Thus $400,-000 remains as *business profits,* the final object of the accountant's effort.[6] The directors decide to use $250,000 of this sum in paying

---

[6] To the accountant, labor is an outside purchase, just as materials are. Thus wages would be deducted as an operating expense at an early point in the income statement. Otherwise, the sequence of deductions followed here is fairly close to the accountant's procedure. The entire return on capital, $500,000 in this case, is called net operating revenue, and the final deduction of interest on borrowed funds gives the net income to the owners.

dividends to stockholders, so that $150,000 is retained as *corporate savings,* presumably to expand the operations of the firm.

Using a mixture of descriptive labels partly from accounting and partly from statistics, we may sum up the activities and the resulting income of the *XYZ* Corporation as shown in the table.

TABLE 3—PRODUCT AND INCOME FROM OPERATIONS OF THE
XYZ CORPORATION

Sales revenue	$5,000,000
Purchases (adjusted) from other firms	2,400,000
Value added by manufacture	2,600,000
Depreciation of durable facilities	200,000
Net product	2,400,000
Taxes	400,000
Income to participating producers	2,000,000
Wages and interest paid	1,600,000
Business profit	400,000
Dividends to stockholders	250,000
Corporate saving	150,000

Of the $5,000,000 of revenue, the people who contribute labor and wealth to the corporation receive only $1,850,000 in wages, interest, and dividends; but the remaining $3,150,000 is not lost to the circuit flow of money and the income stream. The $2,400,000 paid to other firms becomes sales revenue to them and is the basis for a duplication of this analysis. Government bodies will use their $400,000 of tax receipts to pay salaries, interest, and contract costs of public projects. The $200,000 retained to cover depreciation and the $150,000 of retained profits are available for continuing use in replacing and expanding the productive wealth of the business. In fact, as we have seen, $100,000 has already been used in the expansion of inventories. This example of the *XYZ* Corporation represents in reasonably typical fashion the place of the business firm in the production-income process.

National income

Undoubtedly the most useful economic statistics are those that describe production and income from a national standpoint. Such totals provide the best means available for following the economic fortunes of the nation in peace and war, in prosperity and depression. To be well informed, one must be able to interpret such statistics as they appear from time to time in the public press.

National economic performance may be looked at usefully in either of two ways. (1) It may be measured on the basis of all the commodities and services produced in a given year. (2) It may be measured on the basis of the incomes of all the people from their productive activities, together with any income retained by business enterprises. Extensive studies of the national income are carried on continuously by the United States Department of Commerce, and much statistical work is done by various private organizations. We shall use Department of Commerce figures in this discussion.[7]

Figures from this source place the national income of the United States at $202.6 billion in 1947. If we look at this total on the basis of the first of these two ways of viewing national income, its main divisions correspond to the types of productive activity that we considered in Chapter 2. Such an analysis is known as "national income by industrial origin," and appears in Table 4.

TABLE 4—NATIONAL INCOME BY INDUSTRIAL ORIGIN,
1947
(In billions of dollars)

Agriculture, forestry, and fisheries	$20.7
Mining	3.9
Construction	8.0
Manufacturing	61.3
Wholesale and retail trade	38.3
Finance, insurance, real estate	15.8
Transportation	11.1
Public utilities, communications	5.0
Services	19.2
Government	18.8
Rest of the world [8]	.5
Total for all industries	202.6

[7] The national-income studies were published in revised form in 1947, with revised figures carried back to 1929. The totals run somewhat higher than in previous studies, primarily because of the inclusion of the rental value of owner-occupied dwelling. See *National Income—Supplement to Survey of Current Business*, July 1947. The figures for 1947 are from *Survey of Current Business*, February 1948, pp. 9–10.

[8] A nation's economy intertwines the economies of other nations at various points, and statistical difficulties arise in drawing the boundaries. One basis would be to say that only the labor and wealth actually used in the United States should be counted in getting the nation's product. Another basis would be to include productive activities abroad from which persons resident in the United States are receiving income, and to exclude activities in the United States from which persons abroad receive income. The latter basis is used here. Only the net difference gets into the statistics, and part of that difference may be assigned to specific industries.

When national income is viewed as the sum of various kinds of income receipts, it is known as "national income by distributive shares." Table 5 shows the 1947 total broken into its major divisions.[9]

TABLE 5—NATIONAL INCOME BY DISTRIBUTIVE
SHARES, 1947
(In billions of dollars)

Compensation of employees	$128.1
Proprietor's and rental income	47.8
Corporate profits (adjusted)	23.0
Net interest	3.6
Total for all incomes	202.6

But while national income is merely a way of viewing the national product, some care is needed in interpreting total output to make the two correspond. Moreover while national income may be viewed as a total of income receipts, not all income receipts find their way into the hands of individuals to use. At the same time, the income receipts of individuals, in the strict sense, do not equal the funds they have to spend. Further clarification of these national aggregates is necessary.

Gross and net national product and national income. National income is a net figure. If all the final products of a given year are added together at their market prices, together with all government services on a cost basis, the total arrived at is considerably greater than the national income. This larger total, called the *gross national product*, is an important figure, for it represents the entire current economic performance at current prices. In emergency situations, war or a depression, it may tell more about the nation's aggregate economic achievement, high or low, than the national income does. Wherein does the difference lie?

First it should be said that the difference does not lie in any double-counting of current products. Gross production does not imply gross *transactions*. The wood the logger sells is not counted again in the sale of lumber by the mill, again in the sale of lumber by the dealer, again in the sale of furniture by the manufacturer, and once again in the sale of furniture by the retailer. It is counted just once. Accord-

---

[9] Statistics of the distribution of income will be examined in greater detail when we begin the study of the distribution of income in Chapter 24. The figure of $23 billion for corporate profits, it should be noted, was arrived at through an "inventory valuation adjustment" which brought the original figure down from $28.7 billion. The reason for the adjustment is that stocks of goods were used in production in 1947 that had been bought at the lower prices of preceding years. Replacement of these goods at 1947 prices, it was estimated, would have increased their cost by $5.7 billion, and thus profits, as reported by the accountants, overstated by this amount the return from the productive activity of 1947.

ingly, the figure of $38.3 billion for wholesale and retail trade in 1947 represents only the activities of middlemen and does not include the value of goods purchased from manufacturers and farmers. The figure of $61.3 billion for manufacturing similarly does not include materials and supplies purchased but corresponds to the value-added-by-manufacture figure in the example of the *XYZ* Corporation. The $18.8 billion product of government is measured by the service, at cost, of government employees and does not include government purchases from private firms.

Gross national product, however, even after such possible double-counting is excluded, exaggerates the productive activity of the current year. A given year's product must be credited in part to the services of plant and equipment produced in earlier years. In helping to produce the present year's product, these facilities yield up part of their service life through wear and obsolescence, and this fact must be recognized through an allowance for *depreciation*. Only when this is deducted does the total output represent the *net national product* of the year.

For 1947 the government statisticians place the gross national product at $229.6 billion. They estimate that the using up of existing wealth, including residential buildings, amounted to $12.4 billion. Thus the net national product is $217.2 billion.

But this figure is still $14.6 billion above the national income of $202.6 billion. Certainly it would seem that the two should be the same if product and income are but opposite sides of the same coin. Unfortunately the statistical picture is not as neat and simple as one might wish; but nothing in the statistics undermines what has been said of the relationship of product and income. A difficulty arises, however, in interpreting business taxes, and the manner of handling it gives rise to the discrepancy.

The taxes paid by business firms are broken into two parts in the statistical analysis, depending on how closely connected they are with incomes received for particular productive services. Social-security taxes, for instance, are really just a deferred part of the income of employees, and the 1947 figure of $128.1 billion for "compensation of employees" accordingly includes the $5.7 billion of such taxes. Similarly the income taxes paid by corporations may be thought of as coming from the profits of owners, and the $23.0 billion figure for corporate profits includes the $11.3 billion paid in corporate income taxes.[10] But excise taxes, as on liquor and tobacco, and business-property taxes, are

[10] Except for purposes of statistical analysis of income, these taxes were paid from corporate profits of $28.7 billion. See note 9 above.

not assignable to incomes in this way. Instead of coming out of assignable incomes, they may be thought of as sums that are added to the prices of products, so that the national product is sold for a larger amount than the total incomes for all the productive services that go into it. These "indirect" taxes and related charges amounted to $17.9 billion in 1947, and they are viewed as coming out of the net product but not out of the national income. This is larger than the $14.6 billion to be explained; but when some minor adjustments and a technical statistical discrepancy are allowed for, the net national product and the national income are fully reconciled.[11]

Aggregate personal income. We have seen that individuals do not receive all of the income credited to them for their services and the services of their wealth. The national income of $202.6 billion in 1947 included $5.7 billion in social-security taxes and $11.3 billion in corporation income taxes. In addition, $4.9 billion of corporation profits were retained for expansion, so that profits paid to stockholders in the form of dividends amounted only to $6.8 billion.[12] Thus, only $180.7 billion of the 1947 national income passed directly into the hands of individual recipients.

The ability of individuals to buy goods, however, was not limited to the wage, interest, profit, and other incomes received from current production. An important part of the money collected by governmental bodies in taxes is not absorbed in the cost of government services but is paid out in cash to various groups. These *transfer payments,* as they are called, include social-security contributions, welfare and relief payments, and assistance of all kinds to war veterans. In 1947 they totaled $11.6 billion. In addition, *interest payments on government bonds* must be added at this point, since under the prevailing interpretation they are not regarded as part of the national income but as a sort of transfer from taxpayer to bondholder.[13] They amounted in 1947 to $4.5 billion. Thus total *personal income* amounted to $196.8 billion.

Not all of this sum is available for individuals to spend, because

[11] If we were to ask what the contribution of the *XYZ* Corporation is to the national income, we would need to revise the example to show the taxes in two parts. Of the $400,000 of taxes, $150,000, say, representing indirect taxes would be subtracted in getting the "income to participating producers," and the resulting figure of $2,250,000 (instead of $2,000,-000) would be the firm's contribution to national income. Then the remaining $250,000 of corporate income tax would be subtracted from profits prior to the payment of dividends.

[12] Again, it should be noted that corporate saving, based on unadjusted corporate profits, was $10.6 billion, not $4.9 billion. See note 9 above.

[13] It is arguable whether interest on government bonds should be recognized at this point or should be included along with interest on business debts as a return from the productive service of capital. If the latter course were followed, the gross and net national products and the national income would be larger by $4.5 billion.

individuals as well as corporations must pay taxes. Nor is all of the remainder spent for current consumption, since individuals also do considerable saving. In 1947 the $196.8 billion was disposed of as follows (in billions):

Tax and related payments	$ 21.5
Personal saving	10.9
Consumption expenditure	164.4

National aggregates during depression and war boom

These concepts of national product and income enable one to follow the nation's economic performance. They permit one to trace, for instance, those two most striking fluctuations in the nation's history, the depression of the 1930s and the war boom of the 1940s. If we compare the leading aggregates for 1929, the peak year of the prosperous 1920s, 1933, the bottom year of 1930s, 1940, the year before the war boom set in, 1944, the peak of the war effort, and add 1947 to summarize statistics already presented and throw light on the postwar period, an amazing story of economic change unfolds. For these five years, gross and net national product, national income, and personal income behaved as shown in Table 6.[14]

TABLE 6—ECONOMIC CHANGE IN DEPRESSION AND WAR
(In billions of dollars)

National totals	1929	1933	1940	1944	1947
Gross national product	$103.8	$55.8	$100.5	$210.6	$229.6
Net national product	95.0	48.5	92.0	198.8	217.2
National income	87.4	39.6	81.3	182.3	202.6
Personal income	85.1	46.6	78.3	164.9	196.8

Expressed in these figures, during the depression national product fell by nearly half, national income by more than half, and in the war period both totals more than doubled. As they stand, however, these figures exaggerate the real changes that occurred. Further examination of them will not only provide needed corrections but will throw useful light on these crucial periods.

The impact of depression. Consider the depression of the 1930s. The decline was of unprecedented severity, but certainly the indicated decline of 46 percent in gross product (from $103.8 to $55.8 billion) and

[14] One should realize that some of the components of these totals are mere estimates and that substantial statistical discrepancies are sometimes concealed behind them. These inaccuracies, however, do not seriously weaken the comparisons. Figures are from *National Income—Supplement to Survey of Current Business*, July 1947, and *Survey of Current Business*, February 1948.

of 55 percent in national income (from $87.4 to $39.6 billion) greatly overstates its real extent. At least four corrections should be noted, the first three of which operate to reduce the indicated decline.

1. The most obvious correction is for the *fall in prices*. A dollar would buy considerably more in 1933 than in 1929. Wholesale prices had fallen 30 percent and the cost of living 25 percent, so it seems reasonable to assume that the dollar represented at least one third more goods in 1933 than in 1929.[15] If we expand the 1933 totals on this basis to make them comparable with the 1929 totals, it appears that the national product had fallen 28 percent, not 46 percent, and the national income had fallen 40 percent, instead of 55 percent—certainly a much less severe decline. This reduction in output and income was spread most unevenly over the economy. Farm output fell little, manufacturing output by half, and government activities not at all.

2. The decline in national income, and even in gross product, overstates the *impact on the consumer*. During the depression, personal income rose in relation to national income, and consumer spending absorbed more of personal income. Personal income fell from $85.1 to $46.6 billion—or by 27 percent when allowance is made for the fall in prices. On the same basis, consumer spending fell from $78.8 to $46.3 billion—or by 22 percent in real terms.

The change in spending is easily understood. When their incomes fall, people save less and do their best to maintain their plane of living. Thus in 1933 the spending was practically equal to the personal income —which means that individual saving was negative, since personal taxes are paid out of personal income. Past savings were being brought into use.

But why should personal income fall less than national income? Indeed, how could personal income exceed national income by $7 billion in 1933? Perhaps the natural answer is that relief payments were greatly increased in 1933. But actually government transfer payments expanded by less than $500,000 over 1929 and total government expenditures by less than that.

The explanation lies rather in the use of funds by business corporations. In 1929 business corporations retained over $2 billion in undistributed profits, whereas in 1933 *undistributed profits were negative* to the extent of $4.5 billion.[16] Corporations paid out in wages, interest, dividends, and taxes $4.5 billion more than the value of their net product.

---

[15] If prices were three fourths as high in 1933, the dollar would buy four thirds as much.
[16] Again the corporate savings figure is adjusted to absorb an inventory-valuation correction.

How are such payments possible? The most common answer is that corporations have cash reserves from earlier, more prosperous years, and these reserves are used during depression periods. This, however, is only a minor reason. The main reason is that in bad years corporations turn part of their wealth into cash and distribute it. This is done in two ways. (1) Inventories of materials and supplies and of goods awaiting sale are allowed to decline, sales being made in part from existing stocks. (2) Plant and equipment are not replaced as fast as they wear out during depressions. Thus revenues which cover depreciation are available for wage and other payments.

Aggregate declines of 27 percent in personal income and 22 percent in consumer buying are, of course, quite out of line with the experience of many individuals. Unemployed persons were hit much harder than the average person by the depression of the 1930s; and many persons who kept their jobs, and all or most of their pre-depression pay, were actually better off than before, after prices fell.

3. These figures of 27 percent and 22 percent still overstate the impact of the depression on the level of living. As we have seen, it is sometimes useful to separate the *services of durable consumers' goods* from the goods themselves. Only the services of houses are included in the statistics; but during the depression the public continued to have the use of a vast quantity of automobiles, furniture, household equipment, and clothing that were produced and bought before the decline. In 1933 only about one fourth as many cars were bought as in 1929, but the use of cars was still very great. In judging the impact of fluctuations in an advanced economy, the continuing use of durable consumers' goods is an important factor, even though statistics are not available to measure it.

4. The last correction is in the opposite direction. *Population* continued to grow during the depression, and the total income of 1933 had to support about 3 percent more people than the income of 1929. When we recognize this factor and look at personal income in per-capita terms, the decline becomes 29 percent instead of 27 percent. The fall in gross product per capita becomes 30 percent, instead of 28 percent.

The impact of war. From 1940 to 1944 gross product, national income, and personal income all more than doubled in current, unadjusted dollars. During this period, despite price controls, wholesale prices rose by 32 percent and the cost of living by 25 percent. Since much of the production of 1944 consisted of planes and tanks and ships which were not produced in 1940, the expansion in physical output is almost impossible to measure. The striking fact is that, despite war expenditures in 1944 of $88.6 billion, consumer expenditures of $110.4 billion were possible, in comparison with $72.1 billion in 1940. It had been thought that so great a production of war materials would necessitate a severe decline in consumption; but actually more goods were represented by consumer buying in 1944 than in 1940. In part, however, the goods were different, since many consumers' durable goods were not produced during the war.

But despite the increase in consumption, the volume of goods was far below the amount that the public had the money to buy and was anxious to buy. This is the peculiar feature of a wartime economy—a feature that we shall examine later. Money income becomes available in excess of the goods for which it can be spent. This deficiency of goods does not mean that unspendable income yields no satisfaction. Saving—even reluctant saving—is gratifying, especially in anticipation of postwar buying. And there is satisfaction also in the sense of collective achievement in helping to bring the war to a successful close.

In most of its economic aspects, a war period is just the opposite of a depression period, but in one respect they are alike. That respect is the importance of the continuing service of previously produced durable goods. For quite different reasons, automobiles and like products are produced very little in either period. Thus, in describing the level of living that can be maintained during a war, it is necessary to note that the use made of durable consumers' goods is very high in relation to their current production.

National real income as an analytical guide

These several national totals are not only helpful in tracing economic events; they are most useful in analyzing economic practices and policies. Indeed, if one only remembers that total income is rooted in total production, one has probably learned the most useful of all economic lessons. With all the complexities of modern economic organization, it is easy for one's thinking to bog down in a maze of transactions, money flows, and price relationships. But without sufficient knowledge to thread one's way through the maze, it is often possible to gain a sound and simple view of problems by remembering that income, after all, is product.

Consider, for instance, the numerous attempts of particular economic groups to increase their incomes by restricting their output. In a specialized economy, the immediate aim of the group is to increase money income—to get a higher wage, a higher profit, a higher price for its product. By doing this, the group can increase its command over goods. But the apparent successes of individuals and groups in this endeavor can easily mean collective, or aggregate, failure. The only way in which all people can get command of more goods is through having more goods to get command of. The only way in which total income can expand is through the expanded output of particular groups. Whenever industrial monopolists or organized workers restrict output to improve their market position, they are taking the road that must lead to lower national product and income.

Or consider the view that a few extremely high incomes are not harmful because money spent and invested by the rich comes to the rest of us anyway, and we are as well off as if we got it in the first place. The circulating habits of money throw no light on the problem of inequality. If high income means anything, it means that the recipients are able to claim a corresponding quantity of goods out of the total flow of goods from which all people get their means of living. If these few people get more, other people get less. This is plain enough when income is viewed as a flow of products. The persuasive way to justify high incomes is by showing that, because of them, the flow of products is greater.

Or consider the idea that American workmen can achieve the American standard of living only if they are protected by a tariff on imports against the competition of low-wage labor in other countries. That competition, it is said, would force prices and wages here down to the foreign level. The economics of foreign trade, of international prices and exchange rates, is complex, but to the person who understands the nature of income, the answer to this argument is obvious. Suppose that money prices and wages reach whatever level is necessary to meet foreign competition and that trade and industry have become fully adjusted thereto: the level of living in the United States will still depend, as it does now, on the flow of products that the American people are able to produce. Real income must depend on productivity, and productivity can neither be created by act of Congress nor destroyed by the competition of low-paid workmen abroad.

Or consider the frequent confusion of transactions with income in various connections—for instance, the collection of taxes. During the 1930s advocates of the Townsend Plan of old-age pensions contended that $200 per month could be paid to people over sixty with little burden on the rest of the population. It was said that a 2-percent tax on $1 trillion of monetary transactions, a 1929 estimate, would yield $20 billion a year, or enough to pension over 8,000,000 elderly people. A mere 2 percent would seem small to persons accustomed to sales taxes of 3 percent and income taxes at much higher rates. But again the nature of income was overlooked. Twenty billion dollars cannot be given to 8,000,000 people, in real command over goods, without diverting that quantity of goods from the rest of the population. This diversion of goods is the real burden of the tax. If total production is $100 billion, the diversion would amount to one fifth of the flow of products on which the living of all the people depends. The fact that most products are involved in several transactions before they reach the consumer, and that there are innumerable transactions involving deals in securities and real estate and in the making and repaying of loans, has nothing to do with the burden that a $20 billion levy would impose on the country.

These examples must be concluded with a warning. We have applied the national-real-income concept to a number of common misconceptions to show how easily economic problems may sometimes be freed of their complexities and analyzed in a way that is both simple and sound. But this concept is not the key to all problems, nor does it say the last word on the problems just mentioned. No more must be inferred regarding them than has actually been stated. Much remains to be said on the problems of monopoly, unions, inequality, the protective tariff, taxation, and old-age assistance.

Review Questions

1. "The relation between production and income, looked at from the national standpoint in a specialized economy, is about the same as when viewed by a Crusoe." Explain. Show how this relationship, when viewed in detail, is affected by specialization, the use of money, the presence of business firms, the inclusion of products in other products.

2. "Perhaps $50 of transactions will be involved in producing a $10 product, yet no more than $10 of income can be received from all the transactions." Explain.

3. Explain with a diagram the opposite flows of money and of goods in a specialized economy.

4. From a letter published in *The New York Times*: "If *A* receives $20,000 per annum and out of it pays his chauffeur and gardener $1000 each, it is obviously a fallacy to compute the . . . annual income of the three at $22,000 for purposes of estimating the true national income." Criticize this statement. Does it make any difference in what connection the chauffeur does his work?

5. What two obvious errors are likely to enter when we compare incomes simply in terms of money?

6. Show that these errors are avoided when income is thought of either as "real income" or as "command over goods." Give reasons for preferring the latter concept when thinking of individual income.

7. What is the significance of durable consumers' goods from the income standpoint?

8. What is meant by psychic income? Is the concept of any use? What difficulty does it present?

9. What is the purpose of an income statement? Explain in general terms what it does.

10. Use an example to explain the division of the gross revenue of a business into (a) purchases from other firms, (b) recovery of previously invested capital (through the depreciation process), (c) contributions to government, (d) income payments for hired productive services, (e) income to the owners. Show the relation of each of these divisions to the circuit flow of money. What is meant by "value added"? By "corporate savings"?

11. "The fact that product and income are essentially the same from the national standpoint provides two ways of calculating the national income." Explain.

12. How closely do the contributions to national income of the various fields of industry correspond to the number of persons occupied in these fields as given in Chapter 2?

13. Distinguish carefully these national aggregates: total transactions, gross national product, net national product, national income, total personal income.

14. Start with figures of $87.4 and $39.6 billion for 1929 and 1933, respectively, and explain the several qualifications and adjustments that need to be made in order to get a correct impression of the impact of the depression on the consuming public.

15. What are the special difficulties in measuring the impact of war on the economy?

16. "Often big problems may be grasped quite simply, in their essentials, when viewed in terms of national real income—problems that are quite complex when full account is taken of all monetary relationships." Develop this point with illustrations.

17. "An industry consists of all the people and all the wealth engaged in producing a particular kind of product or in performing a particular kind of productive function."

"The tourist industry is now the second largest industry in Michigan."

On the basis of the first statement, can you fit the "tourist industry" into a classification of industries containing retail merchandising, hotels, etc.? If the "tourist industry" is measured by the amount of money spent in a state by people from outside the state, does that money represent "value added" by a certain kind of productive activity? What would be the effect on the "tourist industry" if the people of the several states interchanged their buying across state lines to a greater extent? What would be the effect on the national product?

Wealth

Economic goods have been viewed thus far as products and as the basis of income. They may also be viewed as wealth, and in this guise too they have an important role in economic life. Indeed, the word "wealth" is one of the most used economic terms. It is the term we use when we speak of economic *possessions,* just as the terms "production" and "income" are used in speaking of economic performance.

Wealth and income

In the discussion of production and income the word *flow* has been used repeatedly to convey the idea of something in process, something becoming available. As part of a flow, economic goods must be thought of as a quantity in relation to time. Like the flow of a river, which is measured by the amount of water moving during a period of time, so production and income must be measured in time units. Income statements of business firms and statistics of national product and income usually represent a year's performance.

Wealth, on the other hand, is a *fund* of economic goods, not a flow. Like water in a tank, it must be measured as a quantity in existence at an instant in time. We shall mean by wealth the quantity of economic goods possessed at a given moment. The possessor may be an individual, a business firm, a government, or the people of a nation collectively—as when we speak of national wealth.

The word "wealth" is not always used in this precise sense. Sometimes it is made broadly synonymous with economic goods, and then people may speak of flows as well as funds of wealth. It is in this loose sense that Adam Smith inquired into the causes of the "wealth of nations" and that people now refer to the "production and distribution of wealth." But the word is useful in economic analysis only when it is restricted to the fund, or possessions, sense.

Common and unlike components of wealth and income. Very largely, but not entirely, the same goods may be viewed either as real income or as wealth. Pairs of shoes, as they emerge from the factory, are part of the flow of products of the period. The same shoes, as part of the stock on a dealer's shelves, are included in his wealth at a given time.

But some products can never become part of a fund of wealth. Nonmaterial products, such as an orchestral concert, must be consumed at the instant in which they are produced. One's stock of wealth never consists of accumulations of concerts, lectures, physician's services, and like goods. Economic goods, we have said, consist of things which have utility, scarcity, and transferability; but wealth must also be *material*.

On the other hand, economic goods which are not producible can be wealth but not income. Natural resources, in particular, never appear among the products of a certain year, but they are an outstanding part of the nation's wealth. Only the services of these resources appear in the year's output.

Mutual sources of each other. Thus income derives in part from wealth. Production is carried on by combining human effort with wealth of natural and human origin, and wealth must be credited with a large, though not a dominant, role in production. Several of the chapters in Part II will deal with the productive contributions of wealth.

But in a sense, also, wealth derives from income. It comes from income in so far as we consume less than we produce. However much we produce, if we consume goods as fast as we produce them there is no increase in our fund of wealth. The increase is brought about through the excess of production over consumption. In this sense, wealth comes from income.

Expansion of wealth

Wealth, then, expands through *saving*—which is the word used in economics to denote a rate of consumption lower than the rate of production. It is in this way, as will be shown more fully in Chapter 6, that expansion takes place in industrial structures and equipment, in the stocks of goods used in production, in the volume of residential housing, and in the quantities of other durable goods.

Natural wealth, on the other hand, is producible only in the sense that it may be added to through discovery. Savings may thus be used in prospecting for minerals or otherwise in finding natural resources. But the chief expansion of natural wealth is not through an increase in the quantity of it that is physically available but through an increase in the value of the existing quantity. Population grows, and the demand for the services of natural wealth expands, so that its value rises. It is mainly in this way that farm and urban land have come to represent the great aggregate of wealth that they do today.

This expansion of wealth through an increase in the value of physical things already in existence is known as *appreciation*. It is to be contrasted with saving, which causes the quantity of physical things to expand. Appreciation may take place in wealth of human origin, but it is distinctively the source of expansion in natural wealth.

Just as wealth may expand in these two respects, it may also contract. Goods may be consumed faster than they are produced, as when equipment and inventories are used without replacement during a depression. And both natural wealth and wealth of human origin may decline in value, as they did very decidedly in the United States beginning late in 1929.

Capital gains. Appreciation of wealth raises one serious question of policy that is rooted in the meaning of terms. When the owners of wealth sell it for more than they paid for it, is the gain income? Should it be taxed as income? Professional speculators in securities and real estate make their living through these gains—*capital gains* as they are called—and the net return certainly appears as income to them. On the other hand, it certainly does not represent any part of the flow of products which constitute the real income of the nation and which determine the level on which people may live. This flow of products reflects the services of land and industrial facilities, and the change in value of these facilities, from which some people profit, should not also be counted. Thus, strictly speaking, capital gains are not income, but a case can be made for taxing them as income, nevertheless. Practices differ. In the United States they are taxed, but not as other income is, whereas in Great Britain they are not taxed.

Measurement of wealth

Quantitatively, income and wealth are quite distinct. Income, expressed as a flow during a period, tells us nothing about the wealth we possess at the end of the period. If we have consumed as fast as we have produced, we possess no wealth at all because of the production of that period. Wealth, on the other hand, since it is a static quantity at a given moment, tells us nothing of the events of the preceding period. The wealth we have is the accumulation of the long past.

Wealth from the private and the social viewpoint. As with income, the measurement of wealth depends somewhat on the point of view adopted, whether the limited viewpoint of the individual or firm, or the broad viewpoint of the whole society. Individuals and firms count as wealth not only the economic goods in their possession but also the amounts owed them by other individuals and firms, as well as some other items that are not wealth from the social viewpoint. In computing their wealth, they set against these *assets* the amounts they owe, their *liabilities,* to other individuals and firms. Their *net worth* is set forth through an accounting device known as a *balance sheet,* of which we shall make some use in Chapter 9.

From the social or national viewpoint, nothing should count as wealth except material economic goods, and, when totals are based on measures of private wealth, care must be taken to avoid double-counting and to exclude certain "intangibles." *Debts* in the form of notes and accounts payable, mortgages, and corporate bonds should cancel out, since the asset of one person is the liability of another. But the *stocks of corporations,* which represent shares of ownership, are not debts. Stockholders view them as wealth, and the corporation regards as wealth the land and facilities and inventories that they represent. Both the actual wealth and the titles to it must not be counted if exaggeration is to be avoided. Wealth is not increased by issuing securities against it, or, as in the case of holding companies and investment trusts, by issuing more securities to represent the first ones.

The *intangibles* are such private assets as patents, franchises, and good will. They may be thought of as wealth from an individual, acquisitive viewpoint, but they are not wealth in a social sense, and they should not enter into any total of national wealth. They are simply values assigned to advantageous market positions and reflect a subtle, though perhaps legitimate, invasion of the pockets of others.

Should *money* be counted as wealth? This may seem a foolish question, for money is often regarded as the very essence of wealth. To the uninformed, the wealthy person is the person with a "lot of money," even though, in fact, a very wealthy person may have little or no money. Certainly money, in whatever form, is wealth from the private standpoint. It is the most flexible, adaptable form of wealth. But in getting a measure of national wealth, much of the money supply should not be counted. The nation cannot become wealthy by running the presses in the Bureau of Printing and Engraving and expanding the number of "tickets" with which a given quantity of economic goods is to be purchased. If a billion dollars of paper money were destroyed, the loss would be no greater than the cost of replacing it. Metallic money, on the same basis, should be counted as wealth to the extent of the value of the metal that goes into it, and this may mean its full monetary value. But there is no more dubious form of wealth than an addition to a stock of monetary gold or silver that is already large enough for all monetary purposes.

National wealth. Statistics of wealth are much less adequate and dependable than statistics of income. This is due in part to the fact that they are far less important. Only occasionally has an effort been made to measure the wealth of the United States.

A study completed just before World War II placed the wealth of the United States at $321 billion in 1922, $428 billion in 1930, and $388 billion in 1938.[17] The main wealth categories, for 1930, are summarized in Table 7. Of the 1930 total, about 45 percent was used in private production and the remainder in consumption or by governmental bodies. Of this same total, about 30 percent was natural wealth and 70 percent man-made.

A study by the Federal Trade Commission[18] estimated that national

[17] Robert R. Doane, *The Anatomy of American Wealth,* Harper, 1940, pp. 116, 146.
[18] *National Wealth and Income,* 1926.

TABLE 7—WEALTH OF THE UNITED STATES, 1930
(In billions of dollars)

Farm wealth, except houses	$ 50
Industrial and commercial buildings, equipment, and land	81
Railroad facilities, including land	24
Public utilities, including land	25
Residences and residential land	115
Public land and buildings, naval vessels	36
Motor vehicles	6
Stocks of goods	27
Household furnishings, personal effects	59
Gold and silver coin and bullion	5
Total	$428

wealth in 1922 was $353.6 billion. One used by the Brookings Institution placed the total at $460 billion for 1929.[19] In dollar terms postwar wealth is higher because prices are higher.

Review Questions

1. "The essential difference between wealth and income is the difference between a fund and a flow." Explain.

2. A Detroit newspaper reported that a prominent local radio speaker, "supporting his statement that the New Deal had concentrated and increased poverty, . . . cited Government figures to show that in 1929, 7 percent of the people, with incomes of $5000 or more a year, obtained 40 percent of the national income, and that in 1937, according to the *Federal Reserve Bulletin*, 1.7 percent of the people 'owned and controlled 90 percent of the wealth. This condition under the New Deal is even worse and more acute than it was under the old deal,' he declared." Apart from the accuracy of the figures, what is the error? To what do you attribute such obvious errors?

3. "Wealth and real income both consist of economic goods; but each one includes goods that the other does not." Explain. What quality must goods have if they are to be accumulated?

4. "In one sense income comes from wealth. In quite a different sense, wealth comes from income." Explain.

5. Distinguish the two ways in which wealth expands. Relate them to the two main categories of wealth.

6. What are capital gains? Why may they be thought of as income to individuals but be excluded from the national income?

7. Various percentage relationships are commonly employed in speaking of wealth and income. Assume that Smith has $100,000 invested and that in a given year he receives interest and dividends amounting to $5000, that his

[19] See Harold G. Moulton, *The Formation of Capital*, Brookings, 1935, p. 187. Data are reclassified from a study by W. R. Ingalls.

salary is $10,000, and that he saves $3000. Explain these percentages: (*a*) the return on his investments averages 5 percent; (*b*) he is adding to his capital at the rate of 3 percent; (*c*) he saves 20 percent of his income. To accumulate wealth, need a person have income from wealth?

8. A prominent United States Senator of a few years ago often said that this country is too liberal in regulating the return to the owners of public utilities. It is unreasonable, he said, to allow utilities to earn 6 percent when the annual average increase in wealth throughout the nation is only 3 percent. Show wherein he was confused.

9. Explain the danger of double-counting in the measurement of wealth. What items of private wealth are excluded from totals of national wealth? Why?

10. "Money is the very essence of wealth." "Most money is not wealth at all." Straighten out this difficulty.

- 4 -

Framework and Problems
of the Economic System

THE aim of this chapter is to show what an economic system is and what it does, and especially to sketch the outlines of the system called *capitalism,* or *free enterprise,* the leading problems it faces, and the nature of the response to these problems in the United States.

This is the third of three chapters presenting from different angles a broad view of economic organization and processes. Chapter 2 dealt with the occupational structure and the relationship to economic progress of a complex arrangement of industries. Chapter 3 examined the flow of production and income on which economic welfare depends. This chapter will center attention on *economic control*—how responsibility is placed and direction provided in a complex economy.

As never before, the people of the United States are conscious of the possibility of different schemes of economic control. The present political weight of Russia in promoting its type of collectivism, a totalitarian collectivism, is perhaps the main reason for this awareness. But the progress of socialism in Great Britain, the nursery of modern capitalism, is an equally startling fact. In the United States, concern over the future of capitalism was aroused by the depression of the 1930s and intensified in many minds by the New Deal policies that were adopted to combat depression and reform the economy. The broadest and most basic questions of economic organization have become matters of common discussion.

For such discussion to be fruitful, an orderly approach is necessary. Phrases such as "free enterprise," "capitalism," "the American way," as they are ordinarily used, convey no definite idea of the arrangements by which economic activities are knit into a system. Hence they provide no basis for judging whether specific practices or policies fit into any given system. Can large corporations, for instance, or labor unions be reconciled with the main elements of order in the American economy? What about the New Deal policies? Do they serve, as Mr. Roosevelt contended, to establish a more stalwart capitalism, or do they undermine the American system, as most businessmen have insisted? Or, leaving such broad matters, is it socialistic, as one United States Senator declared, to require manufacturers to put grade labels on canned goods; or is it acceptable in a free system for Mr. Petrillo to keep his musicians from making phonograph records? Solemn pronouncements on such issues may indicate merely that people view with alarm whatever disturbs them personally and rationalize broadly whatever is beneficial to them. But to be worth while, serious judgments must be made in light of some understanding of how the economic system is supposed to work.

Functions and Processes of Economic Systems

The necessity of an economic system, as the term is used here, grows out of the specialized organization of production. A Crusoe is hungry and proceeds to get food for himself. But how is Green in the food industry induced to provide food for Brown in the clothing industry? Why does he bother about Brown's hunger, and why does Brown extend himself to make clothes for Green? And if a dozen other people work with Brown in making clothes, what keeps them at it? What hold does Brown have over them?

How, indeed, did it happen in the first place that it is Green who provides food and Brown who provides clothing, and that some millions of other people are engaged in their particular tasks? And how is it decided just what kind of products they will turn out, and what quantities of each of a thousand different things they will produce? And since all of them consume the products of others, by what process is each person assigned the share he is to have in the total product?

These are problems of economic organization—not the only problems, but the ones with respect to which economic systems differ. Those matters of organization which were discussed in Chapter 2—occupational structure and the relationship of activities in a modern economy —need not differ among systems. In those matters Soviet Russia has been doing its best to ape capitalist America. But in placing responsibility for production, in controlling the use of resources, in dividing the product, Russia has moved along different lines.

When people specialize, they become dependent upon each other. In a broad sense they must cooperate with each other. The task of an economic system is to cause them to cooperate in an effective and orderly way. It is plain that specialization would mean chaos if no arrangements were present to give impetus and direction to the action of individuals. The greater the variety of goods that an economy produces, the more advanced its technology, the more numerous the people who are interdependent, and the wider the areas over which they are spread, the more difficult is the task of an economic system.

One aim of the present section is to explain the nature of this task and to break it down into a number of subtasks or *functions* that any economic system must perform. The starting point in analyzing a system must be a concept of what is expected of it.

The other aim of this section is to sketch the main *principles* and *processes* by which an economic system may perform these functions. In this sketch we shall talk about the characteristic arrangements of a *free economy* and of a *managed economy*. The essentials of a free system are that it is spontaneously organized and, in a sense, automatically controlled. In contrast, a managed economy is consciously planned and authoritatively controlled. We shall not be discussing American capitalism directly, or the actual collectivism of any country, but simplified models that can be used in analyzing actual systems. The main purpose will be to provide a systematic basis for discussing American capitalism.

Enterprise and incentive function

The first task of an economic system is to get people to undertake the production of goods and carry on the work of production effectively. Two aspects of this function should be distinguished, although they are closely related. One involves the placing of responsibility for production, the type of enterprise relied on; the other involves the incentives by which people are induced to perform energetically, progressively, and with reasonable continuity. The free and managed economies can be distinguished more clearly and sharply with respect to their enterprise than their incentive arrangements.

Enterprise. There will be no production unless some person or some organization assumes responsibility for it. In the Crusoe situation, it is clear who must act if anything is done, but where (1) people specialize in producing different goods for each other, and (2) considerable amounts of labor and of wealth must be brought together in producing certain goods, a problem of initiative and leadership arises. Certainly one would not expect various human and material resources to combine spontaneously in establishing an automobile factory in Detroit or a hydroelectric plant on the Columbia River. Some arrangement is necessary in any system through which productive projects are undertaken and organized.

In a completely *managed economy,* government is the *enterpriser,* or entrepreneur. Representing society collectively, it takes responsibility for initiating and running the farms, factories, railroads, stores, and other projects. All workers are government employees, and all land and equipment are presumably state property. Government acts through such bureaus or industrial departments as seem to be indicated by the technical features of industries and the problems of administering them. The direct economic management may be responsible to a political dictatorship or to elected government officials.

In a *free economy,* production is undertaken voluntarily by individuals in a private capacity, acting singly or in such associations as partnerships and corporations. In part this is what the phrase *free private enterprise* implies. Individuals make the decisions and supply the necessary material resources. Private ownership of the means of production is a characteristic of this type of enterprise.

Under private enterprise a problem of authority arises within the specific productive project, or *business firm* as it is called. In projects of any magnitude there are likely to be a number of owners, and there are certain to be workers who are not owners. While production may be organized spontaneously for the whole economy as between different firms, it must be planned definitely and managed with authority within the firm if operations are to be efficient. Among the several owners of a business, a problem of responsibility arises which is often solved through the *corporate form* of organization.[1] For workers who are not owners, the solution is to subject them to a management selected by the owners.[2] Subordination of workers to owners is a feature of economic organization implied by the term *capitalism.*

Incentives. When people participate in production, there must be an incentive to do so. Again, in the case of a Crusoe, the connection is close between effort and satisfaction. If he does not catch the fish, grow the crop, construct the shelter, he suffers. But the producer in a specialized economy—the enterpriser under a free system and the employee under any system—finds no adequate inducement in his own production. He may get some pleasure from it, but there are few occupations in which people will put forth long hours of consistent effort

[1] Discussed in Chapter 8.

[2] It is conceivable that labor should hire wealth rather than wealth hire labor, but not at all probable. Responsible hiring requires possession of wealth, else there can be no assurance of regular payments for the services hired. The role of the entrepreneur-capitalist will be discussed in Chapters 8 and 28.

merely for the direct satisfaction derived from working. Some positive scheme of rewards and penalties is needed to induce vigorous production.

People may be led to act under a variety of impulsions. They may be reduced to slavery, and, through failure to perform as they are told, they may incur the lash, the concentration camp, or even the firing squad. They may be put in a labor army and subjected to military discipline. Their incentive may be the fear of such penalties as these, or it may be the lure of various honors or medals or of promotions within a hierarchy of ranks.

One associates these inducements with state enterprise and centrally managed production. But under any system, appeals to patriotism may be used to expand production, especially in time of war; desire for popular approval and prestige may stimulate activity, especially in public service and the arts; so also may a sense of duty, however inculcated. On the other hand, economies where state enterprise prevails, such economies as that of Russia, may operate pretty much as free economies do in getting people to work.

The *incentives of a free system* lie mainly in the connection between performance and income. Production in a free society is a matter of voluntary inclination, and individuals may work energetically, half-heartedly, or not at all. They are subject to compulsion neither as soldiers nor as slaves. But their welfare depends on what they do, and they are prodded by the fear of poverty and by their desire for the comforts and luxuries of life and the standing and sense of achievement that go with income. They may be impelled also by a desire to serve, and society may gain thereby. But while any system must justify its existence by its success in ministering to the desires of all men, a free system seeks this goal mainly by dangling before each individual the prize of personal gain and satisfaction.

The problem of incentives, it must be remembered, involves much more than getting good service out of hired employees. In a free system the primary need is to induce people to initiate and organize productive projects and risk private wealth in undertakings that may not succeed. Thus income in the uncertain form of *profit* has a key place in a free economy. The profit motive need not differ from the wage motive: both involve economic gain. But profits are linked with successful enterprise in a way for which there is no parallel in a managed economy. There the enterpriser is that abstract entity, the state, and the decisions are made by salaried administrators.

Production in a progressive economy requires an accumulating stock of machinery and the other instrumentalities of modern industry. It requires also a continually advancing technology, a growing knowledge of methods of production. Again, incentives are needed. Where enterprise is private, the return from productive wealth must induce the development of wealth, and improvements in methods are similarly rewarded. Where material resources are state-owned, government must develop them as state officials decide and state finances permit. In any system much of the technical progress is attributable to research workers whose rewards may bear little relation to their achievements.

Two aspects of production should also be noted, two exceedingly vital aspects that involve the nature of enterprise and of incentives but for which the ordinary income inducements of a free economy are not adequate. One of these is the need of *careful, foresighted use of natural resources,* especially minerals, forests, and the exhaustible elements of the soil. In pursuing present income, people are not sufficiently concerned with the requirements of a fairly remote future and consequently use resources wastefully. The other is the need, if an economy is to achieve the most for its people, of *continuous high-level use of its productive power.* The profit incentive allows production to sag seriously at times. Free enterprise implies freedom not to produce, and depressions occur when enterprise is not suitably rewarded.

The function of guiding the use of resources

The most complex task of an economic system is that of assigning particular resources to their specific uses and of channeling the resulting flow of products. How an economy performs this composite task is perhaps its most distinguishing feature and the one most influential in the everyday lives of its people. To be appreciated fully, it must be approached with imagination.

First, it involves the *guidance of production,* or *allocation of resources, among different products.* In the United States there are about 145,000,000 consumers for whom goods must be produced and many thousands of products among which the human and material resources of the nation must be divided. Each person desires many things, and tastes differ from one person to another. These are factors that an economic system must take fully into account if it is to use resources to best advantage. Ideally, no person should have to consume something he wants less in place of something he wants more, within the total of goods that he can have.

Second, the assignment of resources to their uses involves a recognition of the *fitness of each unit of them to serve in specific ways.* The 60,000,000 people who make up the working force of the United States differ widely in individual aptitudes and abilities. They differ also in their preferences for different kinds of work. Natural resources are present in a bewildering variety of soils and climates and mineral, forest, and other attributes, and they must be used in the locations where they are. There are also all the railroads, factories, power plants, and other produced facilities. For each unit of each resource there is the question of the product for which it is best suited, and of the particular way of using it that is best, in view of its characteristics and the technology of the industry. Questions of the *location* of certain activities and the *scale of operations* also enter the general problem of the most effective pattern of production. These are all elements in the task of guiding the utilization of resources faced by every economic system.

Thirdly, because resources do not serve their final purpose until, in the form of products, they enter the possession of consumers, an economic system must guide and adjust the movement of products to the persons who will have them to use. Two aspects of this control should be noted. For one thing, *specific goods must reach the right persons,* and some procedure of assignment or selection is necessary. For another, *goods must move fast enough, but not too fast,* into the hands of the users. Especially in the case of farm products that are produced periodically, the rate of use must be adjusted so that the supply will last throughout the crop year.

Guidance in a managed economy. It is conceivable that the use of resources and products should be controlled through comprehensive planning and compulsory execution of plans. This would mean, first, that some sort of council or commission would decide what products to produce and what the relative amounts of them should be. It would decide how many pairs of shoes to make and what kinds, how much wheat to grow, what amusements should be provided, whether women should have cosmetics and men chewing tobacco, and so on for all the goods that are possible in a modern economy. The state industries would function accordingly.

The commission, secondly, would inventory all resources, analyze their characteristics, and assign them to particular industries and to particular uses in those industries. It would decide whether this man should be a farmer or an actor, that man a laborer or an executive. It would need to choose among the alternative uses to which each piece of land might be put, whether less fertile areas should be cultivated, where factories should be located and cities developed.

The commission, thirdly, would establish some sort of rationing scheme by which each family or other consuming unit would receive specified amounts of particular goods—at rates adjusted to the available supplies.

Of such a nature would be the system of control in a fully managed economy. It is important to realize how formidable the task would be. If the planners actually tried to take account of all the preferences of all individuals for all different products and different kinds of work and of the fitness of all units of labor and other resources for many possible roles in production, the task would probably come as close to requiring omniscience as any conceivable human undertaking.

Indeed, as thus stated, it would be impossible to carry out, and the management of the economy would modify it in either or both of two directions. One expedient, as implied above, would be for the planners to control production not on the basis of the actual preferences of people but according to some idea of what people ought to have, probably from a fairly limited range of products. Rationing would consist in giving people those products, presumably with little choice. Such a procedure would involve serious sacrifice of the primary economic goal, as we view it, of promoting individual welfare.

The other expedient would be to move in the direction of a free system and depend in part on market processes to control the use of resources and products.

Guidance in a free economy. The system of control in a free economy is the most important thing to understand about it. It is control without anyone doing the controlling, guidance without a guide. It operates through markets in a quasi-automatic manner. Goods are exchanged voluntarily, and the decisions of many individuals are depended on to govern their production and use in a mutually satisfactory way. At first glance, it seems that the apparently independent decisions of millions of persons must create a chaotic situation—one in which production bears little relation to the preferences of people, in which resources are used without regard for their fitness, in which products are consumed by the wrong persons in ill-adapted amounts. But, on the contrary, chaos is avoided and order established through the fact that all decisions are made on the basis of a common principle, a comparison of values or prices that reflect the significant aspects of products and resources. The attitudes of consumers and producers are reflected in values, and these values in turn control the actions of consumers and producers.

In controlling the *relative production of different goods,* buyers indicate by their purchasing the quantities they will take at different prices, and enterprisers thus learn of the revenues that may be derived in different fields of production. Enterprisers know also the costs they must incur, the prices they must pay for labor and the services of other resources. Thus their quest for profit leads them to produce only those goods that are worth as much as the resources used in producing them. As demands for products change or the costs of producing them shift, production is adjusted without central planning or direction.

Similarly, *resources are fitted to specific tasks* partly through the liking of people for one kind of work rather than another and partly, perhaps mainly, through their desire to use their labor and wealth in ways that will bring them the largest income. Enterprisers, being anxious to keep costs down, try to combine labor and other resources in the most effective ways and in the best locations. Thus the best opportunities for income are found in situations where resources are used to best advantage. A free economy depends on the suppliers of resources to discover these opportunities without central guidance, but with the beckoning aid of the enterprisers who want to use the resources.

On the same principle, *products are rationed without planning or authority*. Individuals are free to spend their money for the products that please them and to indulge their preferences to the full extent of their incomes. But these products can be had only at prices that reflect the demands for them and the available quantities. If, for instance, the output of apples falls off or the demand increases, a higher price restricts the rate of use; and the price moves as high as the needed adjustment requires. Thus the use of apples is controlled automatically.

Under this principle of control, then, the individual is free from external authority, except the authority of the employer within the particular firm. He may consume what he pleases and produce what and where and how he pleases. But he reaches his decisions within limits that markets set, and his activities are thus coordinated with the activities of the numerous other people in the system. This principle of coordination is the heart of a free economy, and it has long been viewed by economists as central to an understanding of any system that, even in part, is freely organized. Some features of it will be examined further in the next section, and it will be considered in greater detail in Part V of this volume.

The distribution function

The last of the major tasks of an economic system is the division of total product and income among the individuals and groups that comprise the economy. Individual well-being depends directly on the share that the individual gets and not on the total product. However productive a nation is, some persons suffer poverty, and, however low its total output, conspicuous luxury may be the fortune of a few. Distribution is thus the aspect of organization that is most likely to arouse feelings of injustice.

In analyzing the structure of economic systems, as this section is undertaking to do, one should observe that the distribution of income may either be separated from the other functions of a system or integrated with them. If a system depends on income to provide the main inducement to production, then the incentive and distribution functions are combined. If, in addition, income reflects the value of productive services, then the division of income is likely to be combined with the fitting of resources into an efficient organization of production.

Only in a *fully managed economy* can the distribution of income be separated from these other functions. In such a system it is conceivable that all persons should receive the same income or that they should be supported according to their needs, while some other scheme of incentives is relied on to spur them to activity, perhaps some plan of honors and punishments. And they could be assigned to their places in production through a separate analysis of their usefulness in different capacities. Such a separation of functions is at least conceivable, but again it is likely that some concession would be made to the principle of free organization.

Under the *free principle,* the distribution of income cannot be separated from the other aspects of organization. It is an integral part of the whole scheme of market processes and value relationships. Incomes, which fix the individual's share in distribution, are also the chief inducement to production. In addition, incomes reflect the prices that must be paid for the services of labor and of productive wealth; it is on the basis of these prices that enterprisers organize resources into an efficient pattern of production. These incomes, moreover, determine the quantities of goods that people can buy; it is on the basis of the resulting demands for different goods that producers decide what they will do.

In addition to the discussion of these matters in Part V, distribution viewed as a social problem of inequality will be the subject of Part VI.

Review Questions

1. "Russia and the United States are essentially alike in their occupational structure, their pattern of production, but quite different in their economic systems." Explain carefully.

2. Do you think that popular discussion of the merits and defects of cap-

italism is wholesome and should be encouraged? Should the intelligent believer in American capitalism want to see its characteristics analyzed, and
honest comparisons made with the characteristics of other systems, or should
he view such analysis as disturbing and subversive?

3. "The situation of a Crusoe calls for economy but not for an economic
system." Explain. Show that the need of a system rests on specialization.

4. What is an economic system expected to do? Distinguish the principal
functions and subfunctions of an economic system.

5. Distinguish carefully the operations of a free and of a managed economy in the performance of these functions. At what points is a managed
economy likely to adopt features of the operation of a free system? Have you
seen any reason so far why some central management might enter a system
that, on the whole, is free? (The problems of a free economy will be brought
out in the following section.)

6. Distinguish several labels that have been applied to the free type of
economy and the particular characteristics to which they refer.

The Free Principle—Some Criticisms, Requirements, and Problems

American capitalism may be described as a modified free-enterprise
system. It developed when ideas of economic freedom ran strong; and,
though restrictions have entered through public and private action, it
has continued to rely mainly (1) on voluntary private enterprise and
effort in the production of goods and (2) on control through market
processes of the use of resources and the division of income. This conception of organization provides the most useful basis for analyzing the
working of the American system and considering its problems and the
policies they have induced.

This is not the place in our study for a critique of the system; that
must come, somewhat incidentally, as we go along. But as a basis for
the continuing appraisal of the economy that all students of it should
attempt, certain observations should be added to the sketch of an
idealized free economy in the preceding section. There are some
misconceptions that should be disposed of now, some essentials of
sound operation that should be stressed, some leading problems that
should be kept in mind as our study proceeds. This section is a miscellany of such matters.

Selfish aims and social interests

Capitalism has often been attacked on ethical grounds, and certainly
it has displayed features that have deserved the attention of moralists.

Perhaps the most fundamental attack has been aimed at its heavy reliance on private pursuit of income to cause individuals to act in the social interest—a central feature of the free principle of organization, as just discussed. Religious leaders especially have found it deplorable that self-seeking activity should be relied on, and even acclaimed, as the basis of social well-being, and they have often called for a change. When motivation in a free system is described as "intelligent selfishness," as it often is, the language at least is provocative. It is easy, moreover, to cite cases in which individuals, pursuing their private ends, have not been "led by an invisible hand," in Adam Smith's famous words, to promote the interest of society.[3]

This sort of attack is mentioned here not to introduce a discussion of the ethics of capitalism but because persons who sympathize with the criticism should realize how far-reaching it is. Sometimes they probably do not. It is mentioned also to make sure that the objection is not merely to certain provocative phrases but to the actual features of the economy to which the phrases refer.

From Adam Smith down, what economists have meant can be seen best by imagining the opposite situation. Absence of self-interest would mean that John Doe, the typical husband and father, does not work hard and does not spend money carefully because he desires to better his lot and that of his family. Instead, he is equally concerned over the well-being of all other families, of people he knows and of people he does not know. In trying to make the best possible use of his labor and his wealth, he acts impartially on behalf of everyone. He decides what use is best not on the basis of the income he gets from that use

[3] The concern of religious leaders over the fundamentals of capitalism has been voiced frequently in recent years. As one example, an important church conference in 1947 resolved that "The Christian church should oppose the classic doctrine as defined by Adam Smith 'that the individual in pursuit of his selfish gain will be led by an invisible hand to work the good' as an unsatisfactory answer to present economic problems." In stating his general argument against restrictions on imports, Adam Smith said: "Every individual is continually exerting himself to find out the most advantageous employment for whatever capital he can command. It is his own advantage, indeed, and not that of the society, which he has in view. But the study of his own advantage naturally, or rather necessarily, leads him to prefer that employment which is most advantageous to the society." In developing the point Smith says of the individual producer that in directing "industry in such manner as its produce may be of the greatest value, he intends only his own gain, and he is in this, as in many other cases, led by an invisible hand to promote an end which was no part of his intention. Nor is it always the worse for the society that it was no part of it. By pursuing his own interest he frequently promotes that of the society more effectually than when he really intends to promote it. I have never known much good done by those who affected to trade for the public good." *An Inquiry into the Nature and Causes of the Wealth of Nations,* Book IV, Ch. II. This passage is quoted in order to suggest that the student searching for an economic philosophy may accept everything that Adam Smith says about the fundamentals of economic control and still hold that a good deal of supplementary governmental control is necessary in dealing with present economic problems. Adam Smith would probably agree, for he was a realist.

but through some sort of judgment as to what society as a whole requires.

Economists who speak of the role of self-interest may merely be observing that John Doe does not appear to act in this way, and so they describe how an economy seems to operate on the basis of the way he does act—that is, their analysis may be quite neutral, neither approving nor disapproving what they see. But many like Adam Smith have gone farther and expressed the view that it would be unfortunate for everyone if John Doe were to act in the way the preceding paragraph suggests. They have said, in effect, that such conduct would mean (1) a weakly motivated and (2) a badly organized economy. Whether one agrees or not, one cannot ignore either point.

First, these economists have doubted, despite the seemingly opposite view of some moralists, whether ordinary human beings will work as vigorously and effectively on behalf of the unseen millions as they do on behalf of themselves and their families. People show a depth of concern over births, deaths, and illnesses in their own families that they do not feel over like episodes, even millions of them, in other families. And it seems just as natural for them to feel greater concern over feeding, clothing, sheltering, and otherwise aiding their families than other families. If so, then most people can be expected to work harder and more faithfully to promote immediate private interests than general social interests. In holding this, the philosophers of free enterprise have not preached selfishness but have said that it seems wise to adapt institutions to dominant human traits.

On the second point, economists have doubted whether the economy will be controlled effectively if people act with the unselfishness imputed to John Doe above. We have seen how difficult would be the task of an all-powerful commission that tried to plan the most effective use of all resources, but this is the very kind of judgment and from a poor vantage point that the unselfish John Doe would have to make. Undoubtedly he knows much better what is best for his family than for all families, and if he and millions like him go into the market to get what seems best for the people they really know about, the result is a better guidance for producers than a diffused altruism would provide. And if he tries to sell his labor where he can get the most for it, he seems to have the best chance of using it where other people think it most valuable. Or if, as an enterpriser seeking profit, he produces what people are most anxious to buy and pay for and tries to keep his costs down by using labor and other resources as efficiently as he can, he is likely to be acting rather well from the social standpoint. This, at least, is the point that Adam Smith was making when the "invisible hand" entered his discussion.

To reject the role of self-interest as economists have viewed it is to reject these ideas of motivation and control. Rejection implies a belief that individuals can be made to work as well for society in general as for their own families. And it would seem to call for a completely managed economy to take the place of the quasi-automatic control that rests on the limited value judgments of individuals. In other words, those who disavow self-interest should realize that they are taking a very radical position, in the popular sense of that word. On the other hand, acceptance of the role of self-interest does not mean approval of a system that is subject only to automatic controls. It does not mean approval of unscrupulous and antisocial self-seeking. One may still favor many policies to correct abuses and strengthen the economy. But the analysis on which such policies rest does not involve general condemnation of self-interest.

Opposite misconceptions of economic control

As these remarks suggest, it is essential to understand the structure of an economy before diagnosing its ailments. The common tendency is to think in too general terms and to obscure specific problems with blanket diagnoses and prescriptions or with blanket defenses of the status quo.

An example is found in the popularity of the idea of *economic planning* as a general and undefined solution of economic ills. A depression comes, as in the 1930s, and numerous people declare that the reason lies in the absence of comprehensive control over individual activities. The obvious solution, they say, is to establish order where there is none, and this means central planning. Presently a war arises and prosperity returns, and it is noted that a War Production Board has a good deal to say about the use of resources. This is planning, so, along the same line, it is urged that we establish a Peace Production Board to maintain future prosperity.

The student with no more knowledge of economic organization than this chapter has presented has no difficulty in criticizing such an approach. He would note first that an economy without central planning and authoritative control is not therefore uncontrolled. Until war shortages developed, there was a rather remarkable correspondence in the United States between what was produced and what people wanted to buy—a correspondence which, in view of the vast number of producers and consumers involved, could not possibly be accidental.

Certainly there was a degree of order that gave proof of a far-reaching and effective system of control. But production had bogged down badly, and unemployment was high, so that something was amiss in the processes of the economy. The problem was to ascertain specifically where the trouble lay. When war came, there was some positive redirection of activity to war purposes, but why should production of goods as required by government mean greater prosperity than production of goods as ordered by consumers? Very likely the expansion in total buying explained the improvements and not the positive direction of it or the planning of it. Since the purpose here is not to analyze depressions but to illustrate the defect of ill-defined diagnoses and prescriptions, we may end the example.

No less superficial is the attitude of many conservative people who, in opposing government interference with business, reveal a mystical faith in the beneficence of free processes. Somehow, in ways not open to vulgar prying, it seems that an inexplicable economic providence orders things for the best. Such a view of economic control is dangerously negative. The "invisible hand" lauded by Adam Smith has nothing providential about it, despite the poetry of the language. It consists of a definite set of processes which may or may not operate, depending on conditions. Nor are these processes sufficiently recognized by saying that "supply and demand" will take care of everything if given a chance.

In the mechanism of control of a free economy, values and prices may prove to be a defective regulator of the actions of sellers and buyers, and markets may not maintain the conditions necessary to effective control. In approaching the problems of the economy, something further should be said here regarding values and markets.

Values and prices

Three criticisms of the role of values and prices in economic organization as observed in the United States are worth considering briefly at this point, both to re-enforce what has been said concerning economic control and to show the roots of certain major difficulties.

1. Should other units be substituted for value units? The first is a fundamental attack that would displace values altogether as the basis of economic decisions. During the 1930s a group of people who called themselves Technocrats gained publicity for the idea that the depression was due to the central place of value in the organization of economic life. They proposed to substitute units of energy for units of value. "The cause of our troubles," they said, "lies in the fact that during these years, instead of thinking of our well-being and of the operation of our

country in terms of energy, we have thought of it in terms of something
purchasable with dollars." And again:

> Fundamentally the economists, Marxians, and all are as archaic as the
> bankers, for they are tied hand and foot to a conception of price. What does
> price mean in a country where 0.44 of a single pound of coal can do the
> work that the average man can do in eight hours? It matters not a rap what
> men think, wish, or desire. We are face to face with a law of nature. . . . It
> is plain that we must get for ourselves a new series of standards if we are to
> deal with this highly intricate social mechanism that technology has built.[4]

As in many utterances of this kind, we find here a sincere groping for
the source of economic ills—but with little idea of the functions and
processes of economic control as rooted not in outworn institutions but
in the very nature of economy. The problem of economic control is that
of coordinating the actions and preferences of innumerable producers
and consumers so that resources will serve effectively the interests of
human beings. The heart of the matter is what people "think, wish, or
desire." The consumer decides whether to buy this steak, this coat, this
automobile, not on the basis of the energy it represents but on the basis
of its importance to him, its value in relation to the values of other
things. The producer must be guided accordingly. Not even in matters
that involve the use of energy can he be governed by energy calculations. If he were, he might freely substitute for the pound of coal an
amount of radium releasing the same energy. Only a consideration of
value, or cost, would preserve the radium for its essential uses. The
essence of economic control must be a comparison of values.

The Technocrats were disturbed by those *general changes in prices*
which we refer to as inflation and deflation, or changes in the value of
the dollar. They failed to distinguish these general changes, which may
be very bad, from the changes in the relative prices of particular products and services, which are the basis of all economic calculations. The
prices of particular goods must be flexible if they are to reflect the shifting desires of people for goods, the shifting methods of producing them,
and the other factors that create a continuing problem of control. The
energy equivalent of an automobile, perhaps the number of man-hours
required to produce it, may be the same whether the total output is two
or four or six million cars per year. But values depend on quantities,
and only in them does the producer find a guide to the quantity he
should produce.

[4] "Technology Smashes the Price System," an article prepared under the supervision of
Howard Scott, leader of the Technocracy movement, *Harpers Magazine*, January 1933, pp.
130, 141.

2. Are values distorted by the scarcity element? Control must rest on values, but do markets soundly represent the true value of things? More disturbing than the criticism of the Technocrats is the charge that prices are distorted and fail to reflect the interest of society in products and services. How foolish, it has been said, is a valuation process that attaches more importance to an evening's violin playing by a Kreisler than to a whole year's work by a coal miner or puts a higher value on the work of movie actors than that of teachers in the public schools! In the face of this criticism, it is necessary (1) to defend the general basis of market values and (2) to admit the existence of a real social problem.

The defense is that values, if they are to play their part in economic control, must reflect both of the basic elements in economic situations pointed out in the preceding chapter—both the *utility* and the *scarcity* of things. The essence of value is importance, but the importance that counts is the *importance of particular units,* not the general importance of goods. Air and water, for example, are indispensable, because of the nature of the human wants they serve, but, if they are not scarce, no one need be concerned over specific units of them, and no economic decisions have to be made regarding them. It is right, therefore, that they should have no value in the economic sense. Manganese and tungsten, on the other hand, are far less important goods in the general sense, but the quantity of them is so small that each unit of them is important, and their value must be high to insure that they will be used economically in the special processes for which they are fitted.

This is the Kreisler-coal-miner situation. No practical question arises as to whether coal mining is more important in its entirety than violin playing. But there are practical questions as to the use of the services of particular coal miners and particular violinists. Such questions must be decided on the basis of the importance of a coal miner, more or less, and of a Kreisler, more or less. From this standpoint, a substantial difference in value is indicated.

The social problem springs from the fact that these market values are also the basis of incomes. Thus, if the values of people's services differ greatly, their incomes must also differ greatly. Kreisler can live far better than the coal miner. This is the problem of *inequality in the distribution of income.* Many critics of capitalism believe that the inequality which exists is wholly indefensible and should be remedied, if necessary by drastic means. But whatever the merits of the issue, there can be no question that inequaliy is a major source of discontent and bitterness.

Inequality is thus inherent in the valuation of people's services and is unescapable in any economy that bases incomes on such values. But not all the inequality arises from this source. Part of the inequality of income under capitalism arises from the private ownership of land and capital and from the inequality that prevails in the ownership of wealth. Part of it also grows out of imperfections in the operation of markets which distort values in a sense quite different from that under discussion here. Whatever the source of inequality in the distribution of income, we should view it as one of the fundamental economic problems.

3. Is income in value terms a sound economic goal? The scarcity element in value gives rise to another serious economic problem. Producers may often increase their incomes by creating artificial scarcities —that is, by restricting the supply of their products and services to increase the value of what they sell (or the net value after subtracting costs).

This, of course, is contrary to the social interest. In a specialized society, producers do not consume what they produce but depend on the products of others. They get command of the products of others through their money incomes, a matter of values, and they want these incomes to be as large as possible. But at the same time, the interest of all producers taken together is in having the largest possible total real product, not the largest monetary total. Thus, if they restrict output to increase their individual money incomes, they defeat collectively the interests of everybody. This amounts to saying that values, while a necessary *guide* to producers and consumers, can be a defective *goal* of economic action. This, essentially, is the point the socialists are making when they contrast "production for profit" with "production for use." They say that in a free economy, the pecuniary goal obscures the true goal of satisfying human wants. But their phrase "production for profit" is not adequate, since wage earners as well as enterprisers may restrict output to increase income.

Are the possibilities very great of increasing money income through withholding output, either in quantity or in quality? Those who say yes believe that preoccupation with money return must mean serious sacrifice of production. But defenders of a free economy say that the best way to make money is to serve the customer to the fullest extent. Actually the answer must depend on the way in which markets operate.

Conditions necessary to effective control through markets

Market processes, the "supply and demand" of the businessman, provide a fully satisfactory scheme of control only under certain market conditions. These conditions cannot be assumed to be present. This is not the place to discuss them, but we must take note of them because of their relation to the structure of a free system.

Competition. The specialized producer certainly finds it to his monetary advantage to skimp his product and charge a stiff price for it, provided he can do so and maintain his sales. This danger, however, is largely avoided if buyers have adequate opportunity to turn to competing producers. Under competition, the individual producer is bound to respect the interests of the buyer as to quality and price, under penalty of serious loss of patronage if he does not. He cannot create artificial scarcities unless the other producers act in concert with him—unless, in other words, some degree of monopoly is present.

Thus it is on competition that a free economy mainly depends to insure that production for profit is also production for use. Competition should thus be thought of as an integral part of the quasi-automatic system of economic control. Values and prices provide the basic regulator, and competition is relied on to keep prices and profits from being excessive. It is relied on also to keep prices sufficiently high, especially in the case of labor and materials and foodstuffs, so that jobholders, farmers, and other primary producers get a fair return. Competition is viewed, moreover, as an essential element in the scheme of incentives. Especially as an inducement to improve products and adopt more efficient methods, the desire to get ahead of other producers or at least to keep from being outdone is regarded by the defenders of a free system as among its important virtues.

Knowledge and mobility. Competition may be defined broadly so as to include all the characteristics a market should have, but for the present, at least, it is better to state separately two of the conditions that should be present in a freely organized economy. One of these conditions is that buyers and sellers should have thorough knowledge of the commodities and services they deal in and of the opportunities for obtaining them and disposing of them. The other condition is that buyers and sellers should be able and willing to take full advantage of this knowledge in establishing contacts throughout the market and in exploiting only the best propositions. Economic adjustments require mobility.

If the consumer is a poor judge of the goods he buys, producers will be inclined to take advantage of his ignorance. Goods will be represented as better than they are, and prices may be higher than they should be. But, whatever his knowledge, the consumer will suffer if he buys carelessly and does not shop around to compare the offerings of sellers.

The ordinary worker is in a similar situation. To get the most for his labor, he needs wide knowledge of employment opportunities, of compensation and working conditions on different jobs. It is important also that he be able to shift from one locality to another to take advantage of the best income possibilities. Consumers, workers, investors, all economic groups, can do the best for themselves, and do the most in goading others to perform effectively, only if they are informed and enterprising in what they do.

Markets for products and productive services in the United States are of many kinds. They differ greatly in the degrees of competition and monopoly that prevail in them and in the effectiveness with which various groups of buyers and sellers exploit their opportunities. We need not be concerned at this point with the details of these matters; we need only recognize that an economy can be free in the negative sense that it is not centrally managed and still be a poor example of free organization on the basis of markets. It is in the interest of competitors to restrict their competition; there are situations in which competition cannot be made to work; all parties are likely to take advantage of ignorance and inertia where they can.

Unemployment of resources

We have thus identified two areas in the operation of a free economy where serious problems arise: (1) inequality in the distribution of income and (2) monopoly and other defects of markets. A third area—and perhaps the most dangerous—is the sagging in total production that often occurs, involving depression and unemployment.[5] What depression can mean to the country was shown in the preceding chapter in the discussion of the effect of the depression of the 1930s on national income.

Depressions, as was pointed out on page 73, grow directly out of the voluntary nature of enterprise and the uncertainties of profits as the inducement to make use of resources. Behind these uncertainties lie a complex of forces that cause variations in the total demand for goods, variations related to the voluntary nature of buying and investment in a free economy. These are matters that will be discussed in Part IV.

At this point one should be impressed with the irony of a situation in which millions of people want both goods and jobs—a situation in which they live on a low plane for lack of goods that they have the ability to produce and are anxious to have the chance to produce. This is

[5] In analyzing the problems of capitalism, it is useful to differentiate these three problem areas, even though they overlap at quite a number of points.

clearly the kind of situation that is most likely to provoke demands for government action.

Unemployment and economic analysis. Since the purpose of this chapter is to provide a useful framework for analyzing economic problems, this is a good place to call attention to a pitfall into which the unwary often stumble when their minds are on unemployment. To recognize that it is a pitfall, one should have in mind the meaning of *economy* and *economizing* as these words have been used so far. Economizing has meant getting the most out of something. The enterpriser is economizing in getting the most product he can from the labor and materials he uses. The consumer is economizing when he divides the money he has among different goods and between present and future needs so as to get the most satisfaction from it. The whole economy deserves to be called an economy only as it promotes the most effective allocation of resources in view of the desires of consumers, the characteristics of the resources, and the prevailing technology.[6]

Compare this conception of economic behavior with the ideas that often seem to prevail when unemployment is extensive, as in the 1930s. At such a time many people deplore technological progress on the ground that, instead of adding to output, it adds to unemployment by displacing labor with machines. Machines already in use may even be put aside, as when hand labor is substituted for power-driven equipment in road building. Hours of labor are reduced to spread work among job applicants, even though their real preference would be to work more hours for the sake of more income. Public money is spent on "boondoggling" projects to create jobs, even though it is recognized that the results may not be worth their cost. In such an atmosphere, people begin to think that the real object of economic organization is to provide jobs. The job, not the product, seems to be the goal. It is as if economy were promoted through absorbing more effort in getting a given output, rather than through getting more output from a given effort.

To anyone who views the matter from the standpoint of wartime and early postwar experience, such a trend in thinking seems absurd. World War II made it clear that national interest depends on getting the most product from resources and that the real shortage is of resources rather than jobs. High income since the war has confirmed the view that economic welfare depends on using resources as effectively as possible

---

[6] No confusion need arise from the common practice of using the word *economy* to mean (1) a process, as when one speaks of practicing economy, and (2) an economic organization or system, as when one speaks of a capitalist or socialist economy. The economy (in the latter sense) is the means of achieving economy (in the former sense) from the social standpoint.

in producing goods. But even during this period of high production, make-work practices have continued to some extent, and in some trades restrictions have been placed on the output of labor.

It is imperative to remember, despite the seeming superfluity of resources during depressions, that the long-accepted meaning of economy is the sound and proper guide and that judgments of what is good and bad for the nation, from the standpoint of its permanent health, must be on the basis of getting the most, not the least, out of resources. Policies and practices that limit output and use resources wastefully must, in general, be condemned.

At the same time, we must recognize the exceptions as important. A policy that is basically uneconomic may sometimes be justifiable as an emergency or short-run measure. If a depression is severe, and if there is no prospect of early recovery, measures may be useful in caring for the unemployed—such measures as reducing working hours to spread work among more persons—that should be condemned as permanent policy. Thus great care is necessary in all economic analysis to distinguish the ideas which are applicable in a long-run and fundamental sense and the ideas that can only properly apply to immediate and special situations. Unemployment may be all too common, but it must not be allowed to influence thinking so that the creation of jobs rather than the production of goods seems the essence of economic behavior.

Freedom and Authority in the American Economy

Having in mind (1) the functions and processes of economic systems and (2) the main problems that a free economy encounters, one can appreciate the modified sort of free system that American capitalism now seems to be. In order to characterize it, a number of developments and policies will be mentioned in this section, not to invite consideration of them individually but to fit them into a general picture.

Government policies that control private economic behavior have, for the most part, been adopted in the United States only in the face of heavy opposition. The tradition of noninterference has been strong. This tradition is rooted is the philosophy of natural rights and personal freedom that became dominant in the late eighteenth century and in the related belief, in the economic sphere, that free enterprise and free markets are the best means of promoting progress and general welfare. The doctrine of economic freedom was never accepted as fully on the continent of Europe as in Great Britain, and its sweeping acceptance in the United States was qualified in the case of international trade. The policy of restricting imports was established early and without the difficulty encountered in pushing later interfering measures. Apart from the drastic controls of war periods, the depression of the 1930s has been the only period of quick adoption of extensive reforms.

In considering modifications of the free type of system, one should not assume that any governmental interference with private action violates the principles of a free economy. Violations are as likely to be found in the private practices of businessmen and other economic groups, and government action may be merely corrective. Much government interference has been aimed at bolstering rather than modifying the processes of a free economy. The phrase *laissez faire* has commonly been used in referring to a hands-off governmental policy, and the early advocates of a free system often had a rather extreme *laissez faire* in mind. But now it is recognized that *laissez faire* may mean the breakdown of a free system and that various types of government action are necessary to give it a chance.

Basic government functions in the economy

Government has a number of functions of an economic character which are generally looked upon as its distinctive responsibility and which raise no question of interference with the private economy.

Government is the accepted enterpriser with respect to such undertakings as national defense, preservation of internal order, provision of highways, educational facilities, and various institutions for defectives, administration of national and state forests, and so on. In 1947, as noted in the preceding chapter, some $18.8 billion out of $202.6 billion of national income were credited to the productive use of resources in government undertakings. Only when public enterprise gets over into such fields as electric power is it thought of as invading the domain of private industry.

Government must also provide the legal structure, the rules of procedure, for private activity. With private wealth an essential element in the economy, *property rights* must be defined and individuals protected in their use of wealth. With production carried on and goods transferred through innumerable private transactions, *contractual relationships* must also be defined and enforced.

Notable in the organization of private business has been the role of government in developing the *corporate form of organization*. The *patent system* also reflects the responsibility of government in encouraging private activity. Of outstanding importance in implementing private business is the establishment of a *money unit* and a *currency system*.

Market policies

Public policies that are thought of as interfering with and controlling private economic action have been most conspicuous in the market sphere. Policies in this sphere are to be expected in view (1) of the central role of markets in economic control and (2) of the need, if markets function satisfactorily, of competitive and other conditions that are not necessarily present.

For the most part, these policies make no attempt to substitute government control for automatic control through free markets. Under them, government does not set prices, tell enterprisers what, how, or how much to produce, or ration goods to consumers. Instead it attempts, as through the antitrust laws, to keep markets competitive, through the Federal Trade Commission and the Pure Food and Drugs Administration to prevent misrepresentation of products and to improve the character of competition, and through the Securities and Exchange Commission to protect investors from deceptive invitations to invest. The purpose is not to have government perform the essential functions of economic control but to maintain markets that can be depended on to perform these functions.

This type of policy, however, is not deemed adequate in all areas of the economy. Particularly in the case of railroads, power companies, gas companies, and other so-called public utilities, monopolistic tendencies are strong, and some degree of monopoly is useful. Thus government has undertaken positively to regulate the prices charged and to control production in various ways.

In recent years, prompted by the experience of the 1930s, a serious distrust of free markets has developed, not because they fail to protect consumers but because they are believed to be too harsh on producers. Thus there have been many attempts to get government aid in establishing some protection from the rigors of competition. A number of policies reflect this attitude, the most important being the assistance given farmers under the Agricultural Adjustment Act.

Labor policies

The first revulsion from the extreme *laissez faire* of the early nineteenth century developed in the interest of labor. Whatever might be the merit of unsupervised markets in other respects, they did not work to the advantage of ordinary working people. Men, women, and children were subject to intolerable factory conditions, and there was no real corrective in the mere refusal of individual employees to work under those conditions. Thus there began a mounting series of laws dealing with health, safety, hours, minimum wages, and so on.

Labor unions, organizations of workers formed to protect their interests, are of long standing, but only in recent years has there been positive governmental encouragement of unions in the United States and of collective bargaining as a means of settling differences with employers. For our present purpose, the important thing to note is that collective bargaining is a method of control quite different from the processes of a free market. It involves the principle of setting one private organization against another, whereas in a free market there can be no substantial concentration of private power. Bargaining, however, works only within limits set by more fundamental forces.

These labor policies may be viewed as an attempt to improve the distribution of economic welfare. But they are not unique in this purpose, since it is one of the objects of the market policies mentioned above and also of the administration of government finance.

Banking, depressions, public finance

Government influences the working of American capitalism at various other points and in other ways. Frequently policies that are quite separate in some respects converge in others, as in attacking the depression problem from different angles.

Banking is an industry that has long been subject to government control. One reason is that bankers use the money of other people, and safeguards are needed to insure safe keeping and safe handling. Another reason for the control is that banks, through extending credit, provide part of the money supply, and the provision of money is basically a government function. But banking policy, under the Federal Reserve Act, is aimed also at the general problem of economic instability, the problem of depressions and recovery from depressions.

How far government should go in trying to maintain prosperity is still a debated issue. But one noteworthy development in the field of government finance has been that government spending, taxing, and borrowing are now viewed, in part at least, from the standpoint of their effect on general prosperity. At the same time, these financial activities of government are viewed also from the standpoint of their effect on the distribution of income.

But despite all of these policies and despite the pressures of private organizations, the American economy still follows broadly the model of a free system in its reliance (1) on voluntary private enterprise and pursuit of income for the production of goods and (2) on market forces and prices to coordinate the activities of the producers and users of goods.

Review Questions

1. "Economic organization rests primarily on the desire of people for personal well-being and advancement. This may be an unsound basis of organization, but those who condemn it are under some obligation to show how the system they advocate would operate and perform its necessary functions." What does the first sentence mean? (Develop two main points.) Does the second sentence represent a reasonable attitude toward advocates of economic reform?

2. "Economic planning is the obvious cure for the inevitable chaos in an economy in which everybody does as he pleases." As a student interested in a constructive approach to the weaknesses of American capitalism, in what ways would you criticize this statement?

3. "We should depend on supply and demand to control our economic affairs, not the government." Answer the same question as under 2.

4. "If we produced goods and exchanged them on the basis of the man-hours required in their production, rather than so elusive an element as their values, we would have a much sounder economy." Criticize.

5. "If values are to perform their regulating function, they must reflect scarcity as well as utility." Explain and illustrate.

6. "In reflecting scarcity as well as utility, values are the root of the inequality problem." Explain and illustrate.

7. "Because values reflect scarcity as well as utility, they make it possible to increase income without contributing to economic welfare." Explain and illustrate.

8. "If, in a free economy, money income is to be attainable only through serving society, certain conditions must prevail in markets." Explain. Do these conditions exist automatically because an economy is free?

9. What appear to be the leading problems or problem areas of a free economy? What is the special irony of the depression problem?

10. "Economizing consists in spending less." "It would be uneconomical for a family with a $2000 income to save $1000." "To economize is to choose." Do you accept each of these statements as consistent with the meaning of economy as that word is used in economics? Explain.

11. "The chief requirement of economic welfare is to have plenty of jobs." Is creating jobs equivalent to promoting economy? Explain. What difficulty in economic thinking arises in this connection? Relate the terms "long run" and "short run" to it.

12. "Departures from *laissez faire* do not necessarily constitute departures from the free principle of economic organization. They may even support that principle." Explain.

13. If American capitalism is described as a modified free-enterprise system, what seems to be the nature of the modifications?

PART II

Productive Power
and the Methods
of Capitalism

What is the most important economic problem?
Many Americans, recalling the 1930s, would say it is the problem of
unemployment, of failure to make use of available productive power.
Other Americans, observing the often bitter controversies over wages
and profits, would say it is the problem of dividing the national income
among contending groups. Colin Clark, summarizing his comparative
study of economic progress throughout the world, declares: "In conclusion, we must again remind ourselves that, for the greater part of
the world, and indeed ultimately for the wealthier countries too, the
most important problem remains the problem of increasing productive
power." [1]

For a ten-year period, half prosperous and half depressed, he found
that annual income per worker in the United States averaged just below $1400. In the same period, and with their output adjusted to the
same dollar unit, Canada, New Zealand, Great Britain, and Switzerland
also had incomes above $1000 per worker. Australia, the Netherlands,
France, Sweden, Germany, and Belgium ranged from $1000 down to-
ward $500. Czechoslovakia, Greece, Hungary, Japan, Poland, Italy, and

[1] *The Conditions of Economic Progress*, Macmillan & Co. Ltd., 1940, p. 16. The figures in
the following paragraph are from Ch. 2. Statistical comparisons of this sort are necessarily
difficult, in view of deficiencies of data in many countries and the differences in money
units and in the commodities typically produced. But with every allowance made for possible error, the contrasts remain sufficiently striking. Few investigations of this kind have
been undertaken, and Mr. Clark's studies will be drawn on at a number of points in the
following chapters.

Russia ranged below $500 toward $200. More than half the world's people, including India and China, produced less than $200 of goods per worker per year. Between the most and the least prosperous nations, a fourteenfold difference prevailed.

In 1942 Sumner Welles, the Under Secretary of State, said: "The problem which will confront us when the years of the postwar period are reached is not primarily one of production. For the world can readily produce what mankind requires. The problem is rather one of distribution and purchasing power. . . ." [2] On the contrary, the main effort of the United States, in the early postwar period, has been to produce enough to keep world destitution from breeding world revolution. It has made this effort with a recognized deficiency of capital equipment and an ominous dwindling of oil and iron reserves. For the longer postwar period, world needs must be met, and American economic ambitions realized, very largely by the same means that brought a near trebling of per-capita output in this country between 1870 and 1930—that is, an expansion in productive power.

This is not to say that the more controversial problems that lie ahead, the more politically explosive problems, are not found in the fields of employment and distribution. But it is to say that fashions in popular emphasis need to be reviewed, and the balance occasionally adjusted.

Part II will deal with the conditions on which productive power depends: basic resources, human and natural; capital equipment and its expansion; the organization of production in plant and firm and industry; and also the corporate and financial processes through which productive enterprise operates under capitalism.

---

[2] Quoted by Kenneth E. Boulding, *The Economics of Peace*, Prentice-Hall, 1945, p. 102. Professor Boulding observes: "The black mass of grinding poverty under which a half to three quarters of the world's people subsist is not due primarily to exploitation, or to bad distribution of income, or to lack of purchasing power. It is due to the sheer unproductiveness of the mass of human labor."

- 5 -

Natural and Human
Resources

However complex the organization of production becomes, it rests at bottom on resources found in external nature and in qualities possessed by human beings. These *primary resources,* as they are called, are the ultimate basis of productive power.

In the terminology of economics, these resources are referred to commonly as land and labor. The word *land* is used broadly to cover everything that nature provides—not only the surface of the earth and its fertility but also its minerals and original forests, its potential water power, its fish and other wild life. *Labor* is likewise used broadly to include the entire human contribution, whether of hand or brain, whether unskilled manual effort or the activity of artist and executive.

Often we shall speak of resources as *factors* or *agents* of production, but sometimes it will be necessary to distinguish land and the service of land, human beings and the services they perform. Strictly speaking, it is land service and labor service that are the factors of production, not the qualities of land and people from which they come. But the meaning will be apparent from the usage, and no special emphasis is needed to avoid confusion.

A theme running through this chapter, and also the two that follow, is the great progress that has taken place in *technology*. Whether we speak of the primary natural and human resources or of capital goods, which are a sort of secondary resource, or of the complex modern organization of production, productivity depends on knowledge of how to produce. Technology is not a separable topic but an essential, integral aspect of all of these topics.

Man and external nature will be discussed in separate sections of this chapter—separate but for the fact that, in economics, external nature is only what man understands it to be. Between these two sections will be one that relates man quantitatively to the natural setting in which he operates. This is the age-old problem of population. The only idea in the chapter that can be called an economic principle—the principle of diminishing returns—will be developed in discussing this problem.

Natural Resources

The economic dependence of man on external nature is evident. Nature contributes, first of all, the substances of which all material products consist. Man can manipulate matter but not create it, and his dependence on nature is therefore fundamental. Elements from soil and air and water combine in the plants and animals that yield foodstuffs and textile fibers. Metals from the earth are the distinctive materials of the machine age, and other minerals enter glass making, ceramics, and building construction.

The earth yields also energy resources—the coal, petroleum, natural gas, and water power—which are basic to modern production. Merely through its surface area, the earth gives man the place and space for his activities, his work and his recreation, sites for his towns and cities, for his roadways and flying fields.

No economic theory is needed to describe the positive role of natural resources in production. The main problem is that of the adequacy of resources to meet the needs of high and expanding production. The United States has been generously endowed, but its natural endowment has now largely been brought into use and at many points has become seriously depleted. Does further progress therefore face inescapable natural limits? Are the backward countries of the world doomed by nature's niggardliness to a continuing low level of production?

Adequacy is, of course, a relative term. In an absolute sense, no resource that is economic is adequate. Its scarcity limits output. Adequacy is relative to the level of living hoped for. It depends also on the number of people for whom that living is sought. The aim in this section is to distinguish some of the factors on which the adequacy of natural resources depends, apply them briefly to the United States, and view the problem just a little from the world standpoint. The relationship of population to natural resources will be deferred for discussion in the following section.

Factors governing the adequacy of resources

To interpret nature's contribution to production, one must view it from several angles. The following deserve consideration:

The basic fixity of nature. The natural environment in which man operates is fundamentally outside his control. This is what is meant by calling it natural. This environment appears, moreover, not to have been designed to meet his particular requirements—certainly not his changing requirements. Nature has furnished man a setting and framework for his activities and a rich outfit of things for him to use, and to this situation he must adjust himself.

Labor power, in contrast, is adjusted automatically, though not always perfectly, to the need for it. Additional mouths to be fed and bodies to be clothed bring with them additional hands and brains to produce needed goods. Machines and all man-made instruments of production are inherently expansible and adaptable to meet requirements. But only one earth, with its surface area, soil, climate, minerals, and running water, is available for use.

This comparative fixity of the natural environment is the basic factor in appraising the adequacy of resources. It is a notable influence also in the distribution of income, as will be shown in Part VI.

Resources responsive to knowledge. Although the natural setting is fixed, the resources themselves may expand greatly in an effective economic sense. Natural resources depend as truly on man's knowledge as they do on his natural endowment. In an economic sense, natural resources consist not of the things that nature provides but of the things man knows about and can use. Deer and buffalo were a resource to the American Indian, but pools of oil beneath the earth's surface were not. Coal became a resource when people learned that it would burn and still more of a resource when the steam engine was invented.

Thus natural resources expand through *discovery*. Explorations which have revealed new land areas have been major economic, as well as political, events. But long after settlers have invaded the areas, the finding of mineral deposits has continued to expand productive capacity. Today, as "wildcatters" locate a new oil field or prospectors find veins of metallic ore, nature is enabled to play a larger role in production.

Resources expand also through *scientific progress* and the applications of science. The waterfall that once merely obstructed navigation came presently to turn a water wheel and later an electric generator. Coal, petroleum, the metals—all the natural elements in modern industry—became significant resources through advances in technology. These advances continue.

In this expansion, *transport development* has played a distinctive part. Not only must the presence and the uses of resources be known, but they must also be accessible and at a cost that is not prohibitive. It was once said that Germany would never have a great steel industry because the essential elements, iron ore and coal, were too far apart. Actually nineteenth-century transport progress easily solved the modest geographic problem. More strikingly, the Great Lakes freighter and the modern freight train successfully overcame a far greater distance barrier in bringing Lake Superior ore into contact with the coal of Ohio and Pennsylvania and made possible the American steel industry. Undoubtedly a great mineral potential in the mountain areas of Asia, Africa, South America, and perhaps even in the Antarctic, still faces the transport barrier. Important Canadian discoveries are being opened to use.

But discovery, technology, and transportation, it must be remembered, work only within a setting that man cannot expand or redesign. A shortage of natural resources cannot be overcome as can a shortage of locomotives or turret lathes. The prospector, the scientist, and the road builder may increase the supply, but only within boundaries that nature has set.

Depletion. Natural resources may thus expand, but they may also contract, and many of them do. Adequacy at one time does not mean continuing adequacy. Natural resources may be classified in various ways, but probably the most significant basis in distinguishing them is their susceptibility to depletion and exhaustion.

At one extreme in such a classification are those resources that completely escape contraction through use. The best example is the service of land as sites for buildings and roadways. Land is not used up through supporting office buildings and railroads nor is its future serviceability reduced. This circumstance, combined with the fact that so little of the land area is used in this way—less than 1 percent is occupied by towns and cities in the United States—means that manufacturing and commerce, the chief urban activities, do not suffer directly through pressure on the land supply. These aspects of the natural-resource situation, which we take for granted, are particularly fortunate for such densely populated countries as Great Britain.

In some other instances, depletion need not be a factor. The flow of water in streams does not decline through installation of electric generators, though it may decline or become highly irregular if the tributary area is denuded of trees and heavy grass, so that rain water runs off rapidly rather than in a delayed and steady flow. Likewise, the fertility of soil can be maintained indefinitely through wise use, but excessive cropping can deplete it, and erosion from wind and water can remove tons of top soil per acre every year. Contour plowing, interspersing strips of unplowed land, growth of windbreaks, well-planned drainage, and other procedures help greatly to conserve the soil.

The original forests are an exhaustible resource, and lumbering in this country has been conducted largely as an extractive industry with little regard for future needs. But trees are growing things, and depletion is not inevitable. By maintaining conditions favorable to growth and by adjusting cutting to the rate of growth, forests can be utilized as a permanent resource without diminution. The same can be said of wild life. The fur industry might easily destroy the stock of seal, beaver, and other fur-bearing animals, and edible fish may be taken from rivers, lakes, and ocean more rapidly than reproduction occurs. With wise practices, however, wild life is a continuing resource.

Depletion is most crucial in the mineral field. Each barrel of oil, each ton of metallic ore or coal that is taken from the earth is a net subtraction from the stock in nature's custody. An industrial civilization that rests on a vast use of metals and earth-borne sources of energy faces here its most serious threat. Wasteful extraction and wasteful use must be strongly opposed, and further discovery, improved utilization, and the development of substitutes strongly encouraged.

Trade as a natural-resource factor. Transport development has been mentioned as a factor in the natural-resource supply. A related but larger point is that regions and entire nations are not dependent merely on the natural resources within their own borders. As long as materials and products are readily traded in, the productivity of an area is not doomed by its own particular deficiencies. In effect, regions and nations may combine their resources to their mutual advantage.

Some natural limitations cannot be escaped through trade. Land as a site for buildings must be used where it is. In the downtown area of every large city sites are extremely scarce, and nothing can be done about it except to build taller buildings and incur the cost of congestion. Or, where a backward people are committed to providing their own foodstuffs, the size and quality of their own area of crop and grazing and hunting land must closely limit their output. This is the situation of China and India today.

But a region may concentrate on manufacturing and merchandising, as New England has done, and support its people on a high level even though it must depend on other regions for much of the food and raw materials that it requires. Entire nations, as Great Britain has shown, can do the same. With raw cotton from the United States, Great Britain developed a great textile industry with markets throughout the world. Similarly a nation like Australia may obtain automobiles and machinery not through operating mines and factories but through raising wool for export. Or, like Switzerland, it may make its scenery bring it goods of a more substantial kind.

Natural resources, we have seen, are relative to the knowledge and skill of people. They are relative, also, to the scheme of interregional specialization that has developed. This is a basic fact to which we shall often return. Indeed we shall stress it once again in the present section.

Natural resources of the United States

Without a full statistical survey, a few features of the natural-resource position of the United States should be kept in mind.

Agriculture. Of the two billion acres of land in the United States, about half is in farms. Of the farm area about half, a little over one-half billion acres, has been classified as available for crops. Typically in recent years about two thirds of this crop area has actually been planted and harvested.

Little of the land not now in farms is eligible for farming. It is mountainous, incurably arid, badly eroded, or a needed part of the permanent forest domain. Several million acres of farm land are abandoned each year, and additional areas should be retired from cropping and used only for pasture. It is estimated that more than half the crop acreage has been impaired appreciably by erosion.

At the same time, the area actually planted to crops can be expanded considerably. Some suitable farm land is idle, some pasture land plowable, some cutover forest land worth making into farms. Some arid land is practicable to irrigate. A recent Twentieth Century Fund study puts the potential crop area, after appropriate subtractions and additions, at 460,000,000 acres, or more than 100,000,000 acres above the area harvested in 1943.[1] Nearly half that expansion, it is suggested, may well take place by 1960. Land that becomes available through expensive clearing, draining, and irrigating should be regarded as only in part a natural resource and in part a man-made productive facility like a machine or a building.

But farm output may be increased not only through using more land but through making better use of land. Technology has advanced strikingly in agriculture and may be expected to improve further. From the early 1920s to the early 1940s, output per acre for a variety of cereal crops, fruits, and cotton appears to have risen by 30 percent

[1] J. Frederic Dewhurst and Associates, *America's Needs and Resources*, Twentieth Century Fund, 1947, pp. 610–612. This is an extensive study based on a wealth of underlying material, especially government publications. Chapters 23 and 24 have been drawn on considerably in the present section. Important sources of information are the United States Bureau of Mines and the Forest Service, the Soil Conservation Service, and the Bureau of Agricultural Economics in the Department of Agriculture. For a number of years the National Resources Planning Board was a fruitful source of publications in this field.

or thereabouts on the average. A large increase took place also in the ratio of livestock products to the number of animals on farms. The rise in output per acre may be attributed in part to the retirement of inefficient acreage, but it is to be credited mainly to better plant and animal breeding, better fertilizing, and better soil practices in general.

The striking fact is that this improvement took place without an expanded use of labor. It is true that there was an increase in the use of farm equipment and of fertilizer, and both of these require labor and other resources to produce. But between 1920 and 1940 the labor directly involved in farming fell by 1,500,000 persons. If soil-conserving practices are pushed, it seems likely that a moderately expanding population can enjoy an improving farm output for a good while to come, and with probably a continuing decline in the fraction of the labor force used in agriculture.

Forests. Between a fifth and a fourth of the area of the United States was classed before World War II as forest land. Less than half, or about 200,000,000 acres, of this area contained saw timber suitable for lumber. The western states, with 37 percent of this acreage, had 70 percent of the saw timber.[2]

The forests of the northeastern, central, and Great Lakes states were cut ruthlessly, and cutting proceeds in excess of growth in the South and West. The remaining saw-timber stand was estimated at about one and three-fourth trillion board feet before the war. Cutting and depletion from fire and pests were taking about one-half billion board feet annually, and new growth was believed to restore about two thirds of this loss. Much of this restoration was in the South, where growing conditions are most favorable.

The contraction of forests, their greater remoteness from leading markets, and the reduced availability of saw timber have raised the cost of lumber and restricted its use. Peak consumption occurred in the first decade of the century, a 20 percent decline took place between 1929 and 1940, and a further decline of 25 percent has been predicted by 1960. The heavy wartime demand did not reach the 1929 level. Other materials have been substituted for wood in building construction, the making of furniture and vehicles, and other uses. To some extent wood waste has been used in various synthetics. The use of wood has been economized by applying preservatives to fence posts, utility poles, and railroad ties. At the same time there has been a great increase in the cutting of trees for pulpwood.

With continuing improvements in the use of wood and in conservation practices, it seems that the minimum need for forest products to

[2] *Ibid.,* pp. 591–593.

accompany a rising plane of living can be met; but the improvements need vigorous promotion.

Minerals. The mineral situation is less hopeful. Among the nations, the United States is by far the biggest user of most minerals, and, while its resources are prodigious, they are becoming dangerously low at important points.

Before the war the United States produced one third of the world output of coal, iron ore, and copper, nearly two thirds of the petroleum, about 90 percent of the natural gas. Exports of molybdenum, sulphur, and phosphate rock were substantial fractions of its output, and smaller fractions of its coal, petroleum, and lead were sold abroad. There was a small import balance in the case of iron ore and zinc, a substantial balance in the case of bauxite (for aluminum), and most of the tin, nickel, manganese, and asbestos was imported. By 1948 it appeared that the balance in the case of petroleum was shifting to the import side.

Except for some elements taken from the air and sea water, mineral resources are exhaustible, and depletion has become serious in such major instances as petroleum and iron. It is difficult, however, to measure the degree of exhaustion and predict when it will become complete. In any forecast, assumptions must be made regarding the future rate of use, further discoveries, and the type or grade of the resource that it will be commercially feasible to exploit.

The war cut deeply into the reserves of iron ore, and in the high gross output of the postwar period products of steel have been a large component. It seemed when the war was over that the better grade of Lake Superior ore would run short within two decades, but large reserves of low-grade ore would remain. In the case of petroleum, also, war demands were extremely heavy, but by 1947 consumption exceeded the wartime peak and was 50 percent higher than before the war. Railroads were installing oil-burning locomotives, homes were being equipped with oil furnaces, farms were being mechanized, highway transport was expanding, and military uses remained high. Short-term shortages were appearing and long-term prospects were uncertain, though, so far, new reserves were still being found as rapidly as extraction occurred. Known reserves of zinc, lead, and bauxite in the United States had scarcely more than a decade to go, and domestic copper would soon run short.

The situation, however, is not without its hopeful features and alleviating circumstances. We should note:

1. Coal, which has continued to account for nearly half the energy produced, seems adequate for thousands of years, though with increas-

ing difficulty of extraction. Water power, which is not subject to exhaustion, is open to further development. So far it has accounted for less than 5 percent of the energy output.

2. Discovery of mineral resources continues. Another Butte or Mesabi is not likely to appear, and new oil pools are declining in size and harder to discover. In the nature of the case, however, hidden minerals are not quickly nor completely revealed. Thus sedimentary areas suggest that as much as fifty billion barrels of oil may still be discovered in the United States.[3]

3. As the consumers' goods and industrial equipment made of metal expand, the volume retired from use each year increases, and a mounting quantity of scrap metal becomes available for use. By no means all the used metal is recoverable, but in such lines as steel it may provide a third or more of the material currently used.

4. Technology moves ahead in achieving given results with smaller quantities of minerals, in bringing lower grades of ore into effective use, in finding substitutes. In twenty years the coal consumed in generating a kilowatt-hour of electricity fell by more than half. Alloy steels have attained great strength with a declining weight of metal. Progress in utilizing certain clays containing aluminum and brown ores containing iron can yield vast quantities of these metals. Methods of obtaining oil from natural gas and coal are known, and to some extent in use. The possibilities of nonmilitary use of atomic energy are being explored. Plastics are being developed which may displace metals in many uses.

5. The United States is not limited to the mineral resources within its borders. Imports are already important and are certain to become more important. Great deposits of leading minerals are present in regions that as yet make little use of them. While foreign sources are not always dependable, improvement in trade relations is not a hopeless prospect. It is possible, moreover, to stock-pile minerals to last through periods of interrupted trade, especially if they are free from deterioration and not required in great quantities. Canada, a dependable source of important minerals, is likely to serve the American economy increasingly in the future.

Two further optimistic general observations should be made. One is that, despite the heavy reliance on metals and mechanical power in

[3] *The New York Times,* February 8, 1948. This view was expressed in a discussion of the immediate advisability of embarking on an extensive synthetic oil program, involving an investment of $9,000,000,000 to produce 2,000,000 barrels daily. Postwar consumption was running about 6,000,000 barrels daily in the United States. For a fairly optimistic "Look at the Oil Situation," see *The Lamp,* March 1948. This is a publication of the Standard Oil Company of New Jersey.

an industrial civilization, the use of minerals in this country has been expanding less rapidly than the gross national product. An advanced economy develops most in the tertiary lines. The other is a reminder that the fraction of the working population engaged in extracting minerals and in processing them for use is very small. Though it should require double the present effort to supply them or their equivalent, the added burden might easily be outweighed by other factors in economic progress.

At the same time, dependence on present mineral sources is so vital that prevention of waste and improvement of use should be major national concerns.

Public policy in the natural-resource field

With its free-enterprise tradition, the American economy never expands the area of government control without opposition. But government is deeply involved in the utilization of natural resources, and a good case can be made for expanding its influence.

Basis of government action. Government enters first of all through the fact that much of the land area in a new country is originally subject to governmental disposition. Early policy, if one may judge by American experience, is likely to consist in encouraging private settlement and exploitation to hasten economic and political development. But presently the need appears of tempering this policy in the interest of a fair distribution of the benefits from land resources, since ruthless frontier practices are likely to enrich a few people without corresponding public gain. Loose regulations and land frauds in this country brought a belated tightening of controls in the interest of keeping opportunity open for as many people as possible.

Finally the problem of depletion and conservation becomes crucial. The logic of public action in this sphere is compelling, even though the free-enterprise tradition is strong. Free enterprise, as the preceding chapter pointed out, is an acceptable system only if certain basic functions of economic control are performed satisfactorily through the more or less automatic processes of the market. In the case of exhaustible resources, control through markets is necessarily inadequate.

For one thing, the market is too shortsighted to take account of scarcities that will not become serious for decades or generations. In a free system, it is expected that anticipated scarcities will send prices up and thus restrict the use of goods and conserve the stock. This restraint may control the use of wheat between harvest seasons, but it can have little effect on the cutting of timber and the extraction of minerals. Even today, with prospective shortages generally appreciated, much timber is cut without regard for future growth, and ores and oil are removed in ways that, while immediately low in cost, leave a needlessly large fraction in the earth. Only government can take the long view that the problem requires.

Control through the market works poorly also because the scope of individual action is too limited. The removal of forests and heavy grass affects the run-off of water, bringing floods and soil erosion, in ways so indirect and over areas so wide that private action cannot possibly meet the problem. Likewise, if pools of oil are reached by the wells of different operators, private interest dictates the hastiest possible operation of each well to get the largest possible fraction of the pool before it is exhausted.

Obstacles to government action. Although public action to conserve exhaustible resources is indicated, the standards and principles which should govern that action are not clear, and there is bias on the side of doing little. There is no objective method of weighing present interests against future interests, and when a choice must be made between them, the future, especially the remote future, is bound to suffer. Our desires for gasoline to run our cars, for oil to heat our homes, for wood and metal in many forms are pressing, persuasive desires in comparison with which the interests of posterity have only a shadowy existence. Thus often the consuming public is on the side of the business interests who are opposed to restriction of their activities.

There is also the difficulty that the seriousness of future shortages is uncertain. Past estimates have sometimes proved too pessimistic, and new discoveries and scientific advances make drastic conservation methods seem unreasonable. It is not feasible politically to impose serious present sacrifices to forestall future emergencies that may never occur. Nevertheless, in an economy dependent on iron, oil, coal, timber, and soil fertility, the sheer folly of tolerating needless waste of these resources is readily apparent. Some important steps have been taken to conserve and improve the nation's resources.

American policy. Federal conservation policy was initiated late in the last century, but received little impetus until the presidency of Theodore Roosevelt. It has centered in the administration of the great public domain, where government has been free to improve and protect the forests, conduct lumbering scientifically, control the grazing of privately owned cattle and sheep, manage wild-life development, and create parks and recreational areas. Public mineral lands have been subject to lease on a royalty basis. Many states have moved along similar lines.

The federal government has engaged also in extensive river-valley projects for purposes of irrigation and flood control as well as for power and navigation. Its research activities in problems of soil, forests, water flows, minerals, and wild life have been enormously useful. Much demonstration and other educational work has been done to improve private practices. Bonuses have been paid to farmers to promote soil conservation along with other ends. An interstate compact, with federal cooperation, has served somewhat to limit the extraction of petroleum; steps have been taken toward the "unitization" of oil fields. Both state and federal governments have acted to conserve game animals and fish.

But government control has not reached the heart of the problem and the obstacles are great. Property rights and competitive practices that are basically unsuited to the exploitation of exhaustible resources have been changed but little. Resources in the public domain are inferior and meager, and the right of private operators to cut trees and extract minerals wastefully on their own land has been little modified. Practices improve, but the improvement is slow. The authority of state and federal governments is imperfectly coordinated, and the states are often lax. Private interests exert pressures to curtail existing restraints, notably in matters of oil and grazing rights on public lands. Certainly students of the problem would agree that government responsibility for future public interests in this sphere has not been accepted in a firm and effective way.

Natural resources and international relations

Natural resources are involved in international as well as domestic policy. One theory of the explosive situation before World War II was that world resources were unfairly divided among the "have" and "have-not" nations. Germany, Italy, and Japan made the most of this theory and rationalized their aggressiveness accordingly.

As to the inequality of natural endowment among nations, there can be no question. Certainly the United States has been conspicuously fortunate, with its fine farm land, great forests, rich mineral deposits, and usable water power. In contrast, such countries as Italy and Japan have tried to support large populations on narrow strips of generally inferior land.

Unquestionably the economic ambitions of a nation may be seriously impeded by lack of natural resources, just as a region within a nation may be handicapped. But for a high level of living, it is not necessary that a region or nation should be blessed by nature in a rich and varied way. More important is the skill with which a nation uses the resources it has as well as its success, as noted above, in associating itself with other nations in an effective scheme of specialization and trade. Nor need it use aggressive means to gain sovereignty over the areas with which it trades. The relatively high income of such nations as Switzerland and Sweden, in comparison with Russia, for instance, cannot be credited to a more generous nature nor to imperialistic control of richer lands.

The problem of international relations, in which natural resources are a factor, will be discussed in Chapter 32. The point to be stressed here is that satisfactory trade policies will contribute greatly toward solving the natural-resource problems of nations. The United States has a large stake in international relations from this standpoint.

Review Questions

1. "Land has a fixity that other resources do not possess. Yet the expansion of natural resources has been a vital feature in economic progress." Explain both sentences in this statement.

2. Classify natural resources on the basis of their exhaustibility.

3. "Developments of the last two hundred years in effect incorporated in the British economy vast new areas opened up in the Americas and other continents." Explain.

4. "The capacity of American farm land to provide a growing population with a rising level of living must depend on the outcome of conflicting factors." Explain.

5. If timber is cut and otherwise depleted at the prewar rate, about how long should the lumber supply last? Distinguish the extractive and genetic approaches to the forest industry.

6. What are the most critical points in the mineral situation in the United States? On what grounds can it be hoped that minerals will continue to be available for continuing industrial development?

7. "The typical controlling mechanism of a free-enterprise economy is conspicuously inadequate in the natural-resource sphere." Explain. What basic difficulties oppose the development of a conservation policy?

8. What has been done governmentally to conserve natural resources in this country? What are the main inadequacies?

9. How closely do the income levels of different countries appear to correspond to the abundance of natural resources within their borders? What conclusion is suggested regarding economic progress? Regarding international relations?

Population and Natural Resources

The adequacy of natural resources must be judged in relation to the number of people who depend on them. If there is a natural-resource problem, there must also in some sense and in some degree be a population problem. Within the boundaries of the United States there were 5,000,000 people in 1800, 23,000,000 in 1850, 76,000,000 in 1900, 140,000,000 in 1945. This expansion took place in a new country. But during the nineteenth century the number of people more than trebled in such a settled area as England and Wales, more than doubled in Europe as a whole. The numbers that a given natural setting accommodates must, in some way, be a factor in economic welfare.

As a matter of fact, the size of population can influence the level of production in several ways. (1) If essential resources are exhaustible, a greater population hastens their depletion or compels a lower per-capita rate of use. This is obvious and requires no elaboration. (2) Apart from exhaustion, a greater population requires a more intensive use of the soil and other resources, with a possible adverse effect upon output. This changing proportion of labor to land has been the main reason for fearing overpopulation. It will be the occasion in this section for explaining the principle of diminishing returns. (3) A denser population alters the organization of production from the standpoint of manufacturing, marketing, and transportation. Thus the population problem is more complex than the natural-resource problem. (4) Some recent writers have held that a growing population is more likely than a static or declining population to cause a high aggregate demand for goods, one that will hold production at capacity. Since the present discussion is concerned with the factors that explain productivity rather than the employment of productive power, this question will be deferred to Part IV.

It is important to understand how changes in population exert pressure on the level of output. It is also important, and quite a different matter, to sense the factors that influence population growth. It is important, further, in interpreting historical developments to remember that many forces are likely to be working together and that it is difficult accordingly to sort out their individual effects.

The question of optimum population

The object in this discussion is not to render critical judgments. But it should be recognized that all opinions regarding overpopulation or underpopulation imply some standard as to how large population ought to be.

Reference was just made to the effect of population on the level of output and on economic welfare. The viewpoint implied is the typical viewpoint of the economist. That viewpoint, as stated with appropriate qualification in Chapter 3, is that economic welfare depends primarily on per-capita output and income. Economic progress means a rising plane of living, more real income per person. From this standpoint, the right population for an area is that number of people, in relation to material resources and technology, which will cause the flow of products per capita to be the highest possible.

This, plainly, is not the only standard that can govern judgments. One may hold that it is not the quality of human living that should decide but rather the quantity, that it is better to have more people living on a tolerable level than fewer people living on a higher level. Or one may hold that artificial restraint on propagation is morally so objectionable as to outweigh any economic benefit. It is sufficient to say that convictions along these lines do not rest on economic grounds. Holding them necessarily affects one's views of population policy but should not affect one's acceptance of the economic analysis of the effects of population growth.

There is also the common view in aggressive nations, especially the dictatorships, that population should expand to increase national power, whatever may be the effect on individual well-being. Additional people mean greater total output, even though per-capita output is less. They provide military man power as well. It is not hard for a Mussolini to subsidize large families while conquering outside areas to relieve population pressure at home.

From a defensive standpoint, similar considerations may influence the thinking of peoples whose ideal is a high plane of living. The white race fears that it will be outweighed in world affairs by non-Caucasian races; Western nations fear Slavic expansion; Canadians of English stock fear the faster multiplication of French-Canadians.

The effect of population on per-capita output will govern the discussion that follows.

Overpopulation—the Malthusian theory

Multiplication of human beings beyond the means of supporting them is one of the world's oldest and most general problems. Its desperate nature largely explains the practice of infanticide through many centuries in many lands even among the more civilized peoples. In Western countries in the last few decades the fear of overpopulation has largely passed, but little over a century ago it infused economic thinking with an almost complete hopelessness regarding human betterment.

The classic statement of population theory appeared around 1800 in the writings of Thomas Robert Malthus. His views provide an excellent basis for summarizing the problem, because they are comprehensive in scope and his pessimism was voiced near the beginning of a period (1) of spurting population growth and (2) of a rise in the plane of living probably without precedent. No prophet, basing his views on the long past, could seem to have been more wrong in predicting the imminent future. Yet the Malthusian doctrine was not wholly demolished by events.

Briefly stated, the doctrine is that population tends strongly to outrun the means of subsistence. It is biologically possible for numbers to double every 25 years, and the impulse to propagate is strong. The food supply—Malthus stressed the essentials of living—can be expanded only at a much lower rate from a fixed land area. Thus the growth of population must somehow be checked. Since growth arises from an excess of births over deaths, the principal check may be either a low birth rate or a high death rate. Malthus, especially in his later writing, saw some possibility of voluntary limitation of births, but his chief stress was on the pressure of population in causing poor nutrition, disease, and war. These, respectively, he called the "preventive" and "positive" checks. The Industrial Revolution was under way, with its promise of expanding productivity, but Malthus and other writers of his time believed that the power of numbers was so great that larger output would mean merely the support of more people, not a higher level of living. Examination of this theory discloses the main elements to be considered in analyzing the population problem.

Potential population. There can be no question that the biological possibilities of expansion are so great as to make some check on numbers necessary. With population doubling in successive 25-year periods, the descendants after 1000 years, or 40 generations, of one man and one woman would number in excess of two trillion, or a thousand times the present population of the earth.[4] With the more modest rate of expansion that took place in England and Wales during the century following Malthus, the present world population would rise sixfold by the year 2100. We may envisage that prospect by imagining that the present population continues but that the earth in all its aspects shrinks to one sixth its present size. Certainly the possibilities of population growth as evidenced fairly recently indicate that the earth may easily be overrun with people. Malthus was right that population must somehow be checked.

Downward pressure on output. In explaining how the growth of population depresses output, Malthus provided no satisfactory theory. He noted that population tends to expand in geometric ratio (2, 4, 8,

[4] The 41st power of 2.

16, etc.) and said that, in contrast, the food supply expands by only an arithmetic progression (2, 4, 6, 8, etc.). There is no basis for the latter view, and while his general description was more realistic, no satisfactory principle was developed.

The principle of diminishing returns, which is applicable here, will be explained below. Its effect is not to modify the conclusions reached by Malthus but to modify his explanation of the process.

The checks on population. His conclusions, at least as grounds for predicting events in the Western nations since 1800, seem to be most seriously undermined by his views on population checks. He recognized the "preventive" checks and attached some importance to them, but he could not foresee the great change that would take place. Actually population has grown more rapidly since Malthus than within his experience. But the increase has occurred largely through a fall in the death rate and in spite of a decline in the birth rate that has averaged about 50 percent in western Europe and about 65 percent in this country.

The striking fact is that this great fall in the birth rate occurred when production was rising rapidly and people were able to live much better than ever before. Malthus saw evidence that births might be limited so as to hold the plane of living a little above a bare subsistence, but he saw no evidence that births would be restricted enough to sustain a large improvement. Actually, births have fallen so greatly that population in France became practically stationary some years ago. A few other countries have approached that condition. Projection of the curves for birth and death rates indicates that the population of the United States will reach a plateau between 1970 and 2000. For eastern Europe and much of the rest of the world, no such striking revision of Malthus's view is required.

The explanation of the falling birth rate is complex and only in part economic. Increased knowledge of the means of restricting births and acceptance of an ethic that supports use of the knowledge have been indispensable. The democratic environment, with its emphasis on individual interests above governmental power and ecclesiastical authority, has been influential. The need of a longer, more expensive education to succeed in a complex world has made it seem more important to raise a few children well than to have large families. Occupational changes have brought a vast migration from the farm, where children can be helpful, to the city, where they are a burden. New products have raised the conception of how life can be lived if children are not substituted unduly for material comforts and luxuries.

In this connection the concept of the *standard of living* should be introduced. The *plane* of living is the level on which people actually live. The standard is their compelling ideal of how they ought to live, a fairly realizable ideal that may be achieved by working hard and perhaps by postponing marriage and limiting offspring. Thus we may say that a rising standard of living has provided a powerful preventive check that Malthus did not foresee.

The pace of industrial change. Malthus's observation of the early Industrial Revolution could not disclose the swift developments that lay ahead. Population would have needed to move fast to cancel the expanding output per person that was to come. But it is not enough to say that during a given historical period skyrocketing production outdistanced population growth. There is the added fact that the rate of population growth declined. Perhaps, just as Malthus thought, a moderate improvement in production would have been canceled by increased numbers. Perhaps the very great improvement that took place was necessary to provide time for social forces to establish the preventive check as a powerful influence.

Certainly very important is the fact that the Industrial Revolution changed the occupational pattern. The rise in productivity greatly reduced the fraction of the population engaged in producing foods. More people, relatively, worked in manufacturing and commerce, fields in which the force of diminishing returns does not have the same damaging effect as in agriculture. This change, like the principle of diminishing returns itself, must be examined.

The principle of diminishing returns

This principle states more acceptably than Malthus did the effect on output of applying larger amounts of labor to the same land area. But it is not limited in its application to the population problem. It operates in all cases in which productive resources or factors of production are used in changing proportions and in which time is allowed for the most economical adjustment to be made. Thus it applies to situations in manufacturing in which more labor is used in relation to plant and equipment or more capital goods in relation to labor. It is important for its bearing on the population problem but is equally useful in analyzing the distribution of income. The present explanation, therefore, has uses beyond the present one.

Meaning of diminishing returns. Negatively, it should be said that diminishing returns has nothing to do with the exhaustion of natural resources. Minerals are exhausted in time even though they are taken from the earth at a constant rate, with no increase in the labor used in mining. The soil of farm land is depleted without intensification of use, if land is used improperly. On the other hand, with no exhaustion of the soil, the more intensive use of land by applying more labor to it, affects the rate of output. It is only through a change in the proportion of factors that diminishing returns appears.

Also, negatively, it should be said that diminishing returns is not an altogether apt phrase—although it is the conventional one—and it may suggest the wrong idea as to what diminishes. It does not imply, when more labor is used on a piece of land, that the total output will decrease. The total output must increase, otherwise the use of additional labor would serve no purpose. Diminishing returns refers to the output per unit of the labor or other expanding factor. It refers to the relation, the proportion, between the expansion of the labor and the expansion of the output. The principle is sometimes called the *principle of nonproportional output,* and this may be a better name for it.

The principle merely says that when a productive agent, such as labor, is applied in increasing amounts to another factor of production, such as land, a point will be reached after which output will increase less than proportionally to the expanding agent. This is exactly the same as saying that the output per unit of the expanding agent will fall. The principle does not say how fast the average output will fall. There is nothing in it comparable to Malthus's point about arithmetic and geometric progressions, for the rate of decline must vary from one case to another.

While the idea is a simple one, it is worth while to sharpen the statement of it with an example. In Table 8 a case is assumed in which different amounts of labor, from one to ten units, are used on a given land area. At one extreme so little labor is applied as to be wasteful, and at the other the amount of labor is so great as to be similarly wasteful. Growing conditions are the same for each application, and tools and other assisting factors are left out of account.

Three stages in the more intensive use of labor on land can be distinguished here. In the first, called the *stage of increasing returns,* output increases faster than the amount of labor, and output per unit of labor rises. This stage ends when the third unit of labor is applied and output per unit reaches its maximum of 13.3. This is the *point of diminishing returns,* and from it the *stage of diminishing returns* sets in.[5] In this stage output increases, but less than proportionally to the labor, and output per unit of labor falls. Total output reaches its peak

[5] Diminishing returns may be thought of also as the declining *additions* to output rather than as the declining average. This meaning is used in the treatment of value and income distribution, and the principle is then usually referred to with the phrase "diminishing productivity" or "diminishing marginal productivity." In the present connection, it is

TABLE 8—EXAMPLE OF DIMINISHING RETURNS

Units of land	Units of labor	Units of output	Output per unit of labor
1	1	10	10
1	2	26	13
1	3	40	13.3
1	4	53	13.2
1	5	65	13
1	6	75	12.5
1	7	82	11.7
1	8	85	10.6
1	9	83	9.2
1	10	79	7.9

with the eighth unit of labor and falls thereafter. *Absolutely decreasing returns* set in. The first and third stages round out the explanation, but only the stage of diminishing returns is of any practical importance.

Logic of diminishing returns. How do we know that output behaves in this way as factors are used in different proportions? So far as the declining average output from an expanding factor is concerned, ordinary observation and common sense provide a sufficient answer. One cannot put more and more coal in a small furnace, getting proportionally more heat, so as to heat a large building. If this could be done, no one would install a large furnace. Proportionally more power, indefinitely, cannot be obtained from a motor by injecting more fuel into it. If it could, a small motor would drive the *Queen Mary*. But it is just as unreasonable to expect to go on expanding output proportionally from a piece of land by applying more and more labor to it. Were it not for diminishing returns, the farmer should select the best single acre on his farm and apply all the available labor to it. The proportionate increase in output from more intensive use of the best land would be a greater output than inferior acres could yield.

The point is that, when more labor is applied to the same land area, each worker gets less assistance from the land. Both the labor and the land help to produce the product, and the use of relatively more labor means exactly the same as the use of relatively less land. If land is an economic resource, and therefore scarce, each unit of it is important; reduction of the area that a given amount of labor has to use must reduce the average output of the labor. Increasing the amount of labor

the average output that matters. In any case, the point at which the additions to output begin to decline is not significant, because it falls within the stage of increasing returns as here defined.

that must use a given amount of land must have the same effect. Thus labor applied to scarce land must operate in the stage of diminishing returns.[6]

Labor, of course, is best off if land is not scarce. Output per worker is highest at the point of diminishing returns (the third combination in Table 8). If land were abundant, an increase in population and in the number of workers would simply lead to the use of more land and not to a more intensive use of land. Thus the highest output per person would be maintained.

But to say that land is abundant is to say that land of the first quality—in fertility, location, etc.—is abundant so that inferior land need not be used. Output per worker on inferior land is lower, and thus inferior land is worth using only when the best land has become scarce and is used somewhat intensively.[7] If one asks whether the United States has to use its farm land beyond the point of diminishing returns, the easy answer is found in the fact that much inferior land is used in the United States. If land below the best is worth using, then the best land is worth using beyond the point of diminishing returns.

But it is not economical to use land prior to that point—that is, with so low an intensity as to be in the stage of *increasing returns*. Increasing returns may have a pleasant sound, but so light an application of labor to land is a mistake. In Table 8 the first and second combinations are in the stage of increasing returns, but output per unit of labor is less than in the third combination. Rather than to use labor in the first combination and get an output of 10 per unit of labor, it would be better to spread it over only one third as much land and get an output of 13.3 per unit, thus using it at the point of diminishing returns. Doubtless when new areas are opened to settlement, there is a temptation to spread labor too thinly in order to get possession of as much land as possible. But the effect on output is bad. Actually the stage of increasing returns is just like the third stage, that of absolutely decreasing returns. In the former, so much land is used that total output is reduced; in the latter so much labor is used that total output is reduced. To avoid the former, some land should be left idle; to avoid the latter, some labor should be left idle. If a country ever had so many people in land-using activities that they got in each other's

---

[6] It is equally true that land used with scarce labor is operating in the stage of diminishing returns. To apply more land to the same labor—that is, spread the labor over more land—must reduce output per acre. It follows that all scarce resources, when combined most effectively, must be operating in the stage of diminishing returns. In reality, this is just a corollary of the fact that they are scarce.

[7] This matter will be gone into further in the discussion of land rent in Chapter 28.

way and interfered with the growth of crops, a reduction of work
would raise the level of living.[8]

Regional differences in land use. Probably nowhere is land cultivated
with so devastating an intensity as this, but the ratio of labor to land
is extremely high in Japan, India, and China, and it is high also in
much of Europe and in parts of the South. As one would expect, output
per person is low in these areas. From the international statistical comparisons of Colin Clark, it appears that output per person in agriculture in Australia and Argentina has been 10 times as high as in Japan
and India and more than 10 times as high as in China. The density of
farm population runs from 25 to 100 times as high in the latter countries. Both in the density of rural population and in its productivity,
the European countries occupy an intermediate position. Regions
within the United States vary roughly in accordance with the same
pattern.[9]

In such comparisons one must be careful not to confuse *output per
acre* with *output per person*. In the hypothetical example used in
Table 8, labor output is highest when only three units of labor are
used, but the output of land is highest when eight units of labor are
used. One would expect that output per acre would be greatest in
countries where land is cultivated intensively, and, apart from dissimilarities in natural conditions and human skills, this is the necessary
result. But a high level of living means that the output per person is
high. It is people who must be fed and clothed, not acres of land. A
high output per acre obtained through the intensive activities of a
dense rural population is not a situation to be desired.

Offsetting effect of technological progress. An increased output per
acre, gained through better plant and animal breeding and generally
better techniques of land utilization, is, of course, greatly to be desired.
Through an improvement of techniques, a growing rural population
may offset, or more than offset, the effect of numbers.

Nor does this mean that diminishing returns has ceased to be a
factor. It remains a factor, but is counteracted by other factors. A rising
output, when improved methods offset a rising population, has about

[8] Selection of the most effective combination of two or more scarce factors must be made
on a value, or cost, basis—a problem for later consideration. The least costly combination
must be within the stage of diminishing returns, whichever factor is regarded as variable,
and production will be within this stage if the factors can be combined flexibly. Sometimes,
in the short run, this may not be possible.

[9] Colin Clark, *The Economics of 1960*, Macmillan & Co., Ltd., 1942, Ch. IV. Statistics
of this nature necessarily reflect other factors beside diminishing returns, notably differences in products, in soil and climate, and in techniques and use of equipment. But the
relation between density and output nevertheless seems clear. For the countries studied it
appears, roughly, that output varies inversely with the square root of density. That is, a
quadrupling of the people per unit of land cuts the output per capita in half.

the same relation to diminishing returns as an airplane propelled upward has to gravitation. Diminishing returns, like gravitation, is an important influence, but not the only one. Also, like gravitation, it can be seen most clearly when other influences are not present.

When methods of land use improve, however, a growing population is not likely to use land more intensively. Instead, people go increasingly into the secondary and tertiary pursuits through which, with the expanded output of primary industries, a large and varied final product can be obtained. This has been the course of progress in the Western nations, notably in the United States. When foodstuffs and other materials are obtained with the same, or fewer, workers, there is no occasion for diminishing returns to operate in agriculture. Added workers enter other fields where resources are differently combined.

Growing population in manufacturing and commerce

The point, with respect to the secondary and tertiary industries, is that population can grow without seriously affecting the proportion of labor to other resources. There is no lack of land on which to put factories, stores, and railroads, because the use made of land is slight. The principal material factor is not land but plant and equipment, buildings and structures and instrumentalities of all kinds. These are man-made, and they grow with population. While increasing them may not be easy, as the following chapter will show, they have in fact expanded more rapidly than labor has in most recent decades in such countries as the United States. Thus labor has more facilities to work with, not less. Diminishing returns operates, but not to the disadvantage of labor.

It is true that expansion in secondary lines means more demand for materials that come from land. Farm land would have to be used more intensively were it not for progress in techniques. Exhaustible minerals are depleted more rapidly. So far, this depletion has not worked hardship, and, as noted in the preceding section, a considerable increase in the cost of materials could easily be outweighed by other elements in the economy.

As a matter of fact, a growing population is likely to increase per-capita output in manufacturing and commerce. With large numbers of people, it is easier to organize mass-production industries and to market products produced by large-scale, low-cost methods. Transportation is less difficult when many people live close together. Merchandising services can be provided in cities which would be far too costly in rural areas. Some of these aspects of the organization of production will be considered in Chapter 7.

Thus a relatively high density of population can be supported well in areas in which manufacturing and commerce are leading pursuits. Crude comparisons of population densities among nations, without regard for industrial differences, mean nothing. England may prosper with 600 people per square mile, and China be badly overpopulated with a third as many. Economic progress means not only that increasing numbers of people can be supported on a rising plane but that increasing numbers become, in the nature of their effect, less of a barrier to progress.

Current aspects of the population problem

Thus industrial developments and the decline in the birth rate have largely removed the fear of overpopulation in Western countries. In the United States there is greater fear of a static or a declining population. This fear has several aspects. There is the possible relation, already noted, of a growing population to a high sustained demand for goods. There is the danger, if population falls, that an organization of production adapted to larger numbers of people will be disrupted. There is the shift, already apparent, in the components of the population, with relatively fewer children and young people and relatively more people who are old and thus interested in retirement support. There is the fear that a decline will take place through a disproportionate falling off in the offspring of the "best" families, with a resulting deterioration of the population.

The United States not typical. But the problem as seen in the United States is not the problem as it appears in much of the world. Half of the world's peoples live in backward and largely agricultural economies in which population is too dense to permit a high level of output. Families cannot support themselves well on three or four acres of land, as most families in India, China, and the Nile valley must do. Basically there are too many people, and despite a terrifically high death rate the pressure does not relax.[10] Directly, it is no solution to suggest that people be shifted out of agriculture, for there is already too little food, and fewer farmers with present methods would produce less. But the hope is that improvements in plants, animals, and soil techniques will expand output and thus both improve the food supply and release

[10] The fear has been expressed frequently since the war that the world will not be able to support its population. A vivid statement is that of C. Lester Walker, "Too Many People," *Harper's Magazine,* February 1948. "India's Insoluble Hunger," by John Fischer, *Harper's Magazine,* April 1945, states the situation in that country. A fuller statement of the pessimistic view, based both on the rapidity of growth of world population and the wasteful use of resources, is that of Fairfield Osborn, *Our Plundered Planet,* Little, Brown, 1948. More commonly, in recent decades, it has been the fashion to belittle the Malthusian fear.

workers for other activities. The institutional obstacles to be overcome, however, are often very great.

Migration as a solution. With population distributed so unequally over the earth in relation to economic opportunity, would not the real solution lie in vast migrations? Certainly it would seem that a large increase in world output would take place. Migration has played a notable part in world development, an indispensable part in American development. The desire to emigrate is common among depressed peoples, and opportunity to relieve population pressure is a common theme of aggressive rulers.

Migration is not a promising solution, however, and the political obstacles to large migrations are serious. People who migrate ordinarily better their lot, but little relief is likely to result in the areas that they leave. No large fraction of any population will move, and the room left by emigrants is soon filled in a nation subject to continuing population pressure. The source of the difficulty is not removed. On the other hand, the areas that receive immigrants presently erect barriers. The established occupants are not willing that their land should remain an open and unlimited refuge for the discontented of other countries. Under present world organization, the right to control immigration is a basic attribute of sovereignty.

Until after World War I the United States generally encouraged immigration except for Asiatics and individually objectionable persons. During the 1920s a quota system was developed that greatly limited total immigration and, through a formula based on the number of residents of specific national origins, modified the flow in favor of northern and western Europe, as against southern and eastern Europe from which the more recent immigration had largely come. The limitation does not apply to nations of the Western Hemisphere. Immigration restriction is the only major policy of the United States in the population sphere. It has the political support of workers with whom immigrants are likely to compete for jobs, but its main support reflects the difficulties of social and political assimilation of foreigners.

The Quality of Human Resources

In relation to natural resources, population must be viewed quantitatively, but its qualities have an even more important bearing on productivity. Within a wide range of variation, the characteristics of people determine their effectiveness as producers and the level of income they can extract from a given physical setting.

What are these characteristics? If, by some magic, the whole population of the United States were transferred to a vast undeveloped area, what would that area acquire for its development? It would acquire 145,000,000 people with their basic physical and intellectual qualities. It would acquire their knowledge and their skills, their understanding of natural resources and how to use them, of complicated mechanisms and how to make and run them, of complex productive organizations and how to set them up and manage them. The modern revolution in technology would thus enter this new land. It would acquire the habitual attitudes of the people, their desire to live better, and their conviction that energies should be devoted to this end. It would acquire their institutions, their scheme of government, and their system of private enterprise and of incentives and rewards. Undoubtedly capitalism would enter this new area, for it resides in the thinking of people. Thus broadly viewed, human resources seem plainly to be the supreme determinant of productive power.

Much that human resources encompass—the bodies and minds and institutions of people—lies within other fields of study. But economics must take note of the significant productive qualities of men and women and of the conditions on which they seem to depend.

Basic personal qualities

The individuals we observe daily differ widely in the inborn features of mind and body that fit them for particular tasks. In such conspicuous qualities as musical and athletic talent, the differences are striking, and similar differences in native qualification for given activities are everywhere present. People differ in their capacity for prolonged heavy physical labor, in qualities of nerve and muscle that make for dexterity, in aspects of intellect essential to understanding processes and relationships and to contriving new methods, in characteristics of temperament and personality that make for leadership and enterprise.

Individual differences are evident; the debatable question is whether large groups of people differ on the average in their inborn qualities. Do basic human resources differ by races, nations, and economic classes within a society? What is the situation as to Negroes and Caucasians, Italians and Englishmen, high- and low-income groups? It is enough to observe here, without extending the range of the present discussion, that a serious lack of personal productive capacities would constitute the most discouraging economic handicap that a people could face.

Apart from qualities that are innate and hereditary, personal capacities seemingly differ as a result of climate, which may be stimulating or enervating, conducive to health or to recurrent ailments. Undoubtedly productivity in some tropical countries is seriously restricted by the prevalence of malaria and hookworm. Diseases, from tuberculosis to the common cold, reduce output. Inadequate nutrition means low energy and low spirits, and low standards of sanitation and hygiene also help to sustain the low productivity from which they largely result.

Doubtless the native qualities of human beings can be improved by selective breeding, as sheep are bred for wool or mutton. But eugenic proposals run into disagreement as to the qualities that should be developed, and they entail methods of social control that few people probably would be willing to accept. But much progress is possible in overcoming weaknesses due to climate, disease, ignorance, and low income. The difficulty is in initiating improvement and giving it momentum. Outside help may be necessary, as through the notable work of the Rockefeller Foundation in attacking malaria and other diseases in numerous tropical areas. This is constructive work in the development of human resources. But the problem is not limited to backward areas. There is much to be done in the United States in improving health, reducing accidents, and, in general, expanding the working life and strength of the population.

The development of abilities

Basic human capacities become effective in production through acquisition of skills and knowledge. Primitive and modern man may differ little in native physical and mental power, but in their mastery of methods of production, the gulf between them is deep and broad. Economic progress means the crossing of that gulf.

How human beings achieve control over their environment is one of the large questions of social history. By slow innovation, improvement, selection, and transmission, ways of handling materials and of organizing activities are developed. Each new level builds on earlier levels, and thus rises above them. The pace of progress varies among peoples and between periods. It accelerated sharply in the eighteenth century, and the industrial changes since 1750 are one of the most spectacular of human achievements. Once people become conscious of economic progress, they may organize to promote it, as through the research now carried on by business enterprises, universities, and government agencies in the United States. Great forward steps in developing human productive power must come through the work of a few people, but the detailed improvements are the work of many people.

At each stage, however, the main task of most producers is to learn prevailing methods or a small segment of them in some specialty. Education for production comes in part through general contact with business and mechanical matters, in part through learning on the job, in part through formal education. Most present jobs are learned, without long apprenticeship, through actually doing the work that they entail. But special schooling is necessary for some trades and some business activities and especially for engineering, medicine, and other professions.

General schooling is fundamental to all production. As the armed forces reject men on grounds of illiteracy, so, in effect, do the armies of production. Competence in communication, in the use and understanding of the basic tools of expressing descriptions and quantities, is needed almost everywhere. An economically effective people must be one of broad general education as well as one that is specifically trained in the arts of production. Indeed, so largely is modern industry a matter of organization, personal dealings, shifting situations, and general judgments that the best training for people at the top, both in industry and in the economic relations of government, need not be highly specialized and technical.

An undeveloped country need not pioneer in learning how to produce effectively. It has the example of more advanced nations before it. But its task is difficult, nevertheless. It may achieve the general literacy that is required—though this is not done easily, because in a country of low production the investment in education must prove burdensome. It may import the necessary leadership, the engineers and managers, from advanced nations. But an industrial army also needs its numerous lieutenants and sergeants, its foremen and bosses at various levels, as well as its higher officers. These are found readily only in an environment in which modern processes of production are matters of common experience. Ordinary workers, the privates in the ranks, also need this background to be effective.

Work in factories, particularly in close relation to machines and in the routine of mass production, requires a persistent, unrelenting uniformity of action, a consistent conformity to an impersonal process, for which even the more arduous forms of farm work and handicraft may be inadequate preparation. A population does not suddenly acquire work habits of this type. In large plants and firms the relation between action and result is indirect, and the proper sense of relationship on the part of the individual worker is not easily acquired. Thus one writer, a man long familiar with the Chinese people, finds that a major obstacle to the industrialization of China lies in the prevalence of family and village behavior patterns, patterns quite the antithesis of the "instinct toward cooperation in large numbers" and the "concept of loyalty to an abstract organization" required in the operation of a modern factory or railroad.[11]

Attitudes, institutions, and motivation

Basic capacities and training of various kinds are not enough to give human resources a high productivity. Much depends also on the social climate from which human attitudes and incentives largely come. Prevailing hopes and values, and the political and economic framework within which work is done, greatly influence output.

If people are to produce more than bare subsistence requires, they must think it worth while to do so. The people who achieve most in the economic sphere are usually people who regard highly the goal of better living and the standing that income and wealth confer. The good life, as we have noted, has many aspects, and they need not be economic. What people esteem, and what they must do within their culture to command esteem—whether pursuit of luxurious living, or wisdom, or saintliness, or nothing more than being on easy terms with their neighbors and with nature—must affect their economic behavior. One road to "freedom from want," some one has said, is to achieve freedom from wanting, but it is not a road that leads to high production. In many lands productive activities have been approached with a casualness and a devotion to leisure quite foreign to Anglo-Saxon culture.

But, though better living may be desired strongly, it will be pursued effectively only where social, economic, and political arrangements bend people's energies toward it. Where caste lines and other barriers hold sons within their fathers' occupations and even to their fathers' established procedures, enterprise is weak. Where government fails to maintain conditions essential to dependable dealings and calculations, motivation is undermined. Where business enterprises and economic groups find it possible to expand their particular income without expanding output or even by restricting it, the arrangement is plainly faulty. Reward must be tied to productive contribution. Producers must not be protected from the danger that others will outdo them, even though some insecurity results. But needless dangers and burdens must be avoided, and each producer interest must be sufficiently protected so that it can remain loyal to the system under which it works.

Discussing institutional obstacles on both the business and labor

[11] John Earl Baker, "Industrializing the Good Earth," *Fortune*, November 1945.

sides to progress in the house-building industry, a recent writer notes the similarity to the medieval guilds, where "technical progress was seen as disloyalty," and goes on to say:

The greatest thing that ever happened to improve man's material welfare was the overthrow of feudalism by capitalism—the lifting of what Alfred Marshall, the great Cambridge economist, called "the cruelty of the yoke of custom and rigid ordinance." This is not a partisan view. Even Karl Marx said of capitalism that it "has been the first to show what man's activity can bring about. It has accomplished wonders far surpassing Egyptian pyramids, Roman aqueducts, and Gothic cathedrals . . . during its rule of scarce one hundred years, it has created more massive and more colossal productive forces than have all preceding generations together." [12]

Some may wish to argue that Russia has found a superior scheme for evoking production, but the issue is not relevant here. What is relevant is that human resources are not seen completely except as they are seen in the setting of human institutions in which they operate, because that setting has much to do with their productivity.

Review Questions

1. If a person concludes that there is no danger of overpopulation, he may mean (a) that adding people to an area does not exert downward pressure on the level of production. Or (b) he may be predicting that there will be no appreciable increase in the number of people. Or (c) he may mean that scientific progress will maintain productivity despite population pressure. Show that these are quite different reasons for the conclusion stated. They furnish a good example of the need of precision of thought and expression on economic matters.

2. What, in principle, is the best size of population from the usual economic standpoint? Distinguish several other viewpoints that may influence attitudes and policies.

3. State the main elements in the Malthusian view of population. Explain why it constituted a pessimistic view of the prospects of economic progress.

4. Is there basis for saying that population tends to expand in geometric progression? The food supply in arithmetic progression? What do these rates of progression mean?

5. How does experience since Malthus's day bear on his views regarding the positive and preventive checks? How does it bear on the outlook for economic progress?

6. What does standard of living mean? What is the significance of the concept?

[12] "The Industry Capitalism Forgot," *Fortune*, August 1947. The quotation regarding guilds is from Henri Pirenne, a Flemish historian.

7. 'Industrial progress since 1800 has not only outstripped population growth during this period, but apparently it has also reduced the menace of expanding numbers for the future." Explain.

8. Distinguish exhaustion and diminishing returns. Show that the concept of diminishing returns is not limited in its application to the case of labor and land.

9. Using the hypothetical example, show that a "declining average output" means the same as an output "increasing less than proportionally." Distinguish increasing, diminishing, and absolutely decreasing returns.

10. Why would it be illogical to suppose that additional labor can be added in considerable amount and under constant conditions to a given land area without reducing output per worker? Show, in so far as more intensive use of land does not reduce the average output from applied factors, that land must be a free good.

11. Why is it uneconomical to produce in the stage of increasing returns?

12. As between countries with dense and sparse rural populations, what is the expected difference as to output per person? Output per acre? On which basis should a high output primarily be sought?

13. "Farm output in the United States has increased as population has grown. Thus the so-called principle of diminishing returns must be false." Show (a) that this conclusion would not follow even if land had been cultivated more intensively; (b) that, in general, added population seems to have been absorbed without cultivating land more intensively. What conclusion do you reach regarding the proper application of an economic principle or of any other principle?

14. Explain (a) why, so far as the proportioning of factors is concerned, added population may be employed in secondary and tertiary lines without reducing output per person; and (b) why output per person in these lines may be increased by the expansion of population.

15. On what grounds do people fear a static or a declining population in the United States?

16. Does it seem to you that overpopulation is a serious problem in the world today? Has the United States an interest in the situation in backward countries? Does it seem to you that there is any practical way in which an overpopulated country can escape from its predicament?

17. Distinguish the probable effects of migrations on the three groups involved: the people who migrate, the people remaining in the area that they leave, the established population in the area to which they go.

18. What is the nature of the immigration policy of this country? What reasons do you see for it?

19. When the term human resources is used, what characteristics of people are covered by it?

20. Does it seem probable to you that any race or nation is disqualified for high economic achievement by the inborn physical and mental qualities of its members?

21. What are the several problems of training that a backward country faces in preparing its people for modern industry?

22. What are some of the aspects of motivation that must be provided through social attitudes and arrangements if people are to be effective producers? What are the main features of the American economy in this connection?

~ 6 ~

Capitalistic Production

In MODERN production the wealth that is most conspicuous is not the wealth that nature provides. Rather, it is wealth that is produced—but that is produced to serve, like land, in producing other goods. Nations differ greatly in natural endowment, but they differ even more in their possession of the man-made facilities used in farming, mining, manufacturing, and other fields.

To know what is necessary for present purposes about the physical nature and use of these *capital goods,* as they are called, ordinary nontechnical observation is enough. But to learn the economic nature of these goods and of the *capitalistic process* which they represent and of the *capital* invested in them, careful analysis is needed. Consideration of these matters will throw light on the basis of modern productive power, the present topic, and also on the problems of unemployment and income distribution, which will be considered later on.

Capital Goods and the Capitalistic Process

The essence of capitalistic production lies in the *indirectness* or *roundaboutness* just noted. When labor and natural resources are used capitalistically, they do not enter directly into final products for immediate consumption. They are incorporated, instead, in intermediate forms of wealth that assist in producing final products. Indirectness has no merit in itself but is important because it is bound up with the provision and use of improved methods of production. It is bound up also, as we observed in Chapter 2, with the growing complexity of economic organization.

One way to view the capitalistic process is by examining the kinds of capital goods through which it operates. Another is by examining production in terms of time, because capitalistic methods lengthen the period that production requires. Whatever the approach, the capitalistic process should be seen as part of the whole organization of production.

Capital goods and progress

Knowledge of production resides in people, but ideas, to be effective, must ordinarily take tangible form in physical instrumentalities. The point is that improvement in methods of production is not simply the result of human inventiveness; it is also the result of producing and accumulating the capital goods in which ideas are embodied. In discussing capitalistic production, we are discussing an essential part of technological progress.

Early man, in his first steps to control his environment, found that stones could be used for killing, pounding, and grinding and that pieces of wood could be fashioned into weapons, levers, shovels, and containers. Ideas took the form of tools, and human effort had then to be apportioned between getting food and making the tools that would assist in getting it. Provision of hand tools has never absorbed very much productive effort, but modern machinery, through which hammers, knives, and other tools are applied to materials with the speed, precision, and power that typify modern industry, is more demanding. Machines and the engines that drive them are themselves leading products. Of the gross national product of the United States in 1947 the sum of $17.9 billion represented "producers durable equipment." [1]

The connection between the advance of modern technology and of capitalistic production is fundamental, but the two are not identical nor completely parallel. Much capital is invested in buildings which house both people and productive operations. The use of walls and roofs and floors for this purpose is an old idea; although construction methods change, the principle of employing sheltered space has not changed noticeably. Private construction of all kinds in the United States in 1947 amounted to $10.7 billions.[2]

All new methods do not require capital goods for their application. Developing knowledge of crop rotation, soil fertilization, and breeding of animals does not have to be embodied in physical equipment. Improvements in synthesizing and processing materials may require no expansion in facilities. The arts of management may advance without any addition to productive wealth. Moreover technical progress in designing equipment may make it simpler to produce, and thereby permit less wealth to do the same work.

[1] *Survey of Current Business*, February 1948, p. 6.
[2] *Ibid.*

But, despite these qualifications, it is true that progress in methods of production and expansion in the stock of capital goods have moved along together with considerable interdependence. Thus, in studying the difference in productive power among countries or the progress in particular countries, the quantities of man-made productive wealth are doubly significant. Directly (1) these quantities show the extent to which the primary resources—man and nature—are aided by an accumulation of produced facilities—the sheer volume of material assistance that labor has. Indirectly (2) they indicate how fully a nation has taken advantage of advancing knowledge of how to produce—the degree to which it employs modern methods.

The value of capital goods per worker probably exceeded $15,000 in the railroad and electric power industries in the United States before the war and approached $10,000 in manufacturing. These are highly mechanized fields and represent a use of capital, and of the mechanical power that capitalistic production implies, well above the national average. But the average is several times greater than it was a century ago and far larger than it is today in those backward countries in which most labor is supplemented only by a few tools and some use of animal power. No other difference in the physical aspects of production throws as much light on differences in productivity.[3]

Types of capital goods

One way of viewing the capitalistic process is through distinguishing leading types of capital goods and observing the different ways in which resources may enter indirectly into the production of final products. For this purpose we should distinguish the fixed and circulating types of man-made wealth.

Fixed-capital equipment and structures. The examples already used and the ones usually associated with modern production belong in the *fixed-capital* category. Buildings and machines used in manufacturing are capital goods of the fixed type. So also are store and office and storage buildings. In transportation much fixed capital is found in the alteration of the earth that results when roadways are graded, fields leveled, canals dug, harbors dredged, but more is found in rails, concrete surfaces, bridges, locks and wharves. Locomotives, trains, motor vehicles, ships, and planes are fixed capital, however mobile their use may make them. Nature's gift of farm land is made usable by clearing and draining, and farms require machinery, barns, fences, and other struc-

[3] The close connection between the expanding quantities of capital equipment, mechanical horsepower, and output per worker in the United States has been traced for a long period by Carl Snyder. See "The Capital Supply and National Well-being," *American Economic Review*, June 1936.

tures. Animals raised through outlay of labor and materials, and used to yield milk or wool or to pull wagons and cultivators, belong among the durable capital goods. So do the mines and the equipment by which minerals are made available. Perhaps fixed capital is most prominent in producing hydroelectric power, with its elaborate requirement of dams, generators, and transmission lines.

The significant feature of these capital goods is that they are durable and give off their services over a considerable period of time. They are *many-service goods*.[4] Labor, material, and already existing capital goods are used to produce them; then, along with more labor and material, they yield a flow of products during their lifetime of use. The resources embodied in them thus enter indirectly into a stream of final products. It is in connection with such goods that depreciation must be allowed for, so that a proper part of the resources embodied in them will be charged against the products that they help to produce in each period.

Circulating capital—stocks or inventories. Fixed capital is most characteristic of modern production, but the indirectness of capitalistic production appears also in great quantities of produced wealth of quite another kind—wealth in the form that accountants, when they prepare the balance sheets of business firms, refer to as *inventories*. The manufacturer needs plant and equipment, but he also must have his piles of raw materials and fuels, his accumulation of purchased parts and office supplies. In addition, he will have a considerable stock of "goods in process," of partially manufactured goods moving through the successive operations of his plant. Finally, he will usually have on hand a stock of finished products from which orders can be filled. Measured in dollars, these various stocks are a large item in the manufacturer's wealth. Many a balance sheet shows a higher total for inventories than for fixed capital.

Such stocks are present in all lines of production. In wholesaling and retailing they outweigh the fixed facilities. In farming and the handling of farm products, they are also large. Everywhere they figure prominently in the total of capital goods.

The reasons for these stocks vary. Primarily, goods are found in

[4] The durability pertinent here is of a special sort, and it is present in varying degrees. Coal will last a long time in a pile but yields its full service in a single act of use, so it lacks durability in the fixed-capital sense. A motor truck, on the other hand, may not last very long, but it is productive through the stream of services that it gives off. It is durable in the present sense. Many machines are more durable than motor trucks and remain in use for twenty or thirty years, and buildings commonly yield services for half a century or more. Finally, however, most durable goods wear out and have to be replaced if production is to continue, or they are replaced because improved methods have made them obsolete. Only a few types of man-made wealth, such as graded fields and roadways, may be viewed as permanent.

them because of the sheer impossibility of producing physical products instantaneously, including all processes from the mining or growing of materials to the final sale of finished products. But stocks must also be larger than otherwise because successive steps in production cannot be coordinated perfectly, and reserves must be available to draw on at each stage to insure continuous operations. Moreover stocks are necessary, especially in merchandising, to permit customers to be served promptly and to have some choice in their buying.

Inventories as expressions of the capitalistic process. What is the nature of the capitalistic process in the use of stocks of goods? Wherein does the indirectness consist? Materials in this case are not embodied in durable forms like machines that assist over a long period in producing final products. The very materials enter the final products or are used up once and for all in making them. The commodity in the merchant's stock is the very physical thing that will one day be consumed.

To see these things as capital goods, one must see the difference between a stock of goods considered as an aggregate and the particular commodities that make up the aggregate. It is the difference between a river, which may remain unchanged, and the molecules of water in the river, which are forever changing. A merchant may own continuously throughout a year a stock of goods that approximates a value of $30,000; yet the items that constitute that stock may be replaced three or four times during the year. It is the difference, with which we are familiar, between a fund and a flow. The stock is a fund of wealth; it need not be altered by the flow of commodities into or out of it. Thus commodities which are physically of the nature of consumers' goods or are in process of becoming consumers' goods make up great aggregates of wealth essential in production. When they reach the consumer, they will serve the purposes of consumption. But while they are in producers' stocks they are elements in the productive process.

Though differing superficially, these stocks reflect the indirect use of primary resources pretty much as machines and buildings do. Just as some labor and materials are used to make equipment, thus entering final products indirectly through the services of the equipment, so other labor and materials are used to build up the inventories that also serve as facilities of production. As long as stores and factories operate, primary resources must continue to be embodied in both types of capital goods.

The time dimension

The indirectness of capitalistic production may thus be thought of as consisting in the use of resources to produce producers' goods and, through them, consumers' goods. But the essence of the process may be thought of also as lying simply in the passage of time—in the presence of an interval between the application of resources and the appearance of the final products to which they contribute. Equipment and inventories are both reflections of the time element. In very few instances do labor and materials enter a product at the instant it reaches the consumer. For the most part they enter the productive process days or months or years before that instant. Their earlier application may arise from the succession of operations through which materials must pass. Labor and materials may enter at the mining stage or the planting stage or anywhere along the line in manufacturing or merchandising. Or they may enter the process through being embodied in a machine or a building and continue to emerge in final products over ten or twenty or fifty years.

Capital goods are in a sense the result of this time interval. If time elapses between the application of resources and their emergence as final products, they exist in the meantime as part of an aggregate of wealth. The longer the average interval between application and completion, the greater must the stock of produced wealth be in relation to the final product, and the more capitalistic the productive process must be.

While the time aspect of capitalistic production throws light on the nature of the process, and—as we shall see later—on the role of the capitalist, it provides no basis for *measuring how capitalistic* production is. The difficulty is that it is impossible to trace the production of any good back to the very beginning. The mining of the material, for instance, was not the beginning, for back of it was the making of the mining equipment and back of that the production of other materials, an endless series.

To measure the use of capitalistic methods, it is better to think in terms of quantities of wealth than of periods of time, or a combination of them. Thus we may say that in a country such as the United States perhaps $4000 of capital goods is available per worker, whereas in China the amount is not a tenth so great. Or we may say that in producing $1,000,000 of product one manufacturing industry requires the use for a year of $1,200,000 in equipment and inventories, whereas another industry requires only $600,000. Then we can say that production is about twice as capitalistic in the former as in the latter.

Consumers' goods and capital goods

Capital goods have been spoken of as if they were always producers' goods and thus distinguishable from consumers' goods. Is it desirable to associate capital goods exclusively with processes that take place before products enter the possession of consumers?

Certainly the main use of capital goods is in production in the ordinary sense, but there are good reasons for not defining them rigidly on that basis. In the actual functioning of resources in serving human ends, the point at which they pass through sale into the hands of the people who will use them is somewhat arbitrary. In a Crusoe economy there is no such point, but it still makes sense to distinguish instruments and final products. In our society the functions of consumers and producers, and of their wealth, are not separable in a clear and uniform way, and it may be sounder to classify goods according to their use than according to who owns them.

Thus the automobile serving the business and pleasure of its owner performs the same transportation service as the automobile that is part of the capital equipment of the drive-yourself agency, or even as the bus or passenger train. The cook stove in the home and the cook stove in the restaurant are functionally alike. The home itself has the same economic role as the apartment house that brings its owner an income.[5] Stocks of food and supplies in the pantry or basement serve about the same purposes as merchants' stocks.

Moreover, from the standpoint of the formation of capital, which will be discussed in the following section, the wealth of producers and of consumers is hardly distinguishable. Its common origin is a matter of positive importance in analyzing saving and investment and their bearing on general prosperity.

But, despite these considerations, we are justified in associating capital goods mainly with the activities of persons producing goods for sale. Earning a living and using products are motivated somewhat differently, and it is in earning income that people make the more significant decisions regarding the capitalistic use of resources.

Productivity of the capitalistic process

Capitalistic methods are used extensively in countries, such as the United States, in which production per person is high, and they are little used in countries of low productivity. But does it follow that production is necessarily made more effective by making it more capital-

---

[5] Sometimes capital goods are defined so narrowly that apartment houses and drive-yourself automobiles, though constituting man-made wealth used to bring in money income, are not included but are treated as part of a broadened category of consumers' goods. With this definition, the dividing line is between goods that yield satisfaction to consumers and goods that are purely instrumental such as a machine in a factory. This usage would make the category of capital goods much narrower than the field of capital investment. If one desires always to distinguish capital goods from end products, it can be said that the *service* of the apartment house is the end product.

istic? Does the use of resources to expand the quantity of capital goods necessarily expand the flow of final products?

The answer is no. A more indirect use of resources is not in itself advantageous. A further shifting of labor from making consumers' goods to making producers' goods need not increase the output of consumers' goods. Lengthening the average period between the use of resources and the appearance of their final product does not automatically increase the final product. A more capitalistic use of resources is advantageous only in so far as it makes possible the use of methods which are superior—the employment of labor-saving machines, of generated power, of stocks that improve the coordination of processes. Undoubtedly, with present knowledge of the arts of production, most countries have fewer capital goods than they ought to have. But, with any given state of the arts, there is still a limit to how capitalistic production ought to be.

This is just another way of saying that capitalistic methods are costly, and the costs must be set against the immediate advantages. A workman with a power-driven machine can do much more than by hand methods. But the machine has to be produced and maintained; the power to drive it, in the form of engine and fuel, must be provided; the machine method probably concentrates production geographically, and more transportation of materials and products is necessary. So the question is whether the workman who runs the machine, and with him the other resources involved in the machine process, together turn out a greater final product because the machine is used. If they do, the more capitalistic method can be said to be productive. Although there is much room in the world, and even in the United States, for the more capitalistic use of resources, the possibilities must be viewed in the light of these costs.

If capitalistic methods, where appropriate, make a net addition to product, why do not all nations adopt them to the fullest desirable extent? Is there not a free choice between the direct and the indirect use of resources, and it is not foolish to make the less productive choice? This question will take us into the most important aspect of the capitalistic process: the conditions which govern the origin and accumulation of capital goods.

Review Questions

1. "Progress in production is partly a human matter, partly a material matter." Explain.

2. What is meant by saying that capitalistic production is indirect or roundabout?

3. Capital goods of the fixed type have been described as "many-service" goods? What is meant?

4. Explain the functions of the stocks of goods that make up the circulating capital of enterprises in various fields. Using the distinction between a fund and a flow, explain the nature of this type of capital good.

5. Show that both types of capital goods are alike from the time standpoint. Explain how an increase in the use of capital goods of either type increases the average interval between the use of primary resources and the emergence of the final product.

6. On what basis, or bases, can statistical comparisons be made between countries to show how capitalistic production is in them?

7. "The same physical thing can be both a consumers' good and a capital good." Do you agree? Explain.

8. "The fact that a workman can do more with a machine than without one does not prove that the machine method expands production." Explain. What condition must be met if more highly capitalistic methods are to expand production?

The Formation of Capital

The accumulation of capital goods is an economic process, as the origin of primary resources is not. Geological and biological factors explain the presence of land and human beings, but capital goods result from the way in which economic life is organized and carried on. The distinction is not always sharp, but it is fundamental.

Capital goods are produced as other goods are, but possession of the means of producing them does not explain their presence. They come into being, and accumulate, only when society produces more than it consumes and takes the difference in the form of capital goods. The exact process varies, but, in one way or another, saving and investing are the essential features of the formation of capital.

Saving and investing

Saving and investing are closely related and in practice may be combined indistinguishably. But their roles are different, and in our society they are likely to be performed separately.

Saving, from either the individual or the social viewpoint, consists in holding consumption below the level of the total net income and product. Thus the effect of saving is to release resources from the production of immediately consumable goods. If total consumption were as great as total production, then all employed resources would be used in providing goods for current use. Saving permits part of the total productive power to be used to add to the stock of buildings, equipment, and inventories.

In backward countries, the difficulty of saving is the basic obstacle to the use of capitalistic methods. If most Chinese barely get enough food of the plainest sort, and other necessary things are in very meager supply, it is impossible to release much labor power from current uses in order to produce capital goods. Even if all the technical knowledge required for modern production were available, the difficulty of saving, and thus of diverting resources to capital-goods production, would remain.

While saving *permits* the use of resources for capital purposes, *investing causes* resources to be used to expand the volume of capital goods. There are several ways of doing it, but true investment always causes this expansion of capital facilities.

Different relationships between saving and investing. In the simplest situation, saving and investing are a single process. The two are combined, for example, when a Crusoe diverts part of his labor from producing food for consumption to making a boat for fishing or a shelter for storage. By a single act he saves and invests. The farmer who devotes part of his time to building fences or a barn likewise combines the two processes. In simple societies much capital formation is of this type.

A similar merging of the processes of saving and investing appears in completely *managed economies.* Through its central authority, a nation may assign part of its resources to enlarging its capital stock, and by that very act it accepts a smaller volume of consumers' goods than its total production makes possible. Actually the people as a whole do the saving, and the authorities do the investing, but both the saving and the investing arise from the act of the authorities in diverting resources to capitalistic use.

Under *modern capitalism,* capital formation is largely decentralized and specialized. From the individual standpoint, saving and investment usually appear as separate processes. Typically the individual decides how much of his money income he will spend for consumption and how much he will save. Immediately, he keeps the saving in cash or adds it to his bank balance. In the same way, business corporations retain part of the net income that they might use for dividend payments. All these acts of saving restrict the purchase of goods for consumption and, therefore, the use of resources in producing such goods. Then, through a different set of decisions, often made by different people, savings are used to pay for new buildings and equipment and to expand inventories. Thus resources are devoted to capitalistic ends.

When the actual investing is not done by the savers, savings may change hands through personal and bank loans, through purchase of corporate securities, through payments of insurance premiums, and in other ways. Elaborate *financial machinery*, which we shall consider presently, assists in transferring savings from savers to investors. In addition, there is the capital formation that takes place when people pay taxes, or buy government bonds, and government uses the funds, not for current public services, but to develop highways, waterways, and hydroelectric projects, to build schools and post offices, or for any of the capitalistic ends entrusted to governments.

In these cases the saving and the investing are quite separate. Yet, from an over-all collective standpoint, the connection is still close. The part of total production that is in excess of total consumption takes the form of additions to the stock of capital goods. If the annual net product of the country is $100 billion and consumption is at a $90 billion rate, then we can say that society as a whole is saving $10 billion and that, at the same time, $10 billion of resources are being devoted to capital formation.

Consumer wealth in the form of houses, cars, and household furnishings is built up in essentially the same way. There is the same withholding of income from immediate consumption and its expenditure for goods that expand wealth. Consumers may not think of these outlays as investments, because no money return is expected, but a return is expected in the form of a stream of services that yields direct satisfaction. Consumer investing is done by the same people who do the saving, but either act may come first. If consumers buy cars and other durable goods before they have the necessary savings, loans enter the process temporarily.

"Investment" in new and old wealth. In everyday speech we often say that a person invests his savings when he uses them to buy a piece of land or an old house or already issued corporate securities. From the standpoint of the economy, however, these purchases do not constitute investments, since they do not cause an expansion in the stock of capital goods. They merely transfer the ownership of existing wealth, and the savings pass into the hands of the sellers of the wealth. The savings remain uninvested, in a true economic sense, until they are used to hire labor and other resources to produce goods that will constitute an addition to the stock of wealth. Both in understanding productive power and in considering later problems that involve capital, investment should be understood in this sense.[6]

---

[6] When savings are truly invested, but one person provides them and another uses them in constructing a building or in buying equipment, which one is the investor? If the sav-

Gross and net capital formation

The investment so far considered is *net investment*. It involves the use of savings from net income to make net additions to wealth. Now we must recognize that new capital goods are purchased in part to make replacements and maintain the volume of them already in use, as well as to expand that volume. *Gross investment* is a term that covers the purchases both for replacements and for additions. Gross investment corresponds to *gross saving,* which not only includes net saving but also funds recovered through selling products for enough to cover depreciation.

Thus we may add to the previous example, with its total net product of $100 billion and saving of $10 billion, the fact that the total gross product is $108 billion and depreciation $8 billion. Gross saving is then $18 billion, and a gross investment of $18 billion both offsets the decline in value of old capital and increases the previous amount of capital by $10 billion.

Gross saving and investment are a larger fraction of gross product ($18 billion out of $108 billion) than net savings and investment are of net product ($10 billion out of $100 billion). This view of the capitalistic process in gross terms gives a more adequate impression of the demands on a nation's productive power, if it is both to maintain and expand its reliance on capitalistic methods. As nations become more capitalistic in their methods, and their accumulation of capital goods grows, the replacement factor has increasing importance. We shall stress it again in Part IV in dealing with the employment problem.

The processes of saving

It is evident that the use of capitalistic methods can present a difficult choice between present and future well-being. Resources that may be used to meet immediate needs may also be used to build up productive power for the future. Thus a question is raised—a question most serious in backward countries—regarding the rate at which wealth ought to be accumulated by saving present income. How the question is faced depends on the way in which saving is done.

Voluntary and forced saving. Saving may be left up to the individual,

---

ings are made available through a bank, perhaps most people would call the borrower the investor rather than the depositor. But if the saver buys a bond of a corporation that puts up the building, he would often be spoken of as the investor. Something can be said for this usage, but it is likely to promote accuracy of analysis in this situation if we speak of the corporation as the investor. Owners of firms both invest their own capital and capital that they borrow.

to decide for himself on a voluntary basis. Individuals may not be wise, even from their own standpoint, in using money income, but at least it can be said that, when saving is done in this way, the rate of saving is one that the people approve. But saving may not be voluntary, and then questions of policy enter. Doubtless the ordinary Russian would prefer that less productive effort should be devoted to building factories and more to running them to turn out consumers' goods.

Under free institutions, as we have described them, saving is mainly voluntary. But even there it is not altogether voluntary, and, though voluntary in a sense, it may not result directly from the decisions of the individuals who bear the burden of it. Thus when corporations retain part of their profits in good years instead of disbursing them all in dividends, the stockholders are not able to decide individually whether to spend or save the earnings on their shares of stock. The decision to pay dividends or retain profits is made directly by the directors of the company, and the directors represent, or are supposed to represent, the majority of the stock. In consequence this decision may run contrary to the wishes of many individual stockholders.

The involuntary element is more serious when governments collect taxes in excess of the amounts needed for current purposes and use the surplus for road building and similar capital developments. People have no choice regarding the payment of taxes, and this saving has, therefore, a distinctly involuntary aspect. Unlike the corporate stock-holder, the taxpayer retains no personal equity in the wealth accumu-lated, but has only the general interest of the citizen in public property; his willingness to save for roads or waterways in remote sections of the country may be slight. But again we should observe that, if a nation is democratically controlled, the policies of government are the policies of the citizenry collectively, even though they do not conform to all individual preferences. Only a partial compulsion prevails. When, as is often the case, public investments are financed through sale of bonds to individual citizens, the initial saving at least is quite voluntary.[7]

Saving by types in the United States. These are all aspects of the saving that occurs in our society. How much of it arises through in-dividual action in this country, and how much through corporate and governmental channels? According to the National Bureau of Eco-

---

[7] We should also note that a form of forced saving occurs when the money supply is increased, especially through expansion of bank credit, and the holders of the additional money use it for investment under circumstances that force up the general level of prices. Resources are thus bid away from consumption uses, and people are compelled to save not through handing over money they receive but through having the purchasing power of their money incomes cut down.

nomic Research, savings of these various kinds in the United States were as follows for the average of the years 1919–1928 (in billions of dollars and percentages of total savings) :

Type of savings	Annual average	Percentage
Individuals and unincorporated firms	$5.5	69.6
Corporations	1.0	13.0
Government	1.4	17.4
Total	7.9	100.0

When the period is extended to 1938, so as to include the years in which corporate profits were low or negative, average corporate savings become negative for the entire twenty years, and individual savings become 95.4 percent of the total.[8] This result is abnormal in one direction. If we go on to the next eight years, covering 1939–1946, we find that corporate savings averaged $4.5 billion annually and that, when allowance is made for excessive valuation of inventories, they averaged $3.1 billion.[9] Thus the war years appear to be abnormal in the other direction.

Saving under collectivism. In socialistic countries, in which industry is owned and operated by the state, saving may also be done in more than one way. If the system rests on a fully developed exchange economy, with government paying wages to workers and selling consumers' goods to them, the government may make enough on its sales to pay the workers in the capital-goods industries. The products of these industries, then, are not sold but are retained in building up the state industries. Or it may retain no such margin in the consumers'-goods industries, but instead tax all workers a sufficient amount so that it can pay the workers in lines that do not yield a saleable product. There is the third possibility that workers will save voluntarily and make their savings available to the state through state banks or purchase of bonds. Payment of interest on such loans introduces an element of property income into the working of a socialist economy. Even in Russia there is some private income-yielding saving of this sort. In case a collectivist economy approximates pure communism, none of these procedures would be followed, for the machinery of exchange in the ordinary sense would be absent. Resources would be assigned directly to capital purposes without resort to the money mechanism.

It is possible to imagine a strictly democratic socialist state in which, through the franchise, the citizenry decide how much of the total in-

[8] Simon Kuznets, *National Income—A Summary of Findings*, National Bureau of Economic Research, p. 21.

[9] *Supplement to Survey of Current Business*, July 1947, p. 19.

come will be saved, what fraction of productive power will be used capitalistically. Perhaps British socialism will prove to be of this sort. But in totalitarian economies, such as the Russian, we find the clearest case of forced saving. Since the revolution of 1917, a large part of Russia's productive effort has been devoted to building up productive plant and equipment. So far the objectives seem mainly to have been military, but the declared goal is an eventual high level of consumption. Whatever the end, the decisions respecting saving and investment are imposed by the dictatorship. Undoubtedly much less saving would have been done if the Russian people had had a free choice in the matter, especially if they had had access to information regarding consumption in the Western nations.

Conditions governing accumulation; size of income

The great obstacle to capital accumulation is, of course, low income. People with little to live on will not save voluntarily. A study made during the depression of the 1930s indicated that the bottom two thirds of the families in the United States, arranged according to size of income, had, in the aggregate, negative savings. They spent more than their income. Thus the savings of the top third exceeded the total savings of all families.[10] With incomes at a much higher level in 1946, the top 10 percent of the families, with incomes ranging upward from about $5000, accounted for over 60 percent of the total individual saving. The bottom 60 percent of the families contributed nothing to the total, the dissavings of some offsetting the savings of others. Individual savings in 1946 are shown, by income classes, in Table 9.[11]

TABLE 9—CONSUMER SAVING AT VARIOUS INCOME LEVELS, 1946

Income before taxes	Percent of total spending units	Percent of total income	Percent of total consumer saving
Under $1000	17	3	−7
$1000–1999	23	12	2
2000–2999	25	21	9
3000–3999	17	20	21
4000–4999	8	13	14
5000–7499	6	11	16
7500 and over	4	20	45

[10] From *Consumer Expenditure in the United States,* a study by the National Resources Committee based on 1935–1936 data. The data are for spending units, which include families and individuals living separately. Savings for the top third were 24 percent greater than total savings.

[11] "Survey of Consumer Finances. Part III. Consumer Saving in 1946 and Ownership of Selected Nonliquid Assets," *Federal Reserve Bulletin,* August 1947.

While it is clear that, in any one country at any one time, relatively more is saved from the larger incomes, it does not follow that, if all incomes rise in a country, relatively more will be saved. If incomes rise generally, the standard of living can be expected to rise, and families receiving, say, $5000 may save no more than families previously did at the $4000 level. On the same principle, persons in the other nations, in which incomes and the standard of living are somewhat lower than here, may save about as large a fraction of their total income as we do. But this point can be pushed too far. Saving must be extremely small in countries where incomes are so low that only a bare subsistence is possible for most people. Then there is no choice between saving and spending. Countries of low productivity thus are caught in one of the most baffling of circular difficulties: because product and income are low, little can be saved; because little is saved, capital accumulation is slow and productivity is difficult to increase.

Other factors affecting saving. Apart from the size of incomes a variety of factors seem likely to affect the amount of capital accumulation in different countries and at different times. Accumulation is encouraged by political stability, since wealth that will not be protected is hardly worth building up. It is also encouraged by confidence in the economic future. On the other hand, the uncertainty of the individual regarding his personal future, and the knowledge that he must depend upon himself, induce him to save. Accordingly it seems possible that social-security programs, especially old-age benefits, will reduce saving of the "rainy-day" sort. Prevailing popular beliefs regarding saving may also have some influence. If thrift is thought virtuous, as it long has been, saving is likely to be stimulated, whereas a fear of oversaving, now often voiced, may promote the opposite attitude.

Capital accumulation and fluctuations in production

Now we must note a more complex aspect of capital formation. Thus far we have identified accumulation with saving. We have also assumed that the expansion of producers' goods must cut into consumption. Now we must qualify these assumptions. It is true, of course, that resources cannot be used to expand the stock of capital goods and, at the same time, be used to promote current consumption. But it is possible to use for capital purposes resources that would otherwise be idle. Thus, if a farmer spends his evenings building a fence instead of resting, he expands his productive facilities without reducing his command over consumption goods. Much after-hours and off-season effort leads directly to capital formation. In such cases there is saving in a sense, but it is saving from an expansion of output that would not appear except for the production of capital goods.

This possibility of increasing capital formation without reducing consumption has a much more important application. It appears whenever business depressions bring unemployment of labor and other resources. When resources are unemployed, putting them to work in making producers' goods does not curtail current consumption. On the contrary, the very employment of idle resources brings recovery from depression, and with recovery there is expansion in the production both of consumers' and producers' goods. In one theory of depressions, oversaving is viewed as their main cause; thus less thrift, or more investment, is looked upon as the way to get more of all goods.[12]

The soundness of this theory need not concern us now, but the facts are clear. When there are general fluctuations in business, an economy can accumulate plant and equipment without sacrificing consumption. Both types of production rise and fall together. This possibility, however, depends on the presence of idle productive power. When resources are fully used, the rate of capital formation cannot be increased without reducing current consumption.

International investing

We have noted how difficult it is to accumulate capital when income is low. This is the difficulty faced by undeveloped nations. Effective production is needed to permit the capital accumulation necessary to effective production. The most direct escape from this predicament is through calling upon developed nations for assistance, and this has been the common course. Capital formation thus becomes an international task. Great Britain, the nation in which modern industry first attained a high level, became the leader in developing other lands. Through British investment, railroads, factories, and mines were financed and equipped in the United States, Canada, South America, Africa, and the East. In the present century the United States has shifted from a debtor to a creditor position, and American investments are now large and widely distributed.

Apart from economic backwardness, the vast destructiveness of modern warfare has created a special need for foreign capital in recent years. Nations have also hastened their industrialization to provide the economic basis of military power. Capital demands in these postwar years are very high.

Countries that seek foreign capital ordinarily lack savings for invest-

[12] These matters will be discussed in Chapter 14.

ment, but the lack of savings usually reflects a lack of resources to produce capital goods. Such countries are likely also to lack the technical competence to produce needed equipment and to install and operate it. Thus foreign investment has a number of aspects. It means providing funds to foreign firms and governments, but the funds are commonly used to buy equipment in the nation that supplies the capital. That nation, moreover, is likely also to supply along with the equipment engineers and managers, who may take charge of the foreign operations. The government of the lending nation may become involved in insuring conditions favorable to the investment. Thus international capital formation can be of far-reaching importance in international relations.

Capital and Capitalism

This section is mainly terminological. The words *capital* and *capitalism* crept into the preceding discussion, but no real use was made of them. *Capital goods* and the *capitalistic process,* however, were discussed extensively. When a verbal family shows so obvious a common parentage, the resemblances may imply a closer relationship than exists, and thus obscure differences that should be recognized. For complete clarity, some differentiating should be done in this case, and the word capital should come to the fore as a leading concept in economics.

Capital

The terms "capital goods" and "capitalistic process" were applied to the physical, or "real," aspects of the use of primary resources in various intermediate productive forms. Writers on economics have often used the word capital in the same way, recognizing no distinction between capital and capital goods. In this usage, a machine would be an example of capital. This meaning, however, has made little progress in popular or business usage. Instead, the word capital has been used mainly to refer to the value (or money) element in capitalistic production, and its chief use in economics is of this nature. But capital is a troublesome word, at best; even in this value (or money) area it has several meanings.

Capital as money savings. In the money sense, capital is not the medium of exchange as such but a fund of money available to be invested. Savings in liquid form would be capital, and banks would provide capital through their credit-creating machinery. It is in this sense of the term that there exists a *capital market* through which loans are made and investment funds obtained and in which interest rates are determined. While this meaning is common, adherence to it gives capital a very limited relation to capitalistic production. According to it, we would have to say that the use of capitalistic methods in a Crusoe or a communist economy would require no capital, for money capital would not be present. And even in our society, once funds had been used to buy the labor and materials that go into capital goods, capital in this sense would cease to exist. The money would remain, but it would have passed into the hands of workers and others as a medium of exchange, so that the investable fund would have disappeared. Capital goods would remain, but not capital.

Capital as a fund of value. In this money sense, the word "capital" fails to qualify for its principal use in economics. We cannot accept the idea that capital vanishes when it ceases to be a sum of money. If we invest $100,000 in a building and equipment, we want to say that we still have our capital of $100,000. But what meaning must we give the term to have it serve this purpose? What is the nature of the capital to which we refer? If we mean literally that our capital is the physical facilities, we are adopting the capital-goods meaning of the term, but we cannot accept this meaning and still maintain that we had capital before we invested the $100,000. Capital may arise from saving, or it may arise from the activities of construction workers and machinery manufacturers, but not from both.

What we undoubtedly mean when we say that we have the same $100,000 of capital before and after investment is that we have the same *fund of value.* It arose through saving, was held temporarily in money form, then was embodied in the building and equipment. Presently, through use and the passage of time, the value of these physical items will decline, but, if their use has been successful, the sale of product will have returned to us a sum corresponding to this decline in value, as determined through depreciation accounting. Thus the same fund of value, the same capital, will still be ours. This fund-of-value meaning is the most generally useful one to attach to the term "capital" in economics.

This meaning is close to the more common business usage, but the latter is looser and departs from it in several respects. When a manufacturer says that his capital is $1,000,000 he is probably including only a small amount of money and is referring mainly to his plant and equipment and his inventories. But he does not distinguish natural and man-made wealth, and the value of his land is included. Moreover, he may include the value of such items as patents and good will, which we have described as wealth in a private, acquisitive sense but which do not represent elements of productive power from the social standpoint.

The figure he gives may have little relation to savings actually invested but may reflect mainly the value of the enterprise on the market, in view of the income it yields. This conception of capital is widely useful, but should not be confused with the one stressed here. The capital that arises through saving and is embodied in capital goods through investment corresponds to an expansion in productive capacity in a real sense. Mere variations in the value of existing items of wealth, whether land or capital goods, have a different significance.

The term "capitalism"

"Capital," "capital goods," and "capitalistic process" are terms that are useful in discussing certain aspects of production under any economic system. Capitalism, on the other hand, has come to be the label of a specific type of economic system. It is a system in which production is directed by private owners of capital, or their representatives, rather than by the state or by individuals in their role as workmen. Private owners of capital are called capitalists, but not all capitalists participate in the direction of industry. Capital may be hired like labor, and the position of its owners remain wholly passive. Under capitalism, control of enterprises is in the hands of persons who are enterprisers as well as capitalists.

Capitalism is sometimes associated with the Industrial Revolution or with the modern era of economic development. But, in principle, it goes back as far as private enterprise does or at least to the earliest period when workmen were employed by owners of capital goods. What has happened in recent centuries is that capital goods have become more prominent in production and have been owned in larger amounts and mobilized in larger firms. Active capitalists have thus enjoyed expanded power.

A country such as Soviet Russia, it should be seen, departs sharply from capitalism in its scheme of economic control, but it is distinctly capitalistic in its methods of production. Indeed Russia has proceeded with great vigor, and somewhat ruthlessly, to extend its use of capitalistic methods.

Later uses of capital concepts

Capitalistic production is of great importance in economic analysis, as references to later uses of it have indicated. We have considered it here mainly for its bearing on production and the conditions of productive power, but the discussion of some points has been expanded to assist in later applications of them. The present analysis will be stressed in two later connections. One of them is the treatment in Part IV of booms and depressions, the problem of underutilization of productive power. Capitalistic methods, oddly enough, are both a main element in that power and in the complications that cause underuse of it. The other is the study of income distribution in Part VI. To analyze the income from capital, it is necessary to understand its role in production.

Review Questions

1. "If there were no saving, the total net product would have to consist of consumers' goods. Saving releases resources for the production of capital goods." Explain.

2. "I invest my savings in land and in the well-seasoned stocks of established companies." Explain the economic function of investment and show that it is not illustrated in this statement.

3. Contrast the relationship between saving and investment in a Crusoe economy and in modern America. Then show the similarity from an over-all standpoint.

4. "Savings have to be invested both in maintaining and in expanding the plant and equipment of industry." Is this statement accurate? Explain the difference between gross and net capital formation. Which gives the better idea of the extent to which resources are used capitalistically?

5. "Even in our system not all saving is completely voluntary. In other systems, little of it may be." Explain. Of what significance is the statement?

6. How do the main categories of saving in this country compare in relative amount as between periods of prosperity and depression?

7. "Profit . . . is also the only source of the new capital equipment without which expansion would be impossible. New capital can only be created by keeping resources or their products for future use—that is, out of a margin between total production and production currently consumed. This margin is the profit margin." [13] Show that profit need not be the source of capital expansion under capitalism and that there may be profit without capital expansion. Do you think the profit margin means what this statement implies?

8. In raising themselves to a higher level, "countries of low productivity are caught in one of the most baffling of circular difficulties." Explain. Show the bearing on this difficulty of international capital movements. What do such movements involve?

9. "Under stable economic conditions, expansion of the rate of capital formation cuts into consumption. Under unstable conditions, it is not likely to." Explain. Is it your impression that consumption usually suffers in the United States in years of heavy investment? Is a country fortunate to be in this situation?

10. "The capital a business uses may be constant, even though great changes occur in the capital goods it uses." Explain.

[13] Peter F. Drucker, *Concept of the Corporation,* John Day, 1946, p. 232. This book is primarily a study of the General Motors Corporation as an example of large-scale enterprise.

11. "You cannot take a whiff of 'free enterprise' or of a 'way of life' and start a factory with it. To start a factory and provide jobs, you have to have money-capital. The word upon which to fix the national mind at this time is simply, outrightly and frankly capitalism." [14] Comment critically on the use of terms in this statement.

[14] From an address by Eric Johnston when president of the United States Chamber of Commerce.

- 7 -

The Organization
Of Production

PRODUCTIVE power depends not only on human and material resources, as discussed in the two preceding chapters, but on how they are arranged and coordinated in specific uses. A modern economy, as surveyed in Chapter 2, is a complex of primary, secondary, and tertiary activities involving many products, many occupations, and wide interrelated areas. This complexity in the whole economy is the resultant, and the complement, of the use of high-output methods in producing particular products. How these methods call for certain arrangements of resources in the plant, the firm, the industry, and the whole economy constitutes the problem of organization of production as studied in economics.

In approaching this problem, the units just mentioned must be distinguished clearly. The *plant,* or *establishment,* is the integrated physical unit through which a productive project is carried on. It may be a factory, a store, a mine, a railroad, a farm. It includes both material facilities and workmen at all levels.[1] The *firm, enterprise, company,* or *concern* is the owning and controlling unit, the business organization. When a firm operates a single plant, there is no point in distinguishing plant and firm in an analysis of production, but when a firm operates two or more plants, failure to distinguish them may lead to serious confusion.

An *industry* consists of the various firms producing a certain product or a closely related group of products. It is a less precise term, in that the boundaries of an industry are often not easy to define. Thus the automobile industry may be thought of as including, or as not including, the firms that make automobile parts. The term *economy*

[1] Sometimes the plant is defined as the *physical unit,* and the establishment as the *plant plus the workmen.* In the present discussion this distinction is not needed.

is applied to the aggregate of industries, or activities, serving the same group of people. Again the boundary is not precise. We speak of the American economy, but, because of international dealings, we also speak of the world economy.

The aim in the first part of this chapter is to develop the logic of organization in fundamental terms that apply to any type of economic system, capitalist or collectivist. The second part, while still dealing with fundamentals of efficiency, will particularly discuss plants, firms, and combinations of firms as they appear in the United States and will combine description, explanation, and some criticism. Stress will be placed on the size of producing units, in part because size and efficiency are connected and in part because size, especially the size of firms, is related to various problems of a public nature. These include problems of competition, new-enterprise possibilities, and labor relations.

Processes, Plants, Industries, and Markets

Specialization, or the division of labor, is the condition on which the organization of production rests. An individual producing all the goods he consumes is not a specialist, and there is no organization. The narrower the activity in which the individual engages, the more specialized he is, the larger the number of people who must cooperate in producing specific products and products in general, and the more complex the organization of production must be. What is said of people can be said with little change of pieces of land and equipment.

Machines and land are clearly marked for specialized use by their fairly inflexible physical characteristics. But since man is broadly adaptable, what are the reasons for the fairly specialized use of labor? What connection is there between the specialization of resources and their use in plants of various sizes, from the typical small farm to the typical huge steel plant? How does the growth of industries, apart from the size of plants, affect the efficiency of production? How does the geographic pattern of production influence the volume of output? How do markets and factors like transportation which govern the extent of markets affect the manner of using resources? These are leading questions that must be answered in developing the underlying logic of the organization of production.

Specialization of labor

The degree of specialization varies by minute gradations, but two general types are distinguishable. One corresponds to entire products, the other to particular operations in producing products.[2]

---

[2] These two types of specialization are sometimes designated as *external* and *internal*.

The medieval craftsman who made cloth or hats or shoes was a specialist of the first type, or, more broadly, he was a specialist in using a material, such as wood or leather. This type of specialization is approximated today by the barber or house painter, the infrequent custom tailor, and the more versatile house builder. But the more typical specialization of labor at the present time is of the second type. With the entire plant forming the unit that specializes on a product, the individual worker performs a limited operation at machine, bench, counter, or desk. In the large modern factory this may be a very small operation repeated hundreds of times a day, such as drilling a hole in a casting or adding a bolt, spring, or bearing on an assembly line.

This distinction throws light on the Industrial Revolution, since it was manifest, in part, in a striking subdivision of tasks. But the difference between specialization by products and by operations is especially significant in defining the place of the business firm in the modern organization of production. In a free economy, specialization by products is organized through the play of market forces, with each producer guided by the demands for his product and the costs of required resources. But specialization by operations is organized through the deliberate planning and authority of heads of firms and plants. The nicety of coordination required where numbers of people work closely together in turning out a product necessitates the existence of the plant and the firm as areas of conscious direction in the organization of production.[3]

Adam Smith begins his *Inquiry into the Nature and Causes of the Wealth of Nations* with this sentence: "The greatest improvement in the productive powers of labour, and the greater part of the skill, dexterity, and judgment with which it is anywhere directed, or applied, seem to have been the effects of the division of labour." With the far greater specialization of the present, it is certainly no less important than in 1776 to examine the reasons for this view. Why does specialization expand the output of labor?

Facilitation of learning. The most obvious gain is through the principle that "practice makes perfect." The more narrowly tasks are specialized, the more frequently are they repeated. Frequency of repetition usually increases the speed and accuracy with which work is done and improves the judgment of the worker and the completeness of his understanding of his job. This gain is expected whether the process is

---

[3] Graphically described by D. H. Robertson as "islands of conscious power in this ocean of unconscious co-operation, like lumps of butter coagulating in a pail of butter milk." See his *The Control of Industry*, Harcourt, Brace & Co., 1923, Ch. VII. This passage is quoted and the subject developed by Norman S. Buchanan, *The Economics of Corporate Enterprise*, Henry Holt & Co., 1940, Ch. I.

wielding a shovel, running a lathe, stringing utility wires, operating a typewriter, keeping accounts, designing a machine, setting a broken bone, or making an executive decision.

Narrowing a workman's duties not only raises the level of his performance but also reduces the time required for attaining a satisfactory level. The early craftsman devoted an apprenticeship, commonly of seven years, to learning a trade. Much of the work in the more highly specialized modern industries can be learned quite thoroughly in a few hours or days. Breaking in workers is still costly, and formal training and apprenticeships are necessary for skilled work. Management requires long experience, and professional activities lengthy schooling as well. But specialization reduces the time and cost of learning or—what is fully as important—increases the proficiency attainable. It is easier to become a welder than a general mechanic, a highway builder than a master of the whole field of engineering, an expert on tropical plants or Spanish history than a scholar who, like Aristotle and Bacon, takes all knowledge as his province.

Adaptation of work to abilities. When tasks are defined somewhat narrowly, the workman can spend all of his time doing the things for which nature and training especially fit him. Perhaps only a few operations in making a shoe require great skill, but the early shoemaker performed all operations, and thus his special talent was wasted much of the time. Productivity is greatly increased when work that can be done by persons low in strength, coordination, intelligence, or training is assigned to persons with these deficiencies, so that abler people can give their full energy to tasks that challenge their abilities. The skilled bricklayer should not have to bring up his materials, nor should the able executive spend time driving a truck and waiting on customers.

Saving of time in arranging work. In plants where many people work, much time can be saved and confusion avoided if each workman is restricted to a specific task. The workman who engages in a succession of tasks, perhaps with different tools, needs a warming-up period for each one as he is getting into the swing of it. If a change of work requires movement to a different spot, time is lost in shifting and in getting adjusted, and the shifting of many workmen in a plant breeds disorder. Some changing about is unavoidable, and machines must be reset for different operations, but it is the essence of mass production that these changes are reduced to a minimum. Operations are performed thousands of times with undeviating repetition.

Encouragement of labor-saving developments. An observation of Adam Smith, as the Industrial Revolution was getting under way, was that specialized workmen performing limited tasks are more likely to find mechanical substitutes for their efforts than are craftsmen who make entire products. It does not occur to a shoemaker that a machine might do his work, but the performer of a single operation in shoemaking may see the possibility of a machine method. Thus specialization of labor becomes a contributing factor in the mechanization of industry.

Complement to machine methods. Finally it can be said that specialization of labor is necessary to high production simply because power-driven machines perform specialized operations, and their operators must be correspondingly specialized. The gain does not arise through any virtue of the specialization of labor as such but through the vast effectiveness of the machine to which labor is adjusted. However mechanized industrial processes become, human action remains part of them. As machines become more complex and comprehensive, combining operations that had been performed separately, the machine operator is no less a specialist. Indeed, his task may be narrowed through greater dependence on automatic controls.[4]

Weaknesses of specialization. The advantages of specialization, however, are not unqualified. Efficient work depends on motivation as well as on dexterity and regularity, and jobs may be too simple and monotonous to be challenging. Lack of interest leads to careless performance, restlessness, and frequent absences. Even in the more mechanized jobs where the machine sets the pace, there is latitude for human nature to assert itself. Thus management has sometimes found that broadening the task, perhaps by having the workman set up the operation and inspect the product, may improve the performance.

But the main attack on narrow specialization has not been on grounds of efficiency. Economic satisfactions come not only through having products to consume but through life on the job, and it is said that intense specialization and mechanization have made work less enjoyable and more irksome. More serious, it has long been charged that human life is degraded by the narrow and repetitive character of work. Karl Marx, in his broad criticism of capitalism, quotes Adam Smith to the effect that a "man whose whole life is spent in performing a few simple operations . . . generally becomes as stupid and ignorant as it is possible for a human creature to become [and that] the uniformity of his stationary life naturally corrupts the courage of his mind." Marx expands upon the theme.[5]

[4] Machines were developed fairly early that reduced the number of separate specialized operations. Karl Marx wrote of an envelope machine that combined the tasks of several workers and turned out 300 envelopes an hour. In laying the foundation for his theory of capitalist exploitation, Marx reported many details of early machine processes. See *Capital*, (as translated from the third German edition) Chs. 14 and 15.

[5] *Capital*, Ch. 14. Smith is quoted from Bk. V, Ch. I, Art. II, the section in which he discusses education.

This viewpoint should be part of any rounded appraisal of modern industry but should not dominate the appraisal. Critics easily forget that a great many people prefer jobs that are routinized and involve little responsibility. Nostalgic references to the "golden age of craftsmanship" neglect the fact that before the modern era most people were serfs and menials rather than craftsmen, and that interesting work is probably more common now than it was then. It is significant that the more arduous, back-breaking aspects of labor have largely been removed by modern equipment, that working hours are greatly reduced, and that people thus have more energy and time for life outside the job.

Actually, without modern specialized and mechanized methods, it would be impossible to support at a high level the great populations that have developed in the last century. Those who prefer socialism to capitalism do not propose abandonment of these methods. The practical problem is one of improving the character of jobs within the framework of the modern organization of production.

Plant size and specialization

Specialized workmen and equipment must be combined in a deliberately coordinated fashion to turn out a product. The producing unit through which this coordination is achieved is the plant or establishment. It may vary in size from the one-man farm or shop to the $100,-000,000 steel mill. The size of plant necessary for efficient production depends largely on the extent to which labor is specialized and specialized equipment is used.

Thus, if the making of a product is divided into 100 operations, and no workman performs more than one operation, at least a 100-man plant is required. If resources would be used more effectively with the work divided into 1000 operations, a 1000-man plant is indicated. Similarly, an increase in the number of mechanized operations from 20 to 100 would mean more machines and a larger plant. So also would the use of larger and more complex machines. With greater use of labor and machines in the direct manipulation of materials, and a greater resulting product, office and other supplementary facilities and the indirect-labor force must also be larger.

Coordination to use factors fully. The gain from specialized labor and machines is easily nullified if these resources are not kept occupied quite fully and continuously. An efficient plant requires a nice adjustment of specific processes to each other, if full use of all productive agents is to be realized. The result is that any specific degree of specialization calls for a larger plant than at first appears necessary. Perhaps 100 operations are performed by different workmen, but some of these operations are broader and slower than others, and more than one workman must be assigned to them. Thus more than 100 men must perform the direct labor of the plant. Machines present the same problem. Machine A may perform its operation 10 times an hour and is kept busy when the flow of output is at that rate. But machine B can handle 15 units an hour and machine C 25 units, and their capacity would be wasted seriously with a 10-unit rate of production. In this situation, the ideal solution is to produce at a 150-unit hourly rate, since 150 is the lowest common multiple of 10, 15, and 25. But this rate calls for batteries of machines: 15 of A, 10 of B, and 6 of C. Somewhat artificially, this example shows how the problem of utilizing specialized agents fully can be solved only through expanding the size of the plant.

Large indivisible factors. In every establishment there are overhead elements that, within certain limits, do not expand proportionately as the size of the establishment is increased. If the concern provides its own power, its generating facilities may double their output without doubling the required investment and the fuel used. Similarly, top officers and executives may be able to manage a larger volume of operations without a corresponding expansion in their number or in outlay required to hire abler men. The special facilities and knowledge and research involved in using a particular material—say, wood or rubber or copper—involve costs that can be spread advantageously over a larger output. It may even be desirable to diversify operations by producing several different products from this material. Thus the scale of production is increased.

Perfect utilization unfeasible. It would be unreasonable to expect that a plant could be planned so that all the elements in it, with their different capacities, would be used fully or that, even if such planning were possible, continuous full operation could be maintained under the changing conditions to which all industries are subject. Nor is full use necessary to achieve substantial economy. Considerable idleness can be tolerated in the case of a power-machine, for instance, if the alternative is a method which, though it keeps resources busy, still requires more of them. A well-patronized railroad carries freight at an average cost of 1 cent per ton per mile, but a railroad may still be justified in a particular area even though traffic is so light as to make the cost 10 cents per ton per mile, provided the alternative to the railroad is carriage by horse and wagon at 25 cents per ton per mile.

But fairly full use of specialized agents is necessary to the highest economy. Thus in industries that employ modern methods in using labor and equipment, plants are likely to be characterized by large investment, numerous employees, and a high volume of output.

Industry variations. The average size of plant, or establishment, varies widely from one industry to another. Plants differ greatly in size also within industries. From the standpoint of efficiency, some are smaller than they should be and some are larger than they need to be. Getting fairly full use of specialized processes and equipment, adjusted as well as possible to the nature of the product, is not the only element that influences the typical size of plants in different industries, but it is undoubtedly the most important one. Differences in plant size among industries can be explained very largely on the basis of it.[6]

In some industries certain equipment items necessitate a large plant. A railroad cannot carry freight and passengers between New York and Chicago without having tracks that go all the way, and the plant is inevitably large and costly. A power company must extend its transmission lines over the whole area that it serves, and, until its generating facilities are quite large, their cost per unit of capacity declines. A modern steel mill with blast furnaces, open-hearth furnaces, and rolling equipment designed for uninterrupted processing is necessarily a huge affair. Large and complex products like automobiles, locomotives, and bombing planes can be mass-produced only in plants with much space, numerous employees, and an impressive array of equipment.

But such manufacturing industries as textiles, shoes, and furniture employ equipment units of modest dimensions and are able to coordinate specialized factors effectively in plants with a few hundred workers. In much of the clothing industry equipment is still less of an item, and identical repetition of operations is less the rule. Thus establishments may be small and still be efficient. In the extreme case of the now rare old-type custom tailoring shop, the characteristics that relate efficiency to size are all absent. Table 10 indicates the great differences in plant size among manufacturing industries.[7]

In agriculture the specialization of labor cannot go far. Specialists in feeding livestock, milking cows, plowing land, sowing crops, or threshing grain would be idle much of the time. Operations must be performed in series, if labor is to be fully occupied. Not only do the absence of standardization and repetition deprive specialization of its advantages, but they make difficult the supervision of large numbers of employees, and this difficulty is increased by the size of the area that must be supervised. On the other hand, farm equipment is expensive in

[6] Other economies of size will appear in the following section of this chapter, in the discussion of business firms in the United States.

[7] Based on Census of Manufactures data from the *Statistical Abstract of the United States,* 1946. For 184,230 establishments with products valued in excess of $5000, the average "value added by manufacture" was $134,000. The 50 percent of the establishments of smaller size accounted for less than 5 percent of all manufacturing production, and the largest 5 percent accounted for 60 percent of the production.

TABLE 10—NUMBER AND SIZE OF ESTABLISHMENTS IN SELECTED
MANUFACTURING LINES, 1939

Industry	Number of establishments	"Value added" per establishment (thousands of dollars)
Cigarettes	35	$6,480
Steel	253	4,535
Rubber tire and tube	53	4,365
Cane sugar refining	27	2,073
Wool carpets and rugs	43	1,840
Motor vehicles (including parts)	1,054	1,251
Cement	160	775
Cotton textiles	1,248	459
Footwear (excluding rubber)	1,070	323
Women's dresses	2,916	75
Flour and grain mill products	2,143	67
Bakery products	18,399	41
Cheese	2,682	6

grain farming and some other lines, and much of it is necessarily subject to long periods of idleness. Many farms are too small to use it even as efficiently as is possible. But cooperative use of threshing equipment by the farmers of an area—or, better, the provision of threshing services by separate companies which follow the harvest from Texas to Canada —achieves some degree of economy in this aspect of agriculture. Other comparable services are coming to be provided in agriculture on a contract basis.

In merchandising large establishments are not needed because of the use of expensive equipment or repetitious types of labor. Thus small independent stores persist and seem likely to continue. Nevertheless, size yields some advantages—in the firm more than in the plant. These will be discussed later.

Plant size versus *industry size*

When the demand for a product grows and a whole industry assumes an expanding place in the economy, as the automobile industry did through several decades, growth may take place in the form of more plants, larger plants, or both. If plants are not already large enough to use equipment and specialized labor effectively, larger plants are advantageous. If more plants appear, they may follow the pattern of earlier plants, or they may carry further the principle of plant specialization. In either case, but especially the latter, economies are likely to result from industry growth.

Specialization of plants. A complex product, such as an automobile, is assembled from a great number of component parts, ranging from the motor and the body down to wheel bearings, gas gauges, and windshield wipers. These parts may conceivably all be made in a single plant, but it is probable that many of them will be made in separate plants and then brought together for assembly. The assembly, even, may not be in one plant but in several plants located in different market areas.

The advantages of the smaller, highly specialized plant are notable. For its limited product it is able to carry mass-production methods further than they could go in the final assembly plant. Such a plant may make batteries, spark plugs, tires, speedometers, heaters, or even motors or automobile bodies for quite a number of assembly plants and also for replacement purchase. Thus its volume is greater than could be attained merely by a department of a single automobile factory, and it can realize more fully the advantages of specialized labor and equipment. Some products, moreover, such as bolts, bearings, and plate glass, may have a market outside the automobile industry and enter other uses.

In the last few decades it has become increasingly feasible to rely on separate plants for parts and subassemblies. Especially promoting this result have been developments in the power and transportation fields. Use of electric power to propel machinery has made unnecessary the former type of central power equipment, with its elaborate system of shafts and belts, and important gains in flexibility have resulted. Efficient highway transportation permits the prompt movement of parts from plants in the surrounding area. Moreover, the labor supply in smaller communities can be utilized to advantage, and, on the average, employees can live closer to their jobs.

This specialization of plants applies not only to making the parts which go into larger products but to other related activities. Special equipment, such as spinning and weaving and shoemaking machinery, can be mass produced for numerous plants that will use it. Waste materials can be reclaimed from plants in the same field and turned into by-products, as the bones, cartilage, horns, and hoofs of animals are used in the meat-packing industry.

From these cases it becomes plain that the economies of mass production must not be identified crudely and superficially with the size of plants. A fairly small plant making spark plugs or ball bearings can go further in specializing labor and using appropriate equipment than can the great plants that do the final work on elaborate products. For the specific product the volume is greater in the specialized plant, provided it serves a number of other plants. Since plants making parts and equipment withdraw important functions from the plants that they serve, the net effect is that a fuller use of modern methods can be accompanied by some general reduction in the size of plants.

Industry size and technology. Methods of production are likely to advance rapidly in growing industries. In the more highly specialized plants that industry growth encourages, management and technicians focus attention on a small production area, and improvement in products and processes is stimulated. The management of a battery plant, for instance, has a keener interest in improving batteries than has the management of an automobile plant.

But entirely apart from the specialization of plants, a growing industry provides a climate conducive to progress. It provides a field of opportunity for enterprising engineers and managers. It commands the attention of equipment manufacturers, who focus on its problems. Trade associations and publications become active and supply information to its members. Universities and government agencies contribute to its advance.

The essential point is that these gains derive from industry growth, not from the growth of plants and firms. They are present even though that growth takes place entirely through expansion in the number of plants and not at all in the size of plants. They have sometimes been called *external economies* to indicate that their source is outside the plant and the firm and in the industry as a whole. These economies are often neglected in discussions of large-scale production and big business, but they probably belong among the leading advantages of economic growth.[8]

Geographic pattern of production

Thus far we have neglected one basic aspect of organization: the geographic arrangement of productive activities. Within the United States 60,000,000 people are engaged in farming, mining, manufacturing, transportation, and other lines of work, and the location of every one of these producers has some bearing on the effectiveness of what he does. Location is most obviously vital in the primary industries, be-

---

[8] Colin Clark concluded: ". . . examination over a long period of American and British production statistics shows that increases in production per head in any industry are largely dependent on the relative rate of growth of the industry as a whole. The increasing specialization between firms thus made possible appears to be the most deep-lying cause of industrial progress." Regarding plant size as such, he says: "A careful comparison of production statistics, industry by industry, in five countries showed no correlation whatever between average size of plant and high output per head." *The Conditions of Economic Progress*, Macmillan & Co., Ltd., 1940, p. 11. External economies have also been stressed by Alfred Marshall and F. W. Taussig.

cause they depend directly on soil, minerals, and other features of the land. Other industries have greater latitude in finding locations, but their efficiency in using resources must depend on their relationship to the primary industries, to markets, and to each other.

The term *geographic specialization* may be applied to any instance of concentration in an area on a particular product, but it is applied most commonly to the specialized use of natural resources in the primary industries. Thus we speak of wheat, corn, cotton, and citrus-fruit belts and of lumber, oil, and coal-mining regions. One advantage of the specialization of labor, we saw, lies in the fitting of tasks to the innate qualities of the resource. This, of course, is the reason for specialized use of land, but in the case of land the range of adaptability is usually less and the superior use more clearly indicated. Undoubtedly a major source of high productivity in a nation lies in the specialized use of each land area for products for which it is naturally fitted, with other areas depending on it for those products. But such specialization also has its drawbacks which must be taken into account. Resources may become depleted and markets may prove undependable. Thus some diversification, as when cotton farmers also raise other crops, may be a security measure.

The term *localization* is most often applied to geographic concentration in the manufacturing field. Well-known instances, some less pronounced than formerly, are the production of steel in and about Pittsburgh, automobiles in the Detroit area, shoes and cotton textiles in certain Massachusetts cities, clothing in New York, cigarettes in North Carolina. For most important products there is more than one producing area, but localization persists. Its advantages are largely related to the reasons for plant specialization already discussed. When several plants of the same industry are located near each other, other plants are encouraged to develop in the area to provide parts for the product, manufacture special equipment, and utilize waste materials. Moreover, a labor force develops which is acquainted with the work of the industry, and buyers find it convenient to come to a community where a wide choice is possible in obtaining the product. These are reasons for localization apart from the natural condition that nearness to a necessary source of materials or power may be a compelling influence and lead to a bunching of plants.

Complexity of the location problem. These advantages of geographic concentration are evident enough, but actually the problem of efficient location of production is an extremely complex one. The economies of concentration must be set against the more extensive transporting and handling of products that are necessary to achieve them. The cost of transporting wheat would be less if people in each part of the country grew their own wheat, but the cost of growing it would be higher than when most of it comes from the Missouri Valley. If textile mills were scattered throughout the country, the transporting of textiles would be reduced, but there would be more transporting of raw cotton and wool, and the economies of manufacturing on a large scale would be sacrificed. In the case of steel, both transportation and scale of production are still weightier factors. The problem of location is the problem of minimizing all of the costs taken together—of getting the largest output from resources used in transportation and marketing as well as in farming, mining, and manufacturing.

Needless to say, an ideal solution is never achieved, even though producers are constantly seeking better opportunities and improved locations. People settle first in the most accessible areas, as American colonists occupied the eastern seaboard, and they become firmly established before their prospects are fully apparent. Thereafter adjustments are slow. Manufacturing may start in a community through the accident that a particular enterpriser lives there, and presently the industry is "localized" for no reason other than "the momentum of an early start." Transportation and methods of manufacturing are constantly developing and natural resources are being depleted, so that the factors in the location problem are never sufficiently fixed for a slow process of solution to catch up. But whether present geographic arrangements are close to the ideal solution or not, they are an important aspect of the whole organization of production.

Extent of markets

In a sense all the aspects of organization on which productivity depends—the machines, the specialized use of labor and land, the large plants and industries—rest on the capacity of markets to absorb products. As explained earlier, the aim in coordinating operations within the plant is to get full use of specialized agents, but what can be used fully depends primarily on the market.

Thus a small, isolated frontier community cannot have the service of a full-time shoemaker, even though good shoemaking calls for a specialist. A factory worker, if sales are only 50 units a day, cannot be put on an operation that he would perform on 100 units of product a day, even though that degree of specialization is technically best. One machine may have twice the output of another on a given job and involve costs only 50 percent higher, but the seeming economy of the faster machine must be foregone if the market will absorb only the output of the slower one. One of oldest propositions in economics is that *specialization is limited by the extent of the market*.[9]

Markets expand as population increases, as we noted in Chapter 5, and thus there is some offset to the effect of diminishing returns. But the greatest influence in broadening markets has been the *progress in transportation*. It required the modern railroad to make the United States a single-market area for basic commodities and most manufactured goods, and the modern steamship became the basis of world markets. Paradoxically the cheapening of transportation did not make it a smaller element in the final cost of goods; rather it became a larger element. Products travel on the average much farther than they did, but in doing so they permit production to be concentrated in great plants and in areas best fitted by nature, and the total effect is a reduction in costs. Thus the geographic pattern is altered to take advantage of modern methods.

But the benefit of low-cost transportation, as the basis of wide markets and specialized production, can easily be nullified by *artificial trade barriers*. If the United States were cut into economic segments, as France and Germany once were by provincial and local tolls and tariffs and as Europe has continued to be through national trade restrictions, this country could not have developed the markets and the economical methods that it has.[10] In providing against interstate tariffs, the framers of the Constitution contributed more to economic development than, in the late eighteenth century, they could fully realize.

Trade among nations involves many difficulties, as will be recognized later in this study, but it is pertinent here that the presence of different governments does not alter the basic economic factors on which the efficient use of resources depends. If, through some catastrophe, different flags should come to fly on opposite sides of the Mississippi River and trade across it become international, that trade would have exactly the same role as at present in promoting the effective use of resources between the oceans.

Review Questions

1. "Under modern capitalism, the labor of individuals must be coordinated in an ascending series of producing organizations—the plant, the firm, the industry, and the economy as a whole." What is meant in economics by the organization of production? Distinguish these units of organization.

[9] Developed at length in *Wealth of Nations*, Bk. I, Ch. III.

[10] For interesting accounts of early trade restrictions and their effect on economic development, see Clive Day, *A History of Commerce*, Longmans, 1928.

2. "One type of specialization is the basis of the kind of economic control which operates in the whole economy. Another is the basis of the kind of control which operates within plants and firms." Explain. Why is the latter type of control necessary?

3. "Even without the use of machines, there is a great gain in subdividing the operations in making a product." Why? Give several reasons. Why should specialization have increased the use of women and children in industry? How has education been affected by specialization?

4. "Specialization of labor may promote the development of machinery, but in any case it is necessitated by that development." Explain.

5. Specialization has been criticized as going too far for efficiency and as being harmful in other ways. Develop the criticisms and state your reaction to them.

6. If the operations in making a man's suit are more minutely subdivided than in making a woman's dress, what is the logical effect of this difference on the size of plants in the two cases? Can you formulate a general principle covering this situation?

7. If the machines required for four different operations on a product perform at the rate of 8, 12, 15, and 20 units of product an hour, on what basis can these four machines be coordinated efficiently in a plant? Are you applying the same principle as in question 6?

8. To get the possible advantages of specialized processes and equipment, compare the need for large establishments in railroads, motor trucking, steel manufacture, textile manufacture, farming, retail trade, electric power, and other fields.

9. "Plant specialization permits the advantages of mass production to be extended without increasing the size of plants." Explain. What developments encourage plant specialization?

10. What are the "external economies" of size? Size of what?

11. Agriculture in the United States may be organized on the basis of a highly specialized use of land or, on the other hand, with little regional concentration of products. Contrast the advantages of these schemes. What is the actual situation?

12. If a manufacturing industry is to be located in the most effective way, what are the factors which must be taken into account in selecting the location? Inasmuch as the object is to get the highest output from resources, can you see why the problem must be solved in value terms?

13. What are the advantages of "localizing" a manufacturing industry in a specific urban area? Of having activities localized within sections of cities such as financial districts and wholesale districts?

14. "It is obvious that the pipe line and the tank steamer have promoted the specialized use of certain land areas. Just as truly, but not so obviously, the refrigerator car has increased the specialization of operations within meat-packing plants." Explain, tracing relationships carefully. What principle explained by Adam Smith is being exemplified?

15. "The United States provides outstanding proof of the benefit of keeping trade restrictions at a minimum." Explain. Do you know of any state policies that violate the principle?

Business Firms in the United States

What has just been said regarding machines and specialized processes, the size of plants and industries, the geographic pattern of production and the size of markets has general application. These aspects of the organization of production affect the level of output in about the same way under capitalism and collectivism. What will now be said regarding business firms in the United States will, in part, also apply to any modern situation. Most of the economies, and also the weaknesses, of large owning and controlling units may be associated either with private firms or with the government corporations or state trusts that operate industries in a socialist system. But the descriptive material will apply to the American scene, and the discussion of the origin and nature of large firms and combinations will be relevant mainly to an analysis of capitalism.

In understanding the economy of the United States, it is important to have a clear picture—though not necessarily a detailed one—of the characteristics of business firms and the reasons underlying their development. In the present section emphasis will center on the size of firms, chiefly as size bears on economy in production but with a glance, also, at its significance in other ways. "Big business" is a controversial matter and a balanced view of it must take account of many things.

Size of firms in different fields

The relative size of producing units, whether plants or firms, depends a great deal on how they are measured. Measured on the basis of its *gross assets,* the total wealth in its control, a $2,000,000 power company is twice as large as a $1,000,000 manufacturing company. But so different is production in these fields that, if size were measured on the basis of *number of employees,* the manufacturing company would probably appear at least twice as large as the power company. Or an intermediate figure might be reached by comparing them on a *product* or *value-added* basis, although for general use the statistical difficulties of this measure would be greater. In all economic measurements, one should remain aware of what units are employed and how they may influence the result.

Responsibility for production in the United States is in the hands of a very large number of enterprises. Some of these enterprises are not ordinary business firms but governmental bodies—federal, state, and local—or nonprofit private organizations such as prevail in the religious and educational fields. Typically about 15 percent of the working population are employed by such enterprises as these. The large remainder are involved as proprietors and employees in, perhaps, 10,000,000 private undertakings. Of this uncertain total, about 5,000,000 are farms, over 1,500,000 are retail and wholesale businesses, a similar number are in a miscellany of "service" lines—hotels, theaters, barber shops, bowling alleys, medical and legal practice—over 500,000 are in building construction. In such an aggregate, the 150,000 firms in manufacturing and the smaller number of railroads and power companies do not seem important.[11]

Figures such as these may indicate where the opportunities for new enterprise are best, but they tell little regarding the scope of business activity in these various fields. A total means little in which a one-man barber shop has the same weight as the United States Steel Corporation. Probably nine tenths of all firms, according to prewar estimates, have five employees or less, but they account for no more than a third of total employees. Not a firm in a thousand, on the other hand, has as many as 1000 employees, but such firms may employ as many as a quarter of all workers.

A comprehensive view of the size of enterprises in the main fields of activity in the United States can be gained through careful examination of Table 11. For each type of industry the figures show the percentage of total productive activity performed by unincorporated firms, which are mainly very small, and the percentages performed by each of four groups of incorporated firms, arranged by sizes. The size of corporations is measured in gross assets, and productive activity is measured just about as national income is computed. The leaning toward bigness in transportation and other public utilities, manufacturing, and mining is apparent from these figures, as is the preponderance of small firms in agriculture, trade, construction, and the service lines.[12]

In Table 11, 594 corporations are represented in the group with

[11] Useful sources of such data as are included here are: Adolph A. Berle and Gardiner C. Means, *The Modern Corporation and Private Property,* Macmillan, 1933, Ch. III; National Resources Committee, *The Structure of the American Economy,* Pt. I, 1939, Ch. VI; Temporary National Economic Committee Monograph No. 27, *The Structure of Industry;* T.N.E.C. Monograph No. 21, *Competition and Monopoly in American Industry;* Department of Commerce, *Statistical Abstract of the United States.* The 150,000 figure for manufacturing does not include undertakings with an annual product below $5000.

[12] Alfred L. Bernheim (ed.) *Big Business: Its Growth and Its Place,* Twentieth Century Fund, 1937, p. 95. The figures are for the early 1930s, but the percentage relations have probably changed little except for the fact that rising prices have thrown more corporations into large-size groups.

TABLE 11—PERCENT OF PRODUCTION OF MAIN INDUSTRY GROUPS

Industry	Unincorporated firms	Corporations with total assets			
		Less than $1,000,000	$1,000,000–5,000,000	$5,000,000–50,000,000	$50,000,000 and over
Agriculture	94	3.1	2.9		
Mining	4	19.8	15.4	60.8	
Manufacturing	8	24.3	14.3	20.0	33.4
Construction	67	23.4	5.0	4.6	
Transportation and other utilities	14	6.5	2.9	11.1	65.5
Trade	37	37.0	9.5	9.1	7.4
Service	67	19.3	5.0	8.7	
Finance	44	16.0	9.0	14.0	17.0
Miscellaneous	62	28.2	9.8		
All activities except government	38	21.8	8.6	11.6	20.0

gross assets in excess of $50,000,000, but for statisticians who investigate big business 200 is for some reason the favorite number. Several studies have been made of the 200 largest nonfinancial corporations in the United States—that is, in fields other than banking and insurance.[13] They extend in size—or did before the war—from less than $100,000,-000 of gross assets to about $4,000,000,000 in the case of the American Telephone and Telegraph Company. Almost half of the 200 are railroads and other utilities, and the greater part of the other half are manufacturing companies. Nine railroads, headed by the Pennsylvania and the New York Central, are in the billion-dollar class, and along with A.T. and T., the public utilities include five billion-dollar power and gas companies—or did before certain dismemberments took place. There are three billion-dollar manufacturing companies—Standard Oil of New Jersey, United States Steel, and General Motors. In merchandising, along with the numerous small firms, three types of large enterprise have developed: the mail-order house, the chain organization, and the department store. Representatives of each category appear among the 200, but none, unless recently, has exceeded a quarter-billion of gross assets.

[13] Three such studies are: Berle and Means, op. cit., National Resources Committee, op. cit., and T.N.E.C. Monograph No. 29, The Distribution of Ownership in the 200 Largest Nonfinancial Corporations. Gross assets are not a suitable measure of the size of financial corporations.

Measured in gross assets, the size of firms increased sharply during the war period, partly through acquisition of real assets, partly through expanded holdings of cash and government securities, partly through the rise in prices. A study made of 1000 large manufacturing firms, representing fully half of all manufacturing, showed that their total assets in 1946 were 50 percent greater than in 1939. Only a small part of this increase, and none of it up to 1945, was in the value of plant and equipment.[14]

Firms may be measured also, not in absolute units, but on the basis of their *relative size in relation to the industry* of which they are a part. Thus it could be said before the war that one firm in each field produced most of the aluminum, nickel, molybdenum, magnesium, shoe machinery, and glass-container machinery; two firms most of the bananas, plate glass, electric bulbs, electric accounting machines, and sulphur. The four largest firms in each industry produced more than 90 percent of the chewing gum and cigarettes; more than 80 percent of the motor vehicles, explosives, linoleum, rubber tires, and tin cans; more than 70 percent of the oleomargarine, soap, farm implements, and matches. At the other extreme, the four largest firms produced less than 5 percent of the women's and children's clothing, fur goods, printing and publishing, and lumber products, and less than 10 percent of the men's and boys' clothing, furniture, housefurnishings, and jewelry.[15] This method of measurement is less significant in analyzing the economies of size than in appraising the degree of monopoly and competition in industry. It is applicable to the discussion of the latter problem in Part V.

Multi-plant firms; combinations

From the operating standpoint, the firm needs to be distinguished from the plant only when it operates two or more plants. The vast majority of firms are of the single-plant type, and firms may grow large on this basis. But most of the very large firms are multi-plant. Of the 150,-000 manufacturing firms before the war, 15 percent operated more than one plant. The average was five plants for these plural-unit firms, and the largest 200 of them averaged more than 25 plants each.[16]

Multi-plant firms may expand through ordinary internal growth just

---

[14] K. C. Stokes, "Financial Trends of Large Manufacturing Corporations, 1936–1946," *Survey of Current Business,* November 1947.

[15] These data are from T.N.E.C. Monograph No. 21, *op. cit.*

[16] Multi-plant firms in manufacturing are analyzed in detail in T.N.E.C. Monograph No. 27, *The Structure of Industry,* with a larger number of types recognized than here. Almost two thirds of these combinations seem to be of horizontal nature. In the present discussion the word "firm" is applied to organizations under a central control, even though some of the plants may be operated directly by separate, but subsidiary, corporations.

as single-plant firms do. A chain-store company may establish additional retail outlets, or a manufacturing company may build a new factory to provide materials or parts. But most of the multi-plant firms have come about through combination of already existing independent firms. One company may buy outright the properties of another company or buy enough of its voting stock to get control of it, or a new corporation may be formed to control the existing firms. These corporate matters will be dealt with in the following chapter.

As a producing organization, the main feature of a multi-plant firm is the relationship that exists between the constituent plants. The possible relationships are numerous, but they may be grouped in three categories: horizontal, vertical, and diverse-product. It will be convenient to speak of all of them as combinations, whatever the origin.

Horizontal combination. The most common type of multi-plant firm consists of establishments that perform essentially the same productive function. The relationship is that between the different automobile-manufacturing plants in General Motors, the refineries in Standard Oil, the food stores in the Atlantic and Pacific chain, the power plants in Commonwealth and Southern. The products of the different units need not be identical; there may be some plant specialization on the basis of size, style, or quality of product. The essential point is that the plants are at the *same level* in the progress of the product toward completion. If they were not combined and were selling in the same market, they would be at least partially competitive.

Vertical combination. Plants may be combined which produce at different levels or stages in turning out the same final product, so that the relationship is successive or vertical. Thus a furniture company may operate a lumber mill and also engage in timber operations. Such a company as United States Steel sees its material through from mines to final saleable form as sheets, bars, beams, and other products and operates railroads and steamships in the process. Parts plants run by automobile companies bear the same relationship to the final product—though between two parts plants the relationship is properly described as convergent rather than successive.

Diverse-product combinations. The plants in a combination may turn out distinct products that never converge, and yet there may be an operating relationship, or some sort of functional relationship, between them. It may rest on a *common material*. One plant in a combination may use cotton yarn in weaving cloth and another in knitting underwear. One may use leather in making shoes and another in making luggage. Several by-product plants may be offshoots from a single basic process, as when a meat-packing company enters the business of making glue, gelatine, fertilizer, and soap.

A looser relationship exists when only a *common type of processing* is present. Thus a company may operate separate plants making woolen, cotton, and rayon textiles. Still looser is a combination of food plants processing breakfast cereals, coffee, salad dressing, yeast, and baking powder, for which the only common element seems to be the possibility of some *unified effort in marketing*.

But the history of corporate combinations is such that one should not feel obliged to discover a clear operating logic in every case. When a company unites plants producing airplanes, farm machinery, kitchen sinks, chemicals, and electric power, as has in fact been done, the explanation must be found elsewhere.

Economies of large firms

When the question is asked why firms have become so large in many industries, the first answer invariably is that size is necessary to efficiency. Within limits this is a sound answer. The conditions of high productivity cannot be understood without examining the claims to efficiency of the large business firm, especially the multi-plant firm, as it has developed in the United States. But it is equally important to see that the advantages of size are limited and that they depend on the manner and form in which size is achieved.

The preceding section explained the relation between *plant* size and what may be called *technological economies*. If certain pieces of equipment represent the most advanced technique in an industry, the plant should be large enough to install them and keep them busy. If labor is most effective when operations are specialized and arranged in a certain way, the plant should be large enough to make full use of its various specialists. The full and highly repetitious use of specialized machines and labor is the essence of mass production. Since the business firm must embrace the entire plant which it operates, it can be said that the firm also must be large enough to achieve these technological economies —that they are an advantage of a firm sufficiently large to achieve them. The present question is whether there are additional advantages in a firm that is larger than these particular economies require.

To make the problem clear, let us assume that in a certain industry a $4,000,000 plant is large enough, in light of present knowledge, to realize fully the benefit of machine techniques and specialized processes. Firm *A*, with $4,000,000 of capital, operates such a plant. Firm *B*, with $8,000,000, builds a plant twice as large as *A*'s in every respect. Firm *C*, also with $8,000,000, has two separate plants, each identical with A's. Finally Firm D, again with $8,000,000, carries the combination idea farther and has four $2,000,000 plants, also on the horizontal principle. On the assumption made, a firm must have $4,000,000 of capital to be efficient in this industry. The question is whether it will be more efficient with $8,000,000, and if so, why. The question, further, is whether any additional economies depend on the form that the expansion takes.

Confusion of plant and firm. The problem is stated in this way because there is much loose talk about the economies of size. When people think of the producing units that provide goods in the United States, they think ordinarily of companies such as Allied Chemical and Bethlehem Steel and not of the plants these companies operate. At the same time, popular ideas of the advantages of bigness seem to spring from impressions of power-driven machinery and swiftly repeated processes. So people are likely to say that great firms are a fine thing for the country because of the efficiency of mass production.

Firm D, just described, was designed for people who think in this way. It is twice as large as Firm A, and from what one might read in the newspapers about it, one could suppose that it has traveled much farther along the road of large-scale progress. But, in fact, the four plants that Firm D operates are each only half as large as the one plant that A operates; and our understanding is that a plant must be as large as A's to enjoy the technological economies of size. D is a big firm, but a backward one.

Nor, under our assumption, are Firms B and C any better than Firm A with respect to these basic technological economies. If A's plant is large enough, B's is no better through being larger. And whatever the technical character of A's plant, C does not alter that character through having two such plants.

This confusion of plant and firm—set forth just a little too simply and sharply with this example—is the most common and least excusable mistake in ordinary appraisals of the trend toward bigness in industry. There is no close correspondence between the size of firms and the technological advantages of size, since most large firms are multiplant firms. The United States Steel Corporation is ten times as large as some of the members of the group known as Little Steel, but each firm in this group is large enough to operate one or more modern steel plants. The great size of United States Steel, due mainly if not wholly to the larger number of plants it has combined, does not in itself indicate a superior technical efficiency.

Distinctive economies of the large firm. But are not other economies realized by the large firm that do not depend on plant size? Are there not other respects in which Firms *B, C,* and *D* are superior to Firm *A*—respects that inhere in the size of the firm, whether it operates one plant or more than one? Certainly quite a few such advantages have been claimed. Five will be noted briefly.

1. One of the most important is the economy of *buying* and of *selling in large volume.* When materials and supplies are purchased in quantity, the handling and paper work are likely to involve less expense per unit than with smaller quantities. If the suppliers do any special processing for the particular buyer, savings can be realized on large orders. Likewise, in marketing products, advertising and other selling outlays are not likely to increase proportionally as the volume of output expands. But no simple rule can govern this situation. It may be that marketing becomes progressively more difficult and costly to get the additional orders to dispose of an expanded volume.

Economies of this sort are most important in fields in which buying and selling are a large part of the total function. This is the position of the middleman. Thus any advantages that chain stores enjoy in comparison with independent merchants arise mainly, it appears, in their large-scale buying.

But one must be sure, in speaking of the economies of large-scale buying, that the economies are genuine. *Real economy always means that a given result is achieved with a reduced outlay of resources.* When a small supplier of materials or parts becomes dependent on a certain large buyer, that buyer may be able to bludgeon him into lower prices than are charged others, not because of savings in handling and processing but because of the seller's dependence on the large customer. Lower prices, then, do not reflect lower real costs. A situation is created which belongs, as we shall see later, on the edge of the monopoly problem.

2. A similar advantage claimed for large firms is in *financing* their activities. In borrowing from banks, and more particularly in issuing and selling securities, there are costs which are not proportionally greater as the sums involved become larger. In addition there is a prestige factor which may affect the cost of capital. A well-run large firm, though fundamentally no better than a well-run small firm, may, because it is better known, be able to borrow at a lower rate of interest or obtain new stockholders on the basis of a lower expected return.

One must be careful, however, not to claim too much for financial power. It is an elementary mistake to say that the big firm can produce more cheaply than the small firm because it has more capital and thus can afford to buy better equipment. Equipment can be *afforded* by those who can use it fully and to advantage. The main condition to be met is one of volume and plant organization, not of financing. In our example, Firm *A*, with $4,000,000, can afford better equipment than Firm *D*, with $8,000,000.

3. Larger firms, whether they operate one plant or several, have an advantage in the *technical research* carried on to improve their products and reduce their costs. Research can be carried farther, and conducted at lower cost per unit of output, when its results affect a large volume of output. Industrial progress comes mainly not through accidental discoveries but through systematic investigation in such great firms as Du Pont and General Electric.

4. Larger firms may also be able to improve some of the processes of *management*. It was noted in the discussion of plant economies that a good manager is one of those rather large, indivisible specialized units that present a problem of full utilization and may not be fully used unless the plant is larger than most items of equipment require. But the managerial problems of the business firm extend beyond the technical supervision of the plant. They involve questions of markets and selling, financial and legal matters, relations with labor unions, with government, and with the public. There is a place for high-grade managerial specialists, and it is economy to make the fullest use of their services by giving them as broad a scope of activity as they can effectively handle.

5. Finally, it should be noted that firms become larger and achieve advantages through *diversification of their products*. Examples used in preceding pages may have gone too far in suggesting that plants and firms usually confine themselves to single products or closely related groups of products. Some do, but many firms—often in the same plants —turn out a number of products which are quite different in physical character. The aim may be to have a full line of goods to meet the convenience of a certain type of buyer. Thus the manufacturer may undertake to produce a complete line of plumbing supplies or household appliances or school furniture and manual-training equipment, however different the manufacturing problems for the items in the line. Or the aim may be to have staple items of steady sale to balance specialties or seasonal items that, by themselves, would cause costly irregularities in operations.[17]

In most of these respects Firms *B*, *C*, and *D* may have some advantage over Firm *A*. They may not carry the principles of mass production any further, or even as far, but they can achieve other economies. The point is that for one aspect of a firm's activity, say the use of certain machines,

[17] For a full discussion of the product structures of large manufacturing corporations, see T.N.E.C. Monograph No. 27, *op. cit.*, Pt. VI.

one size of organization is adequate; for another aspect, perhaps an efficient marketing program, another size is best; and the ideal is a size of firm that will accommodate them all, or achieve the best compromise among them.

Distinctive economies of combination

In part the advantages claimed for multi-plant firms are simply these general advantages of size. Especially in the case of horizontal and diverse-product combinations, the main economies must be found among those mentioned. Combination is simply a way of becoming larger, and it is much the most direct and the easiest way for firms already in existence. But are there distinctive economies of combination as such—reasons why Firms C and D may be more effective than Firm B which is just as large? And what reason may there be for a Firm E that enters this industry with one $4,000,000 plant and four additional $1,000,000 plants which make various materials and parts that the other firms purchase from outside companies? Several economies may arise from combination under a variety of circumstances.

It can be said in general that, where any diversity of product exists, there is some advantage in producing the different items in separate plants so that the operating management can concentrate on a more limited range of activity. This point is most applicable to vertical and diverse-product combinations. But it is also possible in horizontal combinations to devote each plant to particular styles and types of the product, as the different divisions of General Motors turn out different makes of automobiles.

If the products are sufficiently diverse so that they are made of different materials, growth through combination permits each item to be produced in the location most advantageous to it. Quite obviously United States Steel must do its iron mining and coal mining in different spots, and neither location is ideal for steel mills. It is also said that horizontal combination can save transportation by placing plants in different parts of the country and filling orders from the nearest plant. But whether or not this is a consideration of importance, it cannot be reconciled with plant specialization. If plants specialize, orders must be filled not from the nearest plant but from the plant making the style or type of product that is ordered.

A horizontal combination may also improve products and reduce costs by making available to each plant the exclusive processes and patented devices developed by hitherto competing firms. Each firm has the best ideas about certain details, and the pooling procedure helps them all. But this point carries us afield into complex patent matters and the whole problem of competition to which horizontal combination is directly related.

Vertical combination is held to be advantageous through enabling a firm to be independent of the market in getting materials, supplies, and parts. If a manufacturing firm has subsidiary factories and mines, it is not troubled by variations in market prices which might make its costs uncertain, and it never suffers through refusal of some outsider to supply it. Its peculiar specifications, as for alloy metals and parts, may also be complied with more precisely. But against these considerations must be set the disadvantage of depending on a single source of supply. It may be a better practice to buy from independent suppliers, thus keeping several sources open.

An economy often mistakenly claimed for vertical combination is that several intermediate profits are avoided when one firm develops a product through all stages from beginning to end. This supposed benefit must largely disappear under examination. Normal business profits are not based on the number of transactions but on the amount of capital devoted to production. A net return must be expected on the wealth committed to production at each stage regardless of whether this wealth is owned by different firms or by the same firm. In a vertically integrated firm, the cost of production at each level must be viewed as including a return on the capital used.

The most serious weakness in vertical combination is that it often runs counter to the basic advantage of plant size. A plant making steel sheets or batteries or carburetors will have larger volume and can carry mass-production methods further if it is supplying a number of automobile companies than if it is merely an integrated part of one company. Benefits of combination are dearly bought if expansion of the firm reduces the size of the plant.

Weaknesses of large firms

When the advantages of large firms are presented in this way, they gain in impressiveness through the sheer number of them and the multiplication of detail. They are likely to make too strong an impression. Actually these gains may be realized only in particular situations, under the administration of particular individuals, and the situation conducive to one advantage may preclude another. Many of the items of cost to which the savings apply are minor items, and the savings from expansion are likely to be very minor fractions of these items. Certainly the most important advantages are the technological economies of large plants, and these are not likely to be realized more fully merely by combining more plants into larger firms.

Moreover, as size increases, either in the single- or multi-plant firm, *economies can be realized at best only at a dwindling rate*. As we saw in the case of the *plant,* expansion of volume brings full use of more and more specialized workers and machines, and, when full use is once achieved, there is no further gain from still greater size. Similarly, growth of the *firm* becomes adequate progressively for more and more items in its organization, so that less can be gained through further growth. Even for a certain item whose cost is being spread over more units of output, the rate of gain keeps declining. As annual output rises from 100,000 to 200,000 units, the cost per unit of hiring a $100,000 executive falls from $1 to 50 cents, but as output expands from 1,000,-000 units to 1,100,000, that cost falls only from 10 cents to 9 cents.

Not only do the advantages of size run out, but *positive disadvantages creep in*. They lie mainly in the field of administration. Those persons at the top who are most strongly motivated toward economy and most able to promote it have, of necessity, a looser and looser relation to the activities under them as plants and firms expand. They reach decisions not through direct observation but on the basis of statistics, accounts, and reports, and the intervening judgments of a supervisory hierarchy. It is through this hierarchy, moreover, that their decisions must be given effect. Communication is imperfect, and competence is bound to be uneven. Loyalties are divided, and devotion to the governing aims at the top is not uniformly high. Inertia and inflexibility inevitably attend an elaborate structure, and prompt adjustment is difficult as conditions change. Passive conformity and routine avoidance of mistakes may offer the surest road to advancement in the organization.[18]

It is true that able management may infuse a large organization with high morale. It is also true that progress in the arts of production takes place in the managerial field as elsewhere, and methods improve in handling large organizations. The personal element in administration is the dominant element—so important that, within wide limits, the differences among firms seem to depend more on the quality of management than on the volume of operations.

Factual evidence of economies

Certainly, from such statistical studies as have been made, there is much evidence that this is the case. While, in fields such as steel and automobiles, small plants cannot be efficient and small firms succeed, there are both efficient and inefficient firms among the relatively large and the relatively small in all fields. The evidence fails rather completely to support the idea that efficiency varies directly (and without

[18] See T.N.E.C. Monograph No. 11, *Bureaucracy and Trusteeship in Large Corporations.*

limit) with size and that whatever is bigger in business organization must therefore be better.

The Federal Trade Commission studied this problem on several occasions before the war, and there have been a number of private studies.[19] To some extent, production costs have been examined directly, but, for the most part, the rates of profit of companies have been compared— on the assumption that, among competing firms in an industry, the more profitable must have the lower costs. To the extent that any single generalization is supported, it is that the most efficient firms in most industries are neither the largest nor the smallest but an intermediate group.[20] Often the most profitable single firms in industries are fairly small, but the least successful are also small, so that the average performance of small firms may be rather poor. The evidence seems quite convincing that the largest firms are likely to be only moderately efficient, at least not outstandingly so, but it is not conclusive that bigness positively reduces efficiency. Other factors than size may account for their frequently modest showing. A summary of manufacturing profits since the war shows no clear connection between profitablity and size but again indicates that, if there is any advantage, it lies with the middle-sized firms.[21]

Substantial, but not necessarily great, size makes a better showing when the 5600 multi-plant firms in manufacturing before the war are compared with the 140,000 single-plant firms.[22] On the average, output per worker in the former, measured on a value-added-by-manufacture basis, was nearly 20 percent higher than in the latter, and wages were almost correspondingly higher. This is a striking difference, but its exact significance is not certain. It may mean that *combination* is advantageous or that, entirely apart from combination, *firms* with an average

[19] The earlier studies are reviewed in *Recent Economic Changes in the United States*, the report of the Hoover Committee on Recent Economic Changes, McGraw-Hill, 1929, pp. 188–194. The later report is T.N.E.C. Monograph No. 13, *Relative Efficiency of Large, Medium-sized, and Small Business*. See, also, Wm. L. Crum, *Corporate Size and Earning Power*, Harvard University Press, 1939, and Twentieth Century Fund, *How Profitable Is Big Business?*, 1937.

[20] In 11 tests of groups of companies in different industries on a cost basis, the Federal Trade Commission concluded that the middle-sized companies had the lowest average cost in 10 instances and the largest companies in 1 instance. In 21 tests of rates of return on capital, the middle-sized were first in 14 instances, the largest in 3, and companies classed as small in 4. Similar tests of the efficiency of plants also indicated that the middle-sized were most efficient. T.N.E.C. Monograph No. 13, *op. cit.*, pp. 12–13.

[21] See "The Economic Report of the President," as transmitted to Congress, January 14, 1948, Appendix B, Table XXV. Manufacturing corporations were arranged in five groups, the smallest with assets below $250,000 and the largest with assets of $100,000,000 and over. The smallest firms made the weakest showing in the first half of 1947 when profits were related to sales, and the largest firms showed the lowest rate of return on stockholders' capital. On the latter basis, the intermediate classes made a distinctly better showing, especially the firms between $1,000,000 and $5,000,000.

[22] T.N.E.C. Monograph No. 27, *op. cit.*, pp. 142–143.

of 780 employees are more efficient than firms averaging only one twenty-fifth that large. Most likely it simply means that *plants* with an average of only 30 employees are generally too small to be efficient in manufacturing and that plants with 170 workers—the average size in the multi-plant firms—are likely to be better. Certainly there is no evidence here in favor of the industrial giants to contradict what was said above. The 5600 multi-plant firms include more than half of all manufacturing, so that the only sure conclusion is that the half of production conducted on a larger scale is more efficient than the half conducted on a smaller scale.

It is necessary, further, to be careful about cause-and-effect assumptions. Firms prosper because they are well managed, entirely apart from their size, but when they prosper, they nearly always expand. Moreover, when they are well managed and prosper, they are more likely to be drawn into combinations and become components of still larger firms. To a considerable extent, therefore, we must say that size is the result of efficiency, rather than that efficiency is the result of size. Inefficient firms, on the other hand, are likely to stay small, but even if they are failures they usually drag along for some time. Thus, though many small firms are efficient, the average efficiency of small firms is seriously reduced.

As one economist observed, it is quite possible for persons of different views to examine these studies and come out with the ideas with which they started, but it is at least a plausible position to conclude with this writer that "beyond a relatively modest scale of output the economies of large scale production are in general quantitatively unimportant." [23] Certainly firms of fair size that are bent on reducing costs should find that the surer road lies in improving their management rather than in increasing their size.

Reasons for size other than efficiency

It is not only true that firms grow because they are efficient and that they do not merely become efficient because they grow, but it is also true that they grow for reasons that have nothing to do with efficiency. One of the most serious illusions is that bigness is purely the result of an evolutionary process by which the fit survive and become great. One cannot understand the development of business enterprise in the United States without appreciating the reasons for growth which are unrelated to efficiency. Three reasons will be noted here, of which the first is really a composite of factors.

[23] George J. Stigler, "The Extent and Bases of Monopoly," in the *American Economic Review Supplement* containing papers relating to the Temporary National Economic Committee, June 1942, p. 13.

We may call it the *momentum of growth*. It lies in part in the natural circumstance that expanding demand for goods falls heavily on firms that are well established and whose products are well known. Only in part does industry growth take place through the starting of new firms.

The tendency for established firms to expand is accentuated in mass-production lines such as steel. If it requires $50,000,000 to build an efficient plant, the industry is not one in which new firms can readily get started. From the investor's standpoint, the risks are much smaller in providing capital for existing firms to construct new plants, even though these firms do not become more efficient through becoming larger.

Such expansion would not occur if the heads of existing firms actually opposed any expansion that would not reduce costs, but this is not likely to be their attitude. On the contrary, the heads of firms are likely to be ambitious men who seek wider horizons for their talent and stronger evidences of their success. Expansion is a challenging procedure, and it is plainly more impressive to be head of a larger than of a smaller firm. Even if a firm is only moderately efficient in its operations or is as large as efficient administration should permit, there is a bias in favor of keeping profits in the business instead of paying them out in dividends to stockholders. When large stockholders are in control, this bias is often strengthened by the desire to avoid personal income taxes on corporate earnings. These motives of business leaders enhance the momentum of growth.

A second reason for size, not related to economy, is the desire to *restrict competition* and control markets. Firms that are very large in relation to their markets are usually able to buy more cheaply and sell more dearly than they could if competition were more thoroughgoing. Whatever the general virtue of competition, it nearly always appears restrictive and painful to those whom it immediately affects, and they do what they can to reduce it. The development of the corporate form of organization (discussed in the next chapter) provided a means of combination which was easy and effective. In its more extreme form, the combination movement is simply the "trust" movement against which the antitrust laws were directed.

It should not be assumed that combination to restrict competition necessarily means the ruthless pursuit of profit which nineteenth-century cartoonists loved to depict. It may mean merely a softening of competition which the perpetrators describe as stabilizing the industry and insuring against losses. These are matters to be discussed later.[24] The present point is that some degree of market control is a leading aim in

[24] In Chapter 22.

forming large enterprises, especially through the combination process.

The third reason involves the corporate form even more directly. It is that there is great *profit* through the machinery of corporation finance *in forming combinations*. Forming and financing corporations is a business in itself. It would be an important, though a limited, business if it undertook merely to provide expanding facilities for the expanding production of goods. But it can be made a far larger business through reorganizing corporations and combining them into larger corporations, even though there is no expansion at all in productive facilities. When times are good, corporate securities are bought readily in large volume, and promotion of combines is a flourishing activity. It has attracted much high-grade business talent and fortunes have been made in it. It has been estimated that the Morgan partners and associated firms in 1901 made about $60,000,000 merely in forming the United States Steel Corporation out of existing steel companies. Vast sums were made in the 1920s. Thus, even without the prospect of economies or monopoly control, the motive is strong to form large corporate firms.

Actually, in the growth of great enterprises in the United States, motives have been mixed, just as human motives usually are. It is difficult to analyze any multi-plant firm so as to learn the exact reasons for its existence. But there is no question that such firms have altered the organization of production in this country. They have altered it usually in the direction of increased efficiency, but they have also created problems of broad importance. Where great firms are preponderant, the processes of a free-enterprise system are changed, both in the opportunities that individuals have to become enterprisers and in the controls which guide industry in the public interest. Relations are altered between the owners of businesses and the people who actually run them, and between employers and employees. To analyze these problems and the policies that affect them, we must understand what the connections are between size and efficiency and what additional reasons underlie the expansion of enterprises.

Review Questions

1. With what measuring units might a railroad company be compared in size with a manufacturing company? How would you expect the choice of unit to influence the comparison?

2. Which fields of industry seem to be mainly in the hands of small firms? Large firms? Where are the billion-dollar enterprises found?

3. Distinguish, with examples, the main types of multi-plant firms or combinations. Do you know of firms that represent more than one type?

4. "Size is a factor in efficiency, but some economies depend on the size

of the plant, some on the size of the firm. It is possible for two firms to be so constructed that one is superior with respect to one group of economies and the other with respect to the other group." Give an example which meets the requirements of this statement and explain the leading economies of size on the basis of it.

5. Are the reasons for product diversification, strictly speaking, reasons why larger firms produce more efficiently? Explain.

6. In a case some years ago before the Federal Trade Commission, the facts indicated that Sears, Roebuck bought tires in quantity from Goodyear at from 29 to 40 percent less than other buyers paid, and that only part of the difference could be explained by differences in quality and in costs re-lated to quantity. How would you explain these price differences? What more do you need to know in order to judge the economy of large-scale buying?

7. Are the economies claimed for horizontal combination simply the general advantages of large firms or are there also special advantages? If the latter, do they seem important?

8. A business leader writes: "Try a simple experiment on the next ex-cited opponent of Big Business, whether he be a political bigwig or a street-corner orator. Ask him whether he would, if he could, abolish Big Business; whether he would split each of the great aviation and automotive organiza-tions into a thousand small pieces. . . . It will appear quickly enough that the political medicine men want to eat the cake of American large-scale productivity and distribution and to have it. They want the fruits of mass production while destroying the roots of the great business aggregations which make mass production possible." [25] As an unexcited analyst of the economies of size, what points would you make in commenting on this state-ment?

9. Another businessman, who believes that combinations throttle enter-prise, would allow manufacturing firms with over 1000 employees to deliver their final product only from a single point. Plants might grow to any size and separate plants might be operated to supply materials and parts, pro-vided they sold to no outside customers.[26] Analyze this proposal from the standpoint of mass-production economies.

10. On the question of profit-saving in vertically integrated firms, a gov-ernment study quotes a writer who says ". . . that the final real cost of the product sold by an integrated industry will, ordinarily, be less than the final cost of a nonintegrated product by the cumulative amount of these profit margins." Beside this quotation the study sets another: "When two capitals are joined, it still remains necessary to pay the normal interest on both." [27] Which seems to you the sound position?

11. Give two reasons why the advantages of greater size are attainable only at a diminishing rate.

[25] Eric Johnston, *America Unlimited*, Doubleday Doran, 1944, pp. 151–152.
[26] Fred I. Raymond, *The Limitist*, W. W. Norton & Co., 1947.
[27] T.N.E.C. Monograph No. 27, *op. cit.*, p. 194.

12. What is the chief positive disadvantage which larger plants and firms encounter? Does it seem a serious factor? Is it possible that the multi-plant firm may be useful in achieving certain advantages of size while limiting its disadvantage?

13. "So far as their size is concerned, firms covering a fairly wide range in particular industries seem able to survive and prosper, and their differences in efficiency within that range are not likely to correspond closely to differences in size." Do the facts seem to support this position?

14. "Firms grow large for highly important reasons which have nothing to do with efficiency." Develop these reasons. From a general public standpoint, why are they important?

- 8 -

Business Enterprise
and the Corporate Form

In ANALYZING production it is conventional to classify
the productive agents, or factors of production, as labor, land, capital,
and business enterprise. It is also conventional, in a parallel analysis of
the distribution of income, to put all income into four corresponding
categories known as wages, rent, interest, and profits. There is some
oversimplification here, and at various points, especially in treating distribution, we shall depart somewhat from convention. But the classification is broadly useful, and we are deferring to it in the present chapter
in examining the leading features of enterprise under a system of capitalism.

It is in examining enterprise that we first look seriously into those
aspects of production that set capitalism apart from other types of economic systems. Natural resources and capital instruments are used in
the same way in producing goods, whether the system is one of capitalism or socialism. Essentially the same use is made of labor service. As
noted in Chapter 4, these are, in a sense, passive agents which must
somehow be put to work and organized along lines which their qualities
and prevailing technology require. But the responsibility for putting
them to work can be assumed and carried out in various ways. It may be
assumed by persons in a private capacity, acting individually or in
groups, or it may be assumed through political government. Thus the
nature of enterprise largely determines the nature of the economic system. In this chapter we shall limit the discussion to private enterprise,
or business enterprise.

In this discussion several aspects of enterprise will be considered.
First of all, we shall examine the basic concept of enterprise, the nature
of the enterprise function or functions, to see what it means to be an
enterpriser, or *entrepreneur.* Then, because most of modern industry is

carried on by associated enterprisers rather than by businessmen acting separately, we shall consider the leading forms of association: the partnership and the corporation. Since the corporation has become the dominant form, we shall be particularly concerned with its peculiarities and the reasons for its extensive use. And we shall especially need to appreciate, when many persons become associated in the larger corporations, that the manner of performing the enterprise function is so altered as to introduce one of the distinctive features of modern capitalism. Corporate securities, which constitute the special means of representing the financial participation of associated persons, take one into the broad field of corporation finance, and we shall give that field a brief, introductory survey in Chapter 9. Also in Chapter 9 there will be a short discussion of the public policies adopted in this country to deal with problems that have arisen through the corporate organization of enterprise.

The Nature of Enterprise

As compared with the other factors of production, *enterprise* is not easily defined. For purposes of economic analysis, labor is sufficiently described as human service, whether of hand or brain, and land as natural resources in general. Capital goods are viewed as man-made productive wealth, and capital as the fund of value derived from saving and invested in such wealth. Enterprise, however, is not quite coordinate with these other factors nor is it completely and sharply separable from them. On the one hand, it is linked with labor, since it is through the effort and intelligence of human beings that the enterprise function is performed. On the other, it is related to capital, since, except under unusual circumstances, there can be no enterprise without investment. Thus we may reasonably regard it as only a special expression, a joint expression, of the services of labor and capital.

At the same time, its positive role in production is so peculiarly vital and distinctive that we should set it apart if possible. Labor and capital may be hired to perform their functions. It is enterprise that hires them and puts them to work. Labor, capital, and land may be paid for through fixed, contractual rates of wages, interest, and rent. But enterprise, since it does the paying, must be rewarded with an income in the residual, profit form. The nature of enterprise will be apparent if we examine its labor and capital aspects, its relation both to the control and to the ownership of business firms.

Labor or control aspect

In its labor aspect, enterprise means the initiation of productive projects and the exercise of final authority in running them. The men who start farms, stores, and factories are enterprisers, and so are the men who, in last analysis, control their operations. Day-to-day management of the more routine sort is not enterprise, but major decisions which determine the extent and character of an undertaking are entrepreneurial. When the owners of a business delegate major responsibilities to hired officers and executives, as is commonly the case in large corporations, the owners are still technically in final control, for in exercising their power to appoint and to replace the active management they are assuming final responsibility. But if this final control is, in fact, no more than a passive ratification of the acts of hired officials, as often happens, some shifting of the enterprise function may be said to have occurred. Enterprise, on the labor side, means effective leadership in causing and guiding the use of productive resources; wherever that leadership exists, there is an element of enterprise.

It is futile to try to say exactly where enterprise leaves off and labor in the ordinary management sense begins, nor can the persons who are enterprisers be identified with certainty. In small business, such as the ordinary store or farm, the owner-operator serves as enterpriser, routine manager, and plain worker, and the roles are not distinguishable. In large corporations all ordinary labor and much of management belong plainly in the hired-labor category, but the division of responsibility among stockholders, directors, and top officials is usually so complex and so lacking in uniformity from one firm to another that no general statement can be made regarding the exact location of final control.

This uncertainty in defining the limits of the enterprise function and in picking out the persons who are enterprisers need not disturb us. As in most classifications, the boundaries between categories may be hazy without undermining the usefulness of distinctions. In this case it is sufficient to appreciate the central role in production of persons who do the initial planning of the use of resources and who take the positive action that puts plans into effect.

Capital or ownership aspect

In reality, such positive action means investment of wealth as well as the making of decisions, so that the two sides of enterprise, while separable to a degree, cannot really be divorced. Assuming responsibility for production means assuming financial responsibility as well as responsibility in the control sense. Financial responsibility is distinguished by the investment of capital in circumstances in which all or part of it may be lost. Without capital, factories cannot be built and equipped, stores cannot be constructed and stocked, railroads and power plants cannot be established, nor can farms and mines be developed.

Every new enterprise involves considerable chance of failure, and this danger is the chief obstacle to new undertakings. Thus, among the decisions involved in initiating production, the decisive one is the decision to risk capital by those who have it. The making of all necessary decisions and the committing of the capital constitute jointly the performance of the entrepreneurial function.

It is true that capital can be hired for a fixed rate of interest, just as labor is hired for a predetermined wage. But only a part of the capital of a business can be hired with any certainty of return. Agreements to pay wages and interest mean little unless there is capital out of which to make the payments when current revenues do not cover expenses. It is capital, in other words, which does the hiring. Thus, when we say that enterprise takes the initiative in production and hires the other factors, we are identifying capital in part with enterprise. Someone must assume financial responsibility in order to give meaning to the hiring of factors at fixed rates of return. As will be observed later in the chapter, there may be a sort of specialization in performing the enterprise function, and the same person need not in every instance combine responsibility in the control and in the financial sense. But this is to say that such a person performs only part of the enterprise function.

Varying emphasis on the aspects of enterprise

In thinking of enterprise, should we regard the control or the risk-taking aspect as more important? Logically, since both are indispensable, we cannot place one ahead of the other, but in the particular areas of economics that we study, sometimes one, sometimes the other, is more directly pertinent to the analysis.

Here in Part II, as we consider the conditions on which high productivity depends, both, of course, are important. In the discussion of capitalistic production in Chapter 6, we were examining not only the technical advantage of employing man-made wealth but also the service of those who make wealth available to industry. Now we stress the uncertainties of investment. In Chapter 7, in discussing the organization of production, we were closer to the control side of enterprise. But the enterpriser, we are now emphasizing, should not be thought of as a routine planner of production but as a dynamic person, possessed of daring and imagination, who envisages productive projects, undertakes them, and through personal force and good judgment sees them through.

In Part IV, when we deal with the problem of depressions and unemployment of resources, the investment side of enterprise will be emphasized. The willingness of capitalists to risk their savings will be seen in relation to the maintenance of general prosperity. Vigorous enterprise will imply not the dynamic leader but the daring investor. In Part VI, when we consider the distribution of income, a possible conflict will appear over the division of business earnings when some specialization exists in performing the control and risk-taking functions. Most small businesses and many large ones are owned and run by the same persons and escape this conflict, but it is of some importance in many large corporations.

Forms of Business Organization—Mainly the Corporation

With few exceptions, the enterprise function is organized in the United States through three business forms: the *single proprietorship*, the *partnership*, and the *corporation*. In point of number of firms organized, the single proprietorship is by far the most conspicuous, because most farms, stores, and service establishments are organized in this way as are a substantial number of firms in all fields except railroads and the other public utilities, which are almost entirely incorporated. But only in the farming, retail-trade, service, and construction fields is as much as half the total business done by unincorporated firms, including both single proprietorships and partnerships.

The relative importance of these three forms, both in number of firms and in volume of business, is shown in the accompanying table for manufacturing, retail and wholesale trade, and the service fields.[1]

TABLE 12—COMPARATIVE IMPORTANCE, IN PERCENT, OF FORMS OF ORGANIZATION *

Field of Production	Proprietorships		Partnerships		Corporations	
	Firms	Sales	Firms	Sales	Firms	Sales
Manufacturing	32	4	15	3	52	93
Wholesale trade	37	13	12	11	49	74
Retail trade	77	40	11	12	12	47
Service	86	49	10	13	4	38

* Percentages do not total 100 in four instances because of the omission of certain inconsequential forms of organization.

In 1946 the national income of $178.2 billion was accounted for as follows: by business corporations, 49 percent; by single proprietorships and partnerships, 29 percent; by a miscellany of enterprises such as

[1] The figures are from the Censuses of Manufacturers and of Business, 1939, and are taken from the more extensive presentation in Harry G. Guthmann and Herbert E. Dougall, *Corporate Financial Policy*, 2d ed., Prentice-Hall, 1948, pp. 10–11.

mutual financial institutions, cooperatives, and owner-occupied homes, 5 percent; by nonprofit religious, educational and like organizations, 3 percent; by governmental bodies and publicly owned businesses, 12 percent.[2]

The enterprise function has thus come to be performed outstandingly through the corporate form of organization, but the emphasis it will receive in the present discussion is disproportionate even to its prominence in the economy. Just as large organizations claimed our chief attention in the preceding chapter in studying the basis of efficiency, so now we must study the corporation as the legal form through which large-scale business is carried on and as the source of some of the problems associated with "big business." There is much more to be said about the corporation than about the other forms.

The single proprietorship—virtues and limitations

In a sense, a firm in which one person takes responsibility both in decision-making and capital-risking is not a business organization at all. An individual simply proceeds with the operations of farming, retailing, or some other line, and, without special act on his part, a single proprietorship is said to be born. Doubtless, if all production were carried on in this way, the topic of this section would never have occurred to anyone.

It is this very simplicity, this absence of organization, that is the special virtue of the single proprietorship. There being no rights and duties to define, no basis exists for the clashes of interests and diffusion of responsibility that associated enterprisers often face. But this simplicity, it should be understood, relates necessarily only to the enterprise function—the present topic—and not to the processes of production. If Henry Ford had had a little more capital when he entered the automobile field, he might have developed his vast business as a single proprietorship, because it grew through its own earnings and he was presently able to buy out his associates; but he would still have had to face all the complications of a billion-dollar project. Simplicity in handling enterprise responsibilities should not be confused with the quite different simplicity that arises because productive operations are small.

The virtues of simplicity operate necessarily in a limited sphere and are easily outweighed. One reason why an enterpriser may seek associates in his undertaking is that presumably they will have something to contribute personally. An enterprise is strengthened as varied abilities are combined in running it—as one man may contribute technical or managerial ability, another selling or financial skill. The only basis on

---

[2] *Supplement* to *Survey of Current Business,* July 1947, Table 12.

which the needed people can be obtained may be through giving them status as enterprisers with an interest in the profits—although more commonly the required talents can be hired, and enterprise need not be divided for this reason.

The main reason for business association is not the need of diverse abilities but the need of capital. For projects of substantial size, it is usually necessary to draw on the capital of a number of persons, perhaps a great many of them, and then some less simple form of organization becomes necessary. The partnership is such a form, but we shall make the discussion of it somewhat incidental to our primary interest in the corporation, now the outstanding means of achieving a considerable size.

The corporation, as contrasted with the partnership

The partnership is simply an agreement among individuals to act together in conducting a business enterprise. By private contract they fix the capital each is to contribute, the responsibilities each is to have, and the share in earnings each is to receive. The essential point is that these individuals constitute the partnership. The firm consists of the partners, as individuals, cooperating in a joint undertaking in which they mutually assume responsibility for each other's actions in dealing with customers, employees, suppliers, and creditors in general. With the partnership as thus described, the corporation must be contrasted in a number of respects.

Process of forming the corporation. The corporation is not merely an association of individuals. Legally speaking, it cannot come to exist simply through their agreement to associate nor conduct its operations through their common action. Its legal existence arises not through private contract but through the grant of a charter by governmental authority. Charters are obtained in this country through application to designated officials of state governments. The corporation is often referred to, in a legal sense, as a "creature of the state."

Separateness from associated persons. What is it that the state creates? What sort of operating entity arises when a charter is conferred? The essential point, again, is that the corporation is not merely an association of individuals. It is commonly spoken of as a "legal person," as having a life that, in a legal sense, is independent of the lives of the natural persons who cause it to be formed. Once formed, its continued existence does not depend on the connection with it of any particular person or set of persons. The property it owns in the conduct of its operations is not the property of the associated enterprisers; its obligations are not their obligations; the very decisions through which it performs its economic functions are not viewed, in the ordinary situation, as their decisions. Plainly a disembodied figment of the law has no biological existence—and in reality cannot by itself act as human beings act—but in numerous connections, significant both in economics and in law, it is treated as if it can.

This separateness of the corporation from its stockholders is evident in many ways. Thus if certain persons form a corporation to develop a subdivision in the environs of a city, they do not own a nickel's worth of land. The corporation owns the real estate, and they own personal property in the form of shares of stock. In one famous case in which land was owned on terms which forbade its sale to Negroes, a group of Negroes who formed a corporation which bought some of the land for an amusement park were upheld by a Virginia court on the ground that the corporation, a separate entity, had no racial characteristics.[3] In Great Britain a law which said that only British-owned vessels could fly the British flag was circumvented by a group of foreigners who obtained a charter under British law to form a corporation which they financed and controlled.[4] As a separate entity, the corporation was strictly British. These are extreme instances that do not reflect the invariable action of courts on such issues, but they suggest the degree to which the corporation may differ from the partnership.

One of the most important examples of this difference is in the field of income taxation. If a given firm is organized as a partnership, its net income is treated directly as the income of the partners, whether it is used by them in current consumption or in expanding the business, and is thus subject only to the personal income tax that the partners have to pay. But if this same business, with exactly the same physical characteristics and income, is organized as a corporation, its income is first subject to the corporation income tax and then the part of the income that is paid to stockholders in dividends is subject, in addition, to their personal income tax. Since there is only one source of income, there is evidence here of double taxation. But if earnings are retained in the corporation, they add to the stockholders' interest in it without being subject to the personal income tax.[5]

It is apparent that difficult legal and economic situations arise from recognition of the corporation as separate, in important ways, from its stockholders. Many legal obligations have been escaped through incorporation, and some questionable burdens have been incurred. Thus

---

[3] *People's Pleasure Park Co.* v. *Rohleder,* 109 Va. 439. Cited by I. Maurice Wormser in *Disregard of the Corporate Fiction and Allied Corporation Problems,* Baker, Voorhis, 1927.

[4] The case of *Queen* v. *Arnaud,* also cited by I. M. Wormser, *op. cit.*

[5] Thus, for stockholders whose personal tax rate runs higher than the rate on corporate income (38 percent on corporate income in excess of $50,000 in 1948), there is some avoidance of taxation when income is retained by the corporation.

there exists the difficult problem of permitting the separateness of the corporation to serve its useful purposes but without letting it run to harmful extremes. Courts and legislatures have made progress in dealing with this problem, but it is by no means completely solved.

Size and number of members. The corporation and the partnership differ *inherently* in the ways just described. But they do not differ inherently with respect to certain obvious characteristics often associated with them. Thus it cannot be said, in describing their distinctive features, that corporations are necessarily large and partnerships small. In 1933 more than 50 percent of the nearly half-million corporations in the United States had gross assets of less than $50,000, a sum well within the usual capacity of single proprietorships and partnerships.[6] On the other hand, there were great firms, including the investment-banking house of J. P. Morgan, that were partnerships.

Similarly it cannot be said, as a distinguishing difference, that numerous persons are associated in a corporation and only a few in a partnership. A partnership must have at least two members and some have a score or more. A few states, on the other hand, permit incorporation with only one stockholder, though three is the more common minimum. A majority of all corporations are of the "closed," or "family" type, and have never sought capital through sale of stock to the general public.

But while the forms of enterprise cannot be distinguished in terms of size and numbers, the economic significance of the corporation lies unquestionably in its relation to large-scale enterprise. Most corporations may be small, but it is the large corporations that account for most of the production in a number of fields. Before the war, corporations with gross assets in excess of $5,000,000 accounted for a half or more of the total output in manufacturing, mining, railroads, and electric power and for almost a third of all private economic activity in the United States. Corporations whose gross assets exceeded $50,000,000 did a third of the manufacturing and provided two thirds of the transportation and public-utility service.[7] In the 200 largest nonfinancial corporations, half the stock issues were in the hands of from 10,000 to 100,000 persons, and one firm, the American Telephone and Telegraph Company, had over 600,000 stockholders.[8] So far as the public interest in the corporate form is concerned, its advantages appear mainly in the forma-

[6] Alfred L. Bernheim (ed.) *Big Business: Its Growth and Its Place,* Twentieth Century Fund, 1937, p. 5.

[7] *Ibid.,* p. 95. These facts are from the table reproduced in the preceding chapter on p. 168.

[8] For data of this type see *The Distribution of Ownership in the 200 Largest Nonfinancial Corporations,* Temporary National Economic Committee Monograph No. 29, 1940.

tion of large corporations that obtain capital from a considerable number of people.

Advantages of the corporate form

When we speak of advantages, we must be clear as to the viewpoint we are adopting. Business projects may be incorporated, as we have seen, to escape legal restrictions and avoid taxes. They may be incorporated to limit debts, facilitate shady promotions and stock-jobbing schemes, or promote monopoly. These are simply purposes of private gain, and pretty dubious ones. Since incorporation is a governmental act, the advantages that justify it must be public advantages.

The specific advantages are all subordinate to a general one. The underlying reason for the corporate form is that it is *needed for efficient production under modern conditions.* If firms have to be large to be efficient, a way of forming them is necessary that makes it reasonably easy to achieve the needed size and to handle it when achieved. A legal form produces nothing, but indirectly it can be the basis of efficiency.

The primary reason why the corporate form is useful in realizing the economies of size is that it facilitates the amassing of capital. Two of its attributes especially promote this result: (1) the joint-stock principle of dividing ownership and (2) the limitation of investor's liability. In addition, (3) the corporate form gives to enterprises an essential continuity, and (4) it makes possible a necessary unification of control when numbers of people are associated. We shall consider each of these matters. These advantages, it will be observed, are all logically consistent with the legal separation of the corporation from the stockholders.

Proprietorship through shares of stock. The joint-stock device—which had its first use in unincorporated joint-stock companies several centuries ago but is now an integral aspect of the business corporation—arranges the ownership of an enterprise on the basis of small equal shares. Thus a corporation seeking $1,000,000 of capital may divide the total proprietorship into 10,000 units, each representing $100, or into 100,000 units, each representing $10. Persons interested in participating in the enterprise may buy as many of these standard units as they please, from a single one to several thousand. The number of shares determines the interest, or *equity,* of the particular owner in the enterprise. So effective is this device that it has been described as one of the great inventions of modern times.

In arranging the interests of many persons in an enterprise in this way, an extraordinary simplicity is achieved. In a partnership each owner's participation is a personal matter which is arrived at through negotiation and set down rigidly in the partnership agreement. If there were many partners, such a procedure would be time-consuming and difficult to carry out, and it would appear seriously forbidding unless a person desired a substantial and continuing interest in an enterprise and was willing to be personally involved in it. The share of stock, on the other hand, is a standard and impersonal unit, on the basis of which numerous individual participations can be readily arranged.

With an ownership unit that is small and with little difficulty in obtaining it, persons become stockholders who have too little capital—or too little inclination—to justify their going into business in any other way. Persons of greater wealth are likewise enabled to diversify their investments and their risks among a variety of industries and firms. Thus much capital is mobilized for productive enterprise that would otherwise not become available.

Corporate shares are readily transferable. They make it easy not only to participate in the enterprise function but also to withdraw from participation. Especially in the case of stocks listed on the securities exchanges, disposition of one's holdings at the prevailing market price may be accomplished with remarkable promptness. Even for unlisted stocks a ready market is often available. The possibility of easy withdrawal is an important factor in causing investment to be made in the first place, since a commitment seems less serious the less prolonged it has to be. Thus the *marketability of shares* is one of the reasons why the joint-stock device facilitates the amassing of capital.

We should note that this principle of dividing capital contributions into small standard parts is applied by corporations to borrowed capital as well as to capital supplied by owners. Bonds, issued in denominations of $1000, $100, or even less, are simply evidence of fractional parts of larger debts which may run into many millions of dollars. The same advantages of tapping small savings and permitting diversity of investment arise from the bonds of corporations as from their stocks.

One effect, when bonds enter the financing of a corporation, is that the supplying of capital is divided not only quantitatively into small divisions but also qualitatively into different kinds of relationships between the suppliers and the firm. This development of a *variety of securities,* which we shall examine in the following chapter, is also useful in attracting capital. When corporations have both bonds and stocks, and perhaps several kinds of each, they are able to appeal to investors of different tastes and inclinations—from those who will take large chances for the sake of large returns to those who prefer safety to the uncertainties of rapid enrichment.

Limitation of liability. It was traditionally supposed that when an individual incurred obligations, he should stake his entire wealth and earning power in protecting his creditors against loss—although, indeed, with some chance of escaping a hopeless situation through bankruptcy. The businessman who bought labor and materials or borrowed capital faced the possibility, if events turned against him, of losing not only the property he had committed to his business but also such other wealth as he might possess. If he entered a partnership and it failed, the creditors could take both the assets of the business and also his personal wealth up to the full extent of the debt. If he was the only partner with wealth outside the business, he might be held for the entire debt; for partners were, and are, "jointly and severally" liable for business debts. It is consistent with the theory of the partnership, which is merely an association of individuals, that partners should face unlimited liability in the sense just described.

There is nothing unfair in this arrangement. Indeed, not to hold persons fully responsible for their debts may be thought unfair to creditors. But whether fair or not, unlimited liability ceases to be workable when the persons associated in an enterprise are numerous and loosely related to it. A prudent investor may reasonably risk his entire wealth in a project with which he will be intimately connected; most people have confidence in their own judgments and in their ability to protect their interests against the carelessness and bad faith of others. But a prudent man is unwilling to risk capital in a project of which he is one of many owners, and with which he will have no active connection, if failure of the enterprise could mean loss of the personal wealth he had not committed to it. Thus, as a practical matter, if capital is to be obtained with reasonable ease from numerous persons to conduct great projects, liability must somehow be limited.

One of the most vital features, therefore, of the modern business corporation is the limitation of liability which now, though not always in the past, is inseparable from it. *Limited liability* ordinarily means that stockholders can lose no more than they actually invest, provided they pay fully for their shares of stock. Thus the investor does not imperil the remainder of his wealth when he invests capital in a corporation. This limitation, it should be noted, applies to the stockholder, not the corporation. In case of default, creditors may take all of the property of the corporation, but they cannot go against the stockholders to make up any deficiency.

Unquestionably limitation of liability is of tremendous importance in the financing of projects requiring many investors. But under existing laws limited liability is not restricted to these large undertakings.

The privilege attaches to small, "family" corporations as well as to those that raise capital by selling stock to the general public. Indeed, it is the advantage of limited liability which constitutes about the only reason for incorporating hundreds of thousands of small enterprises. While debtors may gain thereby, is there any social reason for thus limiting the rights of creditors? The reason, in family corporations, cannot be that limited liability is necessary to get outsiders to invest. The justification —if there is one—must spring from the belief that our society suffers generally from deficient investment and that encouragement of it is desirable through limiting business risks, even though the corporate form is not called for in other respects.

Enterprise continuity. The amassing of capital for large projects is the chief positive virtue of the corporation from the public standpoint. But this gain would prove illusory unless the corporate form proved able to meet the serious difficulties that arise when sizeable groups of people are associated as owners.

One such problem is that of maintaining a continuing enterprise despite the changing membership of the owning group. The partnership is inherently unsuitable in this respect when the associated owners are numerous. In the partnership the title to property resides in the individual members who, in their persons, constitute the firm. The partnership originates through a contract among these persons; if one of them dies or decides to withdraw, the partnership is automatically dissolved, and a new contract must be agreed upon if the enterprise is to continue. If the partners are few, such changes are infrequent; if harmony is preserved, the difficulties are not excessive. But if partners were as numerous as stockholders are in many corporations, the constantly changing membership would be highly disturbing and might threaten the continuity of the enterprise. To justify the type of investment required in much of modern industry, assurance of a long period of continuous operation is necessary, and there is need of a form of organization that will obviate the interruptions that partnerships encounter.

The corporate form meets this difficulty through the simple fact of its existence in legal separateness from the stockholders. Legally speaking, the corporation owns the property and conducts the operations; the stockholders do not. Stockholders may die and leave their stock to their heirs, or they may sell to whomever they please, and the existence of the corporation is not affected. Its life depends on the charter granted it by the state and not on the relation to it of particular natural persons. Charters may be·perpetual, or they may be granted for stated periods fixed by statutes, such as 25 or 30 years, but provision is made for easy renewal whenever the useful life of a project has not reached its end.

Unification of control. When there are many owners, a more serious problem is that of unifying the direction of an enterprise, of *centralizing responsibility* for its operations while still enabling all of the associated enterprisers to participate in the control. Again the partnership form is poorly fashioned to meet the difficulty. The trouble with it is that all the partners can take an active part in the business, and the transactions in which they engage are binding upon it. The partners, of course, agree among themselves as to their respective functions, but if they act outside their designated sphere, or act in ways not approved by other partners, the firm is still bound by their acts. One need only imagine a very large partnership—supposing, for instance, that the Pennsylvania Railroad, with its 200,000 owners were organized in partnership form—to appreciate the chaos that would prevail if every partner could act for the firm in hiring workers, buying supplies, borrowing money, and directing train operations. For the partnership form to be effective, it must be limited to a few people who understand each other and are willing to cooperate.

The corporate form, on the other hand, brings control to a sharp focus. Stockholders may be numerous and their views divergent, but they are not the corporation and cannot speak for it. Corporate action takes place through the decisions of officially designated persons, and the firm cannot be bound by the acts of other persons, even though they are large stockholders. The stockholders have no part in management, but they do participate in control through electing a *board of directors*, commonly from among their number, and through voting on other major matters, such as authorizing an issue of preferred stock or setting up a retirement plan for executives. Ordinarily each share of stock carries one vote, so that the weight of the stockholder in the voting is proportional to the shares he holds. It is not supposed that stockholders as such will be expert in running the business, but it is the theory of control in the corporation that they will be able to cause a major overhauling of policies when results are not satisfactory and that they will have the last word on expanding or contracting the undertaking.

The board of directors is not continuously active but meets at frequent intervals to consider important questions of policy. It selects the president and other top officers who are in continuous charge of the business. One or more of these officers are members of the board and thus keep it in close touch with the activities of the firm. The board, in turn, is expected to provide general guidance and to insist, in behalf of the stockholders, on effective management.

Thus, by funneling control from stockholders through directors to active managers, complete unity of direction is achieved despite wide diversity of ownership and owners' views. This centralizing of responsibility is attained in principle without depriving the rank and file of owners of that participation in control which, along with the assumption of risk in supplying capital, is the essence of enterprise. Whether this arrangement appears in practice as it does in principle is a matter that we shall need to consider in the following section.

Review Questions

1. "The enterprise function cannot be distinguished sharply either from management or the supplying of capital, yet it has a distinctive place in the economy which makes it more than either of these." Explain carefully.

2. How important relatively are the main forms of business organization in the economy? Relate them to specific fields of production.

3. Explain the merits and limitations of the single proprietorship.

4. In which of the following respects would you say that the partnership and the modern business corporation differ *inherently*: legal origin; size of business; liability of associated persons; number of associated persons; relation of associated persons to the firm; conditions of permanence; means of dividing the financial interest of the owners? Explain what is meant by calling the corporation a "separate entity," or a "legal person."

5. Is the corporation or the partnership the better form in which to organize a $10,000,000 business? Explain carefully each of the advantages of the corporation.

6. "The leading advantages of the corporate form are all logically consistent with the conception of the corporation as separate from the stockholders. The advantages may be said to be supported by this conception." Explain.

7. "Limited liability" is certainly an advantage to the man who goes into business, but it should not be regarded as an advantage from the social standpoint." Criticize this statement with regard to the public interest in efficient production.

8. What is meant by a "qualitative division" in the supplying of capital to corporations? How does it help to attract capital?

9. Explain the relationship between stockholders, directors, and officers in the running of a corporation. In principle, does this seem to you to be a democratic arrangement?

The Problem of Control within the Corporation

Leading students of the corporation have publicized the view that capitalism is undergoing fundamental change through developments in corporate control. Their central point is that a splitting of the two parts of the enterprise function is occurring in large enterprises, a "separation of ownership and control." This change is seen as having a variety of consequences, all the way from weakening the interests of investors to undermining the foundations of the economic system itself.[9] In considering a number of features of the control that now prevails in large corporations, we shall have this viewpoint in mind.

Nonvoting securities

We shall begin with something less drastic than a full *separation* of ownership and control. We may speak of it as a *concentration of control,* a concentration in the hands of persons who supply only a minor part of the capital but still a control that is attached to ownership. Many suppliers of capital are separated from control, but not all.

In corporate financing, one leading source of this concentration lies in the extensive use of securities that carry no voting power. When persons who are active in starting an enterprise must go to the general public for the greater part of the capital they need, they naturally do not want to yield control to outside investors. One way to keep control is to give no voting rights to the outsiders. The sale of bonds serves this purpose, and preferred stocks also often lack voting rights.

In the 1920s a movement got under way of issuing two classes of common stock: one with and one without voting power. The smaller issue, with voting rights, would be retained by the initiators of the enterprise, and the larger, without such rights, would be sold to the public. Thus nearly all the $130,000,000 required in 1925 to purchase and reorganize Dodge Brothers was obtained from the public, and the investment banking firm that handled the transaction was able to keep control through retaining shares of Class B common stock which carried sole voting rights.[10] Nonvoting common was, however, so obviously a violation of the whole enterprise tradition that it met early discouragement, largely through action of the New York Stock Exchange, which refused to list it.

Nonvoting bonds and preferred shares have been most prevalent in the public-utility field. In many of the great railroad promotions, bondholders put up practically all of the capital, frequently, it appears, under some illusion as to what the stockholders really were contributing. Bonds have been similarly prominent in the capital structures of power and gas companies. Another field in which bondholders often supplied

[9] Adolph A. Berle and Gardiner C. Means in *The Modern Corporation and Private Property*, Macmillan, 1933, provide the best-known statement of this problem.

[10] This transaction was prior to the absorption of Dodge Brothers by the Chrysler Corporation.

practically all the capital was the construction of apartment houses and office buildings as they were financed during the 1920s.

A bondholder is technically a creditor, not an owner. But to be a creditor in the full economic sense and not primarily a participant in the risks of enterprise, his position should be made relatively secure by the presence of a substantial amount of stockholder's capital which, in case of adversity, must bear the brunt of the impact. So protected, a bondholder is not properly viewed as an enterpriser, and it is reasonable that he should not participate in control as long as his contractual claims are met. But when, as has often happened, the bondholder supplies most of the capital, then much of the risk is his also, and, in accordance with the nature of the enterprise function, he should participate in control.

The holding company

Various legal devices, of which the chief is the holding company, have been used to concentrate control in the hands of suppliers of a minor part of business capital. The holding company is simply a corporation, but a corporation which is peculiar in the nature of the property it owns. Its assets, unless it happens to be a mixed holding and operating company, consist not at all of plant, equipment, and inventories but only of the securities of one or more other corporations. These securities are usually voting stocks, and through them control is exercised over the other corporations. They are said to be its subsidiaries. The holding company, like any corporation, has its own securities outstanding, and through them it is controlled directly and its subsidiaries indirectly.

The holding-company principle can be seen best through an example. To see the principle clearly, one must avoid confusing it with the effect of nonvoting securities as just considered. Thus we shall use an example in which the only securities are common stocks with voting rights. We shall assume that Smith, Jones, and Brown have $1,000,000 which they want to invest in the electric-power industry. With this sum they would be able to buy half the stock of Company A, a $2,000,000 concern which operates in a small community. But they see certain advantages in combining the operations of Company A with those of Company B, another $2,000,000 concern in a nearby town. This result they can accomplish with their $1,000,000 through forming Company X, a holding company, which has $2,000,000 of capital stock. They put their $1,000,000 into Company X, and then they sell the other $1,000,000 of X's stock to the general public. With their one-half interest they elect themselves directors and officers of the holding company. Thereupon they use the

$2,000,000 of X's capital to buy half of the stock of Companies A and B. Now X has a controlling interest in A and B. At this point, Smith, Jones, and Brown, as the board of directors of X, elect themselves, or persons friendly to them, to the boards of A and B. Thus with their $1,000,000 they have brought under their control electric-power operations involving a capital of $4,000,000.

This example explains the holding-company principle. By having a controlling fraction of a controlling fraction of the voting stock of an operating company, the ratio of controlled capital to controlling capital is raised, at the very least, to four to one. The principle can be applied further by inserting additional holding companies—*pyramiding* it is called—between the operating companies and the capital that finally controls them. Thus, by inserting Company Y, another holding company, Smith, Jones, and Brown can extend their control over two additional $2,000,000 operating companies, C and D, so that the ratio of controlled to controlling capital becomes eight to one. Schematically, the situation is then as follows:

Smith, Jones, and Brown with $1,000,000
own half the stock of
$2,000,000 Holding Company X which
owns half the stock of
$4,000,000 Holding Company Y which
owns half the stock of
$2,000,000 Operating Companies $A, B, C,$ and D ($8,000,000 in all)

It is apparent, in this holding-company system, that the general public has provided $7,000,000 of the capital ($4,000,000 invested in $A, B, C,$ and D, $2,000,000 in Y, and $1,000,000 in X), and that Smith, Jones, and Brown have provided only $1,000,000. But these outside stockholders cannot muster a majority vote at any level and, with some of them certain not to vote, are bound to fall well short of it. Smith, Jones, and Brown are securely in control. It will be noticed, also, that a total of $14,000,000 of securities is outstanding in the whole scheme, but some of these securities represent other securities, so that only $8,000,000 of wealth is represented. If the operating companies earn a fair return on this $8,000,000, there will be income enough for all the security holders.

We should now observe that the two ways of concentrating control already considered—the use of nonvoting securities and the use of the holding company—can be effectively combined, and that a very high degree of concentration can thus be brought about. If we suppose, modifying this last example, that only half the securities at each level are common stocks with voting rights and the other half are nonvoting preferred stocks, Smith, Jones, and Brown can make their $1,000,000 control $64,-000,000 of operating capital. At each level all of the preferred stock and half of the common stock is sold to the outside public.[11] The remainder of the common stock is held by Smith, Jones, and Brown or by holding companies which they control. The holding-company pyramid now looks like this:

Smith, Jones, and Brown with $1,000,000
own half the common stock of
$4,000,000 Holding Company X ($2,000,000 common and $2,000,000 preferred) which
owns half the common stock of
$16,000,000 Holding Company Y ($8,000,000 common and $8,000,000 preferred) which
owns half the common stock of
Operating Companies A, B, C, and D (each with $8,000,000 common and
$8,000,000 preferred, or $64,000,000 in all)

To have each dollar of capital at the top control $64 of capital at the bottom is to carry concentration pretty far but not so far as to be unrealistic. Concentration went even farther in the case of the Allegheny Corporation in the railroad field and in the case of several of the great electric-power holding company systems.[12] In some of these structures there were several more layers of holding companies than we have shown and even more use of nonvoting securities. In general, the holding companies in manufacturing have been less elaborate and spectacular, but this device has been widely used in effecting industrial combinations.

For our present purpose it is unimportant whether there is one company at the operating level or more than one. We are concerned with seeing how control within a single operating organization can rest in the hands of people who supply only a minor part of the capital. But one reason for this rather extended discussion of the holding company lies in the later use we shall make of it in the analysis of monopoly. There our interest will be in the *control of the industry* rather than in the *control within the enterprise*. The holding company is the most ef-

[11] In practice, much of the stock of holding companies is exchanged directly for the stock of operating companies or subsidiary holding companies rather than being sold to get cash to buy these stocks.

[12] For an extended treatment of this subject, see J. C. Bonbright and G. C. Means, *The Holding Company*, McGraw-Hill, 1932.

fective instrument with which to get a secure control of competing corporations in order to dominate a market.

Control with a minority of voting shares

So far we have assumed that control of a corporation requires half the capital represented by voting securities. So indeed it does, or fractionally more than half, to insure absolutely that no combination of dissident stockholders can seize the reins. But, in fact, within large corporations that have many stockholders, ownership by one or a few people of much less than half of the voting shares is usually adequate. The reasons are (1) partly psychological, (2) partly geographic, (3) partly contained in established voting practices and related internal procedures.

1. The bulk of the shareholders of large enterprises did not buy their stock with a view to active participation in control. The same faith that led them to risk their capital leads to a continuing reliance on the active leadership in corporations as long as it is not obviously incompetent. The holder of a millionth or a thousandth part of a corporation is not justified in spending the time in studying its affairs that would be necessary to enable him to vote his stock with insight and intelligence or to participate in the discussions at annual or semiannual meetings. Even if he were disposed to devote time to this purpose, he would find it difficult to get the necessary information, for corporations do not disclose to numerous ordinary stockholders—in effect, to the general public and to their competitors—the intimate details of their affairs and of the problems that they face. Thus the ordinary stockholder, if he votes at all, votes on the advice of insiders who are better informed than he.

2. The fact that the stockholders of large corporations reside at scattered points means that few of them find it worth while to attend stockholders' meetings. The extent of their interest, and the influence they could exert if they attended, do not warrant the outlay of time and money. Thus the attendance is ordinarily small, and, for the most part, only the large holdings are personally represented. In these circumstances, the vigorous pursuit of control by persons bent on having it, but having only a small part of the stock, is likely to be successful.

3. The main assurance of success lies in the system of absentee balloting used by corporations. To elect directors and do other business a quorum of stock must be voted. To assure a quorum, so-called *proxies* are sent out to the stockholders by which they are given the opportunity to assign their votes to certain designated persons. The proxy is not a ballot which lists rival slates of candidates for the board of directors, with descriptions of the policies for which they stand, so that the voter

can make a choice. His choice is between voting and not voting, and if he votes, the stockholder ratifies, in effect, the policies of the dominant group already in control, because they send out the proxies. Occasionally there are rebellions in corporations, and outside stockholder groups solicit proxies in opposition to the present management. Occasionally they succeed in seizing control, but the odds are against them. Ordinarily concentrated minority holdings, perhaps involving only 10 or 20 percent of the voting stock but buttressed by control of the proxy machinery, can maintain continuing control of a large corporation if most of its stock is well scattered.

Complete separation

The phrase "separation of ownership and control" implies something more than we have so far discussed. Not only may control be in the hands of persons who supply only a small part of the capital; it may even be exercised very largely in established corporations by persons who supply no capital. The officers of the corporation, who technically are only hired employees, may be able to use the proxy process to select directors who will do their bidding and adopt the policies that they desire. This is most likely in cases in which the largest shareholders own a tiny fraction (perhaps 1 percent or less) of the total stock, and in which these shareholders are persons (perhaps second-generation owners) with no active interest in the enterprise. In a legal sense, the stockholder still controls when he votes his stock or assigns his voting right; in a legal sense, also, the directors are obligated to act along lines that informed stockholders can approve. But the economic reality may be that an officer group is performing an important segment of the entrepreneurial function—albeit through sufferance of numerous persons who, conceivably, may throw them out.

In a study by the Securities and Exchange Commission of the 200 largest nonfinancial corporations, the conclusion was reached that 42 of them, or about one fifth, were controlled by an individual, family, or organization holding a majority of the stock; 37 were controlled by a predominant minority holding from 30 to 50 percent of the stock; 47 by a substantial minority with 10 to 30 percent; 13 by still smaller minorities. Thus a remainder of 61 corporations out of 200 showed no dominant stockholder interest, and it may be presumed that active control in them was exercised by officers who were able, quite effectively, to maintain themselves in power.[13]

[13] Figures from T.N.E.C. Monograph No. 29, as interpreted by Harry L. Purdy, Martin L. Lindahl, and William A. Carter, *Corporate Concentration and Public Policy*, Prentice-Hall, 1942, p. 76. Such classifications of types of control should be accepted only in a

Significance of concentration and separation

It is sufficient to indicate three areas in which these developments in the control of corporations have been thought, by various observers, to be significant.

1. There is the danger that the interests of owners will be prejudiced when they lack an effective voice in control. Enough legal looseness exists in the corporate framework so that particular interests, perhaps holders of nonvoting securities or outvoted minorities, may suffer infringement of what they thought were their rights. Centrally placed persons may cause their salaries and bonuses to be questionably high or may cause the corporation to patronize supply houses and banks in which they are interested on terms too beneficial to these outside interests. They may be biased, for a number of reasons, toward retaining profits for expansion when most stockholders would prefer dividends, and this bias may cause investments that would not be made on the basis of a free comparison of alternatives.

Sometimes these abuses are serious, but a recital of them easily creates too unfavorable an impression. Whatever the type of control, some restraint is present in the latent power of stockholders to assert their rights, in the need of maintaining a willing source of capital, in the traditional legal obligations of directors, in the general standing and influence that owner interests enjoy under capitalism.

2. Another fear is that enterprises will be less effectively run with respect to productive efficiency when active control is in the hands of men whose financial stake is slight. The problem is one of motivation. Long ago Adam Smith observed of the early joint-stock companies that, when managers use "other people's money," they display less vigilance than when they risk their own. A more recent writer has called it the "golden rule of capitalism" that control should be exercised by persons who stand to gain most from the successful operation of projects and to lose most from their failure.[14] We saw in the last chapter that a tendency in business toward bureaucratic sluggishness must be combated. While this tendency is more the result of sheer size than of any split in enterprise functions, it may be intensified when officials lack an ownership interest. At the same time, there is real advantage in having men selected because of their special competence as business leaders and not

qualified way. Control is not a precise concept, and the lines that it follows are difficult to trace, even when corporations permit themselves to be investigated. For an earlier study, see Adolph A. Berle and Gardiner C. Means, *op. cit.*, Chs. III–V; for a later one, R. A. Gordon, *Business Leadership in the Large Corporation*, Brookings Institution, 1945.

[14] See D. H. Robertson, *The Control of Industry*, Harcourt, Brace, 1923, pp. 88–91.

merely because of their financial interest. And again we should recognize that the split between ownership and control is not likely to be complete.

3. Finally these changes in the control of corporations have impressed certain observers with the need of a broad reformulation of the philosophy under which capitalism operates. The tradition that owners are entitled to the net return from business is challenged on the ground that owners no longer discharge their duties. Control not rooted in ownership is attacked as illegitimate. Changes are urged whereby, if control of the corporation does not rest on ownership, it should be in the hands of persons named to represent workers, consumers, and the general public as well as investors.[15] While the problem is impressive, the discussion of it thus far has moved mainly in the philosophic realm. Very likely the discussion will remain there. Broad changes in the economy seem more likely to come through failure to solve specific problems in the wage and employment fields, for instance, than through developments in the relationship of control to ownership within large corporations.

Review Questions

1. To what extent must nonvoting securities be used to enable a person with $1,000,000 to retain a secure legal control of a $5,000,000 business? Would you characterize the result as a *separation* of ownership and control?

2. "At the very least, use of the holding-company device should permit control to be exercised with only one fourth of the invested capital." Tell what a holding company is and explain this statement. Explain the further effect (a) of pyramiding holding companies; (b) of combining the holding-company principle with the use of nonvoting securities.

3. "The more widespread and democratic the ownership of large corporations, the less democratic is the control likely to be." Explain, developing several reasons why minority control may be effective—why control may even rest in the hands of persons who own no stock.

4. How may the types of control in corporations be classified?

5. Distinguish a number of viewpoints from which developments in the control of large corporations may be said to have public significance.

[15] For a leading statement of this view, see Adolph A. Berle and Gardiner C. Means, *op. cit.*, Bk. IV.

- 9 -

Finance

This chapter is in part a continuation of the preceding one, developing the financial side of the corporation, but it will go beyond the corporation to sketch more broadly some of the leading features of finance.

Finance serves production as the means by which resources are mobilized for specific projects. Once an enterprise is under way, receipts from the sale of products pay for the labor and materials bought currently, cover the depreciation of its facilities, and presumably yield some additional return. But at the outset there are no sales revenues, and outlays must be made for land, buildings, and equipment and for the initial stocks of materials and supplies. If these outlays are large, they probably exceed the savings of the persons starting the project. Funds must be obtained somewhere else; in other words, financing must be done.

Three parties are involved in the processes of finance: (1) the firms that require funds, (2) the persons who have savings to invest, (3) the institutions that assist in transferring funds from savers to users. The study of finance deals mainly with these institutions and with certain of the arrangements within corporations. While financial institutions supply none of the final products that the term production usually implies, they are a vital part of the organization of modern production. Partly their remoteness from the ordinary consumer, partly the hocus-pocus and chicanery long rampant in the field, have won them a dubious status in the popular mind. Finance in America has been a field of spectacular doings—and also of considerable government action—but its role in production is clear.

Continuing the discussion of the last chapter, we shall begin by examining some of the financial features of the corporation and of the markets through which corporate securities pass. Then we shall survey more broadly the uses of funds and the agencies that provide them. Finally, the leading financial problems as the public sees them will be sketched, together with the main policies which have developed in this country.

Corporate Securities and Financial Structures

In explaining in the preceding chapter why the corporate form aids in amassing capital, it was noted that many corporations have other kinds of securities beside common stock. Securities are contracts between the corporation and the investor, and these contracts differ as to the *risk* the investor incurs, the *claim to income* he acquires, and the part he can play in *controlling* the corporation. These three aspects of securities have been called the "incidents," or attributes, of ownership. Since there are many ways of specifying the details of each of these attributes, the variety of security contracts involving all the possible combinations of the risk, income, and control features is very great. Thus the everyday labels applied to securities, such as "preferred stock" and "mortgage bond," do not represent clearly defined types but designate broad classes of securities that have important common features but many differences in detail. The names of securities are seldom adequately descriptive.[1]

We shall examine briefly the significant features of the leading security types.

Common stock

In every business enterprise, whether incorporated or not, there must be an ownership interest that is residual and final. This is the interest in such income as remains after all operating expenses and all contractual obligations are met and the interest in the assets of the enterprise after allowing for all prior claims. It is the interest to which final legal authority attaches in running the business. Typically, under the corporate form, common stock represents this residual equity and this ultimate power of decision. It is the kind of security, in other words, that corresponds most directly to the enterprise function, the role of the entrepreneur. Corporations need have no other kind of security, but *in every case they must have common stock.*

Placed in this residual spot, the common stockholder feels the full impact of the varying fortunes of the enterprise. If there are losses, they strike him first, even to the extent of wiping out his equity; if the gains

[1] Perhaps the best-known work on the financing of corporations is Arthur S. Dewing, *The Financial Policy of Corporations*, Ronald Press, 4th ed., 1941. A leading text is Harry G. Guthmann and Herbert E. Dougall, *Corporate Financial Policy*, Prentice-Hall, 2d ed., 1948. A work with less of the vocational approach is Hiram L. Jome, *Corporation Finance*, Henry Holt & Co. 1948.

are great, only he can enjoy their main effect. The fortunes that have been built up through ownership in highly successful corporations have gone to the owners of common stock. Whether large corporate income is paid out in dividends or kept within the business to expand it, the common stockholder is the chief beneficiary.

Preferred stock

Preference stock has many variations, but it is distinguished by one main feature: a dividend must be paid on preferred stock at a specified rate before any dividend is paid on common stock. If a corporation has 1000 shares of 5-percent preferred stock, par value $100, no dividend can be paid on common stock until $5000 of the corporation's net income has been paid to holders of the preferred. Beyond this requirement, the preference imposes no obligation on the corporation. It may pay no dividend on any class of stock, even though there are large earnings. It does not default thereby in meeting its obligations, as it would if it failed to pay interest on bonds.

The main question, in describing the subtypes of preferred stock, is whether the holders have a continuing stake in unpaid dividends or whether they are permanently lost. Ordinarily the preference is *cumulative,* so that, when preferred dividends have not been paid for one or more years, no subsequent dividend can be paid on the common until the accumulated dividends on the preferred have been paid. If the corporation in the above example passed its preferred dividend for four years, then, to pay a dividend in the fifth year on the common, it would first need to distribute $25,000 to the preferred stockholders. When preferred shares lack this cumulative feature, they are called *noncumulative*.

If a corporation is liquidated and there are funds to be distributed to stockholders, preferred and common stockholders share in some cases on the same basis and in other cases the preferred stockholders receive the full par value of their stock before the common stockholders get anything. In the latter case, the preferred stock is said to be *preferred as to assets* as well as to earnings. We have already seen that preferred stock may or may not carry voting power. Moreover it may have voting rights in some situations but not in others.

Bonds

Whether or not they are active in corporate affairs, all stockholders are owners in a legal sense. Bondholders are merely creditors, which means that they are outsiders who lend capital to the corporation. This means that a share of stock has no maturity date and implies no obligation on the part of the corporation to repay the stockholder; a bond, on the other hand, is an agreement in which the corporation promises to pay back the principal at a specified future time and to pay periodically for its use at a fixed percentage rate. This latter payment, ordinarily annual or semiannual, is spoken of as *interest,* not as a dividend. Failure to pay interest or principal when due constitutes default in the legal sense and may be the forerunner of the bankruptcy proceedings through which firms are either liquidated or reorganized. In both of these situations, the claims of bondholders stand ahead of the claims of stockholders. As outside capitalists, bondholders do not participate in control—at least as long as their claims are met.

Bonds are classified as secured and unsecured. In the same way that a loan to a farmer or a householder may be secured by a mortgage on a farm or a house, so an entire bond issue of a corporation may be secured by a mortgage on the roadway or terminal facilities of a railroad, on the generating plants and transmission lines of a power company, on an office building or apartment house, or (less likely) on a factory. Such obligations are called *mortgage bonds.* Or a corporation that owns the stocks and bonds of other corporations may use these securities to secure its own *collateral trust bonds* through which it obtains capital. In case of default, the holders of secured bonds may, through proper legal channels, take possession of the securing property and dispose of it.

Bonds not secured by specific properties are commonly called *debentures.* While they are called "unsecured," they actually depend for payment, as does any other obligation of a corporation, upon the revenues from its operations and the sums that can be realized through liquidating its assets. Hence, if no secured bonds stand ahead of them, debentures are on practically the same footing as secured bonds would be. But if there are mortgage bonds, they have priority to the extent of the pledged assets. When corporations fail, the right to appropriate specific items of wealth and liquidate them is likely to have little value under modern conditions, because more can usually be salvaged through reorganizing a business and continuing it than through disposing of its assets separately. On reorganization the bondholders, according to the priority of their claims, receive securities in the new enterprise instead of the proceeds of a liquidation sale.

A hybrid type of security which is placed in the bond category is the *income bond.* The interest on such a bond has to be paid only if the corporation has income to cover it, and thus the interest obligation cannot cause default. Income bonds most commonly appear when bankrupt corporations are reorganized, as part of a financial plan designed to avoid further default.

Effects of fixed-income securities

Leading reasons for complex capital structures, in which corporations combine several types of securities, were pointed out in the preceding chapter. It was recognized (1) that capital may be obtained more readily, in view of the varying attitudes of investors, if securities are offered which combine risk and income prospects in different ways; (2) that the organizers of a business may keep control more easily if outside capital is obtained through sale of nonvoting securities.

We should now see, in addition, that the organizers favor a means of obtaining capital which will divert the minimum amount of earnings to outsiders. The use of bonds and preferred stock is thus made attractive by the fixed nature of their income provisions, at least on the upper side. However profitable a corporation may be, the holders of bonds and preferred stock will get no more of the net return than the specified interest and dividend rates provide. When men start a business, risking their own capital in it, they must have considerable confidence that the return on that capital will be higher than in some safe investment with little of the enterprise element in it. If they are right and their project yields 8 or 10 percent and if they have got outside capital for 4 or 5 percent, the return on the capital they have supplied will be more than 8 or 10 percent. But if, as often happens, they turn out to be wrong, reliance on bonds or cumulative preferred stock makes their position worse than if they had financed entirely with common stock. Thus the use of fixed-income securities creates a sort of "financial leverage" which amplifies both profits and losses to the common stockholders. To hold common stock in this situation is often referred to as *"trading on the equity."*

Financial leverage. An example will bring out the point. Let us suppose that a business project requires $1,000,000 and that the organizers have $500,000 of their own to put in (see Table 13). They take common stock for their contribution, and the other $500,000 may be obtained through selling (1) additional common stock or (2) 5-percent preferred stock. Let us observe the effects of these two capital structures in each of three years, in the first of which the net return on the $1,000,-000 of capital is at just the 5-percent rate called for by the preferred stock, in the second at twice that rate, and in the third at one half that rate.

If the only security is common stock, all the earnings apply to the common, and the organizers get the same rate of return that is earned on the entire capital—5 percent, 10 percent, and 2½ percent, respectively—in these three years. Likewise, as shown in the first year, if the

TABLE 13—EXAMPLE OF FINANCIAL LEVERAGE

Capital structure	First year		Second year		Third year	
	All com.	Half pref.	All com.	Half pref.	All com.	Half pref.
Sales revenue	$800,000	$800,000	$1,200,000	$1,200,000	$685,000	$685,000
Operating expenses	750,000	750,000	1,100,000	1,100,000	660,000	660,000
Net operating revenue	50,000	50,000	100,000	100,000	25,000	25,000
Preferred dividend	—	25,000	—	25,000	—	25,000
Return on common	50,000	25,000	100,000	75,000	25,000	0
Return to organizers	25,000	25,000	50,000	75,000	12,500	0
Rate on common	5%	5%	10%	15%	2.5%	0%

entire capital earns at the 5-percent rate called for by the preferred stock, the return on the common is also 5 percent whether or not preferred stock has been issued. But when earnings on the entire capital depart from the rate specified for preferred shares, as in the second and third years, the rate of return on the common fluctuates more widely when preferred shares are present. Thus doubling the return on the entire capital (to 10 percent in the second year) triples the return on the common (to 15 percent); halving the rate on the capital to 2½ percent in the third year) reduces the rate on the common to zero. The higher rate of return that financial leverage makes possible is matched by the lower return that, on the average, is probably just as likely.

Financial leverage through the holding company. This principle of financial leverage can be applied more strikingly by the holding company, *provided bonds or preferred shares are used at the holding-company and not merely at the operating-company level.* Let us return to the case of Smith, Jones, and Brown in the last chapter (page 202) and make some necessary additions to the example. Let us assume that operating Companies A, B, C, and D earn 10 percent on their $64,000,000 of capital, that their preferred stock carries a 4-percent dividend, that the preferred of Holding Company Y calls for 5 percent, and that of

Holding Company X for 6 percent. If we also assume that all available earnings are paid out in dividends, we can easily compute the return to Smith, Jones, and Brown, as shown in the table.

TABLE 14—PROFIT CONCENTRATION THROUGH THE HOLDING COMPANY

10% on operating capital of A, B, C, and D	$6,400,000
4% on preferred stock of A, B, C, and D	1,280,000
Return to common of A, B, C, and D	5,120,000 (16%)
One half to Holding Company Y	2,560,000
5% on preferred of Holding Company Y	400,000
Return to common of Holding Company Y	2,160,000 (27%)
One half to Holding Company X	1,080,000
6% on preferred of Holding Company X	120,000
Return to common of Holding Company X	960,000 (48%)
Return to Smith, Jones, and Brown	480,000 (48%)

Thus we see that holding companies do not merely concentrate control. When financed in part with fixed-income securities, they concentrate earnings also. When the operating capital yields 10 percent in this example, the operating common yields 16 percent, the common of the first holding company 27 percent, and the common of the second holding company 48 percent.

Pyramiding is equally potent in the opposite direction, magnifying the effect of low earnings. If the operating capital yields 4 percent instead of 10 percent, Smith, Jones, and Brown make, instead of 48 percent, exactly nothing. If the operating return is 3 percent, a respectable return in a poor year, the return will not even pay the preferred dividend of the first holding company and will yield nothing to its common stockholders or to either the preferred or common of the top company. Thus it is apparent why holding-company systems financed in part with bonds or, as in some instances, with bank loans are likely to be pretty shaky structures, quick to collapse in the first economic storm, as many did during the 1930s.

Even in the case of ordinary operating companies, dependence on bonds in obtaining capital, or even extensive dependence on cumulative preferred stock, is "fair-weather" financing unless there is reasonable assurance that earnings will be adequate in poor years to meet the requirements of these fixed-income securities. Fairly extensive reliance on bonds may be warranted in such a field as electric power but has been carried much too far in the railroad industry. Bonds are used much less in the manufacturing and merchandising fields, but considerable use is made of preferred stock. In view of the great uncertainties in the extraction of minerals, practically all financing in this field is done with common stock.

Some Financial and Accounting Concepts

Many terms of corporation finance have entered everyday use. From both the private and the social viewpoint, there has been an expanding interest in the financial affairs of corporations. Millions of people own corporate securities, and many others recognize the impact of corporate financing and earnings on the entire economic structure. The financial pages of newspapers are widely read. Nevertheless, the terms and concepts are not widely understood. To the preceding discussion of the kinds of securities, we shall now add some of the concepts used in speaking of their value, of dividend practices and the retention of earnings, and of corporate capitalization. Incidentally the essential nature of the balance sheet will be explained, as a necessary tool in this and later connections.

Accounting expression of financial status

The *ABC* Corporation, let us say, is organized to undertake a manufacturing project that will require $1,000,000 of capital in plant, inventories, and cash. Ten thousand shares of common stock (par value $100) are issued, partly for cash and partly in direct exchange for an old but usable building. The building is then equipped in satisfactory fashion, materials and supplies are purchased, and a sufficient working force hired to begin operations.

At this stage, in simplified form and in round numbers, the situation of the *ABC* Corporation is as follows:

ASSETS		LIABILITIES AND PROPRIETORSHIP	
Cash	$ 25,000	Capital stock	$1,000,000
Inventories	375,000		
Plant and equipment	600,000		
	$1,000,000		$1,000,000

Operations are begun, and are carried on successfully. Over a considerable period a substantial volume of product is turned out and sold, partly on credit. Materials and supplies are bought, wages paid, and other expenses incurred. Equipment is added, and additional funds for working capital are borrowed at a local bank. Some purchased materials are not paid for fully. At the end of this period, the financial position of the *ABC* Corporation has changed in important respects, as its balance sheet shows:

ASSETS			LIABILITIES AND PROPRIETORSHIP	
Cash		$ 40,000	Accounts payable	$ 35,000
Accounts receivable		50,000	Notes payable	45,000
Inventories		455,000	Capital stock	1,000,000
Plant and equipment			Surplus	75,000
at cost	$690,000			
Less depreciation				
	80,000	610,000		
		$1,155,000		$1,155,000

How are these statements to be interpreted?

The balance sheet. In Chapter 3 income and wealth were distinguished as the difference between a flow and a fund. Income is measured for a period of time, wealth at an instant in time. The two principal financial summaries on which business enterprises depend—the *income statement* and the *balance sheet*—correspond to this distinction. The income statement was presented, in an approximate sort of way, in Chapter 3 as a tool which is useful in explaining the meaning of income from both the business and the national standpoint. The meaning of wealth was explained also at that point, but its expression in balance-sheet form was deferred for consideration here, where the balance sheet finds its chief application.

The balance sheet tells nothing directly of a firm's revenues and expenses. These are matters covered by the income statement, although some inferences regarding them can be drawn by comparing successive balance sheets. The object of the balance sheet is to state the wealth position of the firm, and it does this by viewing the same set of facts from two different angles: the asset angle and the liability-and-ownership angle.

Assets are all the valuable things possessed by the firm—wealth in the private sense. Assets include the *fixed facilities,* the buildings, equipment, and land, and also the *stocks* of materials, partly finished goods, and products awaiting sale—items we have called *circulating capital.* Assets include *cash,* whether in the company safe or in a bank balance. They include also various *claims* against other individuals and firms, such as the "accounts receivable" item above, which represents sales for which payment has not been received. Assets may also include *in-*

tangibles such as patents, but none is shown in this example. Accrued depreciation is recognized as a partial offset to certain property accounts.

The *liability-and-proprietorship* side of the balance sheet—referred to as "liabilities" or "equities," for short—looks at these same properties from another vantage point. There is nothing accidental or contrived in the fact that the two totals are the same. Everything valuable owned by the corporation is *owed* to someone, or else it represents the interest or *equity* of the owners, the stockholders. The right side of the balance sheet represents all the claims against and interests in the assets, and thus necessarily must give rise to exactly the same total that the assets do. At the outset all the assets of the *ABC* Corporation were obtained through issuance of stock, and thus the owners possessed the only interest in the assets. After the period of operation, certain suppliers ("accounts payable") and the local bank ("notes payable") have acquired claims against the assets. The remainder, represented by "capital stock" and "surplus," constitutes the equity of the stockholders.

The *surplus* item should be noted especially, since understanding it is something of a test of one's understanding of the balance sheet—of the basic meaning of assets and equities. This surplus item results from the successful operation of the firm, the fact that it has made money.[2] But the surplus is not cash, nor does it represent cash. Cash is an asset, something valuable in the possession of the company, but surplus is listed on the other side. It belongs with the claims against and interests in the assets. It is simply an extension of the interest of the stockholders, a supplement to the capital-stock account. The company has profited, which means that its assets have increased in comparison with its debts, and this increase in the net assets of the company expands the interest of the stockholders in it. Among the assets the increase can be found in new machines, larger inventories, expanded cash and accounts receivable; among the equities, it appears as surplus.

In the case of the *ABC* Corporation, assets expanded by $155,000 during the period shown. Of this increase $75,000 is from profitable operation, as shown by the surplus; $45,000 is from borrowing at the bank; $35,000 represents supplies not paid for. These sources of the expansion cannot be paired with specified assets that have increased, but all of them together explain the total increase.

Book value and dividends

Of the three value concepts associated with corporate securities—book, par, and market value—book value can be understood directly

[2] This is the principal way in which surplus arises, but there are other ways. One is through selling stock at a price above par. Another is through recognition of appreciation in the value of assets.

on the basis of the preceding discussion. The book value of stock is measured by the *net assets per share*, which can be computed from the balance sheet.

At the outset the total assets of the *ABC* Corporation are $1,000,000, and, because there are no debts, this figure represents net assets. With 10,000 shares of stock, each share represents $100 of assets. The book value of a share, then, is $100. In this case the book value equals the sum received for the stock when issued.

After the period of operation, total assets are $1,155,000 and debts are $80,000. Thus net assets (represented by capital stock and surplus) equal $1,075,000. That sum, spread over 10,000 shares, makes their book value $107.50.

Cash dividend. Thus far we have assumed that the company's earnings are retained for expanding its operations. But the company's directors may now decide that earnings should in part be distributed to the stockholders. Accordingly a dividend of $3 per share is declared and paid. The effect of this payment is to reduce cash by $30,000 and to reduce surplus by the same amount, because the equity of the stockholders is necessarily smaller by the amount that assets are transferred to them by the corporation. With the surplus now reduced to $45,000, the book value of a share becomes $104.50, smaller than before by the $3 received.

Stock dividend. Let us next assume that a long period of successful operation passes by, with a large part of the earnings retained to expand the business, so that the surplus becomes $550,000 and the book value of a share $155. In this situation the directors, perhaps after approval by the stockholders, may decide that it would be well to have the net worth represented by more shares of stock. The object may be to have it appear that the corporation is not quite so profitable, through having more shares to spread the earnings over; it may be to reduce the market value of shares so that trading in them will be easier. Whatever the reason, a so-called stock dividend of 50 percent is declared. Such a dividend involves no cash. It simply involves giving each stockholder one extra share for every two shares he has already. The previous holder of 100 shares now has 150 shares.

How does such a dividend affect the balance sheet, the book value of stock, and the position of the stockholder? Clearly it does not affect the assets. The corporation has received nothing and parted with nothing. On the equity side the total interest of the stockholders, instead of being represented by $1,000,000 of capital stock and $550,000 surplus, is now covered by $1,500,000 of capital stock and $50,000 of surplus. With no change in assets or in debts, their total interest must be the same. But with that total represented by 15,000 shares, instead of 10,000, the book value of a share has become $103.33, instead of $155. The equity of each stockholder, however, is just what it was before. One hundred and fifty shares now represent the same equity that 100 shares did previously. The holder still has 1 percent of the total interest of all holders. Since, in reality, nothing has passed from the corporation to the stockholder, a stock dividend is not income—either in economic analysis or in the eyes of the income-tax collectors.

Par value and capitalization

A second value concept associated with securities is their par value. It is an element in the capitalization of corporations.

In the case of bonds, the par value states the amount of the debt to the bondholder, the amount the corporation agrees to pay on the maturity date. In the case of preferred stock which is preferred as to assets, it provides a basis for the stockholder's claim in case of liquidation. In the case of common stock, par value can have no such meaning, because the common stockholder, being in the residual position, has a right only to whatever is left when other claims are satisfied.

Par value of common stock is significant merely as the sum, in money or property, that the original stockholder agrees to turn over to the corporation in payment for his stock. Thus it is the amount of wealth which creditors may assume the corporation has received, or is to receive, for each share of stock issued. But even this meaning, in the development of American· finance, could not with certainty be attached to par value, since ways were discovered of issuing securities with a total par value greatly in excess of the true asset values received for the stock.

Stock need not have a par value, and in the last quarter century numerous issues of so-called *no-par stock* have appeared. While we may pass over the several virtues and defects attributed to it, we should see that the absence or presence of par value does not affect the essential nature of the common stockholder's interest in the corporation. In either case he has merely a fractional equity in its earnings and assets. Given a corporation with certain physical facilities and a certain earning power, the holder of 100 of the 10,000 outstanding shares of that corporation has a 1 percent interest in it, whether or not a par value appears on the stock and whatever such an expressed value may happen to be. A figure on a stock certificate will not affect the ability of the company's facilities to produce or of the product to sell. Thus par value gives no indication of the worth of a security to the owner.

Capitalization of a corporation. The word "capitalization" in the present connection refers collectively to the securities of the corporation as they appear in the balance sheet. A statement of the capitaliza-

tion of a company tells what securities in what amounts have been issued to obtain its *capital* (its assets or its wealth) and to represent the
interest of stockholders and bondholders. Because securities are recorded on the books at their par values, par value is the basis of capitalization. In the case of no-par shares a "stated value" is recorded which
represents, at least in part, the capital received for them.

Capitalization in this sense is the basis of the concept of *overcapitalization*. If a corporation were to issue stock with a total par, or stated,
value of $1,000,000 in exchange for property worth no more than $500,-
000, the corporation would be described as "watering" its stock, and
the result would be described as overcapitalization. The corporation
would list the property among its assets as being worth $1,000,000 rather
than $500,000, so that a false impression would be created as to the vol-
ume of wealth committed to the enterprise. Thus overcapitalization
means an overvaluation of assets.

There are many lurid pages in the history of American corporation
finance, and on these pages overcapitalization has a prominent place. As
to the seriousness of its effect, there is room for argument at many
points, but it seems clear that the general looseness promoted by unrestricted issuance of securities and valuation of assets was an important
factor in the serious abuses which have prevailed.

Market value of securities

In the strict sense, par value and book value are not value concepts
at all, because they do not rest on the market forces which determine
values. The market values of securities, expressed in the prices at which
they are bought and sold, reflect the current consensus of the buyers
and sellers of them. Book values look to the past, market values to the
future. Book values rest on records (more or less accurate) of the assets
acquired and debts incurred. Market values rest immediately on many
superficial factors, but basically they depend on the earnings which
ownership of securities can be expected to bring. If all invested capital
were to earn continuously just a normal rate of return, the book and
market value could be very close. But the uncertainties of enterprise are
such that actual earnings may be a very high or a very low percent of the
capital invested or may be negative. What the purchaser of a going concern, or of stock in a going concern, may properly pay is not determined
by the amount of capital that in the past was put in. It is rather the sum
on which the prospective earnings would give a reasonable rate of return.[3]

Thus the *ABC* Corporation may have a capital of $1,550,000, ob-

[3] The arithmetic process of computing the value of property on the basis of prospective
earnings is another meaning given the word "capitalization." It will be explained in
Chapter 29.

tained through original sale of securities and retention of earning, and its 15,000 shares may have a book value of slightly over $100. But if an annual net income of $200,000 is anticipated, its shares may be worth $150 or $200—or whatever amount is justified by earnings of over $13 a share. Or if adverse changes have reduced its prospects, so that an income of no more than $50,000 a year is expected, shares may be worth only $40 or $50.

Indeed, variations of this size in expected income are likely to cause even greater fluctuations in market values, for the market is sensitive to an exaggerated degree, subject to irrational waves of fear and of optimism. Under boom conditions shares are likely to be overpriced and in depressions they may fall ridiculously low.

Review Questions

1. Explain carefully the place of finance in the processes of production.

2. "The great variety of corporate securities can be appreciated best by sensing in how many different ways the incidents of ownership can be combined." Explain.

3. Why does common stock correspond most closely to the nature of the enterprise function?

4. Many corporations failed to pay dividends on their preferred stock during the worst years of the 1930s. When earnings revived, how was the position of common stockholders affected by whether preferred stock was cumulative or noncumulative? How would the situation have differed if the preferred stock had been bonds?

5. You have invested $1000 in the only bond issue of an electric-power company. Does it matter, so far as your legal rights and the strength of your position are concerned, whether the bond is a debenture or represents a mortgage on generating equipment and transmission lines? Explain. What other kinds of bonds are there?

6. You are able to supply $100,000 of the $300,000 you require in developing a new business. Distinguish several reasons why you are inclined to sell bonds rather than stock in obtaining at least part of the $200,000 you must raise.

7. "Because bonds call for a steady rate of return, one reason for issuing them is that they add to the financial stability of a corporation." Is this one of the reasons you gave in answering question 6? Should it be?

8. Explain what is meant by financial leverage and how it operates (a) through the presence of different kinds of securities; (b) through the holding company.

9. Explain the two sides of the balance sheet in such a way as to show why, logically, they must be equal.

10. "Surplus results from profitable operation, but it is not cash and does not represent cash." Explain.

11. A company with 1,000,000 shares of stock outstanding shows in its balance sheet a capital-stock item of $10,000,000 and a surplus item of $4,000,000. What is the book value of a share of stock? A stock dividend is declared and paid in the form of a 25-percent increase in the number of shares. What is now the book value of a share? What has happened to the book value of the shares held by any one stockholder? After the stock has been increased, a $1 cash dividend is paid. What is now the book value of a share? At what point or points in this succession of events does the stockholder receive income?

12. "The interest of a stockholder in a corporation should be thought of in terms of numbers of shares and not in terms of par value. The absence of a par value does not affect his interest." Explain. What is the significance of par value? Why may book value depart from it?

13. If you were to describe the capitalization of a corporation, what facts would you include?

14. Why should the market values of securities depart from their book values?

The Marketing of Securities

Much of the financing of corporations is accomplished without the aid of financial specialists. Corporations of the "closed," or "family," type obtain their capital—as single proprietorships and partnerships do—without a public offering of securities. Other corporations of modest size may dispose of securities through the personal effort of individuals in them. In addition, corporations of all sizes get capital and expand through retaining their own earnings.

Much financing is done in these ways, but much is done also through the specialized activity of security dealers who act as middlemen between corporations needing funds and savers desiring investments. In addition the marketability of stocks and bonds is enhanced by the trading in them on securities exchanges. The role of these financial institutions will be considered in this section, ordinary banks and related institutions in the following section.

Investment banking

The term investment bank is the common name for financial houses that act as middlemen in transmitting securities from corporations to investors and in transferring savings from investors to corporations. The term covers a range of institutions. At one extreme are the large, conservative houses, such as Kuhn, Loeb and Company and the old J. P. Morgan and Company, that specialize in financing well-known and well-established corporations or combinations thereof. Primarily they deal in bonds. At the other extreme are the small houses that assist in financing new and speculative undertakings, the new oil wells and gadget-manu-facturing promotions.

Middleman operations. An investment banking house may be the sole merchant in disposing of a security issue, negotiating with the issuing corporation, on the one hand, and placing securities in investors' hands, on the other. Or it may be part of a more extensive marketing arrangement. Often, in the case of a large security issue, a number of houses will form an *underwriting syndicate,* a sort of temporary partnership, to dispose of the issue. A leading house conducts the dealings with the issuing company and acts as syndicate manager, and the other members undertake to dispose of specified amounts of the issue. A kind of wholesaler-retailer relationship often prevails.

The buyers of securities from investment bankers are frequently not individual savers but financial institutions which are indirectly investing the funds of savers. If the rather severe legal standards can be met, securities may be sold to ordinary commercial and savings banks. These banks, in turn, may be thought of as middlemen committing the funds of depositors. Likewise, high-grade securities may be sold to insurance companies, which, again, may be regarded as middlemen placing the funds of policyholders. The trust companies that handle estates are also an important market for securities. However, the large institutional buyers may get the securities directly from the issuing corporations. To an increasing extent in recent years the investment banks have been by-passed through the direct sale of bond issues to insurance companies.

In disposing of security issues, investment houses may assume quite different degrees of responsibility. Formerly they acted merely as agent of the issuing corporation, disposing of such part of an issue as they could sell and providing the corporation with that much capital and no more. In recent decades they have usually served as *underwriters,* in the sense that they guarantee to dispose of the entire issue and provide the company the full amount of capital it is seeking even though buyers are not found immediately. There is thus much less risk to the issuing corporation and more to the middleman.

The return for this merchandising service varies widely. In handling large bond issues of well-known companies, the investment bankers may get no more than 1 percent of the proceeds. But in the marketing of stock of new companies, 20 percent or more of the investor's capital is likely to be absorbed in the marketing process and thus never reach the issuing corporation.

New securities without capital formation. It would be a mistake to suppose that the investment banks are wholly concerned with the financing of real capital formation, as we have used that term. Although it is true that numerous new issues are sold to provide funds to expand plant and equipment and inventories, many new issues merely take the place of old issues or indirectly represent ownership of old issues. New bonds may replace—*refund* is the word—old issues that reach maturity and must be paid; family corporations that have been closely held are sold to the general public arrayed in new suits of financial clothing; holding companies and investment trusts are organized to buy and hold the outstanding securities of existing corporations. In these transactions the investment houses are often more than mere middlemen; they are frequently the active promoters of the transactions which yield the new securities that they sell. In 1929, an active year, of the total of $10 billion of new corporate securities marketed both with and without the assistance of middlemen, over half belonged in these categories which brought no expansion in productive wealth.

The stock exchanges

Not only are many new securities representative of old wealth, but much financial machinery is not even concerned with new securities or concerned only a little. In particular the stock exchanges, the segment of the securities market best known to the general public, serve mainly in the transfer of outstanding securities from which issuing companies have already received their capital. These exchanges are highly organized market places with a definite membership eligible to trade in them, with a specified list of securities to trade in, and with a defined procedure through which buyers and sellers carry out transactions. By far the most important is the New York Stock Exchange, and second to it in this country is the New York Curb Exchange. The securities, both stocks and bonds, of most of the leading corporations are listed on one or the other of these two exchanges. Small exchanges operate in quite a number of other large cities. In addition to the organized exchanges a so-called "over-the-counter market," made up of several thousand dealers, provides trading channels for innumerable issues of securities not listed on the exchanges.

Brokerage houses. Except for the small number of persons who hold memberships in the exchanges, trading in them is done indirectly through brokerage houses. These houses account for a large fraction of the memberships. Branches of the brokerage houses are located throughout the country, and customers' orders are communicated by direct wire connection to brokers' representatives on the exchanges. The exchanges themselves are not engaged in buying and selling securities, and the brokers, when acting strictly in a brokerage capacity, are not principals in the trading. The exchange is merely the market, and the broker simply acts as agent in executing the customer's order. For his service the broker receives a commission which varies with the price of the security but is quite independent of the customer's gain or loss.

An important part of the patronage of the brokers comes from persons who have savings they wish to invest in known securities and from persons who wish to liquidate investments they already hold. But an even greater part of the trading is by speculators whose chief interest in securities is not in the incomes they yield but in the fluctuations in their values on the market. *Speculative trading,* mainly in stocks, is carried on for the sake of the capital gains which result from correct anticipation of price movements. In speculative trading the period during which a security is held is often a matter of weeks or days or even of hours. The securities traded in do not reach the safety-deposit boxes of the traders but are held by the brokers for their customers.

Speculation for the rise and the decline. Since security prices may move in either of two directions, there are two types of speculative transaction, known as *long* and *short.* Much the more common is the purchase of a security that is expected to rise in price with the intention of selling after the rise occurs. This is a *long* transaction, and the speculator is spoken of as a "bull" on the market.

If a security is expected to fall in price, a holder of it may profit by selling it, and then, if he is correct, buying it back later at the lower price. Thus he has the same holding and some cash beside. But to profit from the decline, it is not necessary to be a present owner of the security. The speculator may *"sell short"* a security that he does not have and buy later when the price has fallen. How can a trader sell something he does not possess? The answer is that the broker executes the selling order at the first end of the transaction by delivering shares which are in his name or which he borrows, thus placing the customer in debt to him for these shares. Later, at the other end of the transaction, the customer must place a buying order for the shares and repay the broker. In such a deal the trader loses, of course, if his prediction is wrong, and the price goes up before he covers. Speculators who trade on the basis of anticipated falling prices are known as "bears."

Marginal trading. In the past much of the speculative trading in securities was conducted on a credit basis, known as *marginal trading.* On an order to buy 100 shares of United States Steel at, say $80, the customer might put up $2000 of the required $8000. This $2000 would be his margin, and the broker would supply the remaining $6000 either from his own funds or by borrowing at a commercial bank with the securities as collateral for the loan. If the price went up as the trader expected, rising, let us say, to $100, or by 25 percent, the gain on the 100 shares would be $2000 (minus interest on the loan, the broker's commission, and a small tax), so that the gain on the speculator's funds would be nearly 100 percent. If, on the other hand, the stock should decline to $60, the loss would be 100 percent, and the trader's capital would be wiped out. Through this multiplication of gains and losses, marginal trading explains the quick fortunes and bankruptcies for which the stock market is famous. In recent years credit trading in securities has been largely restricted through federal regulation. At times a 100-percent margin has been required, so that the trader pays cash.

Economic benefits and abuses. What place have the securities exchanges in the financing of production? Corporations get capital only when they sell their securities in the first place, and no matter how furious the rate at which their stocks and bonds are subsequently traded "secondhand" among investors and speculators, not an additional nickel comes to the corporation. Are the exchanges, therefore, nothing more than glorified gambling houses in which large sums are bet on the price movements of already issued securities?

Certainly the staunchest defender of the exchanges must concede that, except for some minor marketing of additional securities by established companies, they do not directly provide capital for industry. But he will make the point that the willingness of investors to buy securities when first issued depends greatly on their marketability. Organized exchanges provide that marketability and thus play an important indirect part in the formation of capital. Whether this indirect function requires so great a volume of speculative activity may be open to question.[4]

Against this economic service must be set the evils of speculative excesses. These are of two types. One is the manipulation, the rigging of the market, in order to create artificial price movements from which the manipulators can profit. By starting rumors as to developments within a corporation, or, even more, by placing heavy buying and selling orders for a stock to give the impression of a movement from which the public will seek to profit, sharp operators have often made large and thoroughly illegitimate profits.

The second evil springs from the peculiar volatility of a speculative market, the stampeding urgency with which speculators (especially the amateurs) join general price swings, either upward or downward, with serious aggravation of their extent and the violence of the ensuing cor-

[4] This is only a partial statement of the economic services claimed for the securities exchanges. For an analysis of these markets and their functions, see C. A. Dice and W. J. Eiteman, *The Stock Market*, McGraw-Hill, 1941. A popularly written critical treatment is John T. Flynn, *Security Speculation*, Harcourt, Brace, 1934.

rections. Undoubtedly these extreme movements in the securities market accentuate somewhat the fluctuations in production and employment which have been a major disease of our economy.

Credit Demands and Loan Agencies

We shall now turn to the main areas of financing other than the supplying of the permanent capital of corporations through sale of stocks and bonds. We shall deal with some of the additional capital requirements of business, as well as the needs of consumers and governmental bodies, and with the lending agencies that meet these needs.

Short-term business borrowing

The bulk of business capital is supplied on a fairly permanent basis by the owners, including stockholders, and by such long-term creditors as investors in bonds. But business firms, whether incorporated or not, are commonly financed with permanent capital to an extent that falls somewhat short of their maximum requirements. For this there may be reasons of expediency, such as unwillingness to take in additional partners or stockholders who would share in the profits and the control or an unwillingness to saddle a business with long-term indebtedness such as a bond issue entails. A more basic reason, however, lies in the economy of short-term borrowing.

The capital requirements of a business are not uniform. While the investment in fixed assets takes no short-run dips, the investment in inventories and the need for funds for wage payments and like purposes fluctuate a good deal. Important purchases of stocks of goods by retailers and manufacturers come intermittently, and other outlays do not correlate perfectly with sales revenues. A firm with $100,000 in fixed assets may find that its working-capital needs—for cash and inventories and extension of credit to customers—vary from $30,000 to $50,000. If a permanent capital of $150,000 is provided to meet maximum needs, idle capital, on the average, may amount perhaps to $10,000. Capital may be economized, therefore, if only $130,000 is committed permanently, and additional sums are borrowed as needed.

This variability in capital requirements is a major element in some industries. In farming, for instance, much expense is incurred in the spring of the year when planting is done, and revenues are concentrated in the period following the harvest. A building contractor makes heavy outlays throughout the period when projects are under way but gets paid in large sums at wide intervals. In such instances the average capital needed falls far below the maximum.

Whether it is desirable to depend on short-term loans to meet these fluctuating requirements is a matter of cost and risk. If relatively permanent capital can be obtained cheaply, the economy is slight. If there is uncertainty about getting loans when needed, or danger of having to make repayment at embarrassing moments, provision of adequate permanent capital may seem the sounder course. There has been some evidence of a trend toward greater reliance on permanent capital and less on short-term borrowing. But there seems, nevertheless, to be a substantial place in the economy for short-term business financing and for the institutions that provide it.

Nonbusiness borrowing

In this chapter, as throughout Part II of this volume, we are dealing with the organization of production, chiefly as carried on through private enterprise, but it is appropriate to recognize at this point that the need of financing is not limited to business. Calls for funds beyond those derived from current income come also from individuals in their capacity as consumers and from governments, national, state, and local. Financial machinery has developed in some degree to meet these demands.

Consumer borrowing. Perhaps the chief role of consumer credit is in enabling people to enjoy the use of the more expensive, durable consumers' goods before they have accumulated sufficient savings to purchase these goods. Few people have sufficient savings to buy a house at the time when it seems most important to own one. Most automobiles are paid for only in part at the time of purchase. Credit also plays a big part in the purchase of furniture and of such household equipment as refrigerators, washing machines, stoves, and radios. Even goods of more limited durability, such as clothing, are bought in large volume on a credit basis.

Much consumer credit is undoubtedly a reflection of shortsightedness and poor management of personal finances, but there is obvious logic, in the case of highly desired durable goods, in having the use of them if possible during earlier rather than later periods. It seems at least as sensible to pay for these goods while using them as to pay for them before the use begins. But against the advantage of earlier use must be set the cost of the financing, and it sometimes runs very high, much higher than consumers are likely to realize.

Apart from durable-goods purchases, the other chief need of consumer financing arises from personal or family emergencies, such as illnesses, deaths, and interruptions of earnings. Except for relatively few persons at the top of the income scale, most people cannot maintain a cash position sufficient to cope with large, unanticipated needs.

Public borrowing. Government borrowing, which has ranked first in volume in recent years, may also be put largely in the two categories of durable goods and emergencies. In ordinary years, the outlays of governments for current purposes are generally met with current revenues from taxation. But it is often both necessary and sound from a financial standpoint to borrow to build schools and water and sewage systems and to develop roads and waterways. These are projects from which benefit will be derived for many years, and the people who benefit will share the cost.

The largest public debts arise, however, from emergencies of two sorts: depressions and wars. A severe depression such as that of the 1930s cuts tax revenues on the one hand, and, on the other, creates a great new demand for funds to care for the unemployed and to promote recovery. The requirements of modern warfare quickly outstrip even a greatly increased flow of tax money, and the government must borrow heavily. In 1929 our federal government had a total gross direct debt of $16 billion, mainly the result of World War I. During the 1930s this debt expanded by 150 percent; from the new enlarged base it grew another 600 percent during the war years that followed, reaching a pinnacle of about $280 billion.

The problem of public indebtedness will reappear at several later points in our study.

Commercial and savings banks

With these credit demands in mind, we may note briefly the credit institutions that meet them. Of these, the best known and most important are the ordinary commercial and savings banks which are found in all communities and which assist in financing business, consumers, and governments.

Differences exist between commercial and savings banking, but most banking houses are engaged in both activities, and the line between them is not sharp. It is sufficient if we note (1) that checks used in making payments are drawn against commercial, but not against savings, deposits, and (2) that the short-term 30-, 60-, and 90-day loans to businessmen are peculiarly of a commercial character, whereas longer-term mortgage loans on real estate fall typically in the field of savings banking. In Part III we shall consider at length the role of commercial banks in creating part of the funds they make available, but for the present we may think of banks primarily as middlemen receiving the funds of depositors and making them available to borrowers.

Business borrowing grows largely out of the practice, described above, of depending on short-term borrowing for working capital. Firms that need funds in varying amounts may be involved in an almost continuous sequence of borrowings and repayments. These commercial loans may be unsecured, based only on the credit standing of the borrower, or they may be secured by stocks and bonds, real-estate mortgages, or warehouse receipts and bills of lading which represent commodities in storage or in transit.

Loans for three months or less do not meet fully all the business needs not met through permanent financing, and banks have increasingly extended business credit for periods of a year or more. Beside this longer term lending, banks assist in business financing, as already noted, through investing in sound corporate securities.

While bank loans go mainly to producers, *loans to consumers* are substantial. Of the numerous loans secured by real-estate mortgages, many are made to householders to assist them in the purchase and construction of homes as well as for other consumer purposes. With suitable collateral, individuals may borrow at the banks to meet any consumer need. As a matter of fact, there is no sharp line between financing production and financing consumption when credit is extended to consumers. The result is about the same whether banks lend directly to consumers to enable them to make purchases or whether business firms extend credit to customers, perhaps on an installment-payment basis, and then in turn borrow working capital from the banks for this purpose. Involved also in this process are many so-called *finance companies* which provide funds for the purchase of automobiles and other durable consumers' goods and in turn depend largely on the banks for their capital.

Banks also play a major role in *financing governments.* Indeed, in recent years, the total investments of banks in government bonds and notes have exceeded the total of their loans to private borrowers. Apart from these investments, banks have acted as agents in selling government bonds to individuals.

Miscellaneous private lending agencies

The boundary is indistinct between banks in the ordinary sense and other lending agencies. *Building and loan associations* receive deposits, as do savings banks, and make loans to home owners and builders. *Industrial* or *Morris Plan* banks specialize in unsecured consumer loans. *Credit unions* or *cooperatives* receive savings from their members and make loans to them. *Insurance companies* not only receive funds from policyholders but lend to them, and they invest heavily in mortgages and corporate bonds.

Persons with poor credit and without acceptable collateral have al-

ways had difficulty in getting money when they needed it. Their victim-
ization by sharp-dealing private lenders led long ago to the condemnation of lending at interest. Most jurisdictions now have usury laws to
prevent excessive interest charges. Loan sharks, nevertheless, still find
opportunities among desperately needy and ignorant people. The risks
of such lending are necessarily high, and even when it is conducted le-
gitimately, as by the *personal-finance companies,* funds are very expensive to the borrower when judged by ordinary interest rates. Rates may
amount to 30 percent or more on the unpaid balances of debts. Costly,
also, are funds obtained through sales of personal property to *pawn-
brokers,* with the privilege of repurchase at an increased price during a
stated period.

The government as banker

Loan making has been mainly a private activity in the United States,
but in the last third of a century the federal government has come into
the field. Government participation has had a number of aims and has
followed a variety of methods.

In its banking activities, the federal government has concentrated on
needs for funds not fully met through private banking machinery.
Often it has seemed desirable, on broad public grounds, to make loans
that do not meet the credit tests which private bankers impose. Bankers
are necessarily restrained by their obligation to their depositors and by
their investment as stockholders. Similarly government may make funds
available for particular purposes at lower interest rates than are charged
by private banks. In some instances also, the aim of government has
been to develop types of credit facilities that seemed needed by certain
classes of borrowers, for example, farmers.

Governmental banking activity has been incidental commonly to
larger policies. As part of the program of relief in a depressed period or
of promoting recovery, loans have been made to farmers and house owners so that they would not lose their mortgaged property and to business
firms to prevent bankruptcy. Government activity in this field has been
part also of the general policy of aid to agriculture and of improving the
standard of housing in the United States. Extensive loans to foreign governments have been an aspect of high policy in the international sphere.

Federal participation in the lending field has been partly direct,
partly indirect. To some extent government has stood as a middleman
between private borrowers and the final sources of funds in the taxpaying and bond-buying public. To some extent it has helped borrowers,
especially farmers, in cooperating to develop their own credit facilities.
Sometimes it has aided borrowers to get funds from private banks by
guaranteeing repayment.

The agencies that operate in this field are numerous. Under the Farm Credit Administration in the Department of Agriculture are such institutions as the banks for cooperatives and the federal intermediate credit banks; also in the Department are the Commodity Credit Corporation and the Rural Electrification Administration, which are loan-making agencies. Under the Housing and Home Finance Agency are the Home Owners' Loan Corporation and the federal home loan banks. The Reconstruction Finance Corporation has made loans of many types for many purposes. The Export-Import Bank makes numerous international loans.

What the final place will be for government in the financial sphere remains uncertain. There are observers who believe that, by making finance more largely governmental, the health of private capitalism in other fields can be promoted, but others view such a move as certain to strengthen a trend toward socialism.

Corporation Finance as a Public Problem

Finance is one of the economic areas in which government has interfered most extensively, both at state and federal levels. Unless they are restrained, dealers in money, whether in lending to small borrowers or in holding and using the funds of investors and depositors, have wide latitude for practices both loose and sharp. Popular suspicion of financial people—from the local loan shark to the Wall Street banker—is traditional, and laws to control them find ready support. Regulations have been aimed first of all at the protection of individual victims, but recognition of the general role of finance in economic organization has broadened the objectives of government control.

Of least general significance are the state laws that aim to protect small borrowers against fraud and usury. In the present discussion we need only recognize their existence; nor will anything be said of the laws that control insurance companies in handling the funds of policyholders. The regulation of ordinary banking will be considered in Chapter 11. The policies most pertinent, in concluding our discussion of production, are those which apply to the financing of business corporations. We shall note the leading reasons for public interference and the major policies that have developed.

Grounds for government action

Public control in this field is aimed at specific abuses and problems, some of which have been mentioned. But it reflects also the general belief that financial power, centered in Wall Street, had become excessive and should be curtailed. Policies should be viewed with a sense both of their specific aims and their general background.

The duping of investors. Corporate securities are perhaps the most difficult goods to buy intelligently. Ordinary consumers are amateurs in their buying and get less than they should for their money in the form of cars and clothes and groceries. But at least they actually see these things, handle them, and profit through experience in judging them. But a corporate security is an entirely different sort of thing to buy. The ordinary investor never sees the structures, equipment, inventories, and land that it represents and could not appraise them if he did. He buys a piece of paper that represents a certain fractional share in them and in the prospective earnings from them. He has little to go on, in new projects at least, beyond the glowing predictions of the promoters and security salesmen. He cannot be perfectly sure that the security represents anything at all.

Horse traders and real-estate operators have been notorious for sharp practices, but no other field has been as fertile as security trading for duping the public. Billions of dollars have been taken through outright fraud and through promotion of misrepresented projects and security issues. But the problem is not primarily one of dealing with outright swindlers. The financial virus is insidious, and in times of general optimism sober spokesmen of reputable houses make extravagant claims for the flimsiest of propositions.[5]

The perils of the investor are not limited to the purchase of securities in newly promoted mines, oil wells, and factories. Undertakings may be well established, but changes in organization may yield fancy new security offerings that no ordinary investor can interpret. Or securities offered in such corporate superstructures as holding companies and investment trusts may represent the underlying properties in a variety of obscure ways. Likewise, as we have noted, security markets may be manipulated so as to distort prices, and corporations may be run by "insiders" in ways harmful to the ordinary investor.

The mushrooming of finance. Contributing to these difficulties of the investor, and to other problems also, has been the peculiar capacity of financial institutions to make business for themselves and grow large upon it. All industries do their best to popularize their products and expand their sales. But finance, dealing not in final products but in claims to wealth, has been most skillful in multiplying its activities. Its chief role in the economy is to assist in mobilizing resources so that produc-

[5] Extensive evidence of the practices of leading firms in the 1920s was revealed by the Senate investigation that followed the stock-market collapse. Ferdinand Pecora, the chief counsel for the Senate investigating committee, gives a popular account in his book *Wall Street under Oath,* Simon and Schuster, 1939.

tion can go on—a subordinate but essential task. It has a place as well in keeping outstanding securities marketable. But a good part of the business of finance, as it reached its peak in the 1920s, was in refinancing existing productive facilities and in piling corporations on corporations and finding new and more intricate claims to wealth with which to represent existing claims. The profits were large, and the zeal to do these things accordingly great. In the furor of activity it was sometimes hard to find the kernel of real capital formation that was the justification of it all.

This development helped to set the stage for thrusting many dubious securities upon a hopeful public. It absorbed the effort of many able people in activities of questionable usefulness—a form of inefficiency from the social viewpoint. In the public-utility field it combined numerous power and gas companies in great holding-company systems which sometimes made no sense at all from the operating standpoint. Moreover, the layers of holding companies at times burdened the operating companies financially and interfered with the state commissions that regulate utility rates. Even in performing their essential services, the great investment banking companies were in position to gain influence over many companies that they helped to finance. The charge of "money monopoly" was often heard, and fears were long expressed that these houses were acquiring a dangerous power over the use of resources throughout the country and were causing a general impairment of competition in industry. Such charges have always been denied, but whatever their merit, their political influence is plain.

With the depression of the 1930s, financial developments were most criticized for their effect on general financial stability. Shaky financial structures, tottering holding companies, exaggerated movements in security prices seem to increase the vulnerability of the economy to depression and unemployment. Certainly they spur Congress in such a period to establish control over financial institutions.

Public policies

Regulation in this field is not an instance of government interference with something that might conceivably go its way without public action. The corporation itself is a product of government, and the securities it issues and the powers its officers possess result from provisions in the *state corporation laws* under which charters are granted to business firms. Leading abuses result from weaknesses in those laws and could be corrected by changing them. But corporations are formed selectively in states where satisfactory charters can be obtained, and general strengthening of the corporation laws of forty-eight states is not likely. Corrective legislation largely follows other lines.

Control of the sale of new securities. To protect investors—and indirectly to reduce financial excesses—there are statutes controlling the sale of newly issued securities. These include the state *"blue sky"* laws and, more important, the *Federal Securities Act of 1933*. The principle of these laws is extremely mild, though it may be applied severely. They do not forbid the sale of the securities of any corporation, however speculative or unlikely to succeed, nor do they insist on sound financial principles in planning the capital structures of corporations. All they do is to require that, when securities are offered for sale, all significant facts be disclosed fully and truthfully to prospective buyers. Control of this type does not violate the principle of a free economy but rather helps to apply it, for markets are not expected to provide satisfactory guidance, in the quasi-automatic working of the system, unless buyers and sellers are well informed.

Extensive governmental machinery is necessary to insure "full disclosure" in the sale of securities. At least, if control is exercised seriously, as it is by the federal government, extensive information must be required and examined before securities may be offered, and the manner of offering them must be supervised. Administering the Act of 1933 is one of the major tasks of the Securities and Exchange Commission.

Control of the sale of old securities. In one section the Act of 1933 provides against fraud in all securities sales, but it required the *Securities Exchange Act of 1934* to deal specifically with the markets in which outstanding securities are traded. These markets include both the organized stock exchanges and the over-the-counter dealers. This Act, like that of 1933, promotes full disclosure of facts, and in addition it gives broad discretion to the Commission to prevent market manipulation. It also empowers the Board of Governors of the Federal Reserve System to take certain steps, including control of marginal trading, to prevent excessive speculation. Furthermore, the Act of 1934 contains provisions aimed at mitigating the problem created by the tendency for control in large corporations to be concentrated in few hands and to be divorced from ownership. There is, for instance, an attempt to improve the proxy system of voting.

Holding-company and miscellaneous controls. In the public-utility field, in which the holding company has been most abused, pyramided organizations producing electric power and gas are subject to more drastic interference by the Securities and Exchange Commission. The SEC may positively require changes in badly balanced capital structures. It may order the complete elimination of layers of holding companies where pyramiding is excessive. Systems that are scattered geographically may be broken down into more cohesive units. The provisions of the *Public Utility Holding Company Act of 1935,* which grants these powers, aim not only at the financial problems which we are examining here but also at some of the difficulties of public-utility regulation with which we shall deal in Chapter 23. In the railroad field a similar control over corporate structures and financing is exercised by the Interstate Commerce Commission.

Other powers of the SEC relate to the reorganization of insolvent corporations, a highly technical problem in connection with which there have been many abuses. Special authority is exercised also over such matters as investment trusts and investment advisory services.

Government interference in the financing of business has not removed the need of wide knowledge and sound judgment on the part of investors, but it has removed some of the pitfalls which beset all but the most wary and sophisticated. More broadly, it has served somewhat to reduce the power of the great financial houses and perhaps to soften the impact of finance on the economy as a whole. But, since attacks on Wall Street and corporate doings in general are the stock in trade of demagogues and indiscriminating reformers, it is important that a watchful public should guard financial institutions in the performance of their necessary functions.

Review Questions

1. "It is a mistake to assume that the machinery of finance provides corporate business with all the capital it uses." Distinguish the other means of getting capital.

2. What is an investment bank; an underwriting syndicate? Explain their economic function.

3. "The volume of new securities handled by investment bankers is much greater than the volume of capital formation for which they can claim credit." Explain.

4. In August 1947 a news report stated ". . . that the experts violently disagreed on whether the upsurge in stocks in the last two months was a short term upswing in the bear market that had started last fall, or a new, rampaging bull market." [6] Explain what this statement means. What light does it throw on the stock market as a source of easy riches?

5. When the stock market crashed late in 1929, many speculators were wiped out, but some made fortunes from the decline in prices. Explain, showing what short selling involves.

6. Why are speculators wiped out by a decline? Why are they not simply the holders of less valuable securities? Explain marginal trading.

[6] *Time,* August 4, 1947.

7. If the stock exchanges are primarily markets for old securities, how can it be said that they aid corporations in obtaining capital?

8. The exchanges are among the most widely attacked economic institutions. On what grounds?

9. Distinguish the permanent and temporary capital needs of business. Why may short-term borrowing be economical? What institutions provide this assistance?

10. What are the principal demands for funds, other than for financing production? Are they important? Through what institutions are the funds obtained?

11. For what reasons may government enter the banking business?

12. Why should the financial field offer exceptional opportunities for ill-gotten gains? Why should it come to assume a disproportionate place in the economy?

13. Distinguish the three main acts administered by the Securities and Exchange Commission and relate them to the problems they are intended to solve.

PART III

Money and the Making of Payments

Money is what we are all after. For better or worse, it is the supreme economic goal. It should be the first object of economic study."

"Economics is concerned with human wants, with the products that satisfy them, with the use of resources in getting the products. Money is just a minor tool in the organization of economic life."

"Economic well-being depends on goods, not money. But it is money that makes the economy run well or badly."

These are sharply conflicting views on the place of money in economic life and on the emphasis it should receive in the study of economics. To justify serious study of money, we need not grant it a prominence as great as pecuniary matters have in everyday affairs; the dollar sign may be stamped on our every reference to income and to wealth, but the essential economic task is still the using of resources to provide the goods that people want. Yet, even as a mere tool in handling transactions and making calculations, money has so important a place in a complex society that its nature and operations deserve careful study.

But we should go further in according to money the place it has actually come to occupy. It is not merely a passive instrument, performing as directed certain essential but subordinate roles. It has a pervasive influence throughout the economy. Through its behavior it may raise or lower the general level of prosperity and change the apportionment of income among the people. Money is not the only force that has these impacts, but it is an important one and should be studied with these broad effects in mind.

237

Money enters at this point in our study because it relates directly to what has preceded and what will follow. Money is part of the organization of production viewed socially. Thus the ensuing discussion will supplement Part II. Money is also an element in the problem of depressions and business fluctuations, which is the topic of Part IV. In Part III we shall consider the nature of money in its various forms, the arrangements by which it is provided, the disturbing changes in its power to command goods, and its operation in making international payments.

- 10 -

Exchange Media: Hand-to-hand Money

IN ITS everyday sense, the word money designates the stuff that passes from hand to hand in a multitude of familiar transactions. It consists of the coins and the engraved bills and notes which are found in pocketbooks of individuals, cash registers of merchants, and tills and vaults of banks. It is what the word *currency* ordinarily implies. To make its identity unmistakable, we may call it hand-to-hand money.

It is not the only money. Indeed, in point of volume, it plays no direct part in the great bulk of all transactions. Its main role is in small dealings. When large sums change hands, the money generally used is the commercial deposits of banks, the balances against which checks are drawn. In sheer extent of use, *deposit currency,* as we shall call it, is the principal money. There are writers who hesitate to say that banks provide money but prefer to view deposit currency as a mere substitute for money. We shall need to recognize that it lacks some features that government gives to money, but we shall find it desirable, on the whole, to view deposit currency as money.

The role of banks will enter this chapter only incidentally. Here we shall deal with money matters of a more general nature and with the arrangements by which hand-to-hand money becomes available. These questions will be discussed: What are the features of economic organization that make money necessary, and how does money do the tasks assigned it? What qualities must money have to perform these tasks acceptably, and along what lines has it evolved in developing these qualities? What are the distinctive types of modern money systems and standards, with their various recognition of gold and silver and the money-printing power of government? As a basis for viewing the un-

certain future of monetary arrangements, at bottom what is the essential nature of money to which any good system must conform?

Functions of Money

In Chapter 2, in distinguishing the main features of a scheme of
production based on specialization, we noted the place of money in the
complex exchange of goods. In Chapter 3 we saw the necessity of
measuring product and income in value terms, and in Chapter 4 we saw
that value calculations are central in the whole scheme of economic
control. Values are ordinarily thought of in money terms. The basic
functions of money require further statement.

Money as medium of exchange

Even when goods are few and simple, direct barter is a crude and
awkward method of exchange; when thousands of goods, produced by
involved methods, are exchanged over wide areas, it is an impossible
method. Very seldom are the parties to transactions seeking mutually
each other's products. The textbook publisher cannot pay his workers
with volumes on calculus and economics nor can he buy his groceries
in this way. The lawyer would do badly if he had to wait for clients who
could provide the clothes he needs and the education he wants for his
children. Even when the coincidence of reciprocal wants occurred, the
values involved would be embarrassing. The automobile dealer might
want a book on salesmanship, but he would not want enough of such
books to pay for a car. Seldom could products be equated properly.
It is clear, then, that under barter modern specialized production could
not go on.

A medium of exchange that is readily acceptable and easily divisible
is the device that directly meets this situation. Through it, producers
translate their products into general purchasing power. Customers buy
their products, and what these customers have to sell is of no consequence. Enterprisers get labor and materials from workers and suppliers, and whether these people want their particular products does
not matter. With a satisfactory medium of exchange, resources can be
utilized and products disposed of with utmost facility, and consumers
can adapt their purchases flexibly to their tastes. Except under the
most primitive conditions, no instrumentality is more essential in the
effective use of productive power and satisfaction of wants. Money fills
this role because it is the one thing that everyone will accept in any
quantity at any time.

Money as a measure of value

In serving as a medium of exchange, the money a seller accepts and a buyer parts with must, of necessity, stand for a certain amount of value. If value is represented by the exchange medium, it is natural that the medium should be used as the measure, or yardstick, of value. Modern money performs both roles, and they are commonly so linked that the distinction between them is not recognized.

They are separable, however. Goods may be exchanged directly without a medium but with money still serving as the value standard. When a farm is bartered for a house in town, or corporate shares are exchanged directly for mining rights or a factory building, the basis of exchange is most conveniently arrived at in dollars and cents. Comparisons are simplified and negotiations facilitated if all products are reduced to common units.

The calculations which call for value measurements are by no means limited, moreover, to the actual exchange of goods. In most of the planning that we do, alternatives are compared in value terms, and money is the usual measure of value. If the consumer budgets his expenditures, he applies money measurement to the various lines of outlay. The producer, in deciding what and how much to produce, and what methods to employ, projects his revenues and costs in money terms, and makes up his mind accordingly. Individuals choose their occupations, in part, by comparing the probable values of their services in various fields of work. Public bodies map their policies respecting revenues and expenditures through monetary calculations. Record keeping, whether in business, government, or economic analysis, is done preponderantly in value terms and money units. Such units are the common tools of the accountant and statistician. Thus money is said to serve as a unit of account.

Money and the passing of time

Economic arrangements commonly have a time dimension. When money is viewed as a device for improving adjustments that extend through time, its services can be more fully appreciated. Two situations should be distinguished.

Storer of value. To the defects of barter, as pointed out above, another should be added. In barter a producer parts with his product and at the same time receives the product of another producer. But commonly it is more satisfactory to receive purchasing power at one time and use it at another time. The farmer may dispose of most of his year's output during a few weeks, but he must consume throughout the year. For most purposes the worker wants his return to come regularly and at short intervals, but he requires part of the return from many periods to buy furniture or a car.

A medium of exchange breaks the exchanging process into two parts, which may be separated in time. Products are sold for money, and the money can then be used at whatever rate the possessor pleases in buying the products of others. Money provides a reservoir of purchasing power, serving, it is sometimes said, as a "storer of value."

Standard of deferred payment. Time enters also through the fact that it is often advantageous to acquire goods before having the means of paying for them. Goods, we say, are obtained on credit, or else a loan is arranged in order to pay for them. In either case it is usually preferable to state the obligation in terms of money units rather than in units of some good of more restricted utility. Credit could scarcely play its important part in economic life if money were not available as a means of measuring values through time. In this role, money is often referred to as a "standard of deferred payment."

Evolution of Money

It is convenient to view together (1) the requirements that money must meet to perform these functions well and (2) the development of money in meeting these requirements. In the broad sense of a conventionally accepted exchange medium, money is a very old economic institution, extending back before recorded history. Physically it has consisted of many things with widely varying degrees of adaptation to money use; chronologically its story is mixed and lacking in order. Some aspects of money deemed valid today were recognized in ancient times, and some of the cruder exchange media are of recent use. We shall be less concerned with the sequence of these developments than with their logic.

Monetary qualities and the emergence of gold

Primitive moneys come into existence in spontaneous response to the inconveniences of barter and the need of a common value unit. But such moneys are crude in a number of ways, and money has had to undergo many changes in acquiring the qualities now thought necessary. We shall take note of the qualities that have seemed essential and of the early stages in achieving them. These qualities, it should be said, are not fully separable and coordinate.

Acceptability. Commodities of common use—things generally desired—seem always to have constituted the primitive moneys, for the first quality a money must have is ready acceptability. When a person parts with his product, not in barter for a good he expects to use but for a medium he expects to pass on to someone else, he must be confident this medium will be accepted by others. A money that emerges naturally and operates by custom must spring from the established activities and desires of the people. Accordingly, sheep and cattle served early pastoral peoples as money; wheat has similarly provided the medium in areas that produced it extensively. Less common but much needed goods such as salt and iron have also been used as money. Tobacco by the pound was a medium readily at hand in colonial Virginia, and beaver skins served on the American frontier. In their own qualities such goods carry assurance of acceptability.

These are unspecialized moneys whose service as a medium was incidental to their primary commodity role. Very likely the early steps toward a specialized medium appeared in the use as money of nonessential, ornamental goods which were prized on their own account but were easily transferable in their symbolism to the money role. After all, the shells, stones, and bits of metal that have ornamental value become even more admirable when they represent a general command over wealth. Thus various trinkets such as the wampum of the Indians seem to have achieved special standing as the accepted means of acquiring other goods. Convention or custom may supplement the ordinary utility of a good in making it acceptable as money, but complete divorce of the exchange medium from other uses is not likely until government takes over.

High value, divisibility, and the superiority of gold. For a number of reasons gold—and next to it, silver—survived the long process of selection as the commodities best suited to money use. Gold possessed universal acceptability. It was also superior in other pertinent respects —at least in comparison with other ordinary commodities.

For one thing a money should permit the handling of large transactions without embarrassment from the sheer bulk of the medium required. The precious metals have been so highly prized and so limited in quantity in relation to demand that their value has been great per unit of bulk or weight. Cattle and wheat are inferior, indeed ludicrously so, as the money to employ on shopping expeditions. For convenience in handling, gold has ranked very high among ordinary goods. A related requirement is that a satisfactory money must be nicely adaptable in amount to the values involved in transactions. Possible money materials that have high value in relation to bulk may not be divisible without loss of value. Four quarter-carat diamonds, for instance, are not equal in value to one one-carat diamond. Gold is perfectly divisible and meets this test excellently. It is also necessary that a money material should have the physical durability essential to preservation of value. Convenience of trade requires that purchasing power be kept in money form over considerable periods. The precious metals again meet this test, for they do not corrode or otherwise deteriorate.

These are the requirements of money that seem most likely to be appreciated by traders and thus most likely to explain the dominant position that gold achieved among monetary commodities.

Stability of value. A further quality—one increasingly recognized as economic life evolves—is the need of stability of value in the money unit. To be acceptable at all, money must have value, but to be a satisfactory medium, it must have a fairly steady value. Stability becomes important as the time element becomes a larger factor in economic arrangements.

From this standpoint also gold has seemed to be about the most satisfactory ordinary commodity, partly because of the durability just mentioned. Because gold is durable, the existing stock of it is large in comparison with current production, so that its supply has no sharp variations. Stability of supply helps to stabilize the value of gold, but it does not mean that the value of a money based on gold will be adequately stable. Instability of the value of money is a major problem to which Chapter 12 will be devoted.

Defects of "natural" money—the role of government

When money, in the early stages of its evolution, is merely an ordinary commodity used as a medium of exchange, government has no part in it. But as money comes to meet more exacting demands, government is called upon in a variety of ways to improve it. Governmental authority has been used to influence both the physical features and the legal status of money. In consequence, money has lost most of its character as a spontaneous development through special use of an ordinary good and tends to become simply an economic tool that government provides.

Standardization of metallic money. The most elementary function of government is in overcoming the defects of even such a money material as gold when used in its ordinary commodity state. When used without official action, gold must be measured and its quality appraised in each transaction. This is a great inconvenience; it is enough to have to judge goods without having to judge money also. The solution is to make government responsible for transforming money material into money. By standardizing the relation of pure gold and the appropriate alloys, by defining a standard money unit as a given amount of this standard metal, by stamping it into distinctive and readily recognized pieces or coins, and by giving these coins a design to deter the removal of bits of metal, government contributes greatly to the monetary qualities of the money material. Only when government performs these functions can money be accepted with confidence and used with dispatch.

Small coins and paper money. While government adds in this way to the convenience of the ordinary commodity that serves as money, it does not modify the nature of the medium; but, once government has entered the money sphere, there is a great deal more it can do and is likely to do. Once people look upon the government imprint as the basis for accepting the standard money material without hesitation, that imprint may be used on other materials. Thus, for small transactions in which coins of gold or even of silver are too small for convenience and safe handling, cheaper metals may be made into coins and given official status. For large transactions even so valuable a metal as gold becomes bulky and inconvenient to handle. It was a great step forward, therefore, when governments undertook to engrave paper certificates in a range of denominations to serve in lieu of the standard metallic money to which their equivalence was guaranteed.

The legal-tender requirement. In proceeding along these lines, government assumes the function of declaring what money is, what constitutes it. It endows coins and bills with full monetary stature by making them *legal tender*. Then they must be accepted when offered in payment of obligations. The result is that the acceptability of money comes to rest directly on an entirely different basis from the ordinary usefulness of the commodity of which it is made. What convention and custom do in some degree, government does completely and with authority.

Deposit money. From this it does not follow that people have to use official money in doing business—and they may not, if other money seems superior and they want to accept it. As a matter of fact, as already noted, most business in the United States is done with checks drawn against bank deposits. Just as paper money is superior to gold in important ways, so deposit money is often superior to engraved bills and notes. Deposit currency makes it unnecessary to carry around large amounts of money in order to be able to make substantial payments. Orders for payment may be drawn conveniently in the precise amounts that transactions require. These orders permit easy and relatively safe payments to persons at a distance. They are not legal tender but are enforceable to the extent that any private business promise is enforceable.

The changed nature of money. With this extensive use of paper money and deposit money, exchange media bear little resemblance to the moneys that develop spontaneously in primitive situations. Doubtless people's thinking regarding the nature of money changes also. Money becomes less obviously an ordinary commodity drawn into special use as a medium and appears increasingly as a specialized instrumentality established through government action for exchange purposes. Has its essential nature changed? Does its value rest on a new basis? Has the place of gold become merely formal, unrelated to essential monetary requirements? These are questions that lie at the bottom of monetary policy.

Before considering them further, we should examine more specifically the ways in which modern monetary systems are, or may, be constituted.

Money Standards and Systems

We shall consider briefly the gold standard in its traditional form and its application and evolution in this country, the varied place of silver in modern currencies, and the reliance at times on paper money not redeemable in standard money. Examples will be taken from American experience.[1]

Traditional gold-coinage system

In its underlying philosophy, a gold-standard system belongs in the cattle, tobacco, beaver-skin monetary tradition. A generally desired commodity is made the medium of exchange and measure of value; government enters to regularize the relation between gold and the money unit and to provide certain of the refinements that modern exchange requires; but, at bottom, the money is what it is because gold is what it is and not because government creates a medium or fixes its value.

Government decides on a name for the money unit—in this country, the dollar. Government links this unit to a specified amount of gold—in this country, for many years, to 23.22 grains of pure gold, or 25.8 grains of gold nine-tenths fine. Governments are likely to charge for

[1] A fuller treatment of these matters, as well as of those just discussed, may be found in such books as Raymond P. Kent, *Money and Banking*, Rinehart, 1947; Lester V. Chandler, *The Economics of Money and Banking*, Harper, 1948; Rollin G. Thomas, *Our Modern Banking and Monetary System*, Prentice-Hall, 1946.

the assaying and refining; they may impose a charge, known as *brassage,* to cover the cost of coinage; they may even impose a larger charge, known as *seigniorage,* to make the coinage function a source of public revenue. In the United States charges have been levied to cover costs, but seigniorage has been limited to silver and the baser metals which exchange in coins for considerably more than the value of the metal in them.

Free coinage. What is the procedure by which the value of gold as money is linked to its value as a commodity? On the surface it may seem that establishment of a dollar containing a specified amount of gold insures an equality of value between the dollar and this amount of gold, but such is not the case. Separation of value is quite possible and has occurred. To prevent it, free movement of gold must be maintained from one form to the other, so that, if either monetary or commodity gold tends to exceed the other in value, gold may flow from the less valuable to the more valuable use. Government provides for this freedom of movement when it establishes the scheme known as *free coinage.* Free coinage means that any one is free to bring gold in any quantity to the mint for coinage and also to melt gold coins for resale as metal. As long as a two-way movement is possible, gold must have the same value as metal and as money. Free coinage with 23.22 grains to the dollar means a price of gold of $20.67 per ounce, since an ounce contains 480 grains. Because gold is mined outside the money system and an expanding money supply is needed in a growing economy, the usual movement is toward the money system rather than away from it. The word "free," it should be noted, applies only to the freedom of movement between uses and not to the absence of a charge for coinage.

Paper money under the gold standard. It is apparent, then, that under the strict gold standard the quantity of money is not a matter of government policy but is determined by the decisions of persons who have gold and want money or who have money and want gold. If paper money is preferred to gold money as the actual medium, monetary gold can be held by the government and paper certificates issued to represent it. This is the nature of the gold certificates in American currency. Such money, which has been described as "warehouse receipts" for gold, in no way alters the money supply in actual circulation. However, various other moneys, which have long done the bulk of the active money work in our system, have been made available by the government or by banks in less rigid relation to gold. While they have usually kept equal in value to gold, so that the gold standard has been formally maintained, they have involved departure from the gold standard, in the strictest sense, by undermining the "automatic" character of the money supply. These other moneys will be considered presently.

Gold-bullion standard and the present place of gold

Once a community prefers paper to gold money for exchange purposes within the country, it is no longer necessary to turn monetary gold into coins. Gold is bought by the government at the same fixed price in any amounts offered and kept in bars of standard size and fineness. These bars are used to redeem circulating money on demand in appropriate amounts—not less than 400 ounces when Great Britain followed this policy between 1925 and 1931. The gold bars are used to make payments in foreign areas where the paper money of a nation is not accepted. Under this arrangement, which is known as the gold-bullion standard, money is linked to gold just as truly as under the gold-coinage system.

Present system in the United States. In 1934 the United States adopted a money structure which has been described as a "modified" gold-bullion system. In the previous year, as part of the Roosevelt policy of combating depression and price deflation, the nation had left the gold standard altogether. Everyone in the country was required to surrender to the Treasury both gold coins and gold certificates, and other moneys were issued in their place. An embargo was placed on the export of gold. It was not intended, however, to detach the dollar permanently from gold, and the President was given power to establish the dollar on a new and reduced gold basis. He might reduce the weight of gold per dollar by as much as 50 percent below the figure of 23.22 grains; in other words, he might raise the price of gold to double the prevailing $20.67. This change was commonly spoken of as *devaluation*. The President used his authority to the extent of raising the price of gold to $35 per ounce, and it has remained at that figure. Thus the dollar is equivalent to 13.71 grains, about 41 percent less than before, or to 15 5/21 grains nine-tenths fine. The effect of this devaluation was to raise the dollar value of the gold holdings of the Treasury by about $2,800,000,000.

Under this arrangement the gold purchased by the Treasury is not coined but is held in bullion form. Since the government will purchase as much gold as is offered at the price of $35, the effect is to hold the value of gold in the market up to that figure. On the other hand, the government does not undertake to release gold freely in exchange for money. It is for this reason that the scheme is characterized as a "modified" gold-bullion standard. The ordinary citizen is not entitled to redeem currency at will in gold bullion, but gold will be released under license for use in meeting foreign balances and for use in the arts and other nonmonetary employments. Thus, while the mechanism is present for preventing a rise in the dollar above the value of one thirty-fifth of an ounce of gold, there is no binding arrangement to prevent a fall in the dollar below that value or a rise in the price of gold above $35 per ounce. During the years following 1934 this gap in the full gold-standard character of the system had no effect, because the natural flow of gold, especially with a large expansion in gold production, was toward the Treasury rather than away from it. If there should be a tendency for the dollar to fall in relation to gold, the government may see fit to act to maintain the $35-per-ounce relationship.

The place of silver

Silver has had a varied career as a money metal and one of generally declining importance. In some periods and countries, it has been preferred over gold as the material of standard money, or it has been used along with gold in a system known as *bimetallism*. But by the time, in the depression of the 1930s, when the nations generally released their currencies from their metallic anchorage, the pre-eminence of gold was so well established that China was the sole conspicuous instance of departing from silver, rather than from gold. Mexico, in one way or another, has kept silver prominent in its money system.

Silver fractional coins. The real function of silver in the money of the United States became long ago the limited one of providing fractional coins—the dimes, quarters, and half dollars of our currency. In principle, silver in this role has no closer a relationship to standard money than have the baser metals used in nickels and pennies or the paper used in printing bills. Under the gold standard all of these moneys are tied to gold and have greater value than the material in them is worth. What the silver in silver coins is worth is of no monetary consequence unless its market value happens to become greater than the value of the coins as money. In that case they are likely to be withdrawn from circulation and melted down to recover the silver. Then, as in one instance in our history, it becomes necessary to reduce the weight of silver in the coins to protect the circulation.

Bimetallism. When Washington became President, the dollar was defined in terms of silver, but during his first term the dual system was adopted of recognizing both gold and silver as standards. The ratio between them was 15 to 1—that is, the pure silver per dollar was fifteen times as great by weight as the pure gold. The system of having two metals freely coined at a fixed ratio is known as *bimetallism*. While, from time to time, changes were made in the ratio, bimetallism remained officially in effect until 1873, when Congress provided that the unit of value should be the gold dollar of 25.8 grains, nine-tenths fine. The primacy of gold was further clarified in 1900.

To say, however, that bimetallism was officially in effect for several decades, with both metals freely coined, is not to describe the standard actually in operation. It is inherently extremely difficult (1) to keep each of two metallic moneys equal in value to their respective bullions and at the same time (2) to keep them equal in value to each other as moneys on the basis of a fixed weight ratio. Their relative values as commodities keep changing, as do the values of other goods, but the law which fixes their relationship as money cannot be adjusted continuously. Congress may fix the money ratio at 15 to 1 at a time when an ounce of gold is actually worth fifteen ounces of silver, but changes in the rate of production of the two metals—and in their nonmonetary uses—will shortly alter their relative values in the market. It may develop, for instance, that an ounce of gold becomes worth only twelve ounces of silver, although an ounce of gold provides the same number of perfectly equivalent legal-tender dollars as do fifteen ounces of silver. Under this condition, then, no one would take silver to be minted, and monetary silver would be withdrawn for commercial use. Gold, the metal that was overvalued as money, would tend in fact to become the single monometallic standard. When, in 1896, William Jennings Bryan sought to re-establish silver as standard money metal on a 16-to-1 basis, its market value was much less than one sixteenth of the value of gold. Had Bryan been successful, silver would undoubtedly have become the dominant metal in the currency.

Gresham's Law. We are here recognizing a principle long known as Gresham's Law, in deference to the sixteenth-century observation of Sir Thomas Gresham that people keep underweight coins in circulation and hoard full-weight coins. Whether the moneys involved are coins of different weight, freely coined gold and silver under bimetallism, or metallic and paper money, the principle applies. If two moneys are legal tender on an equal basis, so that they must be accepted equally in payment of debts, but if one of them comes to be recognized for some reason as more valuable than the other, people will make their payments with the less valuable money. The more valuable, under bimetallism, can be sold as bullion, or, as in the case of gold and depreciated Greenbacks during the Civil War, the gold may be parted with only at a premium. Prices are quoted in the less valuable money, which circulates more readily, and it becomes in fact the standard. All of this is what one should mean by the popular statement of Gresham's Law that "bad money tends to drive out good."

The silver-purchase policy. It was said above that, when gold was established as the standard money metal, silver was left with the minor function of providing subsidiary coins. Silver, however, has actually retained a more prominent place in the American currency than this limited function would imply. An act was passed in 1878 (and another similar to it in 1890), which required the purchase by the Treasury of large amounts of silver and provided for the coinage of so-called "standard" silver dollars. These silver dollars have not resembled standard money in principle, since free coinage was not established, and the silver dollars, instead of being tied in value to the metal of which they were made, have been kept at par with the other moneys which are attached to gold. There was never a provision for their redemption in gold, but the act of 1890 made it the duty of the Treasury to maintain all moneys at parity. The 371.25 grains of fine silver in a dollar have usually been worth far less than a dollar. Silver dollars have been a popular medium in the West—though scarcely on grounds of convenience—and silver certificates representing purchased silver have been a conspicuous part of the paper currency in the lower denominations.

An act of 1934 provided for expansion of the purchase of silver until it should constitute in value one fourth of the entire stock of money metal. Since then vast purchases have been made, but, with the gold stock tripling in amount by 1941, this goal has remained remote. Newly produced silver was bought at figures well above its price on world markets, although generally well below its monetary value of $1.29 per ounce. The effect, directly in line with the main purpose of the act, has been to raise the price of silver and improve the market of the silver industry. The industry is a minor one, but its political influence has long been great.

"Other" moneys and the money supply in the United States

To maintain at parity with gold the moneys which actively circulate, it was long ago discovered that the gold reserve need not approach 100 percent of the active medium. Since few, if any, of the holders of paper money are likely to be interested in redeeming it, the money supply can be made much larger than its metallic base without endangering its parity with gold. Taken as a whole, circulating media have only *fractional reserves.*

The gold certificate, which is the only exception in this country, no longer circulates legally but itself serves as reserve in the Federal Reserve banks. United States notes, a legacy of the Greenback era, are retained in the currency to a maximum of about $347,000,000, with a gold reserve of something over $150,000,000. National bank notes, also of Civil War origin and long a leading type of ordinary money, were secured by government bonds, supplemented by a 5-percent redemption fund. An act of 1935 called for the retirement of these bonds with the aim of removing the notes from circulation. The corresponding purpose of elevating Federal Reserve notes to the dominant place in the currency has now been conspicuously achieved. Before 1945, these notes required a 40-percent reserve of gold certificates, together with government bonds or other eligible obligations sufficient to raise the total reserve to 100 percent. Now the legal minimum reserve of gold certificates behind Federal Reserve notes is only 25 percent. Silver certificates have full silver backing on the basis of 371.25 grains per dollar, but since this amount of silver is not worth one dollar on the market, the reserve is actually fractional. Silver dollars and the fractional coins are in the same situation. As will be explained in the next chapter, the bank deposits which circulate through writing checks may be several times the size of the reserves that support them.

Money in circulation

Money is said to be in circulation when it is outside the Treasury and the twelve Federal Reserve banks. The shifting place in the total circulation of various types of money in this country is shown in the accompanying table.[2] The bearing of changing legislation on the cir-

TABLE 15—MONEY IN CIRCULATION IN THE UNITED STATES
(In millions of dollars)

	1929	1933	1940	1948
Gold	$ 368	$ 321		
Gold certificates	935	265	$ 67	$ 46
Silver dollars	44	28	46	154
Silver certificates	388	362	1,583	2,011
Silver subsidiary coin	284	257	384	903
Minor coin	115	112	169	342
United States notes	262	269	248	310
National bank notes	653	920	165	100
Federal Reserve notes	1,693	3,061	5,163	23,489
Federal Reserve bank notes	4	126	22	361
Total	$4,746	$5,721	$7,847	$27,716

[2] Figures for 1929, 1933, and 1940, which are for June 30 of each year, are from the United States Treasury as reported in the *Statistical Abstract;* 1948 figures, for April 30, are from the *Federal Reserve Bulletin,* June 1948. Treasury notes of 1890 are included with the silver certificates. Federal Reserve bank notes have been used at various times as an emergency currency. To save printing costs in the war period, a considerable quantity was issued that had been stored since the emergency issue of 1933.

culation of gold and silver and bank notes can be seen easily. It is also worth noting that the depression saw a rise and not a decline in the volume of hand-to-hand money in use. The war brought an enormous expansion, attributable primarily to the great growth in production and the methods of war financing, together with the related general rise in prices. The most striking part of the increase was in the circulation of Federal Reserve notes.

The money stock not in circulation. Apart from the money in circulation, the Treasury in 1948 had over $23 billion in gold—a figure more than five times as great as the total gold in the money system of the United States in 1929. This gold is the final reserve for the hand-to-hand money in circulation and also for bank deposits. Representing the gold were approximately $22 billion in gold certificates, most of which was held for the Federal Reserve banks. The Treasury also had about $2 billion in silver bullion. Silver in all forms, in and out of circulation, was about four times as great as in 1934 before the purchase program began.

Significance of fractional gold reserves. All of these circulating moneys, with their fractional reserves, are interchangeable. All are full legal tender and circulate at par, despite the lack of equivalent gold. (Such limitations as had existed in a few instances on legal-tender qualifications were removed in 1933.) As growing trade calls for expansion in the money supply, reliance on fractional reserves is a measure of economy, because other money materials are less costly than gold. Money provided at less than cost affords the government a "profit" which is available for meeting public expenditures. But the most significant fact is that such reliance creates latitude for government monetary policy to operate. The amount of the circulating medium is not controlled "automatically" by the quantity of gold offered to the Treasury but depends, within wide limits, on public authority and even, as we shall see presently, on the action of private bankers.

Inconvertible paper money

It is quite possible for a money system to go farther and remove completely the connection between the money in circulation and any underlying commodity such as gold. Money is then said to be *irredeemable, inconvertible,* or *fiat.* Irredeemability has usually resulted from financial emergencies, especially in war periods, when governments have exhausted their taxing and borrowing ability and have resorted to printing-press money to meet expenses. Prices shoot upward, and, if redemption in gold is not suspended, the gold stock is quickly exhausted.

The Continental currency of the American colonies followed this course in the Revolutionary period; so did the United States notes, or Greenbacks, issued during the Civil War. These were mild examples in comparison with more recent instances abroad. In the inflation following World War I, German marks fell by 1923 to less than one trillionth of their previous worth. Following World War II the Chinese dollar fell to the point by the summer of 1948 where it took 6,000,000 of them to equal one American dollar.

On the surface, at least, this experience suggests that fiat money is bad and should be avoided. Perhaps this is the conclusion that should be drawn, but it does not follow necessarily from the experience. Very possibly the trouble has arisen not from inconvertibility as such but from the financial collapse that caused resort to the printing press and expansion of the currency. Perhaps inconvertible money, if adopted deliberately under normal conditions, would be quite satisfactory. Conceivably a completely irredeemable and nonautomatic medium, created by public authority and skillfully managed, would be better than a commodity-based currency that is, after all, but the descendant of cattle, wampum, and beaver skins.

To make even a little headway with this issue, it is necessary to look farther into the essential nature of money.

Opposing Views of the True Nature of Money

The question is: Is the nature of money such that it has value only because it is attached to some nonmonetary commodity? Or does its value grow out of its use as money, and the action of government in controlling its availability? Two sharply opposed theories permeate thinking on this issue.[3]

The commodity theory

To one who looks at money in the light of its evolution, the conclusion may seem obvious that money is accepted and valued only because it consists of, or stands for, a commodity of nonmonetary importance. Indeed, without knowledge of history, one may easily believe that no one of good sense would attach value to a money not backed by real wealth in the possession of the government. From this standpoint, the logic of money seems to be that some specialized commodity, be it gold or cattle or tobacco, is prized for its own sake as an article of ordinary

[3] These theories have many variations, since the precise nature of money is one of the most elusive subjects in economics. The subject is dealt with intensively by Howard S. Ellis in his *German Monetary Theory, 1905–1933*, Harvard University Press, 1934.

use or ostentation, and, having value on this account, it confers this value on money made of it or exchangeable for it.

In presenting this idea of money, one writer first accepts the fact that the medium which passes directly in exchange consists almost entirely of "promises made by our governments or by our central banks" but then says: "These promises perform all the functions of real money only because they are promises to give real money, and because the promises not only are believed, but under ordinary circumstances are invariably fulfilled." As to what real money is, he reaches the conclu·sion, after surveying the survival value of various commodities: "The indisputable fact about our modern world is that everything else we use as money can be so used only because it consists, at one or more removes, of promises to deliver gold in a stated weight and of a stated fineness." [4] With minor variations, the same view is found in much writing on money.

From this conception of money it follows logically that a reduction in the gold equivalent of the dollar, as in the "devaluation" of 1934, must bring a corresponding fall in its value. If the money unit, as represented in paper bills and notes, becomes wholly separated from gold, the basis of its value disappears and it can be worth nothing except for the speculative possibility of later redemption. To those who hold this view, the idea that a sound currency can consist of inconvertible paper, however managed, is pernicious nonsense.

The nominalist or ticket theory

According to the other view of money, the presence of such a commodity as gold in the money system is a distinctly subordinate fact and not at all essential. It is not the exchangeability of the circulating medium for gold that qualifies it as money, but its exchangeability for goods in general. Money, like other goods, is desired and has value because it serves the purposes for which it is designed, not because it serves other quite different purposes. Money is desired as a medium of exchange and as a handy form in which to hold purchasing power. These are indispensable functions in a complex economy, and anything which will perform them is extremely useful, whether it is made of glass, leather, paper, or gold. It is no more remarkable that a tool of exchange should be valuable than that a tool for cutting wood or drawing water should be. And if this tool of exchange happens to be made of gold, or exchangeable for gold, one does not say it is valuable because gold is valuable as a commodity useful in jewelry or dentistry.

[4] From the highly readable book by Harry Scherman, *The Promises Men Live By*, Random House, 1938, pp. 256, 257, 271.

These are irrelevant facts. One says it is valuable because it performs the essential function of serving as a medium of exchange. Money is valuable simply as a *claim* to goods, a *ticket* used in exchange. This has been called the nominalist conception of money.

A medium, of course, must qualify rather unmistakably for this role, if it is to be acceptable and valuable because merely of capacity to perform it. The physical features of a hammer qualify it obviously for pounding, and lack of those features disqualifies other objects. The requirements of an exchange medium do not so clearly point toward some specific object as the one thing that will serve. Money lacks natural earmarks, and people are suspicious that spurious moneys, or moneys of declining value, will be foisted upon them. Thus it is necessary that some recognizable thing, or a number of recognizable things, should achieve money status and that other things should be disqualified. This may be accomplished by convention, by common public agreement on some object, such as wampum for instance, as money, or it may be accomplished more positively by having government establish a money and make it legal tender, so that people have to accept it in trade. It may be made of paper but, if it is the particular thing that is to serve as a medium, it will be accepted and valued because a medium is needed.

The value of things depends on their scarcity, and one trouble with a paper medium is that the quantity of it is easily increased. A money rigidly tied to gold, on the other hand, is not readily expansible. Thus, if an inconvertible money is to work at all satisfactorily, there must be some assurance that the money system will not be made the victim of every financial emergency into which the government runs. The printing presses can ruin a paper money, just as gold money would be ruined through an alchemy that readily transmuted plentiful materials into gold. But this danger has nothing to do with the nature of money, only with principles that should govern the management of money.

The commodity view of money still has staunch adherents, but it is this second, the nominalist view, which, as one writer says, constitutes "the living tradition of British-American writings on the subject." [5] On first contact, a little readjustment may be necessary in one's habitual thinking to appreciate that a dollar may be acceptable and valuable because it is a dollar and not because it represents a certain amount of gold. But if, in fact, people want dollars for use as dollars and not for conversion into gold—if, indeed, they are quite indifferent to the

[5] T. E. Gregory in his article on "Money" in the *Encyclopedia of the Social Sciences,* Macmillan, 1931.

possibilities of conversion—it is this view which would seem to be supported by common sense.

It is not strange that inconvertible money has broken down when wildly inflated. (Indeed the past breakdowns should first be charged to the gold-based currencies which did not stay convertible.) Any currency must yield in this sort of situation. When, however, the separation of money from gold has not been accompanied by overissue, there is evidence that its value is likely to be maintained. Thus, when Great Britain went off the gold standard in 1931, the domestic value of the pound remained extraordinarily steady until World War II. Likewise, when the United States' dollar was detached from gold in 1933 and related to a reduced amount of the metal the following year, its value did not behave as the commodity theory would have it. Indeed, it seems more accurate to say that gold became more valuable as its price rose to $35 per ounce than to say that the value of the dollar fell.

Nature of money and monetary policy

What may we conclude from this discussion of the nature of money? It seems that we should recognize the possibility of establishing a money on the basis of its service as money as well as through monetization of a commodity. Through its monopoly of money, a government can create distinctive exchange media, give them standing as money (presumably through making them legal tender), and adjust their quantity to the needs of trade, and a money system in every sense of the word will thereby be established. But we should not conclude from this discussion that a money so established is superior to one based on gold. That question remains open. The future place of gold in the money system of the United States and of other countries also remains undecided. However, it is clear that for a long time gold has not governed the money supply in any automatic way. With the fractional-reserve system in effect, the quantity of money attached to a given amount of gold is subject to wide variation. It may be modified by the government and it may be modified also by the banks. The role of the banks in supplying money is the topic of the following chapter.

Review Questions

1. What is meant by hand-to-hand money? From what other main type of money should it be distinguished?

2. Distinguish the main difficulties of barter, and show how they are overcome through the use of money.

3. "It is natural that the need for a medium of exchange and a measure

of value should be met with the same device. But one of these functions may, nevertheless, be performed without the other." Explain. Point out several uses of a measure of value.

4. Show how the usefulness of money grows in part out of the time factor in economic life.

5. Distinguish the leading qualities that should be possessed by a satisfactory money. Does gold possess these qualities in a superior degree (*a*) as compared with other commodities of ordinary use; (*b*) as compared with the moneys now used in transactions in the United States? Is there any point in distinguishing the qualities of a satisfactory money *material* and of a satisfactory money *system*?

6. "The first monetary duties of government are in improving the usefulness of the standard money material, but government has gone much farther than this in developing the money supply." Explain. Show the significance of giving money legal-tender status.

7. Explain the central place of free coinage in maintaining the traditional type of gold-standard system. Why is the money supply said to be automatically controlled? Was the money supply really controlled automatically in the United States before 1933?

8. How does the gold-bullion standard differ from the traditional gold-standard system? How does the present system in the United States differ from the gold-bullion standard? In what circumstances might the dollar depart from its present relationship to gold? Would the price of gold go above or below $35 per ounce?

9. Distinguish three roles that silver has had in the money system of the United States. Does its role under the Silver Purchase Act of 1934 seem essential? How is the policy to be explained?

10. "Bimetallism may be established by act of Congress but, in fact, history indicates that only one metal is likely to function as the standard." Why should this be the case? Apply Gresham's Law to this situation.

11. What have been the major changes in the types of hand-to-hand money in use in the United States in the last twenty years?

12. How is it possible to keep the entire money supply at a parity with gold without having it attached to a 100 percent gold reserve? What are the advantages (or effects) of fractional reserves?

13. What is fiat money? How successfully has it ordinarily worked? Distinguish two possible explanations.

14. "The government is knocking 40 percent out of the value of the dollar. If your product has brought you 60 cents, you will have to get $1 for it now to get the same return." Does this statement, which might have been heard in 1933–34, reflect a commodity or nominalist conception of the value of money? Explain carefully. If you were to explain why gold mining was more profitable after devaluation than before, which conception of money would you use?

~ 11 ~

Exchange Media:
Deposit Currency

BEYOND question the great majority of transactions have as their medium the ordinary, hand-to-hand money that government supplies. These transactions include innumerable small purchases at retail. But in dollar amount a major part of the aggregate of transactions is carried out through the use of the deposit currency which banks provide. These transactions include many of the larger purchases at retail, the buying of materials and supplies by business enterprises, much of the purchase of labor, and nearly all the transactions involving real estate, securities, and other forms of wealth and claims to wealth. The vast dealings of governments, also, are handled by means of checks. Probably 85 or 90 percent of all business in this country involves the use of the deposit medium.

Regarding it a number of questions must be considered. What exactly is it that circulates when checks are used as means of payment? How, if this medium does not consist of legal-tender money, can it be made to circulate as a substitute for, or supplement to, such money? Since it is made available by banks, how is it related to the operations of banks as financial middlemen? What is the process by which this medium comes into being and is permitted to expand far beyond the reserve that supports it, making it a highly variable element in the money supply? What limits govern its amount and how, if at all, can that amount be controlled in the public interest? These are the questions with which the present chapter deals.[1] In considering them we shall be concerned with the money mechanism directly, and indirectly with the bearing of money on general economic stability.

[1] There are many books which deal at length with the relationship of banks to the money supply. Among them are the books by Raymond P. Kent, Lester V. Chandler, and Rollin G. Thomas cited in Chapter 10, note 1.

The Banks Involved

In Chapter 9, in considering the service of banks in mobilizing resources for production, we recognized three types of banks or banking functions: investment, savings, and commercial. Now, in inquiring into the relationship of banks to the money supply, we shall be concerned solely with commercial banking. Only banks doing a commercial business carry the demand deposits against which checks are written and therefore contribute directly to the money supply. Behind the commercial banks stands the Federal Reserve System, whose task it is to relate private action to public policy. A few facts regarding these institutions should introduce our analysis of their functions.

Commercial banks

Of 14,714 banks reported to be in operation in this country on December 31, 1947, all but the 533 which belonged in the category of mutual savings banks did a commercial banking business and carried demand deposits. Of these 14,714 banks, 5005 were organized with federal charters under the National Banking Act. These national banks, together with 1918 state banks that had acted by choice rather than legal requirement, constituted the membership of the Federal Reserve System. This total of 6923 member banks accounted for 85 percent of the total demand deposits of the banking system.

Federal Reserve banks

While the deposits used in making private payments are found in the banks just enumerated, the power of the banking system to expand deposits depends in considerable measure on the 12 Federal Reserve banks. These banks, which are the focus of the credit facilities of the 12 regions into which the country is divided for banking purposes, are often referred to as bankers' banks.[2] They do not conduct an ordinary banking business, but they hold as deposits the reserves of the member banks and make loans, as called on, to the member banks. In addition they perform other important services which we shall note as we proceed.

The Federal Reserve banks are owned by the member banks, which subscribe the capital on a basis fixed by law. Six of the nine directors of each Federal Reserve bank are selected by the member banks of

[2] In the order in which the regions are numbered, the 12 Federal Reserve banks are located in Boston, New York, Philadelphia, Cleveland, Richmond, Atlanta, Chicago, St. Louis, Minneapolis, Kansas City, Dallas, and San Francisco. In most of the districts, these banks have one or more branches located in other cities.

the district, and the other three by the Board of Governors of the Federal Reserve System. This Board, consisting of seven members appointed by the President of the United States, exercises a dominant control over Federal Reserve policy. It is through the Board that government exercises its main influence over the supplying of exchange media by banks.

Deposit Currency—Nature and Circulation

To appreciate the role of banks in providing a distinctive medium of exchange, it is first necessary to sense the exact nature of the medium provided and to understand the manner of its circulation.

Nature of deposits as a medium of exchange

Confusion is common as to what a deposit is. When it is said that payments are made by writing checks against deposits, the deposits referred to are *bank debts*. They are promises on the part of the bank to pay depositors specified sums on demand. These sums constitute the balances, or checking accounts, of the depositors. A deposit is nothing more than an obligation of the bank to the depositor. This point is stressed, because deposits are often thought of mistakenly as money in the bank or as money put in the bank.

It is true that a deposit may be established by bringing currency into a bank and leaving it there, although most deposits do not arise in this way. But even when deposits are created by depositing hand-to-hand money, the money does not constitute the resulting deposit. The money that is deposited adds to the cash of the bank and is reflected on the left-hand side of the bank's balance sheet in an increase in the *asset* cash. The resulting deposit, on the other hand, is reflected on the right-hand side of the balance sheet in an increase in the *liability* deposits. Since deposits arise in other ways than through the deposit of currency, the size of the deposit item tells nothing at all as to the amount of legal-tender money held by the bank.

It is these deposits, these obligations of banks to make payments, which constitute the medium of exchange with which we are now concerned. A check transfers a portion of the depositor's claim against the bank to another person whose name appears as payee on the check. The check itself is not the medium of exchange but simply the device through which deposits circulate, just as the transfer of hand-to-hand money makes it circulate. When statistics appear of the total money supply on a certain day, beside the figures for hand-to-hand money in circulation (see page 252) appears the total of deposits subject to check. The checks written on a given day would not be significant in such a total.

Deposits as a credit medium. The word *credit* is often used in various ways in speaking of the use of deposits as a medium of exchange. The process is sometimes called credit exchange or the medium is called credit currency or bank credit. These are not terms we shall use, but the warning is called for that the medium we are discussing has no relationship to credit in the postponement-of-payment sense. The only connection is verbal, but lines of thinking often become snarled through verbal resemblances. A deposit, if one pleases, may be thought of as a credit claim against a bank, but the use of it to make payments implies nothing at all as to whether goods are paid for when received or later.

Thus the man who buys a $100 radio on a $10-down-and-$10-a-month basis and makes each payment with a $10 bill provides an example of credit in the sense of obtaining goods prior to possession of the cash to pay for them, but he does not provide an example of the use of credit as a medium of exchange. His medium is hand-to-hand money. Another man who buys a like radio and pays for it when he gets it, giving the merchant a $100 check, exemplifies the use of the credit medium—deposit currency—though there is no extension of credit to defer payment to a later time. We are concerned with credit as deposit currency.[3]

Separateness of the deposit medium. One other point should be stressed as to the general nature of deposit currency as a medium of exchange. Its use as a medium actually displaces, or obviates, the use of ordinary money. Deposits are claims to ordinary money, and so are the checks written against them, but when we speak of deposits serving as a medium for a certain volume of transactions, we mean that ordinary money is not used for those transactions. The process is not one in which checks pass from hand to hand in the foreground with similar movements of ordinary money occurring somehow in the background, shadowy duplicates of the surface phenomena. When deposit currency performs fully its function as a medium, ordinary money does not move. Its transfer is obviated now and later. The transfer of deposits is the fulfillment of payment.

The clearing principle

Thus we are confronted with one of the important questions presented by the use of deposit currency. How can mere claims to legal-

---

[3] When we speak, as we shall presently, of banks *extending credit* to customers, we shall have the lending function of banks in mind. The borrower is to pay the bank at a later time, and the bank has a claim against him.

tender money circulate in such a way as to make the movement of currency unnecessary? The answer is found in the process by which credit claims are made to offset each other—in other words, through the operation of the *clearing principle*.

Let us look at this process first from the standpoint of a person employing deposit currency as the medium of exchange. Such a person receives payment for his services or product in the form of checks drawn by other persons against their deposits. These checks he deposits, and against the account thus built up he writes checks to pay for the goods he buys. In principle he uses his claims against others to meet the claims of others against him. In the process these claims are all converted into claims against banks—that is, into deposits—and payments are received and made through the transfer of deposits.

Let us look at the process next from the standpoint of the banks and of the mechanism established by them to make the clearing principle operate. This mechanism should be viewed at several levels, distinguished according to the number and the location of the banks involved. The first level is that of payments between persons who do business with the same bank. Here the procedure requires only the regular bookkeeping operations of the bank. When checks change hands, the sums specified on them are deducted from the balances of the persons who write them and added to the balances of the persons who receive and deposit them. The second level involves payments between persons who patronize different banks in the same community. Here we have the operation of the so-called clearing house. The third and fourth levels, involving payments between persons in different communities, are distinguished as to whether the parties are in the same or in different Federal Reserve districts. For these transactions the Federal Reserve System provides the principal clearing mechanism. There is finally the clearing of payments between persons in different countries, which we shall consider in Chapter 13.

The clearing house. The several banks of a community are ordinarily organized in a clearing-house association. The clearing house is an arrangement through which each bank is able to use the checks received and honored by it but drawn on other banks in the association to offset the checks drawn on it but received and honored by the other banks. The checks thus received are brought by a messenger from each bank to a common meeting place, and here a balance is struck, usually once every day.

Suppose on a certain day that Bank *A* receives checks totaling $40,000 drawn on Bank *B* and checks totaling $31,000 drawn on Bank *C;* that *B* receives checks totaling $48,000 drawn on *A* and checks totaling $34,-

000 drawn on *C;* and that *C* receives checks totaling $26,000 drawn on *A* and checks totaling $37,000 drawn on *B*. Then the situation, including the totals owed to and by each bank, is as follows:

	Owed by *A*	Owed by *B*	Owed by *C*	Total claims
Owed to *A*	$.. ...	$40,000	$31,000	$71,000
Owed to *B*	48,000	.. ...	34,000	82,000
Owed to *C*	26,000	37,000	.. ...	63,000
Total obligations	$74,000	$77,000	$65,000	$216,000

The checks brought in by each bank constitute its claim against the clearing, and the checks on it brought in by other banks constitute its obligation to the clearing. For any one bank a perfect offset is unlikely. Thus, in this example, Bank *A* owes the clearing $3000 ($74,000 minus $71,000), Bank *C* owes the clearing $2000 ($65,000 minus $63,000), and Bank *B* is owed a net balance of $5000 ($82,000 minus $77,000). Thus practically all of the claims of the banks against each other are canceled, and deposit currency provides the final means of payment for a large volume of business.

For the total of $216,000, only $5000 is needed to settle the balances. This sum might be transferred in the form of currency but probably will not be. There are several ways of avoiding this small use of hand-to-hand money, one of which is resort to the Federal Reserve mechanism used in intercity payments.

Intercity clearing. There is no clearing house in the sense just described to apply the clearing principle when checks are used in transactions involving persons in different communities, but the principle is applied nevertheless. Formerly it depended on a system of balances in correspondent banks—a matter we need not go into. Now it is carried out chiefly through the clearing arrangement that is one of the services of the Federal Reserve System. Each member bank of the System keeps its reserve in the form of a deposit with the Federal Reserve bank of its district. When an out-of-town check is deposited by one of its customers, it sends the check to the Reserve bank and the sum is added to its deposit balance there. If the check was drawn on another bank in the same Reserve district, it is only a matter of bookkeeping to deduct the sum from the balance of this other bank. Then the check is sent to the bank on which it was drawn, and the sum is substracted from the balance of the person who wrote the check.

If the check was drawn on a bank in another Federal Reserve district, the clearing of it entails payment from one Reserve bank to another. This is accomplished also without the transfer of hand-to-hand money through a shifting of balances in an *Interdistrict Settlement Fund* maintained by the 12 Federal Reserve banks for this purpose. Since both member banks and Reserve banks are involved in a steady flow of claims in both directions, the clearing process largely eliminates the movement of currency.

Deposit Currency—Expansion and Limitations

The first step in understanding deposit currency is to see what it is and how it circulates. The second step—and the primary one in importance—is to see how commercial banks create deposit dollars and thus expand the money supply. A related matter is the limitations that banks must recognize in expanding deposits—the problem of bank reserves and reserve ratios.

Loans as a source of deposits

Commercial banking expands the volume of exchange media by combining demand deposits with lending operations. It is important to see that this *money-creating function* does not lie in lending operations alone nor in the nature of demand deposits alone but in the combination of the two. This point becomes clear if each is examined with the other, and then they are combined.

Loans without demand deposits. Suppose that banks perform their role as financial middlemen, receiving deposits and making loans, but that the deposits are *saving* or *time* deposits, not the *demand* deposits against which checks are written. Then when A makes a cash deposit of $1000, he gives up the use of that money until the deposit is withdrawn. The bank lends the $1000 to B, and he, instead of A, has the use of the money. In effect A's savings are spent by B, and no additional money becomes available through the operation of the bank.

Demand deposits without loans. Suppose, on the other hand, that the deposit is of the demand variety against which checks are drawn but that the lending operation is absent. C has $1000 of currency but wants to use checks in making payments, so he deposits the currency and is given a credit suitable for his purpose. He then has the use of $1000 in deposit currency, but the $1000 of ordinary money is kept as reserve by the bank. Thus it is retired from active circulation, and again the total medium in actual use is unchanged.

Combination of demand deposits and loans. The creation of additional currency by commercial banks came about when it was discovered that a 100-percent reserve of ordinary money need not be kept behind deposits, even though they are payable on demand. It is no more necessary than a 100-percent reserve of gold in keeping paper money at par. Demand deposits are but slightly withdrawn in the form of hand-to-hand money, and the checks drawn against them are usually in turn deposited, so that the reserve is mostly idle. Why, then, should banks not use this money or part of it in profitable lending operations?

Accordingly the bank that receives C's $1000 proceeds to lend part of it. It lends $500 in currency to D. The result is a 50-percent increase in the circulating medium. C has $1000 to use in deposit currency, and D has $500 in ordinary money—both equally effective as exchange media. The bank, in other words, has added substantially to the money supply in the course of its operations.

More typically, however, the borrower does not want his loan in the form of ordinary cash. When D borrows, he wants a checking account. So the bank writes up his balance, giving him $500 of deposit currency to use. Again, the result is a total money supply of $1500, whereas there had been only $1000 before. But a vital difference appears now in the power of the bank to make further loans. When the loan of $500 to D was in currency, the reserve of the bank was reduced by $500, but when the loan is made in the form of a demand deposit, the power of the bank to make loans appears on the surface to be undiminished. There are limits, we shall see presently, but it is apparent that the power of banks to expand the currency in this way is very great.

Investments as a source of deposits

Loans in the ordinary sense, evidenced by the promissory notes of borrowers, are only one of the ways in which banks extend credit and thus expand the money supply. Another outstanding way is through investment in bonds. The bonds may have been issued by business corporations, but for the most part bank investments are in government bonds. If it is recalled that a bond is simply evidence of a small fractional part of a large loan, it will be clear that there is not much difference in principle whether banks made loans or investments.

The point to be appreciated is that the loans and the investments have the same effect on deposits and the money supply. The seller of the bond, governmental or corporate, usually does not want hand-to-hand money but wants instead the use of a deposit. Thus the bank need not part with cash reserve in paying for the bond but makes the payment, just as it makes an ordinary loan, in the usual deposit form. This deposit becomes part of the total exchange medium and proceeds to circulate as checks are drawn against it and are in turn deposited by the recipients.[4]

[4] Immediately, a bank may part with funds in buying government bonds, drawing on its reserve balance in paying for them. But, if it does, the funds are presently spent by the government and, when deposited, become part of the bank reserves again. The deposits

The most striking change in commercial banking in the last twenty years is the relative decline of short-term commercial loans and the relative expansion of investments. The great increase of bank credit during World War II occurred mainly through the purchase of United States government bonds by the banks. Deposits credited in the first instance to the government were checked against to pay for ships and planes and munitions, and, in turn, were used by the supplying firms to make income payments to the owners and workers of industry, who could spend or save them as they saw fit. Thus investments should be stressed as much as loans in explaining the expansion of deposit currency.

Immediate and ultimate sources of deposits

Most additions to the deposits of any one bank are not directly the result of loans and investments it has made. To an observer standing at a teller's window in a bank, it would appear that most deposits are made by bringing checks and ordinary money to the bank. But these deposits do not *expand* the quantity of exchange media available for use. They merely represent a step in the circulation of existing media. Merchants receive ordinary money and deposit it at the bank. Other persons cash checks to get ordinary money to pay to merchants. Recipients of checks deposit them, and the result is a transfer of deposit currency from one person's balance to another's. Demand deposits are subject to much activity of these kinds—without any expansion in their aggregate amount. But when banks make loans and investments, writing up their customers' balances in the process, they do add to the circulating medium. These deposits may be only a small part of the total a given bank receives, but they are the significant part from the standpoint of the money supply of the nation.

Banking operations

This monetary function of banks may be appreciated better if we look briefly at the nature and peculiarities of commercial banking as a type of business. Consider a simplified example.

Let us suppose that certain persons start a bank by contributing a capital of $125,000 in payment for 1000 shares of common stock (par value $100) at $125, thus creating an initial surplus of $25,000. After $30,000 has been invested in the necessary physical facilities, $95,000 remain for banking operations. This sum, held partly in cash and partly in deposits in other banks, will serve as till money and provide

---

which result from bank investments continue as part of the money supply with no corresponding reduction until the bonds are retired.

a reserve to meet obligations that develop. At this stage a balance sheet of the undertaking appears as follows:

Assets		Liabilities and Proprietorship	
Cash and due from banks	$ 95,000	Capital stock	$100,000
Building and fixtures	30,000	Surplus	25,000
Total	$125,000	Total	$125,000

Banking operations commence, and a number of deposits are made by persons who are shifting their balances from less convenient banks. These total $15,000. Assets in the form of cash and claims against other banks increase; liabilities in the form of deposits increase correspondingly. A merchant borrows $1000 to enable him to pay for merchandise, and accepts the loan in the form of a deposit. To the bank the loan is an asset, since it is a claim against the merchant. Offsetting it is the merchant's right to draw $1000 from the bank.[5] After these transactions, the balance sheet reads:

Assets		Liabilities and Proprietorship	
Cash and due from banks	$110,000	Capital stock	$100,000
Loans	1,000	Surplus	25,000
Building and fixtures	30,000	Deposits	16,000
Total	$141,000	Total	$141,000

Operations of the bank continue to expand. It performs numerous small services, as in making collections and in receiving and paying out cash to meet the convenience of its customers, both in their capacity as businessmen and as consumers. As it proves its usefulness and grows in the confidence of the community, its deposits expand considerably, both through further shifts of funds from other banks and through its extension of credit to customers. Along with its loans, it acquires earning assets in the form of the bonds of corporations and governmental bodies. As it expands, it gains in cash and in the balances it holds in other banks. But funds flow from it as well as toward it, and when grown to what will be its normal place in the community, it finds that funds flow in and out at about the same rate. This means, in particular, that claims against it in the clearing process just about equal its claims on other banks. After a period of development, its condition is as follows: [6]

[5] Commonly interest is deducted in advance—the borrowers' note, in other words, is *discounted*. Thus, if the merchant borrows $1000 for 90 days at 4 percent, he receives $990.

[6] In this simple example there is no separate recognition of savings deposits nor of the undivided profits that would appear as a supplement to the surplus account as net earnings are retained in the business. Various minor items are also ignored.

Assets		Liabilities and Proprietorship	
Cash and due from		Capital stock	$ 100,000
banks	$ 260,000	Surplus	25,000
Loans	335,000	Deposits	950,000
Investments	450,000		
Building and fixtures	30,000		
Total	$1,075,000	Total	$1,075,000

At this point the bank joins the Federal Reserve System. In doing so, it must invest funds equal to 3 percent of its capital and surplus in the stock of the Federal Reserve bank of its district, thus becoming part owner of that bank. It must also place with the Federal Reserve bank a balance equal to the minimum legal-reserve requirement for the class of bank to which it belongs—a matter to be considered presently—and only this balance will be counted as its legal reserve. Beside its reserve, it will have available a sum of cash in its own vaults and tills and certain balances with other banks that it will see fit to retain. The "cash and due from banks" in the above statement may now be more specifically assigned as follows:

Cash	$ 16,250
Due from Federal Reserve bank	200,000
Due from other banks	40,000
Federal Reserve bank stock	3,750
	$260,000

Risk and profit ratios. Two striking features of banking operations may be seen clearly in this example. One is the typically low ratio of the cash assets of a bank—the "cash and due from banks" ($260,000 in this case)—to the deposit liabilities ($950,000) which the bank is obligated to meet in cash whenever called upon. It is because of this low ratio that a "run," a sudden movement of depositors to demand cash, can "close" the strongest bank very quickly. This fact testifies to the general high faith that people have in banks and to the strong preference they have for keeping their cash balances in the form of checking accounts.

The other feature is the typically high ratio of the earning assets of banks—revealed in the loan and investment accounts ($785,000)—to the capital provided by the owners—reflected in capital and surplus ($125,000). Banking is outstandingly a business conducted with "other people's money" and with funds which emerge from the banking process itself, so that the owner's equity appears strikingly small when comparison is made with other fields of activity. It is sometimes asked how a bank can get a gross return ranging from perhaps 6 percent to less than 1 percent on its loans and investments, defray from this interest income the considerable expenses of its operations, and then perhaps be able to pay dividends to the owners of 10 or 20 percent, as the more profitable banks often do. The answer lies, of course, in the great difference between the magnitudes to which these percentages apply. Two percent net on $785,000 is more than 12 percent on $125,000.

Practical limit on deposits—need of reserves

If borrowers take their loans in the form of deposits and recipients of the checks drawn against these deposits in turn deposit them, so that the deposits go on circulating without being converted into cash, the possibility of credit expansion is very great. Since banks get their incomes from lending, they are naturally inclined to expand this process as fully as they can, and the possible expansion on this basis seems to have practically no limit.

Actually, however, though deposit dollars have an amazingly prolific source, their expansion is subject to severe practical limitations. Demand deposits are what the name implies. The depositor may convert his claim against the bank into cash at any time and often does so. Similarly checks drawn against deposits are often cashed by the recipients. More serious is the possibility for the individual bank that checks drawn against it and deposited in other banks will exceed the checks drawn on other banks that it receives. Adverse clearing balances thereby arise which require payments to other banks.

Thus a bank must face the practical question of how large its deposits may safely become in relation to its cash resources. Whether these considerations should cause a bank to hold its deposits to a multiple of twenty or ten or five or two times its reserves cannot be decided on abstract grounds but only on the basis of experience. Any answer, moreover, is a compromise. A complete collapse of confidence would embarrass a bank unless its cash resources approximated its demand liabilities. But human beings do not organize their affairs with an eye to the most catastrophic possibilities; instead they proceed by balancing dangers against the advantages of less cautious courses of action. Good judgment ordinarily implies behavior that works most of the time. In banking it should imply a conservatism that makes losses to depositors extremely rare.

Limits imposed by law—legal reserves behind deposits

A sufficient prudence on the part of bankers in expanding loans and deposits would render unnecessary the enforcement of legal restraints.

There are countries in which the law has imposed no requirements; but so great is the temptation to expand earning assets and, in consequence, deposits that, on the basis of American experience, it has seemed desirable to enforce restrictions on credit expansion. Restrictions take the form of stipulated minimum reserve ratios.

A reserve ratio is a percentage relation between the legal reserve of a bank and its deposit liabilities. Prior to the Federal Reserve Act, banks might count as part of their legal reserve both the cash in their vaults and, within limits, the balances they held in correspondent banks. Now, in the case of member banks, no cash is counted and only the balances held in Federal Reserve banks. The reserve ratio fixes the maximum size of deposits in relation to the legal reserve. If the ratio is 10 percent, deposits may be 10 times the reserve; if the ratio is 20 percent, deposits may be 5 times the reserve.

Loans and reserves. It will be noted that loans and investments do not figure in the reserve ratio. They are assets, and no reserve behind assets is necessary. But the legal reserve ratio restricts, nevertheless, the expansion of loans and investments. When a bank provides funds to borrowers or bond issuers, its actual reserve ratio is reduced, either because it loses funds or because it expands its deposits. It may lose funds because it draws on its reserve in paying for bonds. Similarly the larger deposits resulting from loans mean more checks going to other banks and loss of funds in the clearing process. The enlarged deposits that stay with it directly reduce the ratio of its reserve to its deposits.

In the above example, a reserve with the Federal Reserve bank of $200,000 and deposits of $950,000 give an actual reserve ratio of slightly over 21 percent. Expanding loans and investments would probably both reduce the $200,000 and increase the $950,000. Either change would reduce the ratio. Thus if the legal minimum ratio of this bank were 20 percent, it could expand its earning assets only slightly. This figure of 20 percent is hypothetical, but it is fairly representative. Legal reserve ratios differ among classes of banks, and for any one class they are adjusted from time to time. Data regarding them under the Federal Reserve System will appear in the following section.

The individual bank versus the aggregate of banks

We must now examine a paradox which lies at the heart of the process by which loans and deposits are expanded. A bank subject, say, to a 20 percent reserve requirement and possessed at the moment of more reserve than it needs cannot safely expand by five times the amount of its excess reserve. Its expansion is limited approximately to the amount of its excess reserves. And yet that bank may safely have deposits that are five times its reserves. More important, banks in the aggregate, when they have reserves above the prescribed minimum, may expand by five times the excess, or by whatever multiple corresponds to their average reserve requirement. How can these statements be reconciled?

The answer lies in the clearing relationship, in the danger faced by the individual bank of losing part of its reserve to other banks. When a bank has found its normal place in the community, it neither gains nor loses funds on the average in the clearing process. But if, when in this position, it expands its loans and deposits, it will lose funds. Borrowers use the funds they borrow, and most of the checks they write are likely to go to people who trade with other banks. Thus a bank may lose reserve to the full amount of its new loans and deposits. A bank, then, cannot safely lend more than its excess reserve, because its reserve may be diminished by this full amount.

But when the funds it loses are deposited in other banks, they acquire excess reserves, since their required reserve is only a fraction of the deposits transferred to them. Thus they may expand their loans and deposits. It is only from the standpoint of the individual bank that excess reserves are lost, not from the standpoint of the aggregate of banks. An addition to the reserve of one bank, not immediately paralleled by additions in other banks, will spread among the banks much as water, poured at one point into a pond, spreads evenly over the entire pond. Since banks are required to hold only fractional reserves of perhaps 10 percent or 20 percent, deposits may go on expanding among the aggregate of banks until they become the permitted multiple of any addition to reserves. This result for the aggregate of banks is achieved through each bank following the conservative rule of lending no more than its excess reserves but continuing to lend that much as long as excess reserves appear.[7] The individual banker, lending funds as they come to him in excess of his reserve requirements, may be quite unaware that he is part of a process by which the banking system creates a medium of exchange greatly in excess of the reserve on which it rests.

Strengthening of the reserve position—credit contraction

We have been discussing the expansion of bank credit. Contraction may also sometimes be necessary in the interest of safety and the meet-

[7] This process can be illustrated by assuming that a bank with a 20-percent ratio receives a cash deposit of $1000, for which it requires a reserve of $200, leaving a free reserve of $800. It lends the $800 in the form of deposit balances, and in the clearing this sum is lost to other banks. For their $800 of deposits they need a reserve of $160 and can lend $640. Continuing this series, with successive numbers declining by one fifth, a total of $5000 is finally reached, or five times the cash originally received.

ing of reserve requirements. How can a bank, faced with an inadequate reserve, improve its position? It can do so by reducing its earning assets. With numerous short-term loans outstanding, some of which are maturing every day, it can refrain from making new loans as old ones are repaid. Or it can sell some of the securities in which it has invested. The effect of such action is likely to be both a reduction in its deposits and an increase in its reserve—an improvement, that is, in both ends of its reserve ratio.

Such protective action may seem easy, and perhaps it ordinarily is from the standpoint of a single bank acting by itself. But if the general business situation has taken a turn that puts many banks in the same position, where will a bank find buyers for the securities it wants to sell? If many banks are offering their holdings for sale, an adequate market may not be available and such sales as occur may involve sacrifice prices that threaten the fundamental solvency of the banks.

And what is the effect when many banks terminate loans without replacing them? To find the answer one needs only to reverse the analysis of loan creation. As the making of loans expands the volume of deposit currency in circulation, so loan contraction reduces the volume. As the creation of deposit currency enables borrowers to buy additional goods, so its contraction reduces their ability to buy goods. The proceeds from the selling of products have to be used to repay the banks. Deposit dollars vanish from the scene with effects that may be most serious, intensifying progressively the business situation that first caused the banks to contract.

Reserve requirements are necessary, but the limitations they impose may be harmful, especially when credit is contracted to strengthen the reserve position of banks. It was to cope with problems of this nature that the Federal Reserve System was created.

Review Questions

1. Among United States banks other than investment banks, how numerous are commercial banks? Are national banks? Are member banks of the Federal Reserve System? How important are the latter among all banks? What are the Federal Reserve banks?

2. "Ordinary money may be deposited in a bank, but deposits are not ordinary money. Use of deposit currency means the circulation of bank debts." Explain.

3. "Deposit currency is a credit medium. Therefore, to say that 85 or 90 percent of the business done in the United States is done with deposit currency as the medium of exchange is to say that payment is postponed in that volume of business." Show clearly the nature of the error.

4. "It is all very well to speak of bank deposits serving as money, but they are not legal tender, and ordinary money still has to move behind the scene." Show the error.

5. "Deposits circulate through the operation of the clearing principle—the offsetting and canceling of claims." Explain, showing how the principle is applied in intracity and intercity transactions.

6. Explain how the lending operation of banks, in combination with the use of deposit currency, enables banks to add to the money supply.

7. Show that the investments of banks have the same effect on the money supply as loans do.

8. "A run can close the strongest bank." Explain.

9. We saw in Chapter 9 how corporate enterprisers gain financial leverage through the capital they borrow. Show that banking provides an extreme example of such leverage.

10. "If people who receive checks deposit them, there is no limit to the possible expansion of deposit currency." What is the point? Show that there are limits.

11. "It is a safe condition for a bank to have $1,000,000 of deposits and $200,000 of reserve. Therefore, if a bank receives $10,000 in cash deposits, it can lend $40,000, provided borrowers accept a write-up of their balances." Discuss critically.

12. What is a legal reserve ratio? Why does a reserve ratio limit the *loans* of a bank?

13. "The individual banker, in lending only as much as his excess reserves, is part of a process which expands deposit currency to several times the reserve on which it rests." Explain. What is the significance of adverse clearing balances?

14. The following items appear in the balance sheet of a member bank: demand deposits, $3,800,000; cash, $700,000; United States bonds, $2,200,000; surplus, $500,000; balance with Federal Reserve bank, $900,000; capital stock, $1,000,000; loans, $1,500,000. Assuming these are the only items, arrange them in balance-sheet form. If this bank is subject to a 20 percent reserve requirement, how large is its excess reserve? How much can it safely expand its loans? Show the effect on its balance sheet. What expansion is possible if all other banks are in the same position and expand along with this bank? Explain.

15. Explain what happens to the total volume of deposit currency when banks reduce their loans. Can you explain what happens when the United States government retires bonds held by commercial banks?

The Federal Reserve System

Among leading nations the United States was slow in unifying its banking resources and establishing central control over bank credit.

Financial crises with widespread bank closings had occurred repeatedly when, following the panic of 1907, studies were initiated that led to the passage in 1913 of the Federal Reserve Act. The plan adopted was a compromise which undertook, through twelve regional banks, to recognize the dissimilar interest of the various parts of the country and, through a single governing Board, to achieve a central unity. The functions and powers that we shall consider were assigned with this dual objective in mind.[8]

Service functions

The twelve banks are large institutions with extensive responsibilities apart from or incidental to their main task of improving and controlling the money supply. As described above, the Federal Reserve banks operate a nation-wide clearing system which entails handling innumerable checks and adjustment of the balances of thousands of banks, member and some nonmember, as required by the clearing process. Holding as deposits the reserves of member banks, the Reserve banks serve the needs of the members in providing and receiving ordinary money, much as the member banks accommodate their depositors. At certain times—the Christmas season for instance—member banks require large amounts of hand-to-hand money, and at other times they wish to rid their vaults of surpluses. In this role the Federal Reserve banks provide the channel through which the federal Treasury puts money into circulation, and they are the source of Federal Reserve notes, now the leading form of ordinary money.

The Reserve banks hold the principal deposits of the federal Treasury, which are built up mainly with receipts from taxes and bond sales and drawn down as checks are written in meeting federal obligations. It is in handling federal funds that the Reserve banks become the natural channel for putting coins and silver certificates into circulation. Gold certificates representing newly purchased gold do not enter circulation, but they expand federal deposits and become available as banking reserves. In their capacity as financial agent of the Treasury, the Federal Reserve banks assist also in floating and retiring federal bond issues and in paying the interest on them.

The Reserve banks, furthermore, assume part of the responsibility of inspecting member banks to insure compliance with banking regulations. In institutions to which great sums have been entrusted, sums largely payable on demand, the highest standards of performance must be maintained. In the federal sphere, supervision of banks is shared by

---

[8] The Board of Governors have provided their own compact explanation of the role of the Reserve banks. See *The Federal Reserve System—Its Purposes and Functions*, 1947.

the Comptroller of the Currency and the Federal Deposit Insurance Corporation; state banks are subject to state authorities. This division of supervisory responsibility is quite unsatisfactory, both from the standpoint of the banks and of the public.

The foregoing functions of the Federal Reserve System need not concern us further, except as they relate to the central credit-providing processes.

Defects to be overcome

For a long time before the Federal Reserve Act was adopted, evidence had been accumulating of defects in the machinery by which both ordinary money and deposit currency were provided. Of the former it was said that the money supply was *inelastic*. By this it was meant that the quantity of hand-to-hand money did not expand and contract in close relation to the needs of trade. Gold and silver did not enter the money system in a manner at all responsive to business requirements, and with national bank notes secured by government bonds, no reason existed for expanding the quantity of them when more money was needed.

Perhaps the most common criticism of the banking structure was that *reserves were scattered* in the individual banks and there was no way to coordinate them to make them serve the credit needs of the country. One result was that some banks, or banks in some areas, might have exhausted their lending power at a time when other banks, or banks in other areas, had idle reserves, and there was no means beyond informal and spasmodic interbank lending to correct the difficulty.

But the utilization of reserves was bad in a much more vicious way— a way that *positively invited money shortages* and periods of sharp contraction. In general the banks of the country, except those in great financial centers, kept half or more of their reserves in the form of deposits in other banks, finding an inducement to do so in the interest they received and in services that correspondent banks could perform. Thus banking resources funneled toward the larger cities, especially New York, where funds not otherwise employed were used to finance security speculation. When additional funds were needed in the interior of the country, the withdrawals caused a sharp and destructive contraction of credit in New York and other centers. When the reserves of big-city banks were fully employed in supporting deposits, part of which were reserves of other banks, withdrawal of these reserve deposits precipitated a collapse.

A key element in this situation was the normal inclination of bankers to expand loans and investments to increase banking profits and thus to *use reserves fully* when business is normally good. The result was that means were lacking to deal with emergencies and meet abnormal demands for funds. Perhaps a milder reform could have prevented the pyramided use of reserves, but what was mainly needed was a reservoir of credit that would not be drawn on in ordinary banking operations and would be available to meet extraordinary demands. A new type of bank was called for that could buttress the lending power of all ordinary banks and that would be motivated in its operations by broad economic considerations and not by the immediate desire to increase profits.

Plainly, banking of this type would have to be instituted by government action. Moreover, it would not be sufficient merely to have a new type of bank set up to act in accordance with rules and standards prescribed by Congress. Operations would need to be under the control of an administrative authority which could exercise a broad discretion in adjusting the money supply to the requirements of economic health.

It was to overcome these defects and to meet these needs that the Federal Reserve System was established.

Mobilizing and expanding reserves

By requiring that member banks should keep their reserves with the Federal Reserve banks of their districts, the Federal Reserve Act directly brought about a pooling of reserves on a regional basis. Beyond this, the Act provided for interdistrict borrowing among the Federal Reserve banks, under the authority of the Board, and thus the banking reserves of the entire country were effectively pooled.

New member-bank reserve requirement. The new reserve requirement meant that balances kept with correspondent banks could no longer be counted as reserves, and the concentration of funds in large centers was thus reduced. The new requirement also excluded from the reserve category the cash that a bank must keep to accommodate its customers. These changes reduced the absolute amount of legal reserves, but a major reduction in legal reserve ratios, the required percentages of reserves to deposits, more than maintained the volume of demand deposits that members' reserves would support.

For reserve purposes the member banks are grouped in three classes. There are, first, the banks in "central reserve cities," meaning New York and Chicago, second, the banks in "reserve cities," consisting of about sixty important centers, and third, the remainder of the member banks, which are ordinarily referred to as "country banks." Prior to the Federal Reserve System, the legal reserve ratios for these three classes of banks were, respectively, 25, 25, and 15 percent on demand deposits.

The Reserve Act reduced these ratios to 13, 10, and 7 percent and established a ratio for savings, or time, deposits of 3 percent. These have remained the basic ratios, but the Board of Governors of the System has been granted authority to make limited upward adjustments as occasion requires. In 1935 the Board was authorized to increase the required reserve ratios up to double the previous figures—that is, to 26, 20, and 14 percent on demand deposits and 6 percent on time deposits. In 1948 temporary authority was granted to make further increases up to 30, 24, and 18 percent, and 7.5 percent.

Loans to member banks. The Reserve Banks not merely hold the reserves of member banks but possess the power to increase their reserves by lending to them. This power to provide reserves is not limited to the lending to certain banks of the unused portions of the reserves of other banks. It lies in the power to create, in the aggregate, additional reserve dollars. Reserve banks possess the same power as member banks of expanding loans and investments and thereby expanding deposits. But in the case of the Reserve banks, the customers are the member banks and the deposits are the reserves of the member banks. As in the case of member banks, the deposits of Reserve banks do not require a 100-percent reserve behind them in lawful money. Member-bank reserves may be expanded until they greatly exceed the lawful money held by the Reserve banks to support them. It is through this dollar-creating power of the Reserve banks that the Federal Reserve System mainly overcomes the limitations of previous banking arrangements.

This power of Reserve banks to lend to member banks provides a true reservoir of credit for meeting exceptional demands. Whereas ordinary banks want all the business they can handle, Reserve banks are not concerned with seeking customers but are interested only in seeing that member banks get the reserves that it is best for them to have. Since the members pay interest on the reserve funds that they borrow, they are prompt to relinquish unnecessary reserve obtained in this way. Thus the supplementary reservoir of credit provided by the Federal Reserve System is not likely to be brought into use in meeting ordinary business needs.

The loans made by Reserve to member banks may be handled in either of two ways. The borrowing bank may select certain eligible notes and drafts which it has received in extending credit to its customers and endorse them over to the Reserve bank, receiving a write-up of its reserve balance equal to the maturity value of such notes and drafts minus interest for the period they have still to run. This process is known as *rediscounting*. Or the member bank may give its own promissory note for the loan, securing it with collateral in the form of the same sort of eligible commercial paper, certain kinds of federal securities, or other acceptable assets.

Reserve bank investments and open-market buying. Reserve banks, like member banks, can extend credit through making investments as well as through loans in the usual sense. Through the investment process the Reserve Banks can take the initiative in improving the reserve positions of member banks in general, without receipt of specific loan applications. Such investments may take the form of the open-market purchase of federal securities and of various types of commercial paper evidencing credit transactions. These purchases expand the reserves of member banks whether they are made from banks or from other firms and individuals. If made from member banks, the reserve balances of these banks are written up directly in making payment. If the purchases are made from other parties, these parties deposit the Reserve-bank checks they receive, and the member banks collect the sums as additions to their reserves.

Expansion possibilities—Reserve bank reserve. Whether the reserves of member banks are expanded through direct borrowing or through the open-market investments of Reserve banks, the effect is to make possible an increase in deposit currency several times as great as the increase in reserves. Reserves obtained through extension of Reserve bank credit are exactly as potent as reserves established through the deposit of lawful money. The possible expansion for member banks as a whole is simply governed by the legal reserve ratio to which they are subject. If the ratio is 10 percent, the addition to the circulating medium may be 10 times the new reserve; if 20 percent, the addition may be 5 times the new reserve.

How far can the Reserve banks go in thus extending credit to member banks? What is the size of the reservoir? When banks came into the Reserve System, they contributed sufficient cash to the Reserve banks to establish a 100-percent reserve behind members' reserve deposits. But as the Reserve banks issued Federal Reserve notes and made loans and investments to expand the members' reserves, this ratio fell below 100 percent. How far might it fall? The Federal Reserve Act provided originally that the Reserve banks should hold in "lawful money" a reserve of 35 percent behind their deposits, which are mainly the reserves of member banks, but it allowed emergency deviations below this minimum. The reserve in recent years has had to consist of gold certificates, and in 1945 the required ratio was reduced to 25 percent. Thus member banks' reserves may now become four times as great as the final reserves behind them. In other words, Reserve-bank credit may supply $3 of additional reserve for each $1 of ordinary money deposited.

Federal Reserve notes

These possibilities of credit expansion require illustration, but, before we undertake it, we must bring Federal Reserve notes into the picture. Hand-to-hand money, as well as deposit money, must be adequate and responsive to the needs of trade, if exchange media are to serve the economy properly. It was a fitting recognition of the essential unity of the money mechanism that the Reserve Act should undertake to insure an elastic currency while introducing banking reform. In empowering the Reserve banks to issue Federal Reserve notes, the Act established a new money which could be brought into being and retired in direct response to the fluctuating demands of member banks in meeting the needs of their customers. On request of members for ordinary money, Federal Reserve notes, as well as moneys of Treasury origin, could be supplied, the sums being deducted from the members' reserve balances. As banks overstocked with till money returned the surplus to the Reserve banks, causing a write-up of their reserves, the Federal Reserve notes turned in would not only pass from circulation but, in effect, would pass out of existence.[9] It was provided that Federal Reserve notes would in time displace the national bank notes, and they have now become the principal form of hand-to-hand money.

The elasticity of the notes grows out of the fact that they are not rigidly attached to an inflexible base. The old national bank notes had to be secured 100 percent with government bonds and thus did not expand when more currency was needed. Originally, under the Act, the Federal Reserve notes required a 40-percent gold reserve, so that the volume of them might expand up to two-and-one-half times the money of Treasury origin behind them. In 1945 the reserve requirement for the notes, as well as for Reserve bank deposits, was reduced to 25 percent—permitting a multiple of four in relation to the reserve.

While only a fractional reserve of gold certificates is required, the notes must in other ways be given 100-percent collateral. But the additional security for the notes may consist of commercial paper that arises from business operations, and therefore becomes available in increasing amounts when more money is needed in circulation.

Credit resources of the banking system

We are now in a position to examine as a whole the credit-expanding and money-providing possibilities of the Reserve and member banks.

[9] Since they are liabilities of the Federal Reserve banks, return of the notes simply cancels the liability.

A broad view of deposit currency furnishes striking evidence of the small proportion gold may be of the total circulating medium in a system supposedly based on it and evidence of the wide range within which that proportion may vary.

In viewing the dollar-creating power of the system, a good point of observation is the standpoint of the reserves of member banks, from which we may look forward to the customers' deposits based on them and backward to the reserves of the Federal Reserve banks behind them. Let us assume that the aggregate reserves of the member banks of a Federal Reserve district are $1 billion, and that they support the maximum of member-bank credit and reflect the maximum extension of Reserve-bank credit. Let us suppose also, that 20 percent is the average of the reserve ratios applicable to demand deposits in all classes of banks. Then, if we exclude savings deposits from the example, the patrons of member banks can have $5 billion of deposits for use as means of payment. At the same time, the $1-billion reserve of the member banks, viewed as the deposits of the Reserve bank, requires $250,-000,000, or 25 percent, in gold certificates behind it. This sum is only 5 percent of the $5 billion of deposit currency. In other words, $20 of circulating medium rests on $1 of reserve in the Federal Reserve bank.

The items in this example may be seen in proper relation in the balance sheets of the banks involved:

Aggregate of Member Banks

ASSETS		LIABILITIES	
Due from Fed. Res. Bank	$1,000,000,000	Deposits	$5,000,000,000

Federal Reserve Bank

ASSETS		LIABILITIES	
Gold certificates	$250,000,000	Deposits	$1,000,000,000

The significant relationship is that the two appearances of the billion-dollar figure refer to the same thing—the reserves of member banks as seen from two standpoints. To the member banks these reserves are an asset; to the Reserve banks, a liability.

This example indicates the peak possibility of expansion and does not give a balanced impression of the monetary picture. Dollars of final reserve cannot on the average support so large a circulating medium. Much of the ordinary money, including at present most of the coins, silver certificates, and United States notes, is in actual circulation and does not serve as bank reserves. A part of the reserve of member banks must act as reserve for time deposits, which do not circulate through the checking process. A part of the reserve of Reserve banks must be held, on a 25 percent basis, to secure Federal Reserve notes and thus is outside the pyramiding of ratios which applies to deposits. But the possibilities of expansion are still great.

Let us modify the preceding example to take account of time deposits and Federal Reserve notes. If we assume that the Reserve bank in question has $400,000,000 of notes outstanding, the required 25-percent reserve absorbs $100,000,000 of its cash holdings, leaving $150,-000,000 as reserve for member banks' reserve balances. If maximum credit is extended to member banks, this sum will provide a 25-percent reserve for members' reserves of $600,000,000. Now if we assume that the member banks of this district have time deposits of $2 billion and that a 6-percent reserve (double the original 3 percent) is required for time deposits, they will take $120,000,000 of the total reserve for all deposits. The remaining $480,000,000 will support $2.4 billion of customers' demand deposits on a 20-percent reserve basis.

As before, these items can be related most easily in balance-sheet form.

Aggregate of Member Banks

Assets		Liabilities	
Due from Fed. Res. Bank	$600,000,000	Deposits:	
Loans and investments	x,xxx,xxx,xxx	Demand	$2,400,000,000
		Time	2,000,000,000

Federal Reserve Bank

Assets		Liabilities	
Gold certificates	$250,000,000	Fed. Res. notes	$400,000,000
Loans and investments	xxx,xxx,xxx	Deposits	600,000,000

Counting as circulating media the member banks' demand deposits and the Federal Reserve notes, we find now that the ultimate reserve of $250,000,000 supports a money supply of $2.8 billion.

Use of credit resources

To explain the outside limits of credit expansion is not to describe the actual use that has been made of the credit resources provided by the Federal Reserve System. There has, in fact, never been full use of these resources, but the limits have been approached. On important occasions the expansion of credit and currency has greatly exceeded the capacity of the previous banking structure.

The new system was introduced at a fortunate time—just prior to the heavy monetary requirements of World War I. Demand mounted sharply following 1914, still more sharply when this country entered the War, and reached a peak in 1920. The reserves of the Reserve banks rose absolutely, but in relation to the combined note and deposit liabilities of these banks they declined from 100 to 40 percent. Thus the twelve banks together almost reached the legal maximum in their expansion, and some districts were compelled to borrow from other districts.

Thereafter reserves grew considerably, and during the prosperous 1920s Reserve-bank reserves remained in the neighborhood of 75 or 80 percent of combined notes and deposits. With the depression of the 1930s the ratio fell, due to cash withdrawals and emergency note issue, and reached a brief low of about 50 percent in 1933.[10] In the years directly following, the gold holdings of the Treasury were expanded tremendously, with a corresponding deposit of gold certificates in the Federal Reserve banks. As a result, their reserves grew by 1940 to more than six times the 1930 volume. Reserves of member banks became so large during this period that they were in position, without Reserve-bank assistance, to finance a highly inflationary expansion if the demand for credit developed. It was to meet this emerging danger that Congress amended the Reserve Act in 1935 to enable the Reserve Board to expand the required reserves of members up to double the prevailing ratios. But despite extensive use of this authority, at the end of the decade the total reserves of member banks were nearly twice what were required for outstanding deposits.

With these expanded reserves, the heavy demands of World War II were met with relative ease by the banking system. With only a small increase in their reserves and with their required reserve ratios kept high, the member banks nearly trebled their demand deposits and doubled their time deposits over a five-year period. Loans expanded 50 percent and investments, mainly in government bonds, quadrupled. The Reserve banks more than quadrupled the note circulation. They had little occasion to lend to member banks but did invest substantially in government securities. Holdings of gold certificates declined somewhat, and the effective reserve of the Reserve banks fell toward 40 percent, behind both notes and deposits. It was this pressure that led to the reduction of the required reserve ratios to 25 percent. Some of the main changes between 1940 and 1945 are shown in Table 16.

By the end of 1947, peacetime expansion had added $10 billion to the loans of member banks, but their investments were reduced by nearly $20 billion. Demand deposits were down by $10 billion; but since wartime government deposits had been nearly eliminated from member banks, the more significant fact was a $10 billion increase in

---

[10] Strict eligibility requirements kept the Reserve banks from extending to member banks the assistance that would have been necessary to prevent widespread bank closings.

privately held demand deposits. Demand deposits were thus two and one-half times the prewar volume, whereas hand-to-hand money in circulation had risen to three and one-half times the level in 1940.

TABLE 16—WARTIME CREDIT EXPANSION—SELECTED ITEMS
(Year-end figures, in billions of dollars)

All Member Banks

Assets	1940	1945	Liabilities	1940	1945
Loans	$15.3	$22.8	Deposits:		
Investments	21.8	84.4	Demand	$33.8	$91.8
Reserves	14.0	15.9	Time	12.1	24.2

All Reserve Banks

Assets	1940	1945	Liabilities	1940	1945
Reserves	$20.0	$18.1	Deposits:		
Credit outstanding (including U. S. securities)			Members reserves	$14.0	$15.9
			Other	2.1	1.5
	2.3	23.4	Federal Reserve		
			notes	5.9	24.1

Means of credit control

Emphasis has so far been placed chiefly on money and credit resources and the capacity of the banking system to expand them. The role of the Federal Reserve System, however, is not merely to expand these resources but to control their use. Economic stability may be undermined by monetary excesses as well as deficiencies. The preceding discussion has brought to light the main devices by which the Reserve authorities may exercise control, but they should now be set down together and recognized specifically as means of influencing the expansion and contraction of credit.

The original Federal Reserve Act provided two devices for this purpose. One of these was the authority to *adjust rediscount rates*—or, more broadly, the rates of interest at which member banks borrow from Reserve banks—so as to encourage or discourage borrowing. A lower rediscount rate makes it more profitable for member banks to borrow additional funds to extend credit to customers. It makes possible lower interest rates to the customers, making it worth while for them to borrow for purposes that would not justify higher interest payments. In the same way, a higher rediscount rate makes borrowing by the banks less profitable and increases the cost of loans to their customers.

The second of these devices was the use of *open-market* dealings to control the reserve position of member banks. We have seen that the *purchase* of commercial paper and federal securities by the Reserve banks has the effect of increasing members' reserves, whether the purchase is from banks or individuals. In like fashion, the *sale* of such obligations by the Reserve banks absorbs members' reserves and reduces their ability to make loans and hold deposits. Open-market operations are directed by a special body known as the Federal Open Market Committee. It consists of the members of the Board of Governors and five representatives of the Reserve banks.

A third means of credit control is the power given the Board in 1935 to increase the legal reserve ratios of the member banks, up to double the basic rates of 13, 10, and 7 percent on demand deposits and 3 percent on time deposits. Doubling the reserve ratios has the same effect on the ability of banks to expand loans and deposits as would cutting the reserves in half. During most of the war period the ratios were 20, 20, and 14 percent on demand deposits and 6 percent on time deposits. Under the additional authority granted in 1948, reserve ratios were promptly raised to 26, 22, 16, and 7.5 percent to combat the mounting inflation of prices.

Besides these broad instruments of credit control, the Board has been given specific authority over such matters as the use of bank credit for security speculation and, during World War II and again in 1948, over the extension of installment credit to consumers. In addition to all of these statutory weapons, the Board may use its prestige, through *warnings* and *suggestions* to the banking community, to influence policy along the lines it deems desirable.

Limits to control. Whether these powers of control should be thought adequate depends on what is expected of them. It is to be noted that they operate mainly through the adjustment of member banks' reserves. Through rediscount rates, open-market operations, and alteration of reserve ratios, the Reserve authorities may modify the ability of banks to make loans and establish deposits that may be used in the purchase of goods. Reserves as an instrument of control are like the string of a kite. The string does not cause the kite to rise but limits the height to which it may go. Control of reserves, if employed vigorously, can prevent unwarranted expansion of credit and retard buying based on it. But making additional reserves available does not mean that banks will expand credit. Customers may not want to borrow, or bankers, appraising customers' prospects, may not want to lend. Indeed, persons who already have deposits may not use them, and buying may languish despite the most liberal of credit policies. When free to act, as they were not when assisting in the Treasury's wartime borrowing, the Reserve authorities may apply brakes to inflationary trends and with some hope of success, if member banks are not blessed with large excess reserves. But in the opposite situation, the authorities can do no more than provide a basis for expanded credit; they cannot actually establish it, certainly not cause its use.

Banking policy in general

It would be out of place in the present discussion to go into the complexities of banking policy, but perspective will be improved if, in conclusion, we note its broader features.

From our survey of the role of banks, it must be clear that banking belongs in the group of industries to which extensive public control must be applied. The free play of market forces cannot be relied on to govern its activities. There are several reasons.

Even if banks served only as middlemen for savings, lending funds deposited with them, higher standards of performance would be necessary than are required of business in general. It is one thing to take chances with one's own capital and with the capital that associates commit in recognition of risks incurred, but it is quite another matter to jeopardize funds deposited primarily for safekeeping. Behavior in keeping with such a *position of trust* does not come automatically through market pressures. Regulation is necessary.

Commercial banks do serve as financial middlemen, but much more is involved in their activity. *Demand deposits,* judged by volume of use, are the *principal form of money.* Their volume is directly the result of the lending and investing activities of private bankers. The United States Constitution places in Congress the power to provide money and control its value. If, in fact, much of the exchange medium is privately provided, government is obligated at the very least to direct the process.

We would reach this conclusion even if money were merely a passive medium of exchange with no requirement to meet except that of adequacy for business transactions. But actually the operation of the money mechanism is tied up with the broad *problem of economic stability*—stability of the price level and of production and employment. A responsible government cannot allow money and credit arrangements which actively contribute to instability. On the contrary, arrangements should be maintained that positively promote prosperity and stability.

Deficiencies of control; further expedients. Although the need of government control is obvious, even the more limited objectives have been hard to achieve. It has been difficult to establish regulations and a scheme of supervision that would prevent flimsy banking structures and bad banking practices. The history of American banking, even under the Federal Reserve System, is filled with bank failures that have caused great losses to depositors. Even when the assets of banks are fundamentally sound, a general decline in business obstructs payment of obligations and stimulates withdrawals of cash. Numerous defaults that have meant no final loss to depositors have caused temporary closings, and, for a time, have suppressed the purchasing power that demand deposits represent. The added reserve power that the Federal Reserve banks supplied has succeeded in meeting credit demands well beyond the capacity of the older banking structure, but the Reserve System did not prevent the general closing of the banks in 1933, when exceptional emergency measures became necessary to give the country a medium of exchange.

One outcome of the collapse of the 1930s was the establishment of a system of *deposit insurance* which, while not a cure for basic weaknesses, has largely prevented losses to depositors in insured banks. Nearly all commercial banks and some others pay the prescribed premiums to the Federal Deposit Insurance Corporation and thus protect all deposits up to $5000. The standards imposed and inspections conducted by the Corporation, together with its power to expell banks guilty of unsound practices, are a further influence toward banking improvement.

But reforms which protect depositors and reduce the damage done by depressions need not strike at the causes of instability. From this standpoint, the power of the Reserve System to expand and control credit has yielded disappointing results. Inflationary expansion of business may be checked if the Board is willing to pursue a vigorous policy, but contraction cannot be prevented. It is significant that the greatest of depressions occurred with the Federal Reserve in full operation. It may be said that the Reserve System was never really expected to do more than offset certain credit deficiences and excesses and that Reserve policy should be conceived in limited terms on the basis of business needs. But it is reasonable to combine a modest view of the System's powers with the belief that they should be used to the fullest, in conjunction with other policies, in pursuit of the broad goal of sustained prosperity.

It may well be that monetary and banking reform cannot reach the heart of the depression problem. But to persons who think it can, more drastic changes in the provision of deposit currency appear as a possible solution. Giving private bankers the power they now have over the money supply has seemed a mistake to some authorities. Thus it has been proposed to do away altogether with fractional reserves for deposits. If all demand deposits were required to have a 100-percent reserve of government-provided money, the limits of deposit currency would be set by government action. This proposal has been called the "100-Percent Plan." [11] But some would go farther and make banking itself a government function.

Review Questions

1. What are the duties of the Federal Reserve banks in relation to the federal Treasury? How are their duties related to its monetary functions?

2. What major defects of the money supply before 1913 are implied by the terms "inelastic currency," "scattered reserves," "pyramided reserves?" Explain carefully. Why cannot private bankers be depended on to maintain reserves to handle extraordinary credit demands?

3. What provisions of the Federal Reserve Act were aimed at each of these defects? How did the Reserve System provide an additional reservoir of credit on which the banking system could draw? How may member banks obtain funds from Reserve banks? How do Reserve-bank investments add to the reserves of member banks?

4. "One dollar in gold certificates can operate as reserve for $4 in Federal Reserve notes or $20 in deposit currency." Explain. What assumption regarding reserve ratios is involved?

5. Why do Federal Reserve notes constitute an elastic currency?

6. In what circumstances have the credit resources of the banks, under the Federal Reserve System, come closest to being utilized completely? Explain.

7. Distinguish the three methods by which Federal Reserve authorities can promote an expansion or a contraction in the volume of deposit currency in use. To expand bank credit, should the Reserve banks buy or sell government securities?

8. Is Federal Reserve control likely to be more effective in expanding the use of credit or contracting it? Explain.

9. Distinguish the main reasons why commercial banking should be a regulated industry.

[11] The best known advocate was Irving Fisher. See his *100 Percent Money*, Adelphi Co., 1935.

~ 12 ~

The Changing
Value of Money

CHANGES in the buying power of the money unit are both frequent and troublesome. They occur in many circumstances, most sharply in war periods and major booms and depressions. When income is received in money form, what it means in human welfare depends on the power of money to command goods. When contracts and arrangements that run through time are fixed in money terms, shifts in the value of money can upset expectations and weaken incentives. American reaction to rising prices during and after World War II should give some indication of the situation in other countries where inflation has been many times as great.

In this chapter we shall consider the changing value of money from the standpoint of its meaning and measurement, its effects, the reasons for it in various circumstances, and some of the policies that have been tried or proposed for controlling it.

Meaning and Measurement

Money presents a unique value problem because it supplies the unit in which most values are expressed. Hence there is need of considering exactly what changes in the value of money mean and how they can be stated and measured.

Meaning of the value of money

The value of money cannot be expressed in its *price,* as values of other goods are expressed. When wheat becomes more valuable, so that the farmer needs less of it to buy a truck or a tractor, this fact is expressed in a higher price for wheat. But because money provides the measuring unit in which values of goods are expressed, its own price does not change. The price of a dollar is always a dollar. Sometimes when the value of money has changed, we hear such expressions as, "We now do our buying with a 60-cent dollar," but this idea cannot be literally valid, for, whatever happens to its value, we always have a 100-cent dollar.

Thus, when the dollar, like wheat, acquires greater power to command other goods, we have no short-cut way of thinking and speaking about the change. We can only say that the value of money is its *purchasing power,* and by its purchasing power, we have to mean its ability to command goods in general. This is a cumbersome procedure. We cannot say *absolutely* that the value of a dollar is a certain composite of goods expressed in physical quantities, but it is possible, as we shall see, to measure *changes* in the quantity of goods a dollar will buy and thus measure changes in its value.

Prices of goods and the value of money. To measure changes in the value of money, the changing prices of goods must be used. These necessarily are prices of specific goods, since there are no prices of goods in general. But changes in specific prices ordinarily do not imply a change in the price level. A short wheat crop sends the price of wheat up, and we say merely that wheat is more valuable, not that money is less valuable. A change in the value of money occurs only when there is a general movement up or down in the prices of goods, a significant average change.

The point to bear in mind is the familiar one that, when a general movement does occur in the prices of goods, the value of money moves in the opposite direction. If prices generally are rising, the power of money to command goods—its value—is falling. If prices are falling, the value of money is rising. The relationship is simple, but we must be careful how we conceive it. It should not be said that a rise in prices *causes* a fall in the value of money (or vice versa). A rise in prices *is* a fall in the value of money. Yet the two sides of this single phenomenon must be expressed in terms of movement in opposite directions. We may employ as interchangeable concepts a falling price level and a rising value of money, likewise, a rising price level and a falling value of money.

When we express the relationship in figures, we must also be careful. The arithmetic is simple but may be a little beyond the Congressman who said that automobile production in the depression fell off by more than 400 percent. When prices rise on the average by 25 percent, the value of money is not reduced by 25 percent. If it were, we would conclude when prices double, or rise by 100 percent, that the value of money must have fallen by 100 percent. In that case the dollar would have no purchasing power at all. When the price level rises by 25 percent, or to five fourths of what it was, the value of money has become four fifths of what it was, or has fallen by 20 percent. This is the way with reciprocals, as students in junior high school know.

Value of gold and value of money. Perhaps the person who spoke of a 60-cent dollar was thinking not of its buying power but of its so-called devaluation in terms of gold. On this question, the position we should take is clear. If a reduction in the gold equivalent of the dollar is not paralleled by a like decline in its command over goods in general, it is the latter, not the former, that is pertinent to a discussion of the value of money. Among the goods for which money is spent, gold is relatively unimportant. What money will buy in bread, coal, steel, or gasoline is far more significant than the amount of gold for which it can be exchanged. Its value must be judged by its command over the whole range of goods. This, essentially, was the position taken by the Supreme Court when Congress in 1933 abrogated the clauses in out-standing corporate and government bonds that called for payment in gold dollars of standard weight and fineness. The new dollars repre-sented less gold but did not deprive bondholders of the purchasing power that the gold clauses aimed to protect. Indeed the dollar was more valuable after devaluation than it had been in the 1920s, when many of the bonds were issued.

The question of the relationship of gold to the value of money was raised in Chapter 10 and will be discussed further below. There is ample evidence that money does not follow a parallel course in its re-lationship to gold and to other goods. Great changes in its purchasing power have occurred with no change in its relationship to gold, and its relationship to gold has been changed drastically with little, if any, change in its command over other goods. In our conception of the meaning of the value of money we could practically forget about gold were it not for the international-exchange situation among gold-standard countries. Among such countries, a change in the relationship of a money to gold will alter its command over other moneys and over the foreign goods that can be bought with them. We shall leave this problem to Chapter 13 and concern ourselves here with domestic matters.

Index numbers

The price level—or, reciprocally, the value of money—is measured by means of a statistical device known as an *index number*. Index numbers are used for various purposes in economics, including the measurement of the physical volume of production, but their most common use is in measuring general price movements. They are employed where a group of related items reveal a common trend, but where the individual items do not move to the same extent, or certain of them even move counter to the common direction. An index number may be defined as *a measure of the average change in a group of related variables*. The making of index numbers is technically complex, but enough can be said quite simply about their construction so that they can be understood, and their limitations appreciated, in their now very common popular use.

An index number never gives the price level, or the value of money, absolutely for a given time. It merely expresses the average of prices for the time under consideration as a percentage of the average in a base year. To say that wholesale prices in 1940 were at 78.6 (1926 = 100), according to the much quoted index of the Bureau of Labor Statistics, is to say that they averaged 21.4 percent below the level of the base year 1926. Then, observing that the index number for 1945 was 105.8 (average for 12 months), one can say that wholesale prices rose by about 35 percent during the war period, or that the average buying power of the dollar in wholesale markets fell by about 25 percent. The even more familiar cost-of-living index is also the work of the Bureau of Labor Statistics. Cost of living is expressed as a percentage of the average of prices in the period 1935–1939.

In calculating a price index, the first step is the *selection of the goods* to be included. The goods should be chosen in light of the end in view. Thus house rent should appear in a cost-of-living index but not in a wholesale-price index, and the opposite is true of hides, pig iron, and raw tobacco. For statistical accuracy nowhere near all the relevant commodities need be included. In measuring wholesale prices the Bureau of Labor Statistics uses about 800 commodities, but a quarter of that number would easily meet statistical requirements. Indeed the Bureau has maintained a daily index based on 28 commodities, and even fewer have been used where promptness was the main object or an exaggerated sensitivity was sought.

With prices behaving differently for the particular goods that are included, the next step is to decide on an *averaging procedure*. One problem is to select a suitable formula, since there are several possible methods of calculation by which a single figure can be made to stand, in the representative way an average should, for all the figures in a group. Another problem is to determine the relative importance, or weights, of the commodities, so that each will have appropriate recognition. If an index for June 1940 is sought, with 1926 as the base, one procedure is to express the 1940 price of each commodity as a percent of its average 1926 price, thus getting a collection of so-called price relatives. With such a figure for each commodity, an average can be calculated. In getting the average, the commodities may be given different weights. If the price relative for one good is 75 percent and that for another good is 95 percent, but the former good is twice as important as the latter, the 75 should enter the average twice to once for the 95.[1]

Perhaps the simplest way to calculate a reasonably accurate index number is by the *aggregate method*, which is used by the Bureau of Labor Statistics. It involves no computation of percentages for individual commodities, but only a summation of items for each of the two years and a comparison of the totals. The weights used consist of representative quantities of each commodity entering into trade, and for each commodity the price for each of the two years is multiplied by the same quantity figure. The total of the amounts (prices × quantities) for the year under investigation is expressed as a percent of the total for the base year.

With a very small number of commodities we can illustrate the principle of the aggregate index and see how it is computed. Table 17 pro-

TABLE 17—EXAMPLE OF AGGREGATE TYPE OF INDEX NUMBER

Commodity	Unit of measure- ment	Quan- tity (in mil- lions)	Price (base year)	Price (given year)	Outlay (base year)	Outlay (given year)
Wheat	bushel	800	$ 1.20	$ 0.68	$ 960	$ 544
Cotton	pound	7000	.12	.09	840	630
Coal (bituminous)	ton	500	2.00	1.90	1000	950
Steel rails	ton	3	43.00	40.00	129	120
Lumber (oak)	1000 bd. ft.	2	38.00	26.00	76	52
Total					$3005	$2296
Index number (given-year total as percent of base-year total)						76

vides an example that in method and substance approximates the whole-sale-price index of the Bureau of Labor Statistics. Only five commodities are used, as against about 800 in the actual index, but the quantities of the various goods have some relation to those actually traded. The prices used for the base year are close to those prevailing in 1926, and those for the given year are not far from the 1940 prices. There is, of

[1] Both the weighting and the averaging processes involve many complexities. See Irving Fisher, *The Making of Index Numbers*, Houghton Mifflin, 1927.

course, an accidental element in the closeness of the result to that cited above.[2]

Difficulties with index numbers. Calculating and interpreting index numbers involve many difficulties outside the proper mathematical manipulation of data. Price data are hard to get in a dependable way, especially in markets characterized by classification of buyers, complex arrangements regarding discounts and terms of sale, various supplementary services that accompany transactions, and higgling and undercover pricing in particular deals. Many commodities, to an extent not suggested in the above example, are quite unstandardized, and the characteristics and qualities of many goods shift from year to year. The proportions in which they are used also shift, and no refinement of weighting methods wholly meets this difficulty. The indicated rise of less than 30 percent in the cost of living during World War II understated the actual rise. Quality deteriorated; important low-cost goods were hard to get and more expensive articles had to be substituted; goods were not available in clearance sales at special low prices.

Along with these difficulties is the general one of adapting the measure of prices to the purpose to be served. When we speak of the price level, do we have in mind only the prices of goods bought at retail, or shall we also take account of many products that do not reach final consumers, or shall we be still more inclusive and recognize prices of real estate, securities, and other objects of investment outlay? The purchasing power of money becomes definite only when the point of view from which we consider it is clearly defined; but even when a point of view is adopted, it may be hard to agree on the grouping of goods most appropriate in affording the view that is desired.

Past movements of the American price level

Current difficulties in measuring the changing value of money are exceeded by those encountered by the statistical historian who investigates the remoter past. Price data become sparse and irregular, and changes in the character of goods make uncertain the comparability of prices. But despite the difficulties, the wholesale price picture has been reconstructed quite convincingly for a long period in the United States.

---

[2] When the aggregate method is used, weighting is indispensable. When an average is based on price relatives and no weights are introduced, each commodity has the same weight. But if the aggregate method is used without planned weighting, the result is a grotesque set of weights created by the different units of measurement employed for the different commodities and the typical prices per unit. In the above example, steel rails, which are measured in tons worth $40 or more, would vastly outweigh cotton, which is measured in pounds worth 12¢ or less. Actually cotton should outweigh steel rails by more than five to one, as judged by the amounts spent for these two goods.

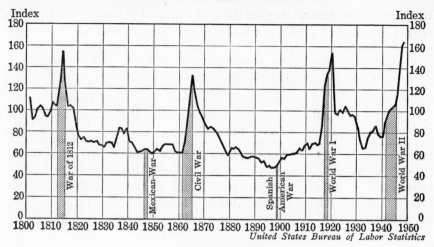

United States Bureau of Labor Statistics

WHOLESALE PRICES
Yearly Average
1926=100

The general price profile, as shown in the accompanying chart, reveals both major and minor swings, like small waves on larger. For
each major war there are high crests, with broad valleys in between.
In the War of 1812 prices rose by more than 50 percent—to a peak of
150 when past figures are converted to the 1926 base of 100. This was
a lower peak than had been reached during the Revolution when the
Continental currency was in use. Prices ran in the 60-to-70 range during
the decades of the 1840s and 1850s, and then shot up to about 130 when
Greenbacks were used to finance the Civil War. The long dip that followed carried as low as 50 in the middle 1890s. Then a marked peacetime advance moved prices nearly 50 percent higher by the beginning
of World War I, and a still sharper advance brought a further doubling
of the level by 1920, when the average rose above 150. After a decided
break, prices were quite steady, in the neighborhood of 100, during the
1920s. Hope was just emerging that a continuing stability was in prospect when the great collapse came that carried the index down to 60 in
early 1933. Thereafter, as we have seen, a level close to 80 was attained
before World War II began; then, despite drastic controls, wholesale
prices rose nearly 30 percent, to 105.8, in 1945. The sharpest advance
waited for the removal of controls in 1946, and by June 1948 the index
reached 165, or more than double the prewar level.

The *cost of living*, which had dipped somewhat less than wholesale
prices during the 1930s, also rose nearly 30 percent during World War
II and by the fall of 1948 was more than 70 percent above the prewar
level. Table 18 shows the dissimilar movements of different categories

of living expenditures during these periods.[3] The small rise in house rent is explained by the continuing government controls.

TABLE 18—COST OF LIVING—DEPRESSION, WAR, AND POSTWAR
(1935–1939 average = 100)

	All items	Food	Apparel	Rent	Fuel, etc.	House furnishings	Miscellaneous
1929	122.5	132.5	115.3	141.4	112.5	111.7	104.6
1933	92.4	84.1	87.9	100.7	100.0	84.2	98.4
1940	100.2	96.6	101.7	104.6	99.7	100.5	101.1
1945	128.4	139.1	145.9	108.3	110.3	145.8	124.1
1948 (November)	172.2	207.5	201.4	118.8	137.9	198.7	153.9

Effects of Price-level Changes

It may seem contradictory to say that the trouble caused by shifts in the price level really comes not from the general change itself but from altered relationships among particular prices. But this is, in fact, the case. If all prices and payments, including those fixed by contract, changed simultaneously to exactly the same extent, and if this perfect parallelism were perfectly anticipated, shifts in the price level would have no effect at all. The big swings are disturbing because specific prices respond unevenly, and strains and distortions result.

Price changes *versus* **production changes.** The direct effects of price-level changes are readily understood, but there is one complicating factor in approaching them: the changes, at least the short-run changes, usually come along with a rise or fall in the total volume of production. If prices climb—some faster than others—while total output is expanding, it is hard to separate the effects of disarranged prices from the effects of greater output. The former affect relative incomes, and the latter means larger total income and fuller employment of resources.

The tangle of price and production factors may go farther. If, as some believe, shifts in the value of money are a major cause of booms and depressions, then the effects of production changes can be charged indirectly to price-level changes. If the price level drops—with some prices falling more than others—and the disturbance causes a decline in output, there are two sets of effects: those due directly to disarranged prices and those attributable indirectly to the impact of prices on production and employment.

[3] The figures are from the *Federal Reserve Bulletin,* in which they are published each month.

While the separation is somewhat artificial, we shall deal only incidentally in this discussion with the problem of shifting general prosperity. It constitutes the topic of Part IV and involves much more than can be developed here.

Characteristic differences in price flexibility. Various patterns are traceable in the unequal responsiveness of specific prices to general movements. On the whole, it can be said that prices of goods in the early stages of production swing more violently than do prices of more fully produced goods. Farm products and such mineral products as are sold in fairly free markets are highly sensitive; manufactured goods are less so. Wholesale prices move faster and farther than retail prices. Industrial monopoly checks price reductions, and often, as a matter of deliberate policy, restrains advances in an inflationary period. When government interferes with prices, the effect is likely to be stabilizing. In the case of farm products, government control has operated to restrain declines rather than advances, except as advances must be less when declines have not occurred. Regulation of rates of railroads and other public utilities has promoted a high degree of rigidity.

It has long been observed that wage rates are less flexible than product prices, slower both to advance and to decline, and this view of them is sound, so far as fundamental market factors are concerned. Organized controls may, however, alter the relationship. When workers are strongly unionized, they may be able in times of rising prices to cause wage increases to equal or outstrip the product-price advance.

The most inflexible prices are those fixed by contract for considerable periods. A salary, such as a schoolteacher's, that is set in advance on a full-year basis, is necessarily slow to move. Rentals under leasing contracts stay unchanged throughout the period of the lease. Most strikingly stable are the interest payments on long-term mortgages and bonds, which remain constant despite wide variations in the value of money. Likewise passage of time does not alter the principal sum involved in debts.

Effect on debtors and creditors

When the price level goes up (or the value of money falls), people gain in so far as their product, service, or wealth rises in price by more than the general rise. They gain also if they spend considerable money for things that rise by less than the general rise. Conversely, when the price level declines, the fortunate people are those who sell at relatively stable prices and buy at prices that are highly flexible.

The most striking application of this general statement is in the case of debtors and creditors. With rising prices, debtors typically get more money for their labor and their products but need no more money than before to make the interest and principal payments on their debts. The debt burden is reduced. To the same extent, their creditors are worse off. They get no more money, and what they get will buy less. Farmers have generally favored a cheaper dollar, as evidenced by their support of "free silver" in 1896 and their opposition to wartime price controls. With inflation, their product prices rise rapidly, and, with their farms usually mortgaged, fewer bushels of grain or pounds of meat are needed for payments to their creditors. But when prices fall to a low level, farmers suffer seriously, and many farms are lost through foreclosure of mortgages.

Rising prices are harmful—and may be disastrous—to endowed institutions, such as colleges and religious and charitable organizations that depend on a fixed income from investments. Others who suffer are widows and old people who are trying to get along on small fixed incomes. The life-insurance industry has proclaimed its product as the safest investment, but nothing is more vulnerable when inflation occurs than the fixed proceeds from insurance policies and annuities. Wild inflation may wipe out the whole creditor class and change the economic, and perhaps the political, complexion of a society. In 1924 all the bondholders of the German railways could be paid off with the equivalent of an American 25-cent piece.

When the United States government during the war urged the people to buy E Bonds, with the solemn assurance that they would be the safest of investments and yield an attractive 2.9 percent return, there was lacking the one essential guarantee of a sustained buying power for the dollar. Perhaps investment of $750 would yield $1000 in 10 years, but if prices meanwhile had risen by one third, the effective interest, in terms of the goods it would buy, would be zero, not 2.9. For carrying the vast war debt with its annual interest of $5 billions, higher prices would ease the load on government and taxpayer, the debtors. On this ground, some urged deliberate, moderate inflation. We should appreciate the weight of this view, but, at the same time, we should see that it involves a judgment that the gain to the debtor outweighs what is, in effect, a partial default in the meeting of the obligation to bondholders. In any event, it is clear that a deflation that would return prices to the prewar level should be opposed from the standpoint of government finance.

Effect on wages and profits

In the case of labor, in so far as wage rates move less freely than product prices, it would seem that a lower price level would be good. Statistics show that labor has usually improved its relative position when prices are falling, but at this point we should recall that general price changes often accompany general changes in production and employment and may be influential in causing them. Those workers who remain employed and sell as much labor as before are better off when prices fall. But if total output, real income, and employment are down, the *absolute* position of all labor will be worse, even if it gets *relatively* more of the total income than it did. Conversely, during a boom period, increases in employment may more than offset a lag of wage rates behind rising prices.

The owners of businesses are commonly benefited by rising prices. Wage cost may lag behind product prices; depreciation remains fixed on equipment bought before the rise; the presence of borrowed capital gives the business owner the usual advantage of a debtor when the value of money is falling. Profits are not a price, but they depend heavily on the two sets of prices that enter revenues and costs. Business owners also gain, of course, if increased volume accompanies rising prices, and they can make fuller use of their facilities.

Some enterprises depart from this general rule because their selling prices are inflexible, and they make heavy use of flexibly priced raw materials and supplies as well as of labor for which wage rates vary. The public utilities, with their regulated rates, are a leading example. In their case, however, the problem of inflexible price is at least partially offset by the fact that their financing is done largely through bond issues. Then their debtor position is an advantage when prices rise and a menace when they fall. For all business it must be said that a wild inflation, while temporarily profitable, is likely to bring disaster in the end. But here again we are relating price-level influences to production and employment.

Review Questions

1. If an abundant potato crop sends the price down, what conclusion, if any, do you reach regarding the value of money? What is the point?

2. Explain the relation between the price level and the value of money. Which, if either, causes changes in the other? If prices, on the average, rise by 50 percent, what happens to the value of money?

3. When the dollar was devalued in 1934, an owner of a $10,000 Liberty (World War I) bond sued to collect $16,931.25 in new gold dollars. If the Supreme Court had been chiefly concerned with maintaining his capital, should it have awarded him this sum? Explain.

4. Assume prices for two years for a group of commodities and compute an index number to measure the average change. What change is indicated in the value of money? What are the main questions to be settled in computing an index number?

5. A weekly news magazine reported in 1947 that average weekly earnings of factory workers had risen 91.3 percent since January 1941, whereas the cost of living had risen only 62.5 percent. Relating these figures, the magazine concluded that the average worker was 46 percent better off than before the war. Accepting the data, show as a matter of arithmetic that the magazine gave its readers a badly exaggerated impression of the rise in real wages.

6. Why did workers contend that the cost-of-living index understated the rise in the cost of living during World War II?

7. Sketch concisely the major changes that have taken place in the value of money in the United States since the Civil War.

8. Explain the typical effect of inflation on debtors, bondholders, farmers, business owners, beneficiaries of life insurance, wage earners. Has the position of wage earners in the recent war period been typical, as judged by boom periods in the past?

Explanation of Price–level Changes

We must now engage in the strange task of explaining the value of the unit in which values are measured. In physical measurement, the standard units are unchanging. A yardstick is of constant length, the gallon a constant volume, and the pound a constant weight, but value is inherently a different sort of thing. The values of goods reflect their changing importance to human beings and their changing quantities; and the money unit that is used to measure values is necessarily dominated by similar value factors.

But while the shifting values of other goods in relation to each other are the nerve center of the whole scheme of control through which production is organized, the changing value of money, manifest in the average change in all prices, is largely a disturbing element that calls for control. Policy to control the value of money must rest on an understanding of the factors that cause it to change. These factors, in a modest way, are our present concern.

Explanation of the changing value of money is not easy and is, in some respects, controversial. The problem may be approached either by fixing attention on the value of money itself or on its other, reciprocally related side, the price level. We may talk about the demand and supply of money or we may talk about the over-all demand and supply of goods. The two are essentially the same: offering goods is demanding money; offering money is demanding goods. Because our usual habit of thinking is to look on goods as the object of demand and on money as the means of making demand effective, we shall emphasize the price level, though with reminders that the buying power of money is our problem.

Flows of money and of goods

As a concise formulation with which to begin, we may say that the price level depends on the relationship between spending and production. A somewhat better statement is to say it depends on the relationship between the rate at which money is offered in markets for goods and the rate at which goods are offered for sale. These elements combine in a simple formula:

$$\frac{\text{flow of dollars into markets}}{\text{flow of goods into markets}} = \text{average of prices.}$$

If the numerator of the fraction expands in relation to the denominator, prices rise on the average (or the value of money falls); if the numerator contracts relatively, prices go down (or the value of money rises). If, during a period, $1 billion are paid out for one billion units of goods, the average price of goods is $1. If $2 billion come to be paid for the same quantity of goods, the average price becomes $2, and the dollar is half as valuable as before. If the money spent remains at $1 billion and twice as many goods become purchasable with that money, their average price must be 50 cents, and money is twice as valuable as in the first case.

The numerator: flows of money. What does it mean to say that the flow of money into markets during a period is $1 billion? Does it imply that the circulating medium is $1 billion? Certainly it does not mean that $1 billion of hand-to-hand money are in use. If we have in mind such an economy as that of the United States, probably $4 or $5 of demand deposits are employed as a medium for every $1 of currency.

Neither does it mean that the total of money of all kinds is $1 billion. We are speaking of a flow, and each dollar, whether of currency or of deposits, changes hands repeatedly. If the period is one year, perhaps each dollar, on the average, is spent 20 times. That, then, is its rate of turnover or *velocity of circulation*. A dollar makes payments totaling $20 a year. If only $10,000,000 of currency and $40,000,000 of deposits are in circulation, and the average turnover of both is 20 times a year, then the flow of dollars into markets amounts to $1 billion in a year.

Following common usage, we may call the quantity of hand-to-hand money M and its velocity of circulation V. Then MV represents the total payments made with hand-to-hand money. Similarly we may call the volume of demand deposits M' and their velocity V'. With these symbols the numerator of the left-hand member of our formula becomes $MV + M'V'$. Now we can say that an expanded flow of money, or volume of payments, comes about through expansion of M, V, M', or V', or through the expansion of any combination of them. More money of either kind may be in use, or it may be spent at a faster average rate.

Just what does it mean to say that the rate of spending is faster? What is the meaning of *velocity?* A person receiving a wage or salary check every month or every two weeks cannot spend this money faster than he gets it, but he presumably has a certain cash balance of hand-to-hand money in his pocket or in a checking account. He may expand his spending by dipping into this balance and then proceed thereafter with a smaller average balance in relation to his income and his spending. If many people make this change in their money habits, the result is not that there is a smaller total of money in people's balances, because all money, except in the instant of transfer, is in someone's balance all the time. The result, instead, is that there is a larger total of spending in relation to the total of balances, or the total of money. This is what happens when the velocity of circulation of money increases. Thus the numerator in the equation rises, and the price level rises.

The denominator: flows of goods. The denominator of the left-hand member of the equation is an expression of the total money work to be done. If more goods flow into markets, money has more work to do. What we need to observe is that the volume of goods, in this connection, depends not only on the volume of end products—goods that pass into consumers' hands—but also on the number of times each good changes hands before it reaches its final user. If there is greater specialization by stages, involving separate firms, the number of transactions grows, and there is more work for money to do, just as there is when there are more end products. The opposite occurs when the steps are reduced in getting goods to the final consumer. This is the effect when much of the total buying is done by government, as during a war, since goods bought by government do not pass through the hands of middlemen. We should also observe that a large volume of transactions involves dealings in old wealth, such as real estate and securities. Many transactions, also, are purely monetary, as in the making and repayment of loans. To stand for the whole volume of transactions of all kinds, the letter T is used in the equation.

The equation of exchange. Letting P stand for the average of prices, or the price level, we may now rewrite the full equation as follows:

$$\frac{MV + M'V'}{T} = P$$

This equation has become part of the standard equipment of exposition in economics and provides a useful framework for explaining the value of money. But it is no more than a framework. It tells nothing about the causal relationships among its symbols. So far as the equation is concerned, changes in M or in T or in any other member of the left-hand side may cause changes in other members of the left-hand side rather than changes in the price level. Likewise, causation may run from prices to the other factors. Nor is light thrown on the economic developments which lie behind the symbols. But the formula does help us to see in simple fashion the bearing that developments in money and trade may have on the value of money, and it fixes our attention on the other factors that should be watched when any one factor changes.

Disturbances which change the value of money

If no changes took place either in the volume of money flows or of transactions, or if perfectly parallel changes took place in both of them, the value of money would remain constant. Despite the wide movements of the price level to which we have grown accustomed, such an equilibrium should not be viewed as abnormal. Indeed it is a natural result of the underlying unity of the source of spendable dollars and of the goods on which they are spent. When a producer adds $100's worth of his product to the total flow of products into markets, the $100 he receives enables him to add that same sum to the total flow of dollars into markets. If the national gross product requires $200 billion to buy it at present prices, its sale provides the $200 billion necessary for its purchase.[4]

But while there is real foundation for equilibrium in the factors governing the value of money, there are also many disturbances which are likely to upset the balance in the flows of money and of goods. Three principal sources of price-level changes will be considered: (1) long-run changes in the money structure and supply in relation to the growth of output, (2) inflationary wartime financing, and (3) the succession of booms and depressions.

Money structure and money supply. Price-level movements are caused by monetary changes of the kinds discussed in the two preceding chapters. Often the legal arrangements and established processes by which both ordinary money and deposit currency are provided are potentially inflationary. If the money system is one of free coinage or unlimited purchase of gold at a fixed rate, and at that rate large quantities of gold flow to the Treasury from mines or from abroad, the volume of money grows appreciably. The 50 percent rise in prices be-

---

[4] This summary statement passes over the complications that arise from taxation and government spending and from saving and investment. They will be developed in the treatment of aggregate demand in Chapter 14. It is sufficient to note here that they do not invalidate the present statement.

tween the middle 1890s and World War I is commonly attributed to a great increase in gold production and a tripling of the monetary gold stock during that period. Had free coinage of silver been adopted during that same period, a far greater expansion in the money supply would have occurred. Monetization of silver without free coinage has the same effect, but on a smaller scale. We have already noted the fear of inflation caused by the more than quadrupling of monetary gold, in dollar terms, between 1933 and 1940, and the steps taken to combat the danger.

Changes in the money structure which raise the ratio of the circulating medium to the gold base are similarly inflationary. Paper money and deposit currency with fractional reserves reflect this sort of development. When gold certificates are reserve for Federal Reserve notes on a 40 or a 25 percent basis, the quantity of money is greater than if the gold certificates themselves circulated. When a Federal Reserve Act reduces the required reserves for demand deposits and establishes a great supplementary reserve, a great expansion of money is made possible.

At this point a warning is necessary. There is a big difference between the presence of money and the spending of money. It is the spending which causes prices to go up. If there is more money, but individuals, firms, and governments are not induced thereby to spend more, the numerator in the price equation does not increase. A reduced average velocity offsets the greater quantity of money. Indeed, new arrangements such as the Federal Reserve System do not even cause more money to exist but only make it possible.

Nevertheless, these expansionary elements in the money structure facilitate, and may promote, inflation. They not only create one of the conditions of greater spending, but they invite it. When government buys money metal, the purchase is not like other government buying. To buy gold, the government need not take money out of the pockets of taxpayers. Suppliers of gold are paid with checks drawn on government deposits, and the deposits are built up with gold certificates issued to represent the gold that is acquired. The suppliers have more money to spend, and no one else has any less. Presumably they will spend it. Similarly, when private bankers have larger reserves, either because the gold stock is greater or the legal reserve ratio is smaller, they are in position to encourage spending. They profit through making loans, and presently the volume of deposit currency in use is likely to expand.

But while changes in the money system may increase the numerator in the equation and pull the price level up, it is quite possible for the money supply to expand less rapidly than the amount of money work to be done. With population growing and technology advancing, T in the equation may grow faster than M and M'. Then, if the velocity of circulation does not increase, money has to be spread over relatively more goods, and prices on the average must fall.

During the period from the Civil War to the middle 1890s, although the circulating medium expanded considerably and its rate of circulation also rose, there was a downward trend in prices which is usually attributed to the still more rapid growth in production and in the work that money had to do. If equilibrium is sought in the price level, it must be a moving equilibrium in which spending and production keep step.

Wartime financing. The sharpest advances in price levels have been caused by the methods used in financing wartime expenditures. Such financing is quite outside the ordinary operations of money structures, and, when extreme, causes the collapse of those structures. It means that government expenses are met not through the normal process of taxation, which takes as many dollars from taxpayers as the government spends, but through creation of additional dollars for government use. In many instances these dollars have been paper currency obtained through the simple process of printing it; in other instances, as in American financing of World War II, they may consist of deposits that are obtained through the sale of bonds to commercial banks. The effect of bank investments in adding to the money supply has been explained (Chapter 11). Government deficit financing is not inflationary to the extent that bonds are bought by individuals and firms from current income, but when bonds are bought by banks through creating deposits or by individuals with idle reserve funds, the price-level equilibrium is upset.

Recent American wartime experience can be appreciated best if attention is focused on consumers' goods. Of the 1944 gross product of $200 billion, government took about half for war and nonwar purposes, leaving the other half for private purchasers. Of the $200 billion of purchasing power resulting from the sale of the total product, the federal government took possession of considerably less than $100 billion. Taxes yielded about $45 billion, and perhaps bond sales absorbed as much as $30 billion of current income. With only about $75 billion of current receipts taken by the government, $125 billion were left in private hands to buy the $100 billion of goods not taken by the government. The difference of $25 billion exemplifies what came to be known as the "inflationary gap." It provided a rough measure of the degree to which financing was inflationary.

Inflationary financing, however, was partly offset by other influences, and the price-level advance was moderate. The effective "gap" was not so great as it appeared to be, for there was much saving not reflected in war-bond purchases. It was patriotic to restrict spending to combat inflation; anyway, the goods one might want were more likely to be available after the war than during it. Savings deposits expanded, and people used funds to pay their debts. Business firms, moreover, were saving to meet the anticipated capital requirements of postwar conversion. These brakes on spending supplemented the direct price control of the war period, but, because they meant a piling up of dollars for later use, they provided an explosive element that would help to shoot prices up after the war.

It is a feature of inflationary financing that *higher prices do not relieve the pressure that causes them*. There were observers who advised that prices should be allowed to go up and thus absorb the surplus of dollars. The trouble, however, is that when prices rise, raising the gross product in money terms, say, from \$200 to \$220 billion, current money incomes rise to the same extent, and, on top of the current income, there are still the extra dollars arising from the continuing deficit financing.

The check must come through stopping the creation of dollars. This the government succeeded in doing by 1947, when the budget was brought into balance. Indeed the bond holdings of commercial banks were reduced considerably, a deflationary influence. But prices continued to rise, in part through the spending of wartime accumulations in addition to current income dollars.[5]

The more sensational kind of wartime inflation that reduces the value of money almost to zero, and finally makes the printing of it scarcely worth while, occurs when war causes general collapse, and government makes little pretense of orderly financing. In Germany at the end of World War I wholesale prices were less than three times as high as just before the war; in the chaos that followed they rose by the beginning of 1923 to nearly 5000 times the prewar level and were up over a trillion times by the end of that year. Similarly, following World War II, prices in China rose until they were millions of times higher than before the war. In Hungary, to escape the weight of zeros in ex-

[5] These accumulations were largely held in the form of savings deposits and war bonds. Both are highly liquid and are sometimes treated as part of the money supply. We have not treated them in that way, because they do not directly serve as exchange media. To be used to buy goods, they must ordinarily be converted into hand-to-hand money or checking accounts. If reserves are adequate, they then result in an increase in M and M'. In any case they cause an increase in V and V', since people who hold reserves in the form of bonds and savings deposits do not need so large cash balances in hand-to-hand money and deposit currency. Sometimes bonds and savings deposits are spoken of as "near money."

pressing prices, a new money unit was introduced equal to one million of the old.

A striking feature of all violent inflation is that *prices rise much faster and farther than the volume of money does.* Knowing that money will be worth less tomorrow than it is today, everyone hastens to translate it immediately into goods. With the frantic effort to get rid of cash balances, V and V' in the equation go up along with M and M', assisting the skyrocketing of the numerator. Midyear in 1923 the turnover of German marks was 50 times the prewar rate—a velocity which was substantially reduced in the next six months by heroic multiplication of the marks in circulation more than 50 million times. Even when an advance in the price level is moderate, the rate of use of money is speeded up.

Booms and depressions. The third class of disturbances are those that accompany cyclical fluctuations in business activity. During recovery from a depression, and until the next break in prosperity occurs, buying increases, and the trend of prices is usually upward. With no assistance through government deficit financing, dollars are put into use faster than they are received from current output, and the price equilibrium is upset, or tends to be. The sources of these additional dollars have already been examined. In part they come through bank loans and the expansion of deposit currency, for the situation is one in which business people want to borrow and bankers feel confidence in lending. Credit buying by consumers is responsible for part of this expansion. In like manner the need for hand-to-hand money is met through greater issue of Federal Reserve notes. Individuals and businesses also dip into their cash reserves to make purchases, with the effect, as we have seen, of speeding up the rate of circulation. There is both more money to use and more use of the money that is available.

It is one thing, however, to explain how this expansion occurs, and another to explain why it does. On the latter question we shall, for the present, limit ourselves to an answer which is vague and incomplete, because the problem will be dealt with in Part IV. It is enough to recognize now that total buying seldom proceeds very long at an even rate, or at an even rate of increase. Wide variations take place in the outlook for business profits and the justification of making capital commitments. Consumer expenditure for the more expensive and durable goods, including willingness to go in debt for them, fluctuates with income prospects that respond, in turn, to business prospects. Given a favorable outlook, total spending increases and, for a time, the price level is likely to rise.

This, at least, is the situation when business expansion is well under way. But increased spending always has two outlets: one in raising prices and the other in *calling forth a larger volume of production*. In the early stage of recovery from a depression, the latter result, for a time, is likely to be the principal one. When labor is unemployed, plants idle, and other resources incompletely used, the first response to increased demand is a fuller use of productive power and an expansion of output. If more goods become available as rapidly as more dollars are offered for them, prices need not rise at all. A completely parallel expansion of T and the numerator of the equation is not likely; but for months, or even years if depression has been severe, recovery may occur with little advance in prices. As American industry responded to the terrific wartime demand of the early 1940s, upward price pressure was not great until 8,000,000 unemployed workers had been drawn into production. The slack had first to be taken up.

We cannot say, however, that as long as there is unused productive capacity, the impact of increased spending will be all on production and not at all on prices. Idle capacity and expanded demand do not dovetail neatly. The industries and areas from which more products are wanted are not necessarily the ones best prepared to expand output. Prices start upward at some points, while unused resources remain at other points. But it is still true that the seriously inflationary phase of a boom period develops only when increased spending has no other outlet than to send prices up.

Breaks in the price level, more or less sharp, come with a break in prosperity and the decline in activity called depression. Depression may follow either the artificially stimulated boom of a war period or an ordinary business boom. Wars have generally been followed by reaction, well exemplified by the sharp decline in 1920 of more than one third in wholesale prices. A further fall of one third characterized the depression following 1929.

The causes of such price breaks are the causes of depression itself. The immediate impetus is a reduction in aggregate buying, reflected in the numerator of the equation. Equilibrium is upset through a decline in spending below the level of current output. The decline appears especially in buying of the future-looking sort—that is, industrial investment and consumer buying of such durable goods as homes and cars. Less confident of the future than they were, people undertake to pay off their debts and expand their cash balances. Production, employment, and prices all fall together.

Again we should note the *cumulative* nature of a general price change. Falling prices themselves become a reason for further declines.

Individuals and firms postpone buying in expectation of lower prices, and this very postponement is a factor in the reduction in demand that brings lower prices. It is at this point that a changing value of money appears at its worst—as a disturbing, indeed a destructive, economic force.

Relationship of the value of money to its gold equivalent

In the first chapter on money two opposing views of the fundamental nature of money were presented. According to the commodity theory, money is valuable because it is tied to a commodity, such as gold, that is valuable outside the money sphere. According to the nominalist theory, money is valuable because of its usefulness as money and be· cause of the fact that the supply of it is limited.

The present discussion of the changing value of money, it should be observed, is in line with the nominalist view. The evidence of a fall in the value of money is a general rise in prices, and such a rise occurs as relatively more money is offered for the available goods. In 1920 the dollar represented 23.22 grains of gold (just as it did in 1914), but spending had expanded in relation to production and the dollar would buy only half as much. In 1933–1934 the gold equivalent of the dollar was reduced over 40 percent. A corresponding decline in its value would have been evidenced in a price rise of nearly 70 percent, but no such rise occurred. Wholesale prices averaged 65 in 1932 and 1933, touching a brief low of 60, stayed near 80 in 1935–1936, reached 86 in 1937, and were below 80 during the next three years. The dollar was still more valuable than in 1929 when it represented nearly 70 percent more gold. The rise in prices following 1933 was not extraordinary for a recovery period, even with no change in the relationship of the dollar to gold. Moreover in this case, beside devaluation, there had been such price-lifting measures as the Agricultural Adjustment Act, the codes of the National Recovery Administration, and heavy deficit spending by the government. Following 1940 the value of the dollar fell more sharply, though it remained attached to 13.71 grains of gold, but by the end of the war it was still worth more than it had been in 1920, when it represented 23.22 grains of gold.

Effects of devaluation. The sense of these observations is not that devaluation does not affect the value of money but that its effect is not in keeping with the commodity theory. By permitting the same amount of gold to serve as the basis for more hand-to-hand money and more deposit currency, it causes prices to rise when, and if, the additional money is offered for goods. But a similar increase in the amount of money, combined with a similar disposition to use it, would have about the same effect with no change in the relation to gold. Devaluation is a quick device for expanding the gold basis of the currency, but in 1934 this effect was largely prevented through the setting aside of $2 billion of the additional money in a special fund for stabilizing the foreign exchanges.

It should also be noted that devaluation may have some effect through the very belief of people that it will. Expecting higher prices, they speed up their buying, with the usual effect. The commodity theory throws no light on the process. Prices are not marked up so that goods will be worth the same amount of gold, but there is an ordinary speeding up in the velocity of circulation. Only in international trade among gold-standard countries does devaluation by one of them directly affect the prices of goods.

The quantity theory

From the foregoing discussion, the value of money appears as the resultant of all the factors which determine (1) its amount, (2) the use people are disposed to make of it, and (3) the amount of work it has to do, as affected by the volume of production and transactions in general. But is it possible to sort out one or two key factors as the critical ones that initiate changes? If this can be done, a great contribution would be made to the control of the price level.

The so-called quantity theory of money is the best known attempt to achieve this end. It simply stresses the relationship of the amount of money to the amount of goods. The stress is on the amount of money itself, rather than on the spending of money which is a composite of many elements. Thus the theory, in its usual form, assumes that the disposition of people to spend money is a relatively constant factor. Velocity of circulation, which depends on the size of the balances people keep in proportion to the amount they spend, is viewed as a matter of well-established habit and subject to little change. Since productive power changes little from year to year, the dynamic element is the quantity of money. It may change sensationally, as when printing-press money is used to pay for a war, or more slowly but still with marked effect, as when greater gold production expands the money base. The word money has not been given uniform meaning by quantity theorists. In the strictest sense the theory means monetary gold, and there is the further assumption that all hand-to-hand money bears a fixed relationship to gold and that deposit currency bears a fixed relationship to bank reserves. In a looser sense, the theory recognizes that the proportions among exchange media may change and takes account of them all.

The quantity theory provides a useful explanation of some price-level changes, but not of all of them. It explains the long-run impact of expanded gold production and the effects of printing-press money. In the latter case, it does not take account of speeded-up velocity, but this factor can be regarded as secondary to a price rise initiated by the additional money. When buyers, including the government, are eager to use such money as is available, more money means higher prices; less money, lower prices. The great weakness of the theory is its failure to explain a volume of spending below the level made possible by the available quantity of money used at a normal rate. The decline in demand that brings depressions finds no adequate explanation in a lack of money, and recovery from depression is more than a monetary matter. Despite a quadrupling of monetary gold during the 1930s and a large increase in ordinary money in circulation and in demand deposits, total demand remained so low as to leave the economy in 1940 with great unused productive capacity and with prices well below the 1929 level.

Nonmonetary, nonspending factors

Certainly the quantity of money does not fully explain the flow of dollars into markets. But when all influences which affect that flow are included, may there not still be gaps in the explanation of the price level? Throughout the discussion we have assumed that average prices are the result of the relationship between spending and transactions, the numerator and the denominator of the left-hand member in the equation. But may there not be other factors not in the equation at all which affect P directly, with the left-hand member adjusting itself thereto?

Perhaps widespread *industrial monopoly,* extensive price agreements among producers, set prices over so broad an area that the average of all prices is substantially affected, and the quantity of money and its velocity of circulation become adjusted to handle any given volume of transactions at those prices. Perhaps *labor unions* which are able to increase costs of production in great industries affect prices in the same way. Perhaps, similarly, *direct governmental price fixing* is the dominant force determining the price level and the value of money.

On this question opinions differ. The view held by some economists is that the impact of such direct influences on the whole average of prices is slight and, at most, temporary. If some prices are held down, more money will be spent on other goods, and their prices will be higher. If all commodity prices are held down, as under the price ceilings of the Office of Price Administration, there will be "black-market" operations and heavy speculation in real estate and securities. If some prices are pushed up through arbitrary power over markets, less will be available to spend on other goods, and the average of all prices will be no higher.

While this view stresses important factors, it appears to go too far. Perhaps direct price controls cannot nullify a general movement caused by a spending trend, but they can retard that trend or accentuate it. Price ceilings can be enforced with sufficient severity to make people slow down their rate of spending and build up their cash reserves. Such a policy as that enforced by the National Recovery Administration, with its numerous codes restricting price cutting, can limit a general price decline. Action by industrial monopolists can retard the average decline in a depression and may, as a matter of policy, restrain the advances of a boom. When buying pressure is high, as during the war and postwar period, wage demands by unions unquestionably promote the upswing of prices, just as do the price-raising policies of industrialists. When the economy is in a buoyant mood and demand is high, an advance in prices for such reasons as these stimulates expansion of the money and velocity factors in the price picture. A higher P in the equation must be supported by a larger M and M', or V and V', in relation to T. But the real occasion for the advance may be some direct, and perhaps arbitrary, impact on prices.

Present interest in monetary factors. It is one thing to get prices higher by pushing them from behind, putting as it were taller props under them, and quite a different thing to have them pulled to a higher level by the volume of spending. Similarly, prices that are low because they are held down should be viewed in a different light from prices that are low because of a low level of spending. Whatever the cause of changes in the price level, they are still changes in the value of the money unit. But the distinctive problems of the value of money are those related to the monetary and banking structure and to government financing. When we use the word *inflation,* we ordinarily have in mind not any general price rise but a rise due to the pressure of the volume of spending; deflation is likewise associated with slackened spending. This is the area in which public policy in the money sphere mainly operates.

Policy respecting the Price Level

In the federal Constitution, as noted earlier, Congress is granted power not only to coin money but to "regulate the value thereof." If, as commodity theorists might urge, this function means only that the money unit should be defined in grains of gold, its performance should be easy. If it means a full control of the purchasing power of the dollar, with the gold ratio only one indirect element in the process, the power is more easily granted than exercised.

In this section we shall deal briefly, and quite incompletely, with the ends sought in controlling the value of money and with some of the methods that have been tried or considered.

Objectives

Broadly, the object of price-level control is a fairly high degree of stability in the money unit. Important changes in its power to command goods should be prevented. No restriction should be imposed on the variations in the prices of particular goods as the relative demands for them shift and the conditions of their production change, but any serious movement in the level of prices, reflecting the relationship of money to goods in general, should be stopped. Both the inequities that such movements create among economic groups and their disturbing effect on production are reasons for this objective.

Short-run aim. There is agreement on this main objective, but it is debated whether absolute stability of the price level should be the goal. At this point the distinction between short- and long-run fluctuations is again important. In so far as depressions are bad—and such virtues as have been assigned them are not impressive—the price declines which accompany them and aggravate them are also bad. In so far as a high, continuing level of prosperity is good, price jumps when there is already high production are wholly harmful.

Long-run aim. The debate concerns long-run price-level policy. On the one hand, it is argued that the proper aim is to *stabilize money income,* not product prices, and that, as improved technology increases per-capita output and reduces the cost of goods in terms of resources used, prices should drop correspondingly. The main reason is that only in this way can people with quite rigid money incomes share in economic progress. If prices fall as productivity rises, there can be improvement in the position of retired persons, of the beneficiaries of life insurance, of endowed institutions. Along with these groups, the owners and workers of industry would take their gains, not in higher money incomes but in lower prices of goods.

On the other hand, there are important reasons for *maintaining stable product prices,* on the average, and having money incomes rise as productivity increases. The public is served best when productive power is fully used, and its full use is stimulated when prices behave in the interest of enterprisers rather than of bondholders and annuitants. The relationship between selling prices and costs, on which profit prospects depend, is less favorable when prices in general are falling and relatively fixed money costs require more output to meet them. Indeed, it has been argued on this ground that public policy should aim not at stable prices but at a *gradually rising price level,* or falling value of money. On the conflict of interest between debtors and creditors, a good case can be made for favoring the former, especially when account is taken of the debtor position of government and therefore of all taxpayers.[6]

These are some of the refinements that should be weighed in defining the goals of price-level policy. But in view of the past antics of the dollar, a sufficient test, perhaps, is that policy should be able to prevent conspicuous shifts in the price level.

The place of gold

If we faced only the long-run problem, involving mainly the adjustment of the money supply to the expansion of production, the general level of prices would be quite manageable. It becomes difficult, if not impossible, to control when the fluctuations are bound up with wars and depressions.

It was once thought that an automatically operating gold standard would achieve sufficient stability. Gold is durable and the total stock changes slowly. Gold production is stimulated when the price level falls, giving gold with its fixed mint price greater power to command other goods. Thus the money supply is increased and upward pressure on prices generated. Similarly, rising prices make gold mining less profitable, and the money supply lags behind the production of goods. International gold movements would operate also to stabilize prices in individual countries.

As a matter of fact, even if only the long-run problem were present, it is quite improbable that the automatic gold standard would keep the value of money constant. The "free-silver" movement may be construed as a fairly sensible, though crude, attempt to offset the failure over a long period of a gold-based currency to keep step with a rapid expansion in production. It was made pointless, however, by the unforeseen gold discoveries in South Africa and the Klondike-Yukon region and by the development of the cyanide process of recovery—events entirely foreign to any conception of automatic adjustment of the gold supply to the monetary need.

[6] General analysis of the depression problem supports this view, but the statistical evidence is not clear. One study of price-level trends over a long period indicates that when prices are rising, periods of prosperity are longer and depressions shorter than when prices are falling. But there is also some evidence that per-capita real income in this country nas risen most rapidly in certain periods of generally falling prices. See R. G. Thomas, *Our Modern Banking and Monetary System,* Prentice-Hall, 1946, pp. 470–473. This problem will be viewed from the standpoint of labor and wage policy in Ch. 27.

In the face of wars and depressions, the gold standard imposes little restraint on variations in prices. The customary—and probably inevitable—methods of financing wars cause spending to increase in relation to production, and prices rise whether the money unit keeps its connection with gold or not. Possibly, as some believe, depressions would be less severe if money were more solidly based on gold or at least not based on bank credit, but the decline in spending occurs mainly for reasons which the mere availability of dollars of whatever type cannot correct. Indeed, close attachment of money to gold may intensify severe depressions, because, when people seek in fear to expand their cash holdings, gold is the most desired thing to hoard. Under the automatic standard it can be withdrawn without limit; and the effect is to remove the foundation of currency and credit and precipitate collapse. Likewise in critical periods, an outflow of gold to other countries may cause severe deflation. It was in this sort of situation that the United States joined the procession of nations departing from gold in the early 1930s.

The "stabilized-dollar" proposal. In light of such experiences, it is interesting to look again at one of the older proposals for control of the price level, the so-called "stabilized dollar" of the late Irving Fisher. This scheme was to operate through frequent changes in the amount of gold represented by a dollar, as indicated by a general price index. Gold would not circulate but would be represented by certificates that would entitle the holder to changing amounts of metal. A small rise in the index, indicating a declining value of money, would lead promptly to a small increase in the gold equivalent of the dollar, and this increase would presumably raise its value or cause prices to decline. Conversely, falling prices would be corrected by a reduction in the gold equivalent.

What has been said regarding the devaluation of 1933–1934 applies to this proposal. To one who takes the commodity view of the value of money, such a plan must seem promising. But, on the basis both of logic and experience, it would seem more reasonable to expect that at least the immediate effect of such changes would be to alter the market value of gold rather than to change the buying power of money in terms of goods. Less directly—and this was Professor Fisher's belief— one would expect on quantity-theory grounds that an upward or downward change in the gold equivalent would lead to a downward or upward change in the quantity of money and of bank reserves and thus to a change of prices. Along these lines a slow, corrective pressure might be exerted which would operate in offsetting gradual changes in prices —though even here some critics have said that speculation in the changing price of gold and speculative international movements would up-set the process.

The scheme assumes, in any case, an automatic character in the gold system that has long been absent. Wide discretion resides in the Treasury, the Federal Reserve authorities, and the private bankers to change the volume of circulating media based on any given amount of gold. For the device to take hold firmly, this discretion would have to be removed and a much more rigid system introduced. With present arrangements, considerable control can be exercised over the volume of money—more directly than through a changing relationship of money to gold. But, however such control is exercised, it does not prevent the deflation of depressions nor offset the consequences of wartime financing.

Advantages and disadvantages of gold. Should the gold standard be retained in some form or be re-established? The answer must be reached by weighing various pros and cons. It does not lie in any fundamental law that for money to have value it must rest on some commodity such as gold. A reverse alchemy by which all the gold at Fort Knox was changed to baser metals would not cause the collapse of dollars that are now used in general indifference to the fact that gold is there. Yet there are psychological reasons for keeping gold somewhere in the money picture. One reason is the very belief of many people that gold has an essential place. In all use of money there is an element of faith, else goods would not be exchanged for it; if gold will help sustain that faith, it has some claim to use. Regard for popular beliefs, as every politician knows, cannot depend wholly on their validity.

A more important reason perhaps is that a gold basis for the dollar may protect it a little from political manipulation. A purely managed currency invites political management, whereas even a pseudo-automatic gold standard may make Congress hesitate to interfere with it. At least interference becomes a dramatic event—as in 1933–1934—and is not to be undertaken lightly.

There are also some practical considerations on the other side. While control by the money authorities of the actual currency can largely offset any failure of the gold supply to adjust to currency needs, there is still some problem of adjustment. With a wholly managed currency, there is no such problem. Particularly when a disproportionate part of the world's gold supply is in one or a few countries, as it has been, the gold standard is not an appealing device to countries short of gold. There is also the matter of cost. A great expenditure of resources was needed to take from the earth such a quantity of gold as was returned to the earth at Fort Knox. Except on grounds of making work for otherwise idle labor, such use of resources, if sound money does not require it, is waste.

Some of the more important pros and cons are related to international payments. Gold is an accepted medium in backward areas where a nation's money is not known or where it is in disrepute—though this is only a reason for having gold and not for basing a system on it. The main argument is that gold gives stability to exchange rates and provides a dependable basis for international trade. But on the other hand, it ties the economies of nations to each other in a way that aids the spread of disturbances and depressions. We shall return to these matters in the next chapter.

Monetary offsets to severe deflation

The point has been made that the sort of price decline that accompanies a depression cannot be stopped by monetary methods. With or without a gold basis, just making dollars more readily available will not cause them to be used and thus preserve a prosperity level of investing and consumer spending. We saw that this is a weakness of the Federal Reserve approach. We also noted the more far-reaching view that private bankers should be deprived of their power to vary the volume of loans and deposits in relation to reserves. An M' that is less collapsible when danger threatens would be an advantage; a 100-percent reserve requirement is a possible line of reform.

Probably much, or most of the problem lies outside the sphere of currency reform, whether hand-to-hand or deposit. The value of money will be stabilized by any policy that helps to sustain prosperity. One such policy, sometimes classed as monetary, is increased spending by governmental bodies to offset the decline in private spending. In a sense it is a monetary policy in that it is likely to involve deficit financing through expansion of credit, just as in war financing. Its main significance, however, does not lie in the creation of dollars but in the positive spending of them that government undertakes to do. The effect is the same if government gets the funds by borrowing or taxing idle money, so that in the equation of exchange only the velocity factor is increased. A raised velocity is not a monetary force but only the statistical resultant of forces causing an expanded demand for goods.

Offsets to wartime inflation

Probably the only way to stop wartime inflation is to stop wars, but, if wars must be fought, they should be financed as far as is feasible by noninflationary means. During World War II the United States Treasury used all the pressure it could muster to get Congress to levy higher taxes and did its best to sell bonds to individuals and business firms other than banks. It also used every art of persuasion to induce people not to spend. These measures may be thought of as the *Treasury policy* of holding prices down.

Since the policy succeeded only in part—doubtless an inevitable outcome—and a large volume of bonds had to be sold to commercial banks—thus expanding the money supply—the Federal Reserve authorities were not able to use their power to check inflation. Such action as employing rediscount rates and open-market operations to reduce bank reserves would have obstructed the sale of bonds. The major end of financing the war could not be sacrificed to the subordinate end of holding prices down. Thus wars not only are inflationary but may rule out the use of the existing controls over prices.

Direct price controls, such as were conducted by the Office of Price Administration in World War II, are designed in part to keep shortages of specific goods from causing hardship or increasing the cost of war through skyrocketing prices. But even without such specific shortages, the control of prices and also of wages would be necessitated by the over-all surplus of spendable dollars. Treasury policy, described above, may be viewed as reducing the steam pressure behind inflation, whereas OPA policy is merely a process of sitting on the lid to hold the steam in. Inevitably some steam escapes. Inevitably, since the nature of the control involves innumerable regulations and much policing (all developed quickly by a large staff created overnight), the control is extremely irritating, often unjust, often the source of maladjustments in the economy.[7] But it is necessary.

With this combination of policies, price advances in the United States during World War II were not so small as they might have been, but they were still moderate in relation to the terrific impact of the war. With the end of the war this nation, with an economy unbroken by the conflict, was able quickly to get its budget under control and end the inflationary surplus of income dollars. But there remained the pent-up demand for goods and the accumulated liquid savings that could be spent in addition to current postwar income. Thus the inflationary pressure was still present. The power to control was, however,

[7] Much was said about the corn-hog and milk-butter price relationships, and there were many others that influenced production quite illogically but in a way hard to rectify because of the repercussions of each change. It was even observable that OPA policy could work at cross-purposes with Treasury policy. Thus OPA joined the fight before the Michigan Public Service Commission to cause a big refund to customers of revenues collected by the Detroit Edison Company. But excess-profits taxation was such that $6 out of every $7 returned to customers came from the federal Treasury rather than the company. OPA helped to transfer tax dollars to individuals to spend.

reduced. Ideally wartime taxation should have been continued, but the public demanded lower taxes. Price and wage controls should have been reduced no faster than the pressure subsided, but again public demands, or at least the demands of important groups, were persuasive. At best, the picture was confused, and competent persons disagreed. When mistakes were made, such as the encouragement of wage advances right after the war, prices had to give, if production was to get under way.

One lesson was clear. Except in an emergency, direct price control is a dubious way to maintain the value of money. While the aim is to control the price level, the actual control applies to thousands of specific prices. In the American economy, it is these prices and the relationships among them that underlie the innumerable private decisions through which the use of resources is controlled. A general freezing of prices, even with such specific revisions as are possible, cannot be reconciled with a freely working system and is certainly no substitute for it.

In economies that are broken by war, as in Europe after both world conflicts, the end of hostilities does not bring a balancing of government budgets. Instead, with war spirit dissipated and faith lost in institutions, an intensification of deficit financing is likely. We have seen the sort of wild inflation that may come. For such a condition there is no normal corrective that can establish stability on the prewar basis. New structures, political and economic, must be created, and the old currency replaced with a new money unit, perhaps on some fantastic basis like the trillion-to-one ratio in Germany in 1924. But the real solution lies not in the new currency but in the balancing of the budget, so that the volume of currency can be held in reasonable relation to the needs of trade. There is also the problem of placing the new money in a workable relation to the moneys of other countries, so that international dealings can go on.

Review Questions

1. "The equation of exchange does not explain changes in the value of money, but it marks the channels through which forces operate in altering the value of money." Explain the equation in terms of money and goods flows. Explain each of the terms in it. Then develop the meaning of this statement.

2. "There is no possibility of paying the national debt. It is several times as big as the total of all the money in the country." What is the error in such a statement?

3. How is the equation affected: by borrowing at banks by merchants; by production of gold; by technological progress; by vertical integration of production; by the belief that prices will rise?

4. State the condition necessary to a stable price level along with an expanding national output. If businessmen borrowed an additional $1000 at the bank for every $1000 increase in production, would a stable price level be promoted?

5. "There is no inflationary effect when the government buys monetary silver, because it must take money from circulation to pay for the silver." Is this correct? Explain.

6. The two pronounced price movements between the Civil War and World War I are often explained in terms of the production of goods and the production of gold. How?

7. "The critical factor in the wartime rise in prices was not the great volume of government buying. Rather it was the sale of bonds to banks." Explain. What is meant by the "inflationary gap"?

8. A news commentator said during the war: "The natural way to stop inflation is to let prices go up. Then the surplus purchasing power will be absorbed." What do you think of this prescription?

9. How are the cases of extreme wartime inflation in other countries to be explained? Do prices rise more or less than the quantity of money? Explain.

10. "During the upswing of business from the depths of a depression, the expansion of spending has two outlets." Distinguish them and explain the situation in which price inflation develops.

11. "A downward movement of prices is likely to be cumulative. In the equation, this is expressed mainly in a smaller V and V'. But changes in V should never be viewed as real causes of changes in the value of money. V and V' are merely statistical resultants of all the factors that influence spending—which may not be monetary." Explain.

12. Compare the value of the dollar with the amount of gold it represented in the years 1914, 1920, 1935, and 1948. What conclusion is suggested?

13. "The chief cause of rising prices since the war has been the pressure of unions for higher wages and the resulting increases in costs." If unions cause the price level to rise, which way does causation run in the equation of exchange? Do you conclude that unions can raise the price level without some secondary participation by monetary factors?

14. In defining the goal of policy, does it seem better to aim at a steady, gradually rising, or gradually falling price level? What considerations are pertinent?

15. What was the "stabilized-dollar" proposal? Does it seem to be a promising method of stabilizing the value of money? Explain.

16. "One may hold, according to the nominalist view, that gold is not a necessary part of a money system and yet believe that a system is better if money is tied to gold." Explain. What is to be said on the other side?

17. Reviewing Chapter 11: How would the Federal Reserve authorities undertake to halt a rise in prices? Check a decline? Were they able to use their power to halt inflation during the war? Explain.

18. Contrast the Treasury and OPA policies of combating wartime inflation.

19. Did this country from 1945 on proceed as vigorously as it might in stopping postwar inflation? Explain.

20. How does the inflation problem differ in countries whose economies are disrupted by war?

- 13 -

International Payments

In the summer of 1944 representatives of allied and friendly nations gathered at Bretton Woods, New Hampshire, to do some major planning for the postwar period. In part they dealt with a capital problem—the setting up of banking arrangements through which world recovery from war could be financed. The result was an International Bank for Reconstruction and Development. In part their concern was with a money problem—stabilizing the relations among the moneys of all countries so that together they would constitute an effective medium of exchange for international trade. The outcome was an International Monetary Fund. This chapter discusses those basic aspects of international payments which must be understood if one is to appreciate the second of these plans.

Fundamentally there is no special economics of exchange for situations in which the trading areas fly different flags, but the presence of different moneys alters the process of payment and creates complications, both for the trader and the student. The legal-tender powers of any government get little recognition outside its own territory, and most international dealings involve the conversion of one money unit into another. When the Frenchman buys goods in the United States, he pays finally in dollars, not in francs. However satisfactory money arrangements may be within a country, it may still be difficult to get command of needed foreign moneys. Whatever may happen to the value of a money at home, its power to command goods abroad may follow a different course. Moneys connect the economies of different countries, and the kind of balance that exists in international payments relates prosperity—or the lack of it—at home and abroad. The power of each sovereign state to adjust the international position and use of its money thrusts this problem into the arena of world affairs, in a critical political sense.

We shall not deal until later with the broad problem of international trade and trade policy.[1] This chapter deals only with the mechanism of international payments and monetary relationships.[2]

The Process of Payment

Ordinary money and personal checks have little place in international payments, and money metal plays only a minor part in normal, peacetime trade. Payments are made directly with drafts of various kinds, such as are used in some domestic dealings. Behind these drafts are balances kept in foreign banks, and through these balances the clearing principle operates much as it does in domestic trade. In effect, the people who sell abroad provide the means of payment required by those who buy abroad.

Some variations in procedure

Uniformity of principle is combined with variety of detail in the manner of making payments. One variation is in the money used. While finally the international seller is paid in the money of his country and the buyer makes payment in his, either money may be employed in negotiating a transaction or in making out the instrument of payment.

Likewise either party may take the initiative in making payment. In domestic dealings the buyer of goods, or the payer of a debt, ordinarily makes out a check or buys a bank draft to remit funds to the seller or creditor. In like manner an importer may buy from his bank a draft drawn upon a foreign bank in favor of the seller. But, on the other hand, international payment is often initiated through action of the exporter. He may draw an order upon the foreign buyer to pay himself or some designated party. Such an order, when accepted by the person or firm on whom it is drawn, becomes an effective means for transferring funds. It may be called a draft, but is commonly spoken of as a *bill of exchange*. The term "foreign exchange" is applied collectively to all the means of making payment in international dealings.

Bills of exchange may make immediate payment, as a check does, or they may include the features of a promissory note and make payment as of a future date, perhaps a month or two away. In the latter case, banks are likely to hold them during the interim and receive the interest. Bills may be drawn either on the importer himself or on the importer's bank, according to instructions in a letter of credit. They

[1] In Chapter 32.

[2] Useful references in this field are Lester V. Chandler, *The Economics of Money and Banking*, Rollin G. Thomas, *Our Modern Banking and Monetary System*, and Raymond P. Kent, *Money and Banking*, mentioned in Chapter 10, footnote 1.

may be accompanied by documents which insure the shipment and make the exported goods the security for payment. These details need not concern us.

Exchange rates are involved in all international dealings. They are ratios between the money units of countries, the price of one money unit in terms of the other as when it is said that the British pound is $4 in New York. If an importer pays for goods in the money of the exporting country, what the goods cost him in his money depends in part on the exchange rate. If the exporter is to receive payment in the money of the importing country, what he gets depends in part on the exchange rate. If a bill of exchange calls for payment only after a period of time, the holder may gain or lose because of a change in the rate during the period.

Bank balances and international clearing

The international clearing machinery is not formally organized, as in a local clearing house or the Federal Reserve System. It is provided by a small number of banks which maintain balances with correspondent banks in the financial centers of other countries. The essence of the clearing process is that exports and like transactions build up these foreign balances and imports and similar transactions draw them down.

Suppose an American cotton exporter draws a bill for £1000 against a British buyer. With the exchange rate $4 to the pound, the exporter sells the bill for $4000 to a New York bank. The bill is sent to the correspondent of this bank in London and is collected through the British clearing system. The correspondent bank adds £1000 approximately to the balance of the New York bank. With the transaction completed, the American exporter has been paid for the cotton in dollars, and the English importer has paid for it in pounds. No money or money metal has passed between the countries, but the American bank is out $4000 in New York and has increased its London balance by £1000.

In the same way, suppose that another American buys diamonds from a British firm for which he agrees to pay £1000. He goes, let us assume, to the same New York bank and pays $4000 for a £1000 draft drawn against the London correspondent in favor of the diamond exporter. The draft is mailed to this exporter, and when received is collected through the British clearing from this London bank. In this case, again, the buyer pays and the seller receives the money of his own country. Neither money nor gold travels, but the American bank has gained funds at home and lost them from its foreign balance. These traders in cotton and diamonds do not know each other, but through the banks the foreign balance built up by the sale of cotton finances the purchase of diamonds. For their services the banks receive a small return which alters the sums slightly from those stated.

Though details may vary, the example shows the essential nature of international clearing. Various complications are met through the cooperation throughout the world of the banks handling international exchange. Thus there is no serious difficulty if one bank in New York is building up foreign balances beyond a useful size while another bank is running short, nor even if the United States, while balancing its claims and obligations in dealing with other countries as a whole, has in-payments running ahead in dealing with some countries and out-payments running ahead in the case of others. The United States can use the excess of its London balances, for instance, arising from heavy exports to England, to meet the deficiency in its dealings with South American countries or the Malay States from which its imports are heavy.

Under a freely working gold-standard system, or under such a modified system as prevails here, gold *may move* as needed to build up balances abroad or bring home balances that are excessive. It is specifically in this connection that gold movements mainly occur. One should not think of importers of goods as boxing up gold and sending it abroad to pay for goods. Goods are paid for with orders drawn on banks and importers. Gold movements come about through such needed adjustment of bank balances as is not taken care of by the transactions out of which payments arise.

The Balance of Payments

International dealings are not limited to the importing and exporting of physical commodities. A large part, sometimes a major part, of the payments are for other purposes. There are internationally purchased services of shipping and insurance companies, royalties on motion-picture films, expenditures of travelers, sums sent to relatives and friends abroad or brought back home by persons who have been working abroad, interest and dividends on foreign investments, the lending of funds and making of investments and their repayment, the placing of balances in foreign banks and their withdrawal. There are also the movements of money metal which are thought of as settling balances arising from other transactions. In any discussion of the balance of a nation's international payments, all transactions must be considered.

The term "balance" in different senses

Apart from its use in speaking of bank balances, the word "balance" is used in a variety of ways in analyzing international dealings. It often denotes a *difference*, as in the mercantilist phrase "favorable balance of trade." In this phrase the word "trade" refers strictly to physical commodity movements, and the *balance of trade* is the difference between the values of exports and imports. Such a balance, one way or the other, is a natural condition; with other items prominent in a nation's dealings, no tendency exists for commodity imports and exports by themselves to be equal.

In the same sense of "difference," it is sometimes useful to speak of a *balance on current account*. In arriving at such a balance, all transactions are included which involve ordinary sales of commodities and services or which give rise to remittances respecting which the sender will exercise no further claim. In other words, the current account excludes loans and investments and such short-run capital transfers as the building up and drawing down of foreign bank accounts. It also excludes gold movements regarded as settling balances. A nation with a deficiency on current account is either assuming a debtor position or losing gold. Current sales and gifts received do not equal current purchases and gifts made.

The other, and quite different, use of the word "balance" is to denote an *equality* rather than a difference, as when we say an old-fashioned scale is in balance. When all of the international dealings of a nation are included, and when statistics are accurate and complete, balance in this sense must prevail. Current items by themselves are not likely to establish a balance in this sense, but when current items plus gold flows plus capital and indebtedness items are all taken together, a balance has to result.[3]

The balance-of-payments statement

Statisticians sum up the international dealings of the people of a country with respect to the payments they entail in a systematic classification known as a balance-of-payments statement. The form of the statement suggests a balance sheet, but the device bears no relation whatever to either type of accounting statement, the balance sheet or the income statement. Unlike a balance sheet, which summarizes assets and liabilities as of an instant in time, the balance-of-payments state-

[3] In a statement of the balance of payments of a country, there is always a figure for "unexplained items" or "errors and omissions." Statistics for some kinds of transactions are poor, but so unassailable is the logic of the matter that when discrepancies appear, one can assume that something has been omitted or misrepresented.

ment is a record of transactions extending through a period of time, usually one year. Unlike an income statement, it tells nothing about a nation's gains from international dealings. An analysis of such gains is an entirely different kind of problem. All a balance-of-payments statement does is to summarize the international dealings of a nation during a period and classify them as to whether they call for payment by or payment to the people of that nation. Those transactions which call for in-payments are conventionally known as *credit* items; and those transactions which call for out-payments are called *debit* items. Again, the warning is appropriate that the words "credit" and "debit" must not be given any accounting significance. They are arbitrary labels for the two types of transactions.[4]

The need of care in classifying items. While the principle of classifying transactions is simple enough, careless application of it leads easily to mistakes. No difficulty arises in the case of *commodity exports* and *imports,* which are, respectively, the leading credit and debit items. Nor do *tourist expenditures* create a problem. For the United States in peacetime years, an important debit item arises from the travel by Americans in foreign countries, which require large remittances for hotel bills, railroad tickets, and numerous other purchases not counted among the commodity imports.

Capital transactions are more likely to be confusing. In the 1920s the *loans we were making to foreigners,* while establishing us as a leading creditor nation, were a major debit item in our balance of payments. They were a debit item because the making of a loan involves a remittance from lender to borrower, an out-payment by the lending nation. *Repayments of loans* are a credit item, as are *interest payments* on loans that we have made previously. Mounting tension in Europe during the 1930s caused a vast outflow of European funds to safer spots. Large investments were made and deposits created in the United States, introducing, as we became indebted to these Europeans, an important credit item in our balance of payments. These transactions called for payment to us.

In this abnormal period, the vast *inflow of gold* was the leading *debit* item in the balance of the United States. Gold imports are debits in the same way and for the same reason that other imports are, but in this connection, as in others, money metal seems peculiarly likely to distort thinking. Because a nation with a credit balance from exports

[4] It would be well to apply new labels to these two classes of transactions, but good substitutes are not easily found. The terms in-payments (for credits) and out-payments (for debits) have been suggested, but they are positively misleading. What is being classified is not the payment but the transaction that calls for payment. With these labels, an inflow of gold might easily appear as an in-payment, or credit item, whereas, as we shall see, it is a debit item.

may receive gold in payment, the gold may be viewed mistakenly as a credit item, instead of as the offsetting debit which it is. The exports pay for the incoming gold, just as the gold pays for the exports. For a gold-producing country, such as the Union of South Africa, an outflow of gold is a major export, or credit, item.

Balance of payments of the United States

The history of the international dealings of the people of a country can be traced through the items in its balance of payments over a period of years. Examination of balance-of-payments statements throws considerable light, moreover, on the operation of the clearing principle in the international use of money. No one recent year gives a representative picture for the United States. Two years are included in Table 19: 1929 to show the culmination of a prosperous peacetime dec-

TABLE 19—UNITED STATES BALANCE OF INTERNATIONAL PAYMENTS
(In millions of dollars)

Type of transaction	1929		1939	
	Credits	Debits	Credits	Debits
Current transactions				
Merchandise	$5241	$4399	$3157	$2318
Shipping and freight	390	509	303	367
Travel expenditures	139	483	135	290
Personal remittances	51	339	36	144
Interest and dividends	982	330	541	230
Government items	261	152	44	99
Silver	83	64	14	91
Miscellaneous (net)		85	21	
Gold movements				
Exports and imports (net)		175		3575
Earmarked (net)	55		556	
Capital transactions				
Long term				
Change in U. S. assets abroad		636	113	
Change in foreign assets in U. S.	358			86
Short term				
Change in U. S. assets abroad		200	211	
Change in foreign assets in U. S.	196		1259	
Unexplained items		384	789	

ade, and 1939 to show the last year that was largely free of the impact of World War II.[5]

Most striking, perhaps, is the vast inflow of gold in 1939. Movements of money metal, as in 1929, are normally small in comparison with total international payments. The great movement of gold to the United States in the 1930s was doubtless due to a number of factors, but one should note that it began in 1934, the year when the dollar was devalued. Also striking in the statistics for 1939 is the large short-term capital movement to the United States, reflecting the eagerness of people to get their money out of Europe. It requires this item plus a large export balance plus several other items to offset the gold inflow.

In 1929 the merchandise export balance and the net return on foreign investments paid for shipping services, travel expenditures, and a substantial increase in American investments abroad. This situation is to be contrasted with an earlier period in American history when foreign capital was flowing in to develop American industry, and the resulting credit item was offset by an excess of imports.

During World War II the United States developed a tremendous commodity export balance, amounting to $11 billion in 1944. This was offset by the "lend-lease" arrangement. In the postwar year of 1947, the export balance remained at the high figure of $10 billion, representing capital investments primarily and gifts to a considerable extent.

Exchange Rates and International Adjustments

The equality between debit and credit transactions which appears in a balance-of-payments statement is deceptive. It is a purely formal equality that reflects the reciprocal nature of dealings but is no reflection of real equilibrium. Such balancing factors as shifting bank balances, gold movements, and short-term loans and debt relations keep the two sides of the statement from diverging. At the same time, changes may be occurring in imports and exports or in capital movements which create stresses of a most disturbing nature in the international position of a country. Such stresses, even when minor, cause exchange rates to rise and fall, moving within a range that depends on the money system in effect and the government controls in operation. All persons making or receiving payments in foreign moneys have their positions bettered or made worse by the movements of exchange rates. If the underlying stresses are serious, they operate through exchange

[5] The figures in the table are adapted from the Department of Commerce study, *The United States in the World Economy*, 1943. A table is included in this study covering the entire period 1919–1939.

rates and other factors to bring about readjustments in the dealings from which the stresses come. Such readjustments often react on the internal economies of nations. These are interrelated matters that require some disentangling.

Expression of exchange-rate changes. Since movements of exchange rates are at the center of this discussion, we must be certain the language we use is clear. Confusion may easily arise from differences in ways of stating rates and from the possibility of looking at any rate from the standpoint of either of two countries. When we in the United States say that the price of a pound sterling is $4.02, we are stating an exchange rate as the amount of our money required to buy one unit of a foreign money. But when the British say the rate is $4.02, they are expressing it as the amount of a foreign money that one unit of their money will buy. Accordingly, if the rate shifts from $4.02 to $4.00, the change is properly described here as a fall in the rate on London, but the change is properly described in England as a rise in the rate on New York. Pounds cost us a little less and dollars cost them a little more.

When prices rise or fall abroad, the value of our money in foreign markets changes, just as its value changes at home when the price level moves. But it is not this kind of change—the kind we use index numbers to measure—that is usually meant when we speak of a change in the international value of money. The ordinary meaning of that phrase is simply a shift in exchange rates, because such a shift directly causes a change in the buying power of money when used abroad. The dollar is a more valuable money internationally when exchange rates here go down, or foreign moneys become cheaper. The dollar depreciates internationally when exchange rates here go up, so that more of our money is required to equal a unit of foreign money.

Movements of exchange rates

Exchange rates are prices and therefore behave in general as prices do. In the absence of artificial stabilization, they are highly flexible prices, responding readily to market changes. Their behavior is described by saying that, like other flexible prices, they rise with an increase in demand and fall with an increase in supply. No knowledge of the intricacies of markets is necessary to understand their movement. The only difficulty lies in seeing clearly what is meant in this connection by demand and supply.

The example used above to explain the clearing process in international trade will show what happens when changes occur in demand and supply in the exchange market. Two levels of phenomena may be distinguished. On the surface, demand and supply are to be connected with the purchase and sale of bills of exchange. The American cotton exporter in that example made out an order in pounds against an English buyer and took it to his bank to sell. In doing so he offered on the market a claim to foreign money and thus added to the supply of exchange. To the extent that one small transaction may exert an influence, he depressed the price of pounds sterling, the rate of exchange in New York on London. *Exporting, we may conclude, adds to the supply of exchange and tends to force exchange rates down.*

In like manner, *importing adds to the demand for exchange and tends to lift exchange rates.* The American importer of diamonds went to a bank to buy a sterling draft drawn on a British bank in favor of the British exporter. This offer to buy constituted an increase in the demand for pounds and helped to raise the rate in New York on London.

International bank balances and exchange rates. As we go below the surface to the second level of phenomena, our concern is with bank balances. It is the foreign balances of banks which receive the impact of the selling and buying of exchange. When the cotton exporter offers the New York bank a bill drawn against a British buyer, he is offering it an increase in its London balance. Purchase of the bill will add to the supply of pounds at the bank's command. With demand the same, such an increase in supply will reduce the price in the United States of English money, for foreign balances are of little use except in the selling of exchange against them. Exporting thus depresses rates because it expands the foreign balances of banks of the exporting country.

In the same way, importing reduces those balances and pushes exchange rates up. In offering to buy a bill to pay the foreign seller, the diamond importer is asking the bank to part with a portion of its foreign balance. As such demands put pressure on foreign balances, banks are able to increase the prices they charge for foreign moneys.

Rates from the foreign standpoint. If we had assumed that the initiative in making payment was taken by the British traders in this example, the effect on exchange rates would have been the same. Had the importer of cotton bought a dollar draft to pay for it, upward pressure would have been exerted on the price of dollars in London, the equivalent of the downward pressure on pounds here. Or if the British diamond exporter had drawn a bill against the American buyer and sold it, the cheapening influence on dollar exchange in London would have been the equivalent of the advance in the price of pounds in New York.[6]

[6] Is it not possible for pounds to be dear in New York and for dollars, at the same time,

Nonmerchandise transactions and exchange rates. Exporting and importing of physical commodities usually account for the largest volume of international payments, but other items in the dealings of a country can be used equally well to explain the movements of exchange rates. When, for example, Americans do more traveling abroad, their demand for exchange exerts the same upward influence on rates that importing does. Expanded lending by this country to foreigners has a like effect, since outgoing remittances are required. When fear of the future stampedes the people of a country into sending funds abroad, the international value of that nation's money may be sharply depressed. Foreign moneys are demanded for remittances, and the prices of them go up. All transactions on the credit side have a downward influence on exchange rates in a country and an upward effect on the value of its money; all debit transactions have the opposite effect.

Effects of movements of rates

How do these movements in exchange rates look to the people who are engaged in international transactions and who buy and sell claims to the moneys of foreign countries? Do they want to see foreign moneys rise or fall in price? The answer, as one would expect, depends on whether a person is receiving payments or making them.

The exporter wants to see exchange rates high in his country and foreign moneys expensive. If the American exporter receives £1000 for his cotton, the bill of exchange he draws on the British importer yields him $4000 if the rate on London is $4 but $5000 if the price of pounds is $5. A high exchange rate has the same effect as a higher price for his product. If the rate is rising, moreover, he may quote a lower price in pounds to the foreign buyer, thus promoting sales without having to take a smaller return in dollars than he has been getting.

This is equivalent to saying that a fall in exchange rates is good for the importer. If pounds are dearer here, dollars are cheaper in

---

to be dear in London? The answer is that exchange dealers are alert to observe any discrepancies between rates as they develop and prompt to take advantage of them, thereby correcting them. Suppose that, both in London and New York, most persons with foreign obligations to meet proceeded to buy exchange instead of waiting to be drawn upon. Demand would seem to run ahead of supply in both centers. But if dollars were high in London while pounds were high here, American dealers would request their London correspondents to sell dollar exchange, adding the proceeds to their balances, so that more pounds could be sold here. London banks would do the same. Such transactions would continue until rates were in harmony. Similar transactions eliminate inconsistencies among three or more countries. If francs are too high here, in view of the rate here on London and the rate on Paris in London, American banks can easily increase their Paris balances by having London correspondents purchase francs for their account. Dealing to make a profit from such price differences among markets is known as *arbitrage*.

London. If a shift in the price of pounds from $4 to $5 leads the American exporter to quote a lower price in pounds for his cotton, the British importer obviously gains from what is—to him—a lower rate of exchange. Or if the importer pays for his cotton in dollars and buys $4000's worth, the cotton costs him £1000 when the exchange rate is $4 to the pound and only £800 when the rate is $5 to the pound. In the same way, the American diamond importer would gain if the pound fell from $4 to $3.

In stating the effects of changing exchange rates, just as in giving the reasons for them, we can say that participants in service and capital transactions are in the same position as exporters and importers of commodities. Americans who travel abroad, being like importers, incur heavier expenses when exchange rates go up in this country. They must pay more dollars for pounds and francs and pesos. Foreigners who borrow dollars from Americans want the dollar to be expensive, just as foreign exporters do, since they want to convert their dollar exchange into as many units of their own money as they can.

Effect of instability of rates. Apart from these specific gains and losses from exchange rate movements, there is a general loss from serious instability of rates. Economic change, when not fully predictable, means uncertainty, and uncertainty upsets calculations and burdens transactions with a special cost. Great uncertainty regarding the value of foreign moneys unquestionably discourages dealings and reduces the total volume of activity. Exporters, though benefited by higher rates, would be willing to forego that gain for the assurance that rates would not fall and wipe out ordinary trading profits. Importers would similarly forego the benefit of lower rates. Fluctuating exchange rates transform foreign trade into a speculative game that the nations should be at great pains to avoid. But the problem of exchange-rate control is tied up with the nature of money systems and with the role of flexible rates in international adjustments and must be considered in a broad setting.

Exchange rates under the gold standard

As mentioned in the preceding chapter, one of the main arguments for the gold standard is that, if adopted by all trading nations, it stabilizes exchange rates and removes some of the uncertainty from international dealings. But in doing this, it causes other difficulties.

Stabilizing effect on rates. Under the gold standard, exchange-rate fluctuations are held within narrow limits, because gold movements act as a quick offset to an imbalance in other transactions. As payments arising from trade, travel, or loans run ahead on either the credit or debit side, the very first impact, as we have seen, is on the foreign balances of banks. The cushioning capacity of these balances, however, is limited, because they readily become exhausted or excessive. It is at this point that gold movements enter as a means of building up deficient balances or of bringing home foreign balances that have become too large.

The costs of transferring gold fix the narrow limits within which exchange rates can move under the gold standard. The costs include transportation, insurance, and loss of interest on the funds during the period they are in transit. Quite typically the cost of shipment between this country and England is about one half of 1 percent of the value of the gold. Before England left the gold standard in 1931 the pound sterling was convertible into 113 grains of pure gold. With the dollar then equal to 23.22 grains of gold, the gold parity of the countries, or *par of exchange,* was $4.8665 to the pound (113 divided by 23.22), so that a cost of about 2 cents was involved in moving enough gold to alter the London balance of an American bank to the extent of one pound. If heavy exporting caused exchange rates to fall here and balances to rise abroad, the rate on London could not fall far below $4.85, because at such a rate banks would find it profitable to buy all the exchange offered and pay the cost of bringing excess balances back in the form of gold. Thus a rate near $4.85 would constitute the *lower gold point,* or gold import point. Similarly heavy importing would not push the rate on London above $4.89, for at that rate it would be both possible and profitable for the banks to sell all the exchange demanded, paying the cost of sending gold across to establish the needed balances. Thus a rate near $4.89 would be the *upper gold point,* or gold export point.

Readjustments in transactions. But just as international bank balances can only absorb a small imbalance in payments, so gold movements also must prove inadequate if the imbalance is large and long continued. Only a country, such as South Africa, that mines gold in great quantities can sustain a heavy continuing outward movement. Thus readjustment in the balance must come about in other types of transactions, so that the reason for the gold flow is removed. Temporarily it may be checked by borrowing funds abroad to build up the balances needed in making payments, but finally an adjustment is required in the current transactions, especially imports and exports, that govern the direction of payments.

The gold standard was long relied on to provide these adjustments automatically. The explanation of the matter rests on the quantity theory of the value of money, as presented in the preceding chapter.

If the trading nations are on the gold standard and the United States, for instance, has heavy exports, with exchange rates pressing against the lower gold point, the resulting inflow of gold expands the reserves of the money system and the banks. The condition is thus created for credit expansion, greater spending, and higher prices. Indeed, the very excess of foreign buying acts to push some prices up. As a higher price level is reached, it can be expected that foreign buying in the country will decline somewhat and exports will fall off. At the same time, in the foreign countries that are losing gold, the opposite chain of events is taking place. Monetary reserves and bank credit contract, and reduced spending and lower prices result. These lower prices abroad intensify the reluctance of foreigners to buy in the United States, with its rising prices, and increase the desire of Americans to buy abroad. Forces are thus present under the gold standard which tend to offset the causes of gold movements. It is through these adjustments, finally, that rates are held between the gold points.

Defects of readjustments under the gold standard. For any moderate maladjustment the automatic working of gold movements may provide a satisfactory corrective—it seemed to work well enough for several decades prior to World War I. But the mechanism fails to cope with the great and sudden imbalance caused by wars and severe depressions. The outflow of gold from a nation may be so severe as to deplete its stock and force it from the gold standard. Moreover, the effect of gold movements on prices is necessarily slow and uncertain when, as was discussed in Chapter 12, the money in actual circulation is highly variable in relation to the gold reserve. Indeed, monetary authorities (as in the Federal Reserve System) may act to neutralize the effect of gold movements, using their power to offset the inflationary effect of gold imports and to avoid the deflationary effect of gold exports. Thus automatic adjustments in the balance of payments are weakened and slowed down.

Ironically, if the automatic control does work under highly disturbed conditions, its effect may be worse than if it failed. This, at least, is the view of some authorities. In the countries receiving gold, an unhealthy inflation may be generated. In the countries losing it, deflation may depress the economy, reducing production and employment. The experience of Great Britain in this regard has come to have great weight in international policy respecting gold. In the late 1920s and early 1930s, with exchange rates on the old gold basis and with the British price level high in relation to prices in countries with which the British were trading, British exports were too small to bring equilibrium in their international balance. A lower price level might

have stimulated exports, but its first effect, it seemed, would be to
deepen the depression. Accordingly it seemed best to the British to
discard the automatic gold mechanism, stop the outflow of gold, and
let exchange rates rise freely above the gold export point. Unstable exchange rates seemed less painful than the domestic stresses for which
the gold movement was blamed.

Exchanges under inconvertible currencies

How, then, do exchange rates behave when moneys are not convertible into gold? Are there limits to their movements? Through what
readjustments, if any, may equilibrium be restored when shifts occur
in a nation's dealings? How acceptable is the situation from the standpoint of persons making and receiving payments, and from the broader
standpoint of general economic health? These questions can best be
discussed together.

When gold movements are outlawed and claims to moneys are not
redeemable in gold, movements of exchange rates are not held to any
such narrow range as the gold points establish. Rates rise and fall
freely as variations in trade and other transactions expand the demand
for bills of exchange or the supply of them. The fluctuations may be
wide, but they are not without restraint, even in the absence of government action. This restraint—the very same that operates in all markets
—lies in the unwillingness of sellers to sell or of buyers to buy when
the market goes against them. It operates both to restrict the movement
of exchange rates and to adjust the underlying transactions that are
responsible for exchange-rate movements.

The explanation lies in the reasons for exchange-rate movements
and the effects of them, as already set forth. We have seen (1) that increased exporting forces exchange rates down and that greater importing causes them to rise. We have also seen (2) that exporters gain from
higher rates, importers from lower rates. Thus expansion of payments
in either direction affects rates to the disadvantage of those responsible
for the expansion. At the same time, it works to the advantage of people
who engage in the opposite type of transaction. We find in these circumstances the mechanism through which both exchange rates are
adjusted and international dealing controlled when nations leave the
gold standard.

If, for instance, a heavy foreign demand for American goods, accompanied by a decline in American purchases abroad, creates a shortage of dollar exchange in foreign countries, importers there will have to
pay more for dollars and American importers will pay less for foreign

moneys. As a result, foreign buyers will have to be satisfied with fewer American products and Americans will find it worth while to buy more foreign products. With freely moving exchange rates, there is no question that an imbalance, however great, can be eliminated. Dollars can easily become so high priced that foreigners cannot afford to buy American goods, and we cannot afford not to buy theirs.[7]

The two kinds of international adjustments. Adjustments under gold and with inconvertible paper money stand in sharp contrast. Under gold, the exchange rates are highly stable, and fundamental readjustments in transactions must come through changes in the internal price levels of countries—changes induced by gold movements. With inconvertible paper moneys, exchange rates move freely, and the exchange-rate movements themselves cause adjustments in the underlying transactions. There is little need for change in internal price levels. The *international value of money*, as expressed in exchange rates, is far more stable under gold than under inconvertible money systems, but the *domestic value of money*, so far as international influences are concerned, can be more stable with inconvertible money than with gold.

Monetary chaos and exchange control

During the years between the wars monetary relationships among countries were chaotic in the extreme. New moneys replaced those destroyed by inflation following World War I, and there was a general return to gold during the early 1920s, though with some currencies, notably the franc, greatly cheapened in relation to gold. But foreign markets on which nations depended had shifted, as a result of the war, and resulting stresses were vastly intensified when the great depression came. An epidemic of abandonments of the gold standard began which swept the world during the early 1930s. In part the abandonments were due directly to gold hoardings and international withdrawals that reduced the monetary gold stocks of many nations; in part they reflected the inability of nations, with prevailing exchange rates and domestic prices, to maintain their foreign markets and sell enough abroad to pay for necessary imports. Moreover, as the value of a nation's money fell internationally, many of its people, fearing inflation at home, shifted funds to other more stable countries—a so-called

[7] Exchange-rate adjustments cannot establish equilibrium in international payments when the source of the trouble is the internal collapse of a money unit, as in Germany following World War I. As long as the printing presses of a country pour out money, it will be used to buy foreign moneys that are stable, and rates will rise without achieving a balance. Exchange rates are likely to rise faster than the domestic price level.

"flight of capital"—thus creating an artificial demand for foreign exchange and speeding the depreciation of the money of capital-exporting nations.

Conflicting policy aims. Under these circumstances the exchanges become a major object of government policy, and policy respecting them easily becomes a large, and perhaps a very disturbing, element in international relations. The aims of policy, at best, are mixed, and they vary with the nature and intensity of the strains to which particular nations are subject. The aim may be primarily to stabilize exchange rates, perhaps on a new basis that will promote international dealings and establish the most effective type of world economy. But countries in desperate economic plight or countries no longer devoted to the principle of a world community readily adopt emergency or purely nationalistic objectives. Even so, no one clear course is indicated. Oppressed by unemployment, a nation may cheapen its money aggressively in the exchanges, thus hoping to expand its exports and reduce its spending abroad. But, as other nations lose markets as a result of such tactics, they fall in line, and a progressive, competitive depreciation of moneys occurs. Even if successful, however, a nation pays heavily for its added markets. Its cheaper money means that it pays a higher price for imports, and in a country that depends heavily on foreign sources for food and raw materials, this is a major loss.

The controls employed. Without going into details of the matter, country by country, one may say that the policies followed in the 1930s reflect all of these considerations combined in various ways. To give continuity to exchange rates at least between major adjustments, the device of the *stabilization fund* was extensively used—and still is. It represents the mildest conception of control and has been relied on extensively by England, France, Switzerland, and the Netherlands since they left the gold standard. The United States established such a fund in 1934. It involves the simple principle of having the government enter the exchange market on the weak side to bolster it. If pounds are tending to slip in value (or rates on other countries to rise in England), foreign moneys owned by the British Exchange Equalization Account are offered to Englishmen who have foreign payments to make. In other words, the excessive demand in England for dollars or other moneys is met with a specially provided supply. Plainly the scheme can work only within limits set by the resources of the fund and cannot combat fundamental maladjustments. The stabilized exchange rates must be approximately in line with the requirements of equilibrium in the balance of payments. The stabilization-fund device may be used, however, in moving rates to higher or lower level and not merely in "pegging" them at one level.

To achieve a more basic equilibrium, the transactions themselves—the merchandise, service, and capital items—must be brought into balance. Letting exchange rates reach their natural level may serve this purpose. But if the cheapening of a country's money promotes a flight of capital, thus making equilibrium a more remote goal, a nation is likely to take steps to stop the outflow of funds. And if necessary imports would be painfully expensive at the equilibrium rate, a policy of holding a country's money on a somewhat higher level may seem necessary. Such a policy requires positive control of imports and possibly the stimulation of exports by means other than cheapening the nation's money.

To achieve these results, Germany and other nations imposed a tight control of foreign exchange, so that all foreign balances arising from exports passed into government hands. Exchange was sold against these balances only under license for approved purposes. This is *exchange rationing*. It may be combined with a scheme of *multiple exchange rates* under which claims to foreign balances have one price for certain purposes, another price for other purposes. Going farther, pairs of nations made *bilateral exchange arrangements* by which they agreed to take equal values of each other's products, so that no payment problem would arise—essentially a barter system. Finally, outside the exchange field, the whole arsenal of direct trade controls—tariffs and quotas on imports and subsidies on exports—was used to avoid such a cheapening of the money unit as would result from a free movement of rates. The problem is only incidentally one of money, which is our present concern, and is chiefly one of trade policy, with which we shall deal in Chapter 32.

Postwar exchange control

The foregoing, while only a summary discussion of the foreign-exchange problem, has brought out the main elements that entered the planning of postwar money arrangements among the nations. To most nations it had become clear that a satisfactory situation must exclude the continuing manipulation by individual governments of exchange rates and of the underlying transactions in the international balance. But it was apparent that the old automatic gold standard, with unchanging gold parities among the moneys, cannot withstand severe dislocations and, moreover, that its effect, in so far as it does operate, can be seriously deflationary to nations that lose gold heavily.

On the other hand, it was seen that the free movement of exchange rates with inconvertible moneys imposes on world trade a damaging burden of uncertainty arising from the changing values of foreign moneys. The problem was one of extraordinary difficulty.

When the nations came together at Bretton Woods in 1944 to find an answer, the United States and Great Britain, the leading trading nations, took opposite positions on the main issue. The United States favored the closest feasible approach to the old gold-standard system, with maximum stability of exchange rates. With the United States starting off with the greater part of the world's monetary gold, such a solution would have given it a strong strategic position. Great Britain, while desiring short-run stability, would not accept the rigid relationship between her economy and others that fixed gold parities would impose, with the attendant danger of deflation at home through loss of gold. The plan agreed on was a compromise.[8]

Its main feature was an International Monetary Fund of $8.8 billion to which all nations would contribute designated shares, the United States almost one third of the whole. Each contribution was to consist in part of gold. At the outset exchange rates based on gold would be agreed on for all the currencies. Then if, at these rates, any nation found itself unable to command the money of any other nation that it needed in making payments, it might borrow some of the money of that country from the Fund. Limits to such borrowing were set. Nations that seemed unlikely to be able to balance their payments at the established rates might depreciate their money units in relation to gold up to 10 percent. Still further devaluation would be possible with the approval of the Fund authorities. In accordance with this collective control, the previously existing regulation of exchanges by individual nations was to be abandoned, though only gradually over a period of several years. Some pressure might be imposed by the Fund authorities on the participating nations to adapt their domestic policies, especially in such matters as the protective tariff, to the requirements of international balance. These proposed arrangements were agreed to by representatives of the allied and friendly nations, and though opposed in some quarters, especially by certain banking interests, they received the necessary ratification from the several governments.

By the end of 1946 the initial par values of money units had been announced—the pound, for instance, at $4.03, the Mexican peso at 20.6 cents, the franc at 0.839 cents, and so on. Russia, whose contribution to the fund was to be the third largest (Great Britain was second) had not

---

[8] For a brief treatment of the International Monetary Fund, see Alvin H. Hansen, *America's Role in the World Economy*, W. W. Norton, 1945.

joined, and it was apparent that a satisfactory international monetary situation was some distance away.

Review Questions

1. Use an example to show how exports provide the means of paying for imports. Explain the operation of the clearing principle through use of international bank balances.

2. Distinguish "balance of trade," "balance on current account," and "balance of payments." What does a balance-of-payments statement accomplish?

3. The following items sum up the international dealings of the people of a small country during one year: They import commodities amounting to $2,800,000 and export $3,500,000's worth. They spend $300,000 in travel abroad; and foreigners resident among them send away $100,000 to families and friends in other lands. They lend $1,000,000 to foreign borrowers, and receive $500,000 in interest on earlier loans. Gold moves sufficiently to establish a balance. Calculate the gold movement and prepare a statement of the balance of payments. Is the gold movement a debit or a credit item? Explain.

4. If the only international transactions of a country are commodity imports and exports and loans, would it have an import or an export balance (a) when it is borrowing abroad; (b) when it is repaying what it has borrowed; (c) when it is lending abroad? Explain.

5. In speaking of exchange rates, what does it mean to say: "Rates on London have advanced"? "The dollar is cheaper in Paris"? What does a cheaper dollar mean with respect to rates in New York? How would you define the term "rate of exchange"?

6. "Exchange rates move with supply and demand as other prices do. The problem is to see what is meant by supply and demand." Explain what would cause an increase in the price of British pounds in New York, taking account of import and export transactions, dealings in bills of exchange, and changes in international bank balances.

7. Other things remaining the same, what is the effect on foreign-exchange rates in New York if Americans do more traveling abroad? Less investing abroad? Return to Europeans some of their American bank balances? Explain.

8. "The direct effect of a movement in exchange rates is contrary to the interest of the people responsible for the movement." Explain, showing the effect of rate changes on importers, exporters, borrowers, travelers, and so on.

9. Explain the limits to exchange-rate movements under the gold standard.

10. Explain the limits with inconvertible paper money, applying the analysis in question 8.

11. Contrast the fundamental readjustments in international payments

with gold and paper currencies. Show that one requires an unstable domestic value of money and the other an unstable international value.

12. What possible gains and losses must a nation consider in reducing the value of its money internationally as a deliberate policy?

13. Contrast the stabilization-fund device with more drastic controls.

14. In what sense is the International Monetary Fund a compromise?

PART IV

The Problem of Business Depressions

IT IS one thing for a nation to have great productive power. It is another thing to use that power fully and continuously, so that its people live as well as their resources make possible. In Part II we examined the conditions of productive power. Now, making considerable use of matters studied in Part III, we shall inquire into the problem of underuse of productive power—the problem of unemployment and depressions.

This country has endured many periods in which the economy moved in low gear, output was low, and unemployment extensive. But the menace of economic collapse was never fully sensed until the 1930s. Probably as great an output was lost in that decade through nonuse of resources as was required by the war effort in the decade that followed.

The threat of depressions is not merely economic; it is also political. People who lack food snatch at panaceas, however dubious, and may be induced to trade their liberties for bread and hope. Other countries have shown what the danger is. Though the United States even in the 1930s was relatively well off among nations, a willingness to try drastic measures was apparent. While the war years have brought a high level of production, depression still looms as a serious future threat.

_ 14 _

Total Demand and
the Depression Problem

To say what a depression is, stress must be placed on the underuse of productive power and the resulting loss of real income. To say how depressions are caused, inquiry must be made into the total demand for goods to see why it is low.

Depressions must be explained in this way, because production is carried on, under capitalism, to obtain money income. Fundamentally, goods are produced to satisfy wants, but, when specialized producers supply goods for others to consume, their direct inducement is the payments they receive. These payments must cover their costs and a return for their risks; they will produce no more than markets will absorb on this basis. This is what is meant by saying that production is governed by the prospect of profits. Thus the demands for goods—the amounts that will be bought at profitable prices—directly control output. To understand depressions, we must understand the total demand for all goods and its weaknesses.

This is not easy. There has been considerable popular theorizing about the capacity of markets to absorb products and about the sources and the adequacy of purchasing power. Most of this theorizing is not very helpful and much of it is confusing. Consequently a careful path must be followed to avoid pitfalls and stay on solid ground. But even when we have cleared up a number of prevalent errors and have the main tools of analysis in hand, we shall encounter disturbing disagreements among the experts that leave the problem in a somewhat unsettled state. Final answers to important questions are not yet available; but we may nevertheless proceed with confidence that enough has been learned so that policy problems, in leading respects, can be approached constructively.

344

Varieties of Slack

First, to get our bearings, a sweeping glance is called for over the whole area of underutilization of productive power—of economic slack, as we may call it for short. In the broadest sense, slack includes more than unemployment of resources; it includes every failure to achieve perfection in using resources. Thus it includes all that the word "inefficiency" implies, whether on the part of managements or of ordinary workmen. Inefficient employment of resources is quite different from lack of employment, and we shall ignore it except to note one point: the two overlap in this respect that, when workmen fear unemployment, they are likely to work slowly to make the job last. Thus inefficiency may spring in part from the same source as unemployment.

Unemployment, moreover, is not all due to depressions, though the most serious part of it is. Resources often are idle in particular situations when there is no deficiency in the total demand for goods. Various maladjustments in using resources account for considerable unemployment even in prosperous periods. Such unemployment we shall call *frictional* to contrast it with *depression* unemployment attributable to weaknesses in total demand.

Frictional unemployment

Change is present everywhere in economic life, and adjustment to change is slow, or at least not instantaneous. Resources are made idle at one point and do not shift immediately to other points where they could be absorbed. The various obstacles to perfect coordination may be thought of as frictions.

Seasonal unemployment may be put in this category. Seasonal interruptions arise both on the supply side and the demand side of markets. Such industries as farming, fruit and vegetable canning, and building construction in some degree are made seasonal by conditions governing production. The summer demand of tourists for hotel and other services and the heavy winter demand for coal reflect the seasonal nature of buying. Unemployment is reduced if products can be stocked in anticipation of seasonal demands, and if activities with different seasonal peaks, such as the coal and the ice business, can be dovetailed. But, despite these expedients, seasonal factors are responsible for much idleness of resources.

Seasonal unemployment follows a regular pattern. In addition, there is much unemployment due to *irregularities* in the economy. Irregularities are of several types: (1) Some are, in a sense, normal to particular industries, as in the loading and unloading of vessels. (2) Some appear in unpredictable interruptions due to floods and transportation tie-ups and to strikes that stop the flow of materials to dependent industries. (3) Then there are shifts of demand away from industries, as from the making of buggies or kerosene lamps, and time is lost before displaced workers find new jobs. (4) Labor-saving innovations are adopted, and, though total demand may be high, an interval of "technological unemployment" results. (5) Regions exhaust their timber or minerals, and jobs are deficient until new industries develop or people move away. (6) The very turnover of labor, as workers shift about in quest of better opportunities, is a source of unemployment. If, for example, workers changed jobs on the average of once a year and an average of five days elapsed between one job and the next, this factor alone would account for an unemployment of almost 2 percent.

While frictional and depression unemployment must be distinguished, they are not unrelated. Each may affect the other. When total demand was abnormally high during World War II, adjustments were hastened and frictions overcome, so that unemployment of labor fell almost to 1 percent, well below the usual level of frictional unemployment in periods of peacetime prosperity. On the other hand, the economic changes that cause frictional unemployment may bring lapses in buying that combine into a general slackening of demand. This possibility will be examined at the end of the chapter.

Chronic versus cyclical depression

As we turn to depression slack, we are confronted with two different and highly significant ways of interpreting it.

Depressions have been studied most extensively as a phase of the *business cycle*. Most of the older general works on economics dispose of depressions and unemployment in a single chapter on the business cycle. The cycle, as ordinarily viewed, is a fairly repetitious ebb and flow of activity, a sequence of boom and depression. Cycles can be explained quite satisfactorily as the cumulative result of a variety of tensions and distortions that develop in a dynamic economy, causing fluctuations in the total demand for goods but not implying any basic inability of capitalism to remain prosperous if these disturbances can be ironed out.

Chronic depression or stagnation implies a more fundamental weakness. Depression can be expected because, ordinarily, markets are basically unable to absorb the volume of goods that would result from a capacity level of production. During the nineteenth century occasional writers expressed this view, among them Karl Marx and his followers, but the view was not peculiar to socialism. It was not widely held until the 1930s, when a number of theories of chronic weakness entered general circulation. At that time and in a number of ways it came to be said that the public is ordinarily unable to buy the output it is able to produce, and thus production must proceed much of the time on a disappointing level. Such old phrases as overproduction, underconsumption, oversaving, and deficient purchasing power became part of the common currency of speech, and expert attention came to focus on the alleged lack of investment opportunities in a "mature economy."

A complete separation of the cycle approach and the stagnation approach would not be accurate. One may accept the idea of a cycle, with a fairly prosperous period now and then and with a variety of factors promoting ups and downs, and still hold that booms must come to an end because demand is basically unable to remain on a high level. But in theories of the cycle, as we shall see, this chronic weakness is commonly subordinated and is likely to be recognized only to be denied. The real point, for our present purpose, is that depressions can occur without cyclical fluctuations, provided stagnation factors are present. Thus, for simplicity in studying the matter, it is useful to examine the stagnation possibility without allowing the cyclical ups and downs to intrude and complicate the problem.

Unlike measurement of cyclical and chronic depression

The difference between these two approaches is sharpened if we consider how, on the basis of each of them, we would go about measuring the extent of underuse of productive power.

From the cycle standpoint, we may visualize the course of activity as represented by a wavelike line (arrived at, as will be indicated in the next chapter, through elaborate statistical procedures). The peaks in the line represent booms and the valleys, depressions. The severity of depression, then, is measured by the difference between the boom and depression levels. By this procedure, we might conclude (as someone has) that production during depressions often runs 15 or 20 percent lower than in boom periods but that the slump of the 1930s attained twice that severity.

Such a procedure, it is plain, does not show how far our economy falls short of producing the amount that it has the resources and the techniques to produce; it merely compares depressions with booms. But perhaps we fall short even in the best periods of what we ought to produce. The ordinary boom may only rise part of the way toward the level of full production and then fade away as its meager impetus subsides. What is needed is a measure of capacity production, with which actual output can be compared in absolute terms. One who suspects the economy of chronic weakness must insist on this approach; others not committed to any theory must recognize its value.

The great difficulty, however, is in determining what is *capacity production for the whole economy*. It is difficult, even in the abstract, to define the capacity of the economy in a satisfactory way. But, having a definition, getting the data to apply it remains a tremendous task. Attempts have been made, nevertheless, to measure capacity, and the results are significant, even though they are not entirely consistent.

The casual observer is likely to get an exaggerated impression of the productive power of a modern economy such as ours. He is likely, as we have noted, to think of production merely as "making things" and to view the dramatic achievements of highly mechanized, automatic processes as indicative of how things, in general, are made. Much manufacturing, of course, is not of this nature at all, and quite a bit of it is devoted to providing and servicing factories and their equipment. Most production, however, lies outside of manufacturing, in providing raw materials and fuels, in transportation and marketing, in producing non-material services—and much of this production is not highly mechanized. Spectacular, but unbalanced, pictures of productive capacity can easily distort popular thinking on policy matters.

To the informed investigator, the problem is in part that of gauging the output each industry is typically capable of when the market will take all it can produce. What it is typically capable of is not its theoretical maximum output, since allowance must be made for breakdowns and shutdowns for repairs, for adjustments to new models and revised processes, for seasonal factors, for labor difficulties, for interruptions in the flow of materials and parts for transportation or other reasons. Modern production is complex, and perfect coordination of all of its elements cannot be maintained. Bottlenecks will appear and have their repercussions.

But the problem of measuring the productive capacity of the whole economy is not just a matter of adding up the capacities of separate industries. Allowance must be made for the simultaneous operation of all segments of the economy. Even if each branch of industry could overcome the obstacles to peak production, all industries could not together operate at their collective peaks. The labor supply would not be sufficient to man the physical plant. Thus it cannot be assumed that two- and three-shift operation of facilities will be general. Moreover, some plant capacity that is inferior and obsolescent will have to be excluded, except in cases of unusual demand for certain products.

Probably the leading study of productive capacity in this country is that completed by the Brookings Institution in 1934.[1] In this study the investigators, making what seemed a reasonable allowance for the obstacles to perfect performance, concluded that in 1929, the peak year of the prosperous 1920s, the American economy produced about 20 percent less than was technically feasible. Another study, made at about the same time but with a different concept of capacity, concluded that about 45 percent could reasonably have been added to the production of 1929.[2]

World War II has provided the best practical demonstration of what the economy can do when markets quickly absorb all that is produced. When this country began its war effort, it had emerged only part way from the depression of the 1930s and had available an unused capacity (including 8,000,000 unemployed) much greater than in 1929. From the level of 1940, the country was able by 1944 to double the gross national product in dollar terms. As we noted in Chapter 3, to interpret this increase accurately in real terms is probably not possible. The difficulty is not merely that prices had risen—for standard goods a price correction is quite easy—but that so much of the product consisted of planes, tanks, ships, guns, and other special war products that cannot be translated into ordinary goods. Millions of persons shifted from stores and farms and southern hills to factories where a high price was set on their services, and these costs, along with other special factors, entered into the prices paid by the government. So-called "industrial production," including factories and mines, is supposed to have risen nearly 90 percent above the 1940 level.[3] But whether output for the whole economy increased by as much as 50 percent, perhaps no one will be able to say. In addition, allowance must be made for the abnormally high productive effort during the war, due partly to the millions of persons who took jobs who ordinarily do not work and partly to the exceptional hours of work. Peacetime capacity cannot assume so great an effort. But against this factor should be set the rather low value put on the services of men in the army and navy. Moreover, it is proba-

[1] Edwin G. Nourse and Associates, *America's Capacity to Produce,* Brookings Institution, 1934.

[2] *Report of the National Survey of Potential Product Capacity,* prepared, in 1935, under the sponsorship of New York City's housing and relief agencies. This study, unlike that of the Brookings Institution, assumed changes in the structure of the economy in estimating its capacity. The difficulty with such an approach is that, when changes are assumed, it becomes problematical what other changes would necessarily follow. If competitive duplication is eliminated, what, one must ask, is the effect on industrial incentives and enterprise? Statistics of the use of productive power are useful only in gauging the performance of the system to which they apply. They throw no light on whether production could be increased, for example, by turning to socialism.

[3] The Federal Reserve System each month reports an index of industrial production. See the *Federal Reserve Bulletin.*

bly true that, under the pressures of the emergency, activities were not so well coordinated as they would be if the same expansion occurred more slowly.

The presence of slack, even during prosperous peacetime years and after allowing for unequal efficiency and various frictions, does not prove that the chronic-stagnation theory is correct—we should leave that issue open—but it strengthens the need for understanding the foundations of prosperity. Accordingly, we shall now consider the meaning and the possible weakness of the aggregate demand for goods.

The Total Demand for Goods

Two opposite misconceptions of total demand are common—opposite in theoretical nature and opposite in the conclusions they point to regarding depressions. In one of them, the more popular one, demand and the purchasing power behind it are rootless and capricious, easily upset and easily manipulated. In the other, the product of an older economic orthodoxy, total demand is so firmly and inflexibly rooted that it should neither suffer lapses nor respond to control.

In the first view, which is not a formulated theory, production and demand seem to have independent sources and travel independent roads. Thus, in one version of it, production is said ordinarily to outstrip demand because of the high productivity of modern industry. With modern power-driven machinery, the economy turns out products faster than it provides purchasing power to buy the products. A variant of this idea emphasizes the displacement of workers by machines and the accumulating unemployment that must result. In another version that stresses the consumer side the idea may be simply that we are now able to produce more than we can consume. The more common version is that there are plenty of wants but that the people who have the wants do not have the money; it is in other hands.

In the second view, the older orthodox one, production and demand not only travel the same road, they practically merge. As stated in a recent version, "demand and supply are merely two sides of the same coin. They are the same thing looked at from different directions. Supply creates demand because at bottom it *is* demand." [4] The wonder is, from this viewpoint, that depressions should take place at all.

The difficulty in studying total demand is that there is a grain of truth, or more than a grain, in each of these ideas. But the truth depends on a particular construction of the idea, with certain necessary conditions stated. Without the correct interpretation, the idea may

[4] Henry Hazlitt, *Economics in One Lesson,* Harper, 1946, p. 16.

lead to conclusions that are completely wrong. We shall proceed, in this connection, by considering (1) wants, (2) purchasing power, and (3) total demand.

Wants

It is first necessary to dispose of the idea that in modern America we can produce more than we want. Inadequate buying is not often explained on this ground, and certainly it should not be. But it is well to see how completely false the idea is.

Commonly it is brushed aside with the observation that human wants are unlimited. "Mankind's desires . . . are insatiable," says one writer. "The prince's luxuries of today are the pauper's demands of tomorrow." [5] Perhaps nothing more need be said, but since we cannot prove that human wants are infinite, it is better, and quite adequate, to say that they greatly exceed what we can produce in the foreseeable future, even in America. With high wartime employment, the net product available for consumption averaged somewhat more than $1000 per capita at prices current then. This is a substantial quantity of goods, but most people could approach much closer to the level of living of the wealthy without feeling surfeited. Even present desires would easily absorb an output several times as large as the largest we have had.

Any notion that more can be produced than people want probably arises from the lack of perspective we have noted regarding productive capacity. Too much attention is paid the direct productivity of automatic machines. Specialists, moreover, are likely to be unduly impressed by the great output in their specialties. Alaskans, for instance, must be appalled at the thought of consuming all of the salmon they catch. It is startling to think of six billion glass bottles finding a market in one year in this country. The wanting capacity of 145,000,000 people is not easy to grasp.

It is quite possible, also, that the trend in consumption will be somewhat away from mass-produced goods. As incomes rise, relatively more is spent on travel, professional services, products of the arts, and on other amenities of living. The rise of the service occupations was noted in Chapter 2. When human desires are compared with the means of satisfying them, it must be assumed that productive capacity is adapted to the kinds of things that people will spend their money for.

Purchasing power

Let us grant, then, that there are sufficient wants. Since to get goods it is necessary not only to want them but also to pay for them, can we

[5] William L. White, "Report on the Russians," *Readers Digest*, December 1944.

assume that the economy provides enough purchasing power to buy its product when that product becomes very large? In answering this question, one of the most important lessons of economics is to be learned. The idea that an economy can turn out goods at one rate and purchasing power at some different rate is basically false. It runs counter to an underlying unity in economic processes that should be seen clearly. Production and purchasing power are linked together because they arise from a single source.

The point appears sharply if we assume that goods are exchanged through *barter*. If commodities are traded directly for other commodities, then each commodity in the very process of being offered on the market as part of a supply constitutes the means of buying another product of like value. The offer to sell is identical with the offer to buy, and the good offered is the purchasing power used. If we use our imaginations and see the whole society as a collection of specialists producing goods for each other, the idea of aggregate purchasing power is simple enough. It is the aggregate of products offered in exchange.

When we turn to the modern world in which goods are exchanged for money, we find that purchasing power is governed by exactly the same principle—though now we must be careful not to conclude too much. Each product, whatever the price at which it is sold, yields an amount of purchasing power exactly equal to that price. This sum (1) goes in the form of wages, interest, rent, and profits to the persons connected with its production or connected with the production of the materials and supplies used in producing it, or, in part, it (2) stays with the various firms involved to be used for replacement and expansion, or it (3) goes to government in taxes. Somebody, somewhere, gets every cent of the receipts—no more, no less—and has that amount to use. These receipts are just sufficient to buy that product at that price or some other product of like value.

Again, if we take the over-all view that includes all products, we see that the receipts from the gross national product will just buy the gross national product. If that product amounts to $200 billion at prevailing prices, its sale yields $200 billion to all parties (plus the government) concerned with its production—exactly enough to buy that output. This relationship holds however much we mechanize industry and expand production and however income is distributed between owners and workers. *The sale of any quantity of product at any set of prices yields a money return sufficient to buy that quantity of product at those prices.*

But now let us return to the warning not to conclude too much. We are speaking here of purchasing power, not of the use of purchasing power, not of the actual spending, the demand for goods. At this point, the barter case and the money case must be distinguished. Under barter the producer can dispose of his product only through buying another's product. Obtaining income and using it are identical. But when money is used, the exchange through which a specialized economy operates is broken into two parts: (1) the sale of one's product for money, and (2) the use of the money to buy other products. This is a fact of tremendous importance, for it permits the individual to receive purchasing power at one rate and spend it at another rate. So we shall not say, as the author quoted early in this section did, that supply and demand are the same thing. For unless one makes this statement with conscious reservations, it conceals the essential difference between purchasing power and the use of purchasing power.[6] This is the gap that we bridge in turning to the topic of aggregate demand.

Total demand

Continuing production depends not on the presence of purchasing power but on its use. If the funds derived from a given volume of production are spent at the rate at which they are received, they will sustain that volume of production (assuming constant prices). It is thus entirely possible for a very high level of output and income to be maintained. In the processes of a capitalist economy, there is no mechanical reason why the high level should not continue.

At the same time, there is no assurance that it will continue. Spending of the receipts from production may slow down. Spending is a matter of free choice, and the total of individual and business decisions regarding the use of purchasing power may cause a reduction in the rate of outlay. If this occurs, production will also fall, because no more will be produced than can be sold profitably. If production falls, then the amount of purchasing power that is becoming available must fall to a like extent. Thereupon the new level of receipts will only buy the new level of product. It is in this way that a recession sets in.

Now let us examine the use of funds more analytically. The main use, except for persons with very large incomes, is in buying commodities and services for *consumption*. Following the usage in Chapter

---

[6] The principle that supply and demand are both rooted in production and that the supply of goods is, in the aggregate, the demand for goods, is known as Say's Law. It has performed a useful service in combating some fallacious notions that would divorce demand from production. But it has been applied in an undiscriminating manner to situations where the essential problem is the rate at which people choose to use their purchasing power. Business depressions are the most important of these situations. Thus we shall stress the distinction noted above and merely say that any volume of products is *able to buy* itself, not that it *will* buy itself. Certainly we shall not say that the purchasing power derived from production in one period will buy an equivalent product in the succeeding period.

6, we shall say that the remainder is *saved*. By saving we merely mean that income is not used for current consumption; the use it is put to, if any, is another question. Of the saving, a part is "compulsory," in the sense that it is taken in taxes by federal, state, and local governments. Presumably most of this "compulsory saving" is spent by these government bodies for current purposes and thus is not saved from the social viewpoint, but some part of it is likely to be used for capital outlays, such as schools and post offices, highways, waterways, reclamation and other projects. The rest of the savings, the part remaining in individual hands, is either invested or hoarded.

Investment, we have seen, means capital formation. It means the use of funds to pay for the labor and materials that go into the manufacture of equipment or the construction of buildings, including residential housing.[7] The saver may use his funds in this way. But if he puts his money in the bank or in life insurance, or if he buys real estate or securities representing already existing wealth, the effect, as far as his action goes, is that of hoarding. He is not using his purchasing power to buy the services of productive resources. If total spending is to be maintained, it will be up to borrowers from the bank or the insurance company, or up to the seller of the real estate or securities, to use the savings in real capital formation.

In the case of *business enterprises*, the division and use of gross receipts are a little more complex. Most of the receipts arrive finally in the hands of individuals as wages and profits and other forms of income. Even the payments for materials, fuels, and utility and other services largely have this destination. But part of the receipts also go to governmental bodies in tax payments. The remainder, as described in Chapter 6, constitutes the gross savings of business enterprises. These gross savings consist of net savings in the form of undistributed profits and of funds which reflect the recovery of previously invested capital—funds which offset the depreciation of existing wealth.

As in the case of individual savings, we must ask what becomes of the gross savings of business firms. The mere fact that they are retained tells nothing of their use. They may be put in the bank and, for the time being, left there; they may be invested in structures, equipment, and inventories. Investment, up to the amount added to the depreciation reserve, merely maintains the value of present facilities. Investment beyond that sum expands the aggregate real wealth of the enterprise.

---

[7] The line between consumption and investment spending is not sharp, and classification, as usual, is a little arbitrary at the boundary. Consumers save to buy such expensive consumers' goods as automobiles, but their purchase is treated by the statisticians as consumption spending. The purchase of new housing, on the other hand, is classed with investment spending, whether the housing is to be used by the owner or rented to others to use.

The two together make up the gross investment of the business. Only the latter constitutes net investment and absorbs net savings out of income.

Importance of saving and investment. Taking account of individuals, firms, and governments, we can sum up what we have said in this way:

1. Total receipts from the gross national product (total purchasing power made available) fall into three parts:

    a. Funds allocated to private consumption;

    b. Taxes paid to various governments;

    c. Private gross saving.

2. Total spending falls into three corresponding parts:

    a. Private consumption spending;

    b. Government spending;

    c. Private gross investment (including replacement and expansion of wealth).

It is easy to see that while the receipts from a given volume of output can buy that volume of output, the rates of spending and receiving funds need not be equal. The spending may lag, or, as we shall see presently, it may speed ahead. Sub-items *a* in the two cases are so defined that consumption spending will not be less than the funds assigned to it, though it may exceed the funds from current receipts. As for the *b* items, government is likely to spend all that it receives in taxes, though it may not. Again, it may spend more. Thus, the possible time gap that will mainly concern us is between the *c* items. Gross investment may fall behind gross saving, or it may move ahead. It is when the rate of investing lags behind the rate of saving that depression sets in and the level of the national product and income falls. We may say, then, that the relationship between saving and investment is the crux of the problem of utilization of productive power.

The "national-budget" approach to total demand. All of this may be clarified with an example. Using assumed figures which may be reasonably in line with the facts for some postwar year, let us look at the gross national product from two angles: (1) the breakdown of the purchasing power it yields into the main funds to be used and (2) the breakdown of the spending necessary to maintain that gross product.

We have depicted here an equilibrium situation in which total spending is just sufficient to maintain total production and each category of spending corresponds to the provision made for it. Neither of these conditions needs prevail. The total may fall, and production with it, or it may be maintained in other ways.

TABLE 20—NATIONAL AGGREGATE OF RECEIPTS AND EXPENDITURES
(In billions of dollars)

Receipts from Gross National Product		Total Spending	
Sum for consumption.........	$140	Consumption spending........	$140
Taxes (federal, state, and local)..	35	Government spending..........	35
Private savings (gross)		Private investment (gross)	
Reserve to maintain		Replacement.......... $ 9	
capital............. $ 9		Expansion............. 16	25
Net saving, individuals.. 11			$200
Net saving, corporations. 5 25			
	$200		

If the rate of consumption spending falls from $140 billion a year to $135 billion, raising the rate of gross saving to $30 billion, and if the rates of government and investment spending remain unchanged, the gross national product of $200 billion will not be bought and production and income will fall. If investment falls, the same result takes place.

But a decline in one department of spending may be offset by an increase in another. The reduction of $5 billion in consumption is not likely to be offset by an increase in investment, but it is possible that government will spend $5 billion more than before to close the gap. In doing this it must not raise taxes—unless a tax could be designed to fall only on savings—since the effect would be to reduce private spending still farther. This, in brief, is the logic of public deficit spending to maintain prosperity, a controversial matter that we shall consider presently.

This approach to the problem of total demand is now widely used by economists (including some in government) as a framework in making estimates regarding future economic activity and the requirements of prosperity. It is called the "national-budget" approach—a term which must not be confused with governmental budgets. This is budgeting for the whole economy to assist in following the course of events and perhaps to serve as a guide to public policy.

Two questions are suggested by the foregoing:

1. If total spending tends to lag—if investment ceases to absorb savings—how serious is the effect? Does the appearance of a $5 billion gap cause a $5 billion fall in total production, a $15 billion fall, or perhaps a $50 billion fall?

2. If production falls way below capacity, how can it rise again? Or how can expansion occur in any circumstances, since the proceeds from a given volume of product will buy only that volume of product?

These are additional aspects of the total demand for goods which we shall consider in the next two subsections.

Effect of saving-investment divergence—the multiplier

How much is total production affected when the rates of saving and investment diverge? In Table 20, what would be the effect of a fall in private investment from $25 billion to $20 billion a year? In answering this question, we shall observe: (1) that the effect is greater than the disturbance which causes it—some multiple of $5 billion in this case; (2) that the movement stops when saving and investment reach a new equality.

A fall in investment of $5 billion has an effect greater than $5 billion because a chain of reactions is set up in the purchase of goods. The *primary* effect is a decline of $5 billion in the purchase of buildings and equipment from capital-goods industries, causing a decline of $5 billion in their production. This includes the impact on the construction and machinery industries and on the steel and lumber and related industries that supply materials.

In addition, there are *secondary* effects on consumer-goods industries. Owners and workers in the capital-goods fields suffer a loss of income that approaches $5 billion, and they will reduce their purchase of consumers' goods, though not by $5 billion. But the total effect on consumer-goods industries will probably go well above $5 billion, for there is not just one wave of impact but a series of declining waves, as workers in these industries also lose income and have to spend a smaller amount for consumption.

Theory of the multiplier. To describe this sort of effect more precisely, a so-called multiplier theory has been worked out—a theory stating the relationship between changes in investment and changes in total production, assuming the same inclination to consume and save.[8] Without the details, the idea can be put briefly. In the above example, with gross product of $200 billion, consumption spending was $140 billion, or about two thirds of the total; saving, including compulsory tax saving, was about one third. *If this relationship holds,* the effect of a $5 billion decline in investment will not die out until the gross product has fallen by about $15 billion. When gross product has fallen by $15 billion, consumption will have fallen by $10 billion and saving by $5 billion, and equilibrium will be restored between saving

[8] The most notable work in the development of the modern theory of total demand is that of John Maynard Keynes, *The General Theory of Employment, Interest, and Money,* Harcourt, Brace, 1936. Less complex treatments are: Theodore Morgan, *Income and Employment,* Prentice-Hall, 1947, and Lawrence R. Klein, *The Keynesian Revolution,* Macmillan, 1947.

and investment. In this case the multiplier is said to be 3. The fall in gross product is three times the fall in investment. If saving, in this broad sense, were half of the total, the multiplier would be 2, and a $10-billion fall in gross product would restore equilibrium.

The principle may operate in the opposite direction. When resources are unemployed and production is on a low level, the developments needed to restore prosperity are the major issue of the day. In depression, profit prospects are poor and investment is low. What is needed most is some spending on plant and equipment, or, in lieu of that (many would argue) an expansion in government spending, using funds not taken from current income. But how much investment is needed? If $200 billion represents full production, and activity is now at a $170 billion level, it will not require an initial outlay of $30 billion to achieve prosperity, since outlays lead to other outlays, as we have seen. With a multiplier of 3, an increase of $10 billion in the investment rate would lift the gross national product from $170 to $200 billion.

This multiplier relationship, as we have put it, is plainly over simplified. *Two important qualifications* should be noted:

1. As spending expands or contracts, the chain of reactions does not stop with the secondary effect on consumer-goods industries. If capital-goods and consumer-goods industries contract, then they will reduce their demand for equipment for replacement and expansion. Thus there will be an additional reduction in investment beside the first fall of $5 billion which started the trouble. This additional reduction will also have primary and secondary effects to which the multiplier principle applies. As a matter of fact, an accelerative principle operates in this connection that can be most disturbing. We shall examine it in discussing booms and depressions in the next chapter.

2. The other qualification works in the opposite direction. As incomes fall, people are likely to reduce their rate of saving. Let us assume that with the fall of $5 billion in investment, an individual who has been making $3000 in the steel industry suffers a cut to $2400, or by 20 percent. If he has been spending $2700 on consumption and taxes and saving $300 beside, it is not likely that he will cut each item by 20 percent. On the contrary, he may now spend the whole $2400 and save nothing except his compulsory tax saving. If this happens generally, a smaller decline in gross product is necessary to bring the reduction in saving that will offset the reduction in investment. But if the percentage of saving falls as incomes are reduced, it seems likely that the percentage will rise, at least in the short run, as incomes expand. If so, investment must expand more rapidly than total income.

Thus it is impossible to arrive at a figure for the multiplier that is an exact working tool. Statistical studies have been made of the relationship between investment and total production through periods of boom and depression, and there is some evidence that a multiplier of 3 is as representative as any. But such statistics are the resultant of a variety of factors and reflect much more than the simple primary and secondary effects first noted. The qualifications just mentioned would enter the result.

The expansion of purchasing power

Perhaps additional investment of $10 billion will raise total product by $30 billion, but how can the additional goods be paid for? In fact, where can money ever be found to pay for an expansion of output, either in recovery from depression or in long-term growth? How can people who are getting their incomes from one volume of output go into the market and buy a larger volume?

This is the dilemma of expansion. A given output, as we have seen, will pay for itself but not for more than itself. To buy more product, people must have more income. But they cannot get more income until they produce more, and they will not produce more unless the product can be sold profitably—which requires that people have more money to buy it. If there is any problem of aggregate purchasing power, this is it.

As a matter of fact, there are three possible escapes from this dilemma:

1. *Spending may be speeded up,* the velocity of money increased. What this means, as we saw in Chapter 12, is that, for a time, individuals and business firms decide to get along with smaller cash balances in relation to the amount of buying they do. In other words, they draw somewhat on their liquid capital to expand their purchases. Thus a greater volume of product can be bought than the volume from which current income is coming.

2. *Prices may fall,* so that more goods can be exchanged with the same flow of money. Purchasing power increases not because there are more dollars or the dollars change hands faster but because each dollar buys more.

3. *Credit may expand.* Consumers may make purchases that their incomes do not cover, and merchants turn to the banks for funds to replenish their stocks. Firms may borrow also to expand their inventories and to buy equipment and construct buildings. In consequence, there is more money in circulation, first, through the expansion of bank loans and deposits and, second, through the release of hand-to-

hand money, especially Federal Reserve notes, as small transactions expand.

Does this violate the proposition that purchasing power derives from production? The answer is no, except in a superficial, immediate sense. Expanded production will be necessary to repay the loans. If production did not expand, the new buying power would prove illusory, for it would be dissipated in rising prices. Thus we can still say that purchasing power must have its basis in production. When resources are idle, credit provides an immediate means of payment that serves excellently in getting them back to work, so that additional products can appear and provide the ultimate means of payment.

Short-run and long-run expansion. These three ways of expanding purchasing power and production are not equally useful in all circumstances. Consider the two principal situations: recovery from depression and the long-term growth of the economy as population increases and technology improves.

In the *recovery case,* expedients 1 and 3 both serve, but 2 does not. During a recovery period, we expect to find that cash balances are brought into use which have been idle during depression; as a boom develops, the rate of use of money expands considerably. We also expect a large expansion of credit buying and an increase of money of all kinds in circulation. But we do not expect prices to fall. On the contrary, some advance in the price level is characteristic of recovery and boom periods. Declining prices, in the short run, squeeze profits and discourage expansion.

In the expansion of purchasing power required for *long-run economic growth,* bank credit has an important part, as do other elements in the money supply. But an increasing velocity of money, through reduction of cash balances, is not likely to be a long-run factor. Changes in velocity occur with changes in prosperity, but there is no reason to suppose that people's habits will change in such a way that output expansion over long periods can be paid for in this way.

In the long run, there is some possibility that a greater output will be absorbed through a fall in prices. If methods of production improve, so that more goods can be produced with the same resources, prices can fall without a fall in profits, and more goods can be absorbed with the same total expenditure. Whether this is the best way for expansion to occur, as we saw in Chapter 12, is doubtful. The view has gained headway that, even in the long run, a fall in prices is likely to have a dampening influence. An expansion in the money supply would then be the main reliance.

Overproduction and make-work beliefs

The most troublesome ideas in the field of economics are the every-day, popular beliefs regarding total demand and job opportunities. They are troublesome in theory and in their effect on behavior. These beliefs, with their variants, are numerous, but they make up a well-knit family in which the central thought is that the economy cannot produce efficiently and keep its labor employed.

Among them are these ideas: that machines and improved methods take the jobs of workers, causing an accumulation of unemployed, and should therefore be opposed; that workmen should cut down their speed to spread work and make jobs last, and unions should compel the hiring of unnecessary men; that married women should not work because they take the jobs of heads of families; that all persons who can afford it should hire someone to mow their lawns, shovel their walks, do repair work in order to make more jobs; that earthquakes, fires, and floods are good because destruction creates demand and work; that profits are evil because profit income is largely saved, and savings do not buy goods and provide jobs; that, in short, overproduction is the cause of our troubles, and everybody's duty is to combat it.

Basic error of these beliefs. We have referred to these ideas before—and shall do so again—because the attitude they engender, as a factor in economic motivation, creates a major problem. We mentioned them first in Chapter 4 in discussing the basic meaning of economy. Economy consists in getting the most out of resources to the end that people may enjoy the highest possible level of living. Economy calls for the highest possible ratio of product obtained to work done. But these ideas mean the minimizing of product in relation to work, or—the same thing—the maximizing of work in relation to product. If they were carried out to their logical end, the effect of technological progress would be nullified, and we would be living the life of primitive man—or that minority would so live who got enough to live at all.

This fundamental point cannot be made too strongly, but it is not the one to be stressed here. The point to be stressed now is that these ideas, as they are often stated and understood, reflect a seriously distorted view of the nature of purchasing power and total demand. From our discussion of these matters, it follows that:

1. There is no such thing as general overproduction in the sense (*a*) that more goods will be produced than we want to use, even if we produce all we can, or (*b*) that more can be produced than can be bought with the spendable income from that product. Of course, too

much of some goods can be produced in proportion to other goods; that is another story, and we shall not go into it now.

2. No one is justified, therefore, in assuming that human desires are so limited that, if a man mows his lawn or paints his house, he will find no other use for the money he could have used in hiring out these jobs, or that floods and other catastrophes must destroy part of what we already have in order to suggest things to buy. Our level of living is plainly improved if we keep what we have and use our buying power for other things that we want.

3. Nor should any one oppose efficiency on the general ground that "there is only a certain amount of work to be done," and that if women do it, men cannot, or if some men do too much of it, others must be unemployed, or if machines are used, the jobs for human beings are fewer. There can be no fixity of employment when wants and purchasing power are as expansible as, by nature, they have to be. The logic is compelling. So also is the lesson of history. Despite the Industrial Revolution, with all its power-driven machinery and growth in productive power, employment has maintained about the same average relationship to population. In some fields jobs have been reduced, and thus labor has become available for the numerous new products that have been developed; in other fields in which mechanization has been great, reductions in the cost of products have so greatly expanded sales that increased employment right in those fields can be credited to the labor-saving methods.

4. Profits are spendable income, just as wages are. There is serious confusion behind the idea that workers must be paid enough to buy the total product. What is received by all parties involved will necessarily be sufficient to buy the product or its equivalent. The fact that money income is saved does not imply that it is not spent. We have been careful to say that saving consists in not spending for consumption. The normal destiny of savings is their investment in the production of goods which become part of the aggregate of wealth—buildings and capital equipment. Spending for these purposes is, dollar for dollar, as effective a part of total demand and as creative of employment as spending for current consumption.

The element of truth in these beliefs. There is no question that confusion, tremendously harmful confusion, lurks in these overproduction and make-work ideas. But when it was stated above that these are troublesome ideas, more than this was meant. They are troublesome also because they can be so interpreted that elements of truth appear along with the error or that their reasonableness is arguable in some respects. Mistaken ideas are seldom dangerous unless they contain elements of truth; then it is difficult to be fair to them without conceding them more merit than they have.

In pointing out the essential error of these views, we have been stressing their bearing on the whole economy in long-run terms. They are most plausible when applied to specific individuals, groups, or localities or to the special circumstances of limited periods.

Certain workers, through strenuous effort, may shorten their employment in some particular capacity or reduce the number that will be hired. In an economy with the frictions we have described, no other work may be immediately in sight, and the uncertainty of the situation may suggest that a slow pace is beneficial to the individual and his fellows. It does not follow that aggregate employment will be greater or even that total shifting about will be less; and a smaller output and real income is the certain result. But from a narrow viewpoint, the slow pace still seems a security measure. Most individual decisions are made on this level.

Machines do take the place of particular workers, sometimes rob them of the value of their skill and reduce their wages, and often cause the inconvenience of going elsewhere to find work, with probably an interval of unemployment. When professional musicians fight the use of recorded music by demanding that stand-by musicians be hired, they need have no theory whatever regarding aggregate employment. They are simply opposing, in an especially highhanded way, the kind of readjustment through which all progress in using resources has been brought about. Such progress is nearly always painful to the individuals directly affected by it. Undoubtedly society should find means of cushioning the impact to some extent.

During a depression job opportunities are low, and there may be no early prospect of betterment. Whatever may be true of aggregate employment in the long run, there is immediately a job shortage, and a case can be made for various methods of work spreading during the emergency. We shall come back to this point when we discuss depression policies in Chapter 16.

But is there no basis for these make-work ideas except in these limited connections? What of the idea suggested earlier that modern capitalism may suffer chronic weakness of demand and stagnation tendencies? We have recognized that the presence of purchasing power does not mean that it will be used. We have suggested that investment may not absorb the funds which are not spent for consumption. If there is some continuing possibility of these difficulties, then there is ground for some continuing fear of unemployment. If that is the case, is there not some broad and permanent justification for opposing machines, spreading work, and encouraging wasteful expenditures?

To this the answer must be that chronic weakness in the economy puts these ideas in a more favorable light. They may be the natural human response to a real situation, but this does not mean that they are a sound response. Even though it should be true that society faces a problem of chronic slack, it is still more fundamentally true that high production is the only road to a high level of living, and these ideas mean restricted production. The solution must be found in some other direction.

These ideas do, however, increase the need of an analysis on which a real solution can rest. The first task, therefore, is to consider why many people now believe that capitalism faces the danger of stagnation and to examine critically the basis of their belief.

Review Questions

1. "Solution of the depression problem would not literally mean full employment." Explain the essential difference between depression and frictional unemployment. Distinguish leading varieties of the latter.

2. Sir William Beveridge, critizing a British plan to promote employment, says it is "an anti-trade cycle policy, not a policy of full employment, because it recognizes only the fluctuations and not the chronic weakness of total demand." [9] Develop the distinction.

3. Point out the difficulties in defining the term "capacity" for the economy as a whole. Of what use is the concept?

4. "We have never come close to producing as much as we can produce." Do you agree? Why is productive capacity likely to be exaggerated?

5. "Productive power is now so great that we can produce in the United States far more than we are able to consume." "The only reasonable assumption is that human wants are insatiable." Do you agree with either statement? Explain.

6. "Our possible output may not be more than we want, but it is certainly more than we can buy. Capitalism is simply unable to turn out enough purchasing power." Do you agree? Explain carefully the basis of purchasing power.

7. "The demand for goods is at bottom the supply of goods. Hence there can be no real deficiency in total demand." Explain what is meant. What distinction is neglected? Explain with an example the segments that make up total demand. Why is stress placed on the saving-investment relationship?

8. If, with a given gross national product, saving tends to outrun investment by a certain amount, why is a decline in total product greater

[9] *The New York Times,* November 9, 1944.

than that amount to be expected? The decline will stop when what condition is reached? State the multiplier idea.

9. "Under capitalism, a prosperous economy means an expanding economy." Why?

10. "Perhaps the proceeds from any volume of output can buy that
volume, but they cannot buy a larger volume. Thus capitalism cannot
prosper." Explain the possibilities of buying an expanding total product.

11. "While all make-work ideas are contrary to the basic meaning of
economy and the requirements of progress, it is understandable that specific
groups should sometimes hold them. But we should not condone the results
to which they lead." Explain leading applications of the make-work idea.
Develop each part of the foregoing statement.

12. "If we are to have capacity production, workers must be paid enough
to buy the full product of industry." Point out the error in this statement.
What must be assumed in order to argue that raising wages at the expense
of profits will increase total demand?

The Economic-maturity View of Depression

As stated earlier, the experience of the 1930s shifted the center of
thinking about depressions in this country. The depth and duration
of slack in that period implied a condition, many people believed,
that could not be explained in ordinary cyclical terms. Whatever
might have been true in the past, it seemed that depressions were
more than mere temporary dips in an essentially sound situation. They
seemed to reflect a running down, a constitutional lack of vigor, in the
economy. Private enterprise might have kept things going while the
continent was being settled and developed; now the economy had ma-
tured, and the great expansion possibilities were gone. True, there
might still be periods of high activity, caused by wars and exceptional
developments like the automobile industry, but chronic underuse of
resources, according to this view, would be the usual condition.

This statement runs in very general, impressionistic terms, such as
might be used by persons untrained in economic analysis. In similar
impressionistic terms, one may reply and declare unlimited faith in
the future vigor of the American economy. We shall try, however, in
this section to put the discussion on a firmer analytic footing. There
are able economists, whose views cannot be brushed aside, who support
each of these views, and, while we shall avoid great technical detail,
we shall attempt to present both positions.

In this approach we return to the preceding analysis of total demand.
Stagnation means that total demand must ordinarily be too low to
justify full production. It means, more specifically, that with full pro-

duction, savings would be too great to find adequate investment out-lets. The issue must be viewed in this way, because savings are the part of money income that is not used for consumption, and private invest-ment along with government spending must absorb this part. Those who take the pessimistic, mature-economy view are saying, in effect, that there are no longer enough profitable ways to invest capital to absorb, year after year, the volume of saving that would appear with a capacity level of income. Those who take the opposite view assume the burden of showing that this is probably not the case.

The older orthodox position

Both positions can be seen more clearly if we begin by considering the way in which this issue was once disposed of by economic theorists. While the idea is old that saving will prove chronically excessive, the main stream of nineteenth-century economics positively excluded this possibility. It was held that saving and investment are kept in equilib-rium automatically by the rate of interest—the rate of return on in-vested capital—however high the level of production may rise.

On the *saving* side, it was said that people do not forego consump-tion because they like to. They do it for the sake of the return on their capital. A high interest rate makes saving attractive, and a low rate reduces the willingness to save. Thus, according to this view, if the need for capital declines, the interest rate falls, and people curtail their saving—even down to the point where they save nothing at all.

On the investment side, interest is viewed as a cost to enterprisers who invest capital in productive facilities and to all persons who build houses. So far as this cost is concerned, it is no more expensive to invest $20,000 when the interest rate is 4 percent than $10,000 when the rate is 8 percent. Accordingly, a high rate retards investment, and a low rate encourages it.

Thus, with any level of production and income, if a tendency de-velops for saving to run ahead of investment, a fall in the interest rate both reduces the saving—that is, increases the consumption spending—and stimulates the investing, so that equilibrium is maintained. If depressions come, they must spring, therefore, from some other source than a basic tendency for saving to outrun investment.

This is indeed a comfortable doctrine on which to rest one's belief in the capacity of private enterprise to maintain full production. But it is a shaky doctrine at a number of points, and the present-day optimists—we may call them the neo-orthodox—do not rely on it. They are likely to agree with the stagnationists that the older doctrine is weak on the savings side, and that, on the investment side, it needs some amending also. But despite common criticisms of older thinking, a wide difference of opinion exists between these groups on the basic issue: the tendency of the economy toward stagnation. We shall consider both aspects of the problem in its modern guise, first the savings side, then the investment.

The issue as to savings

Practically no one now believes that the interest rate—the rate of return on savings—provides an effective control of the amount of saving done. Agreement is general that a very large volume of saving would go on even though the interest rate fell to zero. Most people do not save merely to get income from their capital but to be the possessors of the principal sum which they save. Such a sum adds to their security, and it adds to their prestige. These are powerful motives. If they save for income, they may even save more with a lower than with a higher interest rate, because with a low rate more capital is needed to yield the income sought. At 4 percent, $50,000 will yield a $2000 annual income, but it requires $100,000 at 2 percent. With or without adjustments in the interest rate, one cannot expect, because investment falls off, that consumption spending will expand to fill the gap.

The interest rate aside, there is considerable difference of opinion as to the probable amount of saving with a high national income. Upholders of the oversaving view commonly stress the fact that, as incomes become larger, saving increases not only absolutely but relatively, becoming a larger percentage of the total. If, for instance, $500 is saved from a $5000 income, or 10 percent, and $2000 from a $10,000 income, or 20 percent, doubling the income quadruples the saving. The Brookings Institution concluded, for 1929, that the 2.3 percent of the families with the highest incomes, those in excess of $10,000, did two thirds of the saving that was done by all families. On this basis the Brookings economists reached the possibly ominous conclusion: "The greater the number of persons in the high income groups the larger the percentage of the aggregate national income that will be set aside for investment purposes." [10]

If this view is sound, it plainly follows that the problem of absorbing savings must become more difficult as total income expands. If savings were excessive, and output lagged below capacity, in the 1920s, how much more excessive must they be with full use of an enlarged productive capacity!

[10] Harold G. Moulton, *Income and Economic Progress*, Brookings Institution, 1935, p. 40. More recent data were presented in Chapter 6.

This view of the behavior of saving, which supports the stagnation idea, is disputed both by the neo-orthodox and by various investigators. The reason for questioning it was stated in the discussion of savings in Chapter 6. At one time, in any country, the fraction of income saved rises sharply with income. But when total income rises, and everyone is better off, the standard of living seems likely to rise as much as income does, so that people save no larger a fraction of their incomes than before.

The truth on such issues must be determined statistically, and it is difficult to ascertain, since long-run comparisons are necessary. Some evidence has been found, in the case of Great Britain and the United States, that the percentage of total income saved has declined over long periods as productivity has risen, even though the absolute amount of saving has increased.[11] The amount of saving will be watched closely in the postwar period, especially if production remains on a high level.

The nature of investment opportunity

The investment side of the problem is more complicated. Before stating the opposing views, we shall need to consider the basis on which savings may be absorbed.

Is it not reasonable to assume that investment outlets are unlimited? If people have unsatisfied wants, is there not always room for more productive equipment to turn out more goods to satisfy those wants? Will people not always be glad to live in larger and finer homes which require more capital for their construction? And if a lag in investment should develop, will not a fall in the interest rate so expand the use of capital that, before the rate reaches zero, an unlimited amount can be absorbed?

Unfortunately these questions cannot be answered affirmatively. We must see what is wrong with this approach, why there are limits to the fraction of total income that investment can absorb.

Logical limits of investment. Take first the simple case of investment in *housing* mentioned above. It is true, if the interest rate falls from 8 percent to 4 percent, the interest cost of a $20,000 home is no greater than that of a $10,000 home had been, but there are other important costs. If the owner were borrowing the principal sum and had to pay it back over a 20-year period, it would make a good deal of difference to a person of moderate income, even if interest payments were the same, whether he had to pay back $500 or $1000 of the principal an-

[11] See Colin Clark, *The Conditions of Economic Progress,* Macmillan & Co., Ltd., 1940, pp. 396–398.

nually. If the savings were his own, his calculation would be similar. Other important costs, moreover, especially maintenance and taxes, would be about twice as great on the $20,000 house. Thus it takes much more than a fall in interest to bring a great increase in investment in houses.

In the case of *industrial investment,* we must look into the matter more systematically. Two conditions must be met if investment is going to be profitable:

1. It must seem probable that the entire final product of the new facilities will be bought at a profitable price. Machines and other facilities are made to turn out final products. There can be no profit in investing in machines to make machines to make machines, ad infinitum. The final objective is an expansion in the production of consumers' goods. The demand for machines is derived from the prospective demand for consumers' goods. Thus consumer spending must stay large enough to take from the market the growing final product of expanding industrial facilities. Saving, if it is to be absorbed through private investment, must stay within limits thus set.

2. Investment, to be profitable, must expand the productivity of resources. This point was developed in the discussion of the capitalistic process in Chapter 6. Resources will not be used in the indirect, or capitalistic, way unless it appears that the final product will be greater than if they were used directly. If cloth is to be made by using relatively less labor and materials in spinning and weaving it, and relatively more of them in making spinning and weaving machinery, the reason must be that a larger amount of cloth will be obtained from the same quantity of resources. There is plainly a limit to this diversion of resources. Production cannot be made more and more capitalistic indefinitely and continue to grow as a result. Men cannot be transferred without limit from running machines to making machines with a continuing increase in final product. Thus, even if nothing had to be paid for the use of capital, there is a limit to the amount of it that can be used productively.

An expansion of saving, it will be observed, bears on the investment situation in two ways. More saving means that a smaller part of spendable income is available to buy final products. More saving also means that more investing will have to be done, if savings are to be absorbed, and thus a larger final product will have to be bought.

Effect of declining interest rate. While there is a final limit to profitable investment, short of that limit a lower rate of interest may expand investment somewhat, in line with the orthodox theory. If the interest rate is zero, investment in producers' goods becomes profitable when they earn something more than their depreciation—that is, if they earn back more than the capital invested or more than enough to pay for the resources that went into the capital goods. If interest is 2 percent, they must earn depreciation plus 2 percent on the capital, plus an addition, in order to be profitable; if 4 percent, something more than that. Thus, the lower the interest rate is, the less productive an investment needs to be in order to seem worthwhile. Declining investment opportunity means that additional capital, when invested, promises a smaller and smaller addition to production. Lower interest cost enables investment to be carried farther than otherwise as opportunities decline, but not indefinitely far.

Again, as in the house example, it will be noted that interest is a minor element of total cost in industrial production. It is likely to be less than depreciation and much less than direct labor and materials in most fields. It is likely also to weigh lightly in business calculations in comparison with sales prospects, including uncertainties as to volume and price. In part, the interest element is stressed because it is a factor in the situation that may be controlled.

Possibility of adequate opportunities. But now, if we have disposed of the idea that investment outlets are indefinitely great, have we gone so far as to suggest that they must become exhausted if production remains on a high level? Long before the mature-economy view appeared in this country, there were observers who were sure that capitalism must run down. It could not expand fast enough, they said, to absorb all the savings without turning out final products so fast that people could not buy them with the remainder of their incomes.[12]

This conclusion, however, does not follow from the nature of the investment process. It is true there must be expansion, but the expansion need not take place at so high a rate as to produce the squeeze just described. Expansion may absorb savings without creating a capacity too great for the market for final products.

Areas of investment opportunity. Investment possibilities are very great. Much capital can be absorbed in production through *ordinary economic growth,* even if there are no important changes in the ways of using capital. As long as population grows, an increasing plant capacity is necessary to serve it. New firms appear that require capital, and old firms expand. Moreover, most firms are equipped far less well than the most efficient firms in their industries, so that additional equipment of existing types can be used advantageously. Usable natural

---

[12] Holders of this view need not be socialists, but it is on the basis of it that Marx and his followers contended that capitalism must lead to imperialism, because capitalist countries, to stay prosperous, must find outlets in other lands for their investments.

resources continue to be discovered, and capital is required for their development.

The more striking outlets for savings, however, are likely to come from *technical innovations*. These may be put in two classes: those resulting in new and better products and those providing less costly ways of producing familiar products. The former have a more positive effect on investment. The production of electric power required a great development of dams, generating plants, and transmission lines. Numerous factories have been erected and equipped to manufacture electrical appliances, automobiles, and many other products that were new in recent decades. These developments not only absorb capital, but they stimulate consumption, so that, if there is any tendency for investment to lag behind saving, they exert a powerful offsetting effect.

Innovations that make possible the less costly production of old products also cause much investment in new plant and equipment. But in this case there are complications, and the net effect of any given investment may be less. For one thing, in the absence of new and attractive products, there is not the same stimulus to consumption. For another, there is likely to be some displacement of labor, with immediate unemployment, because a new process that is cost saving must economize the use of resources. Thus, it is more difficult to achieve the expansion in buying required by an enlarged product, and there is more adjusting to be done in putting resources to work.

Even more important, perhaps, are the *nonindustrial possibilities*. There is the housing field, which requires much capital to enable a growing population to live in accordance with a rising plane of living. There is the great field of investment in schools and other public buildings and in public projects such as road development and flood control.

There is, finally, the *international field*. Most nations are not far advanced in their use of capital goods nor have they the means of rapid capital formation. Investment outlets loom much larger when viewed from the world standpoint than when viewed from the standpoint of a single advanced nation such as the United States.

The conclusion, then, from this survey of investment processes and possibilities is that there is no theoretical basis for insisting either that all savings inevitably will be absorbed or that they will not be absorbed. Disagreement among competent observers on the savings-investment issue may rest on little or no difference in their theoretical analysis, but only on differences in the way they view the facts of the situation in modern America. Here there can be considerable divergence of view, as we shall now see.

The mature-economy view of investment outlets

The pessimistic conclusion is that profitable investment outlets cannot remain adequate, year after year, to use the savings from full production. Perhaps while the country was developing rapidly, opportunities were adequate, but now savings have become greater, and the ways of using them are restricted. Three changes are especially stressed as reasons for declining investment outlets—declining, that is, in relation to capacity income.

First, it is believed that *the main task of economic development has been completed* in this country. The geographic frontier has vanished. The great field of investment that appeared as new areas were opened up, as railroads were spread over a vast terrain, as towns were built, as mineral resources were exploited, is now largely gone. At the same time, on the industrial front, the main task of development seems to have been completed. For many years there has been a tremendous accumulation of capital goods, and future additions must be less important than what has been done. True, there will be further inventions and discoveries, and new products and methods will appear. But, according to this view, the rate of change, the amount of development each year, is not likely to be so great in relation to total output as it was when industrialization was young.

Second, there has been *a decline in the rate of population growth.* In the middle nineteenth century, the number of people in the United States expanded by as much as a third in a decade. The growth per decade has fallen perhaps to 10 percent and appears certain to go lower. Capital is required to expand productive facilities to provide goods for a growing population, and the fall in the rate of growth diminishes this demand. This point, it should be said, is not stressed as much as formerly by holders of the mature-economy view.

Third, many inventions are now of a capital-saving nature and promote expansion without absorbing savings. It is usually assumed that additional capital is required when industrial discoveries are brought into use, but their effect may be quite the opposite. Suppose that a certain operation is performed by a machine which cost $10,000 and that when the time comes for its replacement, a new machine of different design is available which also costs $10,000 and can perform this operation twice as fast. The firm's sales have been growing, and it is ready to expand, but, so far as this operation is concerned, expansion requires no additional capital. The original capital, recovered in part each year as revenues covered depreciation along with other costs, is sufficient for the needed expansion. To the extent that this machine is representative, inventions can be said to be capital-saving, and the expansion of industry fails to absorb savings from current income.

Along these lines, the field of domestic industrial investment can be made to look rather meager. If firms save part of their profits for expansion and if replacement has the effect of expansion, established firms may get all the funds they need from internal sources. To this effect, testimony has come from the heads of General Motors, United States Steel, and General Electric that, over a considerable period, these great companies met most of their capital requirements in this way.[13] This means that the funds they obtained through borrowing and sale of stock were relatively small, and thus they provided little outlet for the savings of individuals.

Firms in new industries, new firms in old industries, other old firms as a matter of choice or necessity, go to the capital market for funds and do use individual savings. This is admitted, but the stagnationists hold that capital-saving invention, and internal financing generally, have altered the situation so as to intensify the difficulty of making use of total savings. Ordinary industrial investment, it is claimed, became a diminishing part of total investment after World War I, and more important outlets were found in housing, electric power, and such government undertakings as highway construction.[14]

It is on these grounds that the depression of the 1930s has been widely regarded not as an ordinary cyclical decline but as evidence of the chronic weakness of an old and rich economy that cannot find profitable use for the expanding wealth it must somehow employ to remain prosperous. Wars and the automobile industry, unique sources of demand, should accordingly be credited with most of the prosperity —or pseudoprosperity—of the twentieth century. The future looks dark from this standpoint, except as new means are adopted to sustain the level of aggregate demand.

Attacks on the mature-economy view

This pessimistic view has been rejected by numerous businessmen, publicists, economists, and others. The inherent vigor of the economy has been proclaimed repeatedly, and the mature-economy thesis has been attacked in all sorts of ways, both by those who have understood it and those who have not.

[13] Before the Temporary National Economic Committee in 1939; *Hearings,* Part 9.

[14] This viewpoint is particularly associated in the United States with Alvin H. Hansen. See his *Full Recovery or Stagnation?*, W. W. Norton, 1938. See, also, Stuart Chase, *The Road We Are Traveling, 1914–1942*, Twentieth Century Fund, 1942, and H. Gordon Hayes, *Spending, Saving, and Employment*, Knopf, 1945.

In part the replies of the optimists have been impressionistic, though no less persuasive on that account. Thus the theory has been brushed aside as a natural human reaction to calamity. Borne down by great and prolonged difficulties, people naturally look for explanations that imply major shifts in the course of history. It is observed that this very explanation of depression was used many years ago before a great part of the present development of America had taken place. No attack on the mature-economy idea is complete without a quotation from the *Report* of the Commissioner of Labor in 1886, in which, with much citation of detail, this conclusion was reached:

Industry has been enormously developed, cities have been transformed, distances covered, and a new set of economic tools has been given in profusion to rich countries, and in a more reasonable amount to poorer ones. What is strictly necessary has been done often times to superfluity. This full supply of economic tools to meet the wants of nearly all branches of commerce and industry is the most important factor in the present industrial depression. It is true that the discovery of new processes of manufacture will undoubtedly continue, but it will not leave room for marked extension, such as has been witnessed during the last fifty years, or afford remunerative employment of the vast amount of capital which has been created during that period. . . . Supplying themselves with the full facilities for industry and commerce will give to each of the great nations of Europe and America something to do, but the part of each in this work will be small and far from enough to insure more than temporary activity.

Such views are cited to suggest that the present pessimists are as wrong as those of the past. Certainly they may be, though we should note that there has, in fact, been no long and sustained prosperity to show that this early view was completely mistaken. But in any case it is wholesome to be reminded how prone each generation is to think that it lives at the apex of human progress and that the really good days belong to the past.

There have also been theoretical attacks on the mature-economy view by persons who have only shown how dangerous a little learning can be. As should now be clear, it does not meet the stagnation argument to assert that human wants are unlimited and that, however great productivity becomes, the full product not only can but actually will be bought. But this is quite respectable analysis compared with some. Consider, for instance, the declaration in a popular book on this problem that the vast production of World War II dumbfounded the "mature economists" and proved them wrong—as if they had been doubting American productive capacity. They have only doubted the ability of the country to make use of that capacity without such special spending as war entails. No side of any issue should be judged by the incompetents who support it.

The stagnation view has also been attacked ably by persons who, step by step, have analyzed and found wanting the arguments that support it. This neo-orthodox case rests on historical facts and an attempt at a balanced interpretation of them. Without detail, the nature of the case can be indicated briefly.

England, an older and more mature economy, did not suffer such a collapse as ours during the 1930s. Said the London *Economist* in 1939:

If the United States, with its vast areas, its low debt, its inexhaustible resources, its rising population, is a mature economy, what is Great Britain? And yet our "decadent" economy has contrived, during the decade when America was standing still, to go ahead as fast as on the average of the great Victorian era of expansion.[15]

Indeed, statistical surveys of capital needs in the United States during the 1930s indicated that the depth and prolongation of the depression, whatever their cause, were not due to an underlying lack of investment opportunity.[16]

Regarding the fall in population growth as a reason for declining investments, the point is made that its effect, if any, should have appeared three fourths of a century before the depression of the 1930s. If the passing of the frontier was the cause, the collapse was half a century too late. Why should it be assumed that other great developments would not follow the automobile industry, perhaps not often so big individually but large in the aggregate and fairly continuous? Recent scientific developments are stressed as evidence that the technological frontier can be as important as the geographic frontier. If, moreover, a realistic view is taken of probable savings, then, it is contended, sensational developments are not needed, only moderate growth, to absorb the capital that will be saved. Evidence is also cited to show that the importance of internal financing by corporations has been exaggerated and that private savings still have large outlets through the capital markets for use in industry, housing, and other fields.[17]

[15] As quoted by Ernst W. Swanson and Emerson P. Schmidt, *Economic Stagnation or Progress,* McGraw-Hill, 1946, p. 17. This book is largely a compilation of views which question the mature-economy position.

[16] See the Brookings Institution volumes, *The Recovery Problem in the United States,* 1936, and *Capital Expansion, Employment, and Economic Stability,* 1940, the latter by Harold G. Moulton, George W. Edwards, James D. Magee, and Cleona Lewis.

[17] For an able statement of these criticisms, see George Terborgh, *The Bogey of Economic Maturity,* Machinery and Allied Products Institute, 1945.

Comments on the issue

To the person who wants to see all arguments neatly ended and a conclusion reached, this debate on the stagnation issue must be disappointing, as must most discussion of major problems. Both sides make telling points, but neither seems to prove its case. In a strict sense, neither case can be proved. The real issue, remember, is this: Will the American economy be able, year after year, to find profitable investment outlets for the capital that will be saved with income on a full-production level? To show, however persuasively, that investment outlets are not so great as they once were, is not to prove that they will not still be adequate. To show, however persuasively, that historical facts are badly interpreted in the mature-economy theory is not to show that outlets will be adequate. On the issue as to what did happen in the 1930s, we had better not conclude that lack of investment opportunity was the trouble until other possible explanations have been considered. There is, at least, no compelling theoretical reason why either the optimists or the pessimists must be wrong.

Whatever its real merits and defects, the mature-economy view has been handicapped by language and association. The very phrases "mature economy" and "stagnation" are prejudicial. They antagonize all persons who think well of the American economy, respect its past accomplishments, and expect much of it in the future. They negate the red-blooded attitude most people want to take toward their country. In many eyes, moreover, the theory is condemned by its resemblance to the gloomy Marxish view of prosperity under capitalism. And in the eyes of economists who regard the older orthodoxy warmly, even though they modify it in their thinking, the very idea of oversaving still carries the taint of heresy.

This is said in order to remark that there are many who reject this view when set forth with these phrases but who adopt it, or come very close to it, in their habitual manner of thinking. The person who believes, as many businessmen still seem to, that a highly productive country cannot prosper unless it exports more than it imports really accepts this view—or, at least, this is the most favorable construction that can be put on his thinking. If wants are great enough to encompass the whole product, however large, and investment will actually absorb all purchasing power not used for current consumption, what difference do the exports make? Likewise, the businessman who says that advertising and salesmanship contribute to prosperity because they get people to buy the full product of industry is skating close to the stagnation line. If human wants are naturally so very great, and all product provides purchasing power, total demand needs no artificial stimulus as long as investments are present to absorb all the income not spent for consumers' goods.

This is stated not to support the mature-economy view but to stress the need of grasping the essence of the idea and not merely the phrases in which it is stated. Actually most economists have long doubted these views of businessmen and have grouped them roughly with the make-work notions described earlier.

The real need, if one is not to accept the stagnation theory, is for some other explanation of depressions that is convincing. Some such alternative theory must necessarily be the strongest part of the neo-orthodox approach.

Deficient total demand as traditionally viewed

Whether or not the modern American economy suffers a chronic lack of investment outlets, depressions take place and must be explained. Total demand does not remain continuously at a high level, and great dips occur in production and employment. If the mature-economy thesis is wholly false, the reasons for depressions are still to be stated. But even if there is truth in that thesis, it is not the whole truth. Other factors contribute to slack and perhaps largely explain it. The peculiar rhythm, moreover, with which depressions occur, the cyclical ebb and flow of activity, is itself a feature of the economy that should be examined.

In dealing with depressions, the traditional emphasis of economics has been on the complex and delicately poised character of modern economic organization, its sensitivity to disturbance, the frequency of disturbing change, the difficulties of prompt readjustment. These are inherent features of the economy, but, in a sense, they are less fundamental—less a reason for despair over the future of capitalism—than the weakness of economic maturity.

Balance is difficult to maintain when production is organized through an intricate *specialization* based on numerous industries, firms, and processes. Activity in any field of production depends on revenues from sales to people in other fields. These revenues, in turn, govern demand for the products of other fields. Thus variation anywhere is contagious, and a small decline may have widespread effect.

Into this situation so difficult to balance, upsetting changes enter continually. There are *shifts in tastes* and in demands for particular products. There are also *innovations in methods of production*. Small *changes in revenues and costs* cause larger relative changes in profits, and it is on the basis of *profit prospects* under capitalism that plans are made and production carried on. Variations in the outlook for profit cause still greater *changes in investment*.

Sensitivity to change is increased by the *use of money*. Purchasing power, we have seen, is rooted in production, but it is received immediately in money form. Only slight influences may cause firms and individuals to slow down their use of money below the rate at which it is being received or to speed up its use, especially when credit is employed, beyond the current income rate.

As disturbances arise, readjustment is required, but *readjustment is impeded by various rigidities*. Labor and other resources are not highly mobile, and time is required to shift their use. Prices, through which changes largely influence decisions, may be quite inflexible and aggravate the distortions that occur.

On the basis of these characteristics of modern capitalism, it is not difficult to formulate explanations of deficient total demand and of fluctuating production, which assume no basic lack of investment outlets to absorb savings. Perhaps the traditional type of explanation is not adequate for the catastrophe of the 1930s or for the longer run problem of unemployment which my lie ahead. But whether it is or not, it is essential to a full understanding of economic fluctuations. The following chapter will deal with it.

Review Questions

1. State in general terms the mature-economy view of the relationship between savings and investment.

2. "The rate of interest automatically prevents saving from outrunning investment." Whose view is this? Develop it. Criticize it as an explanation of saving.

3. "Since relatively more is saved from large than from small incomes, it follows that saving becomes increasingly difficult to absorb as average income increases." Does this conclusion necessarily follow? Explain.

4. "As long as wants remain unsatisfied, there must be additional opportunities to invest savings in productive equipment." Show that this statement misconceives the conditions of profitable investment.

5. "It is a mistake to assume that investment opportunities lie entirely in industrial facilities." Distinguish and appraise the main areas of investment.

6. Develop three contentions to the effect that investment opportunities have declined seriously in this country. Are you impressed by them?

7. Along what lines has the mature-economy thesis been attacked? Are you impressed by these contentions?

8. A leading economist wrote in 1947: "An expenditure of about $50 billion would be required to raise capital per worker to the level of 1929

and a considerably larger outlay to raise capital per worker to the level which would be normal in view of the long-term tendency of capital per worker to increase at the rate of about 2 percent per year." [18] What is the significance of this statement?

9. "Many people who berate the mature-economy idea as radical and un-American seem to harbor misgivings of the fundamental adequacy of total demand." Explain.

10. Along what other lines can weaknesses and fluctuations in total demand be explained?

[18] Summer H. Slichter in *The New York Times Magazine*, November 30, 1947.

~ 15 ~

Cyclical Fluctuations

Depressions may be due to some underlying weakness in the source of total demand, as the economic-maturity theorists contend, or to the complexities and irregularities of an essentially vigorous economy, as more orthodox theorists view the matter. But, in any case, the slack which develops in using resources seems to follow a discernible pattern—a pattern not directly implied by either of these views as thus stated. Depressions appear not as spasmodic and separate episodes but as part of a connected series of fluctuations, possessing, it would seem, a compelling internal logic. It is to fluctuations that give evidence of pattern and internal logic that the term *business cycle* has been applied.

The term is both useful and dangerous. It is useful in emphasizing that booms and depressions are recurrent and have coherence and continuity. Booms apparently lead to depressions and depressions to booms; so there is present the circular element that the word cycle implies. But the term "business cycle" is misleading if it suggests a high degree of regularity in the economic ebb and flow. Booms and depressions do not recur with uniform frequency and intensity, nor need the causal factors be exactly identical in successive cycles or operate in precisely the same way.

There is the further danger that the cycle will be studied—as it sometimes seems to be—as if it were itself the object of concern from the social standpoint—as if booms and depressions were, in the same sense, deviations from the normal. The real problem, it should be stressed, is still the problem of depressions, of underuse of productive power. We are simply asking: What can be learned about depressions by viewing them as part of a continuous wave-like movement in the economy?

This chapter has three closely related sections: (1) The nature of the statistical approach to the study of business cycles will be indicated, with some suggestion of the use made of various data. (2) The economic factors will be set forth which seem most useful in explaining the swings in the economy and the termination and reversal of these swings. (3) These factors, brought together in the conventional picture of the cycle, will be contrasted with explanations which stress other causes of fluctuations.

Measurement of Cyclical Fluctuations

The study of business fluctuations has provided a rich field for statisticians. Practically every economic phenomenon is involved, and there are endless tasks in gathering data, sifting and correlating it in order to discover significant factors, and in testing explanatory theories. We shall not clutter the present discussion with displays of data that we shall not use. But our sense of the nature of business cycles will be sharpened if we note the kind of quantitative problem they present and some of the very general facts regarding them.

The statistical problem

The chart on page 382 shows comprehensively the fluctuation of business in the United States during more than a century.[1] Behind any single graph of this kind lies a great amount of statistical effort in obtaining data and analyzing it. Much of the necessary fact-gathering and a good deal of the manipulation of figures are now carried on regularly by agencies of the federal government. Private organizations, such as the National Bureau of Economic Research, have contributed greatly to our knowledge of business fluctuations. Historical studies that carry back before 1900 require a good deal of piecing together of sparse data and sometimes some daring estimates to fill gaps, but excellent work along this line has been done.

The things measured. A graph which conveys a broad picture of fluctuations, such as the present one, is most useful when it measures physical production. This graph, since 1901, represents so-called industrial production—manufacturing and mining—and since 1919 has been based primarily on the much-used Federal Reserve index. For earlier periods a variety of factors enter, but with the same significance. For a more complete picture of the variations in productive activity, farming, construction, transportation, marketing, and service activities would be included. For some purposes—especially as the inquiry gets into causal

[1] This chart presents part of the frequently revised Index of American Business Activity since 1790 published by the Cleveland Trust Company. It is associated with the statistical work of the late Leonard P. Ayres and is explained at pp. 204–205 of his book, *Turning Points in Business Cycles*, Macmillan, 1939.

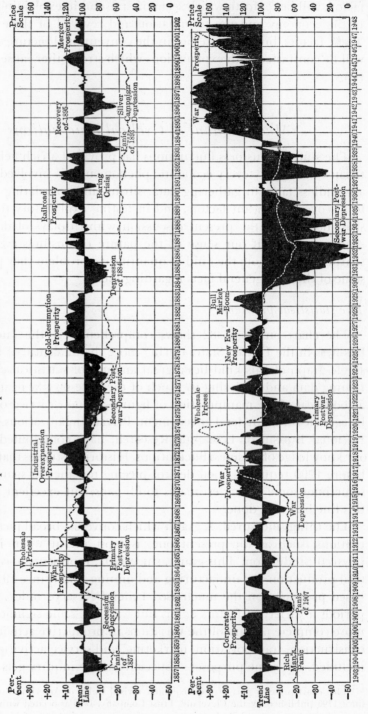

AMERICAN BUSINESS ACTIVITY SINCE 1857

Based on the 21st ed. (April 1948) of the American Business Activity Since 1790 Chart of the Cleveland Trust Company, with supplementary figures. By permission. Such labels on the chart as "Gold Resumption Prosperity," "Silver Campaign Depression," and "Rich Man's Panic" imply theories of business fluctuations which have no necessary place in an explanation of them.

factors—producers' and consumers' goods are separated, also currently used, semidurable, and durable goods. Employment, hours of labor, and overtime work may also be significant.

Output is measured in physical units, such as tons of steel and ton-miles of railroad freight. But often the elements in business fluctuations are most significant when expressed in value terms, such as money income, sums spent in various directions, saving done and investments made. Corporate securities issued, debts incurred, installment buying done, are watched. So are the amount of money in circulation, the deposits in banks, the bank clearings.

Much of the study of fluctuations is concerned with prices. Prices of different categories of goods, at different stages of their production—raw-material prices, wholesale prices, retail prices—are gathered and reduced to index numbers. Prices of city real estate and farm land are followed, and special attention is paid the varying prices of corporate shares. Prices of productive services are important, both as the basis of incomes to the suppliers and as costs to business firms. Data are collected for numerous wage rates and for interest rates on loanable funds in a variety of markets. Profits occupy a central place.

Statistical treatment of data. Such a chart as we have just examined is not the direct result of collecting figures and plotting them on a time basis. To give a general picture of the economy, it must combine and relate a comprehensive mass of data in a meaningful way. The Federal Reserve's monthly index of industrial production, for instance, combines eighteen main divisions (and many subdivisions) in the fields of manufacturing and mining alone. The problem is about the same as that of calculating a price index, as described in Chapter 12. Manipulation of data involves selecting, weighting, and averaging.

But even if the graph represents only a single series of figures, as of kilowatt-hours of electric power, it reflects cyclical fluctuations quite imperfectly unless the raw data receive considerable statistical treatment. Industry is subject to a variety of movements, and those should be excluded which are not associated with booms and depressions. Most raw price and output data reflect *seasonal variations* that go on in good years and bad. Statistical methods are available for removing the seasonal factor, so that a better picture of cyclical change, depicted in smoother curves, is made possible. Likewise, in an economy in which population is growing and productive power expanding, many series of data show a *long-term*, or *secular*, *trend*. Again, a formula can be calculated to measure this trend, and its effect can be removed from the data, so that the resulting figures are more strictly a measure of cyclical change. The horizontal base line in the above graph is the result of eliminating upward trends—at different rates in different periods—from the data.

The statistical procedure in attempting to explain cyclical fluctuations, or in testing explanatory theories, is to seek *correlations*—that is, corresponding movements—between two or more series of figures, representing different elements in the cycle. The correspondence, for example, between profits and industrial output can be measured. A corresponding movement does not prove that a causal connection exists between two elements, but it may suggest relationships worth analyzing or support connections that seem logical on other grounds. More convincingly, perhaps, a lack of correspondence may discredit explanations that, prior to such test, seemed plausible.

Comparison of various series, by showing the relative extent of their fluctuations, indicates their importance in the cycle. Such comparison also reveals that certain series precede others in their movements, reaching turning points more quickly and moving more rapidly, at least in certain phases of the cycle. These *leads* and *lags* may suggest causal connections. In any case, they provide such quantitative basis as there is for *predicting economic changes* a little while before they occur. If, for instance, building construction during a number of cycles reaches its peak several months before the end of a boom, as it did in 1928, then a downturn in building is an indication of a crisis ahead. The stock market is often viewed as a harbinger of economic events.

Periodicity and uniformity of cycles

What does this sort of close, factual study of business fluctuations reveal as to their length and regularity? In the annals of business, certain years stand out as times of crisis and collapse. Among these years have been 1873, 1882, 1893, 1907, 1914, 1920, and 1929. From this experience, the view was widely accepted that a depression can be expected every decade. Cycles seemed typically to run for nine or ten years, but with considerable variation in length and magnitude.

More recent and refined analysis has revealed a much larger number of movements that seem to follow the cyclical pattern, but which, because of their relative mildness, have not measured up fully to the popular idea of booms and depressions. One economist, a pioneer in the scientific approach to cycle study, found nineteen complete cycles between 1855 and 1926, varying in length from 29 to 99 months, and averaging 46 months. If the period to 1885 is excluded—a period in which there were three exceptionally long swings related to the Civil War—the range is from 29 to 52 months, the longest occurring during World War I. Of the thirteen cycles in this period, all but the two at the extremes fall with a range of variation of one year, varying from 34 to 46 months.[2] When these shorter fluctuations are considered, they vary widely in violence of movement. In some of them, only a moderate prosperity is attained at the peak, and in the valleys the loss of output and employment is not severe.

These differences in severity may be attributed to outside events, such as wars and political upheavals, of spasmodic rather than cyclical character. A still more refined statistical analysis would, perhaps, remove such factors, along with seasonal and secular changes, and thus present a cycle picture of greater purity.

Some students of the cycle find an explanation for the varying magnitude of fluctuations right within the cyclical pattern. Their view is that, instead of just one type of cycle being present, there are several types, of quite different durations. Along with a typically three-and-one-half year cycle, there is also a nine or ten year cycle, and even a half-century cycle related to technological changes, wars, and price movements. In this view of the problem, intense prosperity is seen to arise in years in which the peaks of two or more of these cycles occur together; the great depressions take place when the valleys are similarly superimposed.

Measurement of the social impact

With numerous elements in the economy fluctuating and with statistics available for many of them, is there any one series of figures we can single out to stand for the succession of booms and depressions?

The answer should register the social interest in the problem of depressions. The real significance of depressions lies in the failure of the economy to provide the goods which, as demonstrated in the best years, it is capable of providing. The cycle, therefore, is essentially a variation in total production. Movements in prices and other factors are incidental to the variation in production.

Thus, figures for the national gross product, say on a quarterly basis and corrected for variations in the price level as well as for seasonal and secular changes, are probably the best measure of economic fluctuations. Such figures show best the varying success of the economy in do-

[2] Wesley C. Mitchell, article on "Business Cycles," *Encyclopedia of the Social Sciences*, Macmillan, 1931. His book, *Business Cycles, The Problem and Its Setting*, 1927, written under the auspices of the National Bureau of Economic Research, is a pioneering study in the field. A leading textbook is James Arthur Estey, *Business Cycles*, Prentice-Hall 1942. Causal factors are explained in a stimulating way by John Maurice Clark, *Strategic Factors in the Business Cycle*, 1934, also a National Bureau of Economic Research study. Theories of the cycle are analyzed systematically by Gottfried von Haberler, *Prosperity and Depression*, League of Nations, 1939. A useful collection of views on the cycle is found in *Readings on Business Cycle Theory*, selected by a committee of the American Economic Association, Blakiston, 1944.

ing its job, in serving its main purpose. The graphical record reproduced above serves in an approximate way to tell this story. But since even the boom years do not necessarily represent the full performance of the economy, in view of its capacity, the variations in gross product do not fully reflect the weakness that depressions indicate.

Variations in current production, moreover, do not reveal adequately the impact of the cycle on the living of the people. As pointed out in Chapter 3, in the explanation of the national-income concept, the consumption of commodities and services during a depression declines less than the real income that is currently produced. Two reasons were given: (1) the income distributed to individuals is likely to exceed the net national income in years of severe depression, and (2) durable goods produced before the depression continue to give service during the depression years.

Aggregate production and income figures also fail to reveal fully the impact of depression simply because they are aggregates. The impact is not distributed evenly but is concentrated most heavily on the unemployed who lose their main source of income. Thus unemployment statistics, which, unfortunately, are not very dependable, should be given a prominent place. Figures of any kind, however, cannot actually reveal the social impact of depression. The meaning of the depression of the 1930s can be understood only through sympathetic appreciation of the position of the 13 or 15 million who were unemployed.

In contrast with these measures which *express* the performance of the economy and the social impact of the cycle, the data for prices, spending, investment, and so on are mainly useful in helping to *explain* the fluctuations in production and real income.

Explanatory Factors

The business cycle is a problem that may be grasped by a number of handles. Approached in a certain way, one explanation of it seems simple and obvious. Approached in another way, a quite different explanation appears equally plausible. A clever person can spin out any one of a number of theories of the cycle and make it convincing to people who are not competently critical. Depressions may be blamed quite simply on overproduction due to technical progress, on wage payments too small to buy what is produced, on a shortage of money, on the varying value of money, and so on. Whatever the one-track theory, a "cure" based on it is at hand. Herein lies the danger of shallow theorizing in this field.

If anything is certain about the cycle, it is that business fluctuations are too complex for any simple theory or for any theory that seems obvious to uninformed observers. At the same time, there is no one theory that is agreed on by competent students. Instead, a number of explanations have some standing—explanations differing mainly in emphasis but perhaps containing points that cannot be reconciled. In this section we shall, accordingly, pursue a modest aim. We shall not attempt what the experts have not achieved—the formulation of the one correct theory—nor shall we seek a single integrated explanation. Instead, we shall examine a number of explanatory factors that are pretty well agreed on as having some importance in showing why cycles occur.

Procedure; causal factors

To assign causes and say why events occur is an uncertain business in the economic world, as elsewhere. In explaining economic fluctuations there is much of the same sort of difficulty that is often illustrated with the familiar shooting example. When the man was shot, was the cause of his death the bullet, the gun, the pulling of the trigger, the immediate motive in the murderer's mind, or the entire background of the murderer? Causes operate at different levels and in different ways.

Certain of them operate merely by providing the *general conditions* necessary to an occurrence. The characteristics of capitalism which invite instability were sketched at the end of the last chapter. With production carried on voluntarily for private gain, with consumers' tastes and producers' methods constantly changing, with industries dependent on each other in an intricately specialized organization, and with an exchange medium permitting separation between the rates of selling and buying, a continuing demand sufficient to maintain production at a high and stable level is practically impossible. These underlying conditions do not themselves produce a cycle, but they provide the setting in which broad fluctuations can easily occur. As we discuss more specific explanatory factors, these general conditions never cease to be part of the explanation.

In discussing the causes of fluctuations, it is important to distinguish (1) those factors which are an inherent part of economic processes under modern capitalism from (2) factors which, in a sense, operate from outside these processes. We may call them, respectively, *internal* and *external* factors. Interest rates, for instance, are an internal element; weather changes are external.

A cycle that repeats itself with some degree of regularity, a recurrent ebb and flow in the economy, is generally viewed by economists as due to internal factors. It appears as the natural mode of behavior of an economic organism, or mechanism, that fluctuates pretty much as a pendulum swings or a boat rolls. For cycles in the strict sense to continue, the economy must have within it—in its price, money, profit, and output relationships—characteristics that naturally express themselves in a succession of booms and depressions. Its nature must be such that swings in either direction gather momentum for a time and then slow down and go into reverse, somewhat as a pendulum accelerates, decelerates, stops, and reverses.

Study of the cycle, as such, is a search for the principles which govern such a pattern of behavior, as the physicist or engineer studies the swinging of a pendulum or the rolling of a ship. The problem is that of discovering (1) why the particular variations found in a dynamic economy combine into general swings that gather momentum for a while and (2) why these swings slow down, reach a turning point, and are followed by a movement in the opposite direction. For purposes of study, the cycle is customarily broken down into four *periods* or *phases*: *prosperity, crisis, depression,* and *revival.* With these phases in mind, we shall distinguish the accelerating or cumulative factors that operate during prosperity and depression and the checking and reversing factors related to the turning points, the times of crisis and of revival.

We shall stress these internal factors in the discussion that follows, because they throw light on all cyclical fluctuations and because, incidentally, they yield considerable general insight into the workings of capitalism. Such emphasis is justified as long as we remember that cycles are not uniform and regular and as long as we leap at no fixed conclusions regarding their inevitability.

And while we shall not be discussing the *external factors* in this section, we shall remain aware of their importance. Wars and public policies, at home and abroad, weather conditions and natural catastrophes, extraordinary industrial developments and the discovery and exhaustion of resources operate from outside the cyclical process in the strict sense but may influence tremendously the fluctuations that occur.

A variety of explanatory factors will be considered here under five headings: (1) the tendency for variations in certain specialized fields of production to fall in step in general movements: (2) the effect of durable goods and of producers' goods in amplifying these movements and causing tensions; (3) the monetary factors, especially the role of bank credit, in accelerating movements and reversing them; (4) the cyclical shifts in price and cost relationships and their bearing on profits; and (5) the influence of psychological factors, of waves of optimism and pessimism, in intensifying fluctuations.

1. General swings and the interdependence of markets

Let us begin by recalling the underlying fact that, quite apart from general booms and depressions, we are not dealing with a static society. Changes are constantly occurring in particular fields of production. New products are appearing, and old products are becoming more or less popular; new processes are being found, and the availability of resources is shifting; profits rise or fall, and facilities are expanded or curtailed.

As these changes occur, should we expect that some industries will be growing as others are contracting, or that they will fall in step and move along together? Simply as a matter of probability, the former may seem more natural. As a large number of coins tossed in the air tend to fall both ways, heads and tails, so a large number of industries may be expected to meet unlike fortunes. This likelihood is strengthened by the fact that loss of sales in one field may reflect a shift of buyers to some other field.

Certainly these offsetting changes do occur, but undoubtedly the stronger tendency is for industries to move together because of the contagion of good and bad fortune. The fact that, in a specialized situation, producers provide each others' markets is the basic reason for this contagion. When buyers take less of one product, they may intend to buy more of something else, but delay is likely, and the surest and promptest effect is on producers in the industry that feels the curtailment and then on their buying in other fields. This linking of markets through chains of transactions synchronizes the movements in different fields. While other factors strengthen this tendency, the underlying reason for general swings is the interdependence of specialists in a dynamic economy.

2. Durable goods; producers' goods

Such swings would be mild, and perhaps scarcely noticed, were it not for a number of factors that amplify movements and give them cumulative impetus. The disturbing impulses may be small, but the effects may be great. One such amplifying factor in modern capitalism is the prominence of durable goods, and particularly of producers' goods. In this connection several points should be stressed.

Wide variation in durable-goods production. The behavior of durable-goods production is well illustrated by the decline of the early 1930s. In comparing the variations in output of different groups of goods, classified as to durability, several categories should be distinguished: (1) the currently consumable, or perishable, type of physical product, such as foodstuffs; (2) final products in the form of services, which necessarily must be consumed as they are produced; (3) semi-durable consumers' goods, such as many items of clothing, which may last two or three years; (4) durable consumers' goods, such as automobiles, furniture, and most household equipment; (5) producers' durable goods, including industrial plant and equipment and including also, in conformity with statistical practice, all residential building, whether for lease or occupancy by the owner. The decline in these classes of products between 1929 and 1932 is shown in the table.[3]

TABLE 21—PRODUCT DURABILITY AND CYCLICAL CHANGE
(In billions of current dollars)

	1929	1932	Percent of decline
Perishable commodities	$28.5	$18.1	36.5
Services not embodied in commodities	22.5	15.4	31.6
Semidurable commodities	12.4	6.7	46.0
Consumers' durable commodities	9.9	3.8	61.6
Producers' durable goods and residential building (gross capital formation)	20.3	3.1	84.7
Producers' durable goods and residential building minus current consumption of these things (net capital formation)	10.1	−4.4	143.6
Gross national product (total)	93.6	47.2	49.6

The differences in the degree of contraction are striking. Measured in money, the output of currently consumed goods (the first two items combined) fell only one third, whereas for semidurable goods the decline was nearly one half, for durable consumers' goods over three fifths, and for producers' durable goods and residential building over five sixths. Because prices fell greatly, the decline in physical output was much less than these figures indicate. But if they were corrected by the application of the appropriate price index to each group, the differences would be even more striking. The greatest price decline was for perishable commodities, so the correction would reduce the 36.5 percent figure more than it would the 84.7 percent.

Before going into the reasons for these differences, we can make one important observation about economic progress and its bearing on stability. Backward economies, we have seen, devote most of their energies to producing for current consumption. In advanced economies, greater productive power is available, and much of it is used in producing du-

[3] Adapted from Simon Kuznets, *National Income and Capital Formation, 1919–1935*, National Bureau of Economic Research, 1937, p. 85.

rable consumers' goods and plant and equipment. It is the production of these things that falls most in a depression. Thus, even if the sources of disturbance were the same in backward and advanced economies, the latter would suffer more violent fluctuations.

Reasons for durable-goods variations; effects. Why is durable-goods production so highly sensitive? Why does it enter as an amplifying factor in business fluctuations? The first, and the most fundamental, point is readily apparent. The very fact of durability makes it possible to slow down or speed up the buying of goods without changing the rate at which they are used. To the extent that goods are perishable, their continuous use requires their continuous production. If their production ceases, the satisfactions which they afford must also cease. But durable goods need not be replaced at any regular rate. The present house or car or refrigerator may be used, within fairly wide limits, over a longer or shorter period without serious effect on the flow of services to the user. The machine in the factory may be replaced this year or next year or the year following, and the factory will still run. Their purchase is postponable, and their production may be bunched, although their use is continuous.

So it is that small elements in economic calculations may have large effects. In the use of goods, when little depends on whether new purchases are made now or later, small reasons govern decisions. Just a little uncertainty about his job will cause the workman to defer buying the car he was about to get. Just a little brightening of his prospects will cause him to advance the purchase date. A slight weakening of the market will lead the manufacturer to hold off placing his order for new equipment, whereas a slight strengthening of the market may be all he needs to speed up his replacements, even to cause him to begin construction of the new wing on his plant that he has been planning. Substantial sums are involved in these decisions, and the direct effect on the supplying industries is important. More important may be the indirect effects as employment and income are altered through a series of dependent activities.

Thus, if ordinary variations in industries do cluster in general movements, small movements may become large because people postpone or advance the purchase of durable goods.

The acceleration principle. Further light is thrown on the effect of durable goods by the so-called *acceleration principle*. It operates in connection with what is known as *derived demand*. Productive equipment is demanded not for its own sake but for the sake of the products it helps to produce. The demand for spinning and weaving machinery, for example, is derived from the demand for textiles. The acceleration principle states a relationship between the demand for end products (or consumers' goods) and the derived demand for producers' goods.

Let us suppose that the end-products industry—an industry making shoes or automobiles or furniture or radios—is operating at capacity, and that, when so operating, it replaces 10 percent of its equipment annually. The equipment industry that supplies it is just meeting this replacement demand. Then suppose that the demand for the final product increases by 5 percent. This increase seems dependable, so the end-products industry undertakes to expand its equipment by 5 percent in one year. To produce this additional equipment, while still providing for replacement, the equipment industry must thus increase its output by 50 percent, since the expansion requirement is half as great as the replacement requirement. Thus a 5-percent increase in the demand for the final product causes a 50-percent increase in the derived demand for related producers' goods.

This principle may be applied also to certain durable consumers' goods such as houses. The services of houses are demanded by the people who want to live in them. The demand for the construction of houses is derived from the demand for house services. In a community that is not growing, house construction is on a replacement basis. The addition of a few families to the community, causing a small percentage increase in the demand for house services, causes a large percentage increase in the demand for house construction, which may be an important factor in the economic life of the community. Each additional family able to meet a $100-a-month housing outlay may mean a $12,000 construction project.

Thus increases in the demand for final products cause disproportionately great increases in the derived demand for durable producers' goods and residential building. When a boom has been under way for some time, and the capacity of existing facilities is largely exhausted, the rising consumer demand causes great pressure to be placed on the capital-goods industries, and these in turn must expand their facilities. Rising incomes at each stage bring further increases in consumer demand.

Thus the acceleration principle throws light on the cumulative nature of business booms. But it also helps to explain how booms run their course and come to an end. It is a *deceleration principle* as well. When the equipment industry expands by 50 percent to enable the final-products industry to add 5 percent to its output, what condition is necessary to hold the equipment industry at this new high level? The answer, plainly, is that the final-products industry must keep on expanding at about the same rate. If it stops expanding, the equipment industry must decline to a replacement basis. Thus the mere failure of the final-products industry to expand will cause an absolute decline in the equipment industry, with further repercussions on the industries that serve it and that serve the people who derive incomes from it. More than that, a mere falling off in the rate at which the final-products industry is expanding, say from 5 percent annually to 3 percent, must cause a similar absolute decline in the equipment industry. To prevent contraction, not only must the boom go on, but it must go on at an undiminished rate. This is unlikely. When the rate of ascent slackens, the capital-goods lines respond by beginning the descent.

Innovations. Innovations, inventions, technical discoveries have a special place in explaining the wide movements in the production of producers' goods. Technical progress itself does not move with the business cycle. It goes on all the time. Both in booms and slumps, new products and new processes are appearing in laboratories and on drawing boards. But the impact of new ideas does not arise from their discovery; it arises from their actual incorporation in products and in equipment for producing products. Innovation in this full economic sense is not distributed evenly through time but is likely to be bunched at certain times. Why should this be so? One reason lies, no doubt, in the difficulties to be overcome in launching new products and methods and the fact that leadership is needed. Most producers merely fall in line behind the leaders, adding weight to the development. Another reason lies in the risks involved. We have seen that the purchase of known durable goods lags when the outlook is not good and speeds up when it improves. It is even easier to postpone the adoption of ideas on which no one is as yet depending and to mass their practical introduction when prospects are bright. Thus innovations tend to be concentrated in a way that intensifies fluctuations.[4]

Resulting imbalance. The rate of purchase of producers' goods during a boom is a source of tension and requires readjustment. Whether investment is in old-type capital goods, and expands on the acceleration principle, or in new-type capital goods, involving a bunching of innovations, it attains a rate that is too great to continue. It may be too great in relation to a sound long-term view of profit prospects, too great in relation to savings available to finance it without inflation, too great in one industry in relation to another, too great in relation to consumption need without correction of boom-time maldistribution of

[4] Emphasis on innovations is associated with Joseph A. Schumpeter, *Business Cycles*, McGraw-Hill, 1939.

income. It is enough to note these possible lines of distortion without going into them.[5]

The imbalance in production is made worse by the amount of time it takes to complete and equip new plants. Until the new capacity is actually in use, the need for new capacity appears to be present, and investment continues. But whether the distortion is great or small, so sensitive is the response to it that its correction is likely to weigh heavily in terminating a boom.

Distortions in durable-goods output work both ways. Correction of a relatively excessive output is one aspect of the ending of a boom, and correction of an inadequate output is, in the same way, a feature of the ending of a depression. In a severe depression, such as that of the early 1930s, the mere replacement needs for industrial equipment are not being met; houses, cars and other similar goods are increasing in average age and declining in average condition. The purchase of such goods may be posponed, but it cannot be delayed indefinitely without serious effect on the level of living. The factors that bring revival are various, but among them we should include the accumulating need of replacement of durable goods. To this factor we should add the accumulation of new technical ideas that invite practical industrial application.

Similar behavior of inventories. In this discussion, producers' goods have been treated as a division of durable goods. Thus we have had in mind only those capital goods which are of the fixed type—buildings, structures, and equipment. We have not considered the important part of business wealth in the circulating form, the stocks of materials, supplies, and finished products. These are important in most lines of production, but especially important in merchandising.

To a large extent, the goods that make up these inventories are the very consumers' goods and their components which, we have seen, are the least fluctuating element in the cycle. At the same time, producers' stocks of these things vary widely, and their variation works in the same way as the fluctuation in durable-goods output. During a depression, stocks are allowed to decline, with the result that factory production is smaller than the flow of goods to consumers. With returning prosperity and during a boom, stocks are built up; manufacturers and suppliers of materials operate on the basis of a demand that is greater than the demand of final buyers. Thus depression output is lower and boom output higher than it would be with constant inventories.

[5] In speaking of these distortions, we may go farther and say that investment in new plants expands capacity at so great a rate that consumption of resulting products cannot keep up unless saving is reduced so as to limit the expansion and increase consumer buying. If boom-time savings are only at the normal rate for a high aggregate income, this view edges into the pessimistic, mature-economy area.

There are practical limits to the height and the depth to which stocks can be allowed to move. Thus the stimulation in both directions must come to an end. The flattening off of inventory buying to a mere replacement basis may have a critical part in bringing a boom to an end and in starting a recession. The peak that was reached early in 1937 and the sharp break that followed have been attributed to inventory factors. In the same way, the restoration of inventories can be a substantial recovery influence. The changes that take place in inventory buying rest largely on anticipated price movements. Such movements are part of the third explanatory factor, to which we shall turn now.

3. Money and credit factors

In explanations of the business cycle, money is often assigned the leading role. The cause of cyclical swings is found in the exchange media—ordinary money and deposit currency—especially in the source of deposit currency in bank loans and the interest rates charged for loans, and, of course, in resulting changes in the value of money. In examining these monetary factors, we need reach no conclusion as to the degree of their importance in comparison with other factors. That they are significant is generally agreed.

Money phenomena enter the cycle picture hand in hand with the variations in production we have just discussed. If we say that more goods are produced and sold, we are saying, in effect, that more use is made of money. When output declines, the use of money does also. But this is to assign money a passive role, in which its variations are subordinate to transactions in goods. The present topic, the causal influence of monetary factors in cyclical changes, arises from the fact that money is not wholly subordinate. Money enters as a cyclical factor, requiring special discussion, when the nature of money itself (or the manner of providing it) magnifies economic fluctuations, either up or down, or operates to check swings and cause reversals, bringing crises or revivals. It is the business of the money system to provide the exchange media that the level of production requires. Money is a source of disturbance when it overplays or underplays this role, especially the former. It is mainly disturbing through helping to convert prosperity into an unbalanced boom by overstimulating the purchase of goods and promoting the inflation of prices.

Two questions focus attention on the difficulty: Why do prices move upward during a boom and what is the relationship of money to the rise? What are the tensions that develop to precipitate a crisis?

Rising prices during a boom. The money required for exchanging an expanding output of goods becomes available, we have seen, (1) through the greater velocity of funds that firms and individuals already have, arising through a disposition to reduce their cash balances, and (2) through the extension of credit by the banks, mainly in the form of deposits. If the rate at which money is offered for goods expands no faster than the volume of goods offered for sale, prices in general do not rise. Why, when prosperity is under way, is spending likely to proceed at a faster rate? There are several reasons.

At the outset, in getting recovery under way after a depression, some price advances are necessary to make expansion of production worth while. There are price-cost distortions to be corrected and some reassignments of resources to be accomplished. In many situations enterprises require the incentive of higher prices to shake off the inertia of depression. Money must be available to make buying possible at these corrected prices; from the recovery standpoint, its availability is all to the good.

But money also becomes available for buying, or at least for bidding for, goods beyond the capacity of expanding production to supply them. As recovery gains momentum, businesses become anxious to get equipment and to build up their inventories. Consumers want new furniture and cars and houses. The outlays required for such items are large, and the demand for them expands in advance of the receipt of current income from current output to pay for them. Spending moves ahead faster than production, and an inflationary price rise is under way.

In part, especially in the early stages of recovery, expanded spending is made possible through the use of accumulated cash reserves. Even businesses that have undergone losses may emerge from depression in a strong cash position because of their liquidation of inventories and failure to replace facilities. Individuals who have kept their jobs are likely also to have funds. Through use of these balances, total spending can rise above the flow of income from current production.

Expansion through reducing cash balances can occur only in a money economy, but it does not make money itself a positive factor in the situation. Money becomes a positive factor only when the amount of it is increased to assist the expanding buying. Credit dollars play this part. In every boom, consumer credit rises by many billions. Even more, business firms borrow to expand stocks and purchase equipment as well as to finance their extension of credit to customers. This money comes mainly from the banks. How fast total spending expands in relation to the production of goods depends, to a very great extent, on *the rate at which the banks make credit available*.

This rate depends both on the borrowers and on the banks. Funds are not borrowed unless the borrower wants them. But whether he wants them depends, in part, on the interest rate the bank charges and the terms of the loan. More important, the kind of project he gets them for, and the chances he can take in his commitments, depend on the standards of credit risk by which the banks are governed. An easy credit policy on the part of the banks is thus a stimulus to inflation. Such a policy is likely as a boom gets under way. When recovery comes after a depression, the banks are usually in a strong reserve position. Recent lending has been light and earlier loans have, to a large extent, been repaid. Banks are private businesses, concerned with profit; when they are in position to make loans and prosperity is in the air, they naturally try to expand their business. While anxious, of course, to avoid bad loans, they are disposed to take a liberal attitude toward borrowers.

Thus a strong upward pressure on prices is present, explainable partly by the prevailing eagerness to buy and invest and partly by the ability and eagerness of the banks to lend. In this situation, the nature of the buying is important. In part it rests on the judgments—perhaps the too optimistic judgments—of consumers and businessmen as to their real probable requirements. But in part, also, it is purely *speculative,* resting simply on the fact that prices are going up and that there is money to be made from that fact. To some extent, the inventory buying of businesses is speculative, calculated to beat the price rise. But much speculation is divorced from ordinary business. Speculative buying hastens the price rise and helps to create the condition it feeds upon.

Speculative buying, like ordinary buying, is stimulated by the availability of credit, and funds are borrowed for speculative purposes. Rising prices are a boom to debtors, and the speculator deliberately becomes a debtor. He borrows, buys something, sells it later at a higher price, and then pays off the loan.

The rise in the prices of current products is supported by the *rising prices of existing wealth.* Real estate and corporate shares become more valuable, partly because higher earnings are expected from them and partly because they are prime objects of speculation. As they advance, they provide security for larger and larger bank loans and thus promote the monetary expansion.

With respect to this expansion, it should be remembered that credit dollars, once in existence, circulate as other dollars do. The $1000 that comes into being to finance a specific $1000 purchase provides the means of making several thousand dollars' worth of purchases. The increase in spending attributable to the banks greatly exceeds the volume of loans they make.

In viewing these inflationary factors, it is apparent we are doing something more than describing a healthful return to prosperity after a depression. In some degree a rise in prices is desirable. It hastens needed readjustments from the low depression level, stimulates the reallocation of resources, and generally speeds up recovery. But the speed easily becomes too great and new distortions are created. In what ways, then, do these monetary factors help to stall the boom and provoke a decline?

Money factors in crisis and decline. Credit expansion has a leading role in the bunching of durable-goods buying—*overinvestment* it is called—in good years. Overinvestment may be thought of as consisting simply in the disproportionate buying of producers' goods and consumers' durables—in the purchase of them at a greater rate than can be reconciled with a long-run balance among lines of production. But overinvestment means also that, during a boom, the amount of money invested in producers' goods is greater than the savings available for this purpose from current income—or, more accurately, the amount of money so invested is greater than the resources available for the purpose, whether released through saving or unemployed. Thus, in order to command the resources for producers' goods, credit dollars must be obtained from the banks to bid resources away from the making of ordinary consumers' goods. The idea of overinvestment ties the production of durable goods in boom years to the expansion of credit dollars for the purchase of these goods.[6] The credit dollars can be blamed, then, for distortion among lines of production, and need of readjustment, as well as for rising prices.

Credit expansion is also blamed, at least in part, for the peculiarly *shaky promotions* that are the special product of an inflationary and speculative boom. As a boom progresses, the public is increasingly anxious and able to be in on the profit-making, although the sounder developments have already taken place. Then corporations are thrown together and plants and office buildings and apartment houses are constructed with the seemingly sole reason that they can be unloaded profitably on the public. When prosperity assumes these features, it invites an abrupt end.

Rising prices presently generate an uneasy feeling that they have risen too high and must fall. When land and securities are priced higher than the sum on which their earnings can yield an acceptable return,

---

[6] Some writers state this matter in terms of the interest rate. They say that the market rate of interest, governed by the large amount of bank credit available, is lower than a true interest rate would be that really reflected the amount of savings, or the amount of resources, available for capital goods without any inflationary bidding. This artificially low rate encourages the use of funds for capital purposes.

informed persons become alarmed. When important groups, whose incomes are not keeping up, are being priced out of the market, and consumption lags, the end of the rise seems near. Speculative buying eases off, and profit taking increases on commodities and securities. Inventories cease to expand, and some contraction sets in. Perhaps before the public is aware what is happening—even while, as in 1929, the soundness of prosperity is still being proclaimed officially—knowing persons are unloading and selling short. When some striking event, perhaps a break in the stock market, broadcasts the situation, selling becomes widespread, and buying, as far as possible, is deferred. Then the decline may be rapid and hard to stop.

We are not supposing that all booms end in this way, or that these monetary factors solely explain the end of any boom, but we are noting how these factors have operated at times and how they may operate. During the prosperous 1920s commodity prices in general did not rise; they even fell slightly. But inflationary factors seem, nevertheless, to have been present. Technological progress was rapid, and real costs were falling, so that the prices of goods did rise considerably in relation to the resources that went into them. At the same time, funds in great volume poured into the markets for existing wealth, particularly corporate wealth represented by securities, and inflation there was very great. While the collapse was not preceded by the inflation of commodity prices, it was followed by severe deflation, and it possessed monetary features such as we have described.

Contraction of bank credit. For the most strictly monetary aspect of a crisis, let us return to the banks. We have seen that the banks enter a recovery period with large unused reserves and are anxious to expand their loans. Presently this condition passes, and as the boom progresses the banks may find that their lending power is exhausted, except as they resort to central banks which are already frowning on the inflationary trend. Commercial banks may even find that they have gone too far, since cash withdrawals for expanding consumption may continue after business loans have reached a peak. At the same time that the banks become less able to lend, the loan applications of bank customers appear less worthy and appealing. Profits seem less certain, and the credit standing of borrowers is scrutinized more closely. Some loans are not renewed, and interest rates are raised so that they become a more noticeable burden on borrowers.

To repay loans requires cash, and cash is obtained by reducing inventories and restricting purchases. Commodity markets are thus adversely affected, prices decline, and contraction becomes general. If the suspicion is noised about that the banks are seriously overextended, depositors demand cash, and the contraction of loans must, at the very least, be accelerated. At worst, the banks must close their doors, and the condition of general financial collapse is present. But short of any need of contraction whatever, the mere fact that expansion has stopped disappoints profit expectations based on further expansion and causes curtailment. The tensions in a boom seem to be such that when it ceases going forward, it dissolves.

It will be observed, in so far as the money supply is a factor in business crisis and contraction, that it is a money supply that rests on a debt basis. Money as such does not operate in this way. If firms and individuals decide to cut down their rate of spending and hold money instead of goods, the reason for contraction does not lie in the money supply. But if they cut down their spending because their money consists of bank deposits based on borrowing, and it is necessary or expedient to repay the loans, the contraction can be attributed to the nature of the money supply. Debt money contracts in time of stress for reasons we have noted and also because, as prices decline, the burden of debt becomes heavier. The dollars owed are increasingly valuable dollars. Goods are pushed on the markets to pay the banks, and money is retired from circulation.

It is inevitable, therefore, that the extensive use of deposit currency in our economy should be a matter of controversy. Resting on the credit-creating power of banks, its utility as a flexible medium is clear. During recovery from depression and the achievement of prosperity, expanding deposits based on loans serve excellently in providing the purchasing power that must anticipate the expansion of production. But they serve also to finance the inflationary, speculative side of expansion, and in time of crisis they contract in a way that hastens a decline.

4. Prices, costs, and profits

Fluctuations in the use of resources are probable when durable goods, especially producers' goods, have a prominent place in total output. They are intensified by monetary influences, especially the role of bank credit. Further light is thrown on them by the behavior of business profits and the relationship of selling prices and costs behind business profits. Price-cost relationships help to explain the cumulative tendencies in booms and depressions and also the turning points in the cycle.

Profits are the most widely fluctuating element in the business cycle. In the extreme decline of the early 1930s, corporate profits after taxes fell from $8 billion a year to a negative $3 billion a year. Prices, wages, and production showed no such variation. A substantial part of business spending—the most variable part—is governed by profits, actual and expected. While outlays for the labor and materials which go into a product depend directly on the volume of sales, the outlays on plant and equipment—part of the maintenance, most of the replacement, all of the expansion—depend on profit prospects. It is the latter outlays, we have seen, that spell the difference, directly and indirectly, between prosperity and depression.

Why do profits vary so widely? The usual answer is that costs tend to lag behind selling prices, both in boom and slump. In the typical business, profit is a relatively small item in comparison with gross revenue. If selling prices go up, a small lag in cost can cause a large rise in profit. With prices falling, a similar lag can quickly wipe out the profit.

But why should there be a lag in cost? Some outlays, such as bond interest, rentals, and insurance, are fixed in contracts and do not change as long as the contracts run. Depreciation is ordinarily computed on the basis of the cost of existing facilities. Salaries are adjusted at infrequent intervals. Ordinary wages, for a mixture of reasons, tend to lag behind prices. With recovery under way but labor still unemployed, wage rates respond less rapidly to expanding demand than do the prices of products which still have to be produced. Similarly, when a decline sets in, goods are pushed on markets with a pressure not equaled in the release of workers. Doubtless custom is a larger factor in the pricing of human services than of products; perhaps considerations of morale enter. While labor organizations are effective in overcoming the lag when prices are rising, they increase the lag when prices are going down.

But the main reason for the lag in costs is the sheer effect of volume on the spreading of overheads. As fuller use is made of existing capacity, costs related to the plant itself and its administration rise but little in the aggregate, and thus fall sharply per unit of product. But with a decline in output, overhead costs become increasingly burdensome. It is these costs, when they are covered by contracts that call for continuing money payments, which largely account for business failures during a depression.

Cost adjustments and the turning points. Thus lags in costs develop which cause profits to soar during a boom and to disappear during a depression, with decisive effect on the expansion and contraction of business. Equally important is the narrowing of the lag and the catching up of costs in the latter part of a boom, and the adjustments between costs and prices as a depression runs its course. These changes help to explain the turning points in the cycle.

As a boom gathers momentum, costs increase and gain on selling prices. Some of the leading raw-material prices are relatively flexible, and rising demand presently hits them more sharply than it does prices at retail. Labor costs rise as employment is extended and inferior workers are employed and paid standard rates. As jobs become more certain, the discipline of workers declines, and their productivity frequently falls. Wage rates rise more rapidly as pressure on supply develops, and overtime pay adds to costs. As firms approach capacity operation, there is no offset in larger volume; instead, the overheads mount with the rise in wage rates and materials prices. Thus, with costs increasing and the advance in selling prices tapering off, profit prospects decline, investment sags, and the boom draws to a close.

The adverse relationship between prices and costs which develops when business first declines is also modified as the depression proceeds. High-cost contracts run out and are not renewed. Some high-cost firms disappear, and costs are adjusted in others through financial reorganization. Labor productivity improves as inferior workers are discharged and as possession of a job becomes a more compelling incentive. Management is stimulated to increased efficiency. As financial pressures ease, the maintenance of equipment is improved, some worn facilities are replaced, inventories are built up. Credit is increasingly available, and at lower cost, to spur revival. Perhaps profits will be absent or negligible until sales expand, but cost adjustment helps to lay the foundation for improvement.

5. Optimism and pessimism

It is sometimes said that the causes of booms and depressions are psychological. When people feel confident regarding the future, they buy cars and houses and make business investments, with the result that production and employment are high. When they are filled with misgiving, they do not spend, and the economy plods along in low gear. These shifting states of optimism and pessimism control the level of prosperity.

Does such a statement throw any light on the cycle problem? The answer should probably be that its worth depends on what more precisely is meant by it. It may be a wholly unenlightening truism, a dangerous misconception, or a rather useful addition to the preceding analysis.

If it means that the business cycle is not a mechanical thing, pursuing its course like a planet in its orbit (albeit with less regularity), it is a true statement but adds nothing to what we have said. All economic action comes about through human decisions, not through mechanical processes, and the major decisions to buy and invest rest on expectations regarding the future. When expectations are such that commitments are made, one may say, if one likes, that a state of optimism prevails. Use of these words adds nothing to what has been taken for granted as obvious throughout the entire preceding discussion.

But if the statement means, quite apart from objective economic facts, that prosperity and depression are the sheer products of states of mind, we had better beware of it. The psychological approach to prosperity has been tried more than once, but without apparent result. If the later stage of a boom is upon us, we cannot exorcise depression by getting everybody to repeat "business as usual" ten times before breakfast. Nor, if depression is already here, can we achieve prompt recovery by declaring faithfully and often that "prosperity is just around the corner."

Maladjustments in price and costs, in the relations of industries, in the flow and use of credit are real facts which cannot be disposed of by thinking the right thoughts. While they exert influence through human decisions, they have existence outside the human mind. But even if it were true that a collective act of faith would preserve stability, there is no way to cause individuals, in their practical behavior as consumers and businessmen, to conduct their affairs on that basis. The workingman will still have his periods of uncertainty and will postpone major purchases. The manufacturer, foreseeing no demand for his product that his present plant will not meet, will not build an extension, however beneficial the effect might be if numerous manufacturers proceeded to invest in more facilities.

But states of mind do often endow objective economic facts with more significance than they should have. The merit in stressing the psychological side of business fluctuations lies in the fact that prevailing moods of optimism and pessimism cause exaggerated responses to the conditions that actually prevail. We find here another amplifying factor in the cycle. Human beings are shortsighted and readily assume that a brief movement foreshadows the whole future course of events. And they respond to mass suggestion, their hopes and fears being inflated by the presence of like hopes and fears in others. So, when business is good, an unduly favorable construction is put on the facts, and commitments are made which strain credit, inflate prices, and distort industrial development. And when uncertainties develop, or a downturn occurs, both consumers and enterprisers scurry for cover, and needed readjustments are delayed and are made on a lower level than is at all necessary.

The Orthodox Cycle Approach and Its Alternatives

To complete the discussion of business fluctuation, we should contrast the preceding approach to the problem with other leading approaches. We have been considering the elements in what may be called the orthodox or traditional approach. What we have said should first be brought together to present a more unified picture of the cycle as thus viewed. Then, against this conception, or as supplementary to it, we should recognize the view of fluctuation taken by persons who accept the mature-economy theory, set forth in the last chapter, and also the view of those whose emphasis is largely on what we have called "external factors."

Phases of cycle as conventionally summarized

Whatever its deficiencies may be, the traditional cycle concept permits a coherent account of the changing level of activity. Booms and depressions may be viewed as the natural result, under the conditions of capitalism, of those ordinary economic processes which embrace production and employment, income and spending, money and the price level, prices and costs. Viewed in this way, there are no extended plateaus of activity—high or low—but only change. Prosperity is not a stable, though temporary, high level of production but a period of expansion filled with mounting tensions. Depression is a time of contraction in which readjustments take place. Between these periods are times of transition, which may be called turning points—though their length may make *turning periods* a better term. By way of summary, let us combine, on the basis of these periods, the explanatory factors already considered in order to obtain a rounded picture of business fluctuations regarded in conventional cycle terms. One may break into the cycle at any point. Let us begin with the period of rising prosperity.

The boom. As business expands, increased buying spurs production and absorbs idle resources, while, reciprocally, increased production and sales expand buying power. Use of cash reserves and bank credit enables demand to put pressure on production, so that prices rise. Rising prices encourage speculation and further indebtedness. Costs lag, and rising profits stimulate the investment of capital.

All types of durable goods are bought and produced at an abnormal rate, even as judged by the high continuing needs of a prospering economy. Their production reflects accumulated deficiencies from recent lean years, the lag in applying technical discoveries, the accelerated response of "derived demand," the overly enthusiastic reaction to improved prospects and high profits. Presently the deficiencies have been made up, and the more promising new investments have been made. The new plant capacity comes into operation. The rate of durable-goods production declines.

The downturn. Thus the boom tapers off, and the stage is set for a decline. Not only are the more promising investment outlets exhausted, but profits in general fall as costs catch up with selling prices. The price rise slackens, as some prices discourage buying, and then speculative buying eases off and selling commences. In general, those activities that rest on anticipated further expansion fall off sharply. Confidence is shaken, and a cautious attitude develops. When total spending falls below the current income level, the decline is under way.

The change may be dramatized by a sharp break in the stock market and assume a crisis aspect. A more substantial push may come from the contraction of bank credit and the selling of goods that it necessitates. With the downturn, inventories are reduced, and equipment buying goes on a replacement basis, or less. Prices fall, profits vanish, debt burdens intensify, businesses fail.

The depression. Thus production, employment, income, and buying are linked in a downward spiral which closely parallels the previous upswing. For a time the decline seems cumulative, but presently it slackens as the trough is approached. An increasing fraction of the declining output is for current consumption, so that fewer purchases are postponable. Costs are adjusted downward, and firms regain their financial balance. Pessimism moderates as the worst fears appear baseless. Buying reaches the level of current output, and contraction grinds to a stop. The depth of depression has been attained, and with it signs of recovery appear.

The recovery. The roots of revival may lie in the very fact that conditions have ceased to grow worse. If we grant that people prefer higher to lower incomes, that they prefer activity to inactivity, that perhaps they are blessed with a certain basic courage and optimism, the foundation of improvement is present. Labor and plant capacity are available. Costs are not out of line with prices. Needs for goods are great, especially for durable goods that are wearing out, and demand promises to be vigorous if people have the means to buy. Production will provide the means. Much cash, moreover, is lying idle, and large credit resources await the return of confidence. Once the upturn is evident, familiar cumulative forces take hold and recovery mounts.

The foregoing should not be thought of as a particular theory of business fluctuations. It is rather a particular approach, a particular conception of the problem, that has room within it for a number of theories. Within it, the main stress may be placed on durable-goods factors, on money factors, or on price and cost factors. Any one of a variety of causal sequences may be considered dominant. But whichever relationship is emphasized, the general approach is the same. All such theories involve the basic idea of a cyclical ebb and flow due to maladjustments within the ordinary processes of the economy; to explain fluctuations, they do not depend on breakdowns that are due to chronic deficiencies of demand or to outside events that are not an inherent part of the economic system.

Chronic-deficiency theories

In contrast, there is the view of fluctuations which connects them with an underlying, chronic weakness in total demand. In the United States, this view would link them with economic maturity, as we have discussed it. The term "secular stagnation," a somewhat broader term, is also applied to it. The theory is variously referred to as one of underconsumption, underinvestment, and oversaving. Whatever the label, the central idea is that production cannot remain on a high level because the saving from a capacity level of income is greater than investment outlets can continue to absorb. A chronic tendency for saving to outrun investment is the source of difficulty.

The words "chronic" and "stagnation" suggest that the result of oversaving may be a continuing low level of activity, well below productive capacity. So it might, if it were the only factor present. But theories which make oversaving the key influence do not exclude other factors. The sensitivity of durable-goods buying and the credit and price-cost elements are still present, and outside influences such as wars and inventions may still intrude. So the chronic weakness need not be evident in chronic depression, in persisting stagnation. There may be upswings which, at times, even lift the economy to its utmost performance. But entirely apart from other tensions, these periods must end because investment outlets presently run out. All the profitable plants will be built and equipped and all the houses people want to buy will be constructed, whereas saving, with the increased income from expanded capacity, will become even larger if a break does not come. A rest period becomes necessary in which saving falls and a backlog of investment possibilities builds up.

In the more orthodox cycle theories, investment, we have seen, achieves a magnitude and character in boom periods that require correction. The explanation may be that it is financed through bank credit, by means of which resources are bid away from consumption lines. Or the explanation may be that temporarily, with high boom-time profits prevailing, both saving and investment are abnormal. Or the trouble may lie in distorted investment patterns among industries. But it does not arise, in the orthodox view, from lack of sufficient investment opportunities to absorb the saving from a capacity level of income, if boom-period stresses are removed and a balanced prosperity is achieved. In the oversaving view, however, investment must presently prove inadequate and cause depression, apart from other distortions.

As to the merit of this view of business fluctuations, nothing need be added here to the discussion of the mature-economy idea in the preceding chapter.

External factors

Wars and like events, which are clearly no part of the cycle as usually regarded, greatly affect the course of activity. Their influence may be variously construed. They may be thought of (1) as merely modifying an inherent economic rhythm, causing booms and depressions to be more or less violent, to start earlier or later, to last for longer or shorter periods, than they otherwise would; (2) as providing initiating pushes and pressures without which fluctuations would not take place at all; even (3) as having a rhythm of their own, of which the economic rhythm is the result. Persons who stress the inherent sequence of cyclical change in explaining business fluctuations quite logically construe outside factors in the first of these ways. Persons who adopt the oversaving viewpoint may see in wars and outstanding discoveries the only reason for relief from chronic stagnation.

Among such events, wars are the great disturbers. After the several feeble recoveries of the 1930s, the very high level of output and employment in the 1940s came plainly as the result of war. More specifically, on the demand side, it was the result of a vast volume of government spending, financed in part with credit dollars. Past wars and wars in other countries have had similar effect, though the exceptional economic lift in the 1940s can be assigned to what is known as "total war."

Perhaps equally important is the aftermath of war. Transition from war to peace requires adjustments that may cause a temporary dip. Wartime price inflation seriously disturbs the economic balance. But weightier, and on the other side, are the accumulated demands for durable consumers' goods that could not be produced during war and the accumulated buying power from high wartime earnings that could not be spent currently. There are also war-created technical ideas waiting peacetime application. Thus, outside of countries impoverished by war through physical devastation or in other ways, conditions are present for a high level of postwar prosperity. But these abnormal elements in prosperity are likely to create abnormal tensions which will presently assert themselves.

War affects prosperity in part through channels of international trade and investment. But war is only one influence acting through these channels, so we should recognize as another major external factor the *international economic policies* and actions of nations. International dealings are disturbing because of the peculiar relationship that exists among the economies of different countries. Nations neither operate as separate economic units nor as indistinguishable segments of a world economy. National economies are insulated in some degree— by transport costs, by immobility of labor and capital, by use of different moneys, by restrictive policies—but dealings between nations are sufficient to subject each nation's economy to important impulses from abroad. These impulses are made spasmodic and undependable by policy changes and other special circumstances.

Many believe that the billions lent by the United States to other nations following World War I, and the exports paid for with those loans, contributed greatly to the level of American prosperity in the 1920s. In any case, there is little question that the sudden ending of those loans and exports in the late 1920s was most disturbing. Since World War II American production for foreign nations has been on a much larger scale, and thus the prospect of its termination carries even more of a threat. Changes in trade policy—by tariffs, exchange controls, and other means—may alter suddenly the foreign markets on which a nation's industries depend. Export controls may affect the sources of materials needed in other countries. When a nation is as much involved in international dealings as Great Britain long has been, changes in its investment, markets, and sources of supply can largely govern its domestic prosperity.

But the policies that affect prosperity need not be in the international sphere. *Ordinary policies within a country,* dealing with taxation, public projects, industrial relations, business regulation, and a host of matters, can encourage enterprise or depress it. Even anticipated policies, connected with shifts in the party in power, are supposed to be influential. Were public policies not important, it would be futile to look to government for assistance in maintaining prosperity or recovering from depression. External factors in this category will constitute the topic of the following chapter, which will deal with public policy in the interest of high production and employment.

Among the external factors, we should also include instances of *exceptional technical progress,* sensational inventions and discoveries. Here a distinction is required that is not clean-cut. Among the basic features of modern capitalism that cause instability, we included the changes that take place in methods of production. In a static economy, fluctuations would not occur, and technical change is a major dynamic element. Its presence should be assumed in any theory of cyclical variation. But, quite apart from the usual procession of innovations, there are occasional developments so outstanding that they have a special impact. Such, for example, were the railroad building after the Civil War and the extensive adoption of motor transportation after World War I: in both cases the investment, direct and indirect, amounted to many billions and necessarily had a powerful effect on the whole economy. Of like effect, also, are *discoveries of rich natural resources* and the *opening of new areas* to settlement.

Developments which cause *long-run movements in the price level* exert a special influence. If, as is generally believed, the great expansion of gold production in the 1890s caused an upward trend in prices, the cycles superimposed on that trend could be expected to have longer booms and shorter depressions because of the favorable effect on profits.

A different sort of external factor is the *weather* as it affects agricultural output. Much has been written on the relationship between farming and business in general, but there is no unanimity of view. No single generalization is possible as to how weather affects agricultural prosperity, since favorable conditions both expand crops and reduce prices. While fluctuations in agriculture for natural reasons may cause changes in the rest of the economy, the prevailing judgment probably is that agriculture is more the beneficiary, or the victim, of developments in the remainder of the economy than it is the source of them.

The external factors, as already indicated, may be construed, in orthodox cycle theories, as modifying and intensifying factors or, in oversaving theories, as stimuli that prevent a continuing dead level of stagnation. But they may also be regarded as the basis, in their own right, of systematic cyclical variation. Thus the most curious construction of the weather factor has been the attempt by various writers to erect a full-blown cycle theory on the basis of it. It is sometimes called the "sun-spot" theory, since cycles of weather are correlated with cycles of spots on the sun, and a chain of effects is traced from the sun through the weather to agricultural output and, finally, to the general level of prosperity.

Business fluctuations have been the fertile source of theories, some quite mystical, regarding rhythms that find economic expression. This segment of economics seems to appeal especially to persons who would find remote causes for economic events. Pulsations are sought in the universe or in this planet or in the nature of man—quite outside the relationships of prices, output, income, and spending—to explain the cycle. Less remotely but no less alien to conventional thinking, various cycles with various periods are discovered within the economic sphere —overlapping, interfering, re-enforcing. Many minds lean naturally to theories which possess a mechanical neatness and inevitability but which, if there is real hope of combating depressions through public action, we are bound to reject.

Review Questions

1. "The phrase 'business cycle' implies more than the mere presence of variations in total economic activity." Explain.

2. What types of economic data are used in measuring and analyzing cyclical fluctuations? What bearing have seasonal changes and secular trends on the problem? What are leads and lags? What is meant by saying that cycles differ in amplitude and duration? What seems to be the typical length of cycles?

3. Review the main points from Chapter 3 that are useful in measuring the social impact of business depression.

4. As elements in the process of explaining business fluctuations, what are the phases of the cycle? What is the difference between internal and external factors?

5. "Variations in production of durable goods suggest that small differences in expectations may have large effects." Explain, bringing out the facts regarding the variability of output of different classes of goods. What light is thrown on the instability of advanced economies?

6. "During the upswing of the business cycle, a decline in the rate of expansion of consumption demand can cause an absolute decline in the demand for producers' goods." Explain and illustrate. Apply the acceleration principle to residential building.

7. "Even though technical knowledge does not advance in cycles, its application occurs in a way that intensifies fluctuations." Explain.

8. How is the use of durable goods connected with revival from a depression?

9. "Variations in inventory investment accentuate variations in total demand." Explain. Relate to price changes.

10. "Monetary expansion during a business upswing is necessary. In some degree, a rise in prices is desirable. But monetary expansion and rising prices easily become part of the maladjusted production and misleading profits that make prosperity highly unstable." Develop each sentence.

11. "A $1000 increase in total production, while not requiring a $1000 expansion in exchange media, is likely to cause a $1000 expansion when

financed with bank credit." Explain. What is the significance of this point?

12. "Just as credit expansion provides more dollars to buy goods than are received from current sales, so credit contraction means that current income dollars are used to pay the banks, and less money is available to buy goods than current production provides." Develop this point as a factor in business decline.

13. Explain the lag in costs as a factor in the cumulative aspect of booms and depressions; the readjustment in costs as a factor helping to terminate booms and depressions.

14. "Booms and depressions are not just matters of optimism and pessimism that can be dealt with by psychological treatment, but they are probably intensified by popular states of mind." Explain.

15. Summarize the causal factors we have considered on the basis of the four phases of the business cycle.

16. Distinguish the oversaving explanation of cyclical fluctuations from more orthodox explanations.

17. "External factors may enter cycle analysis as reasons for the unusual amplitude or duration of particular cycles. But they are sometimes viewed as the prime reasons for fluctuations, without which booms and depressions would not occur." Develop the distinction.

~ 16 ~

Idle Resources
and Public Policy

Is BUSINESS depression, with heavy unemployment and loss of income, to be accepted as inevitable and endured with such grace as the public can muster? Or is it to be the object of collective, governmental attack? What organized attempts have been made to avoid depressions or to escape them? What lines of action are possible, and what are their merits and defects?

These are unavoidable questions in an economy as depression-conscious as the United States has been since 1929. They raise issues on which many volumes have been written, and on which many more will be before agreement regarding policy is reached. In dealing with so large a topic, we shall be able only to review the main lines of public action that have been, or may be, followed and to note certain critical considerations that bear on them.

It is helpful to keep several distinctions in mind. From a policy standpoint, it is one problem, as in the 1930s, to *escape from a depression* already present; it is quite a different problem, as in the 1920s or after World War II, to *maintain a prosperity* already enjoyed. Each situation presents its subproblems. In a depression, some policies aim at *relief*—that is, making unemployment endurable to the victims of it. But the main policies aim at *recovery,* the restoration of production and employment. During a prosperous period, some policies aim at *preventing the tensions and distortions* that bring collapse; other policies seek to *counteract crises* when they develop and threaten imminent recession.

This chapter will first review briefly American policy and the ideas that have influenced it. Then recovery and relief policies will be considered and policies designed to maintain prosperity. The latter will be grouped as to whether they grow out of traditional business-cycle thinking or out of misgiving regarding the basic adequacy of the total demand for goods—the oversaving, underconsumption approach. Deficit spending by government will be introduced briefly at several points and considered somewhat critically at the end. A number of the policies that enter this chapter will be dealt with at length in later chapters, since they are more than depression-fighting policies. Discussion of them here will be cursory, and reference will be made to later discussions.

American Experience and Attitudes

It is one thing to agree that depressions are bad and quite another to do something about them. The American tradition has generally stood against governmental intrusion in the domestic economy, and conditions have had to be bad in a dramatic and arousing way to bring action. A number of nineteenth-century movements reflected economic discontent, but policies specifically to combat recurring depressions were slow in coming. Policy in this sphere belongs to the twentieth century and has been of an emergency and piecemeal nature. The pros and cons of what should be done, the responsibility government should assume, remain controversial.

Policy in the United States

The break in business in 1907 took the form of financial collapse and panic and led to the view that action to strengthen the money structure, and establish control over the use of credit, would help to maintain stability. The Federal Reserve Act resulted, and it still provides the main continuing policy in this field.

The succeeding break in 1914 was quickly overcome by European demands for American goods. After World War I, the severe, but brief, depression of 1920–1921 brought no positive action, but a number of studies and reports on the problem resulted from the President's Conference on Unemployment of 1921. The last of these, the *Report of the Committee on Recent Economic Changes,* appearing early in 1929 under the chairmanship of Herbert Hoover, concluded with the happy, but purposeful note: "Our situation is fortunate, our momentum is remarkable. Yet the organic balance of our economic structure can be maintained only by hard, persistent, intelligent effort." Pointing toward the need of governmental action, the *Report* stated: "To maintain the dynamic equilibrium of recent years is, indeed, a problem of leadership which more and more demands deliberate public attention and control." [1]

The "marked balance," the "dynamic equilibrium," noted with so much satisfaction by the Committee, contained flaws more serious than were suspected. Mr. Hoover had been President only a few months when the stock market crashed and the great depression began. It was too late then for action to maintain stability, but, to prevent catastrophe, the President exhorted business to carry out its plans for production and capital outlay. Whatever the response, the decline continued and reached catastrophic depths. Credit controls, which had been applied weakly before the break to limit speculation, continued to be used to soften the decline. The main step taken was the establishment in 1931 of the Reconstruction Finance Corporation to keep railroads, banks, insurance companies, and other enterprises from failing. Business failures, however, were numerous.

By 1932 economic distress had created a mood of desperation which, from a political standpoint, made strong action imperative. Brief dips of 15 percent or 20 percent in national real income might be endured but not dips twice as great lasting for several years. Mr. Roosevelt was elected in November, inaugurated in March, and by summer of 1933 a swift series of enactments and orders had come from Congress and the White House aimed at the emergency. They included:

1. Emergency banking legislation. Industrial output had expanded late in 1932 but had relapsed when the banks, borne down by declining asset values and heavy withdrawals, were finally closed by general order. Action to open and strengthen the banks was necessary to prevent paralysis of the economy.

2. Departure from the gold standard, followed (in January 1934) by a reduction of 40 percent in the gold equivalent of the dollar. The aim was to stop the outflow of gold, improve the situation for exports, and raise prices generally.

3. Aid to farmers through the Agricultural Adjustment Act. Prices of farm products had fallen most heavily, and the aim, both in the interest of relief and recovery, was to raise these prices and increase the incomes and purchasing power of farmers.

4. Industry-wide agreements through codes approved under the National Industrial Recovery Act. These agreements sought to bolster prices and adjust output to the market.

5. Wage-and-hour agreements under the same act. The aim was to spread work, raise wage rates, and increase consumer buying.

6. Large federal expenditures for relief and recovery. Under Title II

[1] *Recent Economic Changes in the United States,* McGraw-Hill, 1929, pp. xxii and xx.

of the National Industrial Recovery Act, $3.3 billion were authorized for public-works projects. Federal expenditures had exceeded revenues for three years under President Hoover, and President Roosevelt's first intention of bringing the budget into balance was quickly supplanted by a deliberate policy of deficit spending to promote recovery.

The years which followed have been interpreted in a number of ways and with an objectivity often diminished by politics. Opponents have blamed the Roosevelt policies for the depression, though with some confusion of dates, since the decline began more than three years earlier. They have argued—and with more substance—that the upturn in the United States began in 1932, as it did in most other countries, and that the bank closing was merely an interruption. On this basis the improvement appears as an ordinary cyclical revival, not as a result of government action. By adopting this view and then pointing to the slow speed of recovery, with 8,000,000 still unemployed as late as 1940, the opponents have been able to argue that natural recovery processes were impeded by the Roosevelt program.

But it is also arguable, in view of the state of prostration, psychological as well as economic, which had developed, that only the leadership and drastic policies of President Roosevelt could have brought the upturn that began in 1933. Clear proof or disproof of this view is plainly impossible. And it is almost as difficult, to one who accepts it, to show which of the several New Deal policies deserves credit for the improvement. It may be attributable to all of them or to certain of them and in spite of others. Their effects were merged. In the next section we shall look a little into the probabilities.

The war brought more than recovery; it brought a level of activity without precedent in the United States. Surpluses of labor turned to severe shortages, and popular concern over the depression problem subsided. But neither wartime nor postwar prosperity has been viewed by thoughtful observers as an indication that the problem has been solved or that it will not reappear with the severity of the 1930s. Studies have been continued by government agencies and organized private groups, including leading businessmen, and plans have been proposed for government action.

Attention after the war centered first on an effort to get Congress to declare a high degree of federal responsibility for employment and to lay plans for large federal expenditures, in peace as in war, to maintain prosperity. A "full-employment" bill was debated, and after considerable whittling the Employment Act of 1946—with the word "full" omitted—became law. It provides for a Council of Economic Advisers to "review current economic trends" and make policy recommendations. While the Act declares the government's responsibility to "promote maximum employment, production, and purchasing power," it remains up to Congress in each instance to act, or not to act, on the recommendations of the Council. The Act does not itself establish a positive, long-range plan to maintain prosperity.

Conflicting attitudes toward future policy

A variety of considerations, both popular and expert, have influenced public action and remain difficult to reconcile in their bearing on future policy.

Traditional fear of positive action. In the past, at least up to 1930, depressions were usually regarded as a disease springing from the excesses of boom periods. Booms brought distortions of prices and costs and shaky promotions and financial structures, and the only solution, it was thought, the only way to re-establish prosperity on a solid basis, was through the purge that comes with general deflation. Depressions, then, were not entirely bad but had their therapeutic value. They should not be checked prematurely by use of artificial props. When they had served their purpose, prosperity would return.

The only thing government might do was to restrain somewhat the excesses of prosperous years, as through the control of credit. According to this view, credit control might be an effective weapon if applied vigorously. But it was becoming apparent that, when times are good, every one is impatient of restraint; it is difficult politically to impose controls when few people are worrying about depression.

It may seem that the experience of the 1930s should have convinced the public that some kind of positive and permanent policy should be adopted, not only for getting out of depressions but for keeping out. It may seem that any belief in the therapeutic value of depressions should have been exploded by a depression as severe as that one. A cure should not have the magnitude of a major ailment—indeed consist of that ailment. Perhaps this reaction would have governed policy if the New Deal had retained its hold after the war. But reasons persisted for moving slowly—reasons which, apart from their real merit, fitted in with the lingering aversion to strong public action.

The disaster of the early 1930s may have shown the need of action, but the efforts to deal with it did not convincingly mark the course that future action should take. Even in the aggregate the New Deal policies were not clearly successful, and the merits of individual policies seemed anybody's guess. Certainly experts were not agreed as to how prosperity might best be maintained. The most insistent demands for action came from people with mature-economy leanings and a predilection for large public spending—ideas that most Congressmen and most businessmen have continued to class with the wilder heresies. Effective action against depressions, moreover, would need to be planned action, promptly taken as need arose. Thus extensive authority would have to be delegated by Congress to administrative officers—not a popular step in the aftermath of war.

Along with government spending, the move for a broad policy was linked with other distasteful ideas. Enthusiasts talked loosely about "full employment" and the "right of every man to a job." Full employment, literally understood, is an impossible ideal in a dynamic society, and a close approach to it may be inflationary and injurious to efficiency. Practical men are not likely to concur in legislation that implies it. More philosophically, these phrases suggest a transfer of economic responsibility from the individual to the state, in a way that runs counter to deep-seated convictions. Perhaps the individual is pretty helpless in a complex economy when it works badly; on the other hand, any system will work badly unless the individual acts as if prosperity were up to him. It is not easy to define collective responsibility in such a way that individual responsibility will remain firm and vigorous. Congress was not ready after the war to attempt a solution.

The case for positive action. Despite these difficulties, the case is strong for a farsighted, determined policy to maintain prosperity. The basic argument is the familiar one: The whole purpose of economic organization is defeated when existing productive power, ready to be used, is not actually employed to give people the level of living it makes possible. Moreover, the distress that comes with long unemployment is the worst of economic disasters. Probably to most persons, serious insecurity of income is worse than low average income. Thus, if any flaw in the economy justifies strong corrective action, it is the presence at one and the same time of people eager for more goods than are being produced and for more jobs than are being provided.

In view of the power of the masses, this point is most compelling when regarded politically. If an economic system falls far short of affording the level of income and the security of income that its resources permit, the people will consider exchanging it for another. Some observers thought this country was close to insurrection in the early 1930s. In other countries unemployment and economic distress had much to do with the rise of dictatorships between the wars. Probably no people that has known freedom will adopt any totalitarian scheme as a first choice, and perhaps not by violent means. But in desperation they will accept the domination that security seems to require. Revolutionaries, whether of the right or the left, do their fishing in troubled waters, and unemployment is the condition on which they most readily thrive.

If this country is to be the force in the world in the interests of peace that most Americans believe it should be, we must maintain prosperity at home. Not only is this necessary to give us the strength we require for essential tasks, but it is necessary also as the basis of prestige and confidence, if other countries are to acknowledge our leadership and be willing to tie their economies to ours. A major weakness in the American position has been the fear abroad of another depression here such as that of the 1930s, because such a depression would bring ruin to countries that are dependent on us.

Thus there are reasons for bold action, provided the direction of that action is clear. Proposals must be examined with care, with an eye not only to the chances of their success and the dangers if they fail but also to their probable impact on the whole economic structure if they succeed. We would not wish to fight depression with weapons that cannot be reconciled in the long run with the kind of society we want.

Recovery and Relief Policies

The more important task is that of preserving a high level of prosperity, once the nation has reached that happy state. This especially is the task that faces the country in the period of postwar prosperity. But before turning to it, let us first consider the problem as we faced it in the early 1930s, of stopping the downward spiral of deflation, getting revival started, setting the forces of recovery in motion. At the same time, the problem of relief, of making depression endurable while it lasts, calls for consideration. Because of the number of expedients tried, the experience of the 1930s provides a useful basis of discussion.

Recovery policies

Emergency banking policy. Action in 1933 to open the banks on a sound basis should, perhaps, not be called a recovery policy. It provided a necessary underlying condition, not only for revival but even for stopping deflation, and would be approved by persons generally opposed to government action. If deposits are the principal medium of exchange, people must be able to use their deposits and have confidence that the banks will pay on demand. The banks must not be calling in sound loans merely to maintain their solvency; on the contrary, they must be able to extend credit for worthy undertakings. Ordinarily, depression does not mean a demoralization of the money and credit structure; if it does, prompt action must be taken.

Price-raising policy—monetary devaluation. On the positive side, the Roosevelt Administration undertook to stop the deflation of prices and start the price level moving upward. This is one avenue along which recovery can be sought. When a boom has got out of hand, some downward price adjustments are salutary, but declines of great magnitude, instead of removing distortions, create them. This had happened in the early 1930s, notably in the case of farm products. Moreover, while low prices can be expected ordinarily to stimulate buying, the expectation of still lower prices causes buying to be deferred and stimulates selling instead. Thus a case can be made for government action when price deflation has gained momentum. Perhaps the bottom had been reached before the Roosevelt policies were instituted, but their merits are nevertheless worth considering.

One method was the separation of the dollar from gold, discussed in Chapter 12, and its later devaluation in relation to gold. While support for the policy rested in part on a crude commodity-theory basis, the popular expectation that prices would rise had the temporary effect of getting people to spend money, instead of holding on to it. Internationally the cheapening of the dollar made American exports more attractive, at least to the point of offsetting the effect of similar action abroad. But the main lesson of the period is that world prosperity requires the avoidance of this type of policy by common agreement.

NRA and related price controls. Permitting firms to bolster prices through the codes of the National Recovery Administration may also have helped to halt deflation, if the bottom was not already reached. Probably, also, the expectation that prices would be raised through the codes helped to cause the flurry of buying that came in the summer of 1933. But while it may sound impressive to speak of the orderly adjustment of production to demand through industry-wide agreement, the idea has little to recommend it from the recovery standpoint. On the contrary, the very means of control was the monopolistic method of discouraging production—a price-raising device quite different from the pressure of the expanding demand on which real recovery must depend.[2]

A somewhat different point should be made regarding industries that are exceptionally depressed, as *agriculture* and *coal mining* were. They lose their relative place in the economy, and the sharp decline in their purchasing power affects other industries that depend on them for

[2] The NRA will be considered further in Chapter 22.

markets. Possibly some improvement of their position by artificial price-raising methods will stimulate them to an extent that is broadly beneficial. This was the theory, in part, of the Agricultural Adjustment Act and of the special acts applicable to the coal industry. The main object of this legislation, however, was probably not recovery but relief, or at least a redistribution of income in favor of the people in these industries.

Wage-raising policy. The NRA codes also sought to raise wages. The theory was that purchasing power would be increased and total buying expanded. Here, as in all instances of trying to increase purchasing power, one must ask where the money was expected to come from. Probably its most likely source was the higher prices that firms might be able to charge under the codes; but if this were the case, the effect of higher wages would be nullified, and purchasing power would be no greater than before. Many no doubt expected that the higher wages would come out of business profits that would thus be diverted to labor. But while some firms had remained profitable during the depression, corporations in the aggregate were billions "in the red." This source, then, of higher wages was not promising.

Moreover, the first requirement, if recovery was to come, was the prospect of greater profits. The buying that is most conspicuously low in a depression is the capital-goods and inventory buying of business firms, and it depends on profit prospects. Wages are income to workers, but wage rates are costs to employers. The most direct and certain effect of higher wage rates is an increase in costs. Replacement and expansion are not encouraged, and further contraction may result. Thus, whatever the merit of wage advances when recovery is well established, the raising of wage rates is not likely to get it started.

One of the most striking, but least fortunate, statements by President Roosevelt was his description of the National Industrial Recovery Act, when he signed it, as probably "the most important and far-reaching legislation ever enacted by the American Congress." He characterized it as "a supreme effort to stabilize for all time the many factors which make for the prosperity of the nation and the preservation of American standards." There may be only verbal significance in the comment that, when a nation is in the depths of depression, what it wants is not stabilization of its economy but dynamic movement upward. But, in substance, there seems to have been little in the code idea that could bring revival. The plan was better calculated to maintain a prevailing status quo. Applied in depression, it did not offer the lift that recovery required, and, if it were applied in a prosperous period, it would not remove the main distortions and weaknesses that bring depression.

During the hectic days of its application, recovery made several starts and suffered several relapses. Whatever the reason, the more convincing improvement did not come until, in 1935, the NRA ceased to operate.

Government spending. Undoubtedly the most potent recovery policy of the 1930s was the spending of large sums by the federal government in relief payments and for various public projects. Such spending is potent because, if properly handled and financed, it provides direct and positive expansion of the demand for goods. Government spending was large during the 1930s, so large that the federal debt increased by $25 billion. It cannot be said, however, that this, or any other policy, actually brought prosperity, since unemployment continued. In some degree, the effect of federal spending was offset by a decline in the outlays of state and local governments, and other factors may have neutralized it. But the incompleteness of recovery is no reason for doubting that a nation can spend its way out of a depression, if it really sets about it. The war years that followed gave a convincing demonstration of the heights to which large public outlays can lift the economy.

Relief in relation to recovery

When a depression is severe and prolonged, a major social problem is the care of the unemployed. The savings of workers are usually soon exhausted, and assistance from family and friends, in most instances, is absent or inadequate. Private charitable organizations are helpful, but what they can do is not enough. Thus society as a whole must act through government, and, when government enters, it must accept the main burden. Its task is not only that of preventing physical hardship but of maintaining morale and self-respect and preventing the deterioration of skills.

Public arrangements to care for persons who cannot earn a living are centuries old. The function was once performed locally, but, with a broadening of the responsibility assumed, it has been shifted in part to larger units, the states and, in the 1930s, the federal government. Methods are various: cash grants; direct provision of housing or of food; work relief, in which the unemployed are used on public projects; social insurance, in which funds are collected, at least in part, from persons who may become the beneficiaries. Government may also encourage the dividing up of available work by reducing the hours worked by individuals, and it may increase the jobs involved in public projects by using hand labor in place of machines.

Relief methods constitute an important problem, but we shall not attempt an analysis of them, except for some discussion of social security at a later point.[3] The present aim is to examine the relation between relief and recovery and to stress the importance of not confusing them.

In some degree, the same policies may serve the ends of relief and recovery. When government spends money for relief, this expenditure, if financed in an appropriate way, also adds to the total demand for goods and raises the level of income. But while the two ends may be promoted simultaneously, it is essential to see that they are distinct ends, for otherwise policies that promote one and not the other will be misconstrued. It is one thing to take care of people on the assumption that there will be no immediate recovery, and something quite different actually to promote recovery.

The distinction can be seen most clearly, and yet is most seriously overlooked, in the case of *work spreading*. To reduce hours or efficiency, so that more persons can be occupied in turning out a given amount of product, provides income for some persons who, in a period of general work shortage, would be idle and without income. But it does not increase the total product and real income. Since the essence of recovery is an expansion in production and real income, it does not promote recovery. In reality, it merely redistributes the unemployment in such a way as to reduce the number who are wholly unemployed. This way of dealing with the situation may be preferable to other methods of relief and thus deserve support as long as no one supposes that prosperity is regained.

If spreading available work were able to bring recovery from depression, it would seem to follow that permanent work spreading would establish permanent prosperity—a very foolish idea. There are several grounds on which one may favor such legislation as the 40-hour week provision in the Fair Labor Standards Act of 1938—but one may hope that little of its support has rested on the belief that it could bring and maintain prosperity. Permanent reduction of working hours means, obviously, nothing more than the regularizing of a reduced use of labor on a continuing basis. It bears no relationship to the full and efficient use of resources on which prosperity depends.[4]

[3] Social-security measures will be discussed in Chapter 30.

[4] Perhaps someone will say that, if work is divided so that some incomes are lowered as work is given to others, there will be less saving and more spending from the same total income. This may be true, but it is unimportant among ordinary workingmen. Moreover, the effect does not come from the work spreading as such. It would be achieved as well if the employed were taxed, and the proceeds given to the unemployed.

It may be said also that when work is divided as through reducing working hours, wages are not reduced in proportion, so that total wage payments are greater, and more can be spent. But this is merely to say that the wage rate—the cost of labor—is higher, and the problem is the one we considered above. Either prices must rise or profits are reduced. If there is merit in reducing profits, the benefit is from that source and could be obtained

It is understandable that the term "full employment" should be used with some hesitancy by economists, not only because the word "full" implies too much but also because the word "employment" focuses attention on jobs rather than output. Jobs are tremendously important to workmen, but mainly as a source of income. Though income to the individual may come, as in a depression, through various makeshift arrangements, income basically is product and can be high only when production is high. High production should mean the production of the most goods—and the most valuable goods—that resources can yield. Thus make-work projects, whether through dividing work or doing things for the sake of the jobs provided, are not consistent with the income goal. So let us say that any arrangement that merely provides jobs is relief and that recovery is the expansion of output toward the goal of *full production,* with jobs the incidental but important by-product.

Policies to Prevent Cyclical Downturns

When depressions come, they should be escaped as quickly as possible, but it is more important to keep them from coming. The prime aim of economic policy should be to promote maximum stability at a high level of production while encouraging the progress through which income can be lifted to still higher levels.

It is sometimes said that the way to prevent depressions is to prevent booms. This is a sound view in the sense that a boom, as usually understood, is a frantic, unbalanced sort of prosperity and that a balanced prosperity should be the goal. But the idea seems sometimes to be that we should avoid the boom level of performance and be content with an aggregate output and income somewhere between the levels of boom and depression. This, surely, is a dreary conception of the economic goal. A vigorous, but balanced, prosperity with full production seems the only worthy aim.

A tendency toward imbalance seems unavoidable. There are cumulative factors in prosperity, as we have seen, that bring disturbing tensions if they are not controlled. If prosperity is the rebound from a recent depression, or if it is spurred by war or by some unusual industrial development or some exceptional activity in foreign markets, stability must mean the continuous overcoming of powerful unstabilizing forces. "Dynamic equilibrium" seems a contradictory phrase, but it describes fairly well the goal of policy. And as the sources of malad-

---

from raising wages without reducing hours. Working hours will be considered along with the control of wages in Chapter 27.

justment are varied, so must the means of control be designed to operate on a number of fronts.

Even if the country manages much better than it has in the past, measures to prevent maladjustments will not always succeed. Threats of recession will arise, and an adequate policy must be prepared to cope with crises and prevent a downward spiral from getting started.

Politically speaking, both lines of attack—both maintaining balance and meeting emergencies—are difficult. It is hard under a representative government to get plans made in advance and machinery set up which will operate promptly when needed. It is, perhaps, most difficult to take action to check incipient distortions before a crisis is really threatened. When conditions are good and most people feel prosperous, they resent restraints. Business and labor are both likely to push their gains dangerously and to oppose the controls that may help to preserve those gains.

The *Report* of the President's Committee in 1929 stated the problem in terms of balance. What is said in this section is in harmony with that viewpoint. This view may not be adequate. Certainly, in the opinion of persons who see depressions as the outgrowth of a chronic weakness arising from oversaving, it is far from adequate. But even in their conception of the problem, the need of balance and of policies to promote it should have an important place. What else may be needed, we shall leave to the next section.

Information, advice, and leadership

The view is well established that information can promote stability. In speculative lines, business people may find it profitable to ride with the boom though they know it will presently collapse. But many decisions prove most profitable when they are most in line with longer run market factors. It is important, therefore, to have access to adequate present facts regarding the economic scene and to the best possible forecasts. It is also important that leaders in business and labor set a conspicuous example of respect for such facts.

Investigations are carried on and information provided through various business services and publications, through trade associations, and through government agencies. The information covers such matters as rates of production and sales, movements of inventories and unfilled orders, technical developments and plant construction, prices and price trends, consumer expenditures, savings, and investments. The usefulness of such information does not lie in the willingness of firms, in acting on it, to work for the stability of the whole economy. Its usefulness lies mainly in the probability that firms, in seeking profits, will slow down their buying when inventories are shown to be running high and defer expanding their plants if labor and materials are likely to be more easily obtained later on. Thus informed action promotes balance. But, beyond such calculations, it is hoped that the heads of very large enterprises will act increasingly in recognition of the impact which their decisions may have on the whole economy. Their influence is substantial and their long-run interests are involved.

Hopes for stability by these means at one time ran high. The Committee on Recent Economic Changes said:

> Research and study, the orderly classification of knowledge, joined to increasing skill, well may make complete control of the economic system a possibility. The problems are many and difficult, but the degree of progress in recent years inspires us with high hopes. . . . Increasing skill and scientific data have made the anticipation of demand far more accurate, and by accurate anticipation the deliberate balance between production and consumption has in a measure been maintained.[5]

That was in 1929, and solutions then thought adequate are properly viewed with misgiving now. But the defect may have lain in their insufficient application. In any case, along with other means, they may still be helpful.

Perhaps knowledge may have more effect when it is given official focus and when it is the result of a vigorous official effort to watch closely the progress and prospects of the economy. This is the service, in part, that is expected of the Council of Economic Advisers established in 1946. But whether or not business and labor heed its warnings and advice, such information as it provides is essential to the more positive steps that government may take.[6]

Monetary policy

In modern economies buying is done with money, and money is made available either by government or by agencies which are subject to government control. The money supply, therefore, affords a natural handle with which government can take hold of the economy to control it. The normal aim of policy should be to make available the quantity of money required by the flow of products, in a way that will positively encourage a balanced expansion and positively discourage inflation and speculation. In addition, in time of crisis there should be provision for such a money supply that forced selling of products to pay debts is obviated.

[5] Pp. xx and xxi of the *Report* cited in note 1.

[6] On the basis of the work of the Council, the President makes an extensive report to Congress twice each year. See *The Economic Reports of the President,* Reynal and Hitchcock, 1948.

Present controls. The existing controls over the money supply in this country should be recalled. Demand deposits, the principal money in use, varies directly with the loans and investments of private banks. The Federal Reserve authorities may influence the volume of bank credit through various pressures on bank reserves: through raising and lowering reserve ratios within prescribed legal limits, through open-market purchase and sale of securities, and through fixing the rates at which banks may borrow additions to their reserves. They may also employ persuasion of a less mechanical sort. In addition, they may modify the margins required in security trading. They have at times had some emergency power over installment credit in consumer buying. Indirectly, control of reserves affects the availability of hand-to-hand money, especially in the form of Federal Reserve notes. The federal government also lends funds directly, commonly in circumstances in which the banks will not supply them.

Deficiencies in Federal Reserve power and its use. These controls are useful, but, as means of promoting stability, they are deficient in a number of respects. In the first place, even if Federal Reserve authority were exercised solely to maintain economic balance, the power over the money supply is inadequate. When commercial banks have large reserves even when the legal-reserve ratios are set at the maximum, they may expand credit to an extent that is inflationary and promotive of speculation with little positive restraint. Effective control requires that credit should be more continuously dependent on government authority than it has been in recent years.

There are critics, it will be recalled, who hold that public control of the money supply should not have to work indirectly through controlling private bankers in making loans and creating deposits. The point of this criticism is not that banking should be a public business, but that the plan of fractional reserves should be abolished, since this plan permits the money in circulation to vary in relation to the money that government provides. A 100-percent-reserve requirement would greatly extend the power of government. Whether it would also impair the usefulness of bank loans as a means of financing the purchase of an expanding output is but one of the questions this proposal raises.

But even within the scope of its present authority, the Federal Reserve System does not operate with an eye fixed on the promotion of general economic stability. In acting as financial agent of the federal government in disposing of bond issues or in guiding the international flow of funds, the Reserve System may follow policies that dilute its general stabilizing influence.

In the stabilization sphere, moreover, it faces inherent difficulties in determining just when and how to act. In retrospect the curves that represent economic movements tell a plain story, and it is obvious when certain pressure should have been applied. But when events are taking place, and numerous day-to-day variations are occurring, it is never clear when a particular movement marks the beginning of a substantial swing. Thus action is likely to be hesitant, and hesitancy is encouraged by the popular and political pressures we have noted.

Emergency banking action. Apart from the controls that aim to minimize boomtime distortions, there is the problem of providing funds to forestall a threatened recession when weakness has appeared in the economy. In this connection the primary concern of private banking with its own solvency is a major defect. While depositors, under the present system of deposit insurance, should be less inclined to withdraw cash than they formerly were at such times, the banks must still refuse to renew the loans of uncertain enterprises, and the effect of such action is deflationary. This is the approach of sound banking, even though, from the standpoint of the whole economy, exceptional risks may well be taken if there is a good chance of preventing or mitigating a downward spiral. Thus there is an important place for federal banking of an emergency nature in addition to the role of the Federal Reserve in supplementing the lending power of member banks.

Basic defect and true function of monetary approach. Present defects in the system of money supply and of controlling the supply in the interest of stability can probably be overcome. But the basic weakness of this method of control will remain. The level of economic activity depends directly on the total demand for goods, and the money supply bears only a loose relationship to total demand. At least within the period of the business cycle, the amount of money and the use of money must not be confused. The distinction seems obvious, and there would be no point in mentioning it but for a common tendency to assign a sort of mechanical potency to the money factor. Making money available, in the sense implied by monetary policy, does not mean "putting money in circulation." The latter means actual spending. Supplying money does not imply that the government uses the money to buy goods or thrusts it into people's pockets for them to use. To suggest, as careless writers have sometimes done, that because total spending is the product of the money supply and its average rate of circulation—MV and $M'V'$ in the equation of exchange—a decline in velocity can be offset by an increase in the amount of money, is to put the money factor in the wrong light. The velocity *is* the spending, and it depends on the whole complex of factors with which we are dealing in these chapters on depressions.

But while making money available does not constitute demand, the fact that money is not available can unnecessarily and dangerously depress demand. Similarly, failure to control its supply can encourage an inflationary upsurge of demand. Thus monetary controls have an important place among policies to promote stability.

Output, price, and income controls

We have seen that tensions develop during a boom through the disproportionate expansion of different industries. In particular, the output of durable goods, and especially of producers' goods, reaches a level inconsistent with continuing equilibrium. Strains arise through distorted movements of incomes among industries and occupations and between wages and profits. Presently some lines lag, opening the prospect of recession and promising further maladjustments if a decline sets in. Are government controls available that aim specifically at these tensions and distortions—controls of the rates of expansion in different fields and of prices, wages, and profits? Apparently something of this sort is contemplated by persons who commend the merits of a "planned economy" as the way to achieve stable prosperity. Wartime experiences are often cited, and high output credited to the wide application of government authority.

Broad effect on structure of economic system. It is evident that extensive control of production and prices cannot be reconciled with the processes of a free-enterprise system. The essence of such a system is that private producers decide what and how and how much they will produce and what they will charge, subject only to the guidance and restraint of the market. This is not to say that such controls should not be adopted, but it does mean that they are most clearly of the type which, in trying to strengthen the economy, would alter its character quite fundamentally. Perhaps advocates of a "planned economy" are not offended by this prospect, but general dislike of it is a reason why such controls are bound to be slow in coming.

At the same time, we should remember that there is already much interference with free markets, of both governmental and private origin. Indeed, it is an old principle that when concentrations of private power gain control of markets, government should step in. Government takes action against industrial monopolies, and there is like reason for interference when labor unions become powerful.

The problem of administering controls. These are broad matters of economic and political philosophy. What about the real usefulness of specific controls of production, prices, and incomes as means of keeping the economy on even keel? Here the defenders of economic freedom can make a strong case. If government were to concern itself with what should be done to maintain balance in each of a thousand industries, it would be taking on a very big job. It would still have a big job, perhaps a larger one, if control in the first place were delegated to industry associations, as under the NRA, since the aims of private combines are difficult to adjust to the requirements of the economy as a whole. Great knowledge and foresight would be required of the public officials involved; and it is doubtful whether they would make better decisions than do individual producers, subject to the restraint of the market, when their incomes hinge on the soundness of their decisions. The magnitude of the task suggests a more modest approach. Perhaps investigations, warnings, and advice are as far as government should go in such matters.

Wartime experience. With respect to price and output control, one should reach conclusions cautiously from wartime experience. It is true that extensive, though not complete, control prevailed during the war over output, product allocation, prices, and incomes, and also that the country was highly prosperous. But the output controls had the simple aim of diverting resources to war ends rather than the complex aim of balancing output in relation to millions of private demands. The other controls arose from special shortages and general inflation. There is little evidence, if any, that these controls contributed to the high wartime level of activity or that similar controls would do so in time of peace. In raising the level of activity, government spending was certainly the principal wartime influence.

Problem of price flexibility. A major issue, in approaching the depression problem, is whether price flexibility should be a leading policy goal. We are thinking now not of flexibility of the price level or of the value of money but of specific prices of different kinds of goods and productive services. As we saw in Chapter 4 and will consider more fully in Part V, the use of resources in a free economy is governed by the responsiveness of prices to changes in demand and in conditions of production, and by the responsiveness of buyers and producers to changes in prices. Many economists have blamed rigid prices and the obstacles to price flexibility for cyclical declines, on the theory that, if prices were quickly responsive, maladjustments in the economy would be corrected promptly and would not build up into major disturbances. The necessary flexibility, according to this view, involves not only commodity prices but also wage rates and particularly interest rates— in their role, pointed out in Chapter 14, of adjusting saving and investing to each other.

From this viewpoint, monopoly is a special culprit, since monopoly prices are usually rigid. The main corrective, among policies that have been followed, is the *antitrust laws,* since they are designed to prevent monopolistic control of markets. Price regulation, as in the public-utility field, has not been helpful, because regulated prices are usually more rigid than prices fixed by private monopolists. Labor unions also have dubious standing in this view of the problem, because they prevent downward adjustments in wage rates that may permit more labor to be employed.

Emphasis on flexible prices is in line with the economic philosophy we have referred to as orthodox. Against this approach, two considerations have received increasing emphasis. One is that the degree of price flexibility required for quick readjustments is no longer possible under the conditions of modern production and markets. Thus it would follow that the main attack on the cycle must follow other lines. The other more fundamental consideration is that the maladjustments which cause depressions mainly lie elsewhere—in factors stressed in the two preceding chapters—and that some of these factors may even be aggravated by flexible prices. Thus, if a general decline sets in and prices and wage rates start dropping, people defer buying until the bottom seems to have been reached. More rigid prices would then seem preferable. If the problem is viewed mainly in terms of investment opportunities and oversaving, price flexibility appears of minor importance.

We shall attempt no final judgment on this issue, but we shall examine it further in later connections.

Wage-profit relationship. Another matter that will also come up later is the bearing of wage and profit movements on prosperity and the policies that should be followed respecting them. We have observed that profit prospects need to be extremely bright to bring recovery from depression, but that, when prosperity is well established, the danger is more likely to come from excessive profits and an inadequate rise in wages. There are two sources of trouble.

One is that very high profits overstimulate investment. Ill-conceived and shaky ventures are undertaken, and plant expansion and building construction so greatly anticipate consumer demand that curtailment becomes necessary.

The other lies in the disproportion between saving and consumption that is likely when profits take a greater fraction than necessary of an expanding product. Even though there is no lack of investment outlets—in the mature-economy sense—some sort of long-run balance is necessary in the production of producers' and consumers' goods, and the division of income between profits and wages and between saving and current spending must be in harmony with that balance. If savings are great enough to finance a bunching of investments in boom periods, they are too great for long-run balance. Some redistribution of income, then, will aid stability, for most of the saving comes from relatively high incomes.

It seems desirable, therefore, when recovery is well under way, for wage income to increase at least as fast as the total product—or to rise more than prices do when total output is expanding. Such an adjustment is not characteristic of uncontrolled boom periods, but it probably should be sought. Without any far-reaching scheme of control, this result can be promoted substantially by the credit controls and anti-monopoly controls that bear on price advances and by the informal part played by government in the bargaining between workers and employers over wages. Taxation, also, as we shall see, is an important means of distribution control.

When markets for goods and for labor are not fully competitive, more restraint is needed on the part of business and labor leaders than they have generally shown, if extensions of government authority are to be avoided. We have stressed that profits may be too high for a balanced prosperity, but so also may wages. Labor leaders must abandon the idea that higher and higher wages, apparently without limit, are not only the right of labor but also the basis of greater general prosperity. Wages may be so high as to squeeze profits and repress enterprise, and they may induce a price-wage spiral that is seriously upsetting. It should be a commonplace of policy that concentrations of private power not exercised in harmony with the public interest should yield to public control or be dissolved.

Compensatory government finance

To forestall tensions and maladjustments is to lay the basis for a continuing high level of demand, but no more than that. Government can influence total demand most directly and positively by adjusting the volume of its own spending and by using taxation to control the spendable income of individuals and firms. Spending during the war showed how powerful this influence can be in raising the level of production. On the same principle, modifications in the amount of public spending and taxing, to compensate for opposite variations in private spending, may be employed to hold activity on a high and stable level.

In prosperous periods, when expansion tends to become inflationary, government would thus spend smaller sums for all purposes than it takes from individuals and businesses through taxation. This would be a restraining and stabilizing influence. According to the theory of compensatory spending, budgetary surpluses should normally develop in periods of vigorous activity.

But this policy would perform its more important service when production threatens to lag and recession is foreseen. Then either or both of two steps can be taken. One is to initiate promptly large outlays on public projects that have been planned for this purpose. The other is to reduce taxes that bear most directly on consumer spending. Both of these steps operate to offset a decline in total demand.

Review Questions

1. Review the main policies that have been adopted in the United States to deal with the depression problem. Relate them to the period of their adoption.

2. Contrast the leading attitudes and viewpoints that have influenced policy since the war. Are you impressed that the depression problem calls for vigorous public action?

3. Compare the Roosevelt recovery policies and evaluate them. Is raising wages a promising recovery method; restricting industrial competition?

4. Distinguish the recovery and relief problems. Show that public spending aims at both but that work spreading is merely a relief policy.

5. "The way to prevent depressions is to prevent booms." Interpret this statement in a way that is acceptable; that is unacceptable.

6. Explain what monetary controls, especially the control of bank credit, can do toward preventing depression; what such controls cannot do. Distinguish, in this connection, maintaining equilibrium and meeting emergencies.

7. "The main source of instability is that prices, incomes, and production can move freely and without central control. Have a general plan and apply it, and everything will move along smoothly." Is there evidence to support this view? Does it seem to be in line with the causes of depressions? Does stability necessarily mean prosperity? What general effect on the economy is implied?

8. What are the opposing views regarding flexible prices? What policies, if any, promote price flexibility?

9. On what ground can it be argued that wages should rise faster than prices in a boom period? What is the danger from wage-raising pressure?

10. In what sense is public spending a more positive method of maintaining prosperity than the methods already discussed? What are the features of a compensatory policy of governmental financing and spending?

Policies to Overcome Chronic Weaknesses in Demand

Policies that aim merely at balance and stabilization must fail, it is widely believed, because of underlying weaknesses in demand. There may be intermittent prosperity, but prosperity cannot last because people, when on a high level, will save more of their incomes than can be invested profitably. This is the oversaving, underconsumption, deficient-investment-opportunity viewpoint. What lines of policy, if any, can cope with such a condition?

Doubtless relatively few people knowingly hold this view of the health and vigor of capitalism in its most pessimistic form—some able students of the problem, some socialists and other radicals, some cranks. But many other people, seemingly unaware of the full implications of their views, take positions on policy questions that rest in part on the oversaving theory. Moreover, there are also many people who see the need of policies to strengthen the investment situation, or to expand consumption, who are confident that proper measures can provide the basis of continuing prosperity. To them the depression problem is, at least in part, a problem of underlying weakness in demand—but a problem that can be solved. What policies are in harmony with this general approach?

Policy ideas of the pessimists

Let us summarize first the main positions that may be taken by persons who see no possibility of a continuing level of private investment high enough to maintain reasonably full production. Three positions will be noted. They may be referred to as resignation, radical change, and perpetual public deficits.

The defeatist approach to policy. A nation may resign itself to a lower level of income than its productive power makes possible. It may assume that prosperity, at best, will be anemic and brief. Thus it may put its relief arrangements on a permanent basis and try to prolong its better periods by not meeting demand at too fast a rate. It may do this by reducing hours of labor, not for emergencies merely but for good times as well, and not because leisure is preferred to income but to spread work among more people over a longer period. It may accept tolerantly the restrictions of monopolists who say piously that they seek to keep output in suitable relationship to demand. It may look with indulgence on the output limitations of workers and labor unions that hold employees to a fraction of a reasonable performance and insist that unnecessary men be hired to do perfunctory tasks. Would we not quickly run out of work to be done if everyone did his best all the time?

This is not to say that workers in particular occupations are thinking about the aggregate demand for labor. When the musicians' union uses its power to control the recording and broadcasting industries and create useless jobs, its leaders are thinking only of the employment of musicians. But underlying the practices of particular groups is the assumption that total demand is inadequate and that there are few alternatives to the jobs now held.

The fact that workers restrict output, oppose improved methods, and promote work-spreading schemes does not elevate these ideas to the level of national policy. But if government adopts a permanent reduction of hours of labor to spread work, that is a national policy. Or if government encourages the development of unions without taking positive exception to restrictive practices, it is concurring tacitly in a calculated underuse of productive power.

The radical approach. The attitude just stated seems the least acceptable response to the pessimistic theory. More commendable is the view of those who say that, somehow or other, society should try to achieve the level of output of which it is capable. The most daring expression of this view is that of the radicals who despair of any solution under capitalism and would make enterprise a collective responsibility. Substitute state enterprise, they say, and investment will not be restricted by profit prospects. With no big private incomes from property, moreover, consumer demand will readily absorb the final output, however large. Without going into the objections to such a course or its other possible merits, we should recognize that this is probably the strongest of the arguments for radical change. Whether the chronic-slack theory is valid or not, state enterprise should be able to utilize fairly continuously the productive power it is able to develop.

Continuing government deficits. But if private enterprise is to continue and if it is true that, with capacity income, saving cannot be held to an amount that private investment will absorb, there seems to be only one way to have a capacity income. Government outlays must be kept high enough to offset the deficiencies in private spending. This will mean more than compensatory spending to fill cyclical dips. While public spending will not proceed at a uniform rate, it will be necessary most of the time. Budgetary surpluses in good years cannot be expected to offset the deficits of bad years. Mounting deficits from year to year will be the rule.

Such outlays may be made through expansion of ordinary government functions in relation to tax revenues, through extension of public-works projects, through subsidies to permit producers to sell below cost and thus expand their sales, or through cash payments to individuals in the form of some sort of "social dividend."

Policies to close the savings-investment gap

But if government is going to accumulate deficits for this purpose, it should keep them as small as possible. It should try, in other words, to reduce the gap that would exist between savings and investment with a capacity level of income. This would be accomplished either (1) by getting the public to spend more of its income for current consumption, thus reducing saving, or (2) by stimulating private investment so that more savings would be absorbed.

Either or both of these courses should be advised by persons who are resigned to mounting deficits. They mark also the lines of policy espoused by those other persons who, while recognizing a savings-investment problem, believe it can be solved at the source. To them, the depression problem is more than a problem of cyclical balance, but it is one that can be solved by creating conditions which favor both private consumption and private investment. As one would expect, quite different and not altogether harmonious groups take this general approach. Businessmen favor measures that encourage investment; their employees stress the need of increasing consumption.

Policies to close the savings-investment gap face one inherent difficulty. To encourage investment, profits must be attractive, but high profits mean greater saving. Wages, on the other hand, are more largely spent for consumption, but raising wages squeezes the profit margin. Wages and profits together, along with rent and interest, must be kept within the value of output. There is no hocus-pocus by which they can remain above it. Thus the solution must be such that, with high-level income, the amount spent for consumption is sufficient to absorb the product of a plant capacity that is expanding enough to absorb the amount of income not spent for consumption. This somewhat involved statement sums up the highly involved condition that must be met. It is the conviction of socialists—that is, of socialists with insight into the problem—that this condition cannot be met. The sensible course for other persons is to assume that there is a solution and to look for it.

A healthy climate for business. In their quest they will consider many matters. One of them is the general attitude toward business that should prevail in government policy. The view was common among businessmen that President Roosevelt and the New Deal were hostile to their interests. They were not convinced by Mr. Roosevelt's assertions that his real aim was to preserve capitalism. Whether the business reaction was justified or not, it probably reduced somewhat the willingness to risk capital. Whatever its sins, business may properly ask that government adopt a positively favorable attitude toward constructive profit seeking. For a society to depend mainly on private enterprise to hold production at a high level and yet to maintain a lukewarm attitude toward the requirements of private enterprise is obvious folly. Those who do not really wish to see private business flourish should have the good sense, the courage, and the honesty to espouse some alternative. Then their opinions will confuse no one. While we depend on capitalism, it should be kept as vigorous as possible.

This does not mean at all, in matters of policy, that businessmen should have whatever they want. On the contrary, they speak mainly as members of particular industries, and their aims are often not consistent with general prosperity. There are numerous abuses, moreover, under capitalism that call for correction. The depression problem, while probably the major problem of capitalism, is just one of several important problems. To protect consumers, workers, and investors, regulations may be necessary that run counter at times to ideal antidepression policy, and compromises among objectives become necessary. But policy should always be clearly designed, as a whole, to make effective the essentials of the system on which society depends.

Favorable taxation. Among specific policy areas, business groups place great stress on taxation.[7] Taxes provide money for government to use and reduce the funds available for private spending. While the sums diverted through taxation are large—perhaps fully one fifth of the gross national product in postwar years—why should this diversion affect the total amount spent? The answer lies in the diverse sources of funds and their diverse uses, if left in private hands. Note these cases:

1. Taxation may take dollars that would have been spent for consumption. These dollars may have been received either as wages or as profits, or in any other income form, but taxes that hit wage earners are most likely to cut into consumption spending. If they do, government spending is substituted for private spending, and, while there should be little effect on the total amount, there is some effect on the direction of buying.

2. Taxes may take dollars that would have been saved, but with no plan by the saver for their use in real capital formation. They are dollars for which private investment would have had to be found, if they were not to lie idle. They appear most often as part of large incomes, but incomes of persons who are not active enterprisers. If any tendency exists for investment to fall behind saving, taxation of such dollars has a salutary effect, because government will spend them.

3. Taxation may take dollars which are part of the return from risk-taking investment. Here we are concerned with the source of the dollars, not what the recipient would use them for. The significance of such taxes is that in some instances the prospect of them may deter the making of investments. Suppose personal income taxes, which apply

[7] The investigations and publications of the Committee for Economic Development have been outstanding.

to unincorporated business, would take half of the additional dollars of income above $20,000 and three fourths of the additional dollars above $60,000 (approximately the 1946 rates). With this prospect in case of success, and no offset in case of failure even if the whole principal sum were lost, this tax could easily be the crucial factor in causing a businessman to decide against making a contemplated investment of several hundred thousand dollars. In this case the tax causes a serious reduction at a critical point in total spending.

From this statement the principle should be clear, even though we do not go into detail regarding specific taxes. In Case 1 the taxes neither hurt nor help total spending; in Case 2 they help; and in Case 3 they hurt. In practice, however, there is great difficulty in aiming taxes at all accurately at the right targets. Income taxes, for instance, may hit any one of the three cases, though ways are available of improving the aim. Thus it is possible to exempt income from new investments from taxation for a period of years or to average profits and losses over a period as the basis for taxes. It will be apparent also, in our fuller discussion of taxation in Chapter 31, that other purposes must influence tax policy beside its effect on the level of the national income.

Readily available capital. Another area affecting investment involves the availability and the cost of capital. We saw in Chapter 14 that there is serious error in the older belief that the rate of interest provides a sufficient automatic adjustment of the amounts of saving and investment. Saving goes on, even though the interest return is little or nothing. On the other hand, there is probably some truth in the idea that the cost of capital affects the amount of investment. The point has often been exaggerated, but projects requiring expensive structures and equipment and projects in which the profit margin is small in relation to gross sales will be undertaken more readily when capital can be obtained at a *low interest rate*. More decisive may be the near impossibility at times of getting capital for new undertakings. Savings may be very large, but so-called "risk capital" may be difficult to get.

Thus it is important that the financial middlemen who stand between savers and the users of savings perform their function efficiently and at low cost. It is important also, in so far as it can be done, that savers be given the security they require while their funds, indirectly, are being made available for worthy but uncertain projects. If other means of solving the savings-investment problem are not adequate, ways should be considered of having government play a larger role in the investment-banking field, especially in getting funds at moderate cost to new enterprises. It may be said, in criticism, that this proposal in itself means a departure from private enterprise. But it is a departure that, conceivably, may add considerably to the total of private enterprise. At any rate, the problem of availability of capital to enterprisers is one that deserves public consideration in the making of plans to strengthen the total demand for goods.

Improved labor relations. Still another area that is important to enterprise is the field of labor relations. The rewards of going into business, and of expanding investment, are greatly reduced if dealings with employees and their unions are unpleasant and troublesome. Responsibility here is shared jointly by employers, labor leaders, and government. Modern capitalism developed in such a way that the interests of workers called for many protections, through legislation and otherwise. The process of educating employers to the need of these protections has been slow. Equally slow has been the education of labor leaders to a recognition that the real interest of workers lies in such a degree of cooperation with their employers as will promote efficiency and encourage enterprisers to expand employment opportunities. Government is in position to exert pressures in the direction of wholesome industrial relationships.

Encouragement of consumption. Favorable taxation, available capital, satisfactory employment relations—all are conditions that businessmen endorse. But important, also, in maintaining a high level of demand, are limitations on profits that tend to be excessive or that are obtained in the wrong way. The final product of expanding enterprises must be sold mainly to ultimate consumers. The power of markets to absorb final products is increased when prices are reduced and the incomes that are spent for consumption expanded. Accordingly, policy should recognize (1) the need of *wages* that are as high as can be paid, since wages are used more largely for consumption than are other incomes, and (2) the need of restrictions on *monopolistic control* of markets. If any tendency exists for saving to run ahead of investment, policy must be concerned with excessive savings as well as lagging investment.

The objection to monopoly is not only that it may yield profits that are unnecessarily high but that the means of getting these profits are at odds with the spirit of expanding enterprise. Monopoly is mainly concerned with sure profits from existing markets rather than with the vigorous pursuit of profit through expansion. Enterprise is at its best when it seeks its return through making its product available in great volume and at low cost, as the automobile industry is often cited as having done under the leadership of Henry Ford. It was through putting automobiles within the reach of ordinary individuals that the great opportunity for investment arose, directly within the industry and in highways and in other subordinate services. But monopoly, it should be said, is a complex matter, and we shall need to give it considerable attention later on.[8]

Through various other policies, which also will receive their main treatment at later points, some strengthening of the total-demand situation may be achieved. One of these is the social-security or social-insurance field. If regular sources of income are available to persons who are unemployed or who have retired or whose income is interrupted through accident or illness, it may be that there will be less saving of the "rainy-day" sort and a more confident and continuous purchase of goods.

Appropriate international policy. A nation's activity in foreign trade and foreign investment may affect the demand for its products in a variety of ways. Sharply divergent views prevail as to whether a more solid basis for full production is provided when trade barriers between nations are at a minimum or when barriers are so high as to cause considerable isolation.[9] International investment also presents a complex situation. When a nation's economy depends somewhat on large exports financed by loans—as this nation's economy has after both world wars—and this activity is clearly temporary, the resulting prosperity is precarious. But if investment opportunities are running low in developed countries such as the United States and are abundant in areas not yet exploited or industrialized, a free and continuing flow of capital between these areas should be mutually beneficial. The area of investment opportunity is then the world, not the single nation.

Can policies be reconciled? Let us suppose, then, that under modern capitalism there are basic difficulties in holding investment high enough so that, along with consumption, it will keep production close to capacity. The reasonable course is to adopt policies which, as far as possible, will promote investment and also consumption, limiting saving to an amount that will be invested. Government, accordingly, would act in matters of taxation, financing, labor relations, wages, monopoly, and other areas to promote this result. But since it will not be equally successful at all times, it should be ready also, in keeping with this policy, to expand public spending when needed. If the more optimistic view of the situation is correct, government should be able in good years to accumulate surpluses to cancel the deficits of the poorer years. But if depressions reflect a weakness too great to be overcome in this way, the deficits will not be offset but will accumulate. Whichever outcome is expected, there can be substantial agreement on policy.

[8] Especially in Chapter 22.
[9] These views will be developed in Chapter 32.

Reasonable dissent, however, would come from two sides: those so convinced that the fight is hopeless that they would replace capitalism with state enterprise and those so sure there is no underlying savings-investment problem that they would encourage maximum saving, so that new capital formation could proceed at the fastest possible rate.

Public Spending and Taxation

Government spending and taxation have been considered briefly at three points in this chapter as a means of controlling total demand: (1) in achieving recovery from depression, (2) as a compensatory device in curbing booms and preventing a break in prosperity, and (3) in providing a continuing offset to a chronic deficiency in total demand. In judging public deficit spending in these connections, one should recognize that it has been attacked as ineffective in achieving its purpose, as dangerous through the debts it creates, and as wasteful in diverting resources to inferior uses. These matters will be considered briefly.

Effectiveness in expanding production

The first question may be put in this way: Is a billion-dollar outlay on public works likely to cause a billion-dollar increase in total spending, or more, or less than that amount? A number of factors influence the result.

Source of funds. One factor is the source of the money that government spends. If the funds are raised through taxation, we have seen that the effect is quite likely to be only a substitution of public for private spending. On the other hand, taxes may take dollars that would have remained idle and cause them to be used. Similarly, if government borrows funds when unemployment prevails or is threatening, public use of them is not likely to displace any immediate private use. Especially if government bonds are sold to commercial banks, one can be quite certain that dollars are not being diverted from other uses.

Extent of effect. If the money spent by the government would not otherwise have been spent, how large is the effect on total buying? Going back to our theory of total demand, we may conclude that the effect of $1 billion of public expenditure should be an increase of several billions in the total. We may think of the dollars continuing to circulate until the savings from the expansion of income equal the outlay, thus retiring this sum from active use.

According to one view, commonly called the *pump-priming theory,* the impact would not only be very great but would probably continue indefinitely after the public spending stopped. This view rests on the supposition that the public outlay provides a push that overcomes an inertia in private industry and that private industry, when thus stimulated, carries on by itself. The theory has been widely questioned. If private activity has been interrupted by cyclical disturbances, public spending may fill the valley until private business recovers, but the real basis of recovery may be quite independent of the public spending. On the other hand, if depression comes because investment opportunities have petered out, an improvement caused by public spending must suffer a relapse when the spending stops.

Competition with private enterprise. The main ground on which the effectiveness of public spending has been questioned is that it is likely, in various ways, to interfere with private activity. One of these ways is through the competition of public undertakings with private. Public power plants compete with private plants; public navigation projects take business from the railroads and other transport agencies. From this standpoint, the best projects are those that cannot possibly compete. The late Lord Keynes noted the virtues of gold mining in this respect, since the product is bought in unlimited amounts at a fixed price and then perhaps buried again in places like Fort Knox. He also commended the Egyptians on their good sense in building pyramids. But schools and battleships and many other objects of public outlay serve almost equally well.

However, even if the objects of public outlay do not compete with private enterprise, there is likely to be competition for certain resources. It may seem that there should not be, since government is supposedly putting idle resources to work. This ideal result may be attained in projects of the leaf-raking sort that were widely ridiculed during the 1930s, but a highway or a building requires more diversified resources, some of which are likely to be bid away from private users or, at least, the price of them to private users will be made greater by the competition, and private enterprise will be dampened by the higher costs.

Effect on business confidence. A more general offset to the effectiveness of public spending is seen in the threat to business confidence arising from the fear of an expanding public debt. Any fear of the stability of government credit must weaken the impulse to invest. This is quite apart from the reasonableness of the fear.

The more damaging fear, however, in its effect on enterprise, is not the fear of public indebtedness but the fear of depression itself. If a sharp falling off in demand is expected within a year or two, investments appear rash that could otherwise be made with confidence. Fear of depression causes halfhearted enterprise, and halfhearted enterprise invites depression. If government were able to guarantee that total demand would remain on a high level, the spur to enterprise would be considerable. If this were the result, there might be little need of government action to back the guarantee. Probably public deficit spending is the only means of providing this assurance.

Danger of growing debt

Fear of deficit spending springs from the belief that a growing public debt must presently undermine government credit and bring financial collapse. Purely compensatory spending within the cycle may be tolerated, but an accumulating debt from an endless battle against chronic stagnation seems a hopeless prospect. How can borrowing continue if past loans are not retired? If the $25 billion of debt accumulated in the 1930s still left us with eight million unemployed and full recovery came only when the war debt reached several times that figure, what chance has the economy of surviving further doses of public indebtedness?

To the natural horror of businessmen at the rashness of "spending our way into prosperity," several replies have been offered. It is said that the capacity of federal credit is much greater than is commonly supposed. Those who thought the credit structure was tottering in 1940 should have revised their ideas when war financing was handled with relative ease. It is pointed out, also, that the people of the United States are, after all, both debtor and creditor and can easily manage a debt to themselves—no doubt a seriously overworked point. It is contended that the principal of the debt need not be paid, that a healthy credit condition requires only the payment of interest, and that interest rates should be extremely low if saving is in fact excessive—a much more telling point. These and other considerations could be evaluated only as part of a more extended analysis of public indebtedness.[10]

The most hopeful feature of a deliberate policy of using public spending as a last resort to maintain prosperity lies in the prospect that the necessary deficits will not be great. The depression of the 1930s was of exceptional severity. The increase in federal spending was partly offset by reductions in state and local spending, and other features of policy, it may be contended plausibly, discouraged private investment. With taxation on a much higher level to defray expanded postwar federal outlays, taxes may be designed to cut deeply into surplus private saving and reduce the dimensions of the problem. A debt that grows no faster than the nation's output would not become increasingly burdensome.

[10] They will receive some additional consideration in Chapter 31.

Waste in using resources

A third objection to deficit spending is that large public outlays to maintain prosperity divert resources from their normal uses so that society gets a greatly diminished satisfaction from its productive power. Schools, post offices, highways, power dams, waterways, reclamation projects, and so on are all very useful, as are the current services that governments perform. But if one fourth, say, of the national product is in these forms, does there not appear to be a serious loss of utility, as we compare them with other goods for which we would individually spend our money to raise our plane of living?

To this an obvious answer is that government expands its outlays along these lines only to bring idle resources into use. Perhaps these resources do not have as great utility as they would in a completely healthy economy, but they have greater utility than when they are idle.

But this is not a satisfactory answer if there are better alternatives. Thus something of a case can be made for cash subsidies of various kinds in place of public works. Subsidies to farmers under the Agricultural Adjustment Act or bonuses to soldiers permit the recipients to use the money for goods of their choice, and the expenditure causes otherwise idle resources to be used in producing these goods. This can be said also for various "social-dividend" schemes under which individuals—old people and perhaps others with low incomes—would receive regular contributions for which they would do no work.

Such schemes, however, are open to other serious objections, even if total demand does need supplementing. Payments other than compensation for services threaten the incentives on which production depends. Moreover, all schemes of regular, continuing income supplements misconceive the nature of the depression problem. Whether or not depressions arise through chronic weakness of demand, they consist in an intermittent, not a uniform, lapse in production. The economy is subject to ups and downs. The regular $200 a month that the Townsendites have advocated or the "$30 every Thursday" that was acclaimed in California would not fit the actual situation at all. If government is going to provide funds to supplement ordinary demand, it must adapt its aid flexibly and promptly to conditions as they arise.

It has also been argued that, if considerable public spending is necessary to vitalize private capitalism, it would be well to mark out for government some additional fields of activity where useful expenditures can be made. If, as an example, the railroads were publicly owned and operated, as they are in most other countries, a large field of productive investment would be made available. In this field government could go farther than private owners will in bunching investments in periods when private investment elsewhere is at the lowest ebb. But such a proposal, again, means some sacrifice of the domain of private enterprise in order to make private enterprise work.

Perhaps the best course, if public deficits are to be incurred, is to reduce taxes rather than artificially to increase spending through use of borrowed funds. If tax reductions are such as will most quickly stimulate spending, the same effect will be achieved without causing a dubious diversion of resources to questionable projects.

In any case, a reasonable conclusion would seem to be that public deficits, however distasteful, are not so dangerous as severe depressions. So serious a threat to established institutions would arise from a repetition of the 1930s that conservative people, those most devoted to established institutions, should be most resolute in finding means of preserving a reasonably high level of prosperity. Since government financing and spending are necessarily a large factor in the total flow of funds in markets, it seems clear that they should be used as fully as possible to offset the fluctuations in private industry. Such a program requires careful and determined planning, and, however effective it may be, it should not supplant the insistent application of other policies to keep distortions from arising.

Review Questions

1. "The one wholly unacceptable approach to the depression problem is the defeatist idea of deliberately restricting output, in good times and bad, so that all output will be consumed." Do you agree? What evidence is there of this defeatist approach?

2. Distinguish two other lines of policy that may be advocated by persons who see the depression problem as a problem of chronic stagnation.

3. "The person who believes that the American economy faces a continuing problem of maintaining investment in relation to savings, but who believes the problem can be solved, may stress either of two lines of policy. Employers stress one; employees the other." Explain.

4. "I'm not a socialist. I believe in private enterprise, but—." This statement can be completed in a variety of ways. What menace does it contain from the standpoint of a healthy economy? Does encouragement of vigorous enterprise under capitalism imply unqualified approval of business attitudes? Explain.

5. Show that taxes, depending on their nature, may increase total spending, both private and public, reduce it, or have no effect.

6. How may the financing of new investments be facilitated?

7. If you were considering going into business, or expanding a business you are in, do you think that prevailing labor relations would influence your decision?

8. What lines of policy approach the saving-investment problem from the side of encouraging consumption? Explain their probable effect.

9. "The monopolistic road to profit is not likely to lead to maximum investment." Why?

10. "If international economic relations are satisfactory, a nation need not worry about the exhaustion of investment opportunity within its borders as long as the world as a whole needs capital." Does this seem to be an important consideration?

11. The effectiveness of public deficit spending depends (a) on the source of funds, (b) on what they are spent for. Develop each point.

12. "Perhaps every dollar the government spends may add as much as $3 to total output. But this is not to say that the pump-priming theory is operating." Develop both points.

13. "Businessmen may fear a large public debt, but this fear is probably not as damaging to investment as fear of depression itself." How do these fears operate? Do you think the statement is sound?

14. What factors should be taken into account in evaluating the danger of a large public debt?

15. On one occasion the London *Economist* said: "Clearly, if it is unsafe to let Tories out of gaol in a slump, the Labour Party ought to be locked up in times of inflation." What is the point regarding each party?

16. Develop the point that deficit spending, in seeking to expand total production, diverts production into inferior channels. What ways of managing a public deficit seem most likely to avoid this difficulty?

PART V

Prices and
Economic Organization

THUS far this volume has dealt mainly with certain economic aggregates and the factors controlling them: with total production and real income, which determine aggregate (and average) well-being; with the developments that have expanded total productive power; with the movements of prices as a whole, or the value of money; with the factors in total demand that cause business fluctuations and depressions.

We shall turn now from these aggregate aspects of well-being to the make-up of the aggregates: to the demands for particular goods and the supplying of them, to their prices and their costs, to the organization of economic life on the basis of markets.

This segment of economics—long regarded by economists as almost the whole of the subject—was introduced in Chapter 4. It involves the essentials of economizing, the making of effective choices in utilizing productive resources and products, both for the individual and for society as a whole. From the social standpoint, the main task of economic organization is to control the placement of millions of workers and many kinds of productive wealth, variously located, so that they perform efficiently and so that the resulting product conforms as well as possible to the myriad desires of the even greater number of people who make up the consuming public. The organizing processes, moreover, must somehow put the products in the hands of the people who will use them, determining how much and what particular products each will get and setting the rate at which scarce goods can be used.

How a society handles this complex of related functions largely determines the kind of society that it is. To understand the nature of a free economy and reach any opinion about it, one must ponder especially the area of organization that will be considered here.

~ 17 ~

The Role of Prices

INDIVIDUALLY we are all enmeshed in a network of value, or price, comparisons and of behavior decisions based on prices. As consumers, we take account of our wants and of the prices of the things available to satisfy them and accordingly try to make the best use of our money incomes. As businessmen, we consider the prices of products and the quantities we think buyers will take at those prices, the prices of labor and supplies and the technology at our command, and make up our minds what is worth our while to do. As workers, we consult our preferences among occupations and the prices we can get for the kinds of service we are able to perform, and thus decide on the work we shall do. As owners of material resources, we make similar decisions.

The tyranny of prices is apparent to all of us. We must adjust our lives to them and suffer the fate they impose on us. But we also influence prices. A single one of a million customers for a product contributes a little toward strengthening or weakening its market price as he decides to buy or not to buy. Collectively as consumers we exert a powerful influence. The businessman, especially if he is a big businessman, is somewhat more aware of his influence, but even the single wheat grower has some effect on prices.

But whether or not we are aware of our influences on prices, we are not likely to think of ourselves as part of the system by which the economy is organized and controlled. Yet, in the absence of central planning and authoritative direction of the production and use of goods, it is through our responses to prices and our influence upon them that the economy is organized. We study values and prices, therefore, as the great regulator through which consumers and producers (1) receive directions and are led into certain lines of behavior and (2) register their preferences and exert their influence on the course of economic events.

Thus, though in Part V we are not concerned with aggregate production, we are still concerned with the economy in an over-all sense. It is only for this reason that prices and markets receive the attention that they do in economics. The big question in the study of markets is not: How are prices determined in the short run, the long run, under this, that, and the other set of conditions?[1] Nor is it adequate to consider the question: How do consumers and producers act, in relation to prices, in various market situations? These questions suggest much that should be looked into but mainly as part of the larger question: How does the whole economy, through markets and prices, undertake to use its resources to best advantage? To this should be added: At what points does it deviate from success in this undertaking?

In organizing economic life, prices are involved, as Chapter 4 explained, (1) on the *production side*, (*a*) in directing producers to produce particular goods, in particular relative quantities, and thus in dividing resources broadly among industries, and (*b*) in assigning particular units of labor and other resources to tasks for which, in view of prevailing technology, they are fitted; (2) on the *distribution and utilization side*, (*a*) in determining the size of the share in total product that each person can have, (*b*) in the selection of the particular goods that will make up each person's real income, and (*c*) in adjusting the rate of use of particular goods to the amounts available. It is important to see how closely related these matters are.

Value and price concepts

It was also explained in Chapter 4 why the organization of the use of resources must rest on values. The services of countless workers and material resources cannot be adapted to the varied desires of consumers except through calculations which consider the *importance* of each item for each purpose. Value, we saw, is merely the importance of particular products and productive services—an importance that reflects (1) the qualities they possess, their utility or serviceability, and (2) the quantities of them available. All decisions regarding the use of products and factors of production must rest on these two characteristics. This is the same as saying that all decisions must rest on their values. Value in its most fundamental sense—often called *economic value*—is simply *unit importance*.

Values must have this role under any economic system but need not

[1] One of the most serious defects in the traditional teaching of economics, it seems, is the presentation of "value and price" as if the job were merely, or mainly, to explain how prices are determined, or tend to be. It is as if it were said: Prices are the core of economic organization; therefore the fixing of prices is the main thing to be explained. The conclusion does not follow. What matters is the scheme of organization of which prices are a part.

operate in the same way. In an authoritative economy, the economic management may be less concerned with the utility of different goods, as the people judge utility, and more concerned with what they, the management, think the people ought to have or with what is good for the state. But their judgments of the importance of goods, and of the relative amounts of them to be provided, are still value judgments; the array of products they decide on cannot be provided effectively unless resources are used in accordance with their productivity and their scarcity—in other words, their value. It is said that the Russians in recent years have come to recognize the need of a better theory of value than they have had to guide them in the control of their economy.[2] In a planned economy, value concepts are working tools of economic management.

But in a free, or partly free, economy, values are not merely the basis of economic bookkeeping and planning; they are objective and conspicuous market facts. As the reflection of market forces and the guide to market behavior, they are spoken of as *exchange values*. The exchange value of a product or productive service is the power that it has in the market to command other goods in exchange for itself. This power arises, of course, from its utility or serviceability and its scarcity. The *price* of a good is simply its exchange value expressed in money terms.[3]

Apart from values which are market facts, there are countless *subjective valuations* by buyers and sellers which underlie the setting of prices or arise in response to them. Seeing that the price of a good is $2, the customer says, "It is not worth that to me; I'd give no more than $1 for it;" and he does not buy it. Or he says, "I'm surprised it can be had for $2; I'd gladly pay $3 if I had to." Such valuations have a major role but are not themselves exchange values or prices.

Value is also used in other senses. A shopkeeper putting on a sale says of a good: "Value $4; priced at $2.98." He implies that its value is what it is really worth—what its price ought to be. Price and value thus are different. But he would be glad enough to get the $4 if he could, and the meaning he gives to value seems no more than a sales device. We shall not distinguish value and price in this way.

There are, however, many occasions in economics for comparing *market prices* with something more fundamental. Often we shall speak

---

[2] This was the report of Dr. Oskar Lange, University of Chicago economist and later Polish ambassador and United Nations representative, on returning from a postwar trip to Moscow.

[3] The word "price," however, implies an actual or possible transaction and is not applied to all monetary expressions of value. One speaks of the *price* of wheat per bushel but of the *value* of the wheat crop.

of *normal prices*. The immediate price charged for a good is likely to depend in part on temporary and superficial factors, so that it is not the price that can be expected to prevail over a longer period. The price that *tends to prevail* in view of the more fundamental factors is the normal price, and it may be more significant than the price actually charged. It is necessary also to have a standard of judgment by which it can be said that a market price is not what it should be. Thus when we say that a monopoly price is usually excessive, the *price that would prevail under competition* is the standard. These comparisons are not between prices and values but between market prices and normal or competitive prices (or values).

The price system as a whole

In succeeding chapters a number of market situations will be examined, and certain principles developed and applied. It will be important to see them in a setting that consists of the price system, or market system, as a whole. An appreciation of the interdependence of prices is necessary to an understanding of policy questions.

The relationships that make up the price system are numerous and complex, but we can simplify them schematically. Individuals perform two roles in economic organization: they are buyers and consumers of products and suppliers of labor and material resources. Business enterprises, which extend from the small store or farm to the great manufacturing or public-utility corporation, are the initiators and organizers of particular productive operations and stand in a sense between these two roles of individuals. On the one hand, they buy labor services and other factors of production; on the other, they sell products to consumers. Thus there are *two sets of markets*: markets for products and markets for productive services. All of these elements are brought together and related in the diagram on the next page.

The elements in this picture are all interdependent and must fit together harmoniously if economy is to be achieved in the fullest sense and resources used to best advantage. No person, under a free system, is compelled to buy or sell in any market if he does not want to; so prices must be related with sufficient nicety to fit the voluntary action of consumers and producers into a coherent system.

To see this fully, let us look first at *product markets*. Numerous products are entering them—hundreds of thousands of products, it is said, when all types and grades are counted. On one side of this market, consumers are buying—or declining to buy—each of these goods, acting in light of their personal preferences and their pocketbooks. Economy requires that all of these goods should be so priced, in relation to each

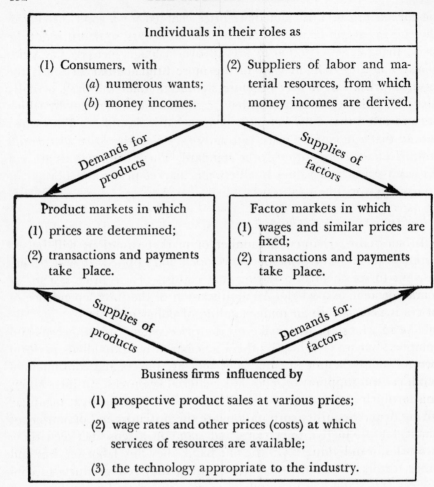

Individuals in their roles as	

(1) Consumers, with
    (*a*) numerous wants;
    (*b*) money incomes.
	(2) Suppliers of labor and material resources, from which money incomes are derived.

Demands for products

Supplies of factors

Product markets in which (1) prices are determined; (2) transactions and payments take place.	Factor markets in which (1) wages and similar prices are fixed; (2) transactions and payments take place.

Supplies of products

Demands for factors

Business firms influenced by

(1) prospective product sales at various prices;

(2) wage rates and other prices (costs) at which services of resources are available;

(3) the technology appropriate to the industry.

other, that all the units of all of them will be bought and used. But it requires also that consumers shall so register their preferences, through buying or not buying, that firms will be led to turn out the most desirable collection of goods that can be obtained from the resources they are using.

Business firms are on the other side of *product markets*. They are confronted with two sets of prices: of products and of factors. The prices of products govern their revenues, the prices of factors, their costs. If products are to be produced in any particular proportion, the prices of all of them, in relation to their respective costs, must be such as to make this the profitable way for firms to use resources.

When we turn to *factor markets* and the dealings in labor and other productive services, we find business firms buying—or refusing to buy —in light of the prices they get for their products, the prices they pay for different factors, and the technology by which factors are combined in all lines of production. There are thus many interrelationships in the demand for factors. On the other side of the factor markets are the workers of all kinds, the owners of agricultural, mineral, and forest land, and the suppliers of capital. All these suppliers, in making resources available for different uses, are influenced by the prices they can get and, perhaps, by other occupational preferences. Relative prices should be such as will encourage the use of all resources and make it unlikely that more desired products will be sacrificed for those that are less desired.

Finally, it will be noted, the returns from the factors (the wages and property incomes) provide the purchasing power of consumers, the money with which they buy final products. The relative amounts they will buy of different products will depend, in part, on the relative incomes of people with different preferences for goods.

Thus the price system underlying the production and use of goods is a far-reaching complex of interdependences. Change the relative prices of two products and the relative purchase of them will be altered with effects on the relative use of different resources in producing them, the relative incomes of different people, and finally the purchase by these people of different products, perhaps including the two we started with. A change anywhere is likely to cause a chain of reactions extending farther than anyone can see. *Equilibrium* is said to prevail when all products and all factors are so priced that there is no tendency for changes to occur.

Price interrelationships. It is not expected that these various relationships will be understood fully at this stage of study. But one should see the main outlines of a somewhat impressionistic picture and get a sense of intricate interconnections and over-all unity. Perhaps one should note most especially the connections between:

1. The price of any product and the prices of the labor, materials, and other elements that go into it. It follows that there must be a compelling connection between the prices of all the different goods produced from the same resources.

2. The markets and prices of any products that can be substituted for each other. Substitutability may be direct, as between butter and oleomargarine, or indirect, as when a family buys new furniture because of the increased cost of taking the usual winter trip to Florida. In a broad sense, all goods are competing for the consumer's dollar.

3. The markets and prices of different productive resources or different intermediate materials and supplies. At many points coal and oil are alternative sources of power. Lumber and brick are mutual substi-

tutes in building construction. Labor and machinery may be combined in many ways in manufacturing.

There are many more relationships of this sort. Certain goods are jointly supplied: for instance, cotton fiber and cotton seed, meat and leather. Other goods are demanded jointly: lumber and plumbing supplies for houses, steel sheets and rubber tires and plate glass for automobiles. The sale of one product may depend on the sale of some quite different product, as when a rising price of wheat brings increased patronage of mail-order houses.

This sketch of the price system suggests the difficulties of *governmental price control*. Even a limited control, as in the public-utility field, has its complications, but a general control, as when the Office of Price Administration established comprehensive price ceilings during the war, is bound to have innumerable unintended effects on the production and use of particular goods. The corn-hog ratio became notorious, because of the difficulty of adjusting prices so as to cause enough corn to be used in pork production, and not too much. Similar difficulties arose in the prices of milk, cream, and butter, various grades of clothing, and in many other connections. Wartime price control, which was necessary in the circumstances, afforded a dramatic popular demonstration of the complexities of the price system noted here.

Some neglected complexities

The purpose of this chapter is mainly to give a useful perspective of market relationships. The more limited situations discussed in succeeding chapters should be seen in relation to the whole system of markets and not as presenting isolated problems. Most of what will be done in Part V can be fitted into the preceding diagram, with its product and factor markets. But it should be borne in mind that the diagram is a simplifying device and that much is omitted from it. An adequate perspective of markets calls for some recognition also of what the diagram omits and for a sense of complexities that only a very lengthy analysis could cover. The chapters that follow will fall far short of a complete discussion of the subject of markets, and an appreciation of diversities not covered will provide a sort of continuing qualification of conclusions that may sometimes be a little too neat and simple.

An obvious qualification is that *business firms are not all at one level,* all taking labor and natural resources and turning them into final consumers' goods. Instead they operate at a number of stages. One firm cuts timber, another makes lumber, another manufactures furniture, another acts as middleman in getting furniture to the user. Along the line are transport agencies and other incidental services. The price system must include suitable margins at all levels to maintain the flow of products.

It also appears from the diagram that the people who get income from labor and material resources use it entirely to buy consumers' goods. But some of it, we know, is *saved* and enters the market for *capital goods*, along with the funds reserved by business firms for replacement and expansion. The capital markets are important not only in the organization and direction of production but in determining the total amount of it, as we saw in Part IV.

Price structures and patterns. For the sake of realism, it is perhaps most important to stress that markets are institutionalized and that goods move through channels and are exchanged at prices that often appear somewhat artificial and arbitrary. Accordingly, it may not be easy to say just what the price of a good is, because it may have a number of prices depending on who buys it, how much he buys, and where he is located. Products become involved in price patterns or structures or "families of prices."

The instance has been cited of a company that sold a particular flashlight cell at 6.5 cents to ordinary retailers, 5.5 cents to department stores, 5.0 or 5.5 cents to industrial users, depending on quantity, 4.5 cents to makers of battery-using devices, from 2.5 to 3.8 cents to toy manufacturers, depending on quantity, and at half price to chain stores if they would sell it under their own label.[4] Such price structures are fairly common in the case of manufactured goods.

Pricing seems also to be somewhat artificial when examined geographically, particularly under zone and basing-point systems. When a manufacturer quotes prices at the factory and lets the buyer pay the transport cost to his location, the arrangement has a natural appearance; when the manufacturer quotes delivered prices which vary with the location of the buyer, but the transportation included is often not the actual transportation from the point of manufacture, the institutionalized type of structure appears. Classic instances of this sort of pricing have arisen in the steel and cement industries.

Price structures appear much more complicated when it is recognized that the product of a firm is commonly not a single, uniform product but a collection of styles, qualities, and sizes among which price relations must be maintained. When prices are viewed on an industry basis, and the somewhat different products of different firms taken into account, an even more involved price pattern appears. Even

[4] Willard L. Thorp and others, *Economic Problems in a Changing World,* Farrar and Rinehart, 1939, p. 196. The price chapters by Theodore J. Kreps are a valuable supplement to the more conventional type of treatment. See also Walton Hamilton and Associates, *Price and Price Policies,* McGraw-Hill, 1938.

for natural products, such as wheat and wool, prices are deprived of easy uniformity by differences in types and qualities.

Probably the most complex price pattern is that governing the sale of railroad-freight service. This service is not a single, homogeneous thing; rates must be quoted for many thousands of commodities and, for each commodity, for thousands of hauls between different pairs of geographic points. Thus the number of railroad rates is truly astronomical, and no one can ever hope to learn all that there is to know about them.

Custom and inertia. The very complexity of these price structures gives rise to price-making influences that we shall largely neglect in the ensuing analysis. Some of these relationships can be traced to elements of monopoly; these we shall consider. But once established, they resist adjustment simply because of the trouble that changes cause. Both sellers and buyers get used to certain relationships, and price patterns continue beyond the life of the forces that brought them into being. We shall stress the main forces that cause adjustments and say little about the factors of inertia and custom that restrain their operation.

Product and industry differences. Insufficient attention will also be given to differences in markets and prices arising from dissimilarities in products and their disposal. There are points of difference, for instance, between farming and manufacturing which are major market factors. To the manufacturer, purchased labor and materials are the main cost items; farm families supply much of the labor used in agriculture, and materials and supplies are a minor item. Farm products may be supplied by hundreds of thousands of producers and manufactured products by only a few firms. Basic farm products are put on a general market for what they will bring; manufacturers supply only the specific customers who patronize them. Farm products are priced in central markets—wheat in Chicago and tobacco at the auction points —and the farmer gets this price less transportation, whereas the manufacturer commonly quotes a factory price and freight is added.

Within these broad areas of production there are important dissimilarities. There is large-scale, as well as small-scale, farming. Some farm products are perishable; some can be stored for long periods; some are sold in local markets, and some in world-wide markets. Most of them, until the government intervened, were sold in free markets, but some, such as citrus fruits and milk, have been controlled by combinations. Some manufacturing industries, such as steel, automobiles, and aluminum, have only a few firms; others, such as clothing and furniture, have many firms. Some products are standardized, such as steel rails and cement, and others differ from firm to firm. Some firms produce for the final consumer and some provide materials and equipment for industry, and thus encounter a different type of purchaser.

Such dissimilarities may be found also in merchandising and other fields as well as in farming and manufacturing. At some points in the later discussion they will play an important part, but there will not be a systematic treatment of them. One should be prepared, therefore, to make adjustments in fitting general conclusions to specific situations.

The ensuing analysis

Part V, from here on, will concentrate on certain key points in the organization of an economy on the basis of markets and prices. These are points at which principles can be said to operate—principles that throw light on the general logic of such an economy. We want to see how buyers and sellers and producers are likely to act under various circumstances and whether the actions of individuals appear to be in harmony with the interests of the whole public. Some generalizations, in other words, will aim to tell how markets operate, and others will provide standards for passing some sort of judgment on how they operate—whether they promote economy, in the broadest sense, in the use of resources and products.

No one should speak up as a defender of the free type of economy unless he understands fairly well these aspects of its operation; nor should he criticize it either, unless he does. Certainly he should not advocate broad economic planning and control unless he understands the task that planners face.

The order of topics that will be followed can be related to the diagram of a price system presented on page 452. In the next chapter attention will center on the market for commodities in the most immediate sense. The interaction of supply and demand will be examined without going far into the nature of either of them. Chapter 19 will look into the demand side of product markets and consider the role of prices as expressions of buyer preferences and as influences on consumer behavior. Chapters 20 and 21 will deal with the producer's side, considering long-run forces that govern the allocation of resources among industries and the shorter run activities of producers in using existing plants.

In these chapters monopoly will have entered at several points, and Chapter 22 will deal more fully with monopoly practices and their significance. Likewise, government policies in aiding consumers and some producers will receive comment as we proceed, and, finally, in Chapter 23, three major United States market policies will be discussed: the antitrust policy, public-utility regulation, and agricultural-adjustment policy. Most of the emphasis will be on products, but the market for productive services will be considered sufficiently to show its role in the whole organization of production. The main discussion of it, however, will be left to Part VI. The prices of productive services are the incomes of workers and owners of wealth, and the controversial subject of income distribution deserves more extended treatment on its own account.

Review Questions

1. A leading economist has written: "There is no more important function of a first course in economics than to make the student see that the whole problem of social management is a value problem." [5] Develop this statement carefully, bringing out the main elements in the problem of social management to which it refers. In your judgment, are there other equally important problems in the economic management of society?

2. Distinguish the main aspects of economic organization that, in a free economy, depend on markets and prices.

3. "Value, in its most fundamental sense, combines in a single quality the characteristics of products and resources on which their effective use depends." Explain.

4. "Values are the basis of any economic system, free or managed, but the values may be arrived at in different ways and reflect different judgments." Explain.

5. When a merchant posts a placard over some merchandise, "Any item $1.49—Values up to $3," is the meaning he attaches to the word "value" that of exchange value, economic value, subjective value, or some other? Distinguish these meanings of value. To which one of them is price most closely related?

6. What sort of comparison is implied when we say that a price is abnormal? That it is excessive?

7. "An economy organized on the basis of markets depends on reasonably coherent relationships among many prices." What are the main relationships that are involved in a coherent system of prices?

8. Suppose that a synthetic textile is developed that is equivalent to wool in all respects. What lines of reaction would you look for, running through various markets?

9. What is a price pattern or structure? How does the presence of price structures complicate the quotation of prices? The explanation of prices?

10. What broad differences are there between farm products and manufactured goods that affect their markets and prices?

[5] Frank H. Knight, *Ethics of Competition*, Harpers, 1935.

11. "It may be that the survival of the free-enterprise system depends mainly on its ability to solve the depression problem. But what it means to the people who are part of it—how it differs from other possible systems—can be understood only through studying its organization on the basis of markets." What does the second sentence mean? Does it seem to be a reasonable statement?

~ 18 ~

Supply, Demand, and Market Price

THE law of supply and demand" is a phrase of the market place as well as of the classroom. No other phrase has been called on so often, or in so many situations, to throw light on economic events. Sometimes it serves only to give the appearance of an explanation without actually providing one. Sometimes, indeed, it is invoked to give respectability to actions that have no place in free markets. A phrase so important, so loosely used, should be examined with care, and its meaning explored. It may lose some of its magic in the process, but the principle of supply and demand will retain a central place in explaining the relations of the producers and users—the sellers and buyers—of goods.

In this chapter we shall deal with the fixing of prices and the effects of prices only in the most immediate market sense. We shall be concerned with the surface behavior of buyers and sellers in the short run, leaving to succeeding chapters some examination of the deeper nature of demand and the conditions governing the supplying of goods. In this chapter two principles of importance will emerge, one called the *principle of single price* and the other, the *principle of supply and demand*. During the discussion we shall consider the meaning of such concepts as *markets, competition,* and *bargaining* as well as *supply* and *demand*.

Markets and Price Uniformity

Behind every transaction is the fact that one person who has a particular good values it less highly than another person who does not have but wants it. This condition makes exchange of the good advantageous to both parties. A highly specialized economy operates through innumerable exchanges, each based on this condition.

The countless people who participate in exchanges fall into two categories: those who buy and those who sell—that is, those who account for the demand for goods and those who account for the supply of goods. Since the factors that affect exchanges are numerous and complex, it is worth remembering that all of them can be grouped into just two categories corresponding to these two sides of the market. Market factors are elements either in demand or in supply.

Transactions take place on the basis of prices. The *primary function of prices* is to define the basis of exchange in a way to reconcile the interests of the parties and confer some benefit on both of them, so that trade can go forward and serve its purpose. This is an obvious but highly important function. It is the only social function of prices with which this chapter is concerned. The more fundamental ones, such as controlling the utilization of resources, will be discussed later.

Prices are determined in markets, and this section will examine the nature of markets and what it means to say, in the full sense, that the price of a good is fixed by the market.

Markets

One is likely to think of a market as a place where buyers and sellers exchange goods, and this is a sufficiently accurate idea if one does not give the word "place" too narrow and specific a geographic meaning. Sometimes a market is a definable spot—the city market, for instance, to which farmers bring their vegetables or the Chicago Board of Trade, where speculators deal in wheat. But usually the relationships between the buyers and sellers of a good extend over a wide area, and it is this whole area of interrelationship that it is significant. Strictly speaking, the dealings in vegetables in the city market are connected in price and other respects with dealings in vegetables shipped from remote points; certainly the Board of Trade is simply the focus of the attitudes of many buyers and sellers throughout the country, even the world. The market area is limited only by the feasible communication and transportation in dealing in the particular commodity. But it is not the physical area that is really important in determining the character of a market; it is the procedures and arrangements through which buyers and sellers are brought together and the relationships among sellers and among buyers.

Concept of an ideal market. When the role of markets in economic organization was introduced in Chapter 4, it was pointed out that markets must have certain characteristics if they are to be effective in controlling a specialized economy. On the basis of these characteristics it is customary in economics to use a conception, or model, of an idealized market in analyzing actual markets. Such an ideal market is one in which the price-making forces reflect supply-and-demand conditions very completely and override the stratagems and strength of particular sellers and buyers. It is a market (1) in which there are many transactions in a standardized commodity (or a commodity of which the units are sufficiently alike to be regarded as interchangeable), (2) in which there are many buyers and sellers of the commodity, with competition among the members of each group, and (3) in which the buyers and the sellers are well informed and active in pursuing their interests.

We shall use this model market in various ways as we proceed, sometimes stressing one aspect of it, sometimes another. Its immediate use is to assist us in bringing out the meaning of a market price, especially the uniformity of such a price for different transactions in the same commodity.

Higgling in a crude market

Markets depart from perfection in many ways and in varying degrees. The characteristics of the ideal market can be appreciated best by considering cases where they are absent, in whole or in part. These cases are also important because they reveal in extreme fashion certain features that are present to some extent in nearly all markets.

Take the case of a unique commodity with, of necessity, only one seller and at the same time only one prospective buyer. An example would be a unique type of house which the owner is anxious to sell and which one other person is anxious to own. Let us assume that the owner, who of course wants to get all he can for it, would rather accept as little as $5000 than keep it and that the customer, who wants to get it as cheaply as he can, would rather pay up to $10,000 than fail to get it. At any intermediate price a deal is clearly advantageous to both parties. Each would benefit from it.

In this situation, the actual price must depend entirely on a process known as *higgling* or *bargaining*—a process that is essentially a game of bluff. Neither party knows what concessions the other can be pushed into making, and each wants to push the other as far as he can without imperiling the transaction. In this situation no principle can be formulated to say where the price is likely to be. The crudity of the market lies in this very fact that there is nothing in its processes to point to a particular price. Over a wide range, one price meets the simple conditions of the market as well as another.

A similar case is that of the corporation executive who is extremely valuable to his employer but whose capacities are peculiarly suited to the needs of this firm and much less valuable to any other firm. What his salary will be may have to be determined within an extremely wide bargaining range. Perhaps he will accept $25,000 in preference to employment with any other firm, but the company may be willing to pay $100,000, if necessary, to hold him. Neither limit is known to the other party, and the outcome is indeterminate so far as any market principle is concerned.

Nonuniformity of prices. The salary agreed on for this executive may be considerably higher or lower than is paid in other corporations to executives who, on the surface, appear to be doing comparable work with comparable skill. Like differences in paying executives probably exist among these other corporations. The point is that the good in question, executive service, is not standardized, and individuals are not interchangeable among positions. Under this condition different prices govern different transactions. This sort of market, then, is crude not only in the sense that price is indeterminate over a considerable range, but also in the sense that there is no uniformity of price throughout the market.

These examples are extreme, but there are many goods and many markets which resemble them in some degree. Various unstandardized products invite higgling over prices and preclude any meaningful uniformity of price. Works of art, handmade commodities generally, and many personal services belong in this category. For such goods, higgling over transactions is an accepted market procedure, unless merchandising methods which exclude it become institutionalized. Travelers in foreign countries, especially in the East, know how little the price first quoted by a tradesman means in the final making of a purchase.

In part, this diversity of prices results directly from the unique qualities of goods. There is no basis for a generally applicable price. In part, it results from lack of knowledge and inferior judgment on the part of traders, especially those who buy. Any novice can make price comparisons between obviously identical goods, and it is therefore difficult for a seller to get more than the prevailing market price or for the purchaser to buy for less. But where dissimilarities exist, lack of experience and training becomes a large factor in markets, and the unskillful are led to pay substantially more than informed customers do. Thus the range of prices is greater than the differences between commodities justifies, greater than would be supported by the appraisal of experts.

In the same way, ignorance and inertia may account for some diversity in the prices even of standardized commodities. Different prices may be charged by different stores in a community or even by a single seller to different customers. All transactions must be interrelated through the knowledge and effort of traders, if higgling is to be eliminated and a uniform price is to prevail.

Uniform pricing in a well-developed market

The more nearly standardized a good is and the better informed the buyers and sellers of it are, and the more energetic in pursuing their interests, the stronger is the tendency toward a uniform price—a price that can properly be spoken of as *the* market price of the good. How these market conditions produce this result can be seen from an example.

Instead of the single unique house considered above, let us consider the market in a community for practically equivalent six-room houses— all built in the 1920s at about the same time and at about the same cost and equally well located. There are a considerable number of owners of such houses and of prospective buyers. To show how the tendency toward price uniformity operates, let us retain our earlier assumption regarding the attitudes of buyer and seller, as the basis of their higgling —that is, let us assume that every seller will take as little as $5000 if he has to and every buyer will pay as much as $10,000 rather than not obtain a house.

Now, if the buyers and sellers know what is going on and act accordingly, there cannot be a range of prices between $5000 and $10,000, depending on bargaining in separate transactions. All transactions are interconnected. A prospective buyer about to close a deal for a house at $8000 hears of another deal about to be closed at $6000. He rushes over and offers $6100 for the latter house, with the result that both the $8000 and the $6000 deals are off. Similarly a seller on the point of accepting $5500 for his house hears of a buyer about to pay $7500. This seller hastens to offer his house to this buyer for $7400, and the $5500 and $7500 deals are off. For the same reason, the $6100 and $7400 propositions will not be accepted, since the seller in the former case and the buyer in the latter, learning what is happening, will proceed as just described. With such fullness of information and energy of action, no seller will take less than other sellers are getting, and no buyer will pay more than other buyers are paying.

This example is unreal not only in the assumption regarding the attitudes of buyers and sellers but also in the wide range through which the correcting of prices takes place. Actually the forces making for price uniformity are continuously in operation and would have been working prior to the beginning of the episode described. Approximate uniformity of prices is the condition to which we are habituated, and the interactions of buyers and sellers which bring it about are a commonplace of free markets.

Principle of single price. This everyday expectation as to the working of markets, sometimes referred to as the "law of single price" or of "one price," deserves to be recognized as one of the principles of market price. We may state it by saying that prices tend to be uniform at any time for the different transactions in a particular good—given competition and full knowledge and the use of it among buyers and sellers. Like all market principles, it represents only a tendency, and operates only to the extent that the conditions are present on which it depends. In the example just used, complete price uniformity would not be possible because houses are not perfectly standardized. Moreover, buyers and sellers would probably not be fully informed regarding other transactions in the market or as aggressive as necessary in using their information. Much greater uniformity of price could be expected in the transactions in a particular grade of wheat or wool. Later on we shall note that monopoly may also upset the uniformity of prices and lead to discrimination in the treatment of different buyers.[1]

But all price differences for particular goods do not represent violations of the principle of single price. A good may be sold under different conditions, involving different costs, and price differentials may then be necessary to carry out the principle and give effect to the forces behind it. An example is the charging of higher prices by stores that extend credit to customers and provide delivery service. The buyer in these stores is getting the commodity plus additional service. Similarly, as between towns located at different distances from the point where a good originates, differences in price reflecting differences in transportation cost are entirely in harmony with the principle of single price.

Price uniformity and price policy. Sometimes the actual uniformity of prices is greater than can be explained by the market forces we have been considering. Markets, we saw in the preceding chapter, are often intricate institutions with established rules and practices and patterns of operation, and there may be considerable concentration of power in them. In these circumstances absolute uniformity of prices, as well as particular relations of prices, may result from deliberate policy. Two quite different cases should be noted.

One of these is the development in the United States and some other countries of *merchandising procedures* which exclude the Oriental-bazaar type of higgling. Goods are commonly offered by dealers on a quoted-price, take-it-or-leave-it basis, and the seller does not try to extract from each buyer the most that he can be made to pay. Doubtless,

---

[1] Discriminatory pricing will be discussed in Chapter 22.

with increasing standardization of products, the possible gains from higgling are outweighed by the costs of slower negotiation of sales. This merchandising policy means directly only that the different customers of *one* seller pay the same price for a good; but with higgling removed, price comparisons among *different* sellers are made easier, and general uniformity throughout a market is promoted.

The other case arises through *agreement of sellers* as to the price they will charge or through market practices equivalent to agreement. Monopoly may mean nonuniform prices, and it may also mean such a perfection of uniformity as could arise under competition only in the ideal market described above. When a city asks a number of manufacturers for bids on drain pipe of certain specifications and the bids which come in are identical to the last cent, one does not marvel at the working of competitive markets. Collusion is the obvious explanation.

The Principle of Supply and Demand

The principle of single price says nothing as to how high or how low the price of a good will be. It disposes of only one of the characteristics of crude markets, the nonuniformity of prices in them. The question remains as to where the single price will be and what forces put it there. Does the market price of a good, in a well-developed market, depend on the bargaining skill of buyers and sellers taken as a whole, or is there some other explanation?

The general answer is found in the principle of supply and demand, which wholly eliminates the bargaining factor under ideal market conditions and greatly reduces its scope under most conditions. In the present section we shall first consider the logic of this principle in a fairly nontechnical way to appreciate its nature and significance. Then we shall examine the concepts of supply and demand and their relationships more carefully to avoid certain pitfalls of usage.

General nature of supply and demand

For supply and demand to set a definite price for a good, the actions of sellers and buyers must depend closely on the possible prices of that good. In the house example, as used above, the actions did not, but in this respect the example was given an intentionally unrealistic turn. Surely all buyers are not willing to pay up to $10,000 for a house and all sellers to take as little as $5000. A range of attitudes can be expected to prevail on both sides of the market. For the sake of concreteness, we shall continue the house example and make some assumptions regarding attitudes.

On the demand side, we shall assume that only one buyer will pay as much as $10,000. Another will pay $9500 if he has to. Because the man who would pay $10,000 will certainly buy at $9500, we may say that at the latter figure there is a demand for two houses. A third buyer enters at $9000, establishing a demand at that price for three houses. For convenience in formulating the example, we shall assume that one additional house will be taken with each successive drop of $500 in the price, until, if the price were as low as $5000, 11 houses would be bought. This is the typical relationship between volume of buying and prices: *the lower the price, the larger the quantity of a good that buyers will take.*

On the supply side of the market, we shall assume that there is only one owner who will part with his house for as little as $5000 but that at $5500 both he and one other owner are willing to sell their houses. More and more additional owners can be induced to dispose of their houses if still higher prices are offered. For simplicity let us assume that one more house is offered at each $500 interval and that at $10,000 the total supply is 11 houses. We cannot be quite so general in saying that this is the typical character of supply, but it is typical for some commodities in all situations and for most commodities in a short-run market sense. What we are assuming is that *the higher the price, the larger the quantity of a good that sellers will make available.*

These facts respecting the market in a community for closely similar six-room houses may be summed up conveniently in the form of *demand and supply schedules.*

TABLE 22—ASSUMED MARKET SCHEDULES FOR HOUSES

Prospective buyers will take:	At a price of:	Whereas owners will part with
1 house	$10,000	11 houses
2 houses	9,500	10 houses
3 houses	9,000	9 houses
4 houses	8,500	8 houses
5 houses	8,000	7 houses
6 houses	7,500	6 houses
7 houses	7,000	5 houses
8 houses	6,500	4 houses
9 houses	6,000	3 houses
10 houses	5,500	2 houses
11 houses	5,000	1 house

To cover only the range of prices from $5000 to $10,000 is arbitrary. It is reasonable to assume that at still lower prices more houses would be bought and that at still higher prices more houses would be offered for sale. In statistical studies of markets, supply and demand are likely to be measurable only fairly close to the market price; in a hypothetical example used to explain a principle, we may suit our convenience as long as we adhere to the essential nature of supply and demand. It is through the fact that supply and demand possess this general character, quantities offered and taken varying with prices, that a particular price can emerge as the one logical expression of the whole market situation.

The pull toward an equilibrium price

With buyers and sellers responding oppositely to price changes, there is bound to be some price at which the amount demanded is equal to the amount supplied. This is the price that tends to prevail in a competitive market.[2] Thus, in the market for houses, we should expect the price to be $7500 and that 6 houses would change hands at that price. This is the *equilibrium price*—in the sense that at this price there is no tendency toward further change under prevailing conditions. At any other price there is a pull toward the equilibrium position.

At any higher price, supply exceeds demand, and there is a downward pressure through the competition of sellers. Sellers, of course, prefer high prices to low prices, but they also prefer selling to not selling—if the price is as high as they insist on getting. At a price of $8000 there are sellers who would like to dispose of 7 houses, but buyers will take only 5 houses. Of those sellers, 6 will take as little as $7500 if they have to, and the price is pulled toward that level by their competition in seeking buyers. At $7500 it happens that 6 houses will be bought, and the downward pressure stops. All who want to sell at that figure are able to.

Similarly, at any price below $7500 demand exceeds supply, and there is upward pressure on price through the competition of buyers. Buyers prefer low prices to high prices, but they prefer buying to not buying—if they can get the good at a price they are willing to pay. At $7000 there are buyers who will take 7 houses, but only 5 houses can be obtained, while at $7500 the 6 houses that buyers will take are available. Thus the upward pressure continues until that figure is reached.

Despite the artificial character of this example, it shows in the fullest sense what is meant by saying that a price is determined in a market through the operation of the principle of supply and demand. Under that principle there is downward pressure on any price at which supply

[2] Demand and supply may also be equal at the prevailing price under monopoly but for somewhat different reasons, as we shall see later.

exceeds demand and upward pressure on any price at which demand exceeds supply, so that *the market price tends to be fixed at the point where the quantities that buyers will take and sellers offer are equal.*

Equilibrium price as promoter of economic interests. The principle of supply and demand is an essential part of the whole system of value relationships through which a specialized economy is organized. Prices so fixed provide a basis for trade that is mutually advantageous to buyers and sellers and, as far as possible, reconciles their interests. The equilibrium price is, in a sense, the only price that meets the conditions that buyers and sellers have in mind. Buyers would, of course, be better satisfied with lower prices, if the goods they were prepared to buy were available, and sellers, similarly, would be pleased if prices were higher. But the price at which supply and demand are equal is the only price at which every participant can do what he prefers to do under the actual circumstances of the market. This being true, the equilibrium price is the one price at which the maximum quantity of a good will change hands.

Competition *versus* bargaining. It was stated above that the principle of supply and demand, when fully operative, removes the bargaining, or higgling, factor from markets. In the case of the unique house with the single potential buyer and seller, supply and demand were equal over a $5000-price range, and there was wide room for bargaining. With many buyers and sellers and demand and supply equal only at a single price, there is no room for bargaining—that is, there is no room for bargaining if the market is competitive. However, combinations of buyers and sellers may bargain within limits in a partly noncompetitive market, for instance, in the collective bargaining over wages in the labor field.

Bargaining and competition are often confused, although they are essentially opposites. It has been said, for instance, that the law of supply and demand operates through the bargaining of buyers and sellers. The relation between employers and workers has even been characterized as competitive, and competition between these parties has been blamed for the trouble in this area. These are unfortunate usages. Clarity will be aided if we think of competition as prevailing among people on the same side of the market—among buyers, on the one hand, and among sellers, on the other—and think of bargaining as the relation between buyers and sellers.

Bargaining, in other words, is a relationship in which each party is trying to advance his own interest. In bargaining or higgling, sellers are trying to get higher prices and buyers lower prices. On the other hand, it is the competition of sellers in markets that pushes prices downward and the competition of buyers that pushes them upward. When it is seen that competition works directly against the interests of those who compete, it is clear why sellers combine with other sellers if they can, and buyers with other buyers, to eliminate competition on their side of the market.

Demand and supply—definitions and usages

Now with the whole picture in mind of the working of supply and demand in fixing prices, it will be useful to look more closely into the meaning of supply and demand and their relation to prices. These concepts should be handled with facility, and some common errors in using them should be avoided.

The essential features of *demand* can be summed up by saying that it consists of *the number of units of a good that buyers, during a period, stand ready to take at a given price,* or, in the schedule sense, that it consists of the whole series of amounts that they stand ready to take at each price in the entire range of possible prices. Similarly, *supply* is *the number of units of a good that sellers, during a period, stand ready to dispose of at a specified price,* or the series of amounts corresponding to the series of possible price constituting a supply schedule.

In speaking of demand, the phrase *"stand ready"* should be stressed because demanding a good is sometimes confused with merely desiring it. The people who demand a good must desire it, of course, but they must also be able to pay for it, and they must be willing to part with their money in order to get it. It is easy to miscalculate demand by paying attention mainly to the needs and desires of people. Probably the postwar demand for private airplanes was seriously overestimated through taking account of the number of war veterans who were able pilots and the growing air-mindedness of the country and through not taking sufficient account of the small number of people who can afford to own and run airplanes. There has likewise been an exaggerated impression of the probable demand for American exports in the backward areas of the world where the need for goods seems great. Exports go mainly to developed countries where incomes are high. Demand rests on two underlying conditions: desires and income.

The phrase *"stand ready"* should be stressed also with respect to supply. At least in the immediate market sense, the supply of a good is not the *stock* in existence nor the *flow of output* from farms, mines, and factories. Wheat, for example, is produced periodically, and great quantities appear at harvest time. These quantities enter the stock which must last until the next harvest. But the supply on a particular day is the quantity that sellers stand ready to part with then at particular prices.

The phrase *"during a period"* in the above definitions refers to an aspect of demand and supply that did not enter the house example used above. Most markets are not like auctions, where a definite stock of a good is to be disposed of once and for all. Dealings in most goods are, instead, a continuing flow. Where a flow is involved, quantities must be measured in terms of time. Thus demand and supply must be expressed as the numbers of units of goods that buyers will take and sellers part with per day, week, month, or year.

It is perhaps most important to emphasize that the quantities buyers will take and sellers make available are *"at a price."* What traders will do at one price, they commonly will not do at another price. It is meaningless to say that demand for a good exceeds supply or that supply exceeds demand without stipulating a price or having one clearly in mind. As seen in the house example, the relation between supply and demand varies widely over the range of possible prices. One should be particularly careful in the use of such words as *surplus* and *shortage*. When producers say that a surplus of their product exists, what they usually mean is that more is offered than is being taken at the prevailing price or at the price the producers think they ought to get. The postwar shortage of steel and automobiles has meant that smaller quantities are available than buyers would take at prevailing prices; there is no question that prices could be raised sufficiently to remove the shortage.

Demand and supply in graphs. The characteristics of demand and supply and their relation to prices can be summed up with desirable brevity, and sometimes clarified, through use of graphs. The conventional procedure in price graphs is to measure quantities of goods on the horizontal scale, or X axis, and prices on the vertical scale, or Y axis. Through this device the entire demand situation for a good can be shown with a single demand line (demand curve) that reflects the quantities that buyers stand ready to take at different prices; a single supply line (or supply curve) does the same for supply.

Thus, on the demand line DD in the following chart, any point such as A tells us that, at the corresponding price OY, buyers will take the corresponding quantity OX. The demand line is made up of a succession of points such as A and thus represents the entire demand schedule and gives the entire demand picture. In the same way, any point A on the supply line SS says that at the corresponding price OY the corresponding quantity OX will be made available by sellers. The supply line tells the whole supply story.

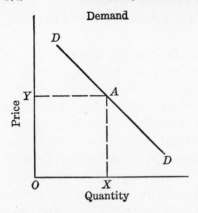

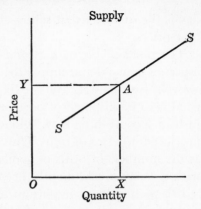

One of the important things these lines tell is the *particular respon-siveness of quantity to price,* as brought out in the house example. In the case of demand, more goods are taken at lower prices, fewer at higher prices; in the case of supply, more goods are offered at higher prices, fewer at lower prices. Thus quantity varies directly with price in the case of supply, inversely in the case of demand, and the demand and supply lines slope accordingly.

The degree of responsiveness of buyers and sellers to price changes varies from one good to another and is known in economics as the *elasticity* of demand and of supply. We shall make use of the concept of elasticity of demand in the following chapter and shall discuss it further there. The demand and supply lines may be straight, curved, or wavy and may tilt at various angles. Here the object is merely to show the direction of variation and not any special characteristic.

Changes in supply and demand and prices

Changes in the prices of particular goods, which are a major element in economic adjustments and disturbances, arise through changes in demand and in supply. If, with the price of a good at the equilibrium point, the demand for the good increases, then at that point demand becomes greater than supply and there is upward pressure on the price. If, in the same circumstances, the supply increases, supply becomes greater than demand at the existing price and there is downward pres-sure on it. These changes can also be shown graphically. (See page 473.)

In the left-hand graph an increase in demand is shown by the move-ment of the demand line from *DD* to *D'D'*. Because demand is the quantity of a good that buyers will take at a price, an increase in de-mand is an increase in the quantity that will be taken at that same price. Thus, at the price *OY*, buyers who were prepared to take quan-tity *OX* before the increase in demand are ready to take quantity *OX'*

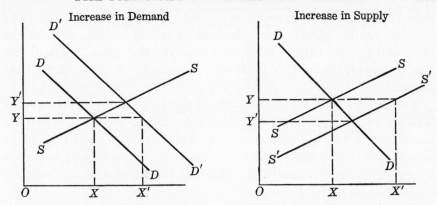

after the increase. Their inclination is presumably to take larger quantities at all prices, and the result is a new demand line $D'D'$ to the right of the old one, although there is no reason for assuming that an equal increase occurs at all prices. The increase in supply, reflected in the new supply line $S'S'$ in the right-hand graph, follows exactly the same principle.

Resulting price changes. With demand DD and supply SS, a price of OY is in accord with the principle of supply and demand. At that price the quantity OX demanded is equal to the quantity OX supplied. Equilibrium is necessarily found at the point where the two lines intersect.

With an increase in demand from DD to $D'D'$, and supply unchanged, price is pushed upward and the new equilibrium is found at the price OY', at which demand and supply are again equal. With an increase in supply from SS to $S'S'$, and demand unchanged, price is pushed downward to a lower OY' in the other graph.

When the demand for a good is said to increase or decrease, we should assume that the supply, as reflected in the supply line, remains unchanged unless the contrary is stipulated. Likewise, when supply changes, no change in demand should be assumed unless specified. The buyers and sellers of a product are distinct sets of persons, acting under their own particular conditions and governed by their own particular attitudes, and a change on the part of one group should not lead one to infer a change on the part of the other group. The demand and supply schedules and lines already tell how buyers and sellers propose to act, in view of their attitudes, at various possible prices. There may be some oversimplification in this statement, but it is a good general rule to follow to avoid confusion. Failure to follow it may involve one in such difficulties as the following.

Seeming circularity within the market. The principle of supply and demand is reduced to apparent futility through such reasoning as this: "Suppose the demand for a good does go up, and the price follows. At the higher price, demand is bound to fall off, and the price will fall, perhaps as low as it was in the first place." Actually, in this statement, the train of ideas runs completely off the track we have just laid.

Throughout this discussion we have been careful to use the phrase "change in demand" in a single, definite sense. We have used it to mean a change in the quantities of a good that buyers will take at the *same* prices. Thus, graphically, a change in demand must be represented by a new demand line. Only in this sense can a change in demand cause a change in price.

But what is called a fall in demand in the second sentence of the above statement is something entirely different. All that is referred to there is the fact that, as the price of a good rises, buyers will take less of it. That fact is shown graphically by following a particular demand line upward, and therefore to the left. The smaller amount taken at a *higher* price does not mean a fall in demand but merely reflects the responsiveness of buyers to prices, the *elasticity of demand*. It is the result of a change in price, not the cause of a change.

Thus, in the chart on page 473, there is a real increase in demand as buyers increase the amount they will take at price OY from OX to OX', and in consequence the price goes up from OY to OY'. Because buying falls off as price goes up, the actual purchases at price OY' are less than quantity OX', though more than OX. But there is nothing whatever in the situation to cause the price to fall below OY', the level to which the increase in demand has raised it.

To avoid confusion, care has been taken in the preceding pages not to speak of the responsiveness of buyers and sellers to price changes as changes in demand and in supply. This responsiveness to prices has been referred to, instead, as changes in the quantities that buyers will take and sellers part with. A real change in demand reflects a change in the underlying conditions that govern the attitudes of buyers and sellers—either in desires or in incomes. Thus, if buyers have more money to spend, they will increase their demand for goods, buying more units at the same prices. But with the same amount of money to spend, they will buy more units at low prices than at high prices.

The whole scheme of control of economic organization through market forces falls, as we have noted, into two parts: (1) how the attitudes of sellers and buyers, in view of the underlying conditions of supply and demand, come to focus in prices; (2) how prices, in turn, control the actions of sellers and buyers. It is evident that confusion of the sort just considered reflects failure to separate these aspects of economic control.

Limitations of supply-and-demand analysis

The house example has been used so extensively, despite certain unreal features, because it avoids complications in the fixing of prices that would carry us beyond the intended scope of this chapter. The discussion of market price should be concluded, however, with some recognition of the type of situation for which the principle of supply and demand is a fairly adequate tool of analysis and of the type of situation that requires considerable further attention.

Supply from existing stocks. The house example got us away from the complicating effect on supply of the continuing production of goods. Since there is no further production of old houses, the supply of them must be from an existing stock and must depend simply on the willingness of owners to part with that stock.

The supply situation is similar for old paintings, antique furniture, first editions of books. But by all odds the most important good in this category is land, because the stock of it, with minor exceptions, is fixed by nature. In all such cases, the variations in demand, through their effect on prices, affect the quantities that change hands but not the quantities available to be sold. Because of the fixity of the stock, the variations in demand can cause very wide variations in prices, in contrast with goods for which price changes would cause variations in output. In the case of old houses, however, a ceiling to prices is provided by the cost of new houses.

Other goods may belong temporarily in the fixed-stock category, and their prices move freely in response to supply and demand. Perishable products may glut a local market, and sellers may throw them on the market for what they will bring. End-of-season sales of merchandise are of the same nature. When a war shuts off the production of automobiles, tires, radios, and other goods, the existing stock becomes the basis of supply, and prices, unless the government prevents, become detached from the conditions that govern production.

The actual markets most often used to exemplify the near-perfect working of competitive supply and demand involve commodities of which the stock is temporarily fixed. One of them is wheat, traded in on the Chicago Board of Trade. Wheat is a produced good, but the fact that a large existing stock must be disposed of after it is harvested means that the price, in the absence of government interference, will move pretty much as we have described. Similarly the corporate shares traded in on the New York Stock Exchange and other exchanges are supplied from a stock that is temporarily fixed, and their prices respond freely to supply-and-demand conditions.

In contrast with such goods as these, all of the goods that are produced fairly continuously depend for their supply on the conditions, especially the costs, of their production. Regarding the supplies of such goods, a great deal remains to be said.

The "setting" of prices by sellers. The house example, moreover, showed a situation in which the price emerged from the market as a whole in the fullest sense. It reflected an equal and coordinate participation of buyers and sellers. No individual or group was in a position to exert any special influence over it. In the strictest sense, it was a *market-determined* price. This situation has ordinarily been present in the markets for farm products and many other raw materials.

It is not likely to be present, however, in the selling of goods by manufacturers and merchants. Products offered continuously on a *quoted-price* basis reflect influences we have not considered—influences which merge into the intricate modifications of competition that prevail in these industries. Supply-and-demand relations still exert powerful pressures of exactly the type we have discussed, but there are other pressures also. Supply and demand in such markets may be equal at the prevailing price, not because price results freely from the interaction of supply and demand but because production is adjusted to demand at a price set by the producers.

Chapters 20, 21, and 22 will develop these aspects of supply, but first, in the following chapter, we shall look further into the demand side of the market.

Review Questions

1. "Countless influences operate in markets and affect prices." "Market analysis is just a matter of supply and demand." Can these statements be reconciled?

2. "The main features that should be noted in describing a market are neither geographic nor essentially physical." Explain.

3. "A market of the Oriental-bazaar type operates crudely in two related respects." Explain. Give other examples. Contrast these crude markets with such a market as the New York Stock Exchange.

4. State the conditions necessary to the operation of the principle of single price, and explain why these conditions tend to establish a single price.

5. If the chain stores sell standard groceries at one price in a community

and independent grocers sell at higher prices, is the principle of single price violated? Explain.

6. "A perfect market insures price uniformity, but price uniformity does not demonstrate that a market is perfect." Explain.

7. "Price tends toward the point at which supply and demand are equal because, at any other point, there is pressure toward the point of equality." Explain.

8. "The pricing of goods in conformity with the principle of supply and demand performs excellently the primary function of prices—providing a basis for the exchanges on which specialization rests." Explain.

9. Contrast competition and bargaining, including the market conditions which they imply.

10. "Because desires are the basis of demand, the greatest demand must come from people whose wants are least well satisfied." Do you agree? Explain.

11. "The demand for schoolteachers is considerably greater than the supply." Amend this statement to make it an accurate expression of the intended idea.

12. Using the house example, assume that demand increases at each price to the extent of two houses, develop a new demand schedule, and explain what should happen to the price. Plot the data and go through the same explanation graphically, using continuous curves.

13. "The demand for a good increases. Thus the supply is reduced, and, as a result, the price goes up." Criticize this method of statement.

14. "Changes in price are largely self-correcting, since any shift in supply or demand causes such a price movement as reverses the shift." Do you agree? Explain carefully, verbally and with graph. Distinguish "change in demand" and "responsiveness of buyers to price."

15. "The operation of the principle of supply and demand can be seen most clearly in the case of goods sold from a fixed stock." Why? What are the leading features of the alternative situation? Give examples.

16. What does it mean to say that a price is determined by the market?

- 19 -

Nature and Role of
Demand and Its Elasticity

In his relation to markets and prices, the buyer of goods is both ruler and subject. His is the dual role of giving orders and submitting to direction. On the one hand, his demands for goods influence prices and guide production; on the other hand, the prices he pays govern his purchases and his consumption and, through him, influence the working of the economy in important ways. In this chapter we shall do some probing into these relations of buyers to markets.

Consumer Choices and the "Consumer Problem"

Primarily, economic welfare means consumer welfare. Consumer welfare depends, first of all, on the money income of individuals in relation to the price level, but it also depends substantially on the wisdom with which spending is done. Consumer choices, in everyday spending and the budgeting of expenditures, lie more within the control of the individual than do the other main factors in his well-being. The logic behind these choices should be examined for the light it throws on market behavior and on the foundations of market demand. It should be examined also as a basis for considering critically the conditions under which consumers do their buying and try to achieve wisdom in their spending of money.

The field of consumer choice

Eskimos, Australian bushmen, South Sea Islanders, natives of central Africa, have a limited range of choice in their selection of goods. The range likewise is not great for most of the people in Asia and even in the countries of eastern Europe. In more productive countries such as the United States, consumers are confronted with a bewildering variety of goods among which they must apportion their money.

But even for people in the United States, fairly regular patterns of consumption appear when goods are grouped in major categories and when consumers are grouped by income levels. An intensive study made for the years 1935–1936, when money income averaged less than half as high as it has since the war, showed, as one would expect, (1) that essential purchases absorb the bulk of the lower incomes, (2) that essential purchases take a declining fraction of larger incomes, and (3) that the absolute outlay for every purpose rises with income. Relatively more is spent on clothes, recreation, and education as income rises—more, at least, as a percentage of total expenditure for consumption. But saving rises so rapidly as income grows that nearly all lines of consumption spending take a declining fraction of income as incomes become very large. Saving, whether for a "rainy day" or to accumulate an estate, should of course be included among the choices that the individual considers in budgeting his income, and it becomes the source of spending in the important capital-goods field. Apportionment of outlay for selected levels of income in 1935–1936 is shown in the accompanying table.[1]

TABLE 23—AVERAGE USE OF FAMILY INCOME AT SELECTED LEVELS, 1935–1936
(Percentage of total income stated in parenthesis)

	Income between $500–$750		Income between $2500–$3000		Income between $15,000–$20,000	
Food	$310	(49.5%)	$690	(25.4%)	$1785	(10.3%)
Shelter	226	(35.9%)	748	(27.6%)	2746	(17.0%)
Clothing	56	(8.9%)	255	(9.4%)	1265	(7.3%)
Transportation (mainly auto)	33	(5.3%)	266	(9.8%)	1318	(7.6%)
Medical care	29	(4.7%)	109	(4.0%)	416	(2.4%)
Personal care	14	(2.2%)	49	(1.8%)	156	(0.9%)
Recreation	11	(1.7%)	81	(3.0%)	486	(2.8%)
Tobacco	14	(2.3%)	41	(1.5%)	104	(0.6%)
Education	3	(0.5%)	30	(1.1%)	537	(3.1%)
Reading	6	(0.9%)	22	(0.8%)	69	(0.4%)
Other expenditures	5	(0.8%)	11	(0.4%)	52	(0.3%)
Gifts and personal taxes	12	(1.9%)	98	(3.6%)	1282	(7.4%)
Savings	−92	(−14.6%)	315	(11.6%)	6915	(39.9%)

[1] Data selected from tables in the National Resources Planning Board Study, *Family Expenditures in the United States*, 1941, pp. 1 and 37. The figures for "shelter" combine the outlays for housing, household operation, and house furnishings.

Statistics of this kind throw light on consumer wants and preferences, but, as with all classifications and averages, the actual situation
is made to appear simpler than it is. At every income range, particular
families differ greatly in their situations and their tastes. For every
category of expenditure, there are many specific goods and many types
and brands among which selection must be made. Mrs. Jones may
have $20 a week to spend on food, but she still has to decide among
steak, frankfurters, and spaghetti for dinner.

Toward explaining the desires or preferences which underlie expenditure patterns and the use of money income, economics has very
little to say. The roots of demand in the nature of human beings have
been left mainly to investigators in other fields. Unquestionably consumer choices are guided in part by physical needs and in part by
social factors. But even with respect to the needs for food and shelter,
specific preferences for one thing rather than another are influenced
by custom, emulation, advertising, the desire to appear to advantage.
As income rises, more wants can be gratified, and specific wants with
more variety and fullness, so that social factors gain in importance.

We shall not pursue this inquiry, but it should be noted that the
amounts spent for various purposes reflect different *types of choices*:

1. For some goods the main choice may be *whether or not to have
the item at all*. Such choices arise at practically all levels of income.
Can the consumer afford a watch or a radio? Should he own an automobile or a dress suit? Should he obtain a college education? Should
he collect paintings or enjoy the luxury of a yacht?

2. For some goods the choice concerns the *number of units to be
purchased* and consumed. How many quarts of milk, or steaks, or
moving pictures should the family's weekly budget cover? How many
suits should be included in the husband's wardrobe, how many dresses
in the wife's? Should the family afford a four- or a six- or an eight-
room house?

3. For most goods there are many *grades and qualities* among
which a choice must be made. A davenport may be obtained for $100
and a much better one for $200, a still better for $300. A suit of
clothes may cost $50 or $100. The family car may be bought secondhand; it may be a new Ford, or it may be a Cadillac.

These various choices, necessarily overlapping in many ways, are
involved in the apportionment of spending. They are complicated by
the fact that outlays for different goods must be made with different
time intervals in mind. Some items such as bread are bought almost
daily; some serve for weeks or months without repurchase; some such
as overcoats and automobiles may be expected to last several years;

some such as a new house or a new watch are bought only at long intervals. To employ one's money income wisely with such alternatives in view is a difficult matter.

Theory of rational choice

Is it possible to describe logically how consumers with given tastes and preferences behave in using the money at their command? The answer must be that a logical explanation is possible only in so far as consumers act logically—as often they do not. But however they actually behave, it is useful to consider the behavior of a rational consumer and then to discuss some of the common departures from rationality.

The consumer's goal. We should recognize, first, what the rational consumer aims at in his spending. If asked, he would probably say merely that he is trying to get the most out of his money or to live as well as he can with the income he has, considering both present and future. Economists convey the same idea when they say that the consumer's goal is to *maximize satisfactions* for himself and his family, or that he apportions his spending to achieve the *greatest total utility* through his outlays.[2] Whatever the language, that aspect of welfare is involved which we recognize, somewhat extremely, in saying that a man with a family and a $2000 income is wiser in spending most of it on food, shelter, and clothing than on liquor, travel, and the theater. In less extreme, more typical situations, a myriad of choices affects well-being, and the rational consumer strives in every instance to make the better choice.

This is a *typical economic problem.* The consumer, having (1) a given set of desires (doubtless a little vague at many points) and (2) a given amount of money he can spend, faces (3) an array of goods available at prices that he is almost powerless to affect. Everything he does with his money, including saving it, precludes doing something else. He endeavors to see that what he foregoes in each instance is less important to him than what he realizes in its place. The movie per week that he gives up should mean less to him than the additional books he is enabled to buy; the car he sacrifices should mean less than having a larger bank balance or making the down payment on a new house. He probably thinks of the *price* he pays for a good as

[2] Since satisfactions and utilities are not actually measured, it may be unrealistic to speak of the total amount of them. Thus economists often prefer to speak only of *scales of preference* and of selecting goods in accordance with these scales. But if choices of goods affect well-being, as certainly they do, then no one need be misled if it is said that goods should be selected to achieve maximum well-being, or maximum satisfaction. These are quantitative concepts.

its cost to him, but its cost, more fundamentally, is the *alternative benefit he foregoes* when he makes the choice.

Diminishing marginal utility. In developing the theory of rational choice, two ideas of considerable importance, not only here but elsewhere, should be understood. One is the principle of diminishing utility or diminishing marginal utility.

If Mrs. Jones, in spending the family income, is confronted with an array of just five commodities—*A, B, C, D,* and *E*—and *A* is recognized as more important than the others, will not her family be best off if all its money is spent on *A?* The answer, we know from experience, is, no, and the question before us is, why not?

The reason lies in the declining benefit we get from additional outlays in any one line of expenditure. The point appears most sharply when a choice must be made between more and fewer units of the same commodity. However important *A* is, a second unit of it will almost certainly be less important than the first, and a third than the second. One suit of clothes, say, costing $50 is highly important to a man, but having one suit, he finds a second less essential. If he has ten suits, it may mean very little to him whether he has an eleventh or not. The same principle applies to the additional movies, additional bottles of milk, additional rooms in one's house, and all the goods of which multiple units may be desired.

But it applies no less where the choice involves the different possible qualities and gradations of goods. The second $50 spent in getting a $100 suit adds less to one's satisfaction than the $50 that enables one to have a suit in the first place. The dollars that enable one to have a finer automobile yield a smaller return than the dollars that enable one to have a car at all.

Thus the additional outlays along any line, whether in getting more units or better units, bring a declining return. It is for this reason that the wise consumer suspends his outlays on even the most important goods and turns to other things. To state the principle more formally, we may say that *successive dollars spent along any line yield less and less additional satisfaction.*[3]

This is the idea of diminishing marginal utility. The word "marginal" is a much used word in economics. A margin is an edge or boundary, and the "marginal utility," as more dollars are spent on a good, is the added utility that the outside or last dollars bring one. *Diminishing marginal utility* is the declining additional importance of what the added dollars purchase. Marginal utility has a key place

---

[3] Again, if one does not like the suggestion that satisfactions can be measured, one can say that as more money is spent on a good there is less and less reason for preferring it to other goods.

in determining the importance of things to us. To the man with ten suits, the importance of a suit of clothes is only as great as the loss he would suffer if one of the ten were taken from him—a much smaller loss than if one suit were taken from the man who has only one. More dollars spent for any good, for more units or better units, thus reduce the importance of one dollar's worth of that good.

Since the principle of diminishing marginal utility applies to each line of purchase, it applies to all lines together and thus to the *consumer's income as a whole*. The first $1000 of income means more than the second $1000, the second $1000 than the third, and so on. It is a common experience that, as one's income grows, the dollar has a declining importance and may be spent for less and less important things. To the poor man, it may have the importance of a week's milk for the children, to the rich man, only the importance of an after-dinner cigar.

Equalizing marginal utilities. The second of the two ideas is that the consumer gets the most from any given income when his outlays along all lines, including saving, are carried to the point where the added benefit from the last dollar is the same.

Good *A* may be much more important than Good *B*, and much more should be spent on it, but the over-all importance of these goods provides no guide as to what the relative outlays on them should be. But if, when $10 per month is spent on *A* and $5 per month on *B*, practically the same additional benefit is derived from the last dollar spent on each, it plainly would not pay to switch a dollar from either good to the other. Subtracting a dollar from the outlay on *A* and adding it to the outlay on *B* would, so to speak, carry one up the utility scale on *A* and down it on *B*, and a net loss in satisfaction would result.

The rational consumer tries to avoid spending a dollar for any purpose that would bring him more satisfaction if used for some other purpose. In this behavior he is thinking in marginal terms rather than judging the total importance of different things. Through such action he tends to equalize the marginal importance of the dollar in all lines of use.

Changing wants, incomes, and prices. In this discussion it has been assumed not only that the preferences of the rational consumer remain fixed but that his income and the prices of goods do also. If his personal *tastes* change, or he gets married or has children, his outlays must of course be adjusted to a new set of wants.

If his *income* rises while his wants remain the same, presumably he will spend more in all major categories and also save more, but the percentage changes will differ. Moreover, he will probably buy absolutely less of certain things. If he now thinks he can afford butter, he will buy less oleomargarine. If he can afford more meat, he will buy less macaroni.

If both his wants and his income stay the same but shifts occur in the *relative prices* of goods, his outlays will also be affected. In the case of goods whose prices fall, he will commonly buy more units or units of better quality. This is the typical responsiveness to price discussed in the preceding chapter. His buying will also change in the case of some goods whose prices stay the same. If butter becomes more expensive, he may buy more margarine at an unchanged price. These goods are substitutes. If green fees for playing golf are reduced, he may buy golf clubs, though their price has not changed. Playing privileges and clubs and balls are jointly demanded.

Are consumers rational?

Do actual consumers behave even remotely in the manner of the rational consumer whose behavior we have been describing? In an approximate fashion, and with great differences among individuals, they probably do. Fortunately it is not necessary to concentrate literally on equalizing marginal utilities. Nor is it even necessary, in debating whether to spend a dollar for one purpose, to compare this purpose with a thousand others that might also claim the dollar. Indeed to make such comparisons would involve such an expenditure of time and effort that superior decisions would hardly be worth the trouble they would require. Rationality, it has been said, can be carried to such lengths as to become irrational.

Probably most of us make reasonably good comparisons implicitly in a rather simple way. As described above, we come to acquire a certain feeling for the value of a dollar to us, in view of the number of dollars we have to use. The more dollars we have, the less important each one is. A little more technically, we may say that the marginal utility of income reflects the marginal utility of dollars spent along all the various lines of expenditure. Thus, with such a sense of the value of the dollar, it is only necessary for the consumer to decide that a particular good is, or is not, worth its price to him, and he is, in effect, comparing it in a rough way with all the alternative goods for which the same money might be used. Through experience, we probably come closer to the goal of rationality than we realize.

At the same time, we should not infer that people get nearly all the benefit they should from the money they have to spend. Indeed, consumer spending is one of the areas in the operation of the economy where great loss of well-being takes place, as judged by what seems possible. Two principal weaknesses seem to be present in consumer behavior, which together account for what has come to be called the *consumer problem.*

One weakness is that people are often *poor judges of their own wants* and do not foresee clearly the extent and the quality of the satisfaction that various purchases will yield. The other is that they are commonly *poor judges of the goods they buy,* and thus their money does not bring them as satisfying products as it could. We shall consider briefly each of these aspects of the consumer problem and note the character of leading efforts to deal with it.

The consumer's judgment of his wants

To say that consumers are human is to say that they will be impulsive in some degree in their spending. They will be governed by the desire of the moment and will have many occasions to wish that they had bought differently. Only a paternalistic control that approached omniscience could offset this weakness. However, if such control were possible, most people would prefer their mistakes to being told what was good for them.

But the institutions of capitalism, it is sometimes charged, have a demoralizing effect on the tastes of consumers. People are unduly concerned with surface gratifications, and the things they are led to want are not the things that prove most deeply satisfying. Modern selling methods and advertising are particularly attacked. The drumming of advertisers is seen as stimulating a futile race with the Joneses and as inducing people to buy, not for positive satisfaction, but to escape artificially created dissatisfactions—through not possessing this or that, or suspecting suggested ailments, or offending in some darkly pictured fashion. People become absorbed, it is said, in a passing panorama of gadgets.

The charge goes further and says that the economy no longer serves genuine human wants but manufactures the wants it chooses to serve. Goods are produced and people are made to buy them. They are not produced because people want them. This charge implies almost a complete reversal of ends and means in the organization of economic life.

Viewed in this light, the consumer problem is broad and fundamental, but the factors in it are imponderable and purely in the realm of opinion. Modern selling certainly has its pernicious, as well as its socially useful, features. Certainly it has power over the minds of people. But despite advertising and related features of capitalism, it is arguable that twentieth-century life in the United States, in its essentials, is pretty much like other significant examples of human living, past and present. It is arguable that the broad channels of human desire are determined, as always, by the physiological needs of people and by their deep craving for comfort, adornment, recreation, and social approval and that they are influenced only in the specific manner of fulfillment within these channels. Even here, selling effort may largely cancel out and experience have the larger say.

But if it seems that social institutions do affect human desires fundamentally, one should remember that a society has other institutions beside the economic. The school, the church, and the home have a responsibility also for the character of people's tastes. Certainly potent voices should speak from these other quarters if the razzle-dazzle of modern selling is to be held in place.

The consumer's knowledge of goods

People may or may not know their wants or want what they should, but in any case they must also know goods if their buying is to be effective. Business enterprises, in purchasing materials and supplies, employ specialists in buying. The federal government relies on the Bureau of Standards to establish correct specifications and test the products it buys. But the ordinary consumer is an amateur in his purchasing; he suffers, and the whole economy suffers, for his mistakes.

The difficulties he faces are great. His purchases are numerous, and he buys so little of any one thing that extensive study of it does not seem worth while. Many of the products he must consider are technically complex. Few consumers have the training to judge competently, in all their significant aspects, the cars, radios, refrigerators, cameras, or even the clothes and food and furniture that they buy. Quality factors are often so elusive that price comparisons are nearly futile.

For each product the buyer is bombarded with the conflicting claims of rival sellers. Much that is asserted is exaggerated, and little is accurately and usefully descriptive. Sometimes there is positive misrepresentation. Often items that carry a given label or trademark vary in quality, so that appraisals arrived at are not of continuing validity. Weights, measures, containers, descriptions may not be standardized and may, in fact, be intended to mislead. Producers find it to their advantage to magnify small differences in products and play up inconsequential merits. Blind buying is fostered on the basis of trade names without comparison as to quality or price, and discriminating judgment is discouraged.

Despite the genuine services often rendered in the selling of goods, there is no question that all of these difficulties confront the consumer in the purchase of many products. What are the *consequences?* If the buyer is unable to judge accurately the characteristics of goods, the purchases he makes will not fit his desires as closely as they should. If he cannot appraise quality in relation to price, his wants will be satisfied less fully than his earning power makes possible.

Moreover, if he cannot judge goods well, he cannot exert the pressure he should on producers—pressure on which the working of a free economy depends. If his price-quality judgments are inaccurate, he cannot reward efficient producers as they should be rewarded and impose suitable penalties on the inefficient. He cannot play his part in making competition an effective force in preventing overcharging and in promoting progress. With some exaggeration, perhaps, but with essential truth, a leading economist has declared: "The fact that consumer buying is largely done by amateurs is undoubtedly the greatest source of industrial waste today." [4]

Reform in the consumer field

Wherever the economic system reveals defects, we naturally ask what remedies are available and what have been tried. Since the main weakness here lies in the consumer's inability to buy wisely, the obvious approach is through increasing his knowledge, training his judgment, and eliminating unnecessary sources of error. Reform in this field, in so far as it seeks merely to enable the consumer to buy more intelligently, is as mild in principle as any reform can be, as devoid of radical qualities. It is elementary, in the theory of a freely organized economy, that buyers and sellers must act on the basis of informed judgments if the system is to work effectively.

It might seem, then, that measures to improve judgment and prevent mistakes, while still leaving producers completely free to produce and to quote prices as they please, would be accepted as readily as any economic reform. In fact, however, the opposition has often been intense. Because of the nature of selling methods, the attitudes of advertisers, their influence with the press, it has been difficult to enact simple requirements of truth-telling to govern the presentation of goods to the public. The opponents of very mild reforms have damned them as socialistic and as destructive of the very institutions they are plainly designed to improve.[5]

[4] Sumner H. Slichter, *Modern Economic Society,* Henry Holt, 1931, p. 542.

[5] An interesting example is the effort of the Office of Price Administration during the war to require the standardized grading and labeling of certain products as a means of preventing concealed price advances through quality deterioration. Such grading may often be impracticable, because of the nature of products, but the opposition, which led to ad-

Nevertheless, over a long period a good deal has been accomplished. Without examining details, we may note that the federal Pure Food and Drugs legislation forbids the sale of many harmful things in the field of foods, drugs, cosmetics, and curative devices. The Federal Trade Commission has extensive authority over misrepresentation in selling and advertising.[6] Various political jurisdictions have enacted laws governing weights and measures and conduct inspections of scales and pumps.

Nongovernmental organizations, such as the Better Business Bureaus, investigate and attack fraudulent practices. Consumer services, available on a subscription basis, analyze products and give ratings and advice. Excellent books and magazine articles appear that aim at consumer education, and the public schools now recognize the problem. The cooperative movement is in part an organized effort to promote consumer interests. But, on the whole, people are inarticulate in their capacity as consumers. Organized producer interests have much greater influence. The conditions under which consumers exercise their choices in translating money income into real income thus seem open to further improvement.

Market Demand and the Control of Production

As an individual, the consumer does his best to adjust himself to an array of products and prices that he cannot control. But, along with other consumers, he is in a powerful position to influence prices and production. A free economy depends very largely on the composite judgments of individual buyers in controlling its use of productive power.

What is the exact relation of individual choices to the market demand for different goods? Is ordinary market demand a suitable device for a society to rely on in registering its interest in the production of bread, movies, automobiles, and a long list of things?

Market demand and individual choices

Demand was defined in the last chapter as the quantity of a good

verse congressional action, largely followed other lines. One Senator was reported as saying: "If anyone desired to standardize or socialize American business, this plan certainly would afford one of the major methods of approach." A newspaper reporting the Senator said the supporters of the plan "hope and conspire to destroy the traditional system of free enterprise in American business." Such confusion on the part of professed supporters of a free economy is unfortunate. The normal processes of such a system are violated when producers are told what and how they can produce and what prices they can charge, but to ask them to state instructively what they are selling is merely to promote the knowledge assumed in the theory of free markets.

[6] The Federal Trade Commission will be discussed in Chapter 23.

that buyers stand ready to take during a period at a particular price —or the series of quantities at a series of prices. Thus the amount of a good that will be bought at any price is simply the sum of the amounts that individuals will buy. It is the summation of such individual attitudes and judgments that is presented in a demand schedule or a demand curve.

But the nature of market demand is not fully revealed by describing it as a simple summation of individual demands. It should be regarded as the reflection of innumerable comparisons of products and prices. Each individual decision to buy a good at a particular price implies the rejection of many alternative ways of using the money involved, including saving it. Thus the market demand for each good rests on a maze of preferences and choices involving many other goods. The demands for goods which guide their production should be thought of as having this extremely complex basis in the comparative choices of individuals.

Merits and deficiencies of this type of control

The import of such a scheme of control is easily lost on people accustomed to it, as Americans are. To appreciate it, they must contrast it, in their imaginations, with a collectivist system of centrally planned production and assignment of products or with an extension of wartime controls.

Certainly heavy reliance on market demand to guide production reflects a view of society as essentially an aggregate of individuals. Moreover, it affirms a belief that individuals are generally the best judges of their interests. There may be dreams as to how resources could be used for the greater glory of the nation, but the market ignores them. Critics may deplore the tastes of the people and long to impose a superior conception of what is good for them, but the market declares the people's tastes.

Certainly, if individual desires are to govern, a demand resting on individual choices seems the only feasible guide. The point was made earlier that no council of planners could adequately take account of individual preferences, but one senses its force only after examining the complex basis of demand in individual choices and comparisons. Only through pressure of individual buying can production really be channeled in accordance with individual preferences. Only through individual buying can products be selected for consumption in accordance with individual tastes. The market, it has often been said, is a democratic arrangement by which people vote with their dollars to guide the use of resources and of products. It should be added that in the market the will of the majority never nullifies minority preferences, which are recognized to the full extent of their dollar support.

The market, moreover, provides a scheme of control unburdened by a heavy overhead of bureaucratic administration. This is what we mean when we call it "automatic." It is a control, furthermore, that operates without the irritating compulsion of authority. In their buying and in their producing and selling, people make their decisions freely on the basis of market facts.

Inequality in the market. In one respect, control through the market has been viewed as undemocratic and unfair. Individuals may influence the market to the extent of their dollar vote, but the dollars available to vote with are more numerous in the hands of some individuals than of others. Thus the $1,000,000 spent by the rich man for a yacht speaks as powerfully in commanding productive services as a like sum spent by thousands of poor families for shoes.

While this is a criticism of control through markets in a free economy, it is not a criticism of the particular feature of that control which we are considering now. It is a criticism instead of the unequal division of income, arising from unequal payments for productive services and the unequal distribution of wealth. Whatever the sharing of income, that sharing is meaningless unless people can go into markets and buy goods with the money they get.

Thus the remedy for this condition—if it should be corrected—must come through changing the distribution of income. But if such a change should come, it would still be as desirable as before to guide the production and use of goods through a market demand that reflects the preferences of individuals. There are leading socialists—persons who would do away with property incomes altogether—who would retain the scheme of market control we are discussing here.

Collective wants. However individualistic a society is, there are collective interests that must in some way be recognized. Thus control cannot be carried out altogether through market demands based on individual preferences. There must be provision for national defense, internal order, education, care of defectives, and for such other purposes as, in the collective judgment, are not met through the response of producers to individual buying. Here government must step in as the collective buyer, and an important area of activity results that is known as the *public economy,* in which appear the problems of *public finance.*[7]

Probably, also, collective judgments will call in other cases for

---

[7] The public economy and public finance will be the topic of Chapter 31.

some modification of the control through markets. Thus the consensus may be that individuals choose to consume too much liquor, and certain restrictions are accordingly imposed. Or it may be decided that the country should have a larger merchant marine than shippers will support, and a public subsidy is voted.[8]

But in a society with the tradition of economic freedom, a prejudice exists against such intrusions of authority, and the burden of proof is on those who propose them. About the only time this prejudice gives way noticeably is during a major war, when, with more or less grace, the citizenry accept sweeping controls over markets to release resources for war purposes.

Review Questions

1. "Statistics reveal certain patterns of consumer spending, but these patterns do not help the individual consumer in spending his money." Develop both clauses.

2. How would you state the goal of the consumer in spending his money income?

3. "The cost of a good to the user is fundamentally the alternative benefit he foregoes when he buys it." Explain.

4. "Even a small income will yield most satisfaction when spread over quite a wide variety of goods." Apply the principle of diminishing utility to this statement.

5. "The importance to us of one dollar's worth of a good or of one dollar of income depends on the marginal utility of the quantity we have." Explain.

6. "To the extent that we equalize the marginal returns from our expenditures in different directions, we shall avoid spending money for the wrong purposes." Explain.

7. "With a rising income, the consumer spends more to satisfy particular wants, but he may spend less for specific goods." Explain.

8. In what different ways may an individual's purchases of one good be affected by the changing prices of other goods?

9. "If the consumer has a sound sense of the value of a dollar to him, he unconsciously compares each prospective purchase with all the possible alternative purchases."

10. "Too largely we are led to buy things not because of any positive satisfaction we hope to derive but to avoid the dissatisfaction of not having them." Develop and evaluate this point.

11. Describe the difficulties faced by the consumer in judging the goods he buys.

12. If the consumer does not select goods effectively, what economic losses result to him and to the economy?

[8] Subsidies will be discussed in the following chapter.

13. Indicate the nature of the reforms that have been introduced in the field of consumption. Do you have an opinion regarding any of them? Do they seem adequate?

14. "In adjusting production to the demands for different goods, producers are necessarily recognizing the social interest in having them produced." What is the nature of the "society" that market demand represents? Explain the relation of market demand to individual preferences.

15. What are the main advantages in a country such as the United States in depending mainly on the demands for different goods to guide the allocation of productive resources? Do they seem to be substantial advantages?

16. "Market demand is a faulty basis of controlling production because demand depends on having money as well as on having wants." Evaluate this criticism.

17. "Even the most individualistic society cannot base its use of resources altogether on individual preferences." Explain, with examples.

Demand Elasticity, Prices, and Economic Adjustments

For produced goods, probably the main controlling function of markets is in causing producers to follow the preferences of buyers. But for all goods, whether produced or not, the rate of purchase and use must be adjusted to the quantities available. This is the problem of *rationing,* in the broad sense of that term. In a free economy, rationing is accomplished typically through price changes, in conjunction with elasticity of demand, although rationing through government authority may be resorted to in emergencies, especially in war periods. The responses of buyers to price changes differ a good deal from one product to another, and these differences bear on the problem of monopoly and on other public problems. The aspect of economic control that will be discussed here has a vital place in the smooth functioning of the economy.

Rationing in a free economy

Rationing in some way is a universal and continuing necessity in any society. If goods are economic, they are scarce; if they are scarce, consumers cannot have all they want of them—all they would take, that is, if their price were zero. Perhaps for such goods as bread little restriction of use is necessary in normal times in the United States, though much is needed in India or in postwar Europe. But for good clothes, for attractive homes and furnishings, for cars and travel, a severe limitation is everywhere required. The wants of most people must remain only partly satisfied, if satisfied at all. Because these scarcities change constantly as tastes and output change, a responsive, flexible control is necessary.

Rationing through prices, and through the reaction of buyers to price changes, is simple in principle. It is only necessary that the principle of supply and demand should have a chance to operate. The needed adjustment is accomplished for any good when its price reaches the level at which there is enough of it, but no more than enough, for the buyers who are willing to pay that price. Such an adjustment is ordinarily possible. Since, for any good, the price can go high enough to stop all buying, it can certainly impose a sufficient limitation on the purchase of the good. Likewise, except in rare instances of miscalculated output, the price can go low enough to bring full utilization of the supply.[9]

This rationing through price adjustments operates more strikingly in some situations than in others. It is least apparent in the case of *continuously produced goods*. When producers, as in most manufacturing and merchandising, are constantly adjusting the flow of products to the changing demands of buyers, there is little need of price changes to adjust buying to the flow of goods. But even here the purchase and use of goods is necessarily being controlled. Produced goods cannot be free, and consumers cannot have all they want. Prices must be high enough to make production worth while, and consumption is limited to the quantities that buyers will pay those prices to get.

Rationing through price adjustments has its most decisive role in the case of goods that are not produced at all and exist in a *fixed stock*. This is the case of land, old paintings, and similar goods discussed in the last chapter. With no adjustment from the supply side, the use of such goods is controlled entirely through having the price reach the point at which every interested person has as much as is worth the price to him, and no one has more.

An interesting situation, in the case of produced goods, is that of *products that appear jointly in fixed proportions* from a single productive process. When cotton is grown, cotton fiber and cotton seed emerge together, but their destinies in the market are quite different. The fiber is used for textiles and the seed for oil and other purposes. The proportion in which the fiber and seed appear when cotton is

[9] The most cited exception is that of fruit which is sometimes allowed to rot on trees. Here the significant point is that the product is only partly produced, and the price is not high enough to cover the additional cost of picking, packing, transporting, and marketing. Exceptions also appear when attention is shifted from the pricing of particular goods to the pricing of goods in general. In a depression it cannot be expected that a general lowering of all prices will lead directly to the absorption of a capacity output.

grown have been determined by nature without consulting human desires for these unlike products. There is no possibility of adapting their production separately to the needs of unrelated markets. Similarly, in designing the beef animal with a certain square footage of potential leather and certain proportions of rib roast, round steak, and soup bone, nature did not think in market terms. But despite the lack of adjustment on the supply side, the purchase and use of joint products are easily adjusted to the relative amounts that become available. When their prices are properly related, joint products are used in the uncontrolled proportions in which they appear.

Another interesting, and a very important, case is that of *products that are not produced continuously* but appear seasonally, as wheat and corn do. While their production is periodic, their use is continuous, and thus there is a special problem of adjusting the rate of use between crops. The large stock available right after the harvest might seriously depress the price of such products. If this occurred, they would be used at a rate that could not be maintained, and a shortage would appear before the next harvest. Meanwhile the price would move from a low point to a high point. Such a course of events is to be avoided, if possible. It would cause uncertainties and embarrassments on the part of millers and other producers who depend on these farm products. It would reduce the benefit that consumers derive from them, because, on the basis of the principle of diminishing utility, the satisfaction from the larger consumption early in the intercrop period would not equal the satisfaction lost later in the period of the resulting shortage.

It is here that anticipatory buying, holding, and selling of a speculative nature play their part in the operation of markets. It is here that *organized speculation* in produce, as conducted on the Chicago Board of Trade, has a substantial economic function. Such a market is the focus of innumerable transactions carried on in light of the size of existing stocks, the expected rate of use, the crop prospects throughout the world. It registers the composite judgment of growers, storers, and millers, as well as of professional speculators who are supposedly most expert in judging future conditions. Since no one sells early in such a market who expects future prices to exceed present prices by more than the cost of holding, the tendency is for prices to rise very little between crops and for the rate of use to be correspondingly uniform.

The speculative markets may not always perform their function well, and they are subject to speculative abuses just as the securities exchanges are, but it is undeniable that the anticipatory dealings which converge on them have a necessary role in controlling the use of periodically produced goods.[10]

The selectivity of rationing through prices. As price changes adjust the use of goods, where does the impact fall? Whose buying is expanded; whose curtailed? In what way, if any, is general economic welfare involved?

Several factors are present in the responsiveness of buyers to prices and affect the elasticity of demand. If, for instance, the quantity of a good increases and its price falls, the expanded buying that results is a composite of several elements. There is (1) the initial buying of people who care less for the good than others do and think it worth the price only when it can be bought cheaply. There is (2) the initial buying of persons of low income who, however great their desire for the good, could not afford it until the price fell. There is (3) the additional buying of persons to whom additional units of smaller added utility appear to be worth the price when the price has fallen. If the price of a good rises, buying is likely to be diminished through the reverse operation of each of these factors.

When a good must be more closely rationed because of a reduced supply, some loss of economic welfare must result, but the loss is not so great as the reduction in quantity. If persons with only a mild desire for the good do not buy it, their sacrifice is small. If persons reduce the quantities they purchase, they will sacrifice only their less important uses of it, and again only a minor decline in well-being results. The greatest hardship is that of persons of low income who want the good intensely and who can no longer buy it when the price has risen.

This hardship is just another phase of the inequality problem commented on above. It arises as an inescapable part of the rationing process in free markets, since in that process the people with more money are free to bid goods away from the people who have less. Thus this situation is ordinarily to be viewed simply as part of the general problem of income distribution and is to be accepted to the extent that inequality is accepted. Only in special circumstances does a free economy see fit to impose a positive, planned rationing of goods.

---

[10] Not only do speculative markets aid in controlling the rate of use of wheat and like products, but, through giving an early focus to market factors, they cause growers to adjust their acreage more quickly than otherwise to the needs of the market. These markets also enable millers, storers, and exporters to "hedge" their holdings against price changes from which they would lose. A hedge is ordinarily a short sale from which there would be a gain if the price fell so as to cause a loss on the stock held for milling and other purposes.

Rationing by public authority

In the United States, governmental rationing has been resorted to only in the face of emergency shortages of essential commodities such as arise in time of war. The case for it then has a dual logic.

Pressure develops for authoritative rationing when exceptionally high prices would seriously divert from low-income people the *usual* foods, fuels, and clothing items on which they heavily rely. If there must be curtailment in the use of essential goods, it appears intolerable from the social standpoint to permit the well-to-do to continue consumption at the usual rate through their ability to bid away the limited supply. Thus government establishes (1) price ceilings and (2) machinery to apportion the available quantity.

Pressure for governmental rationing develops also through the need of drastic action to combat price inflation in wartime. The source of inflation, as we saw in Chapter 12, does not lie merely in the special wartime shortages of particular commodities. It lies in the method of war financing, especially the creation of new money through the expansion of bank credit to buy government bonds. When financing is done in this way, it is impossible for prices to reach the equilibrium point called for by the principle of supply and demand, because at any set of prices there are not goods enough to absorb the dollars offered for them. A general price ceiling is therefore established. Authoritative rationing helps to maintain such a ceiling, since, to bid lawfully for goods, buyers must offer ration coupons as well as money.

Whenever automatic rationing is prevented by price ceilings, planned rationing is the alternative to confusion and inequity. A price ceiling means nothing unless it is fixed at a point lower than the point at which demand and supply would be equal. It is fixed, in other words, at a point at which demand exceeds supply, and aggregate purchases must be less than buyers want to make. In this situation, the apportionment of goods may be left to chance. People may queue up, as they often did for candy, cigarettes, and nylon hosiery during the war, and be supplied according to their patience, idle time, and luck. They may depend on the discretion and the favoritism of distributors. But they may prefer to be subjected to an orderly apportionment planned and imposed by government.

For such reasons as these the United States established authoritative rationing for foods, gasoline, and some other consumption items during World War II and applied even more positive controls to industrial materials. Other countries went much farther. But people accustomed to free markets object to having their buying supervised and favor getting rid of such controls when the pressure eases. They object to the great administrative organization necessary to plan and carry out a scheme of price control and rationing. They object to the "black market" which arises from the persistent bidding for goods outside the controls and the unlawful shunting of supplies to the unscrupulous. Apportionment through ordinary market processes is distinctly preferred as the regular method of control.

Differences in elasticity of demand

Certain effects of price changes, in controlling the purchase of goods, depend on how highly responsive buyers are to them. The degree of responsiveness of buyers to prices is what we mean by the elasticity of demand. Goods differ greatly in the elasticity of demand for them, and the same good may differ in elasticity for different price ranges and time periods.

In *comparing elasticities of demand*, a convenient dividing line is known as *unit elasticity*. Demand has unit elasticity when changes in quantities bought just offset changes in prices, so that at all prices the total amount spent for a good is the same. Thus a good has unit elasticity within a certain price range if a reduction in price from $1 to 80 cents causes an increase in purchases from 800,000 to 1,000,000 units annually. At both prices the outlay on the good is $800,000. If the same price reduction increases purchases to 1,200,000 units, raising the outlay to $960,000, the elasticity is said to be greater than unity, or the demand is merely said to be *elastic*. But if the reduction in price from $1 to 80 cents expands buying only to 900,000 units, with the total outlay on the good reduced to $720,000, the demand has an elasticity less than unity and is said to be *inelastic*.[11]

What *characteristics of goods* cause them to differ in elasticity of demand? In what circumstances will only a little less of a good be bought with a given rise in price—or a great deal less? Elasticity depends on a number of factors, which may unite in their effect in a particular case or which may have opposite influences.

Elasticity is affected (1) by the *nature of wants*. Some *wants seem especially insistent*—for such foods as bread or salt or such habit-forming goods as tobacco—and a large rise in price is necessary to

[11] In the present discussion, we shall find it necessary only to distinguish goods of high and low elasticity of demand, but, where useful, elasticity can be measured more precisely by dividing the percentage change in quantity by the percentage change in price. Thus, with a 1-percent change in price, if quantity changes 2 percent, the elasticity is 2; if quantity changes 0.5 percent, the elasticity is 0.5. This measurement can be applied to elasticity of supply as well as of demand.

reduce their consumption appreciably. Thus their demand tends to be inelastic. In contrast, few people probably feel such an urgency in their desire for melons or ice cream that they are but little influenced by prices.

In this connection (2) elasticity is affected by the availability of *substitute products*. The insistent demand must be for a particular commodity, not merely a kind of satisfaction, if demand is to be inelastic. If fairly acceptable substitutes are available, demand becomes elastic. People may insist on spreading some sort of yellow fatty substance on their bread, but the demand for butter is made elastic nevertheless by the presence of oleomargarine.

Elasticity of demand is affected (3) by the *size of the expenditure on a good in relation to the buyer's income*. If the typical outlay is slight, even in comparison with small incomes, a sharp percentage rise in price will probably have little effect on purchases. Thus demand tends to be inelastic for salt and matches. But however necessary people may think an automobile is, it is so costly that many of them must be deterred by a sharp price rise.

In this fact we find a reason why the demand for goods is often more elastic within lower than within higher price ranges. Within the lower ranges many people with small incomes are buying, and prices and price changes loom large to them. Within higher price ranges, most of the buying is likely to be done by people with fairly large incomes, people whose total consumption outlay stays comfortably within the boundaries of their incomes.

Elasticity of demand is affected also by various other characteristics of goods and their uses. If (4) a good has a *variety of uses,* the demand for it is likely to be made more elastic. The demand for wheat, for instance, would probably be quite inelastic but for the fact that, at low prices, its use as feed for livestock is greatly extended. If (5) a good is used mainly in conjunction with other goods, and *accounts for only a small part of the cost of the combination,* the demand for it will be inelastic. Thus a large increase in the price of thread will have little effect on the cost of clothes and hence will not seriously reduce the purchase of clothes or of thread. A reduction of $10 per ton in the price of steel would be substantial, but the resulting reduction in the price of the automobile in which the steel is used would scarcely be noticed and thus would have little effect on the purchase of steel for this purpose.

Elasticity of demand also has a *time aspect* that is important. Immediately, when prices go up, buyers may persist in using the goods to which they are accustomed; presently these goods appear dispensable and substitutes look increasingly acceptable. This higher long-run elasticity is undoubtedly a major element in markets.

Elasticity and price and income changes

Certain features of the behavior of prices and of business receipts, which grow directly out of these differences in the elasticity of demand, throw light on the nature of economic adjustments and on some problems of public importance.

It follows from the nature of elasticity that it has a *stabilizing influence on prices*. The more elastic the demand for a good, the less the price has to change to establish a new equilibrium after a market disturbance. Elasticity, of course, cannot cause a change in price, because it only expresses the responsiveness of buyers to price changes in view of their existing incomes and preferences. But if a change in demand or in supply occurs to cause a price movement, elasticity governs the extent of the movement.

This can be seen graphically. In the accompanying graph the demand for Good *E,* which has an elastic demand, is shown by demand curve D_eD_e. This curve shows relatively large changes in quantity for given changes in price. In contrast, the demand for Good *I,* shown in curve

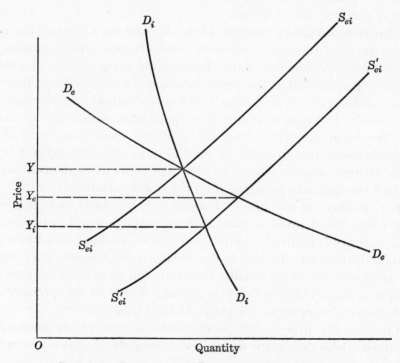

EFFECT OF ELASTICITY OF DEMAND ON PRICE CHANGES

D_iD_i, is inelastic, and quantities change relatively little with given price changes. For simplicity, it is assumed that these two goods have supplies that can be represented identically by the single curve $S_{ei}S_{ei}$. Thus the price for both goods is OY, since it is assumed that supply is equal to demand at the very price at which the two demand curves intersect.

Now an identical increase in supply occurs for the two goods, represented by the new supply curve $S_{ei}^1S_{ei}^1$. As a result, the price falls for both goods, but much more for Good I with the inelastic demand than for Good E with the elastic demand. In the former case, the decline is from OY to OY_i; in the latter from OY to OY_e.

Thus, if the demand for potatoes is inelastic, a fairly small increase in the crop, perhaps an increase of only 10 percent, will cause a large fall in the price, perhaps a fall of 50 percent, because people do not expand their buying of potatoes readily as the price goes down. On the other hand, if the demand for oranges is elastic, an increase in the crop will cause a relatively small fall in price, because buyers will respond readily to a lower price, and a new equilibrium will be reached before the price has fallen very far.

If the disturbing factor is a decrease in supply or either an increase or a decrease in demand, elasticity of demand has the same stabilizing effect on price. We shall have occasion to note later that elasticity of supply exerts a similar influence.

Elasticity and sellers' receipts. If the demand for a product has unit elasticity, gross revenues from sales remain constant, by definition, as prices change. The more elastic the demand for a good is, the more rapidly revenues fall as the price rises, and the more rapidly they increase as the price falls. Similarly, the more inelastic the demand for a good, the faster the revenues from it increase with a rise in price, and the faster they fall with a fall in price. These differences affect fundamentally the attitudes of producers in different fields toward price changes. On the whole, a fairly high elasticity of demand seems to be a fortunate circumstance from the public standpoint.

For instance, in the case of leading *farm products* such as cotton and wheat, the demand is quite inelastic through a wide price range. The industry is naturally competitive, and it is subject to a variety of market disturbances. In view of the inelasticity of demand, when prices go down they are likely to fall a long way, and farm revenues may fall almost as fast. This condition is a major factor in the pressure for governmental support of the prices of farm products.[12]

Likewise the urge to get *monopolistic control* of an industry is strongest where demand is inelastic. A monopoly of such a product as

[12] This policy will be discussed in Chapter 23.

salt is able to push prices up a long way with little decline in volume, and great profits can be exacted from the public. An elastic demand, on the other hand, restrains a monopolist, since sales fall off rapidly as the price is raised.[13] In view of the time element in elasticity mentioned above, it is comforting to have monopolists take a very long-run view of their market.

Flexible prices and the health of the economy

It is obvious that the responsiveness of buyers to prices can play no part in economic adjustments unless prices are allowed to respond to changing market conditions. Governmental controls and the actions of very large firms and of combinations of firms often obstruct the flexibility of prices. This artificial stabilization of prices should be viewed from several angles.

Harmonious adjustments under changing conditions. Flexible prices are an essential part of the mechanism by which a free economy maintains harmony among the constantly shifting demands for different goods and the constantly changing conditions of their production. If the demand for a good increases or its output is curtailed, a higher price is the direct means of economizing its use and should operate prior to any more fundamental reorientation of buying or producing that may presently affect it. Or if demand declines or supply increases, a lower price is the direct means of preventing waste—of making use of the supply and of the resources immediately involved in producing it. Smooth articulation of the parts of a dynamic economy require these adjustments that flexible prices make possible. Buyer responses to prices provide a cushion that absorbs the first impact of change.

Maintenance of general prosperity. But one cannot discuss these matters of allocation, apportionment, and relative adjustment without getting into the question of aggregate production and use of resources. Something was said in Part IV about flexible prices and depressions. The topic is one of the controversial areas in economics.

At the very least, we should be sure not to confuse *price stability* with *general economic stability*. The economy as a whole is stable only when production and employment are stable. Mere price stability often accompanies the most unstable economic conditions. Prices of steel products, for example, have remained almost constant during long periods in which production and employment have ranged from very high to very low.

[13] This statement does not mean that a monopolist will not gain through raising prices above the competitive level if the elasticity of demand exceeds unity. A higher price will reduce his gross receipts, but with smaller volume his costs also fall. Elasticity of demand nevertheless greatly restricts the monopolist's profit possibilities.

Many economists, mainly those who have long been described as orthodox, have regarded this very stability of prices, this artificial stability, as the cause of depressions. Their prescription has been: Let prices fall when there is a weakening of demand, and expanded buying will take up the slack. But the problem is too complex for so simple a solution. One must distinguish (1) the responses to reduced prices in the markets for particular goods and (2) the response when there is a fall in the aggregate demand for goods. In dealing with the latter problem, much emphasis has come to be placed, as we have seen, on the relationship between investment and saving. But one should not conclude that there are no obstacles to general prosperity in distorted and rigid price relations that impede the exchange of goods.

A special difficulty in this connection is suggested by the phrase *"perverse elasticity of demand."* The essence of elasticity, as we have discussed it, is the greater volume of buying at low prices than at high prices. But we have said nothing about the immediate action of buyers *while prices are moving from higher to lower or from lower to higher.* How do buyers react then?

Plainly a buyer does not rush into the market when a price is falling, if he thinks it is going still lower. Instead, he reduces his buying until he thinks the price has reached bottom. For the very reason that he prefers low prices to high prices, he checks his buying when prices start downward. The effect of his action is then to speed the decline. In a similar manner, an upward movement will stimulate buying if it appears that the movement will continue. The increased buying spurs the upward movement.

This response of buyers, not to higher or lower prices but to changing prices, may be temporarily unstabilizing. It is a reason why some economists think that artificial stabilization of prices is not altogether bad from the standpoint of general economic stability.

Flexible prices and progress. In the long run, however, prices must respond to technological progress, if the public is to benefit and the level of living rise. The automobile was first viewed as a luxury product, and early manufacturers, thinking it should continue to be produced on a high-price, low-volume basis, tried to exclude Henry Ford from the industry. But despite patent suits and other obstacles, Ford managed to break in, and his mass-production, low-price policy opened a vast market, with the result during the 1920s that the majority of American families came to own automobiles. The pricing and sale of radios and many other products have followed a similar course. Vision is required to foresee such developments. Ordinarily the safer and more profitable course seems to lie in exploiting the existing market at prices yielding a sure margin of return. But great industries do not develop most certainly and quickly in this way, nor does the economy achieve its final goal of better living.

Review Questions

1. "It grows out of the nature of economic goods that their use must somehow be controlled." Explain what the rationing problem is.

2. What is meant by saying that in a free economy the use of goods is controlled through the combination of flexible prices and elasticity of demand?

3. How do the processes of control differ as between continuously produced goods and those for which the stock is fixed? Show that joint products present an intermediate case.

4. Explain the role of speculative markets in controlling the rate of use of periodically produced goods.

5. "When the use of a good must be more closely rationed because of a reduced supply, the loss to consumers is not likely to be as great as the reduction in quantity." Explain.

6. "The immediate reason for governmental rationing is the fixing of prices below the equilibrium point." Explain, using a graph. What other reasons for rationing lie behind this immediate reason?

7. "Wartime and postwar rent control probably aggravated the housing shortage." What is the reasoning behind this view? Compare the actual rent-control policy with two alternatives: (a) rent control plus planned rationing, (b) no government control at all.

8. If the gross receipts of an industry rise as the price of the product goes up, is the elasticity of demand greater or less than unity? Distinguish graphically an elastic and an inelastic demand.

9. If you were to analyze the difference in elasticity of demand between bread and automobiles, what factors would you take into account? Between automobiles and spark plugs? What other factors affect elasticity of demand in particular situations?

10. "The more elastic the demand for goods, the more stable their prices." Is this correct? Explain, using graph.

11. Why should a monopolist prefer to control a product with an inelastic demand?

12. "Flexible prices are necessary to prevent waste arising from changing supply and demand conditions." Explain.

13. Distinguish price stability and general economic stability. Apply to the steel and wheat industries.

14. "Buyers will take more goods at low prices than at high prices." "Buyers expand their buying when prices move upward." Can both of these statements be true? Explain. Do they suggest the same government policy toward prices in combating cyclical fluctuations?

15. From an advertisement: "Suppose a product is priced to sell at $550. Approximately 5000 people buy it, and total sales are $2,750,000. Now suppose the price of that product can be reduced to $155. Instead of 5000 people, more than *seven hundred times* that number can now afford to purchase it—3,500,000 people. The sales total now goes beyond $542,500,000. As a matter of fact, this is the history of an actual product—the mechanical refrigerator."[14] Put this idea in a general proposition regarding economic progress. Is this proposition so obviously true that we can take it for granted that all industrialists will put it into practice?

[14] From an advertisement of N. W. Ayer & Son, Inc., as it appeared in *Time,* June 9, 1947. This view of pricing is developed extensively by Edwin G. Nourse and Horace B. Drury in the Brookings Institution study, *Industrial Price Policies and Economic Progress,* 1938.

- 20 -

Cost and the Expansion
and Contraction of Industries

Consumers register their preferences as to the use of resources through market demand, but it is directly through the decisions and actions of producers that products become available. In this chapter and the next we shall discuss the supply side of the market—not the immediate offer of goods from existing stocks, as considered in Chapter 18, but the more fundamental adaptation of numerous human and material resources to the demands of buyers and users.

This complicated task of control, which in a managed economy is assumed by the state, is entrusted under capitalism to private businessmen guided only by the markets for products and factors of production. What businessmen aim to achieve, and the circumstances in which they pursue their aims, should be looked into first in approaching the problems of these chapters.

Profits and Producers' Decisions

The behavior of producers, as of consumers, can be understood only through appreciating their aims and the setting in which they act. The producers who concern us here are particularly the people called *businessmen*. The businessman stands at the crossroads in the economic scene, occupying the focal position in responding to the demands for goods and in obtaining and organizing the resources to produce them. We may think of the businessman as an enterpriser, in the strict sense of risking capital and making the final decisions regarding projects, or as a hired executive or official deciding matters of policy in a large enterprise. As we shall think of him, the businessman operates in all fields and in every scale of undertaking. He may be a popcorn vendor, a farmer, a contractor, a mine operator, a manufacturer great or small.

Business aims

The businessman's main goal is said ordinarily to be profit. Whether he owns the firm he manages or acts as an executive on behalf of the owners, he decides most questions with an eye to increasing net income or keeping it from falling. In economics, rational behavior of businessmen is commonly said to consist in running firms so as to *maximize profits*.

From this, as we have already observed, it does not follow that the businessman pursues profit merely as a means of better living. Money-making may be a fascinating game. Great satisfaction may come from the successful control of an undertaking or from building a small or a weak firm into one that is large and strong. The businessman may desire the power, influence, and prestige that accompany business success. But all of these ends are promoted by large profits and usually call for exactly the same business decisions.

Other considerations may qualify the pursuit of profit. Pride in the product may lead to the injection of quality that the buyer may or may not appreciate. Sentiment may lead to the retention of old employees who are not worth their pay. In the interest of workers, a firm may be kept running when, in the interest of stockholders, it might better be shut down. Ideals of decent business behavior may close certain possible short-cuts to profits. Laws may be complied with that could be evaded with fair safety. But none of these factors is likely to cause a large deviation from the profit norm.

Still other considerations may lead the businessman off the direct road to immediate profit but point toward larger or surer *long-term profits*. To maintain sound public relations and foster good will, he must avoid the appearance of overcharging or excessive profit making. Similar restraint may be necessary to forestall heavy wage demands from organized labor or the attraction of new competitors into the industry. Moreover, he must avoid any aspect of profit seeking that is likely to provoke government action and the extension of legal restrictions. Regard for such factors may induce business decisions that seem inconsistent with the pursuit of profit, but which, on the contrary, reflect the most intelligent sort of profit seeking. They may also reflect a mixture of motives, a combination of farsighted profit seeking and a sense of the needs of a sound economy.

Perhaps, for the ensuing analysis, the most serious qualification of the profit norm arises not from any conflict of motives but from sheer *lack of knowledge* on the part of the businessman as to what policy will prove most profitable. When he judges the quantity of a good he can sell at a particular price, he is only making an experienced guess; he is guessing also at the price that competition will permit him to charge. Such uncertainties lead to rule-of-thumb procedures that are sometimes hard to reconcile with the thinking of a perfectly rational profit seeker. Thus, as in the case of the consumer, we find it necessary to distinguish the principles of rational action and the actual behavior sometimes observed in the market place.

Revenue-and-cost decisions

Broadly, the setting of business action is found in the relationships of revenues and costs. To maximize profits, revenues must be made as large as possible in comparison with costs. *Revenues* depend mainly on the elements in demand that we have already considered. They depend on the quantities of particular products that buyers will take and the prices at which buyers will take these quantities. But revenue and cost factors overlap in so far as advertising and other selling costs are incurred to promote sales and greater revenues.

Costs include the ordinary outlays for hired labor, for purchased materials, fuels, and other supplies, for transportation and insurance, for the hire of capital and land, for certain taxes, and the depreciation of facilities. Costs are high or low depending on the prices or rates of payment for these commodities and services. They are also high or low depending on the efficiency with which production is organized and the quantities of resources required for a given output.

One point should be noted in the usage of the term "cost." Ordinarily in economics cost of production is said to include a *necessary return* on the capital supplied by business enterprisers and for the managerial and other labor services supplied by the owners of enterprises. Such a return constitutes what may be called *competitive business profit*. To the businessman, profit is not part of cost; it is something over and above cost. But economics looks at economic situations not from the standpoint of the businessman but from the standpoint of the general public. From the public viewpoint, a necessary payment for the services of enterprisers is as much a part of the cost of goods as a necessary payment for the services of hired labor.

Our analysis of the actions of profit-seeking producers must run largely in terms of the relation of revenues and costs—with costs the chief new element to be studied. But the fact that revenues and costs are approached as elements in the calculations of businessmen does not mean that the analysis applies only to capitalism. The managers of production under state socialism would need also to weigh the values of products to the public and the costs of the resources that go into them and act accordingly. The procedures would differ, but there would need to be no essential difference in principle.

Basic cost and supply situations

The main situations that businessmen face in supplying goods can be classified according to the bearing of production costs on them. But prior to the classification, we must note the manner in which costs affect the supplying and pricing of goods.

No good has value because costs were incurred in producing it. Worth to buyers and users, not cost to producers, is the positive reason for value. Goods are bought for their utility, not their cost. Following the war quantities of costly war supplies were disposed of by the government at their scrap value because they had no peacetime use. Past cost gave them no present value. Various early writers assumed that expenditure of labor gave value to the results of labor, but no amount of labor can give value to a useless result.

Costs govern the pricing and supplying of goods, not because they have been incurred in the past but because they are *a barrier to continuing production*. Businessmen will not devote resources to producing goods that do not promise to be worth as much as the costs that must be incurred in getting them. Thus, in a negative but compelling way, cost becomes a condition of the forthcoming of products and of the prices expected by their producers. With this point in mind, we can appreciate the basic supply situations that businessmen face. Three situations should be distinguished:

1. **Immediate market supply from stock.** The first is already familiar. If the supply of a good is governed by the size of the existing stock rather than by the continuing replenishment of that stock, its supply, for the reason just given, is *not governed by cost of production*. This is necessarily the case with land, old houses, first editions, and other goods that by nature do not continue to be produced. It is also the case with wheat and similar crops between seasons. Whatever their cost may have been, their supply for several months is based on the existing stock, and their price, in a free market, will be such as to clear the market of that stock.

It is the nature of manufactured goods that the output of them can ordinarily be adjusted to the rate at which they are being absorbed. But, immediately, they are being sold from the stocks of merchants and manufacturers, and there are circumstances under which stocks are not closely adjustable to sales. Goods in stock may be out of season or out of style, or they may represent bad judgment on the part of producers. If there is no thought of replenishing the stock, their supply does not depend on the cost of further output; it may be good business judgment to clear them at any price they will bring. On the other hand, it may be impossible for manufacturers to keep up with demand at prices that correspond to cost, and stocks are then disposed of at the higher prices which will ration the supply. Wars create many shortages of this type, although, in wartime, prices may not be allowed to function in this way.

2. Long-run output, or adjustment of capacity. The second situation is that faced by the businessman when he decides whether to enter a certain field of production—whether to clear the land, build the plant, sink the mine shaft, lay the railroad—and, if so, what productive capacity to create. It is also the problem he faces in deciding whether to expand existing projects or to contract them or to terminate them.

These decisions must be governed by the prospect of a revenue sufficient to *cover the full cost of production,* including outlays of every kind and an adequate net return to the owners. All kinds of costs are on the same footing in such a decision. All of them, depending on its outcome, either are incurred or are not incurred.

3. Short-run output, or utilization of capacity. The ordinary decisions of producers, however, do not involve these large matters but only the operation of already existing factories, farms, mines, and stores. Production from existing capacity can vary widely, as more or less labor and materials are used. The output on which the actual supply of produced goods depends is governed by these decisions.

The distinctive thing about them is that, in making them, businessmen need not take account of the full costs of production. Major costs that have already been incurred in establishing plant capacity are not affected by the utilization of that capacity and may be neglected in deciding immediate output policy. If more automobiles can be produced from existing plants, the only additional costs that must be incurred are those involved in a fuller operation of those plants. What prices will actually prevail and what output will be produced are complex questions. The present point is that, in analyzing them, a distinction must be drawn between costs which are fixed and do not vary with the use of capacity and costs which depend directly on that use.

These three situations, with the dissimilar parts played by cost in them, are the basis of the present analysis of supply. The first, into which cost does not enter and on which the principle of supply and demand throws sufficient light for our purposes, has already been discussed. The second, the case of long-run adjustment of capacity, will be considered in the following section of this chapter. The third, the short-run utilization of capacity, will be considered in the following chapter.

Competition and monopoly

Business decisions must be analyzed also with respect to the influence that producers have over the markets in which they sell and buy. Businessmen may have no power over markets and may be concerned solely with adapting their activities to a situation that is outside their control. In other words, they may be in the position of the ordinary consumer who, on the basis of his wants and his income, is adjusting his buying to a market he cannot influence. On the other hand, the businessman may be able to influence the market in some degree because of the extent of his operations, his agreements with other producers, or the uniqueness of his product. Such influence may be large or small. Competition and monopoly, we shall observe more than once, are not two separate, sharply distinguishable market conditions but a range of conditions involving different degrees and types of market control. We shall consider them repeatedly, a little in this chapter, more in the next, and exclusively in the one following.

Prices, Costs, and the Basic Allocation of Resources

Of the long-run and the short-run supply situations just distinguished, the former is more fundamental in the organization of the economy. The general pattern of resource use is governed (1) by the market demands we have already discussed in the preceding chapter and (2) by the decisions of producers, on grounds of revenues and costs, to expand and contract the basic facilities of production in different fields.

On these influences depend broadly the development of farms of different kinds in different areas and the size of the farm population, the investment of capital in different manufacturing lines and the typical working force engaged in them, and similarly the establishment and manning of mines, railroads, wholesale and retail businesses, and other industries and occupations. In all these fields, the *use* of facilities may vary considerably from one time to another. In some instances, on particular farms or in particular factories, shifts may occur in the products produced with particular facilities. But the general arrangement of production is set by the occasional decisions of businessmen which cause the capacity of industries to expand or contract.

The long-run relation of prices and costs

In this central area of economic control there are two related questions: (1) What is the normal basis of the prices of the numerous products among which resources are apportioned? (2) What is the normal basis of the expansion and contraction of industries?

The answer to both of these questions is provided by a principle which ranks with the principle of supply and demand for its importance in economics. It is an exceedingly simple principle, so simple that it was almost brought out in the last section in explaining the way in which cost affects supply. It may be stated by saying that, *under competition, the prices of produced goods tend in the long run to equal their full cost of production, and that industries expand and contract so as to push prices toward that point.*

The logic of this principle rests on the natural behavior of enterprisers who want to make money and who, being unable to dominate the fields they enter, adapt themselves to the market in the most profitable way they can. If a product is selling for more than the cost of producing it, including an acceptable profit, the field is a good one to enter and in which to expand. But the effect of expansion is to increase the supply of the product and to reduce its price down to the level where only a normal profit is realized. In the same way, if the price of a good is below its full cost, producers are led to retire from the field or contract their capacity until an acceptable profit is realized.

This principle is basic to the achievement of general economy in the use of resources. Its effect, in so far as it operates, is to cause each field of production to be developed as long, but only as long, as its product promises to be as valuable as the resources that go into it. The full sense of this statement, it should be said, will not be apparent until we have looked farther into the meaning of cost in the following section.

First, however, this tendency of prices to equal the full costs of production should be interpreted from a number of standpoints. Why have such words as *normal* and *long-run* been emphasized in presenting it? What limitation is implied by saying that it operates *under competition?* What bearing can costs have on the pricing of *jointly produced goods?* What differences are there in the long-run behavior of *costs in different industries?* Each of these questions will now be considered.

Normal versus *actual market adjustments*

When a principle is stated as a tendency, especially a long-run tendency, care is necessary in interpreting it. The normal price of a good, the price at which the long-run tendency points, is not the price one should expect sellers actually to be charging. The normal allocation of resources is not likely to be the actual allocation. Actual market adjustments may be on either side of the norm, and there is no natural, logical relationship between the actual and the normal. The normal would become the actual only if demand and production conditions remained constant long enough for adjustments to them to be complete.

Deviations from the normal are thus due (1) to the frequently changing conditions of a dynamic economy and (2) to the slowness of readjustments to these changes. It is commonplace that demands reflect changing tastes, fashions, and incomes and respond to the appearance of new products. Just as disturbing are innovations in methods of production, developing shortages of some resources, and new discoveries of others. Such changes cause whole industries to rise or fall in profitability and upset the relative positions of particular firms.

Under these conditions, close conformity of prices and production to the long-term norm would require almost instantaneous adjustments. Instead, adjustments are quite slow. Programs of expansion or contraction and major changes in methods are not decided on quickly nor undertaken lightly. Uncertainties are such that abnormal profits, high or low, are discounted as guides to the future, and responses to them are hesitant. Moreover, when changes are decided on, they take time to carry out—months perhaps for expansion and years for contraction—and further disturbances occur before present adjustments are complete. If, furthermore, it should appear that an industry as a whole is in substantial equilibrium—with no tendency to expand or contract on the basis of present prices—one may be sure that great differences exist among the firms in it. For some, revenues will be high in relation to costs, for others, low.

But these deviations from the normal in no way detract from the importance of the long-run tendency we are considering. There is still the pull toward a normal relationship; there are still the stresses and strains from departing from it. Only within limits can prices and industrial capacities defy underlying forces. The occasional decisions of businessmen to expand or contract manufacturing, farming, merchandising, and other facilities still set the general dimensions of industries and the framework within which production must occur. It is to a production thus broadly controlled that actual prices and profits are related. Thus it is a mistake to think of long-run relationships merely as something which might be attained through waiting a long time under the right conditions. *Long-run forces and short-run interferences with them are all operating simultaneously—now.*

The assumption of competition

To be effective, the normal tendency of price to equal cost depends on the presence of competition. Competition is fully present only when producers are unable to control prices but seek profit entirely through adapting their activities to market-determined prices. A normal competitive price would be one at which, with producers acting in this way, the industry would be in equilibrium, neither expanding nor contracting. Such a price would include a *normal competitive profit,* a profit justifying continuation of present investments but no expansion of them.

Through their size, their concerted action, or the peculiarities of their products, producers commonly exert some degree of control over markets and prices. But for such control to affect seriously the allocation of resources among industries, it must include the *power to keep new producers from starting and the present members of industries from expanding.* The more common deviations from strict competition, as we shall study them, do not go this far. Some degree of power to restrict expansion exists, or may exist, in the public-utility field, in industries based on geographically concentrated natural resources, in industries where mass-production methods are such that new firms, to be efficient, must commence operations on a large scale, and also in some situations in which patents are important. But power of this sort is limited by those very dynamic features of the economy that keep market prices from conforming closely to normal prices. In a fluid situation, new techniques provide new channels for breaking into industries, new products are appearing, often close substitutes for old products, and buyers readily transfer their allegiance from product to product and firm to firm.

To the extent that industries are subject to monopolistic control over entrance and expansion, certain *distortions develop in the economy*: (1) Prices persist above the competitive level, and buyers are overcharged. (2) Since resources are not used in these industries to the extent that they would be under competition, buyers are denied goods they would prefer—at a competitive price—to the additional products of those other industries into which resources are diverted. This is misallocation of resources. (3) Profits are greater than necessary, and the distribution of income is distorted. (4) The range of opportunity is restricted for enterprising businessmen. Most of these points will be developed as we proceed.

Pricing of joint products

In the case of certain products there can be no tendency for prices to equal their particular costs, since their costs are not separable from those of other closely related products. This is the situation of those joint products which were mentioned in the preceding chapter to show the special problem of rationing that they present. When seed and textile

fiber grow together on the same cotton plant, no device of cost accounting can arrive at a separate cost figure for growing fiber and for growing
seed. It is just as impossible to assign the cost of raising cattle specifically
to steaks, pot roasts, soup bones, and hide.

In such cases prices tend to be fixed, and resources allocated, for entire groups of related products. Joint productive operations, like other
activities, expand and contract on the basis of anticipated revenues and
costs. But the particular products within a group bear changing fractions of the total cost as the markets for them shift. Thus, if new uses
bring an increased demand for cotton seed, the price of seed goes up.
The increased revenue from seed makes cotton growing more profitable,
and more cotton is likely to be grown. If more is grown, there is an increased supply not only of seed but also of fiber; and no increase in demand for fiber has been assumed. Thus its price must decline. The rule
for joint products would be, then, that (1) the sum of the prices tends to
cover the aggregate cost, with industries expanding and contracting accordingly, and (2) the prices of the individual products reach the levels
at which their quantities are equal to the demands for them.

The distinctive feature of joint products is the *fixed and uncontrol-
lable proportion* in which they appear. There are innumerable cases of
common costs where this fixity of proportion is not present. Thus several products may be produced in the same factory, and costs connected
with the building itself, with some of the equipment in it, and with
some of the employees are applicable to more than one product. Similarly, a farmer uses the same equipment in cultivating and harvesting a
number of crops. A store handles many items of merchandise. Numerous types of freight are carried by a railroad over the same rails, on the
same train, even in the same car. In these cases certain costs are common
to a group of products.

Does the joint-cost principle apply in these cases? The answer is no.
The principle depends on the presence not only of common costs but of
fixed proportions of products. A factory may be operating at capacity
producing desks and bookcases, but an increase in the demand for desks,
if it leads to plant expansion, does not add to the supply of bookcases.
The decision to expand rests entirely on the price and the cost of desks.
If desks are more profitable than bookcases, the company, instead of expanding the plant, may use more space for desks and less for bookcases,
with an effect on supply quite the opposite of that in the cotton example.

Where the proportions of goods are flexible, cost accountants can assign costs reasonably well for long-run adjustments. But there are likely
to be arbitrary elements in the analysis, and the relation between price

and cost is somewhat less firm for goods that are ordinarily produced together. At least in the short run, in the use of existing capacity, common costs increase the latitude that sellers have in their charges, and the extent to which prices depart from long-run norms.

Cost behavior in different industries

We grow accustomed to certain price relationships among the goods we use. Comparatively, within narrow ranges, we expect to pay about so much for various types of food, clothing, housing, house furnishings, fuels, transportation, personal services, and so on. Certain patterns of consumption develop on the basis of customary prices—patterns of which we are hardly aware unless we observe the dissimilar patterns in other countries or are shocked out of our habits by exceptional shortages.

Apart from temporary disturbances, changes in relative prices arising from basic changes in relative costs of production take place with the passage of time and growth in population and demand. The operation of such changes has probably received more attention from economists than their conclusions justify, but the problem is worth noting briefly. The effect of expanding volume will be distinguished from other influences.

Effect of expansion on cost. It has been traditional to classify industries on a long-run basis as *constant-cost, increasing-cost,* and *decreasing-cost,* depending strictly on the effect on cost of expanding the volume of output or, in other words, of growth in population and in demand.

Two main influences are present. Expansion in some fields may bring *economies of large-scale production,* either the economies of larger plants and firms or the external economies of larger industries.[1] Thus growth of markets may lead to lower costs. On the other hand, expansion may intensify the use of certain resources, especially land, and speed the effect of *diminishing returns.*[2]

Conceivably either, neither, or both of these factors may be present in an industry as it expands. In many manufacturing and public-utility lines, scale of production is an important cost factor, and until the economies of size have been exhausted, these industries may be classified as decreasing-cost. But these economies taper off with growth, and presently the condition is one of constant cost, so far as the effect of expansion is concerned. Under the impact of diminishing returns, agriculture is an increasing-cost industry as more output is sought from the same land and use is made of poorer land. Mining may also reveal increasing

[1] See Chapter 7.
[2] See Chapter 5.

costs, though here the main factor is exhaustion, not diminishing returns, and exhaustion operates whether the rate of production is increased or not. Along these lines, the expansion of demand as population grows can be expected to alter the relative costs and prices of products in different fields.

Long-run supply curves. In Chapter 18, in introducing the nature of supply, it was mentioned that the supply schedule based on the old-houses example is not typical of all supply situations. The reason for that statement is apparent as we examine these long-run supply cases in which costs behave in different ways as volume increases. The differences are shown graphically in the following chart. Only in the case of increasing-cost industries does long-run supply show the same sort of elasticity that we observed in the case of the immediate market supply of goods from existing stocks. A sudden increase of demand in all of

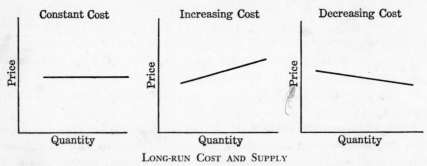

LONG-RUN COST AND SUPPLY

these cases could be expected to send prices up, but if the increased demand brings industrial expansion, cost and supply should presently follow these different lines, as they are pictured, and prices behave accordingly.

Other long-run cost factors. Actually this classification of industries as constant-, increasing-, and decreasing-cost provides a rather poor basis for predicting long-run price changes and industrial patterns. Quite apart from the effect of increases in demand, great changes result from *technological progress,* and these changes occur in all fields of production. In agriculture and mining they may offset, or more than offset, the effect of diminishing returns. Great changes result also, especially in mining, from *discoveries of resources* and from *exhaustion* of known resources—developments which, although perhaps stimulated by an expansion of demand, go on even though demand is constant. The most striking changes in patterns of production and consumption seem likely to result from technological progress and from exhaustion of the better sources of such minerals as petroleum and iron rather than from the factors which underlie the long-run cost curves.

Review Questions

1. "To analyze the actions of businessmen in producing goods and pricing products, it is necessary to know what they are trying to accomplish. Doubtless the best single assumption is that they are trying to run their businesses as profitably as they can." Does this seem a reasonable assumption? If the general aim of businessmen is to maximize profits, does it follow that their behavior in specific situations is readily predictable? Explain.

2. "Because profits depend on revenues and costs, the profit-seeking decisions of businessmen have a key role in promoting economy from the social viewpoint." Explain carefully. If businessmen were not seeking profit but merely aimed at promoting economy in the use of resources, would you expect their decisions to be radically different from what they are? Explain.

3. "In its use in economics, the word *cost* is more comprehensive than in its use in business." Explain.

4. Distinguish the three basic supply situations. Is cost important in all of them? What difference is there in its role in long- and short-run output decisions?

5. Explain the long-run or normal behavior of prices and production. Why is it important?

6. "Normal prices enter the most important decisions that businessmen make, and yet market prices seldom equal them." Explain both clauses.

7. To upset seriously the normal pattern of industrial development, what must be the essential nature of monopolistic control in particular fields? What distortions in economic arrangements result from such control?

8. "If two products are jointly produced, an increase in the demand for one of them tends to reduce the price of the other." Do you agree? Explain. Would the production of spark plugs and batteries in the same factory exemplify this situation? Explain.

9. What is the basis of the classification of industries as constant-, increasing-, and decreasing-cost? What underlying influences explain these differences? What other major factors affect long-run cost relationships and the pattern of industrial development?

Nature and Logic of Cost

To say that prices tend to equal costs is only to say that prices tend to equal prices—the prices of the factors of production. We have assumed that businessmen, in adjusting their activities on the basis of revenues and costs, are promoting general economy as viewed socially. But this assumption is valid only if costs measure what ought to be measured in economizing the use of resources. In raising this question, we are getting to the bottom of the problem of value.

Costs as prices of the factors of production

Below the goods that reach final consumers are layers of costs. Lumber, steel, aluminum, textiles are intermediate products with their own antecedent costs. So also are the buildings, machines, and transport facilities used in production. These intermediate products require materials and equipment to produce them, and again there are antecedent costs.

But, finally, all products can be traced back to factors of production which are not produced in an economic sense. These factors enter the last materials and pieces of equipment, the intermediate products at all stages, the final consumers' goods. They consist in the work that people do, the services of land, with its various qualities, and of capital that is saved and invested. Costs, finally, are the payments for these factors, the wages, the rentals, the interest, and the profits.

All costs, intermediate and final, are fixed by market forces as are other prices. They depend on demand and on supply and on all the influences that enter demand and supply. On the *demand* side, their striking feature is the fact that most resources enter a number of products, perhaps many products. A few do not, for example, coal-bearing land which may be useless except in producing coal. But such materials as steel and lumber enter innumerable goods; such fuels as coal and petroleum are involved in one way or another in producing nearly everything. The ultimate factors, such as common labor, the more general human skills, and uninvested capital, have nearly universal application. Thus the demands for such resources is *a composite of the demands of producers of many different things.*

On the *supply* side, intermediate products are like final products. The industries that produce materials and equipment expand and contract on the basis of revenues and costs. But the ultimate factors of production have no such costs. The costs of labor and saving and risk taking are merely psychological, the reluctance to perform these services. Most important are the natural limitations of supply—in the number of people and the quantities of various natural resources.

Thus, in the case of these ultimate factors which are not produced in the usual sense, values must depend simply on demand and supply—on demand for their services in many uses and on supply, as just stated. The cost principle operates only in the case of products, and the tendency of prices to conform to costs is, after all, only a tendency of prices to conform to values of factors that rest on the principle of supply and demand.

Moreover, it should be noted, the final positive basis of values is in consumers' goods. As we consider products one by one—the food and clothes and houses and cars and other produced goods that we use—it appears, quite correctly, that their prices under competition are adjusted to the costs of producing them. But these costs, the values of factors, depend on demands that derive from all the products into which these factors enter. Factor values depend on product values. Broadly regarded, then, the system of values rests on the desires of consumers and the limited supplies of the ultimate productive resources.

Costs as opportunity costs

The nature of costs should be viewed also in a slightly different way. In discussing consumer choices, we said that the real cost of any good to the consumer is not the amount of money he pays for it but the satisfaction he must forego through not being able to spend this money for other goods. In the same way, the real cost to society of any product is the sacrifice of other products which the same resources could have been used to produce. Factors of production are valuable because of the competing opportunities to use them, and each use of them entails the cost of sacrificing other opportunities of use. It is in this sense of *opportunity cost* that cost of production has its final social meaning.

Just as the consumer, if he is rational, uses his money so that a more important good is never sacrificed for a less important one that costs as much, so a rational use of resources by the whole economy will never allow less important uses to displace more important. It is the function of costs, in the ordinary market sense, to achieve this rational result. This is simply the rationing function, applied to resources, and it operates as in the case of consumers' goods. The numerous purposes for which most factors of production can be used are not equally important or valuable. To obtain a factor for certain purposes, a high price will, if necessary, be paid; for other purposes, a lower price; for still other purposes, a still lower price. Thus a demand schedule is present with quantities responsive to prices in the usual way. The price the market sets cuts out that portion of the demand which would result in actual purchases only at lower prices.

A certain type of lumber may be used for fine furniture, for building construction, or for packing cases. Or, to generalize, let us say that Factor X, which may be most any kind of labor or material, is useful in producing Products A, B, C, D, and so on. At a high price for X, a fair amount of A, a quality product, will be produced, and a little of B, but cost of production is too high for a more extended use. At a lower price for X, more of A, a fair amount of B, and a little of C will be produced; at quite a low price, somewhat more of A, B, and C, and a little of D, a good that serves inferior purposes. Wherever the price of X is, its cost will be high enough to cut out certain potential products altogether and restrict its use for all products, since more units of any of them could be sold at the lower prices which a cheaper X would make possible.

A proper price for X is, of course, a price at which the demand for it is equal to the available supply. Any product, such as D, which can barely be produced and sold at the prevailing cost of X, and would not be if the price were any higher, may be called a *marginal product*. Any units of any product that could not be produced and sold if X were more expensive may be called *marginal units*. As in the case of consumers, when we said that income is spent to best advantage when the marginal utility of outlays for different goods is approximately equal, so we may say now that a productive resource is used to best advantage when units of it have about the same marginal importance in all uses. The logic is the same. Prices of factors so fixed and so followed carry out the principle of opportunity cost.

The whole system of values

The interrelated character of the entire system of values on which the use of resources and products depends is now apparent. This is a good place to be reminded of the unity in economic organization based on markets and prices that was pointed out in Chapter 17.

We have seen that the consumer choices underlying demand reflect comparisons by each consumer of many products. Market demands rest on a myriad of such comparisons. Similarly the costs of the resources that are used in producing different goods reflect the competing demands of numerous competing users of these resources. The price of each product is thus the resultant of interconnections among goods that extend throughout the economy.

Costs, moreover, since they are payments for the services of labor, land, capital, and enterprise, are simply *a way of viewing incomes.* The money that workers and wealth owners have to spend depends directly on these payments. Thus the circle of payments is complete. As suppliers of factor services, people receive incomes which enable them to demand final products, and it is for the production of these products that, directly or indirectly, the factor services are required.

We should observe also that this valuation of productive services, in determining costs that measure incomes, thereby governs the distribution of the national income among the people. It lies at the bottom of the *problem of inequality* which we shall consider in Part VI.

In this broad sketch of the system of values there have been gaps that, in part, will be closed as we proceed. Aspects of the pricing of factors that would merely have confused the present picture can be considered when some use can be made of them in discussing wages and other shares in distribution. Some short-run aspects of cost that we have slipped over will be discussed in the next chapter, together with some further examination of what the assumption of competition implies. Necessarily this discussion has been somewhat abstract and philosophical in tone, as an inquiry into underlying relationships is likely to be. But the philosophy of cost is of great practical importance, as we shall see immediately in considering some of the value judgments that businessmen and consumers are continually making.

The Cost Standard and Public Policy

Business practices and government policies that affect prices and the use of resources concern everyone, and nearly everybody vents his concern in judgments and criticisms. This price, we say, is exorbitant; that one, reasonable; that other, surprisingly low. This public project—this waterway or post office—we assert is a shameful waste of money. That special tax, designed to raise the cost of a certain product, we applaud or deplore, perhaps mainly governed by our particular interest but with a broad rationalization from the public standpoint. In all such judgments, usually without realizing it, we call upon a whole theory of values and of standards in using resources. Literacy in economic thinking requires understanding of the standards used.

What buyers will pay as a test of prices

May not prices be judged without reference to costs? Sometimes it is argued that they can be. A merchant pays $2 for a clock, and, because it is attractive, he puts a price of $10 on it and presently sells it.[3] His mark-up of 400 percent on cost is outrageous; but he argues that the customer is not overcharged since the clock must have been worth $10 to him, else he would not have bought it. What people will pay—"what the traffic will bear"—thus provides its own defense as a basis of pricing.

As so stated, however, it is no basis at all—that is, it provides no standard of reasonable pricing, because, according to it, every price is reasonable at which purchases will be made. The typical demand situation is one in which goods will be bought throughout a wide range of prices—smaller quantities at higher prices, larger quantities at lower

[3] Suggested by a discussion of this point in an article, "They Make Us Gyp 'Em!", by Dane York, *Readers Digest,* January 1934. Cases are cited of mark-ups as high as 2588 percent on imported goods. The author bought a clock for $22 whose "total landed cost" in New York was $1.26. His comment is that the merchant "merely, and cleverly, met my price expectation."

prices. By the standard that a price is all right if people will pay it, any price throughout that range is as reasonable as any other. Plainly value cannot be determined merely by demand; it must rest also on a supply that makes sense from some standpoint.

That standpoint, moreover, cannot be merely the seller's standpoint, if a useful standard for judging values is to be provided. In offering clocks for sale, the merchant is in fact concerned with the quantity he can sell as well as the price he can get. He would like to discover that particular price which, in view both of the margin per unit and the quantity buyers will take, will give him the largest profit. That, at least, is the usual aim of producers and sellers. But adjustments on this basis are acceptable from the public standpoint only if the market imposes suitable restraints. If the seller has much latitude in deciding between higher prices with smaller sales or lower prices with larger sales, the market is not working acceptably. It is defective because of the exceptional ignorance of buyers, as in the clock example, or the absence of competitors who are glad to get business, if necessary, with only an ordinary mark-up. *If markets are competitive and buyers informed, the prices they will pay should ordinarily be regarded as reasonable.* But under these conditions sellers have little latitude for discovering what the traffic will bear. They are pushed instead toward some conception of a normal mark-up. When we look into it, we run at once into cost factors as the real basis of supply.

Cost as a guide

Undoubtedly popular judgments of prices and the use of resources most commonly rest on a cost basis. When the customer says a price is too high, he usually means that he thinks it is too high in relation to cost and that the seller is making too large a profit. When the businessman justifies an advance in his prices, he ordinarily says that his costs have gone up and that he cannot sell at a loss. When the citizen says it is wasteful to spend public money on a certain irrigation scheme or power project, he usually means that the result will not be worth the cost.

It is of great importance that such a theory of the relation of values and costs should be taken for granted and govern everyday thinking. It implies that consumers accept the idea that they are not entitled to goods for which they pay less than the value of the resources required to produce them. This conception is basic to the effective use of resources. It implies, equally, that businessmen are entitled to no more profit than is required to get them to perform the entrepreneurial function. Adherence to this view is the basis of popular opposition to monopoly. Politically it provides the support for those government policies that aim at enforcing competition and at regulating monopoly. But in many connections the popular, common-sense acceptance of the price-cost theory is not adequate. Further understanding of it is necessary if reasonably sound judgments of prices and the use of resources are to be rendered. Interpretations that we have considered in this chapter must enter its application.

Thus the principle is likely to be *misapplied in judging immediate prices and profits* and *profits in particular cases.* It is often overlooked that, under competition, the tendency for prices to equal the *full cost* of production is of a distinctly long-run or normal character. It operates through the occasional decisions of businessmen by which they expand or contract their enterprises. The shifting conditions of demand and production can be expected to make the profits of most businesses most of the time higher or lower than a normal competitive profit. Thus their immediate exceptional profits, positive or negative, need provide no reason for concluding that prices are too high or too low and that something should be done about them.

When the businessman says he is losing money and should get a higher price for his product, perhaps a sounder judgment would be either (1) that under immediate depressed conditions in the market a "normal" price would be far too high or (2) that this particular business-man ought to lose money, since only through imposing losses can markets police the efficiency of producers.

Similarly, when profits are high and businessmen are being condemned for profiteering, the right view may be that the immediate situation calls for more than a normal profit. Perhaps exceptional profits are required to induce needed expansion. Or even when expansion is not justified there may be temporary shortages that, in the absence of government interference, call for high prices to ration the limited supply. Makers of steel and automobiles were enjoying large profits after the war, but their products were being resold by others in the "gray market" for much more than the manufacturers were getting, indicating an immediate market situation in which, by all the principles of free markets, they might reasonably have charged higher prices than they did. In short-run judgments, the tendency of prices to equal costs does not supersede the principle of supply and demand.

The difficulty arises, as we shall see, from the fact that many markets are not free or are only partially free—markets in which government agencies control or large firms have great influence. In these markets a basis of judgment is needed that is immediately applicable to market prices. The relation of prices to the full cost of production is a convenient standard, backed by potent, if not discriminating, popular approval, and it is appealed to even when it is not pertinent.

Our present interest, however, is in the long-run norm itself and in the need of real understanding of it, if it is to be applied properly in many situations. Some of the best examples of this need appear in situations in which government participates in production or acts to alter the costs of private producers.

Costs, when taxpayers assume them

The development of inland water transportation is an interesting case. Waterways, such as the New York Barge Canal, the canalized Ohio River, and the deepened sections of the Mississippi, are constructed and maintained at public expense and provided toll-free to the boat lines that use them. Persons who judge the relative cost of rail and water transportation simply by comparing the rates charged by the railroads and the boat companies are obviously omitting a large element in the cost of water transportation. Water transportation is *subsidized* through the fact that taxpayers meet a substantial fraction of the cost, whereas railroad revenues must cover both the cost of running trains and of providing and maintaining the roadbeds over which they run.

What is not so obvious is what the full cost of water transportation is. This is an important question when government is reaching a decision as to whether it is economical to undertake a projected waterway. The same problem is present when public investment is being considered in highway, water-power, flood-control, irrigation, and other projects. For when government makes investments and causes resources to be used for certain purposes, it is not guided as private business is by the need of foreseeing a revenue from sales sufficient to cover the full cost. There may be no sales, and the taxing and borrowing power of government appears as an inexhaustible source of funds. An honest attempt at economy requires deliberate calculation of the probable value of the results and of the costs that will be entailed. In some divisions of government there has been increasing effort to make such calculations.

One way to get at the costs is simply to ask what outlays the government will have to make. Reduced to an annual basis, such outlays for a waterway would include the costs of dredging and of keeping locks in repair, the interest paid on funds that had been borrowed, and perhaps some spreading of the principal sum over a long term of years. But is this all? If we ask the purpose of the calculation and go back to the nature of cost for guidance, we must say that the real cost of the waterway is as great as any other return, presumably in private industry, that could be obtained from the same resources. This is the principle of opportunity cost, which in private business we expect markets automatically to apply.

When we look at the cost of the waterway from this standpoint, we may amend our calculation. The interest rate of 2 or 3 percent that the government pays is as low as it is, not because the productivity of the waterway is so certain and devoid of risk, but because the vast credit of the government makes the low rate possible. Perhaps the project should be charged with a capital cost of 5 or 6 percent in testing the adequacy of the probable return. Moreover, if the resources were invested in private industry, a substantial tax contribution would have to be made on the basis of them toward the general support of government. The prospective revenue from private use of the resources would have to cover these taxes, and, if government is going to divert the resources to a waterway, presumably its productivity should be great enough to cover them. This is what the principle of opportunity cost implies.

The question then is: If government were to build the waterway and charge tolls for its use sufficient to cover all these costs, with the boat lines adjusting their rates to cover the tolls, would sufficient traffic move in competition with other forms of transportation to make the project worth while? Such a calculation would be reasonably in line with that of the competing private users of resources.[4]

Some waterways doubtless meet this test; others do not. They serve here merely for purposes of illustration. The present object is to see that understanding of the real nature of cost, as discussed in the preceding section, is often necessary if resources are to be allocated economically.

Perhaps the most controversial situation of this kind has been in the electric-power field, in connection with such great hydroelectric projects as those on the Columbia and Tennessee rivers. Government power rates have been lower than private, but private companies have claimed that government rates have not covered all the costs involved. They have noted specifically the low interest rates—artificially low from the standpoint of business risk—at which government obtains funds for these projects and the freedom from the taxes, or a considerable part of the taxes, that private companies must pay. Even with these factors considered, the relative economy of public and private power still remains controversial, but that they are relevant factors seems clear.[5]

[4] But even if government engineers followed this reasoning in judging projects, the railroads would not be satisfied unless tolls were actually charged waterway users. In the absence of explicit charges, the competitive situation is unequal—unequal in the sense that rates do not bear the same relation to actual costs.

[5] Government ownership of public utilities will be discussed briefly in Chapter 23.

Governmental additions to business costs

Thus, through government action, production costs may be borne by taxpayers rather than by the users of products. But government, on the other hand, may act to increase the costs that consumers bear. In doing so (1) it may be making them assume actual costs they would otherwise escape, or (2) it may be imposing an arbitrary burden. This is a basic distinction.

When state governments impose on motor vehicles certain special charges, in the form of license fees and fuel taxes, to pay for highways, the effect is a recognition of actual costs and an avoidance of subsidy. Whether subsidy is completely avoided in this case—an issue debated by railroad and motor-carrier interests—we need not consider, but the principle is clear. These special taxes make the cost of transportation service to the user conform much more closely than it otherwise would to the value of the resources employed in providing it—that is, to cost in the full social sense.

On the other hand, when governments place tariffs on imports to equalize the money costs of production at home and abroad, the imposition is arbitrary. It cancels the gain that comes from international specialization. The tariff is an addition to the costs borne by producers and consumers, not a recognition of neglected costs. Again, our present interest is in the cost principle rather than the merits of the tariff policy.[6]

This same sort of arbitrary addition to money cost appears in the special taxes imposed on the sale of oleomargarine, especially on colored oleomargarine. These taxes represent no failure of the producer to get all the real costs of production into the price of his product but only an effort to handicap him in his competition with producers of butter. The policy violates the principle of open competition in free markets, which requires merely that oleomargarine be labeled for what it is. It can be justified, if at all, only on the ground that butter producers must suffer if consumers choose freely on the basis of actual costs, and that there is special social interest in the prosperity of the butter industry.

Diffused social costs. There are notable instances in which, as in the waterway case, businessmen escape some of the costs involved in their operations but in which the additional costs that society incurs are elusive and perhaps unmanageable. In general, it would still be desirable, if possible, to get these costs into the calculations of the producers and consumers of the particular products, but there is not always a feasible method of doing so.

[6] The policy will be considered in Chapter 32.

A classic example is that of the great expense imposed on the residents of a city by the belching smokestacks of its factories. Laundry bills multiply; clothes wear out more quickly; no doubt human wear and tear increases. Such costs are as truly chargeable to industrial operations as are direct outlays for labor and materials, but the price system does not impose them where they belong. Similar social costs arise from industries that pollute streams or despoil the landscape.

But in some instances costs that appear diffused can be given a money measure and placed on the industry. In a sense this is what has been done in the case of *industrial accidents*. In hazardous occupations serious costs attach to the required medical services, the lost working time, and the destruction of working capacity. Formerly these costs fell almost wholly on the employees involved in accidents. Now, under the system of workmen's compensation, partial coverage is provided on an insurance basis. The direct aim is humanitarian, but in so far as the cost of accidents is made to enter the plans of businessmen and the pricing of goods, it is subjected to the economizing pressures of the market.[7]

A similar cost arises when *labor-saving machines* are introduced, to the extent that a period of unemployment ensues for the displaced workers. Saving labor is socially beneficial only in so far as the saved labor is put to work and a larger total product results. Thus the cost of supporting workers, together with their families, during the period before they are re-employed may reasonably be charged against the machines that displace them. Ideally, this cost should be taken into account by businessmen, along with the cost of the machines, in deciding whether to introduce them. Ordinarily, however, the cost of temporary unemployment does not enter the calculations which govern technological change. It can be made to enter through the device of the *dismissal wage*, a special payment to workers displaced for technical reasons.

The case for subsidies

It is apparent that value-cost relationships may be affected in several ways by public action. Their usefulness as economic guides may be reduced when producers are (1) relieved of valid costs that their activities involve or (2) burdened with arbitrary exactions that have no counterpart in their actual use of resources. But there are situations, on the other hand, when (3) government action is necessary to cause producers to take full account of the costs that, from a social standpoint, they oc-

---

[7] The economizing effect is less if the cost of workmen's compensation causes workmen's wages to be lower instead of increasing the prices of products. The effect is greater, on the other hand, to the extent that the cost to industries and firms is adjusted to their particular accident rates.

casion. Now we must recognize (4) that there are also situations in which the use of resources may be improved by shifting certain costs from producers to taxpayers. These are cases of *justifiable subsidy*.

As the preceding chapter pointed out, the market demand for goods does not always reflect adequately the social interest in having them produced. In extreme instances, such as national defense and common-school education, government itself acts as enterpriser, provides the product, and makes it available without specific charge. In other cases, government subsidizes private production, so that goods can be sold below their full cost and their production thereby encouraged.

Leading examples are found in the transportation field—already drawn on to show the disrupting effect that subsidy may have. Waterways were discussed above from a present-day standpoint, but other considerations applied to their early nineteenth-century development. Railroad builders have received extensive public aid in the United States, both in cash and in land grants.[8] The American merchant marine has been aided through low-interest loans, generous postal payments, and in other ways. Commercial air transport has also received mail subsidies and weather, landing-field, and other aids. Two main reasons for subsidies should be distinguished.

One is the *infant-industry* idea, most often applied to the protective tariff. It may be applied equally well to the use of subsidies—for example, in connection with American railroad development. Building railroads into the West, constructing them before population and traffic developed, was a hazardous undertaking. Early losses were inevitable and forbidding, but it appeared that railroads would pay their way in the course of time. The period of unprofitable operation would be too long for the unassisted private investor, but government, guided by value-cost comparisons for a longer period, could properly act. Thus early subsidization of railroad building seemed justified. Identical reasoning has been applied to air transportation during its developmental period.

The other reason is *political* and *military*. Railroads were necessary to unite the nation and make effective the authority of the government in Washington. The merchant marine is essential as a naval auxiliary in time of war. Commercial air transport is closely related to military aviation, as a continuing reason for plane manufacture, pilot training, and research.

On such grounds as these it is sometimes desirable for government to assume a part of the cost of private production. But if markets are to

---

[8] The land-grant railroads were obligated to carry government freight at less than the established rates. Undoubtedly the early subsidies have been repaid.

remain effective as means of economic control, subsidies should not be used lightly. To justify them, it is not enough to show that society as a whole has an interest in certain lines of production, in addition to the interest of the individual users of products. Such a case could be made for a great many products: a number of industries perform education services, and many of them are essential to national defense. The *compelling reason for subsidy*, however, is not merely the social interest but the fact that, without subsidy, the industry will not develop to the extent that the social interest requires. With most industries, it is enough to accept the social benefits as welcome by-products of private production.

Costs under unemployment conditions. Economizing the use of resources implies, of course, that resources are scarce. No real problem of economy arises unless the use of a resource or product for one purpose precludes the realization of some other purpose. Basically the cost of any product is the value of other products foregone, and the role of money costs, in promoting economy, is in compelling producers to take full account of the interest of the public in other possible uses of resources.

What, then, is the cost situation during a depression when extensive unemployment prevails and the pressing problem is to put resources to work? Money costs remain substantial, even for factors whose supply exceeds demand at those costs; such are the inflexibilities in markets. But real costs, in the opportunity sense, must be negligible for factors whose alternative is idleness. Their immediate use must involve almost no social cost.

It is on this ground that a nation is justified, during a depression, in using resources for projects whose value is less than their money cost. If a dam or post office or highway or some less impressive leaf-raking, brush-clearing, or ground-smoothing project is achieved with otherwise idle resources, society gains through whatever serviceability the result has. The money cost may be high, but the real cost involves only such materials and equipment as would have other use. Critics of work-relief projects may have a point when they stress the difficulties of raising funds for such purposes. This is another case of shifting costs to the taxpayer. But the critics have no point if they imply that there is any real economic waste—in so far as idle resources are put to work.

Even the financial objection largely fades if the workers thus employed would have been on relief in any case. If the public is supporting them anyway, hardly anyone will question the desirability of getting some return. But the real point is not financial: it is that the use of otherwise idle labor involves no cost in the fundamental sense. Thus in bad times the public can afford undertakings that in good times it cannot afford.

In making this point, we are classifying costs. We are observing that, from the social standpoint, the support of people at some minimum level is a fixed public obligation. Cost is incurred whether there is product or not. Thus we are employing in a broad social setting the distinction between fixed and variable costs that is basic in planning the short-run use of particular shops and stores and mines. This is the problem to which we turn in the following chapter.

Review Questions

1. "Costs, in last analysis, are values of factors of production that, in an economic sense, are not produced. Thus these values depend simply on supply and demand." Explain both sentences. What is meant by saying that the demand for factors is composite?

2. "Costs must be viewed as opportunity costs in order to appreciate why they guide producers in a way that is acceptable from the social standpoint." Explain carefully.

3. In the first chapter of Part V a diagram was used (page 452) to give a preliminary view of the system of values on which economic organization rests. Turn to that diagram and point out the relationships, since studied, that it covers.

4. "What buyers are willing to pay provides the best test of what prices ought to be." Show (a) that this test may be no test at all or (b) that it may justify monopolistic extortion. But show, also, that prices may be above or below the full cost of production and still be reasonable by the standards of a free economy.

5. "Popular reliance on costs in judging economic behavior, even if undiscriminating, is of fundamental importance." Why?

6. Distinguish, with examples, the following types of government action in their bearing on the use of resources: (a) harmful shifting of costs to taxpayers; (b) imposing on productive activities costs that they actually occasion but tend to escape; (c) imposing on productive activities arbitrary additions to cost; (d) justifiable subsidy.

7. How does unemployment affect opportunity costs? Apply to expenditures on public works.

- 21 -

Output from
Existing Capacity

 THE capacity of an industry, we have seen, is slow in expanding and contracting. The use of that capacity, however, can change quickly and over a wide range. It is on the use of capacity, of course, that the supply of products directly depends.[1] Large quantities of resources are used in establishing the fixed facilities of production, the farms, factories, mines, railroads, and so on, but even larger quantities are used in operating these facilities. Thus a considerable part of the problem of economy in the use of resources is a short-run problem. And, similarly, the factors directly governing prices and profits are short-run factors. It needs only to be remembered, as the preceding chapter emphasized, that expansion and contraction of facilities provide the setting in which immediate decisions are made.

It is in using their facilities and marketing their products that firms, together or separately, mainly employ the stratagems that profit seeking often involves. Products are given distinctive features to attract customers; agreements are made with competitors to maintain prices or restrict output; pressure is brought on government to permit, or even to support, schemes of market control. The roots of various public issues will be uncovered in this chapter, but with discussion of them postponed to succeeding chapters.

In discussing the use of productive facilities, it is best to transfer our attention to the particular plant or firm and only incidentally to consider industries or the whole economy. The main thing to remember in analyzing the operation of the firm is that the necessary outlays have already been made in providing the buildings and equipment used in

[1] Most directly, as we have seen, supply is from existing stocks. But we are not concerned in this chapter with the errors or temporary shortages that may cause a separation of market supply from the short-run output of goods.

various industries and in clearing land, laying rails, and sinking mine shafts. Our first task in this chapter then, is to examine the behavior of costs when some costs are fixed. When that is done, we can consider how rational and informed profit seekers pursue their ends under conditions of competition and monopoly, as neatly defined. Finally, it will be necessary to recognize that actual businessmen, doing the best they can with imperfect information under prevailing market institutions, present a picture that no simple theory can adequately describe.

Behavior of Costs in Utilization of Capacity

How do fixed and variable costs behave as fuller use is made of existing facilities? What is the resulting effect on cost of production per unit of product? These questions, and related terms, will concern us first.

Fixed costs

Strictly speaking, a fixed cost is one that, in the aggregate, remains unchanged as volume of output expands and contracts. In practice, it is a cost that is relatively inflexible.

It is most commonly a cost connected with buildings, equipment, and land—that is, with the facilities of an enterprise which determine its productive capacity. Bond interest, property insurance, and property taxes provide perfect examples. Depreciation, when calculated as is customary on a time basis, is a fixed cost. Since, in economics, the term "cost" includes the value of all the productive services that must be covered in getting goods produced, a normal return on the owner's investment should commonly be regarded as a fixed cost.

When a cost is fixed in the aggregate, it must get smaller per unit of product as output expands. (Throughout this discussion one must remain alert to the distinction between *aggregate* and *unit,* or *average,* costs.) Not only does fixed cost per unit decline, but it declines at a changing rate—at first sharply and then more gradually but never ceasing to fall a little. Let us suppose that Firm X, a manufacturing business, incurs fixed costs of $500 daily for property taxes, depreciation, return on investment, and similar items. Then, for a daily output of 100, fixed cost per unit is $5; for 200 units, $2.50; for 300 units, $1.67, but for 1300, 1400, and 1500 units the figures are, respectively, 38.5 cents, 35.7 cents, and 33.3 cents. The characteristic behavior of fixed costs is shown graphically in the chart on page 534.

Fixed costs thus become a declining fraction of total costs as output expands. Variable costs, because they increase in the aggregate with a larger output, become a growing fraction of total costs. The fixed costs of an enterprise are much more impressive when it is operating well below capacity than when operating at a high level.

Variable costs

Variable costs involve resources whose use responds readily to the volume of production. In manufacturing the chief variable costs are for labor and materials directly involved in manufacturing processes. In farming, such labor as is hired and the purchase of seeds and fertilizers give rise to variable costs. In mining the main variable cost is the use of labor in extracting minerals.

The chief feature of the behavior of variable costs is that, while they are responsive to volume, they do not vary in the aggregate in perfect proportion to the volume of output. Doubling output is not likely exactly to double them. This is equivalent to saying that they do not remain on a constant per-unit level. In the early stages of using plant facilities, they fall per unit of output; in the later stages, they rise.

Thus, Firm X, we shall assume, was built to produce from 1200 to 1500 units daily. If it is producing only 100 units daily, its outlay for direct labor and materials is $100, or $1 per unit. For 200 units the corresponding figures are $190 and 95 cents, for 300 units, $275 and 91⅔ cents. Thus there is a decline in *variable unit costs*. The main reason for the decline lies in the fact that with a very small output, specialized workers cannot be kept busy at particular tasks, so that dexterity is sacrificed and time is lost in shifting from one job to another. With expanding output, therefore, efficiency improves and cost per unit falls.

Along with aggregate and average costs, we must be acquainted with one other cost concept, namely, *marginal costs*—and this is a good point to insert it. With the first 100 units requiring an outlay for labor and materials of $100, and the first 200 units an outlay of $190, the additional outlay for the second 100 units is $90. If we are thinking of batches of 100 units, we may say that the marginal cost of 2 batches— the added cost from producing the last batch—is $90. Or, thinking of single units of the product, we may say that, when 200 units are produced, the marginal cost is 90 cents.[2] For 3 batches, the marginal cost is $85, and the marginal cost of 300 units is 85 cents. As long as the marginal cost is below the average cost, the average must fall, since the additional units are pulling it down.

Perhaps, when 300 units are being produced daily, the needed degree of specialization has been reached, and greater output does not reduce

---

[2] For simplicity we shall ignore the probability that marginal cost is changing within each batch of 100 units—perhaps from 92 cents to 88 cents as output expands from 101 to 200 daily.

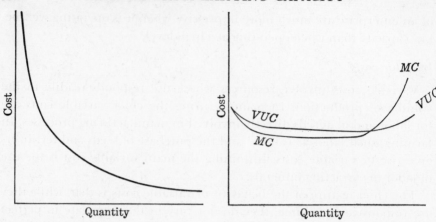

FIXED COST PER UNIT OF OUTPUT   VARIABLE UNIT COST AND MARGINAL COST

marginal cost. Expansion merely means that more specialized workers and more machines are brought into use. Marginal cost, we shall assume, remains at 85 cents until 1000 units daily are being produced. Variable unit cost meanwhile falls to 87 cents. At this point, however, some pressure begins to be felt on the capacity of the available facilities. Further output requires the hiring of more labor than can be used to best advantage with existing space and equipment. Confusion and wastage result, and disproportionate wear and tear accompanied by interruptions to keep the equipment in order. This result must inevitably occur, else productive capacity would have no meaning. If costs did not rise when a certain point has been reached in the expansion of output, increasing demand could be met without limit from existing plants, and additional capacity would never need to be created. In this case, let us say that an eleventh batch of 100 units daily adds to cost at the rate of 90 cents, and additional batches, up to 1500 units, at rates, respectively, of 98 cents, $1.10, $1.27, and $1.55, as pressure on facilities is felt with increasing severity. These, of course, are marginal costs. Variable units costs, with these successive additions above 1000 units daily, moves from 87 cents to 87.3 cents, 88.2 cents, 89.8 cents, 92.5 cents, and finally 96.7 cents. The two curves in the second part of the accompanying chart show, accordingly, the behavior of marginal and variable unit costs. Marginal cost necessarily equals variable unit cost at the point where the latter is at the minimum.

Total unit cost and related concepts

On the basis of this behavior of fixed costs and variable costs, one can see at once how the full cost per unit of output, called *total unit cost*, must behave. Fixed costs per unit go on declining as output expands,

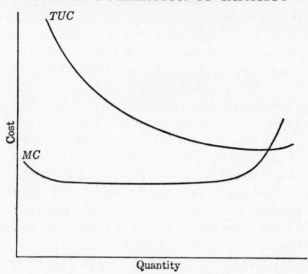

Cost

TUC

MC

Quantity

MARGINAL AND TOTAL UNIT COST

but at a diminishing rate. Variable unit costs fall and later rise. Presently their advance more than offsets the decline in fixed unit cost, and total unit cost, which has been falling, must go up.

In the example used, the product is obtained at lowest cost when about 1400 units are produced. This is the *least cost point*. It can be seen if we compare the situations for 1300, 1400, and 1500 units:

Units produced	Fixed unit cost	Variable unit cost	Total unit cost	Marginal cost
1300	38.5¢	89.8¢	$1.283	$1.10
1400	35.7¢	92.5¢	1.282	1.27
1500	33.3¢	96.7¢	1.30	1.55

For 1400 units the marginal cost of $1.27 has risen to a point where it is approximately equal to the total unit cost of $1.282. If the volume of output corresponding to the least-cost point were more exactly determined, marginal cost would be exactly equal to total unit cost for that volume. In the accompanying chart the curve for total unit cost (*TUC*) combines the fixed and variable costs for each volume of output. The marginal cost curve is repeated from the chart on page 534.

It was said above that Firm X constructed its plant to produce from 1200 to 1500 units daily. When a plant is built, its capacity is planned to enable it to produce reasonably close to minimum cost with the estimated volume of output. It was planning of this sort that was assumed in the preceding chapter in discussing the expansion and contraction of industries. Of course, some latitude should be allowed for growth in business without being compelled immediately to undertake new construction. But if profits are to be close to the maximum, capacity should be planned so that the most probable volume will be forth-coming at a cost close to the minimum—1400 units at $1.282 in this example.

The term "efficiency." This consideration of total unit cost suggests certain comments regarding the use of the term "efficiency," a much used word that we have employed frequently without definition. Greatest efficiency is achieved in operating a plant when output is at the least-cost point. When several factors of production are used together, efficiency is governed not by the output from any one of them but from all of them together. For Firm X, 1400 units does not represent the best result either from labor and materials or from plant and equipment, but it is the best for the combination of all of them.

Thus efficiency is necessarily a value concept. For one factor of production, efficiency may be measured in physical units, as when we say that one motor yields more power than another per gallon of gasoline. But if the former motor is more costly to manufacture, we should not say that it is more efficient unless our comparison takes account of the resources used in making motors as well as the gasoline used in running them. All should be economized. But there is no significant common measure of labor, materials, and fuel except in value terms.

Thus the volume of output at which a plant is most efficient is likely to shift as changes occur in the relative prices of the different factors of production. If wage rates rise for direct labor, it is more important to get a high output per worker, so that, for Firm X, the least-cost volume moves back toward 1000 units daily, where variable unit cost is lowest. If wage rates fall, it becomes more important to spread the fixed costs thinly, and an output in excess of 1400 units may represent the highest efficiency.

The term "capacity." This is also a suitable point to comment on the use of the word "capacity." Capacity may imply definite physical limitations, as when we speak of the capacity of a 12-quart pail. But for complex facilities such as a factory, a store, or a railroad, such a physical limit is difficult to define; in any case it is likely not to be significant. Before the last possible bit of output has been obtained from the fixed facilities, total unit cost is likely to have become so high as to be prohibitive. Production at capacity in such a physical sense would be definitely uneconomic.

Thus the word capacity is more usefully employed in economics when it is used to designate the output for which a plant is designed, the output at which the unit cost will be lowest. The concept in this sense recognizes that output from direct labor is important as well as output from fixed facilities. In this sense, which is the one adopted for present use, output may often rise considerably above the capacity of a plant. It does so through incurring the penalty of higher total unit cost.

Fixed versus variable costs—further aspects

To sharpen this discussion, the distinction between fixed and variable costs has been stated more simply than the facts warrant. The simple distinction will be adequate in most connections, but three modifications of it should be recognized:

1. Costs do not fall neatly into two categories: the absolutely fixed and the perfectly variable. Some lie in between. These include such items as administrative overhead, maintenance labor, fuel and power. Thus it is unrealistic to say of a firm, for example, that half of its costs are fixed and half are variable. But if, with a 20-percent decline in its output, and with particular costs falling from zero to 20 percent, aggregate costs fall by 10 percent, it is *as if* half of the costs were fixed and half were variable. We should bear this point in mind when we use examples that separate costs with simplifying sharpness.

2. Costs which are fixed for small changes in output may become variable with larger changes or changes continuing over longer periods. In the railroad industry, day-to-day fluctuations in traffic may be handled with the same trains and the same station employees. Somewhat larger and more protracted fluctuations, as in the seasonal handling of wheat in the grain belt, cause substantial changes in train and station operations and costs. Still larger and more permanent variations in traffic require changes in the fixed facilities of a railroad, as in double-tracking it.[3] In the long-run problem of expanding and contracting productive capacity, as discussed in the preceding chapter, all costs become variable. The relation between fixed and variable costs has been simplified by distinguishing the long-run problem somewhat too sharply from the problem of the present chapter.

3. Fixed costs may or may not involve a fixed obligation to pay out money. Such costs as interest on bonds and premiums on fire insurance require cash payments; costs such as depreciation of plant and the value of the service of owners' capital do not. The latter, as much as the former, represent continued use of resources as output falls off, but only the fixed costs involving cash outlays cause immediate financial embarrassment when business contracts. It should be noted also, in the case of such items as the services of executives, that there may be no re-

[3] This example is developed in an outstanding study of fixed costs: J. Maurice Clark, *Studies in the Economics of Overhead Cost,* University of Chicago Press, 1923, Ch. 13.

lease of the particular resource as output declines, but a salary cut can achieve the same result from a business standpoint.

These qualifications of the distinction between fixed and variable costs free it of the arbitrary character its simpler statement possesses. But they need not complicate the ensuing discussion.

Review Questions

1. "Variations in the immediate output of goods involve sharply different behavior on the part of different classes of costs." Explain. Why is the word "immediate" inserted?

2. "On a per-unit basis, fixed costs are highly variable, and variable costs are relatively stable." Name the leading costs of each type and explain the statement.

3. Why is variable unit cost not absolutely stable as output changes? Explain the behavior of variable unit cost when output is very small and when it is large in relation to capacity.

4. What is marginal cost? How is it related to variable unit cost?

5. Explain total unit cost and its behavior as output is expanded. What is the least-cost point? How is it related to marginal cost?

6. Explain why efficiency is regarded in economics as a value concept. If direct labor becomes less costly, what is the effect on the point of greatest efficiency in operating a plant?

7. "When plant capacity is defined in the economic sense, it approximates the volume of output hoped for when the plant was built." Explain.

8. One writer has said that two thirds of the costs of railroad transportation are fixed and one third variable. How might you state this idea without implying that costs fall into two sharply separate categories? Can fixed costs remain fixed and continue to constitute two thirds of all costs as traffic varies? Might this statement be truer of some changes in traffic than of others?

9. "Fixed costs are painful as business declines, but all fixed costs are not equally painful." Explain.

The Most Profitable Use of Capacity

If costs behave in the manner just described, what are the guides to business policy in operating existing factories, farms, stores, and like facilities? What considerations govern the volume of output? How are prices determined?

In this section these questions will be discussed within the framework of certain simplifying assumptions. It will be assumed that businessmen are concerned with maximizing profits in a more direct and responsive manner than in fact they are. It will be assumed that they are more completely informed regarding prospective revenues and costs than they can possibly be. While pursuit of profit both under competitive and monopolistic conditions will be considered, these conditions will be stated in a way that does not reflect the perplexing variety of actual markets.

The immediate aim is not so much to describe actual business be- havior as to set forth the logic of adjustments to changing revenues and costs. As in other chapters in this series, the purpose here is not only to convey a picture of the working of markets under capitalism but to develop principles that apply also to other systems and that further a critical understanding of our system. The conclusions reached here will be adapted more closely in the following section to the conditions of actual markets.

The meaning of profit maximization

In using existing plant facilities, maximizing profit must not be con- fused (1) with minimizing costs nor (2) with getting the largest profit per unit of product. The problem, both from the standpoint of the businessman and the Utopian administrator, is to make total revenues as large as possible in comparison with total costs. This should be obvious, but is sometimes forgotten.

We have just seen that for a given plant, with given prices for the variable factors, some particular output will reduce total unit cost to a minimum. We have seen that this is, roughly, the output that is con- templated when the plant is built. But once the plant is built, the most profitable output, or the least unprofitable, may be well below the least- cost volume or well above it. It will *depend on revenues as well as costs* —on prices and the quantities that buyers will take at various prices. Changes in demand are mainly responsible for changes in the use of capacity.

Not only do profits depend on revenues as well as costs, but they can- not be judged by the relation between per-unit revenues and per-unit costs. A firm may have a profit of $1 per unit of output when it is pro- ducing 10,000 units a month, but a unit profit of 90 cents is plainly preferable if the corresponding output is 12,000 monthly. The objective is neither the largest profit per unit nor the largest output that will be profitable but a combination of volume and unit profit that will yield the largest total return on the investment. This same general aim —of making the total value of the product as great as possible in rela- tion to the total cost—should govern from the social, as well as from the business, viewpoint. But from the social standpoint, the business result may be objectionable under monopoly conditions.

Competitive and monopolistic conceptions of revenue

Costs per unit of output vary with volume. Do unit revenues also vary as a firm alters the extent of its operations—that is, does the individual firm get the same price, however much it sells? The answer depends on whether the position of the firm is competitive or monopolistic. By definition, a condition of *pure competition* prevails when the individual firm has no appreciable influence on the price of its product—not enough influence to affect business decisions. Conversely, *some degree of monopoly* is present when the contrary condition prevails.[4]

One should hasten to say that this technical use of the word "monopoly" is not the one in everyday use. Monopoly in the present sense does not imply a great corporation dominating a market. There are deviations from pure competition, and thus some degree of monopoly, in situations that fall clearly within the ordinary conception of competitive industry. The reason for this technical usage—which unquestionably has its unfortunate aspects—is that the decisions of producers are the same *in principle* whether a small degree of monopoly prevails or a much higher degree. There is simply a difference in the latitude within which the monopoly principle is applied.

The case of pure competition is perhaps best exemplified by the wheat farmer, prior to the Agricultural Adjustment Act, who merely tried to adjust his acreage and his purchase of seed, fertilizer, and labor as profitably as he could to an anticipated price that he could not hope to affect. Except that he was not so well informed as he might wish to be, his market possessed the main features of the ideal market described in Chapter 18: (1) he was producing a fairly standardized product; (2) he was one of a large number of similar producers, each small in relation to the market; (3) he reached his decisions independently, not through collusive agreement with other producers in his field. The demand for wheat, as seen by all wheat producers together, is quite inelastic; price responds sharply to changes in output. But to the individual producer, it is as if the demand were elastic in the highest possible degree. He can double his output, or cut it in two, and dispose of it at a market price that, so far as he can tell, is not affected at all. In planning his production, he must estimate what the market price will be, but his decision is uncomplicated by any effect he can have on it.

---

[4] Competition and monopoly are distinguished here on the basis of the seller's side of the market. There may also be departures from competition in the purchase of goods, especially in the purchase by businessmen of the factors of production. Except for incidental references, we shall not consider this possibility until we examine the labor market and the fixing of wages.

Some degree of monopoly appears when any one of these three features of pure competition is absent. (1) The product, as with furniture and automobiles, may be so unstandardized that the products of competing producers are quite different, or consumers may be persuaded that one brand is substantially different from another. Thus the competition among firms is not so close as pure competition requires. This situation has come to be referred to as *product differentiation,* and the phrase *monopolistic competition* is commonly used with reference to it. (2) Whether or not the product is standardized, the number of firms in the industry, as in such fields as steel and automobiles, may be so small that each firm must take account of its impact on the market in considering its output policy. This situation has come to be called *oligopoly.* (3) Some sort of *combination* or *agreement* may exist among the firms in an industry. The making of decisions is thus deliberately transferred from the individual firm to a group large enough to exercise substantial control.

In all these monopolistic cases the particular business decision is made in light of the fact that the quantity to be produced and the price to be received are interdependent. With the unique product, the few firms, or the agreement among competitors, there is some latitude within which a choice can be made between selling more units at a lower price or selling fewer units at a higher price. Thus, as the businessman sees it, *revenue per unit varies with volume,* and this variation must be considered along with the variation in cost in deciding what policy to pursue in using existing facilities.

This does not mean that sales prospects appear to the individual firm as they would to a single great monopolist dominating an industry. The demand that such a single monopolist considers is the entire market demand, with whatever general responsiveness to prices buyers display. To the producer in a partially monopolistic situation, power to influence the price is likely to appear much less. It is as if demand to him were quite elastic, but not perfectly so. To obtain a slightly higher price, a considerable decline in sales must be accepted, and a considerable expansion is possible with a slightly lower price.

This, at least, is what one would expect in situations that lie between pure competition and complete monopoly. Actually, however, these intermediate cases may behave in a variety of ways—ways that, for the moment, need not detain us. We are now concerned with the monopoly principle itself, whatever the degree of its application. We are interested in the fact that the producer must associate different prices with different volumes in deciding his course of action.

Aggregate versus *marginal comparisons of revenues and costs*

The best profit-and-loss situation is achieved when total revenues exceed total costs by the largest possible amount or costs exceed revenues by the smallest possible amount. The problem is to combine the output, cost, and price factors so as to achieve this result.

One way to proceed is simply to *compare the probable aggregate revenues and costs* for corresponding quantities of product through a sufficient range of output and pick the most promising. On the revenue side, the strictly competitive producer merely estimates the market price and assumes that whatever he produces will be disposed of at that price. The monopolistic producer must arrive at his probable revenue by estimating the quantities that can be disposed of at different prices. On the supply side, all producers must estimate aggregate costs for different volumes of output, recognizing variations in unit costs.[5] By comparing aggregate revenues and costs, the best level of operations is discovered.

Another procedure, which avoids all consideration of aggregate quantities, is through *comparison of marginal revenues and costs.* The firm that is already operating—already producing a certain quantity with certain revenues and costs—need not consider a wide range of alternatives. Its problem is merely that of deciding where to go from where it is. It may expand its operations, contract them, or continue them at the present level. All that it needs to consider in such a decision is the relation between the change in revenues and the change in costs. If expanding adds more to revenues than to costs, it should expand; and it should keep on expanding as long as this situation holds. By following this procedure, it will arrive at the most profitable volume of output— exactly the same result as if aggregate revenues were compared with aggregate costs for all possible volumes. Similarly, if contracting is indicated, it should continue reducing its operations as long as the reduction in costs exceeds the reduction in revenues. Again, the best scale of operations will be found.

The difference in revenue from producing a unit more or less is known in economics as the *marginal revenue.* The difference in cost from producing a unit more or less is known as the *marginal cost.* The word "marginal" conveys the same meaning as in the earlier discussion of marginal utility. *Greatest profit is obtained when operations are expanded or contracted up to the limit where marginal revenue just covers*

[5] There is no essential difference in the calculation whether (*a*) aggregate revenue is compared with aggregate cost or (*b*) revenue and cost are compared on a per-unit or average basis. The important contrast is between aggregate, or average, comparisons on the one hand, and marginal comparisons on the other.

marginal cost. This principle, like the principle of supply and demand and the long-run tendency of price to equal the full cost of production, sums up one of the basic relationships in economics.

Its importance does not depend on whether businessmen think in marginal or in aggregate terms. They may think either way, as the next section will show more fully. Nor does its importance arise mainly from the need of understanding how profits are maximized, though that is its present use. It is primarily a useful tool in analyzing the economic use of resources. At the point at which marginal revenue just covers marginal cost, the value of products is greatest in comparison with the value of the resources used in producing them—a relationship that spells economy under appropriate market conditions.

Illustration of marginal principle under pure competition

The difference between pure competition and monopoly can be stated sharply with a hypothetical example. The present Firm *Y* differs from the earlier Firm *X* in that its product is a larger, more valuable unit, and we have knowledge of cost differences by single units as output varies, not merely by batches of units. Moreover, to have unit costs fall and rise in the characteristic way without lengthening the example unduly, we shall telescope the stages of expansion and have marginal costs start rising right after they stop falling. As before, it is assumed that fixed and variable costs are neatly separable, and a $500 daily fixed cost is assumed that includes a normal profit of $100.

TABLE 24—COST VARIATION IN FIRM *Y*

1. Output per day	2. Fixed cost, aggregate	3. Fixed cost per unit of output	4. Variable cost, aggregate	5. Variable cost per unit of output	6. Total cost, aggregate	7. Total cost per unit of output	8. Marginal cost
1	$500	$500.0	$ 145	$145.0	$ 645	$645.0	
2	500	250.0	284	142.0	784	392.0	$139
3	500	166.7	420	140.0	920	306.7	136
4	500	125.0	556	139.0	1056	264.0	136
5	500	100.0	694	138.8	1194	238.8	138
6	500	83.3	835	139.2	1335	222.5	141
7	500	71.4	980	140.0	1480	211.4	145
8	500	62.5	1131	141.4	1631	203.9	151
9	500	55.6	1301	144.6	1801	200.1	170
10	500	50.0	1500	150.0	2000	200.0	199
11	500	45.5	1740	158.2	2240	203.6	240
12	500	41.7	2040	170.0	2540	211.7	300

It appears that total unit cost is lowest at $200, when 10 units are produced daily. At this point marginal cost approximates total unit cost. This is the planned capacity of the enterprise, in the economic sense. Producing 10 units daily and selling at a price of $200, Firm Y exemplifies the long-run competitive equilibrium. If they anticipate any other relationship of price and cost that seems likely to continue, new firms will be drawn into the industry or old firms will drop out. In actual conditions, no firm can expect to be in this position very often, and in no industry will all firms be in this position simultaneously.

If Firm Y is in a purely competitive position, how much will it produce? Since it is able to sell its entire output without affecting the market price, the prevailing market price will govern its revenue, whatever output it decides on. Let us assume that that price is $250. By the aggregate method, we could compute the revenue of Firm Y for each possible output and compare the results, ranging from $250 to $3000 daily for quantities from 1 to 12, with the aggregate costs as given in Column 6. We would conclude that profit would be greatest with a daily output of 11—$510 in excess of the normal profit of $100.

By the marginal method we could have reached the same conclusion by just glancing at the table. *Under pure competition, marginal revenue must be equal to the price.* Each added unit will add to revenue an amount equal to the market price. It is with an output of 11 units, then, that the price of $250 comes closest to just covering the marginal cost, which for that quantity is $240.

Why, with a price of $250, should not a twelfth unit be produced, since the average cost of 12 units is only $211.70? The answer, of course, is that a twelfth unit, while adding $250 to revenue, would add $300 to cost, and producing it would reduce the daily profit by $50.[6]

[6] The relation of marginal revenue and cost under competition can be stated graphically. To the curves for marginal cost (*MC*) and total unit cost (*TUC*) from the chart on page

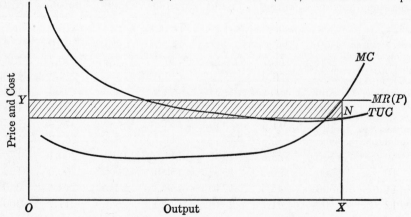

Producing at a loss. Similarly, if the price were $165, the daily output would be 8 units. Marginal cost for 8 units is $151 and is covered by the price. For 9 units marginal cost is $170 and is not covered. Producing 8 units, Firm Y is losing money, $211 daily. Total revenue is $1320 and total cost (now excluding the normal profit of $100) is $1531. But this loss is smaller than would be sustained with a price of $165 and any other volume of output, including no output at all. With a complete shutdown, the daily loss would be $400—the fixed cost without the profit element. We may conclude, then, that both for profitable and unprofitable operation, the best scale of output can be ascertained without considering fixed costs at all. Increase them or reduce them, and the choice of output is not affected.

At first glance, it may seem foolish to go on producing at a loss. Certainly it would be foolish to embark on a new project whose revenues do not promise to cover the full costs of production. But the important thing about *going concerns* is that the fixed costs have already been incurred—are, in a sense, *"sunk"*—so that production is justified *if revenues more than cover the variable costs* and thus earn some part of the fixed costs. We have seen that this situation was so general during the worst years of the 1930s that American corporations on the average were "in the red." It is the situation of many relatively inefficient firms even in prosperous years.

Indeed, a firm may be justified in continuing to operate *temporarily* even though its variable costs are not entirely covered—the costs it could escape by shutting down. It may be wise in incurring additional losses as a sort of investment in keeping itself in shape to operate effectively when prosperity returns. There are two reasons: (1) If it shuts down completely, it loses its market connections. Regaining customers,

---

535, we need only add a line (MR) to represent marginal revenue. In the case of pure competition, MR is a horizontal line at the level of the price (P), which is equal to OY. The price assumed is high, well above TUC at capacity, and is comparable to a price of $250 for Firm Y. The intersection of MR and MC, according to the marginal principle, fixes the output at OX. Total revenue, the product of price and quantity, is shown by a rectangle with dimensions OY and OX. For quantity OX, the TUC is NX. Since a price equal to NX would yield a normal profit for this quantity, the shaded portion of the rectangle represents profit in excess of normal. It will be observed that, if MR and MC are to intersect at any point below the economic capacity of the firm, they necessarily intersect at a price insufficient to yield a normal profit.

Some students of economics are assisted by graphical explanations of this type; others are not. The graph is useful, of course, only in so far as it speeds and improves understanding of the idea presented. It is not an end in itself. Thus nothing is gained here merely by seeing that the graph does, in fact, embody the marginal principle. Graphs are used considerably in the more advanced study of economics, especially in advanced theory; but for persons whose interest in economics is not professional, they may easily divert attention from the object of study. Since the marginal principle may be seen clearly from a simple example, this graph is given footnote status.

once they have slipped away, may be more costly than the immediately avoidable losses it incurs. (2) If it shuts down, its operating organization falls apart and key men drift away. Thus, again, some additional present loss may seem worth incurring. Firm Y, in this situation, might keep going, for example, even though the price of its product were only $137. At no level of output can it cover its variable costs while selling at this price; but with 4 units produced, the revenue of $548 falls only a little short of the variable costs of $556.

Even with no prospect of profitable operation, a firm may keep operating for a long time because a slow liquidation is its least painful alternative. If it liquidates at once, it may get only scrap value for much of its equipment and nothing at all for such investments as have been made in mine shafts and railroad grading. If it keeps operating, its revenue may cover not only its current outlays but enough of its depreciation so that more of its capital can be recovered in this way.

It is the fact, as we saw above, that fixed costs like depreciation involve no cash outlay that enables losing firms to remain solvent over long periods. Bankruptcy occurs only when firms cannot pay their debts. But even with bankruptcy, many firms keep going, perhaps indefinitely, through undergoing *financial reorganization*. In the process of reorganization, fixed obligations are scaled down, with stocks ordinarily substituted for bonds in the capital structure, so that solvency can be maintained on a new basis. Many great corporations, including most American railroads, have been reorganized at one time or another. From the operating standpoint, they may go on much as before.

Under *pure competition*, it will be observed, *a firm operating below capacity in the economic sense cannot be making a normal profit* and is probably incurring a loss, since marginal cost is as large as total unit cost only when output is at capacity or above. Thus profitable operation under pure competition requires a vigorous demand for the product. Firms that operate profitably below capacity must have some control over the market—some degree of monopoly in the present broad sense of that term.

The pricing of competitive output. We have been looking at the relation of output, price, and cost from the standpoint of an individual firm, such as Y. For a moment, let us turn our attention to the entire market in which Firm Y sells its product and ask where the price comes from to which it adjusts its operations.

If a strictly competitive firm expands output as long as price covers marginal cost, we have in this fact the basis for explaining the market supply of competitively produced goods. At any price, a firm will supply that quantity whose marginal cost is just covered by that price. At

$250, for instance, Firm Y will supply 11 units daily, for which the marginal cost is $240; at $200, 10 units; at $175, 9 units; and so on. Firm Y has numerous competitors, and they all contribute in this same way to the total quantity of the product forthcoming at different prices. If we make the simple assumption that Firm Y is a thousandth part of its industry, a skeleton supply schedule for the product is easily constructed. Then if we assume an appropriate demand schedule, the market situation appears as follows:

Demand	Price	Supply
6,500 units	$250	11,000 units
8,000 units	225	10,500 units
10,000 units	200	10,000 units
13,000 units	175	9,000 units
16,000 units	160	8,300 units
19,000 units	150	7,500 units

In this situation, a price of $200 meets the conditions of the market, in accordance with the principle of supply and demand. It is a price to which each competing producer adjusts his operations. Along with all other producers and all buyers, he is responsible for this price. But, since he is in a strictly competitive position, his influence is too small to consider as he decides how much to produce.

It happens, at a price of $200, that Firm Y is just making a normal profit. Other firms, more or less efficient than Y, are making more or less than a normal profit. A price of $200, in other words, is below the total unit cost of some of them, above it for others. But for all of them $200 is not far from the marginal cost of their output, since each firm expands output until marginal cost is just covered.

While Firm Y exemplifies the equilibrium position already defined, we cannot say that the whole industry is in equilibrium. Firms that have introduced the latest methods may be making exceptional profits. If so, we can expect that new firms will enter and that the industry will expand and the price of the product fall. In that event, if Firm Y does not improve its methods, it will presently lose money.

The marginal principle with some degree of monopoly

Departures from pure competition are of various types, and producers behave in different ways under them. However, in considering the essence of monopoly, the essential fact is that the producer must recognize that the amount he sells and the price he gets are interdependent. To have greater volume, he must be satisfied with a somewhat smaller price. To get a higher price, he must be content with smaller volume.

Like the competitive firm, the monopolistic producer maximizes his profit by expanding or contracting his operations until marginal revenue just covers marginal cost. The difference is that, in this case, the marginal revenue is not equal to the price of the product. It is less than the price.

If larger sales are obtained at a lower price, that lower price applies presumably not only to the additional units sold, but to all the units.[7] Thus the revenue from the added units, governed directly by the price, is partly offset by the smaller return from units previously produced. If the direction is reversed and a higher price combined with a smaller output, the same relation holds. The loss of revenue from the smaller output is partly offset by the higher price.

To use Firm Y to illustrate this situation, we must assume what its sales expectations are at different prices. As a starting point, let us say that it can sell 10 units daily at $200 but that at higher prices it must be content with sales that decline as the accompanying table shows. The aggregate revenues corresponding to these prices and quantities appear in the second column, and the successive differences, the marginal revenues, in the third column. To permit application of the marginal principle, the marginal cost of each of these amounts is repeated, in the fourth column, from the earlier table.

TABLE 25—FIRM Y AS A MONOPOLY

1. Sales expectations	2. Aggregate revenue	3. Marginal revenue	4. Marginal cost
6 units at $232	$1392		
7 units at $224	1568	$176	$145
8 units at $216	1728	160	151
9 units at $208	1872	144	170
10 units at $200	2000	128	199

Cast in its earlier role as a strictly competitive firm, Firm Y produces 10 units daily with a price of $200. That price covers the marginal cost of $199. But now, with some control of the market, it will produce only 8 units daily, at a price of $216, under the conditions stated here. The eighth unit is worth producing, since the marginal revenue of $160 covers the marginal cost of $151.[8] But a ninth unit, though the price is

[7] The word "presumably" is introduced because monopolistic firms sometimes get additional business by reducing prices to some customers without reducing prices to others. The result is price discrimination, a matter we shall consider in the following chapter.

[8] The application of the marginal principle under monopoly can also be shown graphically. To a monopolistic firm, sales expectations vary with price, so that such a line as P

$208, is not worth producing, since it would add only $144 to revenue and $170 to cost. It would reduce profit by $26.

With revenues for 8 units of $1728 and aggregate costs (from Table 24) of $1631, Firm Y makes $97 above a normal profit. This result depends, of course, on the particular sales expectations that were assumed. Under other assumptions, its profit could be greater, smaller, or negative. Even powerful monopolies may incur losses, and firms that depart only moderately from a strictly competitive position often do. But it should be noted that Firm Y, with some control of the market, is able to operate profitably below capacity. As a purely competitive firm, it could not have done so.

Comparison with the competitive case. Two general conclusions regarding monopoly—any degree of monopoly—can be drawn from this example, provided we realize the conditions on which they depend. If the same cost conditions prevail as under competition and the same general market situation is present, and if profits are sought with full knowledge of these conditions and are sought by the most direct route, we may conclude that under monopoly (1) the price of the product will be higher than under competition, and (2) the output from existing facilities will be smaller. These conclusions follow from the fact that marginal revenue is less than the price of the product, and thus a higher price, with smaller sales, is necessary to make marginal revenue cover marginal cost.

But while these are sound conclusions regarding monopoly, they

---

is necessary to show the prices that would be received for different quantities. It corresponds to the first column in the table above. Marginal revenue, which is always less than price, is shown by such a line as MR, corresponding to the third column above. The

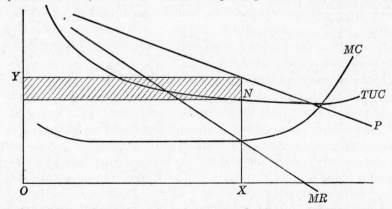

intersection of MR and MC determines the most profitable output OX. For output OX the appropriate price is found at the point on P equal to OY. Again, the rectangle with the dimensions OX and OY shows the total revenue, and the shaded area is the profit in excess of a normal return. In this case a firm operating below capacity has an attractive profit.

throw no light whatever on the extent to which price will be higher and output smaller than under competition. The power of the producer to influence price depends, as we have seen, on the elasticity of demand for his particular product. Even when the market demand for the product of the industry is inelastic, the individual producer may find that a small alteration in his price will be accompanied by a large variation in sales. His degree of monopoly then is slight, and his decision regarding price and output will resemble closely the decision a strictly competitive producer would make. On the other hand, with a higher degree of monopoly, demand appears less elastic to individual producers, and output and price depart further from the competitive result.

Even less can a simple conclusion be reached regarding profits under monopoly. When cast as a monopoly, Firm Y is able to make $97 more daily than a strictly competitive firm would make under like conditions. But this is only the situation of the moment. If Firm Y has only a limited degree of monopoly power and no power whatever to keep other firms from entering and from expanding, the industry can be expected to grow because of the abnormal profit that can be made in it. With expansion in capacity and no corresponding growth in demand, Firm Y is likely to find itself making smaller use of facilities and, though still charging more than a strictly competitive firm, making no more than a normal competitive profit. This can be the logical outcome of partial monopoly.

Review Questions

1. By what test would you decide whether a state of pure competition is present in an industry? Explain the leading conditions that give rise to a departure from pure competition. Relate product differentiation and oligopoly to these conditions. Do these conditions necessarily involve monopoly as the businessman uses that term?

2. State in marginal terms the principle of profit maximization. Explain why it calls for the same degree of plant utilization as a comparison of aggregate revenues and costs for all possible outputs.

3. In utilizing plant capacity, is profit greatest when (a) total unit cost is lowest; (b) total revenue is greatest; (c) price is highest in relation to total unit cost; (d) the greatest difference exists between price and marginal cost; (e) total revenue is highest in relation to total cost; (f) price equals marginal cost; (g) marginal revenue equals marginal cost? Explain in each instance. Is your answer in any instance dependent on the assumption of pure competition?

4. If Firm Y is strictly competitive, how much should it produce if its product sells for $225; for $150? Apply the marginal principle. Assume that

fixed cost is increased from $500 to $800 a day and answer the same question. What conclusion do you reach regarding the bearing of fixed costs on the use of existing facilities?

5. From a student's bluebook: "In periods of low demand, prices are often competitively forced below marginal costs in hopes of at least covering fixed costs." Comment critically.

6. A power dam is undertaken on the assumption that it will cost $1,000,000 and will earn $50,000 annually, which is the minimum return necessary to justify this outlay. When half completed, it appears that the project will actually cost $1,500,000, but with no increase in prospective return. Should it be completed or abandoned? Explain.

7. "The continued operation of a plant is justified during a depression if revenues cover variable costs and may be justified even if they fall below this amount." Explain.

8. A firm that is losing money may be (a) liquidated at once; (b) liquidated gradually through continued operation; (c) reorganized and continued indefinitely. What circumstances would seem to govern the choice?

9. Explain the relationship, under pure competition, (a) between the cost-output situation of the firm and the supply of the product for the industry; (b) between this supply and the price of the product. Show that price can equal marginal cost for all firms while being related in different ways to total unit cost.

10. "Marginal revenue, which is equal to price under pure competition, is less than price when some degree of monopoly is present." Explain.

11. "Because marginal revenue is less than price under monopoly, then, under given conditions, price must be higher and output lower than under competition." Explain.

12. "Though price is higher when some degree of monopoly is present, profits need not be higher." Explain.

Business Decisions in Their Institutional Setting

The price-cost-output behavior of Firm Y reveals certain basic principles but gives only a general impression of how business firms handle questions of production and pricing. In the wide area between pure competition and complete monopoly, there are many market arrangements. Businessmen may call most of them highly competitive, while economists, using the benchmark of pure competition, say that they are essentially, though perhaps often mildly, monopolistic. However they are labeled, they display features not brought out in the preceding discussion.

There is much more to this problem than we can go into, but it is worth observing: (1) that prices often have an inflexibility for which the reasons have not yet been developed; (2) that output, from the firm's standpoint, is controlled commonly by means other than price adjustments; (3) that businessmen seem to do much of their thinking in aggregate and average, rather than in marginal, terms. These points will appear as certain institutional features of markets are noted.[9]

Quoted prices and the selling problem

The monopoly principle, as we have discussed it, makes the relationship between prices and sales seem more mechanical than it is. The concepts of product differentiation and oligopoly, however well they cover most of the situations between complete competition and monopoly, may not suggest how indigenous a certain amount of market control is in the ordinary conduct of business. Let us consider the commonplace fact that businessmen, in fields with which the word "business" is most often associated, give much of their attention to the problem of getting and keeping patronage.

Wheat growers, cattle raisers, cotton planters, producers of many other foodstuffs and materials deal with a market that is essentially impersonal and do not worry about patronage. They have their regular market connections, of course—with certain buyers, distributors, and fabricators—but they are not really dependent on these outlets, because it is the impersonal market that absorbs their products. They have no problem of deciding what price to charge but need only ask what the price is and decide whether or not to sell, or they estimate what the price will be and decide whether and how much to produce.

The typical manufacturer or merchant, on the other hand, depends for his revenue on customers who deliberately decide to patronize him. He deals with them rather than with a market. They must come into his store, send him their orders, yield to his salesmanship. As a basis for disposing of his product, he quotes prices—marks them on goods, prints them in circulars and catalogs, states them to prospective buyers. He may be a small grocer, ice-cream vendor, or laundry operator, or the manager of a great factory, department store, or mail-order house—in any case, his relation to his market confronts him with policy questions at every turn.

In this situation, competition is a conscious, deliberate, active process. Under pure competition, it is not. One wheat farmer does not think of his neighbor as a competitor nor of himself as out to take business from anyone. On the basis of prices and cost, he must make major decisions

---

[9] The aspects of markets considered briefly here have undergone extensive analysis in recent years. A leading theoretical study is Edward Chamberlin, *The Theory of Monopolistic Competition,* Harvard University Press, 1935; a more descriptive study is A. R. Burns, *The Decline of Competition,* McGraw-Hill, 1936.

regarding production. But these very matters of pricing and selling that do not concern him at all are the essence of competition as seen by the merchant and manufacturer.

The monopolist, as exemplified by Firm Y, does make policy decisions related to sales. He must choose among various price-quantity combinations to pick the most profitable, but as we pictured him, he was without sales worries. According to his choice, sales followed automatically. On the other hand, for actual producers with some control over the market, volume of production is not directly governed by such preliminary calculations. The output of the firm must depend directly on the quantities that buyers decide to take at the prices they are quoted. Producers may aim at the combination of price and volume at which marginal revenue will equal marginal cost, but they will produce what their particular customers will buy.

In this situation, pricing is not concerned merely with buyer responses, but with the responses of other sellers—what they will do in light of what you do and what you will do then. Pricing, moreover, is only one means of controlling sales and volume of output. Advertising and all the devices of salesmanship have a major place in expanding and controlling volume. In addition, products are altered—improved or made to appear improved—and packaged more attractively and covered with guarantees and promises of supplementary service. Active competition has many weapons.

Market strategy, pricing, and sales methods

Under pure competition, prices are flexible since they are market-determined. For the price-quoting industries, however, prices move only through the deliberate decisions of sellers and are usually much less flexible. So-called price competition—seeking patronage through reducing prices—is likely to be quite different from the strictly competitive adjustment of prices. Made deliberately, price cuts are distasteful, since they are contrary to the preference of sellers for high prices. The additional business that may be obtained is conditioned on the lower price, and revenue cannot grow in proportion to volume. But, while reductions are made reluctantly, the advancing of prices is commonly a hazardous course, so that upward flexibility is also restrained. The general situation in manufacturing, retail and wholesale trade, transportation, and segments of other fields can be seen best if we consider separately the effects of oligopoly and product differentiation.

Oligopoly. Impediments to price cuts are especially strong in industries that consist of a few large firms. Each firm occupies a conspicuous place and its reductions apply to a large volume of output. Other firms and their customers take notice, and reductions are quickly imitated. This situation is most pronounced in industries with standardized products, because price comparisons are easy and differentials striking. Good examples are found in gasoline, cement, steel, tin cans, and sulphur. It is said that a difference of a cent or two on a barrel of cement will swing patronage quickly from one firm to another.

When price cuts are followed promptly, the initiating firm merely maintains its fraction of total patronage, and the gain, if any, must come through the general elasticity of market demand. Thinking in general market terms, a firm may thus make only such price reductions as promise to increase the profits of the whole industry—in other words, only the price cuts that would be made by a single monopolist if the industry were thus dominated. Along this line it is possible to work out a theory that practically identifies oligopoly with complete monopoly in standard-product industries.

But to achieve the position of a single monopolist, upward adjustments of prices are necessary, as well as the avoidance of downward adjustments. When advances are contemplated, the presence of competitors, even a few competitors, can be a major deterrent. A firm is hesitant to raise its prices for fear that other firms will not follow. If they do not, it both loses sales and suffers the ill will of its customers.

The presence of competitors, though few, may impose even more positive restraints. If profits become exceptionally large, the inducement grows to expand business, even through enlarging plant facilities. Though prices remain constant, sales pressures are likely to increase and customers are enticed by supplementary favors in the form of products and services especially suited to their needs. Indeed, though there is no price cutting on the surface, there may be a good deal of undercover offering of discounts and rebates.

Rivalry of this sort is perhaps most likely to be suppressed, short of single monopoly, in industries in which some one firm is so outstanding that it exercises the influence known as *price leadership*. This has been the position of the United States Steel Corporation in the steel industry, International Harvester in its field, particular Standard Oil companies in various regions, and leading firms in the newsprint, glass container, and other industries. Such a price leader may be followed closely and cooperatively both on downward and upward price adjustments, partly through fear of its power to engage in punishing price cutting when necessary, and partly through realization that, if it takes a "live and let live" attitude toward smaller firms, acquiescence is better than aggressive action.

Studies of price movements show that prices charged by oligopolistic industries fall relatively little when depressions come.[10] But their prices are likely also to be slow in rising during boom periods. Mention was made above of the striking failure, during the heavy postwar demand, of manufacturers' prices of steel and automobiles to rise even to the competitive equilibrium level, thus permitting an extensive "gray market" to develop.

Product differentiation. The directness and sharpness of competition are reduced when the products of competing producers differ substantially or are endowed with special attributes in the minds of buyers. Automobiles, radios, furniture, many types of clothing, and numerous other products avoid close standardization. Such brand and firm names as Coca Cola, Kodak, Frigidaire, Wrigley, Gillette, Kellogg have weight in markets entirely apart from the actual merit of the products they represent. Likewise firms, especially retail shops, may be differentiated by location and exert a special hold on patronage on that account.

To the extent that differentiation is effective, the firm has some latitude within which to choose among price and output possibilities. Prices can be raised without causing a mass shift of buying to competitors. They can be lowered, and patronage attracted, without inducing immediate and equal cuts by other firms. The latitude may be slight or it may be considerable, but within it the typical sort of monopoly decision can be made.

While greater opportunity exists for deliberate price competition than in the case of standard products, there are also greater possibilities of getting business in other ways. There is usually more chance for *competition in quality*. To the extent that quality improvements are costly, their direct effect on profits is the same as if prices were reduced. But quality changes do not so quickly provoke retaliation, and the firm that makes them may for a longer time retain a relative advantage in the market. It is hoped, moreover, that quality improvements will have more effect on sales than equally costly price reductions. Improvements in the appearance of products and the addition of gadgets may have an effect disproportionate to their cost. Improved styling of cars or clothing may be an inexpensive way of promoting patronage.

But as means of expanding volume, these differences in products are not of chief importance in themselves but rather for the basis they provide for *advertising* and *salesmanship*. If products are different, or can be made to seem different, there is something on which the arts of persuasion can work. For some products salesmanship is so much the dominant element that sales at very high prices, with much of the proceeds

---

[10] The results of an extensive study of price flexibility appear in Temporary National Economic Committee Monograph No. 1, *Price Behavior and Business Policy,* 1940.

used for advertising, may exceed sales of the same product at low prices. A cosmetic that costs a few cents to produce may be put in a fancy container, given a fancy name, and with extensive advertising be sold for a dollar or more.

This possibility of controlling sales and output rests very largly on consumer ignorance. It is not often that consumers prefer paying high prices to paying low prices for products of a given quality. Thus, if consumers were all-wise, the firms that would cut out the extraneous factors and sell their products at prices reasonably related to manufacturing costs and merchandising margins would get the business.

Quality improvements and selling pressures may be expensive ways of getting business, but they have the approval of the business world as price cutting does not. In the curious "ethics" of business as promulgated by some of the trade associations, a price cutter is a "chiseler," a rather low person, but the advertiser whose claims exceed the limits of accuracy or good taste may be quite respectable.

Aggregate and marginal revenue and cost comparisons

The marginal principle was presented in the preceding section as containing the logic of profit maximization. It was not asserted that businessmen necessarily do their thinking in marginal terms—only implied that it would be sensible for them to do so. Economics provides no adequate description of how businessmen make up their minds; businessmen themselves might find it difficult to agree on any detailed statement of the process. But certain apparent features of their thinking should be noted—features that may throw additional light on output and pricing, and incidentally on the role of the marginal principle as a business guide.

Recognition of aggregates and averages. Marginal comparisons— comparisons, that is, in which differences in revenues and costs are related to differences in output—probably play little part in the preliminary calculations of businessmen who have prices to quote. Instead, producers are more likely to take account of all elements of cost, fixed as well as variable, and, by relating these costs to the expected output, get an average cost that will guide them in their quotations. This may be done for the sales that would be likely at each of several feasible prices. Such a calculation would be a reasonable first step in deciding what price to quote on a new product or a new model, in setting a price on an old product for the coming year, in quoting on special orders for buildings, machines, and other goods, or in determining the necessary average mark-up in the distributive fields.

Such a consideration of full average costs seems the natural procedure in making plans that affect substantial quantities of output over sub-stantial periods. Marginal calculations may involve large quantities as well as small, but they are most appropriate in planning the small next step, in varying the general course. As a basis for approaching the broader planning of operations, they imply a more accurate knowledge of pros-pective sales at different prices, and of additional costs with different volumes, than it is reasonable to assume. Inaccuracies are less striking when related to large aggregates.

The success of business firms depends on the relation between total revenues and total costs. The surest road to success seems to lie in mak-ing each segment of output bear its proper fraction of all costs and con-tribute to profit. Cost accountants promote this approach to pricing through their assignment of overheads and fixed costs to each segment of output. Trade associations encourage their members to take full ac-count of their costs and to insist that each item of product make its ap-propriate contribution toward the support of the undertaking. Rigid adherence to this procedure must reduce profits in some cases, since products which cannot be sold for enough to cover full average cost may, when there is idle capacity, be sold for more than enough to cover the additional out-of-pocket costs they occasion. But the procedure may still be logical, if its general effect is to reduce competitive price cutting. While marginal calculations yield the same result as aggregrate or av-erage calculations under the same conditions of costs and markets, in-cluding the state of competition, customary pricing procedures may affect the degree of competition.

Volume, average costs, and prices. One aspect of average-cost calcula-tion is especially puzzling. What volume of output shall the business-man assume in figuring his average or total unit cost? Firm Y has a total unit cost of $645 when it produces 1 unit daily, $200 when it produces 10 units, and intermediate amounts for other quantities. The assumed output must be a major factor in arriving at the prospective unit cost of production. Shall it be the actual expected output or some typical or arbitrary figure?

If the cost figure sought is to be a guide to pricing, it should not be arrived at by spreading total costs over the output anticipated in the particular market situation. Such a procedure yields absurd results. On this basis, Firm Y should sell its product at $200 when it produces 10 units daily, $240 when it produces 5 units, and $645 when it produces 1 unit. From the standpoint of the principle of supply and demand, this would mean that price should rise as demand declines. From the stand-point of the competitive recognition of cost, as discussed in this chapter, it would mean that, with marginal cost falling as output drops below the capacity level, price should move in the opposite direction. No monopoly, whether partial or complete, would maximize profit by adjusting prices inversely to demand.[11]

More commonly, in the calculation of average costs, a volume of output is assumed that somehow reflects the sales over a considerable period. Business writers and consultants often speak of a "break-even" point, a volume of output at which revenue covers cost, with no profit element included. This volume is looked upon as a guide in figuring average costs and in pricing products. It might correspond to 40, 60, 80 percent of capacity, as determined in some specified way.

One should sense the arbitrary nature of all such calculations. The higher the prices that are charged, the smaller is the quantity of output at which firms can break even; the lower the prices, the larger the quantity must be. When costs are spread over a volume of output selected on the basis of past prices, average costs depend on those prices and are not an independent basis for deciding what future prices ought to be.

But the present discussion, it should be remembered, is not concerned with the actual fixing of prices in the market. It is concerned with the preliminary calculations by which businessmen develop their ideas as to the prices they ought to quote. As to the prices they will actually charge, such computations are significant but not decisive. If there is any degree of competition in the market, the market price must be the resultant of the cost calculations of all the firms and of their market strategy. A firm cannot simply figure the price it thinks it ought to get and proceed to charge that price. Moreover, since average costs must differ from one firm to another, the market price cannot possibly equal the costs incurred by each one of them. Both prices charged and quantities sold must depart, for individual firms, from the figures in their plans.

Marginal adjustments. It is in these departures, these adjustments to the market situation as it becomes apparent and as it changes, that businessmen make their chief use of the marginal principle. Numerous situations call for it.

A manufacturer may have concluded that $1 is a fair price for his product in view of his costs and his probable sales. But it presently becomes apparent that with a reduction in price to 90 cents he can increase his sales by one fourth. Accordingly, he compares the difference

[11] The final outcome of this principle of pricing would be that a firm whose sales had fallen to 1 unit of product should price that unit to bear the whole load of fixed costs occasioned by the firm's capacity. Serious argument for prices that run inversely to demand is heard most often in the petitions of railroads and other public utilities for rate advances during depressions. The same idea was involved in many "code" applications under the National Recovery Administration.

in his revenue with the additional costs he must incur if he expands his output, and thus decides what to do. Or, again, he has a chance to sell part of his product to a chain organization at 90 cents, and he makes up his mind by comparing the probable additional revenue from this source, the likely inroads into his ordinary sales, and the additional costs. Perhaps he sells on a uniform "delivered-price" basis over a wide region, covering transportation cost in his $1 price. The highest freight cost he is now absorbing is 7 cents per unit, and the question arises whether he should seek business at a still more remote point and absorb a 10-cent freight cost. Again, he must compare the added revenue with the added cost.

Similar comparisons arise when quality improvements are considered. An improvement adding 5 cents to the cost of the product will increase sales, but will the added revenue make the additional cost worth while? Advertising presents the same question. An expanded outlay can be expected to bring more business, but will the improvement in revenue justify the outlay?

Thus in numerous situations businessmen think marginally. But whether their calculations involve margins or inclusive averages, the same conclusions regarding prices and output are indicated, if based on the same knowledge of cost and market conditions. We have stressed the marginal principle because of the clarity with which it shows what profit maximization involves and because it provides a useful means of analyzing and judging the use of resources. Some of these critical judgments, applicable to monopolistic practices, will be considered in the following chapter.

Review Questions

1. "When markets are so organized that products are sold at quoted prices to a particular group of customers, the businessman necessarily becomes a policy maker in price matters. He must assume that he has had some control over his market position." Explain.

2. Distinguish the leading ways in which businessmen undertake to expand and maintain their patronage.

3. How does "price competition" differ from the price adjustments under pure competition.

4. What are the obstacles to price competition—the reasons for inflexible prices? Compare product differentiation and oligopoly in this regard.

5. "Even though an industry consists of several firms, and they act without collusion, its prices and output may be the same as if it consisted of a single monopolistic firm." In what circumstances and by what reasoning may this conclusion be reached? What reasons are there for doubting that it

represents a probable outcome? What is the significance of price leadership in this connection?

6. "Even though competition through sales pressure and quality improvement is costly, it is likely to be preferred to price competition." Why?

7. "It may be true that it is not basically necessary to consider fixed costs in using existing capacity, but producers do much of their planning nevertheless on the basis of total unit costs." Describe the situation in which full average costs are likely to be considered and give the reasons for considering them.

8. At one of the Temporary National Economic Committee hearings, counsel for the Committee asked the president of the American Iron and Steel Institute: "Doesn't your theory lead to this—that as the demand for steel declines and with it the cost increases, of necessity the price would have to keep going up?" Mr. Weir's reply was, "Absolutely." [12] Analyze this statement from the standpoint of competitive pricing; of profit maximization under monopoly (before and after the decline in sales). What conclusion do you reach as to the use of total unit cost as a real guide to the short-run pricing of output from existing facilities? Compare with the long-run expansion and contraction of capacity.

9. Distinguish a number of situations in which it seems quite natural for businessmen to think marginally in the pricing and production of goods.

[12] TNEC *Hearings,* Part 19, p. 10, 652.

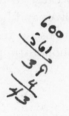

- 22 -

Monopoly and
the Public Interest

U<small>NDER</small> a system that depends on markets to control the use of resources and products, the forces that control markets deserve major attention. Whether such a system works badly or well must depend heavily on these market forces. Most theoretical statements of how markets ought to work if they are to achieve the highest economy and the fairest treatment of everyone proceed on the assumption that an ideal sort of competition exists. But no one really supposes that competition often approaches theoretical perfection; indeed, the deviations are known to be numerous and often striking. Hence some examination of the actual state of competition, and the significance of departures from it, becomes necessary in appraising the present system and the lines that public policy takes.

On the basis of such an examination, the critic of the American economy may take any one of several positions. He may decide (1) that, on balance, markets as they are provide not only a tolerable system of control, but, despite the evidences of monopoly, a better system than any likely alternative. Or he may conclude (2) that the monopoly elements are too serious to be endured, but that, through a vigorous attack on them, we can establish a situation that is adequately competitive. Or, again, he may conclude (3) that the situation is hopeless, that monopoly is so entrenched and so damaging that the whole idea of a free economy should be abandoned, and some other system put in its place. Nor do these positions exhaust the alternatives.

It is the purpose of this chapter, first, to survey the nature and the extent of the departures from competition in the United States, and, second, to set forth the main factors on which judgments of the situation must rest. Because, in neither connection, can points be measured and a balance struck, no final appraisal will be attempted. It is enough to assist in the understanding of a continuing problem. A basis will be provided for consideration in the following chapter of the leading American policies in this sphere.

In a final section the problem of discriminatory pricing will be discussed. References have been made to it at several points, and it should be considered now as a significant aspect of monopoly. It is an aspect of markets that has received a good deal of attention from Congress.

Restrictions on Competition in the United States

The prevalence of monopoly has two dimensions: (1) the extent of the industrial areas, the segments of the economy, in which monopoly is found, and (2) the degree to which markets in those areas depart from competition. Precise information is available on neither of these aspects, but the second, which is the more important, is also the more elusive. Without attempting to be quantitative, we shall examine the sources and evidences of monopoly, considering four categories: (1) departures from competition that are inherent in modern production and selling; (2) loose agreements among firms in the form of price agreements and pools; (3) close-knit, or corporate, combinations; (4) methods used to exclude and suppress competition. These, of course, are not mutually exclusive sources of monopoly but may be combined in various ways in the same industry.[1]

Inherent monopolistic factors

The market factors to be noted under this heading are mainly the elements of product differentiation and oligopoly that we have already recognized in discussing business decisions regarding production and prices. They are referred to as "inherent" because they grow naturally out of methods of producing and selling goods that are commonly accepted and approved without reference to monopoly. Except by economists, they are hardly viewed as monopolistic at all. Indeed, economists long thought on this problem pretty much as laymen did. Only in re-

[1] The literature dealing with monopoly in the United States is extensive. The following are standard items: Temporary National Economic Committee Monograph No. 21, *Competition and Monopoly in American Industry*, 1940; Harry L. Purdy, Martin L. Lindahl, and William A. Carter, *Corporate Concentration and Public Policy*, Prentice-Hall, 1942; Harry W. Laidler, *Concentration of Control in American Industry*, Thomas Y. Crowell, 1931; Henry R. Seager and Charles A. Gulick, *Trust and Corporation Problems*, Harper & Bros., 1929; Eliot Jones, *The Trust Problem in the United States*, Macmillan, 1929; Myron W. Watkins, *Industrial Combinations and Public Policy*, Houghton Mifflin, 1927; William Z. Ripley, *Trusts, Pools, and Corporations*, Ginn, 1916.

cent decades has closer examination of markets revealed that business decisions often follow the monopoly principle despite the presence of competitors. Sharper tests of monopoly have brought increasing awareness of it, just as a biologist becomes aware of new organisms through using a stronger microscope. Thus the generalizations frequently heard regarding the "decline of competition" should be met with the query whether something new has actually appeared or something old has just become apparent.

When industries are characterized by product differentiation and oligopoly, it would be wrong to conclude that competition is fully present; but it would be just as wrong to say that it is absent. If these are the only deviations, certain essentials of competition are present. Industries are made up of a number of independent firms, and these firms act without collusion in matters of output and pricing. They can expand as they please, and no arbitrary obstacles stand in the way of the appearance of new firms. They are confronted by the improvements of other firms in products and methods of production, and by the prospect that other firms will cut into their business if they lag in their methods or overreach their customers. In short, the basis of a substantial rivalry is still present.

Differentiated products. Such monopoly power as arises from product differentiation inheres (1) in the nonstandard nature of products, because of which the products of different firms are not directly competitive, and (2) in the legal protection of company and brand names and the susceptibility of consumers to established reputations based on these names. Certainly product variations are inherent in practically all goods except basic materials, and progressive companies are likely to develop and multiply variations. Governmental protection of trademarks and company names is well established, though not inherent in the same sense. Conceivably a new policy might be adopted under which this protection would be limited, or, going further, government might require standardized grading wherever possible with conspicuous descriptive labeling, so that consumers would be much less influenced by trademarks and distinctive company names. Then one factor in differentiation, for better or worse, would decline.

As to how potent this source of monopoly is, the ordinary observer may judge almost as well as the statistician. Everyone observes that numerous foodstuffs, clothes, house furnishings, and other consumers' goods and even industrial materials are conspicuously associated with particular company labels. The crucial question is whether companies are given much latitude thereby in their pricing policies. If many people will buy a certain brand of asperin or of lipstick at three times the price at which practically the identical article can be obtained under another name, then product differentiation is an important monopoly factor. But as to how prevalent such situations are—whether, on the whole, the profits from valuable names reflect more than extremely minor differences in prices—we have only general observation by which to judge.

Large firms. Oligopoly is inherent in industries to the extent that efficient production requires firms so large that the number of them serving a market must be fairly small. Thus, in Chapter 7 in analyzing the economies of large plants and large firms, we were considering the basis of oligopoly. No one can say definitely how small the number of firms must be, or how large the particular firm must be in relation to the industry, for business decisions to depart substantially from the competitive standard. There are too many variables.

Among the more familiar industries in the United States in which a half dozen or fewer firms supply a major part of the product are automobiles, oil refining and distribution, rubber tires, steel, cigarettes, aluminum, meat packing, soaps, sugar refining, breakfast foods, glass products. But in many smaller industries, or industries less in the consumer's eye, the same situation prevails. In such a list we would find plumbing supplies, enamel ware, surgical appliances, writing ink, linoleum, oleomargarine, dental supplies, bandages and adhesives, fertilizers, washing machines, and many others.

Such instances suggest the influence of modern producing methods in limiting the number of competitors, but it must not be supposed that the degree of oligopoly present in most of these instances is necessitated by the requirements of efficiency. Firms become large, as we saw in Chapter 7, for reasons other than the desire to produce at lower cost. Successful firms naturally expand, so that size results from efficiency as well as efficiency from size. Firms are combined into larger corporations to reap the profits from promoting and financing them. Firms have been combined, moreover, and oligopoly intensified, through the very desire to achieve market control. Thus, so far as the number of firms is concerned, many industries are less competitive than they could be without sacrificing efficiency.

Local monopoly. The number of firms serving a market is often limited by the fact that the product must be provided locally and the local market is small. Thus many communities can support only one bank, one hotel, one newspaper. There may even be room for only one garage, laundry, or hardware store. In communities of nearly every size there are goods that can best be obtained locally for which the number of suppliers is necessarily small. Within limits, then, monopoly considerations govern the supplying and pricing of these goods.[2]

The limits depend, of course, on how advantageous it is to obtain the commodity or service locally, and progress in transportation has greatly reduced the scope of local monopoly. At one time even such businesses as iron foundries, lumber mills, and textile factories depended largely on a nearby market, but the development of railroads in the last century created broad regional and national markets for most basic commodities and manufactured products. More recently the automobile has greatly reduced the dependence of consumers on local business houses and has widened the area of competition.

Students of American business who hold that competition has declined seriously usually stress the growth of great corporations. But there has also been a growth of markets, so that, on balance, it is difficult to say whether more or fewer firms are brought into competition than 75 or 100 years ago. When allowance is made, furthermore, for the greater number of products and for the wider availability of substitutes, a given advantage in a particular product often means less than it formerly did.

Public utilities. Certain businesses are restricted to a market that is covered by their own physical facilities. This is the situation in the public-utility field in which firms must reach their customers with the pipes, wires, and rails that convey the service that they provide. As a result, a considerable degree of monopoly can be said to be inherent in the nature of these public-utility industries.

Loose-knit combinations

If competition is limited only by product differentiation and the fewness of competitors, the rivalry that is present is likely to be sufficient to meet popular expectations. It is when the members of industries get together and agree on prices and the quantities they will produce that the public feels exploited. Combinations are referred to as loose knit when the firms involved remain separate as financial and operating entities and agree merely on matters related directly to the market.

Price agreements and pools. Most commonly the associated firms simply agree on the prices they will charge, or on the minimum prices. Such an agreement may be a potent market influence and may keep prices considerably higher than they would be without it. But price agreements contain an inherent weakness and are likely to be tempo-

---

[2] In the preceding chapter, location was mentioned as an aspect of the differentiated position of different sellers. Now it is mentioned as a reason for a small number of directly competing sellers, for local oligopoly. Either view of it seems satisfactory.

rary in their effect, especially when many firms are involved. When prices are fixed at an especially profitable level, member firms are stimulated to expand their sales, with the result that they offer special inducements to buyers, including undercover price cutting, and the agreement presently breaks down.

The pool is a means of curing this weakness. By arranging in advance the position that each firm is to occupy in the market, the pool aims to remove the urge of member firms to take business from each other. Each firm may be assigned a specified *quota* of the estimated total sales of the industry; or it may be assigned a certain *territory* in which to do its selling; or the *earnings* of the companies may be pooled, with each receiving a prearranged fraction.

The history of business, going as far back as there are records, is replete with schemes to keep prices up and restrict output. They spring naturally from a situation in which sellers' competition means lower prices whereas sellers prefer higher prices. At the local level, price agreements are common, and the prices charged by dry cleaners, coal dealers, electrical contractors, and others are often fixed cooperatively. At the national level, pools and other agreements in cordage, salt, whisky, oil, anthracite, and various steel products drew general attention and aroused public wrath in the years following the Civil War. A continuing stream of such agreements comes before the Department of Justice and the Federal Trade Commission under the antitrust laws.

Means of cooperation. The principle involved in these loose combinations is simple enough. The means of achieving them, however, are varied and often elusive, ranging from shadowy understandings to formal contracts with elaborate arrangements for their execution.[3]

Indeed the primary question is sometimes whether an agreement exists at all, or whether the effect of an agreement is achieved through the spontaneous cooperation of businessmen who think alike and who conform to the customs of their trade. If, for example, the United States Steel Corporation announces prices of steel products and other companies follow its *leadership*, is it necessary to suppose that an agreement preceded the practice or might a sense of common interest have brought it about? Or may the *basing-point system* of pricing develop without collusion, as has often been contended? In the most famous instance of it, the Pittsburgh-plus arrangement in the steel industry, a buyer of steel located anywhere, buying from a steel mill located anywhere, and receiving steel by any means of transport, would pay the

---

[3] The distinction between simple, informal understandings and elaborate, formal agreements does not correspond to the distinction between price agreements and pools. Some price agreements are elaborate affairs, and some pools are no more complex than the agreement of two newsboys to stick to their own corners.

announced price at Pittsburgh plus rail freight from Pittsburgh. Pittsburgh-plus was terminated through federal action, but a multiple basing-point system developed in the steel and other industries that involved the same principle, though with less grotesque results. Whether such an arrangement is the natural result of competition in the sale of standard products under conditions of oligopoly, or whether it must be explained by unlawful collusion, is an issue that has reached the Supreme Court.[4]

Trade associations present a similar difficulty. There are some 2000 national organizations in the United States in which members of industries are associated to promote common interests. These groups may be concerned with public relations and legislative lobbying, conducting joint research and advertising projects, standardizing sizes and types of products to promote convenience and economy, exchanging credit information, developing accounting methods, organizing statistical services, outlawing misrepresentation in selling. Such activities may not only be entirely legitimate, but certain of them are clearly of public benefit.

But when trade associations conduct campaigns among their members to prevent price cutting and "spoiling the market" through excessive production, it may be hard to tell where education leaves off and monopolistic collusion begins. When accounting instruction seeks to insure that every possible element of cost, even with a moderate use of capacity, will be covered in the prices charged, the competitive operation of markets may be threatened. When statistics are gathered and circulated regarding members' orders, prices, stocks on hand, and like matters, it may be argued that the sole aim is to promote the perfect knowledge that ideal markets require, but collusion by indirection seems sometimes a better interpretation.

Views differ as to whether effective cooperative action can take place without definite agreement. The government view has been that it cannot. Be that as it may, outright agreement regarding prices and production is common enough. Since it is unlawful under American statutes, it is kept as inconspicuous as possible. Often there is no written record, but only a *gentlemen's agreement*. On the other hand, agreements may contain many details and stipulations, with penalties for cutting prices or overstepping quotas. Where loose combinations have flourished with governmental approval, as was long the case in Germany, common sales agencies have sometimes received orders for an entire industry and apportioned them among the members.

[4] The multiple basing-point system in the cement industry was contested for years before the Federal Trade Commission and in the courts. Finally, in 1948, the highest tribunal found that it violated the antitrust laws.

The word *cartel* has sometimes been applied to this sort of arrangement, sometimes more generally to any type of loose agreement. Recently it has been associated with agreements involving firms in different countries. So-called international cartels have been active in many fields in dividing world markets and maintaining the prices of goods sold internationally.

Close-knit, or corporate, combinations

Because combinations of the loose type are based on firms that retain managerial independence, they are often short-lived and imperfectly carried out. For assured uniformity of action in the market, competing firms must be brought under a single managerial control, usually as part of a single corporate organization. Corporate combination has sometimes gone so far in the United States as practically to include whole industries. It did once in oil and tobacco and more recently in shoe machinery and aluminum. But usually it has fallen well short of complete monopoly and has only created an oligopolistic situation, as in the fields mentioned above. Apart from the direct effect of oligopoly, the reduction in the number of firms makes it easier to carry out effective market agreements.

In achieving combination under a single management, *intercorporate stockholding*, chiefly through the *holding company*, has been the leading device.[5] Through it, combination can be brought about gradually, as shares of stock are acquired, and complete domination achieved without complete ownership. Often, however, the controlling company comes, sooner or later, to own all of the operating properties directly rather than through subsidiary corporations. Such ownership establishes a *consolidation*. The terms *merger* and *amalgamation* are sometimes applied to particular types of consolidation, sometimes to corporate combination in general.

Early efforts, especially in the 1870s and 1880s, to achieve positive unification of competing companies took the form of the *trust*, in the technical legal sense of that word. Under this device, shares of stock of competing companies, with their voting power, were assigned to a common board of trustees. The early Standard Oil Company was a trust in this sense but later was reorganized as a holding company. The trust form was found to be unlawful when used in this way, but the word "trust" has carried over to the present in such phrases as "trust problem" and "antitrust laws," implying monopolistic combination in general.

[5] Explained in Chapter 8 above.

Exclusive practices

Firms that are out positively to get control of markets are seldom content merely to absorb competitors in a peaceful way or to enter into friendly agreements with them regarding prices and output. Effective monopoly must be both inclusive and exclusive. Aspiring monopolists must use pressures to prevent the appearance of rivals and to suppress or absorb them when they appear. Many ways have been found to make life difficult for competitors, especially if they are small.

Sometimes there is some strategic point in the production of a good that provides a simple basis for exclusive control. The required *raw material* may have a restricted geographic source, as diamonds or even anthracite, and control of that source means control of the industry. At some stage the product may require *special transport facilities,* and control of those facilities establishes domination. Ownership of pipe lines was a major factor in the supremacy of the early Standard Oil Company. *Special marketing facilities,* such as the stockyards in the meat-packing industry, may be the basis of control. It was sometimes charged that the power of Wall Street bankers to stop the flow of capital to rivals of the firms in which they were interested was a broad means of restricting competition.

Patents have often been the basis of exclusive methods. Fundamentally, patents legalize a limited monopoly with the aim, as the Constitution puts it, of promoting "the progress of science and the useful arts," and thus of furthering one of the purposes of competition. But it has been difficult to dissociate this limited monopoly from monopolistic methods that are no part of its intent. A firm with a patent on one vital idea may require its customers to obtain from it other products that can equally well be bought elsewhere. In this way, the United Shoe Machinery Company long required shoe manufacturers to use its whole line of equipment if they used any of it, even though it lacked exclusive rights to some of the machines it produced. Similarly a large owner of patents may license their use under conditions that control the output of the licensees and the prices they charge. The glass-container industry has been dominated in this way. Research, moreover, has been carried on by large firms not to improve their products but to anticipate, and patent, improvements in competitor's products. Patents have often been bought up merely to suppress them.

The *boycott* is a loose combination designed to exclude firms from markets. Thus certain distributors may agree not to patronize manufacturers who sometimes by-pass them in the sale of goods or who sell to price cutters. Similarly building contractors and unions in the building trades have conspired to deal only with each other and thus exclude competitors to the advantage of both groups.

The methods of bludgeoning competitors and making life miserable for them have been numerous. Large, strongly entrenched companies may cut prices ruinously until young and weak competitors are destroyed or will sell out cheaply. Harassing and highly expensive litigation, often based on patents, may be brought against smaller competitors. Products of competitors may be misrepresented and even tampered with when in use. Special processes may be spied on and key employees bribed. Bribery may be applied also to the purchasing agents of companies. Such methods are among the devices of monopoly. But, short of monopoly, they have the effect of making success depend not on efficient production and fair dealing but on sheer power and unscrupulousness. These methods belong under the heading of *unfair competition*, in the proper sense of a much misused term.[6] Quite a number of these exclusive methods are much less prevalent than they formerly were, primarily as a result of policies that we shall consider in the following chapter.

Monopoly on the buying side of the market

Market power is sought by firms not only in selling their products but in buying materials, supplies, and factors of production generally, including labor. Instances often cited are the strategic position of a few large tobacco manufacturers in dealing with many tobacco growers and of the large meat packers in buying from many raisers of meat animals. In the matter of terminology, the phrase *buyers' monopoly* is often used; however, since the root of the word "monopoly" implies selling, the term *monopsony* has been coined to designate concentrated control on the buying side of the market. To indicate the effect of fewness of buyers, *oligopsony* is used.

Market control in buying receives much less attention than in selling and is less important. For consumers' goods, buyers are numerous, and departures from competition only affect supply. Many materials, such as lumber, and many services, as of ordinary labor, are purchased by producers of many products, so that firms are likely to be more competitive in their buying than in their selling. Moreover, the basic materials and fuels may have relatively few sellers in a given market, so that any concentration in buying is offset by a similar concentration in selling. The result is not a competitive market, but one whose operations need cause no public concern. In the case of labor, however, the demand sit-

---

[6] For an interesting collection of examples, see William H. S. Stevens, *Unfair Competition*, University of Chicago Press, 1917.

uation is of peculiar interest, because employers commonly have an advantage in hiring individual, unorganized workers. The labor market, therefore, will receive special attention later on in this study.[7]

Uncertain extent of monopoly in the United States

As the observer casts his eye over the whole field of industry, noting in manufacturing the wide differences between steel or aluminum and clothing or furniture, the contrast in mining between bituminous coal and anthracite or copper, the presence of great firms and many small ones in merchandising and construction, the millions of competing farms and the paucity of competing utilities, the picture seems varied and confused. And even if he has the scholar's contact with an abundance of statistical and descriptive information about the working of industries, he will still be a long way from a clear characterization of American production as to the prevalence of significant market controls. Quite likely he will agree with the author of a leading survey of competition and control in American industry: "The most that can be said today is that competition is far too common to justify the thesis that the competitive system is approaching extinction; and that monopoly is far too common to justify its treatment as an occasional exception to the general rule." [8]

The public should be concerned not with the surface indications of monopoly but with the extent of its effect—how far the actual flow of products and the pricing of goods depart from an acceptable standard of public interest. For this purpose no very usable tests are available. There is no way of translating into a measure of monopolistic distortion the number and size of firms, the standardization of products, the availability of substitutes and other elements in the elasticity of demand, the technological unrest within industries, the cooperative inclinations of business leaders, the activities of trade associations.

Even though normal prices and normal profits are necessary concepts in economic analysis, it is difficult to apply them in judging the extent of monopoly. One firm makes large profits at prices at which another firm loses money. Nearly all firms lose money during depressions and prosper during booms. In such a period as has followed World War II, the backlog of orders may make profits embarrassingly large even at prices too low to equate demand and supply. In growing industries profits may have to be high to bring the expansion the public demands, and the able and fortunate—a Henry Ford with his Model T—may amass quick fortunes in fields that many enter. At the same time, producers

---

[7] In Chapter 27.
[8] T.N.E.C. Monograph No. 21, *op. cit.*, p. 308. Clair Wilcox is the author.

elsewhere may profit only moderately while exploiting monopoly power to the utmost.

But though generalization is difficult regarding the status of competition in the United States, its health or its decline, the elements in the picture must be sensed if one is to weigh the factors on which policy must depend.

Review Questions

1. "Competition has declined seriously in the United States since the Civil War." What evidence would you cite in supporting this view; in questioning its validity?

2. "Partial monopoly, in the form of product differentiation and oligopoly, is inherent in modern production and marketing." What is meant by calling each of these conditions inherent? Are they inherent in all respects, or in the degree to which they are present?

3. How do pools differ from price agreements?

4. Why is it difficult to decide whether actual agreement governs some pricing practices? The ways in which trade associations influence prices and output?

5. Distinguish several forms of close-knit, or corporate, combinations.

6. "A patent confers a legal monopoly. Therefore it cannot be the means of improper monopolistic control." Do you agree? Distinguish several means by which firms may exclude competitors.

7. Explain monopsony; oligopsony.

8. "To identify evidences of monopoly in American industry is not to appraise the seriousness of monopoly in the United States." Explain. Why is this point important?

Factors in Judging Market Controls

The distorting effects of monopoly have been described as consisting in (1) the overcharging of buyers, (2) the misallocation of resources, (3) the amassing of unreasonable profits, and (4) the restriction of business opportunity.[9] The public may not be excited by misallocation and the broader distortions in the system of economic control. But every consumer is aroused when he feels exploited by profiteering sellers; every worker is incensed over the profits he can attribute to sheer exercise of power; every small businessman resents the pushing around he often gets from large competitors, suppliers, and customers. The lauded tradition of free competitive enterprise should exclude such pressures as these.

[9] See Chapter 20 above.

Monopoly is in bad repute, but it is common talk also that competition is wasteful, and the ordinary observer sees a dubious multiplicity of gas stations, milk trucks, and grocery stores. It has been dinned into him also that competition is "cutthroat" and "destructive," that something should be done to stabilize industries and adjust production to demand, and these impressions combine with his worry over depressions and unemployment and the need of action to prevent them. At the same time, and not quite consistently, he is impressed with the power of corporations, and he wonders whether competition really has a chance. Competition has been likened, moreover, to warfare, and he may doubt whether a properly organized society should retain it.

On such considerations, the rather ill-formed public opinion in this major field of policy seems to rest. The leading factors will be discussed briefly.

Levels of monopoly advantage—prices and profits

American policy may be summed up by saying that monopoly should be prevented or regulated. This is a simple way of putting the matter and as useful as any as a general guide. But it implies a neat cleavage of markets into two categories, the monopolistic and the competitive, whereas in fact the kinds and degrees of departure from ideal competition must defeat so simple an approach. So the real task is to decide what types and conditions of monopoly make it so harmful that it must be prevented or regulated.

Layman and expert would in general agree that power should not rest in private hands to control effectively the *long-run expansion of industry*, with the influence on prices, profits, and enterprise that such power implies. This is the aspect of monopoly that was touched on in Chapter 20. Power of this kind exists in the public-utility field and leads to positive regulation. It may arise also in other fields through the formation of great corporate combinations, especially if they obtain a strategic control of raw materials or special facilities of transportation or marketing, or if they employ highhanded methods toward all incipient competition. The old oil and tobacco monopolies are conspicuous examples, and there have been a number of others. In such cases profits may remain high over long periods.[10]

Should *price agreements* and *pools* be viewed in the same light as cor-

[10] Eliot Jones concludes that the old Standard Oil Company paid dividends between 1882 and 1906 that averaged 24 percent on the investment, with almost 40 percent in the last 10 years of this period, and that a considerable part of the profit was not distributed to stockholders. *Op. cit.*, p. 89. There are other notable instances of high profits among the early "trusts," but some of them failed notably both as monopolies and as efficient producers. See Arthur S. Dewing, *Corporate Promotions and Reorganizations*, Harvard University Press, 1914.

porate combinations? Unless government positively supports them, they are not likely to limit expansion very much, although sometimes they may try to. But they do hold prices up and restrict output, though seldom with the great and continuing effect of a single monopolistic producer. Their aim is plainly to prevent the competitive control of markets, so, in a system that depends on competitive markets, they must clearly be condemned and action taken against them. But here a complication enters. The common claim of firms that form these loose combinations is that their aim is not to reap an unreasonable profit but merely to stabilize their industry and insure an adequate return. This viewpoint has received such emphasis that we must give it separate consideration below.

But what about the *oligopolistic industries* such as steel, oil refining, automobiles, and many others? Firms compete in these industries, and there may be no collusion among them. If new firms want to enter, they need encounter no inherent obstruction, nor any arbitrary, highhanded treatment. But the fact is that effective firms must be large, and it is difficult to start large. Thus the entrance of such a producer as Kaiser-Fraser into the automobile industry is a major event. Moreover, as we saw in the last chapter, it is possible for a few firms to interpret the market and each other's actions in such a way that they act in matters of output and prices almost as a single monopolist would.

It is respecting this area of monopoly that opinions differ most widely. Some hold that monopoly power is so extensively exercised and so inescapable that government should step in and regulate prices and production. Others believe that while the public is exploited in some instances, the restraints are not inherent and their sources can largely be removed. From this standpoint, practices such as the basing-point system that make it easy to avoid price competition should be outlawed; collusive action should be more vigorously sought out and attacked; such special advantages as arise from control of raw materials or the improper use of patents should be removed. Still other observers think there is little cause for concern in existing conditions. These persons, if they view the matter analytically, stress the competition that goes on in the quality of products, the appearance of new products which are often close substitutes, the fact that new firms do enter and old ones expand, and the threat that capacity will grow depressingly if profits are excessive. Firms, moreover, are concerned over public relations and the danger of government interference, even if no interference actually develops.

The partial monopoly which results from *differentiation of products and the* reputations of established firms is seldom viewed as a public threat. Undoubtedly the development of new competition in such fields as the manufacture of cigarettes or of automobiles is made much more difficult by the reputation of existing firms, both through real confidence of buyers in their products and the quite illogical sway that names exert. Undoubtedly, also, exceptional profits sometimes result from these advantages. But the institution of trade names is well established, and most people are willing to concede to firms the gains that their reputations bring them. The consequences may not all be good, but, after all, buyers act voluntarily, not through the absence of alternatives caused by exclusive practices and price agreements.

Monopoly and the use of resources

Markets must be judged in part by the prices and profits they enable producers to get. They must be judged also by their effect on the use of resources. Their effect on resource use involves not only the matter of allocation—that is, the direction of use—but also the fullness of use, the efficiency of use, and progress in use.

Waste in use of existing facilities. In contrasting monopoly and pure competition in the preceding chapter, we saw that the firm with some choice between selling more at a lower price and less at a higher price is likely to make less use of capacity than a firm that cannot influence the price. To the monopolist, marginal revenue is less than the price he receives, and output must be restricted to make marginal revenue cover marginal cost. This more limited use of facilities is unfortunate from the standpoint of strict economy in the use of resources. Once a firm has its facilities, with the cost of them already sunk, they should be used as long as the added product is worth enough to cover the cost of added labor, materials, and so on. This is to say that the strictly competitive relationship of price and marginal cost is the most economic. Ordinarily much of industry makes less use of its facilities than this rule requires, though actual use deviates in any market from the theoretical norm.

Long-run allocations. This smaller use of capacity under monopoly would be expected, in varying degrees, under the most secure monopoly, under price agreements, and under the various conditions of oligopoly and product differentiation. But in the long-run adjustment of capacity to demand, an important difference exists between monopoly which can control expansion and monopoly which cannot. As noted in Chapter 20, monopoly that can prevent expansion reduces the employment of resources in a particular industry and diverts them into other industries. A social loss results to the extent that the public would rather have more product from the monopolized field, at a competitive price, than the additional products obtained from other fields. But in meeting the demand at the price it charges, the secure monopoly presumably introduces only such resources as are actually required. From the long-run standpoint, there is misallocation, but without waste.

Partial monopoly, lacking power to control entrance, differs in both of these respects. As we saw in the preceding chapter in considering Firm *Y,* the very presence of monopoly prices and profits invites expansion. The monopoly principle in using facilities causes the creation of more facilities. The tendency, then, is for expansion to occur until profits are no more than normal. But if profits are at the competitive level while prices are above it, one must conclude that revenues are supporting considerable unnecessary, and therefore wasted, capacity.

It is an interesting fact that the layman's examples of competitive duplication and waste are likely to be cases of partial monopoly, or monopolistic competition, operating in this manner. The apparent excess of gas stations and milk wagons exemplifies it. Different refining companies, for example, want their seemingly differentiated products to be sold through stations that bear their names, whereas completely standardized gasoline of competing companies could be sold through the pumps of the same station, just as the wheat of different farmers goes into the same elevators.

This wasteful expansion of facilities that results normally from partial monopoly should be distinguished from the waste that may come through the ignorance of small enterprisers and through their enthusiasm over having their own businesses and being their own bosses. It is so easy to enter small-scale fields such as farming, retailing, motor trucking, and so on, that, if we assign no value to the satisfactions of independent enterprise, resources appear to be wastefully used. But in these cases, once the commitments have been made, there is a good chance that facilities will be used quite fully, though perhaps unprofitably.

Monopoly as a means of avoiding waste. Monopoly is often advocated as a means of avoiding competitive waste, whatever its specific source. Plainly, to accomplish this result, monopoly would need to be comprehensive and secure, with power to control expansion. If it were established under a system of private enterprise, the idea of free enterprise would have to be abandoned; if exploitation of the public were to be avoided, extensive regulation would be necessary. Something of this sort was sought in Great Britain before the war in the movement for "rationalization" of industry—though doubtless the aim of "profit security" was involved as well as prevention of waste. The chief advocates of complete monopoly are the socialists, who would get rid of private enterprise altogether. Systematic avoidance of the wastes of competitive, unplanned private enterprise is an aim often proclaimed by socialists, though economy in using resources is not the main objective of socialism.

A related waste charged to competitive capitalism is the extensive effort expended in selling products. Again, one should remember that selling cost is a feature of monopolistic competition, not of pure competition. It does not burden the wheat or cotton grower. But complete monopoly, nevertheless, would greatly reduce it. With a single organization producing cigarettes, radios, or automobile tires, salesmen and advertising would have no place in pushing one brand against another. Private monopolies would still be interested, as firms are now, in getting people to use their kind of product—for instance, to ride by rail or to paint their houses—without regard for particular companies or brands, and there would be some advertising of this industry character. Moreover, advertising would still be necessary to inform buyers regarding products and their availability. Perhaps, under socialism, selling would take only the latter form, although propaganda might be used to influence the direction of buying.

But these economies of monopoly should not be exaggerated. When advertising carries much of the cost of radio programs and of newspaper and magazine publishing, these services should enter any calculation of its costs. Its informative role is substantial, though often seemingly only a by-product. Even looseness in adapting capacity to demand is not wholly deplorable. A calculated stand-by capacity is commonly necessary to meet the peak requirements for goods, and peak requirements are uncertain. A nation with war emergencies to consider might "rationalize" itself into impotency.

Monopoly and efficiency of size. The highest standard in using resources requires that waste should be kept down, whether caused by monopolistic restriction of the use of facilities or needless duplication of them. It requires also that production should be organized so as to use the most advanced technology and that producing organizations should be large enough for this purpose. In considering how monopoly and competition are related to the problem of size and efficiency, two familiar points should be recalled.

The *first* is that plants and firms should be distinguished and the limits to the economy of size should be recognized in formulating policy. Whenever more strenuous enforcement of the antitrust laws is sought, the cry is heard that a blow is being struck at the great producing organizations on which American efficiency depends. Mass production is eulogized, and government action is seen as threatening to destroy it. But such protests, for the most part, are baseless. Mass production, as

Chapter 7 explained, is mainly a matter of plant size and does not depend on combining more and more plants, in diverse ways, into ever larger corporations. No one has seriously proposed to limit the size of plants. Multiplant firms may achieve additional and relatively minor economies not attained by large plants, but in explaining combinations, these economies seem to be outweighed by other purposes—among them the desire to control markets. It seems a reasonable judgment that the United States might long ago have imposed more severe restrictions on combination with little, if any, adverse effect on efficiency but with the result that today competition would be considerably more effective than it is in many industries.

The *second* point is that modern methods of production necessarily prevent a close approach to pure competition in many fields. If reasonably effective competition means pure competition, then the country should quickly reconcile itself to a drastic change in its system of economic control. Competitive control, however, has never meant pure competition to legislators or businessmen, and, though economists use the concept as a benchmark in analyzing markets, few of them would make it a guide to policy or suppose that a fairly adequate degree of competition requires it. But whether adequate competition can be reconciled with existing oligopoly is an issue, as noted above, on which the views of competent observers differ.

Monopoly and progress in the use of resources. Effective production means not only that the better techniques already known should be employed but that new techniques should be devised, products improved, and new products developed. No one questions that factors of competition and monopoly influence progress, but there is disagreement as to the exact nature of the influence.

The point most often made is that competition provides a powerful incentive to progress. The monopolist, assured of his market, becomes lethargic, whereas the competitive producer knows that he can better his market position if he improves his processes sufficiently—indeed that improvement is necessary even to stay where he is. Very likely, for example, a secure monopoly in the automobile tire industry forty years ago would have hesitated to introduce improvements that would increase tire mileage ten or twenty times, with a probable reduction in sales. Similarly, if means are found of producing truly run-resistant stockings for women, one may have reasonable doubts regarding the fate of the idea if it is left to a monopolist to develop. Patented ideas have been suppressed often enough to justify the doubt. It is easy for monopolists to follow the safe road to profits by "leaving well enough alone."

But the monopolist who does this must feel quite sure of his market. Even some of the public utilities have been vigorous in improving their methods and products, though others, notably the railroads, have shown signs of complacence when free from competition. Certainly there is no reason to suppose that progress requires a close approach to pure competition. Indeed it is probable that with partial competition, as when product differentiation and oligopoly are present, progress is most likely to be vigorous.

There are several reasons for the latter view. One is that firms need to be large to afford the research on which technical progress largely depends. Another is that when a product carries the firm name and the reputation of the firm rests on it, greater zeal in developing it is likely. Still another is that the risks of innovation are so great that some protection from competition is necessary to justify the expense. The patent policy itself reflects the belief that restriction of competition is necessary to encourage progress. If markets were so competitive that every new idea were immediately known and generally adopted, the incentive to progress would largely vanish.

Believers in competitive capitalism, with its mixture of market characteristics, contend that its achievements in advancing the arts of production far outweigh the looseness and waste that advocates of planned and orderly production are anxious to correct.

The "destructiveness" of competition

The problem of markets, as generally viewed, is that of keeping sufficient competition to prevent excessive prices and profits and insure effective use of resources. But what of the opposite view that the danger is not too little competition but too much? What of the belief that competition must be restrained or it will be ruinous—that agreements among producers should be regarded not as a means of gaining excessive profit but any profit at all?

Usually, perhaps, the grumbling of businessmen about too much competition is no more than a build-up of sentiment against price cutting, a justification of the work of trade groups, an argument for a tolerant, understanding kind of antitrust enforcement. But sometimes this viewpoint blossoms into a full-fledged program for the revision of economic control. Such a program, calling for formal industry-wide decisions regarding output and prices rather than decisions by individual firms, is sometimes referred to as "industrial self-government." What it amounts to is an officially approved cartellization which aims to "adjust production to demand" on a profitable basis. The chief move in this direction that has been made in the United States was the establishment of the

National Recovery Administration in 1933. Hundreds of industry-wide "codes" were approved which undertook in various ways to put floors under prices and restrict competition.[11] The NRA was terminated in 1935, but a scattered progeny still display its stamp. The same idea was long dominant in Germany and gained great headway in England between the wars.

The case against pure competition. The chief reason why competitive pricing may mean serious losses appears from the analysis in the preceding chapter. A strictly competitive price is equal to marginal cost, and marginal cost is not so great as the full average cost of production, including a normal profit, unless output is at the capacity level, in the economic sense of capacity. If fixed costs are substantial, marginal cost is some distance below total unit cost for a volume appreciably below capacity, and the loss, if price equals marginal cost, can be severe. If it is also true—and considerable evidence indicates that it is—that most firms are likely to be operating below capacity most of the time, a strictly competitive market must cause losses most of the time. Because private business cannot operate generally on a losing basis, pure competition, despite its merits in other respects, appears as a ruinous controlling force.

On this ground it may be argued that the actual markets in most industries that are only partially competitive are preferable to completely competitive markets from the public as well as the business standpoint. Perhaps the educational work of trade associations, the differentiation of products, even the restrictions due to the fewness of competitors, are useful, within limits, in making competition a practicable controlling force.

The case against cooperative control of industries. But it does not follow at all that industrial self-government, with prices and output controlled cooperatively on an industry-wide basis, is a necessary or desirable step. Acceptance of some softening of competition does not imply approval of extensive monopoly under any set of euphemisms.

Business groups are likely to overstate their hardships under competition. Restraints are always distasteful, and competition cannot do its work if it does not keep sellers from charging the prices they would like to charge or making the profits they would like to make. Moreover—and this is harder to take—competition cannot do its work unless it causes losses rather frequently. Profits should remain something to be striven for, with penalties for picking the wrong field or producing inefficiently or unprogressively. If control is to operate through markets,

[11] See Leverett S. Lyon and others, *The National Recovery Administration*, Brookings Institution, 1935.

capitalism must be not merely a profit system but a profit-and-loss system. Whenever the members of industries get together to control prices and output, rewards are too easy and poor performance is treated too tenderly.

It is true that losses are general, and for many firms disastrous, in severe depressions such as that of the early 1930s. A case can be made then for establishing emergency price floors for distressed industries. But the inherent deviations from competition arising from the nature of markets in price-quoting industries, with their differentiated products and small number of rivals, ordinarily provide adequate protection. Emergency cooperative arrangements, such as the NRA codes, are difficult to keep temporary and should be avoided if possible.

Monopoly and the causes of depressions

Protecting business from the impact of depressions is less important than preventing depressions and hastening recovery from them. In dealing with the depression problem in Part IV, we noted in several connections the bearing of monopoly upon it. Here, in discussing monopoly, it is well to review the points made there.

Views have differed, both in policy and theory. President Roosevelt signed the National Industrial Recovery Act in 1933 with a flourish of optimism that industry-wide agreements would shortly achieve prosperity and stabilize it for the future. But three years after the codes had vanished, antitrust-law enforcement was raised to a new level of vigor, and New Deal spokesmen were blaming depression on the high prices and restriction of output attributable to monopolistic market control. Such a reversal may seem amusing, but it must be said that economists provide no clear consensus on the problem.

They would agree, however, that the depression problem is not to be solved by letting firms get together to adjust output to a set of prices most likely to provide profit security. This idea of stabilization appeals to businessmen, but it is commonplace that stabilizing prices and profits does not mean stabilizing production and employment. Persons who like the idea of economic planning may assume it would be well to assign each producer his place and tell him what to do, whether through supervised monopoly or more positive regulation. But the resulting stabilization is as likely to be that of stagnation as of high prosperity. There is nothing in the process of adjusting the output of each product to demand, at a price somehow determined, that should cause total production to go forward on a prosperity level.

The orthodox view, as we have seen, is that monopolistic controls must be the death of prosperity, since flexible prices and responsive adjustments are the key to a soundly operating economy. Much can be said for this theory, but if a prosperous capitalism really depends on a high degree of price flexibility, the outlook is not good. Competition may be substantial, and adequate for many purposes, without overcoming the rigidities often present in markets.

With emphasis shifting toward the savings-investment analysis of depressions, less is said about flexible prices—indeed some rigidities appear virtuous—and competition and monopoly are scrutinized for their effects on the inclination of people to save income and invest savings. From this standpoint, pure competition and perfect markets may not seem so important, but monopoly is still the villain. On the one hand, by increasing profits and aggravating inequality, it tends to increase the amount of saving out of a given national income and thus expand the amount of investment necessary to maintain prosperity. On the other hand, monopoly seems likely, to the whole, to weaken the spirit of enterprise on which investment depends.

On the latter point it may be argued that, during a depression, some action to prevent severe losses and maintain solvency will speed the replacement of capital goods and hasten recovery. But it cannot be true, in general, that profits from monopoly stimulate production and investment, because the way to get them is through restricting production. Great industries develop best when profits are sought through large volume sold at low prices and with small profit margins. Competition seems the best assurance of such a business policy. The characteristic monopoly approach to profit seeking is essentially timid and unenterprising. It follows the course of making the most of existing markets, apportioning such business as there is, and seeing that it is done at profitable prices. A substantial degree of competition, then, seems necessary to high and continuing investment.

Ethical attack on competition

It may be asked finally, in surveying the factors by which market controls are judged, whether competition can be reconciled with the ethical standards by which society should govern its affairs. Critics of capitalism assert that competition is a jungle force, antiquated and uncivilized. It would be better, they say, for people to cooperate in economic matters rather than be governed by essentially warlike attitudes.

There are elements in this view that do not bear on the present problem. We are not considering now whether society would be better if men were unselfish and labored only for the common good. It is easy to believe in the superiority of such a society, though control of activity in it would be difficult. As we observed in Chapter 4, individuals know more about their own situations than the needs of society as a whole, so that a decentralized control in which each individual registers his desires in markets has decided merit.

The moral issue presented by competition is, however, much narrower. It arises in a situation in which individuals seem, in fact, to be much more concerned with the welfare of themselves and their families than with that of other individuals and other families, and in which employees have a special interest in wages, businessmen in profits, and farmers in the prices of their products. The issue is whether, in these circumstances, it is better to have individuals act separately (or perhaps in small groups) in getting what they are after, or to have them pursue their ends in groups so large and inclusive that competition does not restrain them in promoting their interests.

Critics of competition seem often to have the wrong thing in mind. They may even cite the quarreling of employers and employees over wages as evidence of the evils of competition. But competition, we have seen, takes place among persons on the same side of a market, employers competing with employers, employees with employees. The antithesis of competition is often referred to as cooperation—an appealing word—but it would be better and more accurate to use the word "monopoly" in referring to the cooperation of people on the same side of a market. Then the critics who oppose competition would need to be more explicit as to what they advocate. As always, those who attack one arrangement in a responsible manner should be prepared to be fairly specific in setting forth the opposite arrangement that they espouse.

It should be added that competition is not necessarily warlike. In its pure state, as exemplified by the wheat farmer, even the sense of rivalry is practically absent. Only in the quoted-price area does the pursuit of patronage become bitter. Even here, its less attractive features are widely apparent only in periods of general slack and low demand. These features, as we shall see in the next chapter, may be made the object of special governmental restraint.

Review Questions

1. So far as their effect on prices and profits is concerned, can you see any justification for a difference in public attitude toward (a) complete monopoly that can control industrial expansion, (b) price agreements and pools, (c) oligopoly without collusion, (d) product differentiation? Explain.

2. "Ideal economy in the use of resources requires that plant facilities should be used up to the point where price just covers marginal cost." Develop the point.

3. With respect to the public interest in (a) the expansion of plant capacity

and (b) the use of that capacity, compare pure competition, partial monopoly that cannot control expansion, and complete monopoly that can.

4. "So-called competitive waste may arise from the ignorance and enthusiasms of unguided producers, or it may result from the incompleteness of competition." Develop the distinction. Where does advertising fit in? Do you view it as wasteful?

5. How does the distinction between plant and firm bear on the problem of oligopoly?

6. As inducements to industrial progress, how would you rate complete monopoly, pure competition, something in between? Explain.

7. "Under pure competition firms could not expand their plants in anticipation of expanding demand, nor could they endure the ordinary variations in demand." Develop the point. What conclusion regarding policy does it suggest? Is "industrial self-government" a plausible solution?

8. Review the leading ways in which monopoly and competition are believed to bear on the problem of business fluctuations.

9. From an ethical standpoint, does it seem desirable to allow the members of particular economic groups to cooperate in trying to increase their incomes, or is it better to require them to compete?

Discriminatory Pricing

Prices may be objectionable, not because they are *excessive* but because they are *out of line relatively*. Often the chief complaint of a buyer is that the price he is paying is higher than rival buyers are paying. Discriminatory pricing is related to monopoly in two ways: it is a weapon of monopoly in getting and keeping control, and it is a consequence of monopoly in maximizing profit. It should be considered at this point because of its prominence in policies that the next chapter will discuss.

If a seller charges one buyer a price of $1 for his product and another buyer $1.10 for the same quantity and under the same circumstances, his pricing is discriminatory. But if the former buyer is taking a larger quantity and there is an actual saving of 10 cents per unit in supplying this larger amount, then the differential does not make the pricing discriminatory. Indeed, not to have the differential in this case would be discriminatory against the larger buyer—at least it would in the *economic*, though not necessarily in the *legal*, sense of discrimination.[12] Discrimination exists, in other words, when the different buyers of a

[12] Legal interpretations of discrimination often diverge in several respects from the meaning developed here. In the case of railroads the concept of "relative unreasonableness" covers many objectionable rate relationships which do not qualify technically as discriminatory.

product pay prices not related as the costs of providing it are related.

A discriminatory price, then, need not be excessive in relation to cost. The *preferred* buyer may be undercharged, and the result is discrimination just as truly as when the *prejudiced* buyer is overcharged. Many cases of discrimination arise, especially in the railroad field, in which there is no evidence of overcharging.

Examples of discrimination will appear as we consider three aspects of it: (1) the conditions necessary to its occurrence, (2) the reasons for it from the business standpoint, and (3) its public significance.

Conditions necessary to discrimination

Discrimination violates the principle of single price explained in Chapter 18. It cannot exist under the ideal market conditions which give effect to that principle but may enter if any of those conditions are absent.

Thus *ignorance of market facts* gives rise to widespread discrimination of an irregular, unsystematic character. In markets in which higgling is present, markets of the Oriental-bazaar type, different prices are charged for goods in accordance with the bargaining ability of customers. Differentials of this sort may even exist in the sale of goods supposedly priced on a uniform basis. An astute purchaser of an automobile, at least before the war, might get a radio and a heater thrown in without extra charge, whereas another would pay fully for all extra fittings. Salesmen of industrial supplies may be somewhat flexible in the discounts they offer from list prices, depending on the resistance of buyers. The less standardized products are, the easier it is to have price differentials which are not supported by cost differences.

For continuing and systematic discrimination, however, a substantial degree of *monopoly* is necessary. Under competition a firm cannot consistently overcharge certain customers without losing them to competitors. Nor can it consistently undercharge others without being so overrun by customers that undercharging is foolish. This is the process by which uniform prices tend to prevail. But to the extent that a firm is a monopoly, customers must stay with it despite the prejudicial prices they pay. They must accept the discrimination or go without the product.

If the monopoly is only partial, the possible discrimination is accordingly limited. One buyer may knowingly pay more than another for his favorite brand of a product, but probably not very much more without being led to turn to another brand. Because he is well-to-do, a patient may pay higher fees to his favorite doctor than other patients do, but there is a limit to the discrimination he will accept without looking else-where for medical service. If, however, all other doctors follow the same discriminatory practice, it is as if he were confronted with a market-wide price agreement involving differential fees, the equivalent of a substantial degree of monopoly.

But monopoly alone is not a sufficient basis for systematic discrimination. There must also be an effective basis of *classifying buyers*. A seller may be sure that some buyers will take his product at $1.50, that others will pay no more than $1.25, and still others no more than $1, but he may have no way of sorting his customers and charging them according to what they can be made to pay. A merchant in a monopoly position, unless he were willing to bargain lengthily with his customers, could not charge them on a differential basis.

How may this classifying be done? The bases used vary with products and the circumstances under which they are sold. To some extent, especially in consumers' goods, it may rest on nothing more than differences in *customer gullibility*. Thus a standard soap with some added perfume and a fancy wrapper may be sold at twice the standard price to persons who think a higher price must represent a correspondingly superior product.

A more substantial basis of classification is the *location of the buyer*. Under the old Pittsburgh-plus basing-point system of pricing steel, a Detroit buyer from a mill at Gary, Indiana, would pay less than a Chicago buyer, since freight from Pittsburgh to Detroit is less than to Chicago. But the net price to the mill, after deducting transportation cost, would be less from the Detroit sale than from the Chicago sale. It is as if different prices were quoted to buyers at Detroit and Chicago, with the buyer paying the freight. In this way discriminatory pricing is common under the basing-point system.

Buyers are most easily classified in the *public-utility* field. Customers of electric-power companies fall readily into groups as domestic, commercial, and industrial users. Shippers of the thousands of types of freight that move by railroad are easily put into classes according to the characteristics of goods and how they are packed; different charges can then be imposed for equivalent use of railroad facilities. The location of shippers and destination points is a still easier basis of classification; or when rates are judged on a distance basis, different movements of the same kind of traffic often appear to be charged quite unequally.

In such cases discrimination is made easier by the prevalence of *common costs*. When different kinds of traffic move over the same rails, on the same train, even in the same car, it is inherently so difficult to assign costs logically to specific items of traffic that there is a special temptation to spread them unevenly, provided positive reasons for discrimination are present.[13]

A final condition necessary to systematic discrimination is that *resale* of the product should be difficult. A monopoly may be able to classify its customers, but, if buyers who pay the lower price can turn around and resell to those who pay the higher price, the differential charging would largely be defeated. This, again, is a reason why discrimination is common in the public-utility field; such services as electric power and transportation cannot easily be resold by the buyer. An interesting example of this limitation is found in case of export *dumping* in foreign trade. Firms often sell more cheaply in foreign than in domestic markets —dumping their products abroad, it is said—but unless a protective tariff is present to prevent the importation of goods that have been exported at low prices, the extent of such discrimination is greatly restricted.

Reasons for discrimination

To understand the conditions that make discriminatory pricing possible is not to see why sellers want to discriminate. The main reason springs directly from the nature of demand—the fact that some buyers are willing, if necessary, to pay more than other buyers are. If a firm charges a single uniform price for its product, that price must be low enough to attract the marginal purchasers, those to whom the good is worth no more than the price and who would not buy if the price were any higher. But if the conditions which permit discrimination are present, these marginal buyers can be put in one class and charged the price that will hold them, while other buyers are put in separate classes and charged such higher prices as they can be made to pay. By this means a larger total revenue is obtained from the same volume of product. By using this system of *class price,* a monopolist can expand the profit that his position makes possible.

The urge to discriminate is strongest in industries that not only are monopolistic but that also (1) have large fixed costs and (2) are commonly operating well below capacity. Firms in this position find it difficult to obtain enough revenue to cover their costs, and it is necessary to get all they can from their limited sales, piling their costs disproportionately on their customers according to what they will bear. Accordingly some will be made to pay far more than the full average cost. Others

---

[13] Sometimes railroad rates are treated as a case of joint costs. Actually the different kinds of traffic are seldom carried with that fixity of proportion that the theory of joint cost requires. The situation is rather that of desks and bookcases, the example of common costs used in Chapter 20. Additional business is sought at low rates when there is unused capacity, not otherwise.

will pay considerably less, since, under the specified conditions, marginal cost is well below total unit cost, and additional business is desirable as long as it more than covers the added cost of doing it. In these circumstances prices may be spread over a wide range.[14]

It is in this situation that dumping goods abroad at a low price occurs. But, again, the railroads probably provide the best example. Their fixed costs are large, and in the United States they were commonly built in advance of traffic, so that their unused capacity was usually considerable. In this situation the additional cost of carrying additional tonnage is small in comparison with the full average cost of moving freight. Thus it was logical to develop a rate structure in which traffic that could bear high rates would have to pay them, and other classes of traffic would pay graduated rates down to the point where out-of-pocket costs were barely covered.

[14] It is possible and perhaps helpful to show graphically how discriminatory charging, on the class-price principle, may enable a firm to make money when any single monopolistic price would not bring sufficient revenue to cover its costs. The situation is that

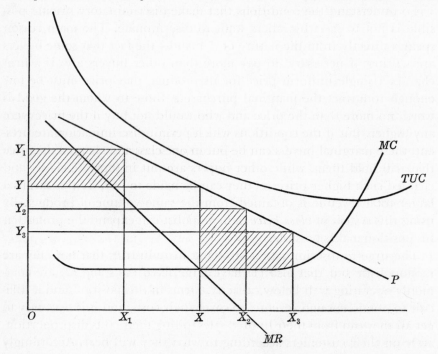

shown in note 8 on page 549 except that the price P for every possible quantity is less than the total unit cost TUV for that quantity. The smallest loss would be with price OY and output OX (at which marginal revenue MR equals marginal cost MC). But by charging price OY_1 to certain selected buyers, additional revenue (represented by the upper shaded area) is obtained without additional cost. And by quoting prices OY_2 and OY_3, which are well below total unit cost, to certain potential buyers, additional sales are made which improve the earning position to the extent of the excess of the additional revenue over the additional cost (shown by the lower shaded area). Total output becomes OX_3.

Discrimination to gain monopoly. The foregoing are reasons why business firms, under the right conditions, can improve their profit position through discrimination. But discrimination is a means not only of taking advantage of monopoly power but of achieving it. Two possibilities of this sort were suggested in the early part of this chapter:

1. Large firms may cut prices locally to destroy new competitors which are springing up. When they do this, prices are likely to be held at a higher level elsewhere, so that the arrangement is discriminatory. Similarly, large buyers may be able to push suppliers into charging them lower prices than are charged their competitors—lower by more than any difference in cost due to quantity. In this way an advantage is derived that may be ruinous to the competitors.

2. Such discriminatory pricing schemes as the basing-point system make it easier to avoid price competition. If it becomes common practice in an industry to charge prices governed by one or a few basing points, with railroad freight from the appropriate basing point included, then the delivered prices at all points are fixed for all companies without the necessity of an elaborate price agreement. A situation is created in which it is hard to tell whether uniform prices are spontaneous or achieved through collusion.

Discrimination from the public standpoint

If the purpose of discriminatory pricing is to establish monopoly, it must be condemned from a social point of view. Nor does discrimination to make the most profit from a monopoly position seem, on the surface, to be any better. But in connection with chronic unused capacity, a case can be made for it—though not an unqualified case.

If adjusting prices to the amounts different buyers can pay causes fuller use of facilities, with a lowering of the average cost of the product, a social gain results. This may often happen. Indeed it may happen in such a way that the prejudiced buyer, the one paying the higher price, pays absolutely less than he would without the discrimination. A railroad rate of $2 per ton may be the best single rate on traffic from A to B, but the amount of traffic at that rate may leave the railroad seriously under-used and losing money. By quoting rates of $1.50 and $1 for types of traffic that will not move at the $2 rate, revenue may be so increased, with small addition to cost, that the top rate need be only $1.75. Discrimination results, but average cost is lower, facilities are more fully used, the prejudiced traffic pays less than before, and the railroad remains solvent.

But this argument for discrimination assumes that there is some basic reason for the unused capacity. The railroad is built with a standard gauge, and it must run all the way from A to B, so that, to have a railroad at all, a capacity is fixed that traffic does not justify. In manufacturing, on the other hand, firms can start small and sell over a wide area, and there is not the same inherent reason for a capacity out of line with demand. Only if the market is not large enough for a single plant of efficient size does economy result from establishing such a capacity that only a discriminatory set of prices can cause it to be used. This condition may often be present in the electric-power, as well as the railroad, field.

But even where discriminatory pricing is justified on the grounds of causing fuller use of facilities, it can still be highly objectionable. It is arguable that because of water competition, railroads should charge lower rates on traffic from New York to San Francisco than they do on traffic from New York to Salt Lake City. If the transcontinental traffic obtained thereby pays something toward the fixed costs, rates can be absolutely lower to intermediate points. But distributors in Salt Lake City reply that the absolute rate is not what concerns them, that they are competing with distributors in San Francisco and should not incur a higher transportation cost for a shorter haul.

This is an example of the difficulty created whenever prices depart from a cost basis. Middle western buyers of steel supplied the pressure to overthrow Pittsburgh-plus. Why should they pay prices based on Pittsburgh when they actually bought from Gary? From the social standpoint, the effect is to cause an uneconomic location of industry when producers at different points do not bear the actual burden of costs that they occasion. The same situation arises when the more efficient of two competitors is compelled to pay a higher price for his raw material, thus preventing production from being carried on most economically. As we saw in discussing the principle of opportunity cost, the prices of resources should promote their use in the best way and by the best users, but discrimination can undermine this system of control. The result can be the same as when government subsidizes certain producers and not others.

Thus, from the policy standpoint, discrimination presents a difficult problem.

Review Questions

1. "Price differences for the same good are necessarily discriminatory." Do you agree? In your answer bring out the meaning of discrimination. Why is the basing-point system of pricing discriminatory?

2. Distinguish irregular and systematic discrimination and the reasons necessary to their existence. Show that the conditions necessary to systematic discrimination are peculiarly present in the public-utility field.

3. "Discrimination may enable business firms to maintain and strengthen a monopoly position, but it is primarily a means of increasing the profit from that position." Explain both clauses. Why is the motive to discriminate strengthened by the presence of large fixed costs and unused capacity?

4. "Discrimination may be socially beneficial if it brings fuller use of capacity and lower average cost; but there should be some fundamental reason for the unused capacity." Explain.

5. "Discriminatory pricing tends to undermine the role of cost in promoting the most effective use of resources." Explain.

- 23 -

Market Control Policies
in the United States

THE preceding chapters in Part V have dealt with the very heart of economic organization. How a nation adjusts the use of its resources to the desires of its people determines the kind of economic system that it has. In every system control must rest on some scheme of values and on some method of giving them expression. The dominant idea in the American system has been that the controlling values should emerge freely in markets and that activities of producers and users of goods should be governed by private responses to these values. At the same time, government has intervened extensively in markets, notably through such measures as the Sherman Anti-Trust Act, the Interstate Commerce Act and similar state public-utility laws, and the Agricultural Adjustment Act. The central place of markets in economic control assigns to these measures a central place among government policies.

Their importance must not lead one to exaggerate their scope. In no major policy, except in wartime, does government displace the preferences of buyers, backed by their purchasing power, as the general basis of assigning resources to industries. In no major policy does government hold that the scarcities of resources, in light of existing technology, should not govern the manner of using them. In no major policy does government impose an alternative to the price-cost calculations by which private producers take account of demand and supply conditions in organizing production.

But government has assumed a large responsibility, nevertheless, with respect to the *operation* of these underlying factors in control. Its approach has varied with the defects that have appeared in markets, as seen by Congress and state legislatures. Three major approaches are clearly distinguishable, and all three are represented in the major policies mentioned above.

The most sweeping policy is that embodied in the Sherman Anti-Trust Act and supporting laws. This is the dominant policy outside of agriculture and the railroads and other public utilities. Its primary aim is *to insure that markets will be adequately competitive.* The occasion for it lies in the desire of all producers to throw off the restraints of competition if they can. It involves no regulation whatever in the strict sense. Under it no governmental body has authority to fix the price of any product or to tell producers to expand or contract their facilities or the use made of them. It aims merely to control the character of the markets within which producers and buyers make their decisions.

The opposite policy, from one standpoint, is that applied to the railroads and other utilities. It recognizes that competition cannot be an adequate regulator in these industries and that an attempt to enforce it would impair efficiency. A substantial degree of monopoly is unavoidable, and the policy is that of *substituting positive regulation for competition as the principal regulator.* Control centers on prices, so that they will be neither excessive nor dangerously discriminatory, but extends also to other aspects of production as necessitated by the absence of competition or the presence of price control.

The third type of policy is, in a quite different sense, opposite to antitrust policy. It rests on the diagnosis that *competition,* instead of being inadequate, is sometimes *excessive and should be restricted.* Output appears too large and prices too low, and government supplies a corrective. This, essentially, was the policy under the National Recovery Administration between 1933 and 1935. Bituminous coal, viewed as a "sick industry," has also been subject to this policy. But its outstanding continuing application has been agriculture.

Sections of this chapter will be devoted to the antitrust laws, public-utility regulation, and agricultural adjustment policy. Much of the analysis of preceding chapters is applicable here and will be introduced by brief reference. The essentials of policies will be stated briefly without elaboration. The aim will be to set forth sharply their main provisions, their underlying logic, their strength and weakness, within the general framework of the control that operates through markets.

With respect to the logic of such policies as these, a preliminary word is needed. Economic policies are seldom, if ever, instituted on the basis of a clearly spelled out economic analysis. They are enacted by legislative bodies, because large groups of people, with many votes to cast, feel that a condition is bad and that government should correct it. At the outset policies need at least to be plausible from the general public standpoint. If they continue in effect, they are subject to an evolving interpretation. The theory of them is clarified, and they are likely to be amended in light of it. But it would distort history seriously to read the analysis of this chapter in its entirety into the minds of legislators and the popular supporters and opponents of the policies discussed.

Antitrust Policy

The policy that has its chief statutory expression in the Sherman Act has been described as "our economic common law," "an elastic procedure backed by tradition to prevent the private seizure of industrial power."[1] Broadly, it has been accepted as few policies have been and violated also as few have been. Its real meaning, unfortunately, is often not understood by those who acclaim it in principle but demur whenever its more effective enforcement is urged.

The main difficulty is the one noted in Chapter 4 in introducing the idea of a freely organized economy. Too commonly the word "free" implies that the producer is at liberty to do as he pleases and that any government interference is per se a violation of freedom. But a free system, all students of it seem to agree, must not be defined negatively as the mere absence of government interference. As a workable economy, a free system requires the positive presence of conditions which cause the actions of private producers to serve the interests of the whole public.

One essential of freedom, in this positive sense, is that new producers shall be able to enter industries and introduce new products and methods, free from arbitrary obstruction by powerful existing firms and combines. Another essential is that the prices of products and materials shall not be subject to any serious degree of organized private control. Positive control over the use of resources and products is expected to operate through prices, and it is a critical violation of the freedom of a free system to distort seriously the price relationships that underlying supply and demand conditions require.

The antitrust laws and their supplements are the chief legislative embodiment of this philosophy of a free economy. In part, they must be judged along with the philosophy itself, since they are scarcely separable from it. In part, the laws must be judged from the more detailed standpoint of the wisdom with which legislators have phrased them, courts have interpreted them, and executives enforced them.

To speak of them as antitrust laws is to defer to popular usage. The

[1] Thurman W. Arnold, *The Bottlenecks of Business,* Reynal and Hitchcock, 1940, Chapter 5. The second phrase is the title of this chapter. Mr. Arnold headed the Antitrust Division of the Department of Justice during its active period just before World War II.

policy aims (1) to maintain a substantial degree of competition in industry and (2) to improve the character of competition.

The Sherman Act

In the period following the Civil War popular wrath mounted against the ruthlessness of business combinations in their treatment both of competitors and customers. Provisions to restrain them appeared in state laws and in state constitutions, and pressure in Congress led in 1890 to the adoption of the Sherman Anti-Trust Act with but one dissenting vote. These laws did not establish a new policy, since monopolies and market restrictions had long been viewed as against public policy and had often been attacked in the courts on common-law principles. But it had become apparent that the "trusts" could be restrained only through positive enactments, enforced through systematic public prosecution of offenders.

Provisions; early interpretation. An extraordinary feature of the Sherman Act is its extreme brevity. Apart from enforcement provisions, it simply condemns as misdemeanors (1) all contracts, combinations or conspiracies in restraint of trade among the states or with foreign nations and (2) the act of monopolizing or attempting to monopolize any part of such trade.[2] These are general phrases, and it was not apparent from them just how they could be made to fit the complex array of combinations, loose-knit and corporate, that had developed and all the practices used to get control of markets. Plainly the law had to get its precise meaning from the courts in the process of enforcement.[3]

The beginning was not auspicious. In a decision in 1895 involving the American Sugar Refining Company, the Supreme Court made it appear that manufacturing is distinct from commerce and that a combination of manufacturers could not be outlawed under the federal power over interstate commerce. Because most of the combines at which the law was aimed were in manufacturing, this was a heavy blow.

Another threat came from the holding company. As a method of combining companies, the technical trust had been made useless through attacks at common law, and corporate combinations were taking advantage of a New Jersey statute of 1889 that permitted one corpo-

[2] The enforcement provisions provide criminal penalties and authorize courts to issue orders that dissolve combinations or require improved behavior. It also provides that private parties who are injured by violations may sue for triple damages.

[3] Among the standard works that tell this story are Harry L. Purdy, Martin L. Lindahl, and William A. Carter, *Corporate Concentration and Public Policy*, Prentice-Hall, 1942; Henry R. Seager and Charles A. Gulick, *Trust and Corporation Problems*, Harper & Bros., 1921; Myron W. Watkins, *Industrial Combinations and Public Policy*, Houghton Mifflin, 1927. For valuable treatments of various aspects of this problem, see *Readings in the Social Control of Industry*, selected by a Committee of the American Economic Association, Blakiston, 1942.

ration to hold stock in other corporations. It appeared that a corporation chartered by a sovereign state could perform the normal act of buying property, even stocks of another corporation, without danger of criminal prosecution. Accordingly, in the years around 1900 most of the old trusts, as in oil and tobacco, were reorganized in the holding-company form, and many new ones, such as United States Steel, were organized. This was the first great period of corporate combination since the Sherman Act was adopted, but not the only one.

Presently, in the first years of the century, the courts made it clear that the Act did not possess the fatal weaknesses attributed to it. It was applied successfully to manufacturing, on the sensible interpretation that a manufacturing combination cannot achieve its object without restricting sales and raising prices, which are in commerce. It was also applied to holding companies. The Supreme Court declared that restraint of trade and monopoly are what they are, whether the form of combination is a technical trust, a holding company, or something else.

But the courts have never been able to give a clear, sharp meaning to restraint of trade and monopoly, as used in the Sherman Act; nor has Congress stepped in to provide legislative clarification. The interpretation has been reasonably satisfactory in the case of loose combinations but not in the case of the great corporate combines.

Application to loose-knit combinations. In the case of price agreements, pools, and boycotts, the general rule is simple. Evidence that they exist, at least in any substantial part of an industry, is sufficient for conviction. It does not matter whether the resulting prices are reasonable or not. The agreement itself is the misdemeanor, not the effect of it.

There is often great difficulty, of course, in proving that an agreement exists. Firms do not display the records of meetings at which they knowingly violate the law. Greater difficulty arises, as in trade associations, when general pressure is put on members to restrict output and hold prices up, but no explicit agreement is reached. Such action may be viewed as tantamount to agreement, and convictions sometimes follow. But circumstantial evidence of an economic nature has never had the weight it should. Prices may behave in a way that could not be accidental, but justices who know the legal language of conspiracy and improper intent are unimpressed by monopolistic price patterns.

Application to corporate combinations. For corporate combinations the law has had no clear meaning. The most notable cases that arose during the "trust busting" campaign of Theodore Roosevelt involved the great Standard Oil and American Tobacco combines. Both resulted, in 1911, in orders by the Supreme Court for dissolution into a few large companies. One result of these decisions was a lesson in the difficulty of achieving a real separation of the parts of a closely knit combine. Another result was the continuing influence of some incidental remarks by Chief Justice White, since known as the "rule of reason," to the effect that the courts possess a fairly wide latitude in deciding whether market restrictions really violate the law. Scholars have argued as to the more precise meaning of these remarks, but they at least fit into a picture of rather lenient treatment of corporate combinations.

If firms constituting half of an industry were to agree on prices, there is no question that the law would be violated. But if these same firms became part of a corporate combination, with much greater power over the market, the law as interpreted would probably not be violated. To agree on prices is itself unlawful restraint of trade; to buy the property of another company has not seemed, by itself and without further evidence of wrongdoing, to constitute either restraint or monopoly. If the combine has used highhanded methods to rid itself of competitors, there is evidence of evil intent. Indeed the word "monopoly" in its traditional legal sense has usually implied action to *exclude* competitors, not merely combination with them. If the combine has not used unfair and exclusive methods, and it claims that greater efficiency in production was the real reason for its formation—a claim not applicable to price agreements—its chances for acquittal have been good.

Certainly the idea of oligopoly—that large firms which constitute substantial parts of industries, but much less than the whole of them, can greatly influence markets—has scarcely entered judicial thinking. The United States Steel Corporation, which at the time included about half the industry, was adjudged a "good trust" in 1920, though by the closest of split decisions. Combinations involving larger segments of industries survived attack in cases involving United Shoe Machinery, National Cash Register, International Harvester, and American Can. The law was found to be violated in some of these instances, but the courts merely required a minor sloughing off of parts or good future behavior. A theory has prevailed in the courts that great power over markets can remain unexerted and is then not unlawful. But the chief evidence whether power is exerted must lie in the behavior of prices and production, and these have scarcely been considered in the decisions.

Enforcement. Entirely apart from the interpretation of the Sherman Act, its enforcement has been weak and spasmodic under most administrations. To do its work, the Antitrust Division of the Department of Justice should be a fairly large organization, able to keep closely in touch with all major industries and to bring numerous suits when violations are suspected. Commonly it has had funds for only a fraction of the work it should do. Quite vigorous enforcement seemed to be getting under way just before World War II, when the New Deal, abandoning its NRA excursion, came to believe that almost all economic evils, and not only the usual monopoly abuses, lay in "the concentration of economic power." War interrupted the effort, but it was resumed with some vigor when the war was over.

The Clayton Act and the preventive principle

The Sherman Act, the basis of antitrust policy, has been supplemented in important ways. Early experience led to the view, which was voiced by Woodrow Wilson, that if markets are to be free and competitive, the surer method is to prevent monopoly, rather than to rely on breaking up combinations that have developed. President Wilson was convinced that great combines are not natural growths, rooted in efficiency, but the result of arbitrary acts. Policy, then, should aim to prevent those acts. This was the idea of the Clayton Act, passed in 1914, and it was part of the thought behind the Federal Trade Commission Act of the same year.

Holding companies and interlocking directorates. Perhaps the most promising provision of the Clayton Act was the attempt to *outlaw intercorporate stockholding,* including the holding company, when it involves companies that should remain competitive. The intention was that the act of forming the combination would constitute the offense, and the problem of appraising its subsequent behavior would not arise. But the provision was highly disappointing. It was loosely worded in several respects, but mainly in the fact that it could be evaded simply through buying directly the assets of competing corporations, without holding their stock. The Federal Trade Commission has repeatedly recommended that the section be strengthened, but Congress has not been impressed with the need. Even less useful has been a related provision that aims to keep the same men from being on the boards of directors of competing corporations.

Exclusive agreements and patents. Another provision struck at the use of "tying clauses" in contracts to get control of markets. Thus a large firm with one or more outstanding products in a field may require merchants, if they are to handle any of its products, to handle its whole line and handle none of its competitors' products. Or, like United Shoe Machinery, it may require that manufacturers who use any of its equipment must use only its equipment. Such arrangements were outlawed if they tended seriously to reduce competition. The effect has been beneficial.

It should be noted that *patents* are usually the basis of tying contracts and that this is only one of the situations in which it is difficult to reconcile patent policy and antitrust policy. While the one aims at competition, the other creates a limited monopoly that is meaningless unless some privileges go with it. In the abstract the two can be reconciled. The patent law rests on the clause in the Constitution which states that the purpose of the exclusive right is "to promote the progress of science and useful arts." This aim is quite in harmony with the purpose of competition. But the limited patent monopoly can be extended, as through tying contracts, to achieve a control of markets not intended by patent policy; it can be used also to suppress new ideas and forestall the progress of competitors. Present laws can be made to cover certain situations that arise, but not all of them, and there is still a difficult legislative problem in the patent field.

Price discrimination and the Robinson-Patman Act. The Clayton Act also condemned discrimination in prices, if the effect is to promote monopoly. Of the many forms that discrimination takes, the one that Congress particularly had in mind was drastic local price cutting to kill off small competitors while holding prices up in other areas. There was little occasion to apply the law to this type of situation, but the provision came presently to be applied in cases where large buyers get an unfair advantage through being quoted lower prices than their competitors pay. Here the threatened monopoly is in the buyer's field, not the seller's.

The latter situation grew in importance, and there was increasing pressure on Congress, largely from independent merchants, to outlaw discrimination more sweepingly without the need of proving that monopoly is imminent. This was done in the Robinson-Patman Act of 1936, which amended the Clayton Act. In general, price differences were made unlawful that could not be defended on the ground of differences in cost or in services rendered. There is much to be said for this principle, but in practice the Robinson-Patman Act has been difficult to enforce, hard to reconcile with some quite proper merchandising practices, and an obstacle to the piecemeal whittling of prices which may be the only kind of price competition under oligopoly.

Unfair Competition and the Federal Trade Commission

Apart from creating the Commission, the main provision of the Federal Trade Commission Act is its sweeping declaration that unfair methods of competition are unlawful. In part, this provision is identical in purpose with the Clayton Act: it aims to prevent practices that will lead to monopoly. But it also has the purpose of *improving the general character of competition,* whether monopoly is threatened or not. Thus it applies to small firms as well as large, and a good share of the many cases under it arise in the case of small firms that are never suspected of potential monopoly. Policy in this sphere, as stated earlier, seeks not only to preserve competition but also to lift it to a higher plane.

Broadly this means that business firms should expect to succeed only on the basis of their efficiency and the quality of their products and that any other basis of taking patronage from competitors is objectionable. Decent businessmen should not be forced to stoop to the methods of unscrupulous competitors. In practice, the Commission does not have the discretion to interpret the word "unfair" quite as broadly as these statements suggest. For a time it was limited considerably by the courts, but later interpretations have given it a wider latitude, and its power has been considerably increased by a 1938 amendment known as the Wheeler-Lea Act. It may now act specifically on behalf of consumers who are the victims of "unfair or deceptive acts or practices," and it is charged with responsibilities that directly supplement the Pure Food and Drugs Act.

While the Commission deals with many dubious practices, the bulk of its work concerns the *misrepresentation of products,* especially false advertising. Some misleading claims involve objective facts, as in saying that a cotton garment is half wool; they are easy to handle.[4] But general claims as to the merits of products are harder to judge, especially when phrased warily to suggest an idea without actually stating it. Despite difficulties, the character of competitive methods has undoubtedly been greatly improved.

The Commission has exclusive responsibility for enforcing the Federal Trade Commission Act, and it shares with the Department of Justice the task of enforcing the Clayton Act. It does not enforce the Sherman Act, though it manages, through a generous interpretation of its powers, to treat price agreements as unfair methods of competition. It does not impose penalties for past infractions but issues "cease and desist" orders with which firms must comply or suffer penalties. Beside its enforcement activities, the Commission conducts many investigations.

Resale price maintenance and other limitations on antitrust power

From the beginning, questions have arisen as to the range of economic activity to which the antitrust laws apply. Are farm cooperatives

---

[4] A special supplementary statute, the Wool Products Labeling Act of 1939, was passed to deal with this particular situation.

subject to them, labor unions, railroads, and so on? At various points the scope of the laws has been delimited, either by the courts or by legislation.

Farmers' cooperatives are not to be attacked as combinations in restraint of trade, though they must not raise prices to unreasonable levels. *Labor unions* have sometimes been treated as violators but seem now, through inconclusive legislative and more conclusive court decisions, to be exempt in all their ordinary activities. *Railroad combinations* have been prosecuted successfully, despite the fact that positive regulation is relied on chiefly to protect the public from exploitation. Since 1918 competing firms have been allowed to form combinations, under Federal Trade Commission supervision, to aid them in their *export trade*.

The National Industrial Recovery Act of 1933 gave brief general exemption to approved industrial agreements, and, had it continued, would have changed basically the conception of economic control from competition to supervised cartelization. With the passing of NRA, the idea that price competition could be harmful continued to get spasmodic official recognition. A limited example was in the coal industry; a more general one was the legalizing of resale price maintenance.

Resale price maintenance is said to prevail when the manufacturer fixes the final selling price of his product and thus controls the margins of wholesalers and retailers. The practice was long regarded as an unlawful restraint of trade and an unfair method, but much pressure to exempt it came from independent retailers and some manufacturers. The former objected to the small mark-ups, and especially the "loss leaders," of the chain stores; the latter wanted the public to associate particular prices with their branded products. In response, many states passed so-called "fair-trade" laws authorizing the fixing of resale prices, and in 1937 Congress passed the Miller-Tydings Act, an amendment to the Sherman Act, to exempt interstate transactions when they involve states that have these laws.

The effect is to reduce competition in merchandising. Manufacturers must remain competitive, as before, in fixing their prices, but if particular manufacturers name the final selling prices of their products, merchants are not at liberty to compete for business with smaller mark-ups. Resale prices operate widely in the case of books, liquor, cosmetics, and many other items, but there are important areas of merchandising where they are seldom applied. Chain organizations and department stores are still able to get their private brands, often manufactured by the same firms that set resale prices on their better known brands. But for its limited application, resale price maintenance would seriously restrict the competition of middlemen. Even so, most believers in the competitive principle disapprove this concession to NRA thinking.

Another concession is found in the *"unfair-practices"* acts of some of the states, which forbid the selling of goods below cost. From the practical standpoint, these laws are hard to administer, because the relevant costs are difficult to define, and their application is mostly to local situations. But, in principle, they reflect the same unwillingness to accept the verdict of free markets in pricing goods and can scarcely be reconciled with a real belief in a competitive system.

An interesting feature of legislation in this field is the frequent use of the words "fair" and "unfair." Behind it is the propaganda value of words that carry favorable and unfavorable connotations. "Unfair competition" is an old common-law phrase, and, as used in the Federal Trade Commission Act, its meaning is consistent with, and supplementary to, the purposes of the Sherman Act. But the "codes of fair competition" under the NRA were legal arrangements to depart from the competitive control of markets and had to be specifically exempted from the Sherman Act. Likewise the "fair-trade laws," which permit resale price maintenance, and the "unfair practices acts" are frank departures from the established conception of the competitive control of markets. It is a mark of one's knowledge and clarity of thought to avoid being imposed upon by the vague implications of words, as in the varied uses of "fair" and "unfair."

Criticisms of antitrust policy

Antitrust policy may be appraised from various standpoints and criticized on various grounds. Many persons question whether it can continue to be the dominant basis of control in a modern economy, but continuing dependence on it is probably expected by the majority of observers.

Attacks upon it are from quite different angles. From one side, competition is regarded as too weak a controlling force, under modern conditions, and not likely to be greatly strengthened. Great corporations seem to dominate many industries, and oligopoly is viewed as equivalent to monopoly. The urge to control markets, through trade associations and in other ways, is looked upon as irresistible.

From the other side, competition appears not as something we cannot have but as something we do not want—a wasteful, unsettling economic force. Cartelization seems superior in "rationalizing" the use of resources and avoiding violent upheavals.

Either position can be made quite persuasive by marshaling selected facts and arguments. Either can be weakened considerably, as the preceding chapter sought to show, by examining critically the analysis on which it rests. Informed persons can still look hopefully on the future of a modern economy organized, on the whole, through the fairly free operation of markets.

Even under modern conditions, the control that competition can exert has not been used to the limit. Antitrust law enforcement has commonly been halfhearted and sporadic. It can be greatly improved without becoming oppressive, if there is a will to improve it.[5] Nevertheless, it should not be judged by the apparent number of violations. The test of enforcement should lie in the unmeasurable extent to which it has deterred violations. It is evidenced by the restrained behavior of violators who are anxious not to arouse action against them. Neglect of more serious enforcement has many causes, but one cause undoubtedly has been a sense that it has not been needed.

Certainly one's faith in antitrust law policy must depend on one's conception of what its goal should be. If competition, to be adequate, must be the simon-pure variety, or something close to it, then, of course, an acceptable competitive system is impossible. But persons who judge the working of markets by the theory of pure competition have little sense of what should be expected. That theory is a useful benchmark in the analysis of markets, as we have said, but not a direct policy guide. If firms are to survive under modern conditions and be enterprising and progressive, a limited control over their market situation seems essential.

From this it does not follow that competition works adequately. The oligopolistic industries, in particular, present a major problem, but evidence increases that their behavior is more restrained than the bare theory of oligopolistic pricing would suggest. Further restraint appears possible, short of positive regulation. The question is whether price-cost relations and output decisions can be kept sufficiently free to cause the handling of resources, and the rewarding of services, to operate reasonably in the general interest.

At least that is the question except to those persons who regard a competitive system, even at its best, as inherently bad. Their viewpoint is one that it is best to defer to the concluding chapter. For the present, it is enough to insist that those who would discard competition must be aware how closely competitive control is tied up with the processes of a free system and how much they would have to discard before they could establish a substitute control.

---

[5] See Temporary National Economic Committee Monograph No. 38, *A Study of the Construction and Enforcement of the Federal Antitrust Laws,* by Milton Handler.

Review Questions

1. "Governmental control of markets does not take the place of values and prices in the scheme of economic control." Explain.

2. In what sense are antitrust policy and public-utility regulation opposites? Antitrust policy and agricultural-adjustment policy?

3. "A free economy cannot be a laissez-faire economy." Review this point, which was first stated in Chapter 4.

4. Give examples of "the private seizure of industrial power," as you interpret that phrase.

5. "Antitrust policy" is not an adequately descriptive phrase. State more fully the purposes of the policy.

6. Why should a federal statute such as the Sherman Act apply the anti-monopoly principle more effectively than the common law as carried out mainly through private suits? Than state laws?

7. "Restraint of trade and monopoly have depended on the courts for their meaning. Judicial interpretation has been simpler and more severe in the case of loose-knit combinations than of corporate combinations." Develop this statement. What does the "rule of reason" imply? What was the fate of the oil, tobacco, and steel combines?

8. "The Clayton Act embodied the preventive principle." Explain.

9. If a large firm wants to absorb a competing corporation, does it matter whether it buys the stock of that corporation or its plant and equipment?

10. If the Radio Corporation of America, which owns many patents used by makers of radio receiving sets, were to require that all licensee companies install R.C.A. tubes in their products, though other tubes were available, what legal difficulty might it encounter? (This was the situation in a suit that R.C.A. lost.)

11. Why is it difficult to reconcile patent policy and antitrust policy?

12. How may price discrimination promote monopoly in the seller's field of business? The buyer's field? What statutes have dealt with discrimination in manufacturing and merchandising? What general rule is supposed to govern price relationships?

13. What is unfair competition, as distinguished from restriction of competition? Are they related? Need they be? What authority exists regarding unfair methods?

14. Would it be equally difficult for the Federal Trade Commission to establish that advertising is "materially misleading" in cases in which the producer claims (a) that a mild antiseptic will cure dandruff, (b) that a brand of motor oil is the best on the market, (c) that a radio is worth twice its price, (d) that a veneered table is solid mahogany, (e) that a tooth paste makes teeth 50 percent brighter?

15. Name some important areas of combination to which the antitrust laws do not apply or are applied in limited fashion.

16. Distinguish resale price maintenance from the ordinary collusive maintenance of prices. Compare their effects on competition. What is the legal status of resale price maintenance?

17. Distinguish the varied uses of the words "fair" and "unfair" and relate them to the purposes of antitrust policy.

18. Antitrust policy is attacked on the ground (a) that it cannot be enforced, (b) that it is an unsound basis of economic organization. Relate to these views the main ideas developed in the preceding chapter.

Public Utility Regulation

The term "public utility" may be used broadly to cover electric power, gas, water, telephone, and telegraph companies, and also railroads and other common carriers. Or the common carriers, at least those operating interstate, may be omitted. The broader usage will be followed here, and, as far as possible, all utilities will be treated together.

The common element in this group of industries is the presence of a sufficient degree of monopoly so that government regulation must replace, or supplement, the regulating force of competition. Such regulation is a drastic departure from the free-enterprise philosophy, and if widely applied would change the character of the economy. Actually, in the United States, only about 7 percent of the working force are in these industries. The percentage of total productive wealth is greater, however, because these activities require a large capital per worker.

The first glimmerings of recognition that industries in this group should receive special control came before 1850. At the outset regulation was attempted through passing laws that fixed rates or through attaching conditions to franchises that permitted use of the streets. But it became apparent that the job of regulation required a specialized, expert body with authority to adjust rates flexibly to dissimilar situations. Thus regulating commissions developed that had discretion to apply rather general laws. State commissions began to appear about 1870 but did not approach their present authority until after 1900. The Interstate Commerce Commission was set up in 1887 to regulate interstate railroad transportation; and there is now a Federal Power Commission to control the interstate sale of electric power and gas, and a Federal Communications Commission to regulate interstate telephone and telegraph service and also radio.

Economic basis of regulation

The industries in this group are often said to be *naturally* monopolistic, implying peculiar characteristics not present elsewhere. The basic feature that sets them apart is the familiar one that firms must extend their physical plants throughout the areas that they serve. Rail transportation can be supplied only where tracks extend, electric power, telephone, and telegraph service only where transmission lines go, gas and water only in areas reached by pipes. For two or more companies to serve the same areas, or connect the same points, much duplication of plant is necessary.

Duplication of facilities. In part, the objection to duplication is from the standpoint of urban convenience and amenities. A city does not want to be cluttered up with more tracks and wires than necessary or have its streets dug up oftener than necessary. But the greater objection is to the waste of resources, and resulting higher costs, when duplication occurs. Of course, as demand increases, even a single company may have to string more wires or lay more pipes or tracks. Thus the related fixed costs, which are high in these industries, are not absolutely fixed. But there is sufficient fixity, and usually sufficient unused capacity in some aspect of these facilities, so that the total cost of supplying the service would be greatly increased if two or more companies entered the same market.

The particular advantage of avoiding duplication in these industries must not be confused with the *general advantages of large-scale production*. The latter are also present, within limits, and may strengthen the case for monopoly.[6] Power for a city of 100,000 can be generated more cheaply by one power plant than by two. This economy would be lost if the city were divided in two parts, each served by a separate company, but this division would not create the duplication that competition would entail. Competition means that each buyer has the possibility of choosing among a number of sellers, so that competitive power would require that each company string its wires along every street. This is the waste particularly to be avoided and the direct reason why competition cannot be depended on as a regulator.

Partial competition in transportation. This factor is so decisive in some cases that the only competition is of the interindustry type, as where electric power competes with gas and both compete with coal and oil. In transportation there is more competition. Most communities are served by only one railroad, or by only one railroad that is useful in reaching a certain destination. But important routes, as between Chicago and New York or Chicago and Los Angeles, may be served by several railroads or combinations of railroads. Thus the competition is spotty, and at best it is competition within a narrow oligopoly. From

[6] The need of extending the physical plant throughout the market limits the market and makes it more difficult to obtain the general advantages of size without monopoly.

the discrimination standpoint, spotty competition is worse than none. The transportation field has also the competition of other carriers. There is water competition on some routes, and highway carriers go nearly everywhere. But the former is limited in extent, and the latter has little effect on long-distance railroad traffic moving at a cent per ton-mile or thereabouts. Intercarrier competition is more adequate in the passenger field.

Certain services are treated as public utilities, at least with respect to some features of regulation, although the duplication factor is not notably present, perhaps no more than in all competitive industry. Thus motor truck and bus lines do not operate on exclusive roadways as the railroads do. It makes little difference from the duplication stand-point whether the hundred vehicles on a route are owned by one company or twenty. Motor-carrier regulation did not spring primarily from the need of protecting its customers from monopoly but from the belief that transportation as a whole must be controlled if the railroads are. Regulation of motor carriers has centered on licensing carriers to op-erate, rather than on preventing unfair charges.

Monopoly to improve service. Wasteful duplication, however, is not the only reason for monopoly, and thus for regulation, in these fields. Services may sometimes need to be unified, in a sense that different furniture manufacturers do not need to standardize their product. The hundred buses on a given route are likely to provide a better service if organized by one company than by twenty. This is even more striking in the telephone field, where if all phones are not operated by one company, or closely integrated companies, the customer's range of com-munication must be limited unless he has connections with several companies.

Legal basis of regulation

If particular industries are to be singled out for restrictions that do not apply to all industries, adequate legal justification must be found. At least in a country where the tradition of economic freedom is strong, and constitutional safeguards reflect that tradition, a solid legal basis is necessary, or regulation will be viewed as deprivation of liberty or property or equal protection of the laws.

Much of the necessary basis is centuries old in Anglo-Saxon law, much older than the industries to which it is now applied. Long ago the courts came to recognize certain activities as *"public callings,"* or businesses *"affected with a public interest,"* and to impose special obli-gations on them. The reasons for such treatment were stated in various ways, but one element was likely to be present—that the customers of these businesses had little choice among suppliers. The traveler was likely to find at nightfall only one inn at which he might stay, or the sender of some article to another town would find only one carrier that could serve him. Thus, in a limited way, monopoly was present.

In these circumstances the supplier might easily be highhanded in his treatment of the patron, denying service or charging unreasonably for it. Injustices gave rise to suits, and gradually the courts developed legal principles that still apply in such circumstances. The first obligation, which now applies to all public utilities and common carriers, is that they must *serve all applicants,* up to the limit of their capacity. A grocer may refuse to sell to a would-be customer, for any reason or for no reason at all; but a power company must supply service to all who want it within the area that it undertakes to serve.

This first obligation requires little regulation to enforce it, but the other obligations do, or may. They are (1) that the company must provide *reasonably adequate service,* (2) that it must charge no more than a *reasonable price,* and (3) that it must provide the service impartially, *without discrimination.* Even if there were no regulative laws and commissions, these obligations would be recognized by the courts as applying to the utility industries. Enforcement through private suit is weak, but the principles provide the legal basis for positive regulation.

Other legal grounds are also available for imposing special restrictions on these industries. When a company asks the privilege of *using the streets* for pipes or tracks or poles, it is easy to attach certain conditions regarding service and charges. Similar conditions may be attached when permission is granted to use the right of *eminent domain* in obtaining a continuous right of way or to use the public highways in operating vehicles for profit. But these are mere legal excuses for regulation, it must be remembered, and not a positive reason for it. The positive reason is economic and lies mainly in the element of monopoly power that these utilities have.

Diverse elements in regulation

Public authority is now applied not only to the rates charged by utility companies, but to other important features.[7] One should see the logic of each phase of regulation and its relationship to the policy as a

[7] Standard works on the regulation of public utilities, other than railroads, include Irston R. Barnes, *The Economics of Public Utility Regulation,* Crofts, 1942; Emery Troxel, *Economies of Public Utilities,* Rinehart, 1947; Leverett S. Lyon, Victor Abramson, and associates, *Government and Economic Life,* Brookings Institution, Vol. II, Ch. XXI by Ben W. Lewis. Chapter XXII by Charles L. Dearing deals with transportation. A leading transportation text is D. Philip Locklin, *Economics of Transportation,* Richard D. Irwin, Inc., 3d ed., 1947.

whole. In particular, one should be clear as to the exact connection between regulation and monopoly.

Sometimes it is said that the purpose of regulation is to protect these industries from the wastes of competition. This is a serious distortion of the purpose. The primary aim, as the history of regulation shows, is to protect the public, the customers, from abuses that arise from monopoly. With or without regulation, a high degree of monopoly is unavoidable, and competitive control is inadequate. Thus government steps in. But when the public is protected by regulation, there is much less reason for trying to preserve such competition as would develop. It is feasible to grant *exclusive franchises* to insure that there will be no wasteful duplication or to require that *certificates of public convenience and necessity* be obtained. Protection of the company from competition is certainly a subordinate, almost an incidental, purpose.[8]

In protecting the public, the main emphasis always has been on *rates*. Regulated industries set their own prices in the first place, just as firms in other industries do, but regulating commissions review rate changes, especially when the change is upward, and they act on customers' complaints. It is helpful to look at rate regulation as having two objectives. One aim is to prevent excessive profits, while seeing to it that company revenues are adequate to attract needed resources. This is the problem of the *rate level*. The rates charged by a company must, *on the average,* be high enough, but not too high.

The other aim is to insure a fair *rate structure*. This problem is concerned with rate relationships or differentials, including discrimination. Regulation must see to it that particular rates are fair as between different classes of customers—for instance, between domestic and industrial users of power, between shippers of different kinds of freight, between shippers located in different towns. This problem of relative charges exists even though company earnings are just what they should be. All state and federal regulatory laws deal with both of these problems. They will receive further consideration below.

In addition to rates, *service* is regulated in various ways. In one category is the control over the thermal content of gas, the voltage of electricity, the utilization of freight cars. In another is the control over the *extension* and *abandonment* of service. In part this control has the aim

---

[8] The point is stressed because, if the public-utility concept is to remain useful, it must be applied in economics to situations of a consistent nature that call for a certain type of policy. When emphasis is placed on protection against competition, the concept merges into the vague area of thinking from which the NRA and like policies have sprung. As a legal concept, the category of industries affected with a public interest has been stretched so that it should no longer be identified altogether with regulation in the present sense.

of preventing wasteful duplication, but its scope is much broader than this. A company that is the sole supplier of a utility service in an area may be unenterprising and negligent, and it may therefore be ordered to fulfill the responsibility it has assumed. Or, on the other hand, a company may want to withdraw service that it claims is unprofitable; again, it may not do so without permission. This is a difficult type of situation. A company cannot be expected to go on indefinitely supplying a service that is not worth its cost, but it has a responsibility that the law recognizes toward the people who have settled in an area and depend on the power or transportation that it supplies. In ordinary industries companies can drop out without creating this problem.

If service is to be adequate and economical, the public is interested also in the way in which the utility companies are organized, especially in the *combinations* they effect with other companies. It is not feasible to permit railroad companies to consolidate merely on the basis of their particular interests and without regard to the effect on the whole network of railroads. Thus the Interstate Commerce Commission has extensive power over railroad combinations. In the power and gas fields great holding companies were formed that were only incidentally concerned with operating efficiency and mainly sought to make money in other ways. Operating companies were often weakened and state regulation impeded. The Securities and Exchange Commission, through the Public Utility Holding Company Act, was given extensive power in 1935 over these combinations.

Partly to assist in rate regulation and partly to maintain financial stability, regulation has a good deal to say about the *capital structures* and *security issues* of companies. This is also the responsibility of the Securities and Exchange Commission, as well as of the usual regulating commissions. Also incidental to other features of regulation is extensive control over *accounting methods* and the *provision of statistics*. All control must rest on adequate records.

The rate level

Rate regulation to prevent excessive profits is now most important in the case of the local power and gas utilities and the telephone industry. In the case of railroads, the main problem has been to maintain their financial strength; and most of the broad rate-level cases before the Interstate Commerce Commission have involved applications to raise rates, especially in the face of rising prices.

Since rate-level regulation focuses on the net return on capital, one must see first how this net return relates to a company's revenues as a whole and thus to the rates charged. Actually the net return can represent only a small part of revenue, since most receipts must go to cover wages, supplies, depreciation, and taxes. Regulation can do little about these items. A power company with revenues of $4,000,000 may have a net return of $1,000,000, which would give it a 5-percent return on $20,000,000 of capital, and the other $3,000,000 would go for operating expenses and taxes. Thus, if the company asks for a 20-percent increase in its net income, or $200,000 more, it is asking for only a 5 percent increase in its total revenue. Or, conversely, if it asks for a 5-percent increase in revenue, it is really asking for 20 percent more for its owners.[9] In any case, the regulating commission has real control over only a small part of what the rates must cover, namely, the net return.

The net return is the product of two factors: (1) the sum of capital on which it is recognized that the company should earn a return and (2) the percent earned on that sum. The former is called the *rate base* or *valuation;* the latter, the *rate of return.* The power company may get a 20-percent increase in its net income by persuading the regulating commission that its valuation should be increased by that fraction, or from $20,000,000 to $24,000,000. Or it may argue that it should earn 6 percent instead of 5 percent on the present base. In either case, its net return would be increased from $1,000,000 to $1,200,000.

The rate base. Valuation of property for rate purposes has been the most confused and controversial aspect of regulation. Conflicting theories have been upheld by the experts, and what the commissions have wanted to do from one standpoint, the courts have often found unconstitutional from another. Three ways of measuring the earning capital of a utility should be distinguished.

On the surface, it might seem that a utility should earn a return on the *market value* of its property. But the market value of a corporation's wealth—which, in practice, usually means the market value of the securities representing that wealth—itself depends very largely on the corporation's earnings. Thus a ridiculous circularity arises. A rate base is wanted to assist in regulating earnings. But a rate base governed by market value depends on earnings. On this basis any amount of earnings can be justified. If the power company is allowed to earn 50 percent more, and its securities then rise in value by 50 percent, the result is that the higher rate base requires the higher earnings. In this situation, valuation for rate regulation must not mean valuation in the ordinary market sense.

How can the circle be broken? The simple way is to say that investors

---

[9] Or a little less than 20 percent, if the increase in rates reduces the amount of power purchased. One difficulty in regulating rates is that any change in them is likely to affect the volume of business.

in public utilities should earn a return on the number of dollars they actually invest in the property—that is, its *original cost* or *historical cost*. Or the base may be narrowed a bit to exclude capital needlessly and wastefully invested. Then the earning capital is called the *prudent investment*. As new assets are acquired or old ones retired, it is a fairly simple accounting matter to keep the rate base up to date.

But what happens when the price level changes? If commodity prices and wages are doubled, should the rate base remain unchanged except as facilities are replaced at the new prices? A view that has been held widely by utility spokesmen, and also by the courts, is that the rate base should not represent what the property originally cost but what it would cost today to replace that same property. This measure of earning capital is known as *reproduction cost*.

Regulation is designed to take the place of competition. Accordingly it is argued that the rate base should change with the price level, since in competitive industry, if prices rise, property values rise and firms normally earn a return on the revalued property. Courts have often overruled commission orders on this ground. Nevertheless, most students of the problem, and most persons experienced in regulation, object strongly to reproduction cost. Indeed, it even fails to apply the competitive standard, since competition recognizes the present cost of modern, up-to-date facilities, not the cost today of reproducing old facilities. Moreover, the rate basis should be measured in a workable fashion whether prices rise or fall. Most of the capital of public utilities is represented by bonds and preferred stock, which call for fixed income payment; if prices were to fall, and the rate base were reduced accordingly, the financial disturbance would be severe. Furthermore, reproduction cost is extremely slow and expensive to determine, and rate adjustments are delayed and bound up in litigation. So the more practical view seems to be to accept original cost as the measure of earning capital, and to make such changes as fairness requires by adjusting the rate of return on that capital.

The rate of return. The percentage that the owners of utility property should expect to earn on their capital also presents a difficult problem. Regulation removes that possibility of large profits which is undoubtedly a major inducement to investment in unregulated fields. Thus a fairly high rate seems justified. On the other hand, the substantial protection from competition, at least in the local utilities, gives a degree of security that the investor in other fields does not enjoy. So a very moderate rate of return may be indicated. Regulation must aim to allow sufficient earnings to maintain the credit of companies and enable them to attract the capital that the demand for the service indicates. This is not an easy standard, either in theory or in practice.

Minimum rates. In controlling the earnings of monopolistic firms, regulation is mainly concerned with the maximum allowable charges. Rates should be no higher than good service and the development of service require. But should regulation ever stand in the way of a company that wants to reduce its rates?

It was long supposed that the railroads and other utilities could be depended on to protect themselves from undercharging, but now the utility laws commonly give the commissions the power to set minimum rates. Where competition is present, it may cause drastic rate cutting when the high fixed costs are accompanied by unused capacity. There is thus occasional use for the minimum-rate power to prevent rate wars that would weaken utility companies. This situation is most likely in the transportation field.

The rate structure; discrimination

A company's charges may on the whole be right, and its earnings what they should be, but it may treat particular classes of customers unfairly. Rail transportation, electric power, and other services are not sold at single uniform prices but on the basis of complex rate structures. A railroad carries thousands of commodities, in different quantities and with different packaging, and each of them may move different distances, between different pairs of towns. This is the most complex case, and the one for which regulation of the rate structure is most important. A power company, similarly, establishes quite an array of charges for ordinary householders and commercial and industrial users, depending on the amount of electricity they buy. Other utilities have similar rate situations.

Where rate differentials are explainable on grounds of *cost,* no problem of regulation ordinarily arises. Many differentials meet the cost test. A railroad may charge only one-half cent per ton-mile for moving coal in carloads on a certain haul, and ten or fifteen times as much for carrying package freight. But there is no discrimination in favor of coal if, as is likely, the coal rate is fully as high in relation to cost. Unfairness arises only when rate relationships are not on a cost basis. In adjusting rate differentials, regulating commissions ordinarily exert pressure in the direction of the cost standard.

As explained in the preceding chapter, monopolistic firms, if not prevented, are inclined to apply the *class-price principle* in maximizing profits. Discriminatory pricing goes especially far in the utility field because fixed costs are relatively large and because rigid facilities, like railroad tracks and power dams, often have considerable unused capacity. Business that can be got only at very low rates may be worth getting; other business that can be kept even at very high rates is charged accordingly. This is the principle of *"charging what the traffic will bear."* Thus the rate relationships that develop in the absence of regulation are commonly not on a cost basis and may depart widely from it.

The resulting problem of regulation is one of the most difficult. It would not do simply to condemn rate differences that are not supported by cost differences, as the Robinson-Patman Act does. Utility companies must have some flexibility in adjusting charges so as to make use of their capacity. The result is beneficial to the public, if the larger volume of business reduces the average costs. Indeed the very customers who are discriminated against, the ones who pay relatively high rates, may pay less than they otherwise would, since the additional low-rate business still adds more to revenue than it adds to cost. On the other hand, some limits to this flexibility are necessary. Competing towns or regions or types of traffic should not be compelled to contribute in a seriously unequal way toward the costs of the railroad service they receive. Household users of electricity should not be made permanently to subsidize the competition of electric power with coal for use in factories.

Policy is necessarily a compromise, and it is difficult, if not impossible, to define the correct standard. The laws merely condemn "undue discrimination" and "undue preference and prejudice," and the regulating commissions must use their judgment as complaints arise.[10]

Effectiveness and soundness of regulation

In preventing the immediate abuses of monopoly, regulation, when well administered, can be an effective substitute for competition. It can prevent excessive profits and check the inherent injustices of rate differentials. Sometimes it has worked badly because state laws have been weak and the personnel of regulating commissions inferior. These weaknesses can be corrected, if government itself is sound. The Interstate Commerce Commission has been the outstanding administrative agency of its type, and, on the whole, has been able, effective, and respected.

[10] Some writers have used the phrase "value of service" in a sense that implies that a definite standard other than cost of service can be defined to govern rate relationships. But value, as worth to the buyer, means merely the value of the quantity that will be bought at a particular price. Either a lower or a higher rate corresponds to the value of the service that will be bought at that rate. But costs provide no basis for definite rate relationships when the costs are *joint* and a difficult basis when they are *common* in any degree. See Chapter 20 above.

But preventing abuses does not amount to a full performance of the functions of competitive markets. Regulation has the positive responsibility of fitting the regulated industries into the economy as a whole. Here it has not always done well and is probably not likely to. Even flexible administration usually operates within quite static conceptions. Rates are adjusted to give existing utilities a reasonable return on existing facilities, with little regard for the role of profit in promoting or deterring expansion. Regulation is no better than unregulated monopoly in dealing with cyclical changes. Monopoly is charged with holding prices up arbitrarily when demand falls off. When business declines and earnings fall, the regulating commissions often actually raise utility rates. On the other hand, when business is booming and prices are rising, the principle of only a fair return holds utility rates in check. The economic principle that competitive prices tend to equal the inclusive costs of production has validity, of course, only in a long-run sense. But commissions make it a short-run guide, and perhaps they can do nothing else.

Moreover, there is nothing in regulation to stimulate progress. Despite monopoly, some utilities have made great technical advances; dynamic leadership can operate anywhere. But by World War I the railroads seemed to have got badly into a rut, and their later improvement is probably as traceable to highway competition as to anything else. It would be meaningless to suggest that regulation be abandoned in favor of competition in the utility field, where much monopoly is inherent. But all of these considerations bear on the wisdom of extending the public-utility category to include other oligopolistic industries.

In addition, the sheer task of regulating is difficult and quite costly. Accordingly, the question has been raised whether it is worth while to continue private enterprise at all in industries where private management must be paralleled by extensive government control. Would it not be better to have government take over and do the whole job?

Government ownership and operation

In view of these special problems, public enterprise in the utility field should not be identified with the general philosophy of state socialism. The railroads and local utilities have often been public undertakings in other countries that relied for the most part on private enterprise. In the United States the provision of water, once usually a private business, is now commonly municipal. Many cities operate power and gas plants as well as buses and street railways. The federal government is engaged extensively in generating hydroelectric power, notably under the Tennessee Valley Authority and on the Columbia and Colorado Rivers.

Movements have developed at various times to make the railroads a federal enterprise.

The case for government ownership of utilities, in a country devoted on the whole to capitalism, has many angles. It is said that the usual advantages of private enterprise and management are largely sacrificed in any case, because of monopoly and regulation. It is said that government can reduce costs and rates, as evidenced in the case of public power plants, because no profit need be earned on private capital. It is said that transportation and other services can be supplied, and charges adjusted, with broad public ends in view, as has been done in the case of the postal service. Likewise, projects can be undertaken, as in the Tennessee Valley development of flood control and navigation along with power, that are more sweeping than private business can encompass. Finally, investment can be controlled to smooth out business cycles and combat depression and unemployment.

These considerations are impressive, but they are by no means conclusive. Despite regulation, there is much scope for private initiative and management in the utility field. The spirit of enterprise is generally much stronger than within the routine of government agencies. True, private capital must be rewarded, but capital that is cheaper because the taxpayer is the risk-taker yields little over-all economy. Moreover, utility spokesmen point out, public enterprise can charge less because it does not pay the usual taxes toward the support of government. Then there is the general objection, where the spirit of free enterprise continues, to subjecting more of the economy than necessary to political jurisdiction and making more people than necessary employees of government.

There is plainly no need of applying any one view to all situations. Opponents of government ownership can concede that such projects as TVA have been useful and are not suitable private undertakings. And they may concede that instances of public ownership here and there, as in the power field, may cause private utilities to bestir themselves to demonstrate their superiority, and provide regulating commissions an additional "yardstick" in measuring costs and judging rates. Equally stimulating comparisons operate in the opposite direction. Any influence that will upset the static character of a secure monopoly or of a government agency is worth while.

Review Questions

1. What industries are usually included in the public-utility group? How important are they in the American economy?

2. Explain the peculiar duplication that competition causes in the case of these industries. What are the objections to this duplication? Distinguish the special advantage of avoiding duplication from the general advantage of size in the case of a power company.

3. Are the grounds for regulation the same in the case of railroads and motor carriers? What is meant by saying that the nature of a service sometimes calls for monopoly, entirely apart from any saving in cost? Give examples.

4. What are the traditional legal obligations of businesses affected with a public interest? Why should these obligations be imposed on some activities and not on others? Distinguish the logical basis of these obligations and certain legal excuses for them.

5. "In principle, public-utility regulation is pretty much like the NRA. Each recognizes the wastes of competition and applies a corrective." Criticize this statement. What aspects of regulation seem to give it some support?

6. Distinguish several features of the utility industries that are subject to regulation. Show that all phases of regulation arise directly, or indirectly, from the basic characteristics of these industries.

7. Distinguish the rate-level and the rate-structure problems. Explain what regulation involves in each case.

8. "For a utility company to ask that its property be valued at a figure 25 percent higher is the same as asking for a 25-percent increase in rates." Do you agree? Explain.

9. Distinguish three methods of measuring the capital on which a utility company should be allowed to earn a return. What special points of strength or weakness should be associated with each measure?

10. "Utility companies strongly support the reproduction-cost base when the value of the dollar is falling but change their tune when the dollar rises in value." Would this be a logical position to take? Explain.

11. "The rate of return a utility company should be allowed to earn should be just sufficient to enable it to provide the service that will be purchased at rates which will yield that return." Is this a reasonable conception of what the rate of return should be? Is it easy to express as a definite percent?

12. "Rate differentials are not necessarily discriminatory." Explain.

13. Review the main reason for discrimination, as presented in the preceding chapter, and apply to the railroads and other utilities.

14. A railroad wants to charge higher rates from New York to Salt Lake City than from New York to San Francisco. How would the railroad justify such rates to the public? What would be the reply of a wholesale house in Salt Lake City that distributes goods west of there? What do you conclude regarding the standards that must govern regulation of the rate structure?

15. "Utility regulation seems to be guided in the short-run by the long-run normal relation of prices and inclusive costs." What is meant? Apply to regulation during cyclical changes. Is there any objection to such regulation?

16. "The case for government ownership and operation of public utilities is not the general case for state socialism." To what extent does this seem to be a fair statement? What considerations that bear on the government-ownership issue impress you most?

Agricultural Adjustment Policy

It is curious, in an economy that depends mainly for its control on competitive market forces, that drastic government action should be thought necessary in the field that is naturally most highly competitive. But a drastic scheme of market control has been applied to agriculture since 1933. Should one conclude that competition, when unrestricted, is too strong economic medicine? Or that truly competitive industry must have too unhappy a time in an economy in which competition has been dulled somewhat for most industries? Or that agriculture has unique characteristics that call for an exceptional policy? Or simply that farmers cast many votes? Discussion of agricultural policy is worth while even though it does not lead to a clear choice among these alternatives.

Farming is an important industry—in one sense the most important —but it is not discussed here for this reason. This book does not analyze particular industries for their own sake. Agriculture simply presents the leading case of an important type of public policy. In the present discussion, therefore, the broad field of agriculture will not be broken into its somewhat dissimilar parts. We shall be aware of, but shall not dwell on, the fact that market problems may differ for cereals, cotton, tobacco, meat animals, dairy products, fruits, and vegetables. We shall not stress differences in the positions of farm owners and of farm tenants—the latter operating nearly 40 percent of all farms in the United States and a much larger percent in the South. Nor need we distinguish farm owners from farm workers in general, a minority of whom are hired employees. The agricultural adjustment policy should be associated primarily with staple products such as wheat, corn, cotton, and tobacco, which are sold on national and international markets, but it applies also to a wider, and a varying, range of products.

In approaching this problem, the most striking surface fact is that, during each decade of the half century from 1880 to 1930, income per worker in agriculture averaged only about 45 percent as high as in the American economy as a whole.[11] Events during and following World

[11] See Simon Kuznets, *National Income: A Summary of Findings*, National Bureau of Economic Research, 1946, p. 43. While data are not adequate, the results are strikingly uniform. For the five decades agriculture's share in the national income ranged from 44 to 46 percent of its share in the total working force of the nation.

War I gave this situation a new political expression, from which the adjustment policy resulted.

The problem has been approached as if it were primarily one of redistributing income in favor of agriculture. In studying, in Part V, the organization of production on the basis of value relationships, we have been reminded now and then that prices are the basis of incomes, though the income aspect of markets is deferred for consideration in Part VI. In dealing with agricultural adjustment policy, we shall observe how income reform may distort the price mechanism that is depended on to organize production efficiently.

Price and income variability

What are the market factors that affect adversely the farmer's position? In analyses of this problem, stress is usually placed (1) on characteristics of leading farm products that cause their prices, and the incomes from them, to be highly variable from year to year and within the business cycle—responsive especially to downward pressures; (2) on longer term influences that obstruct the normal market adjustments which supposedly keep any economic group from remaining permanently in an inferior position. In dealing now with the first of these, we shall consider (a) the sensitivity to disturbance of the prices of leading products, (b) the upsetting market changes and resulting price movements, (c) the short-run income variations.

Causes of sensitivity. Farm products were used several times in earlier chapters as examples of high responsiveness to changes in supply and demand conditions. A major element is the *inelasticity of demand* characteristic of leading farm products, especially essential, low-cost foods like wheat and potatoes.[12] When demand is inelastic, upward price movements caused by shifts in demand or supply are not halted quickly by curtailed buying of these products and go far before they are stopped. Likewise downward movements are not checked readily by expanded consumption, and depressing influences have maximum effect on the seller.

A similar *inelasticity of supply,* at least when prices tend downward, accentuates the effect. Farmers are slow to curtail output in the face of falling prices. Of the cost elements that must be covered by a normal price, the greater part—the taxes, return on investment, and labor of the farmer and his family—are reduced very little by producing less. Prices must fall pretty low before they fail to cover such items as fertilizer, seed, and hired labor—or before farm income is improved by contraction, as the individual farmer sees it. Of course, if only one farm

[12] See Chapter 19, pp. 499–500.

product has fallen in price, elasticity of supply may appear in a shifting to other products, but with a general fall in prices of farm products, the elasticity is low.

The contrast with other industries is magnified by the different ways in which markets are organized. Inelasticity of demand and supply have their full effect only in the case of truly *market-determined prices*.[13] Manufactured products differ from farm products not only in the higher elasticities usually present but in the *quoted-price* basis on which they are sold. Manufactured goods are seldom put on the market for what they will bring, but the production of each firm is closely adjusted to its sales at prevailing prices. With any element of product differentiation or oligopoly present, prices are relatively insensitive to given changes in the conditions of demand or supply.

Market disturbances. Sensitivity does not by itself cause prices to fluctuate. Disturbing changes must occur in the relationship of demand to supply. In graphical terms, as we have seen, the tilt of the supply and demand curves does not cause prices to change; only a movement of the curves to right or left can do that. More or less must be demanded or supplied at given prices. Are farm products particularly subject to such changes?

On the demand side the basic farm products are usually quite stable, more so than most manufactured goods. Eating, smoking, and clothes-wearing habits change very slowly for the mass of people. Even when average income falls off rapidly during a depression, demand for staple foods and tobacco holds up relatively well; the sharper changes in the demand for a nation's farm products occur when wars and the termination of wars affect the international situation.

On the supply side, however, changes in weather and the conditions affecting crop growth cause frequent sharp variations. Over a stretch of a few years the output per acre of a specific farm product may vary 10, 25, or even 50 percent. Thus farmers not only put their output on the market for what it will bring, but they cannot control closely the amount of that output, as manufacturers can.

Price variations. Market disturbances have been sufficient, in conjunction with the sensitivity factors, to cause farm products to fluctuate much more in price than manufactured products and most other products do. This is apparent when price movements are compared, as in Table 26, for the depression, war, and early postwar periods of the 1930s and 1940s.[14] Thus, in the depression drop from 1929 to 1932, all commodities fell at wholesale by 32 percent, farm products by 54 percent.

[13] See Chapter 21, pp. 552–553.
[14] Figures are from the wholesale price index of the Bureau of Labor Statistics.

In the war and postwar rise from 1940 to the middle of 1948, all commodities rose by 112 percent, farm products by 193 percent. The movement for the more volatile farm products, such as wheat, was considerably greater.

TABLE 26—WHOLESALE PRICE MOVEMENTS, ALL
COMMODITIES AND FARM PRODUCTS
(1926 = 100)

	All commodities	Farm products
1929	95.3	104.9
1932	64.8	48.2
1940	78.6	67.7
1944	104.0	123.3
1948 (June)	166.7	198.4

Income variations. Incomes of farmers depend, of course, on the quantities they sell as well as on the prices they get. Incomes may fluctuate either more or less than prices. If price changes are *due to changes in output,* the two factors offset each other, at least in part. At a lower price, farmers have the larger quantity to sell that has caused the lower price. Thus if a commodity has unit elasticity of demand, the gross return from it remains constant as price and quantity move in opposite directions. But if, for instance, a 10-percent increase in the potato crop causes a 50-percent fall in price, potato growers suffer a serious decline in income. This is an extreme assumption, and some observers hold that farm products on the average have an elasticity of demand close to unity. If this is true, restriction of output will not by itself increase farm revenue.

On the other hand, when prices fall in a depression because of a *general decline in demand,* farm income falls because of a reduction both in prices and in quantities sold. Thus income falls sharply. But even so, it does not follow that farming is harder hit, on the average, than manufacturing is. Prices of farm products fall more, and volume less. The main disadvantage in farming is from the enterpriser's standpoint. The typical farm operator must keep on supporting most of his labor force when business gets worse, whereas the manufacturer discharges unnecessary employees. The brunt of depression falls more heavily on urban workers.

Table 27 shows that aggregate farm income fell less, in percentage terms, than aggregate manufacturing income from 1929 to 1932 and

rose less from 1932 to 1940.[15] But in view of the adjustment of manufacturing employment to the volume of output, income per worker
was steadier in manufacturing in each of these periods. However, if the
table were carried through the war period, agriculture would show the
greater percentage rise both in aggregate and per-worker terms.

TABLE 27—RELATIVE INCOME VARIATIONS OF FARMING AND MANUFACTURING
(Aggregate figures in billions of dollars. Percentages show change
from preceding year in table.)

	1929	1932	1940
Aggregate income:			
All activities	$ 87.4	$ 41.7 (−56%)	$ 81.3 (+95%)
Farming	7.8	3.0 (−62%)	6.4 (+113%)
Manufacturing	22.0	7.2 (−67%)	22.3 (+210%)
Income per employed worker:			
All activities	$1911	$1121 (−41%)	$1691 (+51%)
Farming	911	353 (−61%)	839 (+138%)
Manufacturing	2084	1066 (−49%)	2032 (+91%)

So, if we conclude that farm income is exceptionally variable, we
must place the responsibility as much on the inflexibility of the working
force as on the flexibility of prices. But agricultural labor imposes a kind
of cost that at least in part is very easily borne. Food grown on the farm
and consumed there is equally nourishing, whatever its market price.
The costs which are most damaging when revenue declines are taxes
and interest, which involve out-of-pocket outlays. Farms have commonly
been mortgaged. When they have been bought at highly inflated prices,
as in the period right after World War I, the interest and principal payments on debts become extremely onerous when product prices fall
sharply, as they did in 1920–1921. This is the old story of the position
of debtors when the value of money rises.

Depressed farm income in the long run

The short-run variability of prices, and to some extent of income,
may create a special problem worthy of government action, but not a
very fundamental one. It may be thought of as a problem of insecurity,
though actually security is greater in agriculture than in urban occupations afflicted with more variable employment. Perhaps the greater insecurity is that of the consuming public who depend on a variable out-

[15] These figures are from *National Income*, the July 1947 Supplement to *Survey of Current Business*. While 1933 appears to have been the low point in the depression for all
industry, as indicated in Chapter 3, 1932 was the low point for agriculture and manufacturing.

put of essential products. No doubt with both uncertainties in mind, Henry Wallace, as Secretary of Agriculture, became spokesman for an "ever-normal-granary" program that would try to even out the incomes of farmers and at the same time even out the flow of products to market, despite the variability of crops—a program which in principle involves a milder type of adjustment policy than the one actually in effect.

Mainly, however, the farm problem is not one of short-run variability but of long-run downward pressure on farm income. Perhaps the most striking fact in the above table is that in 1929, at the peak of a prosperous period, farm income per worker was less than half as great as national income per worker. This condition had prevailed, as already noted, for half a century or more. How is it to be explained?

Certainly the market sensitivities, the inelasticities and the market-determined character of farm-product prices, are part, but only a subordinate part, of the explanation. They accentuate the effect of long-run downward pressure, as of short-run disturbances. But the main explanation must lie in the long-run pressure itself and its causes.

This pressure arises from the *need of curtailing agriculture in relation to the whole economy*. Farmers tend to expand their production beyond the place it can have in a balanced total production of goods. It is the nature of agriculture to expand as other industries do, whereas, relatively, it must decline. Indeed, with a general falling off in population growth, it seems that agriculture must decline absolutely also— not in output or probably in acreage, but in number of farmers. Such an adjustment, if left to market forces, must be painful to those involved. If the need of adjustment is chronic, as it seems to be, the painful effect must be continuous.

This pressure has several sources. One of them lies in the much *higher birth rate* on farms than in cities. City populations would decline were they not replenished from rural areas. Thus, even if agriculture expanded as fast as the rest of the economy—which it must not— migration from the farms would be necessary. Unless an economic system introduces an authoritative scheme of assigning workers to jobs, such migrations must be spurred by income differentials.

Pressure arises inherently from *technological progress* in a field of production that, in general, has shown *little versatility as to products*. Output per worker in agriculture is said almost to have doubled from 1910 to 1944.[16] Output rose similarly in some other fields, notably man-

---

[16] Arthur C. Bunce, "Our Agricultural Policies," p. 8, in *Agricultural Adjustment and Income*, No. 2 of the Postwar Economic Studies, Board of Governors of the Federal Reserve System, 1945. For other discussions of farm policy, see Chapter XXIII of the Brookings study *Government and Economic Life*, cited above; also Karl Brandt, *The Reconstruction of World Agriculture*, W. W. Norton & Co., 1945.

ufacturing, but in these other fields producers seem to have wider horizons of opportunity. Despite improvements in diet, food consumption per capita has limited room to expand in comparison with the possible uses of manufactured goods and personal services. Very seldom are there important additions to the list of textile fibers and other nonfood farm products. We are simply observing again the familiar point that economic progress depends largely on reducing the fraction of total productive effort that is expended in the primary fields. Technological progress in these fields requires a shifting of workers that, again, must be induced by income differentials.

Other factors have accentuated this relative excess of farm output. Farming, on the whole, has remained a field of small-scale activity and has been *easy to enter*. Thus it has had special appeal in an economy in which truly individual enterprise has suffered from large-scale methods. As long as usable land remains unplowed, expansion is likely. Such expansion is spurred in war periods when demand is high, and the amount of readjusting to be done is thus increased.

Likewise there has been a *long-run decline in the fraction of American farm output sold abroad*. The decline has been striking in the case of cotton, tobacco, and wheat, which have depended most heavily on foreign markets. This decline is attributable to the development of such export areas as Canada, Australia, and Argentina, to the efforts of some importing countries to be more nearly self-sufficient, and to American policies that have discouraged trade.

Farm income is depressed by these pressures only to the extent that adequate readjustments fail to take place. *Quick mobility* would keep the income differential small. But, in fact, the required adjustment is large and farm personnel is inclined to shift slowly. The break from farm to city is sharp, sharper than in most occupational changes. Farming, as has been said, is a way of life, and its appeal to many people is not reflected fully in ordinary economic rewards. With unemployment frequent and serious in the cities, the certainty of roof and food supply is not easily abandoned.

Perhaps this means, when all is considered, that the true income differential, the psychic differential, is much less than the statistics imply. The statistics, as presented above, are defective also in that they present only the aggregate, or average, situation for the United States as a whole. While farm income, except in war periods, has averaged only half as high as income for the entire economy, much of agricultural output has come from farmers whose incomes have been fairly satisfactory in most years. Average farm income is pulled down by the fact that half the farmers in the country are packed together in the southern states and by the number of small and inefficient operators in all areas. These groups account for only a minor part of total output, but they seriously depress average output and income. Were allowance made for the dissimilar conditions behind the average, the conclusion would be modified in two respects: (1) an even greater need would appear for shifting a large number of low-output farmers to other fields; and (2) the case would be weakened for subsidizing the farmers who are responsible for the bulk of the output.

Development of public policy

Perhaps there should be no governmental policy, at least none involving the degree of market interference that now prevails. It is certainly arguable, as we shall see presently, that the whole agricultural adjustment policy is basically wrong. But it is arguable also that a large segment of the population, with an indispensable economic role, should not be doomed to a permanently inferior status. It is arguable that automatic economic adjustments have failed and must be supplemented. There is no touchstone of economic logic by which one can choose convincingly between these views. In practice, the final choice must be political.

Agrarian discontent is of long standing. It was vigorously expressed in the related Granger, Populist, and Free-silver movements after the Civil War. Improvement following the low point of the 1890s raised farmers' hopes, and the years just before World War I were relatively good. War brought an agricultural boom, and then hopes, which had run speculative riot, were cruelly dashed in the depression of 1920–1921. General recovery was quick, but agriculture did not reach the prewar level, and proposals for far-reaching reform took shape. Depression in the early 1930s provided the marginal, backbreaking straw.

Mild aid to agriculture has long been provided. The Department of Agriculture and the state governments have furnished many useful services. For more than thirty years special credit facilities have been developing to meet the needs of farmers in buying land, obtaining equipment, and planting crops.[17] Farmers' cooperatives have been encouraged, to bring economies in buying and selling and to reduce the rigors of too complete a degree of competition.

By the later 1920s the idea had made progress that government should enter the market for staple farm products and control it. Twice a Republican Congress passed a McNary-Haugen Bill to have domestic

[17] Discussed briefly in Chapter 9, pp. 230–231.

prices pushed well above the world level, with surpluses sold abroad for what they would bring. President Coolidge vetoed it on both occasions. In 1929 a Federal Farm Board was set up to promote orderly marketing. But when depression set in, the plan of stabilizing the market turned into a large-scale but futile attempt to support the market through government buying, and the result was an accumulation of big surpluses in federal hands. It became obvious that control of the market would have to mean control of supply and the prevention of surpluses. Republicans and Democrats made similar proposals along this line in 1932, and the Agricultural Adjustment Act was one of the first major policies of the New Deal.

The Agricultural Adjustment policy

The adjustment policy has become highly complex as it has evolved through a series of overlapping statutes.[18] In its central features, it is a policy of *raising prices, limiting supply,* and *subsidizing farmers.* The essentials can be seen best without the details, although the details sometimes qualify any simple statement of the essentials.

The price standard at which the policy aims is contained in the concept of *parity prices.* Most commonly, the price of a farm product has been said to be at parity when it bears the same relation to the prices of nonfarm products, the prices of things bought by farmers, as it did in the base period 1909–1914. That is, if nonfarm prices at any time average double what they were in the base period, the price of wheat, for instance, should also be double. Farm products were in a relatively strong position in 1909–1914, but, if a particular product was better off in some other period, it may be adopted as the base. The formula has been broadened to include leading costs of farming along with other things bought by farmers.

To achieve this parity standard, the Secretary of Agriculture announces each year a *national allotment* for each controlled commodity, and this allotment is broken down in acreage terms by states, counties, and individual farms. But acreage control does not really control supply, since weather is uncertain, more intensive use of land can raise output, and some producers do not cooperate. Moreover demand conditions vary. Thus, to have more direct control, *marketing quotas* can also be established if two thirds of the producers of a commodity agree —and these quotas become mandatory.

---

[18] The original Agricultural Adjustment Act was declared unconstitutional because of some special tax provisions. Subsequent policy developed on the basis of the Soil Conservation and Domestic Allotment Act of 1936 and the Agricultural Adjustment Act of 1938, with amendments of both. Further modifications were adopted in 1948 to take effect in 1950, after expiration of the special postwar price support.

Cooperating farmers receive *benefit payments* for planting soil-conserving crops—grasses and legumes—instead of the soil-depleting crops which, providentially, happen to be the very cereals, cotton, and tobacco whose supply is to be restricted. Farmers may borrow from the government up to a specified percent of the parity price to hold a product from the market. If the market price never reaches the amount of the loan, the farmer keeps the money and the government takes the commodity that has served as collateral. If the price goes higher, the farmer repays the loan and sells the commodity. Thus *crop loans* contain a subsidy element. Benefit payments may also be made to cooperating farmers simply to fill the gap between the market price and the parity price.

The Surplus Commodities Corporation may relieve the market of excess supplies and use the foodstuffs it accumulates for relief purposes. Export sales at relatively low prices have also been subsidized by the government. Under other features of the policy, needy families have received aid in rehabilitating their farms, and a scheme of crop insurance has been made available.

Some critical reflections on the adjustment policy

We may pass over the abstract question whether, in fairness to farmers, government should apply such a policy as this to improve their relative position in the economy. But the nature of the result, especially as the efficiency of economic organization is affected, should be considered.

One notable lesson is the *sheer difficulty of manipulating great industries* that are made up of many producers. Production is hard to control, and so are markets. Even in the drought years of the middle 1930s, acreage restriction seemed to have little effect on output. Marketing quotas may succeed with some commodities, but only at considerable expense to the taxpayer and with troublesome surpluses to dispose of. Prior to the war, farm-product prices in general did not reach the parity level—indeed were further from it than in the 1920s.

Aid to the farmer, however, is not limited to the raising of prices. There are also the *cash benefits*, including loans that are not repaid. In part, the benefits are tied up with the scheme of controlling supply, but they should be recognized as a form of aid in their own right. Doubtless many observers—including some farmers—while approving the market manipulation, demur at the idea of having taxpayers contribute permanently to farmers' incomes. In any case, the policy should be thought of for what it is, a policy of subsidy, and not obscured by euphemisms, as the tendency seems to be. Subsidy, as we have seen, may be an entirely respectable policy, though usually the taxpayer is asked to support an expansion of production, rather than a restriction.

A policy that aimed merely at *stabilization* and *orderly marketing*—to prevent the variation in crops from causing wide fluctuations in highly sensitive prices and incomes—would perhaps be supported by many who object to long-run support of markets and subsidy of agriculture. This was the intention of the 1929 policy, and it is what Mr. Wallace's "ever-normal-granary" phrase implies. The two types of policy should not be confused, and the attractiveness of stabilization allowed to justify something more far-reaching. Stabilization by itself means that stocks accumulated in "surplus" periods should be put on the market in "deficit" periods. In practice, this policy seems unlikely to be carried out, in view of the political outcry that government is depressing the market whenever it disposes of accumulations. A war period, of course, provides an exception, because the shortage of farm products is severe.

To appreciate the nature of the adjustment policy, one must remember that it was adopted first to meet an emergency and in its essentials is little changed. The plight of many farmers was desperate in the early 1930s, and unrest was developing on a serious scale. Economists who approved the adjustment policy as an emergency device largely condemned it as a method of long-run economic control. The conceptions underlying it are essentially *short-run* and *static*.

The parity-price standard is an example. Why should any product be expected to command in exchange the same quantities of other products over a period of thirty or forty years, as the 1909–1914 base implies? Within this period the labor cost of a bushel of wheat fell by more than half. Is it assumed that technological change must have been parallel for all other products, or that costs should not influence relative prices? Of like nature is the basis of acreage allotments, since they rest, in general, on the use of land in particular regions and on particular farms during the preceding ten years.

These are earmarks of the real weakness of the adjustment policy. The main criticism of it is that, in principle, it largely *ignores the allocation problem*—the central economic problem of organizing the use of resources efficiently. The continuing difference in average income between farming and other fields is not accidental but the result of the relative oversupply of farm products as the economy develops. But the income difference is more than a symptom of a condition; it is the inducement to correct that condition. Perhaps the inducement works in a way that is slow, harsh, and unfair, and its impact should be softened. But it is no solution to say to the farmer, in effect: "Stay on the farm and we will improve your income position. If too much is being produced, produce less, and we will make the smaller output yield you a sufficient income."

If there is chronic pressure of supply on the markets for farm products, sound policy should encourage an economic restriction of supply. An economic restriction has two essential features: (1) the high-cost part of the supply—the inefficiently produced part—should be removed from the market, and the low-cost part retained, so that consumers can enjoy the benefit of efficiency; (2) the labor not needed in farming should go elsewhere, so that it can make a positive contribution to the national income. The adjustment policy, instead of promoting these results, opposes them. In its main features, it corresponds to the effort of any monopolist to raise prices by restricting output, but without the monopolist's urge to obtain his product with minimum use of resources.

This basic criticism has been directed against the policy *in principle*. In so far as the policy has been weak and ineffective, its distorting effect on the use of resources has been relatively small. Since, moreover, the parity objective is a rather modest one and even if attained would leave the average farm income fairly low, the natural adjustment forces are not nullified. One can rationalize the policy by saying that no more is sought than to maintain the necessary stand-by capacity in agriculture to give protection against crop variations and varying demands, without having this capacity seriously depress the market. This conception comes rather close to the more limited stabilization theory stated above.

The policy, moreover, has an *international* side that is one of its most perplexing features. Despite the declining relative importance of the foreign market before the war, exports of farm products have continued to be a significant element in the total sales, especially for such crops as cotton. Other countries have continued to depend on American agricultural exports. But the adjustment policy, in the absence of difficult international agreements, is a domestic policy, and such a policy can be combined with exporting only if exports are commonly sold below the domestic price. Such a *two-price policy* involves continuing subsidies —and it is highly provocative to rival exporting countries to have to meet subsidized competition. Thus the adjustment policy is bound up with the large and delicate problem of international economic policy.

One of the most laudable aspects of the adjustment policy is the effort to combat *soil depletion* and erosion. No doubt this feature entered almost as an afterthought, in order to make crop restriction more acceptable, but it is a worthy part of a major conservation program. If private enterprise in agriculture does not find it worth while to give land the care that long-run economic interests require, some subsidizing may be justified to reconcile these interests. But it would be better if the policy were organized unequivocably from this viewpoint. The coincidence that market surpluses arise from soil-depleting crops can be pushed too far.[19]

Undoubtedly the adjustment policy can be improved. But the best prospect of raising farm income without general economic distortion lies in the possibility of *keeping the whole economy prosperous*. Preventing serious depressions would avoid the crucial situations that a sensitive industry encounters. Despite the relatively steady consumption of basic food products, food consumption as a whole varies considerably with the income of consumers. In 1947 the food consumed per capita in the United States was 17 percent above the 1935–1939 average, with the increase preponderantly in fruit, meat, and dairy products. It was estimated that a growing and prosperous population would require, within a decade, a crop production 25 percent, and a livestock production nearly 50 percent, above prewar levels.[20]

With most of the population growth in rural areas and with farm technology continuing to advance, the long-run problem will reappear. Agriculture must continue to decline in relative importance in the economy. But if employment is high in the cities, a readier mobility from farm to urban activity should narrow the income differential.

One should reflect, in conclusion, on the essential difference between the agricultural adjustment policy, on the one hand, and the antitrust and public-utility-regulation policies, on the other. The latter policies aim to protect the public from monopoly, while giving the producer all that is needed to get him to do his job. In such policies no *conflict* arises, in principle, *between the rewarding of producers*—the income problem—*and the assignment of resources* to their places in an efficient scheme of production. But a policy that undertakes to give producers more than is needed to get them to produce does run into this conflict. Consequently it creates the need of an elaborate and costly control of supply. It invites the setting up of arbitrary standards. Unless more

[19] An irritating feature of the policy has been the mixing of objectives and the frequent adducing of reasons which are not controlling reasons. Thus, since facilitating interstate commerce is an honored purpose, the Agricultural Adjustment Act of 1938 makes a valiant, but not wholly coherent, effort to say that a heavy interstate movement of tobacco obstructs commerce in tobacco: "The disorderly marketing of such abnormally excessive supplies affects, burdens, and obstructs interstate and foreign commerce by (1) materially affecting the volume of such commodity marketed therein, (2) disrupting the orderly marketing of such commodity therein, (3) reducing the price for such commodity with consequent injury and destruction of interstate and foreign commerce in such commodity, and (4) causing a disparity between the prices for such commodity in interstate and foreign commerce and industrial products therein, with a consequent diminution of the volume of interstate and foreign commerce in industrial products." (Sec. 311 *b*). Public policy, at its clearest and best, is not manifest in such declarations.

[20] From the President's Economic Report, January 1948. See *Economic Reports of the President*, Reynal & Hitchcock, 1948.

skillfully designed than the adjustment policy has been, it disrupts the normal operation of markets in controlling production, without providing a substitute.

Review Questions

1. How do each of the following affect the variability of the prices of farm products, in comparison with other products: (a) the degree of elasticity of demand, (b) the degree of elasticity of supply, (c) market organization, (d) the prevalence of demand changes, (e) the prevalence of supply changes? How have the prices of farm products behaved in periods of economic disturbance?

2. Why should the income variations of farmers be distinguished from the price variations of farm products? Have farm incomes been strikingly unstable in the short run? Is unemployment relevant to this question? The debtor-creditor situation?

3. "As the statistics show it, per-capita income has averaged lower in farming than in the American economy as a whole over a long period. No doubt the statistics exaggerate the true income difference, when all psychological factors are considered. But there doubtless remains an important difference that can be explained only by the need of contracting the relative position of agriculture in the economy." Develop each sentence in this summary statement.

4. Along what lines did government provide aid to farmers prior to 1933?

5. Explain the price-parity principle. Evaluate it (a) as an emergency guide, (b) as a long-run standard.

6. Distinguish short-run stabilization and long-run adjustment of the market for farm products. Consider both the objectives and the implied policies.

7. "The agricultural adjustment policy aims to improve farm income (a) by changing the supply and demand relation for farm products, (b) by subsidizing farmers to cooperate in causing this change, (c) by subsidizing them because the change is not adequate." Explain.

8. If government were to promote a truly economic adjustment of agriculture to the rest of the economy, what principles would govern the contraction of farm output? Apply them to the adjustment policy.

9. "Certainly the agricultural adjustment policy is open to criticism from the standpoint of efficient use of resources, but the criticism does not sound convincing when it comes from manufacturers who enjoy tariff protection or labor leaders who support go-slow practices by labor." What do you think?

10. What difficulty does the United States encounter when it promotes an international policy of freer markets and retains the agricultural adjustment policy at home?

PART VI

The Distribution
of Income

Poverty continues despite high production and aggregate income. By achieving great productive power and using it fully, a nation does not insure a good living for all its people. There may still be slums and shanty towns and share croppers. Wherever average income is, a fortunate few at one extreme may live in glittering contrast to millions at the other.

Poverty is a relative concept. It continues, despite absolute improvement, as long as some people fail to achieve the plane of living thought necessary by the society to which they belong. As long as there is striking inequality, poverty will persist.

As long as there is inequality, there will be discontent. Discontent is valuable, as a spur to ambition and productive effort. But it is manifest also in social unrest, class consciousness, and bitter controversy. Perhaps a larger total income offers the surest road to greater well-being. But, to the individual and the group, the particular income share is what matters, and the direct way to increase it is to cut into someone else's income. To this end, workers engage in a constant struggle with their employers, and governmental reform movements enlist crusading support.

Part VI will deal with this major division of economics—the distribution of income. Incomes are fixed in the first instance through the pricing process as it applies to productive services. In part, then, we are continuing the analysis of Part V. But distribution will be viewed as a social problem; and the analysis of wages, profits, and other incomes, and of related problems and policies, will center on questions that reflect the intense, almost universal public concern over the sharing of income.

- 24 -

Inequality—Extent
and Significance

Two foundation tasks must be performed before the division of income can be explained and related practices and policies discussed effectively. The first is factual. Do employees of American corporations receive a quarter, a half, three quarters, or 95 percent of the total income resulting from incorporated activities? Are families in the bottom one fifth of all families in the income scale only 1 percent as well off as families in the top fifth, or one tenth, or one half, or some other fraction? On such questions the wildest of ideas prevail in many minds—even sometimes of persons who would influence opinion on income matters—and the misinformation both obstructs judgment and embitters controversy. This chapter will attempt first to convey a reasonably adequate impression of the actual division of income.

The second preliminary task is concerned with attitudes and analytical approach. How should inequality be regarded? Is it good or bad, avoidable or inescapable? One does not approach such a topic as inequality without preconceptions nor discuss it without rendering judgments. Assumptions of one kind or another are bound to enter, and it is well to bring them into the open by raising pertinent questions and recognizing relevant factors. Distribution is discussed in Part VI within the general framework of capitalism, and it is well at the beginning to ponder the connection between what is desirable and what is possible.

The Factual Picture

This examination of income statistics has two purposes. One aim is to indicate the *extent of inequality* in the United States. The people of the country must be classified on the basis of the size of their incomes in accordance with an appropriate scale. Indeed, for a complete picture, one would need to use a number of scales, and also to make comparisons on the basis of industries, occupations, geographic areas, and such factors as sex and color. The other aim is to give factual content to some of the concepts that will be used in explaining distribution and some of its problems. Information is needed on the extent to which income is received in the form of wages and salaries, business profits, interest, and so on. Major issues relate to the division of income between working and owning, between labor and wealth, and the relevant facts should be known.

As in other phases of economics, the nature of the statistical information should itself be examined closely. One should be aware, for instance, of the income units into which the population is divided. Income data may be gathered and presented on the basis of *spending* or *consuming* units—families and individuals living apart from families —of which there are over 40,000,000 in the United States. Or the income units may be the *income recipients,* the members of the working force, of whom there are around 60,000,000 in the country, plus persons who do not work but receive income from property or other sources. If inequality is measured to show differences in well-being, the consuming unit is the more useful; but statistics based on income recipients show differences in ability to command income.

Similarly the purpose of a statistical study influences the definition of income that is used, and what is included within it. Consumer well-being is affected not only by payments for current productive services but by dollars received in pensions, relief, veterans' allowances, capital gains, and so on; but in the primary breakdown of the national income, the latter are not recognized. Similarly, it is better sometimes to measure income before taxes, and sometimes after taxes are paid. Differences in what is measured may affect substantially the statistical result and may easily confuse the careless observer.

Actual statistics are influenced not only by the ends to be served but also by the figures that are available, which are not always ideal for the particular purpose. Income figures have been improved greatly, but they are far from adequate and are often inexact. But while allowance should be made for elements of estimate in the statistics that follow, the main impressions which they convey are probably quite dependable.

Extent of inequality in the United States

One device in measuring income levels is a scale on which income is shown for classes corresponding to equal fractions of all consuming or spending units. This device is used in the Economic Report of the President to Congress on January 14, 1948.[1] Families, including single individuals, are divided into five numerically equal groups, and the average income for each group is given for three different periods, as shown in Table 28. All figures are expressed in dollars of 1946 purchasing power. From these figures it appears that the highest fifth of the families in the

TABLE 28—FAMILY INCOME IN THE UNITED STATES BY INCOME LEVELS
(In dollars of 1946 purchasing power)

Family income levels	Average money income before taxes			Percent increases	
	1935–36	1941	1946	1935–36 to 1946	1941 to 1946
Lowest fifth	$ 446	$ 498	$ 835	87	68
Second fifth	969	1275	2023	109	59
Third fifth	1515	2243	3050	101	36
Fourth fifth	2284	3225	4201	84	30
Highest fifth	5928	7418	8921	50	20
Average for all	2229	2932	3806	71	30

country can be expected to have incomes that average more than 10 times as high as the average of the bottom fifth—13 times as high in 1935–1936, 15 times in 1941, and nearly 11 times in 1946. The top fifth averages three or four times as high as the middle fifth. Apparently 60 or 70 percent of the families have incomes lower than the general average (the arithmetic mean) for all families. Four fifths of the families are included within a range of $5000 or less, and the top fifth spans a range of more than $1,000,000.

Percentage improvement during the war period, it will be noticed, was strikingly greater in the lower than in higher incomes, but no long-term trend should be inferred from this fact. Indeed, though wage rates were rising relatively fast for low-wage workers, the main explanation of the change does not lie in the rise in wage rates. Low-income families before the war were largely farm families and families affected by unemployment; the war brought practically full employment and high prices for farm products. The bottom fifth in 1946, according to the

[1] The data given here are from, and the page references to, *The Economic Reports of the President*, Reynal & Hitchcock, 1948. The first table, from p. 18, is based on the National Resources Committee study, *Consumer Incomes in the United States*, for the years 1935–1936, a study for 1941 conducted jointly by the Bureau of Labor Statistics and the Bureau of Human Nutrition and Home Economics, and a study for 1946 by the Board of Governors of the Federal Reserve System. Considerable adjusting was necessary to make the studies comparable. See pp. 102–106.

Report, consisted largely of families with small fixed incomes from property, pensions, veterans' allowances, and other public assistance. If incomes were shown after taxes instead of before taxes, the relative improvement of the low-income families during the war would have been even more impressive. Before the war only a small federal income tax was paid on the average income of the top fifth, but in 1946 a tax of $1300 to $1800 was likely to be paid, depending on the number of dependents in the family.

Further light is thrown on the extent of inequality by reassembling these same data to show the *fraction of total income* going to each one fifth of the consuming units. With equal distribution, each fifth would, of course, get one fifth of the total income, and the deviation from 20 percent is a measure of inequality. This table is also from the President's Economic Report.[2]

TABLE 29—FRACTION OF TOTAL INCOME RECEIVED BY
FAMILIES AT DIFFERENT LEVELS

Family income levels	Percentage of total money income		
	1935–36	1941	1946
Lowest fifth	4.0	3.4	4.4
Second fifth	8.7	8.7	10.6
Third fifth	13.6	15.3	16.0
Fourth fifth	20.5	22.0	22.1
Highest fifth	53.2	50.6	46.9

Inequality is shown strikingly when it appears that one fifth of the families receive one half of the national income, but again it should be remembered that the income tax takes a large fraction of the higher incomes.

On the same principle, another study traces for the period 1918–1937 the fraction of total income going to the *highest 1 percent* of the income recipients (not families in this case).[3] The fraction ranges approximately from 12 percent to 20 percent. In this study, capital gains realized through sale of appreciated securities and other property are included as income and are an important element in the rather high percentages for the later years of the 1920s. This top 1 percent of income recipients

[2] *The Economic Reports of the President,* p. 105.
[3] Temporary National Economic Committee Monograph No. 4, *Concentration and Composition of Individual Incomes, 1918–1937,* p. 16.

began at an income level a little above $5000 in the worst years and at about $10,000 in the best years (in current dollars of those years).

Still a different way to show the division of income is to define the income classes, not as equal fractions of total families, but as *ranges of money income,* and then give the varying fractions of families, or other units, at each level.[4]

TABLE 30—FRACTION OF FAMILIES AT DIFFERENT INCOME LEVELS, 1946

	Percent of families	Cumulated percent
Under $1000	12.8	12.8
$1000 to 1999	15.4	28.2
2000 to 2999	19.5	47.7
3000 to 3999	18.4	66.1
4000 to 4999	13.0	79.1
5000 to 7499	13.0	92.1
7500 and over	7.9	100.0

Many families in the prosperous postwar period were living, as the Report points out, "below what can be considered an adequate standard." This was true, certainly, of the one eighth of consuming units receiving less than $1000, and of the more than one quarter, except perhaps for the single individuals included, receiving less than $2000. These, however, are money-income figures and do not include the imputed value of produce raised and consumed by the family or of the service of homes lived in by the owners—adjustments most important in the case of farm families.

Other bases of inequality. To give a complete statistical picture, prevailing income differences would need to be viewed from several other angles that will only be mentioned here.

One should know, for instance, how large a factor *unemployment* and *unemployability* are in the low incomes and to what extent low incomes go to older people who have retired from active work.

Income differences among *industries* are important. The fact that farm incomes usually average only half as high as the average of the whole economy is essential to an understanding of the farm problem. At the other extreme, incomes from banking, insurance, and real estate average more than twice the general average.

Incomes differ widely among *occupations* or *types of work*—among the numerous gradations of unskilled and skilled manual labor, the

[4] *The Economic Reports of the President,* p. 19.

many white-collar skills, the professions, and the various kinds of super-visory and executive work. These differences arise in the main current of income-determining forces, and the following chapter will be devoted to them.

Other striking differentials appear when incomes are examined *geo-graphically*. In most of the northeastern and far-western states the income level is more than twice as high as in most of the southern states. The far greater differences among nations have already been pointed out in Part II in the discussion of productive power.[5]

Still other breakdowns of income data are significant in particular connections. One is *age*. On the average, workers earn more than twice as much at 40 as at 20. Another is *sex*. The pay of male workers seems to average about two thirds higher than the pay of female workers. Still another is *color*. The incomes of white families appear to average twice as high as the incomes of Negro families.[6]

These, of course, are not unrelated facts. Thus, a factor in the lower pay of women workers is their lower average age in comparison with men workers. Low average income in southern states is related to the prevalence of Negroes and the prominence of agriculture among the industries, though the average income of white farmers in the South is also strikingly lower than in the whole country.

Distribution by kinds of income from productive services

The data for family incomes, as we have noted, usually include elements such as pensions which are not a direct return from current productive services. A great deal of redistribution of income occurs through private gifts and charitable contributions and especially through payment of taxes which are used to finance relief, veterans' aids, old-age assistance, and such important elements in real income as public education and recreational facilities. This reassignment of income is commonly called *secondary distribution*. Not all of it gets into the family income figures; if it did, according to one study, the lowest income group would probably be found to consume nearly twice as much income as it receives originally in payment for productive services.[7]

From the welfare standpoint secondary distribution is highly impor-

---

[5] Some of the results of Colin Clark's studies are summarized in the introduction to Part II above, pp. 95–96. Even greater differences in income among nations are indicated in a study by Simon Kuznets. See his article on "National Income," *Encyclopaedia of the Social Sciences*.

[6] Various aspects of the distribution of income are analyzed by Maurice Leven, *The Income Structure of the United States*, Brookings Institution, 1938. See, also, the earlier Brookings study, *America's Capacity to Consume*, by Maurice Leven, Harold G. Moulton, and Clark Warburton.

[7] See *The Income Structure of the United States, op. cit.*, p. 103.

tant, and we shall consider it further at a later point. But it is achieved through various social and governmental arrangements subject to wide modification, and thus it must be separated analytically from the basic economic processes through which income is received in the first place. The main task in studying distribution is to analyze these basic processes, and it is necessary to have some data directly related to them. Income is derived from the *services of human beings* and of *natural and man-made wealth,* and it is received in a *variety of forms.* Extensive information regarding wages and salaries, profits, dividends, interest, and rental income is provided by the Department of Commerce as part of its continuing studies of the national income.

For years that mark the outlines of the main changes from the prosperous 1920s through the war period, the "distributive shares" into which the national income is broken appear as shown in Table 31.[8]

TABLE 31—SHARES IN THE NATIONAL INCOME
(In billions of dollars)

	1929	1933	1940	1944	1947
Compensation of employees	$50.8	$29.3	$51.8	$121.2	$128.1
Wages and salaries	50.2	28.8	49.6	116.9	122.8
Supplements	.6	.5	2.2	4.2	5.4
Net income (adjusted), unincorporated enterprises	13.9	5.2	12.7	27.7	40.5
Business and professional (unadjusted)	8.3	2.9	7.7	15.3	23.5
Farm	5.7	2.3	4.9	12.4	17.0
Rental income to individuals	5.8	2.0	3.6	6.7	7.3
Net interest	6.5	5.0	4.1	3.2	3.6
Net income (adjusted), incorporated enterprises	10.3	−2.0	9.2	23.5	23.0
Net income (unadjusted)	9.8	.2	9.3	23.8	28.7
Tax on corporate income	1.4	.5	2.9	13.9	11.3
Dividends	5.8	2.1	4.0	4.7	6.8
Undistributed profits	2.6	−2.4	2.4	5.2	10.6
National income	87.4	39.6	81.3	182.3	202.6

In this analysis, of which considerable use will be made in ensuing chapters, total income is broken into five main divisions. Along with these divisions, certain leading subdivisons are given. Only such in-

[8] *National Income,* the July 1947 Supplement to *Survey of Current Business,* p. 19; and for the 1947 data, *Survey of Current Business,* February 1948, pp. 5–10. These are the sources of the national-income data in Chapter 3, especially Table 6, p. 55, and the same years are represented at both points. Thus these income figures may be related to the figures for gross and net national product and for personal income given previously.

come enters the total as is regarded as a return from productive services. The national income, as explained in Chapter 3, corresponds to the national net product except for certain deductions from the latter—mainly indirect business taxes—which do not seem to represent the value of productive services. The main divisions call for brief comment.

Hired employees receive the largest part of the national income in all years. Their percentage, for the years given here, varies from 58 percent in 1929 to 74 percent in 1933, and seems typically to represent about two thirds of the total. The percentage is highest in depression years, when wages and salaries are absolutely at their lowest but profits have declined even more. Supplements to wages and salaries, now a substantial item, consist mainly of employers' social-security contributions for old age, unemployment, and other purposes.

The next largest segment is the net income, the *business profits,* of firms which are single *proprietorships* or *partnerships.* This income is quite variable as between prosperous and depressed years, absolutely and in percentages of the total. It includes the income of most farms, of most small businessmen in trade, building construction, and service activities, and of professional people in private practice.

Part of business profit is of the nature of a capital gain (plus or minus) since it arises from fluctuations in the prices of materials and supplies held in stock. Such gains do not reflect the value of current productive services and are not included in the national-income totals nor in the main income divisions. The adjustment referred to in Table 31 involves the elimination of such gains and losses from the statistics. But these gains and losses do appear in accountants' figures for business profits, and they must be recognized here in certain connections.

Thus, the *corporate profits* recognized by the statisticians for 1947, a year of sharply rising prices, are nearly $6 billion less than those recognized by the accountants. But it is on the basis of the latter calculation that income taxes are paid, dividends declared, and undistributed profits computed, as shown in the table. It will be noted that corporate net income is the most widely fluctuating type of income, high in good years and falling in the 1930s to less than nothing.

Much of the income from real estate is included in business profits, but many individuals who are not thought of as being in business receive *rental income;* and the figures for that item in the table include also the imputed rental value of owner-occupied homes and also royalties from patents, copyrights, and natural resources. The *interest* item includes the return from private loans but not from government bonds, since the latter are not looked upon as representing currently productive capital.

Return from labor and from wealth. The foregoing figures correspond mainly to the *forms* in which incomes are received: wages, interest, rents, profits, dividends. They tell less than one would wish regarding the returns for the various *kinds of productive services,* the labor of human beings and the uses of capital and natural wealth. The figures throw some light on the return to these services, but to some extent they are composite and require further analysis. We shall pursue this matter now only with reference to the broad distinction between income from labor and income from wealth, for that distinction is basic to much of the controversy over the distribution of income. Many hold that labor should be rewarded but that ownership of wealth should not be, or at least that the income from it should be severely restricted. This issue will come up repeatedly; here only the facts concern us.

Income from labor service. Compensation of employees is, of course, return from labor. Interest and, for the most part, rentals are return from wealth. Corporate profits should also be regarded mainly as return from wealth because, if the owners are active in a corporation, they are usually paid salaries which are deducted in arriving at the net income (though there is a debatable question here that will be discussed later on). The seriously composite item in Table 31 is the net income from unincorporated firms. Much of the work on farms and in small businesses is done by the owners and their families, and income is received not in the form of employee compensation but in the form of business profits. Much of the income of doctors, lawyers, and engineers is also in this form. Part of this income should be credited to wealth, which in farming and trade is important, but most of it should be credited to labor. What should the fraction be? In corporations, wages and salaries absorb in good years from 75 to 80 percent of the net product, after indirect taxes but before income taxes. Hired labor is a minor element in the typical unincorporated firm; for labor to get as large a fraction as in corporations, about two thirds of the profits would have to be viewed as labor income.[9]

Applying this fraction to the profits of unincorporated businesses in the years covered by Table 31 and adding the result to the recognized compensation of employees, we find the following percents of the total incomes of those years going to labor:

1929	1933	1940	1944	1947
69	79	74	78	76

[9] For the basis of this estimate, see *Supplement to Survey of Current Business, op. cit.,* p. 25. In such years as 1932 and 1933, in which aggregate corporate net income was negative, it would be reasonable to credit the entire net income of unincorporated firms to labor. On that basis the percentage of national income going to labor in 1933 becomes 83.

Judged by the prewar situation, the percentages for 1944 and 1947 are high for prosperous years. One of the several explanatory factors, none of which is necessarily permanent, is the greatly increased part of the total income that is credited to government and the fact that the value set on government services is simply the sum paid to employees.

Interpretation of income from wealth. Do not these percentages overstate the labor element and understate the property element in total income? One reason for thinking that they may, in years such as 1947, is that the figures for business profits do not include the appreciation of inventories. Similarly, the capital gains of individuals from such sources as security speculation are excluded. Capital gains may not be true income from the social standpoint, but they are as beneficial to the recipient as wages or interest. Only persons with wealth receive them. They are important, of course, only in years of rising prices.

Another reason for thinking that the property share of income is understated is that interest on government bonds is omitted. Again, there may be some justification in viewing this interest not as payment for productive service but as a sort of transfer from taxpayer to bondholder, yet the $4 billion is nevertheless an important return to the investors of the country.

But if the interest is recognized, so must the taxes that have to be collected to pay the interest. The income statistics we are considering were arrived at prior to the payment of all income taxes and all other taxes directly paid by individuals. These taxes fall generally on income from labor as well as on income from wealth, but the specific income tax on corporate profits—$11,300,000,000 in 1947—should be viewed as coming out of the income of stockholders. The dividends received by stockholders are subject to the personal income tax, just as wages and salaries are.[10] This personal income tax, which amounted to $21 billion in 1947, is highly progressive, taking higher and higher percentages of incomes as they get larger. Therefore, if we were to consider the division of income between labor and wealth after taxes rather than before, we would need to know how much of the larger incomes derives from each source. Some information of this sort is available.

Property income at different levels. Such information throws light on the tax element in distribution, but it is more important for what it

[10] Part of corporate income, but not all of it, is double-taxed through taxing first the income of corporations and then the incomes of stockholders. That part of corporate income which is taken by the government—38 percent for most corporate income in 1947—cannot be distributed to stockholders as dividends, and a substantial part of the remainder is ordinarily not distributed. For stockholders whose incomes reach brackets which are taxed at higher rates than the tax on corporations, undistributed income pays lower taxes than if the corporate form were not used; for stockholders in lower brackets, it pays more. On the distributed part, the personal-income tax is additional.

tells directly regarding inequality. Do the people with the largest incomes get them mainly from salaries or from investments? Underlying this question is another: Is productive wealth distributed more unequally among the people than labor power is? The answer one would give from ordinary observation is correct: The nature of man is such that all normal adults are able to work, but there is nothing in the nature of man that insures ownership of productive wealth, and most persons own little or none of it. Wealth is subject to accumulation, and there is no natural limit to individual accumulation. The institutions of capitalism favor accumulation by the fortunate and the skillful. Thus wealth is distributed far more unequally than labor power, and the income from wealth is far more unequally divided than income as a whole.[11] It accounts for a large part of the larger incomes.

The accompanying data appear in one of the studies growing out of the Temporary National Economic Committee investigation.[12] For incomes at different levels, component percentages are given here for selected types of income for the years 1929 and 1935. Realized capital gains are treated as income, but, while total income includes these gains, it does not include the undistributed profits of corporations. The figures rest mainly on income-tax returns. The striking difference between

TABLE 32—SELECTED KINDS OF INCOMES AS PERCENTAGES OF TOTAL FOR STATED
INCOME CLASSES

Income class	Employee compensation		Dividends		Realized capital gains	
	1929	1935	1929	1935	1929	1935
Under $5000	73.5	68.7	2.6	2.4	−1.2	.1
$5000 to 10,000	46.8	51.9	9.9	11.5	4.3	2.2
10,000 to 25,000	33.7	38.3	20.0	21.3	10.0	4.4
25,000 to 50,000	23.3	26.9	29.3	32.3	15.8	6.3
50,000 to 100,000	16.0	20.2	34.0	40.1	21.9	7.6
100,000 to 500,000	9.1	11.9	31.3	52.8	36.6	7.1
500,000 to 1,000,000	3.8	2.3	28.3	65.5	49.5	13.0
1,000,000 and over	1.9	.9	24.5	78.0	59.4	9.0
All income classes	63.0	64.7	7.1	5.3	3.4	.7

[11] Such statements as that 2 percent of the people own 90 percent of the wealth have often been made, but there have been no satisfactory studies of the distribution of wealth. The best evidence is found in the statistics of the distribution of income derived from wealth, but there are no data on the distribution of income in the form of services of homes and durable consumers' goods, which are important forms of wealth.

[12] Monograph No. 4, op. cit., p. 48.

1929 and 1935 is the extraordinary amount of profit from speculative activity in the former year, reflected in the realized capital gains. This was the major element in the top incomes, just as dividends were in 1935, but it seems that small speculators did not do well. Actually the capital gains were only 3.4 percent of total income in 1929—which indicates how small a part of total income these largest incomes were.

The main point to be got from these figures is that wages and salaries are of sharply declining importance as incomes become large and that the return from wealth is of sharply rising importance. Wealth may account for only a fourth of the national income, but it accounts for the greater part of the very large incomes. It must also, therefore, be subject to much heavier income taxation than the income from labor is.

In these large incomes, the return from wealth comes chiefly in most years from corporate profits—from dividends, as the table shows—and through the effect of undistributed profits on stockholders' equities. Of the incomes below $5000, the part that comes from wealth is only to a minor extent from dividends. It is more largely from interest, from rentals, and from the property element in the net income of unincorporated firms.[13]

Not only do the largest incomes derive mostly from wealth, but much of the income from wealth finds its way into large incomes. This fact is evidence of inequality in the distribution of wealth itself. The top 1 percent of the income recipients—those with more than $9975 in 1929 and with more than $5800 in 1935—received 5.9 percent of the wages and salaries in the former year, 6.8 percent in the latter. But in these years, respectively, they got 64.7 and 59.7 percent of the dividends, 31.7 and 22.1 percent of the interest, and 12.8 and 10.3 percent of the rents and royalties. Of the net income of unincorporated firms, they received 16.2 and 11.6 percent.[14]

Wealth *versus* **labor as source of inequality.** It is clear from these figures that income from wealth is an important source of inequality, because wealth is so unequally divided. But its effect on inequality in the whole distribution of income can easily be exaggerated. Income from wealth is concentrated, but in the aggregate it is a minor part of total income. If, in 1946, all dividends, all rents and royalties, and all interest including interest on government bonds had been divided equally among all the families and other consuming units of the country, the income per unit

---

[13] Of the 1935 incomes below $5000, which were about 98 percent of all incomes, only 2.4 percent came from dividends, while 3.4 percent came from rents and royalties, and 7.7 percent from interest and miscellaneous property sources. Profits from unincorporated firms, including farms, accounted for 17.7 percent, and on the assumption made earlier, about one third of this would be property income.

[14] Monograph No. 4, *op. cit.*, p. 45.

would have been about $465. But if all employee compensation, all wages and salaries, had been divided equally, the amount per consuming unit would have been about $2700. If the latter distribution took place, the lowest fifth of the families would have had, on the average, $1865 more than they actually received and the next lowest fifth $675— much more than the equal division of dividends, rents, and interest would have given them.[15] Thus, for the whole economy, differences in employee compensation must be deemed the greater factor in inequality. This inequality might largely remain even if the industries of a country were socialized, and private-property income abolished.

Review Questions

1. "In measuring economic progress, income is commonly expressed in per-capita terms, but, in analyzing the distribution of income, comparisons are usually made on the basis of income recipients or of consuming units." Distinguish these bases on which income statistics are expressed. What determines the choice among them?

2. "While all real income arises from production, there are elements of income which must be considered in measuring the well-being of consuming groups which do not enter an analysis of the returns from productive services." Explain. Review the distinction between national income and aggregate personal income as given in Chapter 3. What is secondary distribution? What does it involve that the statistics of family income ordinarily omit?

3. If you were called upon to measure the inequality of income in the United States, how would you proceed? Select three facts regarding income classes and relationships that seem to you most effective in describing the degree of inequality.

4. "Income is so divided that average income—the arithmetic mean of income—is considerably higher than median income—the middle income when all incomes are ranged from highest to lowest." Explain. What would be the form of a graph which showed the number of families receiving each size of income?

5. To describe fully the distribution of income in the United States, what other comparisons would you make beside those between income-level classes?

6. What are the main kinds of productive services from which income is derived? Name the main forms in which income is received. (These forms, as they involve the property incomes, will be explained fully in Chapter 28.)

7. Without giving precise figures, indicate the relative importance of the distributive shares to which the Department of Commerce statisticians as-

[15] Equalizing the pay of all workers would not equalize the incomes of families since many low-income families have no fully employed member, and many families have two or more employed members.

sign segments of the national income. What pattern appears in the relationship of these shares between boom and depression periods?

8. What fraction of the national income seems to be received in return for services of labor and what fraction for services of wealth? In answering this question statistically, what difficulties arise in connection with the net income of unincorporated firms, interest, taxes, and capital gains?

9. A magazine article says that labor gets about 95 percent of the national income, whereas a trade-union publication says that factory labor gets only about 35 percent of the value of its product and that there is much room for wages to be raised. Do you see how figures might be manipulated to give such results as these? Do they suggest why it is important to have some understanding of the facts of distribution?

10. Why should you expect income from wealth to be distributed more unequally than income from labor? Do the facts support this expectation convincingly? Explain.

11. How do the labor and wealth components of income vary as the size of incomes varies?

12. "Property incomes largely account for the very large incomes in the United States, but they do not seem to be the chief source of inequality." Is this a defensible statement? Explain.

Factors in Judging Inequality

The second task of this first chapter on distribution is to examine the preconceptions, the standards, the logic by which the division of income is judged. Too often, on this subject, strong positions are taken without a clearly defined, or even a definable, basis. People assail hazily the injustices of a society in which riches and poverty exist together and blindly espouse almost any proposal that promises to hurt the well off or aid the underdog. Or, with equal blindness, they denounce every serious reform as communistic and defend heatedly every arrangement they find personally satisfactory.

The aim of these paragraphs is to establish as rational an approach as possible to a subject that inspires more emotion than any other in economics. Judgments are rendered constantly, by almost everyone, on wages, profits, taxes, social security, and numerous related matters, and the study of economics should try not only to explain what is but also to improve the basis of these judgments.

Approaches to the problem of inequality

If the total income of a country were to be divided in the most logical way among its people, what would the basis be? At least four bases are present in the judgments people render. They are:

1. That income should be divided *equally*. Equality may mean (*a*) that all individuals should have the same income to use, (*b*) that all families should have the same amount, or (*c*) that all workers or income recipients should get the same return. These conceptions of equality yield different results, depending on the number of persons or of income recipients in families.

2. That income should be divided on the basis of people's *needs*. This is the doctrine of theoretical communism.[16]

3. That people should be paid on the basis of *how hard they work*—their productive effort or zeal in contributing to the total product.

4. That they should receive incomes according to the *value of what they do*—the worth of their contribution, including, under capitalism, the contribution of the productive wealth they own.

It will be noted that the first two regard distribution directly from the consumer's side, the latter two from the producer's. These are four logically distinct bases of dividing income, but it should not be thought that any one of them, in any actual society, will be exemplified perfectly or to the exclusion of others. Indeed, in any society, luck and power and strategy are bound also to play a part, though ideally they should not. These alternative principles are stated here because evidences of all of them lurk in the judgments people render in attacking or defending the division of income.

While distribution is an economic problem, the convictions of people regarding it seldom rest on strictly economic reasoning. Ideas as to how incomes ought to be related grow out of *ethical attitudes* and general social philosophy. Thus, to anyone who has grown up within the democratic tradition, inequality cannot be taken for granted but seems to need defending. It may be unavoidable, but, if human beings are basically equal—equal, as religious people put it, in the sight of God—the differences in their well-being should not be greater than necessary. It is not the business of economics to explain, defend, or question such beliefs, but it must remain aware of them while approaching the problem in its own, rather different way.

Certain ideas on the distribution problem, while perhaps more strictly economic in nature, are more clearly at odds with the usual thinking of economists. When a man argues that he is entitled to all he can get from this farm of his, which he carved from the wilderness, or from this ore deposit which he discovered, or this process which he invented, or this factory which he had the enterprise to build, he implies a certain standard of what is just and right. It may be described as a

---

[16] The phrase "theoretical communism" is used to avoid confusion with the Communist party or with Communist Russia.

reward-of-merit standard, a recognition of just deserts. The same idea may be present when the employer says his thousand employees should not begrudge him his profits, since he is responsible for their jobs. Such views enter the general atmosphere, the climate of thinking, within which income questions are discussed, but they provide no guidance for the person who wants to approach these questions with his feet on the ground.

The approach of economics. Whatever guidance economics provides comes from its insistence that income payments should not be judged abstractly as matters of right or desert but by their consequences. If this approach is accepted, the main job becomes one of tracing the results of particular income arrangements and proposals and of seeing how they relate to the working of the economy. Two kind of results are important: (1) direct effects on consumer welfare and (2) effects on production, which indirectly affect consumers. No income arrangement is ideal unless it enables the consuming public to derive the maximum benefit from the nation's output. But no arrangement is ideal either unless it promotes, or at least is consistent with, the most effective use of resources.

To appreciate the bearing of these two considerations on the problem of inequality, it will only be necessary to review certain ideas that are already familiar. Unfortunately these ideas often point in opposite directions. Distribution to maximize directly the well-being of consumers may obstruct the best organization of production, and vice versa. No easy compromise will appear, but approaching the distribution problem in this way should exclude many emotional irrelevancies and provide a useful basis of judgment at many points.

The case against unnecessary inequality

If the problem of distributing income could be divorced completely from the problem of producing it, there would be little reason for inequality and strong reasons against it. Against it would stand the weight of the democratic tradition, and economic analysis would be on the same side. *Any given total income* can be expected to yield maximum benefit to the consuming public when divided equally or according to needs.

The reason for this conclusion is found in the *principle of diminishing utility*.[17] It lies in the fact that, as a person has more dollars of income, the importance of each dollar declines. Hence the advantage of having more than an average income is less than the disadvantage of having less than an average income. If, for example, Smith and Jones

---
[17] Explained in Chapter 19.

together earn $5000, the satisfactions of the two of them will be greatest if each receives $2500. If Smith were to get $3500 and Jones $1500, then dollars, and the goods dollars would buy, would have unequal importance to the two men—less to Smith and more to Jones. If so, a transfer of dollars from Smith to Jones, up to $1000, would increase the total satisfaction of the two of them.

Some qualifications. This use of the principle of diminishing utility is subject to criticism. When we first considered it, we noted that, even for one consumer, the satisfactions from different quantities of different goods cannot be measured and compared confidently. Much less plausible would be any quantitative statement of the relative satisfactions of different people. But in a rough, common-sense way we do make such comparisons, and they are accepted as a satisfactory basis for policy judgments. As has been well said: "If there is any meaning in saying that to take $1 from a millionaire and to give it to a starving man does more to satisfy the starving man than to dissatisfy the millionaire, then logically we must admit that the feelings of different men are commensurable." [18] This reasoning is the main basis, in economics, for opposing unnecessary inequality.

But though this logic is acceptable in a rough way, we should not push it to the extreme of assuming that all individuals are exactly alike in their wants. Jones may be a quiet soul with simple tastes, and Smith's temperament may call for travel and some degree of luxury. If so, the equalizing of income might hurt Smith more than it helped Jones. We may recognize this difficulty by saying that their needs are different and that the ideal basis of distribution is needs, not equality. But probably no reformer would urge that needs reflecting such personal differences should actually be the basis of policy. Other differences in needs, however, would doubtless be considered. If Smith has a family and Jones does not, an equalization of their incomes would certainly not maximize their total well-being. If equality is to be thought of as the ideal goal, perhaps it should be per-capita equality, rather than per-worker equality.

The argument against inequality on the basis of diminishing utility should certainly be qualified from the short-run standpoint. It may be true in the long run that Smith and Jones, if they have no basic differences in tastes, would get most out of $5000 if it were divided equally between them. But if Smith's living habits are once adjusted to the $3500 level and Jones's to the $1500, equalization is likely to bring more immediate injury to Smith than benefit to Jones. The pressure of wants

[18] J. E. Meade and C. J. Hitch, *An Introduction to Economic Analysis and Policy*, Oxford University Press, 1938, p. 224.

depends largely on what we are used to; retreat from a standard, even a senselessly high standard, is painful. So, against the principle that dollars are less important the more we have of them, we may set the qualifying principle that the accustomed dollar is more important than the windfall dollar. To the extent that the problem is one of dividing a given total income, the former may properly guide long-run policy; the latter should govern the manner and speed of its application.

The basis of necessary inequality

But the problem of practical policy is never merely one of dividing a given income, and judgments on distribution matters should not assume that it is. The problem of dividing income cannot in fact be separated from the problem of producing it. Under capitalism, and perhaps under socialism, incomes are received primarily as payments for productive services. Under capitalism, at least, they are an essential part of the whole system of values through which economic life is organized. The communist prescription for an ideal society—"from every one according to his ability; to every one according to his needs"—implies that production and distribution can be separated, but in this study we shall not speculate on a possibility so remote from any present set of institutions. The two main relationships, now to be reviewed, between the division of income and the production of it should be kept in mind throughout the discussion of Part VI.

Distribution and incentives. Certainly income is not the only incentive to production; there may often be specific situations in which losses of production can be corrected better through improvements in working conditions than through higher pay. But it seems to be true that income provides the chief incentive to production in our society. Few men would work as energetically and effectively as they do, as regularly and for as long periods, if their livelihood did not depend on their performance; nor would they be as concerned with improving their productive powers in order to qualify for better positions. Perhaps even more clearly, the risks of enterprise would not be assumed without the prospect of substantial gain.

If incomes are to function as incentives, they will be unequal. People are not equal in what they do, and what they get must vary with their performance or the incentive will fail. Satisfaction of wants is still the social goal is distributing income, but what people get depends not on their wants or needs but on what they do. The possible immediate benefit through basing distribution on needs is subordinated in order to have a large total income to distribute.

But while we have here an explanation, and perhaps a justification, of inequality, it is not an adequate explanation of the inequality that prevails under capitalism. It would be silly to contend, for instance, that if the executive did not get $100,000 a year, he would not do his work conscientiously. The common laborer may do his best for $1000; and executive work, to the man with capacity for it, is not so exceptionally arduous or distasteful as to require a vastly greater inducement. Doing more and better work, and work that requires more years of training, should bring more income; but actual differences can be explained only in part on this basis. As incentives, it is sufficient to adjust incomes to effort rather than to the values of services.

Distribution and allocation of resources. Inequality under capitalism is explained more fully by the fact that payments for productive services are fixed in the markets that govern the use of human and material resources. If all human abilities and all items of land and capital goods are to be used effectively, there must be some rational scheme of assigning them to particular lines of production and of fitting them efficiently into the processes of production. Unless a central economic authority performs this function, it must be left to the value-cost calculations of enterprisers and the desire of individuals to place their labor and their wealth where it will bring them a satisfactory return. The same payments that we viewed as costs in Part V are the incomes that will concern us in Part VI.

The logic of income differentials is found primarily in the *principle of opportunity cost*.[19] Perhaps the executive would work efficiently for $10,000, but where would he work? He is an exceptionally able person, and a score of firms would like to get him at that figure. He finds the spot where his capacities are really required only through the fact that the $100,000 salary offered him is more than he could be worth to other interested firms. The same principle must operate to cause the most effective use of all kinds of labor, high and low, and the services of all kinds of material resources. The result, necessarily, is a considerable degree of inequality.

Some qualifications and additional income factors. Again, too much must not be concluded from what has been said. Production and distribution may be so related that inequality is inevitable, but it does not follow that all the inequality in the United States, or elsewhere, is explained by the logic of this relationship. Factors of power and strategy and luck, it must be remembered, operate in any system.

Indeed, from the standpoint of *maximum productive power,* some lessening of inequality is often beneficial. Such a gain may come at both ends of the income scale. If there are "idle rich" who refrain from work because wealth yields them large incomes, a reduction of these incomes would expand the working force. If assurance of luxury dampens the ambitions of young men of wealthy parentage, more modest income prospects would expand output. Property incomes which serve as guides in allocating resources may operate badly as incentives to personal service.

At the other extreme, very low incomes may restrict production because they fail to maintain physical and mental vigor. Undernourishment is still common in many countries, and, though most people in the United States have enough to eat, many cannot afford proper care of their health. The degradation of hopeless poverty, moreover, can destroy the spirit and morale of workers. Such a lessening of inequality as will raise the lowest incomes to a health-supporting, morale-sustaining level is, therefore, a means of increasing the total income to be distributed.

These are reasons why inequality may reduce productive power. But more often heard in recent years is the argument that *inequality diminishes total demand* and thus *restricts the use of productive power*. The reasoning, developed first in Chapter 14, is familiar: that when a larger part of total income is in the hands of relatively few people, more of it is saved; and if more is saved, the amount of investment necessary to maintain prosperity is increased, and depression and unemployment of resources are more probable. This reasoning is plausible and not without evidence to support it, but its soundness should not be regarded as conclusively demonstrated, and it is certainly not to be applied in an undiscriminating way. For one thing, it involves the assumption that investment opportunity is limited.[20] For another, it does not recognize that profit, a major source of large incomes, is necessary to induce investment. It has come to be used extensively, we shall observe, in supporting demands for higher wages.

Finally, in obtaining a balanced view of the economic basis of inequality, it should be seen that distribution of income does not depend entirely on the rates of payment for productive services. With any particular set of payments for the services of people, land, and capital, incomes depend on two other major influences:

1. One is the *distribution of wealth*. The ownership of wealth, which may become highly concentrated, governs the distribution of interest,

---

[20] If investment opportunities are adequate to absorb savings, then inequality increases production. Greater inequality means greater saving, and greater saving means more rapid capital formation. This point was formerly much stressed by writers on distribution, but in recent years the safer course has seemed to lie in chancing too small savings, rather than too large.

rent, and profit among the people. It is governed by many factors, some of which are distinctly institutional.

2. The other is the factor of *secondary distribution* mentioned earlier in this chapter. Much income is redistributed, largely through governmental channels, after it is originally received, and thus the distribution of economic welfare departs considerably from the primary division of income in payments for services.

Main elements in a standard of judgment

Plainly the problem of distribution is too complex to be solved through any simple set of approvals and condemnations. Certainly it cannot be handled through stirring catchwords and loose tags of theory. The honest and responsible student will not want to approach it in this way.

But two main ideas will probably be accepted and found useful by most persons in their thinking. One is that inequality per se is not good —that there is a presumption against inequality unless it plays a useful part in organizing the production of goods. The other is that incomes are bound to be unequal in their role as incentives, and still more unequal if they are depended on to guide the economizing of resources.

These two considerations cannot be combined into a single standard of judgment. Sometimes they are in harmony; and if any factor that increases inequality does not contribute positively to the effective working of the economy, some sort of reform should at least be considered. But if economic processes must be disrupted to reduce inequality at any point, great caution, at the very least, is indicated. Some would argue, perhaps, that inequality is itself so greatly the source of unhappiness that some equalizing of income is desirable even if total income is reduced. This would mean, for instance, that it better to receive $2500 in a situation in which no one gets more than that sum than to receive $3000 in a situation in which some get $10,000 and a few get $100,000. Economics provides no basis for accepting or rejecting such a view, though the prevailing assumption as to the nature of economic progress is against it. If the aim is greater income, especially more income for those who have little, the surest course is probably through expanding the total income to be divided rather than through changing the division, though there may well be exceptions. In any case, reforms should be approached realistically, in light of their consequences, and not with a blind sense of wrongs to be righted and justice to be done.

The main task of the next five chapters is to explain the determination of income, primarily under capitalism, and not to pass judgments on it. But many opportunities will be seized to examine the sources of controversy and to look into questions from which disputes arise. The final chapter in Part VI will review the policies that have been adopted to alter and improve the division of income in the United States and some of the further proposals that have been made.

Review Questions

1. Distinguish four principles on which the division of income might conceivably be based. Which do you associate primarily with capitalism, which with theoretical communism?

2. "Equality of income cannot be a practical goal of policy under capitalism, or perhaps under any system. But it is well to remember that inequality is not good in itself, that the presumption is against it and it requires justification." Why is the presumption against inequality? Present both economic and noneconomic reasons.

3. "The heart of the distribution problem lies in the fact that the size and composition of the income pie depend on the way it is divided." Distinguish carefully the principal ways in which the production of goods depends on the income payments to producers.

4. Along what different lines may it be argued that a reduction in inequality may sometimes increase total income?

5. "Rates of income—wage, interest, rent, and profit rates—basically control the division of income, but, these rates being what they are, the distribution of income depends on two other important factors." Explain.

6. Set forth what seem to you the main considerations to bear in mind in reaching opinions on economic practices and proposed reforms in the distribution field.

- 25 -

Inequality in the
Return from Labor

CONFLICTS over wages and profits catch the headlines and sometimes disrupt the economy, but they involve only part of the problem of inequality. Profits and other returns to the owners of wealth account for the largest incomes, but, with labor receiving three fourths of all income in the United States and with labor's income varying widely, much of the inequality problem is just a matter of relative wages.[1]

The incomes discussed in this chapter derive from the whole gamut of human services, from common labor to professional practice and corporate management. The word *labor* is used to include all services of hand and brain. Similarly the word *wages* is applied to the whole income from labor, whether based on hourly wage rates, monthly salaries, year-end bonuses, professional fees, or salesmen's commissions. The discussion will apply, in part, to the incomes of farm operators and other business owners for the work they do, even though received in the form of business profits, but consideration of these entrepreneurial workers will be incidental.

Differences in wages are, in a sense, the most striking aspect of inequality. Property income differs from person to person—from nothing at all to millions a year—because the wealth that yields it is unequally distributed. Since wealth is separate from people and by nature subject to concentration, there is nothing mysterious about the inequality it causes. Wages, in contrast, derive from abilities of people which are inseparable from them; every normal person has two hands, a back, and a brain, neither more nor less. Thus, on reflection, it is a startling fact

[1] As pointed out in the preceding chapter, the lowest fifth of the families in the United States in 1946 would have been helped about four times as much through equal distribution of all labor income as through equal distribution of rent, interest, and dividends.

that some men should earn only a few hundreds a year, and other men tens and hundreds of thousands.

This similarity, this surface uniformity, in the source of wages simplifies the problem of wage differences. Only one theoretical tool will be called on: the principle of supply and demand. When we get into the relation of wages to profits, and to the other property incomes, some further analytical equipment will be necessary, but it is not essential here.[2] The first section of the chapter will apply the elementary logic of supply and demand to the range of earnings among occupations. The second section will note some of the peculiarities of the labor market, some of the pressures, imperfections, and institutional factors that affect wage relationships.

Underlying Market Factors in Wage Differences

Just before World War II labor service brought an average annual return of about $1200 in the United States. The largest single industrial group, the so-called production workers in factories, had an average income not far from the general average. Routine office workers did no better, and employees in stores got typically about $20 a week, or $1000 a year. Common labor might do that well at the average wage of 50 cents an hour if it remained fully employed, but annual earnings ran lower. So also did the earnings of laundry and similar workers. Farm hands averaged perhaps $400 or $500 a year, and household employees were lucky if they could make $500.[3]

As one would expect, incomes from labor service spread much further above the general average than below it—thus making the average, the $1200 figure, somewhat greater than workers typically received. Craftsmen in the building trades were likely to make more than $1500 but less than $2000. Electricians had a good chance of earning $2000, and so did printers. Workers for power and telephone and other public-

[2] The marginal productivity principle of distribution, which will be explained in the following chapter, goes more deeply into the demand for productive services. It may throw additional light on wage differences, but it is not necessary in explaining why they exist or their general magnitude. These chapters aim to focus attention on the leading distribution questions, and to adapt the necessary analytical tools to these questions, without subordinating issues to a theoretical scheme. From this standpoint, the next two chapters are a unit; and it is well to discuss wage differences now, so as not to disrupt the sequence.

[3] Wage and salary data such as appear in the newspapers and news weeklies derive from several sources, mainly governmental. The Bureau of Labor Statistics of the Department of Labor compiles extensive data on ordinary wages and reports through the *Monthly Labor Review*. Information on large incomes has become available through the Bureau of Internal Revenue of the Treasury Department. The Department of Commerce has studied professional incomes by the questionnaire method. For a summary, see *Survey of Current Business*, May 1944.

utility companies averaged $1500 or $1600, but some of the railway trainmen went much higher, and engineers and conductors on good runs might make as much as $3500 a year.

In the professions, at the lower levels, ministers averaged around $2000, journalists somewhat more, and nurses and public schoolteachers considerably less. College teachers averaged $3000, dentists over $4000, engineers possibly a little more, and physicians, lawyers, and certified public accountants around $5000. A few doctors and lawyers reached $25,000 and $50,000 levels, and even higher. What actors typically earn is not known, but the $200,000 or more a year made by some of the Hollywood stars, and the thousands a week of some of the radio entertainers, showed what was possible, though not at all probable, in the profession. A few musicians also had very high incomes.

It is impossible to say what was earned on the average by business executives, partly because there is no way to set them off sharply from lower levels of managerial and supervisory employees. A handful of individuals usually received $500,000 or more in salary and bonuses, and the heads of several hundred very large corporations were paid from $100,000 to $300,000, though railroad presidents were getting considerably less. Perhaps a dozen persons in a big corporation would get $50,000 or more. Salaries of $10,000 or $15,000 were numerous among corporation executives, but salaries of this size and higher were received by only a fraction of 1 percent of all wage earners.

The greatest spread among the members of particular income groups, not only absolutely but also relatively, is found at the higher levels. Pay at those levels is less standardized, and performance is such that individuals may stand out distinctively. But even at lower levels, average figures conceal a substantial dispersion of incomes. Behind the average for all workers in manufacturing, the averages for particular manufacturing industries differ a good deal. Employees of steel and automobile companies were averaging twice as much as textile workers before the war. Within each of these industries the broad category of factory work covers an extensive range of activities. In the steel mills the melters, pourers, rollers, finishers, and welders were often getting three times as much as common labor, and other activities were ranged continuously between.

The impact of war raised the pay for all types of work, and by 1947 had just about doubled the average return, to about $2500. Factory work moved up correspondingly and stayed close to the general average, but the largest gains were commonly made in fields where pay was lowest before the war. From 1939 to 1946 earnings in automobile factories rose by 50 percent, but average pay in the women's clothing industry more than doubled, although after the rise the automobile workers were still considerably better paid. Earnings nearly tripled for farm hands and rose by little more than a third for railroad engineers, but the engineers still got four times as much. Within industries, also, percentage differences declined among occupational levels, largely because a number of flat increases in wages added relatively more at the lower levels. As a result, the most skilled factory workers might not make double the pay of janitors. Percentagewise the executives probably did as well as their employees during this period, but, since we are speaking of earnings before income taxes, the rise at the upper levels has no net significance.

From the foregoing it is clear that there is no simple way to divide the working force into classes for the study of wage differences. It is conventional to speak of common or unskilled labor, semiskilled or typical factory labor, the skilled trades, routine "white-collar" workers, the professions, business executives and managers. But when, as in 1946, nearly 20 percent of the workers classed as professional earned less than $2000 and 10 percent of the manual workers made more than $4000, these conventional labels plainly do not correspond to income levels. Nevertheless, within these broad categories, there are definable types of work for which there are fairly typical, persisting income differentials. This section is concerned with the basic market factors that underlie these continuing differences in return.

Mobility and the pull toward equality

Why should these large differences in earnings persist among occupations? Why should the services of ordinary human beings continue to be rewarded so unequally? In matters of pricing, there is no essential difference between labor service and ordinary commodities; the natural tendency is for the returns from different activities to be drawn together through the mobility of workers. Economic motives, both of those who sell labor and those who buy it, work in that direction. If executives get more than foremen, foremen are anxious to shift to the executive field, and the boards of directors who hire executives welcome the competition of more numerous applicants. The higher pay of mechanics attracts workers from unskilled ranks, and employers welcome the pressure on mechanic's wages. As the mobility of workers reduces earnings in better paid occupations, it increases the pay in fields where the supply of labor is reduced. In so far as markets provide a natural corrective for inequality, this is it.

For this tendency to operate, general mobility of workers is not necessary. To equalize the pay for two types of work, the shifting of a relatively small number, adding to supply in one field and reducing it in the other, may be all that is necessary. Indeed, without any actual shifting, the equalizing tendency is still present, because older workers are continually retiring and younger workers are selecting occupations on the basis of the opportunities they afford. This adjustment cannot offset the effect of sharp changes in the demand for different kinds of service but should be sufficient to counteract the ordinary inequalities.

Certainly forces are present which promote equality of return in markets, but the major differences in earnings among occupational classes persist in spite of these forces. The explanation, then, must be found in the obstacles to an equalizing degree of mobility between the various fields of work.

Equalizing offsets to differences in rates of pay

Part of the explanation may lie in the fact that pay in the ordinary sense, earnings per hour or day or month, does not measure the relative attractiveness of occupations. If compensation tends to be equalized, it is income in a sense that encompasses all of the aspects of jobs which affect their desirability—the income they yield not only immediately but in the long run and the features of work that make it pleasant or disagreeable. Differences in rates of pay that offset other differences in compensation in this broader sense are sometimes referred to in economics as *equalizing differences*.

It seems quite obvious that the immediate rate of pay should not be the basis of choosing occupations when work is highly seasonal or irregular. The bricklayer and the longshoreman should judge their earnings on an annual basis, with some allowance perhaps for the attraction of added leisure. Cyclical insecurity of earnings is a factor that the rate of pay may properly offset. Industries and jobs vary considerably in their fluctuations. In fields in which the average working life is shortened by hazards and diseases, income should be considered on a lifetime basis. The steeplejack should be rewarded for his risks. Hard manual labor is performed best by young men, and the early age at which peak earnings are reached and past should enter into any comparison of jobs. In skilled manual occupations a decline is likely after middle age, whereas in the professions earnings are more likely to remain high until near retirement, which may be in the late sixties. A rational mobility of labor is governed more by lifetime earnings than by immediate differences in pay.

A similar factor is the costs that must be incurred in preparing for certain occupations, especially a profession such as medicine. Extra earnings are necessary to compensate for these costs. Occupations in the public eye, both in business and in government, require exceptional outlays for entertainment and maintaining appearances, and earnings should be viewed in part as an offset to these special expenditures.

Many of the elements that enter job comparisons are nonpecuniary but relate to the agreeableness of work or to the circumstances in which workers live. A scientist absorbed in his research may need only a small money income to feel well rewarded. An artist may need only a slight financial inducement to keep him at his work. A satisfying sense of service rendered may constitute for the preacher and social worker a compensation that is not enjoyed in more acquisitive pursuits. College professors are supposedly rewarded in part by the length of their vacations and the amenities of their environment. "White-collar" positions in general seem to have a nonpecuniary superiority over manual-labor jobs. On the other hand, for coal miners and others who do especially disagreeable work or who must live in dreary surroundings, there are disadvantages for the money income to offset. In so far as money-income differences merely balance these nonpecuniary factors, they are to be thought of as equalizing differences and not as evidence of inequality.

In some of these cases, rates of pay probably do reflect the responses of workers to the relative continuity of earnings, the special costs, the appeal or disutility of the work. But equalizing differences that balance these considerations can operate only within narrow limits. The company executive has a pleasanter and more secure position than the day laborer in his employ, but the executive's pay, instead of being lower to offset these attractive features, is much higher. The significant fact is that the laborer is not in a position to choose to be an executive. Equalizing differences operate only among occupations for which the same people are eligible, so that a fairly free choice is possible. Such adjustments do not affect the relative rates of pay of *noncompeting groups* of workers. It is as between such groups that the main problem of occupational inequality arises. What are the factors that impede mobility between them?

Differences in ability—environment and heredity

The first answer is that lack of ability is the obstacle. Most people do not enter the better paying occupations because they are not able to do the work in those fields. To say that any job requires skill is to say that relatively few are available to perform it. Very few are qualified for professional and managerial work.

But the real question is why the supply of superior abilities is so small. Why should not the qualified applicants for the well-paid positions become sufficiently numerous so that the advantage in earnings would largely disappear? This undoubtedly is one of the chief questions to be asked in the analysis of distribution, and perhaps one of the most important questions in economics. But it is not one to which economics can offer a satisfactory answer.

In essence, it is the long-debated question of the relative importance of heredity and environment in determining the characteristics of people, and of how environment exerts its influence. Is White a corporation president, Brown an engineer, Green a mechanic, and Black a section hand because of qualities of mind, energy, and personality born in them or because of the unlike circumstances under which they developed their abilities and found their economic focus? Few, probably, hold tightly to either explanation to the exclusion of the other, but experts on man and society differ widely in the importance they attach to inborn and social influences.

Education is usually named as the chief molder of abilities. Aptitudes for formal education vary greatly—a fact no more surprising than that people should differ in height, weight, or complexion. Supporting the emphasis on hereditary factors, it is said that any youth with the right qualities can now get an education. But it appears, on the other hand, that the right qualities have more than a biological basis. The basis is partly economic. Children of poor families, living in poor communities, personally acquainted only with workers in poorly paid occupations, may never sense in an effective way the possibility of rising to a higher income level. They go to work as early as possible and choose their occupation on the basis of immediate reward rather than ultimate prospects. This is the more likely if they must help support their families. And if this responsibility is placed on them, young people with some native ability and ambition may fall into dead-end occupations and fail even to develop the more important manual skills. Other young people, no better endowed but more fortunate, get the training they can assimilate and thus advance much further. Whatever the limitations that nature imposes, economic factors limit further the supply of talent for the better positions.

But the number of persons reasonably free from economic handicaps is large in comparison with the number who reach the heights in the better paying occupations. Physicians may have averaged no more than $5000 a year before the war, but particular physicians made much more. Salaries of business executives extend over a range of hundreds of thousands of dollars. Relatively few people receive expensive professional educations or embark on business apprenticeships that may lead to the highest incomes, but the number who have these opportunities is far greater than the number who reach the top. The very fact that there are such income peaks to be reached is evidence of the scarcity of something which environment and training cannot give. The gifts of mind, energy, and personality necessary to reach the heights seem to be inborn, though unfavorable environmental factors may keep them from emerging, and favorable factors may speed the fortunate individual in his climb.

Abilities and earnings

While the relative effect of hereditary and social influences can be debated, it is plain that together they limit the supply of various kinds of labor service. But merely to recognize the limitation is not to define the conditions that make for high and low earnings. How does the principle of supply and demand operate in this area?

First of all, it is well to be cautious about saying that this person has high earnings because his ability is high and that person has low earnings because his ability is meager. By what definition of ability does one say that it is the great ability of the movie star that enables him to earn a hundred times as much as the eminent poet? Earnings may be governed by ability, but, to establish a close correspondence between them, one must resort to the circular procedure of measuring ability by earning power. This does not mean that all of the earmarks of superior ability in the economic sphere must be expressed with a dollar sign. It is often possible to identify directly those less common attributes of intellect, training, and personality that are likely to be well rewarded in different fields. For manual work in factories, job classifications can be worked out on the basis of various measures of difficulty and applied practically in determining pay scales. But it is still true, finally, that there is no basis in economics for saying that a certain kind of labor should command a certain return—no basis except that the particular return is the one at which the supply of that labor is equal to the demand.

Condition of demand necessary to high earnings. Poets, movie stars, and others may have rare qualities, but it takes a certain type of market situation to make a very high income possible. Technically, we may say that the demand curve for the particular service must start high. Where much hinges on the outcome of a single act or decision, people are willing to pay a high price for it. A life hangs on the exact handling of a surgeon's instrument. Numerous dollars of corporate income depend on the soundness of an executive's judgment. The appeal of a movie at box offices throughout the nation is fixed by the brief performance of a few actors. The wisecracks of a comedian enter millions of homes through a national radio hook-up. In these cases the condition of demand is present that makes high income possible. Barbers, bookkeepers, and plumbers have no such chance. Whatever their skill and however small the number who have it, their possibility of reward is limited by the kind of work they do and the restricted stage where they do it.

Ability and pay differences in the same field. Is it possible to generalize regarding the relationship between pay and ability in a given field? If workmen are paid on a piecework basis, and one man can produce 10 percent more than another and gets 10 percent more pay, we can say in a crude objective sense that pay is proportioned to ability. A quantitative comparison of this sort is impossible in most situations, but general observation indicates that very large differences in earnings often accompany very small differences in ability.[4]

Only the highest degree of ability may penetrate the market of greatest promise. A slight superiority in the ability of an executive may be the basis of a big difference in worth to a large corporation, in view of the volume of output. Thus the demand of large corporate employers, concentrating on a limited number of men of top ability, operates to give them high salaries. Small differences in the performance and appeal of two movie stars, subjected to the amplifying effect of thousands of showings, explain a big difference in compensation.

But what counts directly is not the superior ability actually present but the superiority believed to be present. The first requirement is that the executive or actor or surgeon have a reputation for superior ability. Given the reputation, demand may concentrate on the individual in a way that his abilities do not justify. Actual abilities are hard to judge, so, to play safe, we patronize the established person. In the moving-picture industry, where known personalities add greatly to the appeal of the product, publicity is used to build up the reputations of a few stars, and their income advantage expands accordingly. The actor, musician, or writer who catches on with the public—whose audience is slightly boastful over having seen, heard, or read him, and apologetic for not having done so—can expect an income quite unrelated to the difference between his ability and that of the person who just misses catching on.

Necessity of limited supply. But there is no basis in economics for saying that executives and surgeons must be paid more than poets. The condition of demand necessary to high earnings may be present, but a shortage of supply is also necessary. A sufficient supply of qualified persons can cause earnings to be low in any kind of work.

---

[4] This is another of the many situations in economics in which common-sense quantitative comparisons are made without actual measurements. There is no basis for saying that one schoolteacher or one barber or musician or executive is 25 percent better than another, but it is perfectly intelligible to say that one is only a little better than another or a great deal better.

This is a point of great practical importance in considering the problem of inequality. There may be fields in which supply, in relation to demand, is so restricted by the rarity of necessary inborn qualities that high earnings seem certain to persist. In such fields only eugenic control would offer hope of expanding the supply of first-rate abilities. But more often it seems likely that better detection of potential abilities and greater availability of training would add appreciably to the supply. The expected result of a greater shifting of persons from low-paid to high-paid occupations would be to reduce the income differentials between them. Of all the approaches to the problem of inequality, this is the most natural and least revolutionary.

But can the highly unequal returns for different kinds of labor service really be explained in these simple supply-and-demand terms? Can limitations of supply in the better paid occupations be corrected so naturally? Are there not arbitrary factors, elements of power and pressure and special advantage, which must be taken into account? Doubtless there are, and we shall now examine some of the possibilities. This section has dealt only with economic fundamentals. It is important to sense the difference between the necessary basis of income differences in valid market conditions—conditions that call for the economizing of resources through the prices put on them—and the practices and arrangements that lead to arbitrary results.

Market Pressures and Defects behind Differentials

We shall deal briefly here with a miscellany of influences that affect the earnings relationships among occupations or within particular occupations. These are factors that create advantages and disadvantages not inherent in underlying supply and demand conditions. Their nature is such that opinion may vary a good deal as to their importance and as to the best way to interpret them.

"Pull"

Family connections can influence earnings, as we saw above, through their effect on the ambitions and training of youth, but their effect can also be more direct. Without possessing superior qualifications, young men often obtain good positions through family influence in business or political circles. The role of "pull" is restricted by the danger that favored persons will prove conspicuously ineffective in the positions given them. The pressure in business to cover costs and show a profit is a strong deterrent to filling posts with inferior talent, but there is considerable latitude, especially in large firms in which salaried executives pick their subordinates, for selecting persons who are not the best available. The latitude is probably greater in government.

The bearing on inequality is twofold. There is, first, the obvious inequality of opportunity among individuals in obtaining desirable positions. Advantages that arise through influential connections are the most arbitrary element in economic stratification and in the social stratification that goes with it. There is, second, a probable increase in the size of income differences between occupations. When the better positions go to a limited number of favored persons, these positions are likely to pay higher salaries than they would if they were open on even terms to the competition of a larger number of qualified applicants.

Lack of "arm's-length bargaining"

Of similar nature is the special advantage that some men have in influencing their own earnings. As a general rule, payments are suspect when the same persons stand on both sides of a market, as buyers and sellers—when, to use a common phrase, arm's-length bargaining is absent. The higher officials and executives of a corporation who act for it in determining the compensation of officials and executives are, in some degree, in this position. They may be thoroughly scrupulous men, and no one of them may pass on his own salary or bonus. But it is inevitable that, as a group, they should have a high regard for the type of ability possessed by corporate officials and executives and be disposed to assign it a high value. The competition for their positions by able outsiders or subordinates, which in a freer market might reduce their compensation, can hardly be viewed by them without prejudice.

There is likely to be considerable latitude in adjusting these incomes. The salaries and bonuses of the top people in a firm usually absorb only a very small fraction of the total revenue—indeed, in good years these salaries are likely to be small even in relation to net earnings.[5] Just as boards of directors can be fairly flexible in deciding what fraction of profits shall be paid in dividends to stockholders, so also they have considerable discretion in rewarding the officers and executives. Their latitude is especially wide when profits are high and stockholders feel indulgent toward the men who serve them. Only rarely are suits brought against the directors for improper use of corporate funds in compensating the top people.

[5] A report covering a substantial list of corporations in 1944 shows that the total remuneration of officers and directors varies greatly in its percentage relation to net income, but 10 percent is perhaps as representative a figure as any. See *Your Investments*, April 1945. To say that this particular percentage is small is not to say that the top people are not exceedingly well paid. This issue will be touched on in the discussion of profits in Chapter 29.

Labor unions and similar combinations

It is true of the sale of labor service, as it is of products, that the most direct and positive way to increase the return is through monopolistic control of the market. A combination of workers may either increase inequality or reduce it, depending on the income position of benefited workers before their pay is raised, but, in any case, relative wages are altered if the combination is effective.

Labor unions are viewed ordinarily as a means of increasing wages at the expense of profits rather than in relation to other wages. We shall examine them presently in that light.[6] But if the one fourth of the working force in the United States that is unionized succeeds in raising its pay from any source at all, the relationship of wages to that of other workers is plainly altered. The relationship is altered more sharply if the gain is at the expense of other workers, as it may be. This effect is most apparent when skilled craft unions use high initiation fees, arbitrary apprenticeship requirements, and other devices to limit their numbers to the injury of excluded workers.

Professional associations, especially in the medical field, have often been accused of seeking arbitrarily to restrict numbers and maintain fees at high levels. This construction has been placed on the limited admissions to professional schools, the educational standards set up, the licensing requirements, and the emphasis on a "professional ethics" directed against fee cutting and other evidences of competition. It may be that the level of income in the professions can be explained adequately by the need of "equalizing differences" to offset costs of education and postponement of earnings and by the scarcity of people with the necessary abilities. It may be that the restrictions and hurdles are not greater than necessary to maintain proper standards. But whenever an economic group organizes itself in ways that may affect its market position, inquiry from the public standpoint is appropriate.

Custom and the wages of women and of Negroes

It is always difficult to appraise the force of custom in economic situations. From the standpoint of rational economic behavior, no wage difference should persist if there are workers in the lower paid group who can qualify to do the work of the higher paid group. But one may wonder whether certain rates of pay for shovel wielders, mechanics, clerks, or physicians do not become established in the public mind as reasonable and thus acquire a certain resistance to change.

However, though custom may endow earnings relationships with a

[6] In Chapter 27.

certain inertia, they are not likely to persist very long unless supported by fundamental supply and demand conditions or organized market controls. This, at least, is ordinarily a reasonable expectation, but there are exceptions. The two instances in which custom, combined with prejudice, seems most clearly to be a factor in the wage structure involve the earnings of Negroes and of women.

Negroes. Custom and prejudice may operate in either of two ways: (1) by excluding a certain type of labor from the better paying occupations or (2) by maintaining different rates of pay for the same work. The striking inferiority of average Negro earnings in the United States can be explained to some extent by discriminatory pay in given occupations, especially in the South. The larger factor undoubtedly is the substantial closing of many fields to Negro workers, so that they derive their earnings mainly from low-wage fields. It is sometimes contended that Negro workers are undependable and lacking in ambition and that they get, relatively, as much as they are worth. This explanation, however, does not escape the prejudice factor, since Negroes have suffered in educational facilities and since restricted opportunity deadens ambition. More directly, there is no question that the prejudice of employers and of white employees has excluded Negroes, largely or wholly, from many fields. Thus congestion has resulted, and wages made still lower, in the normally low-paying occupations into which they have been pushed. Negroes in business and the professions must largely serve the low-income Negro population. Only in the arts have talented Negroes had a fairly equal opportunity.

The two world wars have expanded the job opportunities of Negroes, especially in the North. Some labor unions have encouraged equal treatment of them. A popular movement against race prejudice has made some headway. Its most definite focus has been in promoting the enactment of "fair-employment-practice" legislation, designed to prevent discriminatory treatment of job applicants.

Women. Women workers have also suffered partial exclusion from many fields of work and have been paid less than male workers in fields in which they are employed. It is perhaps more difficult in the case of women to disentangle the parts played by custom and by restricted productive capacity and limited worth to the employer.

Women were formerly employed almost altogether in offices, public schoolteaching, retail clerking, domestic service, and the lighter kinds of factory work, notably in the textile industry. This concentration expanded the supply of labor in these fields, and, on strictly economic grounds, accounted for low rates of pay. The main question is whether the concentration was due mainly to the physical limitations of women or to prejudice against them in other fields and to prevailing social views as to the proper sphere of women. Both factors have undoubtedly been present, but, again, the war periods have upset established ideas regarding the channeling of the labor force. Women have entered a wider range of factory work, and their activities have expanded in business, government, and the professions.

Logical explanation is most difficult in cases in which men and women are paid at different rates in the same occupation, when they seem to be doing their work equally well. This situation is not common in the fields in which women have concentrated longest, for the reason that the low rates of pay have largely excluded male workers. But there are some instances of perplexing differentials in these fields, and many instances in the fields that women have entered more recently. Since competition should equalize wages where performance is actually equal, it is worth inquiring whether male employees may be preferred for economic reasons that do not appear on the surface. A pertinent reason of this sort is that men are more likely to remain employed for a long period. Young women often view their jobs as temporary, and early quitting increases average turnover and raises the cost of breaking in employees. For the same reason, their disposition to learn may be restricted. Another factor is that the typical male is likely to have a physical strength and a mechanical experience that equip him for emergencies and a more general usefulness. Similarly, in the public schools, some men teachers may be wanted not because they are better in the classroom but for disciplinary reasons and influence with the boys. Or in fields that involve contact with the public, a prejudice in favor of dealing with men may justify greater pay for services essentially no better.

But it seems that the prevailing differentials can be explained only in part on such grounds as these. Thus, we may simply have to say that the labor market works imperfectly or that custom supports employers in what resembles a conspiracy to hold the wages of women down. There being too few women, at prevailing rates of pay, to fill the jobs for which women are well qualified, employers merely take on some male workers at higher rates of pay, rather than engage in costly competition for women employees.

The *needs* factor may play a part, a small part, in the attitude of employers toward women workers. Women usually do not support families, and their need for income is not as great as that of men who do. It is true that there is no place for a recognition of employees' needs in the calculations of employers who are trying to produce at lowest cost and maximize their profits. They are interested only in the largest output for the wages they pay. But if competition allows them a little latitude, they may indulge their human inclination to favor their needier employees. Widespread popular disapproval of the employment of women during depressions, when men are out of work, strengthens the general disposition to favor male workers and, more specifically, causes the earlier laying off of women employees, so that their average annual earnings may show an even greater differential than their rates of pay.

Needs, of course, can be recognized more readily by employers who do not sell their product in a competitive market and particularly by employers who are not concerned at all with net financial return. Thus it is easy for government, both in the public schools and in other areas of employment, to maintain differentials in favor of men.

Wage relationships within occupations

We have seen that earnings vary *among occupations* and *types of labor* because of differing scarcities, arbitrary market pressures, and customary and social factors. Finally to be considered are the pay differences *within occupations* for the same type of labor doing the same work—differences that appear from plant to plant and place to place.

All compilations of wage data show striking wage spreads for jobs that, on the surface at least, appear to be about the same.[7] The reasons lie in familiar market imperfections, but imperfections that in the case of labor are likely to be more pronounced than in the case of commodities. Labor is inherently a relatively immobile type of good, and it lacks the qualities most conducive to the ready operation of the principle of single price. We shall note several of these imperfections of the labor market, both for the light they throw on wage differences and for the evidence they provide that the laws of markets work with even less nicety in the case of wages than of commodity prices.

Ignorance. Wage differences may be due simply to the lack of pertinent information necessary to the shifting of workers from poorer to better jobs. Employers likewise may not know what other employers are paying. An obstacle to effective comparison of rates of pay is the intricate variety of types of work, especially in modern manufacturing, and the lack of standardized job descriptions on which comparisons can be based. Progress is being made in this field, however.

[7] Studies made for the National War Labor Board during the war period show many such variations as these: in the Detroit area in July 1943, plant averages for lathe operators, engine, Class A, varied from $1.10 to $1.87 per hour; for polishers and buffers, Class A from $1.18 to $1.96; for punch-press operators, small size work, Class C, from 77 cents to $1.32; and so on for hundreds of job classes. Individual rates differed more widely than plant averages. One factor behind these differentials was the use of incentive-pay scheme in some of the plants.

Lack of perfect interchangeability of workers and of jobs. Even when differences in pay are known, shifting does not occur in a frictionless manner through the quest of workers for higher wages and of employers for less expensive labor. Labor is not a perfectly fluid thing, and its mobility involves adjustments both for the employer and the worker. Employers prefer to avoid the cost of breaking in new men, and their desire to retain the loyalty and maintain the morale of their workers may deter them from cutting the wages of present employees when new ones could be got at lower rates. To the employee, jobs that appear similar are not identical in their requirements, and, when he is used to his place of work and finds his employer acceptable, the worker may require a substantial improvement in pay to induce him to move. Large wage differences cannot persist through so slight an obstacle to mobility, nor any difference persist indefinitely for truly equivalent jobs, but where an industrial situation is in flux, hindrances such as this sustain a procession of inequalities.

Fear of unemployment. When prosperity has ebbed and unemployed persons are about, workers with jobs are inclined to hang on to them even though pay is relatively low. Moreover, if seniority is a factor in keeping one's job when selective layoffs become necessary, it is well to be foresighted and not shift employers on slight provocation even when times are good. Thus fear of unemployment can be a continuing obstacle to mobility. A period of sustained prosperity, as during the war and postwar years, reduces this fear and probably exerts an equalizing influence on wages.

Profit position of employers. Closely related, as a reason for wage differences, is the state of the employer's net income. In a perfect market the weak employer would not get his labor for less than his strong competitor pays. From the standpoint of long-run efficiency, this is as it should be. But if workers realize, as they sometimes do, that payment of standard wages would cause their employer to fail or to close down, they may accept low pay quite readily, especially if employment opportunities are not plentiful. The prosperous employer, on the other hand, may keep his wage payments on a higher level than the market compels him to. The wise course is not always the one that leads to largest immediate profits; just as products may be sold for lower prices than the market would pay, so higher wages may be paid than the market requires.

Geographic differences. The foregoing are factors that operate even within a single local labor market, say a specific city. But when a worker in changing jobs must also change his residence, mobility is further reduced. To cause him to move, the prospective gain in pay must, at the very least, exceed the cost of moving. In addition, it must compensate the severing of ties to friends and a familiar environment. The greater the change in social arrangements that must be faced in the new situation, the more reluctant workers are to move. When the quest for greater income involves going to another country with unfamiliar language, customs, and laws, the resistance to movement is very great.

Within the United States there have been many instances of the unwillingness of people to leave areas in which economic opportunities have declined, and in the South relatively low wage rates have been traditional. Despite large migrations between countries, international wage differences show no pronounced tendency to disappear. Equalizing migrations are, of course, restrained in part by artificial obstacles. Workers who seek new locations within the country run the risk, if work is not obtained, of not being able to get public assistance for a considerable period of time. Between countries the immigration laws provide a barrier.

Unions. We saw that, as between occupations, labor organizations may restrict mobility and alter wage relationships. They also change the wage pattern within occupations. To some extent, through making seniority a bigger factor in holding jobs, they may intensify wage differences. The desire to maintain seniority, as we just noted, reduces mobility in general. More directly, seniority makes unequal the chance that different workmen have of remaining employed during slack periods and perhaps increases the inequality in annual earnings, while giving a possibly deserved advantage to older employees.

The main effect of unions, however, is to promote a greater equality of rates of pay within the occupation than would arise from market forces alone. When unions bargain collectively with employers on an industry-wide basis, the tendency is to wipe out the effects of market imperfections and establish a general uniformity of return—even to the extent in the soft-coal industry of nearly equalizing wages in northern and southern mines. But even though agreements are limited to particular firms, as in the automobile industry, patterns of adjustment are publicized and uniformity promoted.

Unions, however, go even farther in promoting uniformity. Employers prefer types of wage payment, either piece-work rates or flexible hourly rates, that reflect individual differences and create an incentive for the worker to better his output. Unions, on the other hand, bring pressure to establish a standard rate on an hourly basis for a particular type of work. Such a rate simplifies the process of bargaining and the enforcement of wage agreements. It has the effect also of reducing the competition among workers within the union, who are otherwise interested in outdoing each other to better their individual pay. Such competition weakens the position of the union.

These union policies, as noted before, are not aimed primarily at controlling wage relationships. Instead they are weapons for use in dealing with employers, designed for that more embattled area where wages and profits are at issue.

Review Questions

1. Describe what seem to you to be the more significant "normal" earnings differentials among occupations.

2. "Inequality due to property incomes is not surprising once a system of capitalism is accepted, but the great inequality among working groups must exist in the face of what seems to be a strong, natural pull toward substantial equality." Explain.

3. "Equalizing differences must operate within, and not between, noncompeting groups." What is meant by equalizing differences? By noncompeting groups? Explain the statement.

4. If there are, in fact, noncompeting groups of workers, what are the reasons for them? Compare carefully the inborn and environmental factors. Have you any convictions regarding their relative importance?

5. "Once it is recognized that people possess different abilities, natural or acquired, the problem of wage differences is solved. The people with the greater abilities simply get the larger incomes." Show that this statement oversimplifies the connection between pay and ability.

6. "Doubtless not very many people have the ability to be business executives, but, on the other hand, relatively few executives are required. It is not inevitable that executives should have outstanding incomes." Defend this conclusion, and then explain the supply-and-demand situation which probably accounts for the high incomes of executives.

7. "Small differences in ability may cause big differences in pay." Develop this point.

8. Distinguish several ways in which strategic advantage or power in markets may affect wage relationships.

9. "Custom and prejudice seem to be able to affect relative wages both between and within occupations." How, if at all, can custom and prejudice be reconciled with the working of strictly economic motives? How would you explain the lower earnings of women workers?

10. Evaluate the possibility in our society of recognizing needs in paying for labor service.

11. Distinguish several market imperfections which explain wage differences for different workers of the same type doing the same kind of work. What is the effect of unions on such differentials?

~ 26 ~

Productivity
and Income

Differences in pay for labor service account for a large part of the inequality in distribution, but not the most controversial part. Attacks on the division of income are directed mainly at the returns from property and are evident most often in disputes over the relation between wages and profits.

To deal with problems that involve the whole range of incomes, additional theoretical tools are necessary. A simple supply-and-demand analysis does quite well in explaining wage differences but not in explaining incomes from wholly different types of productive services. As between different services, no "pull toward equality" exists, and thus the solution cannot consist merely in explaining the obstacles to an equalizing tendency. The problem is such, moreover, that we must understand not mere differences, but the *limits*, in a more absolute sense, to which incomes are subject, since these limits are the crucial element in all attempts to reduce inequality by raising wages and in other direct ways.

The problem, essentially, is that of the valuation of factor services— their value in a compelling sense that controls their use and the possibilities of modifying the payments for them. This is the most complex of value problems and also the one most commonly raised. It is present whenever a workman says he is not getting what he is worth or an employer says he is paying a workman more than he is worth. The problem is that of the meaning of worth. When Henry Wallace says, "No wage is too high if the worker earns it—five cents an hour is too high if the worker doesn't earn it," he raises the whole issue as to the criteria which, in the intricate circumstances of modern industry, determine the worth of the services of labor and other factors of production. That is the problem before us.

Essential Meaning of Factor Valuation

Most people probably accept the idea that there must be some connection between what a worker or an item of wealth contributes to production and what the resulting income can be. Such words as "earning" and "worth" are assumed to have significance And yet it is also widely assumed that labor unions and governmental policies can make major changes in distribution. There can be serious and dangerous confusion in this combination of ideas. It is important, therefore, before developing an explanation of the valuation of productive services, to see what it means to say that a factor is paid according to the value of what it does. To study a theory of distribution, or of anything else, is a waste of time unless one sees clearly what its implications are and the kind of thinking that can, and cannot, be reconciled with it.

Basis of incomes in total product

The first point to remember in considering income limits is that all particular incomes are simply claims against the national product. Wages, rents, interest, and profits are received mainly in money form, and the national income is expressed as a sum of money. But this sum corresponds to a certain volume of product and is otherwise meaningless. What is really being distributed is the national output. Incomes have their source in it and constitute claims against it.

This is a familiar idea, but it is forgotten in disputes over particular incomes. The particular worker or businessman seems to be better off if his money income increases, and he focuses on the goal of increasing it. The outside boundaries of income are too remote to restrain his quest for a larger share or even the quest of the economic group to which he belongs. But the boundaries are there, and when all economic groups are attempting to increase their portion, they are playing a game at which collectively they cannot win. This is the broadest, and most elementary, sense in which income is rooted in product.

There is undoubtedly much room for distribution reform in most countries, but, at the very least, reforms must stay within the limits of the total product. To proceed, as some reformers would, by first working out some minimum-income standard, some conception of the requirements of health and decency, and then insisting that no income should fall below that level is to work backwards. It is said that on one occasion a wage commission in Australia, under the extensive wage controls that prevail in that country, investigated what the minimum should be and came out with a solemn proposal that, if applied, would have absorbed the entire national product, with nothing left for more valuable labor services or for property. Reform must stay within the realm of the possible. It must begin with the total product that is available, or can be made available, and work toward the highest income for the masses that is practicable under the institutions which govern economic organization.

Most distribution questions, however, do not involve the total product but only small segments of the total expressed in money terms. The question, then, is whether particular incomes must be related in some compelling way to the contribution of particular services to the total product, and, if so, what the nature of the compulsion is. Unless a satisfactory answer can be found, we should abandon the practice of speaking of the worth of services and whether people get what they earn.

Valuation and bargaining

Despite a good deal of talk about what services are worth, the division of income, especially between enterprisers and employees, is often spoken of as if it were nothing more than a matter of market strength and strategy. The extreme case of this view is that of the labor leader who tells his followers that, if they only organize strongly enough, there is no limit to the height to which they can push their wages. The frequency of great wage controversies, in the coal, steel, automobile, meat-packing, railroad, and other industries, and their settlement by collective negotiation after a period of strikes and other maneuvers, has promoted the belief that income is distributed through a process of exercising power and pressure.

It should be seen that a theory in which bargaining power is the main element is the antithesis of a theory in which factors of production are rewarded according to the value of what they do. Under the bargaining theory there can be no underlying reason why labor should get about three fourths of total income. If its power were less, it might get only one fourth. If its power were greater, it might get nine tenths. One result is as right as another, so far as any concept of worth is concerned. The bargaining theory is a complete negation of the operation of valuation processes in the income field.

The nature of bargaining. Bargaining, in the strict sense, was explained in the discussion of supply and demand in Chapter 18. In the example used there, it was assumed that a certain business executive would accept a salary of $25,000 rather than seek work with another firm, and that his present employer would pay him $100,000 rather than lose him. Bargaining skill would have to settle the rate of pay within these wide limits. We may assume that, as a result of negotiation between the parties, a salary of $50,000 is agreed on, but the significant point is that the salary might just as well be twice this figure or only half of it. Within that range, the amount of executive service hired does not vary with the rate of pay. Thus one man would be taken at $100,000 and no more than he at $25,000. Between these figures, there is no basis in the market situation for saying what he is worth.

Meaning of valuation. If the valuation of factors is meaningful, as a basis of incomes, the values cannot be casual sums that, over a wide range, can be pushed about and agreed upon. They must be expressions of worth on which the use of resources depends. It is only in this sense that particular incomes can be said to be rooted in the productive process, so that there is a connection between what factors do and what they receive. The compulsion behind their receipt of particular rates of pay lies in the freedom of enterprisers to hire, or not to hire, them at those rates and in the freedom of users of products to buy, or not to buy, at prices covering those rates.

The demand for productive services must have some elasticity. The example of the executive is certainly unique in this respect. For most services of labor and of wealth, there are many units to be employed and many uses for them. The natural expectation is that their use will depend in some degree on the price that has to be paid for them, or the income they receive. It would be a more typical example to say that in a certain community 100 house painters find employment at a wage of $1.50 an hour, but that, if they push their wage to $2, with prices in general remaining unchanged, only 85 will keep well employed, and at $2.50 the number will fall to 70. With the higher cost of house painting, people will keep their houses less well painted or do more of the work themselves. To hold that incomes depend primarily on bargaining is equivalent to saying that employers are not influenced by costs in their use of resources. Persons who hold this view should reject the idea of an economy being organized on the basis of values.

But one should see that the compulsion behind the recognition of values is not all-powerful. There is nothing in the above example to keep house painters from organizing to push their wage rate to $2 or even to $2.50. They must simply be content, if they do, with the reduced use of their services. Values may be distorted by arbitrary pressures in either direction, but if they are not, they provide the basis of such a mutual adaptation of different productive services to each other that an effective, economical use of resources results. Basically, to say that a productive service is paid what it is worth is to say that it is priced so that all units of it are brought into effective use. They are neither priced out of the market nor priced so low that they can be used profitably for inferior purposes. Other than this, worth has no meaning. The bargaining theory denies the existence of the problem, or at least that it is in any degree solved through the pricing of factors.

There are three levels at which we may think of productive contribution as influencing income and the use of factors. The *first* is the economy as a whole. As stated above, the money incomes of factors must stay within the value of the total product. The *second* is the division of that total on the basis of products and among firms producing those products. The *third* is the division among the participants within the firm, the workers and lenders and owners, who share in its receipts. We shall now consider the significance of factor values and the elasticity of factor demand in the latter two connections.

Division among industries and firms

Just as the total income of all producers is limited by the total value of all products, so the total income of the producers of a particular product is fixed by its value. The value of the cotton crop, less purchases of supplies and related deductions, determines the incomes of the owners of cotton land and of workers in cotton fields. In the same way, the value of the output of hogs or copper or furniture or medical service fixes the incomes of the persons who provide these products.

But whereas, for the economy as a whole, the total product is the total real income, the product of the particular industry or firm does not constitute the real income of the participants. Producers in each industry consume mainly the products of other industries. Thus the *values* of particular products, in relation to the values of other products, govern the relative income position of producers in different fields. This relative behavior of product values is a major element in the distribution of income, though in theoretical discussion and popular controversy it is obscured by the emphasis on the division among the suppliers of labor and of wealth within the firm. Our main discussion of it was in Part V.

Important variations in the distribution of income take place through the ordinary shifting about of the demands for goods and the changes in the conditions of their supply. When an industry is in the ascendant, as the automobile industry was in the 1920s, owners and workers alike are prosperous. When an industry suffers in its market position, as wheat and cotton did over a long period, incomes fall for all participants.

But variations in distribution among industries take place not only through these ordinary shiftings but also through the organized and arbitrary control of markets. Markets may be manipulated and managed with or without the aid of government. If the owners of steel mills, copper mines, or oil refineries enter into monopolistic combines, they may hold the prices of their products above the competitive level and benefit accordingly. Or if labor unions in the clothing, railroad, or automobile industry succeed in pushing wages up, and these higher wages are passed on to consumers in the form of higher product prices, essentially the same sort of redistribution takes place among producers in different fields. Or, again, if government steps in to put a floor under prices that otherwise would be low, as it has in the case of coal and staple farm products, a similar transfer of income occurs in the direction of the assisted industries.

In these cases the beneficiaries may be either the owners or the employees. Often there is some benefit for both. At the same time, there is no question that a transfer of real income takes place away from al' the persons who use the products that command a relatively highei price. These are mainly the workers and the owners of wealth who are engaged in production in other fields.

Limitations on transfers of income. It is essential to see the possibility of such redistribution, but it is equally important to see the limitations upon it. Higher prices for products reduce the quantities of them that will be bought and thus reduce the employment opportunities for labor and wealth in producing those products. If monopoly power is used to hold the price of aluminum high, those who are actually involved in aluminum production are better off than with a low price, but potential producers of the aluminum that would find wider uses at a lower price must seek their incomes elsewhere. Likewise, if workers in the building trades force wage rates up, thus raising building costs and the price of buildings, houses will be priced out of the reach of some purchasers and some will be content with smaller houses, so that there will be less opportunity for employment of labor and capital in the construction field.

This elasticity of demand for products, and thus for factors, is a substantial offset to the gains from high prices and income rates. While resources employed at the higher prices are better off, there is necessarily some check upon arbitrary efforts to raise prices and incomes. But whether or not this check is as effective as it should be, since producing groups may be shortsighted, it is still a potent distribution factor, because services not used in particular fields receive no income from them. In so far as the problem is that of the efforts of unions to raise wages, we shall continue the discussion of it in the following chapter.

Division among producers within firms

Income is distributed, finally, within specific firms. This division includes not only the broad separation of income into wages and profits but also the division among the suppliers of different types of labor and of wealth. When labor leaders demand higher wages, they usually assume that the increase, if granted, will come out of profits. Although it is more likely to come out of a higher price for the product, we shall now assume that it does not and that a redistribution takes place strictly within the firm.

It is here that the problem arises of assigning values to particular productive services in particular uses. In a sense this is the crux of the distribution problem. Certainly it presents the greatest analytical difficulty, and it is here that upholders of the bargaining idea find most support for their view.

Within the firm and plant, if the use of certain factors is to depend on the prices paid for them, the adjustment must come in the methods of production employed. Enterprisers, always on the watch for ways of reducing costs, must adopt methods that make relatively little use of factors that become relatively expensive, relatively great use of factors that become relatively cheap—as when costly labor is replaced with labor-saving machines.

We shall consider this problem in the following section. Here, in conclusion, we shall observe that the prices put on productive services influence their use chiefly in the two ways we have considered: (1) through affecting the prices put on different products and the use made of them and (2) through affecting the methods of production followed in different fields. Market pressures may alter factor prices but cannot escape the consequences of the distortions they cause. If undistorted values actually govern incomes, we can say that incomes conform to productive contributions and that services are paid what they are worth. But, in any case, these values set limits to the quantities of particular services that find employment and to the incomes they can receive and remain fully employed.

Productivity as the Basis of Incomes

The skeleton of a general explanation of factor pricing appeared in the discussion of the nature of cost in Chapter 20. Prices of products tend, in the long run, to conform to their full cost of production; but what are costs? Viewing them, finally, as the prices of productive services, we observed that the demands for these services derive from the demands for the products. We saw that the demand for a particular factor, perhaps a certain type of labor, usually derives from many different products that it helps to produce. We noted then, as we did in the preceding section, that the use made of it depends largely on the price that has to be paid for it—that at higher prices, it becomes too costly for some of the less valuable products for which it can be used and that its use in all products is likely to be reduced because its cost makes them too costly for some consumers. These derived demands for factors, we said, in conjunction with their supplies, determine their prices. But we did not go into the difficulties of putting values on the services of specific factors when several factors are combined in turning out a product. The theory needs a good deal of filling out.

It should be said that in this discussion we shall be developing a theory of factor valuation and of distribution only in a very broad and comprehensive sense. It is distinctly an explanation of the *normal pricing* of productive services. Normal prices, as we have seen, become actual prices only under conditions that are never fully realized. But a theory of the normal pricing of services provides a perspective of the general income pattern and indicates the direction in which basic forces are pulling. It also provides a viewpoint that is helpful in appraising controversial practices and proposed reforms. In developing it, we shall make use of a number of concepts that are already familiar.

Complex valuations and the marginal principle

We have said that the values of services are rooted in the uses to which they are put and that the use of them must depend upon their cost. But when the economist, businessman, or employee says that a service should be paid for according to what it is worth or what it produces, is he appealing to a standard that has real meaning in the complex condition in which particular factors are commonly used? The question is not merely whether a usable measure of worth is available in a concrete situation but whether there is even a valid theoretical concept behind the quest. We shall look into the nature and limitation of what appears to be the only possible answer.

Difficulty of separate valuation of combined factors. We shall first examine the difficulty to which we have referred. Income is governed directly by physical product only in the case of a Crusoe. His product is his income. When there are several specialized producers, each turning out a complete product, productivity becomes necessarily a value matter, and the income of each producer depends on the value of his output. Changes in a producer's income may not parallel the changes in his physical product, but the market for products solves the distribution problem quite easily.

The real difficulty appears when a number of productive services are combined in producing a particular product. This, of course, is the usual case. In the manufacture of an automobile or a book or a sack of flour or in the running of a railroad, numerous kinds of labor, manual and mental, are involved; land is used, and various structures, types of equipment, and stocks of goods play their parts; likewise various risks and responsibilities are assumed. Somehow a value is assigned to each element in this complex aggregate of services, but is it a value that represents a distinguishable contribution, the worth of what the specific factor does?

The problem can be seen in the simplest of cases. The labor of 5 men is applied to 100 acres of land, and 2000 bushels of wheat result. Every one of those bushels is the product both of the labor and of the land. In no physical sense can it be said that 1000 or 1500 bushels represents the work of the men, and the remainder the service of the land, and that wages and land rent should be fixed accordingly. The problem is the same, but the situation more complex, where many factors of production are used together. Is there any logical basis, then, for saying what a certain factor earns or is worth or, since its physical output is not assignable, what its *value product* or *revenue product* is? If there is not, it must appear after all that the sharing of income is no more than a grand scramble in which strength and cleverness have sway through lack of any better principle.

Business decisions and the marginal evaluation of services. When the problem is so stated, it may seem impossible to assign credit to each of several productive services when all are essential to a given result. But the problem has, nevertheless, a logical solution, and a reasonably effective practical solution also. Indeed, it is in process of almost continuous solution, in an approximate way, through the everyday activities of businessmen and production managers. Management, indeed, consists largely in a series of decisions regarding specific elements of revenue and cost. The successful manager must be astute in seeing to it that particular outlays are justified by their effect upon net earnings. These outlays, directly or indirectly, are income payments to the suppliers of productive services.

The problem of separate valuation of combined services defies solution only when viewed in the lump—5 men and 100 acres producing 2000 bushels. When viewed in detail, almost every productive project is a complex array of specific alternatives. These alternatives involve choices of methods and of the specific quantities to be used of various types of labor and of wealth. Such alternatives are present even in wheat farming, since land can be cultivated with more or less labor, and labor can be used along with more or less equipment and fertilizer. The possible variations in procedure are more numerous in manufacturing and some other fields.

Logically, as was shown in the discussion of the use of plant capacity

(Chapter 21), these decisions are made on the *marginal principle*. Particular units of resources should be used if the added costs they occasion will be adequately covered by additions to revenue (or by reductions in other costs that will no longer need to be incurred).[1] In strict logic, the employment of units of labor, capital, and land depends on a procession of marginal judgments which aim to insure that each unit is worth the income it receives. In the particular situation, each unit is worth, or earns, the value of its marginal contribution—its *marginal value product*.

This is an important conclusion. If services, when used in combination, were not subject to separate valuation in this way, we would be appealing to a theoretical will-o'-the-wisp whenever we speak of their worth in particular uses. The demands for them, with their particular elasticities, would have no real foundation. Thus it is important to see what is meant by the marginal value product and equally important to see the limits to its use and the setting of its proper application.

Marginal value product under competition and monopoly. What is the difference between this concept and the meaning of marginal revenue as discussed in Chapter 21? The difference is superficial. Marginal revenue is the difference in revenue attributable to one unit more or less of *product*. The marginal value product is the difference in revenue (or in cost of other factors) attributable to one unit more or less of a *particular factor of production*. In Chapter 21 we were concerned with products and their prices. Here we are concerned with factors of production and their prices, and a factor, depending on the time unit adopted, may be credited with 10 or 50 or 100 units of output. Otherwise there is no difference.

As in the earlier discussion, we should see that the marginal value product depends on the competitive situation of the firm in which the factor is employed. Suppose a small firm has been employing 5 workers and the hiring of a sixth worker is considered. The output situation appears to be as follows:

Number of workers	Monthly output	Marginal output
5	100	
6	115	15

In this situation 15 units of product may be spoken of as the *marginal physical product* when there are 6 workers. If the price of the product is $10, *and the firm operates in a situation of pure competition,* a sixth

[1] Often the purpose in using more of one factor is not to add to output but to reduce the outlay for other factors. The latter is the primary aim when labor-saving machinery is installed. The marginal relation then is between the cost of the added factor and the savings effected.

worker adds $150 a month to the firm's revenue and $150 is the marginal value product. The sixth worker is worth having at any wage up to $150. We may say that, at a wage of $150, this firm demands 6 workers and participates to this extent in the market demand for this kind of labor.

But if some degree of monopoly is present, the marginal value product will be less than $150. If this firm estimates that its production of an additional 15 units monthly will depress the price of the product from $10 to $9.50, the added revenue from having the sixth man will be only $92.50.[2] Then $92.50 sets the limit to what a sixth man is worth to this firm. Thus the marginal value product is less under monopoly than under competition, but it works in the same way as under competition in setting a limit to the hiring of factors and to the amount that can be paid for a given number of units.

To be sharply contrasted is the case of a firm that is monopolistic (or monopsonistic) in the purchase of labor or other services. Neither type of monopoly implies the presence of the other. A firm may have considerable control of the market in selling its product and yet purchase productive services in competition with firms both in its own industry and in other industries. Or it may meet nation-wide competition in selling its product and have some monopoly power locally in hiring factors. In our example, we may assume that the price of the product remains $10 whether 100 or 115 units are sold but that a sixth man can be hired only through bidding up the wage from $130 to $140 per month. It may seem that if the product of the sixth man sells for $150, he must be worth hiring at $140. But if he is paid $140, then the other 5 workers will shortly have to be paid $140. In that case, the added cost attributable to the sixth worker is not $140, but $190, and he is not worth hiring unless the marginal value product is at least that great.[3] A price of approximately $13 for the product would then be necessary for a marginal physical product of 15 units to yield this sum. We shall consider further in the next chapter the effect of monopolistic hiring of labor.

Marginal value product and factor prices. Whether the markets affecting a productive service are strictly competitive at all points—or whether there is some degree of monopoly in selling the product, hiring the service, or selling the service—the marginal value product, as it appears in the existing circumstances, is the logical basis of what can be paid for any particular quantity of the service. The demand of each firm, as thus arrived at, is only an element in the market demand for the

---

[2] Arrived at by subtracting 100 times $10 from 115 times $9.50. Accordingly, we may say that the marginal value product is less than the value of the marginal product.

[3] Arrived at by subtracting 5 times $130 from 6 times $140.

service, and one may think of a demand schedule made up of the series of quantities that all firms together will take at particular rates of pay. If the market works freely, the actual rate of payment for the service must be low enough so that all units of the supply of it find employment in uses where they are worth what they cost. At this price for the service, each firm will be using whatever amount has a sufficient marginal value product to cover the additional cost it entails. But even if the market does not work freely, or if the total demand for all goods is not sufficient to maintain full employment, the *employed* units receive, logically, a rate of pay corresponding to their marginal value product.

Qualified application of marginal principle, especially in the short run. The preceding discussion involves some of the oversimplification and departure from reality that nearly every explanation of concepts involves. Marginal value product has been stressed as the logical basis of factor valuation, but it does not follow, in practice, that marginal valuations take place either accurately or continuously. We have seen (Chapter 21) how uncertain are the immediate estimates of marginal revenues and costs in operating businesses. Commonly it is impossible to judge the value of small increments of particular services in an effective way. Especially in the case of services that bear only indirectly on the flow of products—such services as the work of maintenance men, office employees, and janitors—the contribution to revenue or to cost reduction can be traced only vaguely. Thus evaluations may be possible only for substantial groups of workers and changes in equipment.

Moreover, since the prices of products in price-quoting industries are usually quite inflexible, and since firms make their plans for considerable periods and produce as much as customers will take during those periods, the critical valuations of factors are made rather infrequently. Indeed, the most critical valuations are made only at long intervals, when new plants are built and major changes made. Only then are all productive services on the same footing, whether they will be tied up in fixed facilities or used to operate those facilities; only then has the enterpriser an unrestricted choice as to the relative use he will make of them. He can decide then, for instance, on processes as slightly mechanical or as highly automatic as he cares to make them. He is able then to give simultaneous and equal recognition, over a wide range, to the worth to him of all the resources he will use.

These are reasons why a general theory of distribution should be conceived in fairly long-run terms as a theory of the *normal* pricing of factors. But these are not reasons for saying that factors do not have separate values in complex situations or that these values do not have compelling force in controlling the use of resources and the payments for services. Whether decisions are made actually in marginal terms—comparing differences in revenue with differences in cost—is of no consequence. A firm may do its planning for 6 months or a year in terms of probable aggregate revenues and costs, and incidentally render a judgment that each factor is worth its cost on the planned basis. In constructing a new plant, the probable aim is to minimize total unit cost when output is at the most probable level; such a calculation, though businessmen may not realize it, involves separate valuation of all factors in marginal terms.[4] It seems fair to say, then, as a broad pattern of valuation, that factors tend to be used and paid for on such a basis that each unit of them, or each recognizable segment of them, appears to be worth its cost. This is the marginal basis.

Diminishing returns, marginal product, and income

We come then to the question: What determines whether the marginal value product of a certain type of productive service will be relatively high or low? Is it to be expected, for example, that a year's common labor will be worth more or less than the service of $10,000 invested in industrial equipment? What underlying force, if any, governs the productive contributions of different factors?

The main answer to this question, undoubtedly, is found in the principle of diminishing returns, or diminishing productivity, as explained in Chapter 5. To the extent that the relative value products of factors, in a long-run sense, rest on a physical-output basis, that basis is found in this principle. The principle of diminishing returns is concerned with the effect on the productivity of factors of the *proportions* in which they are used. Broadly, the relative supplies of labor, capital, and land that happen to exist in a nation at any time must govern the proportions in which they are used, and the changes in these supplies must alter the proportions. If there are no upsetting changes in technology, these proportions and the changes in them fix the normal sharing of income on the basis of productive contributions. When any factor becomes more plentiful, the output per unit of it, as we saw in Chapter 5, decreases, while the output per unit of relatively scarcer factors increases.[5]

It must be remembered that, in the normal sense, this is a principle

[4] When any sort of project is planned so that the full unit cost of production will be at the minimum, it is also planned so that a dollar more or less spent on each of the combined factors will have the same effect on revenue—in other words, so that the same relation between marginal revenue and cost prevails for each factor. For a strictly competitive firm that expands to the point where it makes just a normal return on its capital, while producing at the least-cost point, it can be said that the price paid for each factor equals its marginal value product. These are interesting logical relationships but not essential in understanding the leading problems of distribution.

[5] See pp. 114–119.

of universal application.[6] When the relative quantity of any factor used in combination with other factors is increased, each unit of it must receive less help in production from other factors that are scarce. Their scarcity becomes manifest and significant through the declining output per unit of the expanding factor.

Diminishing marginal product and income. In Chapter 5 the principle of diminishing returns was introduced to assist in the discussion of the population problem. We were interested then in the per-capita or *average* output of labor as population increases. General economic welfare was considered without reference to the sharing of national income among different producing groups. Here we are interested in the sharing of income. In examining the effect of more people in relation to natural resources, we want to know what happens to wages in comparison with the incomes of land owners. We shall not be concerned, then, with average output as population grows but with *marginal* output, because income payments cannot exceed the marginal value products of factors.

The striking effect on income shares resulting from the changing proportions of factors can be seen best with an example. To avoid irrelevant details, let us assume, rather unrealistically, that a backward and isolated region produces only wheat and that a fully occupied land area and an expanding labor supply are the only factors of production. All units of both are of uniform quality and technology remains unchanged.

Table 33 gives the necessary facts. The first column gives the increasing number of workers on a given area of land, say 50 acres, as the population grows. The second column gives the output in bushels, the third the declining average output of labor (with which we were concerned in Chapter 5), the fourth the marginal product of labor (with which we are concerned here). Because there is only one product, incomes are received in wheat. The highest wage a worker can get, the full competitive wage, is equal to the marginal product, since that is the output that would be lost if he were not used. Thus we shall assume that column 4

---

[6] We saw in Chapter 21 that, as the use of plant capacity is expanded from a very low to a very high level, marginal cost may first fall, then stay at about the same level for quite a range, and finally rise sharply. Marginal product, accordingly, would be rising at first for variable factors, and finally falling. But this behavior results from the rigid nature of the plant and of its equipment, which is designed for a certain volume of output. The changing proportions of factors that concern us here are not governed by these short-run rigidities in specific situations. We are not interested, for example, in the problem of the effect on output as the number of ditch diggers to be used in conjunction with 5 shovels increases from 4 to 6. We assume, rather, that the capital represented by 5 shovels is adapted in each instance to the form that is best for the particular number of workers. This illustrates the meaning of "normal" or "long run" in analyzing the use of resources and the basis of incomes.

also gives the wage. Column 5, then, gives the total earnings of labor, and the residue, in column 6, is the return to the owner of the land for its contribution.[7]

TABLE 33—DIMINISHING PRODUCTIVITY AND INCOME

1. Workers on 50 acres	2. Total output in bushels	3. Output per worker	4. Marginal output and wage	5. Total wages	6. Return to landowner
3	330	110			
4	420	105	90	360	60
5	500	100	80	400	100
6	570	95	70	420	150
7	630	90	60	420	210
8	680	85	50	400	280
9	720	80	40	360	360

Effects of diminishing returns on income shares and patterns. Despite the artificial nature of this example, it shows in valid fashion the normal effect on distribution of changing the proportions in which factors are used.

For the expanding factor, whether the expansion is absolute or only relative, the rate of return must fall. It must fall by a greater amount, moreover, than the decline in the *average* output of the expanding factor. For the average to fall, the *marginal* product must be below the average product, and the income rate cannot normally exceed the marginal product.

From the employment angle, it should be seen that the wage must fall as the number of workers increases, if they are all to be absorbed in production. One source of elasticity of demand for factors is the possibility of choosing among methods of production that combine factors in different proportion. If labor is more plentiful in relation to land, a more intensive method of cultivation is called for. But this method will be adopted only if labor becomes relatively less expensive in relation to

[7] Again, this is a short-cut explanation. We explain wages on a marginal basis and then regard land rent simply as the residue after paying wages. To carry out the marginal explanation, we should reconstruct the example, with the same underlying facts, so that a certain amount of labor is the fixed factor and a declining amount of land is used along with it. In this way, we would ascertain the marginal product of land. Would we get the same result? We would, provided we assumed sufficiently small units in measuring labor and land—theoretically, infinitely small—and had each factor get the full value of its marginal product, as it would with pure competition for its services. Such an explanation, for the general student, is not worth the time and trouble it requires. The main point of it is that, when all the combined factors are paid on this basis, their incomes just add up to the total income to be distributed.

land. Any attempt to hold wages up arbitrarily in this situation will cause unemployment. A wage that prevents the use of more labor on land is analogous to a wage in manufacturing that causes more reliance on labor-saving machines.

Labor, the expanding factor, suffers in this example, but not as conspicuously as land, the scarcer factor, gains. For exactly the same amount of land, the income rises 500 percent as the amount of labor applied to it increases from 4 to 9. It may readily happen, as it does here, that a constant resource such as land not only receives a larger absolute income as the supply of cooperating services expands but that it gets a larger fraction of the expanding total income. With 9 workers on the land, landlords, in this instance get half of the expanded product. It should be remembered, as one of the major characteristics of normal income distribution, that *any type of productive service benefits through expansion of the other services used with it.*

The dependence of marginal products on the proportion in which resources are used is the central element in explaining the *general distribution pattern in a country.* Countries differ considerably in the proportions in which labor, land, and capital, in their various forms, are available, and every country varies from one period to another in its history. As population grows, the labor supply expands. The two are not completely parallel, since customs differ as to the working of women, the hours of labor, and other factors in the labor supply, but the supply varies approximately with population. Land is as nature provides it, and plant and equipment develop through saving and investment. At any given stage in the development of the arts of production, the relative supplies of these resources must govern the division of income in its main outlines.

Thus, in densely populated agricultural countries, not only is per-capita income low, but the marginal product of labor is particularly low. The position of landowners, in other words, is very strong; and this is what we find in such countries as China and Egypt and in many parts of Europe. Landowners, in the absence of drastic reforms, get an oppressively large fraction of total income.

The principle applies equally well to other relationships among resources. In manufacturing and commerce, land is of relatively small importance, and in Western nations the rate of population growth has declined greatly. At the same time, there has been a rapid expansion of capital facilities through heavy saving and investment. Thus labor has had the increasing assistance in production of equipment of many kinds. With other conditions remaining unchanged, the expansion in capital goods must reduce the marginal product of capital and raise the marginal product of labor. Thus the rate of return is reduced to capitalists and raised to workers.

What we have said regarding these major categories of resources applies equally well to their subdivisions. Capital is flexible and may take many forms, but land is rather rigidly endowed with certain qualities, and particular types of it may be in large or small supply and be rewarded accordingly. Likewise, in so far as labor is not transferable from one type of work to another, the relative quantities of particular types govern their marginal products. Much of what was said in the preceding chapter regarding wage differences might logically be fitted in here to expand the present discussion.

Product prices and distribution

The wheat example, being designed to illustrate as simply as possible the effect of diminishing returns, excluded two other elements in the distribution picture, both of which affect the relative size of the marginal value products of different factors. One is the behavior of the prices of different products, the other the progress that occurs in methods of production.

The effect of product prices was excluded by having only one product. If we change our assumption and have wheat producers selling wheat and buying other products, then their marginal value product depends (1) on their marginal physical product and (2) on the price of wheat. If population and the labor supply grow in the wheat region, expanding the output of wheat, and if there is no increase in the demand for wheat, wages will have two reasons for declining. As labor, in the example, increases from 6 to 7 men on a piece of land, and the marginal product falls from 70 to 60 bushels, the price of wheat declines, let us say, from $1 to 80 cents. Thus the wage falls from $70 to $48, and wheat workers suffer a serious decline in their relative position in the income structure.

For this situation there is, of course, a partial corrective. Workers may transfer from the wheat industry to other industries. The normal situation would be that workmen of their type would receive the same pay in all fields—though, if one may judge by the migration from farm to city in the United States, the differential may be difficult to remove entirely.[8] But at any rate, shifts in product prices that can be corrected by the shifting of resources need not be continuing influences on distribution. In the absence of monopoly with power to prevent expansion, ordinary labor and capital can move about with sufficient freedom to reduce greatly the distribution effect of relative price movements.

[8] See the discussion of agricultural policy in Chapter 23, pp. 622–625.

But the corrective is only partial, since factors are not used in the same proportions for different products. A major reason why landowners have not in fact gained as much through population growth as many people expected is that demand has shifted to products in which land is a less important factor. With rising average income, relatively less is spent on food and more on manufactured goods, and especially on services for which little land is needed. At the same time, owners of petroleum and like resources have benefited tremendously as demand has shifted to products in which these resources are a large element. According to the same logic, the opening of many coal mines reduced earnings in that industry, and the effect could not be diffused since coal lands generally have no other use.

Thus (1) shifts in demands among products that call for the various resources in unlike proportions and (2) shifts in supplies of resources that enter heavily into particular products greatly influence distribution through their effect on relative prices of products. These are fundamental, unavoidable influences on the marginal value products of factors. But numerous arbitrary market pressures that affect the supplies and prices of particular products and the use of particular factors have a similar influence.

Technological change and distribution

In the wheat example, as first presented, we excluded not only the influence of product prices but also of technological progress. One aspect of progress is the development of new products; the other is the development of new methods of production through which output is expanded from given quantities of labor, land, and capital. The latter raises per-capita income, but our present concern is with distribution of income. How does progress affect the relative rates of return to the various suppliers of labor and of wealth?

In part the effect is of the sort just described. Progress affects the demands for different products and the supplies of them, and through the pricing of products the values of factor services are altered. Popular new products cause shifts in demand from old products and similar shifts in the demand for productive services. New methods that expand the output of particular products may benefit or injure the producers, depending on the elasticity of demand for the product. If, in the wheat example, no expansion takes place in the number of workers but a sensational advance in methods doubles the output of present labor and land, the nature of the demand for wheat will govern the income effect. If the elasticity of demand for wheat is less than unity and the price of wheat falls from $1.25 to 50 cents, the doubled output yields less revenue than before to workers and landowners in the wheat industry. The labor may transfer to other fields, but the land has fewer alternatives.

Physical and value products. This example shows the need of care in relating productivity to income. The explanation of distribution we are discussing is often called the "productivity theory," but it plainly does not follow from this explanation that anyone who increases his efficiency and produces more can expect more income. Productivity must be used in a value sense, and a larger marginal physical product need not mean a larger value product. Expansion in the former seldom, if ever, means a corresponding increase in the latter. If bricklayers could be induced to lay bricks as fast as they formerly did, the public would gain greatly in real income. But the direct effect on the wages of bricklayers would depend on the elasticity of demand for brick buildings and bricklaying.

Progress and factor supply and demand. Technological progress, in other words, adds in effect to the *supply* of particular factors. A second reason why, with the growth of population, the scarcity of land has not become more pronounced than it has, has been the more effective use of land. Improved methods of fertilizing and cultivating land and improved breeding of animals have expanded the output of the area in use. Developments in transportation, moreover, have expanded the area available to be used. For this reason, as well as the shifting of demand to products in which land is a minor element, land rent has not become the sharply rising distributive share that many social prophets, following the logic of our wheat example, have predicted.

But technological progress adds also to the *demand* for particular factors. Indeed, its most common effect is perhaps to increase the demand for capital, since machinery and power-supplying equipment require investment of capital and are the distinctive forms that technological progress has taken. Technological change, as we saw in studying the depression problem, is a major source of investment opportunity. Some developments, we observed then, are capital-saving, but on the whole they are capital-demanding. At the same time, moreover, their effect is commonly to save labor. Thus, in its bearing on distribution, technological progress increases relatively the demand for capital, reduces relatively the demand for labor, and strengthens the relative position of capitalists in the division of income.

From this it does not follow that labor is worse off. Products are cheaper and better, and labor's share, though perhaps reduced relatively, is increased absolutely through being a share in a larger total product. Even the relative decline in wage rates need not take place, if, as is likely to be true, the growth in saving—that is, in the supply of capital—keeps pace with the demand.

Marginal *versus* **average output.** In discussing technological progress a special warning is needed that factors must be rewarded, at least roughly, on a marginal basis. It seems especially easy in this connection to speak in average terms. Over a 30-year period, output per worker in manufacturing rises by 50 percent, and, when wages rise by less than 50 percent, the charge is heard that labor is being deprived of its just due on the basis of what it is producing. But what it is producing is its marginal, not its average, product. If the increase in output is due mainly to technological progress, the marginal value product of labor is likely to rise much less than the output per worker. Indeed, if the new methods are sufficiently labor-saving, the direct value of labor's service may not rise at all.

The utter impossibility of placing distribution in general on an average-output basis should be apparent. In the wheat case the output of 5 workers on 50 acres is 500 bushels. The output per worker is 100 bushels, and, on an average-output basis, 100 bushels should be the wage. But it is just as true that the output per acre is 10 bushels, so land rent should be 10 bushels per acre. Thus the same product is divided twice, and payments totaling 1000 bushels are called for in distributing a 500-bushel product. Only the marginal basis leaves room for all cooperating factors to be rewarded.

The general picture again

It is worth while, in conclusion, to look again at the goal toward which these normal distribution tendencies point. This is the broad viewpoint from which factor values were approached in Chapter 20.

Normal distribution tendencies, as the economist sees them, could set the actual returns to producers only if certain conditions were realized. The basic elements in the economy—(1) the desires of people for different goods, (2) the supplies of different resources, (3) the techniques by which they are used—would have to remain constant for a considerable period. *Unobstructed mobility* would need to prevail for factors usable at more than one point in the economy, together with knowledge as to the best ways of using them. *Thoroughgoing competition* would be necessary. This would include competition in selling products, in hiring factors, and in selling factor services. The *total demand* for goods, with its dependence on investment, monetary, and other factors, would need to be sufficiently great to cause full employment of resources, once they were properly allocated.

In these conditions, each type of productive service would command a uniform return in all its uses in all the industries in which it is employed. That return would equal the full value of its marginal product throughout the whole field of its employment. It would enjoy a stable return, since the conditions of equilibrium in the economy would be met. All units of it would be employed, and no employer would want more of it, because firms would be using resources with maximum effectiveness and making just a normal return on their investments.

With all these conditions met, it could be said in the most fundamental sense that each kind of labor and of wealth was getting just what it earned. Short of the full meeting of these conditions, it can only be said in a qualified sense that a factor is getting what it is worth. In a highly useful way, values can be assigned to given quantities of particular factors in specific situations, and factors used accordingly, but such valuations are just the constituent items in the general market demand for factors. There is finally no test of the worth of productive services except in the fact that the payments made for them promote general economy in the use of resources.

No one should suppose that a theoretical picture of this kind can be a close description of the actual distribution of income, but it has its uses. It does bring together the underlying forces that mold incomes. It is a wholesome antidote for easy assertions as to the returns that workers and owners ought to get. It provides a vantage point from which to view the rigidities and immobilities and the pressures and tuggings in the actual division of income. It is helpful in judging their possible effects. But while it provides useful guideposts for economic analysis, it should not be viewed as defining the practical ideal in policy matters. Perhaps certain pressures and arbitrary adjustments are sometimes desirable in the interest of a socially acceptable sharing of income. But to arrive at responsible opinions regarding reform proposals, one should see them in a setting broad enough to embrace their full effects. This theoretical picture serves this purpose. With it in mind, we shall examine some of the efforts made to alter the division of income in the interest of ordinary workers.

Review Questions

1. "To lift the incomes of the people, it is only necessary to increase their rates of pay. It is as simple as that." Criticize.

2. Contrast sharply the conceptions of distribution (a) as primarily a bargaining process and (b) as a process of valuation of services in the market. Show that the role of bargaining in fixing incomes is limited in the degree that the demand for services is elastic.

3. "To say that incomes rest primarily on bargaining power is to say that costs have little to do with the organization of production." Develop this point.

4. Distinguish, as avenues of redistribution of income, (a) shifts in relative values of different goods and (b) changes in the division of the proceeds from particular goods. Give instances of distribution controversies in both categories.

5. Suppose that the average pay of automobile workers is increased from $1 to $1.50 an hour while prices in general remain unchanged. Distinguish two probable types of reaction, each of which helps to explain the elasticity of demand for the services of automobile workers.

6. "The demand for productive services is usually derived from the demands for a variety of products." Explain, reviewing the discussion of factor demand in Chapter 20.

7. "The main difficulty in telling what particular workers and pieces of equipment and land are worth arises from their joint responsibility for particular products." Explain. Show that a solution is found in the marginal principle but that the principle is most applicable on a long-run basis.

8. How does the marginal value product of a factor differ in these cases: (a) competition both in selling product and hiring factor, (b) monopoly in selling product but competition in hiring factor, (c) competition in selling product but monopoly in hiring factor?

9. "In the immediate use of an existing plant, the marginal product of labor may fall, rise, or remain the same as more labor is used. But the *normal* effect of expanding the relative use of any factor, with technology constant, is to reduce its marginal product." Explain.

10. "No factor can normally receive more than the value of its marginal product. Thus, since all economic factors are subject to diminishing returns, no factor can get an income that absorbs the whole product." Explain, using the wheat example.

11. Show that, even in a prosperous period, unemployment may result from maladjustment in the relative rates of return for different productive services.

12. "If overpopulation reduces average income in a country, wages can be expected to fall faster than the average income." Explain.

13. "As a country develops, landowners are ordinarily in an exceptionally strong position." Explain, drawing an important general conclusion from their position. Show that, in fact, the gains of landowners have been limited by technological progress in the form of better uses of land, new industries, and improved transportation.

14. "Technological progress is associated with the development of capital goods, yet technological progress and growth of capital are likely to have opposite effects on the division of income." Explain.

15. "As the quantity of any productive service expands, its marginal value product may fall faster than its marginal physical product." Why?

16. Suppose that bricklayers speed up their laying of bricks by 20 percent. According to the "productivity theory" of distribution, would you expect a 20-percent increase in the wages of bricklayers? Might it be impossible to raise the wages of bricklayers at all, if the same number are to remain employed? Explain. If this were the result, would you conclude that labor does not gain from increased efficiency?

17. "It may be possible, in marginal terms, to say what a particular quantity of a particular factor is worth to a particular firm. But if the value of any factor is to reflect fully all the conditions that bear upon it, it must respond to influences that operate throughout the whole economy." Explain carefully, stating the conditions in which a factor can be said in the fullest sense to be paid what it is worth.

- 27 -

Wage-raising
Policies and Practices

Of the attempts made to reduce poverty and inequality in our society, the most conspicuous has been the effort, through labor organizations and government action, to raise the wages of ordinary workers. The object has been to lift wage rates substantially above the amounts that the market would compel employers to pay. This effort to change the division of income has been dramatized popularly as the conflict between capital and labor—a conflict regarded widely as the most disturbing, indeed the most explosive, that our economy faces.

Use of every available pressure to raise wages has claimed the support and sympathy of a great many socially minded people as well as of the workers involved. Every possible lessening of inequality seems desirable, and employers and capitalists appear generally to be more prosperous than employees. But thinking on this subject has, unfortunately, been governed too largely by devotion to a desirable end and by the purely private interest of workers and of employers. The problem should be examined in light of the knowledge we have of markets and the pricing of services.

We shall begin by examining briefly the methods employed to improve the position of labor. Then, after a considerable analysis of the possibilities of expanding labor's share of the national income, we shall conclude the chapter by recognizing that, to appreciate fully the aims of labor, interests broader than income in the usual sense must be taken into account.[1]

---

[1] Useful general works on labor problems are: Carroll R. Daugherty, *Labor Problems in American Industry*, Houghton Mifflin, 1941; E. Wight Bakke and Clark Kerr, *Unions. Management, and the Public*, Harcourt, Brace, 1948; Florence Peterson, *Survey of Labor Economics*, Harper, 1947; Harry A. Millis and Royal Montgomery, *Organized Labor*, Vol. III, McGraw-Hill, 1945.

Unions and Labor Legislation

Systematic efforts to improve the position of ordinary workers in the economy may be classified under three overlapping headings: (1) labor unions through which pressure is exerted on employers, (2) laws that aim to facilitate union organization and promote collective bargaining, (3) laws that deal directly with wages, hours, and working conditions. In addition, there are laws which impose some restraint on unions and, in particular, promote the peaceful settlement of disputes. Some outstanding features of union organization and of labor legislation will be sketched in this section.

Labor unions

Union membership in the United States numbers 15 or 16 million workers. Thus about one fourth of the entire working force is organized, and perhaps half of those who may be thought reasonably eligible for organization. The American Federation of Labor (A.F. of L.) has more than 7,000,000 members, the Congress of Industrial Organizations (C.I.O.) less than 7,000,000, and perhaps 2,000,000 are in independent unions. Union membership has doubled in a decade.

Employees may be grouped either according to the *craft* or the *industrial* principle. A craft union is made up of workmen doing the same kind of work, but employed perhaps in a number of industries, as toolmakers are whose work is in various lines of manufacturing. The powerful unions in the building-construction field and the organizations of railroad-train employees exemplify the craft principle. An industrial union is made up of all the workers in a specific industry, whatever the nature of their work. The United Mine Workers union of the coal industry is a leading example.

A union may be national or international in scope, but it is built up on the basis of local units. National unions of both the craft and industrial types are combined in federations. The American Federation of Labor developed mainly as a combination of national craft unions, while the newer Congress of Industrial Organizations has promoted the industrial principle in its constituent unions. In neither, however, has a single principle been applied consistently. In organizing any given group of workers, there is likely to be a conflict between these principles.

Unions which are limited to a single enterprise are commonly frowned on by union leaders. Their limited scope is a source of weakness, and they may be dominated by the employer. They are usually spoken of as *company unions*.

Union aims. If we view unions merely as a device for altering the distribution of income, we must think of income in that broader sense in which it encompasses all of the utilities and disutilities of economic life. The raising of *wages* has been the most conspicuous aim of unions, and most of our analysis may properly deal with it. But unions also try to reduce *working hours* and to improve *conditions of work.* They undertake to increase *security of tenure,* especially through preventing arbitrary dismissals and through establishing seniority rights. Beyond these specific objectives, unions are an expression of labor's general reaction to an industrial situation in which few men can break loose from the ranks of ordinary employees and in which, therefore, other roads must be found to the satisfaction that comes through exerting some control over one's fortunes. Some unions, moreover have shown a radical temper and have aimed at fundamental changes in economic institutions.

Union methods. The chief means of achieving the specific aims of unions is through *collective bargaining.* It is believed that better terms will be obtained in fixing wages and conditions of employment if workers deal in a body with their employers, than if they negotiate as individuals. Their case can be presented more expertly by union specialists, and their concerted refusal to accept an employer's terms exerts greater pressure. The threat of *strike,* a collective refusal to work, is a potent weapon. It is matched on the employer's side by the *lockout,* a refusal to allow employees to work.

When strikes are called, plants are *picketed* to prevent unsympathetic employees from returning to work and to exclude strikebreakers. Picketing is supposedly limited to peaceful persuasion but commonly involves intimidation. With collective negotiation failing or absent, a condition of industrial warfare has sometimes developed, with threats and violence on both sides. To bring added pressure, workers have often employed the *boycott* to cause recalcitrant employers to lose patronage.

From the labor standpoint the requirement for success in collective bargaining is a strong union. At the outset employers have commonly refused to deal with unions and have often discriminated against employees belonging to them. Sometimes employers have cooperated in maintaining a *black list* containing the names of objectionable workmen. The first aim of the union, therefore, is to gain full *recognition* and acceptance by employers and security of status. To this end, it is of great advantage if the employer can be induced to hire only union men or require that all his employees join the union, a so-called *closed-shop* or *union-shop* arrangement. The hold of the union is further strengthened if employers can be persuaded to collect union dues by deducting them from employees' pay, the *check-off* system. With a shop in which membership is purely voluntary, the burden is on union organizers to get workmen to join and maintain their loyalty. The *open shop* is a situation in which no union is recognized for bargaining purposes and union membership is neither favored nor discriminated against.

When unions are organized on the industrial principle, membership requirements are slight, for strength depends on the completeness of organization, but in the skilled trades the policy may be pursued of limiting labor supply by imposing fairly exacting membership qualifications and charging high initiation fees.

Government and unions

In the early nineteenth century combination of workers in unions was commonly regarded as unlawful conspiracy, in the same way that combinations of sellers of goods to raise prices are now. During the past century not only have unions become lawful in themselves, but employers have been increasingly deterred, especially in recent years, from discriminating against workers who are union members. Thus the Norris-La Guardia Act of 1932 asserted the right of the worker to "full freedom of association, self-organization, and designation of representatives of his own choosing," and it specifically forbade "yellow-dog contracts" by which workers were often made to agree, as a condition of employment, that they would not join a union. The antitrust laws have been applied to unions only infrequently, but by World War II they were so interpreted by the Supreme Court as to make them practically inapplicable.

Going farther, the United States government has come to insist that employers recognize unions as freely formed by employees and bargain with them on matters of wages, hours, and working conditions. This policy was introduced in the short-lived National Industrial Recovery Act of 1933 and embodied more fully in the National Labor Relations Act (Wagner Act) of 1935, which is administered by the National Labor Relations Board.

The Wagner Act was adopted frankly as a policy of aiding labor, not of regulating industrial relations nor of striking a balance between the interests of workers and their employers. As such, it aroused intense opposition and provoked repeated demands that union activities be subjected to some degree of regulation. The response, in 1947, was the controversial Labor Management Relations (Taft-Hartley) Act. This measure did not change the essentials of existing policy, but, among other things, it provided for some delaying of strikes, especially in essential industries, permitted employers to sue unions for breaking contracts, and otherwise established the principle that unions, as well as employers, can be guilty of "unfair labor practices," and placed some restraint on making union membership a condition of employment. In part, it aimed to protect union members from arbitrary or dishonest action of union officers. With the return to power of the Democratic party, it appeared that legislation less restrictive of union activity was probable.

The principle of promoting industrial peace by delaying strikes—requiring a "cooling-off" period during which disputes can be investigated and settlements worked out—has been followed in Canada and is embodied in the United States in the Railway Labor Act of 1926. There has been some resort, especially during the war, to government seizure of firms or industries to prevent shutdown through strikes. Mainly, however, the participation of the United States government in industrial disputes has been through the mild procedure of *mediation* and *conciliation,* in which trained persons undertake to smooth negotiations and assist contending parties in reaching agreements. Occasionally disputes are settled by decision of an impartial arbitrator or an arbitration board, and *compulsory arbitration,* by which industrial disputes are subjected in principle to court procedures, has been widely advocated. The chief experience with it has been in Australasia.

Wage, hours, and other laws to protect workers

Governmental aid to workers by promoting unions and collective bargaining is indirect. More direct have been the laws passed by federal and state governments in this country and by the governments of other industrial nations to raise wages and improve conditions of work. During the years since the British, in 1802, required that children should not work more than 12 hours a day in factories, the procession of such laws has been impressive.

Many have dealt with matters of safety. A substantial number have aimed to protect women and children in industry. Wages and hours legislation of general application was long beset with constitutional difficulties in the United States, but these seem to have been overcome. Minimum wages may be prescribed by statute or fixed by wage boards with statutory authority. The Fair Labor Standards Act (Wages and Hours Act) of 1938 established minimum wages that, over a term of years, were to increase to 40 cents an hour and fixed a basic maximum working week of 40 hours. The Act applies to workers in industries that are deemed to operate in interstate commerce. Wage legislation of this type is designed to assist only the lowest-income workers and is not to be thought of as a general plan of government wage-fixing.

The Effects of Efforts to Raise Wages

Through unions and wage laws, is it possible to raise wages relatively to other income, and thus appreciably reduce existing inequality in the division of income? The aim in this discussion is to penetrate beneath the common view that improving labor's income is just a matter of raising wage rates—on the apparent assumption that, if wages are raised, profits are reduced and that is the end of the matter. To this assumption we must apply judiciously the main ideas of the preceding chapter: that use of resources depends on the prices paid for them, and that higher prices, which mean higher costs, commonly result (1) in advances in the prices of products and (2) in adjustments in methods of production to economize expensive factors. We must consider (1) whether wages can be raised out of profits without a chain of reactions that cancel the immediate effect, and (2) what the effects of these reactions are when they occur. These questions must be viewed in a variety of circumstances.

For the most part we shall be concerned with unions and the pressure they exert on wages, though the discussion will also apply to the influence of wage laws on the low-income group covered by them.

Raising wages out of profits

If wage advances are to come out of profits, not only immediately but continuingly, so that a real change in the division of income is effected, workers must now be getting, in some sense, less than they are worth to employers. This means that they are getting less than employers can be induced to pay them without raising the prices of products or altering their methods to get along with fewer workers. There must be some latitude, that we may conveniently call a "bargaining area," within which wages of present workers can be raised out of present revenues from products.

Belief that there is such an area rests mainly on the view that the individual, unorganized worker is at a disadvantage in the labor market and cannot get what he is worth. Our task is to consider the nature of this disadvantage, if it exists, and to ask why employers, in their quest for profit, should not bid as much to get labor as it is worth to them.

Weaknesses on worker's side of market. There is little doubt that the individual employee is commonly in a weak market position, in some respects, in selling his services. In seeking a job he approaches a firm that has tens, hundreds, or thousands of employees. A given employer is much more important to him than he is to that employer. Moreover, the employer who handles numerous placements of workers is probably better informed than the worker regarding rates of pay and employment opportunities and is not likely to offer more than the market indicates, whereas the worker, with limited knowledge and few alternatives, may accept less. The worker, furthermore, usually has little financial reserve to carry him and his family while he shops around for a job. It is more important to him to get work quickly than it is to the employer that he staff his plant immediately to the profitable maximum. Behind this consideration is the fact that labor is, in a sense, a perishable good. If today's service is not sold, it cannot be sold another day, but a material commodity can be held for a time awaiting a better market. It is believed, for these reasons, that the bargaining position of the individual worker is weak.

Defective competition on the employer's side. Accordingly, it is sometimes said that wages, as set by the market, can be no higher than workers, in their necessities, insist on getting. It has even been said that the wages of any type of labor can be no greater than the most necessitous members of the group will accept. But such views as these show lack of understanding of the operation of markets. The lower limit of any price is set not merely by what sellers will take, rather than not sell, but also by what buyers will pay, rather than not obtain the good in as great quantity as is worth having at the price.

The latter limit is likely to support wage rates much better than the former. Perhaps 10 persons are available who will do a certain job at 60 cents per hour, 10 more who will work for 80 cents, and 10 more for $1. If an employer needs 30 persons and is willing to pay $1 per hour rather than not get them, the wage will be $1, and thus 20 workers will get more than they insist on getting. If the relation among employers is competitive in the full theoretical sense, additional workers will be hired, and wage rates will be bid up, until the wage equals the value of the added product. At that wage labor will be getting all it is worth for the quantity hired.

Thus, for labor's weakness in the market actually to depress wages, there must be lack of vigorous competition on the part of employers. They must suspend hiring workers at a point where the marginal product of labor has a value greater than the wage. This, unfortunately, may often be the case. Very commonly employers are in a position where they realize that additional workers can be obtained only by raising the wage rate. If they are, then to raise the rate for additional workers will mean that they must presently pay the higher rate to workers already in their employ, and the additional workers will, in effect, cost not only the wages they receive but the additional wages to present workers. In the example of monopolistic hiring in the preceding chapter (p. 684), hiring a sixth worker at $140 monthly would increase the pay of the 5 present workers from $130 to $140, making the cost of the sixth worker $190. So, though he would add $150 to revenue, the sixth is not hired. Labor in this situation, therefore, is not being paid according to its marginal product, as fully competitive employers interpret it.

A situation of this kind may easily exist in a local labor market. Particularly if the market is small and there are only a few important employers in it, each one is keenly aware of the impact of his hiring on the wages he pays. Thus a situation of oligopoly (or oligopsony) in buying labor exists. Moreover, this awareness is probably not left entirely to spontaneous recognition by individual employers. They may be banded together in an employer's association and restrict their competitive bidding for workers by definite arrangement. In any case, they meet in businessmen's clubs that maintain friendly relations among them and help to keep them aware of common interests.

These features of the labor market are easily taken for granted and their significance overlooked. As with the ordinary departures from strict competition in the sale of products, they are not recognized as involving the principle of monopoly, but clearly they do. Because employees, on the other hand, are more numerous, spontaneous behavior of a monopolistic nature is less likely on their side, and the resulting situation is one in which they are likely very often to receive a wage somewhat less than they are worth.

Wage increases within the bargaining area. Such a difference between the wage paid and the wage which strictly competitive employers would find it worth while to pay, rather than not have the services of workers, constitutes a "bargaining area" in the present sense. It is referred to in this way because wage adjustments within it represent truly the meaning of bargaining, as we have defined that term. In other words, the raising of wages within this area does not tend to reduce employment.

Indeed, if wages are raised within this bargaining area through the pressure of unions or wage laws, the effect may even be an increase in the number of workers hired. The reason is simple. If employers are in a partially monopolistic position, they restrain their bidding for workers in order to hold wages down. Restricted hiring is the means of exploiting their advantage. But once a wage rate is set quite positively by outside pressure or agreement, restricted hiring becomes pointless. When the wage rate is not at issue, profits are enhanced by hiring workers up to the point where the rate is just covered by the product of marginal workers. In the example, if a wage of $145 is set through agreement with a union and the 5 workers must be paid at that rate whether a sixth is hired or not, it is certainly advisable to hire the sixth man, since he adds $150 to the revenue. Technically, in this case, the union keeps the marginal cost of labor from exceeding the wage.

Monopoly in hiring *versus* **monopoly in selling products.** It should be appreciated that a bargaining area is not created by the presence of excessive profit or monopoly profit as such. Labor leaders often speak as if it were reasonable, and quite logical, for employers to raise wages without raising prices whenever profits seem unnecessarily large. But *a bargaining area,* in the strict sense, *exists through monopoly in hiring labor, not in selling products.* When power over the market enables an employer to hire workers at less than the value of their marginal product, that power can be offset by monopolistic combination of workers in selling labor. This adjustment is strictly within the labor market and only within limits set by the worth of labor as we have defined it.

If the same employer enjoys a profitable control over the market in selling his product, that control enters his appraisal of the marginal value product of labor. If he hires additional workers, they will add to his output and thus reduce the price he gets for it—not only for the added units but for all the units. If compelled to pay a higher wage, he is thus in position, through restricting output and charging a higher price, to obtain the higher marginal revenue to cover the higher marginal cost. This, normally, is what he will do. There is nothing in the power of the union to prevent him from doing so.

Short-run bargaining possibilities. Again we have stated the logic of employer calculations with a refinement that, in practice, cannot be realized. We have envisaged an employer who knows the pertinent facts regarding revenues and costs and acts accordingly to maximize profits. Now we must recognize, as we have before, that business managers are unable to make accurate calculations of variations in revenues and costs or to act upon them promptly. Moreover, being sensitive to the probable reactions of competitors to changes in their market behavior, they hesitate to disturb the existing situation as long as the over-all profit picture is fairly acceptable. Thus, with respect to labor relations, various factors of limited and short-run significance determine, to some extent, the possibility of improving wages at the expense of profits. Prices and costs are not so tightly and mechanically related that there is no play, no looseness, permitting modest wage adjustments that escape neat theoretical formulation.

Thus, if an employer cannot measure accurately, in marginal increments, the contribution of a given type of labor, he may be pushed into paying a somewhat higher wage for it without reducing the number of workers he hires or raising the price of his product. Led in any case by uncertainties regarding customers and competitors to pursue profit in a restrained manner, he may accept minor reductions in net income without attempting any offsetting adjustment. Certainly if a wage increase is not industry-wide, applying simultaneously to all his competitors, he cannot pass it on promptly to the consuming public without sacrificing his place in the industry. In time, readjustments can be expected to any specific change in costs, but in a dynamic situation opportunities continue to arise to achieve short-run advantages.

Doubtless the closeness of cost and revenue calculations varies somewhat with the *financial condition of businesses*. A firm that is losing money must figure carefully, but a prospering concern is under less pressure and may take a longer view of its position. Thus, while strict marginal calculations would largely prevent the shifting to labor of profits which arise from a strong position in selling the product, nevertheless the presence of large profits from any source probably leads to readier acquiescence in wage advances and less haste in instituting changes to avoid their effect. With imperfect mobility in the labor market, somewhat higher wages in more efficient and profitable firms is fairly common.

Apart from such differences among firms, *general conditions of prosperity and depression* affect bargaining possibilities. It is characteristic of a depression that total demand at any set of prices is insufficient to employ productive resources fully. With a surplus of labor and with free and fluid competition in the labor market, a persisting decline in wages would be the natural condition. In this situation labor unions, resisting sharp wage cuts, can influence the whole price structure and probably improve the relation of wages to the prices of products.

When business is booming, wages are bid up by employers, in their competition for labor, without union pressure. The biggest increases occur in industries that are expanding the most. During World War I, for example, some of the largest advances took place in the wages of steel and farm workers who had no unions to help them, and farm labor had the same experience in World War II. Detroit, with its developing automobile industry, was a high-wage city long before the industry was unionized. Nevertheless, in boom periods wage rates are not likely to rise as much or as promptly as product prices, or as they probably ought to rise to give labor its appropriate share in the expanding product and real income. Union pressure may serve to overcome the lag and thus improve wages at the expense of profits.

The foregoing are temporary reasons why unions may increase the earnings of labor without causing such secondary adjustments as divert the effect from the pockets of immediate employers. But while the amount of latitude for such short-run adjustments cannot be measured, it probably is not very great.

Abnormal profits and wage policy. Somewhat parenthetically let us turn to another aspect of this matter. Let us ask whether it would generally be desirable, provided it were possible, to increase wages to absorb abnormal profits. It has become the common practice of union spokesmen to play up the "abnormal" profits of employing firms in support of demands for higher wages. It is thus important to look into the logic of the assumption that abnormal profits, if by an appropriate standard they exist, should be diverted to the pay envelope. Mainly it is important to be aware of the variety of circumstances which may account for exceptional profits. Consider the following:

1. They may arise through the deficient competition of employers in hiring workers—the matter just considered. In that case, probably most observers would agree that it is desirable, from the economic and social standpoint, to have an upward adjustment in wages, so that workers get paid as much as employers can afford to pay them.

2. If exceptional profits arise, however, through monopoly in selling products, the logical adjustment is not an advance in wages but a reduction in prices. The workers in such industries have no special claim to the profits, but the customers clearly do. It may be said that antitrust-law enforcement may not bring the needed correction and that therefore union action is acceptable as a second choice. But it is an unsound conception of economic control that it should be left to private groups —to be exercised in their own interest. From the standpoint of the consuming public, made up mainly of ordinary working people, it is about as objectionable to be overcharged for goods, whether the revenue goes to enterprisers or to strategically placed workers who get more than like workers do in other industries.

3. The exceptional profits may be enjoyed only by certain firms in an industry. Should the employees of Firm A, an efficient concern, demand higher wages than like workers get in Firm B, a less efficient and profitable competitor? An affirmative answer is implied when unions negotiate with individual firms, as in the automobile industry, and the profits of the particular company are made the basis of wage demands. It seems, however, that there is little logic in giving workers who are no better a higher wage because management is better. The workers themselves would scarcely accept the logic in reverse and agree to lower wages because management is inefficient. Certainly from a social standpoint it

seems undesirable to penalize efficiency by raising costs above those incurred by less efficient firms. If the efficiency, on the other hand, is attributable to superior performance of labor, it should be rewarded, and management should want to reward it on incentive grounds.

4. As the superior methods of the more efficient firms become generally adopted, there is the question, from the long-run standpoint, whether it is better to have lower costs reflected (1) in a falling price level, with money incomes staying the same, or (2) in a constant price level with money incomes rising. This issue was raised in Chapter 12. There are arguments on both sides. The more probable development, history indicates, is the latter. It has the psychological advantage of making labor more aware of progress in well-being, and it may be more conducive to general prosperity. But this means that wages would rise only in accordance with some measure of average efficiency, not on the basis of the efficiency of particular employers.[2]

5. In any period of general price inflation, as following World War II, profits tend to be high. Even though wages rise as fast as the prices of products, profits rise faster because of the fixity of various costs. Are these profits a reason for a still greater advance in wages? It would not seem so. Inflation is fed by expanding purchasing power, and raising wages merely promotes the upward spiral and beckons the disaster that is likely to follow.

6. It should finally be recognized that profits that seem high may be reasonable from a functional standpoint. If demand for a product is increasing and investment in expanding facilities is called for, attractive profits are necessary to induce that investment. Wages in such a case are likely to be high also, since labor must be attracted too, but wages should not be so high as to remove the incentive to invest.

Indeed, in general, in judging whether profits are so high as to call for a corrective, it must be remembered that they are a highly variable income, low or negative in bad years, and the return in good years must be well above the necessary average if enterprise is to remain vigorous.[3] When profits are used as an argument for higher wages, an unduly short-run view of profit requirements is likely to be taken.

This observation would carry an unfortunate meaning, however, if it were viewed as a general defense of business profits. That issue is not being considered here. The present point is that, if there is a problem of profit control, it should not be subordinated to the problem of wage adjustments.

---

[2] The writer is indebted to Alvin H. Hansen for a persuasive statement of this view. See letter to *The New York Times,* January 6, 1946.

[3] The characteristics of profits will be discussed in Chapter 29.

Wage increases not out of profits

It is important to see that advances in wages may be at the expense of the immediate employer, but even more important to see that they may not be. The secondary effects of economic change are less likely to be recognized than the primary effects, and emphasis of them is the more necessary on that account. Efforts of workers to improve their lot enjoy widespread public sympathy and support. Disruption of production through strikes is tolerated as an incidental feature of a commendable campaign for a more just distribution of income. But public sympathy should rest on realistic grounds, and it is not well grounded in this instance unless it reflects full understanding of the impact of wage advances. As the preceding chapter stressed, there is nothing mystical about the source of income. It arises from production and is meaningful only as a claim to products. If wage advances do not come from profits, they come from somewhere else, and any judgment of them, and of the means employed to get them, should rest on an appreciation of the full picture.

Shifting the impact of wage increases. The key point is that wage rates are costs. Employers incur costs not because they are compelled to but because it is worth while to incur them because of related revenues. Thus the use of labor, as we have seen, must depend on the prices paid for it. Adjustments to wage advances may often be slow, but costs cannot rise without effect. They are the basis of the pricing of products, and wage increase beyond the bargaining range, as we have defined it, can be expected to cause prices to increase. Moreover, since employers are concerned with minimizing costs, means of economizing relatively costly resources are sought and are likely to be introduced whenever adjustments are made in methods of production. These changes may not occur promptly enough for the superficial observer to associate them with the wage advances that cause them, but, to persons who do not believe in magic, it is apparent that adjustments must come through the normal channels in which costs operate.

If higher wages are passed on in higher prices, the gain for the specific workers who get the increase is not canceled. The gain simply does not come out of the profits of the employer; it comes instead out of the real incomes of all persons who consume the product. If the product is yachts bought by the wealthy, a transfer of income from them to the workers in yacht manufacturing seems to lessen inequality. If the product is food or clothing or housing, it cannot be assumed that higher wages passed on in higher prices belong under the heading of distribution reform.

If higher prices of yachts or cars or houses, resulting from wage advances, cause reduced buying of these goods, production will fall in these fields, and employment also. Workers who remain fully employed at the higher wages are better off because of them, but their associates who lose their jobs or work part time are worse off. If the demand for these goods is highly inelastic, sales will decline little, but consumers will have less money to spend for other goods, and the effect will be felt in other markets. Moreover, if the use of labor falls at any point, because of changes in product prices or because techniques are adopted that economize labor, workers must be shunted into other fields. The effect is to increase competition in those other fields, with a tendency to reduce wages there or to create a labor surplus. Along such lines the impact of wage adjustments must be traced.

Unless it can be shown over a period of time that wage increases have caused employers to receive a smaller fraction of the revenue from the sale of goods, it must be assumed that the shift in distribution, often in ways too obscure to follow, has been a horizontal shift among many persons in all lines of activity throughout the economy.

Persistence of wage demands. Should we not conclude then that these repercussions impose automatically a certain restraint on wage demands? Will not unions avoid increases which will not come out of profits, especially if the increases may reduce employment of the workers receiving them? A negative answer seems, on the whole, to be indicated. For the most part the secondary effects are not recognized, though, in an inflationary period such as has followed the war, the proximity of wage and price increases may bring recognition. The main consideration is the fact that the particular workers receiving a higher wage are likely to benefit in a way that is not offset by secondary reactions. Higher prices are diffused over the whole body of consumers, and, in a growing economy, the effect on jobs in the specific industry may be merely a slowing of expansion, not an absolute decline.

It should be appreciated that union leadership is hard headed and intensely practical in these matters. Its object is to do something for the members of a certain union. This is what the members want, and it is through achieving this result that leaders keep their jobs. There may be rationalizations in terms of broad social aims and of claims that the fight is on behalf of the common man everywhere, but the actual policies of unions usually have a limited objective. This limited outlook is best observed in the bitter jurisdictional disputes among union groups over the right to particular jobs. The attitude of unions toward the market is that of producer groups generally, neither more nor less noble. It is wholly unrealistic to suppose that unions will be greatly deterred in their wage-raising efforts by the prospect that their gains will come not out of employer's profits but out of the public generally, most of whom are ordinary workers.

Union types and differences in elasticity of demand for labor. Union members should always consider the effect of wage advances on their jobs, but the need of doing so differs with the circumstances of the market. In discussing the elasticity of demand for products (Chapter 19) we saw that, when different goods are used together, elasticity of demand is low for relatively unimportant items in the combination. A substantial increase in the price of steel, for instance, brings only a small increase in the cost and the price of automobiles. Therefore the sale of automobiles is not reduced very much, nor is the purchase of steel used in making them. This same point is significant in the demand for labor. When wage rates are pushed up for a few workers in a plant, the effect is much less than when a corresponding advance is obtained for all workers.

This distinction may apply to the operation of craft and industrial unions and their effect on distribution. If toolmakers employed in the automobile industry succeed, through a craft union, in getting a large advance in pay, the effect on the total cost of production is necessarily small, and the reactions to the change will be small. Perhaps greater effort will be made to economize the services of toolmakers, but only a slight impact is possible on the relative uses of labor, as well as on the relative prices of goods. If, on the other hand, an industrial union that includes most of the workers in the automobile industry achieves a similar wage increase, the effect on costs is large, and the general effect will be appreciable. We are assuming, of course, that the wage increase goes beyond such a bargaining area as has been described.

To the skilled worker, the craft principle of organization may thus seem preferable, for resistance to wage-raising efforts is likely to vary with the resulting disturbances. But from the standpoint of social interest in distribution, it is difficult to approve an advance in pay for workers who are already relatively well off, if adjustments will occur that are harmful to other workers. The industrial union, on the other hand, is presumably as much concerned with the well-being of its unskilled as of its skilled members. Moreover, if its aims are not revolutionary—that is, if it seeks only to improve the market position of its members within the framework of a private-enterprise economy—it should logically be more restrained in the magnitude of its demands.

Minimum-wage laws and the living-wage idea

Unions have been referred to frequently in the preceding discussion of wage control, but most of what has been said applies in principle to wage laws also. Putting a floor under wages may merely give to workers, without further adjustments, the wages that employers can afford to pay them, but there may also be secondary effects of the type described. The special significance of wage laws is that they are intended to aid the very low-income workers who are least likely to be helped by unions. Thus wage laws strike at the most critical aspect of the inequality problem.

These laws are often defended through appeal to the "living-wage" idea, the belief that employers are socially obligated to pay wages that enable their employees to live decently. Industries, accordingly, are called parasitic if they do not support their employees fully but shift part of the obligation to the workers' families, to private charity, or to public relief. This view is most often stated by labor spokesmen and social reformers but finds expression elsewhere, as in the statement of a prominent manufacturer: "We can honestly say, at least in our country, that man does not have the right to employ his fellow man unless he can pay a subsistence wage." [4]

This view invites the obvious comment that enactment of wage laws does not provide jobs, and only the philanthropic employer will knowingly pay more to labor than it seems to be worth to him. If such laws are applied generally and put a significant floor under wages, they can be expected to exclude many inferior workers from employment. Individuals range continuously from those who are highly competent to those who are completely unemployable, and any minimum sets up a dividing line separating those worth employing from those who are not. Minimum-wage laws, accordingly, are often opposed on the ground that it is better to have workers earn something than nothing. The reasons given are two: first, that workers employed, even at a low rate of productivity, add something to the national product and income, and, second, that it is less costly to taxpayers and others to supplement their earnings than to support them completely.

But it may be said in reply that it is better to have such persons completely unemployed, with the state assuming responsibility for their support, than to have them struggle along with an inadequate wage and suffer neglect. Moreover, the actual public burden may be small. There may be little effect on prices, either because these workers are worth more than they are getting or because their wages are a minor element in cost. Thus little reduction in their employment is likely unless mechanical substitutes happen to be available.

Certainly the employment effect of the Wages and Hours Act of 1938 cannot be great. Industries not in interstate commerce are not subject

[4] Robert W. Johnson, as reported in *Time*, November 5, 1945.

to it, and the minimum hourly rate, unless Congress adjusts it quite fully to the postwar price level, cannot be a very serious factor.[5]

Possibility of raising labor's relative share

We have now examined (1) the theoretical possibilities of raising wages out of profits and (2) the reactions through which wage advances may come to fall on all incomes throughout the economy. It would now be highly satisfactory to be able to judge quantitatively the probable outcome of wage advances as between these two alternatives. How much effect have unions and wage laws had on the over-all distribution of income, and how much effect are they likely to have? How much can wage earners hope to benefit from these upward pressures on wage rates? There is no adequate statistical basis, unfortunately, for answering these questions, but it is possible to form some general impressions.

For one thing, it is most important to get rid of the more extravagant expectations, still widely prevalent, as to the possibility of raising wages by these means. Vain hopes bring needless disappointment and controversy. When instances are cited, and they easily can be, of particular wage rates doubling and trebling through union pressure over a term of years, it is easy for people to suppose that any labor group, or labor generally, can achieve a corresponding gain. Irresponsible leaders may make it appear that they are directing a general crusade on behalf of the oppressed rather than advancing the prices of specific labor services.

It is clear that no revolutionary change in the distribution of income is possible through raising wages. When we view the entire income picture, as we did in Chapter 24, and include as labor income two thirds of the net return of unincorporated firms, labor seems ordinarily to get from 70 to 80 percent of national income. If we limit the scope of our comparison, as we should, and consider only the relation between wages and profits in the area of private business where wage controversies mainly arise, the situation appears to be similar. Aggregate wages and profits for all American corporations in years just before and just after the war were as follows (in billions of dollars): [6]

	1940	1946
Compensation of employees	$32.1	$71.1
Profits before corporation tax liability	9.1	20.8
Profits after taxes	6.2	12.2

[5] The "living-wage" idea in wage adjustments must not be confused with the "cost-of-living" basis. During a war period or whenever prices are rising rapidly, the index of the cost of living is watched closely in wage adjustments, and sometimes wage changes are tied by formula to the index. The aim is to maintain real wages during a period when they might easily fall, but the cost-of-living approach provides no correction of wages that may have been inadequate, from any standpoint, in the first place.

[6] *National Income Supplement* to *Survey of Current Business,* July 1947, p. 25.

Profits before taxes were between one fourth and one third of the compensation of employees in these two years, and less than one fifth after taxes. These figures do not reveal what part of the profit, if any, might have been diverted to wages without serious effect, but the transferable segment could have been only a small percent of the wages actually received.

These figures, however, are only a small sample. In such a year as 1929, when business was booming in a speculative way, or in 1941, when the impact of wartime demand was felt sharply, profits have been higher in relation to wages. In these two years, profits before taxes were, respectively, 29 and 41 percent of wages, and after taxes, 24 and 22 percent of wages. But perhaps the main significance of these figures is that no striking improvement had taken place between 1929, when business interests were notoriously in the saddle, and a prosperous year such as 1941 that followed a period of vigorous union activity. It happens that corporate profits, after inventory-valuation adjustment but before taxes, were exactly the same percent (12.4) of total income from private sources in 1929 and 1947. Compensation of employees, in this period that spans the depression and the war, had risen from 56 to 60 percent.[7] But a single comparison does not establish a trend, and time alone will reveal the possible influence of efforts to raise wages. They may rise a little, but under present institutions it is evident that they will not come to absorb a strikingly larger fraction of the income of the country.

High wages, purchasing power, and total income

Up to this point, the raising of wages has been considered as a means of giving labor a larger share in the national income. Now we should recognize that another quite different argument is often used in urging higher wages. It is argued that labor's buying power must be kept at a high level if the nation is to have a high total income—in the interest of everybody. Spokesmen for labor have not abandoned their primary emphasis on the need of getting for labor its just due, but the purchasing-power argument has been used a good deal also. Thus, at the end of the war, it was urged that wage rates should be raised to offset the decline in over-time work, so that labor's "take-home pay" would continue to be sufficient to buy a high national product. This way of thinking should be viewed in light of familiar principles.

There is, first, the practical question whether employers will in fact be governed by this consideration in wage adjustments—whether they will raise wages but not raise prices correspondingly, since price advances would nullify the added purchasing power. On this point, noth-

[7] *Survey of Current Business*, February 1948, p. 7.

ing need be added to what has been said regarding the wage decisions of employers. Wage rates are still costs, and the business decisions of the individual employer will not really be governed by theories of total demand.[8] At the same time, when decisions are related only loosely to the goal of maximizing profit, managements may possibly be influenced a little by this consideration. Conceivably they may grant higher wages a little more readily or postpone price advances a little longer.

Often, as we have seen, these purchasing-power ideas reflect a rather loose conception of the nature of total demand. Whatever may be implied to the contrary, raising wages cannot increase the total of income dollars in relation to the total goods to be bought. From the sale of any volume of product, there emerges sufficient money income to buy that product—and no more. There was reason for maintaining "take-home pay" through wage advances after the war only if labor, working fewer hours, would maintain the wartime level of output. If it did not, the administration's encouragement of wage advances was well calculated to promote the upward movement of prices that, in fact, ensued.[9]

The income dollars that a given output provides include both wages and profits. It is not true that wages, dollar for dollar, represent more purchasing power than profits do and that redistribution from profits to wages would increase the *ability* of the nation to buy its product. The only point is the familiar one that wages are mainly spent for current consumption and profits are more likely to be saved. So the essence of the argument is simply the idea that savings tend to outrun investment. The considerations that bear on this issue do not require further discussion. (1) If there is a chronic deficiency of investment opportunity, consumption should be stimulated and saving discouraged, and, even if deficiencies are only intermittent, it may be safer to err on the side of maintaining high consumption. But, at the same time, (2) profits are the

---

[8] Slips in reasoning are common in this connection. It is sometimes overlooked that the employees of a particular firm, or even a particular industry, do not spend much of their income on the products they help to produce. Employers cannot cast their bread upon the waters, thinking that it will come back to them, but must depend mainly for their receipts on the bread cast by other employers. Employers are not likely to increase their costs out of faith that other employers will do likewise. Moreover, the nature of the increase in costs is misconceived by advocates of these "boot-strap" methods of maintaining prosperity. Even if higher wages lead to greater sales, the revenue from the greater sales cannot be used to cover the higher wage rates. Mainly it must cover the cost of producing the increase in output, which is costly whether wage rates rise or not.

[9] Another bit of reasoning in this connection was the idea that, while wages should be raised to enable workers to buy a high postwar output, employers could not afford to pay the higher wages unless workers increased their production enough to keep unit costs from rising—in other words, unless labor's income per unit of product to be bought was no higher than before. Simple as it is, the relation between wages as income and wages as cost seems extremely elusive.

inducement to invest, and it is equally serious to curtail them unduly.

Wage and job security. Pressure for higher wage rates to maintain prosperity is only one of many evidences of the concern of labor over continuity of income. Loss of employment is labor's greatest fear. Thus various C.I.O. unions have initiated a movement for the payment of wages on an annual basis to make income more dependable. We shall not go into the complex issues that this proposal involves. Similarly, the various go-slow practices adopted to make jobs last, the pressure to require employment of unnecessary workers, the opposition to technological advance are all evidences of fear that jobs and pay will end. But in their bearing on wages—real wages—such practices are necessarily harmful to labor as a whole.

Other Labor Goals—The Public Interest

Economic progress, as the subject was introduced in Chapter 3, consists primarily in an expansion of the flow of products on which economic welfare depends. Higher wages give labor its share of that expanding flow and may increase its share. But economic progress, it was pointed out, has two other aspects, and perhaps economics says too little about them. One of them is an increasing amount of leisure to enjoy the fruits of production and pursue other human ends. The other is an improvement in those features of work which determine not its output but the satisfactions that people derive during their working hours. The labor movement, while stressing most the size and continuity of wages, has been greatly concerned with *hours of labor* and *working conditions*.

In these and other respects, the labor movement should be viewed from the standpoint of the general public as well as of labor. This public includes labor, of course, but it should be thought of as a body of consumers and a body politic concerned with the working of the whole economy. This chapter will conclude with some observations from this broader standpoint.

Reduction of working hours

During the last century or two, the time spent in earning a living has declined greatly for most workers. The struggle for food and other essentials once required effort extending through most waking hours. The regimentation which came through adapting the working day to the blowing of factory whistles and the unlocking and locking of business establishments gave uniformity to working time and provided a basis on which it could be systematically reduced. A 12-hour day was long common, and important instances of it, even outside farming, continued as late as 1920. But early in this century a 10-hour day became standard for most work. Then the 8-hour movement began, with the goal progressing from a 6 to a 5½ to a 5-day week. Now 40 hours has come to be regarded as the standard working week, and a still shorter week is often discussed as a reasonable objective.

Sentiment for fewer working hours has arisen spontaneously among working people, but quite largely the actual reductions have come through organized pressure of laws and unions. Wages may be adjusted piecemeal on an individual basis, but hours, on the other hand, must be uniform for those who work together, and adjustments must be sweeping when they occur. Thus the place of organized control, as an effective influence, seems clearer than in the case of wages. Several features of the hours problem should be noted:

1. One is that reduction of hours is often tied in with the raising of wages. Indeed an advance in pay is often the real aim when reduced hours are sought. The demand is for fewer hours of work and the same pay per day or week—in other words, an advance in pay per hour. Moreover, the stated hours may not be sought as a limit of work but rather as a basis of overtime pay, so that time-and-a-half or even double time will be paid for hours above the basic number. When wage rates are raised in this manner, they involve no peculiarities not already considered. If costs are increased, employers must act accordingly.

2. Often it is said that costs are not increased. The argument is that, with a shorter working day and week, workmen become less fatigued and, especially in work requiring clearheadedness and nicety of coordination, the standard of performance improves. Thus a common generalization is that as much is done in a short as in a long working day. Within limits and depending on the type of work, this may be true. But clearly it does not follow, because a person may do as much in a year of 60-hour weeks as in a year of 70-hour weeks, that the working week can be dropped successively to 50, 40, and even fewer hours without loss of output. However, in so far as hours can be reduced without sacrifice of production, there is no reason for not reducing them, except on the theory of our Puritan ancestors that the devil is active in occupying idle people.

3. The primary aim from a welfare standpoint, of course, is the realization of this very leisure that the Puritans feared. It is wholly logical, as per-capita production rises in the economy, to take part of the gain in more goods and part of it in more leisure. What the ideal division is must differ with the prevailing culture, since conceptions of the good life are not standardized. And however the matter is decided in an economy, it cannot be decided in a manner satisfactory to all individuals.

What is especially important, when hours' reductions are combined with advances in hourly pay, is for people to realize that any curtailment in output has the inevitable effect of reducing average real income.

4. Recently, especially since the early 1930s, reductions in hours have been associated conspicuously with the employment problem. This has already been discussed.[10] Available work may be spread among more people during a depression if each person works fewer hours. But as permanent policy, hours reduction to spread work has the same logic as working inefficiently or opposing technological progress, with the same end in view. If goods are preferred to leisure, any policy is unsound that deliberately reduces the production of goods. The employment problem can find no satisfactory solution along these lines.

Improvement of working conditions

This phrase is hardly adequate to cover all that is implied by it here. It covers such specific matters as protection against accidents, occupational ailments, and the excessive speeding-up of operations; likewise provision for the comfort of workers and as pleasant an environment as the nature of work permits. But it includes also many aspects of the relation of employees to their employers—all the features of working arrangements that give workers a sense of being regarded as human beings, of being safe from arbitrary dismissal and arbitrary penalties, of being able to state their grievances and have them heard and considered. It means, broadly, making life on the job as pleasant as possible.

Some of these matters have been dealt with through legislation. They have also been included extensively in the activities of unions. Here, again, there is probably greater latitude for improvement through organized effort than in the case of wages. Many employers have been successful, without outside pressure, in maintaining satisfactory relations with their employees; many, on the other hand, have bought labor pretty much as they have bought lumber and pig iron, with as little regard for human factors. And even though enterprisers are well disposed, in big organizations so much depends on the immediate bosses that there is much room for ill feeling to develop. Here unions have had a large field in which to do important work, and their successes redound not only to the benefit of workers but of employers also in the form of greater output. Often, no doubt, they are captious and overzealous, and union leaders are frequently more concerned with establishing themselves as protectors of their followers against capitalist aggression than they are with establishing good feeling and promoting the efficiency necessary to higher wages. But, however handled, the problem is a vital one,

[10] In Chapter 16.

and its solution in large firms seems to depend on some scheme of organized cooperation.

Relation of unions to a free economy

Policies should never be judged by the worthiness of their aims but by a full consideration of their consequences. The policy of permitting workers to act collectively in markets to improve their position, and of allowing them to strike to enforce their demands, must be viewed in this light. In particular, the responsible student of economics must consider the bearing of particular policies and practices on the working of the economy as a whole.

The aim of improving the position of ordinary workers has general support. People are inclined to look favorably on arrangements that seem likely to have this effect. But, at the same time, great impatience has developed in the United States with the inconvenience and loss of production resulting from strikes and with the basic idea of resorting to force to decide the merits of issues. Moreover, constant effort to raise wages in the inflationary postwar period has brought against unions the charge that, in part, they are responsible for the inflation. Indeed, leading economists have doubted whether, if unions are strong, inflation can be avoided whenever employment is reasonably full. More fundamentally, misgiving is expressed whether great aggregations of private power can be permitted to operate in the economy without changing its basic character.

Unions and competition. On the last point, a serious inconsistency of policy is alleged. Why, it is asked, should we permit monopolistic combination in the labor field when our general policy is to rely on competitive markets to control economic behavior? If competition is good in the sale of products and the purchase of materials, why should it not also be good in the sale of labor service? Or if, perchance, the labor market is like the public-utility field, and competition cannot succeed as a controlling force, why should not the same principle of government regulation be applied, instead of relying on the organized but disruptive battling of employers and employees?

The answer given by some observers is that acceptance of unions, collective bargaining, and strikes was all a mistake—that competition should be maintained on both sides of the labor market, and that results would be just as good for labor directly, and better indirectly, in view of the salutory effect on production. But this is not the prevailing view, nor is it the view that will prevail politically. The public is impressed with the weakness of unorganized workers in dealing with large employers—and workers, moreover, have many votes. Doubtless most economists would say, in principle, that collective action by labor violates the nature of a free economy but that an economy conforms only roughly to the model of a free system when corporations have as much power as they do in selling products and buying factors. Some offset to their power on the labor side seems, therefore, to be needed.

This is a persuasive view of the matter, but its logic should be fully sensed. It does not justify any expansion of union power that unions can achieve but only a degree of power sufficient to offset labor's weakness. The prevailing policy in the United States is still one of depending on markets to control the use of resources, and combinations of employers in the sale of products are unlawful. A power on the part of labor equivalent to what is condemned on the part of employers is clearly not called for by the logic that supports unionism. To apply this view of the problem is difficult, for it has many aspects. But it means very plainly that some limitation and regulation of union power should be supported by all believers in a generally unregimented, private-enterprise economy. Otherwise the menace of labor monopoly can be about as serious as that of industrial monopoly.

Output restriction; the closed shop; jurisdictional disputes. Some of the more specific features of union action also warrant public concern. Practices that promote inefficiency by limiting output, requiring unnecessary workers, and opposing improvements in methods deserve condemnation, but the public can expect real improvement in this area only through policies that deal effectively with depressions and unemployment and smooth the impact of economic change. Control by unions of the right to work, through closed-shop and union-shop arrangements, may have serious results. No union interest is as fundamental as the right of the individual to accept any available job for which he is qualified; arbitrary union action, unless restrained, may imperil this right.[11] Again, such developments as jurisdictional disputes represent an aspect of unionism that must be deplored, because quarrels of rival unions over particular jobs do violence to the social reason for permitting unions in the first place.

Specific criticisms along these lines, it should be recognized, sometimes reflect general antipathy toward unions and even toward the

[11] The word "right" is always dangerous, since there are quite unacceptable meanings in vogue that may be attached to it. All that is meant here is that the supreme economic interest of the individual is in being able to make use of his earning capacity. If union officials can deny the individual this opportunity, they are in position to take more from him than they can possibly give him. The right to refuse jobs that are not wanted is fundamental in a society that rejects slavery, but the so-called "right to strike" is on a quite different level. When he strikes, the worker neither gives up his job, since he stops working while claiming possession of it, nor does he act individually but through a type of cooperation that, in other circumstances, is called conspiracy. This is not to say that strikes are not a justifiable weapon but merely that the word "right" has a variety of implications.

struggle of ordinary workers toward a better position in the economy. But mainly the specific criticisms should be taken at face value, as expressing a prevalent conviction that unions have often been guilty of excesses and bad practices. The public as a whole, made up largely of common people, is intensely concerned over the economic progress of common people, and most members of society in all economic classes deem it a major goal to abolish poverty and lift low incomes to a higher level. But broad public concern over the division of income is not a concern over the successes of particular unions or the privileges of labor organizations. The policies of unions are mainly judged, and should be, by their effect on the size of the national income and its distribution among all low-income groups, whether organized or not, and by their bearing on the processes of the economy as a whole.

Review Questions

1. "It is possible that, in the typical situation, a craft union should be able to do more for its members than an industrial union, but an industrial union should be more effective in dealing with the problem of inequality." Develop this statement, bringing out the nature of these two forms of labor organization. What are the A.F. of L. and the C.I.O.?

2. "If unions are to be viewed as means of distribution reform, the problem of distribution must be viewed broadly." Why?

3. What is meant by collective bargaining? Distinguish the leading methods of unions by which they try to increase their effectiveness in the labor market.

4. Distinguish the "direct" and "indirect" methods employed by government in improving the economic position of labor and name leading policies which exemplify them.

5. Show carefully that, in analyzing the effects of unions on the distribution of income, it is important to distinguish the raising of wages (a) within a bargaining area and (b) beyond that area.

6. "The nature of the labor market is such as to place labor, under a system of individual bargaining, at a disadvantage." Develop this statement.

7. "The weak bargaining position of individual workers may explain why they will accept less than they are worth; it does not explain why employers will actually pay less." Develop this point. What explanation does the second clause require?

8. "When employers proceed on the assumption that their hiring of workers affects the wage rates they pay, they are likely to pay labor less than it is worth to them. In this situation, some forcing up of wages may be consistent even with an increase in the number of workers hired." Explain both sentences.

9. "The roughness of employer calculations, the hesitancy of producers to disturb market relationships, the malajustments caused by booms and depression, all create some latitude, of temporary significance, for increasing wages at the expense of profits." Develop these points.

10. Distinguish several situations in which "abnormal" profits seem to call for an advance in wages and in which they do not.

11. Explain clearly (a) the readjustments that wage advances beyond the bargaining area are likely to cause and (b) the effects upon distribution, especially the indirect effects.

12. "If wage increases do not come out of profits, unions naturally do not want them." Consider this view.

13. Show the relation between union types and the elasticity of demand for labor, as wages are raised.

14. What differences, if any, are there between unions and minimum-wage laws, in their purposes and effects? If some workers are incapable of earning enough to enable them to live decently, does it seem to you desirable to set a legal minimum on a "living-wage" basis? Consider the pros and cons.

15. "Over a quarter century, longshoremen pushed their wages up from 35 cents to $1.10 an hour. This shows what unions can accomplish for all labor." Appraise this statement in light of the statistics of distribution and their known behavior.

16. "The main consideration that should guide employers in adjusting wages is that they should put into the pockets of workers enough money to purchase the product of industry." Analyze this view carefully.

17. Review briefly the theory of unemployment according to which it is desirable to transfer income from profits to wages.

18. Distinguish several reasons for wanting to reduce working hours. Evaluate them.

19. A prominent manufacturer said, in effect, during the 1930s: "With smaller sales, I have solved my unemployment problem by reducing the working week from 40 hours to 30. Now as many workers are absorbed as before the depression. I pay the same weekly wage, but, despite this, my costs have not risen, for I find that as much is done in 30 hours as in 40." Show conclusively, as a matter of arithmetic, the inconsistency of these statements.

20. Broadly conceived, what does improvement of working conditions involve? Why may unions be more effective in dealing with hours and working conditions than with wages?

21. "The logic of permitting unions in a freely organized economy does not justify permitting them unlimited strength or unlimited freedom in their practices." Develop the point.

22. "Jurisdictional disputes may be inherent in labor organization, but they serve ends unrelated to the public interest in the betterment of labor's position."

23. A musician's union insists, when an orchestra concert is broadcast by both the regular and frequency-modulation processes, that a second orchestra be hired to stand by. What social problem is the basis of such a union policy? What do you think of this method of handling it? Explain.

24. What are the leading considerations in the closed-shop issue? What is your view regarding it? What is meant by saying that if there is a closed shop, there should be an open union?

- 28 -

The Basis of
Property Incomes

U<small>P</small> TO this point problems of income and inequality
have been approached mainly from the side of labor, as both the source
and recipient of the major part of total income. The possibility of expanding labor's share by cutting directly into other incomes has been
examined. Now attention is shifted to these other incomes.

While the return from wealth amounts ordinarily to no more than
one fourth, perhaps no more than one fifth, of total income, it accounts
for a major part of the very large incomes and is thus the conspicuous
element in inequality. From data in Chapter 24, it appears that wages
and salaries, incomes of hired employees, amount typically to two thirds
of total income. But in two selected years—the figures for 1929 and 1935
being combined—these returns from labor accounted for only 35 percent of the incomes between $10,000 and $25,000, 18 percent of those
between $50,000 and $100,000, 10 percent of those between $100,000
and $500,000, and 1.5 percent of those above $1,000,000.[1] While many
high salaries go to corporation executives and moving-picture actors
and directors, the bulk of the large incomes derives from wealth.

It would be a mistake, however, to think of the income from wealth
as going only to people with large incomes. Numerous persons of small
means, in particular retired workers, widows, and orphaned children,
derive modest incomes from property. Such persons, if they are to be
economically independent and avoid support by relatives, friends, or
the state, must depend on income in the form of interest, dividends, and
rentals, and on the gradual liquidation and use of their wealth. Endowed institutions, such as schools and hospitals, also depend on income
from wealth. So, to a considerable extent, do insurance companies.

[1] These percentages recognize capital gains as income from wealth—a large element in
1929.

Organization of analysis. Analysis of income from property is unavoidably somewhat complex. It is first of all necessary to see that the degree of inequality from this source, with a given aggregate of wealth, depends (1) on the rate of return from it and (2) on the way in which the ownership of the wealth itself is distributed. Inequality would thus be reduced either (1) with a fall in the rate at which wealth yields income or (2) with a more even spreading of the ownership of wealth among the people. Most of our discussion will deal with the rate of return, but the final section of the following chapter will deal with the distribution of wealth.

To analyze the rate of return from wealth, it is necessary to combine two classifications which cut across each other. The *first* of these rests on the distinction between the *two basic types of productive wealth,* wealth of natural origin and wealth produced by man. The *second* distinguishes the *forms in which incomes are received.* There are certain forms which are definite and prearranged, as when a service is provided by one person and hired by another at a stated rate of payment. These we may refer to conveniently as *contractual.* Then there is the form of income that is *residual,* consisting of what is left to the employer when all contractual payments have been made. These two classifications must be combined in our analysis, because incomes from both kinds of wealth are received in both forms.

In dealing with the first classification, the different *types of wealth,* attention will center in part on the physical things—land, buildings, machines, inventories, and so on—and on how the supplies of them affect the values of their services. Analysis of the income from land can proceed altogether in this channel, since we need not inquire into the origin of natural resources. When we turn to capital goods, however, the matter of origin complicates the problem. We must again consider the service of saving and investing, recognize capital as well as capital goods, and look into the role of capitalists and enterprisers to understand the basis of their incomes.

As to the second classification, while the *forms* in which property incomes are received do not correspond to the kinds of wealth, they are related somewhat to the kinds of productive services. In particular, they are related to the division of risk and responsibility among the participants in a project. Income received in the *residual* form—the sum remaining after all expenses, including contractual income payments, are met—is called *business profits.* The recipients of profits are the *enterprisers,* or *entrepreneurs,* who are the prime responsibility takers. The contractual returns from wealth appear in two forms, rent and interest. When the physical item of wealth is owned by one person and used by another, the return for its use is called *rent*. When one person lends money to another, enabling the borrower to become the owner of the desired wealth, the return from the loan (a percentage of the principal sum) is called *interest*.

As owners of wealth used in production, enterprisers are also *capitalists* and *landlords*. But there are capitalists and landlords who are not enterprisers, at least not in a significant degree, who merely make wealth available through lending and leasing it. A part of business profits— the part which equals the return the enterpriser could get from his labor and wealth if he hired them out on a contractual basis—is sometimes spoken of as *implicit* wages, rent, and interest. The rest of business profit, the part that is the distinctive return for the entrepreneurial function, is then called *pure profit*.

Services of labor, land, and capital may be rewarded either residually or contractually. In dealing with labor, we said little about income in residual form, since we were interested mainly in ordinary wages and salaries. But we noted, in examining income statistics (Chapter 24), that the business profit of *unincorporated* firms is largely a return for labor services. The profits of *incorporated* firms, on the other hand, are mainly property income, because salaries have been deducted for those stockholders who are in the employ of the company. The profits of corporations may either be distributed to the owners as *dividends* or retained in the business and represented by *surplus*. In either case they benefit the stockholder; either he gets a money return or his equity is expanded.

While both kinds of wealth, natural and man-made, yield incomes in both forms, residual and contractual, certain differences should be noted. There is more renting of land, or of land plus buildings, than there is of capital goods apart from buildings. There is much renting of land for farming and mining and for a variety of urban uses, but land is also widely owned by the enterprises using it, so that the return from natural wealth becomes a part of business profits. Capital goods, in their characteristic form of productive plant and equipment and stocks of materials and goods in process, are commonly owned by the firms that use them, and thus they yield a return in the profit, rather than the rental, form. As exceptions, there are a few instances of equipment rentals, as in the supplying of shoe-manufacturing machines through lease by the United Shoe Machinery Company and of calculating devices by International Business Machines. During the war much government-owned equipment, as well as factory buildings, was leased to private users. There is also some renting of durable consumers' goods, for instance, pianos, sewing machines, and automobiles. Rentals are usually paid on a time basis, but sometimes the basis is the amount of product derived from rented property. Then the rental is called a *royalty*. Coal land, for instance, is rented on a royalty basis.

The distinction between contractual and residual incomes implies that the one is highly certain, the other highly uncertain. This, on the whole is true, but it needs some qualifying. The risks of producing goods are not borne wholly by the enterpriser, and incomes which may seem definite reflect varying elements of uncertainty. Wage, interest, and rental payments may not be made as agreed on. The use of services may be terminated abruptly, with loss to the persons providing them—perhaps great loss as any unemployed worker knows. In his relation to his employees, the employer takes the greatest risk when he guarantees a full annual salary and the least risk when he hires labor at a piece rate and pays only for each small unit of service that he gets. The tenant farmer may pay a fixed sum of money for the farm he uses but is more likely to pay a third or a half of the crop, causing the owner's rental to vary with the volume of output and the prices it brings. Lenders may enjoy a practically certain interest return or may face real danger of loss of interest and even of principal. These variations alter, but do not change fundamentally, the relation between enterprisers and those from whom they buy productive service.

The treatment of property incomes extends through two chapters. In this chapter the emphasis is on the sources of the incomes—the nature of the services performed and the factors governing the return for them. Since the incomes from wealth are often attacked, we shall view them critically and consider their justification from the social standpoint. In the following chapter, attention will center on the profit and interest forms of income, on the relation between the value of wealth and the income from it, and on the distribution of wealth.

Income Characteristics of Land and Capital Goods

Is it really necessary, in explaining property incomes, to deal separately with natural and man-made wealth? Are there important differences between them that affect the values of their services? Certainly to the enterpriser who is starting a farm, a factory, or a store, land and capital goods appear in about the same light. He acquires them in the same way, governed by the primary aim of making each item of them contribute to his net return. Nevertheless, underneath the business calculations there are differences that are vital in explaining incomes and in appraising them from the social viewpoint.

We shall not care in this section whether income is received in the form of rent, interest, or profits. Moreover, we shall ignore the uncertainty factor. Let us simply think of land and capital goods, the physical items of each, working together with labor in production. Each contributes to the product, and its service has a certain value. It is this service value that concerns us, and we may assume, if we wish, that the market actually gives each factor a return that measures its contribution. We are interested in relating this return, or service value, to the special features possessed by natural and man-made wealth.[2]

For convenience of statement, we need some labels. Accordingly, we shall speak of *land rent* and *capital-goods rent*. The word *rent* will be used not because a return in the rental form is implied but because we are thinking of the service value of physical units of wealth. The share in the product that can be credited to all items of wealth is a *gross* rent. The net return to the owners may be a smaller sum.

Differences in nature of supply. As to the *demands* for their services —the reason why they command a return—land and capital goods may be treated together, along with labor. All that needs to be said was said in Chapter 26. All factors of production are employed and paid for on the basis of the estimated value of their services, and the general basis of this estimate is the marginal value product, as it has been explained. As relatively more of a factor is used under given conditions, its marginal product declines and, as a matter of theoretical possibility, can become zero.

Differences that bear on the service values of land and capital goods have their basis on the *supply* side of the market. These differences arise from the fact that capital goods are produced, and land is not. Two consequences of this fact have important effects: (1) a smaller part of capital-goods rent than of land rent ordinarily can be counted by the owners as net income; (2) income from land reflects extremes of scarcity and abundance, in particular uses, which are not present in the case of man-made wealth. We shall now examine both types of wealth from these two standpoints.

Capital goods

Suppose the item of wealth we are interested in is a machine to be used in a factory. This machine will cost $10,000 and can be expected to last 10 years, with negligible salvage value when it is retired. Under these assumptions it will be installed, we can be sure, only if there is a

---

[2] In explanations of property incomes, the return to capital is commonly analyzed with little regard for the physical wealth in which it is invested. With respect to their place in production, however, all forms of wealth are alike. The return to capital has its basis in the relation of machines and structures to the gross product, just as land rent has its basis in the relation of natural resources to the gross product.

good prospect that it will add at least $1000 a year to the value of the product (or bring equivalent savings in the use of other factors). Otherwise it would plainly represent a misuse of the labor and other resources that went into it. If the machine is not to be installed, it will not, in the typical case, be produced at all, and these resources will be available for some other use. Being of human origin, its existence is subject to control, and it will be produced and installed only if the right conditions are in prospect.

It is apparent, then, that a substantial part of the service value of capital goods is not net income to the owner. Probably the machine will not be installed for the sake of a gross return of $1000; perhaps the prospective gross rent will need to be $1500 or $2000—a matter we shall go into below. But even with a margin of net return, a large part of the contribution of capital goods is absorbed by their own cost, the cost of the resources that have gone into them.

It is also apparent that the adaptability of the supply of capital goods must influence the relative return from the different forms they take and the different industries in which they are used. The supply of capital goods of any type can be expanded whenever the prospective return is high enough to make expansion attractive. Whether the necessary minimum in the foregoing example is a gross rental of $1000 or $2000 or some other figure, the prospect of more than that minimum will cause more of those machines to be produced and used. Thus the return cannot go very high, or stay high very long. Similarly, machines yielding less than the minimum will not be replaced as they wear out, and very low returns will thus not continue to prevail. If artificial obstacles to expansion and contraction are absent, a strong tendency toward uniformity of return prevails in the case of man-made wealth.[3]

As we saw in our earlier discussion of the expansion and contraction of plant capacity, this tendency is strictly of a long-run character. It requires time to expand plant and equipment in a field of profitable use; it takes still longer to retire it when unprofitable, if it is physically quite durable. Thus the return from capital goods may vary considerably from any normal figure. If monopoly power prevents expansion or if government, as in the public-utility field, controls reduction of service, adjustments of supply are still more impeded. Certainly wide variations in the return from capital goods are to be expected. But there is present nevertheless a pull toward uniformity for which no counterpart appears in the case of natural wealth.

---

[3] Gross rentals tend toward uniformity in the sense that they first need to cover the principal sum invested during the life of the equipment, and then any net remainder tends to be the same percent of the investment, allowance being made for differences in risk.

Natural wealth in contrast with capital goods

Such distinctive features as the income from land displays grow out of the freedom of its supply from human control. The earth, with its variety of soil and climate, its mountains, deserts, and fertile plains, its streams and broad expanses of water, is simply here, whether use is made of it or not. No prospect of return called it into being, and it may or may not be used productively. Great areas of it are not used at all. To be used, land need yield no minimum rent but need only give to the labor that is applied to it a chance to earn an acceptable minimum return. Some land, because it is fertile for agriculture or rich with minerals or rightly situated to provide urban building sites, receives the impact of a high demand. It adds greatly to production, and its rental value is high. But no great equalizing force is set in motion by these disparities of return, for the amounts of different types of land cannot be adjusted to the demands.

This is the general difference between land and capital goods, but it can be overstated. Land is nature's gift, but man assists in making it available. Before serving its purpose, land may have to be cleared of stumps or graded or drained or irrigated. Minerals have to be discovered, often only after extensive prospecting effort. Special transport facilities may be needed to make land accessible.[4] Governmental assistance is necessary in defining and protecting property rights. To the extent of such outlays, land resembles capital goods. There must be some minimum prospective rental value to justify the investment; and the making of such investments where the return is especially good has a leveling effect on rents.

There is also some leveling influence on rentals arising from the shifting of land from one use to another. Within limits, agricultural land may be changed over from low-paying to high-paying crops, and similar changes in land use can be made within urban areas. But despite all of these qualifications, the essential difference between land and capital goods still stands. The basic conditions of soil and climate cannot be created for farming; minerals cannot be injected into the earth for mining; additional lots cannot be set down in the heart of cities as sites for more buildings.

From what has been said, the relationship between the gross rent from land and the net income to its owners can be inferred readily. The

[4] Investment in transportation may be regarded as, in part, investment in land, if the only way in which the transportation can be made to pay is by capturing some of the rent from benefited land. This may be done by giving part of this benefited land to the transport agency, as in the subsidizing of American railroads in the West or by assessing land owners to defray part of the cost of the agency.

value of land service reflects primarily nature's contribution to production. To the extent that it does, there is no offsetting cost, as in the case of man-made goods. Thus the gross is net. But in so far as other resources have been expended in making land available for use, part of the return must be credited to them rather than to nature. Where such effort has taken the form of stumping and grading, however, the result is permanent, and the outlay can be spread over an indefinitely long period.

At the same time, nature's contribution may not be durable and permanent, and appropriate allowance must be made for this fact in computing net income. In agriculture, continuous cropping wears out the soil, and considerable expenditure is necessary to keep it near its original fertility. In the extraction of minerals there is no possibility of maintaining the original resource, and a depletion charge is recognized in calculating net income. However, the full rental, before this deduction, is income in the sense that the depletion charge, unlike the depreciation of capital goods, is not a cost reflecting prior productive activity. No initial cost is incurred, as when machines are installed.

Taxes on land are, to the taxpayer, a deduction from rental value; from the social standpoint, they may either represent costs to government in serving landowners or a division with government of part of the net return and, through government, with society as a whole. The latter, as we shall see, is the objective of those who advocate particularly heavy taxes on land and the income it yields.

Income from Land as a Distributive Share

Income statistics are not very helpful in disclosing the return from natural resources. The $7.3 billion of rental income to individuals in the national income of the United States in 1947 include not only the rental return from land but also from buildings and other produced wealth that yields income in rental form. This income includes the imputed rental value of owner-occupied homes and the land on which they stand, and also royalties from patents and copyrights. But it does not cover the return from land that is included in the business profits from farms, mines, and oil wells, or of corporations operating city real estate such as apartment houses and office buildings, which often stand on very valuable land. It would be much more hazardous to estimate the natural-resource element than the labor element in the national income.

But, though elusive statistically, income from land is fairly free from theoretical difficulties that need concern us. Relative fixity of the supply of land means that the return from it is largely explained by the general theory of factor valuation, as we have studied it. Indeed, in Chapter 26, the effect on land rent of an expanding agricultural population was set forth in a hypothetical case.[5] It is sufficient here (1) to examine somewhat farther the relation of land rent to the expanding use of land and (2) to take account of the serious attack that has been made, from the social standpoint, on the place of landowners in the division of income.

Land rent and land use

When pioneers in small numbers first enter an extensive unoccupied area, land yields no rent. Such was the case when settlers penetrated the Mississippi Valley a century and a half ago. The productive power of the land may be unequaled, but even the best grade of land is valueless if it is not scarce. In this situation, output would not be reduced if some of the land were wiped out of existence, nor increased if more of it were added. In other words, while it is productive in a physical sense, it lacks marginal productivity. All the labor available for working it can be employed without pushing production beyond the point of diminishing returns—the point at which the output from applied factors is at a maximum. In this condition, the entire output normally goes to labor and the owners of capital goods, with nothing for landowners.

But presently, as population grows, pressure develops on the best grade of land, and the right to use particular pieces of it acquires importance. This developing scarcity of land is apparent in the price of goods produced on it. These products rise in price in comparison with the cost of labor and other factors applied to land. As the revenue becomes more than sufficient to compensate labor and other applied factors, it becomes worth something to own the land on which to employ them. A segment of income arises that measures the value of the service of the land. If land is used by the owner, this income is kept by him as part of his residual return. If land is worked by a tenant, competition, if present, compels him to pay a corresponding rental to the owner. Land rent rests on this basis, whether land is used for agriculture, mining, or building sites.

Intensive and extensive expansion of land use. When good land becomes scarce and its services acquire value, the use of land is expanded in two ways, intensively and extensively. Land is used *intensively* when the application of labor and capital to it carries its use beyond the point of diminishing returns, so that the output per unit from the applied factors declines. These factors can logically receive no more than their marginal revenue product, so it pays to intensify the use of land as long

[5] See pp. 686–692.

as the marginal revenue product is sufficient to cover the return that labor and capital are getting in other uses. With land used more intensively on this basis, the differential widens between the total revenue and the amount that goes to the applied factors. It is in this manner, as we saw in Chapter 26, that land rent increases as population grows, bringing expansion of demand for the products into which land enters and providing more labor to work the land. In agriculture more intensive use of land is manifest in the kinds of products produced as well as in the methods of cultivation used. In urban activities it appears in the size of buildings and the number of people employed in given areas.

Land is said to be used more *extensively* when additional areas are brought into use. When the best land becomes scarce, labor and capital are applied to land that is inferior with respect to fertility, location, mineral content, and other relevant features. To say that land is inferior is to say that, when used to the very best advantage, more of the applied factors are required to yield a given output—including, of course, the resources used in getting the product to market when land is inferior through being remote. When products sell for more than enough to compensate the labor and capital used on the best land, and thus yield the owner a rental, they bring sufficient revenue to compensate labor and capital at the same rate on somewhat inferior land. Then inferior land is worth using, and the higher the prices of products and the greater the rentals from the best land, the poorer the land it pays to use.

Thus several developments proceed together: with increasing demand for the products of land, better land is used more intensively, pushing lower the margin of its use, and types of land are brought into use that are less and less desirable with respect to their qualities and their location. Rent is derived in varying degrees from all the grades of land in use except the very worst.

Marginal and submarginal use of land. The last statement assumes that the use of land is not extended to an uneconomic degree. Ideally, the poorest land in use yields a product that gives the applied factors as great a return as they can get on better land. The difference lies only in the absence of rent. Land on which labor and capital barely get their normal return is known as *marginal* or *no-rent* land. The output from applied factors on marginal land, without going beyond the point of diminishing returns, equals their output at the intensive margin on better land.

The theoretical goal in using land is to *equalize the marginal return* from the applied factors on all land. In this way the resources of the country yield the largest total product. When labor and capital are used on this basis, any transfer of them from one use to another reduces output more in the old use than it expands output in the new use. Undoubtedly, with natural resources what they are, much land would not be used at all, if this principle were fully applied. One should never suppose that it is wasteful, from the social standpoint, to have considerable unused land.

This ideal, however, is never realized. Much labor and capital are employed over wide land areas where they cannot earn a normal rate of return. Such areas are called *submarginal*. On them the rent is, in a sense, negative. Submarginal-land use may be explained in various ways. There is a large speculative element in opening up new areas, and settlers pour in with an enthusiasm that is not justified by the results. Or resources become exhausted and the occupants fail to depart. The continuing use of submarginal land is striking evidence of the immobility of labor.

These submarginal operations undoubtedly account for a level of national income appreciably below the maximum that would be possible. They account, also, for some of the most depressed sectors in the distribution of national income, notably in certain impoverished farming and mining areas.[6] To some extent, as through the Rural Resettlement Administration, government has taken steps to overcome the existing immobility. But doubtless the greatest progress will come through success in maintaining a high general level of prosperity, since the will to leave backward areas is weakened by the danger of unemployment in higher income industrial areas.

Social justification of land rent

It is one thing to explain land rent but quite another to justify it as a source of private income. Its origin is no more mysterious than the origin of wages, because all resources that aid production and are scarce provide the same reason for payment for their services. But private receipt of land rent accounts for an aspect of inequality that has often been attacked as indefensible. It is an aspect, moreover, that may be extremely important. In agricultural countries where land is intensively worked by nonowning peasants or share croppers, and half or more of

---

[6] Colin Clark, in his *The Conditions of Economic Progress*, concludes that agricultural output per male worker in New Zealand is more than three times as high as in the United States and more than twice as high as in Australia, even though for all fields of production the United States and New Zealand are on about the same level. He finds the explanation in the fact that in newly settled countries only the better rural opportunities have been exploited. It also seems clear that in the United States, especially in the rural South, many persons continue activities of excessively low productivity which reflect a bad allocation of resources. Doubtless much use of land that is submarginal from a national standpoint actually yields rent to the owners, because of locally depressed wage rates.

the crop goes to absentee landlords, land rent is the prime source of economic unrest. A large fraction of the world's population is in this situation. It is found in parts of the United States, but here the most striking rental incomes, in an analysis of inequality, are probably those from mineral resources and centrally located land in large cities. Much has been written on the subject, and one significant movement, promoting the so-called "Single-Tax" program, has sought to eliminate private income from land.

Theory and program of land reform. Niceties of logic are not necessary to support an attempt by masses of people to better their economic position. But in this particular case, the attack is supported by a theory worthy of attention. The argument runs: (1) that private receipt of land rent does not contribute to the effective working of the economy and (2) that society as a whole has a better claim than any individual to income from land. The first point rests on the familiar functional view of income, that its role is not merely to satisfy wants but also to provide inducements to production. Wages are an incentive to work and the source of strength to work. Income from man-made wealth may be defended as necessary to get people to provide it. But land, on the other hand, is not the result of human action nor is it obsessed with a reluctance to give forth its services so that inducements are necessary to evoke them. Its capacity for service, arising from its location, fertility, and mineral content, is there for the using; nothing is added by the fact that someone owns it and says it may be used.

Not only is nothing accomplished by paying owners for the services of land, but, the argument runs, the public collectively has a better claim to the income. This conclusion may be reached on the general grounds, already familiar, that inequality is bad per se unless there is good reason for it. The receipt of private income from land by its fortunate owners is thus condemned by the very lack of any functional relation to the working of the economy. But the conclusion receives positive support from the explanation of the origin of rent, as just presented. It is the growth of population, the expansion of society, that creates the demand for the products and services of land and brings about the scarcity which gives land services their value. Society, it is argued, should receive the income for which it is responsible.

But how can land rent be diverted to the public as a whole? One way would be to *nationalize the land* so that government, deriving the income from it, could use it for the common good. Without going to this extreme, advocates of the *Single-Tax program* would retain private ownership but would subject the income from land to a tax that would take all, or practically all, of it. The name "single tax" derives from the supposition that, if such a tax became effective, it would support government fully, and other taxes could be discarded.

Grounds for questioning proposed reform. In appraising this attitude toward land rent, many persons would agree that private enjoyment of income from natural resources stands on more vulnerable grounds than do incomes from resources of human origin. Many who are not Single Taxers would grant the reasonableness of applying heavier taxes to land than to the buildings and improvements on land. Many conservative Americans have advocated reform in the relation of landlords and tenants in China, Italy, Greece, and other countries. But the proposal of full nationalization raises the broad issue of socialism and invites an opposition that goes beyond the limits of the present discussion. The idea of taxing away the full economic rent of land, within the structure of the present society, suggests a number of critical considerations that are pertinent here.

For one thing, it may properly be urged that land rent is not an altogether functionless type of income. We have seen that human effort often plays a part in giving land its useful qualities. Part of the return from land, a not easily separable part, is required to induce the development of land. Moreover, if land is to be administered wisely, with careful maintenance of soil fertility, harvesting of timber, and extraction of minerals, it should be in charge of persons who have a continuing stake in it and want to conserve it. We have not done well in this country in handling this problem, but it can probably be agreed that the kind of motivation characteristic of tenants, who have no stake in maintaining future values, should not be encouraged.

We should also bear in mind that the value of land services is part of the whole scheme of values by which resources are assigned to their places in production—a function of values quite distinct from the calling forth of services. It would be difficult for this system of control to operate if government took in taxes the entire return that leads landowners to seek the best uses for their land.

On grounds of equity it is also urged that present investments in land were made in good faith, and that now to take the rents which have developed would be as objectionable as any confiscation of honestly acquired property. This objection would, of course, not apply to future expansion of rentals which are not now reflected in property values.

Finally it should be observed that there are other incomes, apart from land rent, which arise from the pressure of social demand and which are not necessary in causing productive services to be performed. Indeed much income from personal services exceeds the minimum necessary to make them available. As a basis for distribution reform, the reasoning applied to land could well have broader application.

Review Questions

1. "Wealth is more important as a source of inequality than the total income from it may suggest." What is meant?

2. "Incomes from both natural and man-made wealth may be received in the rent, interest, or profit form." Explain and illustrate.

3. "The positive reason for a return from capital goods or land is no different from the reason in the case of labor. The same general theory of factor valuation applies." Explain.

4. Capital goods and land differ (a) in the relation between gross and net rent from them; (b) in the tendency they reveal toward uniformity of return. Explain. Are there qualifications?

5. In some respects the supply of land can be altered in response to demand. How? How, then, can land be distinguished from capital goods? When the Dutch go to great expense to recover portions of the Zuyder Zee for agriculture, would you describe the result as land or as a capital good? Explain.

6. Explain the origin of land rent. Show that the same conditions account (a) for the appearance of a rental return from good land and (b) for the pushing lower of the intensive and extensive margins of cultivation.

7. What is submarginal land, and what problem does it present?

8. Develop and evaluate the argument that the income from natural resources should be appropriated by society as a whole.

9. "Payments for land use may not perform the social function of calling forth and sustaining an economic service, but they do perform the function of assigning land to its best uses." Explain carefully what this statement means. Can it ever be applied to labor as well as to land?

The Services of Capital and Capitalists

In discussing the income from land, we considered two questions: (1) How does income arise in the case of a resource of nonhuman origin which is available in the absence of income? (2) Is society justified in assigning part of its total income to the individuals who happen to own land? In considering the income from capital goods, we also face these problems of explanation and justification, but the questions to be answered are not quite the same.

As with land, no one doubts that capital goods, in the form of structures, equipment, and inventories, have an important place in production. But capital goods are of human origin, so income must be considered from the incentives standpoint, as an inducement to provide capital goods.

But mention of incentives raises the question: Incentives to whom? Here we get into the matter of social justification, as well as of explanation, and encounter one of the main challenges of the arrangements that prevail under capitalism. Certainly, the socialist agrees, machines are productive and must somehow be accumulated. But what is a machine, and where does it come from? The traditional socialist answer has been this, that a machine is simply the embodiment of the labor and materials that went into its production, and of the services of prior machines of like origin. Machines, structures, and inventories, are merely "congealed land and labor," so that the productivity of the machine is nothing more than the indirect productivity of the primary factors of production.

In this socialist view of capitalistic production, there is no place for capital and capitalists. They have no function—hence no claim to income. So at this point, the first question we must consider arises. Granting the productive service of capital goods, what, if anything, is the role of the people who own them and get income from them? To answer this question, we shall center attention on the capital invested in capital goods and on the persons who provide it (1) as capitalists in the strict sense and (2) as capitalist-entrepreneurs who take the risk that investment entails. To understand the forces which govern interest and profit, one must first look into the services for which these incomes are received.

The carrying function of capital

The nature and origin of capital were explained in Part II (Chapter 6) in analyzing the bases of productive power. Our present task is to adapt this earlier treatment to the problem of income. It is convenient to consider first the service of capital without the presence of investment risk—that is, the role of the capitalist as such. Then the risk element will be introduced, and the capitalist will be viewed also as an enterpriser.

There can be no question that capital has a distinct role in production. The socialists are right, of course, in saying that the use of capital goods involves the indirect use of labor and materials, but capitalistic production involves more than that: it requires saving and investing, in the formation of capital, and it requires that wealth be allowed to remain in productive use and not be used up in consumption. The capitalistic process requires *ownership through time*, which we may call the carrying function.

Consider a machine installed in a factory to produce shoes. The labor and materials that go into the machine may properly be thought of as entering indirectly into the shoes that the machine helps to turn out. But this indirect process is not instantaneous. The labor and materials enter into the machine in one year, and their emergence as shoes takes place during a long series of ensuing years or until the machine is retired from use.

How does it happen that labor and materials come to be used in this way? We can be sure it is not because a group of workers say: "Let us produce shoes and sell them. But because we must have machines to produce shoes efficiently, let us first devote a year or two to making the machines." Merely as workers, and not as capitalists, they cannot do this, because, as workers, they have to have income during the period in which they are making the machines. It is necessary that someone provide capital, consisting of funds diverted from possible current consumption, to pay for the labor of these workers, and for the materials also, at the time the machines are made. It is necessary that this capital remain tied up in the machines during their period of use in producing shoes.[7]

What has been said of machines and other durable capital goods is equally true of the working or circulating capital of production, which is largely tied up in inventories, or stocks of materials, supplies, goods in process, and finished products awaiting sale. Perhaps the first investment in the leather for the shoes was made when feed was bought for the animals that would supply the leather. Over a long period funds were expended at successive stages in processing the leather, funds which provided current income to workers and others and which would not be recovered finally until the shoes were sold. Viewed in cross section, this process is revealed in the billions of dollars in inventories present in all fields and stages of production. In principle, this case is like that of the machines. In both situations, resources are used in production well in advance of the completion of the final product, and the necessary current payments for these resources are made, we say, by investing capital.

The place of capital and of capitalists may seem, to the uninformed, to be merely a money phenomenon in a pecuniary, or acquisitive, so-

[7] The whole capital does not remain tied up for the full period. As receipts from the sale of shoes cover depreciation, the invested capital is being returned to the owners in installments. This is what is meant by covering depreciation cost. If, however, the shoe factory is to continue in operation, the funds so recovered will have to be invested in new machines to replace the old ones. Funds of capital ordinarily remain in existence, despite the disappearance of the particular forms of wealth in which they are invested, but it is not inevitable that they should. Providing replacements is thus viewed as part of gross saving and gross investment, though not as part of net saving and net investment.

ciety. Actually, the essence of their role is in diverting productive services into those methods of production that require buildings, equipment, and stocks of goods. This diversion means that current outlays must be made with an eye to future returns. From the standpoint of ordinary workers, it is an integral part of their use of modern methods. To be assured of getting capital and thus of using modern methods, they may be wise in conceding the capitalist the right not only to recover his principal which has been spent for the labor and other resources embodied in capital goods, but to get a moderate return beside.

Service *versus* **return from service.** To say, however, that capitalists perform a service, and that they may reasonably be paid for it, is not to say necessarily that this is the best arrangement or, even under capitalism, the inevitable arrangement. The carrying function may be performed collectively as under socialism, with the people saving, very likely, in a diffused and involuntary way. The service is there, but no private capitalist has a claim to an income from it. But even if private capitalists perform it, there is still the question whether it requires a reward. We shall consider this question after we have examined the risk-taking role of capital.

The uncertainty-bearing function of capitalist-entrepreneurs

The carrying function implies no uncertainty regarding the outcome of the productive process. It implies simply that resources are committed to production and are paid for well before the appearance of the final product. Now we shall consider the equally important fact that the outcome usually involves many elements of uncertainty. Postponement of return is accompanied by uncertainty of return. There is not only waiting; there are also risks.[8]

In part the uncertainties are of a *physical* nature. The amount and the quality of product that a given outlay of resources will yield can be foretold only roughly—or even only within wide limits, as in the case of mining. In part the uncertainties are of a *market* character. Demand and sales are likely to vary widely, as are the prices that must be paid for labor and materials. Competitors may introduce new methods of production which necessitate the scrapping of equipment before it has yielded its expected life of service.

It is conceivable that enterprises should be organized in such a way that all participants, workers as well as capitalists, should depend for their return on the varying product and revenue. It is in this way that farm operators are paid for their labor. In this way, all would share in

---

[8] Risk and uncertainty are not quite equivalent terms in economics, but since we shall not use the distinction in this connection, we shall use the words interchangeably.

the enterprise function. But since the biggest risk is in connection with fixed investment, which may be lost, a full application of this idea would require that the workers and others who produce buildings and equipment would not be paid outright for them but would wait for their return during the period that these facilities are in service.

Except within narrow limits, such an arrangement would not be feasible. Workers who could not wait long for their return, even if it were certain, could not wait for an uncertain return. In most projects, at least new ones, the uncertainties are too great to be borne by persons who do not have substantial reserves—that is, who lack capital. Undoubtedly most suppliers of productive services prefer a definite, as well as an early, return from the services they render. Undoubtedly they prefer a certain return even if it proves to be somewhat less, on the average, than they would get by sharing in the uncertain final proceeds. In other words, they are probably willing to concede something to the persons who take the risks; though, again, the question remains as to whether they need to.

Enterprisers, one of whose functions is to risk capital in production, pay definite wage rates for labor, definite prices for materials and for the durable equipment in which labor and materials are embodied, perhaps definite interest rates for some of the capital they use and definite rentals for some items of physical wealth. These commitments, often made long in advance of the sale of the resulting product, may or may not be covered by receipts. The enterpriser provides the buffer, or cushion, between the uncertain final revenue and the returns to factors that are paid on a contractual basis. This is the essence of the risk-taking side of enterprise. The other side, involving the personal service of the enterpriser in supplying initiative and control, will be recognized in the next chapter in the discussion of profits.

Distribution of risks under capitalism. Though perhaps already apparent, it should be emphasized that entrepreneurial risk bearing is necessarily a function of capital. There are writers who speak of the enterpriser merely as one who initiates projects and makes decisions, hiring the services of labor and of wealth. It has even been suggested that it would be as logical for labor to hire capital as for capital to hire labor. But this view is not tenable, since responsible hiring means that the employer must make good on his payments even though conditions turn against him. If the bearing of risks is to mean anything, it must mean that productive factors are actually bought and paid for before revenue is known, or that contracts are entered into which carry substantial guarantees. These payments cannot wait for the final sale of product, and they can depend upon it only in part. They are to be made anyway, else the risk is not actually assumed. The practical difference between contractual and residual returns rests on the ability of those who take the residual position to make good on the contractual payments. For this, considerable capital is necessary in the buffer, or entrepreneurial, position.

It may also be apparent, though deserving of emphasis, that entrepreneur-capitalists do not shoulder all, or nearly all, the burden of risk in our society. There is still the risk of unemployment for hired factors and the interruption of income that it entails. Indeed, workers face a graver risk of unemployment with wages held at definite rates than would be present if they depended for their return on a share in the uncertain revenue from sales. There would then be much less reason to lay them off. But it is certainly true of employed workers that their incomes vary much less than business profits do. And as between good and bad years the aggregate earnings of employees, both those who are working and those who are not, fluctuate less than aggregate profits.

Determinants of Income for the Services of Capital

There can be no doubt that capital assists production in ways that cannot be credited to the labor and materials in capital goods. The saving and investing of capital funds make possible the time-consuming capitalistic process of production, and capital shoulders the risks of enterprise in a special way. But the presence of services does not mean necessarily that they have to be paid for and that capitalists must receive an income from them. They may be so readily and abundantly supplied as to be free. If capital does in fact receive a share in the distribution of income—and we know it does—we need to look farther into the reasons for the return. On what foundations does it rest? Are the conditions which support it likely to continue?

Conditions necessary for capital services to have value

In view of all that has been said on the value problem, it may seem redundant to say more on the matter of scarcity as a necessary condition. But there is often confusion as to what is involved in the statement that, for capital to yield a return, the capital goods in which it is invested must be sufficiently scarce so that they yield a net return. A person may understand the service of capital in making modern methods possible and yet not see that the great output of modern equipment does not prove that the service has value. Two points should be recognized.

Net Product. The first is a reminder that the product directly attributable to capital goods is not net product. The $10,000 machine, in the example on page 728, must add $1000 annually to the value of product to pay for the resources embodied in it. Only as its annual contribution exceeds $1000 is there a return that can be credited to the capital invested in it. Capital goods may often appear very useful without ever being able, in their whole lifetime of use, to earn their original cost. Once they are available, they are used to advantage, but it may have been a mistake to produce them in the first place.

Net marginal product. The second point is that capital goods may have a vast net product in the aggregate without yielding a net marginal product that can be credited to invested capital. That is, capitalistic methods may cause resources to yield a far larger output than would result if the same resources were used noncapitalistically, and still capital goods may merely earn their depreciation. This is no more remarkable than that workmen can produce much more when they have air to breathe than when they do not. The aggregate advantage of having air is great, but it does not follow that air is a scarce resource, with output varying with each unit more or less of it, so that its service has unit importance and can be credited with a share in the product.

Capital goods, and the savings and investment responsible for them, make a great aggregate addition to output, but does capital have unit importance? Like other resources, capital is subject to diminishing returns. With more and more saving, and with more and more capital goods used in production, the additions to output become smaller and smaller, and it is entirely conceivable that *additional* capital goods should finally add no more to output than they cost—in other words, make no net marginal addition at all and earn no net return.

As observed in the discussion of investment in Chapter 14, more and more labor without limit cannot be diverted from running machines to making machines, with a continuing increase in total output. The advantage of extending capitalistic methods must finally vanish, and we must therefore recognize that the continuance of a net return on capital depends on the process stopping before this vanishing point is reached—that is, while capital goods are still scarce enough to. have a net marginal product.

What are the factors, then, which operate to hold up the productivity of capital? They lie, first, in the conditions which promote its effective use and cause it to be demanded; second, in the conditions that limit the amount of it that is invested.

The demand for capital—investment opportunity

On the positive, or demand, side, the return from capital is supported by the opportunities for profitable investment—their extent and their promise. Savings are required for the ordinary expansion of industrial plant, equipment, and inventories, as required by the growth of population and by a rising level of per-capita output. Opportunities are afforded also by inventions and innovations that result in new products which appeal to the public or that provide more economical ways of producing old products. Discoveries of natural resources and the opening up of new land areas also stimulate investment. Rising standards of building construction for all sorts of purposes require a great deal of capital. Public works, both normal and emergency, absorb expanding volumes of savings. All of these influences tend to raise or to maintain the rate of return on capital.

How powerful are they? Opinions differ widely regarding investment prospects in this country. The 1930s, as we saw in our earlier discussion, brought general pessimism regarding the future. Fears were based on the passing of the frontier, the "maturing" of the economy, the slowing down of population growth, the commonness of innovations that expand output without absorbing capital. Other observers have looked upon the stagnation of the 1930s as a special event not indicative of the more permanent situation, and they have foreseen an undiminishing field for profitable investment in developing new industries that research makes possible, and in raising the level of living of the people. Wartime prosperity stimulated hope, but without disclosing the future.

Supply of capital—limiting factors

What factors restrict the flow of funds into investment, and thus limit the quantity of capital goods and hold up their marginal productivity? We may distinguish three such limitations.

Rate of saving. Formerly the belief was widely held by economists that capital was certain to yield a return because people would not save unless it did. With saving governed by prospective income, the quantity of invested capital would never be so great that the net marginal product would fail to cover this necessary return. This view was supported by a theory of *time preference,* according to which people prefer a dollar's worth of present satisfaction to a dollar's worth of future satisfaction. Thus they would save, thereby sacrificing present satisfactions, only if the dollars which had been set aside would grow in number, to offset the declining importance of future dollars. Saving, in other words, would be sufficiently restricted to insure a net return from capital great enough to balance this preference for present dollars and present satisfactions.

Not many would hold today that time preference insures a scarcity of capital. Admittedly the motivation that governs saving is complex. The roots of saving, which lie deep in the habits, accepted precepts, and cultural background of the people, are not fully understood, but it seems clear that much saving occurs without the bait of expected future income. Funds are not only saved to increase income, but they are also saved because the principal sum itself will meet anticipated need and will afford security, and because it permits ostentation and the exercise of power. Indeed, as noted in Chapter 14, if people do save to insure a certain future financial condition, that condition can be arrived at more easily with a higher than with a lower rate of return. Thus the higher return may mean less saving, rather than more. It is also true, when income is very large, that added consumption may have little attraction, so that saving takes place practically without inducement.

On the other hand, saving is held in check by a low return on capital, not because people are disinclined to save but because they have less income from which to save. Much of the saving is done by persons with large incomes, and large incomes, as we have seen, are received preponderantly as a return on capital.

Saving and capital formation necessarily depend on the income level. Poor countries have small capacity to save. New countries, with small populations, can provide little capital and, at the same time, they need much of it for their development. The return on capital is therefore high, and it flows in from abroad. As countries develop and incomes expand, saving increases and some, at least, of the investment outlets contract, so that a declining rate of return takes place. Whether the United States, with a national income of $200 billion, can find use for all its savings at a net return above zero is a matter of debate.

Preference for cash. Thus it is not certain that capital will be made scarce by shortage of savings. But a second limitation on the capital supply lies in the possible unwillingness of savers to make their savings available for use unless they receive a return. They have the alternative of keeping their savings in cash. The view has made headway in recent years that the capital supply is restricted less by lack of savings than by reluctance to sacrifice liquidity.

As between cash and a nonliquid asset that yields no return, people prefer cash. With savings in cash form, the saver is prepared for emergencies of any sort. He can change his mind about retaining his saving and buy the contemplated radio or car. If prices start upward, he is in the best position to convert his savings into forms that will conserve his purchasing power. Thus an investment, even though it is absolutely safe so far as the principle is concerned, is not as attractive as cash if it yields no return. Some return above zero, according to this view, is therefore necessary to induce investment and capital formation. *Liquidity preference,* it is said, sets a lower limit to the return on capital.

Aversion to risk. It seems, then, that capital will perform its *carrying* function only for compensation. But more important, in an analysis of income distribution, is the return that capital expects for *bearing the uncertainties of enterprise.* This is the third restriction on the flow of funds into investment. A saver may be willing to lend at 2 percent if he is perfectly certain both of the principal and of the 2 percent; on the other hand to induce him to accept the full risks of an industrial investment, a prospect of 10 percent may be necessary—an additional 8 percent, that is, because he may get no return at all, or may even lose his savings if things go badly. On this basis, our $10,000 machine must promise a gross return of $2000 to justify the investment it requires.

This is not to say that a 10-percent return will be realized on the average. The average, losses considered, may not exceed 6 or 4 or 2 percent. The very fact of uncertainty means that what is expected and what materializes seldom correspond. But it does follow from this reasoning that investment will be sufficiently restricted so that an inviting possibility is present of a return considerably higher than is acceptable on a risk-free basis. We shall return to this matter in the next chapter in the discussion of profits.

In this discussion we have not gone into the characteristics of the interest and profit forms in which capitalists get their returns. We have dealt instead with more fundamental matters: the services performed by capital, capitalists, and capitalist-entrepreneurs, and whether it is necessary under capitalism that a share in the national income should reward these services. The services, we have seen, are important not only to the consuming public but directly to the workers involved in capitalistic production. We have seen, also, that the services apparently have to be rewarded. It should be noted—relating this conclusion to the problem of total demand as considered in Chapter 14—that if an underlying difficulty exists in absorbing savings and maintaining high production, the difficulty becomes greater when capital, to be invested, must promise a substantial net return.

Review Questions

1. On what grounds has it been argued that, although capital goods are productive, capital and capitalists make no contribution to production for which a share in distribution should be assigned?

2. "The primary factors of production—labor and land—would not be

used as they are, or rewarded as they are, if capital did not perform its carrying function." Explain carefully.

3. "The enterprise function is necessarily in large measure a capital function." Explain, bringing out the relation of this function of capital to the incomes of other factors.

4. "The plant and equipment of industry, the widely varied modern facilities of production, make production so much greater than it could be without them that we can scarcely imagine a situation in which the services of invested capital would not be highly valuable." Criticize this statement, bringing out the sense in which capital must be productive, if it is to yield a return.

5. Show how the controversy over the "mature-economy" issue bears on the return from capital.

6. "No more will be saved than can be invested profitably, because people will not save without prospects of a return." Evaluate this statement. What is the relation of it to "time preference"? What seem to you to be the major influences that limit the amount of saving?

7. "The most certain support of the income of capitalists lies in their unwillingness to invest without a return." Distinguish two bases of this unwillingness. Relate them to the two functions of invested capital. Apply them to the machine example and show what lies behind the suggestion that a prospective gross rent of $2000 may be necessary to induce investment in a $10,000 machine.

8. Show that the income of capitalists is related both to the problem of distribution and the problem of the total income to be distributed.

~ 29 ~

Profits, Interest, and Wealth

I~N ANALYZING~ property incomes, it is first necessary to consider what they are and whether they are necessary. The preceding chapter dealt with these matters. So far as land rent is concerned, we need say no more about it. However, profit, as the distinctive return to the employers of other factors and the one return received in residual form, raises issues of interpretation that should be considered. Interest, too, is a form of income that poses challenging questions, but their slight bearing on the problem of inequality justifies only a cursory treatment. It is desirable, if we can, to reconcile the rates of return on new and old wealth, and that matter will receive attention. Finally, we should not leave the problem of property income without being adequately impressed with the importance of the distribution of wealth as a factor in the distribution of income.

Profits

Next to hired labor, the productive services that claim the largest part of the national income are those of enterprisers. Out of $202.6 billion in 1947, the owners of unincorporated firms received $40.5 billion, and corporate profits (before income taxes, but after an adjustment for appreciated inventories) were $23 billion, though perhaps no more than $35 billion of these two items should be viewed as property income.

To the analyst, the main difficulty in interpreting profit statistics comes from the fact that profits appear as a residual, not as a definite and agreed rate of return. Thus they are highly variable, as between different firms and different times, and, accordingly are hard to compare with other incomes and to appraise. But this is only one of the several difficulties in interpreting them and judging their place in the income structure.

The wage element in business profits

The present discussion is of income from wealth, and profits are viewed mainly from that standpoint. But since profit is a mixed return, especially in unincorporated firms, and an issue arises as to the wage element even in corporate profits, the labor side of enterprise must not be ignored.

The significance of incorporation. To break down national income into its labor and wealth components, we assumed in Chapter 24 that two thirds of the net return of farms, small stores, barber shops, doctors' offices, and numerous other businesses in the single-proprietorship and partnership form should be treated as labor income. The labor includes ordinary work of many kinds and professional and managerial services. The fraction is uncertain, but the point is clear that profits are not comparable between incorporated and unincorporated firms unless such an adjustment is made. Before the profits of corporations are arrived at, all ordinary wages and salaries have been deducted and so have the salaries and bonuses of the top officials, including active stockholders. Thus corporate profits are a return to owners. For the most part, this return to owners should be viewed as compensation for the services of wealth, but, because the wealth is in a position of risk, the return may be construed also as rewarding the judgment of the stockholders. The labor element, however, has additional aspects.

Criticism of the reward of leadership in corporations. In discussing the corporate form (in Chapter 8) we saw that it is possible, when ownership and control become separated, for persons in control to take advantage of their position in the matter of salaries and bonuses. On the assumption that corporations should be run in the interest of the stockholders, it can thus be made to appear that ownership is defrauded. This criticism is in harmony with the traditional view of enterprise, and the view of the law. But a more fundamental and essentially opposite criticism is that when most stockholders are largely passive, concerned only with signing dividend checks and proxies, the whole conception is wrong and their claim to profits should be greatly reduced.

The success of an enterprise, as reflected in its net income, depends greatly on the judgment of the men who initiate it and are active in running it. With millions of dollars depending on their decisions, a plausible case can be made for giving them a sizeable part of corporate income. In some degree this view is recognized in the practice of paying high officials not only substantial salaries but also bonuses that vary with profits. But these sums are usually only a small fraction of the profits available for dividends and do not carry the idea very far. Accordingly the argument is heard for a more drastic change under which so-called "passive capital" would receive only a very moderate return, a sort of capital wage, and the rest of the profit would go to the top personnel.[1]

Because the issue goes to the heart of the enterprise function, it is worth considering. Certainly it is good sense to reward responsible officials with such income as will induce their best efforts, as well as attract them from less worthy employers. But to place them instead of capital in the residual income position would seem to violate the realities of their role. We should note (1) that the nature of their services does not imply so highly variable a reward, (2) that they would probably not want to be in the residual position if given the choice, and (3) that they could not discharge the economic responsibility that it entails.

1. Persons who recommend such a readjustment in the flow of income apparently overlook the magnitudes and the fluctuations involved. As a rather extreme example, the United States Steel Corporation had a profit of $197,000,000 in 1929 and a loss of $71,000,000 in 1932. If a few top men of the company were to occupy the position which would entitle them to the 1929 profit, they should also accept the 1932 loss. But this variation in their incomes, like all major profit variations, would bear no relation to differences in the services they performed in the two years. They might even have worked harder and more skillfully in 1932. The case for placing high management in the residual position is not well supported on the ground that profit variation measures managerial performance.

This lack of correspondence between profits and the merits of entrepreneurial decisions is not limited to general fluctuations in business. As between different business undertakings, profits depend in part on factors that cannot be evaluated in advance or subjected to managerial control. This is the essence of uncertainty, and the outcome must, in considerable measure, be ascribed to luck. Undoubtedly Henry Ford and his early associates should be credited with good judgment and exceptional competence, but the great fortunes that came to them were quite out of line with any excellence that their efforts could possibly have possessed. Able men with good judgment were present in the

---

[1] Beardsley Ruml, the head of Macy's, who has been something of a leader in economic matters, has been quoted as saying that "the residual profit should go exclusively to the one or two individuals whose initiative and judgment is decisive for the success of a business." A similar view is expressed by Edwin G. Nourse in *Price Making in a Democracy*, Brooking Institution, 1944, Ch. 4. The general case for reducing the return to ownership to reflect its "passive" character is developed by Adolph A. Berle and Gardiner C. Means, *The Modern Corporation and Private Property*, Bk. IV, Macmillan, 1933.

numerous other firms that were started in the same industry and failed with heavy losses.

2. Whatever the deserts of nonowning corporate officials with respect to such profits and losses, most of them would probably not want to be rewarded in so uncertain a manner. They may not be as much concerned with security as ordinary workers are, but some certainty of income is important to them. We have seen that it is conceivable to have the suppliers of any, or all, resources share in the residual position, but that it is a distinct and highly valued service of capital that it takes over much of the burden of industrial uncertainty from those who depend for their incomes on the current sale of labor service. In this sale of services, even top executives must, in some degree, be included.

3. But, most important, even if corporate officials and managers were willing to risk the losses for the sake of the gains, they would not be able, as noncapitalists, to meet the financial obligations. To assume the burden of making wage and interest payments in years of low sales, and even of absorbing the loss of the original investment in firms that fail, requires financial competence of a high order. It requires the $2 billion of capital of United States Steel to assume this responsibility, and corresponding investments in smaller firms. As pointed out in the preceding chapter, if the buying and hiring of resources for definite sums is to mean anything, it must be done by persons who supply capital. It does not make sense to place this responsibility on one group and then assign the right of profits to another.

Bases in comparing profits

When corporate profits are viewed as property income, it is possible to present them in ways which will create almost any desired impression regarding their reasonableness. To say that they were $28.7 billion in 1947 in comparison, say, with $9.3 billion in 1940 gives one picture. Vicious profiteering is suggested. When the additional fact is introduced that national income was $202.6 billion in 1947 and $81.3 in 1940 and that wages had risen to two and one half times the 1940 total, the charge is weakened somewhat. When it is recognized that 1947 profits contained a misleading inventory element, and that adjustment for it reduces the figure to $23 billion, in comparison with $9.2 billion in 1940, the increase seems much less striking. If, further, corporation income taxes are taken out, along with the inventory adjustment, the comparable profit figures become $11.7 and $6.4 billion, and it begins to look as if the owners of American corporations were losing out in the economic race. Finally, in defending their profits, business spokesmen stress that a smaller fraction of the sales dollar has represented profit since the war than before it. The consumer, accordingly, should feel that he has been treated with restraint.

These alternative comparisons are mentioned to show that caution is needed in interpreting profit figures. Statistics can be made to serve propaganda purposes, often in a misleading manner. We shall not stop to evaluate these ways of stating profits, except to emphasize that comparisons of profits with sales revenues are especially subject to misuse.

Comparisons on this basis may be useful in showing certain changes that occurred during the war, but they give no indication as to whether profits are basically reasonable or not. All incomes should be judged in relation to the productive services for which they are a return, as when a wage is stated as so much per hour of work or interest as a percent of the sum borrowed. Similarly profits, as a return to the owners of enterprises, should be related to the extent of their ownership—*a percent of their investment rather than of their sales revenue.*

Comparisons of profits with sales and with invested capital give quite different results, as one would suppose from knowledge of differences in the "capital turnover" in different fields. A retail establishment may have a net return that is only 2 percent of its revenues from sales, but if its annual sales amount to five times its invested capital, its return on capital is 10 percent. An electric power company, on the other hand, may have a net income that is 25 percent of its receipts, but if its receipts are only one fifth of its investment, its return on capital is only 5 percent. The figures that are significant in judging profits are not the 2 percent and the 25 percent of the revenues, but the 10 percent and the 5 percent on the capital. The 10 percent, however, may be as reasonable as the 5 percent, because of greater risk in the retail field.

Variability of residual income

Mistaken views of profits are most likely to arise through basing judgments on figures for particular years or on year-to-year comparisons. Heated assertions regarding the relative behavior of wages and profits commonly rest on a wholly inadequate base. The fact that profits are residuals means that they can be expected to fluctuate widely, and their reasonableness must therefore be judged over a considerable period.

A hypothetical case will show the arithmetic of the relationship. In a certain year a firm with sales of $1,200,000 and expenses of $1,100,000 makes a net return of $100,000, or 10 percent on its capital of $1,000,-000. A depression comes and revenues fall by *one fourth,* or to $900,000.

Some of the costs are relatively fixed, including certain wages outlays, so that expenses fall by only *one fifth,* or to $880,000. As a result, profits fall to $20,000, or by *four fifths.* Percentagewise, the decline in profits is several times that in wages.

But now recovery comes, and every revenue and cost factor returns to its former position. Receipts rise from $900,000 to $1,200,000, or by *one third.* Expenses mount from $880,000 to $1,100,000, or by *one fourth.* Wages rise approximately by this same 25 percent. Profits increase from $20,000 to $100,000, or by 400 percent.

During the decline some business people lament their sorry plight and compare the great fall in profits with the moderate decline in wages. During the rise some labor spokesmen protest the 400-percent rise in profits while wages are rising by only 25 percent. Both are equally silly. Both types of income are behaving in the usual way, and the outcome of the two fluctuations leaves the distribution of income just where it was to begin with.

The previously cited case of United States Steel illustrates strikingly the volatility of profits. The fall of profits between 1929 and 1932 from $197,000,000 to negative $71,000,000, or well over 100 percent, occurred with a decline of three fourths in ingot tonnage. By 1935 profits had risen to a little over $1,000,000, or by an infinite percentage, with a doubling of volume. By 1937 they were up to $95,000,000 on a little less than the 1929 volume, a further gain of 8500 percent. Wages, of course, moved by much smaller percentage amounts but were higher in 1937 than in 1929.

Profit theory and the problem of profit reasonableness

Profits, more than other incomes, are being judged constantly as to their reasonableness. They are recognized as necessary, since, without them, prosperity under capitalism is impossible. But they enter so heavily into the larger incomes, and figure so prominently in disputes over prices and wages, that it is widely felt they should be held close to the practical minimum. Unfortunately, the theory of profit is not such as to be very useful in judging particular profit situations.

Pure profit and the necessary return to enterprise. The role of profit is primarily to induce investment under conditions of uncertainty. To clarify this role the concept of pure profit is often employed. Pure profit is the part of the net return of business firms that rewards the enterprise function as such. To determine it, the important *wage* element must be deducted from the business profits of unincorporated firms, and such an *interest* element must be deducted from all business profits as the invested capital might have earned in some other, risk-free use. Only the remainder constitutes the special return for assuming the risks and responsibilities of enterprise. This remainder, then, is pure profit.

The question is *how large pure profit needs to be*. When he commits his capital, the enterpriser must foresee the possibility of a pure profit that is substantial. He will not incur the danger of getting no return for his labor and his time, and even of losing his capital, without seeing the prospect of a return well above ordinary wages and interest. But to say there is uncertainty is to say that hopes must often be disappointed. To say that pure profit is the lure is not to say that on the average the enterpriser will get it. He may be like the people who buy lottery tickets, knowing that collectively their prizes will not equal their outlay for tickets. This outcome is the more likely if many people are of the entrepreneurial type, who temperamentally are not averse to taking chances, and if there are many people, moreover, who would rather work for themselves than for others. Conceivably profit prospects are adequate even though, when the results are all in, actual profits prove to average zero or less than nothing.

Even if this were the case, the prizes would still have to be attractive for the successful and, doubtless, much more common than in lotteries. Likewise, if this were the case, profit would still be an important element in the distribution of income. The profits of the successful in good years would amount to billions, whatever the average position of all enterprisers over a long period. We are not justified, however, in assuming that pure profit does not exist in the average situation. We do not know.

Unsuitability as a profit criterion. But even if our theory succeeded in telling us what profit *prospects* need to be in particular instances and what *average* profits need to be over a long period, we would still lack a basis for judging whether actual profits are reasonable in a specific case at a specific time. Firms are quite certain to make more or less than the expected return, and they are certain to vary in return from year to year. Exceptional profits are always subject to the interpretation that they simply represent those variations without which a residual return would lose its essential character.

But exceptional profits are also subject to the interpretation that they reflect arbitrary control over markets in selling products or in buying materials and labor. This possibility is likely enough so that we should regard *monopoly* as probably a significant element in the distribution of income. But for it, we might dismiss the theoretical difficulty as of little practical importance. Actually, however, there is great need of better criteria for judging industrial profits.

Interest

Much recent analysis of interest rates has been concerned with their bearing on the depression problem. In discussing that problem in Chapter 14, we made use of a simple conception of interest as the price paid for the use of savings. Interest has a prominent place, also, in discussions of banking and the money market. Discussion of interest in these connections readily leads to technicalities that need not concern us here. Our present concern is with interest as a share in the distribution of income, and other features of it may be subordinated. Chiefly, we should see the relation between interest as an *implicit* return from the productive use of capital and the *explicit* interest rates paid on loanable funds.

Pure interest and the use of capital in production

Interest fits into the analysis of the preceding chapter as the *return for the carrying function of capital.* As pure profit is the return for the risk-taking function, we may say that *pure interest* is the reward for making savings available when there is no chance of losing them. If all capital were supplied by capitalist-entrepreneurs, interest would be merged with pure profit as an implicit part of business profit. Interest would thus be received in the residual form and would not assume the distinctive interest form, as a percent of a principal sum.

The return for the carrying service of capital takes the interest form when enterprisers borrow part of the capital they use. Then, out of their demand for capital goods for production, there comes a derived *demand* for the funds needed to purchase these goods. An enterpriser, believing an investment will yield 10 percent after depreciation of the facilities acquired but uncertain of the outcome, will borrow needed funds at 4 percent, let us say, on a well-secured basis. He does not believe he should pay 6 percent unless there is a chance of making more than 10 percent if he succeeds, but he would borrow at 2 percent even if prospects were somewhat worse. Along these lines, it is easy to imagine a demand schedule for loanable funds, with different enterprisers willing to take different amounts, depending somewhat on the interest rate.

On the other side of the market is the *supply* of loanable funds available for risk-free loans. This supply is governed, as we saw, by the amount of saving and by the willingness of savers to part with cash— their liquidity preference. This supply, in conjunction with the demand, fixes the rate of interest, the return for the carrying function of capital. Whatever the rate, enterprisers will recognize it as a return they should receive implicitly in their business profit, with the return for risk-taking something additional.

To this very simple picture, a number of additions must be made to bring out the influences that bear on interest rates.

Interest and consumer and governmental borrowing

A major addition is that the demand for loanable funds comes from important sources beside the desire of enterprisers to expand their equipment and inventories. There is also a great deal of borrowing by *consumers* and by *governments*. In part this demand is about the same as that of business enterprisers, in that it rests on the anticipated productivity of capital goods. The consumer who is borrowing to build a house figures that the service of the house, after deducting all other costs, will be worth enough to cover the interest rate. Governments presumably use capital for highways or hydroelectric developments on the basis of the same calculation, except when the object is unemployment relief.

On the other hand, consumers do a good deal of borrowing for current consumption in excess of their incomes, and governments borrow for ordinary operating expenses or extraordinary expenses as during a war. These uses of savings give rise to no increase of wealth. Some persons save and others use up the savings, so that the aggregate effect is as if the saving had not occurred. But these consumption demands for savings affect the market for funds and the interest rate in the same way that investment demand does.

Interest and the level of aggregate income

With governmental and consumer borrowing added to the demand side of the market, we could content ourselves with a simple supply-and-demand explanation of interest but for one possible difficulty. Suppose the mature-economy people are right and the demand for savings, with a capacity level of total production and income, is not great enough to absorb all the savings available, even when the interest rate has gone as low as it can. Then, as we saw in Chapter 14, total production must fall to the point where savings are absorbed—where total spending equals the flow of funds from production. At this lower level savings are less, and investment is adequate. Now, however, can we properly say that the interest rate adjusts itself to the demand for savings and the supply of them? Probably we can do so only in a very superficial sense. More fundamentally the supply of savings, which depends on the total income, is adjusting itself to the demand for savings at that minimum interest rate—which in turn is fixed by liquidity preference, costs of handling loans, and other factors. Interest, instead of depending on the supply of savings, along with the demand for them, helps to determine the supply by restricting investment and national income.

Interest and commercial banks

Another addition to our preliminary picture of interest is necessitated by the credit-expanding power of commercial banks. If banks, in making loans, add to the supply of dollars (as we saw in Chapter 11 that they do), must they not be viewed as a factor on the supply side of the capital market, supplementing the dollars that come from real saving?

The answer—which we shall only indicate—depends again on whether resources are quite fully used and the economy is operating at capacity. If there are no idle resources, then borrowers from banks must use the added dollars to bid for productive services already in use. The result is inflationary. Money falls in value, and a kind of forced saving results in which many people, whose money incomes lag, cut down their use of products and thus of resources. In the process, the expansion of bank credit reduces the interest rate, but, with prices going up, it takes as great an interest outlay as before to get command of given productive resources.

If, on the other hand, resources are idle, expansion of bank credit is the means of bringing them into use. Bank credit simply anticipates the savings from the expanded production that results.

Cost and risk factors in interest rates

When savings pass through the hands of banks and other financial middlemen, a handling cost enters the interest picture. The borrower from the bank pays a considerably higher rate than the saver receives from the bank. What the saver gets constitutes his income from his capital, but what the borrower pays determines the cost that must be covered to make the investment, or other use of funds, worth while.

Thus, in this case, there are two interest rates: one charged by banks and one paid by banks. But over the whole market for loanable funds there are many interest rates. We have avoided recognizing them by limiting the discussion largely to pure interest, as a return for risk-free loans. Few, if any loans, however, are wholly free of risk, and the degree of risk varies widely, depending on the personal standing and business prospects of the borrower and the value of his assets if liquidated. Many bondholders and other lenders share substantially in the uncertainties of enterprise, though their return does not take the profit form. The interest they receive reflects the risk.

Interest rates also reflect the terms of loans, including such features as the remoteness of maturity dates. They are likewise influenced by the costs incurred in dealing with the borrowers. The federal government, with its high credit standing and compelling market position, may borrow on a short-term basis at less than 1 percent, though it pays 2.5 percent or more on long-term loans. Leading public utilities may pay less than 3 percent. Borrowers on real-estate security may pay 5 percent. Rates mount upward on certain types of credit to the 30 or 40 percent paid on some unsecured consumption loans and to the even higher rates sometimes implicit in the installment purchase of goods.

Importance of interest as a share in distribution

As in the case of land rent, it is difficult to get a quantitative impression of the importance of interest in the national income. Much of the carrying service of capital is rewarded implicitly in business profits and has no separate statistical expression. The $4.5 billion interest return on government bonds is viewed statistically as a kind of transfer from taxpayers to bondholders, and thus is not included in the national income, but it represents return from savings and should be recognized, along with $3.6 billion of interest received in 1947 from other sources, in a discussion of property income. Interest income from private sources has fallen in the last two decades, from a figure of $6.5 billion in 1929.

Review Questions

1. "The net income of the small concern is likely to represent a larger percent on the investment than does the net income of the large concern, yet the enterprise function may be better rewarded in the large concern." Explain.

2. "All residual income should go to the top officials and executives of a firm rather than to the passive group of owners." "The people entitled to profits are the people who take the beating when there aren't any." Evaluate these statements.

3. Show that it is not difficult to manipulate profit figures so as to accomplish a particular propaganda purpose.

4. "A firm with profits that are 2 percent of its revenues may be more profitable than another firm whose profits are 25 percent of its revenues." Explain.

5. "Profits before income taxes of fruit and vegetable canners were five times as great in 1942 as in the years 1936–1939 on less than twice the prewar volume of sales." (From *PM*) Do you regard this as a striking fact? Explain the usual relation of profits and wages during the phases of the business cycle. Why does residual income behave in this way?

6. "American businessmen like to take risks and don't need to be paid for it. Unwillingness to take risks is not a reason for profits." Do you agree? Explain.

7. "Pure profits may be an important element in distribution even though, on the average, they are zero." Explain.

8. "A reasonable profit is one that is sufficient, but no more than sufficient, to induce competitive producers to supply the volume of any product that the market will absorb." Show that such a concept provides no practical test of the reasonableness of particular profits.

9. "In analyses of the distribution of income, interest has commonly been regarded as the return for the carrying function of capital." Explain. What is meant by pure interest? By implicit and explicit interest?

10. Explain the business demand for loanable funds. What other sources of demand are there? Do they lead to capital formation?

11. How is the explanation of interest modified if we assume that total demand is insufficient to maintain full employment?

12. When commercial banks expand the supply of loanable funds, do they reduce the cost of capital to users? Do they reduce the income of savers?

13. Why should the interest received by the saver often differ from the interest paid by the user of funds?

14. Why is it necessary to speak of interest rates rather than of a single interest rate?

15. A "personal-finance" company advertises that a customer can borrow $300 and pay it back in 15 monthly installments of $24.29. About how large is the annual rate of interest on the sum the borrower has to use?

Income from Old Wealth

In discussing profit and interest, we have been concerned mainly with new investment. We have dealt with the problem of the rate of return to be expected from investing savings in equipment and inventories (along with loans to consumers and governments), taking account of such factors as the productivity of capital goods, the amount of saving, the preference for liquidity, and the attitude toward uncertainty. In discussing rates of return, we have neglected the fact that most of the wealth from which capitalists get their incomes is not the new wealth arising from current investment but the accumulation from the long past. Any one year's accretion of productive wealth is small in comparison with the aggregate to which it is added. What bearing has this fact on our analysis?

What we called capital-goods rent, in comparing the services of land and capital goods, seldom turns out to be what was expected. The net return, after depreciation, may prove to be greater or less than nothing.

Because most investments are old, are we to conclude that this un-analyzed range of rates on past commitments is of chief importance in studying the income from capital, rather than the expected rates on new investments which we have been stressing?

A large part, probably a major part, of present investment is not made in new capital goods but involves instead the purchase of old wealth. Investments are made in already existing farms, mines, stores, and factories and in the outstanding securities of established enterprises. Not only do savers put their funds in old wealth, but it is to be noted that this wealth consists of land as well as capital goods, whereas our analysis has thus far related investment mainly to the capitalistic process. Have we failed to take account of an important part of the demand for savings? What complication is introduced when land rent provides the source of income on invested capital? What relation, if any, is there between the wide variety of returns on old wealth and the expected returns on new wealth that we have been discussing?

Old wealth and the utilization of savings

On one of these questions, the effect of investment in old wealth on the market for savings, the answer need only be reviewed from Chapter 6. The effect is negligible. Even though most investing is in old wealth, this is still the answer. The reason is that purchase of old wealth does not constitute true investment but merely transfers savings to the seller, so that they remain to be invested. True investment absorbs savings, in the sense that they are used to buy labor, materials, and other things which are essential to the current production of capital goods. Real investment, along with consumer buying, makes up the total demand for goods that absorbs current production. Buying old productive wealth obviously does not do this. Nor does it necessarily interfere with true investment, since it leaves the savings in the hands of the sellers for them to use for consumption or capital purposes.

There may be some interference, however, with the flow of purchasing. To some extent savings may be drawn into the real-estate or securities market where they eddy around in a whirlpool of speculation, without emerging promptly to buy any new product. They become the working capital, as it were, of expanded speculation. Only in this minor respect can investment in old wealth be said to affect the market situation for savings and the returns to be expected on new investments.

Relation of returns from old and new wealth

In discussing income from capital we have stressed the rate of return from new investments because of its critical relation to distribution and the whole working of the economy. Whether past investments were wisely made or not, they cannot be unmade. The factors governing the returns on new investments tell us what capitalists must receive to get them to perform their functions. What they must receive is a continuing determinant of the division of income. It is also a continuing influence on the aggregate product and income.

Adjustment through expansion and contraction. We should recall, moreover, that returns on old wealth are drawn in the direction of the rate of return on new investment. Old capital goods wear out, and, if replacement is not as promising as investment in other fields, the old facilities are not replaced. On the other hand, in fields in which returns are high on past investments, new investments are likely to be made, with a depressing effect on the income rate. Thus variations in the supply of capital in different fields tend to equalize rates of return. But this is a slow process, and, despite it, big disparities of return are bound to persist.

Adjustment of capital values. There is another entirely different sense, however, in which the returns from old investments are pulled in the direction of current market rates. Let us suppose that new investment is being drawn into a given industry, with a given degree of risk, on the basis of an expected 10-percent return. This is the minimum expectation that attracts new capital. At the same time, there are some established firms in this industry that are earning, and are quite likely to continue to earn, 15 percent on their investment, others 5 percent, and some nothing at all. This does not mean, however, that persons who now invest their savings in these established enterprises will make either more or less than if they invested in new facilities, expecting a 10-percent return. The reason is that the price paid for old productive wealth is adjusted to the present, prevailing rate of return for the type of investment in question. An old enterprise yielding 15 percent on its investment of $1,000,000 will be worth $1,500,000 or thereabouts, and its securities will be priced accordingly. Thus the new buyer will earn only 10 percent on what he pays. The established firm yielding 5 percent on its $1,000,000 will be worth about $500,000, and the man who puts savings in it will get about 10 percent. Thus whether he invests in new or old wealth, he may expect about the same rate of return, a rate reflecting the current market situation for the particular type of investment.

Capitalization. This way of placing a value on old wealth is known as capitalization—one of several meanings attached to that word. Capitalization is an arithmetic process, the object of which is to arrive at the principal sum that, at the appropriate current rate of return, will yield the income that is expected from the property in question. If the income is expected to continue indefinitely into the future, the arithmetic consists simply of dividing the expected income by the appropriate percent. A *fall* in the *expected income reduces* the *capitalized value,* but a *fall* in the *rate of return* at which the capitalizing is done *increases* the capitalized value. When the current market interest rate falls, one is justified in committing a larger sum in order to get an income of the size that the particular property yields.

Here are two properties each promising a continuing return of $4000 a year, and with the same degree of certainty. One may have cost $100,-000 originally and the other $40,000, so that returns on the actual investments are 4 percent and 10 percent. But these outlays are sunk, and the future is all that matters; the properties are equally attractive now. If 8 percent is the current market rate for the risk involved, a fair price for each property would be about $50,000, the sum which, at 8 percent, would yield $4000. Thus, whatever the return received on the original investment, the return to the present purchaser of existing income-yielding property is governed by the present market rate.

These existing properties may be either land or capital goods. If the property is land, it did not result originally from capital investment, but once it yields an income, as explained in the preceding chapter, it acquires a value, and savings are used to purchase it exactly as they are used to invest in any other wealth. For any given income prospect and degree of uncertainty, the price paid will be the same as for other wealth. But, as already explained, savings are not absorbed in the process but still remain to be invested. Land valuation affords the leading opportunity to use the capitalization process.

In determining the capitalized value of old plant and equipment and other produced wealth, greater care is necessary. If the capitalized value is *below* what it would now cost to reproduce the wealth in question, capitalization is a dependable process. But if the capitalized value is *above* the present cost of obtaining new facilities to serve the same purpose, one should hesitate to pay that value for the property. It would be better to buy equivalent new capital goods than to buy old ones. In the absence of monopolistic restriction of investment in the industry, someone can be expected to invest in it, and the return can be expected to fall.

Wealth Accumulation and Inequality

In this long treatment of distribution, attention has fallen almost entirely on the rates of return for different productive services. We have dealt with wages, land rent, profit, and interest. Now, finally, we shall return to the point that the inequality attributable to property incomes arises only in part from the size of those incomes. This aspect of inequality rests also on the unequal distribution of wealth itself. What we shall say about it in a few paragraphs does not reflect its importance at all adequately. To quite an extent the ensuing discussion consists of reminders of points already familiar.

The essential fact is that wealth, by its very nature, invites accumulation and concentration. Labor service cannot be separated from the people who provide it; wealth is quite separate from its owners. An individual can have no more labor power than resides in his mental and physical characteristics, but the nature of material goods presents no limit to the amount of them that may be owned by one individual. Given this susceptibility to accumulation, there are positive reasons for concentrated ownership of wealth. These reasons are found (1) in certain *economic* features of the place and use of wealth and (2) in some of the *institutional* arrangements through which society is organized. This classification of factors cannot be clean-cut, but it is of some expository use.

Economic factors in accumulation

The leading means of accumulation is through *saving* out of income. Here the chief point to be noted is the mutual dependence of size of income and amount of accumulation. The larger the income, the easier it is to save, hence the higher the percentage of income that is saved. On the other hand, the greater the wealth already owned, the larger the income; indeed, as we have seen, the largest incomes come mostly from property. Thus possession of wealth makes for incomes larger than otherwise, and larger incomes make for greater saving and accumulation of wealth. The mutual dependence readily becomes a spiral ascension.

The other principal means of accumulation is through *appreciation in value* of wealth which, in its physical aspect, is already possessed. A land area once of slight value comes to be the site of office buildings and stores in the heart of a city, and the fortunate owners of the land are enriched. Oil is struck or metals discovered, and wasteland or ordinary farmland becomes highly valuable. All wealth is subject to fluctuations in value. But, since the value of capital goods is held in check by the possibility of reproducing them as they become worth more than their cost, appreciation is most significant in the case of natural wealth.[2] Sen-

---

[2] Stock bought at an early stage in an enterprise that becomes highly successful may rise in value many times. But the main factor behind the appreciation is likely to be the investment of the large profits earned—in other words saving done by the enterprise but accruing to the stockholders in the appreciation of their stock. However, an improvement in earning prospects without any physical addition to the wealth of an enterprise will cause the value of stock to advance.

sational increases in value have occurred on only a slight part of the land area. Where they do occur, fortunes may result.

While appreciation accounts for an important part of present wealth, it should not be inferred that the *present owners* of that wealth have gained from the appreciation. Property transfers are sufficiently frequent so that most of the appreciation will commonly have occurred while the resources in question were in other hands. The present owners, unless they used funds received through selling other wealth, acquired the resources with savings out of income. To them natural wealth appears in the same light as new buildings or machines which investment of their savings has brought into being. This fact should be borne in mind, from the standpoint of equity, when an invidious distinction is drawn between acquisition through saving and through being the lucky owner of wealth which has become valuable through appreciation.

A leading economic factor in the accumulation of great fortunes has been the *increased scale of productive operations*. However shrewd and however fortunate the entrepreneur may be, whatever the degree of monopolistic advantage he may attain, his activities are circumscribed by the market in which he operates. A Standard Oil Company or a Ford Motor Company needs a national or international market to build in a few decades the fortune of a Rockefeller or a Ford. And large-scale methods must have developed. Progress in transport and industrial technology serve to amplify the effect of other conditions necessary to profit making and wealth accumulation.

We have seen that large enterprises require the assistance of specialists in their *financing,* notably of investment bankers. Those who handle the savings of the many are themselves in a favorable position to acquire fortunes. The Morgans and the Rothschilds come to mind. We have seen also that the economic basis of large business units is inseparable from the legal. The *corporate form* not only facilitates financing, but it provides a handy system of evidences of ownership that permits dealing in wealth without the encumbrance of its physical possession. The possibility of acquiring wealth, not through saving or passively awaited appreciation but by skill in buying and selling existing wealth, acquires new meaning. The qualities of the horse trader have gained a wider field in which to show their worth.

It is important not to confuse the *ownership* of wealth and its *control*. The house of Morgan or the "sixty families" control much more than they own. The Van Sweringen brothers, while owning a few millions, could control over two and one half billions of railroad property. It is ownership which is the direct basis of property income, not control. But if persons in control of great wealth do not make it contribute in some way to their incomes, they are either quite unskillful or extraordinarily self-denying. Were this not true, there would be no real conflict of interest between persons in active charge of a corporation's business and the thousands of its ordinary stockholders.

Institutional factors

Mention of the corporation leads us to those factors which are less strictly economic and more the outgrowth of political and broadly social developments. The prevailing ideas about *property* and the laws governing its ownership and protection are here of basic importance. The more assiduous a government is in protecting the rights and promoting the interests of property owners, the easier accumulation will be, and the larger probably will be the fraction of the total income going to them. A government dominated by property owners may be lacking in zeal in restricting monopoly or regulating it and may be hostile to the activities of labor unions.

But, paradoxically, a certain looseness in the protection of property may facilitate the accumulation of wealth in particular hands. It is said that the basis of certain early American fortunes lay in privateering and piracy, and modern *racketeering* has been a fruitful means of acquisition. The significance of the *corporation* is by no means limited to its inherent features. Its bearing on accumulation is largely related to the looseness of the laws governing its formation, its financing, and the arrangement of interests within it.

Of the features of our property institutions that are pertinent here, the one that probably contributes most directly to the accumulation, and certainly to the continuation, of fortunes is *inheritance*. What may be accumulated is multiplied when the accumulation of the father becomes the starting point of the son. The degree to which inheritance is an integral part of the institution of private property may be debated, but certainly it is not so inseparable that bequest cannot be looked upon as a special phenomenon, subject to restrictions not applied to other ways of acquiring wealth.

Another important institutional element is the policy of government toward the *public domain* and its transfer to private hands. If, when an area is opened up to settlement and exploitation, land, including mineral rights, can be acquired by individuals at little or no cost, with no obligations to turn over to the state—that is, to society collectively—any part of the income or appreciated value that results except through ordinary taxation, the basis is laid for accumulation of wealth by persons who are fortunate in the land they acquire. Again the policy that may be best is debatable. Undoubtedly men are more enterprising in pushing back the frontier and in developing untapped resources when they have the stimulus of full private possession of the wealth that appears. But rapid development means waste, and the terms of acquisition mean inequality. At any rate, policy in this sphere is a factor in the distribution of wealth.[3]

It should be said again that, *under capitalist institutions,* some advantage ordinarily attaches to the ownership and control of wealth, in comparison with other major economic interests. The automatic controls of the market are potent, and so may be the regulations that government imposes. But there are still innumerable situations where some play prevails in the working of the system, and where, because of their position, the play is more likely to be taken up to the advantage of wealth owners than to the advantage of workers or consumers.

Leading elements in the concentration of wealth ownership

We may conclude regarding the ownership of wealth that, at the points of greatest concentration in the United States, it is now mostly to be explained by (1) the retention of business profits, especially in large enterprises, (2) skill in dealings in titles to wealth, and (3) the fortunate acquisition and appreciation of natural resources. No one gets rich during one lifetime by starting with a small capital and compounding at ordinary interest, but persons rich for other reasons may enjoy large incomes from ordinary interest on wealth otherwise acquired. Even 1 percent of $100,000,000 would afford one of the largest incomes in the country. But the great fortunes come to exist in other ways. We should remember, however, that wealth is an important source of income even when present only in the modest accumulations that saving from wages and salaries makes possible.

Review Questions

1. "Investment in new wealth absorbs savings; investment in old wealth does not." Explain. What is the significance of this point? Should it be qualified?

2. "If wealth wears out and if it is reproducible, the return from investment in old wealth is never detached altogether from the rate of return applicable to investment in new wealth. But whatever the return from old wealth, to the new purchaser of it the rate of return is about the same as from new wealth." Explain both sentences.

[3] Another institution that contributed to inequality was slavery. Slavery not only meant inequality in the gulf it created between plantation owner and slave, but it meant inequality in the gulf nearly as great between plantation owner and those other white men who were too poor to own slaves and who suffered progressive degradation to the "poor-white" level.

3. A small factory that cost $40,000 is yielding its owners a net return, after full allowance for their managerial services, of $10,000 a year. If the current cost of funds in the market and the risks of this particular field suggest that 10 percent is a fairly adequate rate of return, what would seem, according to the capitalization process, to be the value of this enterprise? What consideration might cause you to regard this figure as a gross overstatement of value? Does this consideration apply equally to land?

4. "Neither (a) the income that wealth yields nor (b) the distribution of wealth is, by itself, an adequate explanation of the part played by property incomes in causing inequality. They must be taken together." Explain.

5. "Inequality in the distribution of wealth is continually accentuated by the inequality which already exists." Explain. What do you think of the idea contained in the phrase "from shirt sleeves to shirt sleeves in three generations"?

6. "The development of large-scale corporate enterprise has contributed to inequality in a number of ways." Explain.

7. "The accumulation of wealth is favored by a strong enforcement of property rights, but a certain laxity in such enforcement may enable certain individuals to become wealthy." Explain.

8. Do you agree with the conclusion stated in the last paragraph above regarding the sources of great fortunes? Explain.

~ 30 ~

Public Policy and the Distribution of Income

Most economic policies affect the division of income in some degree. They benefit particular interests and impose restraints and burdens on others. One may not think of conservation laws, immigration laws, or corporation laws and financial regulations as measures adopted to alter the sharing of income, but they have important distributive aspects nevertheless. Antitrust laws and public-utility regulation bear more obviously on business profits and consumer real income, and agricultural-adjustment policy is clearly a means of distribution reform. Public acceptance and encouragement of labor unions, together with the enactment of wage laws and related legislation, are definitely the outgrowth of developing views as to how economic welfare should be shared.

Collective responsibility for the division of income, even within a society essentially individualistic, is evident at many points. It is apparent in measures to care for the needy and in the social-security program. It appears in outlays for education and other services provided at the taxpayer's expense. It is reflected in the acceptance of highly progressive income taxes and the heavy taxation of inheritances.

Some of these policies affecting the division of income in the United States have been discussed in earlier chapters. Others have not. In any case, it is well to bring them together for a brief, but systematic, survey of their bearing on the distribution problem. The nature of their impact, their philosophy of reform, their relation to the structure of the economy, should be examined. Since the problem is controversial, we shall begin by reviewing certain points that seem most likely to narrow the area of disagreement, or at least to clarify the issues:

1. Poverty exists in the United States and inequality is substantial.

768

To say that one fifth of the families get half of the total income, as indicated in Chapter 24, exaggerates the situation when allowance is made for taxes and the use of public money, but income differences, nevertheless, are large.

2. Poverty and inequality *as such* appear to be objectionable. Extremely low incomes are a blight on a nation that takes pride in its economic achievements. Given additions to income mean more to those who have little than to those who have much. To urge complete equality is pointless because it is unattainable, but it seems reasonable to urge a reduction of inequality if means are available that are not themselves seriously disturbing and harmful.

3. The danger is always present that reforms will be seriously disturbing. The main reason is that the division of income cannot be divorced from its production. Especially under a free-enterprise system, incomes perform essential functions (*a*) in energizing productive activity and (*b*) in directing its use in a complex scheme of control through markets. Persons who would reform the division of income should be perfectly clear as to the nature of the system within which their reforms must operate. As observed earlier, the person who says that he does not believe in socialism, but that something should be done to get rid of profits, simply disqualifies himself to be heard on matters of policy. Since past gains in income, even at the lower levels, are mainly attributable to progress in production rather than to changes in distribution, proposed reforms should be scrutinized closely for their probable bearing on the general working of the economy.

4. Existing inequality is not so deeply rooted that it cannot be reduced somewhat without disruptive effect. Important features of inequality reflect the faulty working of the system rather than its essential operation, and general gain would result from correcting them. The system, moreover, is not so rigid that it can stand no modification. Adjustments are possible that do not impair its essential features.

There is the further point that sacrifice of output may sometimes be justified in the interest of a better division of income. It may be desirable to take $1 from a $100,000 income for the sake of adding 50 cents to a $1000 income. Since satisfaction is in part a relative matter, it may even be better to have $2500 in a situation in which no one gets more than $10,000 than to have $3000 in a situation in which some get $100,-000 and more. But these are imponderable matters, and from a policy standpoint it is probably better to err on the side of stressing production, because there is already too much willingness to sacrifice output to make jobs and gain advantage in markets.

5. Reduction of inequality may increase total income. Certainly if

saving tends to outstrip investment at any time, a transfer of dollars from the larger incomes, where they are saved, to the lower incomes, where they will be used for consumption, may expand total demand and total production. The qualification—and it is an important one—is that a diversion of income from profits may reduce the inclination to invest.

6. When high income is undependable and irregular, much of its advantage is lost. Moreover, income from high production is of no direct benefit to the numerous unproductive, unemployable people who have nothing to sell. Therefore measures of social security, of relief, of secondary distribution must be part of the whole distribution scheme. Primary distribution in a free system cannot operate on a needs basis, but ways must be found of recognizing needs if the final purpose of economic organization is to be achieved.

With this review of earlier considerations, we shall survey the main policies that have been adopted and proposed to improve the distribution of income in the United States. We shall consider adjustments in the operations of markets, changes in the distribution of income-earning capacity, social security, and other means of redistribution.

Policies to Alter the Operation of Markets

Because incomes depend in the first place on the pricing and sale of products and services, the most direct and obvious way to control distribution is through control of markets. Raise the prices received by producers whose incomes you would increase; restrict the prices charged by those whose incomes you would limit or whose customers you would aid. But, while this is the direct and obvious approach, it easily runs into complications. As long as any semblance of freedom remains in an economy, producers who find prices too low to make their activity worth while are at liberty to stop producing, and buyers to whom prices appear excessive can refrain from buying. The price mechanism and the activities that depend upon it are easily disrupted. As a result, efforts to control the flow of income break down, or else government action must be expanded further than was intended or than the objective warrants.

Much depends upon whether policies aim mainly at removing inequities arising from defects in the operation of markets or, in a more ambitious way, seek to push prices to levels not supported by underlying conditions of production and demand. This familiar distinction is basic in analyzing market reform. The main policies that influence distribution through markets should be reviewed in this light.

Prevention of exploitation by monopoly

Monopoly in selling products and buying services, if substantial, can be a serious source of inequality. But since monopoly is likely to upset the pricing of goods and the allocation of resources, corrective policies cannot be opposed, in principle, as harmful to the economy. On the contrary, believers in free enterprise should support them, if the methods are appropriate.

Antitrust policy, from the distribution standpoint, may be said to have several interrelated aims: limiting the profits of producers to no more than a necessary amount; enabling buyers of goods to get them for no more than a necessary price; keeping opportunity open for new producers to enter existing industries. For these purposes, no public official is given authority over prices and production, but control is exercised through competitive markets. Despite the policy, inequality has doubtless been greater than a sound valuation of productive services makes necessary, though much less than unrestricted monopoly would have produced.

Public-utility regulation has the same purpose of preventing excessive profits and protecting the real income of consumers, but it operates through governmental price fixing and control of production. It can curb monopoly effectively, and many persons have thought that it should be applied more widely to protect the public against the market power of producer groups in mass-production industries. But such persons are likely not to appreciate the complexity and sensitivity of price relationships and their role in economic organization and adjustment. Wartime emergency price control, with its limited purpose, was sufficiently difficult and sufficiently unsatisfactory. To subject the economy to an enlarged and continuing control of this sort would seem to be a costly way of getting a small improvement in the division of income.

Application of upward pressure to wages

Many wage earners, in the usual sense of that term, have incomes above the average of all incomes, but the great majority receive considerably less. Hence raising wages is generally regarded as a leading means of reducing inequality. Minimum-wage laws strike most directly at very low-wage situations, but greater dependence is placed on labor unions and collective bargaining to improve the position of most workers.

Collective bargaining keeps the control of wages in the market, in a sense, as against depending on government to fix wages. But it means that combination is substituted to some extent for competition as an accepted market procedure. A labor monopoly is, in principle, as objectionable as a business monopoly, but the theory is that some combination is necessary to offset the inherent disadvantage of the individual worker in dealing with the employer of many workers. This is probably an acceptable theory within limits, even though its application often involves use of the strike, which is essentially a jungle method of settling an issue. Unions help to give workers the full value of their service, and to insure satisfactory conditions of employment in other important ways.

The difficulty with the union method of reform is that union power may not be limited to this balancing role in the market. Thus unions may insist on wages that exceed a proper valuation of services in the usual sense. The result is that prices to consumers are raised and employment opportunities altered, with effects on distribution quite different from those directly intended. This outcome is most pronounced when times are good and jobs plentiful; it is then that the lowest level of income recipients, made up largely of persons not aided by unions, suffer most in their relative income position. Union leaders, of course, declare that their wage demands are reasonable and within the capacity of employers without raising prices. But a scheme of control is plainly faulty in which interested private groups can judge such matters for themselves and exert an unrestricted power over markets to reach their goal.

Governmental price control has been suggested as a means of making wage increases fall on profits. But if government establishes price ceilings, it must also control the wages that are being pushed against those ceilings. So great an extension of public authority over markets would constitute a fundamental change in economic organization, and its prospects of success would be doubtful within a system of voluntary private enterprise. Friends of unions express the hope that union leadership will grow in its sense of responsibility and will keep union demands within reasonable limits without compulsion. Since aggregations of private power appear inevitable on both sides of the labor market, progress in economic control must depend in part on the restrained exercise of that power. But economic organization must not rest fundamentally on the assumption that interested groups will be self-denying in their exercise of power. Either the power itself must be limited, or government must control it. The former fits much better into the structure of a free system.

Fixing of prices above or below the market

Wage adjustments cause trouble when they violate the competitive pricing standard, and so does governmental price fixing that is undertaken to improve the incomes of particular groups. This point was made in the discussion of agricultural-adjustment policy. If prices are to be held above the level at which farmers will voluntarily supply sufficient product to meet the demand, the supply itself must be controlled, and public authority must be applied extensively to the industry. Among the methods of distribution reform in this country directed at altering the operation of markets, the farm policy goes furthest in principle. However in practice it may be that the gains of farmers have come more through the subsidies received than through the improvement of prices.

Reform may take exactly the opposite course, holding prices at an artificially low level when the aim is to benefit the buyer. An example is the policy that has been followed to some extent of providing housing to low-income tenants at rentals below the market. With the high-cost conditions that prevail in the construction industry, satisfactory new housing cannot be provided to people of low income at rentals they can afford if the full costs are covered. Housing is a major element in real income, and reduction of the charge for it is a direct method of increasing income. But a simple policy of price control that sets rentals below the cost level cannot yield this result except temporarily, since needed housing will not be supplied. To maintain artificially low rentals, government must either enter the housing field or subsidize private housing. Thus the reform cannot be merely a policy of price control but must involve control of supply and secondary distribution at the taxpayer's expense.

Promotion of market information and mobility

Market policies to improve the division of income may operate in other ways than through adjusting the prices of products and services. Policies may seek also to increase knowledge, prevent deception, and promote mobility to the end that goods can be bought and services sold more advantageously and private enrichment made difficult without rendering service to justify it.

Thus, prevention of deceptive market practices, through such policies as the Pure Food and Drugs Act and the Federal Trade Commission Act, improves the operation of markets. So also does the control of weights and measures and the requirement, where practicable, that products be accurately described and labeled. No one should suppose that markets can provide a satisfactory basis of economic organization unless the people who buy and sell in them are reasonably well informed. To this end, both policing and education are needed.

It may not seem, at first glance, that protection of investors can improve the division of income, since most savings come from the larger incomes. But the modest savings of people with quite low incomes are an important source of security and satisfaction; and it is these savings that are most likely to be lost through unwise handling. It is thus important to curb the fly-by-night security salesman and the purveyor of get-rich-quick schemes, along lines followed in state and federal securities legislation, and to require that investment proposals be described fully and accurately. Perhaps even more, the needy debtor requires protection from loan sharks and the trickery of ruinous credit schemes.

The chief effect of such measures on distribution may be felt in reduction of incomes at the upper end of the scale. Fortunes have been made in finance, but not always commendably. While the essential service of getting together the funds for mobilizing resources must be rewarded, no other field has offered as great possibilities of unjustified return. Businesses have been promoted and corporations piled on corporations for reasons unrelated to the betterment of production. The machinery of corporation finance has often concentrated wealth and economic power without corresponding public benefit. Policies to prevent such concentration, but without restricting essential services, contribute to a sound capitalism as well as to a less provocative inequality.

Along with these market aids to consumers and investors, there is benefit to the ordinary worker if employment opportunities are made known to him and he is aided in taking advantage of them. A good system of employment offices to bring together "the jobless man and the manless job" promotes continuity of income and assists in adapting the type of work to the abilities and tastes of the worker. Indirectly such a system, moreover, enlarges the area in which employers must be competitive in hiring labor.

Artificial obstacles to the mobility of labor are, of course, objectionable. Unions which use high initiation fees and other restrictions to limit membership, and combine this policy with the closed shop, weaken the market position of lower paid labor.

Policies to Promote Equality of Opportunity

The price a person gets for a product or service influences his income directly. A more fundamental factor is his ability to supply the product or service. If all persons were equally able to provide the services of labor and wealth, free markets, except for lags, would give them equal incomes. But personal abilities vary widely among individuals, and disparities in the distribution of wealth exist in far greater degree. Can this situation be altered?

Certainly there are inherent obstacles to changing it. No control exists over the inborn potentialities of people as producers. Wealth is by nature subject to concentration, possession of it promotes further accumulation, and individual fortunes and capacities vary in accumulating it. But it would be wrong to conclude that nothing can be done under private enterprise, or that nothing has been done, to reduce the inequalities of individuals in supplying services.

Development of human abilities

If the supply of labor can be increased for better paying types of work and the number of people reduced who are capable only of unskilled work, inequality will be lessened by natural competitive processes. As indicated in Chapter 24, there is probably more room for improvement here than in equalizing property incomes, because more income is involved.

The greatest possibilities lie in the field of *education*. Alfred Marshall, the distinguished British economist, observed near the turn of the century that within a hundred years the wages of the unskilled had gained greatly on the wages of the skilled, and he attributed the change to a development of education which had sharply increased the fraction of the population capable of skilled and responsible work.[1] In the United States the number of years spent in school has increased by half over a fifty-year period, and the fraction of the people who finish high school has more than trebled. College enrollment has risen correspondingly.[2] Such figures cannot be translated statistically into shifts in the potential labor supply, but the change has necessarily been great.

From the economic standpoint, however, education has still far to go. In the poorer regions of the country, facilities and teacher training remain relatively poor. As more of the nation's youth devote twelve years or more to formal education, the results will depend on the direction that education takes. To increase greatly the fraction of the population who receive the present type of higher education seems more likely to reduce the quality of that education than to meet the needs of persons not clearly fitted for it. What is needed is a better adaptation of types of training to individual capacities and to economic opportunities.

It is especially important, from the distribution standpoint, that inequalities should not be perpetuated through the obstacles that low income places in the way of getting an education. In much of the coun-

[1] *Principles of Economics*, 8th ed., Macmillan & Co., Ltd., Bk. VI, Ch. XIII, 1920. Marshall estimated that, within a century, the fraction of the working force capable only of unskilled work and work involving little responsibility had fallen from a half to a quarter. He drew a distinction between skilled work and work involving responsibility and thought that abilities had developed greatly in the latter respect.

[2] See J. Frederic Dewhurst and Associates, *America's Needs and Resources*, Twentieth Century Fund, 1947, Ch. 13 on Education.

try the children of the poor have a reasonable chance for primary and secondary education, but the gifted youth of low-income families are less likely to get the advanced training that, in their interest and the nation's interest, they should have. Scholarships for promising but needy students seem a practical expression of the tradition of equal opportunity.

But to have an environment favorable to the development of human abilities, much more is necessary than the means of formal education. The home and the neighborhood, the whole *social setting,* should be such as will mold character and spur ambition. Not only criminal behavior, but low-level behavior in general is the product of a depressed environment. The less tangible factors in human development are the most difficult to control and the most likely to be self-perpetuating. Improvement in earning power must depend, in part, on the religious, social, and civic agencies that deal most directly with the lives of people.

Equalization of the distribution of wealth

Wealth, unlike human abilities, is not a part of the individual who owns it. Thus, on the surface, it may seem easy to alter the distribution of income-yielding wealth. This fact, and the great differences in individual accumulations, lead naturally to proposals for reapportionment of wealth as a means of equalizing income opportunities.

Socialists would remove the inequality from wealth by eliminating private ownership of material resources. Without proposing socialism, the late Senator Huey Long promoted a "share-the-wealth" movement in this country in the 1930s. Earlier, Henry George and the Single Taxers sought to remove the natural-resource element from inequality by taxing away the economic rent from land. In nations where great estates have been farmed by rent-paying peasants, the obvious reform has been to get rid of the landlords and give the land to the people who use it.

Short of socialization, the obstacles to reapportionment of wealth in an industrialized nation are apparent. The private income from wealth, and the appeal of accumulating it, are relied on to spur its growth and its effective utilization. While a highly unequal distribution is not essential to the working of capitalism, it appears certain to arise, and, whether inevitable or not, it is difficult to correct when it has occurred. Certainly a political atmosphere in which expropriation and arbitrary redistribution take place would undermine enterprise and reduce the efficiency with which wealth is used.

But it does not follow that property arrangements can never be modified to advantage. What is important is that proposed changes should be judged realistically by their probable results, not metaphysically. Too often private property is viewed in a mystical light as inhering somehow in the nature of things—as sacred and therefore immune to legislative tampering. Private property is a social institution, no doubt more deeply rooted in human nature than some of its critics concede but properly subject, as other institutions are, to analysis and modification on the basis of the way it works. Private property, moreover, is not a single, indivisible thing but a collection of arrangements that may to some extent be treated separately. Thus when a city, through a zoning ordinance, tells a man that he cannot build a gas station on a lot he owns in a residential section or a state regulates the manner in which a landowner may exploit his oil or timber resources, property rights are limited, but the institution of private property is not imperiled. The only real question is as to what the effect of the controls will be, all things considered.

Accordingly if unnecessary inequality is to be avoided, the difference between natural wealth and capital goods is worth considering from a policy standpoint. Investment and continuing reinvestment are necessary to expand and maintain industrial facilities, but not to expand and maintain land, at least in all of its uses. Private receipt of land rent is an incentive to careful use of land in agriculture, and perhaps elsewhere, and the single-tax program would certainly be highly confiscatory. But there may be a limited place for taxing land more heavily than the improvements on land, and for public retention of part of the income from mineral and other resources when they are released for private exploitation.

Particular property arrangements may become unacceptable to a people without pointing to socialism as the alternative. In the regions in which peasant farmers turn over a sizeable fraction of their product to large landowners, the functions performed by the owners are commonly not sufficient to prevent a sense of injustice and frustration on the part of the peasants. Such appeal as Communism has had in rural Poland, Hungary, Italy, China, and other countries rests on this basis. Drastic land reform in the interest of the peasants, even to the extent of giving them full title, may be the only way to preserve private ownership and enterprise at all. There can be circumstances in which capitalism must permit some equalizing of opportunity in order to survive.

Inheritance. Among property rights, the one most questioned in the United States, and hence most restricted, is the right to hand wealth down from one generation to another. Inheritance seems to violate most seriously the principle of equal opportunity, for it means that young people do not start from the same point in pursuit of income but enter a race in which the handicaps are heavy.

Whether inheritance should be limited should not be decided abstractly. The case for limiting it does not lie in the fact that the heir is not responsible for the wealth he receives and does not deserve it; he is not responsible either for the intelligence he inherits. Nor does the case against limiting inheritance lie in the mere fact that a traditional right would be violated. The significant point is that inheritance increases inequality, and, if one objects to unnecessary inequality, the question is whether this disposition of wealth is necessary and useful.

Inheritance is useful if it stimulates production and the creation of productive wealth. Doubtless men are stimulated along these lines by the desire to leave their families economically secure. It is desirable, moreover, that family security should be achieved in this way, rather than through public assistance. But neither of these considerations seems to call for unrestricted inheritance. Primarily men produce and accumulate not for post-mortem objectives but for the sake of income, security, and prestige while they are alive. Inheritance must be a declining incentive as the estate gets larger and the heirs more remote. Large inheritances are not necessary for family security and may be positively harmful to the recipients.

These considerations, plausible but not provable, seem to be widely accepted. At least prevailing policy in the United States is in harmony with them. The simple way to limit inheritance is by taxation, and this is the policy followed. The federal estate tax which became effective in 1942 imposed progressive rates, after an exempted $60,000, ranging from 3 percent to 77 percent on successive additional blocks of wealth. While this was a wartime tax, the rates were not much higher than those already in effect. In addition, taxes on inheritances are general among the states, with smaller exemptions but with lower rates. Death taxes are usually supplemented by taxes on gifts to prevent evasion through transfer of property before death.[3]

There is wide room for difference of opinion as to whether taxation of this kind has gone too far or should go further. It is enough to observe, in the present connection, that some redistribution of wealth has been thought desirable and possible under capitalism. Somewhat less inequality of opportunity is the result.

Review Questions

1. "People may not be able to agree about the policies that affect distribution, but they should be able to agree regarding the aims of policy and

[3] Since these taxes are avoided when wealth is given to educational and other nonprofit organizations, they provide an inducement to make such transfers. Organizations such as the Rockefeller Foundation provide extremely valuable services which are not likely to be performed either by private business or by government agencies. The medical services in tropical countries approach the problem of income in a fundamental way.

the standards that should govern it." Do you think this is a true statement? In the field of aims and standards, what matters seem easiest to agree on? What most difficult? Do you think that production should ever be sacrificed to reduce inequality?

2. In what ways do the following policies affect the distribution of income: antitrust policy, public-utility regulation, prevention of deception and promotion of information in markets, control of security sales, agricultural-adjustment policy, low-cost housing, employment offices?

3. "Controls which aim to fix prices at the competitive level are likely to work better and more simply than controls which would fix prices above or below that level." Explain. Apply to wages and to various product prices.

4. "If any important change is to occur in the sharing of the 75 or 80 percent of total income that is received for personal services, there must be a change in the distribution of human abilities and ambitions." How are education and various social services related to this possibility? From this standpoint, how would you like to see education improved?

5. What, if any, possibilities of changing the distribution of wealth, or of income from wealth, seem to be present under capitalism? What are the obstacles to change? Why is inheritance a vulnerable aspect of property institutions? Does present taxation of inheritances seem reasonable?

Social Security and Secondary Distribution

How well individuals and families live depends primarily on the return they receive from their labor and their wealth. If the primary division of income is to be changed, it must be done, as we have seen, (1) through altering the operation of markets or (2) through lessening the differences between people in their ability to supply labor and wealth. But there is more to the distribution problem than can be dealt with through improving the primary distribution of income.

Poverty is most critical for individuals who receive little or no income directly from production and who lack savings. At all times there are millions of consuming units without a regular wage earner—families consisting of old people, widows with children, defectives, and other unemployables. There are also the numerous families whose regular wage earner is injured, sick, or unemployed. Hardship in many cases arises not only from lack of income but from exceptional expenses caused by illness and injury. Thus, in a society in which income is distributed primarily according to the value of services, it becomes necessary also to divide income, or redivide it, on the basis of needs. The arrangements for doing so must be of a collective, ordinarily of a governmental, character.

Apart from actual want, the fear of want is an income factor. The welfare that an economy affords, whatever its productivity, is seriously reduced if income for the mass of people is highly undependable. The depression of the 1930s dramatized the insecurity factor, and *social security* has been the watchword of reform movements of recent years.

Large issues are raised. How far should a society go—how far can it go—in providing income to people who do not currently earn it? What methods should be employed? Should individuals be required when they are working to contribute to funds on which they can lean in case of need? Or should the general taxpayer pay the bill? Should aid be forthcoming only when need is shown, or as a matter of right when certain situations arise? Should secondary distribution through public channels, relied on mainly to aid the needy, be extended broadly to raise low incomes and reduce high incomes in order to lessen inequality?

In this section American policy will be described briefly, and some of its debatable features will be pointed out.

Approaches to the problem

A society with an individualistic tradition does not readily establish collective means of redistributing income. It assumes that individuals should somehow meet their own emergencies. They should be frugal and have savings to fall back on. Old folk without savings should expect to live with their children, and families should be responsible for their needy members. Outsiders should also be helpful where necessary, and private charity should play a large, if unobtrusive, role. As a last resort, the community should assume an official responsibility and at least maintain a poorhouse or poor farm and perhaps render limited aid in other ways.

The philosophy is very old that the community is responsible in some degree for the support of people who cannot earn a living. Under the feudal system the serf on the manor was entitled to maintenance. In the centuries that followed, though the church was often the main dependence of the poor, relief of the destitute was a leading public problem. The evolution of the poor laws has a prominent place in the history of local government. Provision for the needy was usually meager, and only in recent years has the idea prevailed that it is worth while for the community to prevent the demoralizing effects of destitution. Administration in this country has been mainly on a township, municipal, or county basis, but with expanding supervisory and financial participation by the states and with such matters as public health and the housing of defectives receiving separate attention. Not until the unemployment of the 1930s did the federal government participate, but its work-relief program and other aids then became a major expression of public responsibility for persons in need.

Relief matters have been mixed with other problems. A stamp plan to distribute foods at low prices became part of the disposition of agricultural surpluses. Public-works expenditures were expected to achieve recovery, as well as afford relief. Deficient purchasing power became the popular explanation of economic ills, and people acclaimed proposals such as the Townsend Plan that promised to combine comfortable idleness with high prosperity.

Out of this period of the 1930s came the federal social-security program which undertook to provide in a systematic way for the financial contingencies of old age and unemployment. European countries had already applied features of private insurance to leading problems of income uncertainty, and American states were experienced in handling industrial accidents in this way. Whether or not the Social Security Act of 1935 applied the insurance principle in a strict sense, it tried to place the cost of insecurity on the economic situations where it arose rather than on the general tax-paying public. This is about all that the term *social insurance* means.

Insurance as a device to achieve security

The insurance principle should be considered briefly. Insurance by voluntary private action has a conspicuous role in the economy. Fire insurance, windstorm insurance, automobile insurance, accident insurance, hospitalization insurance, life insurance provide familiar services. The object of all insurance is to promote security of real income: perhaps through compensating for losses which, though infrequent, are severe when they occur; perhaps by providing funds for times when ordinary income stops.

The insurance principle is simple, though its application becomes complex and requires the services of skilled actuaries. It is not known that a certain house will burn in a given year, but it is known with fair accuracy what the fire losses will be for a million houses of the same type. If the owners of the million houses pay enough into a common fund to cover the losses, the cost to each owner will be small, and no owner will suffer a great loss.

Similarly, it cannot be predicted on January 1 that a specific person of a certain age will die during the ensuing year, but for a large number of persons of that age, the number of deaths can be predicted closely. A payment of $1000 to the families of those who die can be assured with confidence if each person in the age group pays into a common fund a small premium that reflects the probable number of deaths.

The insurance principle is applicable where there exists *a large number of practically identical risks, for which the average occurrence of a certain contingency is known.* The participants may be said to pool their risks, with the result that a small certain payment is substituted for a large uncertainty. Those who seek protection from a private insurance company must make a payment that covers the risk itself and also the administration of the fund, the cost of soliciting insurance, and other items.[4] Much life insurance, especially in endowment and annuity policies, is less a strict application of the insurance idea and more an elaborate scheme of cooperative investment of savings.[5] Social insurance may be of this nature.

While private insurance provides for numerous contingencies, its coverage is limited, and it is little used to protect ordinary workers from loss of income through accidents, unemployment, or lack of savings upon retirement. Into this situation social insurance enters, with its broad compulsory coverage under government auspices and its assignment of all or part of the costs, on the surface at least, to the employer rather than the worker.

Whether the worker actually avoids the cost that the employer appears to meet is another question, and not an easy one; but the worker probably bears more of the cost than he appears to. The social-security payment that the employer makes through employing a worker should logically enter his calculation as to whether it is worth while to hire the worker and what he can afford to pay the worker. Perhaps, in the first instance, the premium, or pay-roll tax, enters as a cost into the price of the product and is borne by the buyer; if so, it should enter the buyer's calculation as to the amount he will buy at a particular price. Thus, wherever the cost of security falls in the short run, there is a tendency for it to fall finally on the worker's wages. But, wherever it falls, it is attached to the production and use of the product rather than charged to the public in general taxes.

But this is the case only in so far as the pay-roll levies are adequate to meet claims. Often they are not, and then general government revenues must be drawn on, and the scheme is an ordinary instance of secondary distribution of income.

[4] These other items have sometimes included an unjustifiable margin of profit. In general, casualty insurance has not been well regulated either by competition or by government, but pressure has developed for more effective control. Life-insurance companies are large-scale investment organizations, and there has been extensive public control, as in the case of banks, to insure adequate reserves and sound use of "other people's money."

[5] Life-insurance policies which include only the insurance feature are known as term policies.

Accident compensation

Systematic provision for the income contingencies of workers came first in this country in the case of industrial accidents. It is estimated that more than a million accidents which occur on the job cause loss of working time each year in the United States and that more than 1 percent of these are fatal.[6] The total loss of working time and of production is large, and, unless there is compensation to the worker, the medical expenses and lapse of wages constitute a heavy burden.

Until the present century the only legal recourse of the worker was to sue the employer on grounds of negligence. Proof was difficult and legal action costly, so that, in fact, little protection was afforded. Beginning in 1910 state governments began the enactment of so-called workmen's compensation laws which established regular schedules of payments to injured workers and required employers to take out liability insurance with approved companies or with the state to assure payment. Compensation is received by workers as a matter of right, not through some decision about the responsibility for accidents, and is intended to cover a substantial part of the wages lost and medical expenses incurred, with additional indemnity for deaths. Most, but not all, workers are covered; the state laws vary a good deal in particulars. Federal employees and a few others are covered by federal statutes.

Most industrial accidents are, in a sense, avoidable, and great progress has been made in reducing them—in some degree, no doubt, through the incentive of reducing the cost of compensation. But though avoidable in nature, many accidents are still bound to occur where fallible human beings work long hours with industrial equipment. It is realistic, therefore, to view injuries and deaths as a cost of production, just as labor itself is a cost of production. It is logical that the cost of injuries should enter the price of the product and be borne by the consumer. Whether, in fact, it is so borne is debatable, but in any case there is great gain in diffusing the cost and preventing the severe hardships that otherwise would befall injured workmen and their families.

Unemployment compensation

Unemployment is said to exist only in the case of employable persons who want work and cannot get it. As explained in Chapter 14, unemployment is a normal feature of seasonal and inherently irregular industries and occurs sporadically as a result of many shifts and disturbances in a dynamic economy, but the greatest unemployment is an aspect of

[6] See H. W. Hendrich, *Industrial Accident Prevention*, 2d ed., McGraw-Hill, 1941, for an analysis of this problem.

severe general depressions. The latter are undoubtedly the most harmful and dangerous source of insecurity in the economy.

Unemployment had traditionally meant resort to private resources and general public aid. But unemployment on the scale of the 1930s seemed to call for a broader and more systematic approach and one which, in effect, declared the responsibility of the economic system itself for the lack of jobs. State efforts were unpromising, because no state wanted to burden its industries with costs that other states might not impose, and Congress, in the Social Security Act of 1935, adopted a joint state-federal plan. A 3-percent federal tax was imposed on pay rolls, but employers would be credited, up to nine tenths of the tax, with payments that they were required to make under state unemployment-compensation laws. Thus, since their industries would be taxed anyway, it behooved the states to enact laws that would preserve 2.7 percent of pay rolls for unemployed state workers. In doing so, they had considerable latitude as to the precise provisions of the laws they enacted, but certain general federal standards had to be met. The other one tenth of the federal tax was to be used for administration of the plan.

Not all employment was covered. In particular, the plan did not apply to agriculture, domestic service, government work, and firms with less than eight workers. To be eligible, a worker would need to have been employed in a covered occupation for a specified period, but he would not have to declare that he lacked private resources. He would be entitled to compensation as a matter of right when he became unemployed. Compensation would be only a fraction of the pay he had received, and until World War II it did not reach a $20 weekly maximum in any state. Compensation could be received only for a specified number of weeks—perhaps twenty-six in a year—and after that the unemployed worker, if he could show need, could go on general relief.

To receive compensation, a worker would have to be ready to accept any appropriate job that was offered him, but, to be appropriate, the job would have to be reasonably close to his accustomed type of work and not substandard in compensation or working conditions nor available as the result of a strike. In this connection one of the major difficulties in administering unemployment compensation arises, since employment offices are not likely to act uniformly and there is danger of a laxity that will enable workers to receive compensation when they should be working.

There is difficulty also in continuing to finance unemployment compensation on the intended basis. Ideally the pay-roll tax should reflect average unemployment and yield sufficient money, but not too much, to carry out the specified schedules of compensation over a term of years

In practice, however, unemployment lends itself poorly to the insurance principle. Its average rate of occurrence is not predictable, since it comes spasmodically, sometimes in vast epidemics as in the 1930s. A pay-roll tax adjusted to severe depressions would be prohibitively heavy, but a lighter one means that funds run out when a severe depression comes. This has been the experience abroad. When necessary, payments are continued at general public expense. Though they are still received as a matter of right, their source is the source of general relief.

Though not the insurance scheme that it purports to be, and often inadequate from the workers standpoint, the system has advantages. In principle, it recognizes that unemployment arises for reasons outside the worker's control, and assists him on a dignified basis. Being definite, it removes some of the insecurity that undermines welfare. Being counted on, it may keep consumption expenditures on a more even level and lessen the sharp curtailment of buying that fear of unemployment generates. Thus the whole economy benefits.

Provision for income in old age

Very few ordinary wage earners are able to accumulate savings enough to support themselves and their dependents after retirement. This situation gives rise to an expanding income problem. As a result of the tapering off of population growth in the United States, the percentage of the people who are classed as old is rising sharply. Shortly the number who are over 65 will exceed 10 percent of the population. The movement from farm to city causes added difficulties, because retirement means a sharper break in urban occupations and for manual workers it comes at an earlier age. Income arrangements in the economy must somehow provide for the later years of life.

Ideally each occupation should support its members on a lifetime basis, from infancy to death. To do this, it not only must yield an adequate income but must arrange for a suitable spreading of income over periods in which regular pay is not received. Since ordinary private saving cannot be counted on, one possible arrangement is a *pension system*. Many business firms have established pensions for employees of long standing, sometimes on a definite contractual basis, sometimes more flexibly. Pensions are quite general for government employees, including schoolteachers. The cost of pensions is considerable, if not offset by lower rates of pay, but there is a gain to the employer from greater continuity of service. A few labor unions also have established pension arrangements for their members and have increasingly put pressure on employers to contribute to pension funds. Pension payments are usually small in comparison with previous earnings, but they may go far toward maintaining financial independence in the less demanding later years of life.

Voluntary private pensions are available for only a small part of the population, but something of the same idea is present in the system of *old-age annuities,* compulsory and widely applicable, adopted years ago in many European countries and in the United States in 1935. Coverage in this country is broader than for unemployment insurance, because it is not limited to firms with at least eight employees; but it does not apply to agricultural, domestic, and government employees or self-employed persons. The cost is supposedly shared by employers and employees. It was provided in the Social Security Act that 1 percent should be taken from wages and salaries up to $3000 and an equal pay-roll tax in addition should be paid by employers. Payments were to be increased until they amounted to 6 percent of pay rolls, 3 percent from each party, but Congress on successive dates has so far postponed the increase. This plan is wholly under federal administration.

Annuity payments begin at 65. As originally provided, they were to be closely proportioned to the amounts that individual workers had paid into the fund, but later amendment (1) greatly improved the relative position of low-paid workers and (2) made the annuity depend much less than before on the length of time that the worker had been covered.[7] The basic annuity is not likely to exceed a third of the worker's average pay, but additions are made for dependents, and there is also provision for surviving dependents when the annuitant dies. The plan is referred to officially as "old-age and survivors' insurance." Under the Railroad Retirement Act somewhat more generous provision is made for railroad workers.

It is essential to note that old-age annuities are received as a matter of right, and not on a showing of need. The high-paid executive who is subject to the annuity provision on the first $3000 of his salary is as eligible as any other workman. As originally planned the annuities might be viewed, except for their compulsory feature, as an ordinary business arrangement. Human life is predictable for large groups, and it was intended that pay-roll levies would finance the annuities on a business basis. About the only redistribution of income would arise from the fact that individuals do not stay close to the group average. Some live

[7] The 1939 formula provided that the monthly "primary insurance benefit" should be the sum of the following: (1) 40 percent of the first $50 or less of average monthly earnings in work covered by the Act, (2) 10 percent of the next $200 of average monthly pay, (3) the sum of the two preceding items times 1 percent times the number of years in covered employment. For a worker whose average pay had been $150 monthly during 20 years in covered occupations, these items, respectively, would be $20, $10, and $6, or a total of $36. One half of this primary benefit is added for a wife over 65 and for each dependent child under 18. The family maximum is $85.

longer than others and thus cause the sort of redistribution that is present in all insurance.[8]

Redistribution through the annuity plan. Under the amended Act, however, substantial redistribution results, or will result, for a number of reasons. Workers whose average pay has been low get relatively more in relation to what they have paid in than workers whose average pay has been high. Workers who have paid for only a few years get more relatively than workers who have paid for many years. Needs are thus recognized more fully, but at the expense of the insurance principle.

Moreover, early annuitants, those who come in while the pay-roll levy is low, are favored in comparison with later annuitants who must contribute a higher percent of their wages. From an insurance standpoint, the plan is far from self-sustaining at the lower rate. On the surface, this may seem strange, since much more is being taken in than is being paid out. But the point is that claims will increase tremendously during coming decades, and most of the money coming in during the early years should be accumulated as part of a reserve to meet the payments to annuitants who have years to wait. Later on, the 6-percent levy will be no more than enough. In fact, it will be less than enough, because the fund should have accumulated at 6 percent almost from the beginning to remain on even keel. Thus still another type of redistribution will occur. The deficiency in annuity funds will have to be made up by the general taxpayer.

The reserve problem. Why has the pay-roll levy been kept from increasing quickly up to 6 percent as first planned? Why was the annuity formula changed to favor those who had paid but a short time? The main reason lies in the peculiar difficulty that a government runs into when it goes into the insurance business. To build up a reserve, receipts must exceed payments in the early years, and it is difficult to fit this factor into the processes of government finance. Certainly the government must not take large sums of money from pay-rolls and impound it, for the effect would be highly deflationary.

Accordingly the Act provided that the reserve fund should be invested in government bonds. The government would borrow the surplus cash from pay-roll levies and use it for general government purposes, meanwhile paying interest into the fund which would help build it up. But whatever the accounting, it is not desirable to make general use of billions of dollars collected for a special purpose, and it is a little startling to contemplate a governmental annuity reserve of $50 billion or so made up of government debts. Moreover, if the government is try-

---

[8] There is, of course, some further redistribution in so far as any part of the pay-roll tax remains on the employer or is passed on in higher prices to consumers who are not workers covered by the Act.

ing to use its borrowing, as it was in the 1930s, to stimulate the total demand for goods and promote prosperity, it should borrow idle savings or bank credit rather than funds from pay rolls. From a more general standpoint, it is probably not good politics to be taking large sums from workers in excess of what is being paid them currently. Thus it seemed better to postpone the increase in pay-roll levies and to alter the annuity formula in order to reduce the rate at which the fund would accumulate.

Old-age assistance. The Social Security Act also encourages systematic relief payments to persons over 65 who do not qualify for annuities but are in need. Provision for such payments is left to the states, but the federal government agrees to contribute half of the assistance rendered up to a specified maximum per person. Originally the federal contribution was limited to $15 monthly; later the limit was placed at $20. The standard that must be met in showing need to qualify for assistance, and the amount of assistance provided for, differ from state to state. This plan undoubtedly tends to discriminate against equally needy persons below the age of 65 for whose assistance the federal government gives no special encouragement.[9]

Proposed extensions of social security

The movement to protect people against economic hazards still runs strong, and the goal of cradle-to-grave security embraces considerably more than has been achieved. With the 1935 program well established politically, attention turned to the field of health. Numerous surveys, together with the physical examinations for the armed services during World War II, have shown that people in the lower income levels receive considerably less medical and dental care than they should have. Established public-health arrangements do not serve the purpose. The expanding voluntary cooperative or group plans through which members receive medical or hospital service for small fixed monthly fees seem unlikely to reach the neediest segments of the population.

Accordingly a plan of compulsory federal health insurance, with additional pay-roll levies to cover the charges of doctors and hospitals, has been widely advocated. The proposal is opposed as "socialized medicine" and as certain to undermine desirable features of present medical service.

Extension of social insurance is proposed also to cover loss of income through illness and general disability. Further proposals call for extension of unemployment compensation and old-age annuities to large groups not already covered and for substantial increases in benefit rates.

---

[9] Under the Act the federal government contributes also to the assistance of blind persons and of needy children.

The highly publicized Wagner-Murray-Dingell Bill provided for a 12-percent pay-roll levy for all purposes to be imposed equally on employers and employees.

Some social-security issues

The social-security program is already large, but it can easily reach a size that will make it a major element in the economy, in matters both of personal and of governmental finance. Some important issues are raised. In approaching them, one should have in mind three principles according to which security benefits may be claimed and cost apportioned. They may be called:

1. *The insurance or contributory principle.* According to it, prospective beneficiaries, with their employers, contribute to the funds for unemployment, sickness, old age, or other income contingencies. Benefits are claimed as a matter of right and not through showing need.

2. *The needs principle.* Under it the need for assistance must be shown by the person who is to receive it. Funds are supplied from the public treasury and obtained from ordinary tax sources.

3. *The gratuity principle.* According to it, benefits are claimed as a matter of right under such schedules as social insurance implies. Beneficiaries, however, do not contribute to special funds nor are there pay-roll levies on employers, but general tax sources, presumably the progressive income tax in the federal sphere, supply the needed money.

The needs principle long governed such assistance as government rendered in overcoming the income deficiencies of individuals. Regular provision for contingencies along insurance lines is an innovation of recent decades. But the insurance principle is seldom fully applicable, and there is a tendency for the security arrangements involving it to depend in part on general financing, though without applying a needs test in conferring benefits—a tendency, that is, toward the gratuity idea. Some students of the problem believe that this tendency should be encouraged, even to the extent of abandoning pay-roll levies altogether and placing the cost of social security on the general taxpayer. Whether this should be done is a major issue.

Objections to the insurance principle. One reason for favoring this tendency is the belief that it promises a better security program. The security plans which tie benefits closely to contributions involve elaborate specifications and tend to be rigid in application. They are likely, moreover, to emphasize certain outstanding and easily defined types of insecurity to the relative neglect of other sources of hardship.[10] They

[10] This point is developed and the entire social-security program discussed critically by Lewis Meriam in *Relief and Social Security*, Brookings Institution, 1946. The outstanding

centralize administration, reveal bureaucratic tendencies, and depart from the essentially personal and local nature of the problem.

Another reason is that the insurance principle, as we have noted, is difficult to fit into the processes of government finance. Accumulating a large reserve along insurance lines is objectionable, and a reserve consisting of government bonds is something of an anomaly anyway. If the receipts and outgo of government are to be managed with an eye to promoting and maintaining prosperity, pay-roll levies are an objectionable type of tax whenever depression is present or threatening. More fundamentally, the contributory principle is opposed by persons who would make social security the occasion for an extensive redistribution of income. If the benefits that go to ordinary workers are paid for largely with the proceeds of a progressive income tax, a substantial equalization of income results.

These are important considerations, but they do not settle the matter. Both the needs principle and the gratuity principle call for reliance on general tax sources, but they differ sharply as to the basis and the probable amount of the benefits. It is one thing to say that people in need should be aided by others according to their ability, and quite a different thing to set up elaborate schedules of benefits for various purposes, for which individuals are eligible without showing need, and simply charge them to the public treasury. Such an arrangement may be desirable, but its difficulties must be weighed.

Costs and politics. One difficulty is the matter of cost, and cost is an issue quite apart from the method of financing. The United States has not yet felt the cost of a broad security program. Annuity payments now are around $500 million annually; but under the existing system they will probably exceed $3 billion annually within thirty years and under proposed extensions of the plan would be much higher. In the prosperous year of 1946 about $1 billion were paid in unemployment insurance, apart from the special liberal treatment of veterans. Health insurance could cost perhaps $4 billion; and with disability insurance and an expansion in coverage and benefits at other points, the whole program could easily amount to $15 billion or more. Applied to pay rolls this is a large item. As an item to be met from general tax sources, it appears still larger. Before the war, federal taxes for all purposes were running at about one third of this figure.

No one knows what limits a sound economy must set to redistributions of income. But certainly its policy makers should weigh proposals carefully and move with caution. It is desirable that legislators should

---

spokesman for an inclusive social-security program is Sir William Beveridge. See his *Social Insurance and Allied Services*, Macmillan & Co., Ltd., 1942.

make their decisions in an atmosphere in which they are not overwhelmed by the pressures of interested groups. Under the *needs* principle, demands for extended security are restricted by the basis on which benefits are conferred. No irresistible movement develops for greater assistance to people who lack income. Under the *insurance* principle, prospective beneficiaries must consider the added pay-roll levies that must be met from the value of their particular product. But under the *gratuity* principle, neither of these restraints is present. As the ordinary person sees it, his income contingencies will be met at the expense of the wealthy, and he and others like him are overwhelmingly for the proposed beneficence.

There is great weakness in democratic government when large groups of voters have a direct financial stake in policies. It may be the stake of manufacturers and their employees in the protective tariff, of farmers in price-raising programs, of unions in labor legislation, of war veterans in bonuses, of low-income groups in social-security measures. It took a sharp political fight in California to defeat such a proposal as "$30 every Thursday." Had Dr. Townsend sought $200 every month for everyone over 40, instead of over 60, there is no telling how far he would have got. Few people have the integrity and political maturity to view realistically the proposals that promise to put money in their pockets, and public policy easily descends to the grab-bag level. It is in issues of this kind that the economy faces its greatest danger, and democracy as well. On this ground President Roosevelt, who was an ardent believer in an extensive security program, is said to have insisted that the insurance principle should largely be retained.

Effect on beneficiaries. It is often asked whether collective income arrangements, especially if much redistribution is present, do not weaken the fabric of society. The genuinely needy must be aided, but may not people be hurt more than they are helped by extensive assistance, and productivity undermined? Plainly this is a very fundamental issue and one on which opinions are bound to differ widely.

It is easy to agree that the squalid, degraded living that often accompanies extreme poverty should be abated. Society is at least interested in giving children a chance to become worth-while people. Probably the sympathies of most people call for a standard of assistance that goes well beyond the prevention of suffering and utter destitution. But how far? And since fear of want is an evil approaching want itself, does not economic welfare require some systematic provision against insecurity? And if people who are aided are to retain their self-respect, should not assistance come in a dignified manner, received as a matter of right and not in the spirit of alms? Where do such considerations take one?

Certainly they point to programs that many observers fear. Their fear is that too many will get the idea that "society owes them a living" and then act accordingly. Notions of rights develop readily—property rights, labor rights, and so on—and there is danger that people will too easily assume their right to a job and a decent living. What they should have as a matter of right, they are not likely to struggle to get. If, however, they feel morally bound to make their own way, and their welfare depends on what they do, they are likely to act with energy and ambition. On such an attitude, the argument runs, the productivity of the economy must chiefly depend. But more is involved than output. A society should be concerned over its production of people as well as of goods, and people of spirit, self-reliance, and character should be the goal of social arrangements. Paternalistic measures oppose this result. These, of course, are the sentiments of an individualism that is now often disparaged but should not, on that account, be ignored.

Secondary distribution and public finance

In this chapter some questions of government finance have arisen incidentally. The next chapter will approach systematically the broad problem of public expenditures and revenues, and what has been said here will fit into that discussion. Public action in redistributing income extends well beyond the field of social security and aid to the needy and establishes government as the principal agency of redistribution—far more influential, for instance, than unions and wage laws.

Public action in this sphere includes the payment of billions in subsidies to farmers and in bonuses and other aids to war veterans. More important, it includes the regular provision of primary and secondary education without charge to the direct beneficiaries and of higher education at less than cost. Provision of parks and playgrounds and many other services adds directly to the real incomes of the people.

Redistribution is brought about not only through these payments and services to individuals, but through the way in which the government obtains its funds. Whether money is raised for the purposes mentioned or for national defense and other general functions of government, the placing of much of the tax burden on people of large income promotes equalization. Whatever the policy, the sums that governments handle are now so great that public finance is the outstanding instrument of distribution control within the framework of capitalism.

Review Questions

1. "Income deficiencies are most serious not in the case of persons whose products and services yield a small return but of persons excluded in one

way or another from the usual channels of current income." Who are these people and what are the reasons for the exclusion? Do they constitute a large element in the whole distribution problem?

2. In what respect is the concept of social security broader than the older idea of public assistance? Does a social-security program necessarily involve secondary distribution between income classes?

3. Explain the insurance principle. What conditions must be present if it is to be applied fully? Give examples. In what ways does social insurance differ from private insurance? Can the insurance principle be applied more strictly to unemployment compensation or old-age annuities?

4. Should it be assumed, when an employer pays a pay-roll tax, that the burden of it rests finally on him? Where else may it rest? Explain. (This question gets us into the question of tax shifting which will be discussed in the next chapter.)

5. Why is it reasonable to subject industrial accidents to the insurance principle? What is the nature of workmen's compensation laws?

6. Explain the provision of the Social Security Act regarding unemployment compensation, bringing out the relation between state and federal responsibility. What is the main difficulty in administering such a policy?

7. Why is the financial position of retired workers a growing problem? Explain the annuity plan under the 1935 Act.

8. "The federal old-age annuity plan promotes redistribution of income to an extent not originally intended. This development is largely the result of difficulties in financing annuities on a strict insurance basis." Explain both statements.

9. Explain the system of old-age assistance as contrasted with old-age annuities.

10. Does it seem to you desirable to put health insurance on a compulsory federal basis? What are the main opposing arguments?

11. What are the main objections to financing a social-security program on the insurance or contributory principle? What can be said in rebuttal?

12. Considering specifically the main elements in an extended social-security program, do you think that they are objectionable from a broad economic and social standpoint? How far would you like to see such a program go?

13. "Government is a big factor in distribution both in the way it spends money and in the way it collects money." Explain.

PART VII

Further Areas of Government Action

WITH the distribution of income we complete the last of the major, fairly coordinate divisions of the subject of economics into which this volume has been organized. Economic welfare depends, first of all, on productive power, as considered in Part II. It depends, secondly, on the degree of use of that power, particularly the avoidance of depressions—the subject of Part IV. The most complex requirement of economic well-being is the direction of use of productive power, the allocation of numerous resources among many alternative employments and the assignment of particular products to consumers—the problem of coordination to which Part V was devoted. Finally the problem of distribution and inequality has been considered in Part VI.

Most of the subject can be fitted reasonably well under these headings, although it seemed convenient to pay separate attention to money and the payment mechanism in Part III. But there remain a number of topics which, in various ways, cut across the divisions we have considered and involve questions of policy not properly subordinated to them. This miscellany is now brought together in Part VII.

One of these topics is government finance. Government is not merely an agency that controls private activity, but government itself, with its expenditures and revenues, is the greatest of enterprises and must be examined as a financial undertaking. Similarly the international side of economic organization, dealt with narrowly in Part III, requires broad consideration as a major area of policy. Lastly, in concluding the subject, we should undertake again a comprehensive view of the economy, reviewing the essentials of the American system and contrasting it with other systems that have been tried elsewhere or advocated here.

~ 31 ~

The Public Economy
and Government Finance

Under capitalism, productive resources are put to work mainly by private enterprisers. The main flow of funds is from private firms to the people participating in these firms and from these receivers of income back to the firms in payment for products. The problems of production, employment, pricing, resource allocation, and income distribution with which this volume has dealt thus far have been problems that lie mainly in the private sphere. The *private economy*, in short, has been the object of analysis.

It is true that much has been said about government. We have seen that governments charter corporations, issue money, control banks, set standards of market conduct, regulate utilities, supervise industrial relations. These are instances of the use of public authority to guide the private economy. They enter the study of the public economy also in so far as they entail the using of resources, the spending of money, and the raising of funds in the performance of these functions. But, however important these functions are to the private economy, their weight in the public economy is small because they cost relatively little.

In other words, in the study of the *public economy* we are concerned with governments as employers of resources, purchasers of goods, spenders of money, recipients of income, borrowers of funds. As we look to private enterprise for food, clothing, machines, and so on, so we look to the various governmental bodies for national defense, education, roads, policing, and many other services. Both as consumers of these services and as supporters of them, we are concerned with the way in which governments perform their economic tasks.

Governmental extravagance is a favorite theme of taxpayers, and so we shall begin this discussion by considering the purposes and the extent of public spending, the processes by which decisions are made and economizing done, the reasons for the growing prominence of government in the whole economy. Then, secondly, we shall examine the main source of funds in taxation, together with a number of tax principles, and, thirdly, the supplementary but highly important source of funds in borrowing and the growth of the public debt. Finally we shall review the various impacts of the public economy upon the private economy, not through regulation but through the spending and raising of money.[1]

Government Spending and Economizing

Several related questions will be considered in this section. What are the purposes for which the various governments—federal, state, and local—use resources and raise and spend money? How do they rank in point of cost and how large do they bulk in the whole economy? What are the reasons why these functions are governmentally performed, and do these reasons apply to possible further lines of expenditure? How do the methods of making decisions and economizing resources differ as between the public and private economies, and what are their respective merits? What light is thrown by these considerations on the growing economic prominence of government?

Government expenditures

To say for any given year how big the public economy bulks in the total economic picture is not easy. The problem is not primarily one of statistics but of interpretation. There are degrees of government participation in the use of resources and the flow of funds.

The extent of the public economy. Government is the enterpriser in providing national defense, public education, highways, prisons and related institutions, and some utility services, as well as in performing the general legislative, judicial, and executive functions. But what is the size of the enterprise? Some idea of the prominence of a private industry, say coal mining or textile weaving, is obtainable from its sales revenue. Most government services are not sold, but their cost, for most purposes, is a satisfactory substitute. When we observe, then, that in 1944 total public expenditures in the United States were $103.1 billion, whereas the gross national product was $210.6 billion, shall we conclude

---

[1] Leading textbooks in the field of public finance include Harold M. Groves, *Financing Government*, Henry Holt, 1945; Harley L. Lutz, *Public Finance*, Appleton-Century, 1947. For discussions of the impact of financial methods, see Alvin H. Hansen, *Fiscal Policy and Business Cycles*, W. W. Norton, 1941; Harold G. Moulton, *The New Philosophy of Public Debt*, Brookings Institution, 1943.

that government constituted almost half the American economy? The answer requires some important distinctions.

Certainly $103.1 billion do not measure the productive contribution of government in this peak year of public outlay. Of $95.6 billion of federal expenditures, $60 billion went for products of private industry. If private business is to receive credit for its role in the war effort, that product cannot be credited to government. Just as we ascertain the product of a private industry by measuring the "value added" by it to its purchases from other industries, so we must deduct purchases from private industries in measuring the activity of government.

Certain other items of government outlay must also be deducted if we wish to measure the role of government in utilizing resources. Large sums pass through public into private hands without buying either labor service or the products of private industry. These include the federal funds used for social-security and veterans benefits, farm subsidies, and, as we have seen, interest on the public debt. Similarly, federal grants-in-aid to state and local governments give rise to duplication when all outlays are totaled. Such federal items amounted to $6.5 billion in 1944, and state and local expenditures included similar items.

Thus, with total expenditures by federal, state, and local governments of $103.1 billion, their contribution to total product was only $34.4 billion—a large sum but still only a minor part of the national total. But from this it does not follow that the other elements in public outlays are not significant in appraising the impact of government finance. Privately produced goods used by government represent resources devoted to public ends. They show the weight of government in the allocation of resources. Altogether government spending controlled $96.7 billion of productive activity in 1944. Moreover the funds that are merely transferred through government hands reflect public participation in the division of income and the flow of purchasing power.

Developments in government spending. The cost of government is usually shown in statistics of disbursements which are subject to the interpretation just made. To make them provide a picture of the development of government activity in the United States, they should be analyzed to show (1) the functions or purposes of public outlays, (2) the part played by the different jurisdictions—federal, state, and local—in performing government functions, (3) the changes in public outlays through time. A few figures will give the outlines of such a picture.

Total public expenditures in the United States have risen tremendously—by 1947, to 16 times their 1913 level. Population has grown; and on a per-capita basis, the rise has been from about $27 in 1913 to $88 in 1929, $135 in 1940, and $760 in 1944, with a drop perhaps to $300 in

1947.[2] A truer comparison is arrived at by allowing both for the rising per-capita output of the nation and the higher prices in which that output is expressed. This is done when we say that public expenditures probably did not exceed 8 percent of the gross national product in 1913, but had risen to 10 percent by 1929 and to 18 percent in 1940. After the wartime rise to 49 percent, they had fallen to 19 percent by 1947.

TABLE 34—GOVERNMENT EXPENDITURES IN THE UNITED STATES
(In billions of dollars)

	1929	1940	1944	1947
Federal	$ 2.6	$10.1	$ 95.6	$30.9
State and local	7.7	9.3	8.5	14.2
Total	10.2	18.3	103.1	43.3
Relation to gross national product	10%	18%	49%	19%

Table 34 shows this last comparison, and it also shows the striking expansion of federal, in comparison with state and local, expenditures.[3] In a twenty-year period federal outlays have grown from little more than a quarter to two thirds of total public expenditures in the United States. At the same time, state outlays have risen sharply in relation to those of counties, townships, municipalities, and other local units but have not fully caught up with them.

Both the rise in the cost of government and the more centralized placing of the burden are to be explained by a few developments. The depression of the 1930s required outlays for relief that could not be met by state and local units, and large federal expenditures were undertaken also to promote and maintain prosperity. Federal outlays for relief and public works were about as high in the 1930s as total federal outlays for all purposes in the 1920s. In addition, agricultural aid amounted to about a billion a year, and by 1940 another billion was required for interest on the public debt.

War—past, present, and anticipated—is the great occasion for federal outlays. Defense expenditures were running about $1 billion annually

[2] From *Facts and Figures on Government Finance, 1946–1947*, Tax Foundation, Inc., as reproduced by W. Nelson Page and Walter Krause, *Basic Data of the American Economy*, Richard D. Irwin, Inc., 1948, p. 127.

[3] Data for the first four years are from *National Income*, the July 1947 *Supplement* to *Survey of Current Business*, p. 23; for 1947 from the July 1948 issue of the same publication, p. 18. Data for expenditures are compiled in a number of ways and published figures are frequently not comparable. The figures given here are for calendar, not fiscal, years; they do not include, as expenditures, such items as the loans that governmental bodies make. The totals are corrected so as not to count twice the grants-in-aid from federal to other units.

in the 1930s, and veterans of past wars were receiving a smaller sum. With the vast demands of modern total war, expenditures reached an annual rate of $90 billion in World War II. In the aftermath, a high level of defense expenditure has been maintained, great sums have been paid to veterans, loans and other assistance to foreign nations have been major items, and so also has interest on the public debt. Federal requirements for the fiscal year beginning July 1, 1948, are shown in Table 35 as they appeared to President Truman when he delivered his budget message.[4]

TABLE 35—ESTIMATED FEDERAL OUTLAY FOR FISCAL YEAR 1949
(In billions of dollars)

National defense	$11.0
Veterans	6.1
International finance, including European Recovery Program	7.0
Interest on debt (gross)	5.2
Social security, welfare, housing	2.1
Resource development, including transportation and atomic energy	3.3
Aid to agriculture	.9
General government and miscellaneous	2.1
Tax refunds	2.0
Total	39.7

At the state and local level the major items are education, which took $3 billion in 1946, roads and streets, which required $2 billion, and relief and other welfare items which required another $2 billion. Mounting outlays for these purposes explain the rising importance of state governments, since their financial capacity exceeds that of local units.[5]

It will be noted that little mention has been made of the ordinary expenses of running the legislative, judicial, and executive branches of government, of the cost of law enforcement and regulation of private activity. These fundamental services account for less than 10 percent of the total cost of government in all units. The point is significant when the problem of reducing the cost of government is considered. Any substantial reduction must mean less outlay for defense, debt service, veterans, education, highways, and public assistance to farmers, the aged, the unemployed, and other groups. Demands for government economy expressed in attacks on bureaucracy do not convey the situation ade-

---

[4] These are January estimates. By August the total had been revised upward to $42.2 billion.

[5] See Lewis H. Kimmel, *Governmental Costs and Tax Levels,* Brookings Institution, 1948, pp. 10–11.

quately. The main problem of economy is that of the importance to be assigned these major functions that government has come to perform.

Grounds for assigning tasks to governments

Ordinarily we ask no questions about situations to which we are thoroughly accustomed. Thus we take it for granted that the provision of food, clothing, automobiles, moving pictures, and a vast array of things belongs in the province of private activity and that national defense, highways, primary and secondary schools, and various other services belong in the governmental sphere. But in studying the public economy, this division is the very thing we should not take for granted. We should ask why specific functions are assigned to government and not entrusted to private enterprise. Under capitalism the tradition is that private industry should provide all commodities and services unless there is some positive contrary reason. At a time when the sphere of government is expanding, judgment of the trend requires understanding of the reasons that have operated in the past. In the case of public functions usually deemed basic, several reasons commonly apply.

Social benefit not a test. Government functions cannot be identified by the fact that they promote the general welfare and afford broad social benefits. This is a common criterion, but it is too loose to be meaningful. What, indeed, is a service to society? In their social importance, the provision of food and housing ranks very high, but these have not been included among the peculiarly governmental fields. If national defense is a public function, one can say of the industries which produce steel and planes that they are serving a public purpose, but no one contends that government should take them over for this reason. The argument has been used that general taxpayers should pay for highways, at least in part, because travel is educational and education is a public function. But if this reasoning is valid, the railroads, which also provide means of travel, should put in a bid for tax support. The general welfare must be more specifically defined.

Meeting of collective needs. A basic reason for assigning tasks to government is that the product or service is something which, as individuals, we do not buy. The service is consumed by the public only in a collective capacity. Thus there is no individual demand by which producers of the product can be guided, and on the basis of which they can charge for what they do. Then government, representing the public as a collective group, must register the demand and hire or buy whatever is needed for the performance of the service. National defense is an excellent example of such a collective service. So also is the maintenance of domestic order. That minimum of education necessary to meet the requirements of a democracy belongs here from the standpoint of collective need, though not for lack of individually realized benefit.

Requirement of governmental power. Closely related to the collective significance of products is the need of sovereign power in supplying them. The authority, backed with force, necessary to the national defense or the police system, could not be exercised under modern conditions by private organizations. Even more, it should not be entrusted to any private interest but only to an organization established to act on behalf of all interests. Applications of the police power to business, as seen in the control policies we have studied, require government to administer them. Indeed, in the case of any service that is not purchased voluntarily by the user, government power is necessary to impose the levies through which financing is done.

Inability of beneficiaries to supply funds. Beside the peculiarly collective services, there are others that yield recognized individual benefits which would not be provided to the desired extent if left to individuals to buy. Education is an example. While most primary and secondary schooling is governmentally provided, educational service is also provided and sold privately and was so provided altogether at an earlier time. We have seen that education is necessary from the collective standpoint; so also is the steel industry if a nation is to defend itself. The difference is that the steel industry develops adequately on the basis of private demand, but education does not. Education is expensive, and if all individuals are to have it, they cannot be expected individually to purchase it. Thus government must provide it to the extent thought necessary and finance it other than through the direct pricing of the service. What is true of education is more obviously true of the support of the needy and the care of the insane and other defectives. In the nature of the case, the beneficiaries of relief cannot finance it; if a certain minimum level of living is to be guaranteed to everyone, society through government must assume the responsibility.

These three characteristics—the collective nature of the want, the need of sovereign power to meet it, the necessity of apportioning cost other than on a benefit basis—largely account for the central, the almost never questioned, functions of government. But the public economy has expanded for reasons of two other types, and with invariable controversy.

Control of private economy. One of these is the hoped-for improvement of the private economy through the processes of government finance. By channeling part of the national income through public treasuries, its distribution may be modified or its aggregate amount may be expanded. Taxation, as well as public spending, plays a part in promoting these ends, and it is used also to restrict private lines of action. When government finance is employed not to carry on essential functions of the public economy but to control phases of the private economy, the term "fiscal policy" is commonly applied.

Superiority of public enterprise. The other is the aim of conducting certain industries better and at lower cost. It is on this basis that governments take over power plants, railroads, and other activities. The assumption is that public ownership and operation are more efficient than private ownership and operation. State socialism involves a broad application of this assumption.

As suggested above, these various reasons for government enterprise may be applied in a variety of combinations. The Tennessee Valley project was not made a government undertaking merely because men believed electric power should be a public industry, but because flood control and a broad plan of area development were involved for which government authority was necessary. The post office may seem as appropriate as the telephone to be a private business, but public policy has called for supplying some parts of the postal service on a noncommercial basis. Modern highways can be developed as business undertakings and their services sold, but the highway function originated in the social and political, as well as the economic, requirements of community life.

The processes of control and economizing

These considerations suggest a wide latitude in the expansion of the public economy. It is desirable, therefore, to compare the private and public economies more closely with respect to the processes by which they economize the use of resources.

The difference between them in the manner of registering the interest of the public in different goods was indicated in the analysis of market demand in Chapter 19. Market demand, in the private economy, is the summation of individual demands and reflects, on the basis of dollar votes, the relative interest of the public in having resources used for different purposes. In contrast, voting in the public economy is done with ballots, but usually the specific decisions as to the spending of money are made by representatives of the people, rather than by direct vote of the citizenry. These decisions are made by legislators and other officials on the basis of a broad judgment of collective need for schools and battleships and other things rather than as an attempt to sum up individual demands.

Lack of "automatic" controls. At the basis of market demand there are the comparisons by each buyer of the utilities of the alternative things that he may buy. Getting one thing is likely to entail not getting something else, and judgments reflect fairly close evaluations. The broad judgments in the public economy, on the other hand, are not likely to involve similarly close comparisons, even among the objects of public expenditure, and there can only be a crude comparison of these objects with the things that people would prefer privately to use their money for if taxes did not absorb it.

Behind this situation is the fact that the public appropriation of money for various purposes is not linked closely with the raising of money through taxation to pay the bills. The individual is governed in his expenditures by the money income he has to spend, but government has considerable latitude in fitting revenues to expenditures, since taxation is a compulsory process. It is also the case that the burden and benefit of particular public outlays are differently distributed. To the people in one district, a certain waterway development has great appeal because the whole country will pay for it. Every Congressman has his special vote-getting waterway project or its equivalent, and all Congressmen consider each other's political needs. These peculiarities of public finance are behind the story of the Congressman who, when asked how he managed to be re-elected so many times, replied: "It is very simple. I have made it a point never to vote against an appropriation and never to vote for a tax."

The resulting looseness. If these remarks suggest an unfortunate looseness in the processes of the public economy, one must hasten to emphasize that the system is the only one possible for those central public functions in which the end is the collective good and the cost cannot be imposed on the basis of benefits received. For most of these collective functions, moreover, it is in harmony with the democratic principle to let each person have one vote instead of making his influence depend on the number of dollars he has.

But the looseness is a reason for not applying the typical processes of the public economy where they do not need to be applied. This is not the same as saying that the sphere of government should not be enlarged. It is rather to say that government, where possible, should ape the processes of the private economy. In fact, to quite an extent, it does. Scarcely anyone would argue, when government enters the electric-power field, that legislative bodies should decide the outlays to be made on power production by making broad judgments, as in the case of education, as to how much electric power is required in the public interest. Rather, power is sold to individuals at prices somehow related to cost, and investment is governed, as in private industry, by the demands of customers.

Even in the case of public roads, a traditional government function, there has been some effort to follow the private economy as closely as possible without incurring the inconvenience of toll roads. Highways are developed, in part, on the basis of a close study of particular transportation requirements, and outlays are determined accordingly rather than on general judgments of the importance of good roads. Special taxes have been devised to impose the cost of road service as nearly as possible on the beneficiaries in accordance with the road service consumed. Such an effort should mean a considerable tightening of the processes of the public economy.

Two concepts of economy

The cry of all taxpayers is for economy in government, and most taxpayers believe that government is seldom economical. In considering this view, we should be clear what meaning we attach to the word "economy." Two meanings are possible—both embraced within the general concept of getting the most from resources—and they point toward quite distinct problems.

One is the problem of *choices in the use of resources,* the one we have been discussing. In this use of the term, government achieves the highest economy when the resources devoted to schools, defense, roads, policing, and other purposes are rightly proportioned among themselves and are rightly proportioned also to the resources used in producing food, clothing, household equipment, liquor, and all the other things provided within the private economy. In this meaning of the term, government economy is as likely to call for larger as for smaller public expenditures.

As always in choosing between alternatives, the ideal result carries out the *marginal principle*. Additional resources should be used for any purpose only if they will yield at least as valuable a product as would result if they were used to expand some other activity. More labor and capital should not be applied to education, for instance, if some more highly prized product must be sacrificed.

The special difficulty of applying the marginal principle in this situation is apparent. It is not as if a single buyer were exercising his preferences in using his income. Public officials must set a public purpose against the desires of the tax-paying public for the things that people would individually buy. It is easy to say that everyone would be better off if more were spent on schools and less on liquor and tobacco. But a decision on this basis does not rest on a direct weighing of comparable values by the people involved. Nor does it follow, if schools are expanded and taxes raised, that people will give up liquor and tobacco and not food and church contributions.

The other problem of economy is much simpler in principle. It involves not a choice of ends but the *achieving of given results at lowest cost*. If schools, highways, or defenses are to come up to a certain agreed standard, that standard should be attained with the minimum outlay of resources and the smallest drain on the public treasury. It is in this sense of economy that government is most often suspect. The use of unnecessary labor in manning bureaus and departments, a slow "government pace" in the performance of duties, looseness and graft in dealings with private firms are the common complaints of the critics of public administration. It is conceded that there are loyal public servants whose standards exceed those prevalent among workers in private enterprise, but these complaints reflect the common view as to the general situation.

Unquestionably these charges have some foundation. There are inherent difficulties in getting the utmost from resources when the product does not have to stand the test of salabilty on the open market. It is difficult to have tight administration, moreover, when it is not scrutinized at all points on a profit-and-loss basis. But the seriousness of these weaknesses need not concern us here. It is enough to say that the public economy has a heavy task in promoting economy in both senses of the word.

Review Questions

1. What is meant by the public economy? How does the study of it differ from the recognition of government functions in preceding chapters?

2. In explaining the extent of the public economy, what differences should be recognized between government outlays for (*a*) wages and salaries, (*b*) materials and supplies, (*c*) interest, subsidies, and relief payments? Show their significance in interpreting the impact of government finance.

3. What governmental functions occasion the principal outlays of the federal, state, and local governments? What developments explain (*a*) the rise in the relative importance of the public economy, (*b*) the centralization of functions?

4. "The cost of government is getting out of hand. A general assault on bureaucracy to get rid of unnecessary employees in federal departments and agencies will reduce the cost of government by a third or a half." Comment critically.

5. "Economic activities are ordinarily entrusted to government when they are socially important." Show that this statement is not very helpful in marking the boundary between the public and private economies under

capitalism. What seem to be the distinctive features of government functions?

6. Contrast the processes by which we decide what quantity of resources to devote to education and what quantity to automobiles. Compare the merits of these processes. Do all public outlays need to be controlled as outlays on education and defense are?

7. "Governmental economy is partly a matter of choices and partly a matter of efficiency in realizing accepted ends." Develop the distinction.

8. "In the public, as in the private, economy, and as between the two economies, the aim should be to equalize the marginal return from all uses of resources. But there are inherent difficulties in applying the marginal principle to public expenditures." Explain both sentences.

Government Revenue—Taxation

As traditionally viewed, government finance is a subject with two coordinate subdivisions. One division is the spending of money for various purposes and the administration of the expenditures. This is the topic we have been considering. The other is the raising of money to meet the expenditures.

Governments obtain money in four ways: (1) through levying taxes, (2) through borrowing, (3) through printing paper money, (4) through operating public businesses at a profit. We shall not discuss the last except to remark that there are communities in the United States that meet their local government expenses with the earnings of municipal power and gas plants. Printing of paper money will be considered incidentally in connection with borrowing in the next section. In this section we shall discuss the primary dependence of the public economy on the use of the tax power.

Taxes are compulsory levies. The logic of their use arises from the nature of the principal government functions, as we have considered them. When a recognized government provides services on behalf of all the people as members of an organized society, there can be no question of the obligation of all to contribute to its support. Taxes, accordingly, are obligatory payments for collective services.

Pricing in the private economy, even when it is the pricing of monopolists, leaves the individual free to buy or not to buy at the market price. When this element of choice is absent, and payments take a compulsory form and are not even adjusted to the services received by the individual, special problems arise in imposing the necessary levies. This section deals briefly with these problems. But, first, the system of taxation, or the agglomeration of taxes, in the United States will be sketched.

Taxation in the United States

Taxes are levied on a variety of bases. People may be made to contribute to government on the basis of the income they receive, the property they own, the wealth they inherit, the goods they buy (at home or from abroad), the wages they pay, the special privileges they enjoy. For each basis of taxation, the actual levy may be designed in a number of ways.

Local governments—towns and cities, townships and counties—have long relied mainly on *property taxes*. These are levied as a percentage of the assessed value of property—a value set officially and not necessarily close to the market value. Property taxes may cover only land and the buildings and other immovable improvements on the land, or they may be general property taxes that apply to other forms of wealth. The wealth, beside real estate, to which the general property taxes apply may include only such conspicuous types as the inventories of business firms, or it may include the personal property of householders. So-called intangibles, such as corporate securities, mortages, accounts receivable, and bank accounts, if taxed at all, are likely to be taxed under a separate statute with provisions adapted to their peculiar features. Special problems arise in the case of railroads and other utilities whose wealth is spread throughout a number of taxing jurisdictions.

State governments formerly depended largely on property taxes, but the tendency has been to assign this revenue source mainly to the local units. A majority of the states have come to rely heavily on a *retail sales tax,* usually of 2 or 3 percent, levied on the selling price of goods. It is essentially a gross-revenue tax. The sales tax may apply to all goods sold at retail, or certain goods such as foods may be exempt. The special sales tax on gasoline is a large revenue producer, but the tax is commonly regarded not as a general revenue source but as a means of providing funds specifically for highways.

Excise taxes, in the more precise use of the term, are a form of sales tax levied on specified commodities, quite often at the manufacturing stage. The goods most heavily subject to excise taxes have been tobacco and alcoholic beverages, but many other goods, especially in the luxury category, have been similarly taxed—commonly at 20 percent during the war period. Excise taxes have been used most widely by the federal government, but they have had some state and local use also.

Income taxes are most conspicuous in the federal tax scheme, but many states also impose them, though at much lower rates. The personal income tax is a graduated tax, with certain segments of income excluded under a system of exemptions and deductions and with rising rates applicable to successive increments of income. At their wartime peak the rates were graduated upward to the point where they took 94 percent of all income above $200,000. After several reductions, the rates in 1948 were such as to yield the returns shown in the table in the case of an unmarried taxpayer.[6] An additional $600 of income would be exempt for

TABLE 36—FEDERAL INCOME TAX PAID BY A SINGLE
PERSON, 1948

Size of income	Tax
$ 3,000	$ 351
5,000	700
10,000	1,824
25,000	7,305
100,000	51,122
1,000,000	713,660

each dependent, and married persons, under a new community-property arrangement, could divide family income equally between husband and wife. Thus the tax on $20,000 would be only twice what the tax on $10,000 would be without the community-property arrangement. As an upper limit, the tax was not to absorb more than 77 percent of any income.

In addition to the income tax paid by individuals, there is a federal *corporation income tax*. Corporate income in the lower range was taxed in 1948 at rates graduated from 15 percent, but the vast bulk of income, in amounts of $50,000 and above, was taxed at the flat rate of 38 percent. Interest paid on bonds is deductible in determining the taxable income of corporations.

Beside the basic corporate income tax, two other levies have, at various times, been imposed on the net incomes of corporations. One is a tax on *undistributed profits,* designed to catch that part of income not paid out in dividends and thus not subject to personal income taxation. A general tax on undistributed profits, adopted in 1936, was strongly opposed and shortly repealed. It has been succeeded by a tax on profit unjustifiably retained, for which the presumption is that the aim in retaining it is to avoid the personal income tax on the dividends rather than to provide capital for needed business expansion. The other is a tax on *excess profits,* levied on earnings found to be unduly large through application of one or another prescribed formula. This tax is especially useful in emergencies such as wars, when the need of revenue is very great and the problem of business incentives is not crucial. The

[6] Deductions for contributions to church and charity, interest payments, certain taxes, and other allowable items are assumed in each case to be 10 percent of income.

tax on excess profits in World War II rose to a rate of 95 percent, of which 10 percent was to be returned after the war. This tax was repealed as of the end of 1945.

Death taxes are imposed both by the federal and state governments. Such taxes may be applied to *estates,* the wealth left by deceased persons, or to *inheritances,* the portions of that wealth going to specified heirs. Under the federal tax, estates were taxed in 1948 at rates which ranged from 3 percent, after an exemption of $60,000, to 77 percent, applicable above $10,060,000. A credit is allowed for payment of the estate and inheritance taxes imposed by the states. These death taxes need to be supplemented by a tax on *gifts,* since otherwise they would be avoided through transference of property before death. Rates under the federal gifts tax ranged in 1948 from 2.25 to 57.75 percent.

Taxes on *pay rolls* are levied specifically to finance the system of old-age annuities and unemployment insurance. They were discussed in the preceding chapter.

Throughout the greater part of this country's history, the chief source of federal revenue was the duties collected on goods imported from abroad. The *tariff* still yields substantial sums, but it has become a minor element in the whole revenue situation.

Much revenue is collected by state and local units in the form of special *fees* and *assessments.* These may be privilege fees, such as accompany the issuance of corporate charters and licenses to sell liquor. The proceeds may be used for general governmental support or for particular services, as automobile license fees are used to finance road costs, or they may only cover the direct cost of some aspect of governmental supervision or policing as in the case of drivers' licenses and marriage licenses. Assessments are imposed to cover the cost of outlays of specific benefit to property owners, as when streets are paved, sidewalks repaired, and drains laid. These, like taxes, are compulsory levies, but they also resemble the prices that are paid voluntarily for goods.

Tax collections. The course of tax collections in the United States from the end of the prosperous 1920s through the depression and war periods is shown in Table 37.[7] In the federal sphere, it should be noted, income taxes—personal and corporate—were the main revenue source in 1929 but sank sharply as incomes fell in the depression. With rising incomes and increased rates in the war period, these taxes yielded a vast revenue. Even the excise collections became nearly twice as great

[7] Data for the first four years are from the July 1947 *National Income, Supplement* to *Survey of Current Business,* pp. 21–22; for 1947 from *Survey of Current Business,* July 1948, p. 17. The totals take account of minor tax and nontax receipts and of tax refunds that are not itemized. State and local receipts include federal grants-in-aid.

as total federal revenue in 1929. Social-security levies have also become a large item.

TABLE 37—TAX COLLECTIONS, 1929–1947
(In billions of dollars)

	1929	1932	1940	1944	1947
Federal:	$3.83	$1.70	$8.68	$41.98	$43.86
Personal income	1.24	.32	1.04	17.13	20.45
Corporate profit	1.25	.32	2.68	13.45	11.22
Estate and gift	.06	.03	.34	.56	.83
Excise, mainly liquor and to-					
bacco	.56	.63	2.12	5.26	7.30
Customs	.60	.26	.33	.38	.44
Social insurance	.12	.12	2.01	4.82	5.10
State and local:	7.57	7.31	9.96	10.99	15.26
Property	4.69	4.57	4.55	4.60	5.36
Income	.14	.06	.21	.33	.44
Corporate profit	.14	.06	.20	.46	.48
Death and gift	.16	.14	.11	.12	.18
Sales, general	—	.01	.53	.74	1.32
Liquor and tobacco	—	.02	.31	.44	.66
Sales, gasoline	.41	.52	.86	.67	1.27
Motor-vehicle licenses	.34	.29	.41	.41	.56
Social insurance	.12	.15	.27	.36	.49

For state and local purposes, especially the latter, property taxes have remained of leading importance; but the general sales tax has come to be a major factor in state revenue. The expansion of motor-vehicle license fees and gasoline taxes reflects the prominence of highways among government responsibilities.

Tests of a tax system

In analyzing the pricing of goods in the private economy, we dealt critically with pricing processes. When a scheme of charges is wholly subject to public authority, as is true of taxation, there is even greater need of considering the standards by which it should be governed.

Tax standards are applicable to individual taxes and to the tax system as a whole. But a natural question to ask at the outset is why such a variety of taxes should be used. Why not discover the one ideal tax and depend on it? Such a proposal, we saw, came from Henry George, who thought that a tax on land rent would be the ideal single tax. A more likely candidate, no doubt, would be a tax on income. Because real costs in the public, as well as the private, economy must be covered by the gross national product, why not simply assign to government a portion of the money return from that product?

Multiple tax systems are to be explained largely as historical accretions. Taxes are added but seldom dropped. While a specific logic sometimes explains the adoption of a new tax—as the gasoline tax for road purposes—the usual reason is simply the need of more revenue than existing taxes provide. Pressed for funds, legislators look about them for something new to be taxed. Usually it seems less painful, and more expedient politically, to vary the immediate source of tax money than just to raise rates, even though the ultimate source in income remains the same. With ingenuity, collections can thus be expanded.

We encounter, then, the first test a tax system should meet: It should be sufficiently *"productive"*—that is, should yield adequate revenue for the purposes of government. This test, it should be recognized, is subject to two quite different interpretations. The traditional view, the conservative view, is that the budget of a government should be in balance every year. From this viewpoint, those taxes stand particularly high which are productive in bad years as well as good. A general sales tax, with no exemptions for necessary commodities, meets this requirement very well. In contrast, the view has gained ground in recent years that it is sufficient to balance a budget throughout the whole period of a business cycle, with a deficit during depressions, or even not to balance it at all. Persons who adopt the latter view are free to attach greater importance to characteristics of a tax other than its mere revenue-yielding capacity.

Even if an annual balance is sought, there is usually considerable latitude as to how any given volume of public revenue will be raised, so the other tests enter in any case. One of these, the most important of all, should be thought of as applying mainly to the whole tax system rather than to individual taxes. It is that the public should regard the levies to which they are subject as *essentially fair and equitable*. A sense that the burden of government is distributed justly promotes a general sense of satisfaction with economic arrangements and is also important in itself as a substantial element in the whole distribution of income. Because of its complexities, we shall devote the next subsection to the matter of fairness.

In judging specific taxes, a leading requirement is that they should operate efficiently in providing revenue. This requirement has several aspects. One is that a tax should be *difficult to evade*. As an example, the property tax on real estate cannot be escaped, because land and buildings cannot be hidden. There is a fair chance, on the other hand, of escaping a tax on personal property, and especially on intangibles, simply through failing to declare them. This sort of levy has been described as a tax on honesty. From the evasion standpoint, the income tax is a feasible exaction, but it requires much policing, and evasion cannot be eliminated.

A related aspect of an efficient tax is that the *cost of collection should be low*. Most of the money taken from the taxpayer should become available for the real purposes of government and not be absorbed in tax administration. Taxes differ greatly in this respect. A tax on gasoline collected from a few wholesalers costs little to collect, but the net yield of the income tax paid by millions in the bottom bracket is small after the cost of processing tax returns is deducted.

Taxes should be subjected also to a variety of minor tests that may be put under the general heading of *minimizing the annoyance to the taxpayer*—which, when all its aspects are considered, is not minor. Taxes should be certain as to amount, simple to calculate, low in paper work. They should be convenient as to the period covered by a tax payment and as to the time when the payment is made. The cost of taxes to the taxpayer does not lie entirely in the money that he pays.

Direct and indirect taxes. On one point there is divergence of view as to the standard which should govern. Is the best tax one of which the taxpayer is keenly aware, as he is made to be by the procedure involved in paying his income tax? Or is it better that he should pay the tax almost unconsciously, as is usually the case with sales and excise taxes and import duties that are included in a succession of small amounts in the price of goods? This is the issue between so-called direct and indirect taxes.[8] On this issue the ordinary person, perhaps illogically with respect to the total amount he pays, seems commonly to favor the less conspicuous taxes. This, too, is the preference of the politician, to whom the supreme aim in tax policy, it has often been said, is "to pluck the goose with the least squawking."

On the other hand, many students of tax policy believe that government administration is likely to be improved when more people are conscious of the taxes they pay and thus more anxious to watch the doings of government. Certainly democracy requires an informed electorate, and taxation can be educational. From this standpoint, the property taxes seem to have fostered an attentive citizenry, and an income tax paid by nearly everyone is likely to train the eyes of the public on federal activities.

One may wonder, however, whether the economy promoted by awareness of property taxes is not likely to be a false economy, consist-

[8] Sales and excise taxes may be administered in a way to make them quite conspicuous when levied at the retail level. They may be stated explicitly as part of the customer's bill.

ing mainly in the restriction of expenditures and the starvation of important services or in the shifting of responsibilities to state and federal governments. Or the awareness of a tax—now with a broad-based income tax in mind—may simply mean the voting out of office of the men who favor it.

The question of fairness

Taxes may be unfair in a variety of respects. There may be stupidity, carelessness, and corruption in administering them, so that the individuals subject to them are not treated alike. This, for example, can easily occur in the assessment of property under the general property tax.

Unfairness may arise through the relationships of taxing jurisdictions in this country, either through gaps or overlapping in applying particular taxes. Thus, if some states tax inheritances on the basis of the location of the property which is covered, and other states tax on the basis of the residence of heirs or of decedents, the possibilities of confusion and inequality are evident.

Double taxation may arise in this way, and it may arise also in other ways, some of which are controversial as to their equity. As we saw in Chapter 3, the wealth of the community is not increased by having it represented by corporate securities or mortgages; yet, under property-tax laws, taxes may be levied both on the plant and equipment of a corporation and on the securities that represent the actual wealth.

We have seen also the difficulty that arises in taxing corporate income. Some income is taxed twice when a corporation is taxed on its profit and the stockholder is taxed on his dividends. If the same product and income resulted under the partnership form, only the personal-income tax would apply. On the other hand, if the corporation retains its earnings, no personal tax is paid on them, and stockholders may build up their estates through saving within the corporations in which they hold stock. Much avoidance of taxes has been accomplished in this way by persons in the higher tax brackets.

These are matters of fairness, but they are only incidental matters. The main question involves the central principle which should govern the distribution of the whole tax burden, if that distribution is to be deemed equitable. Individuals differ widely in their incomes, in their wealth, in the uses they make of the services that governments provide. Is there any compelling logic by which we can say what amounts should be contributed by the people in different economic positions?

Limited applicability of the benefit principle. As a starting point, it is usually said that there are two alternative principles, or guides, that are worth considering. The cost of government may be spread either (1) according to the benefits that people derive from the services of government or (2) according to the ability of people to bear the cost. The *benefit* and *ability* principles, we shall call them.

This starting point, however, is mainly useful as a basis for declaring that the benefit principle cannot, in general, be applied. To see why it is usually inapplicable, we need only recall the central characteristics of government functions as presented in the last section. Two of these characteristics are pertinent. If the distinctive feature of a government function is that the public is served not as individuals but in a peculiarly collective sense, as in the case of national defense, then it is futile to try to measure individual benefits. If benefits cannot be measured, even approximately, then they cannot be made the basis of taxation. Even more conclusively, if the distinctive feature of a public service is that it would not be provided if the beneficiaries had to pay, as in the case of relief services and much education, then it would be foolish to consider spreading the cost on a benefit basis.

But while the benefit principle cannot govern the financing of the central functions of government, it has important uses. In the private economy, we deem it eminently fair that the users of goods should pay for them. In the absence of compelling contrary reasons, government services may properly be financed on the same basis. The same people, with the same attitudes are served both by the public and the private economies, and there is no reason why displacement of private by public enterprise should revolutionize thinking in this connection. There is, moreover, the possibility of tighter public administration when utilities and costs, and receipts and expenditures, are connected as closely as is possible. Special fees and assessments have thus an important place in government financing. It seems as reasonable, for instance, to require the users of motor vehicles to pay the highway part of the cost of motor transportation as to expect them to pay the vehicle part of the cost, or to expect the patrons of railroads to pay for the services they receive.

Where the benefit principle is applicable, how is benefit to be measured? The word "benefit," though much used in this connection, has no definite economic content, and it invites looseness. To some it has suggested, for example, that the property owner should pay for the new drain or the road user for the new highway on the basis of the *advantage* he will derive from it. Such an approach launches one on a sea of guesswork, and there is no virtue in it anyway. The logic of the benefit approach is the logic of the private economy. There, as we have seen, prices are deemed just when reasonably related to cost. The beneficiaries of government services will be paying according to benefit, in a realistic sense, when they pay according to the *cost* of the services they receive.

The case for the ability-to-pay principle. Popularly, and in the literature of the subject, it is generally assumed that the cost of government should be apportioned mainly on the basis of the ability of people to bear it. Support for this principle rests mainly on grounds of fairness, but other considerations enter. Its standing is strengthened by the fact that no other alternative to the benefit principle is available and by the fact that tax resources appear greatest when everyone pays according to his capacity.

The positive argument on grounds of fairness is somewhat impressionistic, though still highly persuasive. If government serves the whole people, if it performs functions necessary to the well-being of civilized society, what is more just than that each person contribute according to his ability to the joint enterprise? The logic of the family is thus applied to the community. Under capitalism, the private economy cannot operate along communistic lines; but the public economy is inherently communistic, and everyone, the argument runs, should do what he can according to his ability.

Obviously this is not conclusive logic, not nearly as compelling as the value principles which govern the organization of the private economy under free enterprise. Its strength, as the basis of the tax system, must lie in its appeal to the people as the reasonable, even the necessary, basis. Certainly it does not call definitely for a particular tax structure. A system so based leaves room for innumerable group pressures to escape tax responsibility and affords no sharp test by which they can be condemned. But whatever its limitations, it occupies so central a place in all thinking on taxation that its implications should be considered carefully.

Income as the chief basis of taxpaying ability. Since the ability-to-pay principle provides only a general approach to the problem of tax levies, we must consider how it can be applied. How is taxpaying ability to be measured? In discussing this question, we must not expect a very precise answer.

As a first step, we must observe that ability is best measured by income. Income means command over goods and thus measures the capacity of a person to pay the cost of resources used for general government purposes. Taxes may be levied directly on the basis of wealth or purchases or something else, but the reasonableness of the total of the taxes paid by a person must be judged by comparing this total with his income.

To this there is some qualification. Of two persons with equal incomes, the one who has greater wealth is in a somewhat stronger taxpaying position, for he has a more secure economic situation than the man whose income comes entirely from labor service. Wealth in the inherited form is, moreover, an especially appropriate object of taxation because of its windfall character. Thus death taxes may properly be added to a tax structure that applies the ability principle adequately in all other respects. For simplicity in this discussion, however, we shall assume that current income is an adequate measure of ability.

Justification of progressive taxation. The next step is to ask how taxpaying ability varies with changes in the size of income. There are three general possibilities: the tax burden may be proportional, progressive, or regressive. We need to see what these relationships are and which one corresponds best to the capacity of the individual to assist in the support of government.

Taxes are said to be *proportional* when the tax burden, arising from all taxes paid, varies at the same percentage rate at which income varies. On the proportional basis, if an individual with a $2000 income pays $200, a person with a $5000 income would pay $500, and one with a $10,000 income would pay $1000. Taxes take a constant percentage of income.

Taxes are called *progressive* when government takes a larger percentage of income as income gets larger. If we still assume that the man with a $5000 income pays $500 in taxes, the man with $2000 pays something less than $200, say $150, and the man with $10,000 pays something more than $1000, say $1500. The percentages of income taken by government are then 7.5, 10, and 15 percent as incomes rise through these three levels.

When taxes are *regressive,* the government takes a smaller percentage of income as the size of income grows. Absolutely the tax burden rises with income, but it rises less rapidly than income. If, again, we assume that the tax on the $5000 income is $500, the regressive principle would make the tax on $2000 be something above $200, say $250, and the tax on $10,000 would be below $1000, say $750. Then the percentages, starting with the smallest income, would be 12.5, 10, and 7.5 percent.

Now which of these three relationships is the best measure of ability to pay taxes? The answer by practically all students of public finance is that the fairest tax system distributes the burden progressively. Various theories have been propounded in support of the progressive principle—theories that imply different degrees of severity in the treatment of large incomes. We shall limit the discussion to one that is perhaps the most conservative rationalization of progressive taxation, one most in harmony with the thinking of people who are not seeking to use public finance as a means of achieving economic reform.

This view is that the final burden of taxation, its impact on people's satisfactions, should be proportional. But, for the burden on psychic income to be proportional, the burden on money income must be progressive. The explanation lies in the principle of diminishing utility. Units of goods mean less to us, the more units we have. A dollar that is part of a small income means more than a dollar that is part of a large income. Roughly, we may say that the dollars in the last 10 percent of the $2000 income stand for quite necessary goods, of a $5000 income for nonessential things, of a $10,000 income for savings. If a dollar had the same importance whatever the size of income, proportional taxes would impose a proportional psychic burden. But, because additional dollars mean less as incomes get larger, a higher percentage of larger incomes must be taken to impose a proportional burden.

Adding this point to the preceding discussion, we can say that the logic of progressive taxation, from the most conservative standpoint, is this: The central functions of government cannot be supported on a benefit basis but should be viewed as a collective responsibility, to be borne by everyone according to his ability. While the cost of government reduces the quantity of goods that people can enjoy through individual choice, it need not alter the relative position of individuals. But, if relative position is viewed realistically in terms of actual well-being, it is necessary that taxation should take a larger fraction of people's money incomes as incomes get larger. Thus progressive taxation may be said to mean proportional burden and equal sacrifice.

The degree of progressiveness. If this is the theory on which a tax system is to be made progressive, the next question is: How progressive should taxes be to apply the theory? For incomes of $2000, $5000, and $10,000, should taxes progress at the rate, say, of $175, $500, and $1200, or at the rate of $125, $500, and $2000? Both are progressive, but the rates are quite different. To this question, economics provides no answer. One can be sure that satisfactions do not vary in proportion to income without pretending to be able to measure satisfactions. The next step, if it is to be attempted, is for the psychologists.

As a matter of fact, the answer is probably not very important. We are talking, it will be remembered, about the application of a principle —the ability-to-pay principle—to which there is no compelling need of adhering closely, even if precise measurement were possible. The spread of the tax burden is subject to the somewhat arbitrary decision of public authorities. They are influenced by the pressures of various interests, of persons who are anxious to escape as much of the tax burden as possible. The progressive principle is opposed altogether in some quarters; in others it is supported not on the ground just presented but on the more far-reaching basis of promoting general reform in the distribution of income through carrying secondary distribution as far as possible. Results in the political arena do not rest on nicely formulated standards. But, although we cannot say how progressive taxation should be, it is well to see that the progressive principle follows logically from the most plausible and generally accepted view of the role of government.

Actual distribution of tax burden. There is just one further question in discussing the fairness of taxes: How has the tax burden in fact been spread in the United States? When all taxes—federal, state, and local— are taken into account, has the progressive principle been applied? This is a very difficult question to answer statistically, but a few attempts have been made to answer it. In one of these, based on incomes and taxes in 1941, it appears that taxation was then approximately proportional for incomes below $5000 and progressive above that level. Taxes absorbed from 15.5 to 16.2 percent of income at various levels below $5000, 18.5 percent between $5000 and $10,000, and 28.4 percent above $10,000. More detailed figures for 1938–1939 indicated that taxes took more than 40 percent of incomes of $20,000 and over.[9]

General sales taxes are regressive, since the rate is flat and people of low income spend a larger fraction of their incomes at retail than people of large income do. The only important strongly progressive tax is the personal income tax.[10] When the economy is prosperous, the revenue from income taxes becomes a relatively large part of total revenue. When income-tax rates are raised greatly, as they were during the war period, the whole tax structure becomes much more progressive. Thus the figures given, even if accurate for the prewar situation, fail to show the degree of progress in the wartime and postwar tax structure.

The difficulty of such a study does not lie primarily in obtaining the facts regarding the different taxes, who pays them to the government, and what the incomes of these people are. The difficulty lies in the fact that, very largely, the burden does not finally rest on the people who pay the tax collectors. Taxes are often paid finally in the prices of goods, in housing rentals, in adjustments of wages and other incomes, and a dim trail must be followed by the investigator in tracing the tax

[9] Helen Tarasov, *Who Does Pay the Taxes?*, Social Research, 1942, p. 6.

[10] Taxes on corporate profits should be imputed mainly to large incomes, but they fall at the same rate on the equities of small-income stockholders as on the equities of millionaires.

burden. It is this difficulty which leads us to the concluding topic of this section.

Shifting and incidence of taxes

Little can be known about the distribution of the tax burden unless, for each tax, we know reasonably well (1) whether it is likely to be shifted by the person who pays it initially and (2) where its weight is likely finally to fall—that is, its incidence. Such knowledge is necessary to an analysis of the fairness of taxes. It is necessary also to an understanding of their effect on industrial activity. If, for example, a spokesman for business urges the public to oppose high corporation taxes because, first, the public must pay them in higher prices, and second, they cut into profits and depress business, he may properly be asked to explain whether such taxes are shifted or whether they rest on the corporations that pay them. He cannot have it both ways.

Probably no one supposes that tobacco manufacturers bear the excise they pay on cigarettes. But must the manufacturer absorb the effect of the corporation income tax he pays? And can he get out from under the burden of his personal income tax by shifting it to someone else? And what of the property taxes on land and houses and other things?

A little reflection will show how intricate the problem of analysis is. The whole theory of markets, of the prices of products and of productive services, is involved. Shifting and incidence are governed by relationships which extend throughout the entire price situation. When one considers the variety of taxes and the variety of market situations, with different degrees of monopoly and competition and of elasticity of demand for all kinds of products and of services of resources, the difficulties become apparent. It is a problem on which a great deal has been done by theorists and investigators, but the final answers to many specific questions are not agreed on. While this is distinctly a problem for specialists, one can grasp easily the main clues from which the probable incidence of particular taxes may be guessed.

That shifting, if it occurs, must take place through the pricing process is evident. The taxpayer derives his income from selling a commodity that he produces or from selling his personal services or the services of wealth that he owns. To escape the tax, he must be able to raise the price of his product or service or to reduce the price of material or labor that he buys. If the tobacco manufacturer succeeds in passing the excise tax along to the buyers of his product, the process is known as *forward shifting*. If he transfers it through paying a lower price for raw tobacco, the process is known as *backward shifting*. The former is the more important.

Such is the process. The real problem is to define the conditions under which shifting can be expected. We approach it by recalling that prices are controlled by the forces of supply and demand. For the product of the taxpayer to command a higher price, either the demand for it must increase or the supply must decrease. Certainly there is no reason to suppose that payment of a tax by the producer of a product will increase the demand for it; we must look to the supply side. Thus the main question to be asked in analyzing the shiftability of a tax is: Will it lead the producer of the commodity or service to reduce the supply of it? Let us ask this question in the case of excise taxes, property taxes, and income taxes.

Shifting of excise taxes. What is said of excise taxes can be applied to sales taxes in general and to import duties. The normal, and usually also the short-run, effect of an excise tax is to reduce the supply and increase the price of the product, so that it is shifted, at least in part, to the buyer. An excise tax paid by a manufacturer of cigarettes (or any other producer) increases the cost of each unit of the product in just the same sense that a rise in the price of raw materials or in wage rates increases the cost. If, prior to the tax, the manufacturer has made the most profitable adjustment of price and output to the cost situation, the new cost necessarily calls for a new adjustment. With a higher price for the product, somewhat less will be bought, and the manufacturer must reduce output accordingly.[11]

Backward shifting, if it occurs, is likewise the result of this contraction, but such shifting is more likely to be temporary. Reduce the output of cigarettes, and less raw tobacco will be bought. This reduced demand, as long as the supply holds, must cause the price of tobacco to fall. But if the tobacco output had been adjusted to the former price, the new price is likely in time to cause some contraction in the tobacco-growing industry to restore it to a normal level of profitability. In this case, final shifting is entirely of a forward nature.

The *speed* with which excise and other similar taxes are shifted depends, in part, on the *elasticity of demand*. If demand is highly inelastic, so that a higher price will reduce sales only slightly, the full tax may be shifted right away. But if sales are likely to fall off sharply in response to a higher price, the producer will be slow in raising it. He has a plant adjusted to the market, and drastic curtailment of output would make his profit position worse rather than better. A full shifting of the tax will then have to await the growth of the market, or the dropping out of firms that lose money, or some contraction as equipment wears

[11] In the case of market-determined prices, we would say that the higher cost reduces profits, lower profits cause curtailment of supply, and curtailed supply causes price to rise.

out. Elasticity of demand does not govern the final incidence of the tax but only the speed with which it is achieved.[12]

Shifting of property taxes. To analyze the normal effect of an increase in property taxes, it is necessary to distinguish land from buildings and other forms of man-made wealth. In the short run, if the owner of real estate has been getting as high a rental as the market permits, he will have to absorb the additional tax both on his land and his buildings. Demand is not increased by the tax, and he cannot reduce the supply. But in the long run, the tax on buildings will normally be shifted. The tax cuts into the net return on capital invested in buildings; in time this fact will be reflected in slower replacements or in slower expansion as population grows. This adjustment should continue until investment in buildings becomes as profitable as investment in other fields, or until the return becomes adequate in relation to risk.

In the case of land, on the other hand, the new tax will not cause a reduction in supply, even in the long run. Land rent, in the strict sense, does not arise because capital is invested in land; on the contrary, as we have seen, land commands a price because of the value of its service. Even if the tax took the entire land rent, the land would still be there, and it would still be worth using as long as labor and other applied agents could earn a normal return on it. This, as we saw, is the assumption of the Single Taxers. The tax they propose would take the rent of land and be absorbed by the owner. It would not be a cost that he could pass on to the tenant or to the consumer of the product raised on the land.

Shifting of income taxes. In general, the income tax is like the tax on land and cannot be shifted. It does not affect supply as do excise taxes and taxes on buildings. The income tax does not enter at all as a cost that attaches to particular units of products or services. Thus, in the case of the *corporation,* it cannot be one of the added costs that must be taken into account in deciding whether to produce more or less. It applies only to the net return which is the result of calculations that relate cost, price, and output. If a certain output, with related price and cost, yields the largest possible profit when the income tax is low, then, with the same market, that output will yield the largest profit, after the tax, when the tax rate has been raised. Whatever the amount of the tax, the adjustment that is most profitable before the tax is the most profitable after it has been deducted.

This is equally true in conditions of monopoly and of competition, as

[12] This is true of industries which are constant-cost within the area of adjustment. If an industry is increasing-cost or decreasing-cost, the elasticity of demand will govern the amount of contraction due to the tax and thus affect cost.

long as firms are doing what is most profitable. It is likewise true for the individual in his reaction to the *personal income tax*. To be less productive and thus earn a smaller income to escape part of the tax will mean that income after the tax is deducted is smaller than it was.

This is the main point to be made regarding the shifting of income taxes, and probably the best basis for predicting their effect. But there are important *qualifications* that should be noted.

In our analysis of prices we saw, in industries which are not fully competitive, that prices are likely not to be fixed where they will fully maximize profits, at least from a short-run marginal standpoint. Oligopolists are slow to make changes, and they are influenced by fears of potential competition, public disfavor, and government scrutiny. In a situation in which demand would make possible higher immediate profits, a rise in the income tax may conceivably be the upsetting factor that causes firms to take fuller advantage of the market. Or, facing a situation that contains some basis for price reductions, a fall in tax rates may provide the needed inducement.

There are possibilities of a similar response in the sale of personal services. Physicians' fees may not be all the market will stand, but there is reluctance to raise them until a sharp rise in the income tax threatens the level of living to which doctors have become accustomed. The effect may be similar in those markets in which the prices of distinctive services are fixed within a wide bargaining range. In his dealings with a corporate employer, an executive may drive a stiffer bargain because of the inroads of a higher tax. It may even be that a labor union is influenced in its wage demands by the taxes its members have to pay, even though the secondary effects which should limit such demands are not altered in the slightest by the presence of the tax.

These qualifications arise from the fact that markets do not operate in close accord with neat principles based on simple assumptions. Because of income taxes price adjustments take place which could occur without the tax factor, but do not; or perhaps they merely occur sooner because of the tax factor.

Of a different nature are those other responses to income taxes which say, in effect, that the reward for production, after paying the tax, has fallen so low that productive activity is not worth while. Thus the physician may conclude, when he has reached a certain size of income, that the effort required to take care of more patients is not worth while if government takes 50 cents of each additional dollar that he makes. So he provides less professional service than he otherwise would. Or the investor of capital in new industries, considering on the one hand the possibilities of loss and, on the other, the big part of his profit that must go to the government if he succeeds, may decide that investment is not worth while.

Thus it is possible that the income tax will reduce the quantity of the thing taxed. But the significance of this effect does not lie in a shifting of the tax burden to other economic groups. It lies, rather, in the lowering of the national product and income for which the tax is responsible. We shall return to this matter in the concluding section of the chapter.

Review Questions

1. Distinguish four ways of obtaining money to meet public expenditures. Why may taxation be regarded as the normal way? What is a tax?

2. Distinguish the principal types of taxes used in the United States. Relate them to the government jurisdictions that chiefly employ them.

3. From Table 36 on page 809, calculate the percentage of income absorbed in 1948 by the federal income tax at different income levels. How do you reconcile the tax on, say, a $100,000 income with the fact that the rate on taxable income above $90,000 was 87 percent?

4. Distinguish three kinds of taxes on the incomes of corporations and two kinds of death taxes.

5. How does a fee or assessment differ from a tax?

6. What major changes have occurred in the nature of tax collections in the United States in the last twenty years.

7. What are the main tests that should be met by a good tax and by a good tax system? Where applicable, apply these tests to the leading kinds of taxes used in the United States.

8. State the main considerations on which judgment of direct and indirect taxes should rest.

9. What particular kind of unfairness is likely to arise in the taxing of real estate? Of such personal property as household furnishings or cash? Of inheritances?

10. How does double taxation arise in the case of an intangibles tax? A tax on the income of corporations? How may taxes be avoided when income is earned under the corporate form? Who benefits?

11. Distinguish the benefit and ability principles in apportioning the cost of government. Why is the benefit principle not applicable in financing the central functions of government? In what cases is it applicable? Do you think it should be applied where it can be? How should benefit be measured?

12. State the argument for apportioning most of the cost of government on the basis of ability to pay.

13. "People may pay taxes according to their wealth, their incomes, or their expenditures, but, whatever the tax, their taxpaying ability depends

on their income." Explain. What qualifications should be recognized in judging ability to pay?

14. Distinguish proportional, progressive, and regressive taxation. Does regressive taxation mean that people with smaller incomes pay larger taxes than people with larger incomes?

15. "Progressive taxation may be said to mean proportional burden and equal sacrifice." Explain, developing the logic of the progressive principle.

16. "The extent of progression in the distribution of the tax burden seems to depend largely on the relative dependence on income and sales or property taxes." Explain.

17. "Heavy taxes on business cause harm both through reducing profits and through raising prices to consumers." Should these two effects be added together in showing the harm done by a specific tax?

18. What is meant by shifting and incidence? Distinguish forward and backward shifting.

19. What is the main question to be asked in deciding whether a certain tax is likely to be shifted? Apply the principle involved to sales taxes, property taxes on land and on buildings, personal and corporation income taxes. Why should there be controversy over the incidence of the corporation income tax? In light of this discussion what should be the final incidence of social-security taxes?

Government Borrowing

Taxes are the normal source of funds for government use. They are normal in the sense that they divert to government a portion of the money-income stream which corresponds to the portion of total productive activity devoted to government purposes. Thus the financial side of government is disposed of, once and for all. Taxes, however, may not provide all the money that government needs. As in the private economy, borrowing is resorted to when current revenues are inadequate.

There have been many years when the government of the United States has had small deficits, but the great borrowing episodes have occurred during war periods and in the depression of the 1930s. The federal government entered World War I with a debt of about $1 billion, increased its indebtedness to $25 billion by 1919, reduced it to $16 billion by 1930, raised it above $40 billion by 1940, and to about $280 billion by 1946. The total indebtedness of state and local governments exceeded $16 billion before World War II.

Fear was widespread that federal credit was nearing collapse in the 1930s, but the vast additional borrowing of the 1940s brought a better sense of the credit resources of a sound government. The problem of debt administration left by the war, and a wider awareness of the possible uses of deficit-spending to combat depression, have brought this subject into unusual prominence.

Public borrowing, the traditional view

Most commonly the borrowing of governments has been viewed in about the same light as the private borrowing of individuals and firms. Apart from ·those minor debts which are incurred for short periods simply because revenues and expenditures do not synchronize perfectly, public borrowing has been thought justifiable for two main purposes: exceptional capital outlays and emergencies such as wars.

When a community builds a new school or installs a new water system, bonds are likely to be issued. It is not feasible to expand tax levies to cover such large and nonrecurring outlays. Moreover, it seems fair to spread the cost of durable facilities over the period of their use rather than to impose their cost on taxpayers at the time of their construction. Sound financing requires, in the case of governments as of private firms, that such indebtedness be discharged within the minimum service life of the facilities, so that there can be no future piling up of debts as replacements are made. Likewise, just as individuals may justifiably go into debt to meet special emergency expenses, such as heavy doctor bills, so governments also may borrow during wars and severe depressions. Depression requires large outlays for relief of the unemployed, and, with the fall in production, revenues from income taxes decline sharply, and many people default on their property taxes. This condition arises quite apart from any deliberate attempt to use public spending to speed recovery—a basis for indebtedness that is no part of the traditional view of the matter. Modern war requires outlays which vastly exceed ordinary revenues and may exceed the outside possibilities of current revenue collection—though that is a matter that we shall consider further.

But though public borrowing can be justified on these grounds, it has still been viewed ordinarily as inherently objectionable. The general belief is that, as far as possible, it should be avoided. Doubtless the basis of this attitude lies, in part, in the fear that public administration will become lax, and money squandered recklessly, if outlays do not have to be covered currently by the politically unpopular method of levying taxes. It lies also in the recognition, equally applicable to private spending, that people get less for their money when it has to cover not only the cost of the things purchased but also interest on the sums used.

The aim, accordingly, should be to handle capital expenditures on a current basis. The particular outlay may be large, and the result of it may have a long service life, but most governmental bodies have some capital outlays to make every year, and, if they are carefully distributed over time, ordinary tax revenues can be made to cover most of them. Thus, while the early automobile roads were often built with borrowed funds, highway financing, for major construction as well as upkeep, is now generally handled on a "pay-as-you-go" basis. The smaller the jurisdiction, the less likely it is to be able to follow this policy completely, since the projects it has to distribute are few.

Borrowing for war

Wars require the greatest outlays that governments have to make, but they also create exceptional taxing opportunities. There are several reasons why they do. The great demand for goods invigorates the economy, and production rises above the level of peacetime booms. People are animated by an intense patriotism, both to produce and to assist in financing. While money incomes are high, the consumers' goods on which they can be spent are limited, so taxation imposes little hardship. Thus reliance on current financing seems to be possible. It also seems desirable. Reliance on taxation strikes the inflation problem at its source. It avoids the hangover of debt that has plagued postwar periods. It appears to place the cost of war where it belongs, on the people who make money from it rather than on the fighting men who, after the war, become the taxpayers on whom the burden of a debt must fall.

But, granting that the war situation favors high taxes, is not heavy borrowing also necessary? In 1944 the war expenditures of the United States exceeded $88 billion. With other public expenditures added, the federal, state, and local governments spent a sum approximately equal to half the gross national product and considerably greater than half the national income. Federal taxes, five times the 1940 level, covered half the outlay for war. Could they have been raised twice as high as they were and thus have balanced the budget?

Reasons for borrowing. When the problem is viewed in aggregate real terms, taxation to cover the full cost seems possible. If 50 percent of all productive power is used for war and other governmental purposes, then only 50 percent remains to turn out products for private purchase. The real cost of war lies in the diversion of output to war purposes, and this cost is the same whether financing is done through taxation or the sale of bonds. If the nation, under the impetus of war, is able greatly to expand its total output, then the absolute impact on civilian living is reduced, but, in any case, taxes for the full financing of war would take no more from total income than the war takes from total product. Taxpayers would retain sufficient purchasing power to buy the portion of the product available for them. The problem would seem merely to be one of fitting taxes to this situation, so that dollars would be transferred to government in the most equitable way.

One difficulty, which we shall barely note, is that a critical transition period must be covered before the 1944 situation is reached. War demands arise suddenly, but it takes considerable time for new taxes to be legislated and applied. Immediate sources of funds are necessary. More important, a great shift in industry is required, and, if the inevitable inertia is to be overcome quickly, financial inducements must not be nullified by taxes that leave incomes lower even than before the war.[13] If, furthermore, as in 1940, a nation begins its war effort with a large volume of unemployment and a relatively low total output, it must not expect the revenues from that low output to finance the capacity production that it seeks. Dollars must come from other sources than current production, and, if they appear in such volume that a mild inflation results, the expansion will take place even more quickly. Thus borrowing, accompanied by credit expansion, can be expected at least in the early part of a war.

But the difficulty of relying on taxation does not end with this transition period. What was described as the problem of fitting taxes to the situation in an equitable way is, in fact, a problem that cannot be solved if taxation is relied on to meet the full cost of war. The trouble is that war upsets the distribution of income. Some people profit greatly from it, some a little, some not at all, some have less income than before. It is impossible to adjust taxes to these different conditions. But not to do so, while raising taxes to cover the full cost, would create the grossest inequity. The person who earned $2500 before the war and $5000 during it might pay a 50-percent tax without serious hardship. But the person whose income continued on a $5000 level, and who had prewar commitments almost to the extent of that income, would be completely ruined by such a tax. Even if the inequity were not in itself a sufficient deterrent, its political expression would keep a sensitive Congress from causing so drastic an aggravation of the inevitable tensions of war. From the standpoint of wartime morale, full reliance on taxation would be most unwise.

Thus borrowing for part of the cost of war seems inevitable. But because the arguments for current financing are weighty, some sort of compromise must be reached in which taxes are made as heavy as the

[13] Some would argue that financial inducements are not necessary if industries, like men, are drafted for war service. Undoubtedly maintaining incentives under an industry draft would present a difficult problem.

situation seems to permit. It is noteworthy that, despite the greater economic impact of World War II, Congress relied relatively less on borrowing than in World War I.

Deferment of the war burden. We have just said, in effect, that borrowing, in comparison with taxation, lightens the immediate burden of war. Is this equivalent to saying that borrowing postpones the burden so that it is borne in the postwar period, perhaps for generations? That such is the case is the popular view of the effect of borrowing, but it is a view that has often been flatly denied by economists.

The denial rests on the analysis in aggregate real terms, as presented above. In real terms a war cannot be fought now and paid for later; its cost lies in the diversion of resources to war purposes and the sacrifice of ordinary products that this diversion entails. Borrowing money to pay for these resources does not reduce this sacrifice. Likewise, in real terms, there is no cost in the postwar years when taxes are levied to make interest and principal payments to bondholders. If the bonds are owned within the country, there is merely a transfer of purchasing power from taxpayers to bondholders, and aggregate wealth and income are unchanged. True, the men who fought in the war may be more conspicuous among the taxpayers than among the bondholders, so that there is inequity from the distribution standpoint, but borrowing has not deferred the aggregate burden of war.

This is an important point, but it leaves a great deal unsaid. Economic burdens, in final analysis, are psychological, and here is an instance in which psychic costs and returns are not fully revealed by an analysis in the real terms of aggregate resources—products and wealth. Take the case of the man who saves $1000 during the war and buys a war bond. In a sense he is paying part of the cost of the war, but the cost does not strike him as it would if he were taxed $1000. He gives up current consumption, but only in the sense that people always do when they save and accumulate wealth. He does not feel that he is being deprived of $1000 of income, but rather he has the satisfaction of acquiring a $1000 asset—an asset that may not represent command over real wealth today but that will presently.

Now turn to the situation after the war when taxes are levied to pay interest and reduce the debt. The taxpayer has a definite sense of sacrifice as he gives up part of his income to make these payments. Does the bondholder enjoy an offsetting sense of benefit? Not at all. The interest he receives is not the windfall sort of acquisition that comes when government causes a secondary distribution of income. The interest is rather the payment to which he is entitled for the current service of his capital, just as if it had been invested in industry.

And if taxes are collected to pay him the principal of $1000, is he that much better off? Actually, if the bond was worth $1000, he is no better off. The asset has been converted to a new form, but he enjoys no benefit whatever to match the pain felt by the taxpayer.

Thus, in a highly important sense, borrowing lightens the immediate economic burden of war. It not only overcomes the difficulty that war upsets the distribution of income through keeping war contributions more largely on a voluntary basis conforming to individual circumstances; more fundamentally, it reduces the burden because lending is not viewed as parting with income or weakening one's economic position. To the extent that this is true, there is a shifting of the burden to postwar years, and, indeed, the shifting of an added burden in so far as taxes are levied to pay interest as well as the principal amounts borrowed.

The cost of war, it should be added, is also postponed to some extent in real terms, but this postponement is independent of the method of financing. During a major war, normal plant replacements are not made for the production of civilian goods, and durable goods in general are allowed to wear out. Indeed much productive power is made available for war by transferring capital-goods and durable-consumer-goods industries to war purposes. While some of the special facilities created for war can be converted to peacetime use, especially the shells of factories, there is some net loss of durable goods to be made up after the war. Perhaps even more serious is the vast use in war of such resources as iron and petroleum and the nearer approach to final exhaustion of these resources faced by the postwar world. In the devastated countries the heritage of real costs, in the deterioration both of human and material productive power, is far greater, and the paralysis from broken trade and financial connections may prove to be the most difficult obstacle to be overcome.

Debt capacity and national solvency

The questions most asked concerning the present national debt reflect misgiving as to the ability of the government to meet its obligations. Can the country actually pay off so huge a debt? If it does not, will the bonds that people hold remain good? How big a debt can our federal government handle and remain solvent? On these questions widely different views are held, even among the experts.

A common popular fear was expressed by the distinguished Senator who said: "Our public debt will have to be paid in full or repudiated." [14] But this is not a true statement of the alternatives. It is just as

[14] Senator Harry F. Byrd, quoted in *Readers' Digest,* January 1947, p. 103.

possible for a government as for a business enterprise to have a continuing debt, a debt that is not reduced and that remains perfectly valid and is honored in every particular. All that is necessary is that bond interest should always be paid when due and that additional bonds be marketable to replace those that mature. Sound public credit does not mean the absence of debt but the ability of government to carry its debt.

At the opposite extreme is the view that the size of the debt does not matter so long as it is owed internally—by the American government to the American people. Debts to foreigners create the often difficult problem of establishing balances abroad, but the capacity of a people to owe themselves is unlimited. This view, again, is out of touch with reality. It commits the error, already noted, of thinking loosely in terms of aggregates. Taxpayers and bondholders may be part of the same public, but they represent different interests and manifest different responses. To pay more interest to bondholders requires higher taxation, and most of the income that is taxed is not income from government bonds. Taxes depress industrial incentives as they become severe, and there is unquestionably a limit to the amount of income that can be diverted to governments without reducing total production, on which the collection of taxes depends.

Thus the key to the debt problem is the relation between debt requirements and the size of the national income. If total income is high, a very large debt need not be dangerous, but difficulties can develop either through an increase in debt or a fall in income. The absolute limit is not known. Because debts are expressed in dollars, it is total income in money, and not merely in goods, that matters. With annual interest of $5 billion to be paid, it is better to have a national income of $200 billion than of $100, even though these figures represent exactly the same total product. Thus the rise in prices after the war reduced the debt burden. But it is also significant that the fall in the value of money during and after the war more than wiped out all the interest the investor would get on the savings bonds he bought in response to the wartime fanfare about the excellence of such investment.

The debt burden depends also on the interest rate. It is necessary that investment in government bonds remain sufficiently popular with individuals, banks, and other investing institutions so that the whole debt is absorbed at moderate rates of interest. In the cost of carrying the debt, a decline in average interest from 3 to 2 percent is equivalent to a reduction of one third in the debt itself.

In comparison with the debt at the end of the Civil War, the debt at the end of World War II was 100 times as high in the aggregate, 25 times as high on a per-capita basis. But in relation to the national income, as of 1947, it was only three times as high. Furthermore, when allowance is made for a decline in average interest from about 6 percent in 1866 to 2 percent in 1947, the carrying cost appears about the same.[15]

The Civil War debt was reduced by two thirds by 1893, the World War I debt by more than one third by 1930. The American economy not only has the capacity to pay the interest on the present federal debt but to reduce it, and plans have been discussed for wiping it out over a period of 50 or 100 years. But all such plans are contingent on the avoidance of further wars. They are contingent also on the maintenance of prosperity despite debt reduction, and certainly without resort to further deficit spending to maintain total demand.

Borrowing versus printing paper money

It may be asked why a government should borrow and thus create burdensome obligations when it has authority to create money and endow it with full legal-tender character. It would seem not only cheaper but surely much simpler to employ a device with none of the complications of interest payment and refunding.

The general answer to this suggestion was developed in Chapter 12 on the value of money. To make large outlays in this way would ordinarily be highly inflationary. Since the revenue from any volume of output is sufficient to buy that output at prevailing prices, the injection of new money from outside, when production is already high, must start an upward price spiral that has no end. This is not a burdenless process. On the contrary, it is as harsh as taxation, because it makes little difference whether government takes dollars from people's pockets or dilutes the buying power of the dollars that are there. In addition it creates the maladjustments we have considered and brings eventual collapse.

The logic of borrowing, as of taxation, is that it takes from the income stream an amount of money equivalent to the productive power required for the government functions that have to be financed. Thus the money offered for goods does not increase in relation to the goods available. This is an essential difference, and it must not be obscured by the frequency of statements about the inflationary effect of public debts.

But those statements, though often loosely made, have an important basis. When a large volume of bonds must be sold in a short time, some

[15] These figures, with allowance for the 1946–1947 price rise, are based on data in *Our National Debt after Great Wars*, the first pamphlet in the National Debt Series of the Committee on Public Debt Policy.

of them will be absorbed, as we have seen, through expansion of credit by commercial banks. Additional deposit dollars, arising outside the income stream, are just as inflationary in their effect as additional printing-press dollars. The same effect occurs when bonds are bought with balances that have been idle, thus speeding up the use of money. But, on the other hand, many bonds bought by banks really reflect only the passing of current income through the hands of middlemen.

In addition, there is the possibility that the debt will, in a sense, be converted to money. Many savings bonds, bought with current income during the war, were redeemed in cash after the war, and the money was then thrown into markets in the purchase of goods. Likewise, unless specifically prohibited, bonds may be used as collateral for loans, and liquid purchasing power obtained. Even though only a small part of the total debt is "monetized," an inflationary factor is present.

It appears, then, that borrowing does not altogether avoid the prime weakness of paper-money issue. It may also be, as during the war, that a large monetary expansion is needed to handle the expanded volume of production at prevailing prices, or with such mild inflation as is desired. Within limits, then, it may be asked, why should not the special financing be done with paper money, and the costs of borrowing avoided? Perhaps the right answer is that this should be done. The main contrary argument, and an important one, is that a dangerous precedent is set in tapping this easy source of funds. Once done, it is not likely to be kept within the poorly defined limits just mentioned. It may displace the noninflationary sale of bonds and even reduce the reliance on taxation.

Borrowing within a balanced budget

We began this section by stating the conventional attitude toward public debt. From this standpoint, debt is an evil, though sometimes a necessary evil, and the proper aim in government finance is to try each year to collect enough in taxes to cover the outlays for all purposes. The goal of maintaining a balanced budget is defined accordingly.[16] With the growth, during the 1930s, of the idea that public finance should be concerned more broadly with general prosperity, attempts were made to redefine the balance in a way that would leave room for considerable borrowing and more flexible spending. To some the objective may have been a more scientific view of the budget, to others a means of

[16] It is not quite correct to say that budgetary balance is judged merely by comparing revenues and expenditures. The "payments" include allocations to social-security and other funds for which there may be no corresponding current disbursement. Thus, to balance the budget, the government may have to withdraw more money from the money-income stream than it returns to that stream, or the discrepancy may be on the other side.

disclosing deficits in a more palatable way. Two revised conceptions of budget balancing should be noted.

One of these, mentioned in Chapter 16 in the discussion of anti-depression policies, is that of seeking a *balance on the basis of the full business cycle* rather than on an annual basis. The calendar year is undoubtedly an arbitrary unit of time in many economic connections, especially in situations involving the ebb and flow of total income. Compensatory public spending, involving deficits in the poor years, would have recognized status if budgetary balancing were construed on the basis of longer periods of time.

Such balancing is, in fact, the most that can be expected, and there is point in defining the goal in manageable terms. But, in practice, the idea would not be easy to apply. In retrospect the business cycle presents a neat picture, in which booms and depressions are distinct episodes; currently, the course of events is not easily mapped, and clear guideposts are lacking for cyclical budget balancing. More fundamentally, the objections are the usual ones against deficit spending to promote prosperity.

The second liberalized conception of a balanced budget would stress the *distinction between current expenditures and capital outlays,* and the budget would be said to be in balance when tax revenues covered the former. Current expenditures would include interest on the public debt but would not include new outlays for river developments, reclamation projects, and so on. Support for this procedure is found, of course, in the business practice of distinguishing expenses and investments, and of judging profit and loss by comparing revenues with expenses rather than with total outlay.

The logic of this concept is undeniable, but the business analogy may easily be pushed too far. Public investments often lack the financial significance of private investments. Outlays for flood control increase the national product, but the value of the increase is not collected by the government to defray the cost. The increased productivity, then, is a reason for public expenditure but is not directly a public revenue factor. To overlook this distinction is to confuse the operations of the Treasury with the whole field of public policy. The business analogy would require that the current expenses be expanded to cover the amortization of capital outlays and that revenues of some kind be found to cover this cost.

Opinions differ as to whether it is desirable to promote views of the budget that soften the prejudice against deficits. But these conceptions are useful in encouraging a long-range view of the problem of financial administration. They promote a broad conception of the role of public finance in the economy. Necessarily the financing of government must be viewed not merely as the handling of certain established public functions but as a major force affecting the economy as a whole.

Public Finance and the Private Economy

Public spending and taxing, and the incurring and discharging of debts, affect the economy in many ways. The effects may be intentional, through the planned use of government finance as an instrument of economic control. Or they may be inadvertent, and, for good or ill, mold the private economy in unintended ways. In any case, a fifth or more of the total-income stream cannot be channeled through public treasuries without exerting a powerful influence on the character and direction of activity. Thus even though it should seem best to use this instrument with restraint in achieving positive ends, it would be most irresponsible not to examine all programs for their possible effects throughout the economy.

In stressing this proposition it is necessary only to review a variety of influences, most of which have been considered with more or less fullness at other points.

Public finance and the problem of depressions

Overwhelmingly the most important of these influences is the bearing of public finance on the total demand for goods, and thus on employment and the level of national income. Government spending is a sizable part of the total spending that keeps resources employed, and taxation absorbs a sizable fraction of spendable income. Accordingly many informed persons would manage government finance primarily with an eye to its effect on the general level of production. This may mean the soaking up of spendable income to prevent inflation, but more often it would involve the incurring of deficits to expand total buying. Three ways of viewing public deficit spending were distinguished in Chapter 16: (1) the resort to borrowing, as in the 1930s, to bring recovery from depression; (2) compensatory spending when a break in prosperity is threatened, with the idea that indebtedness will be wiped out in the boom phase of the cycle; and (3) such sustained deficit spending as is necessary to offset an assumed chronic tendency toward stagnation arising from the failure of private investment to absorb the savings from high-level income. In practice, as was pointed out, the fiscal policies that would express these three approaches may be scarcely distinguishable.

Supporters of these policies would probably agree that deficit spend-

ing should be undertaken only as other methods of maintaining prosperity fail. Accordingly, opposition to it rests in part on the belief that
other methods of dealing successfully with the depression problem are
available. But the opposition rests also on other grounds. In part it
springs from doubts as to the effectiveness of public spending in
maintaining prosperity, especially in view of the general attitude of
businessmen. It reflects the fear that economy in government will be undermined—that, once the goal of continuous budget balancing is abandoned, public money will be used carelessly, bureaucracy will expand,
and resources will be devoted to all sorts of trivial ends. It sees the
specter of an eventual collapse of public credit. It questions the capacity of democratic government to administer such an instrument of
control, because greater continuity and greater promptness are needed
than legislative bodies can muster and the delegation of adequate
spending authority to administrative officials seems dangerous.

These objections may explain the lack of a broad fiscal policy to
combat depression; but practically speaking, there is no sharp line between (1) positive fiscal planning of this sort and (2) an intelligent recognition of the impact of ordinary financial administration on the
economy. In any case, public expenditures will be large. Beside the continuous outlays in running the government, large sums will be spent for
roads and schools and post offices and for the development of resources
in particular areas. Grants are likely to be made to war veterans and for
housing and other less regular purposes. To ignore the effect of such
outlays on the private economy—not to plan them with an eye to the
general state of business, whether healthily prosperous, inflationary, or
threatening to contract—would seem, in view of present knowledge, to
show a sort of willful blindness to the nature of government finance.
But if all outlays are planned with regard to their general effects, the
basis is present for a more positive and far-reaching policy to prevent
depressions.

This view of public spending applies to the other departments of
public finance. Taxes need to be judged not only by the criteria already
discussed but also by their effect on total demand. How they bear on
saving and consumer spending is significant. How they affect the incentives to produce and to invest is of major importance. Likewise the
complex programs for social security, especially the old-age-annuity
part of it, should be managed so that the tax collections and benefit
payments, which run into billions, are soundly related to the total-
demand situation.

The same considerations should govern the administration of the
public debt. Transferring money from taxpayers to bondholders may

seriously affect the flow of funds in buying goods. Perhaps use of the income tax to make interest payments has little effect, but collection of taxes to give bondholders the principal of their bonds can be expected to slow up the rate of spending unless private investment opportunities are especially abundant and inviting. Even more, to tax deposit dollars from people to retire bonds held by banks means a wiping out of purchasing power that only a prompt expansion of private loans can offset.

Thus debt reduction cannot be carried out intelligently on a uniform basis, so many billions a year, but must be adjusted to business conditions. It can temper the inflationary nature of a boom, and it can aggravate a recession. Such a period as that following the recent war is most favorable for reducing the debt, since tax rates and public revenues remain high and supplies of goods remain inadequate in the face of the very great private demand. This is a time to keep taxes high and to reduce public expenditures as rapidly as possible. But however important it is to reduce the debt, reduction is not justified that appreciably depresses the national income. The prosperity of the whole economy is of first importance, and it is on that prosperity that ability to bear a large debt depends.

If events should finally confirm the views of the pessimists that some long-run increase in the debt is necessary to enable the government to offset deficiencies in private buying and investing, this need should be judged realistically in comparison with its alternatives, which may be even more distasteful. In that event, some other way of reducing the debt burden should be sought. Since the situation would confirm the oversaving thesis, probably government should explore the possibility of obtaining the use of private savings with no other reward than the safekeeping of the principal, together with maintenance of liquidity for the individual. Without interest, a growing debt would be practically burdenless.

Public finance, income distribution, and resource use

Fiscal policy is most important in its bearing on total production and income. But it has great influence also in two other areas of economic organization and policy: the division of the national income and the allocation of resources to particular uses.

We have seen that distribution may be affected both through public expenditures and through the collection of revenues. Services such as education, parks and playgrounds, and medical and housing assistance, as well as relief for those incapable of self-support, involve large income contributions to individuals at the expense of the general public. The more these functions are expanded, the larger is the influence exerted.

On the other hand, the more progressive the taxes are by which funds are collected for all public purposes, the more pronounced is the redistribution. The progressive principle, as we have observed, may aim at leaving undisturbed the distribution of income in psychic terms, or it may strike much more heavily at the high-income groups to affect a substantial redistribution. Even if redistribution is not the objective, it is bound to result from greatly increased reliance on income taxes, as in the war period.[17] Policy in this sphere may react, of course, on the size of the national income through its effect on consumer spending and on production and investment incentives.

Both spending and taxation also affect the assignment of resources to particular uses. Subsidies granted to railroads and other industries have greatly stimulated their development. Heavy excise taxes and high license fees have been used to curtail certain lines of production and consumption. The aims may be various: to protect the public somewhat against its own bad judgment, as in the case of liquor, or to give artificial protection to a favored industry or way of doing business, as through the special taxes on oleomargarine and on chain stores. Of longest standing is the policy of imposing special tax burdens on imported goods, in order to protect domestic producers. We shall consider this policy in the next chapter.

Review Questions

1. "Government borrowing for capital outlays is logical enough, but it should be held to a minimum, and debts should be retired systematically." Develop the ideas behind this statement.

2. "Wars can be financed entirely through taxation. Such taxation would still leave in the hands of individuals all the dollars they can use in buying products available for civilian use." Show that, despite the force of this argument, there are persuasive reasons for partial reliance on borrowing.

3. "Borrowing does not postpone the cost of war. Its real cost must be borne while it is being fought. Financial arrangements may redistribute the burden but cannot defer it." Develop this argument. Show that, in fact, the burden is deferred by borrowing in an important sense—perhaps in two senses.

4. "Unless a nation repays its debt, its bonds become worthless." "As long as a government owes its own citizens, there is no danger of excessive

---

[17] Allowing both for higher prices and higher taxes, a $2000 income would buy about as much in 1948 as a $1200 income in 1939. Wages, on the average, had risen at more than this rate. But it required nearly $10,000 in 1948 to buy as much as $5000 would in 1939, $61,000 to buy as much as $25,000, and $363,000 to buy as much as $100,000. Before the 1948 tax reduction, over $600,000 was needed to have the buying power of $100,000 in 1939. (Taxes are for a married person with two dependents, and the community-property principle is applied in 1948.) See *United States News*, August 13, 1948, p. 20.

debt." Criticize both statements and state the essentials of the problem as you see them.

5. "Since government has the power to create money, it is foolish to borrow money and pay interest on it." What is the chief objection to financing by printing paper money? Is it a burdenless method? Does borrowing altogether escape its objectionable features? Explain.

6. Distinguish three conceptions of budget balancing, two of which do not involve an annual equality of receipts and outlays. To what extent may government treat capital outlays as a business does?

7. "In taxing, borrowing, spending, and repaying loans, government is necessarily a major factor in the total demand for goods." Explain, reviewing the main considerations that are pertinent here.

8. Review the ways in which the allocation of resources and the distribution of income are influenced by the processes of government finance.

- 32 -

International Trade
and Public Policy

W_{HY}, in a book on economic fundamentals, should
there be a chapter on international trade? Is there anything special to
be said about the exchange of goods because national boundaries separate the people who buy and sell? Such boundaries are political. They
do not determine the resources of areas or the skills of people. Because
governments differ and different flags are flown, can trade be either
beneficial or harmful in some new and special way or call for regulations not deemed necessary for domestic trade?

Many a teacher of economics has wished that the subject of international trade would be approached by students with this reaction. It is
a reaction that squares with the whole emphasis of economics. Moreover, if it were the reaction of all people everywhere, it would reflect
the attitude that the world most needs, for reasons that are not merely
economic. Unfortunately, however, international trade is seldom seen
in this light. Trade with foreigners is generally viewed as a special sort
of activity and subjected, as a matter of course, to ways of thinking that
would be deemed suicidal if applied to domestic trade. Persons whose
firmest belief is that government should leave business alone have been
the strongest supporters, for generations, of the most arbitrary interference with foreign trade.

Perhaps foreign trade does have features that justify special treatment. But whether it does or not, prevalent attitudes toward it and
their political consequences call for special discussion. In no other area
of economics is it as necessary, in appraising policies, to begin by clearing the ground of an underbrush of distorted and emotionally inspired
thinking. Accordingly, we discuss international trade in part because
people think it is different, in part because government action makes it

different, and in part because there are actual conditions which may support these policies.

One such condition, attributable to government but not really a trade policy, is the difference between the moneys of different countries. The analysis of exchange rates and international payments which appeared in Chapter 13 will be applied extensively in the present discussion. A more fundamental economic condition is the relative immobility of labor and capital between countries. The world economy does not differ sharply from the economies of individual nations in this respect, since, as we have observed, there are sectional differences within the United States in the availability of the factors of production and in the returns they receive. But the international differences are larger; more important, it is the habit of people to view them differently and reach different conclusions from them. Thus it is commonly said that a protective tariff is needed in the United States because wages are lower in other countries.

Beside these economic conditions which give rise to policies, the biggest condition is government itself and the international struggle for power that spills over into the economic field. We do not have to decide whether it is more true that national enmities grow out of economic conditions or that nationalistic prejudices merely find economic expression. No doubt both relations are present, and only a simple soul would support a one-way case. The essential point for us is that leading occasions for economic policies, notably those concerned with national self-sufficiency, would not arise except for the national sovereignties.[1]

The United States in World Trade

Before getting into matters of theory and policy, it is well to have some idea of the extent and nature of international trade. Because attention throughout our study has focused on the American economy, we shall look mainly into the foreign-trade relations of the people of the United States.

Extent of American foreign trade

Statistically the foreign trade of the United States looms large or small depending on the viewpoint adopted. In absolute amount it is

[1] General works in this field include P. T. Ellsworth, *International Economics*, Macmillan, 1938; Stephen Enke and Virgil Salera, *International Economics*, Prentice-Hall, 1947; Asher Isaacs, *International Trade—Tariff and Commercial Policies*, Richard D. Irwin, Inc., 1948. Prominent among discussions of postwar problems are: Alvin H. Hansen, *America's Role in the World Economy*, W. W. Norton, 1945; Norman S. Buchanan and Friedrich A. Lutz, *Rebuilding the World Economy*, Twentieth Century Fund, 1947.

large and has a conspicuous place in the commerce of the world. In 1938, the last full year before World War II, the exports and imports of this country totaled $5 billion, second only to the trade of the United Kingdom, which had $7 billion. Extraordinary demands after the war raised the exports alone of the United States to more than $14 billion, far ahead of any other nation.

Relative importance. But this is a large country from a number of viewpoints, and the importance of foreign trade to a nation's economy is a relative matter. On a per-capita basis, American foreign trade is ordinarily not large. Imports and exports together amounted to less than $40 per person in 1938. In comparison, they amounted to $275 for the New Zealanders, and to $150 or more for the Danes, Belgians, Swedes, Swiss, Dutch, Australians, and British, in descending order. At the other end of the scale, imports and exports totaled less than $4 per person in Russia, India, and China.

But total goods per capita vary widely among nations, so a still better basis of comparison in judging dependence on foreign trade is to relate it to national product or national income. This basis diminishes further the apparent importance of foreign trade to the United States. In 1938, the $3 billion of commodities exported were from a gross national product of $84 billion, or only 3.5 percent of the whole. The $2 billion of imports were less than 2.5 percent of the total goods that became available. But the word *trade,* from long custom, applies only to physical commodity exports and imports and does not cover the service items—the services of shipping, insurance, and moving pictures, the services of capital invested abroad, the services performed for foreign travelers—which are conspicuous in international dealings and which are part of the total sale and purchase of goods. With these included, the total current transactions on the credit, or export, side of the balance of payments of this country amounted to more than $4 billion in 1938, and on the debit side to more than $3 billion.[2] These figures do not include capital transfers or the abnormal inflow of gold in that year.

Directly comparable figures are not available for other countries. But it appears that well up toward half of the goods consumed in Belgium and Denmark were from foreign sources in 1938 and that the amount ranged upward from 20 percent in other countries mentioned above.[3]

[2] The balance of payments was explained in Chapter 13.

[3] For the data given above such standard statistical sources have been used as the Department of Commerce materials on national income and the balance of payments; also Chapters 1 and 2 of *International Economics,* by Enke and Salera, *op. cit.,* in which use is made of League of Nations data.

Importance of specific commodity movements. It may be objected on several grounds that cold figures, especially aggregates and percentages based on them, do not actually reveal the importance of foreign trade to this country. It may be more revealing to say that, before the war, this country was depending on foreign sources for all of its rubber, tin, coffee, and silk, and that it drew heavily on foreign production for its sugar, paper, wool, hides, and copper, to mention only major products. The outlay for rubber may have averaged hardly $200 million annually in the late 1930s, but the war showed quickly the great importance of foreign rubber. Likewise minor products, which weigh lightly in the statistics—products such as chromite, manganese, cobalt, nickel, and asbestos—come wholly or almost altogether from abroad and have critical importance in the economy.

On the export side, more than a quarter of the tobacco and cotton was sold abroad in 1938, a substantial amount of wheat and some other farm products, and fractions of various manufactured products, especially in the mechanical lines, that went as high as 25 percent. Millions of people find employment in producing goods for export. It is often pointed out, when the general prosperity is considered, that in many industries these exports mean the difference between profit and loss and thus contribute greatly to the health of the economy. Moreover, as in the case of domestic investment, it is possible that each additional dollar of foreign sales will have several dollars of effect on the size of the national income.[4]

But we must be careful not to carry this sort of reasoning too far. It is only a short-run observation to say that, if our industries lost their foreign markets, they would be unprofitable and many people would lose their jobs. These particular industries have expanded as they have, and many people hold the kind of jobs they do, because of the foreign markets. If these markets were eliminated, we would not get the imports these exports pay for, and we would use our resources in quite different ways. We are concerned here with the long-run significance of foreign trade; and it should be plain enough, though even experienced observers sometimes forget it, that long-run judgments must rest on long-run adjustments.

Reasons for national differences

Whatever the importance of foreign trade to this country, it is of much less importance than to countries such as England that depend on foreign sources for much of their food and raw materials. Why

---

[4] See Chapter 14, pp. 357–359, for a discussion of the multiplier idea in domestic trade.

should it enter so unequally into the economic life of different countries?

The leading reason, without doubt, lies in the *size of countries, in area and population.* Countries that are large and possessed of varied resources, as large countries are likely to be, can develop many lines of production internally and accomplish through domestic trade what smaller countries must achieve through international dealings. The trade among the states and regions of the United States is quite comparable to the trade among numerous European countries. In this respect, Russia, China, and India are similar to the United States.

But *low productivity,* general economic backwardness, is also a reason for a small foreign trade. This factor accounts necessarily for low trade in an absolute sense, both domestic and foreign; it accounts also for low foreign trade in a relative sense if the nation produces its own food. The primary concern of a backward nation with its food supply must then prevent it from producing very much for exchange with foreigners. China and India are striking instances of this situation.

A third factor, since trade is subject to control, is the *trade policy of nations.* Russia, with a state monopoly of trade, seems bent on achieving the maximum degree of self-sufficiency and thus restricts its imports to a few essentials and its exports to the necessary means of payment. Most countries have limited their foreign trade by the barriers they have set up. The pre-eminence achieved by Great Britain in world trade can be attributed, in large degree, to her freedom from trade restrictions for many years prior to World War I. Great Britain was willing to depend on foreign foods and materials and to admit anything else that could compete in her markets; and other countries were thus able to obtain the pounds sterling to buy her products. In this policy Great Britain was undoubtedly influenced by her priority in the Industrial Revolution.

Changes in the trade of the United States

The foreign trade of the United States reflects clearly the entire economic development of the nation. Changes over half a century, ending with the great depression, are shown in Table 38. During this period crude materials and foodstuffs fell from 60 percent to 32 percent of the exports, rose from 30 percent to 49 percent of the imports, while finished manufactures rose from 15 percent to 45 percent of the exports and fell from 36 percent to 22 percent of the imports. At the same time, the totals show that the nation shifted from an import to an export balance, primarily because it was making loans rather than receiving them, but also because of changes in various service items.

TABLE 38—CHANGES IN THE FOREIGN TRADE OF THE UNITED STATES
(Five-year averages in millions of dollars)

Class of commodity	1871–1875		1926–1930	
	Exports	Imports	Exports	Imports
Crude materials	$218 (45%)	$ 93 (16%)	$1144 (25%)	$1484 (37%)
Crude foodstuffs	75 (15%)	82 (14%)	300 (7%)	507 (12%)
Manufactured foodstuffs	95 (20%)	116 (20%)	456 (10%)	398 (10%)
Semi-manu- factures	23 (5%)	78 (14%)	663 (13%)	762 (19%)
Finished manu- factures	75 (15%)	209 (36%)	2126 (45%)	882 (22%)
Total	486 (100%)	578 (100%)	4689 (100%)	4033 (100%)

Specialization, Free Trade, and the "Favorable Balance"

The ideal situation, from a standpoint that is *strictly economic* and *strictly long-run,* is one in which no artificial barriers obstruct trade among the nations and no subsidies or other special pressures distort it. This is the "free-trade" position, and, stated with these limitations, it has been the dominant position of economists since Adam Smith.

Both the makers and the analysts of policy differ in the stress they place on the limitations. Noneconomic factors, especially those that spring from the uncertain relations of sovereign powers, may be allowed to outweigh the merits of free trade. Deviations for short-run reasons may obscure the desirable long-run course. The case for trade barriers, on all grounds worth serious recognition, will be discussed in a later section. Here we shall develop the logic of the free-trade principle, within its appropriate limitations. In doing so, we shall examine certain ill-founded reasons for departing from it—reasons for exalting exports and deploring imports that are worth considering only because of the number of people who seem to be influenced by them.

The "free-trade" case

Specialization among nations expands productivity in all of the ways that operate inside of nations, and trade is essential to specialization.[5] Trade permits the regions of the world to concentrate on products for

[5] The economies of specialization were discussed in Chapter 7.

which their natural resources especially fit them. Techniques and skills develop in high degree when industries have wide markets and expand. For the smaller countries especially, wide international markets are essential to mass production and the economies of plant specialization.

Tariffs and the other barriers to trade affect specialization just as high transport costs do. The advantage of having a good produced at a remote point may be canceled by the expense of transferring it. But whereas transportation involves real costs, and no specialization is justified whose direct advantages do not outweigh them, the trade barriers nations set up are artificial and prevent the most effective production of goods. They are as artificial as a return to antiquated and uneconomical methods of transportation would be.

International investment is involved as well as specialization as such. If capital is not to be sunk irretrievably and profitlessly in other lands, creditor nations must accept goods in payment of interest, dividends, and principal sums. Only as the creditors accept goods can debtor nations obtain the money balances they require. When the United States passed the Smoot-Hawley Tariff Act in 1930, after its heavy lending during the 1920s, it acted in defiance of this elementary point.

It is curious how readily people accept ideas in one situation and deny them in another that is identical. It would not be argued that Brown, the carpenter, should make his own clothes because, with some effort and practice, he could somehow manage to do it. Nor would it be contended that New Englanders should raise the wheat they use, up to the full limit of their power to extract it from New England soil. But it will be argued that a nation should not import anything that it can produce itself, however much better it is at other things. Political boundaries do not upset economic logic in this manner.

It was to ridicule this strange confusion that Adam Smith, back in 1776, discoursed on growing grapes in Scotland:

By means of glasses, hotbeds, and hotwalls, very good grapes can be raised in Scotland, and very good wine too can be made of them at about thirty times the expense for which at least equally good can be brought from foreign countries. Would it be a reasonable law to prohibit the importation of all foreign wines, merely to encourage the making of claret and burgundy in Scotland.[6]

In so extreme a case, the idea of protection must seem absurd to any one. "It is not bananas we want to raise in my district, but only sugar beets," says the Congressman, "and Cuban sugar, without a tariff, can undersell us a cent a pound." But the principle, as *The Wealth of Na-*

[6] *An Inquiry into the Nature and Causes of the Wealth of Nations,* Book IV, Chapter III.

tions goes on to say, is the same whether the domestic expense is thirty times as great, or only a thirtieth or a three-hundredth part more.

The free-trade principle should be easy for Americans to understand. To see its force, they need only imagine that every state is a separate country with a high tariff wall and compare the imagined result with the American economy as it is. If they see the advantage of mass-production of automobiles for a nation-wide market or of the geographically concentrated production of tobacco or oranges or of developing the West with capital and capital goods from older areas, they cannot fail to see the basic argument, from the long-run economic standpoint, against trade barriers.

The "favorable-balance" idea

Policy has been greatly influenced by a wholly different view of the gain from foreign trade, the idea that the benefit lies in an excess of exports over imports. This theory is associated historically with the Mercantilists of the seventeenth and eighteenth centuries, but in a vague, undefined fashion, it still permeates popular thinking. It is a "common-sense" idea, just as anyone can "see" that the sun makes the circuit of the earth once each day. From this standpoint, world trade must be a grand scramble in which each nation restricts its foreign purchases and does its best to make foreigners buy its goods, and all nations, collectively, must fail in their endeavor.

As based on a false business analogy. The "favorable-balance" idea is rooted, it would seem, in the everyday experience of the individual. A person or a business gets ahead when receipts exceed purchases, and, by analogy, so should a nation. Exports bring money in, imports take it out, and the object should be to have a net return. The analogy, however, is wholly false. Profit under capitalism, while instrumental in the organization of production, is not the final economic goal. It would be at least as sensible to say that wages are the economic goal, but, from the firm's standpoint, wages are "money going out." Actually the goal is a high level of real income, and policy should be concerned with promoting it.

Indeed, the individual or firm does not receive net money income with the idea of holding it, Silas Marner-like, in cash. The benefit comes when the money is used to buy goods. By analogy, the nation should use its money balance from foreign trade to buy goods—and that means imports.

As based on the desire for money metal. A closely related source of the "favorable-balance" idea is the notion that money itself is a unique form of wealth, to be prized above all others, and that foreign trade should be manipulated to yield a money balance. Since the currency of other nations is not sought, policy is aimed at producing an inflow of gold and silver, the money metals. Probably this idea is not as appealing now as it was back in Elizabethan days, and a little later, when treasure from the Spanish Main stirred the imagination of Europeans and hoards of the precious metals seemed to expand the power of princes.

When moneys are based on gold, nations that are expanding their production and do not produce gold need a net inflow of gold to increase their money supply and prevent deflation. Because the gold inflow is not counted among their imports, such nations naturally find that their other "debits" are exceeded by their "credits," as these terms are used in the balance of payments, and that they have a "favorable" balance. But the excess of exports needed on this account is small, since little of a country's productive effort is required to supply it with a medium of exchange. To expend more productive effort than necessary for this purpose, producing a great volume of goods for export to bring in gold in excess of the amount required for gold's specific uses, is plainly wasteful. Productive effort should be used to obtain the goods that will contribute most to the level of living of the people.

As involving a confusion of means and ends. Viewed realistically, it is the imports, not the exports, of a nation that contribute to the well-being of its people. If a nation could have its imports without having to send out part of its product to pay for them, it would be better off. It exports because it has to to obtain the foreign goods it needs. As we shall note in examining the short-run reasons for trade controls, desperate need of foods and raw materials from abroad often leads to the use of drastic methods to increase exports and curtail unnecessary imports. The "favorable-balance" idea may be suggested; but, in fact, stress is placed on exports—the means—rather than on imports—the end—because it is known that the imports can be bought provided the exports can be sold.

As an aspect of the unemployment problem. A "favorable balance" may also be sought as a means of getting fuller employment and greater production. If a nation can produce for itself the goods it has been buying abroad, it seems that greater use of its productive capacity will result. We shall see later that there is some short-run possibility of this sort, for some nations, but the ordinary advocate of this idea is not thinking with any nicety of qualification; he is simply forgetting the fact that if a nation does not import, it cannot continue to export. It is through selling to it that other nations get the means of buying from it. Thus, in proposing artificial measures to develop home production in the import lines, he is proposing to sacrifice production and employment in the export industries, in which presumably the nation's resources are most effectively used.

As reflecting the neglect of noncommodity transactions. Undoubtedly the idea that a nation can continue to sell more than it buys is promoted by a confusion of the *balance of trade* and the *balance of payments*. The former includes only physical commodities and omits services which may involve large sums. A nation may have an excess of exports but have total purchases as great as its total sales. A "favorable balance" could not possibly achieve the results claimed for it unless it covered the whole range of current transactions, services as well as commodities.

But it is the capital items in the balance of payments that are most confusing. Loans and investments, and the return on them, affect trade in a variety of ways. When the United States was developing its resources during the last century with the help of foreign capital, we naturally had a balance of trade that was "unfavorable," however beneficial the effect actually was. We were using the proceeds of loans to import needed materials and equipment. When this stage was past, and we were in position to repay some of the loans, it became necessary to develop an export balance to obtain the required funds. Still later, during and after World War I, we became a creditor nation, and we needed export balances for the heavy lending we did. In effect, we lent foreign nations the money to buy our goods.

But an old lending nation, one with a large accumulation of income-yielding investments in foreign countries, will receive a larger sum in interest and dividends each year than the new investments that it makes. It will receive them, that is, if its imports are large enough to give other countries the means of making payment, or, conversely, if it uses its receipts to buy foreign goods. The biggest reason for the large import balance of Great Britain before World War II was a return of well over $1 billion a year from foreign investments. Its balance of trade was highly "unfavorable"—though this scarcely seems an appropriate adjective to apply to a large return on investments.

Fortunately the benefit from foreign trade comes through specialization rather than through having a "favorable balance." If it rested on the latter basis, one nation's gain would be another's loss; half the world would suffer for the benefit to the rest. In strict logic, then, the suffering half should stop buying, and trade should end. Actually the gains of specialization are not denied but are accepted in a blundering way that makes their realization more difficult. It is too bad that they are not seen more clearly, for policy problems in this field are suffi-ciently complex if only the necessary difficulties are admitted.[7]

Measurement of the gain from foreign trade

There is no way of telling how much the world gains, or individual nations gain, from foreign trade. If the gain lay in the relation between imports and exports, we might tell; but no light is derived from noting, for example, that in 1938 the exports of the United Kingdom were 58 percent of the imports, whereas the exports of the United States were 158 percent of the imports. We might tell, also, if the gain lay in get-ting rid of surplus products; but most export surpluses arise, as we have observed, through the fact that they are intentionally produced for for-eign markets. Nor is there anything in a balance-of-payments state-ment that measures a nation's gain.

If, in the absence of foreign trade, a nation would produce at home the same identical commodities it is importing, some measure might be possible. For example, the resources used to produce enough tobacco to pay in foreign markets for two million pounds of coffee might, in the absence of trade, produce one million pounds of coffee here. Then we could say, in that instance, that specialization yielded us one million pounds of coffee.

But, very largely, if we stopped trading we would not produce the things we now import. Some goods, notably some minerals, we could not produce; others would be so costly that substitute products would be preferred. There is no way of comparing the relative utilities of the imports and the substitutes or of measuring the decline in production if certain products, such as alloys used in metallurgy, were not avail-able. But even though we cannot measure it, the gain consists in our preference for the goods we obtain through trade to the goods we would use our resources to produce, if we did not exchange products with foreign nations.

[7] The similarity should be noted between the idea of a "favorable" international balance and the "buy-at-home" philosophy with which town merchants sometimes try to indoctri-nate their home communities. If all the individuals and firms in a community actually received more money from outside it than they used to make outside purchases and invest-ments, money would accumulate in that community and either raise prices or lie idle. If the "buy-at-home" slogan were followed literally by every individual and enterprise, the community would become autonomous and have only the goods to consume that its peo-ple produced locally from local materials. In so far as the slogan does influence buying, the local merchants benefit as they would from any successful advertising, and consumers lose to the extent that they buy less advantageously than they could elsewhere. If prosperous merchants are civic-minded, there may be some gain from that source. But the idea belongs essentially in that popular economic gallery entitled "How we lift ourselves by our boot-straps."

Multilateral trade

When the mutual trade of pairs of nations, as of Canada and the United States, is examined, it is commonly found that one of them is buying much more than the other. Sometimes this imbalance is thought unhealthy, especially for the country that buys more than it sells. In fact, however, lack of balance between pairs of nations is a natural aspect of the most effective world-wide specialization. Just as an individual usually finds that the people who want his product are not the ones from whom he wishes to do most of his buying, so specialization among nations develops most fully on a multilateral basis. It is better for us to buy tin from the Malayans and pay them with the proceeds of cotton sold to the British, while the British get income from the Malayans for managerial services and capital, than it would be for us to try to achieve one balance with the British and another with the Malayans. If each nation achieves a balance with the rest of the world, the conditions of international payment are met, provided all moneys are readily convertible into each other.

From this it does not follow that pairs of nations may not find it economical to intertwine their economies in a somewhat bilateral fashion. Economies may be naturally complementary, as those of Great Britain and Argentina seem to have been. And when this situation is present, its effect is accentuated through the economy of loading ships in both directions and through the friendly relations and naturally expanding activities of the numerous foreign representatives of business firms. But an artificial bilateralism which operates through making nations forego other and better sources for their imports can only reduce the total of trade and its general advantage.

The strong trend toward bilateralism during the 1930s must be deemed, therefore, to reflect weaknesses in the world situation. It resulted in part from monetary confusion and in part from a sense of insecurity whose far-reaching effects we shall presently consider.

Basic Trade, Price, and Wage Relationships

If Robinson Crusoe and his man Friday constitute an entire economy, and if Crusoe is twice as good as Friday at raising vegetables and Friday can catch fish twice as fast, they will expand their real income (or their leisure) by specializing and exchanging their specialties. This is evident and will not be questioned. But should they specialize if Crusoe is better at both tasks, twice as effective in catching fish and four times in growing vegetables? The answer, again, is yes, though it may not be quite so evident. If Friday is only a fisherman and leaves the gardening to Crusoe, the gain in vegetables is greater than the loss in fish.

But suppose we substitute nations for these men, say France for Friday and the United States for Crusoe, and talk about Product X instead of fish and Product Y instead of vegetables, shall we reach the same conclusions regarding specialization and trade? Certainly the principle is the same. But we can be sure that many a protectionist would apply trade barriers under the first assumption, and practically every protectionist would under the second. From the standpoint of the United States, what sense can there be for a country to import a good that it can produce better than the exporting country?

It appears, then, that the basis of specialization should be examined more closely than we have done. We need to define more exactly the condition that makes trade beneficial. The underlying condition is summed up in the principle of comparative advantage, a principle ordinarily stated in real terms.

But this underlying condition is not enough. Trading takes place on the basis of prices in different countries and of the exchange rates which relate the moneys of different countries. The basis of trade must be expressed also in these terms.

Finally, we must see why wage rates differ between countries and how trade is related to them. To see this clearly is the practical object of the present discussion, since the most effective argument for the protective tariff in the United States has been that we need it to protect American labor from the competition of low-wage labor of other countries. A belief in trade barriers can be supported by reasons which are analytically respectable, but this is not one of them.

Comparative advantage, the underlying basis of trade

Trade is carried on by many nations in many products, but the basis of trade and specialization can be defined just as soundly, and much more sharply, if we talk about two nations and two products, and assume that there are no more. The United States and France, as hypothetical producers of Products X and Y, will serve the purpose, and the necessary conditions can be introduced as we proceed.

When Products X and Y are produced in both countries, they are priced as follows:

	France	United States
Product X	20 francs	$1
Product Y	80 francs	2

These prices presumably correspond to the relative costs of producing X and Y in each country. Thus Y, which is the more valuable commodity, is twice as costly as X in the United States and four times as costly in France. Such a difference between the relative prices and costs *within countries* is the fundamental basis of trade. Moreover, such differences are the basis of all trade and specialization, whether of nations, regions, or individuals. The example, as thus stated, has not told us how many francs are equal to a dollar. It has not told us whether the United States is more or less efficient than France in producing these commodities. But on the basis of it we can say that France has a comparative advantage in producing X, the United States in producing Y. If prices within the countries correspond to costs of production, we can say that the *comparative* cost of X is lower in France and the *comparative* cost of Y is lower in the United States. X is only one fourth as costly as Y in France; Y is only twice as costly as X in the United States.

For importing and exporting to develop in the modern way, we need more facts. But to show that the essential basis of trade has already been stated, let us introduce into this situation a questing Yankee trader of the old type who combines exporting and importing in a complete exchange. This trader buys 100,000 units of Y in the United States, costing him \$200,000, loads them on a ship, takes them to France, and sells them for 8,000,000 francs. With these francs he purchases 400,000 units of X, which he brings home and sells for \$400,000. Not allowing for his handling and transportation expenses, he has made \$200,000.

In this example all the gain goes to the middleman. For Americans to depend extensively on France for their supply of Xs, the price must fall below \$1. For the French to substitute imported for domestic Ys, a price below 80 francs is necessary. With these adjustments, which are easily possible with so wide a spread in comparative costs, extensive specialization by each nation in its field of superior productivity can be expected. As a result, Americans obtain Xs more cheaply by producing Ys and exporting them, and Frenchmen similarly obtain Ys with less expenditure of resources than before.

It should be noted that comparative advantage rests on the *comparative costs of producing different goods within countries*, not on the relative cost, in terms of resources used, of producing the same good in different countries. It does not matter which of the two Crusoe-Friday situations is assumed. In terms of labor and capital used, the United States may be more or less efficient than France in producing Xs. What matters—and this is the underlying basis of trade—is that **the United States, as judged by the French situation, is relatively better** in producing Ys than Xs, and France, in relation to the United States, is more effective in producing Xs than Ys. With this condition present, prices will be so related within the countries that Yankee traders can work profitably, and the economy of specialization can be achieved.

Trade, prices; and exchange rates

But modern commerce is not carried on by Yankee traders. The American importer of Xs is not interested in the relative price of Ys either here or in France. He is interested in the price he can get for Xs here, the price he must pay for them in France, and the exchange rate at which he can convert dollars to francs. The French importer is interested in the corresponding facts regarding Ys. No product will be imported unless its full cost in money is lower when imported than when bought at home.[8]

The problem, then, is that of finding a set of prices and exchange rates which will make two-way trade possible. The prices within each country must still be consistent with the comparative cost of the commodities, and the imported commodity must be enough cheaper in money terms to make importation worth while in each country. These requirements can be seen best by assuming first a condition that does not meet them, and then introducing the necessary adjustment.

So, leaving prices as they are in the above example, let us add the one additional fact that $1 is equal to 15 francs. Is the basis then present for normal two-way trade between the United States and France? The answer is no. On this basis it pays the French to import Ys, since a $2 Y costs only 30 francs, as against 80 francs for the home product. But it does not pay the United States to import Xs. With Xs costing $1 at home, it would take $1⅓ to pay for an X priced at 20 francs in France. Without exports, the French would lack dollar balances to pay for Ys, and trade could not develop on a continuing basis.

The condition necessary for two-way trade can be established through either one of the two automatic readjustments, explained in Chapter 13, through which equilibrium in international payments is brought about: (1) If the international gold standard is effective, the French will pay out gold for Ys, with the effect of lowering prices in France and raising them in the United States, until it pays Americans to import Xs. (2) If the currencies are not attached to gold, the demand in France for dollars to pay for Ys will raise the price of dollars, or

---

[8] Students are often misled by the statement that a nation may benefit by importing goods that it can produce at lower cost than the nation from which it buys them. Such a statement applies only to cost in real terms, not to money cost. To avoid this confusion, it is necessary to bridge the gap between real and money costs.

cheapen the franc, until Americans can save money by buying their Xs in France.

We shall assume that adjustment is by the latter process. It is somewhat simpler, and it is more in line with the reality of recent years. Accordingly, we shall assume that the dollar is bid up until its price is 30 francs. With an exchange rate of 30 francs to the dollar, the basis is present for a two-way trade that yields a substantial advantage to each nation. It still pays the French to import Ys, since a $2 Y costs them only 60 francs, as against 80 francs at home. And now it pays Americans to import Xs, for an X priced at 20 francs costs only two thirds of a dollar at the new exchange rate, in comparison with the home price of $1. With no allowance for transportation and handling, there is a saving to the French of one fourth, and to the Americans of one third of the domestic price.[9]

It probably seldom happens that the gain from specialization is divided equally. The stronger a nation's demand for foreign goods, the less favorable the terms of trade will be to it. Thus if the American demand for Xs should increase, so that total American payments would exceed receipts at the 30-franc exchange rate, francs would be bid up so that a dollar would command, let us say, only 25 francs. Then Xs would cost Americans 80 cents, and the French would buy Ys for only 50 francs.[10]

What has been said regarding two countries and two commodities applies equally well to many countries and many commodities. Prices and exchange rates must be so adjusted that the goods in which a nation has a comparative advantage appear cheap to buyers in other countries who buy them with their moneys. Goods in which a nation has a comparative disadvantage must be priced so that they are cheaper when imported. Each country, in addition, will have many goods, such as housing, railroad transportation, and the personal services, which do not enter international trade at all and must be bought at home whatever the cost. When full account is taken of transportation and handling costs, and allowance made for the greater risks of foreign dealing, it is apparent that comparative advantages must often be considerable to make trade worth while. Tariffs and other artificial obstacles operate in addition to these substantial natural barriers.

[9] The further assumption is present that we are dealing with constant-cost industries, so that the production of Xs and Ys can be expanded for export at a continuing cost of 20 francs and $2 respectively. Otherwise expansion would either raise or lower unit costs.

[10] This is the basis for one of the more sophisticated arguments for trade barriers. By stopping some imports the terms of trade may be shifted so that the remaining imports are less costly. The barriers should apply only to goods for which the price at home is only a little higher than abroad, so that only a small sacrifice is made to improve the trading position.

Wage differences among countries

Because the leading American argument for trade barriers is that American industry faces the competition of low-wage labor abroad, it is essential to carry this analysis one step farther and inquire into the basis of wage differences between nations. We can do this once we understand the role of comparative cost and of prices and exchange rates in fixing the terms of trade.

The revenues from products go to the suppliers of labor and capital and the other factors of production. Thus, with the 30-franc exchange rate, if it requires more labor and capital to produce a 30-franc product in France than a $1 product in the United States, rates of money income must be higher in the United States than in France. The same amount of money must compensate a larger quantity of productive service in France than in the United States. Higher money income in the United States is, accordingly, a reflection of higher productivity and higher real income. High money wages in a country must rest fundamentally on the superior productivity of its labor.

When we try to make this point concretely, we run into difficulties. One difficulty lies in the defining of factors for international comparison. Skilled manual labor, or a particular subtype of it, may not mean just the same in the United States as in France or in China. Perhaps only averages can be compared. A second difficulty is that the division of income among the factors of production is likely to differ between countries. In each country, presumably, distribution takes account of the worth of factor services, resting finally on a marginal basis. But labor may be relatively scarcer in the United States, and land relatively scarcer in France, so that comparisons for specific factors may not reflect the general situation.

With these complications in mind, so that we shall not think we are doing more than we are, we may do some drastic simplifying to bring out more sharply the basis of money-wage differences between countries. Let us assume, accordingly, that labor is the only economic factor, the only factor that gets a return, in France and the United States and that there is just one grade of labor in each country. And let us assume also that in one day a French worker produces 6 units of X, and in one day an American worker produces 4 units of Y. Then, at 20 francs per X, the French worker makes 120 francs a day, and at $2 per Y, the American worker makes $8 per day. With 30 francs equal to $1, the French worker gets the equivalent of $4 per day, or one half the wage of the American worker.

It should be realized that this relationship of money wages is as necessary to the trade in Xs and Ys as are the prices and exchange rates already discussed. If wages were raised in France to $8 a day, or 240 francs, the price of Xs would have to be 40 francs, or $11⅓, and Americans would not buy them at that price when they can be produced in the United States for $1. If trade is in balance when $1 equals 30 francs and labor produces at the rates assumed, wages must be twice as high in the United States as in France.

Does this mean that real wages in the United States are twice as high, that Americans in this hypothetical situation can live twice as well as Frenchmen? It would mean this if Xs and Ys were the only goods consumed. But, for our example, we need only assume that these are the only internationally traded goods. Other goods, such as housing, are produced and consumed within each country, and it may well be that American labor is not twice as productive as French labor in turning out these domestic goods. Thus, though higher money wages mean higher real wages as between countries, the real wages need not differ to the same degree.

The wages argument for the tariff

What is the bearing of this analysis on the wages argument for trade barriers? Stating the argument in its most extreme form, the protectionist declares that, but for the tariff, wages in the United States would be forced down to the level prevailing in Japan or Italy or some other low-wage country. Unless wages fell to that level, he says, our costs and prices would be so high that foreign goods would flood our markets and our industries would have to shut down. Hence the tariff is the foundation of prosperity and of the American wage level.

In this form, the argument is obvious nonsense to anyone with the slightest sense of economic reality. It is only necessary to observe, as we did in introducing the income concept in Chapter 3, that a country will have a real income equal to its total product, whatever the situation as to money prices and money incomes.[11] If foreign competition were to have the effect of forcing prices and money incomes down, the money incomes would still buy the product, and the well-being of the ordinary person would still depend on that product. The "American standard of living" rests on American productivity, not on Congressional enactments.

Or we may put it this way that if high money wages are worth protecting, they do not need protecting. If they are worth protecting, they mean correspondingly high real wages and corresponding high pro-

[11] The only qualification is the point that high money incomes are advantageous in buying foreign goods. But this is not the point of the wages argument; it is rather an aspect of the theory referred to in Note 10, above.

duction. And if, in comparison with other countries, the productivity of labor is as high as the money wages are, high money wages do not cause money costs to be higher, on the average, than elsewhere. If money costs are no higher, then this competition from the products of low-wage countries is not even a menace to the general level of prices and money wages.[12]

But the wages argument need not be stated so sweepingly. And when it is applied to a specific situation, appraisal of it requires the analysis of wage-rate relationships just presented. When would-be producers of Xs in the United States declare that they can produce Xs as well as the French, they are stating a fact. Paying an $8 wage, they can sell Xs at $1 each; and French producers, paying a $4 wage, charge 66⅔ cents. Accordingly the protectionist argues that it is pointless to import a good that can be produced better here, and he advocates at least a 50-percent duty on the value of imported Xs to offset the wage difference and equalize competition.

This is a plausible argument, but it contains a fatal flaw that must be evident to anyone who understands the basis of money wages, as between countries. American producers of X find wages too high because American producers of Y make better use of the labor. Producers of Y pay $8 a day and not only keep the American market to themselves but undersell French producers in the French market. But their efficiency alone does not enable them to sell abroad. They can sell abroad, on a continuing basis, only if the French can sell goods of like value here. Since Xs are France's exportable product, they must be priced lower in this country than the competing American product. They must sell below $1 here, and that is why French labor, having the productivity that it does, gets a relatively low wage. The wage must be low enough to thwart the would-be American producers of X, if Y is to be produced for export.

Thus, though Americans can do a good job at producing X, they cannot do a good enough job. True, they can get 8 units from a day's labor, whereas the French get only 6. But a day's labor produces 4 Ys, which bring $8, or 240 francs, and 240 francs will buy 12 units of X at 20 francs each. Thus we get 50 percent more Xs with a day's labor when we use the labor to produce Ys and export them. Crusoe, the better fisherman, takes less time to get his fish through raising vegetables for Friday, since he is still better at raising vegetables.

So it is true in the United States, the high-wage country, that wages are too high to permit the production of X without a protective tariff.

---

[12] It is a menace only to industries which have come to exist solely as a result of trade barriers.

But it is just as true in France, the low-wage country, that wages are too high to permit the production of *Y*. Protection is sought here against low-wage French labor. And protection is sought in France against highly productive American labor. And the real reason in both instances is that, among trading nations, money costs must always be too high to permit production of the goods in which a country has a comparative disadvantage. Likewise they must be low enough to permit the export of goods in which a comparative advantage is enjoyed. For continuing trade, the prices of factors should be at the level where international sales and purchases balance. For such a balance, wages must be high in countries in which the productivity of labor is high.

Review Questions

1. "The United States is outstanding in world trade, but international dealings are of less importance to Americans than to the citizens of most other advanced nations." Explain, giving figures.

2. "While foreign trade plays an important part in the markets of many goods that Americans buy and sell, its immediate role in these instances exceeds its long-run importance." Why?

3. Distinguish the major factors that determine whether foreign trade will have a large or a small place in the economic life of a nation.

4. What are the main changes that have occurred in the international trade of the United States?

5. "The case against international trade barriers rests on the logic of specialization." Explain, applying the several advantages of specialization to international trade. How are trade barriers related to international investment?

6. "Getting money is the goal of international trade. Money is not like other things. A person can have more than he wants of other things, but not of money. The same is true of a community or a nation." Show wherein the analogy breaks down.

7. If it were possible to have exports without imports or imports without exports, which would be better from the standpoint of maximizing a nation's real income? If it were possible to get more than we give in trade, would this result occur with a "favorable" or with an "unfavorable" balance? Explain.

8. "Restriction of imports should be viewed not merely as an attack on industries in other countries, or as the promotion of domestic production in those fields, but as an attack on the nations' own export industries." What is the point?

9. "There is no logic in attaching more importance, dollar for dollar, to the commodity items than to the other items in the balance of payments. To apply the words "favorable" and "unfavorable" to the balance of com-

modity items is to pronounce judgment on the travel of tourists, the making and repaying of loans, the transfer of returns on international investments." Develop the point.

10. "The advantage of foreign trade is that it enables a nation to get rid of its surplus products." Criticize.

11. If the facts were available, how would you measure the gain from trade (*a*) if imports consist of goods we would produce ourselves if we did not import them, (*b*) if they consist of goods we would not produce if we did not import them?

12. Why is multilateral trade greatly superior to bilateral trade?

13. What does it mean to say that a nation has a comparative advantage in producing a commodity or produces it at lower comparative cost? Explain the fundamental basis of trade and specialization.

14. "While a nation may gain through importing goods that it can produce with less labor and other resources than the exporting country requires, it will only import goods that, in money terms, cost less when imported. Prices and exchange rates must be adjusted accordingly." Explain.

15. "Money wages must differ among countries in accordance with the productivity of labor in internationally traded goods. If labor is highly productive in the United States, money wages must be high; otherwise the United States cannot engage in two-way trade." Explain.

16. "High money wages are important only if they mean high real wages. If they mean high real wages, they do not cause high money costs and do not create a need for protection." Explain.

17. "A high-wage country has no more to fear from foreign competition than a low-wage country does, if prices, wages, and trade are in equilibrium." Explain. What would you expect would happen if a backward country, such as Japan was 50 years ago, becomes industrialized, and wages lag behind rising productivity?

18. "The high level of American exports is evidence against the wages argument for protection." Why?

Possible Justifications of Trade Barriers

Thus the informed person will not want to control foreign trade to get the supposed advantage of a continuing excess of exports or because the income level is threatened by the products of foreign workmen. He will know that the reasons why trade expands production are independent of national boundaries.

But he may still be doubtful whether, in the world as it is, a nation should become as interdependent with other nations as its own subdivisions are with each other. And, while respecting the basic principles of trade, he may hold that selective controls can achieve limited, but important, ends. Among informed persons there is much room for difference of view regarding trade policy.

Protection of established interests

Perhaps most troublesome to the free trader is the argument for continuing the trade barriers to which the industries of a country have become adjusted. A manufacturer says:

I employ 300 men in producing my gadget, and I make money while paying them as high wages as they could get anywhere. I am the largest employer in my town, and if I shut down there wouldn't be much of a town left. There is a 50-percent duty on my product, and I have to have it. Without it, there is a firm in Belgium that would undersell me 30 percent right here. With such competition I'd go out of business or have to pay wages that would ruin my workers, wages as low as in Belgium. The tariff protects them, and it protects the whole community. There are thousands of plants like mine in the country. Free trade may be a nice idea, but the fact is that the prosperity of the country really depends on protection.

This argument has no bearing on the reasons why the free trader believes in free trade, but no responsible policy maker can ignore it. It does not say that a nation is more prosperous because it adopted protection in the first place and developed industries which remain dependent on it. It merely says that, once these industries have been developed, it would be very damaging to remove the protection. It describes the situation which would result, in the example used above, if the production of Xs were encouraged in the United States. There would be workers and communities that would come to depend on the X industry. The harm done to them by repealing the tariff would be immediate and certain, whereas the ultimate gain from expanding the more productive Y industry to obtain Xs cheaply through trade would appear remote and uncertain. Makers of policy must give weight to such matters.

To this the reply of the free trader, if he is a practical person, would be that the removal of tariffs should be a gradual process. There should be no vested right to use resources permanently in an inferior way, whether the alternative is foreign trade or the adoption of labor-saving inventions, but improvements should be made slowly to minimize disturbances. Changes should cause as little pain as possible—a rule that applies as well to raising tariffs as to lowering them—but changes that promise more efficient production should, nevertheless, be made in the course of time, whether they involve arrangements within nations or between them. This reasoning is in line with the American policy of reciprocal tariff agreements associated with former Secretary of State Cordell Hull. It is a policy of reducing tariffs, but it recognizes the force of the "vested-interests" argument for protection.

Development of new industries by restriction of imports

John Stuart Mill, who was a free trader, conceded that protection of new industries during the developmental period may be desirable. Even in the fields of production for which a nation's resources are potentially best fitted, normal growth may be slow and difficult if markets are open to the mature competitors of other countries. It was mainly on these "infant-industry" grounds that Alexander Hamilton stated the case for protection in the United States, and Friedrich List in Germany.

The argument has been applied mainly to manufacturing. High efficiency is slow in coming when much knowledge is necessary of processes and techniques and when skills must be developed among numbers of ordinary workers. Time is required to get equipment and expand plants to a sufficient scale, to establish sources of materials and the essential supplementary activities, to create the confidence in products on which adequate markets must rest. Meanwhile, if unimpeded, foreign firms determined to maintain their sales can do much to block this development.

Somewhat more broadly Hamilton and others have argued that the energies of a nation will be released and stimulated by opening new fields of activity. A variety of talents which find no outlet in the primary industries will be discovered, and productive power as a whole will expand. Perhaps in time these powers would find expression without government aid, but there is much inertia to be overcome, and protection of new activities provides valuable encouragement. The encouragement has a cost, but a nation, like an individual, is well repaid for the outlay on its training and development.

This sort of reasoning is properly influential in new countries in which the more complicated types of production are not yet rooted, but it does not justify general protection or permanent protection. It justifies aid only to those industries in which a nation, potentially, has comparative advantage, and only during the period required for their development. Presently the developmental period must end—as List pointed out in advocating protection for Germany—and the proof that the "infant-industry" argument has been properly applied lies in the fact that the protected industries become able in time to proceed without protection. Of course mistakes will be made, even if an honest attempt has been made to apply the principle properly, and "vested interests" in continuing protection must be evaluated.[13] Moreover,

---

[13] There are certain to be high-cost firms in protected as in other industries, and such

even the industries that have grown so strong that they compete in foreign markets will lobby for the luxury of a protected home market and oppose the removal of duties. But, on the whole, it can be said that the logic of the "infant-industry" argument is eventual free trade.

The broader form of the argument also has its limits. Untried talents doubtless need encouragement, and latent energies may be most quickly released in protected fields. But established industries need the spur of foreign competition to keep them vigorous and to give the public the benefit of their efficiency.

Increase of employment through trade controls

When a nation suffers depression and unemployment, there is a temptation to manipulate its foreign trade to provide jobs. If it can induce its people to buy at home instead of importing, and if it can expand its exports, domestic employment will be increased. The total effect, in accordance with the "multiplier" principle, may be considerably greater than the direct shift in the balance of trade.

To achieve this result, a nation may raise its tariff duties, impose more positive limitations on imports, subsidize its exports, or even put political pressure on weaker countries to buy its goods. The stoppage of imports and the subsidizing of exports both involve a money cost to its people. But the point can be made that, if resources are put to work that would otherwise be idle, there is no corresponding real cost —the same reasoning that is used to justify some of the less valuable public-works projects undertaken to provide employment. "Exporting unemployment" by shifting the trade balance was a common aim of national policy during the 1930s.

General weakness of policy. Whatever the morality of such a procedure, its practical limitations are plain. A nation cannot buy less from other nations and sell them more, unless they dip into their gold stocks, use up their foreign balances, or borrow from it the funds to buy its goods. These are temporary, and probably unwelcome, expedients. An excess of exports may be financed longest by means of loans. But eventually, as we have seen, the return from foreign investments, if they are sound, must equal the new investments currently made, and the "favorable balance" on that account disappears. Or the outflow of capital will stop for some reason, as the foreign investing of the United States did in the late 1920s, and the country will be worse off through now having industries dependent on foreign sales financed by its loans. If the investments prove unsound, so that, in effect, a

---

firms are certain to protest vigorously that continued protection is required. Thus in practice, it is difficult to carry out the logic of the infant-industry idea.

nation has given away the money to buy its goods, the export balance turns out to be the most unrewarding of "make-work" devices. Apart from the benefits to other countries, the nation might better have hired its unemployed to engage in any kind of flood-control or re-forestation project that would have had a particle of value to its people.

There are even more positive limitations. A depression is commonly international, and when one nation experiences it, others do also. If all seek to shift their trade balance to export their unemployment, the efforts of most nations must be neutralized. And whether they are disposed to adopt this policy or not, they are sure to resent the trade restrictions and subsidized competition of other nations, and retalia-tion is almost certain. Thus, even in the short run, the policy may bring more bad feeling than it does jobs.

Possible job creation through restriction of imports. It may be ar-gued, however, that trade restrictions will expand employment, even though they have no net effect on the balance of payments. If goods are now to be bought at home which have been imported, investments in new facilities are necessary to produce these goods. Thus, even though exports fall as much as imports do, there is an addition to total demand because of these investments. The point has a certain validity, but one must take account of what is happening in the declining export indus-tries. And one must realize, again, that the effect can only be temporary. A nation cannot go on indefinitely reducing its imports to provide investment outlets. Presently it will have no imports. More funda-mentally, this means of creating jobs is of a piece with that whole class of make-work devices which would expand employment by destroying wealth and putting labor at relatively unproductive tasks.

It is also arguable that the initial spur to production through re-stricting imports may so raise total income that, thereafter, imports can continue on a sufficient level to maintain equilibrium—a sort of pump-priming idea. It may also be possible to create jobs through selective restriction of imports in those fields in which labor is espe-cially important in comparison with land and capital, and substitute such other imports as require little labor to produce. Such a procedure, however, must seriously reduce per-capita output, and thus it also belongs in the category of make-work devices.

The logic of these ideas is tenable to persons who understand the principles of trade. But their contribution to employment is likely to be unimportant in a great nation in which foreign trade is a minor factor. Their total economic effect is dubious, and they are likely to cause international irritation.

Reduction of trade barriers to promote employment. While speaking of trade policy as a means of expanding employment, we should observe that free traders also urge their case to the same end. Reduction of trade barriers, it is argued, will provide new markets in the export fields, and thus nations can mutually promote their prosperity. The Hull program has been widely supported from this standpoint.

In part, this view has the same merit and limitations as the idea that curtailing imports will expand total demand. The new exports, as tariffs are reduced, are not to be added to a nation's previous domestic sales. The purchasing power of its people must be used to buy more foreign goods to the extent that they sell more goods in foreign markets. Nations cannot mutually enable each other to have an excess of exports. But when the removal of barriers expands exports, investment opportunities are created in export industries, just as opportunities are created in import industries when barriers are raised. And again the effect is probably temporary, lasting only while the shift is taking place.

On broader grounds, however, it may be argued that freer trade in a peaceful world will strengthen total demand in a rich country such as the United States. If the nation, as many believe, faces the danger of stagnation because investment will not absorb the savings from a high level of income, this danger is reduced if the field of investment is expanded to include the whole world, and not merely the nation. True, after a time, the return on investments will be as great as new investments made, so that the movement of capital will not permanently finance an export surplus. But the savings that continue to be invested abroad will exceed the savings from the income gained abroad, if part of this income is used to expand consumption, so that the relation of investment to saving is improved. Such a result will be promoted if trade is sufficiently free, so that debtor nations find it easy to sell goods to their creditors in such nations as the United States. Otherwise these creditors cannot be paid, and investment will not go on.

Restriction of the uncertain reliance on foreign markets

Nations also use trade barriers to make their economic life more dependable and more controllable. Specialization means interdependence, and interdependence is not so safe and so satisfactory when trading areas are subject to a diversity of governments. Several applications of this general idea should be recognized.

Insulation from international disturbance. There is the danger that other nations will alter their policies and upset established trade relations. They may raise their tariffs, depreciate their money, or impose quotas on imports. They may subsidize exports, causing them to be "dumped" abroad below cost, or they may place embargoes on certain exports, so as to conserve their petroleum or timber or other exhaustible resources. With similar effect, wars may upset the course of trade, not only during the fighting but afterward. In World War I Great Britain lost markets to the United States, and in World War II she sacrificed much of the shipping and the foreign investments that provided the means of paying for essential imports.

Disturbances which restrict and upset trade may completely destroy the advantages of specialization. Nations benefit by concentrating on products in which they are superior only when the markets in which they sell these products and buy other products in exchange are dependable. Specialization requires large investments in particular industries and in the development of skills and techniques. It prevents the development of competence in producing goods that are bought elsewhere. Foreign markets caused Great Britain to concentrate as she did on manufacturing and commerce and to depend on foreign sources of food and raw materials. Thus she acquired a population too dense for her primary industries to support. For a nation to organize its economy on such a basis and then lose its foreign markets is to see its whole economic life threatened.

In a world, therefore, in which governments act capriciously and without regard to the total effect of their policies and in a world in which nations go to war, the long-run benefits of specialization may seem a dangerous gamble. It is at least arguable that nations are wise in not resting their economic fate on a high degree of interdependence, even though they employ their resources less advantageously than would be possible in a stable world.

Avoidance of excessive specialization. Even without governmental misbehavior, there is a similar danger when a nation specializes so narrowly that its prosperity depends on the market for one or two products. Regions within countries may incur this danger in serving the domestic market, but not in the degree that occurs when a nation undertakes to be the main source of world supply for some product. Thus certain areas in southeast Asia built their economies on rubber, Brazil on coffee, Bolivia on tin, Chile on nitrates, the American South on cotton. Such extreme specialization is dangerous because sources of supply may develop elsewhere or substitutes may be found or excessive production may send the price very low and greatly reduce the imports that can be paid for—imports on which the well-being of the country may depend. To avoid this danger, nations consciously promote diversification of industry by giving artificial encouragement to the production of goods which, if all went well, they could obtain more cheaply through foreign trade. The movement for protection in some of the South American countries seems to rest largely on this basis.

Facilitation of domestic market control. When a nation departs from the principles of a freely organized economy in its domestic markets, it must control its international dealings also. This point was observed in Chapter 23 in the discussion of the agricultural adjustment policy. Wheat and cotton are normally export commodities; if they are to be priced above the world level, it is necessary not only to introduce arbitrary market controls at home but also to prevent imports at lower prices and to subsidize the sale abroad of the surplus not absorbed at home. To avoid this irritating two-price policy, it would be necessary to curtail production to eliminate the exports. The natural tendency is toward a more isolated economic position when domestic policies cannot be reconciled with normal world trade.[14]

When government control goes farther and state socialism supplants private enterprise, this tendency is strengthened. Those who have the complex task of managing the economic affairs of a country want as little as possible to do with trade that cannot be fully managed, as international trade cannot be by any one government. Controlled economies want to be insulated from foreign disturbance. It is ordinary private trade, on the contrary, conducted by traders who are interested only in buying cheaply and selling profitably and not in nationalities, that is the most international element in the world.

Emergency controls. Apart from any long-run desire for economic independence, nations snatch at trade controls to help them in emergencies. Automatic adjustments in the balance of payments are slow and they cause internal stresses. When the nations of western Europe, between the wars, found it hard to sell enough to pay for essential imports, they were not content to let prices and exchange rates find new equilibrium levels. They applied drastic systems of quotas and embargoes, rationed foreign exchange, and licensed importers, so that only necessary goods would have to be paid for. They sought foreign balances by giving bonuses to exporters to cause them to sell below cost, and they made barter deals with other countries, often with the assistance of political pressure. Whatever the disruptions, ordinary foreign

---

[14] The alternative, for basic commodities that must continue to be sold in large amounts on world markets, may be a sort of world AAA. *International commodity agreements,* as in the case of sugar, are a step in that direction.

trade was sacrificed for the sake of some degree of stability at home.[15]

In the postwar world these pressures remain strong to promote "secure" national economies at the expense of international trade and specialization.

Maintenance of military self-sufficiency

The security aimed at may be military and political rather than economic. Escape may be sought from the uncertainties of international markets, not for the sake of economic stability as such but to insure a self-sufficient military power in case of war. If a nation depends on foreign sources for goods essential in war, a severance of trade may destroy its power to fight. Thus Germany in the 1930s developed costly *ersatz* products so that it could go on fighting if its trade were cut off. The experience of World War II has caused the United States to insist that part of the rubber used here come from synthetic plants rather than from abroad. Trade barriers may appear too costly from every strictly economic angle and yet seem justified if success in war and national sovereignty are thrown into the balance. The higher cost of goods, just as the outlay to maintain the armed forces, may be viewed as part of the cost of preparedness for war.

Summary

The difficulty of reaching a judgment on international economic policy should now be apparent. Factors must be weighed that are incommensurable and impossible to relate in any fully satisfying way. When the ground has been cleared by getting rid of common favorable-balance and wage-protection ideas, the real factors enter at different levels and through different channels. The great gain, especially to the smaller nations, of concentrating in fields of superior productivity would, of course, be the dominant consideration in a well-ordered world. But even in such a world a case could be made for measures that would hasten the development of regions. And in the uncertain actual world, nations find both economic and military reasons for cushioning themselves from developments outside. They are driven by emergencies to resort to measures that only the closeness of disaster can excuse.

Against these concessions to nationalistic fears and attitudes must be set the fact that trade barriers themselves provoke ill will and nationalistic sentiment. The policies intensify the reasons for them. It would seem, then, that the final aim must be to conduct world trade in the way, and with the objectives, of trade within nations.

[15] This problem was discussed from the monetary standpoint in Chapter 13.

Methods of Trade Control

In the field of public policy it is one thing to agree on the aims and governing principles. It is quite a different thing to devise ways and means of realizing aims and applying principles. In the field of international trade and investment the methods of control are diverse and complicated. The present discussion will be limited to a few significant points of policy, with interpretative comment.

American policy

Trade policy in the United States has taken the form chiefly of the tariff, or duty, on imports. This policy has served the dual purpose of providing revenue and protecting domestic industry, with the emphasis shifting decidedly from the former to the latter. Most federal revenue came from the tariff before the Civil War, but now the fraction is very small. Rates, which were low and mainly for revenue until after the War of 1812, were modified thereafter in a series of enactments that, despite some downturns, showed a decided upward trend. The peak was reached in the Smoot-Hawley Act of 1930, in which rates of 100 percent of the foreign selling price were common, with some much higher, and with an average rate for all dutiable commodities of 59 percent.[16] Many important goods have remained on the free list, especially nonagricultural raw materials and tropical agricultural products. Most manufactured goods have been subject to protective duties.

Tariffs may accord equal treatment to the imports from all foreign countries, or they may be discriminatory. The general policy of this country is to negotiate commercial treaties containing the "unconditional most-favored-nation" clause, by which, if other countries give our exports as low rates as they apply to third countries, we agree to treat their exports to us in the same nonprejudicial way. In this connection, and also to serve other purposes, tariff laws commonly provide for some flexibility of rates, with the exact rate determined by administrative authority. The United States Tariff Commission, which had been created under Wilson as a fact-finding body, was given the task in 1922 of ascertaining the rates which would carry out the so-called "scientific principle" of equalizing the costs of imported and home-produced goods.

In 1933, in connection with the NRA and AAA programs, the President was given power to raise duties on imports to the extent made

---

[16] Some tariff rates are *ad valorem*—that is, they are expressed as percentages of the prices of goods. Others are *specific,* and expressed in cents per units of goods. If the latter rates are left constant, a period of inflation reduces their percentage weight.

necessary by the efforts to raise domestic prices. In 1934, however, largely through the influence of Secretary Hull, the Trade Agreements Act was passed, authorizing the negotiation of treaties which would reduce rates as much as 50 percent for the exports of countries that made reciprocal reductions in rates on our exports. Such reductions would become immediately applicable to third countries under the most-favored-nation principle. This Act was renewed for three-year periods in 1937, 1940, 1943, and 1945, and, somewhat reluctantly, for a one-year period in 1948.

By 1946, treaties had been negotiated under the Act covering the trade with 28 countries. Then, in 1947, at a general conference of 23 nations at Geneva, agreements were reached covering the duties on more than half the trade of the world, and substantial reductions were effected. It is estimated that the tariff wall of the United States was reduced to little more than one third the height established in the Smoot-Hawley Act. In 1948, in a conference at Havana, a charter was agreed on for an International Trade Organization designed to re-establish a much greater degree of order and freedom in the international movement of goods.

We shall return to the special difficulties of the postwar period after observing a number of characteristics of traditional tariff policy.

Tariffs as taxes

The tariff, as we noted in the preceding chapter, is a tax designed to influence the use of resources. The market processes through which it exerts its influence are quite easy to understand but have been obscured by the oracular character of public discussion of the problem.

Revenue *versus* protection. It should be apparent, for instance, that the two benefits claimed for the tariff, revenue and protection, are not in harmony. Goods must enter the country from abroad to yield revenue; they must be kept out to afford protection. The revenue aim calls for placing duties on goods such as coffee and tin that will not be produced here and will be imported despite a moderate tax on their admission. A tariff that successfully preserves the American market for American producers cannot serve this revenue purpose. The fact that two thirds of American imports entered duty-free before the war is evidence not of a leaning toward free trade but toward duties on dutiable goods that largely exclude them.

Who pays the tariff? As a tax, the incidence of the tariff is like that of any excise. Ordinarily it is added to the price of the product and passed on unobtrusively to the consumer. If the article passes through several hands, the final price is likely to be raised by more than the tariff, since the margins of successive dealers have an expanding base. Backward shifting, at least for a time, is also possible. Rather than accept a reduction in sales, the foreign producer may reduce his price, so that, in effect, he bears part of the duty.

The idea that "the foreigner pays the tax"—to which Mr. Dooley replied that he does if he gets past Ellis Island—has no application at all if the tariff is successfully protective and the goods are produced here. When goods are produced here only because of the tariff, their price must be made enough higher to cover their domestic cost, else there would be no protection. Then the consumer is bound to pay a higher price but without revenue to the government.

Tariff *versus* **subsidy.** It is a proper question to ask, therefore, whether the tariff is the fairest way to give artificial encouragement to industries. If there is, in fact, a broad public interest in supporting an industry that cannot meet open competition, should not the cost of its support be placed on the public as a whole? It is not the wearer of woolen garments who objects to the Australian source of the material, so why should he be made responsible for American wool growing? On this ground it is arguable that a bonus, or subsidy, paid to the domestic producer out of general tax revenues is a fairer way to finance developments that are not self-supporting.

It is also arguable that the subsidy method reflects sounder governmental procedure. To pay a bonus there must be an open appropriation of public funds, with an obvious expansion of the tax burden. The cost of protection is then apparent, and in the light of it the alleged public benefit can be judged on its merits. When the tariff method is used, the cost is concealed in the price of the product, and, since it is imposed by the market rather than through explicit action of Congress, it never enters as it should into a judgment of the merits of the policy. This fact is, of course, a reason why the tariff method is preferred by supporters of high protection.[17]

Duties on exports. Many countries have used export duties, also, as a source of revenue, sometimes with a much greater return than from import duties. Usually rates have been low, from 1 to 10 percent. Taxed commodities which are sold competitively in world markets must meet

[17] In judging the cost of bounties, in comparison with the tariff, several points need to be considered. (1) When part of the supply is imported and part home-produced, as in the case of sugar, the tariff raises the cost of the whole supply, whereas the bounty applies only to the domestic portion. On the other hand, with the tariff the imported portion yields public revenue. (2) With the bounty there should be none of the piling up of dealers' margins, with successive handling, as under the tariff. (3) The bounty would have to be adjusted with more care to the amount of public aid required, so as not to make the aid excessive. Every dollar paid out involves a cost to the public, whereas raising a tariff above the necessary level has no effect, provided there is extensive domestic competition among producers of the good.

the world price, so that the export duty amounts to a gross-income tax on the exporters. When a country is the main source of the world supply, however, much of the tax may be passed on to foreign buyers. This was probably the effect when Chile obtained most of its government revenue from an export duty on nitrates. It is possible for an export duty to be protective, as when the Spanish tax on the export of cork makes the material relatively expensive to foreign competitors of Spanish manufacturers. American experience in this sphere has been prevented by the federal Constitution, which denies to Congress the authority to levy duties on exports.

Tariff politics

It would be a splendid thing to know that public issues were decided through a deliberate weighing of factors pertinent from a broad public standpoint. Actually the pressures of special interests have great weight in the legislative process, and perhaps nowhere more conspicuously than in establishing trade barriers. A tariff act is made up of a very large number of specific provisions, and the policy as a whole is little more than a composite of decisions in the case of individual products. Too largely, the architects of the tariff structure adopt the worm's-eye approach in designing it.

With its numerous provisions, the tariff gives an exceptional opportunity to every Congressman to show the people in his district that he is promoting their interests. In every district there is bound to be some product of local importance that foreign competition can affect and for which protection is sought. The Congressman may even be a free trader in principle. But the problem is complicated and he will be of no help in handling it unless he is re-elected, so he does his best to aid the industries that support his constituents. Since the only way to garner votes of other Congressmen is to support their particular interests by vote trading and logrolling, he helps to make this summation of local interests into a national policy. Perhaps there is an element of caricature in this picture of tariff making, but it is too true to omit in any discussion of trade policy. Whatever the balance of arguments from the social viewpoint, there is a strong political bias in favor of protection.

The "scientific principle"

Perhaps the piecemeal nature of tariff policy would be relieved if there were some general principle to which legislators could refer in their thinking. Perhaps this need inspired the popularity of the "scientific principle" that tariff rates should offset money-cost differences here and abroad. But this principle, unfortunately, is not of the slightest aid in deciding the basic question whether specific commodities should be given artificial encouragement or not. So far as the principle is concerned, grapes in Scotland or bananas in Canada would be as worthy of protection as wool in the United States. If some differences in cost are too great to be offset, or if the protected industry should give some promise of finally becoming self-sustaining, guidance in deciding must be sought elsewhere—not in the "scientific principle." No advantage of international trade and specialization is implied by it, since, instead of enjoying the advantage of buying more cheaply abroad, importers expect, according to the principle, to pay duties that neutralize the possible benefit.

What the principle does is to provide a rule to govern the height of the duty when protection has already been decided on. Possibly in this connection the principle has some value. If applied to an industry protected on infant-industry grounds, it should cause a gradual lowering of the tariff as the industry matures and final elimination of the tariff if the infant-industry idea was correctly applied in the first place. It would mean permanent protection of industries never able to stand alone, but, if it kept rates from exceeding the money-cost differences, it would at least have the virtue of not protecting extortionate prices of domestic monopolies. In practice, however, the principle is difficult to apply, for costs differ among the firms that make up an industry in a country, and costs in foreign countries are hard to obtain.

Such flexible tariff adjustments as were made in the 1920s, as recommended by the Tariff Commission, presumably followed the "scientific principle." Under the Trade Agreements Act of 1934 it was viewed as reasonable to permit some invasion of protected American markets, provided other countries would make similar concessions to our exports. In both cases, the use of the administrative method in making adjustments has provided a partial escape from the high-tariff bias of legislative tariff making.

The tariff versus *more drastic controls*

A protective tariff that serves its purpose necessarily reduces international trade, exports as well as imports. But if applied for limited ends, such as a moderate diversification of industry and the encouragement of potentially effective industries, it may reduce specialization without destroying it. The somewhat limited specialization that it permits can still develop along sound economic lines. Private traders can buy and sell as market conditions dictate, and industries develop to serve foreign markets, just as they develop to serve domestic markets.

The tariff limits trade in the same manner as a high cost of transportation, but differences in comparative cost great enough to offset such obstacles can still provide the basis for a fruitful specialization. As long as tariff rates are changed seldom, and never sharply, a dependable world economy can develop despite them. Such was the promise of the nineteenth century.

A wholly different situation arises when trade control becomes the variable instrument of public policy, as it did between the wars, and is made to serve a variety of short-run political and economic ends. Imposing specific quotas on certain commodity movements, requiring licenses to import and export or to get the exchange to make payments, applying discriminatory barriers to particular countries, subsidizing exports, conducting trade through state agencies, and doing all these things in a shifting and undependable way combine to destroy the basis of useful specialization. When international trade consists of the dealings of thousands of private traders within a framework of stable regulations, it may be almost as dependable as domestic trade; when great segments of it are altered *en bloc* by government decree, dealings are demoralized and dealers frustrated.

Postwar American policy, as expressed at the Geneva and Havana meetings, has promoted lower trade barriers, but it has aimed even more at removing these chaotic factors from world trade. Prime objects of policy have been (1) to restrict state trading, (2) to end the discriminatory treatment of nations, and (3) to re-establish the multilateral basis of trade necessary to effective specialization. The Havana charter embodies the principles of nondiscriminatory and multilateral trade, though with short-term concessions to nations confronted with immediate balance-of-payments difficulties. But the conditions that call for desperate, unilateral measures are not to be corrected easily, and United States policy, moreover, does not invite ungrudging cooperation. High-tariff sentiment remains strong in the United States; the AAA policy has been accompanied by provocative export subsidies; and close interdependence with the American economy seems dangerous until the United States shows more convincingly that it can forestall major depressions.

Imperialism

We shall conclude by mentioning a phase of policy worthy of extended treatment. It has long been the practice of politically strong and industrially advanced nations to project their power into the backward areas in which they have economic interests. They have sought "concessions," "spheres of influence," "extraterritorial rights" or have gone farther and turned such areas into dependencies and colonies. In varying degrees, much of Africa and Asia, parts of Latin America, even portions of Europe, have yielded elements of sovereignty.

The reasons given are often vague, as the German cry for *lebensraum*. There may be mention of surplus population and the need of a place where people can go and be sheltered by familiar institutions. More commonly it is said that markets are needed, markets in which to obtain needed materials and dispose of exports, and the assumption is made that political control of such markets is necessary. It may be charged by the imperialistic country that it suffers from discrimination in the markets of other nations, but more likely its aim is to establish markets in which a preference over other nations will be enjoyed. More solid reasons are found in connection with investments, when capital is placed in areas where law and order are not well established or where capricious government action endangers the security of investments that have been made.

In many respects the benefits to the imperialist powers have been meager. As to population relief, people do not move readily to primitive lands, especially if they are tropical; in any event, the numbers lost through migration are likely to be replaced quickly through population growth at home. The trade of the advanced nations is largely with each other, and the markets in backward areas, especially the export markets, commonly prove disappointing. Prior to the disruptions of recent years, discriminations in international trade were not great, because most trade was conducted by private firms whose interest was in the qualities and prices of goods and not in flags and nationalities. The economies of such countries as Switzerland and Sweden, which have depended heavily on international trade and whose traders have bought and sold without imperialist governments to aid them, are the best commentary on the argument that nations cannot prosper without throwing their political weight around.

Foreign investment presents a more difficult problem. The world gains much when rich nations share their capital, and with it their technology, with nations and regions where production and income are low. But if capital placements are to be in the hands of responsible firms and not of speculators and adventurers, they must be made under conditions that are reasonably secure. Needy areas commonly do not provide these conditions. Thus political supervision and pressure, if not subjugation, often accompany foreign investment.

But imperialism is filled with dangers. The doctrine, as President Coolidge put it, that the citizen and his wealth are "part of the general domain of the nation, even when abroad," becomes "dollar diplomacy" in the eyes of weaker nations.[18] Native labor is likely to be exploited by foreign firms, and actions that are, or appear to be, highhanded arouse resentment in the countries that should be benefited by foreign aid. Even more serious, clashes develop among the great powers as they extend their interests into the same areas. This danger seems to be greatest when the economies of imperialist powers are state-controlled, so that external investments and armed forces are under a single direction. Economic ends pursued in other countries are then directly the affair of governments.

But it should not be assumed that the ends of imperialism are necessarily economic. Political power may be used to gain economic advantage, but the opposite causation is probably at least as likely. Foreign investments and the accompanying concessions are means of political penetration and military strategy, especially as they bring control of oil and minerals and military bases and vantage points from which to influence governments. Power seems often to be the end and wealth the means.

As progress in transport and communication draws the nations closer together, occasions for conflict as well as for mutual helpfulness increase. Both peace and economic well-being will be furthered if it can be more widely understood that nations gain chiefly not at the expense of each other but through trade and investment relationships of common benefit, pursued under conditions of stability and mutual trust. Since, however, controversies are bound to arise in foreign dealings, just as they do in domestic dealings, it seems clear that the means of handling them must be through orderly international arrangements rather than through projections of the power of nations beyond their borders.

Review Questions

1. "There are many firms, indeed many communities, in the United States that would be ruined if the protective tariff were removed. It is absurd to say that prosperity does not depend on the tariff." Reconcile this view with the free-trade theory.

2. Explain the infant-industry argument for protection and the kind of policy that it implies. Does it justify protection of steel and textile manufacturing in the United States at the present time?

3. "A nation with unemployed resources is foolish to import products that those resources can produce, even if domestic production of them would be inefficient." Show that, while this may be a sound application of the cost

---

[18] Quoted from Eugene Staley, "Foreign Investment and War," Public Policy Pamphlet No. 18, University of Chicago Press—a good brief statement of this problem.

concept, it has serious weaknesses as a method of combating unemployment.

4. Point out certain limited connections in which trade barriers may increase employment.

5. May the reduction of trade barriers expand employment? Consider (a) the direct effect on export industries and the use of purchasing power, (b) the encouragement of international investment.

6. "The advantages of specialization require stable trade. The free-trade case breaks down when world relationships are undependable." Develop the point.

7. Does it seem wise for countries such as Chile and Brazil to impose trade barriers to diversify their economic life?

8. Why is a domestic policy such as AAA difficult to reconcile with the free-trade position?

9. Explain the logic of the emergency trade controls adopted by European nations in the 1930s and since the war.

10. Give the military argument for trade barriers. Does it deny the logic of the free-trade case?

11. What is the place in American tariff policy of the United States Tariff Commission; the most-favored nation clause in treaties; the Trade Agreements Act of 1934; the Geneva and Havana conferences?

12. "A tariff act may yield both revenue and protection, but in so far as it does one, it fails to do the other." Explain.

13. "The foreign exporter may bear part of the cost of import duties, at least for a while, but if the tariff is effectively protective, the domestic consumer must bear the cost." Explain.

14. On what grounds is it arguable that subsidies are superior to tariffs as a means of aiding domestic industries?

15. How do duties on exports differ from duties on imports?

16. "Politically the cards are stacked in favor of protection." Why?

17. What is the "scientific principle" of tariff making? Does it provide a scientific basis for deciding whether or not an industry should be protected? Explain.

18. What are the more drastic methods used to control trade in recent years? Why are they more harmful than tariffs to international specialization?

19. On what economic grounds do nations justify imperialistic control of backward areas? Evaluate them, considering the economic programs of various nations.

~ 33 ~

Capitalism
and Collectivism

$\mathbf{A}$s a system of competitive capitalism, the American economy has become an increasingly conspicuous member of a smaller and smaller minority among the national economies of the world. Americans accordingly have grown self-conscious in their adherence to a system that other countries have been discarding, and discuss at length, defensively and critically, what once they took for granted. In contending with Soviet Russia for world influence, we in the United States proclaim the merits of our economy as we have not needed to in the past. But some Americans have doubted whether even so great an example of private enterprise can stand against the tide of state-run and state-regimented economies. More Americans have feared that the forces revolutionizing other countries have been operating here in insidious piecemeal fashion to undermine the American tradition. A few Americans welcome all such evidence and hold that we should abandon our traditional capitalism in favor of a system that, they think, would work better in promoting human welfare.

On such questions—where the American economy is going and where it ought to go—each observer is entitled to his opinion. But in arriving at that opinion he should feel obligated to use fully such knowledge as he can gather of the nature and functions of economic systems and of the problems and policies conspicuous in the United States in recent years. Much of the discussion of specific matters in this volume has been focused on their relation to the economy as a whole. It is useful, in this concluding chapter, to review some of these matters in summing up and appraising the evidences of change in the American economy and in glancing at the alternatives to capitalism.[1]

[1] Among the many books dealing with the alternatives, and with appraisals and defenses of capitalism, are: William N. Loucks and J. Weldon Hoot, *Comparative Economic Sys-*

878

Functions of economic systems

An economic system, as Chapter 4 explained, is a set of arrangements that (1) places responsibility for production and motivates it, (2) coordinates the activities of numerous people with respect to what they produce, the resources and techniques used in each line of production, and the utilization of products, and (3) apportions the total output or income among the people.

In its purely economic aspects, an economy must be judged by its effectiveness in performing these functions. A high level of economic welfare depends, first of all, on the productive power the economy develops: its success in improving the abilities of its people and spurring them to vigorous activity, the use it makes of its natural resources and the amount and character of the capital equipment it accumulates. It should provide conditions that promote skillful management, producing units of efficient size, and, above all, progress in the arts of production.

But high aggregate production depends not only on productive power but also on the fullness and regularity with which it is used. Production should proceed most of the time at a level close to the capacity of the economy. An economic system is fully effective only as it avoids serious depressions and the unemployment and loss of income that accompany them.

In assigning resources to their specific uses in producing different things, a system may be expected either to respond to the actual personal preferences of the people or to register some sort of superior judgment as to what the people ought to consume. Americans, and probably most other people, prefer the former principle. But it is quite proper for critics, if they wish, to argue that people would be better off if their choices were supervised or to criticize the influences through which personal tastes are formed. In any case the scheme of control should cause production to respond accurately to the recognized choices among numerous and changing products, and also as between more income and more leisure, and as between more output and more agreeable conditions of work. The control should assign all units of all re-

tems, Harper, 1938; Arthur G. Pigou, *Socialism* versus *Capitalism,* Macmillan, 1937; Barbara Wootton, *Plan or No Plan,* Farrar and Rinehart, 1935; Joseph A. Schumpeter, *Capitalism, Socialism, and Democracy,* Harper, 1947; Karl Marx, *Capital;* Harry W. Laidler, *Social-Economic Movements,* Crowell, 1945; Harold Laski, *Communism,* Holt, 1927; Marquis Childs, *Sweden, the Middle Way,* Yale University Press, 1936; J. P. Warbasse, *Cooperative Democracy,* Harper, 1936; Kenneth E. Boulding, *The Economics of Peace,* Prentice-Hall, 1945; Walter Lippmann, *The Good Society,* Little, Brown, 1943; F. A. Hayek, *The Road to Serfdom,* University of Chicago Press, 1945; John Maurice Clark, *Alternative to Serfdom,* Alfred A. Knopf, 1948.

sources to the places in production where they will make their most valuable contribution, with due allowance for the occupational choices of individuals.

If a society professes the democratic creed that makes welfare depend on the condition of all people and not merely a select few, it must judge the distribution of income by the breadth of its diffusion among the people. But here, as we have seen, no clear basis of judgment is possible. In all systems, though more in some than in others, income payments are tied up with the guidance and motivation of production; and that maximum meeting of the needs of all people, which is the final goal, is not likely to result if income is divided directly on the basis of needs. The critic of economic organization not only must judge how various systems meet certain recognized tests, but he must decide also among conflicting tests of good performance.

The latter difficulty becomes more acute as economic systems are judged by standards broader than the purely economic, as certainly they should be. It can be said that an economic system should not only provide goods, but it should be an acceptable part of the whole social framework within which people live. People should feel happy in their relation to it; or, if one prefers, it should be good for them in broad cultural, ethical, political, and other significant respects. They should be as free as possible from irritating compulsions. They should have opportunity to develop as individuals in the fullest sense, not in any one groove but in many different ways. Their creative energies should not be crushed but should have every chance to flourish. At the same time, they should feel secure and should feel that they are part of meaningful collective endeavors to which they can give themselves. In their economic pursuits, they should not feel compelled to stoop to mean and petty devices that generate antipathies and smallness of outlook. The economic segment of social organization should not only be in harmony with a well-knit body politic, free of disruptive cleavages, but should also further harmonious relations with other nations. From such standpoints as these many of the critical judgments of economic systems arise. But no one should pretend that these noneconomic ends are themselves altogether consistent and harmonious.

The American economy as molded by government

By these economic and other tests, a system of laissez-faire capitalism must prove defective at many points. The approximation to laissez-faire capitalism that was developing in Western nations in the early nineteenth century has undergone many changes in the United States and more changes elsewhere. These changes have come both through government action and directly through organized group action. Partly they have been aimed at correcting defects apparent by these standards, but partly also they merely reflect the promotion of special interests.

In any case, we should ask where these changes leave us. Can we still say in the United States that we work under a system of competitive capitalism or of free private enterprise? Any single broad answer to this question must be debatable, but the point in discussing it is less to arrive at such an answer than to review the impacts of a variety of developments. It is still the fashion to speak unqualifiedly of American free enterprise; it is also the fashion to say that the New Deal reduced us to the verge of socialism. It is often said, moreover, that we now have a "mixed economy," a phrase subject to a variety of constructions. Ordinarily such characterizations reflect little insight into the essentials either of free enterprise or of socialism or into the public and private actions that have proved disturbing.

Changes in the economy can be interpreted best when set against the model of a free system. Such a system has two primary features: it relies (1) on voluntary private activity to produce goods and (2) on the operation of markets to guide the use of resources and products and to distribute the total income. The first of these essentials implies private ownership of productive wealth, the second, a substantial degree of competition on both sides of the markets in which products and productive services are exchanged. With this model in mind, we shall review first the main lines of government action which have affected the American economy.

Government as enterpriser. In no economy can private enterprise provide all commodities and services. To say that government is necessary is to say that it has functions to perform. At the very least, it must attend to matters of national defense and domestic order, and resources will thus, in part, be employed by the public economy. No one has regarded these activities as an invasion of the purity of private capitalism, nor are fears expressed because government provides schools and highways.

But education and transport facilities are also provided privately. To some it seems only a small further step when government takes over such naturally monopolistic industries as electric power, especially hydroelectric power from navigable rivers. But a line must be drawn somewhere, and at this point a cry goes up against encroachment by the state and the threat of incipient socialism. There are nonsocialists who believe that the public utilities should be transferred to the state. But when the movement extends to such industries as coal and steel, as it has in England, the case is clear and, with some exceptions in the case of coal, only the socialists are for it.

From this standpoint it would seem that the first requirement of a free system—that enterprise be private—has not been violated extensively in the United States. There are some instances such as the Tennessee Valley Authority and other public-power projects, some transport activities such as the federal barge lines and the Panama Railroad, some banking activities such as the Reconstruction Finance Corporation. In one sense, accordingly, the economy may be described as "mixed"; but it may be argued for all of these undertakings that there are special reasons that would not hold for general socialization of industry.

Government control of private activity. Apart from activities in which it is enterpriser, government imposes many controls on the private economy that may give it a mixed, and some would say a socialistic, cast. Here discriminating interpretation is especially necessary. No one views governmental enforcement of contracts, protection of property, or provision of money as deviations from a free economy. It is proper, then, to view in the same light the extension of monetary controls that applies to banks, because banks provide the principal medium of exchange.

But the point most necessary to remember is that government can go much further without violating the tradition of economic freedom— that, indeed, it must go further if a free system is to operate acceptably. One of the most serious errors is to confuse freedom with *laissez faire*. Economic freedom cannot mean the freedom to do as one pleases in all circumstances. It cannot mean freedom grossly to misrepresent products, harm competitors in all conceivable ways, or combine with them to dominate markets. As essential as private enterprise to a free economy is a system of markets through which the use of resources is controlled in the interest of society. In its absence a free system becomes an empty phrase. In such markets competition must be substantial and buyers and sellers reasonably well informed. Entirely apart from the details of policy and its administration, the principles underlying the antitrust laws, the work of the Federal Trade Commission, the Pure Food and Drugs Act, and much of the work of the Securities and Exchange Commission are positive requirements of a free economy.

Government has gone much further, however, than to establish markets which will be effective regulators of private action. Without displacing private enterprise, it has taken over the task of control in certain instances that markets are ordinarily expected to perform. Free markets, in a world sense, are violated when nations establish barriers to the international movement of goods. They are distorted by subsidies and by special burdens and restrictions, as on the liquor industry. The deviation is more pronounced when prices are regulated and industrial expansion and contraction are controlled, as in the public-utility field. Maintaining price floors, as for farm products under the agricultural-adjustment policy or for labor under minimum-wage legislation, reflects unwillingness to accept the verdict of markets. At these points, and in a different sense, the economy may be said to have acquired a "mixed" character.

How seriously a free system is modified in these ways depends in part on the scope of the activities affected. Thus agriculture is a larger element in the economy than the public utilities are. It depends also on the positiveness of the control. A floor under prices is not important if, as in the case of a low minimum wage, it affects relatively few transactions. If it requires rather continuous administration of prices and supply, as it may under the AAA, its significance is greater. Its effect is likewise greater if, again in the case of agriculture, it applies a different principle of pricing and resource use from that operative through free markets.

But such controls need not alter fundamentally the character of the economy until they become so comprehensive that they must be treated not as correctives of particular conditions but as general regulators of price relationships and resource use. Then, without guidance from a freely working price system, government must develop its own structure of values and costs, its own criteria of resource utilization, and assume responsibility for the intricate coordination of all activities. The extent and difficulty of this task should be sensed by reformers who would apply public-utility regulation to a wide range of industries or who would make permanent use of the comprehensive price control and rationing that operated by temporary and arbitrary standards during the war.

Governmental redistribution. Policies which establish collective responsibility for people's incomes deviate in another way from the free-enterprise idea. In a free economy people depend for their incomes on the sale of their products and services and live well or badly according to the value of their performance. Various plans of social security, public assistance, and free government services depart in one way or another from this principle. Collective responsibility for individual well-being, unrelated to individual earning power, is associated with socialism and is the heart of communism. Critics charge that these distribution policies, combined with heavy progressive taxation, have brought a mixture of socialism into the American economy.

Whether this is socialism is a matter of labels, and is not important.[2] The principle of redistributing a portion of income on the basis of needs is an old and well-established part of the American tradition. It is clearly involved in the poor laws and in the provision of education at public expense. Probably no one contends that secondary distribution along these lines should be stopped, however it may offend the theory of individualism.

The problem is one of degree, and the amount of redistribution permissible under capitalism cannot be decided by abstract contemplation of the philosophy underlying public assistance and progressive taxation. The problem is the practical one of the extent to which income can be diverted from its primary channels without weakening the incentives on which capitalism depends. Somewhere along the line, as more and more income is redistributed, the incentives that keep private enterprise going must break down. The economy can be "mixed" in the sense that distribution according to needs is combined, in a secondary and discriminating way, with distribution according to the value of services. But it cannot be "mixed" through any general mingling of the two principles.

Government control of total demand. Can policies aimed at controlling the total demand for goods be integrated with the processes of a free economy? These policies include, on the one hand, offsets to inflation and, on the other, measures to overcome and prevent depressions and maintain employment. If the policies apply to the money supply and the use of credit and seek to modify total spending through these channels, they are mild in principle and are not looked upon as changing the working of the economy in any fundamental way.

Policies that grow out of so-called Keynsian thinking are more likely to be thought radical, and persons careless in their use of terms may call them socialistic. The mature-economy view of depressions is related to ideas found in Marx, and the idea of prolonged governmental deficit spending is offensive to persons devoted to the principle of continuous budget balancing. Accordingly it is important to emphasize that variations in public spending and taxation to stabilize total demand, and

---

[2] Since socialism has come ordinarily to imply state enterprise, it may be better not to apply the term to redistribution policies under private enterprise, even though they embody some of the thinking of socialists. Under socialism, moreover, income may be distributed largely according to the value of services. With respect to progressive taxation, sometimes described as socialistic, it should be recalled that some progression in rates is necessary to make the psychic burden proportional.

maintain it on a high level, need not disturb the essentials of a free economy. While government alters the aggregate flow of funds into markets, individuals are not subjected to restraint or compulsion in their producing, buying, and selling. Voluntary enterprise and market control of the use of resources proceed much as they would in the absence of the policy. If the critics of the policy are right, and government credit must eventually collapse through growth of public debt, drastic change in the economy will finally come. But it need not come directly through reliance on fiscal policy to combat depressions.

Careful interpretation of the whole range of government action in the United States, as it affects the economy, provides a wholesome corrective of various extremes of thinking. For the conservative person who objects in general to government interference with business, an analysis of this sort turns attention to the essentials of the system he is interested in preserving and shows that particular policies bear on these essentials in a variety of ways, strengthening, supplementing, modifying, and perhaps displacing them. To many of the critics of capitalism, it should bring an awareness that their broadly phrased attacks would apply much better to the capitalism of a century ago than to the modified system of today. Present attacks on laissez-faire capitalism are anachronisms.

Group action and economic freedom

In viewing the trend of American capitalism, government action is one of the two main modifying forces to be considered. The other is the pressure of organized private groups. The business corporation is itself a combination of capitalists, and it may become a large and powerful combination not only of individuals but of plants and subordinate firms. Pools and price agreements, though unlawful, are further evidences of the group effort of businessmen, and trade associations promote a variety of common interests. Labor unions are combinations of workmen that may become extremely powerful in their effect on markets. Farm cooperatives and federations, professional associations, and other group organizations have the aim, primary or incidental, of strengthening the market position of their members. These organizations may exist despite government effort to prevent them, with government sufferance or tacit approval, or, as in the case of unions under the Labor Relations Act, with positive government encouragement.

It should be apparent that private organizations large and strong enough to influence markets are, in principle, inconsistent with the nature of a free system. Markets can operate effectively to coordinate the activities of all producers in the common interest only if they are not controlled by particular interests. Prices need to be free of distortion by private groups if they are to reflect continuously all relevant supply-and-demand factors and thus achieve economy in the use of resources and insure incomes that reflect the value of services. Efforts to improve market positions by restricting output are serious obstacles to economic growth and development. Questions arise therefore as to the justification and the effects of organized groups in the American economy.

Roots and influence of private organization. If all organization of competitors to influence markets were simply the result of efforts to gain monopoly power and expand income unreasonably, the proper attitude toward it would be clear. It should be condemned and vigorously attacked. Preventing it completely might be difficult, but an adequate degree of competition could certainly be maintained.

But the appearance of private power over markets is, in part, incidental to other developments. Modern methods of production require large producing units and give rise in some lines to a degree of oligopoly. Trade associations formed for other purposes result almost inevitably in some softening of competition through the close relations of producers of common interests. In addition—and this is the main present point—organizations are formed to influence markets for reasons well short of aggressive, monopolistic exploitation. Among all producers there is a powerful urge to find relief from the harshness of competition and to gain, if possible, some security of income. A free system, even working as it should, leaves the individual producer in a highly uncertain position, buffeted by the shifting demands of buyers and by the appearance of new competitors and methods of production. Whatever, ideally, should be their attitude, producers shrink from quite this degree of self-dependence in a fluid situation, and they seek in organization some protection from the risks they face.

Competition operates unevenly, moreover, in its pressure on different groups. Farmers obtain their incomes in the face of crop uncertainties and volatile prices and spend their money in less competitive markets. Workers must commonly sell their labor to large employers, and they band together to be on equal footing. Markets, in general, are not perfect instruments of economic control. Government steps in at many points to correct abuses and defects, but producers feel that they must exert additional pressures if their interests are to have necessary protection.

A fully free economy, bound together only through market dealings —the "cash nexus," it has been called—is an impersonal, intangible entity, and the producer hesitates to entrust his economic fate to it.

Organization with other producers of like interest gives his position a more manageable quality. It provides something recognizable to which he can feel that he belongs. So, however inconsistent with the principles of a free system these group efforts are, there is basis for them both in objective conditions and subjective feelings, and thus they have firm, and doubtless permanent, footing in the economic structure. People may believe in economic freedom and competition, but it is a qualified freedom and a tempered competition that they want. The advocates of a more positive and complete establishment of the principles of a free economy are not likely to have their way.

General control through group organizations. Recognizing these tendencies to organize, there are observers who urge abandonment of competitive economic control through markets. The alternative may be regulated monopoly, on which we commented above. It may be state enterprise, to which we shall turn presently. Or it may be some sort of negotiated control through the organized groups themselves, presumably with mild governmental supervision. A substitute for competition that can be called cooperative, rather than socialistic, is widely appealing but is seldom presented concretely.[3] It might partake of the industrial self-government, or legalized cartel, idea carried out in the National Recovery Administration, but would presumably involve also a wider application of the idea of collective bargaining as it has developed in the labor field.

Broad proposals, stated in general terms, should lead the student to exercise his critical faculties and draw on his knowledge of the requirements and characteristics of economic organization. He would observe in this case that if occupational groups were all organized, they would no longer be the passive victims or beneficiaries of market fluctuations. Producers, moreover, would have less reason to resort to the predatory methods sometimes used to obtain patronage—the problem with which the Federal Trade Commission is concerned—and the resulting gain

[3] An example of this viewpoint is found in the "Declaration on Economic Justice" signed in 1946 by 122 prominent churchmen and laymen of the Protestant, Catholic, and Jewish faiths. Under the heading, "Organized cooperation of the functional economic groups among themselves and with the government must be substituted for the rule of competition," the statement says: "The function of these free organizations must be extended beyond the traditional limits of collective bargaining for self-protection into an organized system of cooperation for the common good. It is therefore the duty of the state and of society to protect and encourage the organization of men according to their function in economic life.

"Economic life is meant to be an organized and democratic partnership for the general welfare rather than a competitive struggle for individual or group advantage. Accordingly, the industries, agriculture and the professions must voluntarily enter into an organized system of cooperation among themselves and with the government to establish a rational and a moral economic order. The only alternatives to this are competitive economic individualism, private monopoly or excessive governmental intervention, all of which are unacceptable under the moral law." *United States News*, November 1, 1946.

would be both economic and ethical. But self-interest would be in no way reduced—indeed, organization of like-minded producers might strengthen it—and its chief area of expression, in buying goods cheaply and selling them dearly, would be present as before in dealing with members of other occupational groups. The difference would be that the organized group could now exercise greater pressure on prices, declaring collectively that they would not buy or would not sell if they did not have their way. In other words, the condition for monopoly action would be deliberately established.

Extortion would be prevented, presumably, by the fact that the group on the other side of the market would also be organized, so prices and terms would be arrived at by collective negotiation. This would not mean peaceful negotiation, with no interruption of activity, if one may judge by collective bargaining in the labor field, but it should prevent a completely one-sided result. At the same time, it might be a decidedly unfair result, because different producer groups would inevitably vary widely in the strength of their organizations and their basic economic positions. The fatal weakness, however, would be that ultimate consumers could not possibly organize to deal effectively with producer groups in all fields. Thus, in transactions between producer groups, buyers could not be expected to deal staunchly with sellers, since the buyers in turn could pass on their payments as costs to someone else, and only the final purchaser would be stuck—just as employers yield readily on wages when they can pass them on to consumers in higher prices. Advocates of group cooperation should consider also whether this type of organization, when conditions are prosperous, would not prove to be indefinitely inflationary.

A general, but perhaps fundamental, objection to the plan, is that it places emphasis wholly on the distribution problem and not at all on the need of producing a large real income to distribute. It leaves in the economy, and accentuates, the elements that make for restriction of output, since restriction is the basic weapon of organized groups in bettering their return. And it greatly reduces the competitive pressure to improve products and reduce costs, by which real income is expanded.[4] The conflict is inescapable between a primary concern with

[4] A type of group organization that meets most of these objections is the consumers' cooperative. In it the enterpriser and the customer become identical, and there is every reason to maximize output. The cooperative movement has made fine headway in Great Britain but seems to fit less well into the American situation. While control and claims to profits are not arranged in cooperatives as in ordinary corporations, the cooperatives are not essentially revolutionary and can operate usefully within the structure of capitalism. While they usually get some free services from their members that reduce money costs, they do not noticeably economize the use of resources. To succeed they must be able to command adequate capital and competent management and must earn profit—available for customer dividends—in excess of interest on invested capital.

income sharing and income security, on the one hand, and the requirement of growth and progress, on the other.

An economy organized on the basis of broad groups representing
special interests must expect a very large measure of government control to protect the public and keep production going. It seems probable
that government authority must presently outweigh intergroup negotiation in the processes of control—to the extent, very likely, of general
wage and price fixing and direction of resource use. Conflicting group
interests may otherwise have paralyzing effect. The totalitarian organization of Nazi Germany was superimposed on a set of group organizations in labor and industry that seemed ripe for such handling. Mussolini's idea of a "corporative state" involved the same main features.
Such a system retains private ownership of productive wealth and
private management of plant operation; everything else that a free
economy implies is gone.

Group organization under capitalism. There is plainly a difficult
problem of compromise if the pressures toward group organization are
to be recognized and, at the same time, the essentials of competitive capitalism are to be retained. This is a major problem now faced by the
American economy. The market power of corporations is great and so
is the power of labor unions. But if the essentials of a free system
are to remain, organized private power must operate only in a subordinate way within a structure of competitive market processes rooted
in basic conditions of demand and supply. Organized interests can
modify beneficially the sometimes warped outcome of free markets,
and they can contribute something toward security of income. But
public policy must focus definitely on holding private power, both of
labor and of capital, within appropriate bounds if the country is not
to be faced with the quite different problem of regulating group power
that has got out of hand.

State socialism and the main economic problems

To retain private enterprise but subject the economy to comprehensive government control would change it radically, as Americans
view the matter. But radical change ordinarily implies that government
does more than regulate. It becomes the enterpriser and productive
wealth becomes public property. These changes establish state socialism. Socialism may be introduced suddenly by violent revolution, as in
Russia. It may come about democratically, as in Great Britain, through
election of a government that stands for state enterprise and through
the ensuing orderly transfer of industries to the state. It may mean a
complete substitution of public for private enterprise, or only the

basic industries may be socialized, with small traders and craftsmen, and possibly farmers, continuing to own and run their businesses.

Socialism is likely to be advocated by people whose ideas of social reconstruction extend beyond the effective performance of strictly economic functions and include ethical and cultural improvement. But we shall begin by considering briefly the strictly economic arguments that socialists can make for subjecting the processes of production, distribution, and general economic control directly to public authority. Let us deal, in order, with the problems treated in Parts II, IV, V, and VI of this volume. State socialism is set forth most persuasively, in the areas covered in Parts IV and VI, as a means of avoiding depressions and serious inequality.

Socialism and production. With respect to the development of productive power and its efficient use, socialists have their arguments, but it is here that the defenders of capitalism can be most emphatic. The sensational progress in production of the last two centuries has been achieved through a private capitalism that, broadly, has been competitive and free of government restraint. It remains to be seen whether state industry, as in Russia, will be more than imitative in its development of methods. It remains also to be seen whether state employees will display the sustained and vigorous enterprise characteristic of private business. For a time the leadership of a newly constituted socialist state may act with energy and enthusiasm, but there is nothing inherent in the motivation of government employment, or in supervision by the electorate, to maintain the drive that effective production requires.

Sovereign power may be useful at various points in implementing production. The project of a Tennessee Valley Authority requires it. Transfer of people from exhausted and submarginal areas can occur more promptly when the state is the employer. Very possibly modern methods can be introduced more quickly into backward regions when changes are undertaken in wholesale manner by government enterprise.[5]

But the chief argument of socialists in the production field is that various types of waste would be eliminated. Less energy would go into buying and selling and finance—pursuits deemed peculiarly acquisitive. Advertising and salesmanship would be unnecessary except in supplying information to consumers. Competitive duplication would not arise since each industry would be subject to unified control. That there are possibilities of economy in these areas, no one will question, but the

[5] It is contended by some observers, however, that the rate of progress which was occurring under the czars would, if continued, have lifted Russia to a higher level of production than it has achieved through state enterprise.

defenders of capitalism reply that these are minor elements when set beside the vigor and forward urge of private enterprise.

Socialism and depressions. Socialists offer their pre-eminent argument when they point to the depressions and unemployment under capitalism and assert that productive power would be used with fullness and regularity if the state were enterpriser. There would still be seasonal variations, of course, and other frictions would arise. But state enterprise would not be sensitive to profit prospects and to the cumulative effects of changes in them. It would have before it the whole range of industry for investment and could adjust its capital outlays to consumer demands in a way that would hold total demand at a high level. Purchasing power would enter government hands both through sale of products and taxation, and the use of funds could be easily controlled.

Defenders of capitalism should sense fully the force of this contention. Its popular influence will depend on the steadiness of production and employment achieved under private enterprise. It can be conceded that capitalism is superior in developing productive power and still argued plausibly that, with frequent episodes like the depression of the 1930s, average output would be higher under socialism. Even if this were not the case, the masses of people would probably prefer the lower but more certain average income that socialism would make possible. It is the part then of conservative wisdom to put forth all possible effort to prevent serious depressions and maintain reasonable stability at a high level. A responsible defense of capitalism cannot do less.

Coordination of activities under socialism. On the problem of directing the use of resources and products—of coordinating the behavior of millions of producers and consumers—socialists again have less to say, and spokesmen for capitalism can speak out strongly. The best hope of socialism would be to follow as closely as possible the processes of a free economy. This, at least, should be its plan if socialism seeks to fit production to people's wants and not impose on people the goods that socialist managers think people ought to want. The latter course would render the direction of production infinitely debatable, if the system allowed debate. But if individual wants are to govern, the only feasible guide is a market demand which reflects the innumerable comparisons that individuals make. To achieve economy, actual production must be governed by such demands at prices which, in turn, are influenced by costs.

The problem of costs is especially baffling when the services of all resources—of productive wealth as well as labor—are used only in state industries. The difficulty is that of putting a meaningful value on services when values cannot emerge in markets that register competing supplies and productivity in alternative uses. Unless the costs followed by the socialist management are truly rooted in the myriad uses and the scarcities of the thousands of types of human and material resources— if, that is, the costs are arbitrary—the problem of economy from the social standpoint is not solved at all. There can be no easy solution to this problem.

A free economy lets individuals pick their places in production, influenced by income prospects and their liking for different kinds of work. Socialism would have to decide what inducements and pressures it would use and what latitude it would give to individual choice. British socialism quickly encountered this problem. Material resources must be inventoried and assigned without the aid of numerous private owners seeking the most valuable ways to use them.

The use of products, as under capitalism, may be controlled through the prices put on them—prices that express significant costs or arbitrary prices that reflect the views of consumption of socialist administrators. But in a controlled economy, authoritative rationing does not have to wait for wars to justify it and may be resorted to considerably. Any failure of adjustment among prices, production, and people's tastes can be corrected by means of ration coupons.

Thoughtful socialists recognize the great difficulties these problems create, but they can reply that, under capitalism, markets are subject to many distortions that spoil the nicety of the economizing process. They may also reply that a nice adjustment of production to consumer demand is something less of an achievement when demand is molded by producer advertising. But they would have other troubles. Whether the extensive planning and control necessary under socialism could be handled without a burden of administrative overhead mildly suggested by OPA experience during the war, and without endless irritation of a battered public, would be incidental matters of some magnitude.

Distribution under socialism. Traditionally socialism has made its chief bid for support on the ground that it would greatly reduce inequality, if not do away with it. In socialist language, exploitation would end. From the structure of state socialism, one would suppose that the more flagrant inequalities of capitalism would be eliminated. Property incomes, which account for most of the larger concentrations of income and private wealth under capitalism, would presumably disappear, except as a small return on savings out of wages might be allowed. The larger salaries and bonuses would also probably stop. Ordinary people should be able to live their lives without so great a sense, as under capitalism, of being overshadowed by the superior economic blessings of others.

From this it does not follow that equality would prevail. Views differ among socialists as to the principles that should govern wages; but, if one may judge from Russian experience, incomes might differ as much as in the United States within a range that includes the bulk of the population but excludes the most fortunate. If wages are adjusted to performance, in the interest of efficiency and the most effective placement of labor, pay differences must be substantial. In addition, an aristocracy of privilege is likely to develop within any extensive bureaucracy.

Nor does it follow that ordinary workers under socialism would necessarily get a return representing a larger fraction of the value of the products they help to produce. Profits and the payment of management now absorb a considerable, but minor, fraction of the value of American production, but these returns supply a large part of the saving from which the capital of industry is developed. Capital formation and administrative overhead might leave the ordinary worker in no better a relative position under socialism. It is argued by some observers that, when allowance is made for progressive taxes, American labor receives rather cheaply the services that are the basis of much of its productivity.

These are aspects of inequality in the primary division of income. An important feature of socialist thinking, at least in its more humanitarian phase, is the emphasis on collective responsibility for persons who are not able to earn a decent living by prevailing standards. Unemployment should not present the problem under socialism that it does under capitalism, but there is still the problem presented by old people, invalids, and those who are otherwise unemployable or of low earning capacity. It is not inherent in the idea of state enterprise that a more generous standard of public assistance would prevail than now obtains, or is likely to develop, in the United States under capitalism; but one would expect that secondary distribution under socialism would come to provide not only education but medical care and possibly housing. Socialism must face the same danger as capitalism that people who are assured of income are likely to be indifferent producers but it would probably respond somewhat differently to the danger— for better or worse.

Socialization of productive wealth can doubtless have greatest effect on distribution in situations unlike the present one in the United States. Where absentee landowners in backward agricultural countries receive half or more of the crop and in return provide little in the way of buildings, equipment, and livestock, a revolution in land tenure can change distribution fundamentally. When industry invades undeveloped regions, illiterate native labor may be employed under conditions that approach slavery; and nineteenth-century industrialization in the advanced nations was not always much better. But even under capitalism at its best, considerable inequality is inevitable for reasons that state enterprise should remove; so that the best case for capitalism must lie in the clear fact that, in its better examples, it has raised the ordinary worker to a level that other systems, as yet, can only promise.

Socialist philosophy

Socialist thinking is not adequately summed up in the claims made for state enterprise as a superior way to perform purely economic functions. Socialism is a philosophy, or a group of philosophies, of society as a whole, and to many it has been a religion. From Plato on, doctrines of social reconstruction—whether called socialism, communism, or something else—have been numerous and varied, and usually their strictly economic prescriptions have been blended into a comprehensive theory of human living. Our attention to this vast field will be limited to a summary of the views of Karl Marx, the great leader of modern radical thinking, and some observations on the scope of the indictment of capitalism and of the hopes of those who would replace it.

Marxian or "scientific" socialism. Marx was a scholar who knew the economics of his day and philosophy and history as well. His study of mid-nineteenth-century capitalism was intensive and detailed. His writing displays the qualities of the preacher and prophet, as well as the scholar, and provides a model of invective that his disciples have followed. As an indictment of capitalism, his work is impressive, but it is best known for the broad theory of history and society into which his views of the economy are fitted. This theory, buttressed by observation at all points, is the basis of what has been called "scientific" socialism, in contrast with more purely idealistic schools of radical thinking.

Marx developed what is known as the *economic interpretation of history,* an approach since followed by many writers. He saw the whole social structure of any period as the outgrowth of the conditions and methods of production. Laws, customs, prevailing attitudes had this foundation, and the political, religious, and other factors, often viewed as coordinate with the economic in molding the course of history, he viewed as derivative and subordinate.

Economic forces in the Marxian philosophy come to focus in the *class struggle*. It may seem that social classes are numerous and divided along many lines, but Marx saw only two classes of importance and one basis of cleavage. That basis is the ownership of capital goods; the two classes are the capitalists, who own and employ, and the ordinary workmen, the proletariat, who are employed. These classes constitute the exploiters and the exploited.

Exploitation, as Marx saw it, is not the incidental result of a mean acquisitiveness on the part of employers but the necessary result of conditions inherent in capitalism. Marx took from Adam Smith and Ricardo a labor theory of value, and on the basis of it he held that the values both of products and of labor itself are governed by the amounts of labor they represent. Thus employers need to pay wages only equal to the amount of labor required to rear and support workers, but employers get more than this amount of labor from their workers, and products therefore yield an element of *surplus value* which the employers retain. Since only labor, according to Marx, is productive, this surplus value represents sheer exploitation.

Because of it, employers have funds for developing their plants beyond the limits of justifiable expansion. Accordingly there must be crises and depressions, and capitalist countries must become aggressively imperialistic as they seek prosperity beyond their borders. As a result also of this exploitation, and of the mechanization of industry, workers suffer *progressive impoverishment*. A worsening of the position of labor is another essential of the Marxian theory.

But while labor declines in economic status, its potential political strength increases. A further aspect of capitalist development is the *concentration of industry*, with capital accumulating in fewer hands as small shopmen and independent artisans are squeezed out. Thus the *middle class must presently disappear*. As a result, when society consists only of masses of exploited workmen and a few exploiting capitalists, the *proletariat takes over*, the exploiters are expropriated, and an ideal *classless society* results.

This summary of the theory must fail to do Marx justice, for surely the quality of this reasoning and these predictions, as viewed three fourths of a century after he wrote, does not explain the hold he has today on the thinking of millions of people. The value theory of Smith and Ricardo has been superseded, and the exploitation of workers by employers, if they are exploited, cannot be explained in surplus-value terms. The real income of workers, instead of falling, has risen greatly, and working conditions are vastly improved. Despite industrial concentration, the middle class has not vanished, and its political influence continues great. Instead of two classes, there are many economic interests, as many as there are industries and occupations. Except among spokesmen of ideologies and their converts, there is little suggestion in a prosperous United States of a simple general cleavage of the population into the classes that Marx expected. His hold, less strong here than elsewhere, must lie in the need of discontented people for an eloquent indictment and a broad synthesis with which to rationalize their discontent.

Other socialist viewpoints. While many socialists try somehow to squeeze the facts of modern life into Marxian categories, there is no need of doing so in order to be a socialist. One may disavow all ideologies of exploitation and inevitable change and simply hold, as a practical matter, that some sort of collectivism can do a better job than capitalism in avoiding waste, depressions, and inequality. Persons of this approach are perhaps more likely to have constructive ideas on problems of centralized-versus-decentralized control, planning and accounting procedures, useful degrees of market freedom, selection and compensation of employees, recognition and place of unions, types of private wealth allowable, completeness of abolition of private enterprise, general relation of political to economic government, and like matters—problems that must somehow be settled under socialism.

But socialist thinking is likely to be suffused with an idealism not reflected in any statement of practical procedures. In part this idealism is a humanitarian concern over the welfare of little people, the people who fare badly in a freely organized, competitive society. In part it is an expression of moral and religious values, of revulsion against an acquisitiveness that, rightly or not, is associated with capitalism. People's lives should be oriented away from getting and spending and toward more enduring things, and the shift is difficult in a society that glorifies economic success. To the socialist, a change in institutions is necessary to general human betterment.

In some minds there is high optimism as to the possibilities of betterment, if institutions are altered. Human beings will become quite different creatures, selfishness will vanish, and a Utopian existence will become possible. The communist ideal—from everyone according to his ability, to everyone according to his need—can then be realized, and material requirements will fall into their properly subordinate place in human life.

Reactions to radicalism

In a time of change in the world, people struggle a good deal with their own views, trying to arrive at attitudes that are sound and worthy. Young people especially are wondering what stands to take. If formulation of their beliefs is difficult, they should not be impatient. It is perhaps best to feel that the last plank is never laid in one's personal platform. "He in whom the love of repose predominates," as Emerson said, "will accept the first creed, the first philosophy, the first political party he meets. . . . He in whom the love of truth predominates will keep himself aloof from all moorings and afloat." But if one is awake, one must react to proposals for social improvement that are about and react to popular attitudes toward those who hold radical views.

Persons who are satisfied with the American economy and anxious that it should continue defend it in various ways. Of them all, the least intelligent is to deny that there are flaws in it and to be unwilling to discuss those flaws. No one is deceived by this pretense, and the effect is to entrust the analysis of weaknesses, and the devising of correctives, to the enemies of the system, not its friends.

Nor is it an effective defense of the economy to silence the advocates of radical change in it—though the inclination to do so is natural when proposals consist of empty phrases backed by venomous attacks on groups successful under present institutions. To honest and intelligent socialists, of whom there are many, it is a serious blow that the Communist party, based in Russia, should chiefly typify the radical approach. Such socialists are offended as much as anyone by the upscrupulous charges, the intrigue, the denial of democratic processes, the ideological purges, the reliance on secret police and concentration camp, that sweeping economic reform now often implies. Radical thought may reflect the most humane and elevated conception of society, and its spokesmen, far from representing the "lunatic fringe" or a band of devious plotters, may show more grasp of economic problems and express better reasoned views than their name-calling critics usually do.

But believers in American capitalism may reasonably ask that its critics adopt an adequate perspective in appraising it, and no honest critic will want to do less. Despite slumps and inequalities, the economy has brought to ordinary workers an income level unmatched elsewhere. Its upward course in raising production has been sustained over a long period, and the drive seems inherent in the system—not dependent on particular policies and personalities, as in a managed economy. A rich offering of products has become available, and individuals have been free to choose, within their incomes, what products they will consume. Opportunity has not been equal, but there has been exceptional freedom from the arbitrary obstacles that often block choices of occupations and prevent the individual from improving his position and developing his qualities. The economy has not moved in rigid channels but has shown capacity to correct its weaknesses. Much of the harshness of early industrialism, in its treatment of labor and its neglect of the weak, has been removed; numerous reforms, not always wise but broadly in the public interest, have been assimilated. Nothing in the working of the economy seems seriously to threaten the basic political liberties that many look upon as the nation's most prized possession.

The responsible advocate of fundamental change in the economy does not lose sight of its achievements and virtues or try to disparage them. He avoids the error, of which many reformers are guilty, of focusing on present evils and setting against them only the vague and glamorous ideal of a changed society. He remains aware that any system he may favor will show flaws and encounter difficulties that are not revealed even in a careful blueprint of the proposed order. Even if all goes well, he knows that his ideal objectives cannot all be fully realized —that people cannot at the same time achieve the maximum in freedom and in security or in productivity and in equality. It can be said of the responsible reformer, as it was of Lincoln, that he does not confuse the desirable and the attainable.

Responsible is a good word to stress in speaking of social judgments and proposals, because too often they are offered as if no more were at stake than in winning a debate. It is unfortunate that academic people, whose role is educational, sometimes express important views in the spirit of speculative exercise rather than of consequential decision making. Young people in their enthusiasm are likely not to count the terrific cost of fundamental change or to insist that prescriptions must be adequate and apply in a practical way to the essential aspects of problems. The responsible advocate of a proposal should be able to say that if he were in a position of authority and could give practical effect to what he espouses, with its impact on millions of people, he would be for it and would introduce it. If he cannot, his views should be duly qualified.

Economic arrangements must meet more than economic tests. It has been said often in recent years that the economic and political problems of the world must find a moral solution, and religious and moral leadership has dealt increasingly with these matters. Such leadership has an important role in causing people to view their institutions critically from the loftiest standpoint they can attain, and in urging a continuous effort to discover ways to better human living.

But the tendency, when moral standards are applied, is to view present arrangements quite unfavorably, as when the World Council of Churches, meeting first in Amsterdam in the summer of 1948, declared "the Christian church should reject the ideologies of both Communism and capitalism." [6] Such judgments must not be interpreted, it is evident, as advice to the public to reject their present economic order and embrace some other. To go that far, moral leadership would seem to be under a moral obligation to point out the better way and show in some

---

[6] The resolution was finally altered to apply only to laissez-faire capitalism.

detail that it is better. As Wendell Willkie said of liberalism: "Very rarely can it rely simply upon a good heart to determine the merits of its cause." Or if the testimony of one rather far from being a Republican is preferred, Bertrand Russell put it this way: "Moral indignation, unless severely controlled, is seldom a source of wise conduct."

After all, an economic system is not condemned by its defects, moral or otherwise; it is condemned only by the fairly certain superiority of some other system. The economic problem, even when the economy as a whole is involved, is a problem of choice among alternatives, viewed, as closely as may be, in the same realistic light. So the advocate of change, after his criticisms and condemnations, should assume the burden of proving that his plan will work and will remove present evils without introducing equal ones. It is not enough that there is a possibility of its working. Perhaps state enterprise will maintain high production if the right people are in charge and specified steps are taken, but there must be a high probability that these people will be in charge and these steps will be taken. Or, if the prime aim is to enable people to live under less acquisitive conditions, the evidence must be convincing that they will in fact be led to behave differently under the proposed conditions. Speculative possibilities are not enough.

Probably Americans are most sensitive on the question of whether, if their economic system became collectivist, they could retain the democratic political processes, the civil liberties, and the freedom from personal restraint that they cherish. A leading contention of socialists, Communist-party behavior notwithstanding, is that the system they propose would be run much more democratically than the present one. Perhaps it could be, but the question again is one of probabilities. Leading students and observers have questioned the likelihood, and even denied the possibility. Running industries requires greater continuity of policy than most government functions, and elections must not upset it. Heads of state industries would be strongly tempted, as heads of large business corporations are, to adopt a one-party system of voting. Totalitarian elections go only a little beyond the traditional proxy system. Furthermore, with government not merely the referee in economic disputes but with all workers directly dependent on it for their incomes, it might easily be compelled to insulate itself from the pressures that democratic processes entail.

Like-minded observers, holding with Alexander Hamilton that "a power over a man's subsistence amounts to a power over his will," maintain that democracy must disappear when all voters, or most of them, depend on the state for bread and butter. Clearly, moreover, it would require a most generous officialdom, with power over the press and other means of communication, to permit these instruments to be used for its removal. Perhaps all of these obstacles to democracy could be overcome. To the responsible citizen who is otherwise impressed with the merits of collectivism, the question is whether there can be sufficiently conclusive evidence that they will be overcome.

There is need in the United States that all questions of economic organization should be discussed with greater insight than they commonly are. The claims made by radicals are no looser, or more larded with empty phrases, than the defenses of capitalism one often hears. Clear understanding is needed mainly not to assist an open choice between our present system and some other, but to interpret less sweeping changes and proposals. These can be evaluated only as they are seen in the general framework of the system as a whole.

Changes are bound to come. Social institutions have evolved, and it is reasonable to suppose that their evolution will continue. All history condemns a reactionary view. But we should sense what is happening as changes occur and guide them as well as we can in directions that we desire. To this end, an understanding grasp of present arrangements is perhaps the best safeguard of progress.

Review Questions

1. Set forth the tests that seem to you important in appraising the working of an economic system and apply them to the economy of the United States.

2. Classify the ways in which major government policies in the United States bear on the economy, showing their relation to a system of free private enterprise or competitive capitalism.

3. Distinguish several senses in which an economy may be described as "mixed."

4. What are the principal private organizations that seem able to influence markets in the United States? Show that they do not fit into the model of a completely free economy.

5. "Individual producers in all categories hesitate to entrust their fate to completely free markets. And when markets become subject to organized controls at one point, pressure is intensified for similar controls elsewhere." Explain both sentences, with examples.

6. Evaluate, as the basis of general economic control, the collective negotiation of organized groups. Does it seem that a limited amount of such control can be reconciled with the working of competitive capitalism?

7. In connection with which economic problems do advocates of state socialism make their strongest case? On which are the defenders of capitalism most persuasive? Evaluate the respective positions on these issues.

8. State concisely the essentials of Marxian doctrine. What seem to be its points of weakness and its elements of strength?

9. As against an economic interpretation of history and of social conflict, consider this viewpoint: "It is a serious question whether, if all economic limitations and conflicts were removed say, by the discovery of some effective magic for producing all material goods and services without effort or the use of scarce means, social antagonism and conflict would be removed, or even reduced, or essentially changed in form. It appears probable that conflict would be more intense, unless other interests and other traits of 'human nature' were at the same time miraculously transformed, removing all desire to 'get ahead' and all occasion for organized action of any kind." [7] Does this seem a reasonable view?

10. A prominent economist, who formerly at least was a socialist, has said that the modern socialist has no more need of Marx's doctrine than of Marx's whiskers. Along what lines would the thinking of such a socialist run?

11. Certain leaders of radical thought have been described as Utopian Socialists or as Christian Socialists. What would you expect their emphasis to be?

12. What are the differences in the implications of the word "communism" when spelled with, and without, the capital letter?

13. What are the main questions that you think an intelligent socialist should be able to answer in explaining the essential features of the system he advocates? Do these questions differ greatly from the ones an intelligent supporter of capitalism should be able to answer in explaining the system he believes in?

14. What is involved in saying that those who advocate substantial change in the economy are obligated to maintain a responsible attitude? What burden of proof do you think they should assume in their proposals?

[7] Frank H. Knight, *Freedom and Reform,* Harper, 1947, p. 399.

Index